THE MAN WHO KNEW TOO MUCH

Hired to Kill Oswald
and Prevent the Assassination of
JFK
Richard Case Nagell
Is

THE MAN
WHO KNEW
TOO MUCH

Dick Russell

With a Foreword by Carl Oglesby

Carroll & Graf Publishers/Richard Gallen
New York

Copyright © 1992 by Dick Russell
Foreword copyright © 1992 by Carl Oglesby

Library of Congress Cataloging-in-Publication Data

Russell, Dick.
    The man who knew too much / Dick Russell, with a foreword by Carl Oglesby.
        p.   cm.
    ISBN 0-88184-900-6 : $27.95
    1. Kennedy, John F. (John Fitzgerald), 1917–1963—Assassination. 2. Nagell,
Richard Case. I. Title.
E842.9.R87   1993
364.1'524—dc20   92-38491
                                                                                CIP

First Carroll & Graf edition 1992

Carroll & Graf Publishers, Inc.
260 Fifth Avenue
New York, NY 10001

Library of Congress Cataloging-in-Publication Data

Manufactured in the United States of America

This book is dedicated
to all generations
that will fight to create a more honest world
and, in the words of Martin Luther King, Jr.,
"redeem the soul of America."

And to my son Franklin.

Razumov thought: "I am being crushed—and I can't even run away." Other men had somewhere a corner of the earth—some little house in the provinces where they had a right to take their troubles. He had nothing. He had not even a moral refuge—the refuge of confidence. To whom could he go with this tale—in all this great, great land?
—Joseph Conrad, *Under Western Eyes*

Contents

III. The Setup

IV. The Deed

V. The Cover-up

Acknowledgments

I owe a debt to so many people. In the beginning there was Mel. Our long talks together about the spirit of the Kennedys, and the forces that killed them, remain my highest inspiration. Over the years, my close friends Jessie, George, Adele, Faith, David, Etta, Eve, Randy, Owen, Jeremy, and Brian have given me guidance in countless ways.

When I finally began to write this book, my wife Susan was always one step ahead of me. She made discoveries that I could never have come to on my own. She edited what was confusing or superflous. She continually challenged me to find a deeper place to see and write from. Without her, I could not have written the book you are about to read.

I wish that Bernard Fensterwald, Jr., could have lived to see this project come to fruition. His death on April 2, 1991, was a terrible loss to all of us who still seek the truth about what happened to the great leaders of the 1960s. Bud's legacy lives on with his partner, James Lesar, at the Assassination Archives Research Center, Suite 510, 918 F Street, N.W., Washington, D.C., 20006, for those who wish to offer their continuing support to what Bud began.

The brilliant suggestions and editing aid of my friend and fellow researcher Carl Oglesby have been invaluable in helping sort out this complex story. Nor could I have assembled this without Mary Ferrell's indefatigable help in footnoting sources and sharing her peerless storehouse of knowledge on the JFK case.

For starting me on this journey many years ago, I will always be grateful in particular to Richard E. Sprague, Richard Popkin, and my editor at *The Village Voice,* Judy Daniels. And for keeping my interest alive, my deep appreciation to Norman Mailer and other members of the Dynamite Club.

To my playwright friend (and computer wizard) Arthur Kopit, many thanks for teaching me how to keep my program running.

For their direct aid in helping open new doors of investigation about Richard Nagell, my appreciation goes out to constant correspondent Arthur Greenstein and to Vaughn Marlowe.

Special thanks are due to numerous researchers and fellow writers who have devoted so many hours of their time to assisting me, in person and over the phone: Gary Shaw and his compatriots at the JFK Assassination Information Center in Dallas, Peter Dale Scott, Earl Golz, Gus Russo, Joseph J. Trento, Kevin Coogan, Matthew Coogan, Jones Harris, Harold Weisberg, Jim Hougan, George O'Toole, Robert Morrow, Edward Jay Epstein, Fulton Oursler, Jr., Paul Hoch, Peter Noyes, Donald Freed, Jim Marrs, Louis Wolf, Philip Melanson, Henry Hurt, William Turner, Russ Bellant, Gordon Winslow, Scott Malone, Jeff Goldberg, Jeff Cohen, Marty Lee, Penn Jones, Jr., Jerry Policoff, Tom McCann, Anthony Summers, Jack Swike, Jerry D. Rose, and A. J. Weberman.

We are all indebted to a number of former intelligence officials who have opened our eyes to the inner workings of a secret world: John Stockwell, Philip Agee, Melvin Beck, Victor Marchetti, Joseph B. Smith, William R. Corson, Ralph McGehee, and L. Fletcher Prouty. And to those who doggedly pursued the truth in an official capacity: congressional staff assistants Gaeton Fonzi, Ed Lopez, Mike Ewing, Kevin Walsh, and David Marston; and, of course, New Orleans district attorney Jim Garrison.

Several scholars offered important perceptions on the Far East: Chalmers Johnson, Bruce Cumings, Jeffrey Richelson of the National Security Archive, and David Kaplan of the Center for Investigative Reporting. Abram Chayes's perceptions about the Cuban Missile Crisis saved me from making some major scholarly errors.

For their help in making (or trying to make) important contacts in other countries, my appreciation to my friend Mario Velásquez; David Crawford; Professor James Barros of the University of Toronto and his son

Andrew; Brian Litman; and my translator for our adventure in Moscow, Kristen Suokko.

At a number of universities and private archives I received prompt responses to my inquiries beyond the call of duty: Edward J. Boone, Jr., at the MacArthur Memorial Archive; Wesley McCune at Group Research, Inc.; translator Matt Rubiner at MIT; Daniel Brandt with his invaluable CIA Data Base; Chip Berlet of Political Research Associates; Sheryl B. Vogt of the Richard B. Russell Memorial Library at the University of Georgia; and librarians with the Mark Gayn (University of Toronto), Harold R. Isaacs (Massachusetts Institute of Technology), and John F. Kennedy (Memorial Library, Boston) collections.

Finally, my thanks for their insights on particular topics to Richard Goodwin, Tad Szulc, David C. Martin, Michael Scott, Gilbert Offenhartz, Forrest Sawyer, Terry Catchpole, Edward S. Cohen, Linda Hunt, John Marks, Christopher Andrew, and the late Mae Brussell.

And to Oliver Stone, whose remarkable film *JFK* revived the interest of so many people.

Also, to Leonard Peltier and others like him, whose human rights have been assassinated by the same forces that took the life of the thirty-fifth president.

To the "Brooklyn Waiter," whoever you are, my rediscovery of your anonymous missive charted a whole new course.

My apologies if I have inadvertently omitted anyone from this list; literally hundreds of people have supported me in this consuming task, and my gratitude goes out to you all.

Foreword

In May 1992, CIA director Robert Gates told the Senate Intelligence Committee that the CIA could not release certain elements of its large secret file on accused JFK assassin Lee Harvey Oswald because to do so would compromise the security of its collection methods.

Especially compromising, Gates held, would be the release of a secret 280-page report prepared in 1978 by the staff of the House Select Committee on Assassinations. This still-classified document reported the discovery of solid CIA evidence that Oswald was actually impersonated in the famous confrontations at the Soviet embassy and the Cuban consulate in Mexico City a month and a half before Dealey Plaza—scenes adduced by the Warren Commission to show that Oswald was a belligerent radical looking for trouble.

Clearly, if Oswald was impersonated in these episodes, then in the first place they no longer prove the least thing about him except that—point two—he was someone whose name the Mexico City mystery man chose to use, which may be something very interesting to learn about Oswald indeed. A key part of the Warren Commission theory of the crime would crumble, and the guardians of the official theory would have another sinister character to explain away.

But in the third place and much more important, proof of politically motivated impersonations of Oswald so near the moment of the assassination would necessarily and resoundingly raise the question of what in the world was going on. Why might someone want to impersonate a "nobody" and a "loner" such as Oswald and go to such great lengths to establish Oswald's name and a violent image of Oswald to Communist diplomats in Mexico City? Was Oswald not really a nobody?

Is there something more about Oswald we ought to know?

Evidently there is much more. And the work in hand, Dick Russell's *The Man Who Knew Too Much,* takes us farther than we have ever been— perhaps farther than many of us imagined we would ever be able to go—in putting the whole increasingly astounding story of Oswald together.

Russell's reconstruction is based largely on his own unique personal investigation, carried out over a decade and a half, of the mysterious role of a retired Military Intelligence captain named Richard Case Nagell. To say that Russell's achievement is unique is not to imply, of course, that colleagues of his in the great JFK assassin chase have not shared and also tried to substantiate his sense that Oswald was some secret organization's operative. This concept of Oswald as a clandestine agent, for example, was basic to the work of New Orleans district attorney Jim Garrison and to many of the early and more influential critics, such as Mark Lane, Sylvia Meagher, and Harold Weisberg, as well as to a 1975 work of the undersigned. More recently comes Philip Melanson's scholarly and elegant 1990 work *Spy Saga,* a marvel of deep deductions from a tiny data base.

But Russell, chiefly through his complex, long-ripened relationship with Nagell, is the first to take the question of Oswald's secret identity beyond the relatively little that can be established from the documents so far declassified. Russell has actually generated a new JFK text, so to speak, a new body of primary statements about the event, its prelude, and its aftermath by people who were, however obliquely, marginally, or momentarily, actually present on the stage of the JFK assassination drama. Had government censors been given a crack at Russell's original material, we can be sure it would be half blacked out. The book itself would be *samizdat.* It would never have seen a press.

Russell's work with Nagell and a large cast of Runyonesque supporting figures demanded great patience and tenacity, but the payoff proves well worth the effort. *The Man Who Knew Too Much* shows that Oswald was an active counterintelligence agent at the very moment of the JFK assassination, a discovery of enormous implications. The book also shows in equally striking detail the *limits* of this new knowledge. We do not yet know, for example, whether agent Oswald was being run by the CIA or the KGB, by the ONI or the GRU or some as yet unknown bureau of the Cold War, one side or the other. Nor do we know for a fact who Oswald himself *believed* was running him. All we may guess at, according to Russell, is that what Oswald believed to be true and the actual truth might in fact have been two very different things.

This remaining uncertainty about Oswald's actual role in the Dealey Plaza plot is not a serious problem for Russell's current purposes, however. His much more important finding here is the set of clues that demonstrates a secret counterintelligence connection in Oswald's life. Thus Russell has shown that *whether or not* Oswald fired a gun in Dealey Plaza and *whether or not* he knew who was really running him, he was *in any case* present in Dealey Plaza as someone's secret agent. This is virtually the same as saying that he was in Dealey Plaza on orders.

What is so exciting about Russell's work is that his approach to the elucidation of Oswald can have—*should* have—a real impact on the national argument about Dealey Plaza.

The great JFK debate has most classically been joined in terms of the physical facts of the shooting. Two questions have predominated: Was there a shot from the front? Were there more than three shots in all? If either answer was yes, then a basic case for conspiracy existed, and the government would be compelled to reopen the investigation.

The case did indeed move forward in terms of these issues, and the movement to reopen the investigation constantly won new popular support. A huge majority of the American people—over 75 percent of those with an opinion—came to reject the Warren theory.

But popular demands based on the physical evidence of a second gunman were finally inadequate to overcome the government's hostility and inertia. Government experts explained that the backward head snap in the Zapruder film was only a muscular reaction, not a reaction to a front shot. They explained that the shotlike impulses audible on the police audiotape were just random bursts of static, not proof of a second gunman. The critics had much to say in rebuttal, naturally, and were hardly driven from the fray, but it came to seem to many activists and onlookers that all forward momentum for a new investigation had been lost.

And then came the book you are about to read.

—Carl Oglesby
Cambridge, Mass., August 1992

Preface

The assassination of President John F. Kennedy in Dallas, Texas, on November 22, 1963, was a coup d'état in America. The truth has never been told about the real perpetrators, and our nation has never recovered from the conspiracy and cover-up.

In large part, this book is the story of a former Military Intelligence officer and CIA contract agent named Richard Case Nagell.

Nagell is still alive, in Southern California, and his revelations about the JFK conspiracy have until now remained largely unknown.

They include the existence of three earlier plans to assassinate JFK, between September 1962 and November 22, 1963.

They include Nagell's contention that he apprised the Federal Bureau of Investigation in September 1963 of a pending plot against the president's life, with enough details to warrant the arrest of the eventually accused assassin, Lee Harvey Oswald—as well as others.

They include Nagell's allegation that, in his capacity as a double agent assigned by the CIA to penetrate Soviet intelligence, he was ordered by the Soviets to kill Oswald in Mexico City—and thereby prevent the assassination.

Why Richard Nagell failed to carry out his assignment is a mystery I have only partially resolved and that awaits a future official investigation.

Most of the information in this book is new. It is based on several thousand pages of documentation about Nagell's life and intelligence career, interviews over a seventeen-year period with Nagell and many of his former associates, and more than two hundred interviews conducted with other vital witnesses.

Many of these people are speaking out for the first time about their knowledge of the JFK conspiracy. One of them, Vaughn Marlowe, was considered for recruitment as a rifleman in a June 1963 plot against JFK in Los Angeles.

In the course of a journey that has occupied me since 1975, I have come upon new leads that go far beyond what Nagell was willing to say. This book contains considerable previously unknown information about Military Intelligence and CIA operations, particularly in the Far East and in Mexico City. It takes a probing look at several CIA officials who might actually have been KGB "moles," and their connections to Nagell and Oswald.

The reader will also learn about a network of ultraright extremists stretching from Dallas to Washington, D.C., and as far as Europe and Asia. In this context, the role of the H. L. Hunt oil empire is scrutinized, primarily through the eyes of two of its former chief employees. And we will examine the chilling prospect that Oswald might have undergone a mind-control program emanating from the CIA, the military, or the Soviet Union.

As an investigative journalist, I followed a long trail, from the National Archives in Washington, to the teeming milieu of the Cuban refugee community in Miami, to the dingy bars in Los Angeles where I spent many hours with Richard Nagell. In the 1970s I wrote numerous articles about what I found along the way for such publications as *The Village Voice, New Times, Argosy,* and *Harper's Weekly.*

I have waited until now to write what I know about Richard Nagell, in hopes that someday he would agree to go forward with a complete, no-holds-barred account. Although he has never chosen to do this, I decided it was time to put his crucial perspective into the historical record. I have been able to corroborate a substantial amount of his remarkable story through other witnesses. As far as he has been willing to go, Nagell's information is, I am convinced, not only genuine but also absolutely vital to our understanding of what happened to JFK. Through a study of the intelligence milieu that at once compelled and repelled this man, it is also my hope to illuminate an era in American history.

In assembling this vast amount of material, I have combined several approaches: reportorial, personal, and historical. The cast of characters is large, the themes are many and interwoven. The espionage apparatus that surrounded Nagell and Oswald is extremely complex and multilayered. My decision was simply to let the pieces of the puzzle assemble in all their ambiguities, keeping the account chronological to the extent possible.

This book is my attempt to shed new light on the many fingers that pulled the trigger.

Cast of Characters

(* = Interviews conducted by the author)

*NAGELL, RICHARD CASE: Military Intelligence officer, 1955–59. CIA contract agent, 1962–63.

OSWALD, LEE HARVEY: U.S. Marines, 1956–59. "Defector" to the Soviet Union, 1959–62. Accused assassin of President Kennedy.

KRAMER, JOSEPH: Pseudonym of Richard Case Nagell and Mark Gayn.

NOLAN, ROBERT C.: Pseudonym of Nagell with Field Operations Intelligence and CIA.

"LAREDO": Code name used by Nagell in contacts with Soviet intelligence.

HIDELL/HIDEL, ALEK/ALBERT: Pseudonyms of Lee Harvey Oswald.

Nagell's relatives:
GAMBERT, ELEANORE: Nagell's sister. Confidante while he was incarcerated.

*GAMBERT, LOUIS: Eleanore's husband. Visited Nagell in prison.
*GAMBERT, ROBERT: Son of Louis and Eleanore. Acquainted with Nagell over the years.
*GAMBERT, ROGER: Son of Louis and Eleanore. Acquainted with Nagell over the years.
NAGELL, MITSUKO TAKAHASHI: Wife of Nagell, 1958–63.
*NAGELL, ROBERT; Nagell's son.
NAGELL, TERESA: Nagell's daughter.

Nagell's friends and associates:
"MR. BUEHEL": CIA (KGB?) official Nagell saw in New York after his prison release.
*BUICK, ROBERT CLAYTON: Bullfighter in Mexico City, 1962–65; allegedly met Oswald and Nagell at Hotel Luma. Acted as intelligence informant. Incarcerated with Nagell, 1966.
*BROGLIE, WARREN: Manager of the Hotel Luma in Mexico City; friend of CIA station chief Winston Scott.
CARMEN, MARIA DEL: Nagell acquaintance in Mexico City; alleged to have worked for both CIA and Cuban intelligence.
GAYN, MARK: Foreign correspondent, *Toronto Star;* alleged to have been Soviet spy using pseudonym, "Joseph Kramer."
*GREENSTEIN, ARTHUR: Met Nagell in Mexico City, 1962. Recipient of many letters from Nagell while imprisoned, 1967–69.
JOHN, FREDERICK: Kept conspiracy evidence stashed with him by Nagell in Los Angeles in September 1963.
*LYNN, WILLIAM: Investigator for California Department of Alcoholic Beverage Control, in Los Angeles.
*MARGAIN, JOHN: Sergeant under Captain Nagell during the Korean War; friend of Nagell in California.
*MARLOWE, VAUGHN: Executive committee, Los Angeles Fair Play for Cuba Committee, 1963. Alleged by Nagell to have been considered for recruitment into conspiracy against JFK.
*NEW, RICEY: Washington attorney. Assisted in arrangements for Nagell's release from East Germany, 1968.
ROBERTS, STEVE: West Coast representative, Fair Play for Cuba Committee, 1963.
WAEHAUF, FRANZ: Bartender at Hotel Luma, Mexico City. Alleged by Nagell to have been with Czech intelligence.

Individuals involved with Nagell's military career in the United States and the Far East, 1953–59:

*DA VANON, JOSEPH: CIA official, Los Angeles, 1955–56.

DUGAN, MASTER SERGEANT EMMETT E.: Member of Field Operations Intelligence. Body washed ashore in Tokyo Bay, 1958.

FUJISAWA, DR. CHIKAO: Professor, Tokyo University, 1950s. Alleged by Nagell to have been a Soviet agent.

*LEIBACHER, HERBERT E.: Agent in charge of CIA office, Los Angeles, 1955–56.

MURAI, JUN: Head of Japan's Cabinet Research Office, early 1950s. Friend of Nagell.

RAINFORD, COLONEL WILLIAM: Nagell's commander, Counter Intelligence Corps, Tokyo.

*ROTH, COLONEL ROBERT: Staff assistant to Colonel Stanley, Field Operations Intelligence, Far East.

*STANLEY, COLONEL JOHN B.: In charge of Field Operations Intelligence, Far East, 1954–60.

Individuals involved with the arrest, incarceration, and court case of Richard Case Nagell, 1963–68:

*BUNDREN, JIM: Arresting officer in El Paso, September 20, 1963. Told by Nagell, before the assassination, of Nagell's concerns about an upcoming event in Dallas.

*CALAMIA, JOSEPH: Court-appointed attorney for Nagell, spring 1964–68.

*HUDSPETH, HARRY LEE: Prosecutor at second Nagell trial, 1966.

*MEDINA, JUAN L.: Jailer in El Paso.

*MENDOZA, JESUS: Jailer in El Paso.

*MORTON, FRED: Assistant U.S. Attorney, El Paso. Prosecutor of Nagell case.

*MURPHY, EDWARD J.: FBI agent, El Paso. Involved in the Nagell case.

O'ROURKE, RAYMOND: Captain, El Paso County Jail.

*RALLIS, GUS: Calamia's coattorney in the Nagell case, 1964–68.

*RANEY, MORRIS: Chief prosecutor, Nagell 1964 trial.

*ROMAN, CRUZ: Jailer in El Paso.

*SHERMAN, ED: Legal assistant to Calamia, Nagell case.

SUTTLE, DORWIN K.: Judge at second Nagell trial, 1966.

THOMASON, R. E.: First judge in Nagell case, 1963.

*THORNBERRY, HOMER: Judge, U.S. Court for the Western District of El Paso. Presided over Nagell's 1964 trial. Friend of Lyndon Johnson.

*WEINSTEIN, DR. EDWIN: Neurological specialist at Walter Reed Army Hospital. Defense witness at Nagell's 1966 trial.
*WEISHEIT, GEORGE, JR.: Secret Service agent, El Paso. Interviewed Nagell in jail.
*WHITE, THOMAS B., JR.: Lead FBI agent in El Paso on the Nagell case.

Oswald's relatives:
MURRET, CHARLES: Oswald's uncle, New Orleans. Affiliated with Carlos Marcello Mob.
MURRET, JOYCE: Oswald's cousin, New Orleans.
MURRET, MARILYN: Oswald's cousin, New Orleans. World traveler, affiliated with Harold Isaacs's "apparatus."
OSWALD, MARGUERITE: Oswald's mother.
*OSWALD, MARINA PRUSAKOVA: Married in Minsk, 1961. Wife of accused assassin.
OSWALD, ROBERT: Oswald's brother.

Oswald's friends and associates:
*ANDREWS, DEAN: New Orleans attorney whom Oswald visited about his dishonorable discharge from the Marines.
*BOUHE, GEORGE: Member of Dallas's Russian community. Befriended Oswald, summer 1962. May have introduced him to George de Mohrenschildt.
*DE MOHRENSCHILDT, GEORGE: Member of Dallas's Russian community who befriended the Oswalds, 1962–63.
*DE MOHRENSCHILDT, JEANNE: George's wife.
GREGORY, PETER: One of the Oswalds' first friends in Fort Worth, 1962; translator for Marina after the assassination.
MAMANTOV, ILYA: Member of Dallas's Russian community. Translator for Marina after the assassination.
OKUI, YAEKO: Alleged Japanese girlfriend of Oswald in Dallas, 1963.
OSBORNE, ALBERT: Old preacher who rode bus with Oswald to Mexico City. Suspected intelligence agent.
PAINE, MICHAEL: Estranged husband of Ruth Paine. Bell Helicopter employee. Also knew Oswalds.
*PAINE, RUTH: Became Marina Oswald's close friend, March–November 1963.
POWER, HARRY L.: Army veteran. Trotsykite type from San Antonio. Mannlicher-Carcano rifle found in his Indiana hotel room, November 23, 1963.
REILY, WILLIAM: Employed Oswald at Reily Coffee Company in New Orleans. Involved with anti-Castro activists.

SCHMIDT, VOLKMAR: Introduced by de Mohrenschildt to Oswald. Had political discussions, hosted party where Ruth Paine met Oswalds.

*THORNLEY, KERRY: Friend at El Toro Marine base, Santa Ana, California. Wrote novel based on Oswald before assassination.

*VOSHININ, IGOR and NATASHA: Members of Dallas's Russian community. Friends of the de Mohrenschildts.

FBI officials and agents:

*ANDERSON, CLARK: FBI legal attaché, Mexico City, 1962–63.

DE BRUEYS, WARREN: New Orleans FBI agent. Alleged to have met with Oswald.

DELOACH, CARTHA: FBI official in Washington. Involved in postassassination investigation.

*ENNULAT, ALFRED G.: FBI official in communication with Nagell, New York, 1969.

FAIN, JOHN: Dallas FBI agent. Met with Oswald twice in summer of 1962.

HOOVER, J. EDGAR: FBI director, 1924–72. Intended recipient of warning letter from Nagell. Promoter of "lone assassin" theory.

*HOSTY, JAMES P., JR.: Investigated Oswald for FBI, Dallas, 1963.

*KELLEY, CLARENCE: FBI director, 1973–78. In correspondence with Nagell.

MALONE, JOHN: In charge of FBI New York office. Knew Nagell.

QUIGLEY, JOHN: New Orleans FBI agent who interviewed Oswald in jail, August 1963.

SHANKLIN, J. GORDON: FBI agent in charge, Dallas office. Ordered Hosty to destroy note from Oswald.

SOMERSETT, WILLIE: FBI informant who tape-recorded discussion of JFK assassination plan with Joseph Milteer.

SULLIVAN, WILLIAM C.: Chief of Division 5 counter intelligence under Hoover.

"TACOS": Code name used by two Miami FBI agents in meetings with Nagell.

CIA officials, agents, and affiliates:

*AGEE, PHILIP: Former CIA official, Mexico City.

*ANGLETON, JAMES: CIA chief of Counter Intelligence.

BARNES, TRACY: CIA chief of Domestic Operations Division. Alleged to have been involved with Oswald/Nagell activities.

*BECK, MELVIN: CIA undercover operative in Mexico City, 1962–67.

"BISHOP, MAURICE": Contact for Cuban exile Antonio Veciana in anti-Castro plots; allegedly met with Oswald, August 1963.

*BISHOP, WILLIAM: CIA contract agent. Put Cuban exile onto surveilling Nagell in New Orleans. Aware of JFK assassination plot.

"BOB": Nagell's CIA contact, Mexico City, 1962–63.

COLBY, WILLIAM: CIA director, 1973–75. Allegedly contacted by Colonel William Bishop about Nagell, summer 1963.

*CRAM, CLEVELAND: Conducted "mole" study for CIA. Knew of Winston Scott's relationship with Soviet agent.

DAVISON, ALEXIS: Air Force doctor at U.S. embassy in Moscow who examined Marina Oswald at the embassy and provided Oswalds with his mother's name in Atlanta. Involved in CIA's Oleg Penkovsky project.

DRELL, BERNARD: chief of CIA's Office of Research & Reports, Manufacturing & Services Division, early 1960s.

DULLES, ALLEN: Director of CIA, 1953–61. Warren Commission member, 1964.

FITZGERALD, DESMOND: CIA chief of Far Eastern Division, 1957–62. Chief of Cuban Task Force, 1962–64. Alleged by Nagell to have been knowledgeable of JFK conspiracy.

*FLANNERY, JAMES E.: CIA official, Tokyo and Mexico City.

GAUDET, WILLIAM GEORGE: CIA official in New Orleans, 1963. Got Mexican tourist card next to Oswald, September 1963.

GEHLEN, REINHARD: Chief of Hitler's intelligence, World War II. CIA-backed head of West German intelligence through 1968.

GOTTLIEB, SIDNEY: In charge of CIA MK-ULTRA mind-control program.

HARVEY, WILLIAM: Chief of CIA's Cuban task force, 1960–62. Organizer of CIA-Mob plots against Castro.

HELMS, RICHARD: Creator of CIA MK-ULTRA mind-control program. Covert-action coordinator, 1963. Director, 1966–72.

*HIDALGO, BARNEY: CIA officer at Miami's JM/WAVE station.

HUNT, E. HOWARD, JR.: Covert-action chief for Domestic Operations Division, 1963. Alleged to have been in Dallas day of assassination.

KIMSEY, HERMAN: CIA official until summer 1962. Alleged personal knowledge of conspiracy to Hugh McDonald.

KIRKPATRICK, LYMAN: CIA inspector general. Wrote report on anti-Castro plots. Warned about mind control, August 1963.

LEDDY, RAYMOND: Organized CIA's Latin American Division. Friend of Winston Scott.

McCONE, JOHN: CIA director, 1961–65.

*McDONALD, HUGH: Ex-CIA contract agent. Author of two books on JFK assassination.

*MARCHETTI, VICTOR: Former executive assistant to deputy director, CIA, Langley, Virginia.

MARTIN, WILLIAM R.: Ex(?)-CIA agent and member of Jim Garrison's staff. Interviewed Nagell in prison, 1967.

MECOM, JOHN: Houston oilman, associate of Hunts and George de Mohrenschildt. Set up CIA front San Jacinto Fund.

MEYER, MARY: Ex-wife of CIA official Cord Meyer. JFK mistress, allegedly knew of conspiracy and mind-control program. Murdered in 1964.

*MOORE, J. WALTON: CIA official in Dallas. Allegedly instructed George de Mohrenschildt to enter relationship with Oswald.

*MORROW, ROBERT: CIA contract agent, 1960–63, under Tracy Barnes. Allegedly knew of Oswald, Nagell, and assassination conspiracy.

PAISLEY, JOHN: Chief of CIA's Soviet Electronics Branch while Oswald worked at Minsk radio factory. Associate of Nagell, who alleged Paisley to have been a KGB "mole."

*PETTY, CLARE: CIA counter intelligence official who concluded Angleton might have been a mole. Also looked into Winston Scott.

*PHILLIPS, DAVID ATLEE: CIA Mexico City chief of clandestine operations (1962) and Cuban affairs (1963). "Maurice Bishop"?

POWERS, FRANCIS GARY: U-2 pilot shot down over USSR on May Day 1960. Believed Oswald (and/or U.S. officials) may have sabotaged his mission.

SCOTT, WINSTON: CIA station chief, Mexico City, 1956–69.

*SMITH, JOSEPH B.: CIA official, clandestine activities, Far Eastern and Western Hemisphere divisions.

SNYDER, RICHARD: U.S. consular official who met with Oswald in Moscow. Ex(?)-CIA.

*WILCOTT, JAMES: CIA official, Tokyo, 1960–64. Alleged Oswald to have been CIA agent.

WISNER, FRANK: Organized CIA's Gehlen, Eastern European underground networks.

Military officials and personnel:

CANON, COLONEL JACK Y.: Colonel with U.S. Military Intelligence, Far East. Associate of Charles Willoughby.

CARROLL, JOSEPH: First head of Defense Intelligence Agency (DIA).

CRICHTON, JACK: Army Reserve Intelligence, Dallas. Made first arrangements for Marina Oswald's translators after assassination.

*DINKIN, EUGENE B.: Army code breaker who warned of plot against JFK, October–November 1963.

*KLAY, ANDOR: Official at U.S. mission, Berlin. Involved in Nagell's release from East Germany, 1968.

*LANSDALE, MAJOR GENERAL EDWARD: Operations chief for MONGOOSE anti-Castro effort, 1961–63.

PIERCE, ROGER: Pentagon "expert" on assassination. Aware of Nagell and de Mohrenschildt.

POWELL, JAMES W.: Military Intelligence officer in Dealey Plaza, November 22, 1963.

*PROUTY, COLONEL L. FLETCHER: Pentagon focal point officer for liaison to CIA.

QUINN, WILLIAM: No. 2 man at DIA.

*WALKER, MAJOR GENERAL EDWIN: Removed as military commander in West Germany, 1961. Leading member of radical right. Allegedly intended shooting victim of Oswald, April 1963.

WEBSTER, ROBERT: Navy man. Allegedly defected to USSR two weeks before Oswald, 1959. Returned home two weeks before Oswald, 1962.

WILLOUGHBY, MAJOR GENERAL CHARLES: General Douglas MacArthur's chief of intelligence, 1941–51. Leading member of numerous radical right organizations, 1963.

Police officials:

BUTLER, GEORGE: Dallas police lieutenant. Knew Jack Ruby and Hunt family.

MARTELLO, FRANCIS: New Orleans police officer. Interviewed Oswald in jail, August 1963.

*REVILL, JACK: Dallas police lieutenant who apparently received data from Army Intelligence about Oswald, November 22, 1963.

*TROSCLAIR, P. J.: New Orleans chief of police intelligence unit. In communication with Tampa about Fair Play for Cuba Committee, December 1962.

Soviet officials and agents:

ANDROPOV, JURI: Head of KGB, 1962–63.

BOLSHAKOV, GEORGI: KGB liaison to Kennedy administration.

EROSHKIN, COLONEL NIKOLAI: Military attaché at Soviet embassy, Tokyo, 1957–58. Target of CIA defection plan.

GERASIMOV, VITALY: Received Oswald correspondence at Soviet embassy in Washington. Suspected of being Soviet spy.

GOLINIEWSKI, MICHAL: KGB defector, 1959.

GOLITSIN, ANATOLY: KGB defector, January 1962. Convinced James Angleton that the CIA had been penetrated.

KHRUSHCHEV, NIKITA: Premier of Soviet Union, 1956–64.

KORNIENKO, GEORGI: Soviet embassy official, Washington, 1963. Name appears in Nagell's notebook.

KOSTIKOV, VALERY: KGB "Department 13" officer in Mexico City. Met with Oswald, September 1963.

MIKOYAN, ANASTAS: Soviet deputy premier who urged that Oswald's request for citizenship be considered, 1959. Met with George de Mohrenschildt in Mexico, 1960.

*NECHIPORENKO, OLEG: KGB official in Mexico City, 1961–71. Met with Oswald at Soviet embassy, September 1963.

NOSENKO, YURI: KGB defector, January 1964. Claimed that Soviet intelligence never had interest in Oswald.

"OAXACA": Code name of Nagell's contact with Soviet intelligence, Mexico City.

PENKOVSKY, OLEG: CIA spy inside USSR. Exposed at time of Cuban Missile Crisis and executed.

PRUSAKOV, ILYA: Uncle of Marina Oswald. Official with MVD. Rumored to have been targeted by CIA for defection.

SORGE, RICHARD: Leader of Soviet spy ring, China and Japan, 1931–41.

STASHINSKY, BOGDAN: Defected to West, 1961, saying he was Soviet assassin.

VOGEL, WOLFGANG: Lawyer involved in spy exchanges, East Berlin, including Nagell's.

YATSKOV, PAVEL: KGB official in Mexico City. Met with Oswald, September 1962, at Soviet embassy.

Cuban officials and sympathizers:

AZCUE, EUSEBIO: Chief of Cuban embassy, Mexico City. Believes the Oswald who visited was an impostor.

BUHAI, HARRIETT: Believed by Nagell to have been foreign agent. Met with Nagell at time of HUAC hearings, July 1963.

CASTRO, FIDEL: Premier of Cuba since 1959.

DURAN, SYLVIA: Cuban embassy assistant, Mexico City. Temporarily imprisoned for questioning after assassination.

*HEALY, DOROTHY: Leading member of Communist Party, U.S.A.

LAMONT, CORLISS: Author of *Crime Against Cuba* pamphlet in possession of Oswald and Nagell, 1963.

LEE, V. T.: Executive director, Fair Play for Cuba Committee, 1962–63.

*LEWIS, AL: Official with Los Angeles Fair Play for Cuba Committee. Described attempts to link him to assassination.

LEWIS, HARRIETT, aka BARBARA BLAIR: Leftist associate of Nagell's in Los Angeles, summer 1963.

Cuban exiles and associates:

ALBA, ADRIAN: Cuban exile who knew Oswald in New Orleans. Witnessed FBI document package going to Oswald.

ALEMAN, JOSÉ, JR.: Cuban exile who alleged Trafficante threat against JFK in September 1962.

"ANGEL": Cuban exile alleged by Nagell to have been directly involved in plots to assassinate JFK.

ARCACHA-SMITH, SERGIO: Cuban exile leader in New Orleans and Texas. Described by Nagell as "peripheral character" in JFK conspiracy.

*ARTIME, MANUEL: Cuban exile leader for Bay of Pigs invasion. Involved in CIA plots against Castro. May have actually been a Cuban intelligence agent.

*AUGUSTINOVICH, RONALD: Claimed to be involved in CIA penetration effort with Oswald against Cuba.

BANISTER, GUY: Ran private detective agency at 544 Camp Street, New Orleans, which Oswald used as office. Associated with Cuban exiles, David Ferrie, organized crime, right wing.

BATISTA, FULGENCIO: Dictator of Cuba deposed by Castro. Went into exile in Miami.

*BRINGUIER, CARLOS: Cuban exile, New Orleans. Involved in street altercation and debate with Oswald.

*BROSHEARS, RAYMOND: Roommate of David Ferrie. Alleged Ferrie was to fly assassins out of Texas.

CUBELA, ROLANDO: Code-named AM/LASH by CIA. Involved in autumn 1963 FitzGerald plot to kill Castro.

CUESTA, TONY: Miami exile. Connected with Alpha 66. Received funds from Hunt oil family. Indicated by Nagell to have been aware of plot to assassinate JFK.

DEL VALLE, ELADIO: Miami exile, partner of David Ferrie. Investigated by Nagell. Alleged to have foreknowledge of JFK conspiracy.

DIAZ VERSON, SALVADOR: Alleged "disinformation" agent for David Phillips in Mexico City. Leader of global anti-Communist league.

FERRIE, DAVID: Involved in Oswald's activities, summer 1963, New Orleans. Worked with right-wing, Cuban-exile, CIA, and organized-crime figures.

"FUENTES, MIGUEL": Pseudonym for exile alleged to have solicited Garrett Trapnell into anti-Kennedy plot.

GONZALEZ, PEDRO: Cuban exile in Abilene, Texas. Said to have received note in mailbox from Oswald three days before assassination.

*HALL, LORAN: Anti-Castro activist. Alleged by FBI to have visited Silvia Odio.

*HEMMING, GERRY PATRICK: Trained Cuban exiles in Florida. Saw Oswald at Cuban consulate, Los Angeles, 1959.

HERNANDEZ, VICTOR ESPINOSA: Cuban exile arms dealer. Friend of Rolando Cubela (AM/LASH).

*HOWARD, LAWRENCE, JR.: Anti-Castro activist. Alleged by FBI to have visited Silvia Odio.

KOHLY, MARIO GARCIA, SR.: Cuban exile leader, Washington, D.C. Alleged to have foreknowledge of assassination.

"LEOPOLDO": Cuban exile alleged by Nagell to have been Angel's partner in plots to assassinate JFK.

*McKEOWN, ROBERT: Weapons dealer approached by Oswald and a Cuban in September 1963. Also knew Jack Ruby.

*MASEN, JOHN THOMAS: Gun dealer in Dallas. Associate of Cuban exiles and Minutemen. Oswald look-alike.

MASFERRER, ROLANDO: Cuban exile leader in Miami. Alleged to have foreknowledge of JFK assassination.

*ODIO, SILVIA: Angel, Leopoldo, and Oswald came to her Dallas door, late September 1963.

"OSWALD, LEON": Oswald look-alike involved with anti-Castro Cubans.

PEÑA, OREST: Owner of Habana Bar in New Orleans. Reported Oswald at that bar with Latin acquaintances. Friend of Carlos Bringuier.

PORTUONDO, EMILIO NÚÑEZ: Batista ambassador to United Nations. Associate of Charles Willoughby. Monitored phone call indicated knowledge of JFK conspiracy.

PRIO, CARLOS: Batista's predecessor as Cuban leader. Went into exile in Miami.

QUIROGA, CARLOS: New Orleans Cuban exile. FBI informant. Went to visit Oswald on behalf of Bringuier.

RAY, MANUEL: Founder of JURE Cuban exile group. Associate of Silvia Odio.

ROBERTS, DELPHINE: Guy Banister's secretary.

RODRIGUEZ, MANUEL O.: Set up Alpha 66 branch in Dallas. Associate of John Thomas Masen.

*SARGEN, ANDRES NASARIO: A founder of Alpha 66.

SOUETRE, JEAN: French OAS captain. Reportedly associated with exiles in New Orleans. Expelled from Dallas on day of assassination.

*TRAPNELL, GARRETT: Cuban intelligence operative, 1963. Said he was solicited by exile group in assassination plot against JFK. Warned FBI August 1963.

VALDES, RENÉ: Named head of Los Angeles branch of Alpha 66, spring 1963, then dismissed as possible Cuban agent.

VARONA, ANTONIO: Cuban exile leader. Detained by CIA during Bay of Pigs invasion. Involved in CIA anti-Castro plots with organized crime.

*VECIANA, ANTONIO: Leader of Alpha 66. Involved in numerous anti-Castro plots. Said he met Oswald in company of "Maurice Bishop," August 1963.

People affiliated with radical right:
*ANGERS, BRADFORD: Former H. L. Hunt employee. Alleged that Oswald had right-wing accomplices in Walker shooting.

BANDERA, STEPAN: Ukrainian underground leader. Found dead October 15, 1959.

BUTLER, ED: Propagandist for Information Council of the Americas. Debated Oswald, August 1963.

DOBRIANSKY, LEV: Associate of Charles Willoughby.

CAPELL, FRANK: Editor of *Herald of Freedom*. Associate of Willoughby. Many FBI-military contacts.

COURTNEY, KENT: Founder of Conservative Society of America, New Orleans. Friend of Guy Banister.

*CURINGTON, JOHN: Chief assistant to H. L. Hunt, 1960–69.

GALE, COLONEL WILLIAM: A MacArthur commander in World War II. Founder of California Rangers paramilitary group, 1960s.

GATLIN, MAURICE B., SR.: New Orleans associate of Guy Banister.

GRINNAN, JOE: Leading member of Dallas John Birch Society. Involved with black-bordered anti-Kennedy ad.

HARGIS, BILLY JAMES: Head of Tulsa-based Christian Crusade.

HUNT, H. L.: Texas oil billionaire tied with extremist right, Charles Willoughby, Cuban exiles.

HUNT, NELSON BUNKER: Son of H. L. Hunt.

HUNTER, EDWARD: Ex-OSS/CIA agent. Coined the term "brainwashing."

KERSTEN, CHARLES: Ex-congressman. Lawyer in Stashinsky trial. Sent warning letter to JFK about Soviet assassins, November 1963.

MILTEER, JOSEPH: National States Rights Party leader. Discussed plan to kill JFK with FBI informant, November 1963.

MURCHISON, CLINT, SR.: Millionaire Texas oilman involved with Hunt family, Mob figures, Bobby Baker scandal.

OBERLANDER, THEODOR: German leader of Ukrainian Nightingales, World War II. West German minister of refugee affairs, 1953–60. Associate of Charles Willoughby.

OLIVER, REVILO: Professor at University of Illinois. John Birch Society spokesman. Knew Carlos Bringuier.

PICHEL, THOUROT: Leader of Shickshinny Knights of Malta. Nazi sympathizer. Associate of Charles Willoughby.

*RAIKIN, SPAS T.: Secretary-general of American Friends, Anti-Bolshevik Nations. Met Oswalds at boat in 1962.

*ROTHERMEL, PAUL, JR.: Security chief for H. L. Hunt, 1957–69.

SCHMIDT, LARRIE: Founder of Conservatism-U.S.A. May have been involved with his brother Bob and Oswald in Walker shooting.

STETZKO, YAROSLAW: Founder of Anti-Bolshevik Nations.

THURMOND, STROM: South Carolina senator. Strong supporter of ultraright causes.

*WEISSMAN, BERNARD: Associate of Larrie Schmidt. Signer of black-bordered anti-Kennedy ad.

Organized-crime figures and associates:

DAVIDSON, I. IRVING: Washington lobbyist. Involved in Haitian deals. Friend of Carlos Marcello.

GIANCANA, SAM: Boss of Chicago Mob. Involved in CIA plots against Castro.

HOFFA, JIMMY: Teamsters union leader. Alleged to have been involved in JFK conspiracy.

*MAHEU, ROBERT: Howard Hughes aide. CIA liaison to organized crime in anti-Castro plots.

MARCELLO, CARLOS: Boss of New Orleans Mob. Associated with Oswald's uncle, David Ferrie, Guy Banister.

MARTINO, JOHN: Mob/CIA affiliate. Allegedly told business associate how Oswald was set up by anti-Castroites.

MERTZ, MICHAEL: French drug trafficker. Allegedly involved with Trafficante. May have been expelled from Dallas on day of assassination.

RAGANO, FRANK: Lawyer for Hoffa and Trafficante. Believes they were involved in JFK assassination conspiracy.

RUBY, JACK: Murdered Oswald in basement of Dallas police headquarters, November 24, 1963.

TRAFFICANTE, SANTOS, JR.: Tampa-based Mob boss. Involved in CIA plots against Castro. Alleged to have made threat against JFK in September 1962.

Government officials and investigators:

*ATTWOOD, WILLIAM: JFK representative at United Nations. Involved in negotiations to reestablish U.S. relations with Cuba.

BAKER, BOBBY: Protégé of LBJ. Forced to resign in Mob-connected scandal, October 1963.

*EDWARDS, REPRESENTATIVE DONALD: Chairman of House Judiciary Committee on Civil and Constitutional Rights. Recipient of 1975–76 correspondence from Nagell.

*ELLSWORTH, FRANK: Alcohol, Tobacco, and Firearms agent in Dallas. Revealed existence of Oswald look-alike.

*FONZI, GAETON: Miami-based investigator for House Assassinations Committee.

*GARRISON, JIM: New Orleans District Attorney who investigated JFK assassination, 1966–69. Met with Nagell twice in New York, 1968.

*GELBER, SEYMOUR: Miami judge who investigated Joseph Milteer threat against JFK.

JAWORSKI, LEON: Warren Commission counsel, trustee of CIA front operation, LBJ friend, Watergate special prosecutor.

JOHNSON, LYNDON B.: Succeeded JFK as president. Told associates in 1967 he believed there had been a conspiracy to assassinate JFK.

KATZENBACH, NICHOLAS: Deputy attorney general. Sought immediately to portray Oswald as lone assassin.

LODGE, HENRY CABOT: U.S. ambassador to South Vietnam, 1963.

*LOPEZ, ED: Investigator for House Assassinations Committee. Wrote still-classified report on CIA and Mexico City.

*MANN, THOMAS: U.S. ambassador to Mexico, 1961–63. Said Hoover stopped him from investigating assassination.

RANKIN, J. LEE: Staff counsel to the Warren Commission, 1964.

RUSSELL, SENATOR RICHARD B.: Warren Commission member. Chairman of CIA oversight committee. Recipient of correspondence from Nagell in 1967.

WARREN, EARL: Chief justice, U.S. Supreme Court. In charge of Warren Commission.

Journalists and authors:

ANDERSON, JACK: Syndicated Washington columnist. In 1967 broke first story on CIA-Mob plots to assassinate Castro.

BARRON, JOHN: Friend of Winston Scott. Author of *KGB*.

*EPSTEIN, EDWARD JAY: Author of books on Oswald, James Angleton, and counterintelligence.

*FITZGERALD, FRANCES: Pulitzer Prize-winning author. Desmond FitzGerald's daughter.

*GOLZ, EARL: Dallas reporter who uncovered many new leads about conspiracy to assassinate JFK.

*HUDKINS, LONNIE: With *Houston Post,* 1963. Alleged Oswald to have been informant for FBI.

ISAACS, HAROLD R.: Far Eastern correspondent, 1930s–40s. Center for International Studies, MIT. Associate of Oswald's cousin Marilyn Murret.

LUCE, CLARE BOOTHE: Wife of *Time-Life* publisher. Member of Committe to Free Cuba. Disseminated information from anti-Castro exiles after assassination.

LUCEY, THOMAS C.: Ex-CIC officer. Wrote article about Nagell for Overseas *Family,* 1969.

JACKSON, C. D.: Publisher of *Life* magazine. Ex-CIA official. Bought the Zapruder film of the assassination.

MCMILLAN, PRISCILLA: Journalist who interviewed Oswald in Moscow. Later wrote Marina Oswald's biography.

*MARKS, JOHN: Wrote book about CIA mind-control program.

*NOYES, PETER: TV newsman in Los Angeles. Did research into Hunt oil family. Acquainted with Robert Clayton Buick.

OLTMANS, WILLEM: Dutch journalist who "befriended" Geroge de Mohrenschildt in 1960s.

*O'TOOLE, GEORGE: Author of *The Assassination Tapes.* Ex-CIA official. Student of Dr. Chikao Fujisawa, 1959–60.

*SAWYER, FORREST: ABC-TV *Nightline* correspondent who received access to KGB files on Oswald, 1991.

STUCKEY, WILLIAM: Set up WDSU radio debate with Oswald. Provided transcripts to FBI.

*TRENTO, JOSEPH: Investigated Paisley case, James Angelton.

*TURNER, WILLIAM: Ex-FBI agent. Author of books on right wing and Cuban exiles. First brought Nagell story to national attention.

Assassination researchers:

*FENSTERWALD, BERNARD, JR.: Prominent Washington, D.C., attorney for clients including James McCord, James Earl Ray, John Paisley, and Richard Case Nagell. Founder of private Committee to Investigate Assassinations, and the Assassination Archives Research Center.

*FERRELL, MARY: Assassination researcher in Dallas. Discovered CIA document on French mercenary Jean Souetre.

*FORD, ART: Did research for "Lincoln Lawrence" book about possible mind control of Oswald/Ruby.

*HARRIS, JONES: Political researcher. Met with Nagell in 1968.

*JONES, PENN: Dallas researcher who received Oswald's "Dear Mr. Hunt" letter from Mexico City.

*POPKIN, RICHARD: Assassination researcher who met with Nagell in 1975 and brought Nagell to the author's attention.

*SHAW, GARY: Dallas researcher. Conducted first interviews with Colonel William Bishop.

*WEISBERG, HAROLD: Obtained declassification of numerous documents by government under Freedom of Information Act suits.

*WOOD, WILLIAM: Staff assistant to Jim Garrison. Ex-CIA agent.

Miscellaneous personages:

*ALDERSON, LAWRENCE: Interviewed by FBI about French OAS captain Jean Souetre's possible role in assassination.

CHARLES, CLEMARD: Haitian associate of George de Mohrenschildt.

LE CAVELIER, GILBERT: Investigated "French connection" for attorney Fensterwald.

VON KLEIST, RICARD: Provided information to attorney Fensterwald about Nagell.

Organizations and Acronyms

AARC—Assassination Archives Research Center
ABC—Alcoholic Beverage Control (Department of)
ABCMR—Army Board for Correction of Military Records
Alpha 66—Cuban exile organization
ATF—Alcohol, Tobacco, and Firearms (federal agency)
BND—West German intelligence
CI—counter intelligence
CIA—Central Intelligence Agency
CIC—(Army) Counter Intelligence Corps
COINTELPRO—FBI operation against "subversive" groups
CORE—Congress of Racial Equality (civil rights group)
CP-U.S.A.—Communist Party, U.S.A.
CRC—Cuban Revolutionary Council (exile group)
CRO—Cabinet Research Office (Japanese CIA equivalent)
DGI—Cuban intelligence (post-1963)

DIA—Defense Intelligence Agency
DRE—Student Revolutionary Directorate (Cuban exile group)
FBI—Federal Bureau of Investigation
FOI—Field Operations Intelligence
FOIA—Freedom of Information Act
FPCC—Fair Play for Cuba Committee
G-2—Army Intelligence
G-2, Cuban—Cuban intelligence
GRU—Soviet Military Intelligence
HID—Headquarters Intelligence Division (South Korean Intelligence agency)
HUAC—House Un-American Activities Committee
INS—Immigration and Naturalization Service
JCS—Jaggers-Chiles-Stovall
JURE—Junta Revolucionaria (Cuban exile group)
KGB—Soviet intelligence agency
KKK—Ku Klux Klan
MI—Military Intelligence
MK-ULTRA—CIA mind-control program
MRP—Movimiento Revolucionario del Pueblo (Cuban exile group)
NSRP—National States' Rights Party (extremist group)
OAS—French Secret Army Organization
ONI—Office of Naval Intelligence
ROK—Republic of Korea
SWP—Socialist Workers Party
USSR—Soviet Union

Chapter One

The Man Who Got Himself Arrested

Late on the afternoon of September 20, 1963, in the West Texas city of El Paso, a man parked his yellow- and cream-colored Ford Fairlane in an alley between Oregon and El Paso streets. He opened his trunk and took out a .45 Colt automatic pistol, tucking it inside his belt. He was tall and rangy, well dressed in a blue suit, white shirt, and red tie. He walked over to a nearby post office and took five crisp hundred-dollar bills from his pocket. Folding them inside a piece of paper, he slipped the package into an envelope and mailed it to an address in Mexico City.

At the counter, he registered another letter to an official of the Central Intelligence Agency. He carefully placed the receipt in his wallet and, momentarily scrutinizing the circular-shaped ceiling, placed his hand on his pistol. Then, fearing a ricochet that might injure one of the customers, he changed his mind.

It was still a sweltering ninety-one degrees as the man walked across the street toward an old gray-stone building with a facade of roman columns and with eagles above the doors. His mind raced; he was being followed, of this he was certain. Inside the State National Bank, it was now a half hour before closing time. He observed a young police officer standing guard beside a Treasury Department currency display, chatting with a woman. The man approached a teller's window and politely asked for one hundred dollars in American Express traveler's checks.

But as the teller laid the traveler's checks on the counter, the man made no move to pick them up. Instead, he reached inside his suit jacket, drew the Colt .45, turned, and deliberately aimed two shots into a plaster wall just below the bank's ceiling. Then he returned the revolver to his belt and, as calmly as he had entered, walked out onto the street.

He stopped at the corner, looking back to see a few bank employees staring at him from the doorway. He headed down the alley, got into his car, and, for a moment, simply sat there. As he finally pulled out halfway into the street, another driver was motioning for him to pass when the man saw the young policeman, with gun in hand, looking for him in the traffic. He backed his car up onto the sidewalk. When the policeman came over to his window, he said, "I guess you've got me, I surrender," and raised his hands.

Nervously Jim Bundren put on the handcuffs and marched him back to the bank. As he led his prisoner up some stairs toward a set of offices, the man suddenly turned his head and cried out: "Capitalistic swine!" The policeman frisked him in an upstairs office, finding a mere twenty-seven cents remaining in his pocket.

Bundren examined the contents of his wallet: a California driver's license, some kind of U.S. military certificate. There was also a mimeographed newsletter. It was addressed to Richard Case Nagell from something called the Fair Play for Cuba Committee.

Bundren picked up a telephone. Because a firearm had been discharged inside a federally insured building, the FBI would have jurisdiction. Two El Paso special agents arrived at the bank within ten minutes. When they asked what his intentions had been, Richard Case Nagell refused to respond. Then, as he was being led to a waiting FBI car, he turned to Officer Bundren and said: "Why don't you check my car and get that machine gun out of there?"

There was no machine gun, but in the trunk what Bundren found were a suitcase, two briefcases filled with documents, and a 45-rpm record box. The latter contained a tiny Minolta 16-millimeter camera and a small but complete film development laboratory. Also taken from the car trunk was a dark brown suit jacket bearing the label of a clothing store in Mexico City. Concealed inside the jacket's lining were two tourist cards for entry to Mexico. Bundren turned over all of these items to the waiting FBI agents.

On the way to the El Paso Federal Building for further questioning, Richard Case Nagell issued only one statement to the FBI: "I would rather be arrested than commit murder and treason."[1]

Many years later, Jim Bundren, retired from the police force and teaching a course in criminal justice at an El Paso college, would look back and remember: "I was sitting next to Nagell at one of his preliminary hearings. I don't remember the exact date, but I know it was before the Kennedy assassination. Nagell looked over at me and said, 'You're a pretty good cop, aren't you? You know, if I didn't want you to, you'd never have caught me.'

"I said, 'You really didn't want to rob that bank, did you?'

"He just looked at me for a minute. He's got that look that's unusual, the penetrating eyes, that scar down one side of his face. And he said, 'What makes you say that?'

"I said, 'I saw the shots you fired in the bank. With your Army training and everything, I just felt like maybe it was some kind of a diversionary tactic.'

"Nagell just smiled and said, 'Well, I'm glad you caught me. I really don't want to be in Dallas.'

"I said, 'What do you mean by that?'

" 'You'll see soon enough,' he said."

The man who once arrested Richard Nagell shook his head. "When the assassination happened, I didn't think about it right away, because that was a pretty hectic time. We were all on alert, we had to close off the bridges. If you were an American in Mexico, you didn't come back, and if you were in the United States, you didn't go across. Then a few days later, after Lee Harvey Oswald was killed, what Nagell said came back to me. I thought, this had to be what he was talking about. How the hell would he have previous knowledge of it? How would he know what was coming down in Dallas?

"I talked to an FBI agent here about it, but a lot of this was just QT— 'Not at liberty to discuss it.' I was just a young cop, there was nothing I could do. I just feel Richard Nagell knew a lot more about the assassination than he let on, or that the government let on. It's bothered me ever since."

A Meeting in Los Angeles

A West L.A. bar, 1978: The man who fired two shots in a bank is sitting at a corner table, his back to the other customers. He is tall and thin, a little over six-foot-two, slightly stoop-shouldered when he walks. As a young man, he must have been quite handsome; the resemblance to the actor Laurence Harvey remains striking. He is in his late forties now, with a receding hairline and sideburns that in contrast seem too long and rather out of place. Something else is odd about his face. The first impression is one of gauntness. But a closer look reveals an indentation that begins at the skull just above his right eye, tracing a hollowed path from forehead to cheekbone and ending in a deep scar. Apparently because of this, his right eye does not track with his left. To compensate, he must focus hard—and he is not someone for whom such directness comes easily. So even as he sits directly across the table from me, there is a distance about him—a kind of disembodied distance, like someone who is constantly looking over his shoulder.

It is a hot day in L.A. Richard Case Nagell is wearing a light tan suit with a necktie. "I hate neckties," he says, tugging at the knot at his neck but leaving it secured, "but I had to see some people." His long hands move in quick, furtive gestures, reaching to shake a cigarette from a pack of Salems. He lifts a Heineken beer to his lips, takes a swallow, sets the bottle down, lights the cigarette, inhales, reaches again for his drink. Each motion seems anxious for the next. Yet, at the same time, each is achieved with a perfectionist's nervous precision.

One beer passes. At the mention of his two children, now gone off on their own, Nagell shakes his head. It was in part because of them that he had stayed largely silent these past fifteen years, carrying inside himself the secrets of what he alone knew about certain events of that autumn of 1963. Once, Richard Case Nagell might conceivably have changed the course of history.

"I don't think about it much, to tell you the truth," he says unconvincingly. "Sometimes, though, I get thinking and I can't go to sleep. Thinking what I could have done, the mistakes that could have been handled differently. I was young. So idealistic. How could I have been like that? But I was realistic, too. I didn't believe in utopias. I had my own beliefs, my own feelings."

He pauses, then adds: "For what?! I'd really like to cash in my chips, go someplace where nobody knows me, and start over. I'd like to forget everything, get away from it all. You know that song that's on the jukebox now? 'Wasting my life away with margaritas.' That really sums up my situation."

Nagell averts his gaze and stares blankly across some private space, a terrain so inviolable that an observer feels to be an intruder. "I look back now at how goddamned stupid I was," he continues. "Everybody was a double-crosser. Is there any justice? Any honor? You should realize that everybody looks out for themselves in the end. They call it 'plausible denial.' I'll tell you this, I didn't have to go to prison. Four and a half years out of my life. Now I've been dismissed as a psycho.

"So suppose I died tomorrow. Would I go down in history as an information broker? Or as a traitor to both sides? I'm always left feeling someone still misunderstands, someone will say, 'But who were you *really* working for?' That hurts. That does hurt.

"Maybe I want people to say years hence, 'Yeah, I knew that guy and he was not like that, he didn't play both ends against the middle.' I'm not a mercenary, believe me. There are some things more important than money. Sure, I'm set. I have my little deals. But a guy likes to be in a situation where he can be honest with people. I just want to be able to say, I'm Richard Case Nagell, take me or leave me. It's still like being always undercover, and it's a drag. Maybe it's my pride. The commodity of pride . . ."

His voice trails off. He lights another smoke. "I was in a quandary in September '63. I didn't know what to do. There are a lot of people I'm still ticked off at. Somebody tells me, who've you got to blame but yourself? Well, sure, I screwed up, man. I know that now. What did I accomplish? Not a goddamned thing.

"So I'm still hanging in there, with no guarantee, only this faith that there've got to be some people in this world who won't just let me fade away."

News of the Day

I am not alone in my conviction that Richard Case Nagell holds a very big skeleton key that could open the door on who was really behind the death of our thirty-fifth president. The late Bernard Fensterwald, Jr., a prominent Washington, D.C., attorney and founder of the Assassination Archives Research Center, served for a time as Nagell's attorney. "Despite the fact that he was ignored by both the Warren Commission and the House Assassinations Committee," Fensterwald believed, "Nagell is probably the only vital individual who knew the details of the assassination and is still alive."[2] Jim Garrison, the former New Orleans district attorney whose 1967 investigation was among the first to raise the specter of a conspiracy, said simply: "Richard Nagell is the most important witness there is."[3]

Local citizens seeing the banner headline of September 21, 1963—"VETERAN TRIES DARING BANK HOLDUP"—on page one of the *El Paso Times* had, of course, not a clue to such a reality. The newspaper gave the impression, since it had no reason to imagine otherwise, that the thirty-three-year-old "battle-scarred Korean War hero" for some reason went around the bend and, as he would eventually be charged, was attempting to rob the bank. Still, even what was written about Nagell on the morning after the incident must have seemed mysterious to a careful reader.

Detectives and FBI agents going through the suspect's suitcase found photostatic copies of numerous certificates and commendations showing he had acquired an outstanding military record in 11 years of service with the U.S. Army in Korea. A photostat showed he had been honorably discharged from the Army at Ft. Dix, N.J., October 1959 with the rank of Captain.

Other military papers found in Nagell's suitcase showed he had been awarded the Purple Heart three times for wounds received in battle with the enemy in Korea. Other papers also disclosed he had been awarded the Bronze Star for meritorious and outstanding service in Korea. . . .

Speaking to FBI agents and other officers Nagell admitted he had entered the Army as a buck private and was in line for promotion to major when he was given his honorable discharge. He told agents he spoke Russian, Japanese and Spanish fluently.

His army papers disclosed Nagell had graduated with honors from the Army Military Intelligence School, from a special leader's course, and had served in the counter intelligence corps (CIC). He had records showing he had been given top secret security clearance on September 22, 1950.

In one of his commendation certificates was a notation that Nagell was a 'perennial calm and level headed officer of superior intelligence.' . . .

A follow-up article of September 26 described the El Paso U.S. attorney's "preliminary investigation" into Nagell. The newspaper noted "that since his discharge he had visited several FBI offices offering 'highly secret' counterintelligence information. . . ."

Behind closed doors, FBI agents were surely aware that they had a most unusual prisoner on their hands, for, among Nagell's belongings when arrested, there were two small brown spiral notebooks. Each was filled with names, addresses, dates, and meeting places. One of these is either lost, or still in the possession of the FBI. The other was returned eleven years later at the request of Fensterwald, who was then representing Nagell in a lawsuit filed with the U.S. Court of Claims, in which Nagell was seeking full disability compensation from the Pentagon.

Before returning the notebook to Nagell, Fensterwald made photocopies and passed one along to assassination researcher Richard Popkin. One of the early critics of the Warren Commission's conclusion that Oswald had acted alone, Popkin had written a 1966 book, *The Second Oswald.* It was built around the intriguing premise that Oswald was impersonated by someone in the weeks leading up to the assassination, particularly at rifle ranges, as a means of making his presence known as a sharpshooter—which in reality Oswald was not. Also a well-known professor of philosophy and author of *The History of Skepticism,* Popkin, in 1975, was among a handful of citizen investigators who had managed to touch base with Nagell. They had met once, and communicated several times by telephone. That June, I learned that Popkin was prepared to go public with some vital information, and *The Village Voice* sent me to San Diego to find out what he had unearthed.[4]

The Professor's Trove

Inside the Popkin household, a motley collection of armchair detectives were gathered around the bearded professor at a dining-room table. Busily dashing off telegrams to high officials in Washington ("Dear President Ford—I know who killed JFK," one began), Popkin arrived at *two* divergent scenarios for what happened on November 22, 1963. One revolved around a young Puerto Rican named Luis Castillo, arrested in the Philippines in 1967 for allegedly planning to assassinate President Ferdinand Marcos. Castillo was placed under hypnosis by a Filipino government specialist in an effort to discover his motivation. Suddenly, in deep trance, he confessed to being a programmed "robot gunman" in Dallas. Although word was starting to seep out about the CIA's MK-ULTRA program, an intelligence operation that utilized drugs and other "mind-control" techniques on unwitting victims, this notion was still a bit far out for most people to take seriously in 1975.

Popkin's second hypothesis concerned Richard Case Nagell. Popkin said Nagell was an ex-CIA man who had served four and a half years in prison on a trumped-up charge of attempted bank robbery. According to Popkin, Nagell was working as a "double agent" for the CIA and the Soviet Union's KGB when he had somehow "penetrated" an assassination plot against President Kennedy. He had sent a warning letter to the FBI just before coming in from the cold by shooting two holes into the wall of a bank. Popkin first heard about him via a letter in which Nagell wrote that there was something to his theory about an Oswald look-alike used by the conspirators to spread confusion.

To the assemblage of media representatives who also descended on the Popkin home that summer (including *Newsday,* CBS News, and *Rolling*

Stone), it all came to seem too bizarre for credibility. None of them ended up airing Popkin's "revelations." At the time, though I made a trip at his behest to find out more about Luis Castillo, I didn't know what to make of it all, either. Several months passed before I gave more than cursory attention to a stack of photocopied material I'd brought back from Professor Popkin's archives. Then, one afternoon, I began leafing through his "Nagell" file.

The first document I saw was a photocopy of Nagell's notebook, seized by the FBI upon his arrest in September 1963. Accompanying it was the 1974 correspondence between attorney Fensterwald and the FBI, including a list of thirty-one items the FBI had apparently "discovered" in its Nagell file in El Paso. "They said they are pleased to return it to you and could not understand why it had not been returned earlier," Fensterwald wrote to Nagell. The itemized list itself contained some curious notations:

> Typewritten listing of 30 items starting with #1 "Principles of USA Intelligence" and ending with #30 "Weapons."
> Slip of notebook paper containing three columns of numbers written in red.
> What appears to be a note on a slip of paper taken from a tablet addressed to Mr. Nagell signed Gene Tuggey requesting that he contact Mr. Tuggey or Mr. Griffin, FBI, their telephone number HU 3-3551.

Apparently, then, Nagell was in touch with the FBI before his arrest in El Paso. In his notebook were lists of theaters and restaurants alongside specific dates and times—indicators of rendezvous points, either for the drop-off and pickup of information or for clandestine contacts. There was a notation about the scrambling of words in a reference book (in this case, the 1963 *Information Please Almanac)*—a well-known method of spy code. Then there were the names: two Soviet officials, six individuals under the heading *"C.I.A."* A Los Angeles post office box for the Fair Play for Cuba Committee was listed. So was this:

C.E. MEXICO D.F.
PHONE:
11-28-47

The contents of the address book found among Lee Harvey Oswald's effects after his arrest bore a number of similarities to Nagell's own notebook—Soviet officials, the Fair Play for Cuba Committee, and, atop one page:

> Mexico City
> Consulada de Cuba
> Zamora Y F Marquez
> 11-28-47
> Sylvia Duran[5]

Unless the FBI was totally incompetent, which I knew they were not, Nagell's notebook must have been pored over with a fine-tooth comb.[6] Not that its El Paso field office would necessarily have made any connection between Nagell and Oswald, but surely the FBI would have seen in September 1963 that it had some kind of intelligence operative on its hands. Indeed, it appeared that Nagell was carrying paraphernalia that he *wanted* to be seen by the FBI. He was certainly not concealing his many connections.

Also in Popkin's file was an FBI report he had discovered buried in the National Archives in Washington, D.C. It was dated December 20, 1963, and read:

> RICHARD CASE NAGELL incarcerated in the El Paso County Jail on a complaint charging him with Bank Robbery advised that "For the record he would like to say that his association with OSWALD (meaning LEE HARVEY OSWALD) was purely social and that he had met him in Mexico City and in Texas."
>
> NAGELL stated he decided to "clear the record up" since his fingerprints were taken on December 12, 1963 by Special Agents WHITE and BOYCE.
>
> Although questioned as to where and when his contacts with OSWALD were made, he refused to comment further and said he had nothing more to say.[7]

It was known to the Warren Commission that Oswald traveled to Mexico City in late September 1963, where he visited the Cuban and Soviet embassies. By that point, however, Nagell had already been arrested in El Paso. So he would have to be describing an earlier meeting in Mexico, a visit that did not appear on the historical record.

From the National Archives, too, there was a handwritten letter dated March 20, 1964, addressed to J. Lee Rankin, chief counsel for the Warren Commission:

> Dear Mr. Rankin,
> Has the commission been advised that I informed the Federal Bureau of Investigation in September 1963 that an attempt might be made to assassinate President Kennedy? Was the commission advised that the day

before Mr. Kennedy visited Dallas I initiated a request through jail authority to the F.B.I., asking them to contact the Secret Service Division in
order to inform such agency of the same information, when it became
apparent to me that the F.B.I. believed my revelation to be mendacious?

Richard C. Nagell
El Paso County Jail—El Paso, Texas[8]

Yet the *Warren Commission Report* failed to mention Nagell; his name
did not even appear in any of the twenty-six published volumes of documents pertaining to the commission's investigation.

Finally, among the Popkin papers was a letter written by Nagell from
prison early in 1967 to U.S. Senator Richard B. Russell (no relation to
author) of Georgia. A Warren Commission member and chairman of a
congressional committee assigned to oversee CIA activities, Russell had
eventually expressed his dissatisfaction with the Warren panel's conclusions. In this letter, Nagell wrote the senator:

Mr. Oswald and his activities came under my scrutiny during 1962 and
1963. My inquiries, coupled with data furnished me by reliable sources,
ascertained the following:

Mr. Oswald had no significant connection with the Fair Play for Cuba
Committee. He had no significant contact or relationship with so-called
pro-Castro elements, though he was led to believe he had such. He maintained no significant association with any Marxist-oriented group or
movement. He was not affiliated with a racist group or movement. He
was not an agent or informant, in the generally accepted sense of the
words, for any investigative, police, or intelligence agency, domestic or
foreign. He was involved in a conspiracy to murder the former Chief
Executive during the latter part of September, 1963. This conspiracy was
neither Communist inspired nor was it instigated by any foreign government or organization or individual representative of any foreign government. . . .[9]

"In the generally accepted sense of the words." What did that mean?
Oswald. He was an enigma to end all enigmas. The trail of his own short
life led in so many directions that pursuit of it led the hunter into a
bewildering forest from which there seemed no exit. As a teenager in New
Orleans during the mid-1950s, Oswald had a dual fascination—his older
brother's Marine Corps training manual, and the works of Karl Marx. His
favorite TV program was *I Led Three Lives*. Enlisting in the Marines, he
served as a radar operator at the Atsugi Naval Air Base in Tokyo, a takeoff point for the CIA's top-secret U-2 spy planes. In the fall of 1959,
shortly after receiving his military discharge, he apparently defected to the
Soviet Union. Living there for two and a half years, he married a Russian

woman and then repatriated to Texas, where members of the ultraconservative "White Russian" community took Lee and Marina Oswald under their wing. He found work at a photo shop that did classified work for the Army Map Service while he simultaneously corresponded feverishly with American Communist and Socialist organizations. He adopted aliases, mail-ordered for a rifle, and allegedly shot at the fanatically right-wing General Edwin Walker. Moving to New Orleans, Oswald was seen in the company of rabid anti-Castroites, at the same time assuming a highly visible stance as a Castro supporter. It seems only fitting that photographs of "Oswald" on his trip to Mexico City, sent by the CIA immediately after the assassination to the FBI and Dallas police, were of the wrong man.

The FBI, the CIA, the State Department, Army and Naval Intelligence, the New Orleans police, the Soviet KGB, Cuban G-2 intelligence—all these agencies had files on Lee Harvey Oswald well before November 22, 1963. Yet none of them has ever acknowledged conceiving of him as any kind of threat. J. Edgar Hoover's FBI, which staked its reputation on unveiling the slightest hint of subversion, had not even seen fit to include Oswald among the some thirty-two thousand individuals on its "Security Index."[10] What was wrong with this picture? Had Oswald really been working for, or been used by, one or more of those organizations? Or did anyone know to whose fiddle Oswald really danced?

Apparently Richard Case Nagell was someone who might be able to shed considerable light on those questions. And I knew that I had to find out more about him. Not long afterward, bearing a residence address that Popkin had provided, I would track him down in the L.A. suburb of Manhattan Beach.

The Missing Link

For many years, I looked for a "smoking gun," some official document that might lend credence to Nagell's revelations. Most assassination researchers considered him "kooky." I did not really blame them for this. Until I saw the notebook and other papers that had come into Popkin's possession, and then managed to meet Nagell, I, too, considered the notion pretty implausible that an Oswald-linked spy had taken himself out of the picture by shooting up a bank. And the federal government had made an effort, during the course of Nagell's imprisonment in the 1960s, to portray him as either a criminal or a lunatic. Doubt had been cast on his mental stability, even by his own lawyers. For example, they had brought evidence to the fore that Nagell had suffered "organic brain damage" as the sole survivor in the 1954 crash of a B-25 bomber plane.

So I needed something beyond the belief of Popkin, Fensterwald, Garrison, and myself that Nagell was indeed someone worthy of serious attention. Finally, in May 1986, Nagell mailed me a copy of "Page 2 of 4" from a Military Intelligence "Agent Report" dated May 2, 1969. Nagell said it had been released under a Freedom of Information Act request from his dossier maintained in the Pentagon's Intelligence Records Repository. He said it had been prepared by Special Agent Thomas J. Hench of the 766th Military Intelligence Department. Headed "NAGELL, Richard Case" and listing his birth date and birthplace, the report read as follows:

> During the period from August 1962 to October 1963, SUBJECT was intermittently employed as an informant and/or investigator for the Central Intelligence Agency (CIA). In April 1963, SUBJECT conducted an inquiry concerning the marital status of Marina Oswald and her reported desire to return to the USSR. During July, August, September, and on one occasion prior to this, SUBJECT conducted an inquiry into the activities of Lee Harvey Oswald, and the allegation that he had established a Fair Play For Cuba Committee in New Orleans, Louisiana. SUBJECT stated that while working for the CIA, HE had operated in Mexico, Florida, Louisiana, Texas, California, Puerto Rico, and New York. HE was primarily concerned with investigating activities of Anti-Castro organizations and their personnel in the United States and Mexico. On 20 September 1963, SUBJECT was arrested in El Paso, Texas on the charge of entering a Federal bank with the intent to commit a felony. In May 1964 and September 1966, SUBJECT was twice tried and twice convicted on this charge. The conviction of the May 1964 trial had been subsequently reversed, thus the reason for the second trial. SUBJECT was sentenced to a maximum of ten years imprisonment, but was released after four and one-half years. SUBJECT claimed that HIS conviction and subsequent incarceration was a result, not of HIS supposed intent to commit a felony, but rather as a result of HIS knowledge of Lee Harvey Oswald and the assassination of President Kennedy.

What was so striking about this report was that, unlike any other government file I had seen about him, it stated directly that Nagell had been monitoring the activities of Oswald, his wife, and "Anti-Castro organizations" on behalf of the CIA. The beginning sentences of the report were not phrased in a manner attributable to Nagell. In other words, they did not say "SUBJECT alleged" or "claimed" or "stated"; the facts about Nagell were simply stated as facts. Clearly, the CIA would have contained such information about Nagell in its own files, perhaps having passed it along at some point to the Pentagon. Or the Pentagon may have been aware of it all from the outset, given the fact that Nagell had an eleven-year career (1948–59) in the U.S. Army and its Military Intelligence branch.

Never, in the course of either the Warren Commission, Garrison, or the House Assassinations Committee investigations, had there ever surfaced any direct verification that the CIA was following Oswald's trail in the months prior to the assassination. At last, here it was.

Nagell's Warning to the FBI

Why was Richard Nagell never called to testify before the Warren Commission (1964), which supported the FBI's thesis of a lone, crazed gunman? Why was he never interviewed by Congress's House Select Committee on Assassinations (1977–79), which later hypothesized a conspiracy fueled by elements of organized crime? He was not unknown to either investigative body. Indeed, he wrote letters to both of them. Was what he might say considered too sensitive for further examination?

I received my first experience of the government's stonewalling about Nagell in the spring of 1976, after he sent me copies of some correspondence with U.S. Representative Don Edwards of California. Edwards was the chairman of the House Judiciary Subcommittee on Civil and Constitutional Rights. Nagell had learned that the subcommittee was looking into circumstances surrounding the FBI's destruction, in the immediate aftermath of the assassination, of a note written by Oswald that November to Dallas FBI agent James P. Hosty, Jr. For over a year in 1962–63, Hosty had been keeping occasional tabs on Oswald and his wife, Marina.

On October 23, 1975, Nagell wrote a letter to Edwards in which he concluded: "Now, if you really want to open up a can of worms, direct the FBI to disclose the results of its 'exhaustive internal inquiry' into the circumstances surrounding the destruction of a registered letter that I dispatched to FBI director J. Edgar Hoover in September 1963, informing him of a conspiracy involving Oswald and two Cuban refugees to assassinate President Kennedy." Edwards personally wrote Nagell back six days later, thanking him for his letter and adding: "The Subcommittee would appreciate any further details you might have in your possession concerning the registered letter you state was dispatched to Director Hoover in September, 1963."

Then, on November 21, 1975, Nagell responded by registered mail:

Dear Mr. Chairman:

In response to your letter of October 29, 1975, I am enclosing herewith an affidavit, which gives further details concerning the registered letter that "I state" was dispatched to FBI Director Hoover in September 1963. Until the Bureau makes public its disclaimer regarding what I have stated therein, I have nothing further to say on the subject to your Subcommittee. Rest assured, however, that I possess the capability of substantiating and in most instances proving what I have stated.

You may also rest assured that this entire affair—including the facts about my unjust imprisonment for over four years at the hands of a corrupt judicial system—will not be covered up or whitewashed forever, not by the FBI, the CIA, the Department of Justice or, for that matter, the House Subcommittee on Civil and Constitutional Rights. . . .

The affidavit, bearing the official seal of a notary public in Los Angeles County, reads as follows:

AFFIDAVIT

I, Richard C. Nagell, being first sworn, depose and say:

In September 1963, the exact date of which I am capable of verifying, I dispatched a letter via registered mail addressed to "Mr. John E. Hoover, Director, Federal Bureau of Investigation, United States Department of Justice, Washington 25, D.C." The envelope in which this letter was enclosed bore the same address, in addition to the return address "Joseph Kramer, Apdo. Postal 88-Bis, Mexico, D.F., Mexico," and was mailed within the United States. The letter was neatly typewritten and composed in the style and format used by operational personnel of the Central Intelligence Agency in writing their reports; that is, it was clear and concise, with the names of persons and organizations typed in caps.

In the aforesaid letter, I advised Mr. Hoover of a conspiracy (although I did not use the word "conspiracy") involving Lee Harvey Oswald "to murder the Chief Executive of the United States, (President) John F. Kennedy." I indicated that the attempt would take place "during the latter part of September (1963), probably on the 26th, 27th, 28th or 29th," presumably at Washington, D.C. I furnished a complete and accurate physical description of Mr. Oswald, listing his true name, two of his aliases, his residence address and other pertinent facts about him. I disclosed sufficient data about the conspiracy (citing an overt act which constituted a violation of federal law) to warrant an immediate investigation if not the arrest of Mr. Oswald. I revealed something about myself which incriminated me on another matter. I stated "by the time you receive this letter, I shall have departed the USA for good." I signed the letter with the name "Joseph Kramer," an alias of a known Communist (Soviet) agent then residing in Canada, and also an alias that I had used during my meetings with two FBI agents in January 1963 at Miami, Florida, who in turn used the name "The Tacos."

I am willing to undergo a polygraph examination relative to any and all statements made herein.

Nagell had already told me bits and pieces about his warning letter to Hoover, but the notarized affidavit filled in many more details. And I was sure it would spark congressional interest in Nagell. On April 26, 1976, I phoned Congressman Edwards, who was himself a former FBI agent, to ask him if his subcommittee had received and was following up on the information Nagell had supplied. At first, Edwards didn't remember any such correspondence. "You know, we get just thousands of letters on that, in addition to abortion and busing," he replied. "However, I'm going to call you right back and see if we got it and what we did with it. I'll check my files."

About an hour later, the congressman did call me back. "Yes," he said, "we got a letter from Mr. Nagell dated October 23, 1975. Then we immediately, of course, asked the FBI about it. Now I have a letter here from Clarence Kelley." Kelley had been named director of the FBI in 1973, and Edwards read me his response. Kelley wrote: "For your information, Mr. Nagell's allegation is not new to the FBI. It has been looked into on several occasions over the years since the assassination of President Kennedy. No record has ever been found of receipt of his claimed September 1963 letter."

What about Nagell's follow-up affidavit? I asked. Didn't the congressman receive a second registered package, dated November 21? "Nagell hasn't sent anything more to us, no," Edwards said. "I'm almost certain there was just the one letter, but the lawyer who's in charge of doing our FBI work is ill today and I'll ask him tomorrow and will let you know."

Since Nagell had already sent me a photocopy of the return receipt for his second, registered mailing to Edwards, the congressman's office must have received it. But Edwards never called me again. There the matter rested, although both the Senate Intelligence Committee and the House Assassinations Committee also would take up the question of why the FBI had destroyed Oswald's note to Agent Hosty. Congress would question, as well, the Pentagon's "routine" destruction of a Military Intelligence file that it admittedly once had on Oswald under his alias of "A. J. Hidell."

When I wrote Nagell to tell him the result of my inquiry with Congressman Edwards, he responded angrily:

If Edwards and his staff can't find my letter of 11/21/75 (which accompanied the original copy of my affidavit and a certain 42-page memorandum), this should alert him to other possibilities. Along these lines, FBI

Director Kelley's carefully worded advisement that no record has ever been found of the receipt of my September 1963 letter to FBI Director Hoover shouldn't have been accepted as the last word on the subject, particularly in view of the record of past cover-ups by that agency. Kelley's reply doesn't mean that the letter wasn't sent anymore than it means that the letter wasn't received.

I have the receipts for almost every letter that I've ever sent by registered mail . . . just as I have duplicates of the letters themselves. You can bet on it. And Kelley, Edwards and all the other liars, cheats and double-crossers had better think about that. The fact that I've never revealed the exact date that my September 1963 letter to Hoover was mailed, or the fact that I've never divulged the full contents of that letter, indicates absolutely zilch. The only remaining thing that I have to say on the subject at this point in time is that my 11/21/75 affidavit, and my stated willingness to undergo a polygraph examination, was the last good-faith gesture that I shall ever make to a representative or official of the United States government. (A xerox copy of my affidavit was also sent to Kelley; I never received a response). . . .[11]

The primary focus of this book is what prompted Nagell to write that registered letter to J. Edgar Hoover in September 1963. Despite what he says about having signed the letter with the alias of a "known Communist (Soviet agent)," and despite Lee Harvey Oswald's affiliations with leftist groups, Nagell is adamant that his knowledge was of *"a domestic-inspired, domestic-formulated, and domestic-sponsored conspiracy to assassinate a Chief Executive of the United States."*

In a bank vault in Switzerland, Nagell says there is a "faded Polaroid pic" of himself and Oswald, which Nagell arranged to be taken by a vendor in New Orleans' Jackson Square in September 1963. He has also indicated the existence of an audiotape recording of Oswald, two coconspirators, and Nagell himself, taped surreptitiously by Nagell in late August 1963. If the reader wonders how anyone who knows so much could still be alive, he maintains it is because he carefully stashed these and other items as "life insurance" shortly before his arrest in El Paso. In the event of his demise, Nagell made arrangements for this and more to surface. As will be seen, he was an astute record-keeper.

Summary

From the day of Richard Case Nagell's arrest on September 20, 1963, for firing two shots inside an El Paso bank, an FBI cover-up began. Prior to his action, Nagell had sent a warning letter addressed to FBI director J. Edgar Hoover and a registered letter to the CIA. To the FBI, he revealed a conspiracy to assassinate the president, then scheduled for late September, and provided information on Lee Harvey Oswald and two of his associates.

Whether the FBI's El Paso field office was made aware of Nagell's letter is not known. But Nagell's belongings clearly indicated that he was involved in espionage-related activities. FBI agents were aware that Nagell was a former Military Intelligence officer with a top-secret clearance, in previous contact with the FBI. His notebook listed officials from the CIA and Soviet and Cuban intelligence; he was carrying a leaflet from the Fair Play for Cuba Committee, the same organization with which Oswald was associated.

At a preliminary hearing before the assassination, Nagell let policeman Jim Bundren know that something was about to happen in Dallas. Less than a month after the assassination, Nagell told FBI officials that he had met Oswald in Mexico and Texas. While the Warren Commission was in progress, Nagell wrote to counsel J. Lee Rankin about his efforts to alert proper authorities of a JFK conspiracy. Yet the commission ignored Nagell. Not until 1969 did a Military Intelligence file specifically state that Nagell had been investigating Oswald and his wife, and anti-Castro Cubans, on behalf of the CIA in 1962–63. Even when Nagell sought to communicate with a congressional subcommittee in 1975, his effort again came to naught.

It was left to private citizens Bernard Fensterwald, Jr., Jim Garrison, and Richard Popkin to advance their belief that Richard Nagell was the most important living witness concerning the events of November 22, 1963.

Chapter Two

First Encounters: El Paso/Los Angeles, 1975

En route to Los Angeles to seek out Richard Case Nagell in the autumn of 1975, I first stopped in El Paso looking for additional clues about his September 1963 arrest. I began in the newspaper morgues of the *El Paso Times* and the *El Paso Herald-Post*, which shared a red-brick building downtown. Their early articles described Nagell's being held on $25,000 bond, pleading not guilty to attempted bank robbery, and informing authorities that he did not wish a lawyer to represent him. He was examined by a court-appointed psychiatrist and then came before the court to present a writ of habeas corpus. It was November 4, 1963, when Nagell told federal judge R. E. Thomason: "I had a motive for doing what I did. But my motive was not to hold up the bank. I do not intend to disclose my motive at this time."[1]

Since that was Nagell's first court appearance since shortly after his arrest—and his last court appearance before the assassination—it was also most likely the day when he made his cryptic remark about not wanting to be in Dallas to policeman Jim Bundren.

Under the headline "Says Bank Holdup Try Patriotic," a December 10, 1963, *El Paso Times* story described Nagell's second habeas corpus hearing. "In one petition, dated Dec. 5, he wrote, 'I have always acted from a principle of love for my country and this same principle actuated my conduct on Sept. 20, 1963, however inappropriate or incomprehensible it may appear. God and I, and also the FBI, know that I am not guilty. . . .' "

Then, in a back section of the *El Paso Times,* was a story from January 27, 1964, beneath a three-column headline, "Suspect Says Agents Asked Him About Oswald, Activities Link":

> Richard Case Nagell, charged with attempted bank robbery, said he had been questioned by the FBI and the U.S. Secret Service, regarding alleged subversive activities and also Lee Harvey Oswald, the alleged assassin of President Kennedy.
>
> Nagell made the statement during his arraignment proceeding before U.S. District Judge Homer Thornberry.
>
> Instead of asking for a plea, Fred Morton, assistant U.S. district attorney, made a motion to put Nagell in a federal institution in Springfield, Mo., for psychiatric observation.
>
> Later Morton, Herbert Hoxie, special FBI agent, and George Weisheit, Secret Service agent, would not comment on Nagell's specific allegations.
>
> Weisheit did say he questioned Nagell on a matter at Nagell's request, but Weisheit would not note what the matter concerned.
>
> Nagell's assertions came when he was attempting to have some documents and photographs returned to him.
>
> He said U.S. District Judge R.E. Thomason ordered in December that all of his property be returned to him unless it was evidence in the alleged attempted hold-up of the State National Bank on Sept. 20.
>
> Nagell said he had the articles in his wallet returned but that photographs and documents were held by Morton. He said some of the photographs were of people in a foreign country.
>
> He said the questions about subversive activities have nothing to do with the charge of attempted bank robbery. Nagell said he should be charged with another crime or have the documents and photographs returned.
>
> What the documents and photographs contain is not known. Nagell said they were taken from his person and from his car.
>
> Nagell's testimony added a further air of mystery to his earlier statements. . . .

Nagell's trial did not commence until late that spring, nearly eight months after his arrest. Nobody from the FBI was called to the witness stand by either the defense or the prosecution. In the courthouse files, I found Nagell's testimony of May 5, 1964. The Warren Commission was then in the final phases of its investigation. While there was no mention of Oswald's name in the trial transcript, there were other statements that would later take on great significance for me.

Asked where he had come from before arriving in El Paso, Nagell replied: "I would rather not answer that question, on the grounds that it might tend to incriminate me regarding a matter in which the F.B.I. is very well acquainted with."

Asked to whom he had mailed five hundred dollars from the El Paso post office immediately before entering the bank, Nagell said: "I think that at this time the Federal Bureau of Investigation knows to whom I mailed it but I am not going to state it."

In 1958, Nagell revealed, he had been "loaned" by Military Intelligence to "another intelligence agency" for assignments in Hong Kong, Formosa, Korea, and Japan. That was precisely the period when Oswald had also been stationed in the Far East.

Nagell went on that he had passed through El Paso many times before on his way from Los Angeles to Mexico City. His arrest in the bank, he believed, "would provide a solution however temporary or immediate to a . . . unbearable problem with which I was confronted." Asked about the Colt .45 pistol he fired that afternoon, Nagell said: "I took out this pistol here [indicating], which does not belong to me but the FBI knows who it belongs to."

Then there was this mysterious back-and-forth between the defendant and his court-appointed attorney, Joseph A. Calamia.

DEFENSE: Mr. Nagell, immediately prior to this incident that happened there at the bank, I will ask you whether or not you had the intentions of leaving this—were you going to leave somewhere to travel somewhere?

NAGELL: . . . I was in the process of leaving the United States.

DEFENSE: For what length of time were you leaving?

NAGELL: Permanently. I was planning on going to Mexico City where I would have left Mexico for another destination and I would have gone permanently from this country.

DEFENSE: I see. And did you obtain any traveling document, such as a passport, for that purpose?

NAGELL: Legal or illegal?

DEFENSE: I am referring to a passport right now.

NAGELL: Yes, sir. I had a legal passport and an immunization card which I had had previously, which was still good. Although I will state that

I did not need the passport per se to leave this country because I would have had a visa.

DEFENSE: Wherever you were going you would have been able to gain access to that country?

NAGELL: Without that passport.

DEFENSE: Without that passport, is that what you were going to say?

NAGELL: Without that one [indicating].

DEFENSE: . . . Captain, were you faced with some decision there on September 20th in connection with that proposed trip?

NAGELL: Yes, I was.

DEFENSE: Would you tell us what it was, what was the decision you had to make?

NAGELL: The decision was very simple. If I left the country, I would not be coming back unless I desired to come back and be prosecuted, so it was in my mind that the decision I had to make was either to leave or not to leave, unless I could perhaps make some kind of an excuse not to leave, to satisfy certain individuals. . . .

In further testimony, Nagell continued: "The real reason that I did not want to leave this country at that time was not because of my love for the United States but was because of my children . . . who at that time were quite young. And I will say this, too, that on leaving the country, if I had been allowed to take my children with me, I would have taken them but the circumstances were such at the time that I was told because I was not leaving the country through legal channels I could not take my children with me."

"Pass the witness," said attorney Calamia.[2]

The next day, a jury had convicted Nagell of "entering a federally insured bank with intent to rob." After the verdict, the newspapers reported Nagell leaping to his feet and shouting: "Why weren't the real issues brought out in this court?" As two deputy marshals led him from the courtroom, again he cried out: "They will be sometime!"[3]

Nagell was not sentenced immediately. A month later, court records showed that attorney Calamia filed an appeal based on "crucial evidence newly discovered"—the findings of a neurological specialist at Walter Reed Army Hospital, who had first examined Nagell after the Army captain survived the crash of a military plane in late November 1954. According to Dr. Edwin Weinstein, Nagell suffered from "organic brain damage," which meant that his "judgment and perception of reality was seriously disturbed so that he could not accurately differentiate right from wrong" when he walked into the El Paso bank.[4]

Yet Dr. Weinstein's "evidence" was not "newly discovered." I would later come across FBI files showing that the bureau was in touch with

Weinstein about Nagell back in October 1963. Nagell says he himself mentioned Weinstein to his attorneys several weeks before his trial. Why, then, the delay in bringing him forward until after Nagell's conviction?

Judge Homer Thornberry handed down a ten-year sentence, "with the provision he may be released at any time the U.S. Bureau of Paroles decides"[5]—a provision that, in itself, seemed very odd.

Nagell's conviction was overturned on appeal early in 1966, with a new trial taking place that September. Once again, despite Dr. Weinstein's testimony, Nagell would be convicted and receive a ten-year sentence, with credit given for the three years he had already been incarcerated. Nagell, I observed, did not testify this time in his own defense.[6]

Then, on April 3, 1968, the U.S. Court of Appeals for the Fifth Circuit handed down a second decision. It concluded "that the evidence introduced by the Government is not sufficient to sustain the conviction" and ordered Nagell immediately set free.[7]

Witnesses

The circumstances surrounding *United States* v. *Nagell* seemed bizarre, to say the least. Compiling a list of names from the newspaper files and court records, I sought out some of the people who were involved in his case. This was the first time I interviewed Jim Bundren, who was still active on the police force in 1975 and who didn't know how much he was at liberty to say. A tall, thin, mustached man, Bundren had been named the city's "Officer of the Year" in 1963 for his "capture" of Richard Nagell.

"Nagell wasn't crazy, by no stretch of the imagination," Bundren recalled. "A man insane does not draw up the briefs and writs he filed. He never got disjointed." After some prompting, Bundren added: "Yeah, okay, Oswald's name came up. I can't tell you whether Oswald was mentioned before or after the assassination. I remember Nagell saying something to me about that, and also about this General Walker that Oswald was supposed to have shot at. Nagell mentioned Cuba. He mentioned a lot of things. That's about all I can say."

Others were even more reluctant to talk. Retired jail captain Raymond O'Rourke said only: "I don't want any hard feelings with my retirement. I left down there with all goodwill and I don't want to say anything that might hinder somebody."

At the Federal Building, I waited to speak with Edward J. Murphy, one of several FBI agents who had interrogated Nagell. When Murphy emerged from a meeting, the moment I mentioned Nagell's name a startled look crossed the agent's face. "Well, sir," I asked, "do you remember any mention of a connection between that man and the assassination of President Kennedy?" Murphy's face blanched, and he shook his head rapidly from side to side. "I don't recall anything like that, no. Court records would probably give you as good an insight as anything else." With that, he walked out the office door and disappeared down the corridor.

Juan L. Medina, a jailer in 1963, had moved on to become a bailiff in the City-County Building across the street. He remembered a number of visits to Nagell from both the FBI and the Secret Service. "I think he was getting some checks from the government while he was in jail. He was always walking by himself, back and forth across the floor, thinking. I think there was something in his mind he never did tell anybody."

Fred Morton, the assistant U.S. attorney whom the newspapers said had called for recurring "sanity tests" for Richard Nagell, was by 1975 a successful lawyer in the firm of Calhoun, Morton, and Deason. His wood-paneled office overlooked downtown from the sixteenth floor of the State National Plaza Building. He was a dapper, youthful-looking man who appeared to be in his early forties.

"As long as I was in the case," Morton said with a shrug, "I don't recall any statement by Nagell in any way concerning the assassination. The first I remember hearing this was in some magazine years later. It'll always be a mystery to me as to what the hell he was really doing in the bank that day."

When I asked why he had ordered a "sanity test" for Nagell within a few days after his arrest, Morton raised his eyebrows and said he didn't recall. "Do you recall a notebook or two that the authorities confiscated from Nagell on the day of his arrest?" I continued.

"Yeah, he had a notebook with him, in his belongings. I don't know if it was offered in evidence. The only thing I remember about specifics is that it had the address of that Fair Play for Cuba Committee that Oswald was associated with, from some city in America. I don't know whether they wanted free rum or what."

Morton chuckled at his own joke. I asked if he had ever seen the contents of the notebook. "I think I did, but I don't remember for sure," he replied. "I don't know if anybody gave a damn."

Then the lawyer began to laugh. "When we got to trial, Nagell took the Fifth Amendment when his own lawyer asked him if he was a Communist. Joe Calamia's tactic was to make a wreck out of the guy in the courtroom, try to show that he was crazy. That was his defense, see. Nagell didn't want to assert that defense, Joe did it in spite of him. Joe and I kidded about it since. The guy was really as calm as tea and crumpets. But Joe got him off. It took a long time, but he got him off."

Joseph Calamia had been named by the court to take over Nagell's defense on April 20, 1964, two weeks before the trial began. He replaced another court-appointed attorney, Nagell's fourth. In 1975, Calamia maintained a legal suite high in El Paso's Bassett Tower Building. He was a short, wiry, dark-complexioned man with a brown mustache, who spoke in a near-whisper. And he immediately seemed to be going out of his way to assure me that he had nothing to hide about his former client.

"This man was a real hero in Korea," Calamia said. "A highly decorated soldier. Two Purple Hearts with clusters, wounded several times in battle. This man went through hell in Korea and back. That's why I took such an interest in the case, because I wanted justice done for a real American and war hero. I hated to see him be labeled and branded as a felon. So I stayed with the guy through three years of court appearances. This was prior to the decision that said you were entitled to represent yourself, so the court required a lawyer to sit with you. I was trying to show that Nagell was temporarily insane at the time he went into the bank. Of course, he denied his illness instead of helping his case, but eventually I got him acquitted. It was unbelievable to me that a jury could convict him!"

Calamia did not bat an eye when I asked him about Nagell's notebook. "Oh, they found him with some paraphernalia—Freedom for Cuba or something. Similar to some stuff that guy Oswald had. That's the only similarity I see in these two cases."

There was no evidence that he knew Oswald? "No," Calamia said evenly. Did he ever say he did? I pressed.

"That's a confidential communication," Calamia replied. "I can't do that."

The attorney brought his hands up to his chin and momentarily closed his eyes. When he opened them, he said: "At the trial, can you imagine me defending this man on insanity and the prejudice that existed in the country at that time over the assassination of a president? That was actually an irrelevant matter as far as I saw. Only more prejudice could arise."

What was Calamia trying to tell me? I studied his eyes but could find no sign. "Nagell had a passport for international travel," the lawyer added. "It was returned to him. Now, if you could establish that he was in Mexico City . . ."

Then he stopped and stood up. He had a client to see, he said.

Some years later, when I sought to reinterview Calamia, he refused. But others would prove less reticent. In 1990, Cruz Roman, a retired jailer, would say: "What we heard is, Nagell was trying to cause attention because of the Kennedy assassination. I just heard this from gossip in the bar and whatever. That he was ex-CIA. That he had been in Mexico. That he knew about the plot. But I didn't really want to know inside information like that."

Hoover's FBI

A two-hour flight from El Paso to Los Angeles provided respite for reflection. By late 1975, much had already surfaced in the media to tarnish the image of J. Edgar Hoover. For years, the FBI director had been viewed by the American people as a guardian of democracy, a crime-stopper who tracked down the likes of John Dillinger, a dedicated anti-Communist who ate subversives for breakfast. Insiders knew him as a mean, vindictive man who maintained his fiefdom by amassing secret files on the private lives of public figures. From the mid-1950s until his death in 1972, Hoover's COINTELPRO operation planted "agents provocateurs" among domestic groups the FBI considered "subversive," and conducted illegal break-ins and warrantless electronic surveillance.[8]

At the same time, Hoover scarcely acknowledged the existence of organized crime—perhaps because he counted some of its members among his friends, during his regular visits to the racetrack.[9] In 1961, Hoover's official boss became Robert Kennedy, who as attorney general embarked on a crusade to put the leadership of "La Cosa Nostra" behind bars. How the director must have chafed to be beholden suddenly to a man who was not even born when Hoover became FBI director in 1924!

The mutual antipathy between Hoover and the Kennedy brothers was no secret. It was surely with considerable delight that Hoover invited JFK to a little lunch in March 1962. Hoover had learned of the president's White House liaisons with Judith Campbell, introduced to Kennedy during the 1960 election campaign by singer Frank Sinatra. She also happened to be the mistress of Sam Giancana, a Chicago mobster near the top of Robert Kennedy's target list. For Hoover to possess such information was tantamount to blackmail.[10]

When the assassination happened, it was Hoover who informed Robert Kennedy. "I have news for you," Hoover began his message. "The president's been shot. I think it's serious. I'll call you back when I find out more." A half hour later, Hoover phoned again and said three words— "The president's dead"—and hung up. The director's reaction, as Robert Kennedy later described it to biographer Arthur Schlesinger, Jr., was "not quite as excited as if he was reporting the fact that he'd found a Communist on the faculty of Howard University."[11]

Within an hour of the shots in Dealey Plaza, police had arrested Oswald a few miles away, sitting inside the Texas Theater. Shortly thereafter, before the alleged assassin had been charged with anything, in Washington

Hoover issued an internal FBI memo. It stated that the Dallas police "very probably" had the assassin in custody, an individual "in the category of a nut and the extremist pro-Castro crowd . . . an extreme radical of the left."[12] By the next morning, Hoover would rescind two teletypes dispatched to all FBI field offices urging agents to "contact all informants" and "resolve all allegations." The new memo advised that "normal contacts with informants and other sources" should resume.[13]

In short, Hoover cut off any legitimate FBI investigation before it could even get under way. It was on record that the FBI's awareness of Oswald dated back to the ex-Marine's showing up in the Soviet Union in the fall of 1959.[14] Then, in December 1963, rumors began circulating that Oswald had had some kind of undercover informant-type relationship with the FBI. Not until 1974 did a Freedom of Information lawsuit by assassination researcher Harold Weisberg pry loose from the government the top-secret transcript of a Warren Commission executive session of January 27, 1964. A primary focus of discussion was information received by Texas attorney general Waggoner Carr, indicating that Oswald had been getting two hundred dollars a month since September 1962 as informant No. 179 on the FBI payroll. According to Warren Commission counsel Rankin—the same man whom Nagell wrote to from jail about his own communication with the FBI—the rumors were that Oswald's number had been "assigned to him in connection with the CIA." The commission chose to dismiss rather than pursue the rumor.[15]

Rogue Agency

The CIA's original mission, as authorized by Congress in 1947, was simply to gather foreign strategic intelligence and counterintelligence information. Nothing about covert action, overthrowing governments, or assassinating other nations' leaders. Nothing about domestic spying, supposedly the bailiwick of the FBI.

Yet all this was quietly approved by what came to be known as "the military-industrial complex," whose right arm was the CIA. Insiders called the Agency "The Company," and the phrase was apt. Philip Agee, a former CIA officer and today one of its leading critics, has described the CIA's main mission as one of guaranteeing "a favorable foreign-investment climate for U.S. industry."[16] By the 1960s, in 108 countries the CIA was said to control some thirty thousand agents variously pretending to be diplomats, industrialists, journalists, professors, and technical advisers.[17]

Then there were the fringe employees—gangsters, mercenaries, whatever men and means were deemed necessary to accomplish the objectives.

The officials who had earned their wings with the nation's first overseas intelligence operation, the wartime Office of Strategic Services, rose to the top of the CIA hierarchy during the 1950s. They generally came from wealthy families, Ivy League schools, and lawyer backgrounds—pillars of the Eastern Establishment whose appetite for cloak-and-dagger operations had been whetted for a worthy cause. Flushed with America's wartime success and largely immune from presidential or congressional scrutiny, they began to write their own rules. During the Eisenhower years, foreign policy was in the hands of the brothers Dulles—Allen at CIA, John Foster at the State Department—and few questioned their hegemony. The colossus fueled by World War II required ever-expanding horizons. In the guise of guarding the Free World, the CIA propped up puppet governments whose strings were pulled by American multinational corporations. And it toppled those suspected of leaning toward "the other side"—in Iran, Guatemala, the Philippines, Indonesia, the Congo, and elsewhere.

If the Communist Chinese could master the art of "brainwashing" our POWs in Korea, the CIA's MK-ULTRA and ARTICHOKE programs would seek to go one better via hypnosis and drugs. If the Soviet KGB could maintain a "Department 13" for political assassinations, the CIA would adopt a less superstitious, more elegant title: "Executive Action." Once Allen Dulles is said to have told a relative that he would "tip his hat to the devil himself if it would help him get a clearer picture of conditions in hell."[18] But little by little, Jekyll was becoming Hyde. The reverse image in the mirror became our own.

The two presidents who immediately preceded John F. Kennedy had begun to take notice of all this. Harry Truman would look back and say: "I never had any thought when I set up the CIA that it would be injected into peacetime cloak-and-dagger operations . . . as something akin to a subverting influence in the affairs of other people."[19] In 1956, two Eisenhower aides had strongly urged the president to consider "the long-range wisdom of activities that have entailed our virtual abandonment of the international 'golden rule.' . . . Where will we be tomorrow?"[20] Yet, as Truman wrote of Eisenhower, he "really didn't want to *do* or *decide* anything. He passed the buck, down."[21] More and more, the buck stopped at the CIA, which by 1957 was devoting 80 percent of its budget to clandestine activities. Only in his farewell address would Eisenhower warn the American people to beware the "acquisition of unwarranted influence" by the "military-industrial complex."[22]

By then the legacy had passed to a wealthy Ivy League war veteran named John F. Kennedy.

Whose Reins of Power?

Both Kennedy brothers started out as Cold Warriors, prepared, as the president said in his 1961 Inaugural Address, to "pay any price" to keep America and the world safe for democracy. It was a scary time, the Cold War at its height. The specter of a nuclear confrontation with the Soviet Union was much evidenced by the underground fallout shelters being built in dozens of American backyards—and the "duck-and-cover" drills being practiced in American grade schools. Spy intrigues permeated the mass psyche by way of James Bond movies and such TV series as *Mission: Impossible, I Spy,* and *The Man from UNCLE.* The much-feared Soviet spy agency, the KGB, was rightly assumed to have hundreds of agents recruiting allies abroad.

Still, what set the Kennedys' thousand days apart from any period since was a willingness to change perceptions and direction, in Robert Kennedy's words "to seek a newer world." The Kennedy spirit was undeniable. If the president asked for the moon, it was his—and John Glenn became a national hero. The space gap against the Soviets symbolized our lack of "initiative, ingenuity, and vitality"—so physical fitness and self-improvement courses became the vogue. When John Kennedy said he practiced speed-reading, another national fad was created. In June 1963, a Gallup poll found 59 percent of the people applauding him; his reelection was all but a certainty.

But what the Kennedy family represented—a potential dynasty of three brothers who might dominate American politics for years to come—was also a common front against a power structure grown fat in the postwar years. The Kennedys were of it and yet above it. When JFK took office, 77 percent of the federal budget was devoted in some fashion to military expenditures. By his final days, that equation had begun to alter considerably. The Pentagon's rate of growth was being curtailed, military installations were being closed.[23] A nuclear test-ban treaty with the Soviets had been signed. Withdrawal of the relative handful of American troops then in Vietnam was being given strong consideration. A rapprochement with Fidel Castro's Cuba seemed in the offing. If accommodation was achieved with the Communist world, the American status quo was threatened. Hoover, Dulles, the military-industrial complex—their very raison d'être would become an anachronism. Power, especially the unbridled power that revved its engines through the Eisenhower years, does not go gently into that good night.

Cuba was the crucible. Only ninety miles off the coast of Florida, Castro's successful revolution on New Year's Day 1959 brought the Communist bear awfully close to the land of milk and honey. For years, corruption had dominated the island; greedy dictators lived hand-in-glove with American casino operators. Now a bearded rebel leader was tossing out the money changers. Hundreds of embittered, rich Cubans fled with their assets into U.S. exile as Castro closed the gambling halls, nationalized the assets of American oil companies, and declared himself a Marxist. Fidel stuck in our craw like sandpaper. There were moments, early on, when things need not have come to such an impasse. But, much as America did with our wartime ally the Soviet Union after World War II, Castro was pushed into isolation; sanctions were imposed on Cuba's economy, secret plans were fomented to rid the hemisphere of his menace.

Kennedy inherited the CIA's plan secretly to train and arm a force of Cuban refugees to retake their homeland. On April 16, 1961—less than three months into his administration—the invasion force stormed ashore at a beachhead known as the Bay of Pigs. It was a disaster from the outset; apparently Castro was well aware it was coming. As his own army began rounding up almost the entire thousand-plus crew of Brigade 2506, the CIA hierarchy appealed to Kennedy to permit the use of American fighter planes. But the president, feeling he could not countenance deeper U.S. involvement, refused.[24]

Among elements of the CIA, and particularly many Cuban exiles, Kennedy was despised for failing to provide the air cover they believed would have ensured the invasion's success. For his part, Kennedy publicly took full blame on himself. But privately he was furious at the CIA, since Allen Dulles had led him to believe that the landing would be followed by a mass popular uprising in Cuba. Contrary to Kennedy's orders, CIA officers had landed on the beach with the exiles, even telling their Cuban protégés to go ahead and invade should Kennedy call off the mission at the last minute. Robert Kennedy later termed such actions "virtually treason." The president is said to have stated that he wanted "to splinter the CIA into a thousand pieces and scatter it to the winds." He proceeded to fire Allen Dulles, along with several of his top aides.[25]

It was a watershed event. From here on out, there were largely two separate agendas. While the Kennedys moved to undermine the Castro regime in subtler ways, the remaining old guard of the CIA set out to assassinate the Cuban premier. They utilized elements of organized crime, an alliance first forged by U.S. intelligence during and immediately after World War II. They contracted with Chicago's Sam Giancana, Los Angeles's Johnny Rosselli, Florida's Santos Trafficante, Jr., and New Orleans' Carlos Marcello—all targeted simultaneously by Robert Kennedy for potential prosecution. The Mob served as the CIA's liaison to certain Cuban exiles, with whom they had worked closely when Havana was in their back pocket. John McCone, JFK's appointee to replace Dulles as CIA director, was largely kept out of the loop.[26]

Such efforts did not cease after the Cuban Missile Crisis, a perilous thirteen days in the autumn of 1962 that brought the world as close to nuclear war as it has ever come. The confrontation occurred after American spy planes detected the Soviet Union's construction of offensive missile launching pads on Castro's island. The agreement that ended the crisis brought a Kennedy pledge that the United States would not invade Cuba or seek in any way to overthrow its government. But behind closed doors, the CIA ignored their commander in chief.

What Senator Frank Church would later call a "rogue elephant" was now trampling on morality, ethics, and the Constitution. The American people would not begin to learn about it until 1975, long after both Kennedy brothers had been assassinated.

At the Center of the Whirlpool

The jetliner honed in slowly on midnight Los Angeles. From the air, the city seemed to have no center. It was simply a myriad of lights stretching from sea to surrounding hills and reflecting endlessly off each other. It was possible to imagine that Los Angeles was scarcely affixed to the earth at all—a kind of floating electrical circuitry, or a network of mirror images. A grand illusion, just like Hollywood's creations. Here, where things were never quite what they appeared, seemed a natural spot to find a man like Richard Case Nagell.

One Sunday midmorning in late October 1975, I eased a rented car onto a southbound L.A. freeway. Urban sprawl had only begun to infiltrate the network of little towns that line the Pacific Coast with their soft, exotic names: Hermosa Beach, El Segundo, Manhattan Beach. In the last of these, up a long hill from the ocean, was the address I was looking for.

In the middle of a block, on a tree-lined street of modest white wood-frame homes, stood a house with a screened porch and a few steps leading up to the front door. For a minute, I simply sat and stared. The shades were drawn, and the house looked dark. The whole neighborhood felt empty. I suddenly did not know if I would be able to get out of the car. Finally, leaving my notebook and tape recorder behind, I locked up. Way back in the driveway, I noticed a parked car.

As I rang the bell for a third time, footsteps sounded inside. A dog barked loudly. A door closed; the barking became a murmur. Then, as a handle turned and the front door opened slightly, half of a man's face formed a silhouette against the darkness within. "Mr. Nagell?"

"Yes."

"I'm sorry to show up unannounced like this, but I didn't know how to reach you by phone. I'm a writer from New York, and I've come a long way to see you. I'm looking to help set the record straight about a certain historical event and . . ." I felt foolish, and only silence greeted me. "I know you've been screwed around by a lot of people over the years. All I can assure you is, I'm looking for the truth."

He remained standing with the door slightly ajar. "Well, I don't know. I'm very busy today."

"It's a long way back to New York. . . ."

"Well, all right, come in."

The door opened to reveal a lean, middle-aged man with light brown eyes and short, reddish-brown hair. "I know I shouldn't be bothering you like this on a Sunday morning," I said.

"Actually, you picked a lucky time. My son just went out bike-riding. If he'd been here, I wouldn't have let you in. We can talk until he gets back."

I asked if I could get my notebook and tape recorder out of the car. He agreed, but said he preferred I not tape him—"I've had some bad experiences with that." When I came back to the living room, Nagell motioned me to a couch. The furnishings were Spartan. A small bookcase stood in a corner; a couple of easy chairs fronted the couch; across from me, the doors to two bedrooms were closed and, farther to my right, the entryway to a kitchen revealed a stack of papers piled on a dining-room table.

Nagell stood in a corner beside the front window, adjusting some dials on an audio sound system. "I hope you don't mind," he said, "but I've made a practice of recording all of my conversations about this subject. A lot of things have been distorted by a lot of people over the years. And I've learned that this is one means of protecting myself."

Rather than feel paranoid, I felt more at ease. There was something about him that I instinctively trusted—and a sad, stoic bearing that spoke of a pain too deep to be false.

He took an easy chair across from me. "First of all, I'm curious how you got this address," he said. "It isn't that easy to come by."

I told him about my visit with Richard Popkin. "Yes, Professor Popkin," Nagell said and sighed. "The researchers are all well intentioned. They've got their own theories, and they all write off the top of their heads. If you want my opinion, if anything, they detract from ever getting at the truth. Not that anyone really cares about the truth." He glanced up again. "Well, go ahead and ask your questions. I may not answer them, but you can ask."

For a moment we sat in silence. Then I said, "It's a rumor among some researchers that you're still getting a sizable income from the CIA."

"I have no comment to make about my money, except that any I get is obtained legally." His voice was even. "Where it comes from or the amount, I won't discuss. But I am *not* getting a $2,000-a-month pension from the CIA, as has been written, to remain silent. I do have a substantial income, which is not a pension. But nobody buys my silence."

For the most part, Nagell continued, he had kept quiet because, since he gained custody of his two children from his ex-wife in 1971, he now had them to worry about. Awhile back, for fear somebody might throw a Molotov cocktail through the front window, he had moved their rooms to the back of the house.

"There have been threats periodically. But if I was killed in an accident, you can be sure it would be bona fide. I took out what I call 'life insurance' long ago, and I have certain documents and photographs being kept for me in at least one foreign country. And the material that would be released in the event of my death would prove quite embarrassing to certain people. I'm frankly more worried about somebody on his own deciding to pull a Jack Ruby."

Nagell gave a quick glance at the tape machine. Like his carefully chosen words, his every move seemed purposeful. He wasted nothing. "Go on with your questions."

"May I correctly assume that your action in the bank on September 20, 1963, was somehow related to the assassination of President Kennedy?"

"Well, it had nothing to do with any *alibi,* as some people seem to believe. I didn't have to establish an alibi. I was on my way out of the country, and I did not plan to return. Instead, I walked into a bank and busted two caps. Not because of what I might have known of any plans to assassinate the president, in that sense—but for a reason that I've never disclosed to anybody in the United States."

"Can you tell me anything about what you wanted federal authorities to find in the trunk of your car?"

"I'll tell you that the police officer who testified that I had photos of classified military installations, that was an outright lie. If I was a spy, I wouldn't have been that stupid. There was a photo of a friend of mine next to a sign in a restricted area with a unit designation of 'intelligence.' And I did have ten or twelve photographs of individuals, including a certain fellow who is of interest to you. The FBI hung on to those. They still have them."

From behind a closed bedroom door, suddenly there came a loud scratching. It startled me, and Nagell smiled. "Do you mind if I let him out?" he asked. I grinned back. Before I knew it, a Dalmatian was sniffing at my feet.

"In the notebook the FBI found in your briefcase," I resumed, "there was the phone number of Mexico City's Cuban embassy—the same number that later showed up in Oswald's address book, too."

"That's something I'd rather not talk about." His tone hardened.

"What about your association with the Fair Play for Cuba Committee?"

"Again, I'd prefer not to answer. Yes, I had involvement, but I'm not saying what it was."

Nagell rose and walked over to check the tape machine. Still half a reel left. But he stood toying with the controls, as if wondering whether to shut them down. Then, abruptly, he turned and stared at me. He seemed to have decided something, but I couldn't decipher it.

"Would you like some coffee?" I nodded. He returned with two cups.

Lowering his eyes, Nagell spoke of how the FBI had interviewed his sister and mother after the assassination. His wife and children, as far as he knew, had never been told which prison he was in; the kids thought their father was dead. When he was released from Leavenworth federal penitentiary in 1968, prison authorities drew up an undated visitors' list with names—to make it look, he felt, as if people had been allowed to see him all the time. At the Medical Center for Federal Prisoners in Springfield, Missouri, they forced on him a drug designed to compel him to talk. A psychologist sought to hypnotize him, but he had adamantly refused.

The more Nagell talked, the more he seemed like a man who *wanted* to come clean. He had been the victim of a gross miscarriage of justice, a pawn in a massive cover-up. He would like to name names, let the chips fall where they might. Yet he had lived too long in the labyrinth, where your secrets were your security and you kept your mouth shut if you wanted to stay healthy.

Nagell got up, excused himself, and disappeared into one of the bedrooms. He returned with a small stack of clippings. There were old articles from *Ramparts* magazine, the *Los Angeles Free Press, The New Yorker,* and *The Washington Post.* All contained some reference to Nagell, generally a brief one, and attached to each was his typewritten reply—his efforts, he said, to correct the innuendos and falsities about his actual and presumed intelligence activities.

"Maybe you should read through these sometime. They might show you how my good faith has been abused in the past. I really don't think I have anything more to say today. If you feel the need to contact me again, I'll give you the number of a friend here in Los Angeles. He will always know how to get in touch with me."

Public Record

Alone that night in my motel room, once again I studied the existing record on Richard Nagell. The article from the October 25, 1968, edition of *The Washington Post*—"E. Germany Frees U.S. Ex-Officer"—was the first to grab my attention.

> BERLIN, Oct. 24 (AP)—East Germany has released a former U.S. Army captain it held for four months.
>
> Informed sources said Richard Case Nagell, 38, was delivered at a border-crossing point between East and West Berlin yesterday in the presence of East Berlin attorney Wolfgang Vogel; attorney Ricey S. New of Washington and an official from the U.S. Mission in West Berlin.
>
> A U.S. spokesman said Nagell left by plane today for the United States. Nagell was described as a Californian and a former U.S. Army captain who left the service in 1959. In 1954, he was the sole survivor of an airplane crash near Friendship Airport that killed five servicemen.
>
> Informed sources said Nagell was taken off a train by the East Germans four months ago while he was on his way from West Germany to West Berlin through East Germany. Apparently he made some remarks which the East Germans considered derogatory, the sources said.
>
> Arrangements for Nagell's release were handled by Vogel, New, West Berlin attorney Juergen Stange and various government officials, the sources reported.
>
> The U.S. Mission had not disclosed that Nagell was being held. He was not brought to trial and apparently no specific charges were brought against him, the sources added.
>
> He was reported in generally good condition on his release.

I shook my head in amazement. Only a few months after his release from prison in the United States, Nagell had ended up being arrested and held for four months behind the so-called Iron Curtain! I had heard of East Berlin attorney Wolfgang Vogel. He was the man the Communists always brought in on high-level spy exchanges, such as the American swap of Rudolph Abel for Francis Gary Powers, the downed pilot in the famous 1960 U-2 spy plane incident. Yet, in this instance, American authorities had "not even disclosed" Nagell's disappearance. And the *Post* article mentioned nothing about his previous history, either as an intelligence officer or a convicted felon. Why had Nagell gone to East Germany?

I read on. There was a long document that Nagell had filed with the

U.S. Court of Claims in Washington, D.C. Upon receiving an honorable discharge from the Army in 1959, Nagell had received a 64 percent disability compensation from the Veterans Administration for injuries sustained during the Korean War and in the crash of a military plane. He had long believed he was entitled to full 100 percent compensation, and in 1973 decided to sue the Army to get it in the Court of Claims. Early in 1974, Nagell retained Bernard Fensterwald, Jr., as his attorney. It was an auspicious choice. Not only was Fensterwald the cofounder of the private Committee to Investigate Assassinations, he was also the lawyer for James Earl Ray, the accused assassin of Martin Luther King, Jr. Another of Fensterwald's clients, former CIA officer and Watergate burglar James McCord, had broken open the Watergate scandal by directly linking his operatives to the Nixon White House.

The Pentagon was represented in the Court of Claims case by Carla A. Hills, an assistant attorney general in the Civil Division. (By 1992, Hills was serving as U.S. trade representative in the Bush administration.) She was seeking to have much of Nagell's pleading struck from the court record on grounds that it was "replete with redundant, immaterial, impertinent, and scandalous matter." However, in the record it remained, in Case No. 1-73 of the Court of Claims. On April 16, 1974, Nagell had filed the following paragraphs concerning his background:

> I am capable of producing and willing to produce documentary evidence, including original documents and duplicates of original documents, photographs, negatives, film, recording tapes and other objects to substantiate and/or prove the veracity of most of the statements made herein. I am willing to undergo a polygraph examination relative to any and all statements made herein.
>
> During the period 1948–1958, I was assigned off and on in various capacities as an enlisted man and commissioned officer to various intelligence units and intelligence activities of the United States Army, including combat intelligence, counter intelligence (security), and clandestine positive intelligence (espionage) units and activities.
>
> During the period 1957–1958, as a commissioned officer of the United States Army, I performed intelligence services in behalf of the CIA, in addition to my assigned duties with the Counter Intelligence Corps (CIC).
>
> During the period 1959–1963, as a commissioned officer of the United States Army and as a civilian, I acted off and on as a confidential informant for the Federal Bureau of Investigation (FBI), both at my own volition and upon solicitation by the FBI.
>
> During the period 1962–1963, and prior thereto, as a civilian, I may have performed intelligence services for a foreign nation, after being deceived by signing a contract and by other reasons into thinking that I

was functioning for the CIA. I arrived at this conclusion in September 1963, after conducting investigations and/or inquiries into the activities, status and/or intentions of certain persons, among whom were Franz Waehauf, a Mexican subject of German nationality; Manuel Artime, a leader of the Miami-based Peoples' Revolutionary Movement (MRP); Vaughn L. Snipes, an executive officer of the Los Angeles branch of the Fair Play for Cuba Committee (FPCC); and Lee H. Oswald, later accused as the lone assassin of President John F. Kennedy.

Nagell seemed to be holding over the government's head certain things he was "capable of producing," in order to get what he considered his just desserts from the Pentagon. The reasons behind his long-standing reluctance to open up fully were becoming clearer.

Also included among the papers Nagell provided me was a letter he had written from prison on January 8, 1967, to Robert Kennedy, who, after resigning as attorney general, had become a U.S. senator from New York. It said, in part:

> . . . I want you to know there exists a far-reaching ramification concerning my own inquiry into Mr. Oswald's activities; a ramification which, if exploited and twisted around by interested parties, might create additional doubt in the matter concerned and unnecessarily strain relations between the United States and another country. So I wish to emphasize that any conspiracy of which I had cognizance was neither Communist inspired nor instigated by any foreign government or representative thereof.

As I pondered the meaning of all this, I suddenly realized that my tape recorder and two earlier interview tapes on the assassination were missing. I seemed to remember stashing the machine under the front seat of my car after leaving Nagell's home. I had parked again and taken a half-hour stroll down Manhattan Beach. Could someone have followed me? Was Nagell being watched? Anxiously, I dialed the friend's number he had given me, and asked a man's voice at the other end please to have Nagell call me as soon as possible.

It was noon the next day when the phone rang in my room. Nagell's voice over the phone sounded amused.

"You left some of your property behind. I suppose you'd like to get it back?"

"Yes," I said, trying to sound cool.

"I'll meet you tonight. There's a little bar I know on Sunset Strip."

Second Rendezvous

As instructed, I took a corner table in the dimly lit bar, ordered a beer, and waited. Within five minutes, Nagell walked through the mahogany door. He nodded to the bartender and headed straight toward me. He looked tired, as if he, too, had had a rough time getting to sleep. "Don't worry," he said, handing me the tapes and recorder, "I didn't play them. I *am* familiar with the names you listed on those cassettes, though." Nagell smiled. And I believed him.

He ordered a round and told me that a friend had suggested I might really be a JTO (junior training officer) for the CIA. But even if I was, Nagell added, it wouldn't matter because my journalist's cover would be complete with everything I needed. I assured him that I was no more, or less, than an interested journalist.

Then, as he began to draw comparisons between Soviet and American intelligence agencies, I decided to pick up where I'd left off in my reading —with the "far-reaching ramification" alluded to in his letter to Robert Kennedy.

"I'll only say this," Nagell offered. "I have never stated who I was working for from August of 1962 to September of 1963, other than that I'd thought it was the Central Intelligence Agency. At the time of my arrest, I knew it had not been. And I had a pretty good idea who I was functioning for. I'm not saying that I didn't have bona fide CIA contacts, or that the CIA was not involved in my particular activities. But some things I did were not for the CIA, and I was led to believe they were."

He paused, took a long draw of his beer, gave a quick glance around the bar, and continued. "It's no intricate affair. It's very easily explained and I was perhaps a little stupid not to see through it. But, having worked in clandestine activities, an individual sometimes takes a lot for granted or makes assumptions. If I'd been a little more alert or checked up on some things, I'd have known long before September of 1963. And if there was not so much secrecy in our government, people would not get put in situations like this."

He paused again, probing my eyes to see if I was following him. Then: "The Soviets were actually more interested in Lee Harvey Oswald than the Americans. Because when he was in the Soviet Union, they had considered him emotionally unstable, prone to commit some act that could bring embarrassment to the Soviet Union—long before he was in fact involved in anything like that. It's possible that the Soviets knew about his particular involvement in certain plans before the Americans did."

The bar seemed very still. I looked around. The people were still laughing, the jukebox still playing. But all that appeared to exist in a vacuum. Nagell raised his hand to signal for another round. "But the CIA as such," he added, "had absolutely nothing to do with the assassination. That's not to say that some of their former employees weren't involved."

In a far corner of the bar, a mixed group in their midtwenties had gathered. Nagell caught the eye of one of the girls and called her name. She waved. "I'd appreciate it if you'd not use my real name here," he said, turning back to face me. "Out here, people know me as Vic."

As the beer began to take its effect and our talk moved to lighter topics, his style of speaking changed. Something was "right on," or someone was "hip," or "That's not my bag." Coming from him, the words sounded almost like a foreign language. Gradually, a profound sadness seemed to envelop us. He was remembering an incident from his Army years in the Far East. A Korean father, a suspected spy, was being tortured by the South Korean military. When the man's son had rushed to try to stop it, he was shot to death by the American "observers." When Nagell had reported the event to his superior officer, he had been told: "You have not seen anything."

"That was 1956. It started me thinking, even then. There was a spark of morality in me, I guess. . . ."

He took a sip of his beer. Then another. And another. He reached into his pocket for a cigarette. I tried asking him about what happened in 1968 in East Germany, but he didn't want to talk about it. Finally, Richard Nagell glanced at his watch. It was almost midnight.

"One last thing I can tell you," he said. "I knew Lee Harvey Oswald before 1962. We had a casual but purposeful acquaintance in Japan, when he was stationed there in the Marines. My association with him, then and later, was strictly with an objective."

One final time, Nagell studied my face. Then he smiled, stood up, and extended his hand. "Maybe I can send you some things when you get back to New York," he said, and walked out of the bar.

Over the next nine months, we would maintain an ongoing correspondence. I would write Nagell with questions, he would fill in more gaps. Early in 1976 he sent along several hundred pages of documents, including many personal letters he had written while imprisoned in the mid-1960s. In an accompanying letter, he wrote:

> Enclosed herewith and in five separate packages being mailed today are xerox copies of some documents pertaining to my case, a number of

which are additional pieces to the patchwork puzzle. . . . Many of these documents have not been seen by anybody outside the intelligence-law enforcement community. Some have not been seen or "discovered" by anybody except the recipients and me.[27]

Shortly after that, Nagell provided written authorization for me to access the confidential files maintained by two of his former attorneys, Fensterwald in Washington and Calamia in El Paso.[28] I also sent Nagell a detailed outline of what I believed to be the "highlights" of his relationship to Oswald and the assassination, which he returned to me with typewritten corrections.

Then, not long after my contact with Congressman Edwards concerning Nagell's missing affidavit about his warning letter to Hoover, I received a letter from Nagell dated June 10, 1976:

> I've just received your letter of May 25. . . . This seems an unusually long time for mail to be in transit.
> A number of things have come up since my last writing, which I don't feel it wise to get into here, other than to say that I shall not be able to meet with you or discuss certain matters further until after my current [Court of Claims] lawsuit is brought to a litigated conclusion. . . .

Late that September, another envelope from L.A. arrived, containing recent correspondence between Nagell and FBI director Clarence Kelley:

> Dear Mr. Kelley:
> A recent news item appearing in the *Los Angeles Times* quoted you as stating that there was no conspiracy involved in the assassination of President John F. Kennedy and that such determination will be borne out by a review of the Bureau's investigation.
> Enclosed herewith is a copy of my 3 January 1967 letter to U.S. Senator Richard B. Russell, the substance of which obviously is in conflict with the statement attributed to you.
> Before you make further public comment on the Bureau's investigative prowess in this matter, I suggest that you personally review the sworn statement that I gave to FBI Special Agents Lawrence W. Gorman and Edward J. Murphy on 6 January 1964 at El Paso, Texas.

> Dear Mr. Nagell:
> In reply to your letter of June 28th, with enclosures, I would like to assure you that the FBI conducted a thorough investigation into the assassination of President Kennedy and we furnished numerous reports to the Warren Commission. That Commission, after careful study of these reports and information from other agencies and sources, arrived at the

conclusion that Lee Harvey Oswald acted alone in committing this heinous crime.

I appreciated receiving your views and observations on this matter.[29]

In February 1977 I took a job as a staff writer in the Hollywood bureau of *TV Guide* magazine. While spending most of my time interviewing celebrities, I recontacted Nagell, and he agreed to meet with me periodically. Over the next two years we built a rapport he had never before established with any other reporter or researcher, whom he felt always had a particular "ax to grind" about the assassination—a shoe into which he did not necessarily choose to fit.

This rapport did not go unnoticed. In a telephone conversation in 1979, Nagell described an effort by the CIA to sever our relationship. Two CIA employees had come to see him, he said, claiming that they had sat at an adjacent table from us and monitored my secret tape recording of our conversation. By agreement with Nagell, this was something I had never done, though I sometimes wished I had. I did take notes on nearly all of our conversations, of which Nagell was well aware. He added that the CIA men were so adamant about my alleged taping that he didn't believe them —but obviously there was an ongoing effort to keep Nagell from "going all the way" with what he knew.

After I quit *TV Guide* late in 1979 and returned to free-lance writing on the East Coast, we would be in touch only sporadically. On several occasions Nagell told me to "hang in there" as I waited for him to resolve his Court of Claims case against the Pentagon. But once he won his full disability retirement in 1983, he became even more reticent. And I had to wonder if, whether he wanted to or not, he had cut some kind of deal whereby he would remain largely silent. Finally, I made the decision to try to get in touch with some of his former associates, to learn more about him through their experiences.

And I spent many hours looking through attorney Fensterwald's files, and more material that Nagell had put on record at the Court of Claims. The latter was particularly enlightening about his formative years in the Army, years that altered forever his gung-ho perception about the deeds he was asked to perform in the name of "national security." It was the beginning of a sea change in his outlook, one that had very much to do with his association with Lee Harvey Oswald and the events leading to the death of a president.

Summary

While the Warren Commission was in session in 1964, Nagell's revelations in open court in El Paso continued to be ignored. It came out that the FBI and the Secret Service had questioned him about Oswald, and that Nagell had been with Military Intelligence in the Far East at the same time Oswald was stationed there with the Marines. Nagell also told of his original plans to be in Mexico City in late September 1963, again synchronizing with Oswald's known visit there. Nagell asked that his belongings be returned to him for evidence in his trial, but his request fell on deaf ears. He was convicted in May 1964 of "entering a federally insured bank with intent to rob."

Even in 1975, officials connected with Nagell's case proved very reluctant to discuss it. The prosecutor recalled his action in the bank as a "mystery." Nagell's court-appointed attorney, Joseph Calamia, seemed to have been told by Nagell about his relationship with Oswald but chose not to raise this matter at the trial. A jailer remembered hearing "rumors" that Nagell was ex-CIA and aware of an assassination plot.

In his Court of Claims lawsuit filed by Nagell against the Pentagon in 1973, he set down that he was a confidential informant for the FBI (1959–63) and worked for the CIA in 1957–58. He also described his conclusion in September 1963 that not the CIA, but a foreign nation, may have been his actual employer while investigating Oswald and others over the previous year.

During the author's initial meetings with Nagell, he alleged that Soviet intelligence was aware of a Kennedy conspiracy before the Americans were. Nagell also indicated that former CIA employees were involved with Oswald in the plot.

I
Cold War

It is in the political agent's interest to betray all the parties who use him and to work for them all at the same time, so that he may move freely and penetrate everywhere.

—E. Howard Hunt, Jr.,
The Berlin Ending

Chapter Three

Origins of a Spy: 1948–56

My study of the dozens of documents sent me by Richard Case Nagell in 1976 revealed one thing beyond a shadow of a doubt: During his years of prison confinement, he had one confidante—his older sister, Eleanore Gambert. It was Eleanore who corresponded with attorneys, congresspeople, and even the LBJ White House seeking justice for her brother.

As early as October 10, 1963, three weeks after his arrest, Nagell had written his sister:

> As this letter will be read prior to its dispatch, I shall not go into detail or explanation with regard to the charges. I am certain to be indicted, tried, and convicted because I have refused to offer an explanation as to certain overt acts which would, under normal circumstances, constitute "Bank Robbery." Someday I shall explain everything in detail to you pertinent to this apparent disgrace.

After Nagell's conviction, Eleanore wrote his attorney Joseph Calamia that she was "truly convinced that there is a political conspiracy going on out there." Her brother, she complained, had not been receiving any of her letters. Calamia responded that he disagreed "when you say that Dick has been made the object of some political conspiracy. I do believe a wrong has been done to Dick in that he has been convicted as a criminal, as I sincerely believe that Dick's illness precludes his being held account-able to the criminal laws."[1]

By late March 1966, Eleanore could be certain that "Dick's illness" was not behind the machinations surrounding his case. She wrote her brother on March 30: "I received your very lengthy (22 pages) letter this morn-ing." In the margin of the copy Nagell sent me, he had typed in: "Letter of 3/24/66 Smuggled out of El Paso County Jail for $50.00." His sister contin-ued: "I am answering it immediately, so you will know that it is in my hands. To say the least, I am quite upset over what I read, but am sincerely grateful that you took the time to write it. It certainly cleared up a few questions that have been on my mind for quite some time. . . ."

In that letter to his sister, Nagell had spelled out at least some of the real reasons behind his action in the bank. As he requested, his sister then destroyed it. When I called to ask if I might interview her, Eleanore Gambert politely declined. By the time I did manage to meet with her second husband, Louis, and her two stepsons, she had died a few years earlier after a long illness.

Family Memories

I had spoken periodically by phone with Louis Gambert, an octogenarian retired to the little Gulf Coast town of Tarpon Springs, Florida. And, on a trip to Miami early in 1990, I decided to make the five-hour-long drive across Alligator Alley south of the Everglades and up along the western coastline to the Gambert home. I hoped that the remaining family mem-bers might be able to offer insights into Nagell's past.

Located about twenty-five miles northwest of Tampa, Tarpon Springs is largely a retirement community and, since the Mediterranean Sea ran dry of natural sponges, is also renowned as the sponge capital of the world. Tourists flock to beaches here to watch the sponge-divers come up with their catch and auction it at dockside primarily to European buyers, whose clients still dote in their baths on the spiny little creatures. Originally the town was named for the huge tarpon that came into the bayous to spawn. Along one of these bayous, down a narrow dirt road, the remaining

Gambert family was waiting for me inside a single-story ranch-style house resting on a half acre of palms, tall pines, and Brazilian pepper trees.

Louis Gambert, now eighty-eight, along with his two sons, sixty-two-year-old Robert and fifty-four-year-old Roger, and their wives were all sitting around a dining-room table. I quickly discovered that Richard Nagell was as much of a mystery man to them as he was to me. As Roger put it, "Dick was always very, very difficult to pin down. He was always involved in things he would never let us know about. Partially, I think he just wanted to keep us out of it. He never wanted to put the family in jeopardy."

Indeed, Eleanore had been so protective of her brother that not even Louis was made privy to most of their discussions and correspondence. "My mother was a very close-to-the-vest Norwegian," Roger explained. "My father is Italian, effusive, and boisterous, but my mother was the exact opposite. She didn't say five words many days, just a very quiet woman. For example, she never talked to me about this at all. I guess Dick said he didn't want people to know, and that was enough for her."

I glanced over at a mantelpiece photograph of the tall, statuesque, brown-haired woman who had worked for years in the publications department of Union Carbide in Long Island City, New York. I fervently wished she could have been there that day. Perhaps, with the passage of so many years, she might have felt the importance of assisting in getting to the truth, for the entire family was convinced that Nagell knew *something* of vital importance about the assassination of President Kennedy. Now he rarely communicated with any of them, having become, in Robert Gambert's words, "almost a recluse."

Louis focused long and hard on me through his failing eyesight and said: "He did tell Eleanore and me about having met Oswald, and pictures that were taken of the two of them talking." Louis asked me to shut off my tape recorder, then added that Nagell was supposed to eliminate Oswald before the assassination could happen.

"He was at the time, in many capacities, working for *a* government, or an agency of the government. I know he tried to tell the government that somebody was going to do this terrible thing. He wanted to get arrested—because he knew the attempt to kill the president was not too far away. He also thought there was a plan to shoot some other politicians. In other words, not only Kennedy, but more than just one person."

Louis recounted how he and Eleanore had gone to visit Nagell at the Leavenworth prison. But when they arrived, two other visitors were awaiting them. "Dick told me to take their names, and I wrote down the names of the FBI person and the CIA person, or maybe it was the other outfit that he represented. Somewhere I still have a little card."

At about the same time—probably late summer of 1965 was the family's best guess—two FBI agents knocked on the Gamberts' door on Long Island. The family was packing for a voyage to Europe, but the FBI wanted to see some documents that they understood Nagell had given Eleanore to keep for him. How the FBI knew about any such documents wasn't made clear, but there had been a few references to these papers in the prison correspondence between Nagell and his sister. After some initial reluctance, the Gamberts decided to comply. Louis went to a storage room in the basement and returned with a metal footlocker. For a while, the two agents sat on the couch, looking through the footlocker's contents.

"He had a copy of the letter he wrote to Hoover, I believe, warning about the assassination," Roger Gambert recalled. "I remember one of the agents saying, 'We'd like to make copies of some of this.' My mother said, 'No, not unless Dick gives you permission.' They were very polite about it and they left." Roger also remembered overhearing the FBI ask whether the family was moving; no, Mrs. Gambert had said, just going on a trip.

The next morning, Louis and Eleanore departed for Europe. Roger was then working at IBM. "When I got home that night and put the key in the back door, I heard something fall in the storage room. I thought there must be somebody in the basement. So I ran downstairs and pulled the door shut, it was dark, and I grabbed a knife and stood there. There was a phone right beside the storage room on a little table, and I called a friend who was a cop and lived a few blocks away. He must have gotten there within two minutes. He knocked on the storage room door and said, 'I've got a gun, come on out.' But when we opened it, there was nobody in there. I didn't know anything was missing until later, when my parents came home."

Some of Richard Nagell's effects, the Gamberts discovered, were indeed absent from the metal footlocker. Louis picked up the story. "Some of the things they took, we hadn't even known were in there. I remember Dick telling us afterwards that some of the materials he'd left with Eleanore for safekeeping were hidden inside of others. Very very minute, little things that not anybody would take. Dick said they knew what they were after. Tapes and pictures. We're sure the FBI broke into our home that night to try to find out what he knew."

Robert Gambert, a husky-voiced man slightly stockier than his younger brother, had sat silently through much of the conversation. He was retired after serving thirty years with the Defense Investigative Service, which he described as a Pentagon "passive counterintelligence program which put safeguards in place to protect against industrial espionage." Perhaps due to Robert's familiarity with such activities, Nagell had once spoken to him at some length about his own career. Now he poured another cup of coffee and began to speak.

"Dick played the role of a disgruntled ex-Army officer. This was in Texas and Mexico, the early 1960s. But he was really still operational, in an undercover capacity, for the Army Intelligence."

"Was it Army Intelligence or the CIA?" I asked.

"I got the impression it was Army because he said he was still working for them. But he could have been converted to some other—actually, my familiarity is, you can be an Army or Navy officer working for the CIA. They float in and out. Some CIA agents get their training in the military, then go off and become strictly CIA."

And would the point of his seeming to be a disaffected Army officer perhaps be so that he could take part in operations involving the Soviets?

"Well, yeah. You could use that as a cover. They're not gonna trust anybody who's active military or a friendly retiree. They're gonna trust somebody who's going around griping against the military, against the intelligence operations, against the government. That's more or less what he told me once, a long time ago. It's hard to pinpoint times and dates. In fact, at the time when he was telling me these things, they didn't mean a lot to me."

Early Years

One of the reasons I had come to see the Gamberts was to learn more about Nagell's early background. Like Lee Harvey Oswald, whose father died of a heart attack two months before his birth, Nagell had come from a broken home. His father, Louis, who had emigrated from Norway, was an electrician by trade. "He had also been in show business, a soft-shoe dancer," Louis Gambert remembered. "But he died very young."

Born on August 5, 1930, in Greenwich, New York, Nagell never knew his father and, as he testified at his 1964 trial: "I was separated from my mother when I was four. I lived in various foster homes up until the time I was eleven and then I lived in well, I guess you can call it an orphanage, until I was seventeen."[2]

Eleanore Gambert was also placed for a time in foster care. The family had no idea why Francis Nagell gave up her children at such a tender age. "Eleanore was actually his half sister," Louis went on, "by a different mother. Dick's mother was of German heritage and an active nurse, a $20-a-day nurse in those days." (Ironically, I realized, Oswald's mother, Marguerite, had also been a nurse.) "She always lived in hotels, New York City hotels. Dick still saw her, and when he was a teenager she would always try to get rid of any girls he got interested in."

The foster homes and orphanages in which he was raised, Nagell would recall years later, constituted "a frugal environment with a strict moral code." His religious training was Quaker; active in the Boy Scouts and 4-H Club, he was an average student who excelled in languages and social studies at Albany High School.[3] On his eighteenth birthday, in 1948, he enlisted in the Army, and soon after got assigned to paratrooper school at Fort Bragg, North Carolina.

José Ibarra, Jr., an Army buddy from Nagell's days with Headquarters Company 505 and whom I located in El Paso, recalled him as being "very reserved. He did not go downtown with us and get in fights with the 225th. You always saw him around the barracks reading, which in those days was a little weird. Nagell always had real nice starched clothes, a close haircut, shined boots. I perceived him as a guy that really liked the Army. We were both very active in company activities. And we were sent to a lot of schools —they pump you with all this knowledge to be prepared for any eventuality. Nagell eventually went to work in S-2. When you're in S-2, you had to have your shit together. That is probably where he first got involved in intelligence. He came in as a private, but went up through the ranks real fast."[4]

Nagell said he "went into intelligence at nineteen on a low level. I studied Russian at Fort Bragg and took an extension course from the University of California in Mandarin Chinese. My first five months in the infantry, I used to monitor the [Communist] Chinese technical broadcasts, which were all in Mandarin, along with two Korean guys who spoke the language."[5]

In Combat

In the fall of 1951, Nagell shipped out to Korea, which was then fifteen months into a bloody war. After World War II, the United States and its wartime ally the Soviet Union had agreed to divide the former Japanese colony in half. North Korea, bordered by China and the USSR, became a Communist state, while the Republic of Korea—South Korea—came under American supervision. In 1949, Mao Tse-tung's longtime Communist revolution succeeded in taking over mainland China. Less than a year later, in June 1950, North Korea invaded South Korea along the thirty-eighth parallel, separating the two nations. U.S. president Harry S Truman, who assumed that global communism was monolithic and that Moscow and Peking were dictating the aggression, immediately ordered American troops into battle under the sanction of the United Nations. China, fearing the rapid U.S. advance into North Korea toward its own border, soon entered the war to help drive back the Americans. Eventually nearly 1.8 million Americans served in the Korean War, of whom 54,200 were killed, 103,300 wounded, and 8,200 missing in action. Dissent at home grew as the war became protracted and indecisive, contributing to the 1952 presidential triumph of General Dwight D. Eisenhower.[6]

When Richard Nagell headed off to battle, he was a fervent defender of the faith against the spread of communism. Selected for officer training prior to being sent overseas, Nagell has described himself as "a young idealist" who went to Korea "voluntarily because most of the other officers that had graduated with me went to Europe or various training centers here in the United States." He arrived in Teagu, South Korea, as a second lieutenant. Though Nagell was a qualified parachutist, only one airborne division was then operational in the war, and he was assigned to be a rifle platoon leader with the 24th Infantry Division.

John Margain, who served as Nagell's sergeant in Korea, was living in an L.A. suburb when I interviewed him in 1991. "I'll tell you, he was a top-notch lieutenant," Margain told me. "We were fighting in the northern part of Korea, there were forty men in our platoon. And Nagell didn't ask you to do anything he wouldn't do. He did not know what fear was. Shit, he would jump in the goddamn trench holes and you'd see Chinese coming out of there. That's where he got all the respect of the company. Have you ever seen his body? He's got bullet holes all over him."

Nagell was promoted to first lieutenant on Christmas Day 1951, the same day that he suffered his first battle wound. He was leading his patrol up a hill when he "got a grenade fragment in my leg, a burp gun bullet here in my left wrist, and a bullet hole through my helmet which took the hair off but didn't really injure me." In August 1952 he was rotated back to the United States and assigned to the 82d Airborne Division, "but I went down to the Pentagon and requested reassignment to Korea and so they just sent me right back." On December 6, 1952, Nagell sustained his second wound—hand grenade fragments that hit him in the legs and face when "we were going up a hill and the Chinese rolled grenades down on us, one of them went off too close." After five days in the hospital, he returned to the front lines.

But if Nagell appeared almost obsessed with duty, honor, and country, his relatives recollected that his days in Korea were not always glorious. "I think he had a rough childhood and when he went to Korea so young, it was a traumatic experience for him," said Roger Gambert. "I remember some of the letters he wrote at the time talking about how bad it was. He came home once and told us about a hill where the company he was commanding set up automatic machine guns and just kept shooting at the Chinese coming up. He said they killed hundreds of them, maybe even thousands, and it really shook him up to think that these people had such a low opinion of life to just keep attacking."

In the early morning hours of June 11, 1953, Nagell sustained his third, and most serious, wartime injury. Fragments from a mortar or artillery shell hit him in the buttocks and face, giving him a concussion. He was flown to the Tokyo Army hospital and did not regain consciousness until his arrival there. Yet, once again, in early July he went back to the front. "The Chinese hit two [South] Korean divisions with about seven divisions and when that happened they threw my organization up into the line to try to plug the gap, try to stop them," he remembered.

The Korean War was drawing to a close. Five hours before the armistice was to be signed, Nagell was ordered off the line and took a train back to the South Korean capital, Seoul. His assistant division commander, a General Dunkelberg, was apparently so enamored of Nagell's meritorious service that he backdated Nagell's last promotion to July 15—thus making him the youngest American to receive a battlefield commission to captain during the course of the war. When the war ended on July 27, 1953, Nagell was nine days shy of his twenty-third birthday.

Nagell had seen action on about 175 battle patrols and became the recipient of three Purple Hearts, a Bronze Star, the Korean Service Medal, and the U.N. Service Ribbon. He was a soldier who, as his Bronze Star citation recorded, possessed "outstanding skill, initiative and untiring devotion to duty." He was also a soldier who would never again be able to escape the effects of what he witnessed on the battlefield. Years later, sitting in his cell inside a federal penitentiary, Nagell would reflect on his Korean War experiences in a letter:

My *initial* desire to see combat came from some deep-rooted part of my nature; the same part that belongs not only to me, but to all men. It was *not* a suicidal instinct; far from it. To call it hunger for experience, coupled with a childish obsession to do my share as a soldier, as an American, would be oversimplification but it would be accurate.

After my first wound, I had satisfied that hunger and I felt I had done my share. But strangely, I found no more peace than before. I had the feeling that I had missed the complete experience. So I volunteered again for combat; and again; and again—until the conflict ended. And while I was volunteering I knew, though I would not admit it to myself, that the *complete* experience included the lieutenants, the sergeants, and the privates under my command who were killed. You see, they had received the complete experience. They had gone into the war and out the other side.

Perhaps everyone who comes out of war alive is left with the troubling knowledge that they did not go all the way; that they really did not do their share. And maybe this is why so few infantrymen are willing to talk about the subject except among others like themselves, who, by simply being alive, are equally guilty. . . .[7]

Immediately following his return to the United States from Korea in the late summer of 1953, Nagell received "Special Orders" to report to the Army Language School in Monterey, California, "to pursue a course of instruction in the Japanese language."[8] This particular school was established primarily for personnel slated for overseas service in Military Intelligence. Nagell spent a year mastering Japanese, Russian, and Spanish.

At some point during this time frame, his relatives recalled the *first* time he became the only soldier to live through a military plane crash. "It was an aircraft flying at low altitude, when they had to bail out," said Robert Gambert. "Dick survived because he'd done a lot of parachute jumping, and he had the training to get the 'chute open fast. The others didn't have enough altitude to manipulate their 'chutes in time."

Nagell was not badly hurt and, on July 1, 1954, he was assigned to the Army's Counter Intelligence Corps (CIC) School at Fort Holabird, Maryland.

Sole Survivor

Nagell was in midcourse at the CIC School when he took Thanksgiving leave to visit a girlfriend in San Francisco. On November 28, 1954, he was returning to Fort Holabird in a B-25 bomber, the only Army man in the company of five Air Force personnel. As the plane approached Andrews Air Force Base near Washington, D.C., Nagell was sitting near the bomb bay doors in the rear, listening to a pelting rain and radio communications that the landing field was closed because of the weather. "Seek landing at Friendship Airport in Baltimore," the base said. The B-25 shifted course and headed toward Baltimore on a radar system. The pilot radioed Friendship and gave a position about fourteen miles from the airport. He was not heard from again. At about 10:30 P.M. the bomber, settling into a westerly approach, struck the top of a steep hill, sliced through trees, and bounced to pieces on the ground.

When the plane was overdue, a number of Army, Air Force, Marine, and civilian aircraft, as well as helicopters, were dispatched on a search. But it was eight o'clock the next morning before a Coast Guard plane spotted the wreckage, two miles from the airport in a swampy stretch of woods. A military helicopter flew in low and hovered to guide rescue squads to the site. The terrain was so difficult to negotiate that state police called for packhorses to be brought to the scene. It took more than an hour for rescuers to wade through a hip-deep stream and fight their way up the all but inaccessible hillside through the trees and thick underbrush.

Five bodies were found, two in the wreckage, two thrown forward, and one lying to the rear of the plane. Near that last body, still alive and conscious after nearly twelve hours in an intermittent but freezing rain, was Richard Case Nagell. In deep shock, he could only groan for water.

Barely able to breathe through his mouth or nose, Nagell was given a tracheotomy to open his throat by a state policeman. An attempt was made to lift him into a helicopter, but the trees closing in the wreckage made the effort impossible. Nagell was placed on a stretcher and carried back through the wooded area while other rescuers chopped a path with axes to the first available clearing, a farmer's sheep pasture. Stretcher bearers scattered the animals, waving their coats to indicate to the Marine pilot that he could land. Nagell was transported by helicopter to Bolling Air Force Base Hospital in Washington.

Doctors found his jaw fractured severely on both sides. He was also diagnosed as having sustained a skull fracture and severe concussion, which would leave a permanent depression on the left side of his head. Nagell had gone into a coma. His condition was listed as critical. But, by the next day, the *Baltimore Sun* reported that the captain was "holding his own."

Several weeks after Nagell's B-25 went down, an article in *The Washington Post* revealed the results of an Air Force investigation into the crash. Early speculation was that the plane had run out of gasoline. But the twin-engine bomber had the use of both of its motors, with fuel in the tanks, and was going at full power when it crashed, the Air Force said. What actually happened to the B-25 would forever remain as mysterious as how anyone could possibly have survived its demise. The *Post* noted that "Nagell, three times winner of the Purple Heart, is making a 'remarkable recovery,' a Bolling Air Force Base spokesman said." He had been removed from the "seriously ill" list.

A "Summary-Chart" by military physicians showed that, only days after his hospitalization, Nagell seemed to know where he was and even dictated a letter in the Japanese language he had studied. But Nagell's first conscious memory was of Christmas, twenty-seven days after the crash. Early in January 1955, he was moved to Walter Reed Army Hospital. There he spent the next four months recuperating. Shortly before his release, Nagell was given a thorough psychiatric examination, which cleared him of any possible personality changes related to his injuries.[9] Even in the first stages of his recovery, Army records show that Nagell was approved for assignment and duty with the CIC on December 27, 1954.

And, in May 1955, he reported back to duty at the CIC's intelligence training center.

Recruited for Espionage

During the course of his El Paso trial in 1964, Nagell was asked to describe the CIC. "Well, the mission of the Counter Intelligence Corps, which is part of the Army, is to investigate any matters relating to treason, subversion, espionage, disaffection, that might be taking place within the military establishment or that might be conducted by civilians which are employed by the corporations, factories or concerns which are under military contract. That is their primary mission. And overseas, when they are overseas, they have police powers. . . . In fact, overseas they are just like the FBI in some ways."

On August 12, 1955, a "Confidential" memo from the headquarters of the Army Intelligence Center announced that Captain Nagell had been designated a Counter Intelligence officer. His first assignment took him to Los Angeles, where he has written that he was "assigned as a CIC investigator (Special Agent) operating in civilian clothes." On September 22, Nagell was granted a Top-Secret security clearance. His main task was to interview civilians, including the relatives, friends, and acquaintances of individuals under investigation by the military. But the facial disfigurement that resulted from the plane crash proved both embarrassing and troublesome for him. A wide, conspicuous scar creased the left side of his face, where paralysis of his eyelid and upper lip further distorted his appearance. On several occasions when Nagell knocked on people's doors in the course of his investigations, he was turned away because of his looks.[10]

The Cold War was at its height. Senator Joseph McCarthy's five-year-long witch-hunt in pursuit of alleged Communists inside the federal government, Hollywood, and finally the U.S. Army had only just come to a culmination. After McCarthy's crusade reached into the military in 1954, ostensibly because the Army had promoted a Communist dentist, televised congressional hearings revealed the Wisconsin politician for what he was—a blustering bully. When the Senate censured McCarthy for misconduct in December 1954, his public power evaporated. But the pall of suspicion that McCarthy cast over the nation hardly dissipated overnight —particularly among elements of the military establishment.[11]

Until now, Nagell had never questioned the merits of what he had been asked to do for his country. His first misgivings, he says, surfaced at CIC School in 1954—"when a civilian instructor attempted to justify one questionable counter-intelligence project by blatantly accusing news commentators Eric Sevareid and Edward R. Murrow (and other prominent figures in the news media) of being 'dangerous and well-known Communists' and 'witting tools of the international Communist conspiracy.'"

Then, on duty for the CIC in Los Angeles in 1955, as Nagell recounted it to me, "We opened the mail of civilians with a postal inspector standing right next to us. The CIC and the FBI stole the files of the local Communist Party chapter, just took the whole file cabinet out of their office."[12]

According to a typewritten statement written in 1968, derived from a tape-recorded conversation with Nagell about his military career, something else transpired during his early months with the Army CIC:

> It was during the winter of 1955–56, while assigned as a Case Review Officer with the Counter Intelligence Corps at Los Angeles, that I was initially recruited into the CIA's farflung network of informants and agents, one of a number, I suppose, within the Defense Department's intelligence community who helped the Agency keep an eye on its not always tame competitor. My recruitment was handled by a Herbert [Ernest] Leibacher, an agent of the CIA's Los Angeles office, and a Joe DaVanon, later identified to me through photographs as an official from CIA headquarters, then located on "E" street in Washington, D.C.[13]

The names of "E. Leibacher" and "J. DaVanon" also appeared under the heading "C.I.A." in the Nagell notebook seized by the FBI in El Paso. I verified by telephone with Leibacher, now eighty-three, that he was in charge of the CIA's L.A. office in the mid-1950s, and that DaVanon was his deputy "for a couple years." Asked if he recalled Nagell, Leibacher replied: "The name sounds familiar, but I really don't know why. It's been quite a few years."[14]

Further recalling that era, Nagell continued:

> Motivated by a degree of naivete and the Agency's subtle reminders that I owed a greater duty to my country than to the military establishment, I served as a non-paid, confidential informant off and on until my resignation from the Army in October 1959. A complete description of the information I supplied to the Agency during my military career would only add to what perforce must become a lengthy addendum; may it suffice to say that it did not always seem germane to intelligence affairs, but when it did it consisted mainly of an assortment of data that for so-called discretionary reasons was seldom passed on to the Agency (or for that matter, to our own higher echelons) through regular channels.[15]

Early in 1956, due to the problems he was encountering in interviewing civilians, Nagell was given a desk job at Army CIC "that required little work and less responsibility." He chafed at the inactivity. An officer efficiency report, noting that Nagell's classified assignment found him occupying "a position commensurate with an assistant to a staff officer of a battalion size unit," cited his diligence and imagination but added: "His character can best be described as undecided and spontaneous." The serious head injury he had sustained in the plane crash, the report went on, must have brought about his "lack of self confidence."

Some of Nagell's disfigurement was corrected by plastic surgery. Nagell then wrote to the Department of the Army, requesting overseas assignment with the CIC or even a return to the regular infantry. As an alternative, he also applied for a full-time job with the CIA. Nagell was officially advised that he could not be returned to infantry duties, as he was tied to an "obligation tour" with Military Intelligence. Then, on May 5, 1956, he was notified by letter from the headquarters of the Army Intelligence Center that he was being reassigned to the Far East.[16]

Parallel Reality

That same spring, a sixteen-year-old teenager living in New Orleans dropped out of the tenth grade and made plans to move to Fort Worth, Texas, with his mother. For a time after his father's death, Lee Harvey Oswald had lived in an orphanage with his two older brothers. His mother, Marguerite, remarried, then divorced, and the boy was shuffled to a variety of schools in a number of cities, described by one social worker as an "emotionally starved, affectionless youngster."

As he became a teenager, Oswald developed two obsessions. One was to join the Marines, as his older brother had. He even forged a document altering his age, so that he might enlist at sixteen, but his application was rejected. His other fascination was communism. Years later, he would say that his involvement with Marxism began when an old woman on a street corner handed him a pamphlet protesting the 1953 execution of Julius and Ethel Rosenberg for allegedly passing atomic secrets to the USSR. Oswald began reading voraciously about Karl Marx, making inquiries about Communist Youth Leagues, and, according to a friend who knew him in 1956: "He would say that the capitalists were exploiting the working class, and his central theme seemed to be that the workers would one day rise up and throw off their chains." While praising the sincerity of Soviet premier Nikita Khrushchev, he accused President Eisenhower of "exploiting the working class." Yet, at the same time he was writing the Socialist Party of America requesting information, Oswald avidly memorized his brother's Marine Corps manual. Six days after his seventeenth birthday, he finally succeeded in joining up, enlisting in the Marines in Dallas on October 24, 1956.[17]

By this time, Richard Nagell had already been stationed for several months at the U.S. Army Command Reconnaissance Activities (ACRAFE) Far East headquarters in Japan. This Asian nation of islands, with the Soviet Union not far from its northern shores and South Korea near its southwestern tip, was a strategic bulwark for the United States. After World War II ended with the dropping of atomic bombs on Hiroshima and Nagasaki in 1945, the American military had rushed in to begin rebuilding its archenemy—before the Soviets could make any such inroads of their own. Occupied Japan soon became almost like an American colony. Early in 1950, a peace treaty between the United States and Japan guaranteed long-term American military bases there. Even after Japan regained its sovereignty in 1952, its security was defined strictly within the framework of an American alliance. From Tokyo, the U.S. military's Far Eastern command center spread a wide net.

The nearby Korean situation was still far from stabilized. Although the 1953 armistice resulted in a cessation of hostilities and a prisoner exchange, it had left the two Koreas divided close to the thirty-eighth parallel and really satisfied neither side. North Korea remained a staunchly Communist state, though more closely aligned after the war to Peking rather than Moscow. South Korea began developing into a prosperous if politically divided country, with strong economic and security links to the United States. To maintain that security, U.S. Military Intelligence kept up a vigilant, if intentionally low, profile.

Between May 1956 and April 1957, Richard Nagell found himself assigned to "the clandestine espionage arm" of Army Intelligence. "Sometime in the '50s," according to Robert Gambert, "I remember him telling me something like 'I'm in a secret Army organization.' But he wouldn't tell me exactly what it was."

Nagell had his reasons. He would have been court-martialed if he revealed its name. Until now, almost nothing has been written about the "secret Army organization" of which Nagell became a part. Official records about it remain classified by the Pentagon. But it existed, and Nagell's experiences as one of its operatives were to have a profound influence on his future.

Field Operations Intelligence

When Richard Case Nagell was first being interrogated by the FBI after his arrest outside the El Paso bank, he made a point of informing the bureau's agents that "he had been assigned to Field Operations Intelligence and had taught interrogation."[18] It would be another ten years before Nagell set down, in his case against the Pentagon with the U.S. Court of Claims, what Field Operations Intelligence (FOI) was really all about.

During the 1950s, according to Nagell, FOI was considered sacrosanct by Military Intelligence (MI). Both upon his entry into and departure from the organization, "I was required to sign papers subjecting myself to ten years' imprisonment or a ten-thousand-dollar fine, or both, if I disclosed to unauthorized persons the nature of my duties or other classified information, including the fact that an organization like FOI existed. I was instructed never to mention the phrase 'Field Operations Intelligence' or the acronym 'FOI' outside of a secure place or in the presence of unauthorized persons, even around headquarters.[19]

"On paper, FOI was subordinate and operationally responsible to the Office of the Assistant Chief of Staff for Intelligence, Department of the Army. In function, however, FOI was merely an augmentation to CIA special (military) operations, in effect a covert extension of CIA policy and activity designed to conceal the true nature of CIA objectives. A substantial portion of FOI's financial support came from the CIA, directly or through reimbursement, as did much of its technological support. A number of FOI operations in which I participated or about which I gained knowledge were closely associated with—if not directed by—the CIA (e.g., the notorious Berlin Tunnel Project, often cited by the news media as a CIA fiasco, is more accurately described as an FOI operation sponsored by the CIA)."[20]

In the many books about the CIA and Military Intelligence that I perused looking to find out something about Field Operations Intelligence, I came across only a single reference to it. This appeared in a 1962 book about the CIA, *The Secret War,* by Sanche de Gramont. It was in a section describing the links between the CIA and the military's CIC branch in West Germany:

> The CIC's main task is finding Communist agents in US military installations, such as clerical or kitchen help, and helping to sift agents who

come to West Berlin as refugees. Agents thus found are turned over to the CIA for possible use as double agents. Army Intelligence in West Germany also has an operational espionage group, the mysterious Field Operations Intelligence (FOI). But CIA crowns all other agencies and takes over any case it chooses to handle. . . .[21]

The book's description of the CIA-FOI relationship in West Germany bore a striking correlation to what Nagell had written about the "Berlin Tunnel Project." This was a long, thin tunnel that originated in West Berlin and burrowed below the heavily guarded border into the then-Soviet-controlled eastern half of the city. Completed in February 1955, the tunnel was designed to tap into the secrets of the Soviet military command there. Today a famous signature of the Cold War, it was discovered by the Soviets about a year later. It has long been regarded as strictly a CIA operation.[22]

Victor Marchetti, a retired CIA officer and coauthor of the book *The CIA and the Cult of Intelligence,* confirmed the existence of an organization like FOI operating in the Far East. "I don't remember what they called it," Marchetti told me in an interview, "but yes, there was a clandestine operations branch of Military Intelligence and they were active in Korea, Japan, and all over Southeast Asia in the 1950s. They were like special units, usually offshoots of the CIC."[23]

I also raised the subject of Field Operations Intelligence with a retired Army colonel named William Bishop during an interview in 1991. I went to see Bishop because I had heard from another source that he might possess some knowledge of Nagell's activities. But I was not prepared for Bishop's reaction when I brought up the subject of FOI. "Where the hell'd you hear that?!" he exclaimed, then added, "Let me say this—walk on eggshells on this one. There are some areas you shouldn't deal in, and this is one of them. Because there's nothing there that you could conceivably make any decent story out of, without hurting a lot of people that don't need to be hurt. And to answer your question—no comment."[24]

The Commander Speaks

In his Court of Claims filings, Nagell had identified two men as the commander and chief assistant for FOI in the Far East. Looking in the directory of the Association of Former Intelligence Officers, I found listed the names of John B. Stanley and Robert C. Roth. Both men verified that they had indeed been the top two officials in FOI.

I reached Colonel Stanley, now eighty-one, by telephone at his retirement home in Hawaii. He said he had commanded FOI from the end of 1954 to the beginning of 1960, when he retired after a twenty-seven-year military career. "There's so much to it, you know," the colonel began. "It was independent of the CIC. FOI, generally speaking, had to do with collection of intelligence in denied areas. Anyone considered unfriendly was a target, and we were particularly interested in North Korea, China, and the Soviet Union. The real estate my unit covered went from the North Pole to the borders of India, and Hawaii to the Ural Mountains. I don't think it's any great secret to tell now, but we had some Japanese fishermen who used to go over to the coast of the Soviet Union there, and they would fill us in on whatever requirements we might have. Mostly on ports and so on, because our primary mission was to gather intelligence on early warning signals or troop size. Like if we detected anything about the Chinese massing troops someplace.

"I guess we must have had about seventy-five or eighty officers, sometimes between fifteen hundred and two thousand enlisted men," Colonel Stanley continued. "I don't remember the exact size, because we had units in various places in Japan. I had one in Korea, and there were more in the Philippines, Bangkok, and especially in Taiwan, where the [Nationalist] Chinese were very cooperative with us. We were allowed to put people undercover—I think this was the first time the Army tried it—take them out of uniform and get them civilian jobs."

Colonel Stanley told me that the name Richard Nagell "rings a bell" but that was all he could remember about him. Stanley did substantiate that the FOI worked closely with the CIA. "Theoretically, I'd say we were supposed to cooperate with each other. However, the CIA in those days was not too old and didn't have things established very well; I think we were ahead of them in many, many respects. We did work with them, mostly as of and when they wanted. I had some problems with them, and I guess they figure they had some with me. Also, we collaborated to a limited degree with the FBI. Anything that might have bearing on their own problems was handled for example, in Japan, by the [FBI's] legal attaché there."

In Tokyo, Bill Child was attached to the U.S. embassy as the FBI's man between 1954 and 1967 and from 1969 through 1976. He, too, is retired in Hawaii. With Colonel Stanley's FOI unit, Child recalls that "we exchanged information; Jack's outfit had dozens if not hundreds of people at one time, and they helped us out in so many ways. And we worked closely with the Japanese National Police. They were very professional. They didn't like to give their information to anybody unnecessarily, but when there was an important reason we got full cooperation. I was strictly on the defensive side, handling a large variety of security cases and trying to guard against what hostile countries might be doing against us back in the

United States." Though Child's reports went through an FBI chain of command in Washington, he said he briefed Director Hoover personally at least once a year.[25]

Retired colonel Robert Roth, whom I reached by phone in Virginia, was more reluctant to talk about FOI. "Back in those days, almost everything about FOI was classified," he said. "The initial FOI concept, as I knew it, pretty well speaks for itself. It was to elevate the sophistication of human collection efforts in support of combat forces. The concept was taught at that time at Fort Holabird. But what FOI involved and what evolved from it is an area I would say would probably still be classified."[26]

Tools of the Trade

Nagell was apparently the first really to break the veil of secrecy still surrounding FOI. When I contacted the National Archives, they could find no specific references to it. As a piece of American history that until now has remained untold, Nagell's full account is worth revealing. During his orientation at Far East headquarters in Japan, Nagell has written:

> I was ushered into a vault and familiarized with various tools of the trade, so to speak, including simple and intricate weapons to be utilized in assassinations; so-called undetectable poisons to be used in assassinations; sundry instruments for self-destruction, which I was advised contained hydrocyanic acid and/or potassium cyanide (one of which I was told would cause immediate unconsciousness, followed by death within 30 seconds); disguises; miniature wire recorders; tape recorders; cameras concealed in innocuous-appearing objects and standard cameras of Japanese and German make; radio transmitters and receivers; codebooks, etc. None of this paraphernalia could be identified as being of American origin . . . although I was advised that some of it was manufactured in the United States by the CIA's technical division. The mechanism of one assassination device (purportedly already used successfully), a short cylindrical metal tube, was explained to me in some detail. I was told that I might come across 'this one' in my work. . . .
>
> Also during my orientation, I was provided with various fraudulent identification (though one item was a genuine active duty U.S. Armed Forces Identification Card, No. 5785871, which identified me as Robert C. Nolan, Captain, ASN 01438346). I was advised that in the event I was apprehended, killed or compromised during the performance of my illegal FOI duties, the Department of the Army would publicly disclaim any knowledge of or connection with such duties, exercising its right of plausible denial.[27]

Among Nagell's Army records there is an "Issue Slip" for American cigarettes bearing a date of August 2, 1956, and the phrase "To be expended through US Intelligence [sic] activities." CAPT. ROBERT NOLAN is listed at the bottom as the authorized representative.[28] The accompanying signature, which I have compared with Nagell's, is clearly his. And when Nagell became a CIA contract agent in 1962–63, he used the Nolan pseudonym again, both for the CIA and in contacts with the FBI.

Partly due to his wartime firsthand knowledge of Korean geography, Nagell writes that in 1956 he was assigned to an FOI unit called Team 26:

> Team 26 operational personnel wore no insignia of rank when in uniform, were armed with .38 caliber snub-nose revolvers, and invariably were referred to in private as "spooks" by other American intelligence personnel and the Criminal Investigation Division (CID). Sometimes we wore "U.S." insignias on our lapels to foster the impression that we were Department of the Army civilian employees (DACs). Sometimes we used the CIA and the CIC as a cover in illicit operations. Sometimes we carried "spook cards" . . . stating that the bearer was engaged in intelligence activities "for the United States Government" and enjoining the Military Police not to question or detain us for any reason. . . . On some occasions we carried no identification whatsoever. . . .
>
> Insofar as practical, I used pre-arranged code sheets, that were changed frequently to communicate with Team 26 headquarters about "highly sensitive matters." My other covert duties, of which Team 26 remained unaware, included functions that required me to make frequent trips to Seoul and occasional trips to Japan, and also necessitated that I familiarize myself with all aspects of Team 26 operations, which I did successfully in one way or another.[29]

Team 26, according to Nagell, was "assigned an espionage mission against the ROK government and other covert activities."[30] Its primary role was to furnish intelligence support to the Republic of [South] Korea (ROK) Army's own intelligence branch—then known as the Headquarters Intelligence Division (HID). This, Nagell believes, was "in itself a violation of the armistice ending the Korean conflict." (The HID was the embryonic predecessor of the Korean CIA, later established in 1961 "with the advice and assistance of the American CIA," according to author Tad Szulc.)[31] Nagell's chief undercover duties were as the senior intelligence adviser to the HID. On several occasions, Nagell says he ventured across the Demilitarized Zone into North Korea, carrying no identification and armed with a Soviet-made PPSH submachine gun.[32]

> Since the HID was financed chiefly through FOI . . . FOI controlled most HID operations, the exception being the HID espionage effort

against Japan, which was financed by the ROK government[33]. . . . I kept extensive notes in cipher and evidence of many illegal activities, initially for my own protection in case I was left holding the bag, so to speak. . . .

During my service with the FOI in the Republic of Korea and during my service with the FOI and CIC in Japan, the FOI sponsored, financed, supported or otherwise participated in assassinations, kidnappings, blackmailings and a host of other illicit practices in violation of U.S. federal statutes, the Uniform Code of Military Justice, international law and U.S. treaties and treaty obligations.

These included, Nagell continued, indirect FOI support for an HID plan to assassinate the Republic of Korea's president Syngman Rhee in the fall of 1956, "an operation that was aborted, allegedly on FOI insistence, when it was ascertained that too many Americans, including a U.S. Army Brigadier General, might be killed in the process. I was told that General Pak Chung Hi (Chung Hee Park), the current President of the Republic of Korea, was the prime mover in that plot and in an earlier plot on President Rhee's life in October 1955."[34] One assassination that did succeed, Nagell says, was:

that of Major General Kim Chang Yong ('Tiger Kim'), the head of the ROK Army Counter Intelligence Corps on 30 January 1956, because of his alleged continued interference in FOI and HID activities[35]. . . . There were less significant assassinations within the Republic of Korea that I had definite cause to believe were sponsored by either the FOI or the CIA's Special Operations Group (a cover designation), but about which I possessed no direct knowledge. . . .

On 7 February 1957, I departed from the Republic of Korea for the last time. . . . I stated either to Colonel Stanley or to his Executive Officer, Lieutenant Colonel Roth, that I was fed up with Team 26, that directly or indirectly I had participated in practically every major crime in the performance of my FOI duties, or words to that effect. I was forthwith assigned to headquarters as the Assistant Director of Support, an administrative position. . . . Although Army Regulation 381-104, dated 22 January 1957, classified SECRET (which supposedly governed the missions and functions of the FOI), made no reference to assassinations, abductions, blackmailings, etc., it is inconceivable that such activities were not condoned and determined necessary at the highest levels of MI. In my opinion that regulation was promulgated only as a cosmetic reform of FOI functions.

As I studied what Nagell had revealed about FOI, I thought back to the sad story he told me during our second meeting—the American execution of a Korean fisherman's son, which a superior officer basically told him to pretend had never happened. It was obvious from Nagell's reminiscences about FOI that his "duties" had troubled him deeply. He was a man of conscience amid a military milieu that seemed increasingly devoid of it.

The activities he described, however, came as no real surprise. They seemed, in fact, precursors of revelations, almost twenty years later, about the CIA's involvement in the assassinations of foreign leaders: Patrice Lumumba in the Congo, 1960; Rafael Trujillo in the Dominican Republic, 1961; Salvador Allende in Chile, 1973; and, of course, ongoing failed attempts against Fidel Castro.[36]

Now, in the autumn of 1957, shortly after Lee Harvey Oswald arrived in Tokyo, Richard Nagell would take on a new assignment in the Japanese capital.

Summary

Richard Nagell's relatives not only believed his account but also provided additional details. Louis Gambert recalled Nagell's describing a plot to assassinate not only JFK but other government officials as well. Nagell, he said, was to eliminate Oswald before the assassination could take place. Robert Gambert believed that Nagell was still an Army Intelligence agent when he went to work for the CIA in the early 1960s. The family encountered not only FBI and apparently CIA officials while visiting Nagell in prison but also sustained a break-in to their Florida home, where some of Nagell's documents being held by his sister were stolen.

Nagell had begun receiving intelligence training at age nineteen. Wounded three times in battle during the Korean War, he became the youngest American to receive a battlefield promotion to captain in that war. Assigned to the Army Language School and then the Counter Intelligence Corps, he was the sole survivor of a military plane crash late in 1954 —sustaining severe head injuries that would later be used by his defense lawyers to try to prove "temporary insanity" when Nagell shot up the El Paso bank.

Yet, upon his recovery from the crash, Nagell had gone on to further duties with the CIC and the CIA in Los Angeles in the mid-1950s, then had been assigned to a Top-Secret espionage unit in the Far East known as Field Operations Intelligence (FOI). This military arm worked closely with the CIA on operations such as the Berlin Tunnel. The FOI commander, Colonel John Stanley, described its mission as "collection of intelligence in denied areas." Nagell recalled FOI's having conducted numerous illegal activities, including assassinations. Deeply upset about his role in FOI, he received a transfer back to the CIC early in 1957.

Oswald, a teenager whose dual fascinations were Marxism and the Marines, had enlisted in the Marines in the fall of 1956.

Chapter Four

Echoes from the Far East

On February 7, 1957, at Richard Nagell's request, he was transferred from South Korea back to Field Operations Intelligence's Far East headquarters in Tokyo. Two months after that, the Army captain was reassigned to duties with the 441st Counter Intelligence Corps Group.[1] It was here, beginning in October 1957, that Nagell recounts he "was assigned full time to the CIC file depository in Japan to supervise the review, regrading of security classification, and the destruction of thousands of SECRET and TOP SECRET documents accumulated by the CIC during the years 1945–57."

His assignment, Nagell also wrote, was a response to pressure from the Japanese Diet (Parliament), which had grown increasingly concerned about U.S. Military Intelligence activities on its shores. When a new prime minister, Nobusuke Kishi, began renegotiating a security pact with the United States, he made it clear that his nation expected to be treated more as a sovereign equal. Thus did the Pentagon, with reluctance, make a diplomatic gesture by agreeing to disband the CIC in Japan—"except," according to Nagell, "for a 34-man unit destined to be left behind in secret." And all CIC files were "being systematically destroyed after being placed on microfilm and shipped to the Central Records Facility (now called the Intelligence Records Repository) in the United States."

What was contained in this multitude of papers? They included, according to Nagell, "Agent Reports, Summaries of Investigations, Intelligence Summaries, Periodic Intelligence Reports, individual dossiers (many compiled on U.S. Senators, Congressmen, newspaper correspondents, American businessmen, tourists, and other American citizens who had visited or traveled through Japan over the years) and numerous classified reports" originating with the FBI and "cover organizations of the CIA." What he saw provided Nagell with "additional knowledge about illegal American intelligence operations worldwide."[2]

When I first read through the list of military/CIA "black operations" that Nagell set down in 1974, the names meant nothing to me. Only as I delved into books about the early years of the American occupation in Japan did I learn that the events were real—and that Nagell seemed to know more about them than had ever been revealed publicly. There was, for example, the 1951 kidnapping of a Japanese writer named Kaji Wataru by Military G-2 Intelligence. Handed over to the CIA as a suspected Soviet spy, Wataru had been held incommunicado for over a year and allegedly tortured. When the Japanese press eventually found out about the affair, there was outrage amid its government.

A mysterious American intelligence outfit, based in Okinawa and run by Colonel Jack Y. Canon, was accused of involvement, but hard evidence was lacking. The CIC's intelligence files, Nagell recorded, stated that Canon's "ZED group" was indeed behind the kidnapping; further, that the CIC was advised to stay clear of the project because it was considered to be an "indiscreet" CIA operation.[3]

There was another report, about a high-ranking Soviet intelligence officer, Yuri Rastvorov, whose defection in Tokyo in 1954 had given the Americans a picture of Moscow's designs toward infiltrating Japan.[4] In fact, according to what Nagell came across, Rastvorov had been blackmailed by U.S. intelligence before being flown to Okinawa. And there was more—such as the "TOP SECRET—EYES ONLY" account of the 1956 assassination of South Korea's counterintelligence chief, and a document suggesting that an American tourist named Harry Lister "be dealt with severely" while in Japan.

These Cold War tales apparently did not sit well with Nagell, so recently involved in dirty undercover work for FOI. He has written that "these revelations, among others not herein cited, further intensified [his] emotional stress." What he saw in the Tokyo files seems also to have brought

him to a pivotal decision. Nagell's relative Robert Gambert alerted me to
what next transpired.

An Oriental Puzzle

As my several hours over coffee and donuts with Nagell's sister's family
drew to a close in February 1990, Robert asked if I would care to go out
back and "take a look at the place." At the end of Louis Gambert's
retirement property in Tarpon Springs, the waters of a lovely bayou lapped
peacefully at the shoreline. As we stood together on an old wooden dock,
Robert gazed across to where the bayou emptied into the Anclote River,
then onward to the Gulf Coast, only a ten-minute boat ride away. He said
there was something else he thought I should know, but hadn't wanted to
mention in front of the other family members.

"Dick talked to me one time about his service in Japan," Gambert said.
"You see, he operated intelligence rings over there. In other words, he
had Japanese operatives feeding information back in to the Army Intelligence. They were picking up anything on subversive or Communist or
antigovernment-type activities.

"He also headed up this team that went through all the old Army
Intelligence files in Tokyo. Some of these papers apparently went all the
way back to the prewar years when Japan invaded China [in 1937]—
records that came into Japanese possession in Shanghai. There was information in there about a lot of Communist activities, and Dick told me that
some of the files had to do with American news correspondents who after
the war became very prominent. See, a lot of these people had been
arrested by the Japanese as Communists, and then released by pressure
from the United States before World War II.

"Apparently," Gambert added, "Dick came across some of this information in a secret government file on the Sorge case."

I was vaguely familiar with Dr. Richard Sorge. He was a German who,
between 1929 and 1941, had been the leader of a notorious spy ring operating for the Soviet Union in both China and Japan. The subject of a
number of books, Sorge was credited with having built up one of the most
successful Soviet espionage operations ever, keeping the Red Army fully
apprised of Japanese military and industrial potential and intentions. At
the same time, he was not completely trusted by his superiors. One book
recounted that Sorge also supplied some information to Adolf Hitler's
Nazi spy operation, and sometimes passed along "planted" data that Japan's Emperor Hirohito wanted to see transmitted to Moscow. Although

Sorge was caught by the Japanese shortly before Pearl Harbor and alleg-edly executed late in 1944, the story did not break in the American press until 1948.

Sorge himself had posed as a journalist. One of his suspected recruits was Agnes Smedley, an American newspaper correspondent in Shanghai during the early 1930s. Another of his spy team was a second journalist, who used the code name "Jacob" but whose real identity had never been publicly revealed. He had also reportedly been recruited in Shanghai when Sorge first organized his espionage cadre.

Gambert himself had studied some of the classified U.S. files on the Sorge case, as part of his training with the Defense Investigative Service. "There was a question whether Sorge was actually executed, or exchanged with the Russians," he continued. "Dick [Nagell], from his knowledge of the Japanese, felt that probably he'd been swapped, because the supposed execution had occurred so quietly, without witnesses, whereas the Japa-nese customarily stuck to very dogmatic, rigid procedures in these mat-ters."

Then Gambert revealed what Nagell had done with the information he came across in the Tokyo file repository. "Dick told me he had multiple stashes of documents from those files. He wasn't supposed to have them, but he'd gotten them on film. It was secret information, and I figure he wanted to use it as a lever, by threatening to disclose certain things later on."[5]

It was a curious tale indeed, and one that Nagell had not elected to set down in his Court of Claims case. What did it mean? Had the American military covered up what the Japanese knew about—or had done with—Richard Sorge? If so, why? What of the "prominent" American journalists and their purported Communist backgrounds? In the Cold War climate of the 1950s, wouldn't power brokers such as Joe McCarthy or J. Edgar Hoover have delighted in publicly exposing these people's "subversive" pasts?

By 1990 I had lost contact with Nagell and so was unable to ask him about Gambert's statements. I didn't have any particular reason to suspect that this even bore relevance to the bigger story I was pursuing—except to indicate a distinct alteration in Nagell's attitude toward American intelli-gence methods. For whatever reason, he began keeping a private record of U.S. skulduggery and Communist activities in the Far East. He had stepped beyond sanctioned military procedures, into his own underground realm.

So I found myself suddenly immersed in studying the prewar years in China. For a while, though reading about the Sorge case was fascinating, I felt I was probably on a distant sidetrack. Then two names leapt out at me from the old books and faded news clippings about Shanghai in the 1930s, where Richard Sorge first organized his Soviet spy ring.

The "Joseph Kramer" Connection

One of the names I happened upon—a man who had lived in Shanghai between 1934 and 1940 and who became a prominent American and then Canadian journalist—was Mark Julius Gayn. Nagell, in a complexly phrased sentence he inserted into a 1974 brief filed with the Court of Claims, made his one and only direct reference to Mark Gayn. It was in the context of explaining the aliases that Nagell used while under contract to the CIA in 1962–63:

> In addition to my true name, I used the pseudonyms of "Robert No-lan," one of the assumed names provided me while functioning for the FOI, and "Joseph Kramer," also a pseudonym of Mark Julius Gayn, a known Communist (who, according to a CIC report furnished the FBI, had penetrated several MI organizations in the Far East shortly after World War II), while contacting the FBI by telephone, in person or by registered mail at or from Los Angeles, Calif., Mexico, D.F., New York, N.Y., Jacksonville, Fla., Miami, Fla., Dallas, Tex., and New Orleans, La., during the months of July, September, November and December 1962 and January, July and September 1963, respectively.[6]

The reader may recall (see Chapter One) that it was the name "Joseph Kramer" with which Nagell signed his September 1963 letter to J. Edgar Hoover—alerting the FBI to a conspiracy involving Oswald to assassinate President Kennedy. According to Nagell's sworn affidavit, "Joseph Kramer" was also "an alias of a known Communist (Soviet) agent then residing in Canada." Nagell had listed a return address for "Kramer" in Mexico City, though his warning letter was mailed within the United States. Nagell also used the "Kramer" alias while meeting with the FBI in Miami in January 1963.

And, in a long typewritten memorandum written by Nagell while incarcerated in 1967, he further described the contents of his personal property "seized and confiscated" by the FBI on September 20, 1963. It included "two Mexican tourist cards (one of them for multiple entrance) made out to the names "Joseph Kramer" and "Albert" or "Aleksei Hidel[7] . . . ." Alek J. Hidell was an alias known to have been used by Lee Harvey Oswald in many of his 1963 activities. Nagell was alleging that an Oswald tourist card had been in his own possession.

As his trial approached, Nagell had written J. Edgar Hoover again from his El Paso jail cell. Dated April 16, 1964, this letter said in part:

> My responsibility concerning the then prospective action of Lee H. Oswald (Albert Hidel) terminated with the dispatch of the registered letter from Joseph Kramer to the F.B.I. in September 1963.
> Since the information disclosed in that letter was judged to be mendacious by the F.B.I., as is quite evident, then with whom the responsibility lies for what subsequently happened in Dallas is rather obvious.
> Certainly, F.B.I. files in Washington, D.C. (or Miami, Florida, Mexico City, etc.) reflect who "Joseph Kramer" is. And, such information received from a known Communist who allegedly had been effective enough to penetrate several U.S. military intelligence agencies, should not have been ignored. In this respect, the efficacy of the F.B.I. is the responsibility of its director, regardless of the actions or judgment of his subordinates.

During one of our interviews, Nagell had added this about the crucial September 1963 letter to the FBI: "I have never stated where that letter was mailed from, or that I'd mailed it personally. I've always said I *dispatched* a letter at the instance of Joseph Kramer. I felt sure that if the FBI got a letter signed 'Joseph Kramer' and ran a computer or file check, they would look into it. They would know this was not a crank letter."[8]

A dictionary definition of one meaning for the word "instance" is as follows: "the act of asking or suggesting; solicitation, notion." So if Nagell "dispatched" his letter to Hoover about Oswald "at the instance of Joseph Kramer," the clear implication is that "Kramer" was directly involved in his doing so. And if the "Kramer" name was, as Nagell alleges, also a pseudonym of "known Communist (Soviet) agent" Mark Gayn, then it also follows that Gayn was somehow involved with Nagell. And, it would seem, Gayn was at least cognizant of Lee Harvey Oswald.

It was even conceivable that Gayn himself might have "dispatched" the letter. Nagell's use of the "Kramer" name could well have been his way of letting the FBI know that Soviet intelligence also had foreknowledge of the conspiracy. Nagell says he carefully composed his letter "in the style and format used by operational personnel of the Central Intelligence Agency."[9]

Nagell had never elaborated further with me about Mark Gayn. But his statement that the FBI would have known of Gayn's postwar activities in the Far East by way of "a CIC report" brought me back to Nagell's days amid the CIC's Tokyo files late in 1957. Prominent journalists. . . . the Sorge case . . . Now, as I learned that Gayn had worked for *The Washington Post* and then Japanese and Chinese news organizations in 1930s

Shanghai, Robert Gambert's remarks took on a heightened significance. Nagell most probably came across reports on Gayn in those Tokyo files. Whatever they said, he had secretly filmed and stashed it. Somewhere along the line, he must have encountered Gayn.

Though I didn't know what the circumstances meant, I had stumbled onto a whole new potential dimension surrounding Nagell, Oswald, and the assassination.

The Mysterious History of Mark Gayn

"I'm sure Mark Gayn *was* a Soviet agent," James Barros was saying, "but you'll have a difficult time proving it. Those papers of his at the library, you can be sure, have been very well sanitized."[10]

Barros, a professor of political science at the University of Toronto, was also the author of *No Sense of Evil,* a study of the likelihood that Canadian diplomat E. H. Norman was a longtime Soviet agent before Norman committed suicide in 1957. I had flown to Toronto in March of 1992 to examine the Gayn papers at the University of Toronto. The papers had been donated by Gayn's widow after his death in 1981. Starting in the early 1950s, Gayn had been a leading foreign correspondent for the *Toronto Star* newspaper.

Professor Barros was right. Despite the more than 150 boxes of Gayn's correspondence, diaries, and published works at the Thomas Fisher Rare Books Library, there seemed to be vast gaps in his history—particularly about his 1930s years in Shanghai, and the 1962–63 period. Still, it was not a wasted trip. The papers did contain a few clues that led me to believe I was not on a wild-goose chase. No smoking guns, but a small quiver of arrows pointing in the direction Nagell had mapped out.

I studied the photograph on the cover of the library's *Guide to the Mark Gayn Papers.* Right below a picture of Mao Tse-tung, it depicted a bespectacled, round-faced, balding man with a long nose and a tight-lipped smile, well dressed in a dark suit and offering a sideways glance.

In brief, Gayn's biographical sketch described his birth in 1909 of Russian-Jewish parents in a tiny town near the border of Manchuria and Mongolia. Educated in China, Russia, and at New York's Columbia University, he had begun his journalistic career in Shanghai and covered the Far Eastern sector for *Newsweek* and *Time* during World War II.

But there was one conspicuous blight on a long career during which Gayn traveled constantly to every corner of the globe, specializing in the Communist world. In June 1945 he had been arrested by the FBI on charges of illegally procuring secret government information from America's wartime OSS intelligence service. Sixty classified documents were found in a raid on his New York apartment.

Yet it was an odd thing: A congressional report would note that Gayn "on one occasion . . . was seen to leave the *Amerasia* [magazine] offices with a stuffed briefcase and board a bus with his wife. An FBI agent peered over his shoulder as he sat looking at some papers from the briefcase. They were government documents, classified and so stamped."[11] It seemed almost as if Gayn were looking to get caught.

Also charged with stealing some six hundred more files were two State Department employees, a Naval Intelligence officer, and the coeditors of *Amerasia* magazine. Many of the documents revolved around the battle plans of Chiang Kai-shek, the Chinese leader who was then fighting on two fronts, against the Japanese and Mao Tse-tung's rebel army. The *"Amerasia* case" became a cause célèbre, especially among the zealously anti-Communist "China lobby," which viewed it, as late as 1970, as a classic example of how U.S. officials and journalists contributed to Mao's eventual victory. While four "coconspirators" were indicted, a grand jury did not see fit to do the same with Gayn or State Department China expert John Stewart Service. Gayn then resumed his journalistic career.[12]

After the war, the period when Nagell wrote that Gayn had "penetrated" U.S. Military Intelligence in the Far East, he had indeed been based in Japan and Korea. Though in 1944 Gayn had become an American citizen, in 1953 he immigrated to Canada, according to Professor Barros because of his difficulties with U.S. Immigration authorities over his "leftist" leanings.

Gayn's long obituary in the *Toronto Star,* noting that he had died at age seventy-two "after a difficult illness," described his having "visited Castro's Cuba several times. . . . As he traveled around the world Gayn maintained a long list of impressive contacts in the countries he visited. Even in the Soviet Union he was able to meet high-ranking Communist officials and dissidents in their private apartments."[13]

According to the library's sketch about his life, at different stages of his career Gayn had "often resorted to the use of pseudonyms . . . to protect himself . . . [and] when writing on Communist matters."[14] I found one cryptic reference to a "Kramer" during his time in Tokyo in the late 1940s. Graham Bradshaw, the librarian who organized the Gayn papers, told me he thought he recalled something about the name "Joseph Kramer," perhaps in connection with the *Amerasia* spy case, but I couldn't find it.

What most intrigued me was a trip Gayn had made to Mexico City and Cuba in January–February 1963. Nagell was on record as saying that he himself had been to Mexico City many times between September 1962 and

September 1963. I also knew that Nagell had made, in his words, "an unauthorized trip to Cuba" at some unspecified time in 1963. (All American travel to Castro's island had been severely restricted by the State Department.) But if the two men had rendezvoused in either place, there was no record of it. One page in Gayn's appointment book—for February 11 in Mexico and the following day in Havana—had been torn out. All that was clear was Gayn's interest in the "factional struggle within the Communist Party" in Mexico City.[15]

There was also Gayn's trip to West Berlin and then the Soviet Union in the summer of 1968, simultaneous with Nagell's being taken off a train in East Germany and held for more than four months behind the "Iron Curtain." Noteworthy, too, was Gayn's presence in the Soviet Union in May 1960—when Francis Gary Powers's U-2 spy plane was shot down, scuttling an impending peace summit between President Eisenhower and Premier Khrushchev. Oswald was living in the USSR at the time. But, again, there was nothing among the papers to link any of these events more than coincidentally.[16]

Also evident was Gayn's ongoing scrutiny of both left- and right-wing organizations in Japan, Korea, and elsewhere. In the spring of 1962 he wrote an article about the Minutemen group and their Southern California associates among the American "Far Right." Early in 1963 he visited Strategic Air Command headquarters in Omaha, taking detailed notes on what the American military knew about Soviet and Cuban defenses.[17] And in his 1960 notebook there were some fascinating passages relating to an interview he apparently conducted with CIA director Allen Dulles—whose work and home telephone numbers were also noted by Gayn.

"Dulles was asked if Sovs had penetrated CIA. He said, 'I naturally assume that the Sovs. will attempt to penetrate the CIA. . . . I don't think they're going to find it easy, (but) we are going to keep on our guard all the time.' "

Following this was an account about the American trip of Nikita Khrushchev in the autumn of 1959: "Khrushchev told a film studio pres.: 'your agents in Europe & Middle East give us your code books and then we send false information back to you through the codes. . . .' " Then Gayn set down an exchange between Dulles and Khrushchev that reportedly took place at a White House dinner. "Dulles said to Khrushchev: 'You Mr. Chairman may have seen some of my intelligence reports from time to time.' Khrushchev said: 'I believe we get the same reports. And probably from the same people.' Dulles said: 'Maybe we should pool our efforts.' Khrushchev: 'Yes, we should buy our intelligence data together and save money, we'd have to pay the people only once.' "[18]

It was impossible to do more than speculate on any hidden meaning behind all this. All that was tangible was Gayn's interest in the CIA-KGB spy wars and his appearance in certain locales at interesting times. What I wondered most about was how someone with Gayn's reputation—for the *Amerasia* stolen-secrets case remained a benchmark during the Joseph McCarthy era and even later—could have received such seemingly easy entrée to U.S. defense installations and even to Allen Dulles. Gayn was in the Soviet Union in 1960 and every single year between 1964 and 1970. Twice—in 1947 and 1965—he had gained private audiences with China's Mao Tse-tung; in 1971 Gayn was among a handful of Western journalists authorized to enter Peking.

Conversation with the Widow

Gayn's notebooks for the months leading up to the John F. Kennedy assassination were conspicuously absent from the collection of his papers. By telephone, I contacted Suzanne Gayn, a Hungarian actress whom Gayn had taken as his third wife in 1950. Did she remember her late husband ever using the name "Joseph Kramer"? I asked.

Adamantly, she denied that Gayn had ever used "a stupid name like Joseph Kramer. You can tell whoever told you this that he's absolutely mad. I was his researcher. I knew everything about him. He had no secrets from me."

I quickly changed the subject, asking whether the FBI had hounded him in the years after his arrest in the 1945 *Amerasia* case. "Yes," said Suzanne Gayn, "my husband had umpteen ulcer hemorrhages because of the stress they put on him. But after McCarthy died, things changed. The pendulum went from one side to another, everybody was at his feet. When he went to China in 1971 and *The New York Times* published it on page one, senators, Averell Harriman, everybody invited him to their place overnight."

Had Gayn ever spoken to her about the assassination of President Kennedy? I continued. Though I said nothing beyond that, her immediate response was another adamant "No!" Then she continued: "The strangest thing happened. We were driving through Florida on vacation. We had just had lunch at Cape Kennedy—it was called Cape Canaveral then—and suddenly came the radio announcement [about the assassination]. And my husband, I swear to God, started to cry. He immediately phoned the *Star,* left me in Florida, and flew to Washington. When he met his colleague there, they both embraced each other and cried. His colleague said, 'I never realized how soft you are'—because my husband wrote everything very matter-of-fact. He loved Kennedy. The idea is absolutely ridiculous!"

What idea? I thought. Apparently Gayn's widow thought my question was aimed at inferring that he had some "involvement" in the assassination. Responding to another question about whether Gayn ever traveled to Mexico on journalistic assignments, she replied that he "was never in Mexico," but had made a trip to Cuba in 1961.

I left our conversation feeling puzzled, and with the impression that there was much Mrs. Gayn was not saying. Justifiably so, if Nagell's revelations about "Joseph Kramer" were true. Beyond filing a Freedom of Information request on Gayn with the FBI—which, as of this writing, has yet to produce a response—my quest seemed to have reached a dead end.

Harold Isaacs and Oswald's Curious Cousin

But there was someone else—a man whose life's path for a time paralleled Mark Gayn's so closely it was eerie—whose name Nagell most likely would have come across in the CIC's Tokyo intelligence files. This was Harold R. Isaacs. After the assassination, the FBI had briefly looked into his relationship with Lee Harvey Oswald's cousin Marilyn Murret.

The New Orleans-based Murret family crops up consistently at crucial times in Oswald's life. In 1954 Oswald and his mother had lived for a while with his Uncle Charles and Aunt Lillian—when Oswald first developed a fascination for spy stories and communism. When he moved from Dallas to New Orleans in April 1963, Oswald temporarily resided with the Murrets on his arrival. That summer it was Uncle Charles who arranged to bail Oswald out of jail after his street altercation while passing out Fair Play for Cuba literature.

Most recent conjecture about this relationship has focused on the uncle, who served as a kind of surrogate father to Oswald during his youth and adolescence. In 1963, besides his full-time job as a steamship clerk, "Dutz" Murret was also a prosperous middle-level bookmaker in the gambling network of New Orleans Mob boss Carlos Marcello. This has fueled speculation of a Marcello link to Oswald.[19]

But equally important, in figuring out Oswald's connections, may be his closeness to the Murrets' daughter Marilyn, some twelve years his senior. Shortly before Oswald embarked on the overseas voyage that would take him to the USSR, his cousin had set off on a journey of her own. Deciding to work her way around the world as a schoolteacher, Miss Murret went first by tramp steamer to Japan. According to the Warren Commission, one of the first people she called on there was Oswald's older half brother John Pic. A career serviceman, Pic was then stationed at the U.S. Air

Force hospital in Tashikawa. Pic later told the Warren Commission that he'd asked Marilyn when she last heard from Lee. "Oh, he's in Russia, didn't you know?" Pic remembered her replying. In her own commission testimony, Miss Murret recalled that Pic's wife had informed *her* about this.[20] In any event, at that time nobody in the general public was yet aware of Oswald's arrival in the Soviet Union on October 15. So how did Marilyn Murret know?

An FBI interview with Murret, conducted the day after the assassination, revealed the following about her journeying: That she had returned to the United States in January 1963 after three and a half years abroad; had lived in Japan, teaching all grade-level subjects, for a year; had also traveled to Hawaii, Hong Kong, Australia, New Zealand, Singapore, Thailand, India, Iran, the Holy Land, and England; "that she had visited East Berlin and had been detained there for twelve hours after which she was released."[21]

There was no elaboration on why Oswald's cousin was "detained" in East Berlin. Nor did the Warren Commission pursue the matter with her, focusing instead on what she described as a brief conversation with Oswald about his Soviet stay *after* he settled in New Orleans again in 1963. Late that July, she and other members of the Murret family had traveled with Oswald to a Jesuit seminary in Mobile, Alabama, where another of his cousins was studying for the priesthood. There Oswald gave a speech to the seminarians, recalled as being highly critical of Russian-style communism. After that, the FBI report on Marilyn Murret finds her traveling "through Mexico and Central America by bus" all through August. Oswald himself would enter Mexico in September and probably, as we shall see later in this narrative, in early August as well.

Lonnie Hudkins, a journalist in 1963 with the *Houston Post,* told me that "a high-level source in Washington" maintained that Murret was for a while "a CIA agent assigned to Japan, the person who helped make the contacts when Oswald 'defected' to Russia."[22] William George Gaudet, a now-deceased CIA agent in New Orleans, told attorney Fensterwald in 1975: "She [Murret] may have worked for the agency in New Orleans. They had quite a few here. You know, this was not a small office. I would say fifty people."[23]

The Murret family has consistently declined all requests for interviews. But given the possible Nagell-Oswald-Gayn connections, what I found most compelling was the FBI's statement that Oswald's cousin "was linked in some manner with the apparatus of Professor Harold Isaacs."[24] Another FBI report, which surfaced only when an assassination researcher discovered it misfiled in the National Archives in the mid-1970s, is titled "MARILYN DOROTHEA MURRET." But it contains not a word about her. It is instead all about the background of Harold Isaacs, who in 1963 was a research associate at MIT's Center for International Studies in Cambridge, Massachusetts.[25]

Once more I was drawn back to the distant echoes of the Far East. Between 1931 and 1936, the FBI file said, Isaacs had been living in Shanghai, the young editor of a radical English-language weekly that supported the Communist uprising of Mao. Here Isaacs became a close friend of an American journalist named Agnes Smedley—who, as it happened, was then secretly working for Soviet master spy Richard Sorge. Starting in 1931, according to her biographer, "It was through Smedley that Sorge found most of the Asian contacts who gave him significant information over the next two years."[26]

Yet, by 1935, a rift developed between Smedley and Isaacs. As Isaacs told the FBI, he "gradually came to learn that the Chinese Communists were deceitful and were playing politics, and he became increasingly estranged from them, eventually denouncing them as corrupt politicians." He was then accused by his former comrades of being "a paid agent of the Japanese government."[27]

Two books about the Far East in those years both refer to Isaacs as a "Trotskyist"[28]—that form of Communist/Socialist ideology that, unlike the more insular Stalinism, advocates a global Communist revolution. In the United States, Isaacs told the FBI in 1951, he had become an active member of the Trotskyist Socialist Workers Party (SWP) and "contributed articles to their press." But he indicated he had left his youthful idealism behind by the time he accepted a position at MIT's Center for International Studies in 1953.

The worldview of Lee Harvey Oswald, at least on paper, can likewise best be described as "Trotskyist." In 1962 and 1963, the SWP and its newspaper, *The Militant,* would be those with which Oswald maintained his strongest paper trail of associations. Not that there is anything to tie Oswald to Isaacs (except, apparently, Oswald's cousin)—with one exception: a single, unsubstantiated FBI report in the National Archives.

After the assassination, the FBI interviewed a Canadian businessman, Richard Giesbrecht, who told of a conversation he had overheard in a restaurant at the Winnipeg airport on February 12, 1964. It was between two men sitting at an adjacent table, both of whom Giesbrecht claimed began expressing concern about how much Oswald might have told his wife about the assassination plot. Suddenly one of them brought up the name "Isaacs," saying, "Why should a person with such a good record as Isaacs become mixed up with a psycho?"[29]

Harold Isaacs died in 1988, but, as with Mark Gayn, his papers were donated by his widow to a library archive. Poring through more boxes of faded files at MIT, I discovered the remarkable parallels between Gayn's and Isaacs' careers. Both men had been educated at Columbia University, then ended up as radical journalists in Shanghai in the 1930s. For two of those years in China, they had been there simultaneously. Both men had covered the Far East for *Newsweek* during World War II. Both had been in Tokyo and in Korea in the war's aftermath. Both had gone on to work for the *Toronto Star*, though Isaacs' tenure preceded Gayn's by some years. And both had authored a number of books about Far Eastern affairs.[30]

In addition, both Gayn and Isaacs were acquainted with Agnes Smedley, later accused by U.S. Military Intelligence as having been a member of the Sorge spy ring. In 1933, Isaacs gave the farewell party in her honor in Shanghai[31]; in 1945, Smedley's name was found in Gayn's address book by the FBI. And, though Isaacs' name never came up alongside Gayn's in the *Amerasia* stolen-secrets case, Isaacs' name appeared in both an address book and a list of "Far Eastern personnel" whom Congress was curious about in the *Amerasia* matter.[32] John Stewart Service, the State Department employee acquitted with Gayn, testified before Congress that he had "talked with one Harold Isaacs, whom he knew to be a former Communist" in New York that spring of 1945.

Yet, in none of the Gayn or Isaacs papers that I saw was there anything hinting at an association between the two men. I supposed that this was possible but, given their histories, unlikely. They definitely ran in the same circles. The question was whether those circles extended all the way to the activities of Oswald.

By the time the FBI looked into Isaacs after the assassination, he had been at MIT for ten years. A secretary at the university's Center for International Studies told the FBI that the center "was endowed to a great extent by the United States government" and that much of Professor Isaacs' work consisted of international travel.[33] Indeed, here is the way the MIT think tank was described in *The Invisible Government*, a 1964 best-selling book that provided the first in-depth look at the CIA:

> "Harvard has refused to accept money for classified projects," wrote author David Wise, "but some of its faculty members have done research for the CIA by the simple expedient of funneling their work through the Center for International Studies at the nearby Massachusetts Institute of Technology. The MIT Center, which was set up with CIA money in 1950, has adopted many of the practices in effect at the CIA headquarters in Virginia. An armed guard watches over the door and the participating academicians must show badges on entering and leaving."[34]

Isaacs' specialty was the study of worldwide youth movements and, soon after Oswald's cousin Marilyn returned from her own extensive travels in the Far East, in 1963 Isaacs had embarked on "a long journey of inquiry" to some of the same countries: Israel, India, Malaysia, the Philippines,

Thailand, Indonesia, and finally Japan. A letter among his papers described putting him in touch "with students interested in China" when Isaacs arrived in Tokyo on October 4, 1963.[35]

He was in Japan when the assassination happened, his chaperone being Shigeharu Matsumoto of Tokyo's International House. Isaacs' papers identified Matsumoto as the former head of Domei, the now-defunct Japanese news service for which Mark Gayn had also worked in the late 1930s while in Shanghai. A book I later came across—*Japan's Imperial Conspiracy*—described Matsumoto further. It noted that his International House was "a hostelry where young visiting scholars from abroad are accommodated and watched at minimal expense to all concerned." Watched? I wondered. Author David Bergamimi also recalled Matsumoto as the "best friend" of a fellow named Hotsumi Ozaki when the pair attended Tokyo's Imperial University together.[36] Things were coming full circle. Back in 1930, Ozaki had been introduced to Richard Sorge by Agnes Smedley. Ozaki had gone on to be the Soviet agent's chief source of high-level information about the Japanese government, and was supposedly executed along with Sorge in 1944.

What was it all about? Was I grasping at straws? Or was I peering through the looking-glass at some kind of intelligence network with roots in prewar Japan and China, and tentacles that reached all the way to the death of a U.S. president? If so, whose network was it? Could Isaacs—and Oswald's cousin, as part of what the FBI described as his "apparatus"—have ended up with the CIA? Or a section of the CIA? A section, maybe, with ties to the KGB?

There was one last clue, and it also centered around Isaacs' Tokyo host in 1963, Shigeharu Matsumoto. Among the possessions seized from Nagell by the FBI that September were four small photographs of Japanese. Before his trial, Nagell specifically requested that these pictures be returned to him, saying they were central to his defense against the bank robbery charge.[37] One of these, as Nagell wrote to attorney Calamia, was of "Shogo Matsumoto." According to a Japanese linguist I consulted at Harvard, the Japanese language for given names was not standardized until after World War II; thus it was quite conceivable that "Shogo" could be another form of "Shigeharu."

MacArthur's "Little Fascist"

We come now to a man whose worldview was as diametrically opposed to communism as it is possible to imagine. This was Major General Charles

A. Willoughby, who first brought the Sorge case—and its alleged American conspirators—to the American public. I believe that, just as Mark Gayn and perhaps Harold Isaacs may have come to play an important behind-the-scenes role in the Oswald saga, so might Charles Willoughby.

His name first came to my attention in an anonymous letter, a response to the first article I wrote in 1975 about the assassination. If I wanted to "solve" the great mystery, I was advised to examine the career of someone identified only as "Tscheppe-Weidenbach," born in Heidelberg, Germany, in 1892. It was only recently that I discovered that Adolf Tscheppe-Weidenbach was the original name of Charles Willoughby. In biographies he provided to the Army and to *Who's Who in America,* Willoughby described himself as the son of a German baron and an American woman from Baltimore. Later, *Reporter* magazine would question the nobility of his lineage. A friend from his early days in the United States said that both his parents were German and that Willoughby was a rough Anglicization of Weidenbach (which means "willow brook"). Willoughby told a reporter that he was an orphan and never knew his father. It was a past marked with ambiguity from the beginning.[38]

During World War I, along with future OSS chief William J. Donovan, Willoughby had chased bandit Pancho Villa for the U.S. Expeditionary Force in Mexico. Then Willoughby helped train Allied fliers in France and, in the 1920s, served as a military attaché in Venezuela, Colombia, and Ecuador, where he built a reputation as an expert on military intelligence. In the mid-1930s, while Willoughby was teaching at Fort Leavenworth, he met General Douglas MacArthur. Between 1941 and 1951, Willoughby would go on to serve as General MacArthur's chief of Army G-2 intelligence.[39]

It is not stretching a point to say that Willoughby was a racist, an anti-Semite, and, as even MacArthur referred to him, "my little Fascist."[40] He was an odd, clever, little-known man, fluent in four languages, whose bearing was almost a caricature of a Prussian officer and earned him the nickname "Sir Charles." Willoughby's physically intimidating six-foot, three-inch, 220-pound frame meshed with a character that was both autocratic and arrogant. Aside from MacArthur, his hero was Spain's Fascist dictator Francisco Franco, whom he had first met in the 1920s. In 1939 Willoughby had written of the Italian dictator Mussolini: "Historical judgement, freed from the emotional haze of the moment, will credit Mussolini with wiping out a memory of defeat by re-establishing the traditional military supremacy of the white race."[41] He viewed the Soviet bloc as the great enemy, "the historical continuity of 'Mongoloid-PanSlavism.'"[42]

During World War II, MacArthur and Willoughby successfully staved off all efforts by the fledgling OSS to encroach on their Pacific territory.

As OSS head William Donovan put it, MacArthur insisted on "keeping everything in his theater under his thumb." It was the beginning of a rivalry that would last for many years, as Willoughby fought for hegemony over the OSS's successor agency, the CIA, in postwar occupied Japan and then during the Korean War. When the Korean War broke out and the CIA bivouacked a thousand-man force at the Atsugi base in Tokyo, Willoughby went so far as to put CIA personnel under surveillance by Japanese policemen working for him. As far as MacArthur and Willoughby were concerned, certain elements of the OSS/CIA had a left-wing tinge that could not be trusted.[43]

The 1945 *Amerasia* case was often cited by Willoughby as an example of how the OSS could be so easily compromised, since so many of its Top-Secret documents ended up in the hands of Mark Gayn and his friends. But Gayn had a curious subsequent relationship with Willoughby. After all charges against Gayn were dropped in the *Amerasia* matter, he had gone back to Tokyo as a journalist to cover the American occupation. He was indefatigable. Many of MacArthur's people viewed him with suspicion for asking too many embarrassing questions. His 1948 best-seller *Japan Diary* was severely critical of MacArthur's tactics. At the same time, Gayn's papers reveal that he and Willoughby had a quite cordial relationship. Besides Gayn's making reference to their "friendly terms" in a letter to *Amerasia* editor Philip Jaffe, there was a Christmas 1947 missive from Willoughby to Gayn. And this at a time when Gayn, according to what Nagell learned from the CIC files, was simultaneously penetrating U.S. Military Intelligence on behalf of the Soviets.

In this same period, Willoughby set about secretly remobilizing a private, rabidly anti-Communist army within Japan. According to the 1987 book *Sheathing the Sword: The Demilitarization of Japan* by British scholars Meirion and Susie Harries,

Willoughby believed implicitly in the solidarity of the military caste. Before the war many American professional soldiers had had links with their Japanese counterparts within the ruling oligarchy. During the war, despite being enemies, in a curious way they were bound even closer, as Willoughby put it, by "years of intimate combat association." Now in the aftermath of war Willoughby and many like him were finding that in important respects they had more in common with the remains of the Japanese military hierarchy than with the American civilians in Tokyo. . . . The militarist spirit was kept alight in small cells spread throughout the body of the nation. As for the one man with the power to control Willoughby and his Japanese henchmen, it is not clear whether MacArthur ever knew what was happening.[44]

Willoughby cut deals with everybody. During World War II the Japanese had conducted germ warfare experiments using human beings as guinea pigs. At least three thousand people died, including an unknown number of captured U.S. military personnel. But when the Pentagon determined that the biological research might prove useful in the Cold War, the Japanese responsible for the experiments received immunity from prosecution in exchange for their lab records. Only in 1982 did this seamy story come to light, including the Pentagon's 1947 acknowledgment of Willoughby's "wholehearted cooperation" in arranging examination of the "human pathological material which had been transferred to Japan from the biological warfare installations."[45]

Just as the OSS and later the CIA had forged alliances enlisting New York, Sicilian, and Corsican gangsters in the battles against Nazism and then communism, so did Willoughby hire mobsters for postwar "dirty tricks" against the Japanese Communist Party and others. Yoshio Kodama, future leader of the Yakuza crime syndicate (as well as CIA contract agent and Lockheed lobbyist) bargained his way out of jail as a "Class A" war criminal. Kodama had made a fortune while setting up a Japanese spy network in Shangai, much of it in opium smuggling. None other than Mark Gayn had described in a 1940 article the drug trafficking "used to defray the cost of Japanese aggression," totaling some $100 million in that year alone.[46] After Pearl Harbor, the U.S. Treasury Department had charged Japan with a deliberate campaign to smuggle narcotics into this country. Kodama knew where all the Shanghai skeletons were hidden. In 1947 he made a package arrangement with Nationalist Chinese leader Chiang Kai-shek and with Willoughby, whereby Kodama turned over half of his immediate personal fortune of $200 million to the U.S. Army's Counter Intelligence Corps—thereby gaining his freedom and new employment.[47]

"War criminals sit in the Diet, the Cabinet, and the imperial court," Mark Gayn wrote in May 1948. "War criminals are 'revising' the textbooks, running the press, dominating the radio and moving picture industries. Thought Control agents, purged and purged again, keep reappearing in positions of responsibility—often with American encouragement."[48]

Perhaps most important to this chronicle was Willoughby's relationship with Tokushiro Hattori. Despite the fact that Hattori had been private secretary to General Tojo and a leading figure in Japanese wartime military intelligence, Willoughby allowed him to set up his own postwar spy agency under the cover of the Army G-2's historical research operation. When Kaji Wataru was kidnapped by G-2 in 1951 and handed over to the CIA, the Hattori group was discovered to have aided the Americans and been disbanded by the Japanese government, though Hattori himself kept his relationship with the nation's right wing.

According to *Sheathing the Sword*, "Hattori's mission in life after the war was to exploit the American-Soviet conflict to Japan's advantage."[49] Hattori may have been related to the wealthy Hattori family that was reputed to own some of the real estate in Tokyo's "geisha strip" of nightclubs, where American servicemen—especially those stationed at the Atsugi base—went for their entertainment.[50] Their turf included the Queen Bee, a club frequented in the late 1950s by both Richard Case Nagell and Lee Harvey Oswald, a story we shall examine in more detail.

When author Edward Jay Epstein was researching his 1978 book about Oswald, Jones Harris, then one of his research assistants, set about obtaining the names and addresses of the men who had served overseas with the young Marine. Harris was able to interview, among others, Marine lieutenant John Donovan, once stationed with Oswald in Japan and later at the El Toro Marine Base in California. While at El Toro, Donovan recalled that Oswald had received a visit in 1959 from a member of the Hattori clan. Donovan recognized the visitor as the brother of a Hattori girl he himself had known in Tokyo.

The young man, according to Donovan, was Noboru Hattori, son of the president of the Hattori Watch Company in Tokyo. Harris added that Noboru Hattori was located and admitted having visited the Santa Ana base en route to Chicago, but maintained that his trip was in 1962 (not 1959) and denied ever having met Oswald.[51]

Whether this Hattori family was related to Tokushiro Hattori—or precisely which Hattoris owned the nightclub real estate in Tokyo—I have been unable to determine. But in the 1951 Kaji Wataru kidnapping, and no doubt many other ventures, the Takushiro Hattori organization had worked in conjunction with the mysterious "ZED group" organized by Jack Canon with Willoughby's blessing in the late 1940s. Twenty years later, Nagell would bring up Canon's name with a Garrison investigator. "Jack Canon," the notes of the conversation depict, "rub-out man for CIA." Little else is known about Canon, but by the early 1960s he would become an associate editor for Willoughby's *Foreign Intelligence Digest* and work with the ex-general on the International Committee for the Defense of Christian Culture.[52] And, in 1977, the *London Guardian* would publish an article based on a new book written by a Soviet journalist. The John F. Kennedy assassination, Mikhail Lebedev claimed, had been carried out by an international Fascist cabal; the fatal head shot was delivered by an agent with the alias of "Zed."[53]

The crossover in "Zed" nomenclature may, of course, be purely coincidental. But not so easily dismissed are General Willoughby's links to two other very important features of the Nagell narrative. One was FOI.

"I'm quite sure FOI did start under Willoughby," according to its former commander, Colonel Stanley. "When I took over Combined Command Reconnaissance Activities Far East [CCRAFE], the Korean War was going on and Willoughby was still there. FOI was more of a function rather than the title of any group. Then, after the war, the overall title changed to Army Command Reconnaissance Activities Far East [ACRAFE], and FOI was certainly a prime function of that, as opposed to the CIC."[54]

In correspondence with Allen Dulles, Willoughby described his having "solved" his intramural battles with the CIA in occupied Japan "thru the creation of a J.S.O. (Special Operations) in which C.I.A. had autonomy but co-ordinated with us, in covert operations, to avoid crossing wires."[55] That, apparently, marked the beginning of FOI.

Willoughby also set up the original 441st Counter Intelligence Corps Group, to which Nagell was reassigned in 1957. Under its auspices, Nagell went through the old Tokyo files. This brings us, again, to the Richard Sorge spy case. In April 1951, when President Truman relieved MacArthur of command for defying his directives and pressing forward in the Korean Theater, Willoughby left with him. Coming under heavy criticism because his intelligence service had failed to foresee the Chinese Communist attack that routed the U.N. forces and stopped MacArthur's "win the war" offensive, Willoughby then went on the attack himself. He had, Willoughby said, "a lot of unfinished business with the Pentagon."[56]

That summer, Willoughby went before the House Un-American Activities Committee, with two aluminum footlockers of secret documents about the Sorge ring beside his chair. Willoughby had been building his case for a while. In the spring of 1950, he had passed along copies of his evidence to then congressman Richard Nixon.[57] Dating back to Shanghai in the 1930s, Willoughby said, he had pieced together the Sorge saga from Japanese documents seized after the occupation. This comprised "the largest single crop of Commies and fellow travelers in a single pattern." Besides Agnes Smedley, Willoughby named all kinds of names of supposed American subversives. One of them was Harold Isaacs, whom Willoughby in his book linked with Agnes Smedley among "the more important members of the Shanghai branch."[58]

But in the magazine accounts of Willoughby's sensational testimony—as well as his 1952 book *Shanghai Conspiracy*—there is no mention of any suspicions about Mark Gayn. This struck me, again, as odd, since Gayn's name had just resurfaced again in Senator Joe McCarthy's revival of the *Amerasia* case.

While Willoughby sought to bolster his spy-catcher image in Washington, the Asian network he had left behind was flourishing. "MacArthur, Willoughby, and the CIA had midwifed a string of bone-crushing regimes calling themselves the Iron Triangle," as author Sterling Seagraves has written.[59] These included Chiang Kai-shek's old Kuomintang on Taiwan, right-wing strongman Syngman Rhee in South Korea, as well as puppet governments in the Philippines and Japan. By 1954, elements within South Korea's Headquarters Intelligence Division (HID) and Chiang's own spy net would unite conservatives from across the continent to battle the "red hordes." They called themselves the Asian People's Anti-Communist League (APACL). Their prime mover in Tokyo was Nobusuke Kishi, another war criminal freed by Willoughby along with Kodama; by the time Nagell and Oswald settled in Tokyo in 1957, Kishi would be Japan's prime minister.[60] And his seventy-five-thousand-man National Police Agency, first established by MacArthur and Willoughby, spent much of their time keeping an eye on American servicemen and tourists with possible "subversive" leanings.

Extending the Network

In April 1952, Willoughby had accompanied an American military mission to Spain whose ostensible purpose was to discuss with dictator Franco the question of establishing U.S. air and naval bases there. For three months, the now-retired general stayed on, provided by Franco with government limousines and in constant contact with the dictator's ministers. Spain under Franco was, in Willoughby's words, "a cradle of supermen."[61]

At the same time, Otto Skorzeny came to set up shop in Madrid. A very tall, muscular figure, ex-SS colonel Skorzeny had been Adolf Hitler's "favorite commando," the very embodiment of the Führer's vision of a "master race." When it had become clear as early as 1943 to Hitler's right-hand man, Martin Bormann, that the Germans could not win the war, three different branches of a survival organism known as the "Odessa" were created. One was assembled by Reinhard Gehlen, chief of Nazi intelligence. At war's end, Gehlen bargained his vast network to the OSS's Allen Dulles and to U.S. Military Intelligence officials. The ORG, as it was first known, would become America's anti-Communist warrior force against Eastern Europe all through the 1950s and 1960s.

Another survival arm was Skorzeny's, who set up "ratlines" for resettling leading Nazis in a number of countries—particularly Brazil, Argentina, Paraguay, Mexico, South Africa, Egypt, and Indonesia. With his father-in-law, Hitler's Reichsbank president Hjalmar Schact, Skorzeny organized the third branch—the transport abroad of Nazi assets such as gold, establishing dozens of front companies.

Captured after the war but released from American custody in 1947, Skorzeny settled in Madrid to set up his "International Fascista" five years later. He reportedly kept in close contact with Gehlen, and over the years Skorzeny's name would be linked not only to the CIA but also to Latin American death squads, global illegal arms deals, and assassination plots against French president Charles de Gaulle and Fidel Castro.[62]

There are no records extant on any meetings between Willoughby and Skorzeny in Spain, though the general journeyed there many times over the ensuing years. In 1955, however, Willoughby's "German connections" were the subject of an exchange of correspondence with CIA director Allen Dulles and Dulles's then-deputy Frank Wisner, who was in charge of relations with the Gehlen network as well as the American resettlement of several hundred ex-Nazi scientists under "Operation Paperclip." By now Willoughby was living on Park Avenue in New York. I obtained the correspondence from among Willoughby's papers on file at the Douglas Mac-Arthur Memorial Archives in Norfolk, Virginia.

Dulles to Willoughby, January 17, 1955:

I appreciate your letter of 5 January and its interesting enclosures, which I have sent to some of my people for study. Also many thanks for the interesting books which arrived separately. . . . Regarding your idea of a trip to a certain country for the purpose of writing a book, I find this matter interesting and I shall be in touch with you further about it.

Willoughby to Dulles, March 17, 1955:

. . . I believe in "centralization" of intelligence. In a covert outfit, the command leadership is most important. . . . I would be entirely satisfied to serve with or under you and have every conviction that C.I.A. could not be in better or more responsible hands. . . .

On the "book" idea, I take the liberty of making certain suggestions:

i) I am more interested in Europe or So. America than in the Far East, at this time.

ii) It is true that I have an exceptional entree in Spain.

iii) However, I can develop the same thing in Germany. My father's family (though a divorce took place) is unimpeachable in Wilhelminian society. I am in touch with very high-level people. As you know, I have a fluent command of French, German and Spanish.

iv) I think "rapprochement" with Germany is becoming frightfully important. It can only be done on a personal basis, in the end.

v) . . . I will develop for you a weekly report. . . .

The correspondence continued through the year, with Willoughby offering on October 30, 1955, to aid in setting up "promising . . . social contacts" between young American servicemen stationed in Germany and their counterparts. "The new generation has less to remember—and to resent," Willoughby wrote, suggesting that "In American garrison towns, in Germany, this approach can become the first step in developping [sic] a literary youth-movement, by utilizing existing Karl May clubs." (Adolf Hitler, from his teenage years onward, was a devotee of the Wild West novels of Karl May, a German imitator of James Fenimore Cooper.)

"From the viewpoint of social relations and youth indoctrination," Willoughby continued, "it fits neatly, as you know, into one of the many facets of 'psychological warfare.' It could become the medium by which we can gain young adherents and partisans. Anyway, I am going to try it. . . . However, I do not want to stand alone (though the Germans will take it up) and I suggest that you examine it, from the viewpoint of a 'discreet' penetration and the 'making of friends.' "

Dulles responded with interest on November 20. "I trust we may soon get together for a personal account of your conversations with the German gentlemen. I have also had two very interesting meetings with them, and it might be useful to compare notes. Let me know when you are next in town." One of the two "German gentlemen," mentioned by Willoughby in his previous letter, was General Hans Speidel, chief of staff for Nazi field marshal Erwin Rommel during the latter stages of World War II.

Willoughby seems to have been turned down on his offer to go to work for Dulles, at least on a formal basis. His letter to Dulles of December 3, 1955, concluded bitterly: "I imagine that I am restless and seek outlets for my energies. Since my peculiar talents are not employable in your outfit (which I deplore and consider just a bit silly), I must do something else. I sometimes wonder, if this reluctance is tracable [sic] to the hatreds or prejudice engendered by MacArthur, whom I naturally defended as I would any man whom I work for. . . ."

Old soldiers—and old enmities—apparently never die. As late as 1957, a Willoughby speech before the convention of the American Coalition of Patriotic Societies was still trumpeting his exposé of the Sorge affair. This time his target was the U.S. Supreme Court under Earl Warren, whose decisions Willoughby railed against for nullifying "worldwide evidence of the Russian conspiracy" and giving "aid and comfort to international traitors."[63]

Meanwhile, the Munich-based Gehlen apparatus with which Dulles and Willoughby worked soon extended its tentacles far into Asia, its operatives hooking up with those of the Asian Peoples' Anti-Communist League. On Taiwan in October 1957, an international meeting was held setting the stage for a grand global alliance of such forces. Chiang Kai-shek, Syngman Rhee, and South Vietnam's leader, Ngo Dinh Diem, all sent representatives to the steering committee. German veterans were included, notably Fritz Cramer—a former Nazi Abwehr officer who then headed up a private vigilante group that ferreted out German leftists at the behest of private industry. Its U.S. sister organization was the American Security Council (ASC), a private Washington group set up in 1955 by ex-FBI agents that built an index of over one million alleged "subversives" for major corporations seeking security checks. Willoughby, a friend of Fritz Cramer, eventually sat on the ASC's board. Two other Willoughby associates—Charles Edison of the ASC and the John Birch Society, and Lev Dobriansky, a Georgetown University professor with strong connections to Army intelligence circles—represented American interests at the Taiwan gathering.[64]

This event coincided with Oswald's arrival in the Far East, and Nagell's immersion in the CIC's Japan files. And this tangled web of associations—Gayn, Isaacs, Willoughby, and friends—I became convinced was intrinsic to ascertaining what surrounded, or even motivated, those two men.

Stationed Stateside during his basic training, Marine recruit Oswald had expressed an interest in aircraft maintenance and repair. By the spring of 1957 he was granted a "confidential" clearance to learn radar and air traffic control.[65] Like Nagell during his own first months as a soldier, during his training period Oswald was said to be a loner who preferred his own company to running into town with members of his unit on off-duty hours. That September, Oswald would find himself assigned to a Marine air control squadron at Atsugi, a base just outside Tokyo and where, that summer, a Top-Secret U-2 spy plane operation had been established, primarily for surveillance over the Soviet Union.

In Tokyo the Nagell and Oswald paths were soon to cross for the first time.

Summary

Nagell's review—and private microfilming—of Top-Secret Military Intelligence files in Tokyo made him aware of individuals suspected of working for the Communists in pre-World War II China. These included people who went on to become prominent North American journalists. Two such journalists, Mark Gayn and Harold Isaacs, also came to figure in the Oswald/Nagell saga.

Nagell alleges that Gayn was a Soviet agent who used the pseudonym "Joseph Kramer"—the same alias that Nagell used in warning the FBI about the Kennedy conspiracy. His warning letter, dispatched at "Kramer's" suggestion, was apparently intended to alert the FBI of similar awareness by Soviet Intelligence. The widely traveled Gayn was in the USSR the same time as Oswald (1960) and Nagell (1968).

Isaacs, whom FBI files reveal as being connected with Oswald's cousin Marilyn Murret, had a career path remarkably similar to Gayn's through the early 1950s. Both Murret and Isaacs also journeyed all over the globe. Murret, who was aware of Oswald's "defection" to the USSR before this became public knowledge, is rumored to have been a CIA agent.

The formation of a global anti-Communist alliance in the 1950s was facilitated by U.S. intelligence agencies, which enlisted Japanese warlords and German Nazis shortly after World War II. In the Far East, this originated under Charles Willoughby, Douglas MacArthur's chief of intelligence. Willoughby, who set up Field Operations Intelligence, had wide-ranging connections in Germany and was in regular communication with CIA director Allen Dulles.

Chapter Five

Genesis of a Relationship: Nagell and Oswald in Japan, 1957–58

In the autumn of 1957, Tokyo was the world's second most populous city, after New York. The capital that General Douglas MacArthur's American occupation Army helped rebuild was a teeming metropolis with more· neon lights, more movie theaters, and more traffic jams than anyplace else. Beneath the bustling surface, however, Tokyo was rife with intrigue.

The CIA had begun taking responsibility for many spy operations here by early 1951, after a secret meeting transpired between then CIA director Walter Bedell Smith and MacArthur.[1] There was plenty to occupy the CIA, its military FOI affiliate, and the Army's CIC. Both the Soviets and the Communist Chinese sought inroads in this strategic Asian nation of islands, especially among students and the burgeoning Japanese Communist Party. After the United States and the NATO powers, the KGB made Japan its number one target. By 1960, anti-American riots in Tokyo surrounding the signing of a new U.S.-Japan security treaty would force President Eisenhower to cancel a scheduled visit there. The relationship was tenuous, and while the U.S. troop presence had been halved over a three-year period, in 1957 some eighty-seven thousand American military personnel remained in Japan.

Quite a number of these bivouacked out of the Atsugi naval air base about thirty-five miles southwest of Tokyo. One sector at Atsugi contained an innocuous group of buildings known as the "Joint Technical Advisory Group." These buildings were actually the CIA's main operational base in the Far East. Here was the point of origin for the Top-Secret U-2 spy plane flights, designed to photograph military and industrial targets at altitudes high above the Soviet Union and Communist China. Here, too, was one of only two overseas field stations where the CIA conducted experimental testing on military personnel of a then little-known drug called LSD.[2]

"I went into Atsugi just as World War II ended, taking some of MacArthur's bodyguard in there," says Colonel L. Fletcher Prouty, a former Pentagon-CIA liaison officer (1955–63). "A monstrous stairway went down into caverns, you could drive a truck into it. A huge underground base. The agency used it for a lot of things."[3]

Soon after his squadron's arrival by ship on September 12, 1957, Marine private Lee Harvey Oswald, bearing a "Confidential" clearance, took up his responsibilities as a radar operator at Atsugi. In a largely monotonous task, the eighteen-year-old was on duty in "the bubble"—a hot, crowded radar control room—watching on his "scope" for indications of any penetration of non-Communist airspace by Soviet or Chinese planes.[4]

The Warren Commission would not spend much time focusing on Oswald's Far Eastern tour, beyond publishing his supposedly complete itinerary. Nor was the House Assassinations Committee "able to discern any unusual discrepancies or features in Oswald's military record."[5]

But neither investigative body ever spoke to Richard Case Nagell.

Sighting at the Soviet Embassy

The Japanese National Police Agency, established by MacArthur during the Korean War, was still flourishing in the late 1950s. As Allen C. Willis, then a Tokyo liaison officer between the CIA and Military Intelligence, described it to me, "Most of the KGB officers were pretty well identified, and the Japanese police had them covered like a wet blanket."[6]

Recent research into Oswald's period in Japan, based on the recollections of former Marine colleagues, has shown that Oswald often disappeared into Tokyo on two-day leaves, refusing to discuss his reasons even with his closest friends. On one of these trips he became known to the Tokyo gendarmes.

As Nagell told the story, both to myself and attorney Bernard Fensterwald, Jr., one day a contact of Nagell's in the Foreign Affairs Section of the National Police Agency related to him a curious episode. The agency had observed a young American, whom it thought at first was in the U.S. Army, dressed in civilian clothes outside of Tokyo's Soviet embassy. He was with a friend and was simply walking back and forth just beyond the tall iron gates. Finally both Americans had stopped at the main entrance to the embassy compound and been observed going inside. One was eventually identified as a Marine private from Atsugi.

"The Japanese police had a picture of Oswald," according to Nagell, "although I'm sure they would deny that they took photos of everybody going into the Soviet embassy."[7]

Not long after this, under an assumed name Nagell arranged to be introduced to Oswald.[8] Nagell determined that Oswald had entered the Soviet embassy "allegedly to have some coins identified." But once inside, Nagell learned either from Oswald or other sources that the young Marine had met with a Colonel Nikolai G. Eroshkin.[9] Officially Eroshkin was listed as a military attaché at the Soviet embassy. According to Nagell, he "was also suspected of being the legal GRU (Glavnoe Razvedyvatelnoe Upravlenie) resident in Japan."[10]

While the Soviet KGB was equivalent to a combination of the American CIA and FBI, the GRU was part of the USSR's military intelligence side—more like Army G-2 and its CIC branch. Like the KGB, the GRU's personnel often served overseas in Soviet embassies. A "legal resident" is an officer who has diplomatic cover and, in the event of exposure, diplomatic immunity. An "illegal" GRU operative, such as superspy Richard Sorge had been, works strictly undercover.[11]

This book marks the first time that any known meeting between Oswald and Soviet intelligence in Japan has ever been alleged. Though I have only Nagell's word that it occurred, the name of "Nicolai G. Eroshkin" under a heading of former military attaché at the Tokyo embassy does show up in the notebook taken from Nagell by the FBI in 1963. Nagell maintains that Oswald and the Russian colonel had more than one meeting, though he has never specified what they may have talked about. But Nagell did add that "almost since the day" Oswald first saw Eroshkin at the embassy, the Soviets suspected the Marine "of being an agent of one of the U.S. intelligence services."[12]

Something else was going on around Colonel Eroshkin in 1957 and 1958. The CIA was trying to entice him to defect to the American side. It was November 1957, while Nagell was still supervising the review of (and privately filming) the CIC's massive Tokyo intelligence files, when Nagell says a CIA contact, John Lampert, enlisted his own participation in its Eroshkin project.[13]

As he described it in his U.S. Court of Claims case, Nagell's role was to recruit into the CIA's effort "a well-known Japanese author, linguist and professor emeritus of political science at Tokyo University." Nagell had been introduced to Dr. Chikao Fujisawa while with Field Operations Intelligence, during one of the Army captain's trips from Korea to Japan in October 1956. Nagell had renewed their acquaintance upon being reassigned to Tokyo in February 1957, and, he writes: "Subsequent to my return to CIC duties I had maintained a fairly close relationship and professed friendship with him, mainly because he was an accomplished linguist, but also for other reasons."

Dr. Fujisawa lived in the same section of Tokyo, Setagaya-ku, as the Soviet colonel. The professor was also known to be making frequent visits to the Soviet embassy, "allegedly to finalize an agreement for a cultural exchange program between Japan and the USSR," Nagell says. "Any overtures I made to him were bent on ascertaining the nature of his business at the USSR embassy, whom he met, and how best we could arrange for him to bump into Colonel Eroshkin, who was under constant surveillance by the Japanese police (once he turned around and photographed the plainclothesmen who were photographing him)."

Could Oswald also have been at least peripherally involved in the CIA's targeting of Eroshkin? I realized that such a sensitive matter would not ordinarily involve a teenage Marine. Still, Oswald was a radar operator at a U-2 base that was among U.S. intelligence's most guarded secrets.[14] So it seemed plausible that Oswald could either have been sent to see Eroshkin, or gone to the embassy for reasons of his own. Whatever the nature of the relationship, I came to believe that the Eroshkin project bore important relevance to the bigger picture surrounding what Nagell described as his "casual but purposeful acquaintance" with Oswald in Japan.[15] I arrived at this conclusion sitting alone with Nagell one evening in the spring of 1978 in another of those dark L.A. bars. For Oswald was not only in communication with the Soviet intelligence officer, but also with Dr. Chikao Fujisawa.

Oswald and the Professor

There was not a whole lot more I could pry out of Nagell about Professor Fujisawa. Having read Nagell's court filing about his recruitment of the Japanese scholar into the CIA's Eroshkin affair, I brought up the name offhandedly, not expecting much. "What about this Dr. Fujisawa?" I asked. "Did he know Oswald?"

Nagell signaled to the bartender for another round of Heineken, then let a slight smile escape him. "He knew Oswald," Nagell said. "Or he met him, in my presence. I *think* he met him later."

I stayed mum as Nagell went on: "It was in a German beer hall and restaurant. There were two of those, I keep thinking it was called Rhineland; anyway, it begins with an R. It was in Ripongi, a section of Tokyo not too far from the Soviet embassy."

Nagell thought for a moment, then added: "Fujisawa had a lot of friends. He spoke fluent English. And excellent Russian, along with five other languages. The last time I saw Fujisawa was in 1959 in New York City. He told me he was going to São Paulo [Brazil]. The FBI figured he was just a right-wing politician. But I wonder what the Trenton, New Jersey, [FBI] field office records would show. They had information, copies of his letters to me." Then Nagell changed the subject.[16]

Nagell was not a man who could be easily pressed, and I had to content myself with that. Late that night I went back into the records of his Court of Claims case. There was nothing in there about any Oswald association with Eroshkin or Fujisawa. But there was plenty more Nagell had written about the results of the CIA's defection plan and about the hidden agenda of the Japanese linguist.

What happened with the Eroshkin business said as much about the growing efficiency of Japanese intelligence as anything else. Nagell says that before he could get around to filling Professor Fujisawa in on all the details of the CIA's mission, two Tokyo police officials told Nagell to beware of what was really going on. One was a "Mr. Masui," chief of the Crime Prevention Section of the National Police Agency. The other was a personal friend of Nagell, Jun Murai, head of the Tohoku Regional Police Bureau and formerly the director of the Cabinet Research Office—Japan's equivalent of the CIA, established with American approval in 1952.

Murai, Nagell says, "warned me that the Japanese had penetrated the [Eroshkin] project and believed that it entailed something else, something unlawful that might further strain the already tense relations then existing between Japan and the USSR." Murai made "pointed reference to some unsavory incidents that had occurred over the past several years involving the CIA," including the abduction of the writer Kaji Wataru, which Nagell had read about in the Tokyo files. Nagell's friend "added that the Japanese government could no longer afford to tolerate the mischief caused by the CIA in Japan."

So, on about January 10, 1958, Nagell dropped out of the plans, "as I assume Dr. Fujisawa did, since I made no further effort to recruit him. Had I known that the project encompassed blackmail, an abduction, or other illegal activity, I would not have become involved in the first place, as I had had my fill with those type shenanigans elsewhere."[17]

It would be important to know whether the dates of Oswald's meetings with Eroshkin, Fujisawa, and Nagell overlapped with the CIA's project. Again, Nagell refrained from being more specific. If those meetings did occur prior to Nagell's "dropping out," then it becomes more likely that Oswald himself may have played a part for the CIA. If they happened subsequently, then we enter a realm where Oswald might conceivably have been utilized by Soviet intelligence—wittingly or unwittingly.

That is because, as Nagell says he suspected and eventually knew for certain, Dr. Chikao Fujisawa was really a Soviet agent.

Close Encounter in the Big Apple

It was late April 1959, and Nagell had returned Stateside with a beautiful Japanese wife when a special delivery letter arrived for him at Fort Dix, New Jersey. It bore the return address of a room at the Great Northern Hotel in New York City. Professor Fujisawa, writing in English, began:

> Dear Captain Nagell,
> You will be surprised to know that I am actually in New York City, as I came here a week ago by flight from Tokyo. I wish I could live here indefinitely, because I consider it to be of vital importance to deepen much more *mutual* understanding between the U.S. and Japan. . . . I am firmly determined to render a substantial service in this connection— by laying the groundwork of true and genuine Japan-America friendship capable of weathering any storm likely to happen in near future. . . .

Dr. Fujisawa went on that he wished to become "a cultural and moral *intermediary*" between the United States and its Cold War enemy, the Soviet Union. He was "looking forward to obtaining a permanent position in university circles" while making a series of "popular lectures on some interesting features of Japanese culture." In closing, he wrote: "I am burning to meet you as soon as possible."[18]

Nagell says he went to New York to see Fujisawa, "initially with my wife and subsequently alone at his insistence, because he did not want her present." Their last meeting transpired in early June 1959 at a New York restaurant called The Left Hand—"a place with hands all over it," as Nagell described it to me. "I thought I was getting set up," he recalled.[19] In a document filed with the Court of Claims, Nagell elaborated:

Dr. Fujisawa revealed that he worked for Soviet intelligence, something that I had suspected despite his reputation of being an ultra-nationalist. . . . Upon receipt of his letter, I had notified the FBI at Trenton, New Jersey, of my suspicions, both verbally and in writing, voicing my surprise that he had been granted a visa to the United States. The FBI suggested that I meet him. After revealing that he was with Soviet intelligence, Dr. Fujisawa attempted to persuade me to work for the Soviets, hinting that he had been informed by reliable sources that I knew more about the death of an American CIA agent (actually an FOI Agent Handler) in Japan than I had disclosed to the American and Japanese authorities that had investigated the case. When that threat failed to dislodge my countenance, Dr. Fujisawa remarked that he might create an incident, with dire consequences to both me and my wife (who was Japanese) by informing the Japanese authorities that I had solicited him to participate in the blackmailing and kidnapping of a Soviet diplomat in Japan. Knowing precisely to what he was alluding, I told him to go ahead and do so; that I was bugged [electronically wired] (which I was not) and that in turn I would notify the Japanese PSIA [Public Security Investigation Agency] he had admitted being a Soviet agent. Whereupon, Dr. Fujisawa smiled, said "touché," that he had been joking, and abruptly left the spot at which we had been talking. I never saw or heard from him again. Shortly thereafter, one of the FBI agents to whom I had spoken, approached me at Fort Dix and stated that he (or the Bureau) did not think that Dr. Fujisawa was a Soviet agent. I agreed with him, because I felt it was pointless to do otherwise, and let the matter rest. . . . I have no idea where Dr. Fujisawa got the information that he . . . used in his attempt to blackmail me in the United States.[20]

The Professor's "Master Race" Philosophy

What was Chikao Fujisawa's game? How much did it have to do with Oswald? When both were in the United States in 1959, could Fujisawa also have met with Oswald before the Marine headed for the USSR? I was not going to be able to find out directly. A reporter friend in *The Wall Street Journal*'s Tokyo bureau tried to locate the professor for me, and sent back word that he had died, at age seventy, sometime in 1963.

Strangely, Fujisawa's name came up during a conversation in Washington with George O'Toole, a former CIA officer who ended up writing a probing look at the FBI's cover-up in the JFK case (*The Assassination Tapes*). We were in attorney Fensterwald's office, kicking around the implications of what Nagell had set down in his Court of Claims case, when a stunned O'Toole realized that the Fujisawa whom Nagell was describing was the same man who once befriended him in New York.

O'Toole had been employed in the defense industry, but not yet by the CIA—"Back then, I couldn't even have told you what the initials meant." But in 1959 he had enrolled in a course called "Zen and Shinto" at New York's New School for Social Research, where his instructor, Fujisawa, took a shine to him. O'Toole had graciously chaperoned the frail little man around the city and taken him for dinner at O'Toole's mother's apartment, where a spirited conversation en.●.ed about the works of Charles Dickens. Never had O'Toole gotten any indication that Fujisawa was other than a philosopher-scholar. "I remember driving him to the docks in Brooklyn to load his trunk, around April or May of 1960. He said he was going, I believe, to L.A., to pick up a freighter back to Tokyo."[21]

O'Toole's encounter was, at least, further verification that Fujisawa had been in the United States when Nagell said he was. From there, just as in my probe of Mark Gayn and Harold Isaacs, I was drawn back in time—to World War II.

I found more than passing reference to Fujisawa in the book *Politics and Culture in Wartime Japan.* He was considered one of the country's leading intellectuals. Before the war the professor had been Japan's representative at the permanent secretariat of the League of Nations. In 1940 he wrote a book containing some rather bizarre speculations, including "that Hitler had been influenced by Confucianism through the works of Voltaire and Frederick the Great." Considered a staunchly right-wing Japanese nationalist, as the war unfolded Fujisawa became chief of the Research Department for the Imperial Rule Assistance Association, which, like the Nazi Party in Germany, had become Japan's sole political party. In this capacity Fujisawa "directed propaganda at foreign countries and at American and British prisoners of war."[22]

A major piece of his wartime work was a 1942 booklet titled *On the Divine Mission of Nippon,* printed in English for the widest distribution throughout the Far East. It was reprinted in its entirety as an appendix to the 1944 book *Tokyo Record* as the "most revealing" tale of Japan's true motivation. Fujisawa's subtitle was *A Prophecy of the Dawn of a New Age.* How curious, I thought, for our current catchphrase "New Age" to have such an antecedent. Japan, as Fujisawa saw it, had a "divine mission for the salvation of disoriented mankind."[23]

As Otto Tolischus, author of *Tokyo Record,* summarized Fujisawa's work:

It bluntly announced that Japan was fighting by command of the Japanese gods to "reunite" all nations under the rule of the Japanese Emperor "as it was in the beginning." According to this leading light of Japanese science, Japan was the original motherland of all nations and the cradle of civilization, from which other nations have strayed, and to which they must return. The whole warring world, he proclaimed, must be converted into one large family under the divine rule of the Japanese Emperor, in which each nation will take its own proper place. This, he blandly announced, is the goal of "the divine mission of Nippon," and the objective which Japan has been pursuing throughout her history. . . .

The capitalistic individualism prevalent in the United States, he declared, runs "counter to cosmic truth," and so does the Communism of Russia, but Nazism and Fascism are closer to the "truth." The latter had much in common, Fujisawa wrote, "with the Musubi principle of one in many." And this "spiritual solidarity" of Japan, Germany and Italy prompted "a common front against the desperate offensive launched by those powers defending the old order."[24]

I came across another little book by Professor Fujisawa, called *Zen and Shinto: The Story of Japanese Philosophy,* translated into English in 1959. While any talk of Nazi-Fascist alignment was expectedly absent, his views of Japan's "divine mission" did not seem to have changed that much. He now viewed his country as a bridge between the superpowers. Japan, he wrote, "can reconcile perfectly American capitalism, which emphasizes only too unilaterally *political freedom,* and Soviet communism, which stresses only too unilaterally *economic equality,* into a new pattern of Musubi-economy which renders the unobstructed display of individual creative impulses compatible with the appropriate regulation of production for meeting the requirements of a community as a whole. Under these circumstances, Japan should refrain from siding politically either with the U.S.A. or with the Soviet Union, holding fast to her supreme position transcending all conflicts and divergencies."

Fujisawa continued, "as a preliminary step towards the effectuation of this global project," the Shinto International Academy had been established "for the promotion of *planetary consciousness,* while fostering frequent personal contacts between ideologically conflicting parties."[25]

I took a deep breath and thought about several things. Most obvious, of course, was how Japan's "Musubi-economy" had pretty much come to dominate today's world. More germane to this chronicle was the "worldview" of Lee Harvey Oswald. It was striking how closely it paralleled Fujisawa's Oriental outlook. A Marine buddy of Oswald, Kerry Thornley, had described it this way to the Warren Commission:

"He [Oswald] looked upon history as God. He looked upon the eyes of future people as a kind of tribunal, and he wanted to be on the winning side so that 10,000 years from now people would look into the history books and say, 'Well, this man was ahead of his time.' "[26]

Thornley, when questioned by the Secret Service the day after the assassination, stated that "Oswald was very intelligent and extremely well read; that he spoke Russian, which he [Thornley] understood he had learned while stationed in Japan; that he subscribed to *Pravda* and had also read books written in Russian. He said Oswald professed to be an admirer of the Communist system, sometimes jokingly. . . . He said that Oswald criticized the capitalist system, and once mentioned that the leaders of the two ideologies should 'fight it out on a personal basis.' "[27]

Fighting it out on a personal basis was one radical step beyond Fujisawa's avowed aim of "fostering frequent personal contacts between ideologically conflicting parties." But I could not help wondering if the professor might have had an influence on Oswald's thinking and perhaps even pushed him toward seeking his own "personal contacts" in the Soviet Union. After his return from Russia in 1962, Oswald would tell his older friend George de Mohrenschildt that "he had some contact with the Communists in Japan, and they—that got him interested to go and see what goes on in the Soviet Union."[28]

If Fujisawa was a Soviet spy, he was also a distinctly unique breed, one for whom there existed a "transcendent" philosophy in the sense that Japan was seen as the vital link into the "New Age." But it really remained an extension of the "master race" theory first propounded by Fujisawa during the war. In his context, both sides (capitalism and communism) could and should be played against the middle, where, in the professor's view, Japan resided like a sleeping tiger. History as God. . . . The winning side. . . .

This middle ground was, by design, inscrutable. One's deeper motivations remained concealed. One could play the spy game almost as a kind of private joke. Or, as I believe ultimately happened in Oswald's case, one could end up being manipulated by forces of which he had neither cognizance nor control.

A Link to Mark Gayn

While combing through the papers of Mark Gayn in Toronto early in 1992, I chanced upon yet another link in this odd chain. Gayn, it turned out, had also known Fujisawa. Gayn described their meeting in his book *Japan Diary*, which covered the period when Nagell said Gayn first managed to "penetrate" several U.S. Military Intelligence organizations for the Soviets. Gayn, just back from a trip to Korea, was describing his attendance at a party "given by the counsel of the war criminals now on trial" in November 1946.

He and his wife were watching a geisha show

when a trim-looking Japanese came up and gave me his card, testifying that he was Chikao Fujisawa, Director of Research, Institute of Multilateral International Relations. After that the conversation took a curious turn. Fujisawa said he had spent many years in China, running "a cultural affairs institute," and had just been repatriated. Quite without prompting, he said:

"You know, I'm a famous reactionary, and I've been purged. I admit that. I admit that I've collaborated very closely with the Japanese military until about three years ago, when I decided they didn't follow the correct policy in China."

Now he was counsel to one of the more notorious of the war criminals on trial. "I feel," he said, "that the Japanese military have made many mistakes. But the core is sound. That's the point I always try to develop. Take for instance our monarchy. It's a sound institution. Don't you think so?"

I asked him if he was doing anything else besides his court work, and he said, matter-of-factly, that he was on the faculty of the U.S. Army university here, teaching Oriental philosophy. "I have about thirty Americans in each of my two weekly classes," he said. "Some of the officers I invite to my home, where we can discuss various topics at leisure. I should like very much to have you and your wife come to my place. There're so many things we can discuss. Especially the question of the emperor."

I said I would try. The fact that professors purged by the Japanese as war criminals are hired by the U.S. Army to indoctrinate Americans fascinates me.[29]

I went back to Gayn's original notebooks to see if I could glean more. Gayn noted there that he had provided Fujisawa with his home address. The man Fujisawa was acting as "counsel" for, I saw, was "the notorious Maj. Gen. Kenryo Sato, who almost single-handedly captured Indo-China for Japan, and later ran Japan's politics as chief of the military affairs bureau." Then, at a visit with two Japanese "right-wing" leaders shortly thereafter, Gayn inquired about the professor. He was told that Fujisawa had been "ousted from Kyushu Imperial University back in 1934 for left-wing activities. Since then he has turned around—a cheap opportunist. He has always boasted of his multilingual capacity. Both said 'outrageous' when I said he was now teaching in the US Army university."[30]

There was no further mention of whether Gayn and Fujisawa ever met again. The only other items from this period that caught my eye were notations that Gayn "went to cocktails and dinner at the Soviet Embassy" in Tokyo, and that he had "been trying to get hold of the year books on subversive movements—both Rightist and Leftist—put out by the [Japanese] Thought Police."[31]

In the mid-1950s, the CIA-funded MIT Center for International Studies —out of which operated Professor Harold Isaacs' FBI-labeled "apparatus"—brought over a group from Japan to embark upon a major study of the country's "Science of Thought." It examined how Japan's once-notorious "Thought Police," in a prewar form of brainwashing, had broken down the identities of Communists and brought them around to the imperial viewpoint. Isaacs himself was said to have been closely associated with a linguistics-oriented group of Japanese in Tokyo, as well as at MIT and Harvard, who had long specialized in looking at ideological conversion. Their other interest, as with Isaacs, was student radicalism around the world.[32]

The Queen Bee

If Oswald was a young rebel looking for a cause, in the beginning was the CIA. Richard Nagell was "on loan" to the CIA from the Military's CIC when he first touched base with Oswald. And Nagell has also said that the German beer hall where he introduced Oswald to Dr. Fujisawa was not the only Tokyo night spot frequented by the Army captain and the Marine private. Another was the Queen Bee, one of the three most expensive night clubs in Tokyo. Nagell confided two important things about this period in conversations with Bernard Fensterwald, Jr.: that Oswald definitely "had CIA connections" in Japan, and that both Nagell and Oswald had had girlfriends at the Queen Bee. Oswald's girl was older than he, lived in the suburb of Yokohama, and was named Midorii.[33]

This is not the first time that the Queen Bee has surfaced among assassination researchers. Marine Corpsman Zack Stout told author Edward Jay Epstein that Oswald seemed to have fallen in love with a hostess at the Queen Bee not long after his arrival in Japan. The club, Epstein wrote, "catered to an elite clientele—field-grade officers, pilots (including U-2 pilots) and a few junior officers with private incomes—not to impoverished Marine privates." A typical evening's date there could cost $60 to $100; Oswald was earning less than $85 a month in take-home pay. Yet he apparently dated one woman "with surprising regularity, even bringing her back to the base several times." Naval Intelligence was interested in the possibility "that hostesses from the Queen Bee were being used at the time to gather intelligence and that Oswald was receiving money from someone at the Queen Bee."[34]

David Bucknell, another Marine Corps friend of Oswald, provided more details to author/attorney Mark Lane. Bucknell related that Oswald had told him about being alone in a bar when an attractive Japanese woman approached him. She asked him some questions about his work at Atsugi, and Oswald maintained he reported the conversation to a superior officer, "who then arranged for a meeting on the base between Oswald and a man dressed in civilian clothes. The man, a 'security' or 'security-intelligence' operator, explained to Oswald that he could do his country a great service. Oswald was told that the woman was a KGB contact and that he would be given false information to pass on to her. . . . His liaison with the woman continued; he was given money to spend at the Queen Bee, and apparently encouraged by American intelligence to enter into a sexual relationship with the woman."[35]

Was Nagell the " 'security-intelligence' operator"? I don't know, but if he was, then it would seem their liaison began sometime during the fall of 1957. Corpsman Stout recalled Oswald being unhappy about plans to ship out with his unit on maneuvers to the Philippines, since this meant he wouldn't be seeing his hostess girlfriend at the Queen Bee. On October 27 Oswald was gathering some gear from his locker when a .22-caliber derringer supposedly fell onto the floor and discharged, grazing his left elbow. He had ordered the gun, Oswald had previously told a friend, from a mail-order house in the United States—the beginning of a pattern that would continue into 1963. Some Marines felt that Oswald actually shot himself so he wouldn't get transferred to the Philippines. Two of those who came rushing into his room now maintain that the bullet missed Oswald completely. At any rate, Marine records show that he had to undergo medical treatment for three weeks. Some researchers speculate that the gun incident was a cover allowing Oswald to "disappear" temporarily from his unit for either intelligence training or an assignment. On November 20 he returned to duty in time to depart for the Philippines, and he would not return to Japan until mid-March 1958.[36]

Desmond FitzGerald

By the time Oswald got back to Atsugi, the CIA's Eroshkin defection plan —at least as far as Nagell was concerned—was over. That particular "counterespionage project," Nagell had been told, was supposedly authorized from Washington by the CIA's chief of Far Eastern operations, Desmond FitzGerald. In the autumn of 1962, FitzGerald would move over to run the CIA's anti-Castro task force—where he personally organized at least three plans to assassinate the Cuban leader, in contravention of the Kennedy administration's policy. Indeed, he was meeting in Paris with a Cuban code-named AM/LASH, finalizing a plan to eliminate Castro, at the very moment the president was assassinated.

Of FitzGerald, Nagell would later write: "I did him some favors in 1957, when he was the Agency's top dog in the Far East. Likewise, I did him some favors in Mexico, in the 1962–63 period, when he was ramrod for dirty tricks in Latin America."[37]

Did those "favors" have something to do with Oswald? When Nagell signed his contract with the CIA in 1962, starting him on a "double agent" mission vis-à-vis the Soviets, Nagell says it was a FitzGerald subordinate who would serve as his CIA contact in Mexico City. Since Oswald was among Nagell's "subjects" during this latter period—a story we shall get to in due course—almost certainly FitzGerald would have been aware of Oswald by then. The question is whether that awareness began at the time of the Eroshkin project, which Nagell has also said he personally discussed with FitzGerald somewhere along the line.

According to Nagell, Desmond FitzGerald definitely figures into the Oswald saga—to what degree we may never know, except perhaps through a no-holds-barred official inquiry. A *Time* magazine file would later describe FitzGerald as "one of the most powerful, but least known top officials in Washington." This was shortly after his death at age fifty-seven, when FitzGerald suddenly collapsed of an apparent heart attack on a country-home Virginia tennis court on July 23, 1967, and died en route to the hospital. At the time he was in charge of all CIA clandestine operations.

"Now there is a corpse," Nagell would write, "that should be exhumed and examined by a qualified pathologist."[38]

James Flannery, a CIA colleague who served under FitzGerald in both the Far Eastern and Western Hemisphere divisions, recalled being surprised at his early death. "Des kept himself in good shape," Flannery told me in a telephone interview from his retirement home in North Carolina. "He played tennis constantly. I remember when he made a trip out to Tokyo in the '50s, he had me come see him about seven in the morning and was already doing all sorts of calisthenics."

FitzGerald was a charming, well-connected, redheaded Irishman whose roots derived from the same Boston-Irish background as the Kennedys'. In fact, Flannery understood that his ancestry may have linked up to the FitzGerald side of the Kennedy clan (matriarch Rose Kennedy's father was a Boston-Irish politician affectionately known as "Honey Fitz"). Fitz-Gerald stood about six-foot-two, with strong, rugged features and, Flannery remembers, "the deepest dimples I can remember on a man."[39] Like his mentor Allen Dulles, there was often a ready pipe in his mouth.

My library research into FitzGerald's known history turned up the broad outlines of a man who seemed the very personification of the Eastern Establishment. The son of a prominent stockbroker and himself a Harvard Law School graduate, he was already a prosperous Wall Street lawyer when he married Marietta Endicott Peabody in 1939. She was the beautiful daughter of a founder of Radcliffe College and granddaughter of Endicott Peabody, who established the Groton prep school. After the birth of a daughter, Frances, the marriage would end in divorce in 1947. FitzGerald was, and would remain, a conservative Republican. Marietta, who remarried the British multimillionaire Ronald Tree, was active in New York liberal politics. She and FitzGerald, as she would later write in *The Saturday Evening Post,* had simply entered different worlds during World War II.[40]

Like many other men who achieved command positions in the CIA hierarchy, FitzGerald received his intelligence baptism in the war. He had served on the Army G-2 staff of General Joseph Stilwell as the liaison officer to the Nationalist Chinese Sixth Army, rising to the rank of major. Returning to the practice of law in New York, in 1948 he married again to a lovely Englishwoman who had once also captured the fancy of Joseph P. Kennedy when the family patriarch was U.S. ambassador to Britain. Barbara Kent Green Lawrence, Kennedy thought, would have made a good match for his eldest son, Joseph, Jr., who was killed in an airplane crash during the war.

In 1951 FitzGerald joined the CIA. Almost from the beginning he was the agency's leading spokesman for agents in the field, a staunch advocate of the "can-do" philosophy. He started out as executive officer to Colonel Richard Stilwell, the general's son, who was put in charge of the Far East Division. During the Korean War FitzGerald made his name, smoothly organizing dozens of covert operations from a CIA base in Taiwan. According to ex-CIA official Joseph B. Smith, "I heard in the corridors that Des did not have a very friendly relationship with MacArthur's man Charles Willoughby."[41]

After Korea, FitzGerald moved on to become CIA station chief in the Philippines and then Japan before being appointed the Agency's Far Eastern Division head. He was known as a scholarly sort with a rapt interest in art—as well as an avid enthusiast of CIA covert operations. The Zip code for the exclusive Georgetown section where he lived was, appropriately, 20007.

"My stepfather was motivated by misdirected patriotism," Barbara Train remembers, "as well as a bit of noblesse oblige and the notion that Boston Brahmins must rule, the good-old-boy connection. He was part of a cohort that saw Commies under every bedpost and felt that might is right."[42]

"He grew up in a world where the models were the British," his daughter Frances was saying as we sat in her book-lined apartment overlooking New York's East River in the spring of 1992. "You know, the attitude that a whiff of grapeshot would do. He viewed politics in the Third World as a matter of elites, very small elites, so he simply believed you could change things quite a bit by changing the ruler."

Frances FitzGerald, a redhead like her father and who is today a renowned political author (her book on the Vietnam War, *Fire in the Lake,* won a Pulitzer Prize in 1973), recalled him as being "very reserved, emotionally reserved. One time when I had some problem or other, my stepmother decided I ought to discuss this with my father. She told me later that she'd told him he *had* to do this. I remember the day very well. We went out bird-watching, which was a fascination of his—and he was unable to bring the subject up. Because, I mean, we didn't have that kind of relationship.

"We used to talk politics, but my father always said he didn't believe in parties. He just wasn't very ideological. More than that, I think he saw his cast of people as being above politics. I knew a certain amount about his attitudes, but certainly not anything about what he was up to. Neither did anyone else. That was simply out of bounds. And he didn't care for publicity. It wasn't so much about being secretive, it was just that he believed a low profile gets you someplace."

The Spook's Spook

James Angleton, the CIA's longtime chief of Counter Intelligence, had also known FitzGerald well. On three occasions in the mid-1970s, Angleton agreed to meet with me for wide-ranging interviews at the Army-Navy Club in Washington. For more than twenty years, Angleton had been even more invisible than FitzGerald, a "spook's spook" who stalked the agency's corridors in pursuit of an obsession—that the CIA had been penetrated by Soviet "moles" at a high level. Ultimately his fanatical quest had divided the CIA against itself, and Angleton had been forced to resign in 1974—after then director William Colby leaked word to the media that Angleton had also been in charge of Operation CHAOS, a domestic intelligence program that far exceeded the bounds of the CIA's original charter.[43]

Angleton was one of the strangest men I ever met: tall, bespectacled, stoop-shouldered, his appearance bringing to mind the image of an ostrich whose head seemed, despite itself, to be peering out at the world after a lifetime of seclusion in the sand. He had taken to meeting with journalists after leaving the CIA, as a last-resort means for promoting his viewpoints about the ongoing internal threat he perceived from the KGB. Like Richard Nagell, Angleton felt he had been burned, hung out to dry, by the intelligence world to which he had devoted his life. So, on the one hand, he was compelled to reach out and beseech his justification. On the other hand, as a master spy, his entire training was to hold himself in check. Like Nagell, he seemed a man caught in a "Catch-22" netherworld between the mutually held desires to reveal and conceal. And, just as Nagell did, Angleton always insisted on buying the drinks.

Speaking in clipped, rapid sentences as we sat alone in the plush Army-Navy Club lounge, Angleton reflected on Desmond FitzGerald: "St. Mark's, Harvard, distinguished Irish family, highest social status. Distinguished himself in the Far East Theater [during World War II], working with guerrillas and different people. One of the most energetic men you can imagine. He was, to put it bluntly, a hard-nosed, positive individual who worked himself to death seven days a week. He lacked what I'd call research analysis—the verbal side of discussion for arriving at a decision. But never waffled on decisions. When he made up his mind, there were no ambiguities, no ifs, ands, or buts. Very loyal to his men, extra loyal to the cadre."

The cadre. Strange, I thought, to hear a word I generally associated with the "other side" of the spy world. But then again, espionage exists beyond conventional thinking. The more I learned about the CIA-KGB spy wars, the more I came to see the two groups as a kind of brotherhood. Their ideology was intelligence. In this sense they shared a common politics, a common economy, a common language. They had far more kinship with each other than with the countries they represented. Indeed, sometimes I thought of the espionage systems that developed during the Cold War as akin to those giant mutant creatures that filled the movie screens of the 1950s—unintentionally spawned by the new science and devouring everything in sight.

By early 1958, Richard Case Nagell and Lee Harvey Oswald would find themselves ensnared in the maw of that beast.

Summary

In this chapter, new information has been brought to light concerning Oswald's contacts in Tokyo. While stationed at Atsugi, a Top-Secret point of origin for American U-2 spy plane flights, Oswald was photographed by the Japanese National Police outside the Soviet embassy in Tokyo. Inside, Nagell says that Oswald met with Colonel Nikolai Eroshkin, whom the CIA suspected of being the Soviets' top Military Intelligence (GRU) officer in Japan.

In November 1957 Nagell was recruited by the CIA into a plan aimed at enticing Eroshkin's defection. Nagell was told that this originated with the CIA's Far Eastern Division chief, Desmond FitzGerald. Nagell was to enlist into the project Dr. Chikao Fujisawa, a professor emeritus at Tokyo University. Early in 1958 Nagell was warned to stay away from the project by friends with Japanese intelligence. Somewhere during this time frame, Nagell and Oswald met together with Dr. Fujisawa. Fujisawa, a propagandist for Imperial Japan during World War II, was also acquainted with Mark Gayn. In 1959 the Japanese professor attempted to recruit Nagell to work for Soviet Intelligence.

It is not known whether Oswald was involved in the CIA's Eroshkin defection plan, or the nature of his meeting with Fujisawa. Clearly, this overlapping set of acquaintanceships demands further official investigation. Nagell and Oswald each had girlfriends at an exclusive Tokyo nightspot, the Queen Bee, and a fellow Marine maintains that Oswald was asked by U.S. intelligence to pass along false information to a KGB contact at the nightclub.

Chapter Six

Tokyo Triangles: 1958–63

Counterespionage is, by its very nature, virtually unfathomable. To confuse an enemy, one intelligence service will train and then send someone to an opposing country's intelligence service, pretending to be a traitor to his own country. The false defector will pass along certain information carefully "cooked" by his superiors. His mission is to destabilize, exploit, or ferret out the interests of the enemy. The pinnacle of achievement is to plant agents or informants directly inside the other's spy apparatus.

These people are not dispatched willy-nilly. They have spent time building a "cover" to make them appear appealing to the foe. They may seem to be ideological converts for whatever reason, or simply in pursuit of cold, hard cash for their services. But whether "defecting" from the American or the Soviet sides, their disaffection may also contain more than a glimmer of truth. Both sides are always on the lookout, anxious to "turn" such individuals back against the source that sent them in the first place. A "double agent" may actually be ripe to let himself be "tripled."

Or, depending upon the true loyalty of whoever set them on this winding road in the first place, they might even be used without their knowledge. Deception is, after all, the hallmark of the business. If the "case officer" for a CIA "double agent" is really working for the KGB himself, the agent then becomes a pawn in a much larger arena of distortion.

It is my contention that Lee Harvey Oswald and Richard Case Nagell were swept into such a web, both while stationed in Japan in the late 1950s. Particularly in 1958, Oswald's and Nagell's disaffection with military life independently but abruptly reached often bizarre levels. I believe they were building a "cover" for future intelligence work aimed at the United States' main enemy, the Soviet Union. At the same time, however, their interest in Marxist ideology was not entirely specious. Both the KGB and the CIA were aware of this. And they were almost certainly not the only players.

As I will outline at the end of this chapter, my hypothesis is that the Japanese themselves cannot be left out of the picture. No previous published research into the assassination has mined this particular lode. For both Oswald and Nagell, the influence of the Orient did not culminate in the late 1950s in Tokyo. It continued on into the critical years of 1962 and 1963.

As we enter into the counterespionage maze, the only certainty is that we are following some kind of parallel course with Oswald and Nagell. We will find Oswald, in the fall of 1959, announcing his intent to renounce his citizenship at the American embassy in Moscow—and allegedly bearing U.S. radar secrets for the Soviets. We will find Nagell, in the fall of 1962, announcing his intent to renounce his citizenship at the American embassy in Mexico City—and certainly he, as a high-ranking Military Intelligence officer with knowledge of Top-Secret files, knew things the Soviets would find of interest.

The Oswald Riddle

First, what happened to Oswald in the Far East? Even during his first months at the Atsugi naval air base, he had displayed a keen interest in briefings on classified material held by his unit's intelligence officer. One fellow Marine would later recall Oswald even taking photographs around the base where the CIA's U-2 spy plane flights originated. Somewhere in here, as we have seen, Oswald visited the Soviet embassy, met with Colonel Eroshkin and Professor Fujisawa, began frequenting the exclusive Queen Bee nightclub—and encountered Richard Nagell.

Things began to get curiouser and curiouser after Oswald came back to Atsugi from the Philippines on March 18, 1958. Three weeks later, he was brought up on charges for having possessed an unregistered weapon—the derringer with which he supposedly shot himself the previous October. A court-martial found Oswald guilty as charged and sentenced him to twenty days at hard labor. But any confinement was suspended for six months, on condition that he stay out of trouble. He then put in for a hardship discharge to care for his mother, but was turned down.

After this, Oswald tried to pick a fight with a sergeant whom he felt had assigned him an overload of KP duty. Failing the first time, Oswald then poured a drink over Sergeant Miguel Rodriguez's head on June 20, at the Bluebird Club in Yamato, and military police intervened. Another court-martial found Oswald guilty of using "provoking words" to a noncommissioned officer. His previous suspended sentence was revoked, and Marine records state that Oswald then got sent to the brig for forty-five days.

Following his release on August 13, as Marine acquaintance Joseph D. Macedo recalled, Oswald was "a completely changed person"—cold and withdrawn, associating more than ever with Japanese friends and less with other Marines. On September 14, American forces mobilized after the Communist Chinese appeared to be considering a move against the islands of Quemoy and Matsu, and Oswald was sent with his unit to Formosa (Taiwan). Shortly after his arrival, Oswald was pulling guard duty when Lieutenant Charles Rhodes heard several shots around midnight. He ran to the scene and discovered Oswald, his M-1 rifle in his lap, slumped against a tree. "When I got to him, he was shaking and crying," Rhodes would later remember. "He said he had seen men in the woods and that he challenged them and then started shooting. . . . He kept saying he couldn't bear guard duty."[1]

Rhodes believed that Oswald planned the shooting incident to get himself sent back to Japan. Indeed, he was quickly shipped out, arriving alone at Atsugi on October 5 to receive "medical treatment." Shortly before this, his medical records show that Oswald had already been treated for gonorrhea, a venereal disease that in those days often resulted in disciplinary measures against military personnel who contracted it. Yet Oswald's record bears this very odd notation: "Origin: In line of duty, not due to own misconduct."[2]

With his unit still on Formosa, Oswald was temporarily reassigned to a Marine squadron at Iwakuni, an air base some 430 miles southwest of Tokyo. Owen Dejanovich, who had attended radar school with Oswald, ran into him there—and found Oswald ranting constantly about "American imperialism" and "exploitation," referring to the Marines as "you Americans." Oswald was also observed by Dejanovich and others in the company of a "round-eyed Russian girlfriend," an attractive Eurasian woman whom they had the impression was schooling Oswald in the Russian language.[3] On November 2, 1958, Oswald then boarded a ship in Japan, bound again for the United States.

The Strange Death of Private Schrand

James B. Wilcott, a former CIA finance officer who had served in Tokyo between 1960 and 1964, testified before the House Assassinations Committee in 1978 concerning what a CIA case officer told him shortly after the John F. Kennedy assassination. The CIA, Wilcott asserted, had some kind of "handle" on Oswald, and recruited him "from the military for the express purpose of a double agent assignment to the USSR." The committee, after questioning other CIA agents, found discrepancies in Wilcott's background and testimony and concluded his allegation "was not worthy of belief."[4] Still, I decided to track down Wilcott, and I reached him by phone in California in 1986.

"People who had been with CIA's Tokyo station told me that they had helped train Oswald in Russian at Atsugi," Wilcott asserted. "They actually gave me a cryptonym [a code designation for sensitive projects] that was supposed to have been Oswald's for the [Soviet] project. And they told me that I had paid out funds for Oswald over some period of time for it. The story I heard was that Oswald had been picked up by CIA from the Marines after he'd been compromised somehow. In other words, he'd killed somebody and they found out about it, so CIA had a handle on him."[5]

What was most interesting about Wilcott's allegations was this: On January 5, 1958, one of Oswald's fellow Marines had died under strange circumstances while both were temporarily based at Cubi Point in the Philippines. Oswald and Martin Schrand had been stationed together since their days as radar trainees in Biloxi, Mississippi, and Santa Ana, California. Then, one night, guard personnel in another area heard a shot. Private Schrand was discovered lying on top of his M-12 "riot gun" at his guard post beside a U.S. carrier pier, bleeding profusely. At this location, one of Oswald's Marine colleagues would later tell the Warren Commission, his squadron was temporarily assigned the duty of "closely guarding a hangar for a U-2 aircraft."

Schrand died in the ambulance en route to the base hospital. It was determined that the fatal wound came from his own weapon, a gunshot that entered below his left arm and exited his left shoulder. Not until March 31 did an official investigation conclude that Schrand "died in the line of duty and not as a result of his own misconduct." His death was ruled accidental, with no one else "involved in the incident." Yet regulations specified that no bullets were to be kept in the firing chamber while an M-12 was being used for routine guard duty. Indeed, four unused rounds were found in Schrand's pocket. Apparently Schrand had loaded a single live round in the chamber of his weapon. How it could have "accidentally" discharged under his armpit was never adequately explained.

Donald Camarata, another Marine who had served with Oswald and Schrand, told the Warren Commission of a "rumor that Oswald had been in some way responsible for the death." When, in 1978, the House Assassinations Committee briefly looked into whether the military had conducted any investigation of Oswald after the assassination, it was told by the Office of Naval Intelligence that the only matter looked into was the death of Private Schrand.[6]

The Strange Death of Sergeant Dugan

Another military mystery had occurred soon after Schrand's death—the discovery of Master Sergeant Emmett E. Dugan's body in Tokyo Bay on March 12, 1958. I had first seen cryptic references to Dugan amid the material the FBI seized from Nagell when he was arrested in El Paso. But, like the stories of Field Operations Intelligence and Dr. Fujisawa, more details were spelled out in Nagell's case record at the Court of Claims. Here Nagell writes that in February 1958 he had personally "witnessed the abduction and execution of a U.S. Army intelligence agent (Master Sergeant Emmett E. Dugan) by other American agents, because he was suspected of harboring intentions to defect to the Chinese Communists." Nagell identified Dugan as an "Agent Handler" for Field Operations Intelligence, who had been assigned to work with a Chinese informant from Hong Kong.[7]

When I spoke to Nagell's FOI commander, Colonel Stanley, he said he did not recall the Dugan incident. But, sure enough, library files from the period showed that it had occurred. On March 16, 1958, the New York *Sunday News* carried a page two story headlined "Army Sergeant Slain on 1st Intelligence Job." It recounted how Emmett Dugan's body had been found floating in Tokyo Bay four days earlier. Dugan had last been seen on the evening of February 4, when he left his wife, Maude, at the Osaka Hotel in downtown Tokyo, telling her he had "things to take care of" and handing her his insurance policies. "If I don't return," Dugan reportedly told her, "you'll need these."

Dugan, thirty-nine, had been in the Army since 1942, was captured by the Germans in World War II, and later served in the Korean War. The Army said he had completed a Chinese-language course at the Army Language School in Monterey, California, in June 1957. Japanese newspapers reported Dugan had been investigating Communist activities in Japan. An Army spokesman told the United Press that Dugan was on his first intelligence mission when he disappeared and that he was dead when thrown into the water, though the cause of death was undetermined. Medical examiners noted that his body had been in the water about two weeks. "The possibility of poison is not being overlooked," Army investigators added. "Extensive pathological tests will be conducted."

In 1981, a Military Police report from Nagell about the death of Sergeant Dugan showed up in my mailbox. Covering the period from March 12 to June 17, 1958, the report stated that pathological and toxicological examinations "have failed to disclose the immediate cause of death." Nor had the investigation come up with anything about Dugan's whereabouts in the six weeks preceding the discovery of his body. The report concluded: "This case is closed in the files of this office until such time that receipt of new evidence or investigative leads warrants that it be reopened."[8]

Obviously, in Nagell's view, the case was far from closed. It was the FOI, he alleged, that had killed one of its own. And the truth about Dugan's demise was hidden from both Army investigators and the Japanese police. Yet Professor Fujisawa, when he sought to recruit Nagell as a Soviet spy in 1959, had somehow known about it. As we saw in the previous chapter, Fujisawa had tried to use Nagell's knowledge of the Dugan affair as leverage on him. Did Fujisawa have sources within U.S. intelligence circles?

In other of Nagell's correspondence, I later came across this passage about Dugan: "What else was the Army to do with one of its intelligence agents who was suspected of having been doubled? Try him by a General Court Martial, where the truth would have surfaced and heads would have rolled? . . . Had it leaked out that we were engaged in clandestine activities which flagrantly violated the provisions of the treaty between Japan and the United States, this fact alone could have proved somewhat embarrassing to all concerned."[9]

There is, by Nagell's own admission, much harder evidence tying Nagell to knowledge of the Dugan case than Oswald to the death of Schrand. Still, the pattern of two mysterious military deaths is noteworthy. And the parallels between Oswald's and Nagell's lives extend further: At about the same time Oswald started his assault on military regulations, so did Nagell.

Nagell's Military Offensive

On January 5, 1958, Nagell sent a letter to the Army's inspector general in Washington maintaining that the colonel who commanded his unit was unfit for duty. According to an Army file about Nagell, he alleged "misconduct on the part of other military personnel in the US Army, Japan. NAGELL charged personnel injustices, incompetence, corruption, mismanagement, mal-administration, and lack of opportunity to present fully all matters relative to HIS complaints. He also alleged that Efficiency/Progress Reports submitted by HIM concerning other military personnel had been altered and changed by superior officers."[10]

On January 11, Nagell's commander, Colonel William Rainford, referred Nagell to the U.S. Army Hospital in Tokyo for a psychiatric evaluation. Nagell had recently, and rather abruptly, gotten engaged to a young Japanese woman named Mitsuko Takahashi. The psychiatric evaluation, the Army says, was recommended because of Nagell's "attitude over being reported for having his fiancée in the Bachelor's Quarters." It was the first of a number of such Army hospital stays and evaluations, which would always come at crucial times in Nagell's intelligence career. The Tokyo hospital's clinical record notes "no evidence of a neurosis or psychosis was found," but after his release Nagell was relieved of all "sensitive" duties in his CIC unit.

Then, on February 3, Colonel Rainford recommended another psychiatric evaluation of Nagell. According to the Army, this was "for having written letters to the Department of the Army, U.S. Senator Jacob K. Javits, and Columnist Drew Pearson, complaining of alleged security violations within the Counter Intelligence Corps."

The next day, Sergeant Dugan disappeared.

On February 13, Nagell was again sent to the Tokyo Army hospital, where yet another clinical report states that there was essentially no change from its previous evaluation. On March 3, Nagell was reassigned to the U.S. Army Intelligence Support Center in Tokyo.[11]

Then, on April 21, 1958, Nagell was informed that he had been named in connection with an investigation "into the compromise of classified material in Detachment B, 3d Operations Group" and was warned of his rights under the Articles of War. A subordinate had claimed that Nagell "permitted Japanese Nationals to have unauthorized access to classified defense information."[12]

But an Army report covering his service from March 11 through July 8, when Nagell was assistant chief of administration for the Army Intelligence Support Center, does not mention any such problems. Instead, it recounts: "During his present temporary assignment, he has performed all tasks and details assigned him with dispatch, thoroughness, initiative and meticulous attention to detail. He is a sound, mature officer, loyal, considerate and able to work well under pressure. His morals are above reproach. Recommend this officer attend Associate Advance Course as refresher in his basic branch after completing a tour in a security type assignment."[13]

All of this—the psychiatric evaluations that point nowhere, the contradiction between the Army's accusations and commendations of Nagell—make it appear that two entirely separate records were being built about him. And the worst-case dossier, I realized, could certainly have been used later as a means of proving his "bona fides" to the Soviets. In other words, his bitterness against the U.S. Military Intelligence establishment would have several legs to stand on in a future "double agent" role for the CIA.

A Soviet Agenda?

In the labyrinth of counterespionage, searching for the truth becomes akin to a quest for the Holy Grail. But I have learned enough about Nagell to conclude that he did enter into a liaison with Soviet intelligence while stationed in Japan. Jim Garrison, who had two meetings with Nagell in 1968, recalls Nagell saying that "beginning in the late '50s" he had begun his role as an American "double agent."[14]

The first strong hints about this go back to a mysterious letter that arrived at Fensterwald's law office late in 1968. At the time, the attorney had not yet met Nagell but, as founder of the private Committee to Investigate Assassinations, he was already most curious about Nagell's past. The letter came from a Ricard von Kleist in Upland, California, specifying that his background on Nagell came from another source.

First it mentioned the warning letter that Nagell had written to the FBI in September 1963, which "contains information about Oswald, who was named and referred to as Alex Hydell, and advises Hoover that Kennedy would definitely be killed." Von Kleist then added: "The history of Richard Case Nagell is important. While a member of Counter Intelligence in Tokyo, he was dealing with a Soviet attaché officer stationed with Russian Embassy in Tokyo at that time. He was approached several times and was said to have dealt with said Russian officer as to vital information (classified)."[15]

It seemed that this probably referred to Colonel Eroshkin. Von Kleist went on to say that further insight would be coming on a "Dr. Fujiyama," who almost certainly was Dr. Chikao Fujisawa. Whoever von Kleist was, he communicated with Fensterwald only once more, by phone. Nagell, in his Court of Claims case, would call von Kleist's statement "a distortion." But Nagell also made it clear that the man had indeed been made privy to highly confidential information.[16]

One night, as I sat alone with Nagell, I pursued further the question of his early involvement with the Soviets. It was the spring of 1978, and Nagell was quietly going back and forth over how much of his story he could possibly tell me. I brought out a handwritten letter he had sent me, addressed to him in 1962 from an old Army friend and containing references to their having served together in Japan. I asked him who it was. He named the man, identifying him as "a private detective now, but he's former CIC and FOI."

"Hypothetically," he continued uneasily, "I was doing something for another country and it backfired. I got ID'd, got called in, and I strapped some story on my superiors at the CIC. He [the friend] was aware of this. Finally it was all hushed up about this kind of activity in Japan. This had to do with a Korean who was a suspected Soviet agent, though he was working with a very right-wing group. He was one of our informants, and also an informant for the Japanese police. They wanted to know, why did I contact this guy? They caught me cold. I came out with some preposterous thing that they bought. I blamed it on FOI, doing those guys a favor in Tokyo. But just like the FBI doesn't tell the CIA anything and vice versa, it was the same way with the FOI and CIC. Competitive jealousy. If they'd have checked, I'd have been court-martialed—who are you and what were you really doing? It was one of the few slipups I ever made in my life. The Korean was really a contact and I screwed up."[17]

It was a telling moment, but one that only deepened the mystery about this man. Later, in the files of his court case, I came across a statement Nagell had prepared for an appeal when he was incarcerated on the bank charge. It concerned his Army years and said, in part: "During the period of my military service I had occasion to sign numerous U.S. Government loyalty oaths, and to perform in capacities for which I could now be prosecuted if it were disclosed that I was a Communist at the time."[18]

There was also, in Fensterwald's files on Nagell, a memorandum of a conversation the lawyer had with Nagell in 1978. When Fujisawa attempted to recruit Nagell in 1959, it stated, the Japanese professor apparently did not know that Nagell had *already* worked for the Soviets.[19]

So where did all this leave Nagell's "casual, but purposeful acquaintance" in Tokyo with Oswald? In 1978, Nagell mailed me his "critique" of a recent book titled *KGB*, authored by John Barron. Nagell wrote of the

Soviets' suspicions that Oswald was an agent for one of the American intelligence services—"almost since the day he first met with a GRU representative in Tokyo. . . . Without doubt information regarding this suspicion was passed on to GRU headquarters. And since the KGB had the responsibility of conducting military counter-intelligence (security) operations, it too would have become aware of such information at that time."

Nagell has never said whether he himself played a role in Oswald's eventual "defection." But certainly in Tokyo, Oswald encountered a variety of people from all walks of the spy spectrum—Eroshkin, Fujisawa, Nagell, a "security-intelligence" operator, Japanese Communists, and girlfriends.

Another Oriental Girlfriend

In following a trail that may have originated in Tokyo, Yaeko Okui was a striking young Japanese woman, some six years older than Oswald, who came to the United States in 1959 to study "professional flower arrangement." FBI reports show that she settled first in Dallas, then in New York City. Then, in August 1962, Okui came back to Dallas to work as representative for a Tokyo department store chain, Nippon Services, Inc. Oswald had just returned from the Soviet Union with his Russian wife, Marina. That December the Oswalds were introduced to Okui at a Christmas party.

The party took place at the home of a member of Dallas's White Russian émigré community, which had taken the Oswalds under its wing. George and Jeanne de Mohrenschildt, an older couple grown particularly close to the Oswalds, brought them. They observed that Okui and Oswald spent several hours in intense conversation and that Okui spoke both English and Russian with equal fluency. Later, in her Warren Commission testimony, Jeanne de Mohrenschildt would make a point of emphasizing the possible importance of Okui.

"Do you know about Yaeko?" she began. "She was imported by some American family. . . . She is supposed to be from a very fine Japanese family. She was wealthy. It was strange she worked almost as a servant in some family. . . . To tell you frankly I never trusted Yaeko. . . . It was very strange to me the way she was floating around. . . . Marina told me that Oswald saw Yaeko after, which was very unusual, because I don't think Oswald wanted to see anyone, let's put it that way."[20] The Warren Commission did not elect to pursue the matter.

Marina Oswald later told her biographer, Priscilla McMillan, that she took Lee aside at the 1962 Christmas party and cautioned him against talking politics with Okui. "She may be a spy," Marina sensed. "Don't be too frank with her."[21]

George de Mohrenschildt felt similarly. "I think she works for some government or other, but which one, I don't know," he told Marina. In a manuscript written not long before his mysterious death in 1977 and reprinted by the House Assassinations Committee, de Mohrenschildt recalled Okui approaching him about Oswald as the Christmas party wound down. "He had so many true things to say about Japan," she reportedly said. "He is a very sensitive person and he understood my country. The New Japan is very complex. . . . Where does he work?" De Mohrenschildt said he provided the woman with Oswald's address and phone number at the Jaggers-Chiles-Stovall photo-lithography firm—which, among other tasks, did classified work for the U.S. Army Map Service.

After the party, de Mohrenschildt went on, the two "did communicate . . . and I wouldn't have known about it had it not been for Marina." He recalled a furious Marina dropping by to see him, having found the Japanese woman's address in her husband's pocket. Marina had a black eye. "That Japanese bitch," de Mohrenschildt recalled her crying bitterly, "we had a fight over her! What a bastard, he is having an affair with her!"[22]

Whatever went on between Oswald and Okui, the immediate days after their first meeting marked two things: degeneration of his marriage to Marina, and heightened activism on several fronts. On New Year's Day 1963, Oswald ordered several political pamphlets from the Trotskyite Pioneer Press. From a bookstore in Washington, he soon wrote asking for subscriptions to a number of Soviet periodicals. At the Dallas library, he began checking out books about Marxism, Trotskyism, and American imperialism in Latin America, especially Cuba.[23]

Okui went back to Japan in mid-1964, soon after an FBI interview in which she said she vaguely recollected talking with Oswald merely about *ikebhana* (Japanese flower arrangement). In 1976, when author Edward Jay Epstein sought her out in Tokyo, Okui said she did not remember what she and Oswald talked about but that her one short contact with him had "ruined her life." She would not elaborate further.[24]

More Oswald-Oriental Ties

A fascination with Cuba came more and more to predominate Oswald's life as 1963 wore on. That summer in New Orleans, his highly visible presence passing out Fair Play for Cuba pamphlets became a landmark for his apparent pro-Castro sympathies. When he was jailed after taking part in a scuffle with some anti-Castro Cubans on August 9, the authorities noted that Oswald had on him a calling card for a Japanese hotel. Japanese writing covered the front of the card, alongside the English words "Compliments of the GA-JO-ENKANKO HOTEL—A Special Services Hotel."

On the back of the card appeared the notation "ROSA" and the number "92463."[25] I surmised that these numerals might stand for a date: September 24, 1963. And I flashed back to Nagell's warning letter to Hoover, which specifically stated that the assassination plot involving Oswald was, to his knowledge, scheduled for the twenty-fourth to the twenty-ninth of September. I also had, among my letters from Nagell, his statement that Oswald had "once stayed at the Enlisted Man's Kanko Hotel in Tokyo."[26]

I then located a most interesting photograph in the National Archives of Oswald with his Fair Play leaflets that August. It depicts six other men standing near Oswald in front of New Orleans' International Trade Mart; several of them seem to be looking at the literature. Right next to Oswald and holding leaflets is a Hispanic man, wearing an identical white shirt and tie. He has never been identified, though the two appear to be working together. Then, directly behind Oswald and to his right, stands an Oriental man with glasses, his arms akimbo behind his head. An FBI report dated November 30, 1963, says of him that "a confidential source . . . advised that the Japanese . . . was probably named O'Hari; that he has an office in the International Trade Mart but he has not yet been located for interview."[27]

The Trade Mart itself later came under considerable scrutiny in the Garrison investigation. The Trade Mart was run by Clay Shaw, the New Orleans businessman accused by Garrison (and acquitted in 1969) as a coconspirator in the assassination. The Trade Mart was also the office base of William George Gaudet, a CIA specialist on Latin America who, on September 17 in New Orleans, was standing right in front of Oswald in line to get a tourist card for entry to Mexico. Gaudet's identity would not be revealed—and even then, inadvertently through a bureaucratic error—until declassification of some government files in 1975.[28]

Nagell and the Japanese

Richard Nagell had his own ongoing relationship with the Japanese. First, there was his wife. After a brief courtship, his marriage to Mitsuko

Takahashi took place on March 24, 1958, at the American embassy in Tokyo. She was, as Louis Gambert described her to me, "a beautiful girl, the most beautiful girl I've ever known. When they came over for dinner, I remember asking Dick to put her opposite me so I could look at her."[29]

But there was evidence of more than strictly personal ties continuing between Nagell and Japanese. The papers taken by the FBI from his trunk after his September 1963 arrest were predominated by Japanese names and photographs. On one page of Nagell's notebook was a list of contact points for meetings in a variety of locations—at restaurants in Mexico City, New York, Miami, and Nuevo Laredo, Mexico, during the September 1962 to February 1963 period. At the bottom of that page was this notation: "JAPANESE GOV'T) (R.O.K.)" [Republic of Korea].

Numerous other Oriental references were in the notebook, including the license plate number and job description for an aerospace employee in Burbank, California, "Jack Miyaki (Miaki)." There were also four passport-size photographs of Japanese, which Nagell specifically requested be returned to him in 1964 in order to prepare for his defense at trial. The FBI did not see fit to comply.

The name that cropped up most often among his September 1963 effects was Jun Murai. Besides his being one of the four photographs, Murai's name appeared in his notebook and on a separate slip of paper bearing his address in Japan. Murai was the friend who had warned Nagell to steer clear of the CIA's Eroshkin defection project. The notebook listing appeared on a page directly under Eroshkin's name, and in parentheses identified Murai as "(Cabinet Research Office—C.R.O.) (National Rural Police Agency) (Private Secretary to P.A. Yoshida) (Intelligence Agency in China)—Now in Fukuoka-Shi."

Among the papers I photocopied from the Fensterwald file was an article from a Japanese English-language newspaper dated December 21, 1957. In it Nagell had underlined "Cabinet Research Office" and the name of Murai, whom the story identified as "a veteran police official" who in 1952 had been appointed "to head the newly created Cabinet organ." The article noted that the Japanese government was planning to enlarge the CRO, one of whose principal aims was to "evaluate pertinent information" gathered from Japan's National Police Agency and the Public Security Investigation Agency. It went on that this expansion had raised fears in certain political circles as akin to revival of "the wartime Cabinet Information Bureau." Nagell also underlined that phrase.

The article continued: "The Government, however, wants to redouble its vigilance against Communist infiltration, as communication between Japan and the Soviet Union or Communist China is expected to intensify. . . . After the wartime horror of a police state, however, it seems inevitable that every move of the Government is scrutinized with suspicion, especially when a police official or two comes into the picture. . . ."

What was Nagell trying to indicate? Did he himself have some kind of intelligence connection with a Japanese agency? When Nagell had been with FOI in South Korea, the Top-Secret American group worked closely with, and passed its methodology along to, the republic's own Headquarters Intelligence Division (HID) spy unit. As CIA Counter Intelligence chief James Angleton once imparted to a researcher, one of the agency's biggest weaknesses was knowing what was really going on among Far Eastern intelligence organizations. There was also the Asian People's Anti-Communist League (APACL), set up by the MacArthur-Willoughby partisans. By the early 1960s, the APACL would have an offshoot—the Anti-Communist League of the Caribbean, whose Cuban exile members had Castro as a primary target and with a major base in the New Orleans milieu of Lee Harvey Oswald.

John Margain, Nagell's Army buddy from Korean War days, told me that after Nagell left the service and settled in Los Angeles late in 1959, Military Intelligence still utilized his skills in the Japanese language. "Every time some big Japanese guy would come over [to the United States], they'd pull him out to go with him," Margain said. "Nagell said, 'They're using me, because as soon as an ambassador or whoever arrives, they pull me to be the interpreter—but they really want me to keep an eye on him.' "[30]

During the course of his espionage work in 1963, Nagell also carried an unusual business card. Vaughn Marlowe, then the owner of a left-wing bookstore in Southern California and an executive officer of the L.A. Fair Play for Cuba Committee, recalled for me that when Nagell dropped in unannounced to meet him that spring: "He left a calling card with the name Richard C. Nagell on one side, and the same thing in Japanese on the other side."[31]

And there was a mysterious letter that Nagell dropped in the mail to me in 1978. He had blanked out the sender's name, but the letter was written to him and was dated May 22, 1963. After noting that "You no doubt have more than adaquate [sic] cause for your feeling of disaffection towards the governments," the author continued: "But I think if you take inventory you'll see that your training is broader, and more useful than you realize at present. I would mention your ability to smoothly handle the written language, investigation, Japanese knowledge of world affairs—as things difficult to obtain and useful to employers."

The final and perhaps strongest clue came in another of Nagell's letters, outlining the "advice" given him while in the service of a number of different intelligence agencies—some American and some foreign. Here is what it said:

"Advice given when one leaves service of CIC/FOI: 'Don't tell tales away from home.' Advice given when leaving CIA/DIA: 'We have a strong right arm . . . with parameter.' Advice given when leaving HAI/WAI: 'You are still NASH.' Advice given when leaving CHAOS/XYZ: 'You were never NASH.' "[32]

The acronym "DIA" stands for the Defense Intelligence Agency, a branch of the Pentagon established in 1961 to coordinate all U.S. Military Intelligence activities. Nagell seemed to be saying that his CIA/DIA "advice" was along the lines of, "If you don't shut up, we have ways to deal with that." As for the term "nash," it is a Russian word commonly used in intelligence parlance, and its English translation is "ours." I knew, from deciphering other of Nagell's "messages," that "CHAOS/XYZ" stood for a branch of Soviet intelligence, probably the KGB.

Which left the veiled acronym "HAI/WAI," which seemed to stand for an Oriental intelligence service. "You are still ours," Nagell was told by "HAI/WAI"—which might have accounted for his reluctance ever to talk about whatever services he provided the Japanese. Once, when I asked him if there might conceivably be a Japanese tie-in to Oswald or events leading to the assassination, Nagell replied in more adamant tones than usual: "I have never even *hinted* at anything like that."

But the fact was, the hints existed. He was a soldier who wore a lot of hats.

Japan and the JFK Assassination Probe

Two very strange incidents involving Japan occurred during the early stages of the official investigations into President Kennedy's death. One of these came to light in 1977, when the wife of ex-serviceman Larry Huff contacted the House Assassinations Committee. Huff, it was said, had been a flight crew member aboard a planeload of military investigators who flew from Hawaii to Japan early in December of 1963. Their mission was to look into Oswald's military background while stationed in Tokyo.

According to Huff, on the return trip he had read through a twenty-page typewritten report classified "Secret, For Marine Corps Eyes Only." Its substance dealt with interviews with a number of people in Japan and contained a psychological evaluation of Oswald. As the House Assassinations Committee wrote, "Huff remembered the conclusion being that Oswald was incapable of committing the assassination alone." Huff's former chief warrant officer, Roger G. Morgan, verified from his old logbooks that flights to and from Japan had indeed taken place on the dates Huff specified, though Morgan's letter to the House Assassinations Committee did not outline the purpose.[33]

Not long after the U.S. military's voyage, in January 1964 the Japanese government dispatched a special security agent from Tokyo's National Police Agency to the United States. An article in the June 8, 1964, edition of *U.S. News & World Report* identified him as Atsuyuki Sassa, saying he came to "join quietly with the American FBI in its investigation of the assassination of President Kennedy."

But the article made not a single mention of Oswald's Marine duty in Japan. It consisted largely of quotes from Agent Sassa during a four-hour interview with reporter Glenn Troelstrup in Tokyo. And, coming four months prior to the release of the Warren Commission Report, Sassa's statements served to bolster in advance the official U.S. conclusion: that President Kennedy was the victim of what the Japanese agent termed the "impulsive act" of one man.

Debunking rumors "that Oswald and Jack Ruby were hirelings of wealthy U.S. right-wing interests" as "emotionally imaginative speculations," Sassa told the reporter that "Oswald tried to preserve a small Russia in his home. . . . In Washington, the FBI psychiatrists noted that Oswald obviously hated his father for abandoning him. So, Oswald readily disliked anyone who wielded authority. He probably saw his own father in President Kennedy. . . . Oswald was not a man who could prepare or plan things. He was too unstable."

Asked to explain the unusual role of a Japanese in the American investigation, Sassa replied: "You see, these things usually come in strings. We have had a number of assassination attempts in Japan over the past decade. We feared the next tries would be made with high-powered rifles. So I was sent to join the FBI's assassination investigation."

I found a short follow-up story in the next issue of *U.S. News & World Report*. It stated that "quite a stir" had emanated from Tokyo after Agent Sassa's role was revealed in an American newsmagazine. The article continued: "It [the Sassa story] has been confirmed in all essential details, although it develops that the Japanese officer had no official connection with the Federal Bureau of Investigation's study of the assassination. Sassa did work with various security agencies in the U.S."[34]

The CIA perhaps? I wondered. Was there something about Oswald and Japan that the Japanese authorities knew and wanted to tell the United States? Or did the Japanese want to know what the Americans knew? I thought back to what Nagell had said about Tokyo's National Police Agency—the same outfit that sent Sassa abroad—having a photograph of Oswald taken outside the Soviet embassy. All this could not be innocently explained away.

On August 21, 1992, I located former *U.S. News & World Report* correspondent Glenn Troelstrup in Florida. In a lengthy telephone conversation, Troelstrup recalled that agent Sassa had temporarily been ordered to "disappear" by his superiors when a furor erupted in the Tokyo press following publication of the *U.S. News* story. Troelstrup said he had agreed that his initial conversation with Sassa and another Japanese intelligence official be off the record, and he continues to abide by this.

"Primarily, Sassa was sent to the United States because of Japanese concerns about the safety of the emperor," Troelstrup added. "They also wanted to know, was there a Japanese connection with the apparent killer? How many people were involved, and what were their aims? From the moment Sassa got to Dallas right after the assassination, I know they knew just about every goddamn thing going on with the FBI investigation. Sassa did tell me later that allowing his name to be divulged had put a real crimp in his career. Because after that, he was known, particularly and unfortunately by the Chinese mainland."

Troelstrup also verified Nagell's assertion that "people entering the foreign embassies in Tokyo were regularly photographed by the Japanese."

New Leads to Nagell and the Japanese

The first political researcher to believe that Richard Nagell was a lead worth pursuing was Jones Harris. At the time of the assassination, Harris happened to be working on a book about the Elizabethan world—where assassinations and attempted assassinations had been the order of the day. Privately, he soon shifted his attention to interviewing witnesses in the Dallas area, and in 1967 was enlisted by Jim Garrison to help his staff become acquainted with various aspects of the case.

Having seen a letter sent from Nagell in prison to Professor Popkin, Harris got word to *Ramparts* magazine, which was preparing a long article on the Garrison investigation and which included an analysis of Nagell's potential importance in its January 1968 issue. Getting in touch with Nagell's sister, Harris obtained the complete transcripts of the two El Paso trials. And soon after Nagell arrived by plane in New York after his prison release that April, Harris was the first researcher in whom Nagell confided. He then arranged Garrison's two meetings with Nagell in the city.

Now in his early sixties, Harris leaned across a couch in his apartment and reflected: "I first met Dick Nagell, by his arrangement, on Third Avenue. He did not want to speak in my apartment, though later we did converse in a stairwell outside. My first impression of this thin, emaciated man was that he had just gotten out of the camps but had a chance to feed up for a couple months. 'Do you know what FOI is?' was the first thing he said to me. He quickly realized I didn't. At that time, you had to be really on the inside to know something like that.

"I liked, admired, and felt sorry for Dick Nagell. I found him a remarkably intelligent individual. But to me he was also a perfect example of somebody who'd gotten badly manipulated beyond his capacity to comprehend, let alone deal with it. I could not believe my ears that there came a point in Mexico and beyond when he was part of a mechanism to try to kill Oswald.

"I believe he shot two holes into that bank wall because he became afraid. My impression was, he began to feel nothing was going to stop this thing and if he was on his lonesome, an effort might be made to kill him as someone who knew too much to live. He definitely wanted to come in from the cold. Nagell was attempting to seek shelter for reasons best known to himself, but under the umbrella of the bureau [FBI] rather than the agency [CIA]. He felt he'd swum beyond his depths and it had to be known where he would be on the offending date [of the assassination].

"I gathered from my talks with him and others, and documents that reached me, that he was partially working for the Soviets. He was a Cold Warrior who had a lot of admiration for the Russians—in other words, a bright fellow who felt he could help do the good work of the world by working among these various agencies—and he'd been led into a trap."

Harris was also curious about Nagell's background in Japan, for the researcher had run into a strange brand of stonewalling from the National Archives when he set out to obtain an original print of a photograph in the Warren volumes. In its published form, the picture showed the scene of a press conference held in the Dallas police station late on the night of the assassination. Somehow Jack Ruby had managed to work his way in, and standing near him was an Oriental man. But when the requested print came to Harris, it was an edited version. All it showed was Ruby surrounded by some Caucasian newspeople. Harris wrote back that the picture seemed to be incomplete, then received another print that showed half the face of the Oriental man. Only when Harris went to Washington and insisted that he was literally not being given the complete picture did he finally manage to obtain it. This may have been the same man who was present in the police basement when Ruby shot Oswald two days later. Among a listing of all those present compiled by the FBI, the Oriental was the one person who could never be identified.

Harris also had a number of meetings with a syndicated newspaper columnist in Washington named Paul Scott, the first journalist to express interest in the Oswald-Yaeko Okui story. The most important thing Scott finally divulged to Harris along these lines concerned something Scott had gleaned from the FBI. "The FBI has certain knowledge that Oswald visited the Japanese embassy when he went to Mexico City," Scott told him. Until now, the Soviet and Cuban embassies are the only ones where Oswald is known to have paid mysterious trips while in Mexico City in late September 1963.

This raises intriguing questions about an obscure mention in the Warren Commission's documents. Sylvia Duran, a Cuban embassy employee whom Oswald met in Mexico, also served at the time as head of a "Friendship Committee" between the Mexican-Cuban Institute of Cultural Relations and Tokyo.

The Origin of Oswald's Alias

Before leaving the Far Eastern sector of the mystery, we come to the "Hidell" alias adopted by Oswald early in 1963. His first known use of the name occurred when, on January 27, Oswald filled out a magazine coupon form to Seaport Traders, Inc., of Los Angeles, for a .38 Smith & Wesson revolver with a sawed-down two-inch barrel. He would not actually place the order until March, when he also sent off for an Italian Mannlicher-Carcano rifle with a Japanese scope, under the pseudonym "A. J. Hidell."[35]

The following summer in New Orleans, Oswald would list "Hidell" as chapter president of his local one-man Fair Play for Cuba Committee. When briefly arrested by the police, he would tell an FBI agent that "A. J. Hidell" had asked him to distribute the Fair Play literature.[36] And when he was taken into custody for the assassination, authorities found counterfeit Selective Service and Marine certificate forms in his wallet in the name of "Alek James Hidell."[37]

Some researchers have speculated that "Hidell" was Oswald's own weird composite of "Fidel" and "Lee Harvey." Others think it might even be a combination of "Jekyll and Hyde." Warren Commission files contain a statement from a John Rene Heindel, who had been stationed with Oswald at Atsugi, saying that fellow Marines often referred to Heindel by the nickname "Hidell." The commission's conclusion was that Oswald simply borrowed the name from his old acquaintance.[38]

In my conversations with Nagell, it became clear that the "Hidell" alias had a particular significance. In fact, it was some kind of code name in an intelligence operation. Its origins, once again, track back to the Far East— and go far beyond anything Oswald might have thought up on his own.

We were in Nagell's living room at our very first meeting when he volunteered that he knew "precisely where the name Hidell came from and why it was used." He went on to say that the Warren Commission was way off-base but that neither did the "Hidell" usage emanate directly out of either CIA or FBI headquarters—even though dossiers of both agencies would reveal Oswald's use of several variations of the name.[39]

"The pseudonyms 'Albert' and 'Aleksei Hidel' were given to Oswald," Nagell added, "by whom, could be discovered by CIA authorities by breaking the last name into two syllables and by determining precisely what those syllables meant."[40]

After that I spent a long time puzzling over certain references made by Nagell in some of his correspondence:

- Is "Hidell" a name . . . or does it signify something else?"
- "Who suggested the name *"HID*ell for use by Oswald in his Fair Play for Cuba venture? Why? Did Nagell ever spell his name 'Nagel'? Was Oswald ever furnished a Mexican Tourist Card under the name of Albert Hid*el?* Why? Of what significance is the name 'Albert'? Alek? Aleksei?"[41]

Nagell seemed to be saying that if you dropped the last letter of the "Hidell" surname—or, for that matter, on his *own* name—it bore a different meaning. It was some kind of signal.

Then, in 1978, we had a short discussion about the language of intelligence. Nagell told me that the CIA generally used six-letter cryptonyms to designate certain operations, or even individuals within operations.[42] Yet Nagell implied that the CIA did not *know* the real root of the six-letter HIDELL name. So it followed that some other agency, familiar with CIA cryptonyms, might have made it out to *look* like a CIA derivation.

The KGB, Nagell also imparted to me, sometimes used five-letter words as code names. Drop the last "L" from Hidell, or Nagell, and that's what you have. Since Nagell, as a "double agent," was working several sides of the street, might the variation on the alias depend upon which side he, or Oswald, were communicating with? That is, if Oswald even *knew* who was really behind his use of the name.

I set about dividing the name into syllables. I also noted Nagell's deliberate underlining of the *HID* half. And, in perusing the documents he had filed with the Court of Claims about his early military career, I observed that he had underlined "HID" not only pertaining to Oswald. He also did so in harkening back to his midfifties career with Military Intelligence's FOI branch—when Nagell served as liaison officer to South Korea's own intelligence outfit, the Headquarters Intelligence Division, or HID, forerunner of the Korean CIA.

Also, among the papers seized by the FBI after the bank incident was a typed slip of paper listing sixteen Korean names under the heading

"H.I.D." And, as noted earlier in this chapter, Nagell's notebook accounting of 1962–63 meeting places in a number of cities had "JAPANESE
GOV'T—R.O.K." [Republic of Korea] at the bottom.

Could this be the connection? I arranged to meet with Nagell at a place
in Hollywood called the Raincheck. Early in our conversation, I said: "I
think I know where the Hidell name came from." We were sitting a couple
of feet apart at a corner table. Nagell looked at me with a quizzical expression.

You gave Oswald that name to use," I continued. "HID is derived from
the Korean intelligence outfit that you worked with for FOI. And 'ELL'
are the last three letters of your own name."

Nagell did not reply. He stared back at me, did not deny it, and quickly
changed the subject.[43]

I went back to published sources. In a book called *Kempei Tai: A History
of the Japanese Secret Service,* I found this passage about Japanese spy
operations: "Cooperation with the intelligence services of other countries
was, of course, inevitable and essential in post-war years. Naturally there
was a close relationship with the C.I.A. of both the United States and
South Korea."[44]

The Republic of Korea's military, which went from virtually zero to
some 650,000 men by 1954, was built along the American model to a
remarkable degree. Most of its early officers, after U.S. occupation forces
came in after World War II, were trained at a military English-language
school. Not only did the ROK Army have a counterpart Joint Chiefs of
Staff, but also an Army Intelligence Bureau and a Counter Intelligence
Corps.[45] The HID had emerged from the MacArthur/Willoughby network, and its agents had been the cofounders of the Asian People's Anti-
Communist League. The APACL, in a 1960 pamphlet describing its
"growth and outlook," wrote of its collaboration with psychological-warfare experts in the Pentagon and with the right-wing John Birch Society.[46]

In 1961, when Park Chung Hee took power in South Korea, he made
the APACL an important instrument of his foreign policy. The HID's
successor, the Korean CIA, was established in that same year and, according to the writer Tad Szulc, soon earned "a reputation as one of the most
brutal and venal security services in the world. A State Department official described the agency . . . quite simply as a combination of the Gestapo and the Soviet K.G.B."[47] It wielded more than a hundred thousand
agents, who fanned out through Asia and the United States (with the
approval of American intelligence) and who retained close links with Korea's own organized-crime network. The book *Yakuza* recounted: "KCIA
and the Korean yakuza were certainly intermingled, so it was never certain

what was an official KCIA initiative and what was from a mobster organization."[48]

In another book, *CIA Diary,* by former CIA employee Philip Agee, I came across this: "Stan Watson, the Mexico City Deputy Chief of Station, has been meeting with a South Korean CIA officer who was recently sent under diplomatic cover."[49] Agee was describing a period a few years after the John F. Kennedy assassination, but it still showed a crossover between the pivotal Mexican and Asian scenes.

Finally, there was the Warren Commission testimony of John Graef, Oswald's boss at the Jaggers-Chiles-Stovall photo-lithography firm between October 1962 and April 1963. One day shortly before Oswald left, Graef recalled asking him about a Russian newspaper he was reading. "I said something like 'What is the action on this?' And he said, 'I studied Russian in Korea.' This fit in with his previous statement when we employed him about being in Korea, when he was a Marine. . . ."[50]

Yet there is no official record of Oswald ever having been in Korea. Either he was making it up, or perhaps he had a reason for saying it. Did the origins of "Hidell" go back to an FOI and/or CIA liaison with Korean intelligence in the 1950s, part of an ongoing intelligence operation that hooked into Oswald?

About two years after I confronted Nagell with my thoughts on the "HIDELL" matter, I found an astonishing document in Fensterwald's files. This was a notarized affidavit sworn to by Nagell on July 18, 1979, apparently in response to a letter the CIA had sent him eight days earlier. At that time Nagell was seeking his CIA files under the Freedom of Information Act, and there seemed to be a CIA "requirement" that Nagell list any other names under which files about him might appear. After listing his true name, date, place of birth, and two passport numbers (others had been deleted in the photocopy), Nagell continued:

"In the past, and among other fictitious names, I have used and/or have been documented with the following names and variations thereof: Ben Blum [next name blanked out in the photocopy], Robert C. Corsa [next two names blanked out], Alek Hidell, Aleksei Hidel, Joseph Kramer [next name blank], Victor Nadell, Vic Nadelli, N. Nagel, Robert C. Nolan, Paul Schmedke."

Nagell was admitting that he himself had used the same alias as Oswald, in two different variations! A Garrison memorandum, setting down notes of his conversations with Nagell, added: "A number of people were using the name Hidel."

Officials of U.S. Military Intelligence, more than the CIA, may have the most additional light to shed on the matter. As Lieutenant Colonel Robert Jones testified before the House Assassinations Committee, on the afternoon of the assassination he received a phone call from Dallas "advising that an A. J. Hidell had been arrested." Jones was then an operations officer with the 112th Military Intelligence Group in San Antonio. He said he had quickly located the "Hidell" name in his files, cross-referencing with another dossier on Oswald. But the House Assassinations Committee was informed that these Hidell/Oswald files had been destroyed in 1973 as a matter of Pentagon "routine."[51]

Summary

We continue to find very curious parallels in examining the Far Eastern military careers of Nagell and Oswald. In 1958 both men came under scrutiny for insubordinate actions against their superiors. Both men were in the proximity of two servicemen's mysterious deaths—Oswald with Martin Schrand, Nagell with Emmett Dugan. While Nagell says that Oswald was suspected by the Soviets of being part of a U.S. intelligence agency, Oswald began ranting publicly against "American imperialism." Nagell himself appears to have become a "double agent" during his Tokyo period, suggesting that he may have performed services on behalf of the Communists.

Was there a continuing Japanese connection to Nagell and Oswald? New evidence indicates this may be the case. Nagell married a Japanese woman; Oswald later had an apparent affair in the United States with a Japanese, whom his wife and acquaintances suspected of being a spy. Mysterious Oriental personages appear during Oswald's pro-Castro leafleting in New Orleans, and again alongside Jack Ruby when Oswald met the press the night of the assassination. Oswald is also said to have visited the Japanese embassy in Mexico City in September 1963. Nagell's notebook from this period is filled with Japanese names, and he is said to have chaperoned Japanese officials at the request of American intelligence.

Soon after the assassination, an American military contingent flew to Tokyo to examine Oswald's Marine background. The Japanese National Police—which had photographed Oswald outside Tokyo's Soviet embassy —dispatched a security agent to assist American authorities in a postassassination investigation.

Finally, there is the "Hidell/Hidel" alias used by both Oswald and Nagell. This seems to have been a code name in an intelligence operation, perhaps derived from the last three letters of Nagell's name—and the South Korean Headquarters Intelligence Division (HID) with which Nagell liaisoned during his FOI service. A U.S. Military Intelligence file on Oswald/Hidell has since been destroyed by the Pentagon.

Chapter Seven

California Odysseys: 1958–62

For a considerable time after Tokyo, the paths of Richard Case Nagell and Lee Harvey Oswald seem to have diverged. Four months before Oswald was shipped back Stateside, Nagell had returned to the United States with his Japanese bride on July 15, 1958. Upon recommendation of the Pentagon's Intelligence-Security Department, he was reassigned from Military Intelligence to his basic infantry branch. Nagell's records on file with the Court of Claims show that he immediately took leave from the Army Training Center at Fort Dix, New Jersey—and set about preparing a twenty-four-page typewritten "contestation" addressed to the Pentagon's inspector general.

Among other things, Nagell says this detailed "his allegations of security violations within Military Intelligence and the injustices he felt had been dealt to him by his CIC superiors in retaliation for his 'disclosures' in Japan." On August 28, 1958, he hand-carried his "contestation"—with a cover letter containing information about the alleged execution of Sergeant Emmett Dugan by FOI—to the inspector general's office.

The very next day, Captain Nagell was assigned to understudy a first lieutenant in a basic training company. On October 5 Nagell wrote a letter of resignation to the Army, then withdrew it nine days later. His change of heart, Nagell says, came when he was informed "that the conditions of his current assignment would not be permanent, and that the matter discussed in his 28 August 1958 letter to the inspector general would be investigated." Nagell remained stationed at Fort Dix.

On April 14, 1959, a memo from the adjutant general to the commanding general of the U.S. First Army noted that he "has been declared ineligible for further duty and assignment with the Counter Intelligence Corps. Release of the officer from such assignment is without prejudice or adverse reflection on officer's character, loyalty, and discretion."

Nagell's marriage to a Japanese national was also apparently a source of contention with his superior officers. "As soon as I married a Japanese girl, they [the Army] didn't think I was good enough for Military Intelligence," Nagell's old Army buddy John Margain remembered Nagell once telling him.

On August 31, 1959, Nagell sent another letter of resignation to the Army, stating "a wish to further his civilian education and compassionate reasons of a personal nature." This came two weeks after Lee Harvey Oswald, then stationed in Santa Ana, California, requested a dependency discharge from the Marines to care for his mother. Then, two days before Oswald showed up at the American embassy in Moscow looking to renounce his citizenship, Nagell received an honorable discharge on October 29, after eleven years of military service.[1]

Origins of a Defection

In our examination of Oswald's time in the Far East, we have seen that the young Marine had contacts with both Military Intelligence and the CIA—through Nagell, at least—as well as a Soviet intelligence officer, Nikolai Eroshkin, and a Soviet spy, Dr. Chikao Fujisawa. We have also seen that Nagell had the same contacts, and more, on both sides of the ideological fence. Some kind of plan was being mapped out for Oswald there—by the CIA and/or Military Intelligence, the Soviet KGB or GRU, maybe even the Japanese.

Shortly before Christmas in 1958, after taking a month's leave and staying with his mother in Fort Worth, Oswald reported to a new unit—

Marine Air Control Squadron 9—in Santa Ana, California. Here, for the next nine months, he would be part of a ten-man radar crew. The main function of the El Toro base, as Oswald's training officer John F. Donovan testified before the Warren Commission, was "basically to train both enlisted [men] and officers for later assignment overseas." The base's minimum requirement was a "Secret" clearance.[2] All of this seems a unique situation for a young Marine who twice had been court-martialed in Japan and whose previous foreign-duty extension had been canceled—especially when one considers Oswald's extracurricular interests.

He was considered the outfit oddball by his fellow Marines, who sometimes referred to him as "Comrade Oswaldskovitch." Dennis Call told the Warren Commission that when "many members of the unit kidded him about being a Russian spy, Oswald seemed to enjoy this sort of remark."[3] According to Kerry Thornley, who was so taken with Oswald that he began basing a novel on him (*The Idle Warriors*) *before* the assassination, Oswald identified strongly with Winston Smith, the hero-victim of George Orwell's classic book *1984*. Oswald also compared the Marine Corps to the *1984* society. " 'Be careful, comrade, with Big Brother's equipment,' he would say as we unloaded government-owned gear from a truck." Yet Oswald's unbridled enthusiasm for *1984* also caused Thornley to "have second thoughts about his [Oswald's] commitment to communism," since Orwell offered "a severe criticism in fiction form of socialist totalitarianism."[4]

Thornley and others remember Oswald studying Russian in his leisure hours at the El Toro base. The official record on Oswald makes no mention of his having received official tutelage in any language during his Marine years. However, at a Warren Commission executive session whose minutes were declassified in 1974, chief counsel J. Lee Rankin is quoted saying of Oswald: "We are trying . . . to find out what he studied at the Monterey School of the Army in the way of languages."[5]

California's Monterey School, where Richard Nagell had received his own extensive language training, was still quite active when Oswald was stationed in California in 1959. And in addition to his relative fluency in Russian—an extremely difficult language to learn—Oswald was later known to speak passable Spanish.

This brings us to another of Oswald's interests during that time: Cuba. Even before Castro's takeover on New Year's Day 1959, the CIA had long been interested in his revolution, even sending agents to join with him in the mountains to glean his intentions. Gerry Patrick Hemming was a soldier of fortune who eventually ended up training embittered Cuban exiles in Florida for guerrilla warfare against Castro. But before Castro started nationalizing American assets and looking to the Soviets, Hemming says the romantic aspects of Castro's effort appealed to him. In 1958, the six-foot, six-inch ex-Marine had joined Fidel's men in the Sierra Maestre hills. Later Castro had assigned Hemming to work as an officer-instructor of a parachute regiment, then an adjutant at a Cuban air base. Early in 1959, while in Los Angeles, Hemming says he crossed paths with a nineteen-year-old Marine who was stationed in nearby Santa Ana.

"There had been a shooting incident when Castro's Twenty-sixth of July Movement people took over the [Los Angeles Cuban] consulate in January," Hemming told me as we sat having coffee in a roadside Miami café in 1976. "It was under both physical and photographic surveillance by the local police, at the request of the State Department. One day a Cuban who was coordinating the movement there called me aside. He said there was a Marine who'd come around, saying he was prepared to desert and go to Cuba to become a revolutionary. The Cuban asked if I'd meet with this Marine, check him out. I did. The young guy told me he was a non-commissioned officer. He was wearing sport clothes. He talked about being a radar operator and helping the Cubans out with everything he knew. It turned out to be Oswald."

"What was your impression of him?" I asked. "Did you feel he was sincere?"

"No, he didn't look like he was worth a damn, maybe just trying to create a scandal. I thought he might've been on the Naval Intelligence payroll. You know, a penetrator. I told the Twenty-sixth of July leadership to get rid of him."[6]

Hemming is not alone in recalling an early link between Oswald and Castro's Cuba. Nelson Delgado, a Marine buddy of Oswald, told the Warren Commission in 1964: "He started actually making plans, and how we would go about going to Cuba, you know. At about this time Castro started changing colors, so I wasn't too keen on that idea myself." But Oswald, according to Delgado, believed that "we weren't getting the true facts of what was happening in Cuba." So it came as no surprise when Oswald told Delgado he'd also been receiving correspondence from and visited the Cuban consulate in Los Angeles. Delgado said he observed that Oswald was receiving more letters than usual, and on some of these he noticed the official Cuban seal. One night, Delgado continued, an outsider asked for Oswald at the camp entrance and Oswald was allowed to stand down temporarily from guard duty. An hour later Delgado saw Oswald at the gate, heavy into conversation with a man in an overcoat who looked to Delgado like a Cuban.[7]

According to David Bucknell, another Marine associate of Oswald, he, Oswald, and several others stationed at El Toro were ordered in 1959 to report to the military's Criminal Investigation Division (CID). Here a civilian sought to recruit them for an intelligence operation against "Communists" in Cuba. Oswald, as Bucknell told the story to Mark Lane, was selected to make several more trips to the CID and later confided to him that the civilian had also been his intelligence contact at the Atsugi base. Bucknell added that Oswald also indicated later that he was to be discharged from the Marines and go to the Soviet Union—on behalf of American intelligence.[8]

On August 17, 1959, Oswald requested a dependency discharge from the Marines to care for his mother, who he said had injured herself at work and needed his support. In truth, the Warren Commission discovered, the "accident" to his mother, Marguerite, had occurred the previous December, when a box fell on her nose in a Fort Worth department store and had kept her home for only a week. But Oswald received word a few weeks later that his request would be granted—three months ahead of his scheduled discharge.

That same day, September 4, he immediately applied for a passport, stating plans for a four-month trip to Cuba, the Dominican Republic, England, France, Switzerland, and the Soviet Union. Oswald picked up his passport in Los Angeles on the tenth, got his Marine discharge the *next* day, and then went to see his mother briefly in Fort Worth. He told her that he might go to Cuba and join Castro, then headed on to New Orleans, where, four days later, Oswald set sail on September 20.[9]

Nagell in California

In November 1959, Nagell brought his wife, Mitsuko, and their first child, Teresa Dolores, born at Fort Dix in June, to Los Angeles. The family settled into a house in the Pico Rivera section. On November 20, 1960, a son, Robert Lamont, was born.

Nagell had first applied for a job here with the Los Angeles Police Department. Though he successfully completed written and physical tests, he failed to pass the required medical examination.[10] Nagell then went to work for the state of California, initially assigned as an investigator in the Fraud Division of the state's Department of Employment.

But as Nagell was quoted in a 1969 typed memorandum based on a tape-recorded conversation with him, this was not his only job. "My patronage under the CIA did not end with my discharge from the Army and ensuing employment in December 1959 as an investigator for the state of California; in fact, henceforth I was offered remuneration for my services, however nominal it sometimes was. What my new tasks comprised is of no real pertinence to this addendum or to later developments, except perhaps to mention that one of my contacts said he worked out of 'Domestic

Intelligence,' possibly the forerunner of the present-day Domestic Operations Division [DOD], which illegally keeps tabs on a wide range of American civilian organizations and activities."[11]

In 1962 the CIA would formalize the DOD under the direction of Tracy Barnes, one of the leading architects of the Bay of Pigs invasion. "This new division," as a former CIA contract agent has written, "tailored to accept projects unwanted elsewhere in the CIA, has to this day been shrouded in mystery."[12]

It was John Margain, who served under Nagell as his sergeant during the Korean War, who provided my strongest insights into this continuingly peculiar period of Nagell's life. I knew about Margain from a series of his letters, passed along from Nagell, that Margain had written to him in prison. According to Nagell, these innocuous-appearing letters were withheld by prison authorities and given him only after his release. Since Margain's father had been a member of the Mexican Communist Party, the authorities suspected the letters might contain coded messages. Both Nagell and Margain denied this, and I suppose Nagell sent the letters to me as another example of his maltreatment. At any rate, they bore a return address for the L.A. suburb of Baldwin Park—and that's where I found John Margain still residing in the spring of 1991.

When I showed up unexpectedly, he was standing on a wooden porch festooned with numerous hanging plants. A husky Mexican gentleman in his late fifties, he was employed by a company that makes fire extinguishers for airplanes. At first Margain was reluctant to talk to me, until I showed him Nagell's authorization allowing my examination of his lawyers' files. Inviting his wife, Toni, and a daughter in her late twenties, Belia, to join us, we sat down at a little metal picnic table in the front yard of their modest home.

"Does he still always dress up?" Margain wondered. "I think I saw Dick one time with a pair of khakis. He was always with a suit. And a little pocket book with him to write things down. He came in and out of our lives for years. I had a lot of respect for him—a man with compassion. But he was very mysterious. He used to tell me, 'I can't tell you this, John, I don't want your family to get involved. If they ever make an investigation, your name might come up.' He says, 'If you ever see me on the street, don't say hello. If I'm clear, I will say hello.' We had an understanding for me never to approach him. That's just the way it was."

Then Belia entered the conversation. "Nagell's wife used to teach my sister and me origami, how to make the little animals and swans. She taught us how to eat with chopsticks, and would make authentic Japanese food. But you could see even then that she was uncomfortable. She was always so quiet, which is characteristic of her people, but there was a sadness, too. She couldn't go back to Japan because she was like an out-cast there—after marrying an American military man."

Margain shook his head and recalled something else about the origin of Nagell's relationship with Mitsuko Takahashi. "I think he got a raw deal," he said. "I know the government used him. You know, when Nagell married Mitzi, he had been investigating her dad. In World War II, he told me there was a lot of money which got lost. Mitzi's father was a general or a minister of finance. Anyway, all this money had disappeared and Nagell was investigating that—which is how he met Mitzi."

By this time, nothing about Nagell should have surprised me. But that he had married a woman in the course of probing her prominent Japanese father's background raised still more questions in my mind.[13] I could not help thinking, too, of the parallel with Oswald's equally quick courtship and marriage in the Soviet Union to Marina Prusakova—whose uncle was a colonel in the Soviet internal security agency, the MVD.

Later, I would wonder if the "lost money" Margain mentioned could be the legendary "Yamashita's gold." Toward the close of World War II, that Japanese general was rumored to have secreted away a fortune in booty gained through previous conquests. Some of it was said to have been hidden away in tunnels in the Philippines. The CIA, according to the book *The Marcos Dynasty,* maintained an avid interest in the missing treasure for several decades. As late as 1986, a team of high-ranking U.S. military personnel was reportedly in the Philippines in search of the buried bullion. One of these was General John Singlaub, the CIA's deputy chief in South Korea during the Korean War and later tied into the Iran-contra scandal.[14]

Continuing his Nagell story, Margain said: "He wanted to get into the police force here in internal affairs, as a shoofly. They call 'em shooflies because they're always on you. But they wouldn't take him because of his facial scar, which was very noticeable; somebody would spot you and know who you were. So he ended up working for the state, eventually with the ABC." (ABC stood for California's Department of Alcoholic Beverage Control, to which Nagell was transferred on March 31, 1961.)

"Yeah, old Nagell was a maverick," Margain went on. "He wanted to do things the right way, by the book all the time. And this was not gonna work, because everybody was crooked. When he was with the ABC, people were on the take, and he didn't go for that. We used to go drinking together down in Little Tokyo. I'd see people trying to pay him off, putting bills like this"—Margain made a big fist—"in his pocket. But no, thank you. I remember Dick saying, 'My boss tells me, because of my ways we're gonna have a very poor Christmas.'

"Mitzi was by herself a lot of times, because he was gone. With Beverage Control, his hours were up to two in the morning. He was always fighting this and fighting that. Every time he turned around, he said there was a higher authority trying to push him out of the way. He was traveling all over, stopping here, going back East. We'd go drinking and next morning he'd take off and I wouldn't see him for months. After he and Mitzi broke up, I thought he'd gone to Mexico, or left the country. He kept saying, 'One of these days, I'm gonna write a book.' "

After the late summer of 1962, the next Margain knew of his friend was Nagell's arrest. "I've got relatives in El Paso, and somebody sent me an article about what happened in the bank. I found out he was in Leavenworth, and kept writing to him at the prison. They must have had him incommunicado, because he never answered my letters. Then after that, a guy from New York City wrote me, who was with the CIA, and sent an article that they'd just released Dick out of Germany!"

That would have been the fall of 1968, when Nagell ended up being detained while traveling through East Germany—only two months after his release from prison in the United States.

"But how did you know the article came from someone with the CIA?" I asked.

"The fellow who wrote me said, 'I'm with an agency that Richard Case Nagell has been associated with.' So I figured as much."

At this point I asked if Nagell had ever said anything to the Margains about the John F. Kennedy assassination.

"Yeah, this was when we saw him sometime after he got out of prison," Margain said. "He used to write to me then, from Switzerland, Mexico City. Or he'd call and I'd go see him, pick him up at the airport."

Did he ever mention his warning letter to the FBI? I asked. When the Margains nodded agreement, I showed them a copy of the 1976 affidavit about the letter that Nagell had sent to Congressman Edwards. It concurred with what the family remembered Nagell telling them. "He told me about that letter to Hoover," Margain continued. "He had it registered. They didn't do anything about it, but they had it.

"Nagell was smart enough, he always covered himself. One time he left a suitcase with me. He said, 'Don't ever let it out of your sight. If anything ever happens to me, then open up the suitcase.' I kept it for six months, then he came for it."

And did you believe what he said about his foreknowledge of the assassination? "Yeah, I truly believe him," Margain said. "Because I know him, and he's not a bullshitter. He was there, in the thick of it."

His daughter Belia said, "You think it's something out of a storybook, a plot in a movie."

Margain ran a hand through his thinning dark hair, then added: "I'm just glad he's alive. I wish this could come to a head, one way or another. Nagell knew. There's no doubt in my mind he knew that something was coming down. But they ignored him. That's what I think really killed Dick Nagell—on the inside, I mean."

Troubles at the ABC

During Nagell's tenure with California's Department of Alcoholic Beverage Control he also became friends with a fellow investigator, Charles W. (Bill) Lynn. For almost two years in the mid-1970s, Lynn would be my go-between whenever I wanted to get in touch with Nagell. I would call Lynn, he would pass along the message, and Nagell would phone me. In the summer of 1977, I phoned Lynn to see if he would have lunch.

We went to a Chinese buffet restaurant across the street from the ABC headquarters in West Los Angeles. Lynn said that the restaurant, a pleasant spot replete with fireplace, was once regularly patronized by mobster Mickey Cohen and friends. Cohen had died recently, and when I wondered aloud whether it was really due to natural causes, Bill Lynn said: "The blow on his head didn't help too much. Dick [Nagell] knew the guy who whacked Mickey with a hammer in prison."

Lynn was a big man—about six feet, five inches—with a very deep voice and a square jaw. He said he'd been married five times—"I like diversity" —and was feeling a bit under the weather since he'd tied one on the night before. For the most part I found him very guarded concerning his knowledge of Nagell.

According to Lynn, Nagell was "the best ownership guy we ever had at ABC," meaning that he kept tabs on who owned which bars in Los Angeles by checking on things like paint jobs. Lynn expressed admiration for Nagell's "brilliant mind." They used to go to "J-town" (the Japanese section in downtown L.A.) together and hang out in the bars. Since Nagell could read, write, and speak Japanese fluently, they would eavesdrop on conversations. Once in a while Nagell would say something in Japanese, just to shock the other patrons. "His wife took me to task for supposedly leading Dick astray," Lynn went on.

From examining the records in Nagell's Court of Claims case, I knew that his relationship with Mitsuko had indeed been a stormy one. There had been at least one separation prior to February 1962. That month, upset over what she considered her husband's flirtations with white girls on his ABC job, Mitsuko Nagell had simply taken off with the couple's two young children and moved into a downtown L.A. apartment. In both April and May, Richard Nagell had checked himself into the Veterans Administration Psychiatric Hospital in Brentwood. A May 15, 1962, clinical report by VA psychiatrist Harvey D. Weintraub described Nagell's situation:

He apparently has been doing well in his job in spite of his marital difficulties until just recently when a more acute crisis arose causing him to feel that he could no longer hold his job. He is at present toying with the idea of resigning. His wife apparently is a highly unstable individual who has refused to take care of their two children, has frequently deserted the family for varying periods of time and consistently refuses to seek any help for herself. The patient has consistently felt that a lot of the problem was his fault and has obviously been turning his anger against his wife upon himself. He has had fantasies of killing his wife and/or himself. He complains of a recurrent nightmare which he has been having for the past two weeks in which he is back on a hill in Korea being attacked by the enemy and insistently radioing his superiors for aid and assistance. They refuse to send him any reinforcements and merely insist that he stay on the hill and defend it. This is approximately an accurate description of an actual situation in which he was involved. He complains that he is unable to understand why he is having this type of dream when his current problem concerns his marital difficulties.[15]

Released from the hospital, Nagell then ran into his wife at the New Ginza bar in Little Tokyo on the night of May 31. According to a Los Angeles police report I was able to obtain, he sat down beside her, drank several glasses of saki, then took her back to her apartment on South Union Avenue. An argument erupted when Mitsuko wouldn't let him come in. Nagell kicked in the door. His wife ran outside, with Nagell cursing and shouting as he pursued her onto the front lawn. Overhearing the melee, the apartment manager took her in and phoned the police. When they arrived just after midnight, Nagell yelled at them, "Here I am, over here." Arrested on a "drunk" charge, Nagell refused to give his residence address, birthplace, or place of employment. Mitsuko told the police she was planning "to start legal action for divorce."

Bill Lynn remembered this incident as the beginning of the end for Nagell at his ABC job. A week later, on June 8, 1962, Nagell was dismissed by his state employers "by reason of unsatisfactory service."

Military Intelligence and the FBI, as well as Nagell himself, have alluded to something else being involved besides his marital difficulties and "unsatisfactory service." A 1969 Military Intelligence file on Nagell states that he "was suspended for unauthorized release of information to the newspapers and the Los Angeles Police Department." Nagell, at his 1964 trial in El Paso, basically concurred, saying, "I was dismissed for making a statement to the newspapers." An FBI file has Nagell saying he lost his job after "having been accused of taking a $20,000 bribe," which Nagell maintains he turned down.[16]

All Nagell has added since, in his Court of Claims case, is that the existing record does not reveal "the true nature of [his] civilian employment, the wide range of functions and duties encompassed by the positions classified as 'agent' and 'investigator' by the State of California, the kind of departments—one of them now defunct—in which [he] worked, or, of more pertinence, the reasons why [he] left such employment."

Robert Gambert indicated to me that Nagell's departure from the California ABC focused around an ongoing probe into organized crime. "Dick was involved in an investigation of casino investments," Gambert said during my visit to Tarpon Springs, Florida, "and he'd turned up some information. That's the way he explained it to me. He was looking into some of the people who were investing money into a casino in Lake Tahoe, Nevada. They were trying to determine if it was Mafia money."

At my last face-to-face meeting with Nagell in 1984, he had just managed to obtain his FBI files under the Freedom of Information Act. He was so upset by "all the lies" that he said he hadn't bothered to read through the entire dossier. The FBI, he said, had him tied into a murder and a shooting incident while he was with the ABC in 1962.

Most alarming to him—and most intriguing to me—was that the FBI files also linked Nagell in that period to John Rosselli and Sam Giancana. Both mobsters had been part of the CIA's plots to assassinate Castro; both had been murdered in the mid-1970s in the midst of congressional probes into CIA-Mafia activities and the John F. Kennedy assassination.

"I did know Rosselli at the Friar's Club [in Los Angeles], and a lot of the guys out there," Nagell told me. "But the guys from the agency [CIA] were a lot more involved with Giancana and Rosselli than I was. I maybe met Giancana one time in my life, just to shake his hand."[17]

A Shooting on the Beach

A little over five weeks after Nagell lost his job with California's ABC, another mysterious event transpired. On the night of July 16, 1962, Nagell pulled his 1957 Ford Fairlane into the Wadsworth Veterans Administration Hospital in Los Angeles and walked into the emergency room. He had driven perhaps twenty miles from a beach area near Malibu, where a .38-caliber bullet had passed through his right chest and out through his back. An operation was performed immediately to seal the wound. An FBI report about the incident states that Nagell "refused furnish police details of his shooting by unidentified assailant on 7/16/62 and subsequently filed Civil Rights complaint against police."

Bill Lynn went to visit Nagell in the hospital. "Dick was very close-mouthed about the circumstances," Lynn recalled. "Maybe it was organized crime. Or an L.A. cop. Or a Communist."

"Did what happened that night maybe have something to do with later events?" I asked.

"Maybe so," Lynn replied. "Look, Dick has a historic tale to tell someday."

John Margain remembered: "One day Nagell called me from the Veterans Hospital. Dick said, 'I'm afraid because they've got me in here.' When I went in, he said, 'John, go down and get my gun out of my car and bring it up to me.' Even there, at the VA Hospital, he was afraid of *something!*

"He told me that he'd been investigating some guy with a prison record who was not supposed to have a liquor license. He shot Nagell. But he said it was never reported that he shot the other guy, too."

Nagell's relatives believed that the shooting altercation resulted from his investigation into the Nevada casino situation. Files of Dr. Edwin A. Weinstein, a neurological specialist who interviewed Nagell later in an El Paso prison, described the shooting as having to do with "hoodlum threats."

Neil Spotts, who was then with the LAPD's Organized Crime Bureau, told me the police were never able to come up with anything conclusive. "Different accounts indicated that he'd been shot by a police officer over some kind of Communist thing, or even that it was a self-inflicted wound. It was always something Nagell didn't want to talk about."[18]

Whatever happened on the night of July 16, 1962, Nagell made a rapid recovery. A week later, he bounded into the office of clinical social worker Charlotte Jackson at the hospital, "demanding that the police be contacted regarding the return of his wallet, notebook and car." According to Jackson's report, Nagell "said that he had been shot in his car and that now he would talk to the police and requested that the Internal Affairs Department of the police be notified." But by the time Jackson followed up on his request, getting an agreement from the police that Nagell could have his possessions back, he had left the ward and apparently obtained them on his own.[19]

Nagell soon left Los Angeles and drove cross-country. The Gambert family remembers being shocked to see him show up at their house in Queens, New York, the side of his car riddled with bullet holes. "He stayed with us for a little while to recuperate from being shot," Robert Gambert recalls. "One morning he told me he had to see the FBI. That evening, when he came home, he said he had. They had asked him to cooperate by giving them certain types of information, I'm not sure about what.

"He told me he asked them to help him get a government investigative job, because that was his whole training, his whole career. And that there were many jobs in government that didn't require any sensitivity, any security clearances, or anything of that type. And if they would help him, then he would cooperate. So the FBI then challenged his loyalty to the United States. His response to them was, 'You name anybody who has given as much to his country as I have who is still alive. So don't give me that baloney about loyalty and patriotism.' That's where it ended. He did not cooperate with them because they were not willing to help him."[20]

Shortly thereafter, Nagell drove back to Los Angeles. There, at the Mexican consulate, he would obtain a tourist card for multiple entry into Mexico—a sojourn that would alter the former Army captain's life forever. It was in Mexico that his "double agent" role between the CIA and the KGB would lead him back into the orbit of Lee Harvey Oswald.

But what was really going on in California that propelled Nagell into such a role? He has said that certain contract work with the CIA continued during his tenure as a liquor control investigator and that California's Department of Alcoholic Beverage Control itself had "a wide range of functions" that went beyond what is generally known. John Margain said that Nagell was often still utilized by Military Intelligence in "chaperoning" high-ranking Japanese visitors—despite Nagell's official resignation from the Army in 1959.

It is quite possible that throughout this entire period, from late 1959 through the summer of 1962, Nagell was being "sheep-dipped." The term has a couple of meanings in intelligence parlance. The Senate Intelligence Committee defined "sheep-dipping" in 1976 as the utilization of a military "officer in clandestine operations, usually in a civilian capacity or under civilian cover," while the officer covertly retains his military standing.

That could certainly be one way of looking at Nagell's employment with the state of California. But "sheep-dipping" also has to do with establishing credentials for future intelligence placement. In other words, if Nagell is to make himself appealing to the KGB, his earlier disaffection with U.S. military practices now reaches over into his civilian life: losing his job, losing his wife and kids, even nearly being killed in his car. Whether all or some of this was coincidental or by design, it most assuredly adds to building a plausible "cover."

In California from late 1960 to mid-1962, Nagell certainly had a variety of connections at both extremes of the domestic political spectrum. Arthur Greenstein, who came to know Nagell in Mexico City late in the summer of 1962, remembers him mentioning being acquainted with "an unreconstructed Nazi who owned a club called the Pink Pussycat. I guess the scandal was that the fellow got a liquor license, because he was into many things, many illegal activities."[21]

There was also Steve Roberts, whom Nagell described to me in 1975 as "a friend of mine in L.A. When I first met him, he was a functionary in the Socialist Workers Party [SWP], and I was definitely working for an American intelligence agency. I knew him in both an official and unofficial capacity."[22]

The SWP and the Fair Play for Cuba Committee

The SWP, first established in 1938, was the leading "Trotskyite" arm of the American left wing. Oswald, upon returning from the Soviet Union in June 1962, would soon be corresponding regularly with the SWP and subscribing to its national newspaper, *The Militant.* In its literature, the SWP boasted that it "alone of all the radical groups . . . attracted a dynamic youth movement genuinely interested in revolutionary socialist politics."[23]

Steve Roberts, born in New York City in 1898, was a labor organizer who moved to Los Angeles in the mid-1930s and who was the SWP's candidate for governor of California in 1946. By 1960 Roberts had also been named the "West Coast representative" for a new organization—the Fair Play for Cuba Committee (FPCC).[24] The FPCC made its public debut on April 6, 1960, with the appearance of a full-page ad in *The New York Times* announcing that the organization would provide Americans with "the truth about revolutionary Cuba." Among its earliest supporters were such prominent authors as Norman Mailer, Truman Capote, and James Baldwin. But as controversy mounted over the organization's supposed "pro-Communist" sympathies, eventually the FPCC came down to a hard core of enthusiasts with numerous chapters across the United States.

Both the CIA and the FBI had a keen interest in the FPCC since its inception. One of its New York founders, Richard Gibson, was later suspected of having been a CIA agent all along.[25] The Greater Los Angeles chapter, formed in January 1961, was of particular concern—especially after its news release more than four months prior to the Bay of Pigs helped blow the whistle on the CIA's plans. At a press conference, the L.A. FPCC "called upon Congress to investigate immediately the widespread reports indicating that the Central Intelligence Agency is implicated in the training of armed forces for an invasion of Cuba. Persistent reports from Guatemala, Nicaragua, and Florida of invasion forces in these areas being tied to the CIA raise into question U.S. observance of the principle of nonintervention into the domestic affairs of other countries."[26]

By that spring, Senate Internal Security Subcommittee chairman James Eastland was stating "it is obvious to everyone that the Fair Play for Cuba Committee is a Communist operation" receiving funding from Castro's government.[27] Behind the scenes, according to since-declassified CIA files, in May 1961 a CIA "field survey was completed wherein available public source data of adverse nature regarding officers and leaders of Fair Play for Cuba Committee was compiled and furnished [FBI official Cartha] DeLoach for use in contacting his sources."

In December 1961, the CIA's New York office "prepared an anonymous leaflet which was mailed to selected FPCC members throughout the country for the purpose of disrupting FPCC and causing split between FPCC and its Socialist Workers' Party (SWP) supports, which technique was very effective."[28]

The SWP also became a target of the FBI's COINTELPRO program—"secret action designed to 'disrupt' and 'neutralize' target groups and individuals," as a 1976 Senate report described it. Though action against the Communist Party, U.S.A. had been the initial thrust of COINTELPRO, in October 1961 the FBI also approved forty-five actions against the SWP. One technique was "using informants to raise controversial issues" as well as "to take advantage of ideological splits in an organization."[29] Indeed, during the 1960s an estimated one of every ten SWP members was a paid FBI informant.

There is no doubt that someone with as long a history of radicalism as Steve Roberts would have been on the CIA/FBI lists. In April 1962, Roberts was called before a House Un-American Activities Committee panel that was looking into the FPCC in Los Angeles. He invoked the Fifth Amendment on nearly every question. Afterward he told the *Los Angeles Times:* "The Committee is trying to terrorize citizens by publishing names of witnesses after the hearing. It is on a fishing expedition to find out what kind of organization the Fair Play for Cuba Committee is."[30]

It may well be that Nagell, who befriended Roberts somewhere in this time span, was on a "fishing expedition" of his own. Cuba was soon to be the focal point for Nagell—and for Lee Harvey Oswald.

The CIA's Secret War over Cuba

Back in 1960, with then vice president Richard Nixon serving as the White House's liaison to the CIA's Cuban operations, the CIA had initiated its long series of assassination attempts against Castro. The "cutouts" in the operation started with Las Vegas billionaire Howard Hughes's right-hand man Robert Maheu, who got in touch with organized-crime leaders Sam Giancana, Johnny Rosselli, and Santos Trafficante, Jr. They in turn enlisted the direct assistance of Cuban exiles. But these nefarious conspiracies were not confined to Castro and his chief aides. Before the Bay of Pigs, a CIA faction set out to ensure that Castro's successor would not even be close to the same stripe.

After reluctantly deciding to go along with the already existing invasion plan, the incoming president, John F. Kennedy, asked a team of advisers to draw up a list of exile leaders with liberal views as the best choices to lead a post-Castro Cuba. He did not want the next government to be simply another Batista-style dictatorship. The CIA gave tacit agreement to go along with Kennedy's proposal. Behind the scenes, however, men within the agency laid plans to have these exiles assassinated during the turmoil that was expected to follow the invasion. A secret unit code-named "Operation 40" was established to accomplish such ends while the CIA arranged for its own choices to succeed Fidel.

In 1976, at a press conference called by Congressman Thomas Downing, former CIA contract employee Robert Morrow went public with what he knew about this operation. Morrow described his relationship with Mario Garcia Kohly, Sr., a former Havana businessman who claimed the loyalty of a sizable underground force inside Cuba. Before the 1960 presidential election, Kohly told Morrow that he had met with Richard Nixon at a Washington golf course. They had discussed eliminating the "leftist" exiles after Castro's fall so that Kohly himself could take power. Morrow said the existence of this "deal" was confirmed to him by his CIA case officer, Tracy Barnes. A deathbed statement provided Morrow by Kohly in 1975, and a notarized affidavit by Kohly's son Mario, Jr., offer further corroboration.[31]

Even before Morrow's revelation, it was known that several prominent exiles had been held incommunicado at a CIA "safe house" in Miami as the invasion got under way. Expecting to join the troops headed for Cuba as they had been promised, instead five exile leaders found themselves flown to Opa-Locka, Florida, and taken by the CIA's Frank Bender to a barracks with armed U.S. soldiers guarding the doors. There, Antonio Varona accused his CIA captors of "treason." Reportedly, the CIA's explanation to JFK was the need to keep the Cuban Revolutionary Council leaders under wraps, to ensure that nothing leaked out about the invasion. On April 17, JFK dispatched his adviser Arthur Schlesinger, Jr., to meet with the exile leaders and, after the invasion failed, the president had them flown back to the White House for a consultation.[32]

After that, and the other CIA deceptions over the Bay of Pigs (see Chapter Two), JFK moved to shake up the agency's hierarchy and to try to take much firmer control of all anti-Castro operations. It proved impossible. The Bay of Pigs intrigue not only exacerbated factionalism among the moderate and extremist Cuban exiles, it also set up an unbreachable rift between the administration and the "right-wing" forces within the CIA and the Pentagon. "Operation 40" was not disbanded by the CIA after the failed invasion. Some members of this team would be used in the continuing CIA-Mob efforts against Castro, without the administration's knowledge.[33]

The Rise of the Radical Right

Fueled by the Cuban situation, the radical right came into full throttle during the Kennedy years. The best-known organization—but far from the most militant—was the John Birch Society, named after a young Army captain killed by the Communists on a mission into northern China ten days after World War II ended. Robert Welch, the Massachusetts candy factory vice president who formed the society in 1958, called Birch the first victim of World War III.

The Minutemen, headed by pharmaceutical executive Robert Bolivar DePugh, trained their own private combat militia in bracing for an eventual Communist invasion. As the civil rights movement intensified, the southern-based Ku Klux Klan and the National States Rights Party formed alliances with George Lincoln Rockwell's American Nazi Party.

On some two hundred college campuses there was Young Americans for Freedom, founded in September 1960 at the estate of William F. Buckley, Jr., the well-known editor of *National Review*, and a former CIA official in Tokyo and Mexico City. The leading media propagandists were Texas oil billionaire H. L. Hunt, whose *Life Line* broadcast was regularly carried on more than four hundred radio stations in forty-two states, and the weekly *Manion Forum*, offered by a former Dean of Notre Dame University's law school, Clarence Manion.

And, from the pulpit, Billy James Hargis's Christian Crusade (Tulsa), Carl McIntire's American Council of Christian Churches (New Jersey), and Gerald Smith's Christian Nationalist Crusade (Los Angeles) provided the most strident anti-Communist Bible-thumping witnessed before or since.

Even this was but the tip of an iceberg. A White House memorandum prepared for JFK in mid-August 1963 estimated that the radical right spent as much as $25 million annually, supported by about 70 foundations, 113 corporations, 25 utility companies, and 250 identifiable individuals.[34]

In the thick of it all, and much more, was Charles Willoughby. While his mentor, General MacArthur, passed into quiet retirement and was occasionally sought by Kennedy for advice, Willoughby approached his seventieth birthday with samurai swords placed strategically next to his desk. Willoughby's holy war against the "Red Menace" found him sitting on the boards of most of the major conservative groups, and reaching into Europe and Latin America to start his own International Committee for the Defense of Christian Culture.[35]

Willoughby had maintained his relationship with CIA director Dulles. Their correspondence up until Dulles's firing by JFK was wide-ranging. On May 18, 1960, Dulles wrote Willoughby, who had moved to Washington: "It was good seeing you and I enjoyed very much our talk. I might say that I appreciate your interest in our organization and I am now looking into the possibility of our taking advantage of your offer to be of assistance in our training activities. . . ."

The retired major general responded on May 23, 1960: "In general terms, I have felt that you (and other Federal enterprises) do not make sufficient use of retired specialists. On the other hand, time is fleeting— and I have built my own European contacts, for my own amusement."

At the same time, Willoughby was politically astute. He contributed funds to Kennedy's inauguration, about which he wrote to Texas oilman H. L. Hunt on January 31, 1961: "My identification with the Kennedy group may 'puzzle' you—but I have never been a voting Republican of great enthusiasm. I am aware, however, that you supported the Vice President—and a fellow Texan. As an important figure in the oil industry, certain international concepts must be of interest to you. . . . the political unity of North and South America, control of their strategic raw materials (oil, tin, manganese, iron etc.), security of the Panama Canal and the effective application of the Monroe Doctrine, in order to keep Red Russia and China out of this hemisphere."

After JFK's refusal to provide air cover at the Bay of Pigs and his purge of Allen Dulles, by late 1961 the anti-Kennedy invective was mounting among Willoughby and his allies. The former major general's *Foreign Intelligence Digest* began appearing as a supplement to Billy James Hargis's

Weekly Crusader newsletter. One of Willoughby's first articles was about the CIA, about which he wrote to Allen Dulles on June 2, 1961: "I was pleased to have your reaction to my first piece on the Central Intell. Agency. I could have run it earlier, in timing with the Cuban embroglio but held it pending your approval, as per our gentleman's agreement. It will appear in Issue 33 of the *Weekly Crusader.*"

Willoughby's publisher and friend Billy James Hargis was a short, portly, double-chinned fellow in his midthirties who gained much of his financial support from H. L. Hunt and other wealthy oilmen. From a four-floor office building in Tulsa, Oklahoma, he barnstormed the country in a streamlined, air-conditioned bus with two bedrooms and two baths, warning of treason in high office and Communists under every bedpost. Along with Willoughby, who was his Washington eyes and ears, another of Hargis's advisory committee members was retired lieutenant general Pedro del Valle, U.S. Marine commander in the Pacific Theater during World War II. After the Korean War, del Valle had become vice president of ITT's Latin American operations.

In September 1961 Hargis announced that a secret fraternity to coordinate right-wing activities would soon be formed. Then, on March 21, 1962, a carefully selected group was called together in Washington. "Dear Fellow Country-Savers," Hargis's invitation began. It went on to describe plans for regular briefings "by great conservative statesmen from both political parties on what must be done in the field of education and otherwise to help save our country from internal communism."

No press representatives were allowed at the founding session of the Anti-Communist Liaison, which brought together about one hundred delegates representing some seventy-five right-wing groups at the Washington Hotel.[36] Named as its chairman and operating head was Edward Hunter, a National Advisory Board member of Young Americans for Freedom. A foreign correspondent since the 1920s for various newspapers, Hunter had taken a two-year "sabbatical" to serve as an OSS "propaganda specialist" in World War II. Working undercover as a roving journalist across Asia after the war, Hunter remained under contract to the new CIA.[37] In September 1950, his article in the *Miami News*— " 'Brain-Washing' Tactics Force Chinese into Ranks of Communist Party" —was the first printed use of the term "brainwashing." Hunter went on to churn out a number of books and articles on the subject, coming to be considered the nation's leading expert on it. He wrote,

> . . . the Reds have specialists available on their brainwashing panels, drugs and hypnotism. . . . In brainwashing, a fog settles over the patient's mind until he loses touch with reality. Facts and fantasy whirl round and change places, like a phantasmagoria. Shadow takes form and

form becomes shadow, inducing hallucination. However, in order to prevent people from recognizing the inherent evils in brainwashing, the Reds pretend that it is only another name for something already very familiar and of unquestioned respect, such as education or reform. . . ."[38]

What Hunter did not say, then or later, was that the OSS and Military Intelligence were investigating the same methods, starting in World War II. And that the CIA, starting in the late 1940s, initiated its own wide-ranging "mind control" program, to become known as MK-ULTRA.

Besides Willoughby, also included on the Anti-Communist Liaison's five-person Committee of Correspondence was retired brigadier general Bonner Fellers. Starting out as a military attaché in Franco's Spain, Fellers became a member of William Donovan's original OSS "planning group." Joining MacArthur's staff in 1943, Fellers ended up as the general's military secretary into the first year of the occupation of Japan. An advocate of strong air power, like Willoughby he called for a rollback of communism and disdained the CIA, which in Fellers' view harbored "a group of Marxist-Socialist pro-Communists."[39]

The new group's insider was U.S. representative John Rousselot, a John Birch Society spokesman and Christian Crusade board member from Los Angeles.[40] It also had a Southern California "outsider," Colonel William P. Gale, yet another ex-MacArthur man. A logistical organizer of American guerrilla forces in the Philippine campaign, by 1944 Gale was director of supply to the U.S. Army Forces, Far East. He then spent three and a half years with the occupation forces in Tokyo where, he would later brag, "nobody got a building in Japan without my personal approval."

Gale retired, at only thirty-three, in 1950, going to work for billionaire Howard Hughes's aircraft company as "manager of government property control" in Hollywood and bringing a number of his Far Eastern cronies along. Here Gale also hooked up with Wesley Swift, an evangelist and Ku Klux Klan organizer in the little Southern California town of Lancaster. In 1962, as California state chairman of the Constitution Party, Colonel Gale announced his candidacy for the governorship on a platform calling for the abolition of all income taxes.[41] He also organized, soon after the pivotal springtime meeting in Washington, a paramilitary outfit.

Willoughby, del Valle, and a number of other military officers put together Gale's tactical guide, or manual of arms for the future. It suggested that "patriotic underground armies should be established, named the 'Rangers' who should train to assassinate, sabotage, and overthrow the 'People's Democracy.' "[42]

This came to light in a 1966 book, *Victory Denied*, by Lieutenant Colonel Arch E. Roberts. He had been removed from active duty in 1961 after a Pentagon investigation into a "Pro-Blue Troop Information" program he had authored. This directive, permitting military men to instruct civilians in anticommunism, had then been initiated by Major General Edwin A. Walker as commander of the 24th Infantry Division in West Germany. Walker, too, had been purged from the Army by JFK's defense secretary Robert McNamara—becoming a cause célèbre among the radical right.

A 1965 California attorney general's report, "Para-Military Organizations in California," would describe Colonel Gale's group as follows:

> The purpose of the Rangers is to build an underground network for the conduct of guerrilla warfare. No reliable figures are currently available, but all information indicates a small membership figure. The training program is said to encompass all the different activities which a guerrilla force would be called upon to undertake, ranging from intelligence to actual combat. The members assertedly are instructed to acquire firearms, and to practice in their use. . . . Under Col. Gale's leadership, some of the recruitment effort has been directed toward former military servicemen to serve as an organizational nucleus.[43]

A *Long Beach Press-Telegram* exposé called Gale's Rangers "a secret guerrilla group composed of persons devoted to extremist racial and religious beliefs."[44] Not long after their spring 1962 formation, the Rangers would begin attracting a wide range of wanderers along an L.A.-to-Miami route. Those people's dedicated aim was the overthrow of Fidel Castro. On May 21, 1962, Willoughby wrote to Hargis's Christian Crusade:

> I have just closed a "deal" with the important Bonn (Germany) unit "C.I. Inform." An international organization, it began spreading into South America. They were eying [sic] North America. They have the same purpose, almost the same title as "Christian Crusade." I developped [sic] editorial agreements. We will exchange our materials, articles as desired. It was a fine opportunity to move in. They reacted promptly. . . . they elected Dr. Hargis and myself as *members of the international directorate.*

It was quite a time for Willoughby's old journalist acquaintance Mark Gayn to show up on the scene, authoring an article titled "The Far Right: America's Own 'Ultras,'" for the April 1962 *Canadian Commentator* magazine. The dateline was Los Angeles, and Gayn warned that "The 'Minutemen' are known to have acquired some first-rate automatic weapons, and they thank big business for providing the funds for this. . . ."

It was quite a time for Richard Nagell to reach the end of the line with California's Department of Alcoholic Beverage Control, leave his wife behind, and head for Mexico City.

It was quite a time for Lee Harvey Oswald to return from the Soviet Union with his Russian wife, resettling in Dallas-Fort Worth in June 1962.

To understand how all these forces began to converge, we must now take a long look back at what Oswald's stay in Russia was all about.

Summary

Cuba, where Fidel Castro's revolution succeeded on New Year's Day 1959, begins to play a role in the lives of Oswald and Nagell. Not long after Oswald was reassigned to a Marine base in California, Gerry Hemming reported seeing him at the Cuban consulate in Los Angeles, where Hemming suspected Oswald of being a "penetrator" for U.S. intelligence. Nagell, leaving the Army, moved with his family to Los Angeles and renewed acquaintance with a Fair Play for Cuba Committee (FPCC) coordinator named Steve Roberts. The CIA and the FBI were intensifying surveillance and actions against the FPCC as early as 1961. At the same time, the CIA had formed "Operation 40," basically a "hit squad" of Cuban exiles.

While Oswald received a Marine discharge and embarked en route to the USSR in September 1959, Nagell soon took employment as an investigator for the state of California. His marriage—to a Japanese whose father he had previously investigated—was on the rocks by 1962. That June, under mysterious circumstances, he was fired from his job with the California Department of Alcoholic Beverage Control. Under even stranger circumstances, Nagell was shot in his car five weeks later. These incidents may have revolved around his investigation of organized crime. FBI files link Nagell to well-known mobsters Sam Giancana and Johnny Rosselli, involved in the CIA plots to assassinate Castro, and Nagell admits to having known both Giancana and Rosselli. There is a possibility that Nagell was being "sheep-dipped" in Southern California, in preparation for future intelligence work targeted at the Soviets as a disgruntled ex-Military Intelligence officer.

At the same time, extremist elements of the right wing were forging the new Anti-Communist Liaison. The network of Charles Willoughby extended to several other ex-MacArthur military leaders and all the way to West Germany. Instrumental were Dallas's H. L. Hunt oil family, Oklahoma preacher Billy James Hargis, and intelligence agent-turned-journalist Edward Hunter, who coined the term "brainwashing." A paramilitary arm was established in Southern California under retired colonel William P. Gale.

Chapter Eight

The CIA, the KGB, and Oswald in the USSR: 1959–62

Late on a mid-December afternoon in 1975, two months after my first meetings with Richard Nagell, I arranged an interview with James Angleton in the outer lounge of Washington's Army-Navy Club. "This is very much against my nature," began the CIA's former Counter Intelligence chief. Leafing through a story I had published in *The Village Voice* about the assassination, Angleton lit a Virginia Slims cigarette and took a sip of his martini. "The subject is a far more complex one than reflected in your article," he said.

Back in 1964, Angleton's office had been assigned as the CIA's direct liaison to the Warren Commission. I wondered why. "Because we had the research facilities, knew the mechanisms of the KGB and foreign intelligence," Angleton replied. "We knew every assassination in history, knew more about the sophistication of the Cuban DGI [the intelligence organization known as G-2 through 1963], that type of thing."

So did Angleton have any idea what really happened? Angleton began his reply by dismissing the rumors that Oswald may have been an American agent as "completely false." Then he went on to describe how he had urged Allen Dulles, former CIA director and a Warren Commission member, "not to bring a finality to the investigation. Allen was a close friend, I saw him two or three times a week during that period," Angleton went on. "Because the assassin is dead and the assassin's assassin is dead, no doors of history can be closed. Unless one knows the dossiers that are in Moscow and Cuba, there can be no ultimate determination."

I would come to have three long interviews with Angleton in 1975 and 1976, in the course of which it became clear that he wanted to project suspicion of Soviet-Cuban involvement in the assassination. He was an expert fly fisherman long accustomed to dangling bait, and he often spoke in language just out of reach—yet tantalizing enough for hungry prey to bite. Several times he raised the specter of the KGB's Department 13, which specialized in what those in the know termed "wet affairs." These were defined in a 1964 CIA report from his staff to the Warren Commission as "abduction and murder to combat what are considered to be actual or potential threats to the Soviet regime."

According to Angleton, "the personnel they recruit for Department 13 is not known; they are not connected to other KGB, but housed and trained differently. It's hermetical—you are dealing in a pure science." By way of illustration, he described to me how the KGB had used the Czech intelligence service, which was in turn able to penetrate the Austrian police, in poisoning a defector in Vienna the very morning he was to fly to the United States in 1961. "This showed, number one, the coordination of the [Soviet] Bloc services, where one takes up slack from the other—and number two, the assassination capability." Angleton believed that "Castro and the KGB worked hand-in-glove as equals."

At the same time, he "discounted 1 million percent" the possibility of a domestic assassination conspiracy. This, he added, was "because the Soviets immediately began to spread the persistent rumor that the right wing in the United States was behind it." It was rather flimsy reasoning, I thought, for such a connoisseur of intrigue.

On two occasions I attempted to steer Angleton toward the subject I knew had obsessed him for years: the possible penetration of the CIA, at a high level, by people who actually worked for the Soviets. "I would never discuss that," Angleton said, drumming his long, angular fingers on a tabletop. "Obviously in the OSS period [of World War II] a number of people emerged afterwards out of the woodwork. We had a helluva big cleanup job to do after 1947. But everyone, including myself, has been polygraphed many times. You don't play tennis with the net down. No one ever entered the CIA in my day with the thought they were joining a democratic institution. There were many investigations of personnel."

In future years, Angleton would finally discuss some of those investigations with writer Edward Jay Epstein. Angleton would describe his faith in Anatoly Golitsin, a Soviet defector in December 1961 who convinced Angleton that the CIA had indeed been infiltrated. In the eyes of Angleton and his Soviet "protégé," all other defectors were suspected of bringing "disinformation"—in particular Yuri Nosenko, who happened to arrive on the CIA's doorstep right after the assassination, bearing tidings in January 1964 that Soviet intelligence had absolutely no relationship with Oswald.

The ensuing dispute over Nosenko's legitimacy divided the CIA into warring camps. Those who believed Nosenko came under Angleton's microscope as potential KGB "moles" themselves. After three years in which Nosenko was placed in solitary confinement and subjected to what can only be described as brutal interrogations, over Angleton's fierce objections the CIA ultimately deemed him a bona fide defector whose information should be trusted. And, though the careers of several CIA officials were shattered by Angleton's simultaneous and continuing mole quest, no such traitor was ever unearthed.[1]

I never told Angleton anything about the knowledge I had gleaned from Richard Nagell. But at our second meeting I did ask Angleton if he was familiar with Nagell's name. "I don't know," Angleton replied hastily, shaking his head.

Then frustration seemed to broil up from inside him. "It is a fact that the papers regarding Oswald, turned over voluntarily by the Soviets to the American government, are worthless," Angleton said. "They do not truly reflect KGB files on a Marine defector living in the Soviet Union, marrying a Soviet woman, then leaving the country. It's faceless information, I went through it in about five seconds. Not the kind of dossiers they keep on foreigners, particularly Americans. He'd had special training in the Marines. It would be a matter of intense interest to them as to why he would defect."

Though I was pretty sure that Angleton was looking to manipulate my thinking, it was certainly true that Oswald's two and one-half years in the Soviet Union bore relevance to what happened on November 22, 1963.

Bound for the USSR

One of the big unresolved questions is how Oswald managed to finance his overseas voyage in the autumn of 1959. Before he left the United States, Oswald's bank account contained slightly over $200; the trip cost at least $1,500. His passport showed he had arrived in England on October 9,

1959, then left the following day for Helsinki, Finland. Yet no available commercial flight could possibly have gotten him there by the eleventh, leading to speculation that Oswald must have traveled by private or military aircraft.

Oswald checked into an expensive hotel and went to the Soviet consulate in Helsinki. There, Soviet consul Gregory Golub—a man the CIA suspected of being a KGB officer—issued Oswald a visa in only two days. The Warren Commission would later determine that normally it took at least a week to obtain a Soviet visa. But Golub, as the House Assassinations Committee would later learn from studying American embassy dispatches, had the authority to provide quick visas without approval from Moscow—as long as he was convinced an American was "all right."[2]

Things got even stranger after Oswald's arrival by train in Moscow on October 16. Immediately he was met by an Intourist guide and registered as a student at the Hotel Berlin. After several contacts with Soviet authorities, five days later Oswald was told that his visa had expired. He was given two hours to leave Moscow. His Intourist guide, Rima Shirakova, arrived for a meeting with Oswald in his hotel room—only to find that he had slashed his wrist in an apparent suicide attempt. Oswald reportedly spent the next eleven days recuperating in a psychiatric hospital, after which his guide accompanied him to another hotel, where Oswald spent another isolated three days. No longer did Soviet officials care, it seemed, that he hadn't followed their orders to depart.[3]

Finally, on October 31, Oswald headed for the American embassy, thrust his passport down before a receptionist, and announced he wanted to "dissolve his American citizenship." Oswald was directed to Richard E. Snyder, a U.S. consular official who had previously worked for the CIA.[4] Oswald handed Snyder a handwritten, undated note that affirmed "that my allegiance is to the Union of Soviet Socialist Republics." John Mc-Vickar, another consular official present at the time, would later comment to the Warren Commission that he believed Oswald "was following a pattern of behavior in which he had been tutored by a person or persons unknown."[5]

Snyder testified before the commission that he attempted to talk Oswald out of renouncing his citizenship, and told him to come back after the weekend if he still intended to do so. Immediately after Oswald's visit to the embassy, Snyder sent off a confidential telegram to the State Department that was forwarded to the CIA. It reported that Oswald "has offered Soviets any information he has acquired as [an] enlisted radar operator. Main reason: I am a Marxist. . . . Says action contemplated last two years."[6]

That would take us back to the fall of 1957 in Japan, when Oswald first came in contact with Nagell. Besides his knowledge of the U-2 spy base at

Atsugi, Oswald had had access to privileged information concerning radar installations, radio communications codes, and the deployment of military planes in the western United States.[7] Now here he was in Russia, telling the American embassy specifically how he intended to "betray" his country! Why was he tipping his hand?

Snyder speculated on an ABC-TV *Nightline* program in 1991 that Oswald "thought he was talking to a bug in the wall . . . talking as much to what he thought were his Soviet handlers as he was to me." Which, Snyder added, was probably right; the KGB was customarily known to have bugged the American embassy.

Oswald never returned to see Snyder and formally renounce his U.S. citizenship. For weeks he simply stayed in his Moscow hotel room, writing pro-Communist letters home to his family in which he detailed the alleged reasons for his defection. He also granted Marxism-espousing interviews to two American reporters; one of these, Priscilla McMillan, would eventually write Marina Oswald's 1977 biography.[8]

By December 1959, as far as American authorities say they knew at the time, Oswald had simply dropped from sight—not to be heard from again for over a year.

The KGB: Kid Gloves or Hands Off?

The KGB today maintains that "there was some sort of suspicion [of Oswald] at the very beginning. . . . The KGB thought that man could be an agent of the CIA, for instance." Those were the words of Valentin Kandurian, who allowed *Nightline* correspondent Forrest Sawyer a look at five volumes of hitherto secret KGB files on Oswald in the wake of the failed Soviet coup in 1991. "They tried to do their best to clarify the situation," added Kandurian, and found "no evidence at all" of any Oswald ties to U.S. intelligence.

Nor did the KGB allegedly conclude that Oswald was of any intelligence value to their side. *Nightline*'s Sawyer was shown a "Top-Secret" file dated when Oswald first told the Soviets of his intention to stay. It stated: "Taking into account that the personality of the applicant is absolutely unclear to us, and because the First Directorate KGB and Counter Intelligence have no interest in Lee Harvey Oswald," therefore he should be refused citizenship. According to Kandurian, Oswald was considered "an eccentric sort of person, some kind of adventurer." Despite being aware of the ex-Marine's offer to share information, the KGB says it never debriefed Oswald. Nor was there any mention of his potential knowledge about radar secrets or the U-2 spy plane in its files. One ex-KGB agent described this to Sawyer as a "classic intelligence blunder"—in other words, they had supposedly missed a bet.

Yet, in an episode *Nightline* mentioned only in passing, no less a personage than Premier Khrushchev's chief deputy, Anastas Mikoyan of the Supreme Soviet, is said to have urged that Oswald's request for citizenship be reconsidered. "Clarify your position and submit it to the Central Committee," Mikoyan penned in a note found in the KGB's Oswald files. Soon after this, Oswald was told he could remain in the Soviet Union for a year; he would, in fact, stay for much longer.

"Find employment using his electrical skills," the KGB ordered.[9] The Warren Commission noted that Oswald was soon flown 450 miles south of Moscow to the city of Minsk, where the mayor personally greeted him on January 8, 1960, and promised him a rent-free apartment. His flat, with a private balcony offering a panoramic view of the city, was lavish indeed by Soviet standards. So was the salary he received as an apprentice "metalworker" at the Byelorussian Radio and Television Factory, where, coupled with a stipend he received from the Soviet government, Oswald earned as much money as the factory's director.[10]

But if, as Nagell said, the KGB already knew when Oswald arrived that he had CIA connections, then why the delicate treatment?

Oswald and the U-2

A number of researchers have postulated that Oswald was being rewarded, that the KGB did garner from him radar secrets and greater awareness about the U-2 spy plane. Not long after Oswald began living high on the hog in Minsk, a U-2 came plummeting onto Soviet soil outside the city of Sverdlovsk. The pilot, Francis Gary Powers, was alive and taken into custody. Curiously, it happened on May Day 1960, the revolutionary holiday when the Soviets always put on display their military hardware. It also happened almost on the eve of scheduled Paris peace talks between Premier Khrushchev and President Eisenhower, after which the American leader was scheduled to visit Moscow. The U-2's downing was a diplomatic disaster for the United States. Khrushchev, who had recently stated that Eisenhower was a "sincere" man with whom he could negotiate, canceled the summit and the president's visit. John F. Kennedy, then campaigning for the presidency, told the press that the U-2 affair meant Americans were now "living through the most dangerous time since the Korean War."

The spy flights had been going on for nearly five years high above the USSR. But nobody in the top levels of the U.S. government could say with certainty whether this one had been specifically approved by then secretary of defense Thomas S. Gates, Jr.[11] According to Colonel L. Fletcher Prouty, then the chief liaison officer between the Pentagon and the CIA: "I know . . . from being inside those operations, that the U-2 was an illegal flight. The U-2 operators had been told not to launch any overflights before the summit conference."[12] Interestingly, after the U-2 went down, the price of shares of arms manufacturing companies rose sharply on the New York Stock Exchange, and government military-contract awards increased substantially.[13]

Exactly what happened to the U-2 remains a subject of historical controversy. At first Washington had put out the false tale that this was simply a weather plane that had accidentally drifted into Soviet airspace. Moscow waited forty-eight hours before bursting open the cover story: Its missiles had brought down the U-2 at ninety thousand feet, an altitude that American intelligence was said to believe was undetectable by Soviet technology and well out of range of its missiles. Data collected by the U.S. National Security Agency showed that the plane had actually suffered an autopilot malfunction, causing it to tumble to thirty thousand feet. But after CIA director Allen Dulles made the initial announcement, inexplicably the American government changed *this* story and went along with the Soviet claim.[14]

James Angleton offered this cryptic statement to me about the U-2 incident: "To this day, we have no finite knowledge as to the fate of Powers' mission. The mind would be boggled with trying to consider all means by which it was eventually brought down. You can't discount anything, because the circle of knowledge [about the U-2] was so expanded."

Pilot Powers, who was exchanged in February 1962 for Rudolf Abel, a Russian spy being held by the United States, would tell reporters after the Kennedy assassination that he suspected Oswald of having sabotaged his mission. "He had access to all our equipment," said Powers. "He knew the altitudes we flew at, how long we stayed out on any mission, and in which direction we went."[15]

However, if the Soviets had lacked the ability to detect and shoot down the U-2, nothing Oswald might have said would have enabled them to do so. The plane's Lockheed designer, Kelley Johnson, believed that "the Soviets were somehow able to isolate the radar jamming devices"—something that Oswald's knowledge of radar techniques might conceivably have assisted in. But if Oswald did have a hand in the U-2's demise, one might expect that he would have been high on the lists of the CIA, the FBI, and Military Intelligence for a treasonous act. Besides Powers, he was presumably the only American in the Soviet Union with any awareness of the

U-2. Powers maintained that the Soviets questioned him at length about the Atsugi base and seemed already to know quite a bit about its activities. Yet, while a "net damage assessment" for defectors was standard procedure by U.S. intelligence, none was ever conducted for Oswald.[16] Nor, the CIA claims, did it even bother questioning Oswald after he returned to the United States.

Powers, who at his August 1960 trial apologized to the Soviet people for doing them wrong, was seized upon by psychological-warfare "expert" Edward Hunter as an example for a revised edition of his book *Brainwashing: From Pavlov to Powers*. The ex-CIA agent flatly stated: "Powers was brainwashed. As with his predecessors in North Korea, the Reds did not seek to indoctrinate him, except as this might develop naturally in the softening up process. Just as did our captured men in Korea, he fell into enemy hands with the softening up already begun by his own country."[17]

Psychiatrist William Jennings Bryan, who had headed an Air Force medical survival training program that itself employed hypnosis to prepare pilots to resist brainwashing, echoed Hunter: "Brainwashing hypnosis as apparently used on Powers is vastly different from the permissive type of medical hypnosis." The pilot, Bryan added, "may have even thought himself that he was being treated rather well. . . . only a brand-new type of other powerful technique could have changed his personality in so short a time."[18]

But Powers would cast a different light in his book *Operation Overflight*, which was withheld from publication by the CIA until 1970. His Moscow statements, he wrote, were in accord with his CIA instructions that, if captured, "when questioned, I would tell the truth." Indeed, he went on that he was examined by a West German flight surgeon, acting for the CIA, immediately after being released at the Berlin border. Blood samples were taken from his arm, which Powers was told "were necessary to determine whether I had been drugged. . . . They seemed almost disappointed when I told them I hadn't."

Flown to the United States, Powers spent more than three weeks being debriefed by a team of intelligence analysts and psychiatrists. "In a sense," he wrote, "I had been released by the Russians to become a de facto prisoner of the CIA." When the pilot insisted he had been neither drugged nor brainwashed by the Soviets, he was given tranquilizers—the first drugs he had received since his ill-fated U-2 flight took off from Turkey. The Americans, Powers noted ironically, were much more disposed to the use of drugs than the Soviets.[19]

There was speculation, again expressed by Edward Hunter, that the Communists may have gotten to Powers's plane before it ever took off. "Powers never specifically said his plane was struck by a rocket," Hunter wrote. "This is particularly significant in view of the strange fact of his capture alive, and the capture of so much equipment intact. Was Powers a sitting duck? Had his plane been sabotaged?"[20]

For years Powers insisted his plane had not malfunctioned and then drifted down to a lower altitude. Then, shortly before he died in a helicopter crash in 1977, Powers made a remarkable statement in a radio interview. He said he believed his plane had been *sabotaged on the ground* before his takeoff in Turkey. And, since internal security surrounding the plane was so tight, it "would have had to have been an inside job." The last people to touch Powers's plane were part of the CIA's own Office of Security.[21]

Two novels—William F. Buckley, Jr.'s 1982 *Marco Polo* and Matthew Eden's 1969 *Flight of Hawks*—bear plots that make the same conjecture. Buckley concludes that the CIA brought down its own plane. Eden sees it as the work of a cabal within the CIA and the KGB that wanted to extend the Cold War.[22] This leads us right back to Oswald. In a letter he wrote home right after the Soviets released Powers, Oswald said: "He seemed to be a nice bright American-type fellow when I saw him in Moscow." After Oswald went to work at Jaggers-Chiles-Stovall in the fall of 1962, colleague Dennis Ofstein recalled Oswald mentioning "that he was in Moscow for the May Day parade at one time." All of Oswald's "May Days" are accounted for elsewhere, except for the one when the U-2 incident occurred in 1960.[23]

Hence the nagging question: What was Oswald's relationship to the U-2 affair all about? Was he somehow used in this venture by elements of Military Intelligence, the CIA, the KGB, or some combination of all three? If so, I believe it was an earmark of a pattern that would follow Oswald right up to November 22, 1963.

Oswald's Minsk Employment

Although he was set up nicely in Minsk five months before the U-2 incident, the KGB files say that Oswald was shadowed constantly. Agents tailed him, neighbors and coworkers informed on his activities, his mail was opened, and a bug was placed in his apartment. A simple explanation would be that the KGB wanted to know who the American defector was associating with. Reasonable enough. But was there more to it? Why, for example, did the KGB specifically want Oswald employed where he could use his "electrical skills"?

This is a particularly interesting question because, during the period when Oswald was employed at the Minsk radio factory, the CIA's Office of Research and Reports (ORR) had a branch aimed at ferreting out whatever it could about the Soviet electronics industry. Bernard Drell, former chief of the ORR's Manufacturing and Services Division, explained it to me this way in a 1992 telephone interview:

"The agency, in finding out how strong the opposition was, measured it not only by counting people in military boots, but economically. The Russians published handbooks, from the time of Khrushchev on, showing economic performance and capabilities, but the United States didn't know whether to believe this or not. So the federal government created our own set of national accounts for the USSR. To do that under the circumstances was extremely difficult, especially in a field such as electronics. You could estimate steel or cement production, which were produced in large establishments. But how do you estimate the output of the electronics industry in physical terms—like the number of civilian radio sets they might be producing, or radars and unconventional military equipment? Then how do you convert that from rubles to dollars, and plug it into a GNP set of accounts? So that's what we were trying to do."

When I asked Drell how this might have applied to a city like Minsk, he added: "In particular places like that, it would be real tough. You have no idea how many electronics manufacturing plants there would be in Minsk necessarily. In the intelligence business, you send out requirements. You say, 'Find me someone in that plant, or where the plant is and who's in it.' That was not the responsibility of our office, we were all economists. The clandestine part of the agency had responsibility for that, and it was an extremely difficult thing to do. Naturally, they would send us what they could."[24]

We must assume that the KGB at least suspected that the CIA would make such an effort. So what sense did it make to send a "defector" whom the KGB already knew had CIA ties into the heart of a large electronics factory? None at all, unless the KGB had a private reason of its own.

The Paisley Tie

We come now to a man who died under extremely suspicious circumstances—right in the midst of the House Assassinations Committee's investigation. Early in October 1978 I received a clipping from Richard Nagell in the mail. It was from the front page of the October 3 *Los Angeles Herald-Examiner* and headlined "CIA Mystery Death—Ex-Deputy Director's Body Found Floating in Bay." The subject was John Arthur Paisley, then fifty-five, whose decomposed torso had floated into the mouth of

Maryland's Patuxent River and been discovered by a passing pleasure boat. The body, allegedly identified as Paisley's through dental records, was affixed to diving weights. There was a bullet wound in his head, with police investigators speculating on either a suicide "or an execution-type murder." Paisley had last been seen alive aboard his motorized sailboat the *Brillig* on Chesapeake Bay on September 24. The boat was found aground near his home mooring in Solomons, Maryland, the day after that.

Below the headlines about Paisley, Nagell had inscribed a typed message: "Was he nash? He was nash!" Nagell had drawn a box around one sentence in the article: "Paisley, who lived in Washington, retired in 1974 as deputy director of the CIA's Office of Strategic Research."[25]

Only a few months before this, I had been sitting with Nagell in a West Los Angeles bar when he suddenly said, "Do you know what 'nash' means? The Russians used to use that phrase. It meant he was 'ours' and nobody else's."[26]

When I mentioned "nash" to a couple of sources familiar with the intelligence community, they expressed surprise that I had even heard the term, but reiterated the Russian meaning. One source referred me to a scene in a novel by Herman Wouk called *War and Remembrance,* in which a "General Yevelenko" is having a big party in Moscow. An American, "Buck Henry," is in attendance and, when a KGB man scowls noticeably as the general and the American share a friendly embrace, "Yevelenko" takes the KGB man aside. "Forget it," he says, "he's nash."

Now, in sending the clipping, Nagell appeared to be revealing that John Paisley was "nash"—a Soviet spy inside the CIA.

Officially, Paisley's death was ruled a suicide. But speculation about the activities of this hitherto-publicly unknown CIA official would be rampant among the media in the months ahead. At the time he disappeared, Paisley had been working under a CIA contract to coordinate a Top-Secret government reevaluation of Soviet strategic capabilities and intentions. Now there were grave questions about the sophisticated communications equipment on his boat designed for secret transmissions, and about Paisley's earlier role in the CIA's debriefings of Soviet defectors.[27]

Paisley's widow, Maryann, decided to hire a lawyer to "find out what really happened to my husband." Her choice was Bernard Fensterwald, Jr. I called Fensterwald, who explained that he had known the Paisleys "very well back in the '50s." When Fensterwald was working for the State Department, "we were each involved in liberal politics in Arlington [Virginia] for a while. I knew John was with the CIA, but I pretty much lost track of them for years. I don't think I'd seen John in a long time."[28]

Fensterwald had a reputation for taking on controversial cases and clients (including Nagell and Watergate burglar McCord), and I had no reason to suspect that this was anything other than part of his penchant for rattling the skeletons in the CIA's closets. He had managed to obtain a number of documents about Paisley under the Freedom of Information Act and, after Fensterwald received permission from Maryann Paisley, in 1980 I flew to Washington to examine the documents.

That was when I realized that a possible Paisley connection to Oswald might have dated back to the ex-Marine's time in the USSR.

Paisley and Soviet Electronics

In 1959, the same year Oswald "defected," John Paisley had been appointed chief of the Electronic Equipment Branch, Industrial Division, within the CIA's ORR. Paisley's primary function was overseeing the CIA's assessment of "the problems and accomplishments of the [Soviet] Bloc electronics industry."[29]

Paisley's name never came up during the House Assassinations Committee's investigation. However, one committee report described information received from an ex-CIA employee "that the CIA maintained a large volume of information on the Minsk radio factory in which Oswald had worked. This information was stored in the Office of Research and Reports"—which would have been Paisley's office. The committee report continued: "Another former CIA employee, one who had worked in the Soviet branch of the Foreign Documents Division of the Directorate of Intelligence in 1962, advised the committee that he specifically recalled collecting intelligence regarding the Minsk radio plant."[30]

When Oswald left the Soviet Union in 1962, he brought home with him a "Historic Diary" that was discovered among his effects after the assassination. It covered his entire stay in the USSR, but handwriting experts later determined that the diary was written almost completely on the same paper and apparently in continuous fashion. This led the House Assassinations Committee to conclude that the "Diary" was written in one or two sittings just before Oswald left.[31] In short, it looked to be a fabricated effort. Most of the "Diary" focused on Oswald's seemingly growing disenchantment with life in the USSR, leaving out anything inconsistent with his desire to go home.

The likelihood that someone coached Oswald in his writing is especially evident in a narrative description of life in the USSR that he wrote on the ship home, where Oswald's usually atrocious spelling becomes very correct. One section is a detailed description of the Minsk radio and television plant. Here Oswald carefully noted the number of employees at this "major producer of electronic parts and sets." He also delineated that the factory "manufactures 87,000 large and powerful radio and 60,000 television sets," as well as the plant's size and various shops.[32]

If the CIA became the beneficiary of this information—whether true or falsified—it would almost surely have come to the attention of John Paisley. Could the KGB have been *allowing* Oswald to gather information at the radio factory that would ultimately end up on Paisley's desk for analysis?

The only comment Richard Nagell has made about Oswald's "Historic Diary" is that the KGB was not concerned at all about any of its disclosures.[33]

Paisley and Webster

As I began poring through the several hundred pages on Paisley's background released by the CIA, numerous clues emerged in the direction Nagell had pointed me. Later I would find still more clues through interviewing Maryann Paisley—who, it should be said, firmly avowed that her husband had been a loyal CIA employee—and in the 1989 book *Widows,* which contained an exhaustive review of Paisley's career. One of the book's coauthors was William R. Corson, a former Military Intelligence official.

Born in Sand Springs, Oklahoma, in 1923, Paisley was two when his mother moved out on his alcoholic father and took her three children to Phoenix, Arizona. There young John became a radio buff, working with homemade crystal sets. Later he put that knowledge to work in World War II, as a radio operator in the merchant marine. While helping resupply America's British and Soviet allies, Paisley made at least two trips to Murmansk, viewing firsthand the Russian people's battle for survival against Hitler. After the war, Paisley continued to earn extra money as a radio operator. One longtime friend, Edward Masters, recalled him shipping out to a number of Soviet Bloc countries.[34]

A *New York Times Magazine* article by Tad Szulc, a writer with numerous contacts in the intelligence community, added a fascinating detail. In 1948, the twenty-five-year-old Paisley had gone to Palestine as a radio operator for the U.N. peacekeeping mission. There he came to the attention of James Angleton, who was touring the Middle East recruiting personnel for the infant CIA. "Paisley," Szulc wrote, "was among Angleton's first recruits."[35]

The next year, Paisley enrolled at the University of Chicago, where he would get a degree in international relations, specializing in Soviet affairs. And, in 1953, Paisley went to Washington to join the CIA, immediately entering the branch that monitored Soviet electronics. On his employment application he falsely wrote that he had never traveled to the Soviet Bloc. That Paisley's merchant marine past raised no alarm bells came as a surprise to the authors of *Widows*, who wrote: "According to former CIA officer Robert T. Crowley, radio officers like Paisley were particularly important targets for GRU and KGB recruitment during the war years."[36]

In 1955 Paisley was "loaned" by the CIA to the National Security Agency (NSA), where, among other duties, he analyzed the electronic data coming back from the Berlin Tunnel. Returning to the CIA in 1957, Paisley, who already spoke Spanish, mastered the Russian language to probe Soviet technical journals better. Then, appointed to head the ORR's Electronic Equipment Branch, Industrial Division, he began to travel widely.

On October 17, 1959, the day after Oswald's arrival in the USSR, CIA records noted that Paisley took off "for travel to London, England; Paris, France; and to such other European coasts as may be necessary during the period October 17–December 15, 1959, to participate in economic defense negotiations."[37] Some of this travel, then and over the next two years, included, according to *Widows*, "months in Eastern Europe, usually under State Department cover, trying to learn what Eastern Bloc diversions of Western technology were taking place."[38]

Oswald was far from the only "defector" to the Soviet Union during this same period. *The New York Times*, commenting on the first such defection in June 1959, a Mr. and Mrs. Libero Ricciardelli, stated that "similar cases have been rare" since the 1930s.[39] Yet by late October, Oswald became the *fifth* American defector, and there would be two more by 1960. Six of these seven eventually experienced an apparent ideological disillusionment and returned home.[40]

One of these was Robert E. Webster. A former Navy man, Webster arrived in Moscow consul Snyder's embassy office to renounce his citizenship just two weeks prior to Oswald.[41] Webster had been participating in a trade exhibition in Moscow, as a "plastics technician" with the Rand Development Corporation. When Webster went to see Snyder, Webster was, curiously, accompanied by Henry Rand and George Bookbinder, two Rand Development executives who both had served with the OSS in World War II. In 1959, Rand Development was one of the first private U.S. corporations to undertake negotiations with the Soviet Union for the exchange and purchase of technological information. Like its parent, Rand Corporation, it also held several CIA contracts.[42]

This, too, would have fallen within John Paisley's bailiwick. In the late 1950s, among Paisley's specialties was commercial technology transfer. He was assigned to determine ways to keep the Soviets from buying Western technology on the open market.

Rand Development's Washington representative in 1959 was Chris Bird, a former CIA agent in Japan and psychological warfare specialist for the Army. Bird, who spoke fluent Russian and Chinese, would later become "Biocommunications Editor/Russian Translator" for Mankind Research Unlimited, Inc., a bizarre Washington think tank that specialized in parapsychology and other behavioral sciences. Among MRU's list of "Company Capabilities" were "brain and mind control . . . acquiring on a daily basis, a large amount of unique bio-cybernetics data from Eastern Europe."[43]

Interestingly, the Rand Corporation had long been interested in such techniques. As far back as 1949, it had issued a report that traced Soviet experiments in hypnosis dating back to the early years of Lenin, and suggested an American counterattack. In 1958, the Bureau of Social Science Research—a Rand subcontractor—issued a report to the Air Force titled "The Use of Hypnosis in Intelligence and Related Military Situations." The chief investigator was Albert Biderman, who had been among the project leaders for an Army-Air Force team first assigned to look into brainwashing techniques in the early 1950s.

The new study's author, consultant Seymour Fisher of the National Institute for Mental Health, wrote in his introduction that "hypnosis has long been regarded as a potentially powerful instrument for controlling human behavior. Undoubtedly, the intelligence divisions of many countries have given serious thought to this potential and have done classified research in various areas of hypnosis . . . these techniques could have been used and covered up so successfully that they might be impossible to recognize."

The Rand investigation determined that hypnotic techniques were limited as an "offensive measure" due to "the relatively small percentage of individuals susceptible to deep hypnosis." However, as a training technique for personnel subject to capture:

In defensive applications, subjects can be specifically selected by a criterion of hypnotizability, and subsequently trained in accord with their anticipated military function. . . . Personnel entrusted with particularly sensitive material could be prepared against possible capture in many different ways: (a) by simple hypnotic suggestion, they could be "immunized" against hypnotic interrogation and suggestion by the enemy; (b) with posthypnotic and autosuggestive training, appropriately timed amnesias could be induced; (c) posthypnotic depersonalization and related dissociative states could be built into the subjects so that if they fall into enemy hands, they would no longer function as rational, integrated individuals. . . . There certainly exist numerous potentialities of hypnotic training to aid prisoners in utilizing their period of captivity in a constructive manner—the realization of these potentials can only be determined by sound research and experience.

The report concluded that certain pharmacological compounds could prove useful adjuncts to hypnosis. "It can be seen that the study of combined drug-hypnosis effects represents a direction in which developments may take place which can make hypnosis a valuable asset to an interrogator and a distinct threat to captives."[44]

There is no evidence that Webster's 1959 "defection"—or Oswald's two weeks later—had any direct relationship to the think tank's mind-control studies. But it is quite clear that the military was being urged to find means of countering purported Soviet expertise in such interrogation methods—which might be anticipated to occur with a sudden spate of American defectors, or a captured U-2 pilot.

Robert Webster's odyssey certainly bears an uncanny similarity to Oswald's. Like Oswald, he was put to work by the Soviets in the trade in which he specialized. Like Oswald, he took a Soviet wife and had a child (in Webster's case, it was a common-law marriage, since he already had a wife back in the United States). And two weeks before Oswald came home in 1962, Webster likewise had a change of heart and returned to the States.[45] According to a State Department document, Webster's return was facilitated by "affidavits from Rand."[46]

Nor do the parallels end there. When Oswald first set about arranging his own departure home in 1961, at the U.S. embassy he "asked about the fate of a young man named Webster. . . ."[47] After the Kennedy assassination, a U.S. intelligence check into Marina Oswald's background found an address matching that of Webster's Leningrad apartment building in her address book.[48] And Marina herself, some years later in America, told an acquaintance that her husband had defected after working at an American exhibition in Moscow. The trouble was, *that* defector was not Oswald, but Webster.[49]

Nagell, Paisley, and Soviet Defectors

If John Paisley was a Soviet "mole," then how did Richard Nagell know it? That question haunted me until I had a brief opportunity to raise it during my last personal visit with Nagell in 1984. On this occasion, Nagell felt uncomfortable with my taking notes. I was cautious in bringing up the clipping he had sent me some six years before. "What more can you tell me," I asked, "about John Paisley?"

Nagell turned his head sideways and replied that Paisley had been involved in his own activities. Beyond doubt, he said, Paisley had operated on behalf of the Soviet Union. In fact, he was "one of the lesser ones" who had burrowed into the American government. I thought back to something Nagell had once written down, about the head of the KGB and the State Department. "Is Yuri Andropov still running the show at Foggy Bottom these days?" he had said.

Nagell went on that he had heard about Paisley's disappearance into the Chesapeake *before* the body was identified. At first he wondered if the KGB might have substituted another body for Paisley's and whisked him away to Moscow. But, most likely, Nagell figured the CIA had somehow found out about Paisley—and killed him.[50]

I was unable to press him further. Not about Paisley and Oswald, or about Paisley's CIA role in later interviewing a number of Soviet officials who had defected to the West. Maryann Paisley had told me she understood that her husband was a key figure in "clearing" Yuri Nosenko—the controversial defector who claimed to have reviewed the KGB's entire Oswald file and found nothing to show a KGB-Oswald relationship in it. Also, according to Nosenko, there was *no* KGB "mole" who had ever managed to get inside the CIA.

I had interviewed Mrs. Paisley, a tall, dark-haired woman then in her early fifties, at attorney Fensterwald's office. She, too, had worked briefly for the CIA in 1974, as a computer programmer on the clandestine side. But she said she and her husband rarely talked about their intelligence activities; that was the nature of the beast. "I do know that John, because of his fluency in Russian, interviewed most of the major defectors. A lot of times. Occasionally he would talk about whether you could believe a defector's material. But he never mentioned anybody by name."

Back in the mid-1960s, she remembered Paisley being furious when the CIA refused to publish some of a defector's data in its internal intelligence newsletter. The defector's information corroborated her husband's own analysis of Soviet missile strengths. "What are we here for if we don't do something with this kind of information?" she recalled Paisley saying. He had even resigned from the CIA and accepted a job at the Defense Department, only to reconsider when the CIA finally published the material.

The defector in question, Maryann Paisley added, "would have been Nosenko."[51]

After his release from CIA captivity in 1968, Nosenko had been given a large sum of money and set up with a new identity in North Carolina. Writer Szulc uncovered that "Paisley started visiting him there while sailing up and down the East Coast. Having purchased a thirty-one-foot sloop following his retirement, Paisley registered the *Brillig* in Wilmington, North Carolina, often keeping the sailboat at the Masonboro Boatyard and Marina, not far from Nosenko's home." One Masonboro employee told Szulc that Paisley's final visit there had occurred in the spring of 1978, a few months before his death.[52]

Maryann Paisley confirmed to me that shortly after her husband's 1974 retirement from the CIA, he had indeed registered his new boat in Wilmington, North Carolina. The only CIA file to comment along these lines stated: "There is no official, recorded basis for the allegation of a relationship between Paisley and Nosenko."[53] The wording seemed to me like a highly hedged bet.

On September 22, 1978—the very day before Paisley's last voyage out to sea—ex-CIA director Richard Helms was testifying before the House Assassinations Committee about Yuri Nosenko. Helms said he still did not consider Nosenko "a bona fide defector." Added Helms, "No person familiar with the facts finds Nosenko's statements about Oswald to be credible. . . . Therefore, this tends to sour all the other opinions he maintained."[54]

On September 25, the first man to wade aboard "a boat apparently adrift in the Chesapeake Bay" was Gerald Sword, a ranger at Point Lookout State Park. Sword said he had seen a neatly stacked pile of papers on a cabin table of the abandoned sloop, and more papers in disarray inside an open briefcase. One of these bore the name and address of John Paisley. Sword jotted down the information, drove to a nearby farmhouse, and called the Coast Guard. Sword said a Coast Guardsman later told him that "two CIA agents and a lieutenant colonel from the Pentagon had gone aboard. Apparently the information was of a higher classification than the agents were permitted to handle, so the colonel took possession of the papers."[55] When Maryann Paisley arrived on the scene late that night, any papers were gone.

The only official mention I came across about this was in a CIA memo that read: "Coast Guard personnel found some papers dealing with the Cuban crisis, but Lt. Murray was not sure if they were classified or not."

The only "Cuban crisis" I could think of was the 1962 Missile Crisis—an event I knew had marked the inception of Richard Nagell's official "double agent" role between the CIA and the KGB. The Cuban Missile Crisis. . . . Nosenko. . . . Whatever Paisley was doing in his last years, right up to the moment of his disappearance, it apparently traced back to the Kennedy era. And I did not believe that the timing of his disappearance—coming as it had amid a congressional focus on Nosenko—was coincidental.

I figured if anybody might have been extra suspicious about all this, it would be James Angleton. Maryann Paisley told me that a few months after her husband vanished, Angleton had come to see her. "He asked me if John always wore a beard, because people used so many names. Angleton said he didn't memorize names but looks, and he didn't recognize pictures of John with a beard. I told him that I questioned the identity of the body. The only thing he said was that if it wasn't John's body, he would be able to find out and would let me know. I never heard from him."[56]

But when I phoned Angleton in October 1986—some nine months before his death—he seemed perfectly sanguine about Paisley. "I have no question there was no problem with him," Angleton said. When I asked if Paisley had been involved with Nosenko, Angleton replied, "I don't think so." He added that Paisley "never had any relations with the covert side" —a definite contradiction to what Maryann Paisley maintained two CIA agents told her.[57]

Yet, in his conversations with author Edward Jay Epstein, Angleton apparently said more. As Epstein wrote in his 1989 book *Deception*, "Because Paisley had obtained a crucial overview of the credence given by the CIA to the different methods of assessing Soviet developments, Angleton speculated that Paisley's knowledge would have been of 'great value' to the KGB, and that if they had obtained it they might also have had an incentive to hide this success by disposing of Paisley."[58]

I could not resolve the contradiction. If Angleton had in fact been Paisley's original recruiter in the late 1940s, was the Counterintelligence chief protecting his own possibly poor judgment? The Szulc article said that "Paisley always stayed in touch with Angleton." In 1991, Tom Mangold's *Cold Warrior*, the first full-length biography of Angleton, would reveal that the superspy himself came under suspicion in the CIA's final "mole-hunt" in 1973. Clare Petty, an Angleton protégé, had ended up focusing on his boss after studying his career and also concluding that Angleton's pet defector, Anatoly Golitsin, was probably a "dispatched agent" of the KGB.[59] It was certainly a fact, I thought, that the KGB could scarcely have better factionalized the CIA than Angleton had, in casting clouds of suspicion over so many of the agency's employees— except, oddly enough, John Paisley.

Oswald as CIA (KGB?) Courier

If Oswald was aiding the CIA in the Soviet Union—possibly passing information on the Minsk radio factory to be "cooked" later at Paisley's desk— then how did he manage to do so? I received a glimpse of an answer from a former CIA contract employee named Robert Morrow. And it provided a remarkable tie-in to Oswald's post-Soviet days.

I first became aware of Morrow through his semifictionalized book *Betrayal: A Reconstruction of Certain Clandestine Events from the Bay of Pigs to the Assassination of President Kennedy*. This book, which hypothesized a conspiracy among Cuban exiles and rogue elements of the CIA, inspired New York representative Thomas Downing to make the first call for reopening a congressional investigation into the assassination.

What especially grabbed me was a character in Morrow's book whom he called "Richard Carson Fillmore." This, Morrow wrote, was a CIA man who had managed to penetrate the assassination plot in New Orleans, using the alias "Joseph Kramer." I was stunned by the reference. Somehow Robert Morrow knew quite a bit about the thinly disguised Richard Case Nagell.

Morrow's story of Oswald in the Soviet Union, I came to believe, might be of considerable significance. There seemed little doubt that Morrow had been, as he claimed, under CIA contract between 1960 and 1964. Articles from *The New York Times* and in Baltimore newspapers of October 2, 1963, revealed the arrest of Morrow, his wife, and a Cuban exile leader for plotting "to print counterfeit Cuban pesos and smuggle them into Cuba in an attempt to unbalance the economy of the Communist-led island." They had been foiled by an undercover agent from the Secret Service.

By the time I met with Morrow in his Baltimore apartment in 1976, he had long since returned to his specialty as an electronics consultant. He was a big redheaded man who spoke in low, rapid tones. Picking up from his fictionalized version, the story he related about Oswald in the Soviet Union went like this:

During the Bay of Pigs invasion in 1961, the CIA had flown Morrow into Cuba's Camagüey mountains on "a technical mission to look for missiles or installations." Morrow was "told to go in and take some electronic data from certain signals they were curious about, instrumentation data." His pilot was a New Orleans resident named David Ferrie. Six years later, Ferrie would figure prominently in Jim Garrison's probe of a possible assassination conspiracy.

Later in 1961, Morrow continued, he traveled to Athens, Greece. There he met Ferrie again, in arranging a CIA weapons shipment destined for some Cuban exiles. Going on to Madrid, Morrow received instructions to go to the office of a CIA front company called Permindex and wait for a phone call.

Permindex, too, would later enter into Garrison's investigation: Clay Shaw, brought to trial on conspiracy charges, served on Permindex's Board of Directors in the early 1960s. He was also, by the CIA's own admission, a contact of the agency's Domestic Contact Service, at least through 1956. Permindex's major stockholder was Montreal banker Louis M. Bloomfield, a former major in the OSS; another director was Ferenc Nagy, deposed as premier of Hungary in the 1947 Communist takeover and living in exile in Virginia.

Morrow said that while at Permindex he then "took a call from David Ferrie from either Zurich or Geneva. Ferrie had gotten instructions that I was to go directly to Paris, check into the Plaza d'Athene Hotel, and wait."

"Wait for what?" I asked.

"Some people I describe in my book as the Hampshires. Their name was really Hamilton. They were a couple who lived in Pittsburgh. The reason their name was given to me is because they already knew of me, through a family association. They had just come from traveling in the Soviet Union. I picked up a packet of papers from them. Mr. Hamilton said I was to inform the man I gave these to that this was the latest information from Harvey in Minsk."

"Were the Hamiltons connected with the CIA?"

"No. Well, he may have been. They had spent some time in Russia and he had been connected with the St. Regis Paper Company, which could have gotten him all over the world. As you know, a lot of people in high places in some of these companies do work for *the* Company [the CIA]. But I knew, and was told, that we did use tourists as couriers."

I asked, "So, since Lee Harvey Oswald was living in Minsk at that time, you believe that he and 'Harvey' were one and the same?"

"I'm convinced of it," Morrow said. "When I got into the actual reconstruction of things, looking at various letters of Oswald's in the Warren Commission documents and so on, I was certain. I must confess I was curious, but I never did look at those papers."

"Who did you give them to?"

"My case officer, Tracy Barnes," Morrow replied. "The envelope had his CIA code name on it." (Morrow could not recall the cryptonym.)

Morrow added that both Lydia Hamilton and her husband had since died. Ferrie and Barnes are also deceased. So there was no way to verify Morrow's charge, which linked Oswald not only to the CIA but also to CIA people with a direct hand in Cuban affairs.

Tracy Barnes, like his counterpart Desmond FitzGerald in the CIA hierarchy, was a Harvard Law School graduate and former New York lawyer who earned his wings in wartime intelligence. When the Bay of Pigs operation got under way in 1960, Barnes was chief of the psychological and paramilitary staff for the CIA's clandestine branch—and specifically assigned to Castro's overthrow. After the Bay of Pigs, Barnes had established the CIA's supersecret Domestic Operations Division.[60]

So, if Morrow was correct, Barnes would have been the first CIA official in Washington to receive Oswald's material out of Minsk. After which, for analysis purposes, its next handler would probably have been John Paisley.

I was beginning to learn about the CIA's chain of command.

Lee and Marina

According to Morrow, this was not the only time that "Harvey" came up prior to the assassination. Sometime in the late summer of 1963, Morrow recalled having another conversation with Tracy Barnes.

"It had to do with 'Harvey' being down in New Orleans at that time," Morrow said. "The mention was that he'd done some work for them [the CIA] over in Russia. I was told that 'Harvey' had married a Russian girl for the purpose of trying to get a relative of hers to defect. Understand that I didn't realize Marina Oswald actually was the niece of a Russian colonel. This didn't even come to my attention until after the Garrison investigation. That's when the notion came to me that it might've been the same person. I think it came up in my talk with Barnes that 'Harvey' had come back with her and first gone South to Dallas-Fort Worth."

Not long after Morrow completed his manuscript of *Betrayal*—where he first raised the possibility of a planned Oswald marriage—some fifteen hundred documents on the assassination were declassified by the CIA in 1976. Among them was a brief file dated December 4, 1963: "Source on [deleted] said he saw [deleted]. [Deleted] reported SOVCONGEN told him 30 November that Oswald sent to USSR and married Soviet girl under CIA instructions. [SOVCONGEN stands for Soviet consul general at an unidentified embassy.]"

I might have thought this farfetched were it not for Oswald's earlier possible connection to the CIA's Eroshkin defection plan in Tokyo. Or the story told me by John Margain—that Richard Nagell had taken for *his* bride a Japanese woman whose father he had been investigating.

Another CIA official's memorandum about Oswald, also declassified in 1976 and dated November 25, 1963, referred to "the Harvey story" in terms of a peculiar pattern: "the number of Soviet women marrying foreigners, being permitted to leave the USSR, then eventually divorcing their spouses and settling down abroad without returning 'home.'" The memorandum noted that there were "something like two dozen similar cases" but did not specify when. It concluded: "It was out of curiosity to learn if Oswald's wife would actually accompany him to our country, partly out of Oswald's own experiences in the USSR, that we showed [deleted] intelligence interest in the Harvey story."[61]

The CIA, with its thousands of employees in many different divisions, was highly compartmentalized. So did one branch of the CIA know what another was doing? Not necessarily. Marina herself seems to have had cognizance, at least, about two American "defectors"—Oswald and Webster—both of whose activities in the USSR were of interest to Paisley in the CIA's ORR. Perhaps it was the KGB that really wanted to know if Marina's uncle would take the bait?

The uncle's name was Ilya Prusakov. He was an engineer and also a ranking colonel in the MVD, or Soviet Ministry of Internal Affairs, which had secret police functions. The subsidy Oswald received from the Soviets all during his stay in Minsk came from the MVD, as the "defector" set down in notes he kept at the time. Marina, whose mother's second husband was a skilled electrical technician living in Leningrad, had been living with her uncle since the summer of 1959.

And it was Colonel Prusakov who urged the pretty nineteen-year-old to attend a trade union dance at the Palace of Culture in Minsk sometime in mid-March of 1961, where she first met the young fellow who was introduced as "Alik." At first, Marina would say years later, she believed Russian-speaking "Alik" to be a Soviet citizen from somewhere in the Baltic region—and was surprised to learn that he was really an American named Lee Harvey Oswald.

Shortly after this, Oswald entered the Fourth Clinical Hospital in Minsk for an adenoid operation. This was where most of the couple's whirlwind courtship took place, with Oswald proposing to Marina from his hospital bed. They were married on April 30, 1961, less than six weeks after they met.[62]

Oswald had already written to the U.S. embassy that February, stating his "desire to return to the United States." This occurred soon after his mother, Marguerite, made a trip to Washington. She went by the State Department, demanding to see Secretary Dean Rusk, shouting that her son was a government agent—and why hadn't she heard from Lee in almost a year? Within two days after her appearance there, Oswald wrote her a letter from Minsk. This was either coincidental timing, or someone had a direct means of contacting him.[63]

Two weeks after his marriage to Marina, Oswald wrote the embassy once more: "I would not leave here without my wife so arrangements would have to be made for her to leave at the same time I do." Oswald then flew to Moscow on July 8, 1961, where U.S. consul Snyder promptly returned his passport to him—despite the Passport Office in Washington having specifically told the embassy, in writing, to wait on doing so until after Oswald's travel plans were finalized.[64] Upon recommendation of the American embassy in Moscow, Marina was exempted from the standard quotas imposed by the U.S. Immigration and Naturalization Service

(INS). After initial objections, the INS gave in after the State Department made a "strong case" on Marina's behalf.[65]

All applications completed, the Oswalds simply settled down to wait for approval to leave the USSR. On February 15, 1962, Marina gave birth to a girl, June Lee, in Minsk. Three months later the Oswalds were at the American embassy in Moscow, signing the final papers to send them westward. "It was during this time that Marina noted a cooling in Oswald's attitude toward her," writes Jim Marrs in his book *Crossfire*. "This coolness was to increase after they left Russia. It was almost as if he had made up the story of his love and instead was simply following some sort of orders in his courtship. Afterward, with his assignment completed, he didn't bother to act like his love was real."[66]

Just prior to their leaving Minsk, Colonel Prusakov did have a private meeting with Lee and Marina and then saw them off at the train.[67] But Uncle Ilya never defected. Whether he ever considered doing so, or whether Lee and Marina's relationship was originally part of a CIA or KGB (or both) design, must be left to conjecture.

What's in a Name?

There is no known record of Oswald having adopted in the USSR the full alias Aleksei Hidell/Hidel that he used later. But he was widely known as "Alik" among his acquaintances in Minsk. A 1964 CIA chronology of Oswald's activities in the Soviet Union notes that a hunting license was issued to him on June 18, 1960, in the name of "Aleksey Harvey Oswald." A membership booklet for the Electric Power Plant and Electrical Industry Union in Minsk, dated September 1, 1960, is made out to "Alik Harvey Oswald."[68]

The customary explanation is an innocent one: Oswald adopted "Alik" because "Lee" was a difficult name for Russians to pronounce. "Alik" or "Aleksey" is, of course, one of the most common names in Russia. But Nagell had told me that there was significance attached to both halves of the alias Oswald would later use to order his fateful Mannlicher rifle.

The false name "Alex" was one that the CIA used many times in its Soviet-related counterintelligence projects. "Alex" was also the agency's code name for Yuri Nosenko, who first approached the agency about defecting in June 1962—the same month the Oswalds arrived Stateside.[69] Nosenko would assert when he came over to the Americans right after the assassination that he had personally superintended the KGB's Oswald file from the moment the "defector" arrived in the autumn of 1959.

The "Alex" name was assigned as well to Oleg Penkovsky, a defector-in-place who passed secrets to the West for eighteen months in 1961 and 1962. His CIA case officer, George Kisvalter of the Soviet Russia Division, had the code name "Alexander."[70] And, in Moscow, one of Penkovsky's two American contacts was an Air Force doctor at the U.S. embassy whose true name was Alexis Davison.

Just prior to the Oswalds' departure for the United States in May 1962, Marina was given a physical examination by Dr. Alexis Davison. At this visit the doctor gave Oswald the address of his mother, Natasha Alekseevna Davison, in Atlanta, suggesting that he get in touch with her should he ever pass through that southern city. After the assassination, Captain Davison's mother's name was found listed in Oswald's address book. And after the Oswalds sailed to the United States, oddly enough Oswald picked a New York-to-Dallas flight that made a brief stopover in Atlanta. For some reason, as Robert Oswald would later write in a biography of his brother, Lee and Marina had started for Texas with five suitcases but arrived in Dallas with only two. The other three bags were never accounted for, leading some researchers to speculate that Oswald had performed some kind of courier mission along the route.[71]

Coinciding with Davison's moment with the Oswalds, the doctor was in regular secret communication with Oleg Penkovsky. Penkovsky was deputy chief of the Soviet State Committee on Coordination of Scientific Research; he was also a senior GRU official with the Intelligence Directorate of the General Staff in Moscow. In April 1961 Penkovsky had gone to London to lead a Soviet trade delegation. There he defected to the West, becoming an agent-in-place for the CIA and British MI5, passing along thousands of pages containing the best Soviet military intelligence ever seen in Washington and London. During the Cuban Missile Crisis his information would allow the Kennedy White House to follow the hourly progress of Soviet missile emplacements.

In the midst of the Cuban Missile Crisis, somehow Penkovsky was unmasked by the Soviets. In December 1962, an article appeared in *Pravda* accusing three American embassy officials of "complicity in a spy ring" with Penkovsky. *Pravda* published a photo of Captain Alexis Davison as he inspected a lamppost for a mark, meaning that Penkovsky had made a drop-off in a nearby mailbox. After Penkovsky's confession, he would be executed in May 1963 for high treason. Davison, whose phone number was found on Penkovsky, was declared persona non grata by the Soviet Union.[72] Years later, Alexis Davison would tell the House Assassinations Committee that his only involvement with intelligence work had centered around "Alex," lasting for about a year. The deputy chief of the CIA's clandestine Soviet Russia Division concurred to the committee that Davison's involvement was a "one-shot deal."[73]

This scenario is not to imply that Oswald would have had any knowledge of the Top-Secret Penkovsky operation. It is extremely unlikely that a "defector" heading home would be entrusted with anything pertaining to such a sensitive matter. Still, the timing of the Oswalds' meeting with Davison, and the apparent disappearance of some of their luggage en route to Dallas, struck me as peculiar.

To this day, nobody knows if someone betrayed the CIA's "mole," or whether the KGB picked up on him without assistance. This brings us, one more time, to John Paisley—and the knowledge he may have had of the Penkovsky case.

Victor Marchetti, a retired CIA official who took part in the Penkovsky project, told me that "Paisley was probably involved in the analysis of this material." Could this, I wondered later, have been among the papers about the Cuban Missile Crisis found on his boat immediately after his disappearance? Marchetti added his doubts that Paisley "would have been in a position to figure out who the agent was, or even that there *was* an agent."[74] However, as the authors of *Widows* point out:

> Paisley was famous for demanding the original source of "humint," or human intelligence. . . . If the Soviet Bloc Division would not tell him who an agent in place was, Paisley could figure out a great deal just by considering the type of material to which the agent had to have access. Then, by going out to the National Security Agency, where he was considered one of the boys because of his tour there in the 1950s, Paisley could get the raw intercepts to look at. . . . By using this material, Paisley could supplement his knowledge of what the Soviets were up to and, in some cases, where the United States had agents in the Soviet government.[75]

The KGB-CIA Disclaimers

In 1991, when *Nightline* scored a TV news coup by getting access to the KGB's Oswald file, at first KGB officials indicated they were willing simply to turn over the entire dossier to correspondent Forrest Sawyer. Then, shortly before the hour-long special was to air on November 22, the KGB got cold feet. Sawyer was permitted to look at a portion of the faded material and to interview a few former acquaintances of Oswald. The Oswald that came across was, in *Nightline* anchor Ted Koppel's words, basically that of "an unstable, incompetent dolt."

But Sawyer, in a phone conversation we had two months after the broadcast, expressed some reservations. "I had no reason to believe they had suddenly manufactured documents for me to look at," Sawyer told me. "But maybe they had in 1964, when nobody dreamed that KGB files would ever see the light of day. I think what I saw was absolutely real, but they could have and probably did launder them in the past. It's not at all believable to me that they never debriefed Oswald. All the documents showed was an interminable series of banalities. A synopsis that I saw of all the files was innocuous, a flat recitation of a rather unpleasant, boring defector. They really didn't reveal a damn thing, except that they followed people like Oswald and bugged their houses."

Sawyer added that he was allowed to examine only material from the KGB's Second Directorate, whose function is basically domestic counter intelligence, subversion, and industrial security. His request to see First Directorate files was specifically refused; these far more telling records would be akin to those held by the CIA's Directorate of Operations and would include "active measures, counter intelligence, and analysis" related to KGB missions at home and abroad. "These days," Sawyer concluded, "you can bet that a Russian intelligence agency will not put out anything that would upset the CIA."[76]

For the CIA's part, there has long been a kind of "party line" on the subject of Oswald and the KGB. Richard Helms, in charge of the CIA's clandestine projects at the time of the assassination, said in his 1978 testimony before the House Assassinations Committee almost verbatim what James Angleton had told me. Helms stated: "Until the day that the KGB in Moscow or the Cuban intelligence in Havana is prepared to turn over their files to the United States as to what their relationships to these various people were, it is going to be extraordinarily difficult to tidy up this case, finally and conclusively."[77]

What "various people" Helms was referring to was not elaborated on. Asked whether the CIA ever had an operational interest in Oswald, Helms responded: "Not that I am aware of." Angleton, in our interviews, flatly stated that such assertions were "completely false." John McCone, CIA director when the assassination occurred, told an interviewer in 1970: "I never heard of any rumors that Oswald was a CIA agent. There were rumors that Oswald was an agent of either Castro or Moscow and that the CIA had such information in its files—which we did not have. We knew of his movements, but we knew of no activities of his that would lead us to believe that he was an agent of either."[78]

The statements of these three top CIA officials are, even unto themselves, somewhat contradictory. Helms did allude several times in his testimony to "hypothetical" responsibility for Oswald falling under the military's Office of Naval Intelligence. As with Nagell, it is quite conceivable that the ex-Marine would have had a military cover for any CIA functions. Author Henry Hurt, in his book *Reasonable Doubt*, would recount an unnamed former Naval Intelligence official in Moscow telling him: "I felt that there was a CIA man under cover in the Naval attaché's office that I believe was sort of like a handler for Oswald. . . . There was more CIA connection to Oswald than ever met the eye."[79]

Another ex-CIA employee, whom the House Assassinations Committee did not identify, "claimed that during the summer of 1962, he reviewed a contact report from representatives of a CIA field office who had interviewed a former Marine who had worked at the Minsk radio plant following his defection to the USSR. This defector, whom the employee believed may have been Oswald, had been living with his family in Minsk." Still another CIA memorandum released in 1976, from an unidentified official, stated that "we showed intelligence interest" in Oswald and "discussed . . . the laying on of interviews."[80] Precisely when that occurred, or whether it was pursued, is not indicated. Officially, the CIA—despite its practice of debriefing even a number of American tourists who had traveled anywhere behind the Iron Curtain—maintains to this day that it never debriefed Oswald.

So either the CIA hierarchy is lying or, conceivably, unaware of what was really going on with Oswald and a section of its bureaucracy. If "moles" inside the CIA did exist—and were perhaps part of an Oswald-related operation—for either the CIA or the KGB to reveal this would be tantamount to giving away the crown jewels.

Whatever seeds were planted in the Soviet Union, they would be sown soon enough—as the Oswalds settled down in Texas and as Richard Nagell made his fateful trip to Mexico City.

Summary

Despite official disclaimers by the CIA and the KGB, it appears very likely that Oswald was utilized by both intelligence agencies during his two and a half years in the Soviet Union. Nothing else explains the ease with which Oswald financed his European voyage, and so quickly received his visa in Finland from a KGB official. Nothing else explains the nonchalance of American embassy officials in Moscow when Oswald avowed his intent to renounce his citizenship and provide "radar secrets" to the Soviets.

The strange circumstances surrounding the capture of U-2 spy pilot Francis Gary Powers leads to some very big questions. Was Oswald instructed by U.S. intelligence to pass along information that contributed to the U-2's demise, thus sabotaging possibilities of détente at an Eisenhower-Khrushchev summit?

The KGB must have known of the CIA's interest in its electronics industry, yet Oswald's employment at a Minsk radio-TV factory was cleared at the highest levels of the Soviet government. Nagell's allegation that John Paisley—then chief of the CIA's Soviet electronics branch—was a KGB "mole" makes sense of the Soviets' willingness to provide Oswald with such a job. Any information passed along by the "defector" would ultimately have reached Paisley's desk. Ex-CIA contract agent Robert Morrow says he personally received such data from Oswald, which went next to Morrow's case officer Tracy Barnes. Morrow's contact in Europe was David Ferrie, who would meet Oswald again in 1963 in New Orleans.

The rash of American defections in 1959 is itself highly suspect, particularly the parallel coming (and going) of Robert Webster, whose technological expertise would also have fallen under Paisley's aegis at the CIA. That Webster's U.S. employer, Rand Development, was also connected to military experiments into hypnosis raises still more chilling questions. So does the "treatment" of Francis Gary Powers—by American extremists seeking to link him to Soviet "brainwashing," and by the CIA upon his release.

Equally bizarre is Oswald's whirlwind courtship of Marina from a hospital bed, and the possibility that this may have been a "planned" CIA marriage aimed at enticing Marina's uncle to defect. Finally, there was the Oswalds' curious relationship with embassy doctor Alexis Davison, who was simultaneously involved in obtaining information from CIA spy Oleg Penkovsky. Did John Paisley help expose Penkovsky to the Soviets? If Paisley was recruited by James Angleton—who, despite his suspicious nature, never targeted Paisley as a "mole" suspect—what was Angleton's game?

The only certainty is that much more was involved with Oswald in the USSR than either the Americans or the Soviets have ever been willing to admit.

II
The Mission

Whenever we leave principles and clear positive laws we are soon lost in the wild regions of imagination and possibility where arbitrary power sits upon her brazen throne and governs with an iron scepter.
—John Adams, second president of the United States

Chapter Nine

Double Role in Mexico: Autumn 1962

Mexico City, splendid and squalid, seems to epitomize double images. Twin volcanoes keep watch over the teeming land where Montezuma met Cortez. Ornate colonial buildings blend with the tumbled blocks of ancient pyramids beneath a harsh sun. Multicolored mosaic walls mix with the cold steel-and-glass facades of skyscrapers. Suffering Christian saints and grotesque pre-Christian gods alike adorn old stone carvings. Magnificent mansions and the adobe walls of miserable tenements bear dual witness to the deep, chilling shadows of twilight. It is the oldest city in North America and, already in 1962, was one of the world's most populous.

When Arthur Gilman Greenstein arrived in Mexico City that August, he was twenty-nine years old and still undecided about his future. His partnership in a bar in his hometown of Wilmington, Delaware, was not faring well. But Greenstein had saved some money working at Everfast Fabrics, where his father was an executive, and just completed a summer course in Spanish at Yale University. He thought perhaps he might become a teacher, and he decided to enroll at the National University of Mexico because he had heard it was an easy way to get a master's degree.

Looking at a map, Greenstein selected a temporary domicile for its proximity to the university. Making his way through the bustling roadways to 16 Orizaba Street, he checked into the Hotel Luma. Here, on one of his first lonely evenings, he ran into "these two friendly fellows about my same age group" in the lobby. One of them, Richard Case Nagell, would have a haunting impact on Greenstein's life.

I was sitting with Arthur Greenstein on a crisp February morning in 1990 at a long table in the Wilmington Public Library. He was a husky six feet two inches, wore glasses, and his curly black hair was rapidly receding. He was divorced and, as he put it, "somewhat floundering," pushing sixty and living with an elderly relative, the adult bookstore he had eventually opened in Wilmington having been shuttered by the courts. Things hadn't quite turned out the way he had once dreamed of in Mexico City. Looking back, those were really his halcyon days—filled with lots of pretty girls, fascinating places to visit, strange characters to meet, and intrigue.

The intrigue had everything to do with the tall, scarred, ex-Army captain who befriended him at the Hotel Luma. In 1990 Greenstein had not seen Richard Nagell in over ten years. But out in the trunk of his car he had brought along to our meeting his piece of Nagell's legacy: a briefcase full of papers, many of which Nagell had sent him while in prison on the bank charge, and a little Minolta "spy camera" that Nagell had later given him "for safekeeping."

I had been trying to locate Greenstein since Nagell wrote me in 1976: "I am curious to know whether or not you possess copies of any of the forty-odd letters that I wrote to Arthur G. Greenstein from Leavenworth, most of them written during the period July 25, 1967, through April 20, 1968. . . . The few significant letters that I wrote Art were by necessity, and by design, quite cryptic . . . seemingly silly thoughts under the heading of 'cerebrations,' which was the only safe way that I could get a portion of what I wanted to say out of prison and on the record, so to speak. . . ."[1]

Now, recently Greenstein had gotten back in touch with Bernard Fensterwald, Jr., who first helped him "decipher" Nagell's letters in the late 1960s. Through Fensterwald I obtained his number, and at the end of our long day together Greenstein would provide me photocopies of Nagell's "cerebrations"—allowing me to try my own hand at decoding more pieces of what Nagell once called his "patchwork puzzle."

A Mystery Wrapped in an Enigma

It was August 17, 1962, when Nagell obtained his tourist card for multiple entry at the Mexican consulate in Los Angeles. He listed his age as thirty-two (true), his marital status as divorced (false), and his occupation as "writer" (also false).[2] One week later he drove across the Texas border at El Paso, shortly arriving in Mexico City and checking into the Hotel Luma.

The Luma, which closed down in 1980, was a medium-size, inexpensive abode in a fashionable nightclub area known as the "Pink Zone." It had a bar that stayed open until the wee hours, and a decent musical trio. Not until years later would Nagell inform Greenstein that "it was really a spy hotel—spies coming to town would congregate there. He told me he guessed I was the last to know."

Even at the time, the hotel's resident clientele seemed to Greenstein like characters out of a picaresque novel. There was a mysterious woman who rarely emerged from her room on an upper floor, claiming to be a writer, receiving "all kinds of people coming to visit her." There was a Benzedrine addict named Benny, whose well-to-do parents owned an inn on the outskirts of Houston but who shipped him into exile because he was too embarrassing to have around the house. There was a French-Canadian cobbler named Marcel who, as Nagell would later reminisce in a letter to Greenstein, had for years been "utterly devoted to his job of fastening heels and soles to an endless train of shoes bouncing along on a conveyer belt" for just over a buck an hour—and finally rewarded by his factory with a round-trip vacation to Mexico. And there was a hard-drinking, self-proclaimed cardiologist from St. Louis named Worth Walrod, Jr., who seduced just about any available female ("except he couldn't stand women who don't shave their legs," Greenstein recalls).

It was Walrod who first introduced Greenstein to Richard Nagell. "Nagell and I saw each other just about every day for about two months, daytimes and having meals together," Greenstein was saying, shifting his eyes around the Wilmington library to ensure that nobody was within earshot. "He had all these silver dollars with him, I think he was collecting them. He tried to make a big thing out of that, as if they could be some kind of intelligence signal. I don't know what it was about.

"Once I wanted to borrow his car, which was an older Ford, to take an American girl to the bullfights. He wouldn't let me have it, and it became evident the reason was he had all these documents in the trunk. All these cardboard boxes, he said they were just documents proving what a shafty deal he got out of California's Department of Alcoholic Beverage Control. He told me there was a subpoena out for him in California that he was trying get away from, it had to do with a bribery charge against him. At one point he showed me these bullet wounds in his chest. They were just like little white spots, and he said he'd been shot recently in California."

"Did he ever talk about what that incident was all about?" I asked.

"It was like a little misunderstanding with some of the local hoodlums or something, a little falling-out."

Even in many of their initial conversations, Greenstein realized that his new friend at least wanted him to believe that he was ideologically very left-wing. "He came on real bitter. He didn't say too much about being in the Military Intelligence, but he was bitter over the fact that his wife had cost him his security clearance, being married to a Japanese foreigner. Looking back, that seems like a cover, maybe he had very excellent security clearance all the time. But he talked about some of the senseless battles he had fought, getting people killed charging up a hill in North Korea and the next day they'd give the hill back. He was big on revisionist history, like the alleged fact that South Korea had really started the Korean War by invading the North. And he'd say with a snicker that Hungarian freedom fighters were 'a bunch of Fascists.' He said at least one time that American leaders are nothing but murderers—because of the things he knew about.

"Nagell was, to borrow Churchill's phrase, a mystery wrapped in an enigma. Once we were caught in a rainstorm, standing in the overhang of a store. At that point I got the feeling that I just didn't know him whatsoever. An emotion came over me that he was a complete unknown to me, just unfathomable."

Greenstein shook his head and continued: "Another somewhat amazing incident—possibly just he and I were at this nightclub, and some males came over who he said were not Mafia but hoodlums from California. They wanted him to ride around town late at night. Before he left to go with them, he gave me a phone number on a match cover. I raised the question, is there some danger here? And he said, 'I'll be back, there'll be no problem.' But he secretly wrote down the number, saying there was somebody at the U.S. embassy I should contact."

"In case something happened to him?"

"Yeah. I felt like this was very much on the level."

This was not the only time that the American embassy came up between Nagell and Greenstein. "Sometimes he would say he had to go to the embassy and wouldn't be available for social events. What he told me, pretty early on, was that he came to Mexico to renounce his citizenship. He couldn't do it in the United States, he had to do it there."

Sometime that September of 1962, according to one of the few files about Nagell since released by the FBI, he had walked into the American embassy and advised an unnamed official that "he had been approached for recruiting in Mexico City, refused to elaborate, did not desire to return to U.S., was 'bitter, disgusted, disillusioned, and disaffected.' Said if he did go to some other country it would cost U.S. millions, was 'through being a good citizen' and thought he had gotten 'a dirty deal all around.' "[3]

Being "approached for recruiting" clearly referred to a foreign government. Five years later, from prison, Nagell would harken back to his action at the American embassy in two separate letters to Greenstein. In a short "play," Nagell referred to himself as an "indiscreet, loud-talking, disgruntled" ex-Military Intelligence man "afflicted with red spot on right chest [apparently the gunshot wound] earned vicinity of Malibu for indiscretion, who is currently on a mission for the notorious XXX." He had done "a great job of spreading suspicions of being a spook around while real moves are as subtle as a thumbtack placed on a wooden telephone pole, a feat at which he is also experienced. Subterfuges are well-thought out, well-planned and well-executed."

"Who, in Sep 62," Nagell also wrote, "asked somebody to make application at American Embajada to renounce citizenship, change coats, talk loudly in and about . . . become a provocateur in simple ploy that was so simple it almost backfired—'It's in the vital interests of our national security.' "[4]

Who, indeed, was behind Nagell's citizenship-renunciation trip to the American embassy in Mexico City, similar to the one made three years earlier by Lee Harvey Oswald in Moscow?

Capital Intrigues

The American embassy in Mexico City housed the largest CIA station in the Western Hemisphere in the 1960s. As former CIA officer Philip Agee, who served there slightly later in the 1960s, described it in his book *Inside the Company: CIA Diary:* "Altogether the station has some fifteen operations officers under State Department cover in the Embassy political section, plus about twelve more officers under assorted non-official covers outside the Embassy."[5]

David Atlee Phillips, the CIA's covert action and then Cuban affairs chief in Mexico during 1962–63, elaborated in his 1977 autobiography, *The*

Night Watch: "The reason for a large CIA contingent in Mexico City is to conduct what are known as 'third country operations.' That is, using Mexico for access to the nationals of other countries. Traditionally, Mexico City has been the main outpost of Soviet intelligence for its activities throughout Latin America and, since 1959, for the support of Cuban skulduggery in the Western Hemisphere. The mainland Chinese have an embassy there, as do all the other Socialist countries."[6]

The Soviet Union also maintained its largest mission in the Western Hemisphere (except for its Cuban presence) in Mexico City. According to Philip Agee, of the Soviets' fifty diplomatic officers, twenty-five were known or suspected KGB agents and another ten were with the GRU. Only three blocks away from the Soviets' beautifully landscaped headquarters on Tacubaya Avenue was Cuba's only remaining diplomatic mission in Latin America. Of its thirteen officials, over half were suspected of being with Castro's intelligence network, then known as G-2. They were known to work pretty much hand-in-glove with the Soviets.[7]

Nagell arrived in Mexico City at a particularly auspicious time. On August 31, 1962, an Airgram went out from the American embassy there to CIA headquarters as well as various agencies of the Pentagon. It was headed "Cuban Exiles Report Soviet Troops in Cuba," and it described the information from an "American resident correspondent" that "thousands of Soviet technicians" had recently arrived on the island.[8] At the same time, in Miami, recently arrived Cuban refugees being questioned at the CIA's interrogation center reported seeing truck convoys hauling long tubular objects swathed in tarpaulins through the streets of Havana.

As CIA director John McCone later reflected: "We had lots of reports from informers. . . . Sometimes there were delays in the transmission of this information, because sometimes the information would have to go to Mexico. . . . Some of it had to find its way by way of a traveler going to Mexico and coming out. There wasn't a great deal of instant communication because of the restraints of travel and communication and so forth. So we didn't have the hard information that a constant aerial surveillance would have revealed."[9]

The Cuban Missile Crisis was on the horizon. And the CIA wasn't the only information-gathering body that wanted to know what was going on. Early in 1961, President Kennedy had agreed to establish a new Pentagon branch, the Defense Intelligence Agency (DIA). Its necessity arose out of the conflicting estimates among the CIA, Army, Navy, and Air Force intelligence about a U.S.-Soviet "missile gap." The DIA was viewed as a means of consolidating data gathered from the various MI services. Allen Dulles at first objected vigorously, fearing that the new agency might intrude on the CIA's turf. As told in the 1964 book *The Invisible Government,* "Some of Dulles' advisers suspected that the Pentagon had covert ambitions for the DIA which were being suppressed temporarily for tactical reasons." Dulles would later write of the possibility "that two such powerful and well-financed agencies as CIA and DIA will become rivals and competitors."

By the Cuban Missile Crisis period, that seems to have been the case. Ironically, however, the triumvirate that ran the DIA had stronger ties to Dulles—by then dismissed from the CIA—and to J. Edgar Hoover than they had to Kennedy's new team at the CIA. The DIA's director was Lieutenant General Joseph F. Carroll, who had been a leading FBI assistant to Hoover until he moved over to set up the Air Force's first investigation/counter intelligence section in 1947. Both of Carroll's top subordinates were ex-CIA men who had worked closely with Dulles.

One was Major General William ("Buffalo Bill") Quinn, who had been Dulles's personal courier for information pertaining to Nazi troop movements in World War II, while a G-2 officer with the Seventh Army.[10] After the war, when OSS personnel were reassigned into the newly created Strategic Services Unit (SSU), Quinn was appointed director. Instructed to "preserve the intelligence assets of the OSS and to eliminate its liabilities."[11] Quinn soon found himself besieged by accusations from Army G-2, the Office of Naval Intelligence, and the FBI that his outfit was riddled with Communists. The truth was, none of those three branches wanted a centralized foreign intelligence system to continue beyond the OSS.

So Quinn went to Hoover and personally requested that the FBI check out his personnel. In a fascinating account told by ex-intelligence official William R. Corson in his book *The Armies of Ignorance,* Hoover then proceeded to "penetrate" Quinn's organization with some of his own trusted operatives. Hoover had despised the OSS's horning in on his territory, especially in the Western Hemisphere. Now, in what Corson called Hoover's "grand design," he orchestrated a plan "brilliant enough to qualify as a classic example of how a counterespionage operation—one designed to manipulate another intelligence service—should be run."

The first wave of FBI émigrés into Quinn's postwar group included William Harvey, Raymond Leddy, and Winston Scott. All three would go on to play vital roles in U.S. intelligence after the CIA's formation in 1947.[12] Harvey would become chief of the CIA's Berlin base in the mid-1950s and later, through the Cuban Missile Crisis period, the agency's Cuban task force chief; it was he who spearheaded the CIA's recruitment of organized-crime figures into anti-Castro plots. Leddy would set up the CIA's original operational network in South America, then become the State Department's officer in charge of Latin affairs; at Allen Dulles's request, he would map out plans for the overthrow of the Guatemalan government in 1954.[13] Scott, the CIA's first station chief in London and then its inspector general in Washington, would from 1956 to 1969 be the agency's station chief in Mexico City.

It was William Quinn who set up James Angleton as his man in Italy after World War II. They traveled widely together across Europe and, years later, Quinn would call his old friend "the finest counterespionage officer the United States has ever produced." Within Quinn's SSU, the career of Richard Helms was promoted; Helms would become the CIA's covert operations boss and eventually CIA director.

Quinn had also pushed forward an overseas spy network aimed at the Soviets and run by Hitler's ex-intelligence chief, Reinhard Gehlen. This mushroomed, of course, through the 1950s, becoming a subject of common interest to Allen Dulles and Charles Willoughby. Late in 1956, when it became clear that a German-based Free Europe Committee of disenfranchised Hungarians and other Eastern Europeans was riddled with reactionaries, Eisenhower sent word to Dulles to disestablish it. Assigned the task of closing down U.S. refugee reception centers and terminating subsidies in Berlin were William Harvey and his old FBI sidekick Raymond Leddy. The Gehlen web stayed intact but, by 1958, as Angleton would comment with seeming regret, many of the émigré units were disbanded, "causing great disillusion and bitterness among the members."[14] At that point those units turned increasingly to private support channels, through the auspices of men such as Charles Willoughby and H. L. Hunt —a point that will figure prominently in this narrative.

The knot of associations that originated in the postwar period looked like this in September 1962: People whose original loyalties were to Dulles and Hoover were well positioned inside the new DIA (Carroll and Quinn), CIA counter intelligence (Angleton), the Cuban task force (Harvey), and the CIA station in Mexico City (Scott). Into this milieu now walked Richard Nagell.

Technically, I was told that the military's FOI espionage arm with which Nagell had worked in the Far East, and which extended into Germany, ceased to exist after 1960. Yet Nagell's old connections appear to have persisted. His Florida relative Robert Gambert believed that Nagell used an Army cover when he signed a CIA contract in Mexico in September 1962. The "Robert C. Nolan" pseudonym provided Nagell by FOI became his alias once again during the 1962–63 period. In one of his letters to Greenstein, Nagell wrote: "DIA is Defense Intelligence Agency. Leaving the service? Build new career at DIA. Fringe benefits and plenty of plausible denial. Apply Room 2E239, pentagon-shaped building."

In another letter, Nagell referred to "a certain right-wing clique in the Pentagon"—one that, he added, the CIA ought later to have checked in with concerning Lee Harvey Oswald.

"There was very definitely a right-wing clique in the Pentagon," according to Joseph B. Smith, a twenty-two-year veteran of CIA clandestine work in the Far East and Latin America. "The Army ran its own separate thing, and there was a big problem with [intelligence] coordination. As long as Eisenhower was president, his idea was that clandestine operators abroad had to be under one control or they'd stumble all over each other. But this broke down in the Kennedy years and, after the DIA was established, duplication on operations became more and more of a difficulty."[15]

So it appears that Kennedy's idea of what the DIA should be was exactly the opposite of what it became in reality. It also appears that Nagell may have gone to Mexico at the behest of someone in the DIA. Pentagon intelligence, I was told, was keen on examining some curious goings-on in Mexico City between the CIA and its archrival, the KGB. For, as David Phillips also wrote, "Each intelligence service in Mexico City plays the cat-and-mouse game of attempting to penetrate the other's organization. In short, the Mexican capital is a hugger-mugger metropolis of cloak-and-dagger conspirators."[16]

When Nagell went to the American embassy announcing that he had been "approached for recruiting," he also quickly came to the attention of the FBI. Traditionally, the FBI was supposed to restrict itself to domestic investigations. But just as the CIA expanded beyond its congressional mandate of strictly foreign-intelligence gathering by establishing its Domestic Operations Division, so did the FBI maintain what were called legal attachés in selected foreign localities.

One of these, as we have seen, was Tokyo. In Mexico City, the FBI's scope was quite extensive. Back in the early 1950s, the CIA agreed to allow the FBI's direct participation after Hoover accused the agency of not investigating subversion in Mexico with enough vigor. David Phillips's autobiography noted: "The FBI has had a keen interest in Mexico City since the McCarthy era, when several hundred American Communists transplanted themselves there, and also because the Soviet Embassy is a base for Russian intelligence operations into the United States."[17]

In 1977 it was revealed that the FBI's COINTELPRO operation had maintained a covert "Border Coverage Program" aimed at disrupting the Communist Party of Mexico, starting in 1961 and lasting ten years. Oversight emanated from Washington and the FBI's hush-hush Division Five counterintelligence unit, presided over by William C. Sullivan.[18]

In Nagell's Court of Claims case, where he set down that he was in personal communication with the FBI that September 1962 in Mexico City, he added: "I acted off and on as a confidential informant for the Federal Bureau of Investigation, both at my own volition and upon solicitation by the FBI."[19] Elsewhere in his correspondence, Nagell mentioned both a Harry White and a Harry Johnson as his FBI contacts in Mexico, who worked out of Room 1501 in the State Department's Legal Section of the embassy.[20] (Neither Harry was officially listed as the legal attaché, who was then Clark Anderson.)

"Most of my connection in 1962–63 was with the CIA and FBI," Nagell told me in 1977, "and there was a reason for it. Some have made it look like I was working for those people per se, but that was not the case. In Mexico City and Miami, some of my 'adventures' were done for specific reasons with a specific objective in mind. I wasn't exactly an amateur in those days, and I had a pretty good idea how things functioned on both sides. I had very high moral principles back then."[21]

By "both sides" I believe Nagell meant not only the CIA and the FBI, but also all the machinations going on among the various American intelligence agencies, the Soviets, and the Cubans. If his Mexico voyage was an assignment from Military Intelligence, its originators were undoubtedly aware of his Far Eastern counterespionage work in the FOI-CIA-KGB-GRU netherworld—perhaps even of his previous relationship with Lee Harvey Oswald, just returned to the United States from the Soviet Union.

From prison in 1966, Nagell would write to his sister: "If it does, eventually, become mandatory for me to touch upon the events leading to my sojourn in Mexico during 1962 . . . (where and when *it* began), I shall do so, but only subsequent to being granted immunity from prosecution *and* persecution. Otherwise, the interested parties will have to take my word that I was *placed* in a position to gain cognizance."[22]

Nagell has elaborated only that the principal reason for his trip to Mexico City was to touch base with three people. He described them as "those shadowy figures [out] of the past."[23]

Intrigue at the Hotel Luma

In January 1964, when the FBI was trying to force Nagell into revealing his real reasons for shooting up the El Paso bank, Nagell finally offered a signed statement. It said in part:

"In September 1962, while I was in Mexico City a representative of a foreign government proposed to me that I participate in an act; such act being a criminal offense and inimical to the best interests of the United States. At that time I refused such proposal."[24]

It is quite probable that this proposal took place at the Hotel Luma. The manager of Nagell's hotel residence was Warren Broglie, a Swiss whom Arthur Greenstein recalled as being fluent in four languages. Broglie was also in charge of hotels in Acapulco and along the Yucatán and

Baja peninsulas. One of these was owned by the reclusive billionaire Daniel K. Ludwig, another by American oilman J. Paul Getty. But the modest Luma served for twenty years as Broglie's "home base" because so much of his business was transacted in Mexico City.

Early in 1992, through another writer who had been in touch with him about Daniel Ludwig, I located Broglie in retirement in Florida. He said he did not recall Richard Nagell, but he did "get together socially with Win Scott, the head man of CIA in Mexico. The Scotts had a beautiful home in Chapultepec," Broglie recalled. "I knew what Win's position was, but we never had any conversations about it, and he never asked me any questions either." Broglie said he was also "an old friend" of George Munroe, another ex-FBI agent who in 1962 was the CIA's leading surveillance man in Mexico City, responsible for the electronic bugging of the Soviet and Cuban embassies.

And Broglie had a more-than-social acquaintance with the FBI. "We sometimes had diplomats coming in from Havana," he said. "I think the Cuban embassy felt that the Luma was sort of a hotel where there would not be too much attention, so for a long time they used the hotel to put people up. And maybe some people stayed there from Eastern Europe, too. Then I was asked by the United States embassy to inform them on who was coming. Which I did. I used to talk to one of the FBI's assistants to the legal attaché. Eventually my front office manager must have advised the Cubans I was informing, because suddenly they stopped coming, which I didn't mind either."[25]

Broglie's bartender and relief headwaiter at the Luma was Franz Waehauf. Of German heritage, he had served in the German military's merchant marine during World War II, afterward ending up in Mexico. Though he never gained Mexican citizenship, Waehauf stayed on. By 1962 he had been working at the Luma for more than a decade.[26]

Greenstein recalled Waehauf as being "quite Teutonic in appearance. The resemblance I draw is with the old advertising figure for Stroehman's bread. Franz was medium height, big-boned, and had noticeable hair loss. He tended to speak softly. He spoke English and Spanish well, but with a German accent. I thought of him as middle-aged. I never saw the personality of Franz open up, though Nagell spoke of him as a real nice guy. Nagell and he did a lot of whispering over the bar of the lounge. They were pretty chummy."

It was Waehauf, Greenstein remembered, who "told Nagell how he could dispose of his car—take it to the right place where they'll dismantle it for parts, thus beating the stiff import duty. He felt this would be of help to Nagell in his plan to renounce his citizenship. But according to what Nagell told me, the U.S. embassy was telling him that you were allowed to renounce citizenship only in the continental U.S.A.—which was why he hadn't accomplished it."

Greenstein added: "Later Nagell glibly pigeonholed Franz, or just classified him, saying, 'You know, he's Czech intelligence.'"

Czechoslovakia was, then and since, the official intermediary between the Castro government and the United States. In Washington, Cuba maintained a handful of diplomats out of the Czech embassy. In Mexico City, the Czechs' formal staff was relatively small. But according to Philip Agee, five of its eight diplomats were known or suspected intelligence officers. "This intelligence mission," Agee writes, "is also thought to be targeted against the U.S. Embassy and against objectives in the U.S. proper. As elsewhere they are considered to be an auxiliary service of the Soviets. . . ."[27]

Among several other people, including Oswald, Nagell in 1974 specifically identified Waehauf as having been among the subjects of his investigation after signing a contract with the CIA in the fall of 1962.[28] Luma manager Broglie told me that while he never suspected Waehauf of being a spy, he had dismissed the bartender from his employ sometime around 1965. "I noticed that the bar revenue was not up to par," said Broglie, "so I hired an American hotel detective who posed as a client with his wife, sat in the bar, and caught Franz stealing. I had to fire him, and I lost track of him after that."

Fateful Encounter

Since Nagell has been vague about providing a precise chronology, all that can be known for sure is that someone—perhaps Franz Waehauf—sought to "recruit" him before Nagell made his strange citizen-renunciation attempt at the American embassy. Whether he made direct contact with the CIA before or after his embassy visit is unclear. But one night that September of 1962, Art Greenstein remembers Nagell inviting him along to a party. It was hosted by a group of young women from the Chilean and Colombian embassies, and Greenstein's eyes still light up when he remembers it: "I never saw so many girls."

Greenstein also noticed someone else, a tall American who wore glasses and looked to be in his midthirties. The man introduced himself to Greenstein as "Bob" and said he was a salesman or representative of an American book publisher. Bob spoke "gringo Spanish in an overly slow but grammatically correct way," Greenstein remembered. "The guy was coming on like a real bon vivant, kissing the girls and drinking fairly heavily. But in his remarks he seemed to be a right-wing-type individual."

According to the brief statements Nagell has been willing to make about that night at the party, Bob told him that "he'd been with me in Japan," and they had spent some time together conversing in the Japanese language. Either that night or subsequently, they would discuss Nagell's involvement in the CIA's attempt to get Soviet colonel Nikolai Eroshkin to defect in Tokyo, and Nagell's relationship with Professor Chikao Fujisawa.[29] In such a context it was quite conceivable that Oswald's name would have come up, though Nagell never said so directly.

This was Greenstein's only encounter with Bob. "Afterwards, Nagell made some disparaging remarks about him to me. He said something like, 'There's a typical CIA agent.' "

Nagell said only that Bob would become, for the next year, his CIA "contact." Nagell was instructed to take the bait offered by "a foreign government." Melvin Beck, an undercover CIA agent in Mexico City between 1962 and 1967, later described such assignments in his book *Secret Contenders: The Myth of Cold War Counterintelligence:*

> Mexico City Station's efforts against the Soviets had long emphasized double agent operations, from which it might be learned to what extent the KGB or GRU were pressing their agents to penetrate U.S. circles, or to collect information on sensitive U.S. activities in Mexico or the United States. . . . At times of international stress, flash points of conflict or confrontation, or threatening moves of Soviet policy and power in the world arena, it is the custom to use the double agent operational window on the Soviets to elicit a "Soviet" view of the disturbing events. The theory is that a clever agent (or case officer) will be able to extract inside information from his Soviet contact.[30]

Nagell says that the CIA "double agent" mission he was about to embark on involved his "participation in a 'disinformation' project directed against the Soviet embassy at Mexico City in 1962 at the onset of the so-called Cuban Missile Crisis." This participation, he added, led to his "later indirect involvement in a conspiracy to assassinate President Kennedy and other highly placed government officials in September 1963."[31]

Nagell has said little more about the man who sent him on his mission, except that Bob was a "subordinate" CIA officer whose ultimate reporting reached all the way up to Desmond FitzGerald in the CIA hierarchy. If Nagell knew Bob's last name, he has never revealed it. Nor have I been able to ascertain it, although in contacting as many ex-CIA people as were willing to talk to me, I learned that FitzGerald did indeed bring along quite a few of his Far Eastern staff when he shifted over to supervising anti-Castro activities during the Cuban Missile Crisis period.[32]

Whoever Bob was, he would have worked closely with David Phillips, who was running the CIA's covert action section in Mexico City when Nagell arrived there. Phillips, a tall, ruggedly handsome Texan who was thirty-nine years old in 1962, had been the agency's propaganda specialist for the Bay of Pigs. After coming to Mexico in mid-1961, he was known to have "run" four of the CIA's five full-time "disinformation" agents.[33] Since Phillips had never served in the Far East, I ruled out that he was Nagell's contact. But Nagell strongly hinted in a letter to Greenstein that Phillips had been an "accomplice" in the project. And in Phillips's autobiography I came across an intriguing story dating from his tenure in Mexico.

It concerned a "middle-grade United States military officer" whom Phillips had learned badly needed money, was locked into a bad marriage from which "he could not extricate himself," and who had offered to provide the Cuban embassy "important information on United States military matters." Such information, Phillips says he learned from his sources, was then to be passed along to the Soviets.

Phillips did not name the "military officer," who sounded hauntingly like Nagell after he left his Japanese wife and lost his job in Southern California in 1962. Nor did Phillips provide the specific date of this event. He wrote only that he had in turn alerted Clark Anderson, the FBI's legal attaché in Mexico City.

In 1977 I telephoned Phillips and asked him about this story. "Yeah, I know who the man was," Phillips said, "but I have no idea what happened to him." Could you describe what he looked like? I asked. "Well, that's getting a little tricky," Phillips replied, "because we're talking about a case now that became an FBI case. It's their baby and not mine."[34]

I was never able to find out whether the officer he described was Nagell, or to determine why Phillips told the story. But I wondered whether it could have been a subtle means by a CIA propaganda expert of putting out a message, or of establishing a form of "plausible denial" for something else he may have known—for, as we shall see, Nagell is not the only one to connect David Phillips to the Oswald saga.

Phillips, who was based in Mexico until 1965, became a good friend of CIA station chief Winston Scott. So was Warren Broglie, manager of the Hotel Luma. According to Scott's family, Scott was also very close to Desmond FitzGerald. Several former CIA officials told me that FitzGerald often traveled to Mexico City in 1962–63 from his Langley, Virginia, headquarters base. "A piece of Win died with Des," one of Scott's relatives told me, referring to FitzGerald's death in 1967.

While Nagell never mentioned Scott by name concerning his own CIA involvement, he did tell me in 1977: "The CIA station chief worked out of the American embassy. I wrote his name down the other day, so I wouldn't forget it. So many guys didn't use cover names, they used their own names." When I pressed Nagell whether it was the CIA station chief he was primarily involved with, he responded that it wasn't any one individual. He hastened to emphasize that FitzGerald was the overall head of the CIA's Latin American projects.[35]

It is doubtful that anything as sensitive as Nagell's "double agent" role could have occurred without being cleared by Scott, who, as ex-CIA official Joseph Smith put it, "ran a little principality there. Win Scott became *the* figure in Mexico for years. He was quite an operator, with all sorts of fascinating contacts."[36]

James E. Flannery, who served under Scott and Phillips in Mexico City in 1964–65, added: "Win's contacts were better than the [U.S.] ambassador's usually. I don't know that the State Department liked him too much, because the fact he had so many contacts in the Mexican government made them feel like he was treading on their territory. Win did have a top deputy but, like most guys that are pretty strong chiefs, he didn't use him much. And people didn't bother him much down there in Mexico City. He was sort of like Des [FitzGerald], in a way. He would give you guidance if you came around asking for it. But mostly he turned you loose, let you make your own mistakes and your own victories."[37]

Separate Agendas: Kennedy vs. the Pentagon/CIA

In several interviews and letters, Nagell recounted what happened when, as instructed by his CIA contact Bob sometime in September 1962, he made contact with the Soviets: "I was really involved heavy with the so-called Cuban Missile Crisis. The onset of it was back in July. In my opinion the first Soviet IRBMs (or at least their launching mechanisms) were delivered in late June or early July 1962. *Before* the crisis, the chief Soviet concern (KGB's EEI) was to determine whether or not the U.S.A. would 'act out' or actually conduct a naval blockade, and if so, whether any attempt would be made to board a Soviet ship, any ship, of course including those transporting missiles."[38]

IRBM stands for intermediate-range ballistic missiles. The phrase "EEI," I discovered later, stands for "essential elements of information." As a former Military Intelligence officer, Wayne Barker, described it to me: "It's a military term. When you have agents or units, you're giving them EEI. You don't just tell them to go out and gather intelligence, but specifically what you want them to find: like what units are out there, where are they stationed, and so on."[39]

His own CIA role, Nagell became convinced, was part of "the Pentagon's hopes" to spark a military confrontation with Cuba.

There is quite a bit of historical evidence to back up Nagell's assertions —about both the midsummer "onset" of the Cuban Missile Crisis, and the Pentagon/CIA behind-scenes plans. In July 1962, harbor activity in Cuba was known by U.S. intelligence to have accelerated—large numbers of Soviet freighters arriving with unknown cargoes and wide hatches riding high in the water. At about the same time, the Defense Department drafted a memo listing a number of steps that might involve U.S. military intervention in Cuba. One such step was to "assassinate Castro and his handful of top men."

As revealed by Senate investigations in the mid-1970s, on August 10, 1962, there was a meeting of "Operation MONGOOSE," an interagency team assigned to draw up plans against the Castro government. According to the 1975 testimony of several former Kennedy administration officials, the "liquidation" of Castro and other Cuban leaders was put on the table and pushed hard by elements of the CIA and the Pentagon.[40]

The MONGOOSE operations chief, Major General Edward Lansdale, would recall for the Senate investigators: "At the time, we were getting intelligence accumulating very quickly of something very different taking place in Cuba than we had expected, which was the Soviet technicians starting to come in and the possibilities of Soviet missiles being placed there."[41]

In May 1976 I went to interview Lansdale at his home in McLean, Virginia. He was a legend in intelligence circles. Lansdale had been a psychological warfare specialist under Charles Willoughby in World War II, rising to become head of military intelligence in the Philippines by war's end.[42] In the 1950s he operated as a CIA officer in the Philippines and Vietnam, using an Air Force cover. Lansdale was so auspicious that no less than *three* novels had used him as a central character (Graham Greene's 1955 *The Quiet American,* William J. Lederer and Eugene Burdick's 1958 *The Ugly American,* and Jean Lartéguy's 1965 *Yellow Fever*).[43] In the early 1960s, Lansdale's chief arena of responsibility shifted to Cuban affairs. When I met him, Lansdale was retired and in his late sixties, but he still cut a dashing figure. While his pretty Filipino wife passed in and out of the room and his big black Labrador dog panted into my tape recorder, Lansdale told an intriguing tale of his private war with the CIA.

Lansdale admitted that his own "contingency planning" had included the possibility of assassinating Castro. "Apparently you shouldn't have such horrible thoughts, but at the time we were justifiably concerned," he said. "The U.S. intelligence flow started giving indications very early about missile bases going in there—considerably earlier than what's been indicated in some of these books. I know they were getting bases ready long before the crisis came."

My area of strongest curiosity was the CIA's agenda during the period right before the Cuban Missile Crisis. According to Lansdale, the CIA deeply resented his hegemony over the MONGOOSE program and close relationship with Robert Kennedy. "They wanted to escalate on the commando-type actions," Lansdale said, "which I felt merely stirred things up and didn't lead in any real direction. There were some things I tried to call off and wrote orders in *writing* to do so, but they were carried out anyhow. Some of the economic disrupting the CIA planned would merely cause suffering by the Cuban people, and I thought that was a stupid way of doing things. That's when I got the label of not knowing what I was doing, because I was trying to stop them."

In particular opposition to Lansdale was FitzGerald's predecessor as the CIA's Cuban affairs chief, ex-FBI man William Harvey. "President Kennedy was teasing me once about being a kind of James Bond," Lansdale reminisced. "I said, 'Oh, no, there's another guy who thinks he's James Bond. Would you like to meet him?' And he said, 'Oh, I sure would!' So I explained that William Harvey was working on these Cuban operations for the agency, and I'd bring him in.

"Harvey was convinced that the enemy was after him, so he always went everywhere armed. When we arrived at the White House, I'd forgotten that he carried a gun in a belt in the small of his back. Just as we were going in to see the president, I remembered. I whispered, 'Hey, if you've got your gun there, the Secret Service are all around and they probably have metal detectors. There'll be a loud bell ringing and this could be *very* embarrassing.' So he started taking his gun off right there. And there I was alerting the Secret Service—'Don't shoot this guy, he's just getting rid of it!' Harvey had forgotten he had it, it was so much a part of his clothing."

And what did Kennedy think of William Harvey? "He thought I was pulling his leg. He told me later, 'Ahhhhh, that wasn't James Bond.'" There was a slight pause before Lansdale resumed. "That was part of the conditioning of the period, you know, the novels and the espionage. I know a whole lot of the CIA people were acting out parts and doing things only because it was expected of them. Harvey was one. He was of a type I didn't ever quite trust, and I think it was mutual.

"Harvey played his cards very close to his breast, with me and also his superiors. At times I'd go in and talk about things with his bosses and just draw blanks." As for John McCone, the Kennedy-appointed replacement for Dulles, Lansdale believed "he didn't know enough about what was going on in the agency to take an opinion. He just didn't have that much say in things, frankly."

The battle lines within the administration were being drawn by the late summer of 1962. On August 22, a British freighter under lease to the Soviets crept into a harbor in San Juan, Puerto Rico, for repairs. Headed for a Soviet port and carrying eighty thousand bags of Cuban sugar, the ship had damaged its propeller on a reef. Because of an American embargo on Cuban imports, the sugar was temporarily placed under bond in a customs warehouse while the freighter was in drydock. CIA agents surreptitiously entered the customs shed and contaminated the sugar with a purportedly harmless—but unpalatable—substance. When a White House official came upon an intelligence report about the incident, President Kennedy was furious. Such an operation, he raged, had taken place on our territory and could set a terrible precedent for chemical sabotage. To the CIA's chagrin, Kennedy ordered the doctored sugar not be allowed to leave Puerto Rico.[44]

On September 5, Kennedy aide Arthur Schlesinger, Jr., wrote the president a memo expressing concern about "intelligence reports describing plans for an uprising inside Cuba in the next few weeks." Schlesinger cautioned the president that if the United States supported this, "we would find ourselves in a difficult war in which, so far as we can presently tell, the majority of Cubans (and very likely the majority of the nations of the world) would be against us. . . . It is indispensable to be sure that no one down the line is encouraging the Cubans into rash action." Kennedy responded in writing: "I know of no planned 'uprising in Cuba within the next few weeks.' Would you send me the intelligence reports to which you refer. In any case, I will discuss the matter with the CIA."[45]

Clearly, the CIA was keeping its plans hidden from the president. For a long time, the majority of high-level opinion in the American government was that the missile buildup in Cuba was purely defensive. On September 8 and 15, the first two *known* secret shipments of offensive nuclear missiles arrived by Soviet freighters in Havana Harbor. But according to the extant historical record, it would be almost another month before U-2 spy plane photographs verified the existence of launching sites. Yet, as early as October 1, it is now known that the Pentagon issued secret orders for an air strike option of "maximum readiness" against Cuba by October 20.[46]

Nikita Khrushchev, in his memoirs, would quote from a conversation in Washington during the crucial late October period, between Soviet ambassador Anatoly Dobrynin and Robert Kennedy, who reportedly said: "Even though the president himself is very much against starting a war over Cuba, an irreversible chain of events could occur against his will. That is why the president is appealing directly to Chairman Khrushchev for his help in liquidating the conflict. If the situation continues much longer, the president is not sure that the military will not overthrow him and seize power. The American Army could get out of control."[47]

During the hottest period of the missile crisis, William Harvey ordered teams of more than sixty agents into Cuba to support any conventional U.S. military operations. Robert Kennedy was outraged, demanding to know on whose authority Harvey had acted, at a moment when the smallest provocation might unleash a nuclear war. According to Kennedy, Harvey replied that "we planned it because the military wanted it done." But when the attorney general questioned the Pentagon, they claimed not to know about Harvey's operation. It was after this that FitzGerald was moved in to replace Harvey on the Cuban task force. James Angleton found the ex-FBI man a new post, as CIA station chief in Rome.[48]

Nagell and the Cuban Missile Crisis

Harvey's private maneuvering brings us back to a letter from Nagell written in 1976. "I'm sure that somebody wanted to start a small war," he wrote. "The disinformation project in which I was engaged had more to do with the blockade than the IRBMs themselves, at least so I felt."[49] Nagell would tell me in 1984 that everything had hinged, from the CIA side, on whether the Soviets would try to run an American naval blockade and, from the Soviet side, on whether we would board their ships. From the Soviet perspective, he added, it was a matter of maintaining their integrity. Throughout history, boarding another nation's ship has generally been equivalent to a declaration of war.[50]

"The CIA was in this up to their asses," according to Nagell. "But there was no crisis, not in reality. This had all been settled, all taken care of, by the time Kennedy gave his famous speech." Nagell added that the Soviets "had some guy in Washington—not Ambassador Dobrynin—playing footsies with the top people." Later he elaborated that this was a high-level KGB official who was in direct communication with the Kennedys.[51]

When Nagell first mentioned this to me in 1978, it was not widely known that Robert Kennedy had established a relationship in 1961 with Georgi Bolshakov. Using the cover designation of "information secretary" at the Soviet embassy, Bolshakov was really Khrushchev's personal KGB middleman with the Kennedys. (The Bolshakov-Kennedy liaisons were first publicly revealed in Arthur M. Schlesinger, Jr.'s, 1978 book *Robert Kennedy and His Times*.)[52]

Nagell would not be more specific about his own participation in the Cuban Missile Crisis. I was never able to figure out what he meant by saying that everything had been "settled" *before* Kennedy's frightening speech to the American people on October 22, 1962, announcing the presence of Soviet offensive missiles in Cuba. Nagell seemed to imply that Soviet intelligence had cut some kind of private deal. How he could possibly have known of such a thing, if it transpired, remains very much a question.

But this much seemed clear enough: Nagell had very strong sources inside Soviet intelligence circles. And he appears to have been a key player in behind-the-scenes operations in the pivotal Mexico arena. In 1976 I had written asking Nagell to respond to a claim then being recirculated that the Russians didn't hold up their end of the bargain; that some missiles had actually remained in Cuba after the Kennedy-Khrushchev agreement that ended the crisis.

Nagell wrote back that this was extremely unlikely: ". . . the most offensive of the 'offensive' missiles were taken out during the 'Crisis.' (Translation: visible defensive missiles = offensive missiles.) And why not? The USSR accomplished precisely what it set out to accomplish by putting missiles in Cuba in the first place: (1) it forced the USA to withdraw its missiles from Turkey, and (2) it achieved a guarantee that Cuba would not be invaded by US forces, at least not during the tenure of the Kennedy administration. . . ."

Nagell concluded: "At this point in time, and until these most secret agreements are made public, one can only be certain that both sides enacted concessions . . . and that the USSR did not back down anymore than the USA."[53]

It would be more than a decade after Nagell's letter before some of those "most secret agreements" began to be discussed openly. At a series of meetings between Americans and Soviets who had been part of the negotiations surrounding the Cuban Missile Crisis, it became obvious that *both* sides "blinked"—and blinked hard—in the famous "eyeball-to-eyeball" confrontation where JFK was long thought to have held a firm upper hand over Khrushchev. In exchange for Kennedy's private assurances that the United States would withdraw all missiles in Turkey and abandon any effort to overthrow Castro, the Soviets turned back all ships approaching Cuba and pulled their missiles out.[54]

Had Kennedy's military advisers had their way and bombed out the Soviet missile sites, we would likely have witnessed a devastating nuclear war. As it was, the Cuban Missile Crisis marked the beginning of a real understanding between Kennedy and Khrushchev, the first thaw in the Cold War since 1945. This would result, in August 1963, in the signing of a historic treaty that ended atmospheric testing of nuclear weapons.

But the aftermath of the Cuban Missile Crisis marked something else as well: the beginning of a plot to assassinate the president, who had quietly come to terms with the Soviets. The first people to find out about the plot, as far as Richard Nagell knew, were the KGB.

Summary

With Nagell's arrival in Mexico City, we enter a realm of intrigue whose ramifications lead directly to the death of a president. The Cuban Missile Crisis looms on the horizon, and the split between the Kennedy administration and the Pentagon/CIA "old guard" is rising to the surface. Even Major General Edward Lansdale, a hard-line anti-Communist through the 1950s, finds himself aligned with the Kennedys against forces looking to create what Nagell viewed as an attempt to spark a war over Cuba.

After being approached, apparently by the Soviets, Nagell goes into action: making a phony attempt to renounce his citizenship at the U.S. embassy, meeting with a CIA official known only as "Bob," receiving instructions to take the bait and go back to the Soviets as a double agent. This is part of a CIA "disinformation project" targeted at the Soviets. On the periphery are two CIA officials who will come to play a much larger role as our story unfolds: station chief Winston Scott, and covert-action specialist David Phillips. Nor is this the last we will hear of the Hotel Luma, a "spy hotel" whose manager is a friend of station chief Scott and whose bartender is a Czech intelligence operative.

In the background are the Defense Intelligence Agency, which seems to have dispatched Nagell to Mexico in the first place, and the FBI, to which Nagell will make continual "confidential" reports over the ensuing months. Precisely what Nagell's role was in the Cuban Missile Crisis is yet unknown—but his knowledge of Soviet concerns about the naval blockade adds a new dimension to that pivotal historical event. Whether a private, still-secret preliminary agreement was made between Kennedy and the Soviets is a tantalizing possibility for future scholars to examine.

Chapter Ten

Nagell's Soviet Assignments; Oswald's Return: June–December 1962

Languishing in prison in September 1967, Richard Nagell first put on record the culmination of his autumn sojourn in Mexico five years before. It was in a letter to Arthur Greenstein, and by using a series of "coded" terms, Nagell avoided giving too much away. Later this letter would be pored over by a number of people looking to crack the Kennedy assassination. I, too, eventually added my name to the list of would-be code-breakers. And based on what I had learned directly from Nagell, I was finally able to decipher his meaning. It is offered here just as he wrote it, with my interpretations in brackets where necessary:

It seems that during the first week of October [1962] XYZ [Nagell's Soviet contact] had gotten word or picked up a rumor to the effect that the subject so often adduced to in my memos [the assassination of President Kennedy] was being discussed in earnest by members of a certain group which had branch offices, or affiliates, located in D.F. [Distrito

Federale, or Mexico City] and the United States, besides other places. Its headquarters or main base might have been situated in D.F. also, though I'm not sure. This group, hereinafter referred to as "Bravo," in lieu of its proper designation was, according to XYZ, receiving financial support from La Agencia [the CIA] . . . for what effort or purpose, I had absolutely no idea. I did know, however, that D.F.-Bravo was then engaged in little more than such random ventures as tossing homemade bombs (one of which failed to explode) at or near the facilities occupied by its foe [the Cuban embassy]. And it was this fact, I suppose, that caused a certain amount of anxiety amongst XYZ's *superiors*, lest the "earnest discussions" give form to something more tangible than talk (a potential well-conceived in view of Bravo's demonstrated capacity for violence) during a period when another situation [the Cuban Missile Crisis] was becoming increasingly tense. Not that XYZ's superiors wanted Bravo's purported objective accomplished at any time, mind you; I'm only expounding the sensitivity of things, the priority of things, as I saw them.

Anyway, my new assignment related to this, to assist in ascertaining whether or not the rumor was true, and, if it was, to further ascertain the identities of those involved, the motive, method, etc., etc. It was obvious that I wasn't the only guy saddled with this task, since I had barely started (initiating an inquiry) when I was called to the diplomatic hinterlands [the Soviet embassy]—an unprecedented move in my circumstances—and told the rumor was indeed true, and briefed and furnished a number of photographs and instructed to return to the U.S. This was the cause of my hasty departure from D.F., the cause that I was not able to tell you as we sat munching tacos in that Greasy Spoon on October 19.[1]

Early in 1976, I learned from Nagell what "Bravo" really was. I had sent him a ten-page outline of what I believed were the essential elements of his story, and he mailed it back with numerous typed corrections. In a section I titled "The Identity of the Conspirators," I had written this sentence: "In Mexico, one code name for the group may have been 'Bravo.'" Nagell crossed out the word "code" and also eliminated the "Bravo" reference. Above it he wrote "Alpha 66."[2]

Established in the summer of 1962, Alpha 66 was a well-known Cuban exile organization "with a demonstrated capacity for violence," originally set up and funded under the aegis of the CIA. The first public references to the group, which I found in *The New York Times* from that September, described its "300-man force scattered in small units throughout the Caribbean" and "a war chest of $100,000 in cash and material to carry on its fight" against Castro. As the Cuban Missile Crisis accelerated all through the month, Alpha 66 made a series of hit-and-run attacks on ships carrying supplies to Cuba, including three British vessels. Alpha 66's Miami and Puerto Rico-based leader was identified as Antonio Veciana, "chief of the movement's 'action group' in the anti-Castro underground."[3]

The Soviet KGB and GRU comprised a remarkable intelligence network, and it was not surprising that one of these might have gotten wind of such a scheme against the president. But how much did the CIA know? Or the Pentagon? Or the FBI? And how could Nagell be certain he wasn't being set up himself? The Soviets must at least have suspected that he was a dispatched CIA agent playing a "double" role. Here was the way counter intelligence expert Melvin Beck described such situations in *Secret Contenders:*

> Any case officer contemplating a double agent operation is convinced, or should be, that the opposition probably knows that he is an intelligence officer of the CIA. Indeed, there is always the tantalizing possibility that the walk-in agent is a "plant." . . . If so, that only heightens the competition. What ensues may be likened to a chess game, American Intelligence Service versus Russian Intelligence Service, in which moves and countermoves are studied, projected, and applied. That is probably the simplest description of what double agent operations are—games. . . .
>
> The course of a double agent operation is fairly well charted. It will wax or wane as the case officers on both sides assess the relative costs involved, or, put another way, the relative damage to the other side. Any move by the opposition through "his" agent to tie up the resources of the other side, to instigate costly investigations, to drain money, to pass along "deception" information, etc., is viewed with the suspicion it deserves. The countering case officer will then try to turn the operation in a direction that will have the same effect on the opposing service. . . .[4]

In this instance, the "games" were suddenly being played for the highest of stakes.

Oswald's Welcoming Committee

Monitoring an assassination plot against JFK was not the only assignment Nagell received from the Soviets in October 1962. He was also told to check into a young "defector" who had returned from the USSR four months before. "Oswald was under intermittent surveillance since the day he arrived back in the United States," Nagell told me in 1975.

Soviet intelligence, according to Nagell, "was more interested in Oswald than the Americans. The reason was, when he was in the Soviet Union, he was considered emotionally unstable—prone to commit some act that could bring embarrassment to the Soviet Union. This was before he was in *fact* involved in anything like that."

Around mid-October 1962, the week prior to Nagell's departure from Mexico, he met again with his Soviet contact. "I received instructions about Oswald, and was shown his photograph. But it had nothing to do with Kennedy."[5]

Not yet. Not for some months to come. At that time, Nagell's observations of Oswald and a Kennedy-aimed assassination plot were entirely separate entities. How they came to coincide will be the central theme of the remainder of this book.

Lee and Marina had departed the Soviet Union on June 2, 1962, spending two unexplained days in Amsterdam. When their ship docked in New York, they were met by Spas T. Raikin, whom the Warren Commission described as "a representative of a travelers' aid society which had been contacted by the Department of State." Raikin, as assassination researcher Peter Dale Scott uncovered, was also the secretary-general of a powerful lobbying faction of the international right-wing American Friends of Anti-Bolshevik Nations (ABN). Scott came across Raikin's name in a 1960 publication of the Asian People's Anti-Communist League (APACL), with which the lobbyist was in personal contact.[6]

The ABN had its roots in the pre-World War II Ukraine, where Hitler viewed a group of nationalists as potential allies that might rise up against their Soviet state. The Ukrainian group had an ideology similar to Nazism —virulent hatred of Jews, fanatical racism against ethnic Poles and Russians. Sure enough, in 1941 a large Ukrainian force wearing Wehrmacht uniforms carried out guerrilla warfare in aiding the German invasion of their territory. The "Nightingales," as they were called, assisted in massive exterminations of Jews in the war-torn Ukraine.

With Hitler's defeat in 1945, thousands of these Nazi collaborators ended up in displaced-persons camps administered by the British and Americans. Here, the Army CIC, the SSU, and then its successor CIA recruited "agent candidates." The ABN was formed in 1946, claiming its direct descent from the Committee of Subjugated Nations, formed during the war by Hitler's allies and dominated by Ukrainians. "That many of us fought on the German side against Russian imperialism and Bolshevism was in our national interest," stated a 1960 ABN pamphlet.

By then the ABN, as described by Russ Bellant in his 1988 book *Old Nazis, the New Right, and the Republican Party,* was "the high council for the expatriate nationalist groups that formed the police, military, and militia units that worked with Hitler during World War II." Its fascist underground existed in Hungary, Bulgaria, Romania, the Ukraine, the Baltics, and other Eastern European regions. Its primary focus was psychological and political warfare.

The ABN's founder and leader was Jaroslaw Stetzko, who in 1941 had announced plans to unite with Hitler to "create a New Order in Europe and throughout the world." In 1956, 1957, and 1961 Stetzko journeyed to Taiwan to pursue his long-standing alliance with Chiang Kai-shek and also attended meetings of the APACL.[7] Based in Munich, he often came to visit the ABN branch in New York, where Oswald's "greeter," Spas Raikin, worked with the "American Friends" group. And on the masthead of retired major general Charles Willoughby's *Foreign Intelligence Digest,* Stetzko was listed as his ABN correspondent.

In the United States, Willoughby and Lev Dobriansky were the two leading supporters of the ABN. As researcher Scott noted, both men were associated with U.S. private industry's own espionage network, the American Security Council (ASC), formed by ex-FBI agents, and with interlocking right-wing organizations such as the Young Americans for Freedom Advisory Board. Both Willoughby and Dobriansky were violently opposed to what they considered the pro-Soviet sympathies of the CIA, and had connections with the FBI, the Army, and the Army Reserve.

Dobriansky, a Ukrainian-American and an OSS officer in Germany during World War II, was chairman of the National Captive Nations Committee. He served in 1959–60 as the Republican National Committee's chairman of the Ethnic/Nationalities/Heritage Groups Division. An instructor at the Army's National War College, in 1958 Dobriansky had been named a lieutenant colonel in the U.S. Army Reserve's mysterious 352nd Division for "Military Government Civil Affairs." This was, according to *The Ukrainian Bulletin,* the only such reserve unit of its kind, concerning itself "with military government administration and supervision over countries with populations over 25 million people."[8]

Also in 1958, in Mexico City, both Dobriansky and Stetzko were elected members of a fifteen-man steering committee for a new World Anti-Communist Congress for Freedom and Liberation. Serving on the same board were representatives from numerous Asian and Latin American countries and former Nazi Abwehr officer Fritz Cramer. Alfred Gielen, once a Nazi publicist for Hitler's propaganda secretary, Joseph Goebbels, was named the committee's "regional secretary" for Europe. (Gielen, too, was a Willoughby overseas associate.) Appointed press secretary was Cuba's Salvador Díaz Verson, a military intelligence officer in the pre-Batista government of Carlos Prio Socarras.[9] Díaz Verson lived in Mexico City, where he allegedly became one of David Phillips's agents. After the Kennedy assassination Díaz Verson was among the major rumor distributors of an Oswald link to Fidel Castro.[10]

By 1962, both this anti-Communist alliance and the ABN in particular were profoundly disenchanted with the Kennedy State Department. Secretary Dean Rusk opposed the demands of Spas T. Raikin's American

Friends-ABN for a permanent congressional Captive Nations Committee, not wanting to place the administration "in the undesirable position of seeming to advocate the dismemberment of a historical state" [the USSR]. Bitter polemics ensued—not only over the issue of "rolling back" communism in Eastern Europe, but also over the ABN's desire to create a permanent "Volunteer Freedom Corps" (or United States-supported foreign legion) and an academy for psychological warfare training. Both the APACL and the ASC assisted in the ABN's American lobbying effort, to no avail.[11]

Such was the backdrop for Spas Raikin's meeting the returning Oswalds at New York Harbor in June 1962. When I located Raikin, now a retired professor in Pennsylvania, by phone early in 1992, he insisted that at the time he "was keeping ABN out of my professional life." He did say that he found it quite strange that no official U.S. government agency was on hand to meet the returning defector.

As Raikin told the story, "Oswald tried to avoid me on the ship. He was being paged and asked to come to the purser's office, but apparently he was hiding from me. I finally found him with his Russian wife and baby out on the pier, where the baggage was. I was trying to ask him this or that, and he gave me a wrong story. He said he had been a Marine stationed in Moscow. I knew even then there was something he was holding back."

Raikin said he assisted the Oswalds in finding a hotel in New York City, "and that's where my contact with them ended."[12] The Oswalds were then taken under the wing of Cleary F'N Pierre, a Haitian professor and former employee of the Traveler's Aid Society, who said he "had simply stopped in to visit and been pressed into service since they were shorthanded." Pierre took Oswald around to welfare offices, looking for financial help in getting him back to Fort Worth. (Oswald's brother Robert ended up wiring the $200 needed for the Oswalds' flight.) Then Pierre left Oswald off that evening at Pennsylvania Station, so he could ship some excess baggage by train.[13] Raikin recalled the couple as having been carrying "quite a few pieces of luggage, seven or eight bags."[14]

In his book *Legend,* Edward Jay Epstein noted: "It is possible that Oswald took a train to Washington, D.C., that evening. A psychologist code-named Cato on assignment for the CIA claimed to have interviewed a Russian defector at the Roger Smith Hotel who resembled Oswald. Oswald could then have returned in time to visit the Welfare Department the following morning."[15]

Late on the afternoon of June 14, the day after the Oswalds' arrival in New York, they boarded a plane that stopped over in Atlanta, then went on to Dallas's Love Field.

Settling into Texas

"Not even Marina knows why I came home," Oswald's mother, Marguerite, remembers her son saying the day after his return.[16] On June 26, a Dallas FBI special agent, John Fain, visited Oswald and questioned him about his activities in the Soviet Union. An FBI report dated July 6, 1962, related that "Oswald stated that in the event he is contacted by Soviet intelligence under suspicious circumstances or otherwise, he will promptly communicate with the FBI."[17]

On July 1, Marina wrote to the Soviet embassy in Washington, giving her address in Fort Worth and requesting that her residence permit be registered. In mid-July, Oswald found employment as a metalworker at Leslie Welding. Then, early in August, he, too, wrote to the Soviet embassy, referring to Marina's having forwarded her passport for registration and requesting "any periodicals or bulletins which you may put out for the benefit of your citizens living . . . in the U.S.A."[18]

Both letters, as well as all subsequent correspondence from the Oswalds, were routed at the embassy to the attention of "Comrade Gerasimov" (as the FBI's mail-intercept program discovered). Listed as a second secretary, Vitaly A. Gerasimov was then under close scrutiny by the FBI. "Gerasimov," a CIA report later noted, "is known to have participated in clandestine meetings in this country and to have made payments for intelligence information of value to the Soviets."[19]

While Nagell allowed that, to his knowledge, the Soviets had not sought to recruit Oswald while he was on their territory, "This in no way implies that the KGB would refrain from talking to him, or listening to him talk, or keep him under surveillance subsequent to his return to the U.S.A., particularly after he sent letters to the USSR embassy in Washington."[20]

Early in August, Oswald also resubscribed to the Communist Party-U.S.A.'s The Worker newspaper and then wrote to their Trotskyite rival Socialist Workers Party, inquiring about their aims. On August 16, FBI agent Fain came to see him again.[21] Fain later claimed to have concluded that Oswald posed no security threat and closed his file. The day after that Oswald-FBI visit, coincidentally or not, Nagell had obtained his Mexican tourist card in Los Angeles, departing a week later.

According to an FBI report dated August 23, Oswald informed the bureau that "contact had been made by letter with the Soviet Embassy in Washington, D.C., to advise the embassy of his wife's current address, saying this is something that is required by Soviet law." Another FBI report, of August 30, added: "Oswald agreed to report to the FBI any information concerning contacts or attempted contacts by Soviets under suspicious circumstances."[22]

Links to an International Underground

Very soon after their homecoming, the Oswalds were favored with the attention of a small circle of wealthy Russian patrons. Nearly all of them were part of Dallas-Fort Worth's petroleum engineering industry. If the Oswalds needed a car to go shopping or be moved, the Russian families were there to lend a hand. Most of these émigrés had arrived since 1949 under the auspices of the Tolstoy Foundation, which carefully screened applicants to exclude those of "left-wing" views. The Warren Commission would learn that the Tolstoy Foundation, while maintaining a European headquarters in Munich, received "as much as $400,000 a year subsidy" from the U.S. government.[23]

The foundation's local "godfather," as George Bouhe testified before the commission, was Dallas oil millionaire (and militant anti-Communist) Paul Raigorodsky, whom Bouhe said also performed "confidential" missions in Europe for the United States. Bouhe himself was a personal accountant for Lewis MacNaughton, whose oil exploration consulting service retained numerous CIA contacts. Bouhe did "the organization work" for the Tolstoy Foundation. Others testified before the commission that he "even kept files on new arrivals."[24]

When I telephoned Bouhe in Dallas in 1976, he responded: "I helped Oswald learn a trade, the printing trade. I've been asked so many times why I associate with him. Well, I say, I was following the policy of the United States—helping the poor bastard to get on his feet. I'd hoped with a little money in the bank and a bed for the child, he would put some meat on his bones and become a different person. But all he did was criticize me for being a capitalist with white sidewall tires. I ask him, 'You really want to be chief commissar of the United States?' Lee Harvey Oswald significantly looked at me and said yes."[25]

Through the Tolstoy Foundation, the H. L. Hunt oil family is believed to have funneled considerable money into a West German-based organization known to U.S. and British intelligence as "Nightingale." As set forth by ex-CIA official Miles Copeland in his 1974 book *Without Cloak or Dagger,* shortly after World War II "aging émigrés from Czarist Russia, joined by a smaller number of disillusioned Soviet Communists, formed a near-fanatical secret organization." Though the two sides had their differences, both "saw the advantage of sticking together in dealing with the various U.S. Government agencies that took an interest in them. Their cohesiveness was greatly enhanced by the financial support they got from a multimillionaire American who was involved in a one-man crusade against 'the evils of Communism.' "

Their main value was considered to be an ability to penetrate "denied areas" of Europe's Communist world—similar to the Far Eastern mandate of FOI, as described to me by Colonel Stanley. The CIA's clandestine branch, Copeland writes, "finally got 'Nightingale' leaders to agree, with the approval of their millionaire patron, to submit to a degree of operational direction. . . . Eventually, 'Nightingale' agreed to set up operational bases in various European countries bordering on the Soviet bloc." They would undergo CIA training but would not allow members to work for the CIA as individuals "or to receive pay except through the 'Nightingale' bursar."[26]

This does not seem to be the same "Nightingale" that fell under the Nazi/Ukrainian umbrella during the war. Rather, its roots trace to the National Alliance of Solidarists (NTS), which arose a few years after the Russian Revolution of 1917. British author E. H. Cookridge has written that "it had enjoyed political and financial support from several European governments and from business concerns which had had investments and industrial plants in Tsarist Russia before the revolution, and never gave up hope that the Soviet rulers would one day be ousted."[27]

Like the Ukrainians, thousands of NTS members had collaborated with the Nazis and played a key role in creating the "Liberation" Army of Andrei Vlassov. This Soviet Army general secretly jointed forces early in the war with an anti-Bolshevist underground that had penetrated key departments of Stalin's regime. When the Germans invaded the Ukraine, instead of repulsing them, Vlassov had merged his troops with theirs—and commanded a division against his own country under the flag of the "Great White Russian Reaction for the Restoration of the Czar." After the German advance was pushed back, Vlassov established a secret alliance with Hitler's spymaster Reinhard Gehlen.

Though Vlassov was executed by Stalin after the war, it was remnants of his team—now in exile in Germany—that Gehlen made a key part of his deal with U.S. intelligence. By combining his and Vlassov's forces, Gehlen offered a postwar spy network of White Russian and Central European agents to keep tabs on the Soviets.[28] After a clandestine meeting at Fort Hunt, Virginia, in 1945, Gehlen was sent back to Europe with a $10 million budget. From that moment until his retirement in 1968, Gehlen's Munich-based Org (known as the Bundesnachrichtendienst, or BND, after 1956) became America's primary espionage source against the USSR. His operatives—numbering as many as twenty thousand, almost all of whom were former Nazis—dug the famous Berlin Tunnel and roamed all the way to Asia.[29]

So it was that on October 20, 1961, General Willoughby had dropped a line to Secretary of State Rusk. It was a warning about the crisis over the Berlin Wall, which the Soviets had just erected and which Willoughby viewed as "a contest of will between the Kremlin and the White House." MacArthur's ex-intelligence chief wanted to inform the administration about "the expellees from behind the iron curtain" who are "naturally intensely concerned with the fate of their homelands . . . and the ultimate position of Washington on this question.

"I have been in touch with this group for many years," Willoughby continued. "Their moral cause is unchallengable (the right of self determination); they are a prime source of intelligence; they have been used by all Allied intelligence agencies; they have been used by Gehlen (whom I know well) who, in turn, was used by the C.I.A.—indeed a principal source of Russian intelligence. I have had access to that information, too —but at infinitely less expense than the CIA—I entertained this group, briefly. . . ."

Willoughby was clearly referring to the Gehlen/Vlassov network. The strategy of the NTS was elitist. Its leaders believed that the "battle for men's minds" should be taken right into cadres of the Russian Army and bureaucracy, rather than appeal to dissident minorities such as the Ukrainians. So, while the NTS was said to have successfully planted agents inside the Soviet military, it did not get along with the ABN. Both the NTS and the ABN, however, collaborated closely with the Asian League. And, as we have seen, Willoughby kept a supportive hand in with each.

The NTS had at least one member in Dallas, Igor Voshinin. According to his wife, Natasha, whom I interviewed by phone in 1992, she and her husband had steered clear of Oswald from the beginning. "Igor immediately distrusted and disliked Oswald," she recalled. "You see, Russian émigrés like us, we have a sixth feeling about somebody. This came to the point where we told others not to bring Oswald to our house at all, he stays out! The reason was very simple. We had learned right away that the town in which Oswald lived in Russia had the KGB training academy. And that it took exactly two years to graduate—the exact amount of time Oswald was there. Don't you think that strange? We felt very sorry for his wife, but after we heard this, Oswald was taboo."[30]

It was certainly rumored, particularly after the assassination among the radical right, that the KGB maintained a terrorist special operations school in Minsk. But even J. Edgar Hoover could never prove it. "I don't know of any espionage school at Minsk or near Minsk," he told the Warren Commission, "and I don't know how you could find out if there ever was one because the Russians won't tell you if you asked them."[31]

Making Friends in Mexico

In Mexico City in the early autumn of 1962, Richard Nagell basically adopted his student compatriot at the Hotel Luma, Arthur Greenstein. Not only did Nagell make sure Greenstein was around to witness certain meetings, he also let him in on certain things he was up to.

As we drove through the streets of Wilmington in 1990 in his battered old car, Greenstein reflected: "There's no ready explanation overall for Nagell's actions. You could sort of push him into being an intelligence burnout; the problem is that theory doesn't hold water. You could push him into being a dedicated Communist, but that doesn't seem to hold water. Nothing really seems to hold water."

But had Greenstein suspected in Mexico that his new friend was a spy of some kind? "Well, I wouldn't have been surprised. I'm not sure who he was working for. In some of his letters to me, he mentions some of these people being triples and doubles [agents]. One time over a few bottles of Dos Equis, he even tried to sign me up."

Sign you up for what? "To be a Communist. I don't know if he was sincere, or whether it was just to prove his own credentials. I specifically told him, 'Well, I'll be happy to become a Communist, after the withering away of the state.' Knowing that was Leninist or Marxist doctrine, see. He was taken aback, as if he had studied up on it but he didn't have an answer to that one, because the state had no intentions back then of withering away.

"One little tidbit, he acted like there was one true Socialist country, but he wouldn't tell me what it was. It wasn't China. It was this little game he was playing, but he acted like that was where he would go to live. He also told me the FBI was working overseas when they weren't supposed to be. At one point, after he got out of prison, he said to me, 'I've been running rings around the FBI for years.' "

At the Latin embassy party where Greenstein met "Bob"—and observed Nagell in intense conversation with the alleged book salesman—there was someone else in attendance. "Her name was Maria del Carmen," Greenstein remembered. "She acted like she was infatuated with Nagell, or at least infatuated with his money. She was like a party girl, a Cuban national of about twenty-five. She had a good office job with the Mexican government. Nagell liked Carmen, because he said, 'She's right there.' I thought what he meant by that was, she was really on the left. Nagell said to me, I think later, that their relationship was not romantic, but that she was with Cuban intelligence and was working with him on some kind of unspecified project."

At a meeting with Nagell in 1978, I first raised the subject of Maria del Carmen. Nagell was taken aback—the only time I saw him more on edge was when I had brought up my surmise on the origin of the "Hidell" alias. He asked where I had gotten that name. I told him I came across it in attorney Fensterwald's files, in one of his prison letters to Greenstein. Nagell shrugged and offered a brief response. "She wasn't CIA," he said. "If she was ever CIA, she wasn't *really* CIA. She was a Cuban who worked for the Mexican Treasury Department, and she was pro-Cuban."[32]

I knew, from another of his prison messages, that Maria del Carmen was well traveled during the 1962–63 period. Nagell specifically mentioned her making trips to Miami, New York, and Montreal. She was obviously a contact for Nagell in some fashion. Over the years, I decided to toss out her name in interviews with a few other sources. It was a fishing expedition, and my line did not come up slack.

In 1990 I paid a visit to former CIA officer Barney Hidalgo in Pennsylvania. After an eighteen-year career, he was said to have left the CIA to become a fireman in 1970, breeding Japanese goldfish in his spare time. When I arrived at Hidalgo's lakeside retirement home, the short, dark-complected former undercover operative began by informing me that he planned to write a book titled *Hey Spic!* Explained Hidalgo: "I am a spic. I'm just so tired of hearing, 'Oh, I'm a minority. Why don't they teach me in my native tongue?' It's going to be an extremely controversial book, friends will become enemies, I'm sure."

Our conversation was wide-ranging, embellished by numerous stories of Hidalgo's "dirty tricks" cooked up against the Castro regime. He had used a Military Intelligence cover while serving in counter intelligence, primarily out of the CIA's JM/WAVE station in Miami. He was a case officer for the "ATOMS," former members of the Bay of Pigs invasion force. "In fact, I named it Brigade 2506," Hidalgo said. This man of Cuban heritage also made regular journeys "down to and past the [Florida] Keys," trying to determine which of the exiles then coming out of Cuba were "true refugees, dope smugglers, or Castro operatives."

Desmond FitzGerald was his superior officer at headquarters, but FitzGerald spent considerable time on the road. "He didn't know what I was doing, and I didn't care to know what he was doing," Hidalgo commented. It was the same, Hidalgo said, with his "good friend" David Phillips in Mexico City: "I didn't know Phillips's agents, and he didn't know mine."

Had Hidalgo spent much time in Mexico during the early 1960s? After the Bay of Pigs, he replied that he had made "certain trips," including those to Mexico City. "My reason for going there was to meet a woman agent. In addition to her being part of our embassy group or conclave that was doing Cuban work, she was a high member of the Communist Party in Mexico."

Much later in the interview, I brought up the name of Maria del Carmen. "Yeah, well, that's the one that was mixed up in—she was an 'in' for me in the Communist Party in Mexico City. She was in her early twenties. I just met her in a park one day. She played the part of a hooker and I played the part of a guy picking her up, so that nobody was aware of what was going on. We drove off to a safe house, where she gave me all the details I needed.

"What I was doing there simply was an attack on the Communist Party of the U.S.A. My specialty. When I got through with them, they didn't trust *anyone.* For about three years, they didn't know what was what, they were so disorganized."

Hidalgo still relished this long-ago mission, which he recalled took three weeks of undercover work. "I simply got about ten garbage trucks and about twenty to thirty Mexican police, to whom ten bucks and a quart of liquor was quite a bit. Then, one night, at the same time they raided every single office of the Communist Party. Just walked in and took everything, desks and all, and put it in the garbage trucks. Then they delivered it all to a certain place, dumped it there, and drove off. That was the end of their job."

Did Hidalgo surmise del Carmen was *really* CIA, or Mexican Communist Party? "I don't know, she might have been an agency mole *into* the Communist Party. That's the only way I can think of, because she was introduced to me as someone that can help you. I was told that name. 'You go there and contact her, so she knows you're American intelligence.' If she had been truly Communist Party, she would not have talked to me as a stranger just like that."

Maybe, I thought, unless she was secretly working for Cuban intelligence, as Nagell said.

Before my interview with Hidalgo ended, I brought out a copy of a passport photograph of Richard Nagell, circa 1963, and passed it over to him. "He looks familiar, all right," Hidalgo said, "but I couldn't tell you who he might be."

Shortly before departing Mexico in October 1962, Nagell had made an arrangement with the Hotel Luma's bartender, Franz Waehauf, apparently a secret operative for the Czech intelligence service. Waehauf sent him to a weapons specialist, where Nagell has said he obtained a .22-caliber revolver equipped with a welded-on silencer. The original target, he added, was a well-known Cuban exile leader in Miami named Rolando Masferrer.[33]

A Cuban senator under the Batista dictatorship, Masferrer's private army, known as "Los Tigres," had battled Castro's revolutionary forces in the mountains. He was particularly despised by Castro and his people, and several attempts on Masferrer's life are known to have occurred before he died in 1975—the victim of a bomb that exploded when he turned on the ignition in his car.[34]

In April 1967, shortly before he was to be interviewed by an investigator from Jim Garrison's staff, Nagell wrote a letter from prison to a friend in Los Angeles. It asked him to "please fly down to Mexico City and locate a guy for me, a prospective defense witness, who is quite important to my case. Actually, I need only know whether or not he is still employed at a certain place. Simple, no? It would not be necessary, or even desirable, for you to mention my name or tell him the purpose of your visit."[35]

Later Nagell would elaborate slightly about this, in a letter to Fensterwald. He wrote that his prison request pertained "to my attempt, albeit futile, to contact Franz Waehauf in order to keep him quiet should he be questioned about my referral to a man who handled the equipping of weapons with silencers."[36]

On the afternoon of October 21, 1962, Art Greenstein had stood by as his mysterious friend checked out of the Hotel Luma and got into his 1957 Ford Fairlane. "Yes, I saw him off," he remembered. "His leaving was sudden, quite sudden. I remember I said, 'Will I be hearing from you?' And he said, 'Yes, you'll be hearing something.' I said, 'Or read about it in the papers?' He said, 'Yes.' 'Something big?' I asked him. And he gave a chuckle and said, 'Yes. . . . something big.' "

Nagell drove all night to a Holiday Inn in Laredo, Texas. He was on the freeway the next day when he heard President Kennedy's voice come over the radio "to give his bit about the [Cuban] Missile Crisis." Later that same day, Nagell arrived in Dallas. Here he says he "briefly inquired into the status" of Lee Harvey Oswald, as he had been instructed by the Soviets.[37] By the end of October, Nagell would arrive at his sister Eleanore's home in Queens.

Greenstein himself soon departed Mexico, heading home to Delaware for Christmas that December. There, Nagell came by to touch bases briefly with him again. "He said he had driven through the southern tier of the United States, and he stopped to drop off some presents I had given him to deliver." The next he heard from Nagell, his friend was in jail in El Paso.

Tracking the Cuban Exiles

From the fall of 1962 up to his arrest in September 1963, Nagell has described himself as "an investigator (informant) for the Central Intelligence Agency in an undercover role. . . . Usually I posed as a tourist, an investigator for the Immigration and Naturalization Service, or as a researcher for a private firm, the appropriate credentials being furnished to me by the CIA." His duties also included serving as an intelligence courier and "cutout."[38] The latter is a CIA term referring to a person who is used to conceal contact between members of a clandestine activity or organization.

Nagell's movements during the final months of 1962 remain, no doubt intentionally, very vague. Nagell says that an FBI man, "possibly on a subversive beat," first approached him in New York and "demanded to know the scoop."[39] An FBI file records that the only "scoop" Nagell provided, on November 16, was advising the bureau that "he wanted to expose [the] Department of Alcoholic Beverage Control in California"[40] (Nagell's employer until his dismissal the previous summer).

In New York Nagell commenced his surveillance of the Cuban exile community. A memorandum in the Garrison investigation files, written by William R. Martin after he visited Nagell in prison in 1967, partially describes their conversation along these lines:

> . . . the subject [Nagell] asked me if I was aware of the fact that the Cuban refugees in the United States had formed and organized a great number of movements, organizations, groups, and societies all of which were, in one way or another, dedicated to the overthrow of Fidel Castro. Most of these organizations of Cubans are either formal or semi-formal organizations with elected Presidents and officers and go under a variety of names, such as "Alpha 66." The subject made it expressly clear at that time that none of these organizations, acting as organizations, planned to assassinate, or in fact assassinated, President Kennedy. Rather, he stated, that the Cubans who took an active part in the assassination acted as individuals and they did not all belong to one organization or even to two organizations, even though they had all come together and become known to each other because of these organizations.[41]

Following Nagell's trail through that winter produces a variety of strange events. In his Court of Claims file I found a letter written by Nagell on November 25, 1962, to the adjutant general, Department of the

Army, in Washington. He was seeking to know "if it is again possible for me to obtain a commission in the USAR" [U.S. Army Reserve]. He enclosed his service record, giving his return address as his sister's. He said he wanted to be reappointed as a captain with concurrent active duty in the reserves.

The Army's reply, dated December 7, from infantry lieutenant colonel Louis J. Scholter, Jr., told Nagell he would have to submit an application, but added: "I do not believe that your chances for obtaining a commission with concurrent active duty are very good. This opinion is based upon the efficiency reports you received on active duty. Based on correspondence in your file, I am certain that you are familiar with their contents."

By the time of the Army's reply, Nagell had left New York and traveled to Washington, D.C. An FBI file reports Nagell later informing the bureau that he had been approached in Washington "by individual believed to be working for Soviets" and had "contacted CIA in Virginia for instructions."[42]

Further adding to the intrigue were two names in Nagell's notebook from the period. One was "AMTORG," a Soviet trading agency in New York known to have long been manned by KGB spies given the task of recruiting agents in the United States.[43] The other was the only listing on a page, which read:

GEORGI M. KORNIENKO
SOVIET EMBASSY
WASHINGTON, D.C.

In 1962 and 1963, Georgi Kornienko was the Soviet chargé d'affaires at its embassy in Washington. By the mid-1960s he would be back in Moscow as head of the Foreign Ministry's United States Division. In 1969, the Soviet Union's "America watcher," as *Time* magazine described him, would become part of a six-man Soviet delegation in the first nuclear arms reduction talks. And by 1975, Kornienko was promoted to deputy foreign minister.[44]

From Washington, according to the FBI's files on Nagell, he told the bureau that he was sent to Florida "by his Soviet contact" after contacting the CIA for his instructions. He advised the FBI of this on December 15 in Jacksonville.[45] Nagell later wrote to Greenstein that he had initiated an "artifice" that resulted in his being questioned by the FBI, and "got something off his chest" while sitting in the agents' car.

After this, Nagell described himself (in another letter to Greenstein) as "running scared now, races west to Tallahassee, south to St. Pete." There he checked himself into the Bay Pines Veterans Administration Hospital "complaining of severe headaches, blackouts, and . . . amnesia."

It is on the public record that Nagell was admitted to the Bay Pines Hospital's neurological ward in St. Petersburg, Florida, on December 20, 1962. A report by a clinical social worker describes what he told the VA: "Patient feels his intentions were to go to California, but came to Florida instead. He cannot remember any part of his trip until he arrived in Tallahassee, where the police suggested he come to Bay Pines. He said his travel check showed that his journey to Florida took ten days, having spent two days in Washington, D.C., stop-over in Jacksonville, Florida, and so forth."[46]

Another "psychological report" on Nagell, dated December 28, states: "Recently, he has been visiting his sister in New York City. Following this, the patient is quite vague as to his movements until he came into Bay Pines."[47]

There was, no doubt, a method to Nagell's seeming madness. For, as he described to me, he had managed to infiltrate a Cuban exile team that was discussing "using a concealed bomb near or inside the Miami stadium where Kennedy was to address the prisoners released from Cuba on the Bay of Pigs exchange."[48] It appears that Nagell then checked himself into the Bay Pines VA Hospital to keep a safe distance. Whether he alerted American or Soviet intelligence agencies about what was transpiring, he has never said.

Kennedy in Miami

Amid the thousands of pages of material in the Assassination Archives Research Center in Washington, there is a single-page report that originated with the Miami Police Department. Written by policewoman Mary L. Gilbert of the Intelligence Unit, it was dated January 3, 1963. It said:

> Capt. Napier called this date, and stated that John Marshall of the U.S. Secret Service was anxious to find out some information concerning the following individual:
> A Cuban male, 25 yrs, 5′4, 135–155 lbs, strong muscular build, known only as CHINO.
> He allegedly is a truck driver for Richards Electric. . . .
> On Sat., Dec. 29, 1962, when President Kennedy addressed the Cubans in the Orange Bowl, CHINO allegedly made the remark, "Something is going to happen in the Orange Bowl."

December 29 was a momentous day in Miami. After months of negotiations, the United States had agreed to pay Castro a "ransom" of $53 million in pharmaceutical drugs, medical equipment, and other supplies in exchange for Cuba's releasing the 1,113 prisoners taken during the ill-fated Bay of Pigs invasion in April 1961. Now the Cuban exile members of Brigade 2506 were coming home. On December 27, President Kennedy flew to Palm Beach to meet with a delegation of the returned Cuban captives.

Two days later, a crowd of nearly forty thousand gathered for a rally at Miami's Orange Bowl. The commander in chief slowly reviewed the brigade, passing through the lines of troops, chatting with many of the men. At the speaker's podium, on the fifty-yard line, brigade leader Manuel Artime spoke into the microphone: "Our plan is to return to Cuba. We will come back—when or where I cannot say—but we will return." Then, as the crowd roared, Artime presented President Kennedy with the brigade's flag, which had been hidden by one of the men during the long months of imprisonment and smuggled out of Cuba.

In emphatic tones, Kennedy told the cheering crowd: "Your conduct and valor are proof that although Castro and his fellow dictators may rule nations, they do not rule people; that they may imprison bodies, but they do not imprison spirits; that they may destroy the exercise of liberty, but they cannot eliminate the determination to be free. I can assure you that this flag will be returned to this brigade in a free Havana. The strongest wish of the people of this hemisphere is that Cuba shall one day be free again, and when it is, this brigade will deserve to march at the head of the free column."

As his speech came to a close, the president said: "Submerge those differences which now may disturb you." Then the president's party filed out of the Orange Bowl toward a waiting helicopter.[49]

Not too far away, lying on his bed at the Bay Pines VA Hospital, Richard Nagell listened attentively to Kennedy's speech. The first plot to assassinate the president, Nagell would say years later, "never got past the talking stage."[50]

Summary

From Soviet intelligence in Mexico City, Nagell received his two assignments in October 1962. One was to monitor a group of Cuban exiles, affiliated with a CIA-sponsored outfit called Alpha 66, who were said to be plotting an assassination attempt against JFK. The other was to keep tabs on Oswald, recently returned from the USSR.

While Oswald corresponded with the Soviet embassy and subscribed to "leftist" publications, the people around him from the moment of his repatriation were largely connected to an international right-wing underground. First there was the Oswalds' greeter, Spas Raikin of the Ukrainian Anti-Bolshevik Nations. In Dallas-Fort Worth, the Russian émigré community had links to U.S. intelligence and a post-World War II espionage network in Europe. Charles Willoughby and associates were closely tied to the Ukrainians and other anti-Communist White Russian factions. Also during the summer of 1962, FBI files reveal an agreement with Oswald to provide information on any "suspicious" contacts made with him by the Soviets.

Before leaving Mexico, Nagell began a liaison with Maria del Carmen, whom he knew as a Cuban intelligence agent but whom CIA officer Barney Hidalgo believed was working for his agency. Nagell headed East as the Cuban Missile Crisis captured the attention of the world, communicating with the Soviets, the CIA, and the FBI as he moved from New York to Washington, D.C., and down to Florida. Monitoring a Cuban exile-inspired discussion about killing JFK with a concealed bomb when the president addressed returning Bay of Pigs prisoners in Miami, Nagell ended up checking himself into the V.A. Hospital at Bay Pines. The first plot did not materialize.

Chapter Eleven

Oswald and the Baron: 1962–77

By the early autumn of 1962, Lee and Marina Oswald's relationship was already devolving into constant bickering. Thirteen days before Nagell's arrival in Dallas from Mexico to make some inquiries about him, on October 10 Oswald had suddenly left his job at a Fort Worth metal factory, bid a temporary farewell to his family, and traveled alone the thirty miles to Dallas. Staying for a few days at a YMCA, he opened his first of several post office boxes, Box 2915. On October 12 he suddenly found new employment with the Jaggers-Chiles-Stovall (JCS) photo-lithography firm for $1.35 an hour. From then until he rented an apartment on November 3, bringing his family to join him, it is not known how Oswald spent his evenings or even where he resided.[1]

JCS was an interesting place for a "redefector" from the USSR to find a job. One of the company's contracts was doing classified work for the U.S. Army Map Service. In this context, employees set type for place names on maps of Cuba. Just two days after Oswald arrived at JCS, pictures taken by an American U-2 spy plane would confirm the existence of Soviet missile launching pads.

Technically, only JCS workers with a special security clearance were allowed access to this sensitive material. In fact, the office space was so small that Oswald could readily have seen it. In his address book confiscated after the Kennedy assassination, authorities found the notation "micro dots" written next to Oswald's entry for the JCS firm. Microdots, developed by German intelligence during World War II, are a data-sending method wherein documents are photographically reduced to a size that could be hidden under a postage stamp.[2]

A tiny Minox "spy camera," originally manufactured in Nazi Germany and used by both sides during World War II, was found among Oswald's effects when Dallas police took possession of them after the assassination. Loaded with film, the camera was turned over to the FBI. According to detective Gus Rose, the FBI later pressured the police to change their inventory records to make it appear that only a light meter had been found. Oswald's camera simply disappeared from FBI records.

Then, in 1978, a Freedom of Information Act lawsuit forced the FBI to release twenty-five pictures. The FBI indicated the two rolls it developed were not inside the Minox camera but found separately, in tin containers. Most of the photographs depicted civilian scenes in Europe. Three others showed some kind of military environment, either in the Far East or Central America, inside a barbed-wire encampment where civilians walked outside. Another picture seemed to have been taken from a boat, showing a tanker anchored offshore from some mountainous terrain.

The FBI did not release, but made reference to in files declassified in 1976, photographs Oswald had also taken while in Minsk—of an airport, an Army office building, a polytechnical institute, and a radio-TV factory assembly line. Hundreds of dollars' worth of photographic equipment were also discovered by the Dallas police in Oswald's apartment—three more cameras, a 15-power telescope, two pairs of field glasses, a compass, even a pedometer.[3]

Oswald himself was never known to have been fond of taking long cross-country camera hikes in foreign lands. But someone else was. This was a well-connected Russian émigré some thirty years Oswald's senior, who had befriended Lee and Marina late that August. Both the wife and daughter of George de Mohrenschildt would tell the Warren Commission that it was he who had arranged for Oswald's employment at Jaggers-Chiles-Stovall.[4] Not the Texas Employment Commission, as official records would have us believe.

Background of a Baron

George Sergei de Mohrenschildt is another of those remarkably enigmatic characters whom we find permeating the assassination's landscape. He was born in Czarist Russia in 1911, his father a "marshal of nobility" who served as director of the Nobel oil interests—hence his own title of "baron." He became a world traveler who spoke six languages and boasted membership in both the exclusive Dallas Petroleum Club and the World Affairs Council.

De Mohrenschildt and his fourth wife, Jeanne, were part of Dallas's clique of Russian émigrés, most of whom had settled shortly after World War II on the periphery of the city's oil industry. The baron himself was an oil and mining geologist who, coincidentally, had become a close friend of Jacqueline Kennedy's mother when he immigrated to the United States in 1938.

In the early 1960s, Dallas was still in many ways like a small town. A long ebony table in the Dallas Petroleum Club was inlaid with coins from all over the world. In his extensive journeys, de Mohrenschildt had visited many of those places—everywhere from Nigeria to Venezuela, Yugoslavia to Cuba (in the Batista days). "He was traveling so extensively that it was absolutely impossible to remember everywhere he went," one of his friends, Mrs. Igor Voshinin, would tell the Warren Commission.[5]

The commission took notice that de Mohrenschildt was acquainted with several powerful people in Houston, where he made a number of trips in 1962–63 that Igor Voshinin found suspicious—"like [de Mohrenschildt was] reporting to somebody."[6] Among the baron's Houston associates were several close friends of Lyndon Johnson: oil millionaire John Mecom, and construction industry titans George and Herman Brown.[7] Another de Mohrenschildt friend was Jean De Menil of Schlumberger Wells Services Company, who in 1961 permitted his New Orleans branch to be used as an ammunition conduit for the CIA.[8]

The baron's affinity for people in high places even extended as far as LBJ and another future American president, George Bush. In 1966–67, from residences in Haiti and Dallas, de Mohrenschildt would correspond regularly with the Johnson White House. On file at the LBJ Memorial Library in Austin, Texas, the letters show high-level interest in the baron's proposal for establishing an "Institute of Latin American Resources." Replied presidential assistant Arthur C. Perry: "I feel that the President will be interested in having your views in this regard and I shall be pleased to bring them to his attention at the earliest opportunity."[9]

De Mohrenschildt's personal telephone book, discovered after his alleged suicide in 1977, contained this entry: "Bush, George H. W. (Poppy) 1412 W. Ohio also Zapata Petroleum Midland."[10] President Bush, Zapata's chief executive officer between 1956 and 1964, moved from Midland, Texas, to Houston in 1959. De Mohrenschildt had marked an "X" through the old address. According to investigative journalist Anthony L. Kimery, the Bush-de Mohrenschildt acquaintanceship went back to the late 1940s and continued into 1963.[11]

Such odd coincidences attach themselves to de Mohrenschildt's life with amazing fluidity. He was, for example, born in Minsk—the same Soviet city where Lee and Marina Oswald resided. While traveling through Mexico early in 1960, de Mohrenschildt "became acquainted" with Anastas Mikoyan—who gave the strange order to the KGB to let Oswald remain in the Soviet Union (see Chapter Eight). "Mr. Mikoyan was on a trade mission to Mexico at the time," according to a 1964 article about de Mohrenschildt in *The New York Times*, "attempting to negotiate trade agreements with the Mexican government-controlled oil corporation known as Pemex."[12]

His Warren Commission testimony revealed that at the same time the baron and his wife were in the midst of an eight-month "geological trip" through Mexico and Central America. The pair loved to wander. Soon the de Mohrenschildts told friends they were embarking on another trip, a seven-thousand-mile "walking tour" along "primitive jungle trails" into the heart of Central America. According to de Mohrenschildt, in March 1961 "by happenstance" they arrived in Guatemala City a short time before the Bay of Pigs invasion. On a nearby plantation, for some months the CIA had been training a sizable force of Cuban exiles. The de Mohrenschildts hung around until the invasion's failure on April 16, then trekked onward through Honduras, Costa Rica, Panama, and Haiti. "We led a life close to nature for a whole year," the baron would recall—close enough, he added, "to review all the mining resources of Haiti" before returning to Dallas that September.[13]

Right when Oswald went to work at JCS in October 1962, de Mohrenschildt wrote a letter to the U.S. undersecretary of state offering to submit a slide travelogue of his Central American sojourn. Otherwise, he said he planned to send it to Europe, where some friends abroad thought they might pass it along to the Soviet Union—"where there is a great demand for travelogues and adventure stories."[14]

De Mohrenschildt had a long history of providing one side first crack at his services—before offering them to someone else. Just prior to Pearl Harbor, he had worked with a French counter intelligence operative, helping recruit an agent network in the United States to gather information about oil exports to Europe. At the same time, as de Mohrenschildt later admitted to his wife, Jeanne, he was "playing a double game."

In 1941, de Mohrenschildt formed a documentary film partnership with Baron Konstantin Von Maydell. Maydell was a "distant cousin" who just happened to be the senior resident agent of the Abwehr—Nazi Germany's Military Intelligence arm in the United States. The "Facts and Film" propaganda venture came to an end in September 1942, when Maydell was arrested as a "dangerous alien" and placed in a North Dakota internment camp for four years. U.S. authorities also determined that de Mohrenschildt was then corresponding with Germany through Saburo Matsukata, the son of a former Japanese prime minister who was believed to be the coordinator for German-Japanese spying in the United States.

On his way to Mexico with a lovely Latin lady, the baron was confronted by the FBI while making sketches near a strategic Texas Coast Guard station. He went on to Mexico anyway, only to be expelled nine months later for "possibly subversive activities." After that, de Mohrenschildt returned Stateside, applying for a job in the summer of 1942 with the CIA's wartime predecessor, the OSS. A CIA document notes that de Mohrenschildt "was not hired because he was alleged to be a Nazi espionage agent."

But, as the CIA recounted his history for the Warren Commission, by the time de Mohrenschildt enrolled at the University of Texas in 1944 to get his petroleum geology degree, "he was said to have Communist tendencies." One CIA file noted that "DE MOHRENSCHILDT appears to be a dubious character" and that the FBI had him under investigation "from 1941 through 1948."

Clare Petty, a former official on Angleton's staff, told me that shortly before his CIA retirement in 1974, he was examining a potential de Mohrenschildt link to some Soviet cipher traffic first intercepted by American intelligence in World War II. Known as the VENONA material, "it was only partially broken," according to Petty, "including lots of agent cryptonyms that we never found out to whom they applied. I had started to consider the possibility of whether a certain Soviet illegal [agent] might have been de Mohrenschildt. It was clear that whoever was being described in the codes had been in the United States, went to Mexico during the war, and was a real wheeler-dealer. He also had another nationality; my recollection is that it was Polish."

De Mohrenschildt had, in fact, been raised in Poland after his family fled the Bolshevik Revolution. There, he graduated from the Military Academy of Poland, and he served as a reserve captain in the Polish Army before immigrating to the United States.

Another CIA file noted a background investigation in late 1957 and early 1958 showing "that he was a member of the Communist Party; and that after the war he was sympathetic toward Communism and the U.S.S.R." Yet, simultaneous with that "background investigation," the CIA is on record as having itself been utilizing de Mohrenschildt's services.

In 1957 the baron made an extended trip to Yugoslavia on behalf of the International Cooperation Administration, which was looking for help developing oil resources under what de Mohrenschildt recalled as "some kind of government deal." Upon his return that December, the CIA sent the head of its Dallas office to see him. In the course of several meetings, according to a CIA file sent to the Warren Commission, "the CIA representative obtained foreign intelligence which was promptly disseminated to other federal agencies in ten separate reports." This same CIA official maintained occasional "informal contact" with de Mohrenschildt. According to the CIA's official records, it ceased in the autumn of 1961.[15]

But de Mohrenschildt maintained that the contacts continued. Only a few hours before he died on March 29, 1977, the baron told the story to journalist Edward Jay Epstein. De Mohrenschildt related that, late in 1961, J. Walton Moore, in charge of the CIA's Domestic Contact Service (DCS) in Dallas, had taken him to lunch. Moore described an ex-Marine working at an electronics factory in Minsk, who was soon to return to the United States, and in whom the CIA had "interest."

By that time, the DCS would have come under the larger CIA umbrella of the Domestic Operations Division—headed by Tracy Barnes, the same man whom Robert Morrow alleged to have been the recipient of Oswald's information from Minsk (see Chapter Eight). In the summer of 1962, de Mohrenschildt maintained that an "associate" of J. Walton Moore provided him Oswald's address in Fort Worth, suggesting the baron might want to meet him. De Mohrenschildt called Moore, noting that in exchange for his services with Oswald, the State Department might assist him with an oil exploration deal he was trying to make in Haiti.[16]

Moore, de Mohrenschildt said, then "encouraged" him to pursue an Oswald relationship. Called before the House Assassinations Committee, Moore denied ever discussing Oswald with de Mohrenschildt. But he added that from 1957 onward he "had 'periodic' contact with de Mohrenschildt for 'debriefing' purposes over the years."[17]

De Mohrenschildt gained the confidence of Lee and Marina, encouraging Oswald to write a detailed memoir about his experiences in Minsk. By October 1962, when de Mohrenschildt also landed Oswald his job at JCS, a typed draft of Oswald's manuscript was in his possession. The baron informed Moore. Not long after this, someone broke into de Mohrenschildt's apartment.[18]

Oswald, Nagell, and the de Mohrenschildts

De Mohrenschildt was always vague about who first arranged his introduction to the Oswalds, though a number of Warren Commission witnesses attested it was George Bouhe, the man who "helped Oswald learn a trade, the printing trade." What is most interesting is that, soon after the friendship began, most of the other members of Dallas's Russian community dropped the young couple like a hot potato. "George [de Mohrenschildt] was always arguing with us that Oswald was a decent person," Natasha Voshinin recalled in 1992. "But Igor and I were convinced he [Oswald] was a scoundrel. George himself was a little bit of an adventurer, there was a streak of nice hooliganism about him. Igor and I always thought he might be working for the CIA. He sort of hinted about his travels—but there again, can we trust whatever he said? We never took him seriously."[19]

As de Mohrenschildt eventually wrote in a manuscript about Oswald (reprinted in entirety by the House Assassinations Committee in 1979), his wife, Jeanne, particularly hit it off with the returning defector. U.S. intelligence apparently had previous concerns about Jeanne as well. She was a former fashion model, born in Harbin, China, to the White Russian director of the Far East Railroad. Early in 1957, shortly before she married de Mohrenschildt, her former husband had reported her as a member of the Communist Party to two Dallas FBI agents. One of these, in yet another strange coincidence, was James P. Hosty, Jr., the same FBI man who would later spend considerable time looking into Oswald.[20]

Since Jeanne had lived in a wealthy Chinese family during her formative years, many of her discussions with Oswald focused on the Far East. "She remembered the Chinese as humble and kind people, dismally poor," de Mohrenschildt wrote. "She told him of . . . the Japanese invasion and of the ensuing cruelties, of her flight from the Japanese to the United States. Lee compared her experiences of the old militaristic Japan with the present Japanese movement, which he knew so well. And so both of them got along fabulously well, instructing each other on the Far-Eastern situation thirty years ago and now."[21]

De Mohrenschildt recollected Oswald telling him that while he was in the Marines "I moved around, began visiting places where students meet and established contacts with some more progressive and thinking Japanese—and this is what led me to Russia eventually."[22] Yet, while in Minsk, he found the life "too regimented. . . . Indoctrination of any kind are not to my taste." Oswald had made contact with Cuban students and technicians in Minsk and, according to de Mohrenschildt, "Lee liked Fidel as a representative of a small country, an underdog, facing fearlessly a huge and powerful country like [the] United States." Oswald, he added, was especially enamored of the most radical of Castro's chief revolutionary aides, Che Guevara.[23]

As for the American scene, de Mohrenschildt described Oswald as "keenly aware of the racist cancer eating America's healthy tissues" and speaking of such origins going all the way back to "the hypocritical Pilgrims, through Indian genocide."

After Oswald left his wife and child behind, moving from Fort Worth to Dallas to take the JCS job, it was again the baron who convinced Marina to join her husband in November 1962 at a little apartment on Elsbeth Street. De Mohrenschildt brought the couple to the December 28 Christmas party where Oswald met and apparently went on to have an affair with Yaeko Okui. In so much of Oswald's life until he and de Mohrenschildt went their separate ways in April 1963, the baron could best be described as his chaperon.

In my conversations and correspondence with Richard Nagell, the name of George de Mohrenschildt arose on several occasions. When I brought up his name at our very first meeting, Nagell smiled and said: "Now there's a relationship to pursue. I'm surprised Jim Garrison never really got into that." When we met again two nights later, Nagell elaborated: "There was enough of intermittent surveillance on Oswald by other people whose reports I read, that I have intimate knowledge who he was associating with. De Mohrenschildt's name popped up, not in connection with the CIA, though he may have been."[24]

When Nagell and I began writing back and forth, I once described the de Mohrenschildt-Oswald friendship, half in jest, as one between "the Prince and the Pauper." The allusion, of course, was to why such a man-about-town as de Mohrenschildt would have chosen to "befriend" a young couple living in semisqualor in Fort Worth. Nagell responded in a letter: "The relationship between the Prince and the Pauper is, of course, another matter, but I'm sure that the CIA's knowledge of this hasn't helped [Uncle] Sam get at the truth (apparently it didn't help the Warren Commission), not that Sam is concerned with the truth."[25]

At our next one-on-one meeting in 1977, I asked Nagell to describe de Mohrenschildt's political leanings. He was, Nagell indicated, "so far left he made most leftists look like right-wingers." Yet, in a subsequent discussion with Bernard Fensterwald, Jr., the lawyer's memo has Nagell saying: "Oswald was debriefed by the CIA upon his return to the U.S.A., but it was done by George de Mohrenschildt."[26]

Once more we are left gazing through a looking-glass where U.S. and

Soviet intelligence interests may have overlapped. Just as they did when Oswald was in Japan and the Soviet Union; just as they emerged again in Nagell's "double agent" assignment in Mexico City.

Close Encounter with the Baron

In 1975, shortly after my first meetings with Nagell, I set out to locate George de Mohrenschildt. I began with a phone call to George Bouhe. "We have an old Russian proverb," Bouhe said. "It is, 'The soul of the other person is in the darkness.' But George was pretty close for the months when the plot was brewing in Oswald's mind. He's better equipped than anybody to talk. And he likes to talk, he will for money. Maybe you'll find him listed in the telephone book under Nero, his dog. George likes to play tricks."[27]

I did not find de Mohrenschildt's number listed under his dog. The last anyone knew, a Dallas assassination researcher told me, he was teaching at an all-black college on the outskirts of Dallas. Driving out to Bishop College on a beautiful autumn day, I was directed by some students to Professor de Mohrenschildt's office in the Literature Department. Shortly after a classroom buzzer sounded, a tall, broad-shouldered man of aristocratic bearing emerged from a stairwell, carrying a stack of papers. He had a shock of curly silver hair, though he was balding above the temples. His mouth was tight-set and his eyes penetrating. He looked remarkably fit for his sixty-four years.

When I told de Mohrenschildt I was a writer, his response was quick. "And I'll bet you want to talk about Lee Harvey Oswald." At first he said he didn't care to discuss the subject. "It is all in the Warren Commission. All this new talk is so much lies and bullshit. Nothing will ever be solved, unless somebody comes up with a confession." Then he decided to give me "five minutes," beckoned me to pull up a chair, and tumbled into his own, swinging his legs up onto his desk and motioning me to ask my questions.

"Whatever you write," he said abruptly, "Lee Harvey Oswald was smart as hell. They make a moron out of him." The baron's words came offhandedly, before I could say a word. "Lee was the most honest man I knew. He was—what?"—de Mohrenschildt raised his hand dramatically— "he was ahead of his time really, a kind of hippie of those days. He would have gone to a black school like this one if he could. And I will tell you this—I am sure he did *not* shoot the president.

"I will tell you this, too," he went on. "Lee was too good in his knowledge of the Russian language not to have been instructed by someone before he took his trip to Europe. You hear the way I speak English. I've been here thirty-five years and still I have a foreign accent. And Lee hardly had a foreign accent in *Russian*, a much more difficult language than English."

Finally I managed to get a question in, asking de Mohrenschildt why he thought so many government files about his own life and times remained classified. At first he denied that the CIA would have any files on him. When I insisted they did, de Mohrenschildt raised his eyebrows and continued: "Really? No kidding. Well, I think it's not because there is anything essential in them, but they don't want to annoy people, to destroy reputations. Because I told the truth, you see, about things that have nothing to do with this case."

Baron de Mohrenschildt's eyes seemed to glaze over, and he stood up, indicating my time was up. I had one more question. I wanted to know about something Nagell had told me. "The Cubans," I said, "there were some Cuban exiles that Oswald is said to have associated with. Did you know of them, or who they might have been working for?"

De Mohrenschildt stared blankly into space for a few moments, then said: "Oswald probably did not know himself. I myself was in a little bit of danger from those Cubans, but I don't know who they are. Criminal lunatics. There was an incident which I described to the European press in an interview with Dutch television. I understand the whole film was stolen and destroyed. That's how far it all goes.

"Could I walk you to your car?" the baron added.

We walked out a set of double doors and up an incline toward an asphalt parking lot. My car turned out to be parked directly across from his. He was driving an old Jaguar, vintage 1963.

"So, you don't have any leads for me?" I said as we shook hands.

Baron de Mohrenschildt gave a half smile. "If I knew, I'd go and shoot the son of a bitch," he said. Then he got into his car, revved his engine, and cruised away.

The Final Days

My second, and last, visit with de Mohrenschildt took place on another trip to Dallas, in mid-July 1976. When I showed up unannounced at the apartment complex on Dallas's Travis Street, I noticed the baron staring at me out a big picture window. He answered the door wearing a T-shirt and cut-off jeans, a headband across his forehead. His wife, Jeanne, was sitting at the dining-room table, still in her dressing gown as the noon hour approached. The apartment was small and rather unkempt, but paintings adorned the walls and the fragrance of houseplants filled the air.

I asked de Mohrenschildt if he remembered me and he said, "Yes, from the college." His wife, apparently thinking I was a former student of his, invited me to sit down. When I mentioned my subject of interest, Jeanne pointed to her stomach and said she was "sick of it, it makes me feel like where Oswald got it in the gut." Then she added: "Of course, the truth has not come out. We know it was a vast conspiracy and Oswald did not shoot the president."

I explained I had heard a rumor about twelve hours of taped interviews that George was supposed to have given to a Dutch journalist friend named Willem Oltmans. Were the de Mohrenschildts thinking about possibly releasing them? Jeanne was adamant that she didn't want them out. George wondered aloud how much money they might bring. "I want to burn them," his wife said, shaking her head. In my presence, they decided to write their journalist friend and tell him not to release the tapes under any circumstances.

Jeanne served me a glass of Spanish wine. We moved on to other subjects. I reminded de Mohrenschildt about the two Cubans he had mentioned as "having been in a little trouble with myself" the previous fall. The baron said something in Russian to his wife. "That's a different story," she said, adding that "one must examine the motive of the time, the anti-Castros."

Then Jeanne said she knew that Oswald had been sent to the Soviet Union by the CIA, but her husband abruptly cut her off. The baron began pacing back and forth across the room. Suddenly he was shouting: "It is defiling a corpse! Defiling a corpse! I don't want to talk about it, it makes me sick!"

His wife motioned me toward the door. Recovering his composure, George de Mohrenschildt said, "It's been a pleasure," and shook my hand.

Nine months later, de Mohrenschildt was dead. His final days, as reconstructed afterward in a magazine article by journalist Willem Oltmans, seemed a fittingly Byzantine finish to his strange life. Oltmans had first met de Mohrenschildt in 1967, when he did a series of tapes for a forty-five-minute Netherlands-TV film. In 1974 de Mohrenschildt had written the journalist a letter that said in part: "In case of my removal from the scene—by assassination or otherwise—you will be able to sell the tapes. The proceeds (one-half) are to go to my daughter Alexandra." According to Oltmans, in 1975 the finished film would mysteriously disappear from the Dutch Broadcasting Corporation's archives.

Then, in early December 1976—just as a congressional assassination probe was getting under way—Oltmans says he arrived in Dallas and found that de Mohrenschildt had been committed to the Parkland Hospital Medical Clinic for observation. He was receiving heavy drug treatments, and his memory was reportedly impaired. Many months after de Mohrenschildt's death, Oltmans says Jeanne de Mohrenschildt remarked that she and the family lawyer "had him committed . . . because we knew that one more interview, and he would have had it."

After six weeks, de Mohrenschildt was released from the hospital and resumed teaching at Bishop College. Meeting in a quiet corner of the college library, Oltmans says the baron told him he "felt responsible for Oswald's role" and wanted to talk about it. But he had been receiving death threats for some time and begged Oltmans to take him to Europe.

So he did. On March 5, 1977, while a book contract was being drawn up with a Dutch publishing company, Oltmans says he and de Mohrenschildt took a flight to Europe. They drove together to the Belgian capital of Brussels, where Oltmans wanted "to keep a luncheon appointment with an old friend, the Soviet chargé d'affaires, Vladimir Kuznyetsov." The baron told the pair he was going for a walk, but would meet them for lunch in about an hour. Then de Mohrenschildt simply disappeared.

Ten days later, Oltmans testified about what had transpired in Europe, in a closed session before the House Assassinations Committee in Washington (the transcript has never been released). Then, on March 25, de Mohrenschildt suddenly surfaced at a villa near Palm Beach, Florida, where his daughter was also staying. According to Oltmans, de Mohrenschildt sent him a telephone message, thanking him for his efforts to protect him but saying he had been "too scared to go through with his confession." Instead of contacting de Mohrenschildt again, Oltmans says he informed the House Assassinations Committee where de Mohrenschildt could be reached. "We will have an investigator there tomorrow," committee attorney Robert Tannenbaum reportedly said.[28]

On the morning of March 29, 1977, Gateon Fonzi, the committee's Miami-based investigator, arrived at the villa in Manalapan. He was told by de Mohrenschildt's daughter that her father was meeting with journalist Epstein at a Palm Beach hotel but would be back that night. At 1:00 P.M., de Mohrenschildt left by car and returned to his temporary residence. By 2:21 P.M., he was dead. Authorities determined the time by listening to a tape on which de Mohrenschildt's daughter was recording TV soap operas while she was at work. The official verdict was that de Mohrenschildt had committed suicide by putting a 20-gauge shotgun into his mouth and pulling the trigger.[29]

In September 1978 I contacted Jeanne de Mohrenschildt again by phone. Did she believe that the baron had taken his own life? "Nobody that knew him does, that's my answer," she said. "I have a few other little facts that prove that he didn't." That was all she would say.[30]

At my last meeting with Richard Nagell in 1984, he said he was sure that de Mohrenschildt was murdered before he could testify before the House Assassinations Committee.[31]

I wondered then, and still do, whatever happened to the de Mohren-schildt-Oltmans tapes. Something very weird was going on around de Mohrenschildt in the months after I last saw him. Later, I came into possession of a two-page typed statement, signed by de Mohrenschildt in Brussels on March 11, 1977, in the midst of his having vanished. In it de Mohrenschildt wrote that "while staying at Oltmans I had the impression that I was drugged and later I thought that my travelers checks were exchanged. . . . He wanted to sully me into admitting things I did not do." Then, when Oltmans scheduled a mutual luncheon with a Soviet official, de Mohrenschildt said he called an old friend "in despair and asked him to contact the U.S. Embassy re my whereabouts if more pressure was put on me." He expressed fear that his wife's Dallas lawyer "collaborated with Oltmans."

A few days after de Mohrenschildt's death, Oltmans told newsmen in Washington that de Mohrenschildt had revealed to him: (1) Cubans "who thought that President Kennedy had betrayed them at the Bay of Pigs" had fired the same time Oswald did and (2) de Mohrenschildt had served as a middleman between Oswald and Dallas's wealthy H. L. Hunt oil family. "Mr. de Mohrenschildt indicated to me very strongly that his ties upwards were towards H. L. Hunt and downstairs to Lee Harvey Oswald," Oltmans said in an ABC-TV interview. Beyond that, the journalist refused to elaborate.[32] Later he would retract his comments about de Mohren-schildt and the Hunts.

Gaeton Fonzi, the House Assassinations Committee investigator who never got the chance to interview de Mohrenschildt, told me how Oltmans claimed to have turned over seventy-nine pages of crucial documents— "but it was mostly just a bunch of crap. He said he didn't have the other stuff, it was back in Holland. Then he told other people he wasn't going to give the committee everything, but keep it confidential. Yet he's telling the press that he already did. It stank."[33]

Then I discovered an FBI file reporting that Oltmans had contacted its New York office on April 3, 1967—around the time the Dutch journalist first met de Mohrenschildt. It had Oltmans saying he "had received information from an informant in Western Europe that De Mohrenschildt was the principal organizer of the assassination of President Kennedy."[34] A curious thing for a "friend" to do to the baron.

In the final analysis, Oltmans becomes as much of an enigma as de Mohrenschildt himself. A 1977 New York Times study of the then fifty-one-year-old Oltmans' background found him to have inherited independent wealth and to have received an education at the Dutch Institute for Foreign Affairs, usually attended by potential diplomats. He had worked as a correspondent for both left- and right-wing newspapers and had written a book about a 150-day trip through the Soviet Union.[35]

Nor does the Oltmans story end with the baron's death. While in Europe shortly thereafter, the journalist has written, he was contacted by a Bulgarian who called himself "Donald A. Donaldson." His real name was Dimotor Dimitrov, and he said he was a titular American general. He informed Oltmans that de Mohrenschildt had "contacted the wrong people in Brussels" and, upon returning Stateside, received instructions in Washington to "go to Florida where he would be less exposed. He first traveled to Dallas in an effort to recover some papers which he was afraid would be destroyed by his wife." (Jeanne de Mohrenschildt had left her husband in January 1977 and traveled to California, where she still resides.)

Then, according to "General Donaldson" via the Oltmans account, "de Mohrenschildt was murdered by two men. They first offered him safe conduct to Mexico, and they also asked him to sign a false document drawn up by the CIA. George did so and was killed. After all, these experts know only too well how to make it look like a suicide."

After several negotiating sessions about a TV deal, Oltmans said "Donaldson" disappeared. The Dutch journalist then roamed on to the Soviet Union "for the purpose of conducting a series of interviews." There, he says, the deputy director-general of the Tass News Agency "happened to show me a lengthy cable he had received from his Tokyo office." It concerned a series of articles about the Kennedy case by a free-lance Japanese journalist, Nobuhiko Ochiai, who had reportedly accumulated his data on nearly one hundred trips to the United States. J. Edgar Hoover and Allen Dulles (with the knowledge and approval of Richard Nixon) were named as having "planned and instigated the assassination." The Japanese writer maintained that de Mohrenschildt was killed by Florida gangster Santos Trafficante, Jr., who held close ties with the CIA.[36]

Whatever role Willem Oltmans himself played in the final days of George de Mohrenschildt, he has rarely been heard from publicly since 1977. Perhaps, in trying to figure out the inscrutable baron, whom friends once nicknamed "The Chinese," we should go back to his earliest remarks after the assassination. The first known record of de Mohrenschildt's reaction came in a personal letter to Janet Auchincloss, the mother of Jacqueline Kennedy and with whom he had become friends back in 1938. Dated December 12, 1963, the letter is a kind of apologia in which de Mohrenschildt strangely misspells "Osvald" throughout. Toward the end he wrote:

"Somehow, I still have a lingering doubt notwithstanding all the evidence of Osvald's guilt."[37]

That doubt, as de Mohrenschildt was said to have expressed to one of his children that holiday season of 1963, centered around his belief that "the right wing or FBI" was behind the assassination.[38]

Summary

Who was Baron George de Mohrenschildt? He strides across the international petroleum scene, in touch with future American presidents, Soviet officials, and the CIA. At various times he has been suspected as a Nazi and as a Communist agent. He is in the right places at the right times—Guatemala during the Bay of Pigs invasion training, Dallas-Fort Worth when the Oswalds come home from the USSR. He finds Oswald a job at a photo shop that does classified work for the Army, where Oswald employs "microdot" spy techniques and apparently utilizes a bevy of camera equipment.

As de Mohrenschildt revealed the very day of his alleged suicide in 1977, Dallas's CIA official J. Walton Moore first mentioned Oswald to him late in 1961—when Oswald was still in Minsk, and at the same time that Robert Morrow says he picked up information from Oswald through a CIA courier. According to Nagell and the baron himself, de Mohrenschildt essentially "debriefed" Oswald for the CIA.

During my two encounters with de Mohrenschildt, he was adamant that Oswald did not commit the assassination and admitted having faced problems from some anti-Castro Cubans. His wife, Jeanne, alluded to "a vast conspiracy" but would not be more specific.

De Mohrenschildt's death was as mysterious as his life. It occurred just as he was about to be questioned by a congressional investigator following a bizarre hospitalization and European voyage with a Dutch journalist who is as mystifying a personage as the baron himself.

Chapter Twelve

Nagell and the Cuban Exiles: January–April 1963

After the bomb plot that failed to go forward against President Kennedy in Miami at the end of December 1962, Richard Case Nagell continued his intentional confinement at the Veterans Administration Hospital in Bay Pines, Florida.

On January 2, 1963, a letter went out from the hospital, addressed to JFK. Strangely, Nagell later informed me that, while the signature is his own, the letter was neither composed nor typed by him.[1] This makes it appear that he was being "coached" by someone, for a particular purpose. The letter began:

> Dear Mr. President:
> I doubt if you will ever hear of this letter, let alone read it. However, to satisfy myself that by writing to the top I have exerted a maximum, though futile, effort to obtain a resemblance of justice in my case; also, if by some remote possibility you should read this, to determine whether the Com-

mander-In-Chief possesses a comparable compassion for an American veteran as he so aptly displayed last week during his address in Miami to Cuban veterans . . .

Nagell went on to recite his history in the Korean War, his being the sole survivor of a 1954 military plane crash, and the head injuries he had sustained. "Since then I have never been the same—mentally or physically —although the Army returned me to a general duty status and assigned me to military intelligence. I was aware of my condition but pride made me try to 'hang on.' . . ."

Nagell continued that he had felt he had been "squeezed out" of the Army in 1959. No physical exam, he stated, was given him prior to his discharge. The letter's conclusion read: "I have given as much to this country as many others, and more than most. Now I feel, when the chips are down and I cannot even get the time of day from my own government, what a fool I was! I have a small boy and girl the same age as yours; only they live in a foster home because I cannot afford to keep them with me. I have no job, no home, no future. And, the way I feel right now—no country." (Nagell's children were not living in a foster home. They were then in the custody of his estranged wife, Mitsuko.)

Not only personal bitterness toward the American military establishment but also problems with alleged mental problems and memory loss were set down by Nagell in other correspondence from Bay Pines. A typewritten memo he wrote to the hospital's administrator, Dr. M. L. Schwartz, begins: "If it is possible that I am in the process of what is commonly, and often in diffidence, referred to as cracking up, I believe myself to be cognizant of some of the when-where-why-what-how factors which need to be answered. And even though a rather recent emotional trauma may have pushed me over the brink so to speak, the first factor, the 'when' factor, began much, much earlier. . . ."

Harkening back to his surviving the 1954 plane crash and his subsequent hospitalization for four months at Walter Reed Army Hospital, Nagell described how he had set about "matching wits with the psychiatrists" to cover up his true condition. Otherwise he feared he "would have been barred from duty with military intelligence to which I already had received a tentative assignment. . . ."

Nagell traced the "when" back to the Korean War and his six months on "Outpost" duty, and how, during the latter part of his second year, "something happened. . . . I began to question my orders, many of which I did not consider to be tactically sound or wise." In the last months of the war, while bargaining toward an armistice was ensuing, "I cursed the arbitrators of *both* sides. It was always take a hill, pull off of a hill, push forward, or pull back. And I began to visualize the truth that we were nothing but pawns in a game of power-politics being played at Panmunjon. Also, there were the fruitless and senseless patrols which got men killed because some idiot upstairs desired to create an impression with a superior in order to secure his safe position, or to obtain a medal, or to get a promotion. . . . And when the Graves Registration Section stacked my men up like cordwood, I would be congratulated on a job well done. So, Dr. Schwartz, there is where it began, like it or not, believe it or not. . . ."

Twice Nagell also wrote to Dr. Edwin A. Weinstein, a prominent specialist in neuropsychiatry at the Walter Reed Army Institute of Research in Washington. Weinstein had first examined Nagell during his 1954–55 hospitalization at Walter Reed, had kept in touch periodically thereafter, and would eventually appear as a defense witness after his imprisonment in El Paso.

"Evidently I was self-admitted to this hospital on December 20, 1962 for reasons unknown to me at the present time," Nagell wrote Dr. Weinstein on January 10. "I do not know how long I am supposed to remain here. . . ." The letter concluded: "Right now I remember vaguely about the [airplane] accident, but I distinctly remember *everything* about Korea and my men and my friends who were killed fighting for this so-called democracy."

Then, on January 21, again to Weinstein: "I received your letter dated January 9, 1963 and judge from its contents that I have written to you. If so, I do not recall doing so, however there are many things which have occurred recently that I do not remember. . . ."

The letter then launched into a chronicle of "severe headaches, loss of equilibrium while standing or walking slowly (but no dizziness) and loss of memory for extended periods" that had occasionally plagued him since the plane crash. "I might add here that these same 'occurences' [sic] have happened to me quite recently, have been more frequent and of longer duration, and are the reason why I was admitted to this V.A. Hospital. . . . Another strange thing. I cannot sleep on my back on a level bed without waking up abruptly, usually the result of a nightmare (ie: someone trying to kill me). However, if I rest my head on *two* pillows (or while in the hospital, raise the front of the bed) I can sleep on my back without experiencing the foregoing. . . .

"I am a voluntary patient here, and I do not believe that I will stay much longer. The main reason being because nobody has been able to provide a remedy for my headaches. . . . I have kept many notes during the past eight years and could probably write a book pertaining to 'an account of how I have been since the accident,' but time and headaches will not permit me to do so. Anyway, I sincerely hope that the foregoing information will be of some assistance to you in your research."

What was behind Nagell's seeming "madness"? It is as if portions of what he was saying were a kind of code, designed to be interpreted by appropriate readers, then or later. As Nagell undoubtedly knew, all such correspondence was being duly placed in his Veterans Administration file. Just as was a handprinted, all-capitalized statement Nagell addressed to Bay Pines' neurologist, a Dr. Padron:

> *Cuba es hoy una esperanza de emancipación política y económica para los pueblos de America Latina.*
> *Por El Gran Jefe*
> *Dr. Fidel Castro Ruz*

Translated from the Spanish, his message reads: "Cuba is today a hope of political and economic emancipation for the peoples of Latin America. For the Big Chief, Dr. Fidel Castro Ruz."

"Final Summary" and Departure

A "Final Summary" of Nagell's month-long stay at Bay Pines notes that he was discharged on January 22, 1963.[2] It goes on to relate how Nagell had initially "refused to discuss why he was in the hospital" and refused to attend any group psychiatric conferences "because he did not want anyone to know about his private business." However, after several days of complaining about headaches and constant demands, "a better rapport was established and a private interview was given him. He seemed well oriented in all spheres. Speech was of normal flow and coherent. He showed no flight of ideas. He denied delusions or hallucinations. No suicidal or homicidal tendencies were elicited. . . . During the interview his retention and recall were good. . . .

"Although he smoked continuously during the interview he related quite a story about his Army activities and his domestic situation, but was somewhat evasive about the trouble he was in while in California, especially the trouble involving the F.B.I. and some shooting event." Nagell further related that because he "has a poor memory," he kept everything he had done or said "in a little book." The reason he wished to depart Bay Pines was that "he had a job in mind and was going for an interview."

The summary's "Final Diagnosis and Present Status" read:

1. Chronic brain syndrome associated with brain trauma (by history of) with behavioral reaction characterized by passive aggressive and paranoid features. Treated. Unchanged.
   (a) Precipitating stress: Unknown.

(b) Predisposition: Moderate, by history of, frequent hospitalization and interviews for his present type of behavior.

(c) Psychiatric Incapacity: Minimal. Patient is competent at this time.

The first sentence of that summary, and only the first sentence ("Chronic brain syndrome. . . ."), somehow ended up in the FBI's file on Nagell. How it got there is not known; apparently someone from the VA Hospital must have passed it along. Why the FBI chose to delete the rest of it—including the conclusion that Nagell was in fact "competent at this time"—is also open to conjecture. Was someone inside the FBI intent on portraying Nagell as a crackpot? The file in which I came across the FBI's reference to the January 1963 diagnosis at the VA Hospital appeared in an FBI report of February 4, 1964. A week before that, at his arraignment on the bank charge in El Paso, Nagell had shouted out to the local press that the FBI was in some manner "responsible" for the Kennedy assassination. This was ample reason for the FBI to make him out a man of considerable mental instability.

As for the legitimacy of the hospital's diagnosis, Nagell would later write: "Not only was I not informed of it, but also there was no evidence in my VA file (which, incidentally, arrived at Bay Pines the day I was discharged) showing that the 'brain trauma' was other than a 'brain concussion, cured.' Even that diagnosis was referred to years later by the VA, in writing, as a 'nervous condition.' "[3]

Rendezvous with the FBI

Back in his Ford Fairlane, with "a job in mind," Nagell checked out of the Bay Pines Hospital and drove south to Miami. On January 23, 1963, under a false name, he checked into a Holiday Inn on Biscayne Boulevard.[4] Here he set about to contact "two Miami-based FBI agents who were familiar with the Cuban community and a so-called anti-Castro organization operating there."[5]

The FBI's Nagell file says this much, in very elliptical tones, about his meeting: "Asked FBI in Miami on 1/24/63 if his Cuban or Russian sources gave him a pistol and microfilm would he be permitted to return same to his contact so he could be of further use to U.S. Government. Claimed to be constantly under surveillance."[6]

But, according to Nagell, that wasn't all that happened during his latest liaison with the FBI. In the first place, there was more than one meeting.

Besides the Cuban exiles, what he was discussing with the agents concerned assassination devices known as "tortillas"—"how they are made,
who makes them, etc."[7] The agents, in turn, used the code name "The
Tacos."

As Nagell later outlined it to Art Greenstein, "Taco" was also a code
name for a lethal weapon illegal in the United States—a beer-can-shaped
attachment to a rifle barrel that gives the shooter "a degree of parameter,
like shrapnel from a grenade." The Spanish references, I believed, probably pertained to Nagell's Mexico City sojourn—when Hotel Luma bartender Franz Waehauf put him in touch with someone whose expertise
was equipping weapons with silencers.

So the FBI's "Tacos" were presumably investigating such illegal armaments in the Miami area. "When I wanted to get in touch with these two
agents," says Nagell, "I would call a certain telephone number from a pay
telephone located in a café or restaurant and ask to speak with one of
THE TACOS, precisely as they had instructed me to do. I assumed that
the telephone number given to me was the telephone number to the FBI
field office in Miami."[8]

During his meetings with "The Tacos," Nagell says he used the "Joseph
Kramer" alias[9]—the same name he alleged was the pseudonym of "known
Communist (Soviet) agent" Mark Gayn. As it would be when Nagell
wrote his warning letter to Hoover the following September, the
"Kramer" pseudonym sounds like a tip-off to the FBI that, whatever he
was doing, the Russians probably knew about it.

The Cuban Crusade

There are a number of references in Nagell's notebook to his January
1963 trip to Miami. One lists the address for "SUZANNE'S RESTAU-
RANT." Another page bears notations for the "Miami theatre" and
"Dixie theatre." Opposite that page, under the heading "MIAMI," are
listed several telephone numbers, a locker number in the Greyhound bus
station, and seven automobile license plate numbers: two from Florida,
two from California, one from Texas, one from Massachusetts, and one
from Kansas. All this is bracketed and labeled "JAN 63."

Nagell's mission in Miami, according to a 1969 Military Intelligence file
about him, was "investigating activities of Anti-Castro organizations and
their personnel."[10] At an interview in 1977, Nagell told me: "I received a
list one time of 150 names, with check marks near certain names. Some of
these were individuals *suspected* of being anti-Castro Cubans. The number

I checked out was an extremely small number. A lot of these guys I didn't know personally anyway, even if I had their photograph or home address."[11]

The thousands of Cubans who had gone into exile in Miami and many other American cities in the early 1960s were scarcely a unified band. Dozens of their organizations soon sprang up, each seeking to build its own power base for what they all presumed would be an eventual return to their homeland. They cut across many ideological persuasions. Many had themselves fought with Castro—before he avowed himself a Marxist —to rid Cuba of the oppressive Batista regime. Others stayed loyal to Batista, or his equally wealthy exiled predecessor as Cuban president, Carlos Prio Socarras. Many worked closely with the CIA and even received special training at U.S. Army bases. Some of these same people went into drug-dealing or other illegal activity on behalf of American gangsters they had known in Havana. Soldier-of-fortune types moved in to help train exile commandos at camps in the Florida Keys and New Orleans. And Castro's Soviet-trained G-2 spy network worked diligently to recruit "double agents" and generally keep abreast of all anti-Castro activities. It was a wild potpourri indeed.

It was no secret that Castro was outraged at what he perceived as Khrushchev's lack of backbone during the Cuban Missile Crisis. Things became so heated at one point in October 1962 that Aleksandr Alekseev, the new Soviet ambassador to Cuba, had to convince Castro even to meet Deputy Premier Anastas Mikoyan for discussions. It was revealed in 1987 that Khrushchev had given very precise orders that Soviet officers should take no provocative action in Cuba. But Castro was determined to defend the sovereignty of Cuban airspace regardless and, even after one American U-2 was shot down, the Cuban premier had ordered his antiaircraft artillery to keep firing at any low-flying planes. Had one more American plane bit the dust, Robert Kennedy said later that the United States probably would have invaded.[12]

Castro also felt excluded from the deal cut between the United States and the Soviets. At first he had no reason to trust that the Kennedy administration would make good on any promises to leave his island alone. Yet trust began to build when, soon after the crisis, the White House Special Group on Cuba ordered a halt to all sabotage and other anti-Castro activities emanating from within American borders. Operation MONGOOSE was disbanded. A new interagency Cuban Coordinating Committee was established at the State Department, given responsibility for developing any future covert action proposals.

At the same time, however, the CIA's new Cuban affairs overseer, Desmond FitzGerald, charted his own course. A 1967 CIA inspector general's report—compiled not long before FitzGerald's death that summer—revealed that one of his first plans had called for James Donovan, who was handling the administration's delicate negotiations with Castro for release of the Bay of Pigs prisoners, to "present Castro with a contaminated diving suit." As a Senate report unveiled publicly in 1975: "The [CIA] Technical Services Division bought a diving suit, dusted the inside with a fungus that would produce a chronic skin disease (Madura foot), and contaminated the breathing apparatus with a tubercule bacillus. The Inspector General's report states that the plan was abandoned because Donovan gave Castro a different diving suit on his own initiative. [Richard] Helms testified that the diving suit never left the laboratory."

On January 4, 1963, a week after the Bay of Pigs prisoners came home, Kennedy's national security adviser, McGeorge Bundy, proposed to the president that the United States finally explore the possibility of communicating with Castro. That same month, FitzGerald privately asked an assistant "to determine whether an exotic seashell, rigged to explode, could be deposited in an area where Castro commonly went skin diving. The idea was explored by the Technical Services Division and discarded as impractical."[13]

With such "direction" coming from the very top at the CIA, it is little wonder that the Cuban exiles were confused by the Kennedy administration's dual nature. Even the moderate exiles once protected by JFK from the CIA during the Bay of Pigs began turning against him. In February 1963, Antonio Varona of the Cuban Revolutionary Council (CRC) asserted that the administration was "tying our hands so we could do nothing." By April, Miro Cardona resigned as head of the CRC, denouncing Kennedy for granting Castro "absolute immunity in the execution of Khrushchev's sinister designs."[14]

Robert Kennedy had sought to appease their anger over the new Cuba policy by inviting Manuel Artime to a mid-January 1963 ski weekend in New Hampshire. Artime, known as the CIA's "Golden Boy," was a former Havana medical doctor who had been placed in charge of the Bay of Pigs training camps in Guatemala and Nicaragua. Captured by Castro's forces when he led the brigade ashore, he was released in the December 1962 prisoners-for-ransom exchange.

In 1976, about a year before Artime died at age forty-five of what was termed "inoperable cancer," he recounted the story to me of his visit with Robert Kennedy.[15]

"Bobby made the proposition, I should go to Fort Benning and help train the released members of my brigade inside the American Army," Artime said as we drove in his car through the Miami streets. "I made only one question: 'Mr. Attorney General, do you warrant to me that this training will be in order to land another time in Cuba, to rescue my culture from the Castro dictatorship?' Then he told me, 'Manolo, from the United States you cannot do anything against Castro.' I smiled at him and said, 'But with the support indirectly of the United States, could I make my own Latin American war against Castro?'

"Then he smiled and he told me, 'You are terrible, but I will tell you honestly—if, without using the name of the United States, you can get one country to give you a piece of land and the moral support to attack Castro, we will get you the weapons and the necessary things for doing that.' "

The precise substance of that conversation can, of course, never be known. But that such a ski rendezvous did take place was confirmed in a 1981 book about the exile movement, *The Fish Is Red*. Artime took Kennedy at his word and was soon back on a CIA retainer, making arrangements to establish anti-Castro operations bases in Nicaragua and Costa Rica.[16] Before long, however, Artime also came to believe that "no doubt we were betrayed[17] [by the Kennedys]."

I knew that Artime had been one of Nagell's "subjects" during the course of his double-agent role. Not long after the Artime-Kennedy meeting, at the end of January 1963 the exile leader first came under Nagell's scrutiny.

Nagell has stated: "I conducted inquiries relative to 'dissident' members of several Cuban refugee groups based in the United States; I checked out an alleged connection between a Miami resident named Eladio Del Valle and New Orleans CIA informant Sergio Arcacha-Smith; I investigated an associate of the now deceased right-wing extremist David W. Ferrie of New Orleans. . . . I conducted a surveillance on a man, said to have been an ex-CIA employee, observed talking to [exile] leader Manuel Artime and former Cuban senator/racketeer Rolando Masferrer."[18]

All of these people were prominent names in exile-related activities. All of them have also surfaced before—as having been involved in CIA-backed attempts to assassinate Fidel Castro, or even rumored connections to the assassination of President Kennedy.

Eladio del Valle: Nicknamed "Yito," del Valle had been a young Cuban congressman and city councilman in Havana during the final years of the Batista dictatorship. According to several sources, he had also piled up a small fortune smuggling in American cigarettes and other contraband—in partnership with Florida mobster Santos Trafficante, Jr.[19] As Castro approached the capital, del Valle fled into exile, where he bought a Miami grocery store as a front for various operations.

"Now there was a gun for hire," I was told in 1975 by Al Tarabocchia, then a Hispanic investigator for the Senate Internal Security Subcommittee. "Anything that had to do with smuggling, gun-running, del Valle was with it. Both a bagman and a hit man, mainly involved with people from the Batista regime."[20]

As early as 1960, del Valle was reportedly working with a New Orleans pilot, David Ferrie, in flying clandestine missions over Cuba.[21] In January 1961, shortly before the Bay of Pigs invasion, del Valle told the New York *Daily News* that he had a fighting force of "8,500 men in Cuba and a skeleton force of about 200 working in Miami and Central America."[22] By 1963 he was also a leader of the Committee to Free Cuba, or "Cuba Libre."[23]

On the night of February 22, 1967, del Valle's body was discovered by Miami police, sprawled across the floor of his flaming-red Cadillac. He had been brutally beaten, shot above the heart, and his head chopped open. He was being sought for questioning at the time by Jim Garrison's investigative staff.[24]

David Ferrie: The same night del Valle died, so did his old friend Ferrie. He had already been questioned once by Garrison about his possible knowledge of the assassination. Ferrie's body was found in his New Orleans apartment, alongside two typed notes suggesting suicide. The coroner's ruling said "natural causes," though Garrison suspected he had been poisoned.[25]

Back in July 1955, when Lee Harvey Oswald was living with his mother in New Orleans, the sixteen-year-old had joined the Louisiana Civil Air Patrol—commanded by Captain David Ferrie. In the summer of 1963, when Ferrie was seen by credible witnesses in Oswald's company on more than one occasion, Ferrie was wearing several hats. Besides being an investigator for Guy Banister Associates, a private detective agency linked with the CIA, the FBI, and Cuban exiles, Ferrie was helping prepare the defense of Carlos Marcello, the New Orleans Mob boss whom Robert Kennedy was seeking to deport. The evidence is strong that Ferrie had also been a CIA contract employee.[26]

Sergio Arcacha-Smith: Under two dictatorships prior to Castro, this Spanish-Irish lawyer had served as Cuba's consul to several countries. Going into exile in New Orleans, in 1961 he and Ferrie had set up together the Cuban Democratic Liberation Front. Arcacha-Smith was also an associate of Guy Banister, was reported to have made a number of trips to Mexico in 1962 and 1963, and, some ten months before the Kennedy assassination, moved to Texas—where he often commuted between Houston and Dallas.[27]

In 1967 Garrison was unsuccessful in having Arcacha-Smith extradited from Texas for questioning. The exile eventually moved to Key West, Florida, where he is said to still reside.

Rolando Masferrer: Nicknamed "The Tiger" after his ruthless private army of the Batista era, Masferrer was an ex-Cuban senator and newspaper publisher who reportedly fled the island with as much as $10 million. "A guy who could slit your throat and smile while doing it," as U.S. Senate aide Al Tarabocchia put it.[28]

In Miami, Masferrer was an FBI informant who maintained connections to the Trafficante underworld. His "30th of November" exile organization kept up efforts to eliminate Castro all through 1963 and beyond. Cuba seems to have responded in kind; Castro was known to have a substantial bounty out on Masferrer.[29] As we saw in Chapter Ten, before leaving Mexico City Nagell obtained a weapon, with Masferrer as the original target.

And who was the unidentified man—"said to have been an ex-CIA employee"—whom Nagell observed talking with Artime and Masferrer that January 1963 day in Miami? Based on other material supplied me by Nagell, I believe it was a Cuban exile who used the "war name" of "Angel" (pronounced On-hel). He, along with a partner, would later come into direct contact with Lee Harvey Oswald.

In a ten-page outline of "highlights" I sent Nagell in 1976, returned to me with his corrections, here is what Nagell delineated:

"The two other figures directly involved were known to Oswald by the given names 'Angel' and 'Leopoldo,' and were said to be former CIA employees of Cuban extraction, born and raised in Cuba. Both were connected with a violence-prone faction of a CIA-financed group operating in Mexico City and elsewhere. In 1962, both had participated in a bomb-throwing incident directed against an employee of Mexico's Cuban Embassy. Both were said to be well known to Mexican and Cuban authorities, and of course to the CIA. In Mexico, one name for the group may have been 'Alpha 66.' In Florida, members of their group may have associated with a Cuban exile organization called Movimiento Revolucionario del Pueblo; in Puerto Rico, with a group called 'JURE.' There were, as well, past ties with a group called Movement to Free Cuba, which originally functioned under the auspices of the CIA. In correspondence with one Arthur Gilman Greenstein, [I] cryptically referred to this group as 'Cuba Libre.' "[30]

Nagell also outlined his observations of "Angel" in a letter to Fensterwald, as follows: "Angel was in Miami during the latter part of January 1963. He may have stayed at the Holiday Inn located on Biscayne Boulevard [where Nagell was also residing]. On several occasions he visited a well-lighted Cuban restaurant that was located on Flagler Street. He also visited a small photo shop that was located on a street perpendicular to the long axis of Flagler; this shop had some kind of a connection with the MRP" [the exile group Movimiento Revolucionario del Pueblo].[31]

Nagell added in another letter that Angel also used the pseudonym of "Rangel" or "Wrangel" as a surname on at least one occasion.[32] According to a description furnished by Nagell in 1968 for the Garrison investigation, the exile was twenty-eight to thirty years of age. He stood about five feet, eleven inches or six feet tall and weighed a stocky 180 pounds. He had black hair and hazel eyes.[33]

When I asked Nagell on two occasions whether he knew Angel or his partner's real names, the first time he would say only, "I might have suspected a lot of things." The next time he added: "I know the names that were supposed to be real. I knew names. And their backgrounds."[34]

I knew this much: Somehow I had to learn more about the CIA-backed exile organization known as "Alpha 66."

Inside Alpha 66

In the summer of 1976, *New Times* magazine sent me to Miami to do an article about a series of mysterious murders plaguing the "Little Havana" exile community. It was on this trip that Artime agreed to see me for a brief interview. In a story in *The Saturday Evening Post,* I had also first come across the name of Antonio Veciana, identified as one of Alpha 66's founders. To my surprise, I found his number listed in the Miami phone book. Speaking in halting English, Veciana agreed to meet me downtown outside the Trailways bus station. I was the first journalist to contact him in recent years.[35]

He showed up with a bodyguard, emerging from the passenger side of a blue Maverick, a stocky, handsome man about six feet tall and wearing sunglasses. He was dressed in an open-collar black silk shirt and black slacks. Inside a little coffee shop, Veciana said he had recently been paroled from the Atlanta Federal Penitentiary, after serving seventeen months of what he asserted was a trumped-up narcotics conspiracy charge. He was bitter at certain U.S. authorities about it and had decided to break a many-years silence about his activities. And he informed me that he was meeting regularly with an investigator for the House Assassinations Committee. Then Veciana asked if he could see my "government card." When I succeeded in convincing him I was a legitimate journalist, we drove out to the beachside Shellborne Hotel.

I was not prepared for the remarkable story Veciana unfolded. "I know a lot of secrets," he began. He had been president of a Havana accounting firm when Castro took over Cuba. Embittered by Fidel's turn toward the Communists, Veciana began raising funds for an anti-Castro uprising. Shortly thereafter, in 1960, he received a visit from a man who used the name "Maurice Bishop." It was to be the first of more than one hundred meetings in a relationship that would last thirteen years.

Veciana described Bishop as standing about six feet, two inches, with dark hair, blue eyes, a high forehead, and sunspots below his eyes. He appeared to be in his early forties (in 1962–63). Bishop dressed expensively, spoke fluent French, and carried a false Belgian passport. He told Veciana he was part of an American intelligence service but instructed him not to ask which one.

"Bishop inculcated into us the principles of psychological warfare," Veciana recalled. "We spread false rumors or disinformation. We put out counterfeit bills that were similar to bank notes printed by the government, and we distributed them throughout the country. We wanted to disrupt the Cuban economy to create a spirit of resistance within the people."

When this failed to create the desired result, Bishop used Veciana to coordinate assassination attempts. The first was scheduled as Castro prepared to introduce the Soviet cosmonaut Yuri Gagarin, but was canceled when Bishop anticipated a violent Soviet reaction. The next was planned for October 1961 during a Castro speech, using a bazooka fired from a nearby rooftop. But Castro got wind of the plot, and Veciana was forced to flee Cuba by boat. A month later in Miami, Bishop contacted Veciana again. Together they laid plans to form the group known as Alpha 66. Veciana traveled to New York, where he worked on another plan to eliminate Castro should he come to speak at the United Nations.

Later I would find the first public records on Alpha 66 in the archives of The New York Times. Through the Cuban Missile Crisis buildup period in September and October 1962, the "anti-Castro fighting group" seemed to have wanted to get itself in the news. Veciana was mentioned in several articles datelined San Juan, Puerto Rico, reading "a declaration of war" that included guerrilla-style machine-gun attacks on five British and two Cuban vessels bringing supplies into the island.

Veciana was quoted that all the planning was being done by leaders "I don't even know" but that Cubans of all major exile organizations were backing the Alpha 66 efforts financially. Another article found him saying that his group owned four vessels of various sizes, but admitting only that their base was in "an area of the Caribbean close to Cuba." Said the Times: "Although Mr. Veciana admits founding Alpha 66, he denies he or anyone else is its chief. It is ruled by a small committee of which he is a member. The committee controls all bands and directs military operations through designated commanders."[36]

Clearly, Alpha 66 had been part of the CIA's and the Pentagon's hopes to "start a small war," as Nagell had described the situation surrounding the Cuban Missile Crisis. According to ex-CIA official Barney Hidalgo, after the Cuban Missile Crisis "the word came down that Alpha 66 was not in the American best policies to work with. Politically unstable, too many wildcats, hotheads, shoot-from-the-hip types, and they could get us in trouble by going out and committing assassinations. Well, being an intelligence agent you *should* be able to go hog-wild, achieve your end by whatever means. But unfortunately, the agency said no."[37]

But just as Desmond FitzGerald was going against Kennedy's Cuban policies, so was someone else in U.S. intelligence contravening CIA orders to steer clear of Alpha 66. Picking up his story, Veciana told me that Maurice Bishop organized a series of commando attacks against Soviet merchant ships in Cuban harbors early in 1963.

"As a result of the [Cuban] Missile Crisis, he believed that Kennedy and Khrushchev had made a secret pact to do nothing about Cuba. Bishop kept saying Kennedy would have to be forced to make a decision. The only way was to put him up against the wall. Three ships were attacked in different ports of Cuba. The first one was a mistake in identity; it was a British ship. The other two were Russian. To further make Kennedy reach a point, we held a press conference in Washington to let him know about the commando groups. That was when Kennedy ordered that I be confined to Dade County, Florida."

Veciana's statements were backed up in *The New York Times*'s chronicle of the period. In March 1963 a splinter group of Alpha 66 calling itself "Commandos L" had gone on the offensive. First it infiltrated Cuba and attacked a Soviet military post. Next it shelled two Soviet freighters operating near the Cuban coast. On March 30 both the State and Justice departments announced they were taking "every step necessary to ensure that such raids are not launched, manned, or equipped from U.S. territory." Surveillance of the refugees intensified; certain Miami exiles, including Veciana, were forbidden to travel at all.[38]

It would be the late summer of 1963 before Veciana saw Bishop again, this time in Dallas, Texas—in the company of a silent, unnamed young man whom the exile would later recognize as Lee Harvey Oswald. We shall return to that pivotal meeting in due course.

Whoever "Bishop" was, obviously there was a rogue operation going on with Alpha 66—whose target, by the spring of 1963, was as much the Kennedy administration as Fidel Castro. And with as much finesse as I could manage, I brought my discussion with Veciana around to "Angel," "Leopoldo," and Mexico City.

Veciana leaned back on the hotel lobby couch, cupped a hand to his chin, and answered my question with deliberation. "Angel is a very common name," he replied. "During that time, I never met or knew a Leopoldo. I knew there was a person Leopoldo. I might know him under his real name. We all had other names. I worked under the name of Victor Fernandez. A lot of people knew me as my real name, but a lot also knew me as Victor."

"Tell me a little about Alpha 66's operation in Mexico in the beginning," I said.

"At that time, the only way to get in and out of Cuba was through Mexico," Veciana went on. "We had four people there in the fall of 1962. It was secret intelligence work. Their main job was to inform the movement here in Miami of people who were visiting Cuba, and what the Cuban consulate was up to. They did check up on the personnel of the Cubans, to see if they could bring them over to our side."

As far as Veciana may have been willing to go with his recollections, they appeared to be genuine. But I did not press him further; this might yet be dangerous territory. Instead, I decided to pursue the Alpha-Mexico link by visiting the headquarters the group still maintained in 1976 in Little Havana. The first thing I noticed when I walked into the storefront was a huge gun mounted on one wall alongside a bust of Cuban martyr José Martí. A young, well-mannered man served as my interpreter in speaking with Andres Nasario Sargen, who, like Veciana, had been among Alpha 66's original founders. The war against Castro was still continuing, I was told. Alpha 66 claimed to have some two hundred active members and "one hundred thousand active sympathizers."

I did not tell Sargen that I was seeing Veciana. Mostly, as he went to some length to distance the group from the FBI or the CIA ("the CIA had Cubans try to infiltrate Alpha, to see what [the] CIA needed to know to put us out of business," Sargen claimed), I let our conversation be limited to generalities about Alpha's efforts. But I did ask about Mexico City.

"There were scattered Alpha delegates there in the early '60s," Sargen responded with a quizzical expression. "Some Cubans had gotten out through Mexico and decided to stay there instead of facing an entirely different environment. When we had an office there in 1962–63, there was trouble. The Cuban consulate was on one street and Alpha was close by. This was a very hard time, very trying for our people there."

As I said good-bye, I glanced over again at the office wall. Next to a map of Cuba there was a little plaque. It said:

"Alpha 66
Es La Respuesta"

Or, in English, "Alpha 66 is the answer."[39]

Cuba and the Radical Right

In Washington's Assassination Archives Research Center there is a memorandum of April 4, 1963, written by the chief of the Miami Police Intelligence Unit. It was based on a series of informant reports "concerning the feelings and proposed actions of the Cuban refugee colony." Believing "that the United States Government has turned against them," the exiles were regrouping into new factions and proposing a series of actions. The list enumerated by Detective Sgt. C. H. Sapp was chilling. It included "a complete disregard for Federal, State and local authority" and "the bombing of Federal agencies." The rumor was "that all violence hither-to directed toward Castro's Cuba will now be directed toward various governmental agencies in the United States."[40]

Six days later, on April 10, a notarized statement was sent to Detective Sapp from another detective, Lochart F. Gracey, Jr., who had an informant monitor the annual conference of the Congress of Freedom, Inc. Founded in Omaha, Nebraska, ten years before, the COF's 1963 meeting had taken place in New Orleans on April 4–6, bringing together wealthy radical rightists from across the United States. In various speeches, according to Gracey, "in a generalized feeling, there was indicated the overthrow of the present government of the United States." This included "the setting up of a criminal activity to assassinate particular persons. . . ." The report went on that "membership within the Congress of Freedom, Inc., contain high ranking members of the Armed Forces that secretly belong to the organization."[41]

Also in April 1963, a flyer was circulated among the Miami Cuban exile community. It read: "Only through one development will you Cuban patriots ever live again in your homeland as freemen . . . if an inspired Act of God should place in the White House within weeks a Texan [LBJ] known to be a friend of all Latin Americans . . . though he must under present conditions bow to the Zionists who since 1905 came into control of the United States, and for whom Jack Kennedy and Nelson Rockefeller and other members of the Council of Foreign Relations and allied agencies are only stooges and pawns. Though Johnson must now bow to these crafty and cunning Communist-hatching Jews, yet, did an Act of God suddenly elevate him into the top position [he] would revert to what his beloved father and grandfather were, and to their values and principles and loyalties."

The flyer, dated April 18, 1963, was signed "a Texan who resents the

Oriental influence that has come to control, to degrade, to pollute and enslave his own people."[42]

More and more as the Cuban refugees felt themselves cut off from the Kennedy policies toward Castro, they began turning to nongovernmental sources for help. Charles Willoughby, for one, had been pushing their cause for some time. Back in June 1961, he had written Allen Dulles expressing outrage over the Kennedy administration's choices—Manuel Ray, Miro Cardona, and others—to take over Cuba had the Bay of Pigs succeeded. "On what conceivable ground could ex-henchmen of Castro become the 'hope of liberation'?" Willoughby asked.[43]

His *Foreign Intelligence Digest* warned that "hundreds of former Castro adherents have fled Cuba, seeking 'political asylum' in the United States. . . . This could well be an organized plan to infiltrate and subvert the Cuban refugee movement."[44] Later, Willoughby would also write: "Kennedy used the missile crisis to forbid the Cubans to make attempts to rescue their country."

In Dallas, Willoughby's wealthy oilman friend H. L. Hunt was going beyond polemics. Mario Garcia Kohly, Sr., the right-wing Cuban exile who according to Robert Morrow was the CIA's choice (by arrangement with Richard Nixon) to take command in Cuba after the Bay of Pigs, met with Hunt soon after the Cuban Missile Crisis. A letter from Kohly to the oil millionaire, dated December 12, 1962, began:

> First, let me express my thanks and those of my associates for the very kind reception of Monday night, by you and your charming wife. I also enjoyed very much meeting with your two good friends who were present.
>
> Since speaking with you, I have again been in contact with the Vatican. As you know, they are very interested in my program, so much so that they will finance the greater part of my efforts for the liberation of Cuba. . . . It is my thought, recalling your statements regarding your close friendship with Vice President Lyndon Johnson, that if he would be kind enough to speak to a church authority such as Archbishop Patrick A. O'Boyle, here in Washington to the effect that they urgently transmit to Cardinal Cento in the Vatican Curia the good feeling of the Vice President in respect to our efforts to liberate Cuba and that we would be recognized after we succeeded in overthrowing Castro. This would then accomplish our objective and the help of the Church would immediately be forthcoming.[45]

I could find no H. L. Hunt response in the Kohly files bequeathed to Morrow before the exile's death, but there were dozens of other letters indicating that Kohly's curious effort to enlist the Vatican's assistance continued all through 1963.

Gerry Patrick Hemming, who then worked among the exiles in Florida, remembers: "We had people who dealt directly with the Hunts, but they did not want to know operational plans. Several of the exile leaders were in touch with them—Felipe Vidal's Liberation Front people, Tony Cuesta's Commandos L. After Cuesta broke with CIA, he sought support and Texas money to buy the equipment that started them on their operations."[46]

Tony Cuesta, whose "Commandos L" force was the Alpha 66 offshoot that claimed responsibility for the March 1963 shipping raids against Cuba, worked closely with Antonio Veciana. When I asked about Cuesta, Veciana said that he, too, had been acquainted with "Maurice Bishop."

The first time I pushed Nagell to reveal the true names of "Angel" and "Leopoldo," he suddenly steered the conversation to Cuesta, asking if I knew what became of him. I knew only that Cuesta had been captured on a 1966 raid into Cuba, blinded in one eye by gunfire, and was presumably still in jail. He was with Alpha 66, correct? I asked.

"Yes, and with a couple other outfits, wasn't he?" Nagell replied. "Free Cuba Committee or Cuban Freedom Committee."

The next time I saw Nagell, I specifically asked if Tony Cuesta was important to the Oswald story. Again, Nagell's response was cryptic but revealing. "Did they kill him?" he asked. No, still imprisoned by Fidel, as far as I knew. "He was CIA, there's no doubt," Nagell continued. "An agent, not an officer. You realize the Cuban government did not just throw these guys in jail on suspicion. They had something on these guys."[47]

Kohly, Cuesta, and Felipe Vidal were not the only exiles in touch with Texas money. So was another man on Nagell's January 1963 surveillance list. Sergio Arcacha-Smith, as former security chief for the Hunt oil interests Paul Rothermel recalled, was "a frequent visitor" to the Hunt offices during that period.[48] In 1975, ex-CIA agent William George Gaudet would tell attorney Fensterwald that Arcacha-Smith was "a shadowy figure" whom he believed knew Lee Harvey Oswald.[49]

"I believe that Sergio and General Walker were pretty good friends," Paul Rothermel added.[50]

In April 1963, Major General Edwin A. Walker was about to play an extremely significant role in the Oswald saga.

Summary

In what seemed to have been part of his espionage guise, Nagell's correspondence and actions in the Bay Pines V.A. Hospital were generally aimed at building a picture of instability and anti-American sentiment. Immediately upon his departure, Nagell headed for Miami and contacted two FBI agents whose specialty was illegal armaments. Nagell then commenced investigating several members of the Cuban exile community, whose possible role in a JFK conspiracy has been speculated about by others. One was "Angel," a "war name" for someone whose true identity Nagell has never revealed—a major figure in the JFK conspiracy.

While the Kennedy administration began exploring communicating with Castro, the CIA's Desmond FitzGerald secretly continued scheming to assassinate the Cuban premier. Another intelligence official, "Maurice Bishop," worked with Alpha 66 leader Antonio Veciana in putting together covert actions seeking to force JFK's hand. Bitterness at the Kennedys' hands-off-Cuba policies escalated among the Cuban exiles. By April, violence against U.S. officials was being voiced by both the Miami refugees and by right-wing extremists at a conclave in New Orleans. Some exiles began making friends among ultraright wealthy circles in Dallas, specifically oilman H. L. Hunt.

Chapter Thirteen

The Attack on General Walker: February–April 1963

———————◇———————

Before departing Florida in early February 1963, Richard Nagell renewed his correspondence with the Army concerning the circumstances of his resignation back in 1959. A letter from Brigadier General Kenneth G. Wickham, acting adjutant general at the Pentagon, dated January 24, was a response to Nagell's letter to President Kennedy from the Bay Pines V.A. Hospital. Though the Pentagon's letter arrived at the hospital some days after Nagell checked out, somehow it still seems to have reached him.

"Your resignation was approved only after careful review of your final type physical examination in the Office of the Surgeon General," it said, "and you were found to be physically qualified for separation. When a resignation has become effective, it cannot be rescinded. As you were previously advised, if you believe that there has been an error or injustice in your case, the inclosed [sic] application should be completed and returned to the Army Board for Correction of Military Records. . . ."

On February 3, 1963, Nagell typed out his request to the Army Board that he "be given a complete and adequate physical examination by the Army to include a neurosurgical examination, and if applicable to receive a disability retirement from the Army." Referring once again to his Korean War injuries and the B-25 plane crash, he added that his preresignation physical "was hurried and incomplete to say the least," in that no neurologist examined him. "I have been turned down from many jobs because of my wartime wounds and injuries," Nagell added. "The last time I was employed was on June 8, 1962. . . ." He made reference to records kept by Dr. Edwin Weinstein at Walter Reed, and listed his return address as a post office box at Sanford Station, Los Angeles.[1]

After sending off his letter, the ubiquitous traveler then drove through Florida and Louisiana into Texas. In Dallas, he says he again spent "a few days inquiring" into the status of Lee Harvey Oswald—but Nagell would never say what this inquiry was about.

Shortly before this, on January 27, 1963, Oswald, using the "A. J. Hidell" alias for the first time, had filled out a mail order to Seaport Traders in Los Angeles for a .38-caliber Smith & Wesson revolver. He had also completed repayment to the State Department of a loan made to him in the Soviet Union the previous spring, legally freeing him to seek a new passport if he desired.[2]

Oswald had taken to referring to himself as a Marxist—but *not* a Marxist-Leninist. There was a distinction. The "purer" form of Marxism was embodied in the life of Leon Trotsky, who split with Stalin and went into exile in 1929, only to be assassinated by the Stalinists in Mexico in 1940. Trotsky advocated a worldwide Communist revolution, not a slow-paced development of such principles within Soviet borders. As Oswald claimed to see it, "Cuba is the only real revolutionary country in the world today."

He had been in touch with the Trotskyite Socialist Workers Party (SWP) almost immediately upon his return from the Soviet Union. Late in August 1962, in response to his query, Oswald had received back a fifty-four-page pamphlet from the SWP's New York headquarters "as well as some other material which may be of interest to you." No trace remains of the "other material." The pamphlet speaks of "the Stalinist degeneration [that] welled out of Moscow and began corrupting young Communist parties everywhere." The Trotskyists were different, they were truly ready to "save us from capitalist barbarism and open up a new world for humanity." The day after receiving this, Oswald airmailed to SWP headquarters for *The Teachings of Leon Trotsky.*[3]

At the end of October 1962, soon after opening his Dallas post office box and starting work at the JCS printing shop, Oswald wrote again asking to join the SWP. According to the Warren Commission Report, in November "his application was not accepted since there was then no chapter in the Dallas area."[4] But that December, he would once more offer his services in printing SWP posters while employed at JCS. And he would subscribe to the SWP's newspaper, *The Militant.* As the New Year dawned, he ordered three more pamphlets from the Trotskyite publishing house Pioneer Press. Several pieces of correspondence from Oswald to the SWP, the Warren Commission would find, ended up missing from the organization's files.[5] Nagell was, as described in Chapter Seven, a friend of the SWP's longtime West Coast representative Steve Roberts.

Nagell and Marina

After Nagell's stopover in Dallas early in February 1963, two references in his notebook map out where he went after that.

> NUEVO LAREDO, MEX. (FEB) 63
> CAFE REGIS, CALLE PINO
> SUAREZ

A couple of pages later, under a boxed heading of "NUEVO LAREDO," are listings for several meeting places:

TEATRO ALAMEDA, LA ROCA BAR & RES'T. (DOWNSTAIRS) (1800-2130).
THE GREEN CAT (2400 ONLY)
REFORMA REST. & BAR GUERRERO 806, N. LAREDO (1300–1700)
WATCH TV AT 6:30 P.M.
  ABC MUSIC STORE
  1002 HIDALGO
  LAREDO, TEXAS

Whomever Nagell was meeting with, the rendezvous took place on both sides of the U.S.-Mexican border. In 1978 he would tell me that his own code name for the purpose of checking in with his Soviet contact was "Laredo." Nagell explained that Soviet intelligence often used names such as "Laredo," "Quebec," or "Dallas"—pointing out that a recently captured American sergeant was a KGB spy who had the code name "Quebec."

"It does not refer to the country you're operating in at the time," Nagell said. "I did not use the name 'Laredo' in the United States. There is a Laredo on both sides of the border."

In turn, his KGB contact used the name "Oaxaca." The latter was derived from the Mexican state of the same name. In 1963, Nagell says, "Oaxaca" had never set foot in the United States.[6]

So it seems probable that Nagell may have met with "Oaxaca" in Nuevo Laredo—perhaps to pass along information concerning his January 1963 Cuban exile-monitoring in Florida and then his stopover in Dallas to look into Oswald's latest activities.

Soon after this, Nagell began looking into some new circumstances surrounding Oswald's wife.

Sometime in late January or early February 1963, according to Marina Oswald's Warren Commission testimony: "Lee wanted me to go to Russia . . . and I told him that if he wanted me to go then that meant he didn't love me and that in that case what was the idea of coming to the United States in the first place. Lee would say that it would be better for me to go to Russia. I did not know why. I did not know what he had in mind. He said he loved me but it would be better for me. . . ."[7]

On February 17, Marina wrote a letter to the Soviet embassy in Washington. "I was forced to because Lee insisted on it," she said. "He handed me the paper, a pencil, and said, 'Write.' "[8]

Marina wrote: "Dear Comrade Reznichenko! I beg your assistance to help me to return to the homeland in the USSR where I will again feel myself a full-fledged citizen. Please let me know what I should do for this, i.e., perhaps it will be necessary to fill out a special application form. . . ."[9]

This letter, like the Oswalds' other correspondence, was routed to the desk of Vitaly Gerasimov, the Soviet consular officer then under surveillance by the FBI as the suspected paymaster of an espionage network in the United States.[10] The letter was also first examined by the FBI. On March 8, Reznichenko's consular section replied to Marina that she would need to fill out an application in triplicate, along with similar copies of her detailed biography. "Time of processing requires 5 or 6 months," she was informed.[11]

The FBI had apparently intercepted some of this correspondence before allowing it to proceed through the mail. On March 11, Dallas FBI agent James P. Hosty, Jr., made an effort to call upon Marina at the Oswalds' apartment—only to find that they had moved to an unknown location. Hosty has said he did not pursue further contact at the time.[12] Yet the Oswalds had moved only a block north and half a block west, to 214 West Neely Street, taking the top floor of a rickety wooden two-story duplex. From this address, on March 17, Marina filled out and sent to the Soviet embassy most of the items demanded by them.[13]

At this point Richard Nagell entered the picture. A memorandum by Fensterwald of a conversation with Nagell reports Nagell saying that "the

CIA has pictures of Nagell outside the Soviet Embassy. At least one set was taken in April 1963."[14] Another Fensterwald memo quotes Nagell that the Soviets "put Nagell to watching Marina."[15]

The timing would indicate that Nagell was in Washington, D.C., perhaps receiving his instructions about Marina Oswald at the Soviet embassy, for, according to a Military Intelligence file on Nagell: "In April 1963, SUBJECT conducted an inquiry concerning the marital status of Marina Oswald and her reported desire to return to the USSR."[16]

Nagell says that this latest Oswald inquiry took him back to Dallas and to San Antonio, where, posing as an investigator for the Immigration and Naturalization Service, he met with INS officials concerning Marina. "I believed I was functioning for the CIA for my inquiry into her," Nagell told me in 1975. "I was provided photos of her. I've seen her but never met her. There is a possibility she has seen me with other people. I certainly wouldn't say that this project was entwined with the later thing that happened."[17]

From Texas, Nagell continued to head west. By April 19, an FBI file on Nagell describes his making contact with the bureau on the West Coast. It states that Nagell "advised FBI in Los Angeles on 4/19/63 he had taken former wife to court on same date for failure to comply with court order giving subject visitation rights with children."[18]

After the Kennedy assassination, at Nagell's request a Secret Service agent would come to see him in the El Paso County Jail. The date was January 2, 1964; the agent's name, according to FBI files, was George Weisheit. Under a file headed "INTERNAL SECURITY—RUSSIA," the FBI says: "At the conclusion of the short interview with NAGELL, he advised that he had been acquainted with MARINA, LEE HARVEY OSWALD's wife, and pointed out that OSWALD was having marital difficulties with MARINA."[19]

In 1976 I located Weisheit, who had just retired from the Secret Service and who was teaching at Texas Eastern University's School of Criminal Justice in Tyler, Texas. But Weisheit said he only "vaguely" remembered visiting with Nagell. Even after I read him the FBI report over the phone, he maintained: "Boy, I just do not recall this at all. You'd have to go to my original reports in Washington."[20]

Those reports were not available under the privacy section of the Freedom of Information Act. However, in the mid-1970s, the Secret Service finally released the last of its "protective detail" reports about Marina Oswald when she was in their custody after the assassination. These reports were no more than a chronicle of Marina's daily visitors, both official and personal. And this particular page was the only one that had previously been withheld from public view.

At midpage, under a heading for *"January 18, 1964 (Saturday),"* the report reveals:

"10:00 A.M.—SA Jamison arrived and interviewed Mrs. Marina Oswald re Richard Case Nagell.

"12:00 noon—SA Jamison departed."[21]

Two hours spent talking with Oswald's widow about Nagell seems an awfully long time for casual Secret Service conversation. But Nagell's name would never surface, at least publicly, during the Warren Commission's then ongoing investigation. And his was the only name on the long-withheld page that might have raised certain eyebrows had it been released.

"I wonder why the Secret Service displayed my mug shot to Marina Oswald," Nagell would say after learning about the Secret Service report. "I never stated that I had met her or knew her personally . . . though I sure knew a lot about her."[22]

Oswald and the General

Nagell's Texas inquiry into Marina Oswald would have placed him in Dallas around the time of another event—the night of April 10, 1963, when Oswald is said to have fired a shot aimed at General Edwin A. Walker.

Walker briefly became a household word during the Kennedy era. As commander of the 24th Infantry Division in Augsburg, West Germany, in 1961, he had issued a manifesto declaring communism a "satanic enemy of mankind" that "must be destroyed by a concentrated and determined effort of all God's people."[23] That April, JFK had asked Defense Secretary Robert McNamara to look into Walker's indoctrination of his troops with the beliefs of the John Birch Society. Walker was relieved of his command pending an investigation. In June 1961 McNamara issued a directive stating: "In public discussion all officers of the Department should confine themselves to defense matters."[24]

This was quickly seized upon by the extreme right. Senator Strom Thurmond of South Carolina, once the presidential candidate of the States' Rights party in 1948, called for an investigation "of Defense Department censorship of speeches of officers and of the admonishment of Major General Walker." The John Birch Society quickly echoed Thurmond's plea to end the "military gag rule."[25] In November 1961 Walker angrily resigned from the Army to run for governor of Texas and "throw out the traitors." He ran as a Democrat, with the longer-range goal of challenging

JFK for president in 1964, but finished dead last in the 1962 Democratic primary.[26]

Then, late in September 1962, the general made headlines around the world. James Meredith was seeking to become the first black ever admitted to the University of Mississippi. It was a landmark moment in the fight against racial segregation. Meredith's entry was mandated by a federal court order and, when Mississippi governor Ross Barnett set out to block it, the Kennedys ordered National Guardsmen deployed on Meredith's behalf. That was when General Walker called for ten thousand civilians to march on Oxford, Mississippi, in opposition. Walker was on the scene when rioting broke out against four hundred federal marshals escorting Meredith onto the campus. Despite JFK's nationally televised plea for calm, a melee left two people dead and seventy injured.[27]

The next morning, Walker was arrested by federal authorities on four counts, including insurrection, and flown for psychiatric observation to the Medical Center for Federal Prisoners at Springfield, Missouri.[28] Once again he became a cause célèbre of the radical right. As the Liberty Lobby's December 1962 newsletter put it, the Kennedys were embarked on "a campaign to reduce his prestige, and his asset value to the anti-Communist cause . . . [and] an effort to incarcerate him for an indefinite period on the 'mental health' excuse by utterly illegal 'police state' methods, partly for the sake of establishing a precedent which could be used against other American patriots in the future." There were, the newsletter went on, obviously "pro-Communist influences within reach of the Attorney General. . . ."

Years later, Colonel William P. Gale—MacArthur's guerrilla leader in the Philippines and later organizer of a paramilitary band in Southern California—would make an odd comment about Walker and the events in Oxford to his biographer, Cheri Seymour. Gale, noting that he was himself in Mississippi, where he "was supposed to meet with General Walker," added that Walker "took the Birchers' advice and got himself arrested and put in jail in Springfield." Gale seemed to be saying that Walker's actions were done with some ulterior purpose.[29]

After being held in Springfield for a week, Walker was released on $50,000 bond after agreeing to submit to a psychiatric examination in Dallas. Some 250 enthusiastic followers greeted his return flight to Love Field. That same Sunday afternoon in October 1962, Lee Harvey Oswald made a sudden decision to leave Fort Worth and move to Dallas.[30]

In late February 1963, after a Mississippi grand jury refused to indict him on the government's charges, the resurrected general took off with preacher Billy James Hargis on "Operation Midnight Ride"—a twenty-seven-city coast-to-coast series of rallies to alert the faithful that the Red enemy was upon them.[31]

Oswald's first known thoughts about Walker came in early February. It happened in the course of a three-hour conversation with Volkmar Schmidt, a young geologist acquaintance of George de Mohrenschildt. The baron arranged the Oswald-Schmidt meeting, according to author Epstein, because "he also knew that Schmidt was fascinated with political ideology . . . [and was] a shrewd analyst of human psychology." Schmidt had come over from Germany late in 1960 and gone to work at Magnolia Petroleum, where he also taught classes in Russian.

He and Oswald discussed the Kennedys' Cuban policy, with the ex-Marine lambasting the Bay of Pigs and the Cuban Missile Crisis as examples of "imperialism" and "interventions." Even with the withdrawal of Soviet missiles, Oswald asserted, sabotage and "terrorism" against Cuba were continuing.

Looking to win Oswald's confidence, Schmidt recalled trying to one-up him on his extremism—a technique Schmidt said he had learned while studying and living with Dr. Wilhelm Kuetemeyer, a professor of psychosomatic medicine and religious philosophy at the University of Heidelberg. According to Schmidt, Kuetemeyer had been conducting experiments on a group of schizophrenics when he got involved in a German generals' plot to assassinate Hitler in 1944 and had to go into hiding. Schmidt, who was admittedly very right-wing himself, was also fascinated with techniques of hypnosis, according to his interview with Epstein.

Schmidt said he decided to bring up Walker's name to Oswald, drawing a comparison with Hitler. "Oswald instantly seized on the analogy . . . to argue that America was moving toward fascism. As he spoke, he seemed to grow more and more excited about the subject." Schmidt's own "psychological profile" concluded that Oswald was apparently a "totally alienated individual"—"obsessed with political ideology and bent on self-destruction."

Schmidt told Epstein that he then decided to arrange a small party that might help bring Oswald "out of his shell." Among the invited guests on February 22, along with the de Mohrenschildts and the Oswalds, was a Quaker woman named Ruth Paine. She and Marina hit it off right away. Ruth, who had worked with the East-West Contact Service in facilitating cultural exchanges between the USSR and the United States, wanted to learn Russian. Before long she would take Marina under her wing in much the same way that de Mohrenschildt had done with Lee.[32]

Stalking the General

When I interviewed Paine at her home in Philadelphia in 1976, she contended that her relationship with the Oswalds had been an innocent one. She remained perplexed, and apparently pained, by the terrible events of late 1963. "I got the feeling of Oswald's being a theoretician, following a theory," she said. "From what he said, he hadn't liked being in Russia—didn't think the system was working very well there. And he certainly didn't like what was happening in the United States. He seemed just sort of generally disgruntled, dissatisfied. But he liked to play roles."[33]

When Ruth Paine had dropped by to see Marina sometime in the second week of March 1963, Oswald's wife told Paine of her marital problems and Lee's insistence that she communicate with the Soviet embassy about returning to Russia. Right around that time, as Marina later told the story, on March 10 Oswald journeyed across town to the ritzy Tuttle Creek neighborhood and photographed the alley behind General Walker's house. Marina says Oswald eventually told her that he had measured distances around the home and collected bus timetables that served the area. Two days later, Oswald mailed off for a Mannlicher-Carcano rifle, to be shipped to "Hidell" at his post office box.

After the weapon arrived on March 25, curiously Oswald brought it to his job at Jaggers-Chiles-Stovall and showed it to fellow employee Jack Bowen.[34] At this same juncture, Oswald had just been given two weeks' notice by the firm's boss, John Graef, who later explained that Lee had been making too many errors at work and wasn't getting along with other employees.[35]

On March 31 Oswald asked Marina to take some photographs of him in their backyard. Dressed completely in black, a revolver holstered on his hip and the rifle in his right hand, in his left hand he held aloft two newspapers—Communist Party, U.S.A.'s, *Worker,* and the SWP's *The Militant.*[36] The issue of *The Worker* contained a lead article about how Walker was bidding to be the American Führer.

Also on March 31, came Oswald's first still-existing communication with the New York headquarters of the Fair Play for Cuba Committee. His note to FPCC chairman V. T. Lee described a pro-Castro street demonstration he staged "yesterday." He was writing to request "40 or 50 more" copies of a pamphlet called *Crime Against Cuba* by Corliss Lamont,[37] a well-known radical critic of U.S. foreign policy. Back in 1944, the notoriously anti-Communist House Un-American Activities Committee had labeled Lamont "probably the most persistent propagandist for the Soviet Union to be found anywhere in the United States."[38]

Early in 1992 I telephoned Lamont, now eighty-nine years old, at his home in New York City. Lamont said my call was the first time he had ever heard that Oswald once passed out his pamphlet. He described it as "an analysis of American policy toward Cuba. It was just to defend Cuba's right to live and be free, not subject to American imperialism. I must have also attacked the ban on Americans traveling to Cuba, and the economic embargo the United States had imposed on the country. I wrote it shortly after the Bay of Pigs invasion."[39]

Oswald was not the only person interested in Lamont's little treatise. When Richard Nagell was arrested on September 20, 1963, he, too, would have a copy of *Crime Against Cuba* among his possessions.[40]

Working overtime in his final days at his JCS job, Oswald had made a number of copies of the militantly posed photographs Marina had taken. On one of them he inscribed "Ready for anything," and he told Marina he was sending it to *The Militant.* Though the newspaper never officially admitted having received it, two former *Militant* employees have recently confirmed to an assassination researcher that it did arrive sometime in April 1963.

On another picture, Oswald wrote: "For George, Lee Harvey Oswald," and dated it "5-IV-63." He asked Marina to add in Russian, "The Hunter of Fascism. Ha, Ha, Ha"—after which she was to forward it on to Baron de Mohrenschildt.[41]

On the night of April 2 the Oswalds went to have dinner with Ruth Paine and her husband, Michael, in the Dallas suburb of Irving. The Paines were already separated, but Ruth felt that Michael might be interested in meeting the couple. He was an inventor at Bell Helicopter and, interestingly enough, his father, George Lyman Paine, was one of the leaders of the American Trotskyite movement.

After Oswald suggested to Michael that violent revolution was a necessity in America, Paine, a liberal who regularly attended meetings of the American Civil Liberties Union, told the Warren Commission that he had sought for some common ground by bringing up the name of General Walker. "We seemed to agree at least superficially that the far right was unfortunate in its thoughts," he would testify, but added that Oswald gave no indication he was planning an attack on Walker.[42]

Then, at some point in the conversation, Ruth remembered Oswald "suddenly referred to *The Militant* newspaper. He said, 'When you know how to read it, you can read between the lines and get revolutionary direction, see what they're *really* telling you.' Michael was skeptical and said, 'Well, show me.' But Oswald let the subject drop. Evidently he was very interested in decoding, which I looked upon at the time as non-sense."[43]

Out in Los Angeles, the Hargis-Walker crusade came to a rousing finish on the night of April 3, when an estimated forty-five hundred people turned out at the Shrine Auditorium.

Two nights after that, Oswald wrapped his rifle in an old raincoat and, when Marina asked where he was going, told her, "Target practice." She watched him board a bus and, when he came home two hours later, he did not have the rifle. The next day, oddly after having been given many hours of night overtime *since* his termination notice, Oswald left JCS.[44] He began spending entire days away from home, never explaining his movements to Marina.

On the evening of April 8, Robert Alan Surrey, a printing salesman and associate of General Walker, says he "saw two men around the house peeking in windows" as he drove up. Spotting a dark-colored new Ford sedan without license plates on the street into which Walker's back alley ran, Surrey waited until the men returned to the car and then briefly tailed them. When the car doubled back, Surrey, believing he had been spotted, abandoned the trail. He reported the incident late that night to Walker, just arrived home from his trip with Billy James Hargis. The general says he called the police.[45]

The shooting incident came two nights later. At about 9:00 P.M., while Walker was sitting at a desk in his study, a bullet came whizzing through the window, passed near his head, and embedded in a wall, showering Walker with plaster.

Although the testimony of a teenaged neighbor boy, Walter Coleman, was glossed over by the Warren Commission, the teenager said he observed *three* men outside Walker's house. Two of them sped away down an alley in a white or beige older-model Ford. (It should be recalled that Nagell drove a 1957 yellow- and cream-colored Ford Fairlane all through this period.) Coleman saw the third man put something on the floorboard of a 1958 Chevy in the adjacent church parking lot, then hastily leave the scene.[46]

General Walker's omnipresent bodyguards, some of whom liked to stride around in black jackboots, were mysteriously unaccounted for. Walker told reporters later that evening that he had dashed upstairs to get his pistol, but his assailants had already fled. A photo of Walker, taken shortly after the shooting and appearing in the next day's newspaper, would show the general relaxed, smiling, and drinking a cup of coffee. The crime went unsolved until Oswald's name came up a week after the assassination.

At about 11:30 P.M. on the night of April 10, Marina says she found a note from Lee. It told her how to get rid of his clothes and possessions and how to contact the city jail "if I am alive and taken prisoner." It also asked her to inform "the Embassy" what had happened. "I believe the Embassy will come quickly to your assistance on learning everything," he wrote, apparently meaning the Soviet embassy. He also left for Marina the key to P.O. Box 2915.

Soon after she discovered the note, Marina says her husband came rushing into the house and exclaimed that he had just used his rifle to fire at General Walker. Later Lee displayed to her the reconnaissance photographs and notes he had made in planning the shooting. Allegedly at Marina's insistence, Oswald then destroyed portions of these. But, for some reason, not the photographs or the incriminating note—through which the Warren Commission eventually concluded that Oswald "attempted to take the life" of Walker that night.[47]

Among the pictures found among Oswald's possessions after the Kennedy assassination was a rear view of General Walker's house. Parked outside was a 1957 Chevrolet. Yet, when the Warren Commission published this photo, there was a gaping hole in it. The license plate number had been obliterated. Dallas police claimed the picture was as they found it, that Oswald had apparently trimmed off the plate to prevent anyone from identifying the owner. Marina, however, adamantly insisted that there was no hole when Lee first showed her the picture—*and* when the FBI displayed it to her after the assassination.

When former Dallas police chief Jesse Curry wrote a 1969 memoir of the assassination, he included some previously unpublished pictures from his files. Among them was a snapshot of assorted Oswald paraphernalia as it was first found in his rooming house after he was taken into custody. Visibly included amid the police photo of all Oswald's effects is the picture taken by Oswald outside Walker's house—but with the license plate intact, though its number is illegible to the eye. The implication is that someone in authority, not Oswald, then cut the license plate out of Oswald's picture after the assassination.[48]

A Visit with General Walker

In 1976 I interviewed General Walker on a trip to Dallas. It had taken a good deal of telephone persuasion. When I set out by attempting respect for his military status, Walker said, fuming: "I am NOT a general! I am a FORMER general! I RESIGNED from the service, I didn't retire! Because I was fed up with the NO-WIN WARS!" After probing my credentials and strongly suggesting that anything reputable I would write ought to be in accordance with his ideas, Walker agreed to a rendezvous. We sat down together on a sunny Sunday morning that March, in an empty conference room of the Dallas Hilton.

"They set out to distort this case the day Oswald was picked up," Walker began. "The intention here in Dallas was to cover up from the beginning, even before it got to the Warren Commission! Now"—he held a long pause, then half-whispered—"why all this cover-up unless it was something bigger than anything?"

As the ex-general's eyes bore down hard on my notebook, suddenly he brought up the name of George de Mohrenschildt. "He could tell you the whole story if anybody wanted to get to him. The whole works, what it was all about, and so forth. He did harbor and abet Oswald to the extent of helping him!"

What makes you so sure? I found myself saying.

"We know he's a member of the Russian community of Dallas!" exclaimed ex-general Walker, with hissing emphasis on the "Russian."

In his own way, Walker seemed as impenetrable a man as de Mohrenschildt. On the surface, Walker was as direct as the baron was sleight-of-hand, as down home as the baron was aloof. But there was something elusive and askew about Walker's face. Not the fervent dark eyes so much as the mouth, which drooped to the right side during his most outraged statements and that seemed to send a signal that in turn glazed his eyes. He was wearing his customary blue-gray hat, sitting tall and erect in a blue serge suit. His six-feet, three-inch frame simply begged for medals, and something in his demeanor automatically brought forth an inner salute. His hair, at age sixty-six, had not yet begun to turn gray. Like de Mohrenschildt, who was two years his junior, he could have passed for someone ten years younger. Like de Mohrenschildt, his manner concealed more than it revealed.

Not quite sure if I had grasped Walker's thought, I asked if he believed the Soviets were behind the assassination.

"It's not quite so simple as that," he replied, wagging an admonishing finger. "Oswald was a détente agent. Both sides had him, and neither could release him. He had them caught in a trap. He's working for the FBI and at the same time the Russians know they've got him. He had them where he was working for either one he wants, by his own choice. An agent of the détente. He conned both sides."

Or, I thought, maybe both sides were conning *him*. Silently wondering how Walker could have such "inside" knowledge, I then brought up a subject that had long perplexed researchers. The first mention of Oswald's attempt on Walker had appeared in the *Deutsche National-Zeitung und Soldaten-Zeitung,* a right-wing newspaper out of Munich, West Germany, on November 29, 1963. Yet Marina Oswald would not tell her story to the

FBI until four days later, purportedly the first awareness anybody had of it.

Assassination researcher Peter Dale Scott's look into the newspaper's history revealed that it had several ex-Nazis and ex-SS men on its staff and a long arm into American far-right circles. Its editor, Gerhard Frey, was closely tied in Munich to the Ukrainian ABN, as well as to two men whose names show up among General Willoughby's correspondents (Dr. Theodor Oberlander and Walter Becher).[49]

Just how, I asked Walker, had the Munich newspaper obtained its "scoop"?

"Well, how do you know they published it before Marina Oswald said it?" the ex-general replied testily. I explained the discrepancy in the dates. "That's interesting," Walker said, rubbing his chin. "Of course, the Germans have terrific sources over here. I'll give the Germans credit for the finest intelligence in the world, even to this day. We paid Germany $5 million for international intelligence up to '57. I don't think anybody can beat 'em, except maybe Israel. But it never quite dawned on me that they published this beforehand."

But hadn't the Munich newspaper called him all the way from Germany on the morning after the assassination? Walker had been in Shreveport, Louisiana, at the time, having flown there from Dallas on November 22 to give a speech to the segregationist Citizens' Council of Louisiana.

"Yes," Walker nodded, "they woke me up. I didn't know anything about Oswald shooting at me, I had no idea. And they didn't say a word about that. But I do think it was within a couple days that Marina spilled *something!* They certainly tied something together in there right quick, didn't they? The subject of their conversation was what did I know about Oswald. I said, 'Well, Oswald has said he's a Communist.' They said, 'Well, that answers the question, we can go to print now.' They just said I was the only one in the United States they could think of that would tell them the truth. I thought that was quite a compliment."

Walker went on to quote from the paper, saying that he himself later verified what the story said. It had to do with Oswald allegedly having been arrested the very night he shot at Walker, but being released on direct orders from Robert Kennedy. This, I felt, was absurd, but Walker was adamant. "I heard it from somebody who knew what he was talking about. I know a lot of people in Dallas."

We talked on. "Oswald was chasing the Fair Play for Cuba Committee while I was coming down in every speech against Castro and Cuba," Walker said. He conceded he had personally been to "a student meeting" of anti-Castro Cubans and that "one or two" Cubans had visited his home. "We knew some were no good and some were legitimate," Walker said.

All I knew then about Walker's association with anti-Castro Cubans was on record with the Warren Commission. Walker and a close acquaintance, a "Colonel Caster," were described by one witness as "trying to arouse the feelings of the Cuban refugees, in Dallas, against the Kennedy administration" in speeches to exile groups.[50] The colonel was actually Robert Castorr, who in 1968 consented to an interview with researcher Harold Weisberg. In it, Castorr said he had indeed attended some of the exiles' gatherings and had become "acquainted with Walker eventually through H. L. Hunt."[51]

According to all official versions, including Walker's, the ex-general had never heard of Oswald until the day of the assassination. Yet in 1992, John Curington, H. L. Hunt's chief staff assistant during that period, told me a different version. Curington said he himself "had run across Oswald before the assassination. He was sort of known in certain circles as being an extremist, very vocal about certain issues, and his name had just come up in conversation or some of our reviews."

I pressed Curington to be more specific. "Well," he added, "General Walker was a pretty good friend of Mr. Hunt's and we visited in his home. Walker told us one night that Oswald's name had come up in an investigation of the sniping there against him. I don't remember just when, but this was before the assassination."[52]

De Mohrenschildt and the Walker Incident

Two days after the Dallas headlines revealed that someone had fired, and missed, as the general sat in his study, George and Jeanne de Mohrenschildt showed up unexpectedly at the Oswalds' door on April 3, 1963. According to Marina, the first words out of the baron's mouth were, "How could you have missed, how could you have missed him?" Marina says Lee looked at her with a stunned expression. Since he had told her that nobody except she knew about the Walker attempt, Marina was equally shocked.[53] De Mohrenschildt would later explain to the Warren Commission that his statement was a "logical assumption," since he knew his young friend had a "gun with a telescopic lens."[54]

Then, not long after the Walker shooting, Mrs. Natasha Voshinin recalled de Mohrenschildt dropping by to see them one evening. "He said, 'Listen, that fellow Oswald is absolutely suspicious, you are right.' Thousands of times before, he would say we were wrong. 'Imagine,' George said, 'that scoundrel took a potshot at General Walker. Of course Walker is a stinker, but stinkers have the right to live.' Then he told us something about the rifle. But Igor and I felt Oswald had some connection with CIA.

Anyway, I immediately delivered this information [from de Mohren-schildt] to the FBI."[55]

That last statement seemed to me a remarkable one, for according to the Warren Commission Report, "The FBI had no knowledge that Oswald was responsible for the attack until Marina Oswald revealed the information on December 3, [1963]." Yet Mrs. Voshinin was saying she had alerted the FBI of the possibility sometime back in April. Had the FBI looked into this at the time? Was the bureau's disclaimer of any fore-knowledge in the Walker matter a fabrication, designed to cover up its prior awareness of Oswald?

Not only the FBI but, according to de Mohrenschildt, the CIA knew about Oswald's connection to the Walker incident long before November 22, 1963. On the day of de Mohrenschildt's death, author Epstein asked him whether he had discussed this—and the gun-toting Oswald photograph that Marina passed along to the baron—with his CIA contact, J. Walton Moore. "I spoke to the CIA both before and afterward," de Mohrenschildt is said to have replied. "It was what ruined me."[56]

The Walker shooting seemed to mark a turning point for both de Mohrenschildt and Oswald. Very soon after the baron's visit with Igor and Natasha Voshinin, he pulled up stakes. On about April 19, he and his wife headed East for a trip to New York, Philadelphia, and Washington. Five days later, Oswald departed alone by bus for New Orleans, with Ruth Paine taking his wife into her home until Marina went to join her husband two weeks later.

A CIA Office of Security memorandum, declassified many years later, notes that an agency case officer for an unidentified individual (both his name and the contact's were blanked out) on April 29, 1963, "requested an expedite check of George DE MOHRENSCHILDT for reasons un-known to security."

The memo continued: "It is interesting that [name deleted] interest in de Mohrenschildt coincided with the earlier portion of this trip and the info would suggest that possibly [name deleted] and de Mohrenschildt were possibly in the same environment in Washington, D.C., circa April 26, 1963."[57]

As the House Assassinations Committee found out, de Mohrenschildt's primary business in Washington that spring was with a visiting Haitian banker named Clemard Charles. In mid-March, with the help of the U.S. State Department, a $285,000 contract for de Mohrenschildt to conduct a geological survey had been approved by the Haitian Congress. Ostensibly he and Charles were now discussing the de Mohrenschildts' upcoming move to the Caribbean island. But Clemard Charles was also of interest to Army Intelligence. Colonel Samuel Kail, who worked closely with Cuban exile groups in Miami, contacted a woman with the Army chief of staff for intelligence that spring about meeting with the banker—"because of Charles's relationship to President Duvalier of Haiti and Haiti's strategic position relative to Castro's Cuba."[58]

The woman, Dorothe Matlack, told the House Assassinations Committee that her work included serving in a liaison capacity to the CIA. According to retired Colonel L. Fletcher Prouty, the chief Pentagon-to-CIA liaison officer during that period, Matlack was "from a real black intelligence arm of the Pentagon. It's very strange that she met with de Mohrenschildt."[59]

The committee concluded that Matlack apparently made the Washington hotel reservations for the de Mohrenschildts and Clemard Charles. Then she arranged a May rendezvous for Charles with Tony Czaikowski of the CIA, whom she introduced as a professor from Georgetown University. Matlack testified that it was a "surprise" to her when the de Mohrenschildts accompanied Charles to the luncheon. She felt that the baron "dominated" Charles in some way and, though the pair explained they were in the jute business together, "I knew the Texan wasn't there to sell hemp." She said she was so disturbed about de Mohrenschildt's presence that she subsequently discussed it with the FBI. Charles, she recalled, had seemed "frantic and frightened" during the luncheon—and had urged Mrs. Matlack to get the U.S. Marines to invade Haiti and overthrow dictator François ("Papa Doc") Duvalier.[60]

At precisely the same time, Cuban exiles were fomenting plans to do just that—looking to use Haiti as a staging ground for a takeover of Cuba. In 1983, Bernard Fensterwald, Jr., arranged a meeting in Washington to discuss the Charles-de Mohrenschildt relationship with a twenty-year Army Intelligence officer named Roger Pierce. In the memorandum the attorney then sent along to me, Fensterwald wrote: "It is quite obvious that he is the Department of the Army's 'man' with respect to the Kennedy assassination."

According to Pierce, de Mohrenschildt had "acted as introducer, interpreter, and general foot-rubber" for Charles that spring of 1963. The Haitian banker spent three weeks in the United States "with an unspecified amount of money which he wanted to invest"—and "had a much broader noncommercial objective which would require cooperation from many departments and agencies of the U.S. government. . . . Pierce would not reveal the nature of Charles's objective but said that revelation of it publicly would still raise all sorts of hell in the Caribbean." The banker, Pierce added, had died violently under "bizarre circumstances" in Haiti in 1981; despite a number of inquiries from U.S. officials, "the Haitian government will not divulge the details."

While talking with Pierce, Fensterwald also brought up Nagell's name. "Pierce had known Richard Nagell and knew of his involvement in the case," the memo continued. "He was noncommittal when I said that Nagell had known Oswald in Japan and Mexico. He was also noncommittal about Nagell's monthly check from the U.S. government."[61]

When Fensterwald had asked Nagell previously about the curious Haitian connection, he had responded in a letter: "The only contact that I ever had with Haitians was at a reception given by an exile group in Madrid, in 1969. Serge de Morenschildt (sp) had a number of connections in Haiti at the time he was acquainted with LHO [Oswald] . . . so I was told."[62]

On June 2, 1963, George and Jeanne de Mohrenschildt had departed for Haiti. They would remain there into 1967, except for returning to testify before the Warren Commission, when Colonel Prouty maintains that de Mohrenschildt had several private Washington lunches with Allen Dulles.[63] Two witnesses later told the House Assassinations Committee of hearing that a substantial sum of money—as much as $250,000—had been deposited in George's account in a bank in Port-au-Prince. Then the money was paid out by de Mohrenschildt to someone just before the de Mohrenschildts came back to settle in Dallas in 1967. They had apparently remained close in Haiti to Clemard Charles. Joseph Dryer, a stockbroker who lived in Haiti at the time, told the House Assassinations Committee that Charles was a possible arms dealer with "many connections" to the CIA. Dryer said he also found de Mohrenschildt's behavior "strange." It included following people in his car.[64]

As the baron told the Warren Commission, he had gotten the news that a suspect had been arrested in the Kennedy assassination, while gazing out over the sparkling Caribbean bay at the home of an American embassy friend. Even before any name was mentioned, an image flashed through his mind. It was the photograph of Oswald holding the rifle, dispatched to him by Marina the previous spring. "Could it be Lee? No, it was impossible," de Mohrenschildt says he thought.[65]

In de Mohrenschildt's entire existence, as with so much else surrounding Oswald, we seem to be looking at a kind of voodoo. But stranger still was a story I heard in 1992 as I began to put this book together.

General Walker and the Schmidt Brothers

In October 1962, just when Oswald temporarily left Marina behind and moved alone from Fort Worth to Dallas to take the job de Mohrenschildt had arranged for him, another young man also arrived in Dallas. His name was Larrie Schmidt, and he bore a remarkably similar profile to Oswald:

broken home, military background, assiduous chronicler of his own organizing activities. There was just one big difference: Schmidt seemed as
far to the right, ideologically, as Oswald purported to be to the left. Larrie
Schmidt's once-liberal thinking had undergone a marked shift in 1960,
influenced by Barry Goldwater's *The Conscience of a Conservative* and Ayn
Rand's *Atlas Shrugged*. Where Oswald claimed to see the Bay of Pigs as a
symbol of American imperialism, Schmidt viewed its failure as humiliation
for all those "who refused to lose our identity to a collectivist society."

Schmidt had served two Army tours of duty in West Germany and,
though he was not a native Texan, came to Dallas straight from Munich
after receiving his discharge. He had already mapped out plans in West
Germany for an organization called CUSA, code for Conservatism-U.S.A.
By June 1962, Schmidt had signed up several zealots in West Germany
inside the Military Police and the Counter-Intelligence Corps. As *Look*
magazine later described it, Schmidt "had trained a small, disciplined
band of soldier-conspirators to follow him stateside and do, he hoped,
'whatever is necessary to accomplish our goal.' " That goal was to infiltrate
right-wing groups across the United States and weld them into CUSA,
with the grand design of taking control of American politics. Schmidt's
plan was to gain financial support from wealthy supporters such as Dallas's H. L. Hunt family.[66]

From Dallas, where Schmidt got a job with United Press International,
he corresponded regularly with his cadre back in Munich. His letters were
later reprinted in the Warren Commission's volumes.

November 2, 1962: "Arrangements are being made for me to meet the
heads of the Dallas John Birch, General Walker, and H. L. Hunt. . . ."

January 4, 1963: "I want big men. . . . Believe me if I have a dozen
such men I can conquer the world. I will go down in the history books as a
great and noble man, or a tyrant."

February 2, 1963: "We have succeeded, the mission with which I was
charged in Dallas has been achieved. Friday night I attended a gathering
of the top conservatives in Dallas. The meeting was at the home of Dr.
Robert Morris, President of the Defenders of American Liberty. . . ."
(Morris was Walker's lawyer in fighting the Kennedy administration's
charges over the Mississippi "insurrection.")

"Others suggested using an already existing movement," Schmidt continued, "named the Young Americans for Freedom [YAF], with already
50,000 members. CUSA, as set up in Munich, is now an established fact in
Dallas, only we are calling it YAF. I think you catch on. We are getting
every top name in business, education, politics and religion to endorse
YAF. . . . Change all your records to read YAF."[67]

One of the YAF's leading board members by 1963 was retired major
general Charles Willoughby,[68] who had a daughter living in Texas. Wil-

loughby, I have learned, was also a leading supporter of Larrie Schmidt, and met with him on more than one occasion.[69] As we have seen, Willoughby retained strong connections overseas in Germany. His International Committee for the Defense of Christian Culture (ICDCC) had two branches in Bonn, where its founder was an ex-Nazi turned anti-Communist. The organization's avowed purpose was "resistance against regimes and political concepts contrary to its own." In this context it linked extremists in Spain and Portugal together with Germany, and across the Atlantic to the United States.[70]

One of the ICDCC's leading lights was Walker's early 1963 traveling companion, segregationist preacher Hargis, on whose Christian Crusade National Advisory Committee Willoughby likewise presided. A major ICDCC funder was Nelson Bunker Hunt, son of the oil billionaire.[71] Willoughby's friendship with H. L. Hunt dated back at least to the early 1950s, when the oilman met regularly with Willoughby and other generals in New York in seeking to push a presidential bid by General MacArthur.[72]

Like Willoughby and the Hunts, General Walker was a fervent member of the John Birch Society. Walker remembers meeting Willoughby in the course of his 1963 travels with Hargis but says he did not know him well.[73] Indeed, there seems to have been a noteworthy distance maintained from Walker by both Willoughby and the Hunt family. Perhaps this stemmed from Walker's almost maniacal desire for the limelight; Willoughby's ICDCC, about which little is known, preferred behind-the-scenes maneuvering. Walker was pointedly not among the members of the ICDCC.

Years later, when I asked Walker about his relationship with the Hunts, he replied: "Basically, we crossed. H.L. did everything possible to convince me not to run for governor [in 1962] as a Democrat. He brought the head of the Republican Party here to my house to try to get me to switch, and I wouldn't. 'Course, he didn't know why I was running for governor, which was to get enough following in the state of Texas to make sure Kennedy never got another term. Politically speaking."[74]

Walker's previous "indoctrination" of his troops in Germany had also caused a curious rift with some of his brethren among the radical right. According to a former acquaintance of Larrie Schmidt's, Willoughby had worked with Schmidt in helping expose Walker's activities.[75] In 1961 Schmidt was working in the Army's Public Information Office in Munich.[76] That April, wire services and newspapers around the world quoted a story that appeared in the German-based serviceman's newspaper *Overseas Weekly*. The *Weekly* maintained that Walker had set up a "special warfare" section inside his division "to fight Communism in the U.S." Walker denied the charges, calling the *Overseas Weekly* "immoral, unscrupulous, corrupt, and destructive." But that article prompted JFK's investigation of Walker, leading to his recall.[77] Immediately after Walker departed Munich, Schmidt began quietly organizing his CUSA crusade within the U.S. military there. Schmidt, whose admitted hero was Hitler's propaganda chief, Joseph Goebbels, had apparently scored an organizing coup d'état.

Then, not long after Schmidt's arrival in Dallas in October 1962, his brother Bob began cozying up to ex-general Walker. By October 1963, Walker would hire Bob Schmidt as his personal chauffeur.[78] But the actual purpose of the carefully contrived liaison, according to *Look* magazine, was "to spy on him." Larrie Schmidt's CUSA was infiltrating Walker's own "boys."

All through 1963, Larrie Schmidt continued his correspondence back to his Munich base.

June 13, 1963: "Warren Carroll, our only other recruit to CUSA, is already a PhD and two MS's. Warren is a scriptwriter for Lifeline, the H. L. Hunt television and radio series. . . . Warren is 32, former CIA man. Don't worry, he has been checked out. Hunt checked him out."

October 1, 1963: "I have a lot of contacts, bankers, insurance men, realtors. My brother began working as an aide to General Walker. He is being paid full time."

October 29, 1963: "This town is a battleground and that is no joke. I am a hero to the right, a stormtrooper to the left. I have worked out a deal with the chairman of YAF. The arrangements are always delicate, very delicate. . . . Kennedy is scheduled in Dallas on November 24 [sic]. All big things are happening now."[79]

On November 4, the chief recipient of Schmidt's letters, Bernard Weissman, arrived in Dallas. Weissman was one of five Jews whom Schmidt had recruited in Munich in the summer of 1962. At Schmidt's urging, Weissman said he came "simply to follow through on plans that we had made . . . to develop a conservative organization in Dallas, under our leadership." Now, to coincide with JFK's visit, Schmidt conceived the idea of taking out a full-page "Welcome" ad in the *Dallas Morning News* that would show how the president had gone "soft on communism." It was Weissman's contribution that the ad have a black border around it, "something to bring it out" so readers would not simply "turn the page and pass it by."

Joseph Grinnan, an independent Dallas oilman and volunteer coordinator for the John Birch Society, gave Weissman the nearly $1,500 he had collected to pay for the ad (one of the funders was Nelson Bunker Hunt). Weissman was told to place the ad under "The American Fact-Finding Committee" and list himself, and himself alone, at the bottom as "Chairman."

He did as instructed. Until the rapid capture of the "fanatic leftist"

Oswald, the initial press reports of November 22, 1963, focused on the right-wing-sponsored, black-bordered ad. Its creators quickly decided to go "underground." As Weissman would remember, he and Schmidt had been having a beer when Oswald was picked up. "First, what was said, like I hope he is not a member of the Walker group—something like that . . . because it is like a clique, and it is guilt by association from thereafter." Schmidt said he was afraid to go home. He called Grinnan, who reportedly told him, "Don't say anything, don't do anything, don't get any more involved than you have to, lay low, keep out of it, it is going to be pretty bad."[80]

Schmidt would later say that he hoped using Weissman's name on the ad would provoke anti-Semitic attacks (which it did), thus enabling Schmidt to prove that the right wing "has no monopoly on bigotry."[81] After all, he had previously suggested to "Bernie" that he consider changing his name if he wanted to be considered for John Birch Society membership.

From all the testimony taken by the Warren Commission, Weissman certainly seemed to have no inkling of what was to transpire the day of the ad. When I located him in Indiana in 1992, he recalled this about affixing his name to the ad: "The ulterior motive to the ulterior motive was that I would supposedly attain more strength in our organization. Of course, it backfired. In every political organization, there are always jealousies and points of view that don't mesh exactly. If Larrie wanted to put me in the soup that way, whatever his motives and ambitions were, it's nothing I hold a vendetta against him for."[82]

Of the assassination, Schmidt would tell *Look* magazine that he was driving with Joe Grinnan when the news came over the radio. "I said a silent prayer, that it wasn't true or wouldn't be serious. We knew there was going to be a tremendous witch-hunt. Normal procedure. I had a premonition that this was the end of CUSA."

Which it was. Weissman, who feared retribution for having signed the ad, left Dallas a few days after the assassination. Schmidt quickly departed —Weissman believed he went to Louisiana—and his current whereabouts are unknown. But questioning by the Warren Commission had exposed Schmidt's grand political scheme. "It's such a shame," he was quoted in *Look* magazine. "It would have worked."

The Walker Shooting Revisited

Bradford J. Angers, a former Army security agent and private investigator, today continues to manufacture electronic surveillance equipment in semiretirement in Dallas. For a brief time in 1963 he had been in the employ of H. L. Hunt, until the oilman demanded that Angers pack for Washington and go to work on his *Lifeline* radio project. Angers refused, and walked out of the office.

Then, several weeks after the assassination, Angers says he got a surprise phone call from Hunt.

"He said, 'Brad, I'm sending a guy over to you, I want you to put him to work.' It was like an ultimatum." Angers agreed to do so.

When I spoke to Angers on a tip in the spring of 1992, he refused to identify publicly the person whom Hunt asked him to hire. But it quickly became obvious to me who it was.

Angers recalled the young man as being "a frail fellow, very meticulous. He patterned himself after Joseph Goebbels. He and I used to talk about how Goebbels used syllogistic logic to build the Nazi empire."

Angers landed him a job in Austin, assisting Lady Bird Johnson's radio station in an advertising campaign. Then, suddenly, the FBI showed up at Anger's door. "They said, 'how much do you know about this guy that you just put to work for the president's wife?' I said, 'Well, I know he's a helluva smart guy.' Then they told about CUSA and the black-bordered ad. I had never associated this fellow with the ad. So I tried calling the fellow up, but he'd disappeared. Finally his housekeeper called me and said to come over, that he needed medical care and some money. I went to his apartment in Austin. His face was all bandaged up, he had his arms in splints, and his wife had her leg in a cast. They said they'd had a little accident near Denton County.

"I gave them some money, and then called this old sheriff up in Denton. He said there had been no major accidents there in several weeks. But one of their squad cars did pick up a man and woman who'd been beaten up and thrown out of a car. The sheriff said they gave phony ID, but he gave me a description. So I went back to this fellow and asked him what was up, and he let me tape-record our conversation. He told me that he and his wife had been picked up by the Secret Service. They were told if they even mentioned any relationship with the Kennedy assassination, or the Hunts, they'd be dead.

"Before the assassination, this guy's brother had gotten close to General Walker. Eventually he'd become his chauffeur. It was part of their infiltrating Walker's organization, and it went back to a power struggle in Germany, when this fellow had been in the Army there and started forming his own little group. Apparently this fellow couldn't stand Walker. Neither could his brother.

"Somehow that spring of '63, the brother had made friends with Oswald, who was also trying to get close to Walker. But this fellow I knew had never met Oswald, I don't think, until his brother introduced them that night in April. The three of them got drunk together. They got in a car and the brother said, 'Somebody ought to shoot that no-good son of a bitch Walker.' And this fellow said, 'I've got news for you, I got him kicked out of the goddamned Army in Germany.' Then Oswald said, 'I've got a rifle, let's go hit the son of a bitch.'

"The three of them drove down St. John's Avenue, and stopped the car close to a little stone bridge that went over Tuttle Creek. The brother and Oswald went down the creek, and Oswald laid down on the embankment looking at Walker's house. Remember the great big window Walker had in the front? Walker was a nut, he would turn up a lamp and just pace back and forth reading in the room. They saw his shadow against the back wall and Oswald pumped off a shot. It hit the wall instead. Then they jumped in the car and took off."

Angers's story has never before been made public. The young man he is describing could only be Larrie Schmidt. This would mean that Schmidt, who was in touch with Charles Willoughby and the Hunt family, would have been perfectly positioned to pass the word along about Oswald. Schmidt and/or his brother might even have been acting under instructions in the first place to involve Oswald in the Walker incident. If this account is true—and Angers is sure it is—the implications are staggering.

In the summer of 1992 I recontacted General Walker, now eighty-two, at his Dallas home. He well remembered Larrie Schmidt and his brother Bob. "Larrie had been in a logistics command under General [James] Gavin down in Munich. The Schmidts' objective here in Dallas was to take over a ready-made organization. They started out moving in on Frank McGee's National Indignation Convention. Then Young Americans for Freedom became a good cover for them. Finally, they wanted to take over my organization."

Walker could not remember just when he took Bob Schmidt onto his personal staff, but it was probably before he hit the road with preacher Hargis early in 1963. It was Walker's aide-de-camp, Robert Surrey, who first brought the Schmidt brothers around. "I had six to eight people working for me at the time, and Bob ran a lot of errands," Walker recalled. "I had a station wagon, people coming into the airport, all my publications had to be printed across town. Larrie would hang around, just being a nuisance. Finally I ran him out of my house and told him never to set foot in it again. The dead giveaway was when one day he appeared on the front page of the *Dallas Times-Herald* as a Dallas businessman. I thought he was overdoing it, he didn't seem to have much objective except making a power play. People don't realize how vicious it was; people were sabotaging within the organizations you see, even on the conservative side."

Finally I asked this question: Did Walker think it was conceivable that the Schmidt brothers could have gotten together with Oswald to shoot at him? His reply stunned me. "I've been told that they were," Walker said. "Several people investigated the shooting as best they could, and raised that possibility. They were plenty capable of working with Oswald, sure. I think it's rather natural to suspect they were helping him one way or another."

A Springtime Gathering in Washington

Two weeks after the Walker incident, at about the same time George de Mohrenschildt arrived in Washington, another event took place. It was a two-day "strategy seminar" of the Anti-Communist Liaison, held on April 26–27 at the Washington Hotel.[83] The meeting, which brought together 125 people from all over the United States, was chaired by Edward Hunter, the ex-OSS and ex-CIA man who made "brainwashing" part of the American lexicon. Hunter, along with Willoughby, was a board member of Young Americans for Freedom, the group whose identity Larrie Schmidt's CUSA took on in Dallas in 1963.

Group Research, Inc. (GRI), a still-existing private Washington organization established in 1962 to keep tabs on the American right wing, sent its own "spy" to the Anti-Communist Liaison seminar on April 26. "I noticed people from California, Florida, Texas, Michigan, Ohio, as well as the nearby states and Washington, D.C.," the GRI reporter said.

"Mr. Hunter started off the meeting by talking about the work of the Anti-Communist Liaison Committee and its use of psychological warfare principles to help alert people in the field to the problem. He wants to help people pursue this problem and indoctrinate them in a 'hatred of the communist menace.'"

General Willoughby was part of an afternoon panel that discussed "psywar tactics." On hand to discuss "State Department aims" was the former chief of General MacArthur's joint planning section, Brigadier General Bonner Fellers. Also in attendance was Major Arch Roberts, the original author of General Walker's "Pro-Blue Program" for his Munich-based troops.

The meeting's first speaker was soldier of fortune Alexander Rorke, accompanied by a Cuban exile member of the "Cuban Freedom Fighters." Both men had just returned from a flight over Castro's island, a "bombing mission of Cuban refineries and oil tanks."

"In fighting communism, we should not aim at peace but aim at victory," added another speaker, Madame Anna Chennault. She was the widow of General Claire Chennault, who had fought in China with Chaing Kai-shek during World War II and whose private airline company (Civil Air Transport, later known as Air America, Inc.) served as a paramilitary arm for the CIA for more than two decades in Southeast Asia. "We are making the same co-existent policy mistakes in the United States with Cuba that we formerly made with China, Laos" and many other places, the GRI's on-scene reporter quoted Chennault as saying.

On the same panel was Sarah McClendon, a veteran news correspondent in Washington, who complained that the "American mind was being taken over by managed news" emanating from the Kennedy administration. "We should imitate the 'sword and shield technique' used by the Communists," the GRI report continued in describing her speech, "who try to infiltrate and push an organization to the left, in order to convert people to the conservative cause."

As the GRI concluded, "Hunter has put together a much more effective organization than was previously indicated."

Summary

In the spring of 1963, Nagell received orders to look into Marina Oswald's reported desire to go home to the USSR—something she had expressed in a letter to the Soviet embassy. Nagell (code name "Laredo") met with his Soviet contact ("Oaxaca") across the Texas-Mexico border, went on to Washington for further instructions, then checked out Marina in Dallas and San Antonio. After the assassination, a Secret Service agent questioned Marina for two hours about Nagell—but just the fact that this occurred was withheld from public view until the mid-1970s.

Nagell may have been in Dallas at about the time of another event: Oswald's alleged shooting at General Edwin Walker, a fanatical spokesman for the radical right. It is startling how many times Walker's name came up in conversations beforehand among Oswald and his associates. More startling is that the FBI (through Igor Voshinin) and the CIA (through George de Mohrenschildt) were each aware of Oswald's involvement in the Walker shooting—many months before the assassination.

So much surrounding the Walker incident has never added up: the license plate obliterated (after the assassination) from an Oswald photo taken in Walker's driveway . . . a Munich-based newspaper, with ultraright connections, breaking the news even before Marina mentioned anything about Oswald and Walker to the FBI . . . De Mohrenschildt's apparent awareness, within two days afterward, of Oswald's role, and de Mohrenschildt's subsequent meetings in Washington with two U.S. intelligence officials before moving to Haiti.

The never-before-revealed information about Larrie Schmidt offers a chilling possibility. Was Oswald being observed—even set up—by members of the radical right? Not only do we have the reported "confession" by Schmidt to Bradford Angers, but also Walker's own belief that Schmidt and his brother Bob could well have been connected with Oswald in the shooting. Yet Schmidt's own associations extend to the Willoughby-Hunt circles, within which Walker seems curiously to have been left out of the loop. Before coming to Dallas the same month as Oswald (October 1962), Schmidt had been stationed with the Army in Munich—the same city where the Oswald/Walker story came from on November 29, 1963.

Then, two weeks after the Walker affair, the new Anti-Communist Liaison met in Washington to map "psychological warfare" strategies. Could Oswald have been their pawn?

Chapter Fourteen

The Second Plot to Kill JFK:
April–June 1963

On April 18, 1963, the formation of a Los Angeles chapter of the anti-Castro group Alpha 66 was announced at a press conference attended by about forty Cuban exiles. A man named René Valdes described himself as the local "cell leader." He said he had received the blessing of Antonio Veciana at a meeting in Miami in December 1962.[1]

Around the time of this announcement, Richard Case Nagell also arrived in Los Angeles. Sometime that spring, Nagell received a comprehensive briefing about "Angel" and "Leopoldo," the two exiles who were now the primary subjects of his anti-Castro surveillance.[2] Nagell has never specified whether his briefing came from the CIA, the Soviets, or perhaps Castro's G-2 intelligence apparatus.

Like "Angel," whom Nagell had surveilled in Miami in January, "Leopoldo" was said to be an ex-CIA employee who once lived in Cuba. According to Nagell, Leopoldo had also received training from the U.S. military at Fort Jackson, South Carolina.[3] Early in 1963, Fort Jackson became home base for dozens of the Bay of Pigs invasion brigade recently freed from Cuban captivity. The exiles received special Army courses there, and many went on to work for the CIA in undercover operations abroad.[4] Conspicuously attached to the Miami Police Intelligence unit's April 4, 1963, memorandum citing potential violent acts by the exiles against the U.S. government, was a page-long message "TO ALL OUR FELLOW COUNTRYMEN" signed by the "Fort Jackson Commandos." It states "that we are already organized and fighting again for the liberty (liberation) of Cuba."[5]

In a physical description he provided for the Garrison investigation in 1969, Nagell described Leopoldo as being of Mexican ancestry, between twenty-seven and twenty-nine years old in 1963. "200 lbs.—5'10" or 5'11", black hair, heavy build, Alpha 66," the Garrison memorandum notes.[6]

In a 1976 letter, Nagell elaborated: " 'Leopoldo' was a nom de guerre taken from the name of a now-defunct Mexican restaurant once located at 3675 Beverly Boulevard in Los Angeles (the proprietor's name was Leopoldo Gonzalez)." This restaurant had served as "a sometimes contact point" in 1963.[7]

FBI files from this period show considerable attention being paid to Alpha 66's activities in Los Angeles and elsewhere. Finally declassified in 1984 under the Freedom of Information Act, the names of all sources and/ or informants are blanked out. A May 2, 1963, report described an L.A. radio interview given by René Valdes and Lawrence Howard, Jr. Howard was noted as having been training guerrilla fighters at an isolated camp in the Florida Keys. Valdes "pointed out that none of the [current anti-Castro] raids were from anywhere inside the United States."[8]

A May 8 FBI file described an informant who had recently "had an opportunity to copy the addresses of the [Alpha 66] organization's various branches from available literature." These included Miami, New York City, Chicago, Milwaukee, Philadelphia, Newark, and Union City, New Jersey; Silver Spring, Maryland; Fairhope, Alabama; Toronto, Venezuela, and "Mexico, Central America—620 Apto. 208, Mexico, D.F."[9]

Another FBI report, headed "Unity Efforts" and dated May 18, 1963, described an alliance of five exile groups "signing a pact for joint action": Alpha 66, Second National Front of Escambray (SNFE), People's Revolutionary Movement (MRP), 30th of November Revolutionary Movement, and the Anti-Communist Front of Liberation. The purpose, according to the FBI's source, was "to facilitate the raising of funds, make propaganda, infiltrate men inside Cuba, and carry out guerrilla warfare within Cuba."[10]

There was already confusion about whether Alpha 66 was really just a "front" or "action group" of the SNFE, since the two organizations had first merged during the Cuban Missile Crisis. In retrospect, maybe such confusion was by design. So, perhaps, was the confusion being spread by Alpha's leadership that spring about the loyalty of one of its own men.

On May 19, Alpha 66's "general secretary," Andres Nasario Sargen, traveled to Los Angeles from Miami and presented an exhortatory call to arms at a public meeting of some six hundred exiles. It was in the form of a tape-recorded message from Veciana, then forbidden by the government to travel outside Dade County, Florida.[11] Then, ten days later, Sargen went to the Los Angeles FBI. He said he'd learned that René Valdes was possibly a "G-2 agent" for Castro's government. Valdes himself would tell the FBI on June 22 that two local Alpha members had visited him, inquiring about his Communist leanings in the past. Somewhere in this time frame, Veciana instructed Valdes to step down as the Los Angeles delegate to Alpha 66.[12]

Alpha 66's hierarchy had been well schooled by the CIA in duplicitous techniques. If, in fact, a small cadre of its people were considering ways and means to assassinate Kennedy, the modus operandi would certainly not be designed to point the finger at themselves. The intent of a few of the exiles and their backers, according to Richard Nagell, was to lay the blame at Castro's doorstep and ensure an invasion of Cuba. To recruit a Castro supporter, or supporters, into the project, the conspirators themselves would need to pose as Castro G-2 agents.

I do not know—and am not implying—that the Alpha 66 "fingering" of René Valdes to the FBI was part of such a plan. The true identities of Angel and Leopoldo remain unknown. But Nagell has made it very clear that such a scheme—anti-Castro exiles pretending to be Castro agents—was the one eventually aimed at enlisting Lee Harvey Oswald into the JFK assassination conspiracy.

At the same time Nagell was continuing to probe the activities of Angel and Leopoldo, he was also monitoring the Los Angeles-area left wing. According to a memorandum written by Nagell in 1971, ". . . my records for the spring and summer of 1963 . . . reflect that at the time I had already received instructions to inquire into the then current status of a number of persons (all members of the CPUSA) residing in the Southern California area."[13]

President Kennedy was scheduled to come to Los Angeles in June. According to Nagell, a second plot to assassinate him was being discussed among some Cuban exiles in the spring of 1963—much more seriously than the Miami proposal of the previous winter. "It was to take place," Nagell says, "during the showing of the movie PT-109 at the Beverly Hilton Hotel, Beverly Hills, in June 1963."[14]

The man being looked at for "recruitment" as a shooter was an executive officer of the Los Angeles Fair Play for Cuba Committee (FPCC).

A Man Named Marlowe

Now sixty-one years old, Vaughn Marlowe currently resides in the pictur-esque Pacific coastal town of Newport, Oregon. When I met him in the summer of 1990, he was working out of a little sign shop, writing plays and remaining a self-described community activist—"host at a homeless shel-ter, defending the arts against the assault of the right-wingers and the religionists, stopping a couple of local polluters." (The sign shop and homeless shelter have since closed.)

His true name, back in the early 1960s, had been Vaughn L. Snipes. After he went to work for L.A.'s Pacifica radio station in 1964, he decided to change it. "The station manager told me I was asking for trouble from the listeners otherwise," he would remember, "because Snipes can be an action verb and open for a lot of puns. So my ex-wife and I drew up a bunch of names and she picked Marlowe, after the Raymond Chandler character."

I was aware of Marlowe for many years before we met. It was he who, in March 1967, had sent a letter to Jim Garrison (under the alias "Don Gordon"), informing the New Orleans DA about his peculiar relationship with Richard Nagell. Marlowe wrote of Nagell that in 1963 "he was check-ing me out, slowly, carefully, for a reason unknown to me even today."[15]

In 1976, locating Marlowe through his address on a letter sent me by Nagell, I spoke to Marlowe for about forty-five minutes by phone. Then, in 1986, I was given access to a file of material that Nagell had provided over the years to a since-retired LAPD officer with the Organized Crime Bureau.

Included was a telegram that Marlowe, using the pseudonym "John M.," had sent to Nagell in prison. The Western Union message of April 1, 1964, from Santa Monica, California, looked innocuous enough. Sent care of an El Paso attorney, it read: "Surprised to hear that you did not receive my holiday greeting card. The PO employees must be overworked. I sent it long ago. Good luck John M."

At the bottom of the page was a typed paragraph by Nagell. And what I read stunned me:

> The original of the above xerox copy of a telegram is a significant piece of hard evidence substantiating the existence of a conspiracy to assassi-nate President Kennedy. It contains a coded message and was sent to me at El Paso in April 1964 before my first trial on the merits by Vaughn L. Snipes, aka "John Miller" and "Don Gordon." When Jim Garrison's in-

vestigation was made public in 1967, [Vaughn] Snipes sent a letter to the Orleans Parish DA's office attempting to disavow any unlawful connection with me. Actually, I had investigated Snipes and his wife Priscilla in conjunction with my inquiry about Oswald. One of the two Cubans who were associating with Oswald in August and September 1963 (who also fits the description of one of the two Cubans who allegedly visited Sylvia Odio at Magellan Circle with Oswald the day before his trip to Mexico in September 1963) was witnessed entering the "ON THE BEACH BOOK-STORE" on two separate occasions while he was under surveillance. The bookstore was located in Venice and Snipes was the proprietor. Snipes, who once boasted that he was a good shot with a rifle, was considered for recruitment to hit JFK in June 1963 during his visit to the Beverly Hilton hotel. That "project" never materialized.

I knew that I had to see Vaughn Snipes/Marlowe in person. But he had left the University of Michigan's Flint campus, and none of his university friends knew where he had moved. Finally, someone recalled that he had bought some property along the Oregon coast. That was where I found him in 1990. Marlowe stood a husky six feet, two inches, with a bushy mustache and a shock of brown hair. I decided to wait awhile before bringing up the subject of the telegram—and Nagell's addendum.

Marlowe was an engaging conversationalist whose reminiscences about the wild and woolly days of what he called the "vanguard left" could fill a book in themselves. Born in 1931 in Flint, Michigan, he had become active with the United Auto Workers while working in a factory. Entering the Army the same year Nagell did (1948), Marlowe, too, had served in the Korean War. When I mentioned that Nagell was apparently the youngest soldier to receive a battlefield promotion to captain, Marlowe chuckled and replied: "Far cry from my service record—I might have been the *oldest* soldier promoted to private first class."

Marlowe says he "acquired a fascination with the Chinese during the Korean War, to find out what the hell they were all about. I was an embryonic Marxist. And when I came home to Flint and the factory, I was associating with a number of people who could be called Trotskyists, I suppose. A split-off from the Socialist Workers Party (SWP). Their position was that someday the Soviet Union would break up, and Eastern Europe would fall apart. That was a good thirty to thirty-five years ago, and they're the only people I know who were right about that."

After moving to San Francisco and then Los Angeles, by mid-1962 Marlowe had become a leading organizer for the Congress of Racial Equality (CORE) and an executive committee member of L.A.'s Fair Play for Cuba chapter. He considered himself an independent battler for social justice, bemused by all the ideological infighting. Marlowe was hard-nosed, and all sides knew it. He recalled a FPCC rally at the UCLA campus in the spring of 1963, where both the Communist Party, U.S.A., and the SWP called on him to protect their people "from a rumored attack by right-wing Cubans. I brought a dozen goons into the hall, I mean street people, animals. I remember realizing I had seven ex-cons out of twelve, armed robbery guys and like that. These people were pro-Castro—actually they were social anarchists but they hated the establishment and the cops so much that I could call them out to protect *Communist* speakers! Well, if there was any trouble planned to come out of that audience, nobody moved."

Not long thereafter, a tall stranger suddenly walked into Marlowe's life.

Rendezvous on the Beach

Marlowe began: "My ex-wife and I had opened a left-wing bookstore in Venice [a beach suburb of L.A.] that spring. It must have been sometime in May, I'd been down swimming, and when I came back, the clerk who was running the place for me said there was a fellow who'd just come in and left a calling card. It was an unusual card—the name Richard C. Nagell on one side, and on the other side was the same thing in Japanese. He'd said he would be next door at the Venice West Café for about an hour and would like to talk to me.

"So I went over, and here was this guy wearing a dark blue suit, summer weave, white shirt and regimental tie, highly polished black shoes. Good-looking man, trim, close-shaven. He was no fashion plate, but he could have worked for any *Fortune* 500 listing, you know? His teeth had all been reworked, plenty of gold. I figured that it had to be government work. The only other expensive mouth I've seen like that was on an uncle of mine who was a Ford executive.

"Anyway, the guy looked about as out of place, as Raymond Chandler would put it, as 'a tarantula on a piece of angel food.' I mean, the Venice West was the ultimate beatnik coffeehouse in those days. Even though it was early in the day, I could see people running around whispering, 'Cop, cop, cop.' Well, obviously no real cop would come in dressed like that. He introduced himself, we sat down and started talking.

"He began the conversation by saying he was interested in, and sympathetic to, our organizational activities in the Santa Monica-Venice area. He told me he was an ex-officer with Army Intelligence who had done some hard thinking about his role in the past. He claimed to have friends and connections with various law enforcement agencies, and access to certain files. By way of example, he brought out some information on me that came, he claimed, from the Los Angeles Police Department's Red Squad files. It was accurate, though somewhat dated, and it contained the names of a number of friends who had worked with me on various projects. That's when he offered to help in any way that he could through his 'connections,' saying he didn't want to be as 'active' as we were for 'personal reasons.'

"Well, we had a few beers and I ended up asking him to prove his good intentions by tracing the license plate numbers of two cars that came regularly to the beach. We suspected they were narcotics officers. As a little test, I added in two other numbers of friends' cars that I could see in the parking lot across the street from the coffeehouse. By the next day, he had the information for me, and he fingered a 'narc' from the West Los Angeles Division of the LAPD. The guy's cover was blown. So I figured that whoever this guy was and whatever loyalty he had, it certainly wasn't to the LAPD.

"Our second meeting was at a bar that I chose arbitrarily while driving around with him in my car. Here he showed me various documents and copies of news items sufficient to impress me that he was what he claimed: an ex-U.S. infantry and ex-Army intelligence officer, and a former investigator for California's Alcoholic Beverage Control. One news item was about his being shot in the chest in the summer of '62. And he mentioned this plane crash where he was severely injured, resulting in facial plastic surgery. Again he told me he had many connections that could be of help in our various organizational activities that included the FPCC, CORE, ACLU, and SWP.

"Richard was a charming man, and I held two opinions about him simultaneously. It was odd. I felt he *was* sincerely interested in what we were doing. My wife and I dined with him probably twice, and there was a lot of high-minded talk about the need for democratic socialism and political reconstruction. I had the definite feeling he was disenchanted with American foreign policy. At the same time, I suspected he was also a spook, working for one of the intelligence-gathering agencies and checking me out for some unknown reason. Well, hell, I had nothing to hide. I'd even entertained FBI agents for lunch in earlier years, simply because I was intrigued with all this business of trying to save America from people like me. So I accepted Richard for what he was.

"He volunteered to help us with a little publication called *The Specter*, which was given over to complaints about Chief Parker's LAPD. He even met once with our editorial board in a back room of the bookstore, and showed us a registered letter he'd written to Chief [William] Parker inquiring about the Red Squad. The name he chose to write under was

Robert C. Nolan. And he set about preparing an article about the Red Squad for the paper.

"I remember he talked about Japanese culture at times—he was the first person I ever heard mention sushi. And he told me his wife was a Japanese national, they were separated, and she had taken custody of their two kids. At that time, my wife and I were both quite taken with the Communist Chinese experiment, doing a lot of reading and studying about it. I laughed with Richard once. I said, 'This is kind of unusual, two Korean War vets sitting around talking about the Chinese.' I believe he said something like, 'Well, they made an impression on me.'"

Marlowe remembered the pair discussing Cuba as well, "probably because I was so interested in it," and the fact that the SWP was the organizing force behind the FPCC. They also talked about a nearby foreign capital that both had recently visited: Mexico City. Shortly before the Cuban Missile Crisis—Marlowe guessed it must have been August 1962—he had traveled to Mexico and "spent a few days with Mexican Communists, so-called, and dropped into the Mexican-Russian Cultural Friendship Center." He had also gone by the Cuban embassy "two days running, trying to get the equivalent of a visa to go to Cuba." Marlowe added: "It was years later before I found out that the CIA was operating a listening post across the street, and photographing everybody that was going in. So it's quite possible that's how Richard Nagell got onto me. He eventually told me he'd been down there in Mexico at the same time. We discussed a couple restaurants in common, and he knew the hotel I'd stayed in."

"And did you make it to Cuba?" I asked.

"Well, I can't answer that," Marlowe replied. "Let's just say I didn't leave the Cuban embassy, get on a plane, and go to Cuba. I don't want to say anything more about Cuba. A couple of people I know wouldn't be happy about my saying anything further about it." He said he never raised that subject with Nagell and doesn't know whether Nagell was aware of any such voyage he may have made.

It was illegal (and still is) for American citizens to visit Castro's island without State Department approval, and such unauthorized trips were being scrutinized carefully by the House Un-American Activities Committee in 1962–63. Indeed, many of the individuals whom Nagell was then checking out in Southern California were known to have visited Cuba during that period. So it is likely, since Marlowe was one of his subjects, that Nagell would have been briefed about any Cuban trip he had made. Of his 1963 acquaintanceship with Marlowe, Nagell would later write: "My report on him was 23 pages long, a copy of which I have on microfilm."[16]

Marlowe seemed a straightforward enough person, and I decided it was time to tread into deeper waters. "Why did you use so many different names?" I asked. "It just seems to be kind of a left-wing tradition," he replied. "Keep your opponents off balance any little way you can; if you can't change the way you look, at least change the name. I've even published under different names that I used only once, like a radical 'Call to Arms' that I wrote for a foreign paper. It would open a file all by itself, in that it certainly advocated sabotage and nonhuman terrorism. But that was just part of the kind of busywork I was involved in back then."

The Candidate

All the parallels to Oswald, Nagell, or both felt positively eerie—the pseudonyms, the militancy, the FPCC-SWP-CP affiliations, the trip to Mexico City and the Cuban embassy. Finally I said, "There's something I think you ought to see," and passed over Nagell's description of how Marlowe had once been "considered for recruitment to hit JFK."

A stunned expression crossed Marlowe's face. "This blows my mind," he said in a lowered voice, shaking his head. "Well, I didn't like the Kennedys, but I sure as hell wasn't going to shoot any of them!" We lapsed into silence as Marlowe reread the page several times. Then he said: "You know, what's really weird is, there was a little joke I had for a while. I used to talk about Nagell with the woman I later married and she said, 'What do you think that was all about?' I said, 'I think they were looking for somebody to shoot Kennedy and I was scheduled to be Oswald.' I always thought that was a pretty funny joke—until this moment."

Marlowe conceded he might have looked like an ideal candidate. He made no secret of his criticism of President Kennedy's policies. In the window of his bookstore in 1963 was a large satirical photo of JFK, depicting a distorted presidential profile railing against the Cubans. "I'd even been one of the lieutenants organizing a demonstration against Kennedy when he was supposed to speak in L.A. during the [Cuban] Missile Crisis, until his trip got canceled."

Nor did Marlowe disguise the fact that, dating back to his Korean War service years, he was a good shot with a rifle. "My bookstore was in the middle of a junkie paradise," Marlowe recalled. "The word on the beach was that I was a shooter. I put that out intentionally, because I didn't want to be knifed for my $25-a-day receipts at the end of every night. I saved myself from getting cut up one night by some lunatic, because I had a gun. I just didn't try to hide the fact that there were guns in my bookstore and in my house. It was certainly known to the cops and the FBI that I had this reputation. And Nagell knew it. We talked about it."

Marlowe shook his head again. "There I was, this crazy bastard who'd been to the Cuban embassy in Mexico, helps run the L.A. Fair Play for Cuba Committee, tied into all these left-wing groups. Wow! But I just have no recollection of anybody I knew as a Cuban coming into the bookstore, or my having any contact with anyone who was Cuban."

Understandably, it took awhile for Marlowe to recover his composure. When he did, I asked him about the telegram he had sent Nagell in jail in 1964, which Nagell alleged contained "a coded message." Marlowe gave a long sigh and picked up the story of their relationship.

"He never tried to recruit me for anything, and I never got the idea that he was trying to pump me for any information. He told me in the spring of '63 that he had a job driving a cab, I believe in either Beverly Hills or West L.A., up the street a ways. Which was so easy to check on that I didn't even bother. I figured he either had a cover driving a cab, or he *was* driving a cab. What difference did it make?

"I saw Richard less frequently as the summer went on, and then suddenly in August he sure went out of L.A. in a hurry. I don't think he was planning on it, because he gave no indication that he wouldn't be around to help put out that issue of *The Specter*—the one where 'Robert Nolan' was going to write an article on the Red Squad for us. When he left, he stopped by the bookstore, but I was out. He left a couple things for me. One of the items was in a manila envelope—the cover off of a short-lived publication called *USA,* issue number one. It was a marvelous photograph of Chou En-lai [the Communist Chinese premier]. And there was a cryptic note saying something about contacting me later and that 'certain people in certain circles thought very highly of me'—whatever that meant. I didn't hear from him again for quite a while."

Marlowe looked again at the remarkable piece of paper I had given him to read. "I don't know what he means here by saying he investigated my wife and me in conjunction with his inquiry about Oswald. He didn't ask me about anybody by that name. I don't remember ever hearing of Oswald until November 22, 1963. But—this sounds spooky—when I saw Oswald's picture, I recognized him. In some really strange way. This was before I had any reason to suppose that Nagell had any connection with him. But I said to Ginger, 'I've seen this guy somewhere before.' The only time I was outside of California was the summer of '62, so I couldn't have met him anyplace else except in Mexico City, or in L.A. I don't know where, but I always had this funny feeling.

"Then sometime in the spring of 1964, I came back to L.A. from a long vacation in the Northwest to find in my mail two letters from Richard. They'd been sent at an interval, and they scared the shit out of me. I hadn't even known he was in jail, and he indicated that he'd smuggled them out somehow. The first one was a curious request that, if questioned,

I be sure to attest to his 'right-wing leanings.' And that I take into consideration that the events in 'D' might have been a tragic blunder. He ended with, 'Sometimes things go wrong.' As if something could have been corrected, you see. That's the part that frightened me more than anything. I could only conclude that what happened in Dallas might *not* have happened if something that he was involved in had taken place, which, of course, implicated him in the assassination. If not in its plotting, at least in its execution, because he implied that he was in a position to affect it or stop it.

"The second letter was a request to mail out a series of letters, in the form of a prepared press release, to Earl Warren, Senator Richard Russell, *The Washington Post,* the *L.A. Times,* and *The New York Times*—reporting that he had been overheard to say during his arraignment that 'the FBI held full responsibility for the Kennedy assassination' and that he was immediately led out of the court by 'federal men.' Meaning, as I later came to learn, that he'd attempted to notify the FBI that a domestic plot was in place to assassinate JFK. It also had to do with his being railroaded into his first trial in El Paso.

"Well, I liked him and it didn't even occur to me that he'd be in jail for something he deserved. I'm not at all happy about my response to his letters, I feel that in some way I disappointed him. I think he enclosed ten or twenty bucks, and a form which had to be typed up and mailed out. Amid my confusion and speculation about what his letters *meant,* I only managed to get a couple of the press releases off. But that telegram I sent him at the jail *is* a coded message, sure, a way of acknowledging that I had mailed some of this stuff for him.

"Both of his letters to me had begun with the information that the return addresses on the envelopes were 'phony' and to disregard them. The street names and numbers were identical, and the city was El Paso. But I suddenly recognized the street name as being here in Los Angeles. I looked in the L.A. phone book—nice piece of cop work—and there was a 'Nagell' living two doors away from the return address on the envelope. People will sometimes do that, I suppose, put a familiar address from another city on something, if they're trying to obscure the origin.

"So I called and, yep, it was Richard Nagell's mother. I pretended to be an old Army buddy of his, I think I used the name John Miller. I hated doing this to a man's mother, but I was frightened. I said he'd dropped out of sight and I just got this curious card from him in Texas indicating that he was in some kind of trouble. She was very reluctant to talk, but she was not hanging up on me. I said, 'This is really off the wall, Mrs. Nagell, and I may be crazy, but I got the feeling that Richard somehow knows something about the Kennedy assassination.' There was a long silence. Finally I said, 'Mrs. Nagell, has someone asked you not to talk about this? Has the

FBI gotten in touch with you or someone like that?' Her response to all this was affirmative, but she said she was not free to discuss it. She advised that I'd have to go to the city where the letter came from if I wanted to find out something.

"I did go to El Paso. Less than a year later, March of 1965. I'd just come from the Selma-to-Montgomery [civil rights] march. In El Paso I studied the newspapers for September 1963, and then I talked to one of Richard's dingdong lawyers. Once again, [using a] phony name. I think the lawyer said something over the phone like 'Your friend's insane,' anyway something that led me to conclude he was definitely unsympathetic. I was supposed to meet with the man, but I got spooked. I figured he'd probably already talked to every intelligence agency in the Western world about this. So I caught the next plane out of town. I realized I might be backing off of the story of the century, and I was supposed to be a goddamned newsman at the time. But I had no knowledge of what I might be up against. When I got home, my wife and a friend read all the meager correspondence between Richard and me—and we burned the paper-work."

Marlowe took a deep breath, and we both sat there for a while quietly digesting it all. The strangeness had not ended after a frightened Marlowe burned his correspondence from Nagell in 1965. Not long thereafter, Marlowe discovered someone had broken into a friend's apartment in another city, gone through his briefcase, and stolen only a rubber-banded series of letters from Marlowe. Then there was an incident involving the other friend, whom he had allowed to see his messages from Nagell before disposing of them.

"Tom was an ex-Air Force sergeant who'd gotten discharged after writing a pamphlet, *Cuba Sí, Yanqui No,* in the orderly room during the [Cuban] Missile Crisis. We worked in the movement for a long time together. He had some menial job here in L.A., sometime in the mid-'60s, when a guy came to work there and befriended him right away. Even before I met the guy, Tom said, 'Be careful, he may be a plant.' I said, 'Why?' Tom said, 'His hands—they don't do the kind of work he's doing at the factory.'

"Anyway, the three of us were shooting pool over at Tom's one night, when this guy lies down on the floor and looks like he passes out or goes to sleep. About fifteen minutes later, he rolled over, sat up, and said, 'Boy, I just had the damnedest dream. I dreamt you guys were talking about Jack Kennedy.' I said, 'No, not us.' And he said, 'Yeah, and you were all getting ready to shoot him, you were in this building somewhere.' I said, 'Weird dream, man.' He was around for another week or so, then he quits his job and disappears.

"I'm up in San Francisco a few years later and I go in this real upscale club with a girl. Lo and behold, there's the same guy, this common laborer sitting there in his blue subdued pinstripe. Goddamn FBI narrow horn-rims. I went over and said, 'How you doing?' He looked up. 'Vaughn Marlowe,' I said and he put out his hand, said, 'Oh yeah, Vaughn, how you doing?' I said, 'Did you ever find the guys who killed Jack Kennedy?' Well, he looked all flustered at his girlfriend. I winked at him and went back to our table."

In 1967, Marlowe had written Jim Garrison's office "to alert him that there was a guy out there somewhere who might really know something." Then he had sought to communicate with Nagell in 1968, but his letter was returned as "undeliverable" by prison authorities at Springfield, Missouri. The years went by until, in 1975, he came across "in one of the scandal sheets that pursue the assassination" the name of Professor Richard Popkin, reported as being in touch with Nagell. Marlowe briefly corresponded with Popkin, received Nagell's address, and wrote to him at his L.A. post office box. Opening a little file, Marlowe handed across to me his letter and Nagell's reply. Marlowe had written Nagell apologizing for failing to do more with the "press releases" back in 1964.[17]

Marlowe wrote: "Nobody in the country was saying a word about 'conspiracy.' There was no round-up, no 'red hunt'; there was only lone assassin Oswald blown away by a cheap Chicago torpedo. Case closed. There we were [his wife and he] . . . watching television, organizing picket lines, smoking dope, and wondering about Richard Nagell somewhere in Texas who knew something so goddamned big that if we knew it it could get us killed off quicker than you got thrown in jail. Man, it stank! We went a little crazy. I kept both of my pieces loaded, took to carrying the damn things [and] I included myself out. . . .

"Ginger and I thought a good deal of you, even though we knew you were a cop of some sort," Marlowe's letter continued. "Since you knew so much about me, you obviously knew that I was neither cop nor fink, but was what I said I was: a student of Marxist-Leninist-Maoist thought who hoped, eventually, to have a small part in the smashing of the state. In fine, a revolutionary in a pre-revolutionary society. . . . My wife and I talked to you at first because it was almost flattering to have what might have been our own *mamka* [wet nurse], but we soon felt that you were truly receptive. I have always believed that you were sincerely on the left, or moving there rapidly, and in those days I would have attempted to convert Allen Dulles (I still would!). Somehow I did not buy the notion that you were *only* a cop. . . ."

Nagell responded early in 1976 by sending Marlowe some documents "which may provide a better insight into that fella you once knew in Venice, though you will have to read between the lines to grasp the nuances. . . . Rest assured that I wasn't your mamka back in 1963, nor was I an agent provocateur, notwithstanding the vibes you may have felt in that direction. Precisely what the overfriendly, bungling oaf was up to in those days will have to remain undisclosed at this point in time. Suffice it to say that I was abiding by my principles and ideological beliefs, whatever they were, in the pursuance of an objective to which you and Ginger would not have been totally opposed."

That was the last time they had been in touch. Now Marlowe looked over at me with a puzzled expression. "Well, that 'objective' must have been something other than hitting the president of the United States," he said. "But who could have been looking to 'recruit' me into that? What was it all about?"

Target: Los Angeles

In the late spring of 1963, in his double role Richard Nagell clearly was investigating Vaughn Marlowe for the CIA (and/or Soviet intelligence). Simultaneously, certain Cuban exiles were considering Marlowe as a candidate to be a left-wing hit man. It might have been purely coincidental that these matters overlapped, but Nagell has admitted that he had meetings in L.A. with "Angel" and "Leopoldo" and twice surveilled one of them browsing in Marlowe's bookstore. Nagell also says he took 16-millimeter still photographs of both exiles in L.A. in June, negatives of which he provided "for safekeeping" to a friend that September.[18]

In Los Angeles that June, Vaughn Marlowe was never approached by the Cuban exiles. The "project," as Nagell has written, never materialized. But unlike the first plot in Miami the previous December, Nagell says the L.A. effort "got past the talking stage."[19]

Three days before JFK's trip to the West Coast, on June 4 Nagell requested admission to the psychiatric ward at the Veterans Administration Hospital in suburban Brentwood. It was the same tactic he had employed in Florida the previous December, to remove himself from the local scene. An FBI file on Nagell records: "Subject's condition diagnosed by Veterans Administration, Los Angeles, on 6/4/63 as 'depression, tearful, nervous, rigid.' Would only utter words 'Got to see my kids.' " Nagell was seen by a psychiatrist at the outpatient clinic but this time was not granted admission to the hospital.[20]

A question that arises, in looking back at the press accounts of Kennedy's voyage, is whether the president might already have been alerted that something was afoot. JFK arrived in L.A. on the afternoon of June 7, having just spent eighteen hours aboard two aircraft carriers at California's China Lake Naval Ordnance Testing Station. There, *The New York*

Times noted, he was "given a look at virtually every weapon in the Navy arsenal."[21]

The *New York Herald Tribune* recounted: "At 3:40 p.m. (P.D.T.), as the chopper that brought the President to Los Angeles from China Lake, Calif., was landing on the lot atop a wing of the [Beverly Hilton] hotel, a score of Negro and white pickets from the Congress of Racial Equality marched on the street outside. The signs they bore called on Mr. Kennedy to take prompt, aggressive leadership to halt all forms of racial segregation."[22]

According to the *Times:* "Mr. Kennedy did not go through the picket line, however. He went over it. The president's helicopter landed on the roof of the Beverly Hilton Hotel, where no pickets were posted. The pickets, members of the Congress of Racial Equality [CORE], said they would remain outside the hotel until Mr. Kennedy left."[23]

The president hobnobbed inside with nearly two hundred of the California Democratic Party's big contributors at a closed dinner. "One of those who paid $1,000 to attend the dinner was the motion picture executive Jack L. Warner . . . the producer of 'PT-109,' the film story of Mr. Kennedy's wartime adventures."[24] Guests were shown a preview of the Cliff Robertson-as-JFK role, while outside civil rights picketers set up an "overnight demonstration."

The CORE group outside the hotel was the same one that Marlowe had worked closely with in L.A., though he says he did not attend the demonstration. (Later that summer, in New Orleans, several witnesses would see Oswald also attend a CORE voting-rights registration drive.) As for Nagell, he was apparently driving a cab in the vicinity of the Beverly Hilton. One of his letters to Arthur Greenstein told "of picking up unwanted passenger from those picketing." This, Nagell added, related in some way to the incident of the previous summer when Nagell had been shot in the chest near Malibu. After the presidential visit, Nagell says he quit his job at "Yellow [cab] No. 1."[25]

Late on the night of June 7, the president flew on to Hawaii to discuss civil rights issues at the U.S. Conference of Mayors.

What was Richard Nagell really up to during his springtime of '63 in Los Angeles? One clue appears in the signed statement he gave to the FBI in January 1964 concerning his real motive in firing inside the bank. Here he refers to the September 1962 proposal made to him by "a representative of a foreign government" in Mexico City—"a criminal offense and inimical to the best interests of the United States," and one that Nagell refused to take part in at that time. Then Nagell continues: "In May, 1963, another representative of the same foreign government made the same proposal to me. At that time I agreed to such a proposal."[26]

Nagell has never revealed, either to the FBI or in later years, what this "proposal" was, except to say that it "pertained to Lee Harvey Oswald." I did not know what to make of this. According to Nagell, Oswald had not yet been approached about any plans to assassinate the president. In 1966, Nagell wrote that his knowledge was of a "domestic-inspired, domestic-formulated, and domestic-sponsored conspiracy to assassinate a Chief Executive of the United States and other highly-placed government officials."[27]

So the "proposal" that originated with representatives of a "foreign government" must be about something else. But whatever it was, could the Kennedy conspirators have been aware of it—and somehow used it as a means of manipulating Oswald, or getting close to him?

Vaughn Marlowe is sure "that Nagell was representing some interest other than his own. And yet there was a touch of the idealist about the guy in conversation that led me to suppose, when push came to shove, he would follow his own inclinations—instead of the orders of someone else."

When I next heard from Marlowe, in 1992, he had just finished writing two plays. One of them was an imaginary construction of a conversation between J. Edgar Hoover and his chief assistant shortly after receiving a certain warning letter in September 1963. The other was about a man named Oswald and was titled *The Patsy*.

Summary

A second plot to assassinate JFK, at a presidential visit to the Beverly Hilton Hotel in Los Angeles, was being discussed in the spring of 1963. This coincided with the establishment of an Alpha 66 branch office in L.A. and with Nagell's monitoring of left-wing organizations. Vaughn Marlowe, on the executive committee of the L.A. Fair Play for Cuba Committee, was among the targets of Nagell's surveillance—and was considered for recruitment by a cadre of Cuban exiles into their assassination conspiracy. One of these exiles, "Leopoldo," borrowed his "war name" from a local restaurant.

Marlowe well remembered Nagell's having befriended him. His "anti-imperialist" sentiments—and expertise with a rifle—were no secrets. He had visited the Cuban embassy in Mexico City. In other words, Marlowe fit the Oswald pattern perfectly—for someone looking to make it appear that the assassination was engineered by "Communist sympathizers" or even Castro himself. Like Arthur Greenstein, Marlowe remained spellbound by Nagell for years, especially after receiving word from an imprisoned Nagell that the assassination might be considered a "tragic blunder (sometimes things go wrong)."

Exactly what Nagell's role was in investigating Marlowe is still a mystery. So is the "proposal" that Nagell accepted in May 1963, from a foreign government's representative, to take part in a "criminal offense" against the United States. This does not seem to have been the assassination, but it did somehow relate to Oswald. Did a separate intelligence operation end up being manipulated in a different direction? Was this the "tragic blunder" of which Nagell spoke?

Chapter Fifteen

Fair Play or Foul?: June–July 1963

Six days after the shooting incident at General Walker's home in Dallas, Lee Harvey Oswald stepped up his communications with the Fair Play for Cuba Committee. The Warren Commission observed that Oswald's correspondence with the FPCC did not begin until the spring of 1963. Yet, found among Oswald's effects after the assassination was an empty envelope on which was the FPCC's return address in New York and sent to Oswald at Mercedes Street in Fort Worth. Since the Oswalds lived there only between August 4 and October 8, 1962, the indication is that Oswald was in touch with the FPCC at least six months earlier than the commission perceived.[1]

By 1963, the chairman of the FPCC's New York headquarters was a thirty-five-year-old ex-GI who used the name V. T. Lee. His real name was Vincent Tappin. Ending two years of Army service in 1956, "Lee" had become a merchant seaman. Later he was said to have hooked up with members of Castro's 26th of July Movement and made frequent trips to

Cuba. He had been in charge of the FPCC branch in Tampa, Florida, but departed for New York in the fall of 1962 because, according to a file in the *Time-Life* library archives about him, "he was being hounded to death by FBI agents."[2]

V. T. Lee had traveled to Los Angeles as part of a speaking tour on April 4–5, 1963, shortly before Nagell's arrival in the city. There Lee called a press conference and gave speeches at UCLA's Young Socialists Alliance and the First Unitarian Church. The FPCC's national spokesman told the press: "Cubans today have freedom from hunger, freedom from racial prejudice, freedom to educate themselves. . . . That's much more than they had when the United States dominated Cuba."[3]

Soon after this, Oswald began writing regularly to V. T. Lee. Also soon after this, according to FBI files declassified in the mid-1970s, the FBI intensified its probe of Lee and the FPCC. The parallels are intriguing.

April 16, 1963: Oswald wrote the New York FPCC headquarters that he had passed out FPCC literature in Dallas, and he requested that more be sent to him.[4]

April 17: An FBI file described "confidential source #7" advising that V. T. Lee "had been responsible for directing national office of FPCC for about six months and FPCC had during that time published 8 new pamphlets and prepared 300,000 leaflets for dissemination."[5]

April 19: The New York FPCC office sent literature to Oswald.

April 21: The FBI's New York field office, either through an informant or its mail-intercept program, learned that Oswald had written a letter to the FPCC. But this information would not be reported to the Dallas office until June 27, or to FBI Headquarters until September 10.[6]

April 24: Oswald left Dallas, taking a bus alone to New Orleans, and leaving Marina—now pregnant with a second child—and baby June behind at Ruth Paine's home. Arriving in the Crescent City, Oswald was taken in by his aunt, Mrs. Charles Murret, while he set out to look for work. Her husband, Charles, offered him a $200 loan in the interim.[7]

May 6: The FBI's confidential source #2 advised "that the FPCC participated in the annual May Day celebration" five days earlier in New York's Union Square.

May 7: The FBI's confidential source #1 advised that V. T. Lee "had returned from a 6,500 mile speaking tour through major United States cities in California, Washington, Colorado, Iowa and Illinois. . . ."[8]

May 9: Oswald applied for a job at the Reily Coffee Company as a maintenance man. The company's owner, William Reily, was a wealthy American backer of the anti-Castro Crusade to Free Cuba Committee—an organization formed to raise funds and support for the CIA-backed Cuban "government-in-exile," Antonio Varona's Cuban Revolutionary Council.[9] On Oswald's application, he gave three references. One was his uncle, the shipyard worker who ran a little sidelight as a bookmaker for the Carlos Marcello crime syndicate. Another was "Sgt. Robert Hidell"[10] —a combination, intended or not, of the surname from Nagell's "Robert Nolan" alias and of the "Hidell" name used at times by both men.

Oswald immediately got the job, rented an apartment, and called Marina to bring the family to join him in Bayou country.

May 14: Oswald mailed a change-of-address card to the FPCC.[11]

May 24: Oswald renewed his subscription to the Socialist Workers Party newspaper, *The Militant,* at his New Orleans address.[12] The SWP (see Chapter Seven) was considered the guiding hand behind the FPCC.

May 26: Oswald sent five dollars to the national FPCC office for membership, writing to V. T. Lee: "Now that I live in New Orleans I have been thinking about renting a small office at my own expense for the purpose of forming a F.P.C.C. branch here in New Orleans. Could you give me a charter? . . . Also a picture of Fidel, suitable for framing would be a welcome touch."[13]

May 27: Dallas FBI agent Hosty returned to the Oswalds' Neely Street residence, seeking to interview Marina, and was informed that the couple had moved from the area without leaving a forwarding address.[14]

May 29: V. T. Lee wrote Oswald back, suggesting that he get in touch with the Tampa chapter, which Lee had personally organized. He warned Oswald that "It would be hard to conceive [sic] of a chapter with as few members as seem to exist in the New Orleans area. I have just gone through our files and find that Louisiana seems somewhat restricted for Fair Play activities. . . . We feel that the southeast is a very difficult place to work."[15]

That same day, without waiting to receive Lee's reply, Oswald visited the Jones Printing Company, opposite the side entrance of Reily Coffee. Using the name "Osborne," he ordered a thousand copies of a handbill. It read: "HANDS OFF CUBA! Join the Fair Play for Cuba Committee NEW ORLEANS CHARTER MEMBER BRANCH."[16]

May 30: An FBI file noted that V. T. Lee had indicated to an unnamed source that "he has no intention of permitting FPCC policy to be determined by any other organization."[17]

June 3: Oswald rented P.O. Box 30061 in his own name, giving Fair Play for Cuba as an organizational name and listing A. J. Hidell and Marina Oswald as authorized to pick up mail. The same day, he ordered five hundred offset-printed copies of a membership application blank, using the name "Lee Osborne."[18]

What was going on? The FBI, during the Cuban Missile Crisis the previous fall, had expanded its Security Index, establishing a special "Cuban Section" that included not only names of suspected Cuban agents operating in the United States, but also of people who had participated in organizations or picket lines that supported Castro. Nearly twelve thousand persons were included on the main index and another twenty thousand in two reserve indexes—all of whom were targeted for arrest as "potentially dangerous" in the event of an "internal security emergency."[19]

But despite Oswald's history in the USSR and his flurry of correspondence with the Communist Party, U.S.A., SWP, and FPCC—much of which was known to the FBI at the time—his name was never included on either part of the Security Index, not even after he went on to set up his highly visible FPCC chapter in New Orleans that summer of 1963.

Had the FBI received word from someone to keep a relative distance from Oswald? If so, was it because he was considered part of another intelligence operation? Or providing the FBI with an opportunity to observe, through him, what was going on with the FPCC? Or giving some information to the FBI himself?

As we have seen, all through this same period Vaughn Marlowe of the L.A. FPCC was being "scouted" by some Cuban exiles as a potential recruit for an assassination attempt against JFK.

Oswald on Assignment

What I learned over the years from Richard Nagell does not solve the riddle of Oswald's SWP-FPCC-related activities. But it sheds some light particularly on what they were *not* about.

As far back as 1967, in his letter from prison to Senator Richard Russell, Nagell had written that "Mr. Oswald had no significant connection with the Fair Play for Cuba Committee."[20] Then, at our first meeting in 1975, Nagell elaborated: "I cannot agree that Oswald himself was penetrating anything. His involvement with the Fair Play for Cuba Committee in New Orleans was something entirely different. There *was* no chapter of the committee that he was associated with, not in reality. It was a ploy."[21]

Then, in 1976, Nagell elaborated that Oswald's FPCC chapter in New Orleans "started out as a scam, to establish a 'bona fide' for use in checking on something in another state, strictly tangential. That's all I can say."[22]

Whatever this "scam" was, it shows that if Nagell did not instigate it, he was certainly aware of it. It also shows that Oswald was continuing to be directed by one force or another. As for what Nagell wrote about "checking on something in another state," I came across some unusual correspondence in the Assassination Archives Research Center that pointed in the direction of Tampa, Florida. This was the city where V. T. Lee suggested Oswald "get in touch" with the chapter, and himself continued to make occasional trips from his new base in New York. Almost as much as Miami, Tampa was then regarded as a hotbed for both anti-Castro exiles and Castro's own intelligence agents. It was also home base of Santos Trafficante, Jr., the gangster who admitted to the House Assassinations Committee having worked with the CIA in plotting Castro's demise.

On December 17, 1962, the supervisor of Tampa's Police Intelligence Unit wrote a letter to P. J. Trosclair, his counterpart with the New Orleans Police Department. It referred to a Trosclair letter of December 3 concerning the Fair Play for Cuba Committee. "This unit has not received any information with reference to the New Orleans area," said Sergeant J. S. De la Llama, "however the Fair Play for Cuba Committee is very active in the Tampa area. As you know the Fair Play for Cuba Committee is Communist inspired and all literature is very strong pro-Castro."

The letter went on to describe how V. T. Lee had helped to organize the Tampa chapter before moving to New York. "This unit maintains a current file on the local chapter and its members," continued the Tampa police official. "Please be assured of our cooperation in any matters of mutual interest, and advise if we can be of further assistance on the Fair Play for Cuba Committee."[23]

Why, more than six months prior to Oswald's establishment of his one-man group, was New Orleans' Police Intelligence supervisor so interested in the FPCC? After Oswald's arrest the following summer of 1963, while passing out FPCC leaflets and getting involved in a scuffle with anti-Castro Cubans, Trosclair was apprised of the situation in an August 12 interoffice memo. It described a police interview with Oswald during which "Oswald stated he had talked to Major Trosclair about getting a permit for F.P.C.C. and the Major advised him to consult his attorney."[24]

Yet, when I reached the now-retired Trosclair by telephone in 1992, he claimed to have no recollection of even hearing Oswald's name before the JFK assassination. Nor did Trosclair recall any correspondence he had with Tampa's Police Intelligence Unit about the FPCC. "I only know that members of my [Police] Intelligence Unit interviewed Oswald on the street as he was handing out leaflets or something, while he was in New Orleans," Trosclair said.[25]

New Orleans' Police Intelligence, like many of their counterparts elsewhere, were known to be cooperating extensively with the FBI and even the CIA. So it would be quite conceivable that Trosclair's early interest in the FPCC—and the later contact alleged by Oswald—occurred on orders from a federal agency.

In interviews with congressional investigator Gaeton Fonzi and myself, former CIA clandestine officer Joseph Burkholder Smith spoke of Desmond FitzGerald's possible CIA role with a Fair Play for Cuba Committee operation: "I know that Des's Cuban Counter Intelligence staff was very interested in the Fair Play for Cuba Committee, and getting a penetration into it would have been a high-priority effort. In other words, finding out exactly what they were doing, any ties with, say, the Cuban Intelligence service, and how much if any they were funded by the opposition—from Cuba, or Russia via Cuba, or anybody else."[26]

The China Card

A CIA document declassified in 1976 indicates that the agency was even concerned about possible Communist Chinese involvement with the FPCC. The one-page report dated November 29, 1963, was addressed to "Chief, Chicago Office" from "Acting Chief, [Domestic] Contact Division." Much of the page remained blanked out. But it did state that an unnamed contact "received information that early in 1963 the Chicoms [Chinese Communists] took over the operations in the US for the Fair Play for Cuba Committee. In February 1963 a secret meeting of the Committee was held at [blank], Chicago. At this meeting the assassination of the President of the U.S. was discussed. My contact added that Lee Oswald purchased the rifle that was used in the assassination of President Kennedy in March 1963. . . ."

There is no available substantiation whatsoever for this report, and it could either be another of thousands of rumors that arose after the assassination—or even planted "disinformation." Other since-released CIA and FBI files reveal the two agencies spent many man-hours after the assassination following up an unnamed foreign diplomat's certainty that the Cubans and Chinese, "through intermediaries" in Mexico and Texas, might have had a hand in the assassination.[27] A front-page story in the *New York Journal-American* of December 8, 1963, that pointed a blatantly conspiratorial finger at V. T. Lee made a similar point—that key figures within the FPCC were "oriented to the Red Chinese."[28] And there is no doubt that the SWP's newspaper, *The Militant,* was then the American left's strongest voice on behalf of Maoist doctrine.

As I studied further about this tangled era, I came to consider a little drama glossed over by most historians of the Cuban Missile Crisis. This was the deep rift between Soviet and Chinese communism that surfaced after Khrushchev and Kennedy reached their historic agreement. The gap had been widening for a couple of years, but with the Cuban Missile Crisis, the comrades came to a distinct parting. Peking accused the Soviets of "adventurism" in introducing the missiles into Cuba in the first place, and viewed the accord with the Americans as a sign of weakness. "The capitulation of the Soviet leaders has inflated the aggressiveness and arrogance of the imperialists," an official Chinese statement read in 1963.[29]

At the same time, Mao Tse-tung's China backed Castro to the hilt, praising his "fearless" leadership. "The 650 million Chinese people will always stand by the 7 million fraternal Cuban people in weal or woe, through thick and thin and fight to the end against our common enemy US imperialism," an editorial in the *People's Daily* concluded.[30]

Khrushchev was so concerned that Castro might abandon their own alliance in favor of Peking that he felt compelled to write the Cuban premier a rambling letter on January 31, 1963. Not made public until early in 1992 in Havana, it finds the Soviet leader complaining about "representatives of some Socialist states" who were "distorting" and "criticizing" his actions during the Cuban Missile Crisis. He went so far as to refer to Chinese verbal attacks on the United States as "a paper tiger, dung."[31]

The last straw for the Chinese was the Limited Test-Ban Treaty on nuclear weapons between Kennedy and Khrushchev. Through much of July 1963 in Moscow, the U.S.-Soviet treaty negotiations and Chinese-Soviet talks to resolve their ideological differences had been going on simultaneously. On July 31, 1963, Mao's government issued a statement denouncing the treaty as a "dirty fraud" in which the Soviets had "sold out" the interests of "peace-loving peoples." Their own discussions with the Soviets were postponed indefinitely, and overt polemics erupted on both sides.[32]

The Sino-Soviet split represented a very real danger in what otherwise then seemed a dawning of détente between the superpowers. Shortly before the assassination, there had reportedly even been discussion within Kennedy administration circles of bombing out the Chinese nuclear facility at Lon Nol. The Soviets were said to be privately urging the United States to go ahead. Interestingly, some of the same Joint Chiefs of Staff who had advocated attacking the Soviet missile sites in Cuba now opposed any hit on China. They were afraid such a move would merely strengthen the Soviets' hand, especially among Third World countries in Asia, Africa, and Latin America, where both the Chinese and the Soviets were seeking inroads.[33]

So during the time when Nagell was a "double agent" for the CIA and the Soviets, both sides would have been keenly interested in any goings-on among Cuba, China, and American groups such as the SWP and the FPCC. In combing through the Mark Gayn ("Joseph Kramer") papers in Toronto, I noticed that Gayn himself spent considerable time in 1963 researching an article, "Peking vs. Moscow—Conflict on Two Fronts" (it appeared in the October issue of Canada's *Commentator* magazine). If, as

Nagell says, Gayn was a Soviet agent, he, too, could have been part of a China-watching network.

In 1967, when Nagell consented to a series of interviews in prison with an investigator for Jim Garrison, Nagell first wrote a short note to Arthur Greenstein. The letter served as a letter of introduction for the investigator, William R. Martin. It also harkened back to certain individuals Greenstein had seen in Nagell's presence in Mexico City in the fall of 1962. Nagell wrote:

> I have asked him [Martin] to contact you only in the event I should become deceased.
>
> On this basis, *and only if you know such demise to be fact,* I would ask that you furnish Mr. Martin a description of the following persons, as near as you can recall:
> 1. Maria del Carmen
> 2. "Bob" (the caucasian guy who conversed with me in Japanese at the party given by the Colombian & Chilean girls who worked at those embassies)
> 3. The Chinese guy we met at Sanborn's restaurant one evening, with whom I exchanged business cards.[34]

Whoever those three people were, apparently they were keys to solving the mystery of Nagell's covert activities. As we have seen, "Bob" was Nagell's CIA contact in 1962–63 and apparently had been in Tokyo at the same time that Nagell and Oswald were in the late 1950s. And Maria del Carmen was a Nagell contact with Cuban intelligence, though she feigned allegiance to the CIA.

The "Chinese guy" was more of an enigma. Greenstein said he could no longer remember the meeting Nagell was describing, though Nagell indicated in another letter that the man was an "Oriental Mexican." Ever since I went through the files of Nagell's El Paso attorney Joseph Calamia, something else along similar lines had proved puzzling.

When Nagell was arrested in September 1963, among the "messages" the FBI received in his briefcaseful of car-trunk papers were a series of pamphlets. Three of these pertained to Cuba (Corliss Lamont's *Hands Off Cuba; A Visit to Cuba by I.F. Stone;* and *Speech at the United Nations by Fidel Castro*). Yet five more were all about Communist China (a 1955 issue of the magazine *People's China; Is There a U.S.-China Market?; "Your QUESTIONS About NEW CHINA"*; a Peking Foreign Languages Press publication with an exchange between Chinese and Soviet Communist Parties of March 30, 1963; and a June 14, 1963, edition of the weekly *Peking Review*).

Also eventually returned by the FBI to attorney Fensterwald from among Nagell's seized effects was: "Five pages under the heading of 'Information to Date on Ben Tue Wong.'" When I asked Nagell about the relevance of this, he said that Wong (also known as Shung Wong Yet) was a Chinese he had investigated in 1963—who had nothing to do with the assassination, but who was connected with the Mafia.³⁵ There were rumors afloat at the time that Mao's China was funneling narcotics through Cuba into the United States, something that did not sit well with the American drug lords.³⁶

It was even possible that the mysterious Japanese connections to Nagell and Oswald (see Chapters Five and Six) might relate to this particular picture. In a lengthy Ph.D. thesis I read about the Japanese Communist Party (JCP), it was noted that it had come out strongly on the side of Castro and the Chinese view of events during the Cuban Missile Crisis. By 1963, the JCP was rapidly moving toward open alignment with Peking against Moscow.³⁷ If Nagell was keeping a hand in with elements of Japanese Intelligence, this development could have formed part of what he was looking at.

In that event, all those Chinese and Cuban pamphlets in Nagell's possession when he was arrested would be a tip-off to the FBI—*not* about who he was working *for,* but about a primary aim of his own investigative work—for the CIA, the KGB, and, if all the Japanese names in his notebook were intended to mean something, perhaps Japanese Intelligence. With Nagell's knowledge of all the relevant languages (including Mandarin Chinese), he would have been a logical candidate to serve all three of those outfits where their intelligence interests overlapped.

The radical right, too, was surely keeping tabs on such developments. Truman's 1951 dismissal of General MacArthur as commander in the Korean War, taking Willoughby with him, had all centered around MacArthur's demands that he be allowed to move onto the Chinese mainland against Mao's armies. Willoughby described the "convulsive, bloody effort" by "the Chinese hordes" to discredit his commander. And he never forgot it. Nor did his longtime allies in the "China lobby," who all saw Castro's Cuba as the latest result of American appeasement of communism. Willoughby's friends in the Asian People's Anti-Communist League, particularly Nationalist leader Chiang Kai-shek, had long memories as well.

Nagell and the L.A. Left

While Oswald established his one-man FPCC chapter in New Orleans, much of Nagell's investigative work was focusing on the "leftist" community around L.A. His notebook from the period is filled with their names: Helen Travis of the FPCC; Dorothy Healy of the Communist Party, U.S.A.; Reverend Stephen Fritchman of the First Unitarian Church; officials of the Medical Aid to Cuba Committee. All of these individuals or groups had been the object of scrutiny by the FBI and the House Un-American Activities Committee (HUAC).

Vaughn Marlowe was well acquainted with them. "Helen Travis had the strongest Cuban connection in L.A.," he explained. "She went in and out of Cuba like the rest of us drove in and out of Beverly Hills. I called Dorothy Healy once on the phone for some reason, probably to complain about her party stealing one of my people. It sounded like a goddamn canary cage. I said, 'Dorothy, your phone is tapped heavier than anybody's I've ever heard in my life.' Reverend Fritchman was an FPCC sympathizer, actually the public radical spokesman for the L.A. area with validity, because he was a minister."[38]

There was also Steve Roberts, West Coast coordinator for the FPCC and a SWP functionary (see Chapter Seven). In 1974, Nagell wrote to Fensterwald that a number of items were still missing from the 1963 inventory finally returned to him by the FBI. One was "a typewritten letter addressed to me in my true name at my post office box (POB 76121, Sanford Station) in Los Angeles, signed by one 'Steve Roberts' and dated in July 1963." Another was "a mimeographed or offset-printed newsletter issued by a Los Angeles chapter of the Fair Play for Cuba Committee, concerning in part Steve Roberts' (then) recent operation and hospitalization."[39]

When Roberts died on October 16, 1967, "after a long illness," according to his obituary in The Militant, the newspaper noted he had made "many visits to campuses to talk about the Cuban revolution and to mix with the students as though he was one of them. . . . The tendency to become involved wherever there was action characterized Steve throughout the years. . . . His inclination was to get into the swim, even if the temperature of the water was not exactly right."[40]

Al Lewis, who worked with him on the FPCC's executive board in L.A., told me that Roberts had traveled to Cuba from Mexico City in 1962 "as a guest of the Cuban government."[41] Whether this coincided with Nagell's time in Mexico, I do not know. But Nagell, who says he knew Roberts as a friend and in an "official" capacity, revealed at our first meetings in 1975: "I did contact Roberts concerning Lee Harvey Oswald. In July [1963], I talked to Steve when there was a big meeting of the Fair Play for Cuba Committee. I asked him what he knew about the chapter [being formed by Oswald] in New Orleans. I always considered myself a good investigator, I never went into anything half-cocked."[42]

How much of a part Roberts may have played with Oswald's activities is an unresolved question. My inquiries about Roberts among surviving members of the L.A. "left" detected lingering uneasiness about him, but none recalled anything ever arising in connection with Oswald. Everyone I talked with remembered numerous encounters between themselves and the Cuban exiles. Supporting Castro in 1963 meant being chased with tire irons, ducking smoke bombs, even witnessing an exchange of gunfire with police escorting some FPCC speakers out of a meeting.

In the context of discussing Roberts, Nagell also said: "In early July of 1963, I monitored a witness at hearings of the House Un-American Activities Committee for several days. I'm sure I was photographed by the LAPD."[43]

The HUAC, whose rabid pursuit of supposed Communists came into its own during the McCarthy era, held hearings in L.A. during the first two days of July 1963. According to the *Los Angeles Times,* these concerned "alleged illegal travel to Cuba." Most of the witnesses defiantly refused to answer the committee's questions. The last witness was attorney Harriett Buhai, who invoked constitutional protection twenty-four times.[44] Nagell had first "investigated her in Mexico in September or October 1962," when Miss Buhai traveled with a group to Cuba.

"In the latter part of June or the first part of July," Nagell has written, "I met Buhai personally for the first time in an office located on Crenshaw Boulevard, Los Angeles. As I recall, this was either her office or the office of another attorney, a male negro named Arnett Hartsfield. Anyway, both were present. It was through Buhai that I met the person identified to me in Mexico by name and by photograph as Harriett Lewis, whom Buhai introduced to me as Barbara Blair." Nagell went on that his records reflected that Lewis/Blair "was a member of the Southern California District Committee, CPUSA."

Both Buhai and Lewis/Blair are deceased. Nagell has added only that he felt Buhai was "a representative of the same foreign principal with which I was associated."[45] Again, how this might relate to the Oswald picture remains a mystery.

That midsummer of 1963 was a particularly auspicious moment in the spy wars between East and West. On July 1, 1963, the British government publicly disclosed that one of its own former high-ranking intelligence officers—Harold "Kim" Philby—was really a longtime Soviet agent who had fled behind the "Iron Curtain."[46]

That same day in Washington, the State Department ordered a cultural attaché at the Soviet embassy expelled for having attempted to recruit a Soviet-born employee of the CIA. Then, on July 2, the FBI arrested a Soviet official of the United Nations and a Washington couple on charges of spying for the USSR. Georgi M. Kornienko, the Soviet embassy's chargé d'affaires, called at the State Department to protest that Ivan Egorov and his wife were protected by diplomatic immunity and thus had been arrested illegally.[47]

Then, on July 19, a federal court jury in New York convicted a thirty-three-year-old U.S. Navy yeoman, Nelson C. Drummond, of conspiracy to commit espionage for the Soviets. Drummond admitted to having been recruited while in London in 1959 and having gone on to turn over to Soviet agents numerous documents "relating to the national defense of the United States." Drummond was caught and indicted at the time of the Cuban Missile Crisis (October 5, 1962), but his first trial, in May 1963, resulted in a hung jury. The second time around he was found guilty and sentenced to life imprisonment.[48]

Nagell's notebook reveals that he may have been right in the thick of all this intrigue. Not only does Kornienko's name appear, so does that of "NELSON C. DRUMMOND"—with a line drawn through it. Three lines directly below the Drummond reference had been rendered indecipherable with heavy black ink. Then there was this notation:

ANITA L. EHRMAN
7-30-63 WASHINGTON, D.C.

On that very date, according to *The New York Times* archives, the body of Anita L. Ehrman was discovered in her Washington apartment. Ehrman was a twenty-eight-year-old reporter who had joined *The Washington Post* in January 1963 and then left the paper five months later. Previously she had worked for five years as a foreign affairs correspondent for the Hearst Headline Service, working at the United Nations as well as making "trips to Europe and the Far East on special assignments." The *Times* reported that the police were investigating the death and an autopsy was ordered, though the local coroner "said death was probably due to natural causes." Mrs. Frederick L. Ehrman, Anita's mother, told me in a telephone interview in 1992: "They said she died of asphyxiation. Apparently reporters drink quite a bit. Maybe there were suspicions about something else, but if so, my late husband never told me."[49]

The meanings of the notebook references to Ehrman and the date of her demise—as well as the Kornienko and Drummond names in Nagell's notebook—remain obscure. This is simply another indication that the monitoring activities of Richard Nagell were wide-ranging indeed.

New Orleans Agendas

In New Orleans, the maelstrom of forces around Lee Harvey Oswald continued to build through the summer. On June 18, Oswald went to the Port of New Orleans docks, where he was seen passing out pro-Castro leaflets to sailors aboard the aircraft carrier USS *Wasp*.[50] Sometime in June 1963, according to Marina's Warren Commission testimony, Oswald compelled her to forge the signature of "A. J. Hidell, Chapter President" on his membership card for the local FPCC. "I said, 'You have selected this name because it sounds like Fidel,'" Marina would remember, "and he blushed and said, 'Shut up, it is none of your business. . . . He said that it was his own name and that there is no Hidell in existence, and I asked him, 'You just have two names, and he said 'Yes . . . it is none of your business, I would have to do it this way, people will think I have a big organization and so forth.'"[51]

On June 25, one day after filling out an application for a new passport, Oswald was issued one. He listed his occupation as photographer, gave "England, France, Holland, USSR, France, Findland [sic], Poland" as countries to be visited, and offered his tentative time of departure as "Oct-Jan."[52]

A few days later, Marina finally responded to letters of April 18 and June 4 from the Soviet embassy in Washington, which had requested her reasons for seeking repatriation. She responded that she had had "certain family 'problems'" but her main reason was "homesickness." In October, she added, she was expecting the birth of a second child. "But things are improving due to the fact that my husband expresses a sincere wish to return together with me to the USSR. I earnestly beg you to help me in this." She noted she was enclosing Lee's application "for permission to enter into the USSR."[53]

Unknown to Marina, Lee enclosed a handwritten note of his own in the letter to the embassy. It requested that her entrance visa be rushed so that she could return prior to October. "As for my return entrance visa please consider it separtably [sic]," he wrote.[54]

Getting not only to the Soviet Union, but also to Cuba, was apparently on Oswald's mind. According to a 1974 Nagell letter to attorney Fensterwald: "Oswald had been apprised of the legal requirements for travel to Cuba as early as May 1963, including the travel restrictions imposed by the Department of State, the length of time it would take to obtain a visa from the Cuban government, and the fact that the visa would not be stamped on his U.S. passport, but rather would be issued to him as a separate document."[55]

Yet, according to one witness, Oswald was simultaneously in contact with the FBI. Adrian Alba then managed the Crescent City Garage, next door to the Reily Coffee Company, where Oswald worked. Alba's hobby was gun collecting, and he recalled Oswald making frequent visits to his garage, where Alba loaned him some gun magazines and they talked about firearms.

One of Alba's contracts involved looking after some unmarked cars belonging to the Secret Service and the FBI. One day, Alba remembered, "I was just back from lunch when this green Plymouth came by, which I recognized as an automobile I had let out that morning or the day before. The driver had identified himself as an FBI man, I think visiting New Orleans from Washington. I had the impression he was bringing the car back in. Instead he continued on right past me. He stopped outside the Reily company and I saw Oswald step across the back door and go over to the car. He was handed a good-sized white envelope, and he put it under his T-shirt. Then Oswald went back inside and the car drove off."[56]

On July 19, Oswald was fired from his job at the coffee company. The Warren Commission reported the reason as due to "inefficiency and inattention to his work," because he had spent so many hours next door at Adrian Alba's garage.[57] Upon Oswald's dismissal, Alba says he dropped over one last time to say good-bye. Oswald seemed in good spirits. His parting words, Alba remembers, were these: "I have found my pot of gold at the end of the rainbow."[58]

FBI reports describe ten Cuban exiles arriving in New Orleans from Miami on July 24. They came to join an existing group at a "training camp" north of the city, where they were allegedly awaiting transport to Guatemala for work at a lumber company. That same day, Oswald made contact with Arnesto Rodriguez, a Cuban exile who served as president of New Orleans' Modern Language Institute. Rodriguez was also among the controllers of funds for the Crusade to Free Cuba Committee, among whose primary backers was Oswald's most recent employer, William Reily.

A CIA file originating in Mexico City right after the assassination and declassified in 1976 reported: "Maria Rodriguez de Lopez said her son-in-law ARNESTO was well acquainted with Oswald; runs Spanish Language School, is anti-Castro and 'has a taped conversation with Oswald.' "

Rodriguez, questioned by authorities, denied having any tape but admitted Oswald had sought him out "concerning a Spanish-language course." Interviewed years later by Dallas reporter Earl Golz, Rodriguez added that Oswald also offered his services in training anti-Castro Cubans in guerrilla techniques.[59]

On July 26, the FBI was advised by "Confidential Informant NO [New Orleans] T-1" that Oswald had rented P.O. Box 30061 on the third of June. The FBI described T-1 as "an employee of another government agent."[60] That same day, someone signed "Lee H. Oswald, USSR, Dallas Road, Dallas, Texas" into the register at the Atomic Energy Museum in Oak Ridge, Tennessee. The FBI would later determine that it was not Oswald's signature.[61]

On July 27, Oswald did make a trip by car with his aunt, uncle, and Marina to Mobile, Alabama. Earlier that month, Eugene Murret, an older cousin of Oswald who was preparing for the priesthood at the Jesuit House of Studies there, had written to invite Lee to come speak "about contemporary Russia and the practice of Communism there" to a small group. Those who heard his talk recalled it as being critical of both the capitalist and Communist systems. The following day, the Oswalds and the Murrets drove back to New Orleans.[62]

At many different times between 1975 and 1979, when I was in fairly regular communication with Nagell, I sought to make sense of what Oswald's seemingly contradictory life was all about in 1962–63. Here is what I have pieced together from my notes on what Nagell had to say:

- "He [Oswald] was not an agent or informant for the Soviet government. Nor was he working as such for the CIA or the FBI, at least not in the accepted sense of the words. There may have been unsolicited reports (by Oswald) to the CIA. As for the FBI, he might have been classified as a 'casual informant' as FBI agents interviewed him occasionally, at least once upon his own request. But Oswald was not attempting to penetrate any group, he was just being used."
- "If Lee Harvey Oswald worked for the CIA, he sure didn't know it."
- "If he worked with Cuban G-2, he didn't know it. If anybody did, nobody was telling him. Cuban G-2 is smart, well-trained. That's why anti-Castro organizations are penetrated to the hilt."
- "Oswald got paid by indirect means."[63]

We must read between the lines, as Oswald claimed to do with *The Militant* newspaper, to follow Nagell's meaning. The key point is that Oswald did not know exactly whom he was working for. It appears, though, that the CIA, the FBI, U.S. Military Intelligence, the KGB/GRU, and Cuban G-2 intelligence were all in a position to use him in some fashion. And Nagell himself certainly had ties to people in all those branches.

Genesis of Another Journey

Dean Andrews was a New Orleans attorney who, according to the Warren Commission Report, "stated that Oswald came to his office several times in the summer of 1963 to seek advice on a less than honorable discharge from the Armed Forces, the citizenship status of his wife and his own citizenship status." Andrews also testified "that Oswald was accompanied by a Mexican and at times by apparent homosexuals."

To Warren Commission lawyer Wesley Liebeler, Andrews elaborated about "the Mexicano" in Oswald's company. "They came in usually after hours," Andrews said. The Mexican was "approximately the same height, with the exception that he has a pronounced butch haircut. He's stocky, has what they call an athletic build. He could go to fist city pretty good if he had to. . . . About 26 [years old], hard to tell. [He wore] normally different colored silk pongee shirts. . . . He talked Spanish and all I told him was poco poco, that was it."[64]

Andrews' description is a pretty close match for that provided by Nagell for "Leopoldo" (see Chapter Fourteen). In a series of discussions with researcher Harold Weisberg in 1968, Andrews recalled Oswald and "the Mex" as having discussed passports and means of traveling to Mexico.[65]

For five days after Oswald came back from his Alabama trip with the Murrets in late July 1963, there is considerable mystery about his whereabouts. At three places where he supposedly applied for jobs between July 29 and August 3, each company denied that he had. Some of the firms that Oswald listed with the Louisiana Department of Employment Security, looking to justify his receiving unemployment benefits, did not even exist. On the thirty-first, two books were returned and two more were checked out with Oswald's library card at the New Orleans Public Library.[66] But on that same day, other witnesses believed Oswald may have shown up in Austin, Texas, visiting a Selective Service office about having the Marine Corps Reserve rescind his undesirable discharge.[67]

That decision had been handed down in August 1960, after Oswald's "defection" to the USSR. While he was still in Minsk, early in 1962 Oswald had set about corresponding with the Navy, insisting that his discharge be given a full review. It struck me as strange that both Oswald and Nagell seemed so determined to bring about a change in their military status. It struck me as even stranger that both Oswald and Nagell were officially turned down on the same day, July 10, 1963. Oswald's undesirable discharge was upheld by a review board of officers. Nagell's request to be given a medical examination pursuant to obtaining a full Army disability retirement was denied. If both men had been part of the same service, this coincidence could be explained as the military bureaucracy's finally getting around to processing such requests. But the Marine and Army service bureaucracies did not overlap.

Both men were notified by letter. Oswald received his on July 25. "Careful consideration was given to the evidence presented in your behalf," he was informed. "It is the decision that no change, correction, or modification is warranted in your discharge."[68] A letter dated July 26 from the Pentagon's adjutant general was to have let Nagell know that a review of his records had determined "insufficient evidence" for complying with his request.

Nagell would later maintain "that through oversight, or for other, somewhat more sophisticated reasons, the Army failed to mail the original of the Adjutant General's 26 July 1963 letter, just as it failed to reply to *any* of [Nagell's] communications that were sent directly by him during the period 1960–1969."

Any letter from the Pentagon, however, would not have reached Nagell at that precise time, for, abruptly, he had left Los Angeles. As Nagell would later state in his Court of Claims case: "While [I] may have failed to inform the Army of a change in [my] residence address, when [I] was in Mexico during the latter part of July or the first part of August 1963, it was neither required nor necessary that [I] do so, as the Post Office box was not closed until after [my] arrest on 20 September 1963."[69]

Again, Nagell was headed south of the border. Sometime in late July, Nagell says he contacted the FBI in Dallas, though no record of this has appeared in the meager amount of information about him yet released by the bureau.[70] If Oswald did make an appearance on July 31 at a Selective Service office in Austin—only two hundred miles from Dallas—then it is quite conceivable that he and Nagell could have rendezvoused somewhere in Texas.

I believe they did, and journeyed on together to Mexico City—where certain plans were formulated that would bring Oswald into the Kennedy conspiracy.

Summary

Oswald's flurry of correspondence with the Fair Play for Cuba Committee coincided with intensified interest by the FBI in its director, V. T. Lee. The CIA was also interested in obtaining penetration into the FPCC.

According to Nagell, Oswald's one-man chapter in New Orleans began as a "scam," a means of establishing a "bona fide" for checking on something in another state. A full six months before Oswald set up his chapter, New Orleans' police intelligence supervisor was in touch with his Tampa, Florida, counterpart about the FPCC. Since Tampa was also V. T. Lee's former town—and V. T. Lee himself suggested Oswald get in touch with the Tampa chapter—it is quite possible that this was the locale of whatever the intelligence agencies were looking into.

Of Oswald, Nagell has said that he did not work for the Soviets; was unaware of any liaison he had with Cuban intelligence; might have been classified as a "casual informant" by the FBI; and provided "unsolicited reports" to the CIA. All this brings us no closer to an answer as to what was really going on, but it clearly suggests more of an Oswald intelligence connection than has ever been publicly admitted.

Nagell, meantime, was busy scrutinizing the activities of the L.A. leftist community. With one of its members, FPCC coordinator Steve Roberts, Nagell discussed Oswald's activities for reasons unknown. So many espionage dramas were playing out during the summer of 1963, and Nagell appears to have had a hand in more than one. Could concern by both the Americans and the Soviets about Communist China have formed part of the picture? Given all the Chinese pamphlets in Nagell's possession when arrested, this is something else that must be considered.

After Nagell and Oswald's requests for reconsideration of their military status were turned down on the *same day*, both men pulled up stakes by the end of July 1963. From opposite ends of the country, they appear to have converged in Texas. The Mexican border was a hop, skip, and jump away.

III

The Setup

Thus conscience does make cowards of us all,
And thus the native hue of resolution
is sicklied o'er with the pale cast of thought,
And enterprises of great pith and moment
With this regard their currents turn awry
And lose the name of action.
—Shakespeare, *Hamlet,* Act III, Scene 1

Chapter Sixteen

Oswald's First Trip to Mexico City:
July–August 1963

In the fall of 1977, Richard Nagell agreed to get together with me along Sunset Boulevard inside Schwab's drugstore, where would-be starlets used to go to be discovered. It was early afternoon when he walked in, wearing a light blue sportcoat and a necktie. But he seemed ill at ease in the crowded, noisy restaurant, and I suggested we head down the street. We ended up sitting in an open-air patio outside Little Pietro's restaurant.

Nagell said he had been busy—"you'd be surprised how busy"—doing a lot of traveling. I gently suggested he might be doing some police or investigative work, but Nagell was, as always, noncommittal about his current activities. I told him that the House Assassinations Committee had recently gotten in touch with me, looking to find him. He shrugged and said, "Congress doesn't know what it's doing, nobody there really wants the truth. Everything's become so garbled, nothing will come out of their investigation." He said he really was not interested in testifying.

"I'm not getting any younger," Nagell went on, adding that he wished he could do something different with his life. Now that his two children were in college, and no longer living with him, as they had been when we first met in 1975, he was thinking of leaving the country. "I'd be a hippie," he added, "except they don't exist anymore."

A TV movie called *The Trial of Lee Harvey Oswald* had just aired that week, and I wondered if Nagell had watched it. He nodded, adding that he was amazed how closely the actor John Pleshette resembled Oswald, even in many of his mannerisms. "His facial expressions were really like Oswald. A blank stare. You didn't know if the guy was agreeing or disagreeing with you. That's typical Oswald. I don't think he ever let his emotions get the best of him. Let me tell you, he was a cool customer.

"That's a Freudian slip," Nagell continued, offering a grin. He paused, then continued: "If I was mountain climbing, I would trust that guy to hold the end of my rope in a crisis. He had a lot of control over himself. He was articulate, though you'd never get that impression from reading what he's written, because his spelling was atrocious. He could hold a good conversation on just about anything political. He was cautious. Certainly no raving maniac. Sure, he had problems. He had problems with his wife. She was going to divorce him and go back to Russia. That's something not generally known. But it had nothing to do with what happened.

"On that TV program, they tried to make it appear he did it [the assassination] out of spite. But that's bullshit. It had nothing to do with it. He was no crazier than the rest of us, what can I say? How much do the top psychiatrists know about the human mind? How much of it can you put on the head of a pin?"

I thought back to a letter Nagell had written me in 1976, describing his own motivation. In it, he had referred to himself as "LA Joe" and said: "How would you feel, how would you react, if LA Joe had been more deeply involved than ever mentioned publicly or even behind closed doors? (I'm not saying that he was, per se). What if there had been no big deal, just two or three (or four) 'madmen' out to further their 'just cause,' change the course of history, whatever? What if LA Joe could have pulled the plug then and there, but didn't for whatever reason; could he, this man of principle, apparently dedicated to his own just cause, honestly pass the buck to those who are dead, to the FBI, the KGB, the CIA, to whomever or whatever? Could he ever really explain to anybody, except, perhaps, to himself? Would any rational person accept his explanation as bona fide, his actions (or lack of action) as justified? Think about it."[1]

Nagell looked at me for a long moment through his sunglasses. "Too bad Oswald didn't stand trial, eh?" he continued. "Whether I could be considered directly involved, I won't get into that. There is no statute of limitations on murder, and I won't be an accessory. I will say this: I made every reasonable attempt to report to the proper authorities, even when I was told not to."

I asked him whether the CIA's former chief Richard Helms might have some answers. "Helms couldn't tell you anything more than Yuri Andropov," he replied. I asked who that was. "Supposedly head of the KGB," Nagell said, then went on: "I won't deny that the CIA-Mob plots against Castro had some connection to what happened to Kennedy. That might be applicable as far as motivation is concerned.

"But to come out and accuse the KGB or CIA per se is a bunch of crap. Or the Mafia, because they wanted their casinos back or something. That's not how it happened. Most of the writers present their conclusion, then write something to back up the conclusion."

Nagell studied my face carefully. Then he said: "Look, a lot of people were pissed off that had moral principles, that knew about things different outfits were doing, like the CIA, and knew that the public did not know and that the government would deny it. What do you do when you reach a point you know something's got to be done? What's that old saying? The best-laid plans sometimes go astray."

I had come to realize that Nagell himself seemed to have been deeply enmeshed somehow in the conspiracy, despite his claim that he eventually attempted to avert it by "report[ing] to the proper authorities." He may have been working for the CIA and the KGB. He had been observing Oswald, and the Cuban exiles, for many months in what originally were independent operations. He had had a role in Oswald's adopting the "Hidell" name, and setting up his Fair Play for Cuba chapter for another purpose. In Los Angeles he had befriended FPCC official Vaughn Marlowe, who he says was then "considered for recruitment to hit JFK." Nagell's involvement with "Angel" and "Leopoldo" obviously went beyond mere observation. He seems to have been a kind of go-between for them in casting an eye first on Marlowe and then on Oswald.

Yet all this appeared to be part of an intelligence operation that, in his words, eventually went astray. Or, perhaps, was commandeered from within. Between July and September, Nagell said, most of his time had been spent on "the subject of Lee Harvey Oswald," who was "exploited by various individuals for their own reasons."[2] By the time Oswald stepped "on stage" in midsummer of 1963, as Nagell wrote to Arthur Greenstein, "the motives, method, etc., in fact, everything except the 'team,' in this instance also Bravo [affiliates of Alpha 66] had changed considerably."

The "Bravo Club" team, Nagell continued, got wind in July that the Kennedy brothers had put out feelers through "private" channels aimed at effecting a rapprochement with Fidel Castro. As he phrased it to

Greenstein, "There is huddle. There is chant: 'Remember Cochina Bay!'"
Remember the Bay of Pigs!

Oswald, according to Nagell, was already "well-known to Bravo Club."
Angel and Leopoldo got together with Oswald and convinced him they
were "special emissaries" sent by Castro to deliver a "Christmas present"
to Kennedy. This, Oswald was told, was in retaliation for the ongoing
attempts by the U.S. government to assassinate the Cuban premier. Oswald had been "chosen" to help deliver the message. If he agreed, he
would be furnished "Safe Conduct Pass" to Havana by the Cuban embassy
in Mexico City and "be given proper treatment on arrival" on the island.[3]

Not long after Oswald was approached by Angel and Leopoldo, it appears that Oswald and Nagell went to Mexico City. The known record on
Oswald pinpoints only one trip that he made to the capital surrounded by
the twin volcanoes, during a six-day period in late September and early
October of 1963. Yet Nagell was on record in an FBI file of December 20,
1963, as saying that he had met Oswald "in Mexico City and in Texas."
Nor is Nagell the only person to raise the possibility of an earlier Oswald
trip.

Two Australian girls who were on the same bus with Oswald in September recalled him recommending Mexico City's Hotel Cuba as a good place
to stay—indicating to them some previous knowledge of domiciles there.[4]
In 1977, author Anthony Summers learned from Delphine Roberts, who
had worked as a secretary to ex-FBI man Guy Banister in New Orleans,
that "on the basis of what Banister told her—she knew Oswald had made
more than one trip to Mexico in the summer of 1963."[5]

In the archives of the *Time-Life* library there is a 1975 file from *Time*'s
Washington correspondent Jerry Hannifin. "Lee Harvey Oswald had
made two trips to Mexico," he reported, "calling at the Castro Cuban
Embassy both times, and also attempting to visit the Soviet Embassy."
The correspondent's source was someone inside the State Department.
Time magazine never used the material.[6]

There was also an obscure remark about this subject in the *Manion
Forum* newsletter of March 1964. Its Indiana-based editor, Dean Manion,
was a well-known supporter of right-wing causes, and his interview about
the assassination with a "prominent Cuban exile leader" named Leopoldo
Aguilera, Jr., was clearly aimed at pointing a conspiratorial figure at Fidel
Castro. I wondered, of course, if this might have been the same "Leopoldo" whom Nagell had named, for Aguilera's statements revealed a
considerable knowledge of Oswald, including: "Oswald made two trips to
Mexico, the last one from September 26 to October 3, 1963, and visited
the Cuban Embassy there." What this showed, at the least, was awareness
among some Cuban exiles of an earlier Oswald trip.[7]

Clark Anderson, the FBI's legal attaché in Mexico City at the time, also told me of having heard something about an Oswald appearance in Mexico before September. "This had come to our attention," Anderson said, "but we got it secondhand."[8]

Thomas Mann, then the U.S. ambassador to Mexico, recalled "a rumor" of the same thing. "My memory is that the intelligence agencies had pictures of him entering the Cuban and Soviet embassies," Mann said. "And then probably reports on him, not nearly as convincing, that he had been there earlier, too."[9]

At our first interview in 1975, Nagell responded to my question like this: "Was Lee Harvey Oswald with me in Mexico? Not in September 1963. I told the FBI: He shot at a cactus plant and he couldn't hit the broad side of a barn with a shotgun."[10]

John Margain, Nagell's friend from Korean War days who saw him several times after Nagell's release from prison, remembered: "On Oswald, the only thing he ever told me—he was in Mexico with him one time. They both had some rifles and were shooting at some cactus. He told me Lee Harvey Oswald couldn't hit the side of a barn. Nagell said, 'Don't tell me he could have hit the president twice.' He said Oswald was set up, first for the killing and then they had to knock him off right away. A fall guy."

"A fall guy for whom?" I asked.

"I understood that Nagell was in the CIA or working with the CIA when he was with Oswald, when they went to Mexico sometime in '63. He wouldn't tell me what it was, but it was something like a mission. He said he thought the plot was people from CIA and the Cubans."

The Castro Cubans?

"No, no, not Castro. The other Cubans. The exiles. He never told me about any Mafia being involved."[11]

In Nagell's meetings with Jim Garrison in 1968, the New Orleans DA recalled him "mentioning seeing Oswald in Mexico City and he said something about a woman being with him."[12]

In December 1963, Lonnie Hudkins had broken a story in the *Houston Post* that Oswald may have been a paid FBI informant. Years later, a declassified Warren Commission document revealed that Hudkins had also been aware of an assassination plot against Castro.[13] Hudkins was believed to have extensive sources inside the U.S. intelligence community and, when I met with Hudkins in 1976, he, too, described a fateful Oswald rendezvous in Mexico City.

"Here I go back to sources," Hudkins said. "A very good source, still is. He's deep cover, still active. There was a meeting in Mexico, sometime in the summer of '63. There were no Americans present other than Oswald and one CIA man, from what I've been told. There were also a couple girls there. One posed as a prostitute. Maria del Carmen was not the main one, but she was there."[14]

Maria del Carmen was the young Mexican Treasury Department employee whom Nagell reluctantly indicated was a contact of his with Cuban Intelligence—and whom the CIA's Barney Hidalgo said posed as a prostitute when they worked together in Mexico on a project (see Chapter Ten). New Orleans attorney Dean Andrews also contended that Oswald had been "befriended by a CIA whore in Mexico City."[15]

Nagell's Complaint

In 1974, when queried by attorney Fensterwald about Oswald's September journey to Mexico, Nagell responded in writing with his belief "that Oswald's Mexican trip at that time did not entail his participation in the finalization of any plans at Mexico City to assassinate President Kennedy."[16] I noted Nagell's careful use of the phrase "at that time." The implication seemed to be that an *earlier* visit might indeed have entailed "his participation" in such a plan.

In the material sent by Nagell over the years to Arthur Greenstein, Nagell once enclosed a standard Better Business Bureau "Customer Experience Record." There, under the various boxed headings, Nagell had typed in some most significant information.

Under the heading "DATE OF TRANSACTION," he began by writing: "July 1963." The remainder read:

> DATE YOU COMPLAINED TO COMPANY: Aug 27, 1963
> TO WHOM: Desmond FitzGerald
> SALES PERSON: 'Bob'
> IDENTIFY PRODUCT OR SERVICE: Mrdr [Murder]
> IF ADVERTISED, WHEN: Sept 13/17, 1963
> WHERE: FBI, Wash. D.C.
> FORM COMPLETED BY CUSTOMER: X [in the box].
> RECEIPT OR CONTRACT NUMBER: Unknown
>   COMPANY: Latin American Operations
>   U.S. Central Intelligence Agency
> ADDRESS: (Quien Sabe) (/2%#&**+) ["Who knows?" in Spanish.]
> CITY: (Everytown, U.S.A.)

Then Nagell had listed the CIA's Langley, Virginia, headquarters telephone number. Below that, under the heading "Check Cause(s) of complaint and explain briefly" at the bottom of the form, Nagell had placed X's in the boxes alongside the following items:

"Defective merchandise . . . Guarantee or contract not fulfilled . . . Misrepresentation-Oral . . . Promised adjustment not fulfilled . . . Unsatisfactory service."

It was a curious way of getting some vital matters on the record. Nagell first received a "murder" assignment emanating from "Bob," his CIA contact in Mexico City, in July 1963. Since Nagell did not use the word "assassination," it was impossible to say for certain whose murder it was. Then he "complained" to the CIA's Cuban overseer, Desmond FitzGerald, late in August. Nagell's warning letter to Hoover about the assassination had been dispatched on one of those two September dates. And his "causes of complaint" indicated that Nagell felt he had eventually been left holding the bag.[17]

The Hotel Luma Connection

Between 1960 and 1965, Robert Clayton Buick was a professional bullfighter in Mexico City, residing for a time at the Hotel Luma. The reader may recall the Luma as the residence of Nagell and Greenstein in August–October 1962. The hotel was managed by a friend of the CIA's Mexico station chief, and its bartender, Franz Waehauf, was an intelligence contact of Nagell's.

Bernard Fensterwald became aware of Robert Clayton Buick in 1969, by way of the mysterious phone call and letter that he received from Ricard von Kleist—who professed knowledge of Nagell's activities in Tokyo and Mexico and who spoke of confidential matters that only certain intelligence officials knew about.

Von Kleist described a meeting at the "Hotel Luna [sic: Luma], Mexico City, July 1963." This meeting, von Kleist alleged, was attended by "Alex Hydell, otherwise known as Lee Harvey Oswald; a female attorney who is well known Communist in Los Angeles . . . [and] hotel headwaiter, Frity [sic: Franz Waehauf] . . . who owned a launch believed to be shuttling between Mexico and Cuba. Also believed to be involved—Richard Case Nagell, former Captain, U.S. Army, associated with Counter Intelligence in Japan in 1959 [sic—1957–58]."[18]

Von Kleist had also mentioned Robert Buick as someone who might be able to shed additional light. At the time, Buick was doing a twenty-year sentence at the McNeil Island penitentiary in Washington State, having been convicted of a series of bank robberies. Fensterwald contacted Buick, agreed to become his lawyer temporarily, and visited him twice in prison in April 1969.

Buick said he had indeed been corresponding with von Kleist, who identified himself as a writer from Upland, California, when he first wrote to Buick at the suggestion of a mutual friend. Von Kleist and Buick often played chess by mail, and discussed a subject of common interest: the Kennedy assassination. It was hard for Fensterwald to tell how much of what Buick related he had picked up from von Kleist. But he certainly knew a good deal about the Hotel Luma, which had already come to the lawyer's attention through Greenstein.

Buick showed Fensterwald his own spring 1962 hotel receipt from the Luma, and bullfight posters proving that he had been an American toreador in Mexico City as of September 1963. The attorney's memorandum quotes Buick saying: "I happened to stumble on meetings and accidental things and I became extremely interested at the time. Something too big for me to handle was in the making. In 1963, summer. Hydell [Oswald's alias] was in Mexico before September, 1963. Hydell went once by bus and once by plane. Hydell was mixed up in it to the hilt. The man was used as a pawn all the way through."

According to Buick, Oswald had stayed in a "dingy, flea bag" hotel but also "frequented the Luma." Buick knew the Luma's manager, Warren Broglie, and bartender Waehauf, whose first name Buick misremembered as "Fritz." The bartender, Buick went on, had a "def[inite] personal tie to Broglie, had launch, kept at Vera Cruz. Moved between Vera Cruz and Tampico, big boat, did big with LA shrimp boats."

Buick also knew of Richard Nagell. "Buick stresses Nagell's prior associations in LA," Fensterwald's memo noted. "Nagell's dealings with Russians goes back to Japan. Nagell in a way is a loner, didn't seem to have any close friends, no girl. Another meeting took place right after he [Nagell] was busted in El Paso. Buick would have expected him to be enroute to Mexico for this meeting. 'Nagell was at the border, trying to make up his mind whether to go south or not. . . . He didn't want to go back to that meeting in Mexico City.'

"Buick got married June 29, 1963. [Mexican] Wife related to whole Olivares family, all well connected. Married two weeks, Buick [was] approached by U.S. Agents. Could identify by sight. . . . Wanted Buick to infiltrate and see what was going on. Said 'This was a tremendous bungling or a set plan.' Every other official in Washington should have known about it. U.S. Embassy in D.F. [Mexico City] knew. Why let it go so far?

"Answer to whole thing is in Mexico City."[19]

The Strange Saga of Robert Clayton Buick

At Fensterwald's suggestion, I was able to find Buick through Pete Noyes, a TV news director in Los Angeles who had once written a book about the assassination and been in touch with Buick sporadically. When I first spoke to Buick by phone in 1981, he was still on parole and not particularly interested in discussing the subject. When I asked about Ricard von Kleist, he replied: "I can't answer those questions over the phone, but I'll tell you what they did to him. He's a paraplegic, had polio in his younger years, and when he tried to come see me in the joint, he was turned away. Three days later, they put Ric von Kleist on the sidewalk and pointed him towards Foothill Boulevard in his wheelchair. 'If you ever contact Mr. Buick again, or write a word about him,' he was told, 'you're going right down the middle of the boulevard.' We met at my apartment when I got out in '71. From what I understand, he's since fled into Canada somewhere."

Ten years later, when I met with Buick at his real-estate broker's office in the L.A. suburb of La Crescenta, he had long since straightened out his life. For a time back in 1966, he had been on the FBI's "Most Wanted" list, accused of going on a spree of eighteen bank robberies across California.

As an FBI release described Buick prior to his being apprehended: "Said to be a personal 'playboy type' extrovert who likes attention and the opportunity to boast of his past bullfighting activity, Buick reportedly drinks expensive wines and liquors, frequents good restaurants, nightclubs and beach resorts and likes swimming, dancing, boating, dancing, television and jazz music. He is known to dress neatly and conservatively, to travel by air and private automobile, usually exceeding the speed limit, and to wear a diamond ring, a gold identification wrist bracelet and a gold religious neck medal. Buick reportedly smokes cigarettes, is especially fond of Italian and Mexican food and is fairly fluent in the Spanish language."

When caught in Pecos, Texas, on March 29, 1966, Buick had offered no resistance to the authorities.[20] After his release in 1971, with some financial help from a sister he "bought me a little mini 'hoss-ranch'" and got into raising Thoroughbreds, playing golf, and finally the real-estate field. Even today, Buick still cuts a handsome figure. He is a stocky man of medium height and graying hair who looks considerably younger than his fifty-nine years. Indeed, he bears a striking resemblance to the actor Robert De Niro.

"I went on that bank spree," Buick said, "because I was bitter over the Kennedy assassination, and that nobody was doing anything about it. That's the truth. I figured I'd hit back somehow. I was completely distraught over it. Here's a man that I absolutely idolized. Kennedy was the first president I could really identify with, other than Franklin Delano Roosevelt when I was a kid. And I knew that certain people with U.S. intelligence knew what had gone down with the assassination, and that I myself had been used by them—and nobody was doing jack-shit to get to the truth."

It all started for him, Buick continued, when he began frequenting the Hotel Luma in Mexico City. Buick had stayed there a couple of times in 1962 and continued to pay late-night visits to the Luma's "nice, quaint little bar with the guitars and everything." A number of bullfighters hung out there, drinking into the wee hours.

One night in the summer of 1963, not long after his marriage to a daughter of the wealthy Olivares family, Buick had been imbibing at a nearby bar, the La Ronda. At about 2:30 A.M. he decided to head home.

"I'm wearing a two-and-a-half-karat diamond ring, Rolex watch, the whole bit. And I was well armed, man. I mean, everyone of any substance in Mexico City carried a firearm. It was part of your dress code. I kept a .357 [magnum] under the seat of my emerald-green Cadillac convertible, and I carried a .38 long up-and-over derringer with an ivory handle, just like Patton, under my belt. Pearls for pimps, okay? And as I walked out of the bar, I could feel my hair begin to curl and the goose bumps on the back of my neck. Because out the door come these two dudes, all right? I can feel 'em, they're not walking too fast and I pick up my speed a little bit, and I walk past my car.

"I know there's shops down this next street and all type of little alcoves, with the windows and what-have-you. So the first deep alcove, I jump into it, but through the other pane I can pick them up looking for me. I don't know whether I'm gonna get bludgeoned or what. So as this one guy starts to check the alcove, I just pull the hammer back and lay it right against his temple. And I said, '¿Qué quieres?' Well, they don't speak Spanish. One says, 'I can't understand.' So I say, 'What the fuck do you want?' And I told 'em both to lay their hands straight out or I'll blow the guy's brains out.

"That's when they flashed an ID on me. U.S. government. Guy says, 'Well, we just wanta talk to you.' I said, 'This is fucking two-thirty in the morning and you almost got your friend's head blown off. I've got a telephone. Every morning at ten, you can find me at Plaza Mexico workin' out with the bulls. So what's this all about?'

"Well, one thing led to another. Basically, they hired me. Asked me to check some things out at the Hotel Luma, wouldn't tell me why. I said, 'Why me?' They said, 'You're there at the hotel three or four nights a week, sometimes for lunch during the day.' They wanted to know who was frequenting the place, what their names were, if there was any type of conversation other than ordinary bullshit going on. I got duped into the mom's apple pie and flag-waving shit to go see what's going on."

Buick says he agreed to meet with the two agents periodically in Mexico City's Garibaldi Park. "They didn't want anything written down. They said store everything here"—Buick pointed to his head—"somehow they must have picked up on my retention. Because when I was a bell captain out in Palm Springs, I was also booking horses. But they could never find any slips on me, because everything was in my head."

One of the first people Buick reported back on was the Luma's bartender, Franz Waehauf. "He was way below his station, pal," Buick recalls. "I often wondered what the hell he was doing as a cocktail waiter. Because he seemed to have an awful lot of authority. He was very tight with the manager, Warren Broglie. It was just mysterious to me why Broglie and a simple cocktail waiter were always in these very intense conversations. Waehauf wore glasses, heavy build, about my height. Strictly very Germanic, very Aryan type."

That same summer of 1963, Buick also observed a tall, well-dressed American with erect military bearing in the bar. "I didn't pay that much attention to him at the particular time," he says. "But you can't miss him, because of his scars and what-have-you. And he had a very penetrating look about him. It was only later that things fell into place."

The tall American, Buick would later realize, was Richard Nagell.

There was another American whom Buick said he saw in the Luma as well. "This young guy in his early twenties, he came up to me and said he was interested in becoming a bullfighter. He was cocky, you know. I was kinda throwing him for a shine, because I didn't know what he was up to, or what was happening. I says, 'Hey, you just don't go out there and wave this little cloth at the animal. I mean, there's fundamentals.' He says, 'Well, you did it.' I said, 'Yeah, but I started three or four years ago and beat the bushes. I explained it to him, how you start with the brahmas and then go to the indios and finally the *de toda le costa*—the younger bulls, which are harder to fight because they move faster, turn quicker. Once you get past that, then you get the big time.

"That was some of our initial conversation. Then it went into some political things. And it began to seep in that this guy's philosophical views were erratic. Out in left field somewhere. He was an extremist type.

"He'd introduced himself as Alex something," Buick continued.

Alex Hidell? I asked.

"Yeah, that's it! But then he fucked up, he came back and used another name. That's when I started to say, hey, wait a minute—this guy couldn't remember his own name. Either he's a little kooky, or . . . There was a lull at the bar and I went over to him. I said, 'Hold on, in a prior conversation, when you introduced yourself, it was Alex.' He didn't say anything. Wouldn't talk to me after that."

So Buick watched "Alex Hidell" from a distance, watched as he huddled in conversations with bartender Waehauf and sometimes hotel manager Broglie. "As I recall, 'Alex' wasn't in the hotel very long. I saw him once fleetingly, either leaving the bar or the lobby going out the front door. And I saw him twice in the bar. There was times where him, Waehauf and Broglie, all three of them, were completely out of sight. They never all left together or came back together, but then all of a sudden one would come in. Five minutes would pass, and another shows up. Ten minutes later, the third one comes back into the bar. Sometimes as much as an hour would go by when none of them were around. So what is the conjecture there? Probably meeting in one of the vacant motel rooms, who knows?

"They would talk to some Cubans, too. Well, actually it's very difficult to determine whether they were Puerto Rican or Cuban or from one of the adjacent Caribbean islands. Because the rapidity of their phrasing is almost identical. They were just generally in the picture."

Buick claimed he did overhear snatches of conversations in the Luma bar concerning an assassination attempt against President Kennedy. "And I related this to those gentlemen I would meet in the park. It wasn't so much what I heard at one specific moment, you understand? And it wasn't something that was directly stated, but more implied. Only in retrospect did it all come together for me.

"When Kennedy got hit, the top of my head came off. My whole five or six months went right before my eyes when I saw Oswald's face. It was Alex! I was at a friend's house in Rialto [California]. All the whispering in the Luma bar, all the conversations in Garibaldi Park, it all suddenly fit. Then when I saw Ruby take Oswald out, I started screaming and yelling and trying to get to people. I was naive at that particular point in time, like 'I know something's gonna be done over this.' And then all of a sudden they started lifting the rug and just sweeping everything under it. That's when I decided to start hitting banks."

That was as specific as Robert Clayton Buick would get. It was as bizarre a tale as I had heard along the assassination trail, but a number of pieces fit with what I knew of Nagell and Oswald. The summer trip to Mexico City (Buick was adamant that he saw Oswald there *before* September) . . . The Hotel Luma, and Buick's suspicions about the bartender whom Nagell knew and later sought to locate from prison . . . U.S. intelligence interest in the goings-on at the Luma.

Then, after Buick was apprehended for his bank spree, on March 29, 1966, things got even stranger. Buick says that despite the warrant calling for his extradition from Texas to California, he was not sent there immediately. Instead he was taken first to the El Paso County Jail—and put in the same cell with Richard Nagell! Nagell has also verified that he met Buick while incarcerated for his own so-called attempted bank robbery.[21]

Buick remembers: "California wanted me flown out from Texas right away, you're talking about twenty-two counts. But for some reason they wheel me into El Paso, into a dormitory with a little Australian jockey and Richard Case Nagell. Short hair. The obvious scar. The one eye a little off-set. Tall, thin. Brilliant at times, erratic the next moment. But with a degree of stability that never panicked me. At first I didn't snap that I'd seen him in the Luma three years before. You know, we're talking about county jail clothes and a certain amount of time that had passed. But then we got together and he started talking about his case. He started to confide in me the reason that he got himself busted. Then all of a sudden, everything started coming back.

"At first he seemed paranoid, he would whisper. They had the fuckin' joint wired! As soon as I snapped to who he was, I said"—Buick lowered his own voice to a whisper—" 'you're right.' So we would talk in normal monotone about the horse racing with this little jockey, and kinda splice in other things real quiet. My mind isn't too clear about it, because the whole world was comin' down on me at the time."

So did Buick think that the authorities put him in with Nagell to try to pick up on what they might talk about?

"Yeah, there's no doubt about it. I mean, why else did they stop me over in El Paso for three days? We talked about the Luma. He had a distaste for that waiter [Waehauf] like you couldn't believe. There was no love lost between 'em, as I recall, just complete disdain. I think it had to do with whatever had taken place at that particular time at the Luma. There was just total difference in philosophy between them. They had undoubtedly got into it fairly heavy over certain aspects of whatever was being planned."

Did Buick remember mentioning Oswald to Nagell, seeing Oswald at the same hotel?

"Yeah. I think he asked me when I saw Oswald there. I told him I'd seen him that summer [of 1963]."

Buick added: "Nagell's been fortunate because they've tapped him off as a kook. Well, he's definitely no kook. An absolutely brilliant man—who's been through some shit, I'll tell you."

The CIA and Mind Control in Mexico

In October 1975 I asked Nagell about something that had come to light that June, when the Rockefeller Commission Report on CIA Activities Within the United States was released. The report revealed the existence of a CIA effort begun in the late 1940s "to study possible means for controlling human behavior."

Nagell confirmed that hypnosis was used in intelligence for "compartmentalization of information." He added that sometimes an intelligence "courier"—which was one of his own admitted roles in 1962–63—might undergo such treatment. "You only undergo hypnosis for certain projects," Nagell continued. "It is used by the CIA for any number of reasons. To a degree in the recruiting program, in the Psychiatric Division. It's actually a section of the Security Division, to find out if you're homosexual or have done this or that. In instances, they use hypnosis for real bona fide reasons."[22]

Nagell's comments predated by almost two years the fire storm of publicity that occurred after John Marks, of the private Center for National Security Studies, managed to obtain about a thousand CIA documents on such programs through the Freedom of Information Act.[23] It soon surfaced that the CIA's Office of Security, whose mission was to protect personnel and facilities from penetration, had sent a team to Tokyo a month after the Korean War began—utilizing hypnosis and drugs in the interrogation of some suspected double agents. The project, originally called "Bluebird," was expanded into "Artichoke" by 1953.[24] "Artichoke" was one of four such operations that came under the overall code name of MK-ULTRA.

The New York Times, in February 1978, unveiled the story of a 1954 CIA study wherein a team was asked to "give an evaluation" of a "hypothetical problem." Quoted from the study was the following: "Can an individual of (deleted nationality) descent be made to perform an act of attempted assassination involuntarily under the influence of Artichoke?"

The CIA wondered whether, "as a 'trigger mechanism' for a bigger project," such an act might be induced "involuntarily, against a prominent (deleted) politician or if necessary, against an American official. . . . Access to the subject would be extremely limited." After being drugged, the subject would perform the deed "at some later date," after which "it was assumed the subject would be taken into custody by the (deleted) government and thereby 'disposed of.'"

It appeared that the plan was implemented at least once, for the *Times* quoted a subsequent 1954 memorandum saying: "Herewith the report of Artichoke team on first assignment. Considering the speed with which we had to operate, I believe it went extremely well. We were ready when called upon for support, even though the operation did not materialize."[25]

Such control was the notion behind the best-selling 1958 Richard Condon novel *The Manchurian Candidate,* where a soldier "brainwashed" by the Communist Chinese during the Korean War is later picked up and used—unwittingly to him—in a domestic assassination plot against an American presidential contender.

The CIA's security officer for Artichoke was Sheffield Edwards. Cooperating closely with the CIA was the Federal Bureau of Narcotics (FBN).[26] Charles Siragusa, a Military Intelligence officer in World War II and later the FBN's liaison to the CIA, helped set up the California "safe houses" where numerous MK-ULTRA experiments were conducted on unwitting subjects in the 1950s.[27] Then, in 1960, Edwards approached Siragusa about another project. Given Siragusa's vast knowledge about members of organized crime, Edwards now wanted him to help recruit teams of money-for-hire assassins to assassinate selected foreign leaders. Siragusa would tell the Senate Intelligence Committee in 1975 that he had turned Edwards down. The Office of Security chief then turned to a Howard Hughes aide, ex-FBI agent Robert Maheu, who in turn went to Sam Giancana and John Rosselli to find Cuban exiles willing to eliminate Castro.

The initial anti-Castro plots involved methods developed in the CIA's Technical Services Division, where Dr. Sidney Gottlieb had supervised the MK-ULTRA mind-altering program since its 1953 inception. The idea was conceived that a box of Castro's favorite cigars be treated with a lethal poison. Later, apparently at the suggestion of Giancana and Rosselli, the scheme was altered to put poison pills in a Castro beverage. Two attempts were made, but failed, during the 1961 Bay of Pigs period. With the first, Castro suddenly stopped visiting the Havana restaurant where the CIA's "asset" was employed. With the second, exile leader Antonio Varona got the pills delivered to Castro's personal secretary, Juan Orta, who was suddenly exposed by Fidel as a counterrevolutionary and thrown in jail. Somehow, it seems, Castro was being tipped off.[28]

Late in 1961, the CIA's assassination projects (code-named ZR-RIFLE) passed to William Harvey, who, acting, he said, on "explicit orders" from Richard Helms, then had Edwards put him in contact with Rosselli for more "executive action" planning. It was also Helms who had first proposed to Allen Dulles the creation of a full-blown MK-ULTRA mind-control effort in 1953. Now, in the Kennedy era, Helms was running the CIA's entire clandestine operations program.[29] And, as outlined in

Chapter Twelve, once Desmond FitzGerald took over Cuban operations from Harvey after the Cuban Missile Crisis, his own secret plans against Castro also involved the use of lethal poisons developed by Dr. Gottlieb's Technical Services Division (TSS)/MK-ULTRA branch.

So what we have here is a frightening crossover. The same men who had spent more than a decade overseeing and implementing mind-control techniques—Helms, Edwards, Gottlieb—became the very men who propelled forward the CIA's covert assassination squads, through Harvey, FitzGerald, the Mob, and the Cuban exiles. Gottlieb even dispatched poison to the Congo intended for use against Premier Patrice Lumumba—but a team of CIA-backed assassins got to Lumumba first. Another scheme was discussed about spraying Castro's broadcasting studio with a chemical that produced LSD-like effects.

The Senate Intelligence Committee, in describing Gottlieb's MK-ULTRA program in 1976, reported: "By 1963 the number of operations and subjects had increased substantially."[30]

John Marks, in his 1979 book *The Search for the "Manchurian Candidate,"* added another dimension to the MK-ULTRA story. Marks wrote: "In June 1960 [Gottlieb's] TSS officials launched an expanded program of operational experiments in hypnosis in cooperation with the Agency's Counterintelligence [CI] staff." That, of course, was James Angleton's turf.

"Counterintelligence officials wrote that the hypnosis program could provide a 'potential breakthrough in clandestine technology.' Their arrangement with TSS was that the MK-ULTRA men would develop the technique in the laboratory, while they took care of 'field experimentation.' The Counterintelligence program had three goals: (1) to induce hypnosis very rapidly in unwitting subjects; (2) to create durable amnesia; and (3) to implant durable and operationally useful posthypnotic suggestion."[31]

Mexico City, it turns out, was a primary locale for the new experiments. Melvin Beck, a CIA undercover operative there between 1962 and 1966, told about it in his book *Secret Contenders:*

[Angleton's] CI staff had in tow a young psychiatrist who claimed that he could produce a hypnotic state in an instant of shock to the subject. He had evidently convinced the staff of its feasibility. Such a feat opened up wide vistas of utilization by the staff, particularly in the area of its prime concern—the bona fides of Clandestine Services agents. Under hypnosis, the agent was compelled to reveal the truth, thus putting to rest the doubts that always remained after studying the scattered and elusive evidence contained in a dossier or a file. Best of all, the method of putting the subject under instantaneous hypnosis was practical and adaptable to the agent situation, with the significant added factor that the agent would remember nothing of the experience. The time had come for a field test with an agent.

"The reason that Mexico was chosen for the experiment," Beck continued, "was that the station had a prime candidate, a double agent whose honesty was in question. . . ."

The scenario Beck went on to describe was said to have involved one of his own agents, a Spanish-speaking man who had offered the CIA his services as a double agent against the KGB.[32] Beck provided no date for when this took place. But John Marks's book took note of a similar situation in Mexico City.

Marks says the document about this "field experiment" came to him when a former member of Angleton's staff showed up unannounced in his office. Marks found the timing strange, since it occurred in the midst of national uproar over the MK-ULTRA revelations in 1977. The man told Marks that he had once been a participant in this particular test. It came about, Marks wrote, when "the Counterintelligence staff in Washington asked the CIA station in Mexico City to find a suitable candidate for a rapid induction experiment. The station proposed a low-level agent, whom the Soviets had apparently doubled. A Counterintelligence man flew in from Washington and a hypnotic consultant arrived from California. Our source and a fellow case officer brought the agent to a motel room on a pretext. . . .

"Waiting in an adjoining room was the hypnotic consultant. At a prearranged time, the two case officers gently grabbed hold of the agent and tipped his chair over until the back was touching the floor. The consultant was supposed to rush in at that precise moment and apply the technique. Nothing happened. The consultant froze, unable to do the deed."

Marks's CIA visitor was using this as an example of the inherent limitations in such techniques. "The MK-ULTRA veteran maintains that he and his colleagues were not interested in a programmed assassin because they knew in general it would not work and, specifically, that they could not exert total control." The man admitted "that he and his colleagues spent hours running the arguments on the Manchurian Candidate back and forth." He declared that "Castro was naturally our discussion point. Could you get somebody gung-ho enough that they would go in and get him?" But, in the end, they had decided "there were more reliable ways to kill people," and Marks's walk-in source gave "many reasons why he believes the CIA never actually tried a Manchurian Candidate operation, though he acknowledges that he does not know."[33]

The Mexico City "field test" that Marks's informant/apologist was talking about had taken place during a particularly crucial period in our story

—around July of 1963. And, as we shall see, upon departing Mexico City early that August, the behavior pattern of Oswald took on a highly unusual dimension.

Summary

Sometime in midsummer of 1963, Angel and Leopoldo approached Oswald in New Orleans. The exiles convinced Oswald they were emissaries from Castro, bent on retaliating against the American government for the assassination plots. Oswald apparently went along with their plan that he take part in an assassination attempt against JFK, after which he would be given sanctuary in Cuba. According to Nagell, Oswald's recruitment was part of a plan that somehow went astray.

Many witnesses have speculated on an Oswald trip to Mexico City earlier than his known visit in late September. It is quite probable that Oswald and Nagell rendezvoused in Mexico around the beginning of August, where they are said to have gone target-shooting and Nagell observed what a poor shot Oswald really was. Maria del Carmen may have been present at a meeting.

Bullfighter Robert Clayton Buick was enlisted by U.S. intelligence to keep an eye on the goings-on at the Hotel Luma. There, Buick claims to have encountered Oswald (using the name "Hidell") and Nagell, and observed Oswald in conversation with manager Warren Broglie and bartender Franz Waehauf. Buick reported to his contacts in Garibaldi Park. After the assassination, he went on a bank robbery spree and, when arrested in 1966, was temporarily put in the same cell with Nagell in El Paso.

Author John Marks and ex-CIA undercover agent Melvin Beck have separately maintained that the CIA conducted mind-control experiments in Mexico City. Marks's source pinpointed a July 1963 date. Nagell has said that hypnosis was often used on intelligence couriers. A CIA program to create a "Manchurian Candidate" (programmed assassin) is now known to have originated in 1954. By the early 1960s the same CIA personnel in charge of the mind-control effort proceeded to set up an assassination program aimed at Castro and other foreign leaders.

Chapter Seventeen

Oswald Recruited: New Orleans, August 1963

Tucked away in the Garrison investigation files is a fascinating, very strange statement from Edward G. Gillin, an assistant district attorney for Louisiana's Orleans Parish in the summer of 1963. In his almost Poe-like reminiscence to Garrison, Gillin wrote:

It was in the month of July or early August, 1963, when I had an occasion to speak with Lee Harvey Oswald . . . this person came into the office and asked to speak to the District Attorney. I was on duty at the time and informed him that I was an Assistant District Attorney and was available to speak with him. He came into the private office and stood across the desk, and remained standing, although invited to sit down. He asked if I could advise him on whether or not a particular drug was legal or illegal. . . . I again asked him to be seated, as I thought at this point I would like to develop this line of conversation further, not only because of the unusual inquiry, but because of his demeanor upon entry into the office, which gave every indication of emotional disturbance and lack of personal conviction or a sense of security. He again declined. At this time I asked for his name, and he declined to give this information, saying it was unimportant. . . . I asked him for the name of the drug to which he was referring. I recall that I had never heard of it, but cannot recall the name which he used. . . . He was ill at ease, always looking down, shifting from foot to foot. . . . He kept saying that he must determine the existence of such a drug, and whether it was legal or illegal.

At this point, Oswald said he was reading a book, and in this book the author stated that, if the reader could procure and use this particular drug, the reader would be able to see into the future as he, the author, had seen and envisioned it; and then, and only then, would the reader see that the views and conclusions of the author were correct . . . the subject matter of the book had to do with the socio-economic picture of the world 500 years in the future. . . . At this point he spoke so rapidly that I did not see any great content in what he was saying and I became disinterested . . . however, what struck me the most, when he was "chattering" or "speeling" was that he was apparently emotionally detached from the subject matter itself . . . he was demonstrating a super-imposed indoctrination in which he had no great self-identification. He was spouting words, phrases, and clichés without true comprehension, and without personal persuasiveness, as you might expect of someone who was a dedicated advocate of a cause. . . .

I sought again to determine his identity and asked him "What did you say your name was again?" I cannot recall what he stated his full name was, but I can clearly recall that "Oswald" was a part of it, because at the time I related the name "Oswald" in my mind to that of a comedian or character many years ago on the Milton Berle radio show. I sought again to determine the book which he was reading and he said it was [Aldous] Huxley's *Brave New World*. I told him that if a drug could produce the kind of effects (a view of 500 years into the future) I thought it would definitely be a strong narcotic, or a narcotic derivative, however, since I was not an expert on this subject . . . since the City Hall was next door, I suggested that he go consult the City chemist.

On the night of President Kennedy's assassination . . . while my back was turned to the T.V., I was listening to the voice of Lee Harvey Oswald from this tape. I did not particularly concern myself with the voice until I heard the same speel and chatter-type expressions which I had heard in my office several months before. . . . I became convinced of this before turning around and viewing the T.V. screen . . . his facial features were the same as the man I interviewed. I contacted the FBI and gave this statement to them. . . . No one else has contacted me by way of follow-up. . . . As a passing comment, I observed in the press the following morning, November 23, 1963, that Huxley had died in California of mouth cancer.[1]

Aldous Huxley, British author of a futuristic vision of a totally controlled society of push-button pain and pleasure (*Brave New World*), had
indeed expired on the same day as President Kennedy. Huxley was also
among the first to write widely about psychedelic drugs such as mescaline
and LSD.

Going with the Program?

What so intrigued me about Gillin's statement was not only the timing of
Oswald's appearance in his office but also the description of Oswald as
"demonstrating a super-imposed indoctrination in which he had no great
self-identification." It was eerily similar to the psychological-warfare tactics being discussed by members of the radical right at their Washington
seminar in April 1963—and to the CIA's ongoing mind-control program.

Back in the early 1940s, George Estabrooks, chairman of the Department of Psychology at Colgate University, had been called to Washington
by the War Department shortly after Pearl Harbor. Estabrooks was considered the ranking authority on hypnosis at the time, and his opinion was
sought on how the enemy—Germany and Japan—might be planning to
use it. In 1948 Estabrooks would set down some of his findings in a book
titled simply *Hypnotism*. Discussing the value to intelligence, Estabrooks
wrote:

> There are certain safeguards if we use hypnotism. First, there is no
> danger of the agent selling out. . . . More important would be the con-
> viction of innocence which the man himself had, and this is a great aid in
> many situations. He would never "act guilty" and if ever accused of seek-
> ing information would be quite honestly indignant. This conviction of
> innocence on the part of a criminal is perhaps his greatest safeguard
> under questioning by authorities. Finally, it would be impossible to "third
> degree" him and so pick up the links of a chain. . . .

Estabrooks believed that when it came to counterespionage, "This
would require both care and time to perfect but once working it might
prove extremely effective." He spoke of using "enemy alien stock" and
cited a hypothetical example of utilizing "aggressive Cubans."

Estabrooks continued:

> In hypnotism we would build up their loyalty to this country; but out of
> hypnotism, in the "waking" or normal state we would do the opposite,
> striving to convince them that they had a genuine grievance against this

country and encouraging them to engage in "fifth column" activities. Here we would be coming very close to establishing a case of "dual personality." There is nothing at all impossible in this. We know that dual, and even multiple, personality can be both caused and cured by hypnosis. Moreover, that condition, the Dr. Jekyll and Mr. Hyde combination, is a very real one once it is established.

. . . Through them we would hope to be kept informed of the activities of their "friends," this information, of course being obtained in the trance state.

Strange to say, most good subjects will commit murder. In the writer's opinion there can be very little doubt on this score. They commit a legal, but not an ethical murder, so to speak. . . .

Such experiments, Estabrooks concluded, ought best be left to the intelligence agencies.

In 1950, the same year that Edward Hunter coined the term "brainwashing" in reference to the Communist Chinese, Estabrooks again aired his own views, in *Argosy* magazine. "I can hypnotize a man—*without his knowledge or consent*—into committing treason against the United States," his article began. "If I can do it, so could psychologists of other nations in the event of another war."[2]

The biggest problem with looking to create a "Manchurian Candidate" was lack of control. This was how John Marks's source, who had served on Angleton's Counter Intelligence staff, put it: "If you have one hundred percent control, you have one hundred percent dependency. If something happens and you haven't programmed it in, you've got a problem. If you try to put flexibility in, you lose control. To the extent you let the agent loose, you don't have control."[3]

Could someone have been "loose" and out of control by August 1963? Again, it is oddly coincidental timing that Lyman Kirkpatrick, then the CIA's inspector general, chose that month to write a warning memorandum to Richard Helms concerning his staff's wide-ranging investigation, which had begun that spring, of the agency's Technical Services Division. "Research in the manipulation of human behavior," Kirkpatrick wrote, "is considered by many authorities in medicine and related fields to be professionally unethical, therefore the reputations of professional participants in the MK-ULTRA program are, on occasion, in jeopardy."[4]

In a footnote in his book, John Marks elaborated somewhat on his CIA source's thoughts:

The veteran admits that none of the arguments he uses against a conditioned assassin would apply to a programmed "patsy" whom a hypnotist could walk through a series of seemingly unrelated events—a visit to a store, a conversation with a mailman, picking a fight at a political rally. The subject would remember everything that happened to him and be amnesic only of the fact the hypnotist ordered him to do these things. There would be no gaping inconsistency in his life of the sort that can ruin an attempt by a hypnotist to create a second personality. The purpose of this exercise is to leave a circumstantial trail that will make the authorities think the patsy committed a particular crime. The weakness might well be that the amnesia would not hold up under police interrogation, but that would not matter if the police did not believe his preposterous story about being hypnotized or if he were shot resisting arrest. Hypnosis expert Milton Kline says he could create a patsy in three months; an assassin would take him six.[5]

Picking a Fight at a Political Rally

In the scenario Nagell says was mapped out for Oswald by Angel and Leopoldo wherein he was led to believe he would be welcomed in Cuba as a "revolutionary hero," Oswald first had to prove himself, in Nagell's words, "deserving of great honor." Using his Fair Play for Cuba Committee chapter, he was instructed to pass out pro-Castro leaflets on a New Orleans street corner, to make himself known in the media, and to "start rumble" with some anti-Castro exiles.[6]

All of which, in August 1963, he quickly proceeded to do. After Mexico City, while Nagell temporarily returned to Los Angeles, Oswald's New Orleans persona was about to become a highly visible one. New Orleans: queen of the Mississippi and birthplace of jazz; famed for its creole cooking, the Mardi Gras, the teeming nightlife of the French Quarter. A city of seven hundred thousand population in 1963, it was also the second busiest port in the United States, the Gulf Coast's gateway to Latin America. That was where 70 percent of the imports unloaded in its modern riverside harbor came from. And a dominant factor in New Orleans' trade industry was Castro's transformation of Cuba away from a capitalist economy largely controlled by American corporations.

Besides the business interests and the powerful Carlos Marcello Mob—which, along with its brethren, lost millions when Castro closed down the gambling and prostitution dens in Cuba—New Orleans was the halfway point in a Cuban exile network extending along the coast from Florida to Texas. After the CIA's Langley headquarters and its huge JM/WAVE station in Miami, the agency's largest domestic base was in New Orleans.

One of the CIA's local contacts was Carlos Bringuier. Bringuier had started on his anti-Castro crusade in 1961, as propaganda secretary for the

CIA-sponsored Cuban Revolutionary Council. By 1963 he was the New Orleans chief of the DRE, or Student Revolutionary Directorate. Bringuier had journeyed to Helsinki, Finland, in 1962, "to combat . . . worldwide communism" at the World Youth Festival—which was actually a disruption mission sanctioned by the JM/WAVE station. The DRE's self-avowed goal was to "do battle with" the Fair Play for Cuba Committee in the United States. After the assassination, Bringuier's name and business address, alongside the words "Cuban Student Directorate," were found to have been inscribed by Oswald in his notebook.[7]

On August 5, 1963, the first day that Oswald's known whereabouts can be definitely accounted for in a week, he walked into Bringuier's Casa Roca retail clothing store. "He told me that he was against Castro and that he was against communism," Bringuier told the Warren Commission. Bringuier gave Oswald some copies of the DRE's literature. "After that," Bringuier said, "Oswald told me that he had been in the Marine Corps and that he had training in guerrilla warfare and that he was willing to train Cubans to fight against Castro. Even more, he told me that he was willing to go himself to fight against Castro."[8]

According to the Warren Commission, Oswald was also overheard asking the exile leader "was he connected with the Cosa Nostra." At that time, only the FBI was even aware of the phrase "Cosa Nostra."[9] It would only become synonymous with organized crime that September, when mobster Joseph Valachi went public at a Senate hearing. But on July 31, five days before Oswald came to see Bringuier, an exile training camp in nearby Lacombe, Louisiana, had been raided by the FBI. It was based on land owned by William J. McLaney, a former Havana casino operator with extensive Mob affiliations. Bringuier, says an FBI file, was to assist the arrested exiles in the raid "in getting back to Miami."[10]

The day after Oswald saw Bringuier, he returned to the exile's store and dropped off his Marine Corps training manual as proof of his fighting abilities. Bringuier's store was only two doors away from the Habana Bar, where, two nights after that, bar owner Orest Peña and a waiter reported seeing Oswald in the company of two Hispanic acquaintances at about 3:00 A.M. Coincidentally, Peña says, he had first met Oswald when both went to the New Orleans passport office on the same day (June 24; Peña used his passport to travel to East Germany for "a one-day sightseeing holiday"). Peña earned some spare change as an FBI informant. After Oswald showed up in his bar, Peña reported to the bureau that the two Cubans who accompanied Oswald—posing as Mexicans, Peña noted—had made disparaging remarks about the United States.[11]

Peña also alerted Bringuier, who later that August wrote to the FBI: "Oswald asked for a lemonade and when they collected for it he said that surely the owner had to be a Cuban capitalist. On that occasion Oswald was accompanied by a Mexican. After that the Mexican returned with another Mexican to the Habana Bar. The FBI was making inquiries for them and left word that if they saw them again, to call there." Bringuier said he was told that one of Oswald's companions was a "Mexican Communist wanted by the FBI."[12]

On August 9, the day following the Habana Bar incident, Bringuier says he was tipped off by a friend that "a young man carrying a sign telling 'Viva Fidel' in Spanish" was over on Canal Street. He and two friends picked up their own sign—"Danger. Only 90 Miles from the United States Cuba Lies in Chains"—and went looking for him.[13] It took two tries to locate him and, when they did, Bringuier claimed to have been initially surprised when he recognized Oswald.

According to Bringuier, Oswald smiled and extended his hand. Bringuier became enraged and, as a crowd gathered, said he started "to explain to the people what Oswald did to me, because I wanted to move the American people against him. . . . and I told them that that was a Castro agent. . . . The people in the street became angry and they started to shout to him, 'Traitor! Communist! Go to Cuba! Kill him!'"[14]

Approaching the ex-Marine, one of Bringuier's associates grabbed the Fair Play for Cuba leaflets that Oswald was passing out and threw them into the air. "Okay, Carlos, if you want to hit me, hit me," Oswald reportedly said.[15] At which point the New Orleans police showed up and arrested all four. Habana Bar owner Peña then bailed Bringuier out of jail.

"I think Carlos [Bringuier] went there on purpose," William George Gaudet would tell attorney Bernard Fensterwald, Jr., in 1975. Gaudet, a CIA agent in New Orleans in 1963, insisted he had no personal contact with Oswald. But he added he was sure "the local office of the CIA, with the local operatives that they had, must have contacted Lee Harvey Oswald. They couldn't trust him, but they could get certain information from him. Oswald, obviously, had some information that they wanted."[16]

The police who interviewed Oswald at the station immediately sensed something weird about the street altercation. "He seemed to have set them up to create an incident," said Lieutenant Francis Martello. Sergeant Horace Austin noted that Oswald "appeared as though he is being used by these people . . . and knows very little about this [FPCC] organization that he belongs to and its ultimate purpose or goal."[17]

The likelihood that the street fracas was staged is evident in a letter Oswald wrote to the FPCC's New York headquarters. It was dated August 1 and postmarked August 4—five days before Bringuier accosted Oswald. Oswald wrote:

> In regards to my efforts to start a branch office in New Orleans.
> I rented an office as I planned and was promptly closed three days later

for some obsure [sic] reason by the renters, they said something about remodeling, ect. [sic], I'm sure you understand.

After that I worked out of a post office box and by useing [sic] street demonstrations and some circular work have substained [sic] a great deal of interest but no new members.

Through the efforts of some Cuban-exial [sic] "gusanos" a street demonstration was attacked and we were officially cautioned by police.

This incident robbed me of what support I had leaving me alone.

Nevertheless thousands of circulars were distrubed [sic] and many, many pamphlets which your office supplied.

We also managed to picket the fleet when it came in and I was surprised at the number of officers who were interested in our literature.

I continued to recive [sic] through my post office box inquiries and questions which I shall endeavor to keep answewering [sic] to the best of my ability.[18]

There is nothing in the known record indicating that any Oswald confrontation with Cuban exiles occurred prior to August 9, five days after Oswald mailed this letter. Nor did the FBI uncover any evidence that Oswald ever tried to rent an office. Marina Oswald would offer her opinion to the Warren Commission that her husband set up the FPCC "primarily for purposes of self-advertising. He wanted to be arrested. I think he wanted to get into the newspapers, so that he would be known." The commission added: "According to Marina Oswald, he thought that would help him when he got to Cuba."[19]

When Oswald was arrested, he presented two forms of ID to police officials. One was his FPCC membership card, listing "A. Hidell" as chapter president. Another was his Social Security card, #433-54-3937, "which did not bear his signature," according to the police report.

Years later, Art Greenstein would turn up something amid the papers Nagell had sent him, either while in prison or after he got out in 1968. It was a photocopy of the same Social Security card—except this one did bear the signature "Lee Harvey Oswald." Underneath the card there are four additional signings of Oswald's name—the apparent meaning being that someone was practicing how to do it.

After spending a night in jail, Oswald was interrogated by police lieutenant Francis Martello. At the close of the interview, Oswald requested to speak to a representative of the FBI. Martello called over, telling the FBI that Oswald "was desirous of seeing an agent and supplying to him information with regard to his activities with the FPCC in New Orleans."[20] FBI special agent John Quigley then spent an hour and a half talking with Oswald on a sweltering Saturday morning at the police station. Oswald told the FBI man that "A. J. Hidell" had asked him to distribute FPCC literature two days before the street incident.[21] Quigley later maintained that he had never heard of Oswald before. Yet in 1961, after Oswald's "defection" to the USSR, his Navy file had been reviewed by the FBI in New Orleans, where he was born. John Quigley had handled the case.[22]

Immediately after seeing the FBI, Oswald called Uncle "Dutz" Murret, seeking bail money, but reached his daughter Joyce. She decided to stop by the station, telling Lieutenant Martello that she was very reluctant to get involved in Oswald's release because of his FPCC activities. Joyce also mentioned his "defection" to the USSR. So, Martello recalled for the Warren Commission, he decided to question Oswald again.

Martello said he asked Oswald "if he was a communist and he said he was not. I asked him if he was a socialist and he said 'guilty.' . . . I asked him if he thought that the communist way of life was better than the American way of life and he replied that there was not true communism in Russia. . . . He said they have 'fat, stinking politicians over there just like we have over here' and that they do not follow the great precepts of Karl Marx. I asked Oswald why he would not allow members of his family to learn English [something else that Joyce Murret had informed the policeman]. . . . He stated the reason why he did this was because he hated America."[23]

Meanwhile, Joyce Murret had telephoned Emile Bruneau, an "old friend of the family" and liquor store owner—who paid Oswald's bond. Years later, House Assassinations Committee investigators uncovered that Bruneau had been closely associated with two of mobster Carlos Marcello's top henchmen.[24]

The next day, August 11, Oswald approached the city editor of the *New Orleans States-Item*, asking him to give more coverage to his FPCC campaign. Late that evening, Uncle "Dutz" dropped by his nephew's house and told him: "You be sure you show up at that courthouse for the trial." Lee told him not to worry, he would be there.[25]

By now, Carlos Bringuier had reported his contact with Oswald to DRE headquarters in Miami, which in turn made sure to pass the word along to the CIA.[26] Bringuier invited a WDSU-TV camera team to the August 12 trial, where he described in outraged tones Oswald's "infiltration attempt" of his group, holding up to the judge the Marine Corps manual Oswald had given him. Oswald, who sat on the "colored side" of the courtroom, pled guilty to "disturbing the peace by creating a scene." His uncle, accompanied by an associate of the Marcello mob, paid the ten-dollar fine. All charges against Oswald's Cuban adversaries were dropped.

That night, Oswald wrote again to V. T. Lee at FPCC headquarters in New York—even though Oswald had not heard a word from Lee since the long letter of May 29 cautioning him against setting up an FPCC chapter in such a hotbed as New Orleans. Oswald enclosed a copy of his court summons and a clipping from the *New Orleans Times-Picayune* about his sentencing, and wrote:

"Continuing my efforts on behalf of the F.P.C.C. I find that I have incurred the displeasure of the Cuban exile 'worms' here. I was attacked by three of them as the copy of the enclosed summons indicates. I was fined $10 and the three Cubans were not fined because of 'lack of evidence' as the judge said. I am very glad I am stirring things up and shall continue to do so. The incident was given considerable coverage in the press and local TV news broadcasts. I am sure it will be to the good of the Fair Play for Cuba Committee."[27]

The next day Oswald wrote to Arnold Johnson, information director of the Communist Party, U.S.A., in New York, also sending him a clipping about his arrest.[28] He then called the Long John Nebel radio show in New York, offering to appear at his own expense.[29] He was "going public" in as many ways as he could find.

The Office at 544 Camp Street

Ex-New Orleans CIA agent William George Gaudet said in 1975 that he, too, had observed Oswald doing his street leafleting. "I don't even think he knew exactly what he was distributing . . . [with] the Fair Play for Cuba deal, which was nothing but a front and was one of the dreams of—I think Guy Banister."[30]

One of the pamphlets Oswald was carrying when arrested in New Orleans was Corliss Lamont's *Crime Against Cuba*—the same one that Nagell would be carrying when arrested by the FBI in El Paso. The FBI's Quigley wasted no time in querying the New York office for information on Lamont. But the FBI apparently expressed no interest whatsoever in an address stamped on the back of the pamphlet: "FPCC—544 Camp St.—New Orleans, La.[31]

Five forty-four Camp Street was right around the corner from the Reily Coffee Company, where Oswald had found work earlier that summer. This weather-beaten, gray granite structure also happened to be the office of Guy Banister Associates.

Born in a log cabin in rural Louisiana in 1901, stocky, white-haired Guy Banister had served twenty years with the FBI. Having once helped capture John Dillinger, he received a commendation from Director Hoover and ended up in charge of the FBI's Chicago office. During World War II Banister took time out to work in Naval Intelligence, then left the FBI in

1954 to come to New Orleans as deputy chief of police. Dismissed from that job in 1957 after allegedly threatening a restaurant waiter with a pistol, he went on to found the Guy Banister Associates private detective agency.

At 544 Camp Street, Banister amassed vast files on "Communist groups and subversive organizations." He was a member of both the John Birch Society and the paramilitary Minutemen, and served as "special adviser" to the Louisiana American Legion's "Committee on Un-American Activities." He put out a racist publication titled the *Louisiana Intelligence Digest,* which depicted integration as a Communist conspiracy. And his office provided a haven for numerous Cuban exile groups looking to get rid of Castro, for whom he hired young "infiltrators" to run background investigations on people seeking to join their cause.[32]

Carlos Bringuier's original anti-Castro headquarters had been housed in Banister's building. So were those of Sergio Arcacha-Smith,[33] whom Richard Nagell had "checked out" in Miami back in January 1963. According to CIA records, Arcacha-Smith "maintained extensive relations with the FBI. . . . Two of his regular FBI contacts were [name deleted] and . . . Guy Banister."[34]

Nagell has described Arcacha-Smith as a "dapper, mustachioed, ex-fink for the CIA"—and a "peripheral" character in the assassination conspiracy. "Mr. Smith was strictly right-wing, into everything so-called anti-Castro," Nagell told me. "At one time I think he had a connection with Cuba Libre. He may also have had something to do with [Alpha] 66."[35] Arcacha-Smith, removed from his post with the Cuban Revolutionary Council after being accused of misappropriating funds, then moved to Texas early in 1963[36]—where several times he visited the offices of oilman H. L. Hunt and was said to be "pretty good friends" with General Walker (see Chapter Twelve).

Nagell was well aware of Guy Banister. "He was a real asshole as far as I was concerned," Nagell told me. "A private detective who did a few jobs for the agency. Now there was a guy who was into everything, a guy who should have gone to jail."[37]

In 1978, author Anthony Summers managed to obtain an interview with Banister's former secretary and lover, Delphine Roberts. She remembered Banister as having "access to large funds at various times in 1963—I think he received funds from the CIA . . . I know he and the FBI traded information due to his former association." She also remembered something even more remarkable: Oswald had come into her office, asking to fill out a form for accreditation as one of Banister's "agents."

As told by Summers in his 1980 book *Conspiracy,* Roberts continued: "During the course of the conversation I gained the impression that he and Guy Banister already knew each other. After Oswald filled out the application form Guy Banister called him to the office. The door was closed, and a lengthy conversation took place. Then the young man left. I presumed then, and now am certain, that the reason for Oswald being there was that he was required to act under cover."

Roberts reported Oswald coming back a number of times, using an office on the second floor above Banister's own. That was where Oswald kept his FPCC leaflets, and Banister was incensed when some of this material ended up in his main office. One afternoon, Roberts saw Oswald passing out his literature on the street and reported this to her boss. "Don't worry about him," she says Banister told her. "He's a nervous fellow, he's confused. He's with us, he's associated with the office."

Summers was able to confirm this basic story through several other witnesses. Ivan Nitschke, a Banister business associate and also a former FBI agent, recalled that Banister became "interested in Oswald" in the summer of 1963. Delphine Roberts concluded: "I knew there were such things as . . . spies and counterspies, and the importance of such things. So I just didn't question them."[38]

The FBI did interview Banister three days after the assassination. He was asked about some anti-Castro exiles, including Sergio Arcacha-Smith. But apparently nothing was mentioned about Oswald or the 544 Camp Street address on Oswald's leaflets—even though the FBI was aware of this connection the previous August.[39] Nor was Banister questioned about the allegations of Jack Martin, a part-time investigator for Banister who called Herman Kohlman at the New Orleans DA's office on November 23, 1963, saying he had information linking Banister and David Ferrie to what had happened in Dallas. Martin's statements were then relayed to the FBI.

Questioned by the House Assassinations Committee in 1978, Martin related that he and Banister got into a heated argument on the night of the assassination. Banister accused Martin of removing some files from the office. "What are you going to do—kill me like you all did Kennedy?" Martin shot back. At this point Banister drew a pistol and began beating Martin on the head. Martin believed Banister would have killed him, but for the intervention of secretary Delphine Roberts.[40]

Another of Banister's close associates was Maurice Brooks Gatlin, Sr., who had attended the 1958 meeting in Mexico City that launched the international right wing's global anti-Communist alliance (see Chapter Ten). The Garrison investigation would uncover that Gatlin had, in 1962, funneled $100,000 to a right-wing clique in France that was plotting to assassinate Charles de Gaulle. Gatlin died in Panama in 1965, when he either fell or was pushed from a sixth-floor hotel window.[41]

Still another Banister friend was Kent Courtney, who in June 1962 organized the Conservative Society of America (CSA) in New Orleans with his wife, Phoebe. The Courtneys, who believed that even archconservative Arizona senator Barry Goldwater was "tainted by socialism," were the city's best-known spokespeople for the radical right. In 1960 Kent had run for governor of Louisiana on the States Rights ticket. He became a featured speaker at meetings of Billy James Hargis's Christian Crusade. In 1963 Phoebe authored *The Case of General Edwin A. Walker,* a book-length defense of Walker. An August 15, 1963, memorandum on right-wing groups prepared for President Kennedy noted that the Courtneys' CSA "claims a membership of several thousand, located in 47 states. . . . Among those said by the Courtneys to be identified with the CSA are . . . Major General Charles Willoughby of the District of Columbia."[42]

After the assassination, Revilo Oliver, a professor of classics at the University of Illinois, published a trilogy of articles about it in the John Birch Society's *American Opinion* magazine. "Upon his arrival in this country Oswald took up his duties as an agent of the conspiracy, conspiracy with a cap C," Oliver wrote, "spying on anti-Communist Cuban refugees, serving as an agitator for Fair Play for Cuba, and participating in some of the many other forms of subversion that flourish openly in the defiance of law through the connivance of the Attorney General, Robert F. Kennedy."[43]

On September 9, 1964, Oliver was called to testify before the Warren Commission. Asked about that statement, among many others, the professor replied that "Fair Play for Cuba is very obviously a Communist enterprise." He added that he had "heard a personal account" about this in Tulsa (site of Hargis's headquarters) "from a man who was connected with a Cuban group that Oswald tried to infiltrate." "Was that Carlos Bringuier?" Oliver was asked.

"Bringuier, I believe so, yes. And I also heard from the publisher of the *Independent American* of an attempt by Oswald to obtain employment on that newspaper." The *Independent American* was put out by Kent and Phoebe Courtney.[44]

In 1977, when the House Assassinations Committee sought to locate Banister's files, his widow, Mary Banister Wilson, said she had given them away to various organizations soon after her husband's death from a heart attack in June 1964. Some went to the Louisiana State Police, others to the New Orleans Metropolitan Crime Commission. The House Assassinations Committee "learned several books from Banister's collection went to Banister's associate, Kent Courtney." But congressional investigators were unable to get their hands on any of this material; the contents of the "half filled" file cabinet provided to the state police had been "routinely destroyed."[45]

Interweaving Threads

A man named David Ferrie also worked as a private investigator for Banister. Ferrie was a bizarre character indeed. He wore a red wig and false eyebrows to compensate for a rare ailment, alopecia, which left him bereft of all body hair. He founded his own church, conducted experiments looking for a cancer cure in a laboratory above his garage, and spoke out vehemently against the Kennedy administration's policies. After the Bay of Pigs, when Ferrie gave a speech on Cuba to the New Orleans chapter of the Military Order of World Wars, his attack was so vituperative that he was asked to leave the podium.[46]

In Chapter Twelve we saw that Ferrie probably first encountered Oswald in 1955, when Ferrie commanded the Louisiana Civil Air Patrol in which the teenager took part. Then, in 1961, ex-CIA contract agent Robert Morrow has said that Ferrie was involved in the European arrangements whereby Morrow couriered information from Oswald in Minsk to the CIA (see Chapter Eight). In the summer of 1963, according to Delphine Roberts, on at least one occasion Oswald and Ferrie went together to a Cuban exile training camp near New Orleans to take rifle practice.[47]

Born in Cleveland in 1918, Ferrie had originally studied theology in hopes of becoming an ordained priest, but departed seminary school because of "emotional instability." Hired as a pilot by Eastern Air Lines in 1951, he soon moved to New Orleans. Here, according to the House Assassinations Committee, "Ferrie spent considerable time studying medicine and psychology, especially the techniques of hypnosis which he frequently practiced on his young associates."

In August 1961 Ferrie was arrested twice by Jefferson Parish, Louisiana, police and charged with "indecent behavior with three juvenile boys." The *New Orleans States-Item* reported that "authorities claim he used alcohol, hypnotism and the enticement of flying to lure the youngsters into committing indecent acts."

Sergio Arcacha-Smith, Ferrie's partner in anti-Castro activities, sought to intervene on his behalf. But Eastern Air Lines removed Ferrie from its payroll, and the Federal Aviation Administration opened an investigation into the charges. That was when Ferrie turned to G. Wray Gill, a lawyer for Carlos Marcello in the mobster's fight against conspiracy and perjury charges brought by Robert Kennedy. Gill agreed to represent Ferrie in exchange for his investigative work "on other cases."

Ferrie simultaneously made an arrangement with Banister in February 1962. Ferrie's work included analyzing autopsy reports in exchange for Banister's investigative services on his behalf. According to another of Banister's secretaries, Mary Brengel, Banister was also assisting Carlos Marcello in his fight to stop the Kennedys from deporting him.[48] Arcacha-Smith, too, had a relationship with Marcello. An FBI report of April 1961 indicated that when Arcacha-Smith began seeking funds for anti-Castro activities, Marcello offered a "substantial donation" in exchange for a guarantee of gambling rights in Havana after Castro was overthrown.[49]

Author John H. Davis, in his 1989 biography of Marcello, carefully traced the bookmaking connections between Oswald's uncle "Dutz" Murret and the Marcello syndicate. Shortly after Oswald came to New Orleans at the end of April 1963, Davis describes an FBI informant's report that Oswald received a loan from a top Marcello lieutenant, Joe Poretto, at the Town & Country Restaurant. Davis also raised the possibility that Oswald had served as a part-time "runner" for Marcello's bookmaking operation that summer.[50]

Back in September 1962, Edward Becker, a self-styled private investigator and free-lance businessman, described having attended a meeting at Marcello's sprawling country estate. The ostensible purpose was to obtain investment capital from Marcello for an oil venture. Amid considerable imbibing of Scotch whiskey, Becker made an offhand remark about Robert Kennedy's having packed the mobster off on a plane to Guatemala on April 6, 1961—a deportation effort from which Marcello, after a harrowing two months and a humiliating cross-country trek, had managed to return.

Becker recalled Marcello leaping to his feet and uttering a Sicilian oath: *"Livarsi na pietra di la scarpa!* [Take the stone out of my shoe!]." Then Marcello shouted: "Don't worry about that Bobby son of a bitch! He's going to be taken care of." He then quoted from an old Sicilian proverb: "If you want to kill a dog, you don't cut off the tail, you cut off the head." Marcello, Becker claimed, said the plan was to use "a nut, like they do in Sicily" to take the blame for assassinating the president. Then Marcello sat down again and changed the subject.[51]

The timing of Marcello's alleged statements coincides with when Nagell was briefed that same fall by the Soviets in Mexico City about plans afoot to eliminate JFK. And the Marcello Mob's links to so many people within the New Orleans web surrounding Oswald led the House Assassinations Committee to conclude in 1979 that elements of organized crime were the most likely suspects in a conspiracy.

"I have a friend who is familiar with both John Rosselli and Carlos ('The Little Man') Marcello," Nagell once wrote to Fensterwald. In his correspondence with Greenstein, Nagell also raised this question: "Did the CIA make a hard contract with Carlos 'The Little Man' Marcello (of New Orleans fame) to hit Fidel?"[52]

The Setup Moves Ahead

So, in August 1963, the net around Oswald was tightening—and the FBI was being kept fully apprised about him by the Cuban exiles and others, every step of the way.

On August 16, Oswald reportedly hired two helpers, paying them $2.00 apiece, to help pass out his pro-Castro leaflets near the International Trade Mart. Miguel Cruz, one of Carlos Bringuier's partners during the earlier street altercation, stood idly by this time and simply watched. A photograph of Oswald's second leafleting exists in the National Archives. Standing behind Oswald, also holding the FPCC pamphlets. is a thin, Hispanic man dressed identically to Oswald in a white shirt, black slacks, and tie. He has never been identified.[53]

The leafleters were there for only a few minutes, yet the demonstration was filmed by WDSU-TV, which happened to be on hand—apparently alerted in advance. Jessie R. Core III, the public relations man for the International Trade Mart, also attended the leafleting and alerted the FBI immediately afterward. In the resulting memorandum, which reopened a supposedly dormant FBI case on the FPCC, Core was revealed to be an FBI "source of information relative to Latin American matters."[54]

That evening, one of Bringuier's friends, Carlos Quiroga, dropped by Oswald's house on Magazine Street. As Quiroga later told a Garrison investigator, he "suggested to Bringuier that they try to infiltrate Oswald's organization." Quiroga first came to public attention, though he was not named, in a New York Times interview a few days after the assassination—after Bringuier put reporter Fred Powledge onto his "intelligence agent" for their DRE organization. Quiroga related a conversation with Oswald that, given the verbatim manner in which it appeared in the Times, seemed to have been taped. Under the headline "CUBA EXILE TELLS OF OSWALD BOAST—Reports He Said He Would Aid Castro Against U.S.," the Bringuier/Quiroga story was clearly aimed at casting blame at Cuba's doorstep.[55]

Besides working with Bringuier, Quiroga was also the FBI's "Confidential Informant NO T-5." He is not specifically identified in an FBI file of November 27, 1963 (the same day the Times's article appeared), but the FBI story matches that in the newspaper and the one later told by Quiroga to Garrison's investigator. The FBI report revealed little except that

Quiroga had tried to come across to Oswald as sympathetic to his cause and had gone afterward to New Orleans police lieutenant Francis Martello offering to "report any information . . . in an effort to do away with the FPCC in New Orleans."[56]

The day after Quiroga's visit with Oswald, on August 17 William Stuckey of WDSU Radio called Oswald at his apartment and found him eager to appear on his weekly *Latin Listening Post.* Stuckey admits he had been briefed by the FBI on Oswald's background. Only four and a half minutes of their thirty-seven-minute taped conversation at the WDSU studio ended up being aired. Oswald discussed a wide range of political ideas, including ". . . government agencies, particularly certain covert, undercover agencies like the now-defunct CIA—its leadership is now defunct. Allen Dulles is now defunct. . . . With a little bit different, humanitarian, handling of the situation, Cuba would not be the problem it is today."[57]

That evening, Oswald sent an airmail dispatch to V. T. Lee outlining his wave of recent publicity.[58]

August 19: WDSU Radio turned over a copy of the tape to the New Orleans FBI. Stuckey talked to his news director about arranging a debate. He selected Edward Butler, who helped disseminate anti-Communist propaganda into Latin America through the New Orleans-based Information Council of the Americas (INCA). Butler said he had conceived of this psychological warfare PR unit while serving in a special Army unit "in the quiet little town of Alexandria, Virginia." Butler's propaganda consisted, according to Stuckey, primarily of "tape-recorded interviews with Cuban refugees and refugees from Iron Curtain countries."

Stuckey also contacted Bringuier, "the man who led me to Oswald—I asked him to appear on the show to give it a little Cuban flavor." Then Oswald called up Stuckey and, as they had already agreed, promptly said yes to the debate arrangements. "How many of you am I going to have to fight?" Stuckey remembered Oswald saying.[59]

August 21: As the debate began, interviewer Stuckey and propagandist Butler kicked things off by producing newspaper clippings about Oswald's attempt to renounce his American citizenship in Moscow in 1959. "During those two weeks," said Oswald, "I was, of course, with the knowledge of the American embassy, getting this permission [to reside in the USSR]. . . . At no time was I out of contact with the American embassy."

How had he supported himself in the Soviet Union? Oswald was asked. Did he have a government subsidy? Oswald replied: "Well, as I uh, well, I will answer that ques—uh, question directly then, since you will not rest until you get your answer. I worked in Russia. I was under uh, the protection of the uh . . . of the uh . . . that is to say, I was not under the protection of the uh . . . American government. But that is I was at all times considered an American citizen."

When the Warren Commission published a transcript of this debate, the word "not" was added in the first time. Its version of Oswald's words reads: "I worked in Russia. I was *not* under uh, the protection of the uh . . ." etc. However, a careful listening to an LP record later produced by fellow debater Edward Butler inadvertently reveals otherwise. Oswald definitely can be heard saying, before changing his phrasing, that he *"was* under uh, the protection of . . ." Butler's 1964 album "OSWALD—Self-Portrait in Red" would be disseminated by Billy James Hargis's Christian Crusade.[60]

As the debate proceeded, Stuckey asked Oswald, "Are you a Marxist?" Oswald responded, "Yes, I am a Marxist. . . ."

Bringuier asked, "Do you agree with Castro when he qualified President John F. Kennedy as a ruffian and a thief?"

Oswald responded, "I would not agree with that particular wording. I think that certain agencies, mainly the State Department and the CIA, has made monumental mistakes in its relations with Cuba."

Oswald talked at length about his efforts in "trying to attract new members" to the FPCC. He spoke of how its national director, V. T. Lee, had "recently returned from Cuba." He gave out the FPCC's New York address and noted it had "been investigated by the Senate subcommittees who are occupied with this sort of thing. They have investigated our organization from the viewpoint of taxes, subversion, allegiance, and in general where and how and why we exist. They have found absolutely nothing to connect us with the Communist Party of the United States. In regards to your question about whether I, myself, am a Communist, uh, as I said, I do not belong to any organization." Oswald added that "Hands off Cuba is the main slogan of this committee."

After the radio debate, while Oswald and Stuckey went out for a beer, Bringuier put out a press statement calling for a congressional investigation of Oswald.[61] That night, Oswald wrote again to V. T. Lee at FPCC headquarters.

August 22: WDSU Radio made the debate transcript available to the New Orleans FBI. At the same time, FBI headquarters in Washington sent out instructions to its Dallas and New Orleans offices to look further into the ex-Marine.[62]

Inveterate reader Oswald returned one book to the library and checked out three more (including Ian Fleming's spy novel *From Russia with Love*). The Napoleon Avenue branch library, which Oswald generally visited on Thursdays, was located some distance from his home. Libraries, as noted by the Garrison probe, are often used as "drops" for intelligence operatives. And Norman Gallo, who had gone to work as a librarian on Napoleon Avenue in 1963, had been just that. Fluent in Japanese, Italian, and Spanish, Garrison uncovered that Gallo had started out "in something to do with codes" with Air Force Intelligence in Korea. After continuing in some intelligence capacity in Washington between 1957 and 1959, Gallo then returned to Japan before coming home to his native New Orleans in the spring of 1963.[63]

After August 22 until September 17, when he applied for a Mexican tourist visa, Oswald pretty much dropped from sight. On the day of the assassination, a copy of the incriminating radio debate would be immediately delivered to the national media by Carlos Bringuier's DRE affiliate group in Miami.[64]

The DRE led the charge toward a Castro-used-Oswald scenario. José Lanusa, the DRE's Miami chief, contacted Clare Boothe Luce and Daniel James about Oswald on November 22, 1963. Luce, the wife of *Time-Life* publisher Henry Luce, and free-lance writer James were both board members of the Committee to Free Cuba, which had been established in May 1963. James promptly called the FBI. "LANUSA described OSWALD definitely a communist and a supporter of FIDEL CASTRO," an FBI report states. ". . . LANUSA also advised him that FIDEL CASTRO, in early September at a function at the Brazilian Embassy in Havana, remarked that if the United States causes him difficulty he has facilities to 'knock off' United States leaders."[65]

Luce, a former congresswoman and U.S. ambassador to Italy, waited longer to come forward. Then, during the Garrison and House Assassinations Committee investigations, she made a point of passing along a story that originated with the DRE. Luce said she had gotten a phone call the night of the assassination and been told that the DRE had "penetrated" Oswald's organization after he came around offering his services as a potential Castro assassin. DRE members had worked their way inside his "Communist cell," where Oswald was tape-recorded bragging about being "the greatest shot in the world with a telescopic rifle." Luce said she had instructed the exiles to turn everything over to the FBI. The House Assassinations Committee spent many fruitless hours looking to track down Luce's leads.[66]

In the files of the Garrison investigation there is an interview conducted with the DRE's Carlos Quiroga on January 13, 1967, about a month before the DA's probe was announced in the press. When Garrison staffer Frank Klein asked the exile what he figured they were looking into, "He answered that he believed that we were investigating the assassination of President Kennedy with relation to David Ferrie. I asked him why he believed this and he said that Ferrie had called Bringuier and told him this after Ferrie was subpoenaed by [the] DA's office. He says Bringuier told him what Ferrie had said. He also says that Ferrie is 'plenty scared.' "

Quiroga spoke openly of knowing Ferrie, Arcacha-Smith, and Guy Banister and said that Ferrie had asked Bringuier to attempt to find out Arcacha-Smith's current whereabouts. Quiroga also alluded to ties among the Marcello organization, Ferrie, and Cuban exile groups—long before such information became public knowledge and that, for some reason, Garrison did not pursue.

But Quiroga stuck to his guns that "Castro was the instigator for Kennedy's assassination." Oswald had impressed him as being very intelligent and certainly "not a nut." Quiroga expressed his view that Oswald had been paid "by someone," probably Castro agents.

The interview ends with an underlined note from investigator Klein: "This man knows a lot more than he is telling us." Later, according to Garrison, Quiroga "failed a lie-detector test when he denied knowing in advance that Kennedy was going to be killed, or having seen the weapons to be used in the assassination."

Two days before Ferrie's alleged suicide, which occurred just before Garrison could fully question him, he and Bringuier had a long meeting on February 20, 1967. Bringuier, who still resides in New Orleans, told me in a 1992 telephone interview that Ferrie believed Garrison was trying to frame him. Bringuier says he himself then wrote a letter to J. Edgar Hoover, saying that Garrison was going to postulate a vast conspiracy involving the FBI, the CIA, Cuban exiles, and Lyndon Johnson. After this, Bringuier says the CIA contacted him seeking to learn more of what he knew about Garrison's investigation.[67] The exile followed up by writing a 1969 book about the assassination, *Red Friday*.

Today Bringuier continues to deny that there was anything suspicious about his own contacts with Oswald. "All the evidence," he still says, "points to a Castro plot."

This was, it seems, a number of people's idea all along.

Summary

Everything about Oswald's high-profile August in New Orleans is bizarre. First came his appearance in the office of Edward Gillin, viewed by the assistant DA as an expression of a "super-imposed indoctrination." There is abundant evidence of a CIA (and military) long-term effort to create an Oswald "type" through mind-control techniques. While there is no way to know whether Oswald was ever part of such a scheme, building a programmed "patsy" through a circumstantial trail certainly cannot be ruled out in his instance. David Ferrie, a known Oswald associate during the summer of 1963, was an expert in hypnosis.

All the earmarks of a setup follow Oswald in New Orleans. First he offers his services to Carlos Bringuier as an anti-Castro guerrilla trainer, then is encountered passing out pro-Castro leaflets on the street. While Oswald lets national leftist groups know about his every move, he operates out of the office of Guy Banister—who is all tied in with anti-Castro Cubans, right-wing fanatics, mobster Marcello, and the FBI. No less than five people observing Oswald during this period are reporting about him to the FBI. Oswald himself asks to see the FBI after his arrest for the street altercation. Both the New Orleans police and CIA agent William Gaudet believe that Oswald does not really seem to know the nature of his own Fair Play for Cuba organization. An organized-crime figure posts bond to get him out of jail.

Does Oswald think he is infiltrating Banister's organization? Or is all this part of someone else's big plans to make Oswald the fall guy for the assassination? After his radio debate, Oswald drops out of sight. A few months later, his New Orleans activities will be used by the exiles and the right wing to portray him as a fanatic devoted to Fidel Castro.

Chapter Eighteen

The Third Plot to Kill JFK:
August 1963

◇

At least during the early part of August 1963, Richard Case Nagell and Lee Harvey Oswald went separate ways. After the trip to Mexico, Nagell is known to have returned to Los Angeles where, on August 6, he renewed his passport.[1] Vaughn Marlowe also remembered it as being August when Nagell dropped by his bookstore for the last time. Bill Lynn, Nagell's friend at the California Department of Alcoholic Beverage Control, recalled loaning Nagell his Colt .45 pistol at about the same time. "Dick told me he needed the gun for protection in Mexico," Lynn told me. "I know he was spending a lot of time in Mexico during that period."[2]

Sometime not long after this, Nagell apparently drove to New Orleans. Except for the little he has put on record about Oswald's Fair Play for Cuba chapter, Nagell was generally vague in our interviews and his writings about the nature of his business there. He did tell me that "in July to September, most of my time was spent on the subject of Lee Harvey Oswald." But it was Robert Morrow, the former CIA contract agent who pseudonymously referred to Nagell as "Richard Carson Fillmore" in his 1976 novel *Betrayal,* who helped fill out the picture.

Now in his early sixties, Morrow resides in Cincinnati. When he decided to break his long silence as the mid-1970s congressional probe began to heat up, I met with him twice at his then residence in Baltimore. But not until 1990 was he willing to reveal the full background on how his knowledge of Richard Nagell came about.

In the summer of 1963, Morrow was moving full steam on a CIA project to counterfeit Cuban pesos for delivery into Cuba, in an effort to destabilize the Castro economy. That same summer, he says another assignment came from his CIA case officer, Tracy Barnes.

Morrow alleges that Barnes was the initial CIA recipient of the "defector's" information from Minsk (see Chapter Eight). In 1962, Barnes, who had been second-in-command of the Bay of Pigs invasion, set up the CIA's new Domestic Operations Division. Its purpose, according to author David Wise, was for "clandestine operational activities of the Clandestine Services conducted within the United States against foreign targets." Morrow's Cuban peso scheme fell under its bailiwick, and there was close cooperation with the Cuban Task Force, then under the tutelage of Desmond FitzGerald.

In midsummer, Morrow says that Barnes asked him to purchase several weapons. "I was told specifically to get good ones, 7.35mm Mannlicher-Carcanos. A 6.5mm [the type of Mannlicher-Carcano allegedly used by Oswald] was not an accurate rifle at all, and not to be considered. I remember going to Sunny's Surplus up in Towson, Maryland. They had a whole wall of Mannlichers, Mausers, and other rifles. I picked out four, which I felt were pretty good. When we got them back to the laboratory, I discovered that one of the bolts had been sheared off. So I didn't ship that one. I still have it. I bought some surplus ammunition at the same time."

The rifles and ammo, Morrow says, were then picked up by David Ferrie in a private plane and flown by him to New Orleans. "He flew a Tri-Pacer into Campbell airstrip. That was the last time I ever saw Ferrie." Researcher Gus Russo confirmed with a former airstrip employee that "a funny-looking guy with a southern accent" returned by private plane to New Orleans after loading several guns there during that summer.

Morrow asked Mario Garcia Kohly, Sr., a Cuban exile leader whom Barnes had assigned him to work with, about the intended purpose of the weapons. "Kohly said they were for an operation against Juan Bosch, who was then headman in the Dominican Republic. He was a thorn in their side. This didn't necessarily mean assassination, but possibly a coup, or whatever. For all I knew, they'd been getting weapons from all over the United States. I didn't think too much about it.

"Not long after this," Morrow continued, "Barnes asked me if I'd delivered the rifles to Ferrie. I said I had, and I also asked Barnes what they were for. He said the story he had gotten was: an assassination attempt on Juan Bosch."

Two years earlier, in May 1961, the CIA had played a major role in the assassination of Dominican Republic dictator Rafael Trujillo.[3] Bosch, who eventually took over the Caribbean nation's government, proved to be too far to the left for the CIA's liking. Adding credence to Morrow's story is the fact that Bosch was indeed overthrown, in a CIA-backed coup d'état, on September 25, 1963.[4] He was not assassinated, however. Morrow says he does not know whether the three Mannlicher rifles he sent South with David Ferrie were utilized in the Dominican Republic.

"After I'd delivered the rifles, and Barnes and Kohly had briefly described this operation against Bosch, the subject came up again. I think this was sometime in September. The wild part was, Tracy Barnes mentioned that it may not be Bosch who the group in New Orleans really wanted the rifles for. He said it could be anyone—right up to the President."

The date of the Bosch coup, September 25, coincides with the time frame when Nagell says a third plot against President Kennedy was now scheduled—"for the latter part of September, presumably in Washington, D.C."

Morrow, Nagell, and Tracy Barnes

In *Betrayal,* Morrow wrote that "Ed Kendricks," a pseudonym he used for Tracy Barnes, had briefed "Richard Carson Fillmore" about the strange goings-on in New Orleans. "Fillmore" was told about Ferrie's flight back from Baltimore with the three Mannlicher rifles. "Kendricks" then instructed "Fillmore" to go to New Orleans and register in a hotel under the name "Joseph Kramer." Fillmore was to find out who was running a certain paramilitary operation training Cuban exiles at Lake Pontchartrain, just outside New Orleans. Using a cover as a paramilitary Minuteman, Fillmore was to "penetrate" the David Ferrie-Guy Banister group. Fillmore was also to ascertain whether Oswald, whom Kendricks had utilized before in the USSR, was acting as an FBI informant. Kendricks had arranged for the Pentagon to supply a dossier on "Joseph Kramer" to the FBI, so that when Guy Banister queried his own contacts at the bureau, Fillmore's credentials would be kosher.[5]

Several factors add credibility to Morrow's novelesque account. For one, there is Nagell's own recollection, as set down in an October 1967 letter to Art Greenstein. There, thinly disguising himself as "Triple-Man Zero," he wrote that he had received instructions from someone at CIA headquarters to join a Cuban exile affiliate of Alpha 66 in New Orleans, in the guise of a rifleman, to "find out if things [were] real."[6]

Also, Morrow could not just have plucked out of thin air that Nagell did indeed use the "Joseph Kramer" name as a pseudonym during this period. When I wrote Nagell asking about Morrow's claims, he responded: "I *am* curious as to how or why the author chose the name 'Richard Carson Fillmore,' since I did use the pseudonym 'Carson' on occasion, though not in Louisiana and not in July 1963. And, like practically everybody else who had any dealings with the Cuban community in those days, I *was* cognizant of the goings-on at Lake Pontchartrain."[7]

It also made sense that Nagell could have been asked by the CIA to check out Oswald's possible status as an FBI informant. Throughout Oswald's temporary surge into the New Orleans public eye, we have seen that just about everyone in touch with him that August was reporting to the FBI. Again, it must be asked how Oswald could have been innocently left off of the FBI's vast "Security Index"—unless the FBI was using him for its own purposes.

Orest Peña, the owner of New Orleans' Habana Bar, went public on a 1975 *CBS Reports* program that he had seen Oswald with New Orleans FBI agent Warren de Brueys on "numerous occasions." De Brueys was one of two local FBI men specifically assigned to keep tabs on pro- and anti-Castro activities. While de Brueys denied the allegation before the House Assassinations Committee, Peña maintains that the agent warned him to keep quiet about what he'd observed prior to his testimony before the Warren Commission. After the assassination, de Brueys had been called to Dallas to assist the FBI in its Oswald investigation.[8]

Tracy Barnes was not unfamiliar to Nagell either. In the Garrison files there is a memorandum of an assassination researcher's conversation with Nagell in 1969, recording Nagell as saying that both "Angel" and "Leopoldo" had worked in the past with "an outfit called Movement to Free Cuba, headed by Tracy Barnes." The same memo reported Nagell saying: "[David] Ferrie also knew both [Angel and Leopoldo]."[9]

After I alerted Nagell to the impending publication of Morrow's book, in mid-May of 1976 he sent a certified letter to then CIA director George Bush. Nagell wrote: "I am now advised by *a most reliable source* that while Mr. Morrow claims to have received much of his information about me from people in the Cuban exile community, a substantial portion of his account actually is based on unsupported allegations furnished to him by a CIA official who retired in 1974. (I have been given the name of that official and I am aware of the position that he occupied at CIA headquarters in 1974).

"I would urge that the CIA take immediate steps to have the references to me that are contained in Mr. Morrow's book deleted, for if the book is published in its present form, I fully intend to initiate a libel suit naming the CIA as one of the defendants."[10]

Nagell never filed his threatened libel suit. Nor would he comment further on Morrow's "unsupported allegations." In 1990 Morrow finally revealed to me that Barnes was one of his sources and "evidently was the CIA official who instigated sending Nagell down to New Orleans, because he suspected there was an assassination plot underfoot against Kennedy. The way I got it," Morrow said, "Nagell was working for CIA, or the DIA —it was kind of a mystery. Then something happened, he couldn't get ahold of Tracy Barnes. Barnes was doing something and was unavailable. So Nagell filed an FBI report, is what I heard, which had something to do with a fellow aka [also known as] Joseph Kramer."

That was as much as Morrow knew of Nagell. But that Nagell was still following the movements of Angel and Leopoldo is clear. On August 20, Nagell has written that he took 16mm still photographs of the exile pair, though he did not specify whether this occurred in New Orleans.[11] Four days before that, a man fitting Nagell's description of Leopoldo was observed in Oswald's proximity during the ex-Marine's final round of street leafleting. Miguel Cruz, a friend of Bringuier who was later interviewed by a Garrison investigator, remembered

a strong looking Latin-American type person around 25 or 30 years old who was a little taller than OSWALD and who weighed close to 200 pounds, standing in front of the Maison Blanche Building with a camera and taking pictures of OSWALD and other people. . . . He asked a few people where they were from and seemed interested in what was going on. He was dressed in a suit and tie and wore dark glasses.[12]

As it happens, Nagell was not the only man involved with Cuban exiles who sought to alert the authorities about a Kennedy-aimed plot. Another was Garrett Brock Trapnell, who at this writing remains confined in the federal penitentiary at Marion, Illinois, serving a life sentence for the 1972 hijacking of a TWA jetliner.[13]

The Warning of Garrett Trapnell

It is on record among the National Archives documents on the assassination that, on August 19, 1963, Garrett Trapnell first alerted the FBI that he had been solicited by a Cuban group to participate in what he then

described as a kidnap/assassination attempt against Robert Kennedy. It
was scheduled for September 1963. In 1978, Trapnell would tell me that
President Kennedy was actually the proposed target.

Because of the remarkable parallels to Nagell's own account, Trapnell's
story is worth recounting—not only the September date and then-planned
locale (Washington, D.C.), but also Trapnell's eventual belief that those
who approached him were anti-Castro exiles *posing* as G-2 agents of Fidel
Castro. His description of one of them—a Hispanic male approximately
twenty-eight years old, of medium height, and weighing about two hundred pounds—is also a close match for Nagell's "Leopoldo." And,
Trapnell says, he encountered the conspirators while he was involved with
the exile group known as Alpha 66.

Trapnell is a fascinating fellow in his own right. The black sheep of a
distinguished military family (his father was a naval commander), he was
arrested more than twenty times for robberies and other crimes. Yet he
became so skilled at faking mental illness that he repeatedly got himself
hospitalized and then escaped. Trapnell's exploits are the subject of a
book-length study, *The Fox Is Crazy, Too,* by Eliot Asinof.

For six months in 1958, Trapnell says he was in Cuba, helping train
members of Castro's rebel band. Captured by Batista's forces, he was
temporarily imprisoned and then deported to Miami. There, in the early
1960s, he claims to have begun working for Cuban G-2 intelligence and to
have infiltrated various exile organizations, including Alpha 66. "I'm not a
Communist or a Socialist," Trapnell would later explain, "but I just
couldn't stomach the *gusanos.* I didn't believe in the U.S. putting its thumb
on a Cuban republic trying to do something for itself."[14]

I originally heard about Trapnell from a lawyer friend in 1976. Given his
reputation for fabrication, it would be tempting to dismiss Trapnell's story
—were it not for FBI files from the crucial August 1963 period concerning
interviews with both Trapnell and his wife.[15] Prior to my getting in touch
with Trapnell at the Marion penitentiary, I located Warren Commission
Document 196. It recounted information he had provided to FBI special
agent Francis L. Pearthree on August 19, 1963. At the time, Trapnell was
incarcerated in the Kent County Jail in Chestertown, Maryland, having
been arrested two months earlier "in connection with fradulent checks
issued for the rental of a boat." His wife, Ingrid, had been with him when
he was arrested and had turned over to a policeman "a foreign-make
semi-automatic rifle, make not known."

Trapnell told the FBI that while in Miami in May or June of 1963, he
had met with four Cubans at a building in Little Havana. "He described
these persons as loyal 'Castroites' although all had come to the United
States as refugees from Castro." They drank, smoked marijuana, and
sniffed cocaine. And, according to the FBI file, "The group talked freely

with TRAPNELL and told him that the four of them planned to kidnap and kill ROBERT KENNEDY . . . in an effort to sabotage any relationship between the Cuban Revolutionary Movement and the United States."

The file went on: "The group allegedly exhibited gasoline company road maps of Virginia with marked routes . . . a professional looking floor plan of a house that they claimed to be that of the Attorney General at McLean, Virginia, drawn on white paper approximately 18 inches by 24 inches, and small photographs supposedly of the KENNEDY homes at Palm Beach, Florida, and Hyannis Port, Massachusetts, and of the yacht the 'Honey Fitz.'

"In addition, the group showed him a closet in this building wherein were stored at least 14 rifles, four 38 caliber revolvers, fragmentation and concussion hand grenades and some plastic explosives. . . ."

Trapnell was told that the group had considered an assassination attempt earlier in the spring but "felt that there had been a leak, that the authorities knew of their plot so they decided to postpone the attempt until late August or September 1963." (Trapnell's report of a springtime plot also dovetailed with Nagell's story of the L.A. conspiracy where Vaughn Marlowe was considered for recruitment.)

The FBI report continued: "The group allegedly gave TRAPNELL one of the rifles which he described as a 7.62-millimeter, semi-automatic or full automatic rifle with ventilated ribs extending the full length of the barrel, a tripod under the muzzle, with the wood stock removed and replaced with a removable metal stock. This rifle which was allegedly of Russian make, resembled the U.S. Browning automatic rifle. . . ."

The day after providing this information, on August 20 Trapnell was admitted to the Clifton T. Perkins Hospital in Jessup, Maryland, "for observation and study." The FBI claimed to check Immigration and Naturalization Service records at Miami and came up "negative for all individuals" whom Trapnell had named, except for one. But, the FBI said, "it was determined through interviews that he could not possibly be the MIGUEL AMADOR FUENTES who TRAPNELL said was a party to this plot."

On August 29, two FBI agents reinterviewed Trapnell, who repeated his story and "protested that he was telling the truth and that he really cared for the life of the KENNEDY family." Trapnell's wife was also interviewed. She remembered seeing a Russian-made gun that summer, in their apartment in Baltimore, "and she asked TRAPNELL where the gun came from and he did not answer her. . . . She knows that TRAPNELL had associated with Cubans but he never introduced them to her nor did they come to their house in Miami."

That was where things stood until November 22, 1963. Perkins Hospital

President John F. Kennedy
AP/WIDE WORLD PHOTOS

Richard Case Nagell (right), handcuffed and being led into federal custody in El Paso, after getting himself arrested outside the State National Bank.
EL PASO HERALD-POST

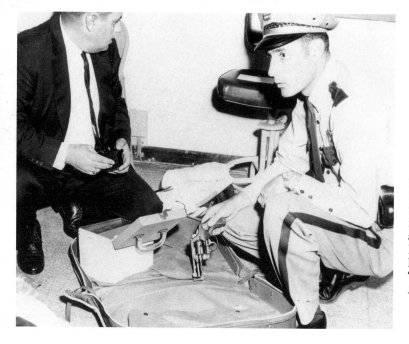

El Paso policeman Jir Bundren (right), going through belongings f in the trunk of Nagell after the bank incide Detective Gordon Bi holding Nagell's Min "spy camera."
EL PASO TIMES

Lee Harvey Oswald, in
ody of the Dallas police
the accused assassin of
President Kennedy.
DALLAS MORNING NEWS

Nagell in the El Paso
police line-up on
September 20, 1963.
EL PASO HERALD-POST

Marina Oswald.
AP/WIDE WORLD PHOTOS

The late Bernard Fensterwald, Jr., Nagell's lawyer for the U.S. Court of Claims lawsuit against the Pentagon and founder of the Assassination Archives and Research Center.
J. GARY SHAW COLLECTION

Nagell's 1968 passport, issued to him shortly after his release from prison, which he was using when arrested by East German authorities that summer.

A Nagell military I.D. card, issued to him in 1969.

Nagell, as he looked while working for Military Intelligence in Tokyo in 1957.

Nagell's two young children, Robert (left) and Teri, isolated from Nagell until he was able to track down their whereabouts in 1970.
PHOTO COURTESY OF ARTHUR G. GREENSTEIN

SOCIAL SECURITY
ACCOUNT NUMBER
433-54-3937
LEE HARVEY OSWALD

Photocopy of an Oswald Social Security card,
sent by Nagell to Arthur Greenstein. (See
Appendix A, page 731.)

swald's Uniformed Services Identification Card,
ized by the Dallas police after the assassination.
ote the Department of Defense overstamp.

A Nagell military I.D. card (top), and another
Oswald Uniformed Services I.D. which was in
Nagell's possession. Note the different
signature, photograph, and lack of Department
of Defense overstamp. (See Appendix A.)

Robert Clayton Buick in 1990. While a bullfighter in Mexico City during the early '60s, Buick says he worked for U.S. intelligence, shadowing Nagell, Oswald, and others at the Hotel Luma.
PHOTO BY DICK RUSSELL

Vaughn Marlowe, as he looked in 1963 when, as an executive committee member of Los Angeles' Fair Play for Cuba Committee, he was befriended by Nagell and considered for recruitment into an assassination plot against JFK.

Arthur Greenstein, pictured at a party in 1990. Befriended by Nagell in Mexico City in the autumn of 1962, Greenstein later became the recipient of many Nagell letters from prison about the assassination.
PHOTO COURTESY OF ARTHUR G. GREENSTEIN

Colonel William C. Bishop, circa 1980. As a CIA contract agent, Bishop worked closely with Cuban exile groups and said he ordered surveillance on Nagell in New Orleans in 1963.
J. GARY SHAW COLLECTION

Robert Morrow, former CIA contract agent, holding on of four 7.35-mm Mannlicher-Carcano rifles that he purchased shortly before the Kennedy assassination fo delivery to a group in New Orleans.

George and Jeanne de Mohrenschildt, who befriended the Oswalds in Dallas; George de Mohrenschildt maintained he was acting under orders from the CIA.
AP/WIDE WORLD PHOTOS

ark Gayn, a Canadian foreign correspondent whom Nagell alleged was a Soviet agent and used the same alias ("Joseph Kramer") as Nagell used when he warned the FBI of a JFK assassination plot.
THOMAS FISHER RARE BOOKS LIBRARY, UNIVERSITY OF TORONTO

Desmond FitzGerald, chief of the CIA's Far Eastern Division in the 1950s and head of the Cuban task force in 1962–63. Nagell says he was warned of the Oswald plot.
THE NEW YORK TIMES

James Angleton, in charge of the CIA's Counterintelligence Division until his dismissal in 1974.
UPI/BETTMANN

Winston Scott, CIA Station Chief in Mexico City, 1956–69, and who may have had a "double agent" role with Soviet intelligence.
PHOTO COURTESY OF MICHAEL SCOTT

John Paisley, high-ranking CIA research analyst and possible KGB "mole."
AP/WIDE WORLD PHOTOS

Tracy Barnes, chief of the CIA's Domestic Operations Division and alleged by Robert Morrow to have early knowledge of Oswald's activities.
PHOTO COURTESY OF YALE UNIVERSITY

David Phillips, head of clandestine activities and then Cuban affairs for the CIA in Mexico City, 1962–63.
PRINT COURTESY OF THE ASSASSINATION ARCHIVES AND RESEARCH CENTER

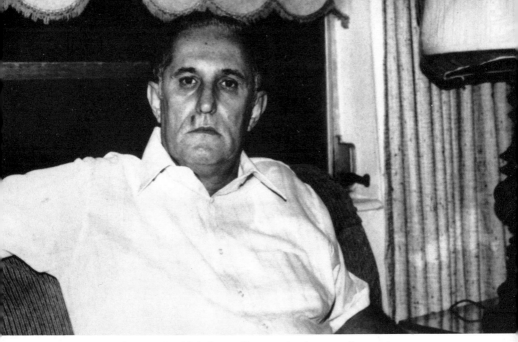

ntonio Veciana, leader of the Alpha 66 Cuban exile organization; says he met
wald in the presence of "Maurice Bishop."
INT COURTESY OF THE ASSASSINATION ARCHIVES AND RESEARCH CENTER

Rolando Masferrer ("El Tigre"),
Cuban exile leader.
J. GARY SHAW COLLECTION

Garrett Trapnell, who alerted the
FBI in August 1963 about an attempt
to recruit him into a Kennedy
assassination plot.   UPI/BETTMANN

uban Premier Fidel Castro.
P/WIDE WORLD PHOTOS

Oswald passing out Fair Play for Cuba leaflets, August 1963, New Orleans. Note Hispanic man (never identified) in Oswald's company, also Asian individual with arms akimbo above his head.
NATIONAL ARCHIVES

Guy Banister, right-wing associate of Oswald, David Ferrie, and Cuban exiles at 544 Camp Street.
J. GARY SHAW COLLECTION

Carlos Bringuier, the Cuban exile who engaged Oswald in the street altercation in New Orleans.
PRINT COURTESY OF THE ASSASSINATION ARCHIVE AND RESEARCH CENTER

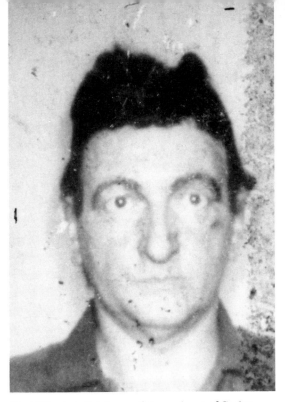

David Ferrie, pilot, hypnotist, employee of Carlos Marcello, and alleged associate of Oswald.
J. GARY SHAW COLLECTION

Carlos Marcello, head of the New Orleans Mob.
PRINT COURTESY OF THE ASSASSINATION ARCHIVES AND RESEARCH CENTER

Sergio Arcacha-Smith, Cuban exile whom Nagell says was a "peripheral character" in the JFK assassination conspiracy.
J. GARY SHAW COLLECTION

Billionaire Texas oilman H.L. Hunt, said by ex-employees to have purchased first copy of Zapruder film and ordered a check on security surrounding Oswald in custody.
PRINT COURTESY OF THE ASSASSINATION ARCHIVES AND RESEARCH CENTER

Nelson Bunker Hunt, the oilman's son and a supporter of right-wing causes.
MARK PEARLSTEIN/BLACK STAR

Joseph Milteer, Georgia racist who spoke with FBI informant of JFK assassination plot ten days before it occurred.
J. GARY SHAW COLLECTION

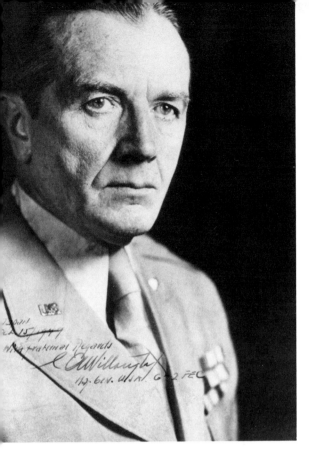

Charles Willoughby, General MacArthur's Chief of Intelligence, right-wing extremist and ally of the Hunt oil family.
GENERAL DOUGLAS MACARTHUR MEMORIAL

Major General Edwin Walker, who believes Larrie Schmidt may have been involved with Oswald in shooting at him in April 1963.
AP/WIDE WORLD PHOTOS

Larrie Schmidt (right), founder of Conservatism-USA and alleged accomplice of Oswald in Walker shooting incident.
PHOTO ORIGINALLY APPEARED IN *LOOK*

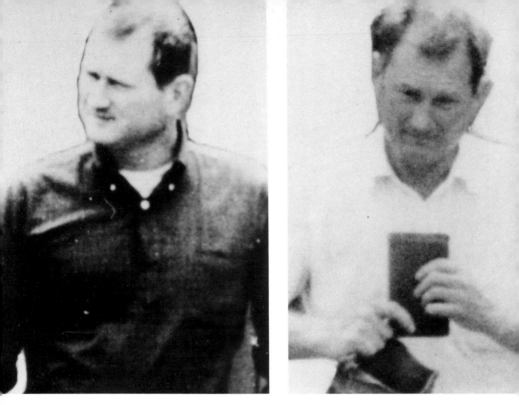

The Mexico City "mystery men" wrongly identified by the CIA as "Oswald" in the autumn of 1963. Nagell says these are two different people.
J. GARY SHAW COLLECTION

Albert Osborne, the elderly "preacher" who accompanied Oswald on the bus trip to Mexico City, September 1963.
J. GARY SHAW COLLECTION

Jimmy Hoffa, Teamster's Union boss.
AP/WIDE WORLD PHOTOS

Santos Trafficante, Jr., boss of the Tampa, Florida, Mob.
AP/WIDE WORLD PHOTOS

Jean Souetre, French mercenary deported from Dallas after the assassination.
J. GARY SHAW COLLECTION

FBI Director J. Edgar Hoover.
AP/WIDE WORLD PHOTOS

STATE OF CALIFORNIA   )
)   **SS:**
COUNTY OF LOS ANGELES)

AFFIDAVIT

I, Richard C. Nagell, being first sworn, depose and say:

In September 1963, the exact date of which I am capable of verifying, I dispatched a letter via registered mail addressed to "Mr. John E. Hoover, Director, Federal Bureau of Investigation, United States Department of Justice, Washington 25, D. C." The envelope in which this letter was enclosed bore the same address, in addition to the return address "Joseph Kramer, Apdo. Postal 88-Bis, Mexico, D. F., Mexico," and was mailed within the United States. The letter was neatly typewritten and composed in the style and format used by operational personnel of the Central Intelligence Agency in writing their reports; that is, it was clear and concise, with the names of persons and organizations typed in caps.

In the aforesaid letter, I advised Mr. Hoover of a conspiracy (although I did not use the word "conspiracy") involving Lee Harvey Oswald "to murder the Chief Executive of the United States, (President) John F. Kennedy." I indicated that the attempt would take place "during the latter part of September (1963), probably on the 26th, 27th, 28th or 29th," presumably at Washington, D. C. I furnished a complete and accurate physical description of Mr. Oswald, listing his true name, two of his aliases, his residence address and other pertinent facts about him. I disclosed sufficient data about the conspiracy (citing an overt act which constituted a violation of federal law) to warrant an immediate investigation if not the arrest of Mr. Oswald. I revealed something about myself which incriminated me on another matter. I stated "by the time you receive this letter, I shall have departed the USA for good." I signed the letter with the name "Joseph Kramer," an alias of a known Communist (Soviet) agent then residing in Canada, and also an alias that I had used during my meetings with two FBI agents in January 1963 at Miami, Florida, who in turn used the name "The Tacos."

I am willing to undergo a polygraph examination relative to any and all statements made herein.

Richard C. Nagell
RICHARD C. NAGELL

SWORN TO AND SUBSCRIBED BEFORE ME THIS 21st DAY OF NOVEMBER 1975.

WITNESS my hand and official seal:

Signature _Albert S. Fujimoto_

> OFFICIAL SEAL
> ALBERT S. FUJIMOTO
> NOTARY PUBLIC - CALIFORNIA
> LOS ANGELES COUNTY
> My Commission Expires Oct. 2, 1976

Nagell's sworn affidavit concerning his warning letter to J. Edgar Hoover September 1963.

attendant Irving Scheuer advised the FBI that shortly before suppertime, Trapnell "had given him a slip of paper on which TRAPNELL had written the type of a gun which TRAPNELL stated had been used to kill President KENNEDY. Scheuer stated that TRAPNELL had been listening to the radio all afternoon following the assassination. . . ." The paper said:

MIKE AMADOR FUENTES
#1 German Mauser
Cal. 7.65 MM or
#2 Tokarev 7.62 MM
11-22-63.

For the first twenty-four hours after the assassination, the initial police reports described the weapon found near Oswald's alleged sniper's nest as a 7.65 Mauser bolt-action rifle. CIA files, as late as November 25, were still calling it a Mauser—although the Warren Commission would conclude that the only rifle Oswald owned was an Italian-made 6.5mm Mannlicher-Carcano.[16] It is quite possible, of course, that Trapnell could simply have heard the Mauser reference on the radio.

But Trapnell's alternate mention of a 7.62mm Russian-made Tokarev is interesting for another reason. Recall Rolando Masferrer, whom Nagell was shadowing in late January as the Miami exile conversed with "Angel." A 1964 FBI file on Masferrer reports that he was contacted during January or early February 1963 (the report does not say by whom) about "furnishing some arms" to an exile group intending to infiltrate into Cuba. Masferrer "had given instructions to [blank], his Miami representative, to relinquish some weapons—including two Tokarevs. Masferrer advised that the Tokarev is a Russian gun of 7.63 calibre, self-loading, which sells for about $40 in the United States and is available for purchase through mail order. Masferrer said that the Tokarev guns obtained by his organization were bought from a gun dealer in California, name not known, which had been obtained from a magazine advertisement."[17]

This may be pure coincidence, but Trapnell's "slip of paper" cannot be dismissed out of hand. Oswald also mail-ordered for a .38-caliber revolver at the same time (the end of January 1963), from a California gun dealer (Seaport Traders) he found through a magazine advertisement. The gun Trapnell says he was personally provided by the conspirators in the spring of 1963 was described by the FBI in August as a 7.63mm Russian-made weapon.

The FBI came again to see Trapnell on December 4, 1963. He said he had first met the man he knew as "Fuentes" while they were briefly stationed together in the Army at Fort Campbell, Kentucky, and then again when both were in the mountains with Castro. Trapnell reiterated the story he told in August, adding, "someone in the group had said, 'We are going to get KENNEDY in the fall.' It was TRAPNELL's impression that ROBERT KENNEDY was the target. . . ."

Trapnell also added the claim that he had been introduced at the springtime Miami planning session to an "Oswaldo," whom he now realized was Lee Harvey Oswald. I found this dubious, given that there is no record of Oswald ever having been in Miami, and Nagell's assertion that Oswald was not brought into the conspiracy until midsummer in New Orleans.

Then, a final FBI interview with Trapnell, on February 11, 1964, brought an apparent retraction. The bureau file had Trapnell "admitting" he made it all up, "that he had invented the story to confuse and complicate the facts surrounding the local criminal charges against him in Chestertown, Maryland."

A Visit to the Marion Pen

Despite Trapnell's 1964 disclaimer, I remained curious about all he had said, and we struck up a correspondence in 1977. Trapnell again began stating definitively that his original story was legitimate. Except for one thing: "The men who attempted to involve me in the assassination of JFK in the spring-summer of 1963," he wrote me, "were not Cuban G2 nationals, or resident agents of G2; they were exiles with the assistance of white adult males whom I assumed were US nationals. . . . [You should] examine the exile's role in conjunction with dissident CIA types."[18]

After I sent Trapnell copies of the 1963–64 FBI files about him, he wrote back that "their reports were 'doctored' to completely change the entire picture of what I originally told them. This is the first time that I've seen this material. . . . Nevertheless, the facts do remain that I did tell them about the approach to me *prior* to the assassination and that they themselves sure seemed to have gone to a hell of a lot of trouble or 'cover-up' for someone they felt was either a lunatic or a liar!"

Trapnell said that neither Nagell's name nor pseudonyms rang any bells. "No, I don't recall the name Leopoldo," he responded to my questioning, "but the name Angel or Angelo comes back to me."[19]

The maximum-security Marion penitentiary is the modern-day Alcatraz. Most prisoners are sent here after "failure to adjust" to institutional life elsewhere. Housing such famous criminals as arms dealer Edwin Wilson, Soviet spy John Walker, and hit man Charles Harrelson, Marion is considered the end of the line for federal prisoners. It was March 10, 1978, when

I drove up along its acres of rolling, manicured lawn about fifteen miles east of the southern Illinois town of Carbondale.

Garrett Trapnell entered the visitors' room, squinting into the harsh daylight that streamed through the windows. He stood about six feet tall, and his slightly bearded face looked drained and older than his forty years. We sat facing each other on folding chairs. Throughout the interview, Trapnell was agitated and hesitant. "I don't want this to come out that I'm any sort of a snitch, you understand?" he began.

Still, he revealed more than he had told the FBI about his purported encounter with the Kennedy conspirators in the late spring of 1963. He reiterated that he had worked for Cuban G-2 intelligence in the early 1960s, "infiltrating exile organizations with harebrained schemes to discredit them and the U.S. government." And he had been asked to come down from Baltimore, to the meeting in Miami, by a Cuban he called Miguel Fuentes.

"His last name wasn't really Fuentes," Trapnell said. "I'm not going to give his real name. The guy exists, believe me. I'm not gonna go into any more than that."

Trapnell ran through basically the same story he had told the FBI fifteen years before—the meeting at a corner building with a plate-glass front on Flagler Street, the discussion about going after the Kennedys, the guns in the closet, and the Russian Tokarev semi-automatic rifle he was given.

"There was a lot of feeling out," he said. "This broad who was there at the meeting did some talking. I did a lot of listening. They talked about hitting Kennedy in Palm Beach at the family estate. If not there, then Hyannis Port, Massachusetts, while he was sailing. They were discussing the best way to do it, and I told them a sniper would be the best way. I don't know what I'm leaving myself open for here but anyway, they all agreed to that. Snipers firing from several different points, and that a main signal would have to be given. You've already pretested the weapons. What you do is have something—a street sign, anything—and a guy standing beside it takes his hat off. He's telling you that your target's right on the money.

"We had several conferences, then I said I might be interested. So I took the rifle. It didn't have a stock on it, but it was a beautiful weapon."

At the time, Trapnell assumed that the "six or seven people" at the meetings were working with Castro's G-2. This was what "Fuentes" had told him. "See, I can't say they were connected. They were fronted, what their ulterior motive was I can't say."

Which group fronted them? I asked.

"I can't remember the group's name. I told the FBI at the time what it was."

Years later, Trapnell would have many questions about the meaning of it all. That spring of 1963, he had been able to penetrate the Alpha 66 group, which he described as "one of the go-getters, one of the real terror organizations." Might Fuentes actually have gotten back in touch with him through their auspices? I wondered. "Well, there were two Americans at the meetings," Trapnell said, "who I definitely think now were U.S. intelligence agents."

Trapnell still insisted that someone "referred to as Oswaldo was there at the second meeting. I told this to the FBI and Secret Service before the assassination. He was looking and nodding yes mostly. As far as talking, he was interested to find that I spoke Spanish. Fuentes was telling them about my experiences, that I'd been in a Cuban prison down there, and this young guy [Oswaldo] asked me a couple pointed questions about Cuba, and I answered, and that was that."

Trapnell said he decided early on not to participate in the plan. Why then, I asked, did he wait several months before he spoke about these meetings to federal authorities? After a long pause, Trapnell replied: "Well, it wasn't a sense of patriotism, it was a matter of business. I was in jail; I contact the FBI and maybe the CIA, thought maybe we could do some trading off.

"The morning after Kennedy got shot, a whole squadron of FBI came to see me, must have been five or six. One told me right out, 'If there's any more of this, we know how to handle you.' I said, 'Wait a minute.' The agent said, 'Don't worry, just be crazy and everything will be all right.' I said, 'Okay.' That's why I said I'd made the whole thing up. A few months after the assassination, I was released from the hospital. I'd received a paycheck while I was in there, so you figure it out. I had no job, you understand? I had so much money when I left the hospital, they had to take me to the bank.

"I think the FBI had their hand and glove in what happened to Kennedy. The fact that they knew about it, and didn't stop it. That's what I believe."

A guard watching us from across the room signaled that our forty-five-minute interview was at an end. A little over two months later, on May 25, 1978, Trapnell's girlfriend, Barbara Oswald, chartered a helicopter and hijacked it, trying to force a landing in the prison yard in an attempt to free him. She was shot and killed in a struggle with the pilot on the approach to Marion. That December the woman's teenaged daughter Robin hijacked a TWA jetliner with eighty-three passengers aboard. She said she had three sticks of dynamite strapped to her chest and threatened to detonate them unless the plane landed at Marion and picked up Trapnell. She surrendered peacefully after holding the plane for ten hours.[20]

Garrett Trapnell was confined to his cell. Still in Marion today, in recent years someone else has struck up a correspondence with him—John Hinckley, in prison for attempting to assassinate President Reagan in 1981.[21] The ironies of recent history never seem to end.

In one of his letters to me, without any solicitation on the subject, Trapnell also said: ". . . Why don't you write to David Atlee Phillips and ask him if he knows Trapnell? I met him in 1963 during one of the interviews after I had stated what I knew . . . we spoke in Spanish and he was very solicitive. He's a gin and tonic drinker and also a Cuba-libre imbiber. He knows all about the place on Flagler!"[22] (the Miami street where Trapnell says the planning meeting took place).

"Maurice Bishop," Veciana, and Oswald

It was a sultry June day in 1976. In a hotel lobby in Miami Beach, Antonio Veciana, the former leader of Alpha 66, had brought his lovely daughter, Ana, to assist in translating his halting English. Veciana proceeded to recount the story of a meeting with his U.S. intelligence case officer, "Maurice Bishop," who was accompanied by a taciturn young man whom Veciana later recognized as Lee Harvey Oswald.

"Bishop had previously contacted me for other meetings in Dallas, other times," Veciana said. "Sometime late in August of 1963, when I arrived at the Dallas airport, Bishop had given me the address to a building, either a bank or insurance company. There I met Bishop in the company of this young guy. The three of us walked to a cafeteria. The young guy did not say one word. He was very quiet, very strange. He was with us only ten or fifteen minutes. Then when I take a cup of coffee, Bishop says to the young fellow: 'I'll meet you in two or three hours.' The guy left and Bishop and I talked about the movement and plans.

"I never knew why Oswald was with Bishop. I didn't even know Oswald was Oswald, until the assassination happened and I saw his picture. After the assassination, the FBI contacted me to ask several questions. At first I was worried, but the agent who interviewed me said it was a matter of routine, nothing important. I didn't tell the agent anything, because I thought it would harm the movement.

"I never asked Bishop about Oswald, because Bishop always told me that in this type of work, you just do things, you don't ask. I had a cousin, Guillermo Ruiz, who worked with the Cuban [G-2] intelligence service in Mexico City. After the assassination, sometime early in 1964, Bishop said to me: Did I think by getting my cousin a considerable amount of money, would he say he'd talked to Oswald, to make it appear Oswald was working for Castro? Because of this, I asked Bishop if it was true Oswald had been talking with Castro agents. Bishop said it did not matter if it was true, what was important was to get my cousin to make that statement. Bishop didn't bring up the topic again. Several months later, I brought it up. Bishop said there was no need to talk about that plan any longer.

"I always thought Bishop was working with Oswald during the assassination. I believe that the CIA wanted to pin the blame for the assassination on Cuba. This is why I believe that Cuba was not involved. I do not think that the agency as a whole was involved, but that certain renegade members were involved. I think that Lee Harvey Oswald, if he didn't work directly for the agency, worked with people connected with it."

It was an astonishing revelation for the former leader of Alpha 66—who admittedly still wanted to get rid of Castro—to make. Veciana had worked with "Maurice Bishop" in a number of assassination plots against Fidel (see Chapter Twelve). The last one had been in 1971, in Chile. At the time, Salvador Allende, who would himself be assassinated (with the help of the CIA) in 1973, was about to come to power.

"Allende was a Marxist and we knew that once he was voted in, Castro would go to Chile," Veciana recalled. "While Allende was still campaigning, Bishop contacted me to talk to several people. Friends of mine among the exiles. We were to prepare to get Castro killed. A lot of the officers of the Chilean Army were very cooperative with me and Bishop. They knew everything—when Castro would arrive, where he was going to make an appearance. The plan was to have TV cameras with machine guns inside. We got two agents, they were able to get IDs as pressmen and would handle these cameras. All this was planned directly by Bishop, from Bolivia.

"We all went to Chile as diplomats, by car through Peru. It was very similar to the Kennedy assassination, because the person Bishop assigned to kill Castro would later himself be killed. He was going to get planted with papers to make it appear he was a Moscow Castro agent who turned traitor—fake documentation that could be recognized as being from Moscow. But it never got off the ground. One of the agents had an appendicitis atack and had to be rushed to the hospital. The other agent said he wouldn't do it alone."

Veciana reached across a little table and handed me a sketch of "Maurice Bishop" that he had been requested to draw by congressional investigator Gaeton Fonzi. When Fonzi's boss, Pennsylvania senator Richard Schweiker, saw the sketch, he was convinced he knew who it was: a CIA official who had "retired" in 1975 to establish the Association of Former Intelligence Officers (AFIO), whose purpose was to defend the CIA against what he termed the "snowballing innuendo" of its media critics.[23]

This was David Atlee Phillips, who in 1962–63 was the CIA's leading anti-Castro specialist in Mexico City (see Chapter Nine).

David Phillips and "Maurice Bishop"

Born in Fort Worth, Texas, in 1923, David Phillips had started out trying to make it as an actor in New York. When World War II intervened, he became a bombardier who, after being shot down over Austria, managed a daring escape from a German POW camp and made it back to the Allied lines. After the war, Phillips bought a small English-language newspaper in Chile and was promptly hired by the new CIA. "It was a 'dangle operation,' " Phillips would later recall. "Other secret agents were supposed to think I was the chief of U.S. intelligence there. They paid me $50 a month, and the first time a Soviet KGB agent approached me, it occurred to me that I should be making $60."

By 1954, Phillips was a "full-time contract man" posing as a businessman in Guatemala, where he helped orchestrate the CIA coup that overthrew the government of Jacobo Arbenz Guzman. Also serving in Mexico, Venezuela, and Lebanon, Phillips was working undercover in Havana when Castro's revolution succeeded in 1959. Moving to Washington to serve as the CIA's propaganda chief for the Bay of Pigs invasion, Phillips then went on to Mexico City.[24]

He was the CIA's clandestine action chief there when Nagell arrived during the Cuban Missile Crisis period. Then, early in 1963, Phillips assumed control of the agency's Cuban operations desk in the capital. His new task, as he described it, "would be to monitor the Cuban embassy in Mexico City." His reassignment occurred when a man he described as one of the CIA's "Knights Templar" came to Mexico "to review the station's Cuban efforts." That man was Desmond FitzGerald.[25]

There were many reasons besides a close physical resemblance to "Maurice Bishop" why congressional investigators came to focus on David Phillips as Veciana's contact. "Bishop" and Phillips both had Texas accents, and both spoke French as well as Spanish. Phillips had been stationed in Havana when Veciana first met "Bishop" in 1960. In Phillips's 1977 autobiography, *The Night Watch,* he had cited a particular Cuban restaurant as his favorite eating spot. It was the same restaurant that Veciana mentioned to Fonzi—more than a year before Phillips's book came out—as being a casual meeting ground between himself and "Bishop."[26]

The fact that "Bishop" was aware of Veciana's cousin, a Cuban intelligence official in Mexico City, made it clear that he was someone quite knowledgeable about the situation there. Then, when the assassination attempt against Castro in Chile was being planned in 1971, Phillips had been promoted to run the CIA's Western Hemisphere Division. In that capacity he was in charge of a task force looking to prevent the election of Chile's Allende.[27]

But the House Assassinations Committee was never able to get a positive identification from Veciana, even after Fonzi brought the exile and Phillips face to face at a meeting of the AFIO in October 1976. Ed Lopez, another congressional investigator who was aware of the encounter, told me: "There was definitely a real look of recognition in Veciana. I have no doubt that Phillips was Bishop, from the way Veciana responded to questions. When Gaeton asked, 'Is it him?,' I remember Veciana saying, 'Does he have a brother?' "[28]

Sometime later, Fonzi confronted Veciana on the matter a final time. "I would like you to tell me this one time very truthfully," Fonzi said. "Would you have told me if I had found Maurice Bishop?"

Veciana smiled, scratched his forehead, and gave the question careful thought. "Well, you know," he said, "I would like to talk with him first."[29]

That a high-ranking CIA official might have been in communication with Oswald in late August 1963 was, of course, of intense, ongoing concern to the House Assassinations Committee. Former CIA director John McCone first said he did recall a "Maurice Bishop" and believed he was a CIA employee. However, when the CIA reviewed its files at Congress's request, the agency concluded "that such a man did not exist, so far as CIA connections are concerned." McCone then withdrew his statement.[30]

Melvin Beck, the former undercover CIA operative in Mexico City, said this when I called and asked what he thought about David Phillips: "Not much. His specialty, as was mine, was propaganda operations—and I thought Phillips had some rotten stuff going on, where all the burdens fell on Third World countries."

Did Beck feel that Phillips was capable of having been involved with someone like Lee Harvey Oswald? "Capable of it? Yes. If there was any way of maneuvering somebody, I think Dave Phillips would have found it."[31]

During the Bay of Pigs planning, Joseph Burkholder Smith had personally supervised Phillips's propaganda role. Smith recalled Gaeton Fonzi showing him the Veciana sketch of "Bishop." "There was no question in my mind, it was Phillips," Smith told me in a telephone interview. "But I know Bishop was not his official pseudonym. Phillips was a pretty gung-ho guy, theatrical, a good self-promoter. The only thing I think subsequently is, when you're handling people, you sometimes say things you think they might like to hear. I know in the period after the Bay of Pigs, there were tremendous problems handling these Cuban exile types. And Phillips, as I say, could be theatrical."[32]

"Theater," of course, was not exactly the word to describe a possible Phillips association with Alpha 66's leader and with Oswald, of which Smith said he was simply not cognizant.

The House Assassinations Committee could never arrive at a definitive conclusion about either Veciana's veracity or the real identity of "Maurice Bishop." Phillips denied under oath ever using the pseudonym. But Phillips had long-standing ties to the other CIA officials whose names have cropped up in our narrative. He and Tracy Barnes went back to the Guatemalan coup that overthrew the Arbenz government in 1954 and then to the Bay of Pigs planning. Phillips was a close friend of Mexico City's CIA station chief Winston Scott and, as Mexico's Cuban expert, worked closely with Desmond FitzGerald in 1963.

This does not necessarily mean that Phillips told his superiors everything he was doing. Officially the CIA had broken off with Alpha 66 not long after the Cuban Missile Crisis. Veciana recalled glimpsing a memorandum that "Bishop" had written to someone who bore the initials "HH."[33] There would be three likely potential candidates for someone with those initials: E. Howard Hunt, Jr., then Tracy Barnes's covert-action specialist in the Domestic Operations Division; the wealthy Texas oilman H. L. Hunt; or even Howard Hughes, the Las Vegas billionaire whose aide Robert Maheu worked with the CIA and the Mob in setting up the early anti-Castro plots.

Was there a connection between Nagell and Phillips? In Nagell's correspondence, Phillips's name had come up on one occasion. This was in a mid-1970s letter to Art Greenstein, *before* Phillips's name ever came up with Congress in connection with "Maurice Bishop." Nagell phrased his remarks in his often customary manner of raising questions as potentialities.

"What's this?" he wrote. "Dave Phillips, titular head of Latin American operations (a position once held by Dizzy Fits: Desmond FitzGerald), organizing former U.S. intelligence officers to defend the CIA against those who attack it? Why the advertisement that he had been station chief in La Republica Dominicana, Brazil, Venezuela? Why nothing said about his capers in Mexico? Was he a mere accomplice in the N-matter?"

It seemed clear to me that the "N-matter" probably referred to Nagell himself. But in my meetings with Nagell, he was noncommittal about Phillips. He would say only that he was curious about the man "with sunspots below his eyes," adding that he would like to know whether the meeting where Veciana said he saw "Bishop" in Oswald's company occurred before August 20.[34]

The other question, of course, is the meaning behind Oswald's being in

"Bishop's" company that August of 1963. We will never know, at least not from David Phillips, who died of cancer in July 1988 at age sixty-five.

As for Antonio Veciana, there is a frightening postscript to his story. I kept my word and did not write about him for some time after our meetings in Miami. Then, in January 1977, someone apparently inside the House Assassinations Committee leaked Veciana's information to syndicated columnist Jack Anderson.[35] "A Mr. X enters the JFK mystery," Anderson's story was headlined—but it would not have been difficult for insiders to identify "Mr. X."

Veciana went on to testify in executive session before the congressional committee. Several weeks before the House report was to be released, in July 1979 Veciana was driving home from work when someone ambushed him in Miami's Little Havana. Four shots were fired, and one ricocheting bullet hit him in the side of the head. Veciana survived the attempt to kill him.

His oldest daughter, Ana, a reporter for the *Miami News*, would write soon after the effort to slay her father that Americans have never really understood "the violence that comes with Latin politics." Veciana has kept quiet ever since about the events of 1963.[36]

Taped Evidence

In March 1967, from his prison cell, Richard Nagell wrote a letter to his sister Eleanore Gambert. Nagell instructed her to contact Jim Garrison's office and inform the DA that he was willing to turn over "proof" of a conspiracy—"a recording tape"—providing certain conditions were met. These included a guarantee of anonymity and "that I shall not be required to disclose how the recording tape came into my possession or queried on any alleged relationship with the individuals whose voices are recorded thereon." Nor could "the person who currently has possession of the recording tape" be identified or questioned "outside of official channels."[37]

If these and other stipulations were met, Nagell would agree to meet with a Garrison representative. The man who came to see him, on April 10, 1967, at the Medical Center for Federal Prisoners in Springfield, Missouri, was William R. Martin. He had recently been hired onto Garrison's New Orleans staff as an assistant district attorney.

Martin's initial memorandum about Nagell to Garrison reveals:

> The subject was able, in some manner which he did not disclose, to infiltrate the assassination plot and, for a reason of his own which he did

not disclose, the subject was able to make a tape recording of four voices in conversation concerning the plot which ended in the assassination of President Kennedy. It is precisely this tape recording which the subject has decided to turn over to Mr. Garrison as soon as he possibly can.

As to how it might be obtained, Martin wrote that Nagell advised him as follows:

The tape in question, along with a variety of other tape recordings, papers and other items highly incriminating to the subject, are in a box or small trunk which the subject left in the safekeeping and care of an intimate and trusted friend. An arrangement was made between the subject and this friend that under no circumstances was this box or trunk or any of its contents to be released to any person whatsoever, other than the subject, unless the friend were to be approached by a person bearing a handwritten letter in the handwriting of the subject, which letter would have to be signed by the subject in a certain secret manner. If anyone were to approach the friend and attempt to obtain the box or any of its contents without first having obtained this letter signed in a secret manner, then, in that case, the friend had instructions to destroy anything and everything that had been left in his safekeeping by the subject.

Mr. Nagell then indicated to me that he was willing to whisper to me the name, address and telephone number of the friend with whom he had left this evidence but prior to doing so the subject asked me to pledge my word that . . . [this] would not be written down in this report . . . [since] copies of this report could conceivably leave this office and fall into the hands of the FBI or the CIA. The subject indicated that if this should happen, he was sure that the FBI would charge in on his friend, kick in his front door, and harass him into turning over all of the aforementioned material. He stated that "this material is my whole future" and indicated that he had to be particularly careful of how it was handled. . . ."

Martin went on that the friend's name and whereabouts were turned over to Garrison "for use at his discretion." Nagell, according to Martin, then "asked that I return to Springfield within a few days to attempt to see him under privileged circumstances since in his own words, 'time is of the essence.' "

Martin concluded that Nagell

is an extremely articulate and well spoken individual who seems to have full command of his senses and total recall of his activities and constantly mentions dates, times and places that pertain to matters concerning this investigation. . . . he also stated to me that the release of his tape recording to Mr. Garrison was his first step in seeing what he could do to "square himself" with this country.[38]

Over the next couple of months, things seemed to be proceeding smoothly toward obtaining the remarkable tape. Martin began functioning as Nagell's legal counsel. On June 7, 1967, he gave Martin a handwritten letter of introduction to his friend in Los Angeles. It instructed Frederick H. John to turn over "one of the small recording tapes," bearing a Houston label, located "in a box (cigar box, I believe) beneath my films on Korea." After doing so, Nagell asked John to "immediately dispose of all tape recordings that were in my trunk in September 1963, and also destroy my passport, and all 'embarrassing material.' "[39]

But by the time Nagell wrote again to his sister, on June 12, something had gone awry. He informed her: "I want you to know that one major cause of the recent setback in my dealing through Mr. Martin stems directly from his advisement that he is a former employee of the Central Intelligence Agency. He could have done no worse by telling me he was an ex-F.B.I. man. Regardless of his reasons for such advisement, I can only say it had the effect of making me extremely cautious and suspicious. . . . I intend to take whatever steps I deem appropriate to protect my interests in the matter at hand."

Martin, according to Nagell's later correspondence, was "an officer of the CIA assigned in an operational capacity to the Latin American directorate and . . . a past associate of Tracy Barnes [and] Desmond Fitzgerald. . . ."[40] Martin's apparent purpose was to ascertain what Nagell would say—and not say—concerning Barnes, FitzGerald, and the Kennedy assassination.

In 1967, Nagell somehow must have gotten word about this development to Frederick John in California. On June 20, Martin wrote Nagell that he had been able to locate his friend "with absolutely no trouble and managed to spend several hours in amiable conversation. . . . Unfortunately, however, the physical evidence that I had hoped to obtain was not available. Apparently it was the subject of a burglary sometime in 1964. . . ."

After this, Nagell terminated his relationship with William R. Martin. On July 8, Nagell wrote once more to his sister and informed her: "I can state with good foundation that if it [the tape] was stolen, it was not stolen in 1964. In the same vein, I can also say that while the item involved may indeed no longer be available, it is not in the custody of the opposition either."

At the time Garrison hired Martin, the DA says he had no idea about the investigator's prior employment with the CIA. Garrison's later suspicions that Martin was a CIA infiltrator on his staff will be examined in a later chapter. As for the tape, Nagell indicated to me that as of the late 1970s, anyway, it remained in safekeeping. I have tried in vain to locate Nagell's friend Frederick H. John.

But Nagell has set down on paper an outline of what is on the tape. Sometime between August 23 and 27, 1963, a meeting took place among four people. One of them was Oswald. Another was "Angel." A third party, by his own admission, was Nagell. The fourth individual remains unidentified.

Unknown to the conspirators, Nagell was making a "small, composite recording tape." The subject under discussion was assassinating President Kennedy in the latter part of September. There was also talk of killing Robert Kennedy and perhaps other "highly placed officials" of the American government.

The beginning of the dialogue was in Spanish, during which Nagell served as an interpreter for Oswald. The balance of the conversation was in English and, according to Nagell, Oswald's voice is audible on the tape. The name of Cuban exile Sergio Arcacha-Smith was mentioned during the discussion. The name "Raul" is also on the tape, a cover name for someone else whose true name Nagell would not disclose. For the most part, cover names were used in describing both persons and places.

In September 1963, Nagell would stash his evidence of a conspiracy, along with other pertinent material, with a friend in Los Angeles "for safekeeping." Its spool bore a "cover label" reading "Houston—August 23, 1962" or "Houston—August 27, 1962." In fact, Nagell says, "the tape was recorded at another location, outside the state of Texas, *between* August 23, 1963, and August 27, 1963."[41]

During those same four days, Oswald's whereabouts are unaccounted for. Twice during this period, Oswald listed himself as having applied for jobs at New Orleans photo studios; both companies deny that he did so. On the twenty-seventh, Oswald's signature appears on a form at the unemployment benefit claims office. But the FBI could not authenticate the signature as being his.[42]

On August 27, Nagell has indicated that, in some fashion, he alerted Desmond FitzGerald about what was transpiring. His "complaint" focused upon his agency contact—and FitzGerald's associate—in Mexico City, "Bob."[43]

On August 28, Oswald wrote a letter to the Central Committee of the Communist Party, U.S.A. He described having sought to "legally dissolve my United States citizenship" while in Moscow and asked for advice on whether, "handicapped as it were, by my past record, can I still, under these circumstances, compete with anti-progressive forces, aboveground or weather [sic] in your opinion I should always remain in the background, i.e., underground.

"Our opponents could use my background of residence in the U.S.S.R. against any cause which I join, by association, they could say the organization of which I am a member, is Russian controled, ect. [sic], I am sure you see my point. . . ."[44]

August 31: Oswald wrote to the managing editor of the Communist Party, U.S.A.'s newspaper, *The Worker*, in New York. Offering his services as a commercial photographer, he added: "My family and I shall, in a few weeks, be relocating into your area."[45]

September 1: Oswald wrote two more letters. To the U.S. Communist Party: "Please advise me as to how I can contact the Party in the Baltimore-Washington area, to which I shall relocate in October." To the CP's rival Socialist Workers Party: "Please advise me as to how I can get into direct contact with S.W.P. representatives in the Washington-Baltimore area. I and my family are moving to that area in October."[46]

Once again, Oswald was making contact with various leftist organizations—this time informing them with a "paper trail" that he was heading East, to the very locale where his involvement in an assassination plot against the president was scheduled.

The clock was ticking. And the ball was about to be passed, for better or for worse, into Richard Nagell's court.

Summary

Many matters began reaching a crescendo as the summer of 1963 progressed. At the same time that the CIA's Tracy Barnes asked Robert Morrow to purchase four Mannlicher-Carcano rifles—supposedly earmarked for a Dominican Republic coup—Morrow says that Nagell was dispatched by Barnes to New Orleans. There he was to infiltrate the Guy Banister-David Ferrie group that the Mannlichers were destined for.

In August, Garrett Trapnell alerted the FBI about an approach made to him several months earlier by a Cuban group targeting the Kennedys. As with Nagell's September warning, Trapnell's information was apparently ignored. Trapnell, an admitted Cuban intelligence operative, had infiltrated the Alpha 66 exile organization. And, late in August, Alpha 66 leader Antonio Veciana says he was called to a meeting in Dallas by his intelligence case officer, "Maurice Bishop"—and was introduced to Oswald.

Was "Bishop" really David Phillips, the CIA's Cuban specialist in Mexico City? Congressional investigators believed so, but Veciana refused to provide a positive identification. Given Phillips's appointment by Desmond FitzGerald, and his longtime association with Tracy Barnes, a Phillips-Oswald-Nagell relationship would certainly fit into a developing pattern.

Late in August, Nagell surreptitiously tape-recorded plans for the conspiracy among himself, Oswald, Angel, and a fourth individual. But when he learned in 1967 that Garrison investigator William R. Martin was a former CIA associate of FitzGerald and Barnes, Nagell got cold feet about turning over the tape. Its existence should be a primary target of a new official investigation.

Chapter Nineteen

Nagell's Cruel September of 1963

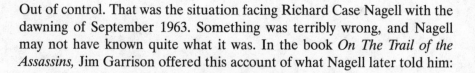

Out of control. That was the situation facing Richard Case Nagell with the dawning of September 1963. Something was terribly wrong, and Nagell may not have known quite what it was. In the book *On The Trail of the Assassins,* Jim Garrison offered this account of what Nagell later told him:

> In mid-1963 he had been working for the United States government, so Nagell's story began, in an agency which he would not identify. The people for whom he worked, a vagueness from which he never departed, were curious about a project involving a fellow named Lee Oswald and some other men. Consequently, Nagell was assigned to spend some time establishing the necessary relationships and observing. In late August or early September of 1963, for reasons he would not spell out, it became apparent that an exceedingly large—he emphasized the word "large"—operation, pointing toward the assassination of President Kennedy, was under way. At just about the time of this discovery, for reasons he would

not explain, the individual who had given him the assignment was moved
to another part of the country, and Nagell suddenly found himself without
a direct contact.

It was a strange tale, Nagell being "frozen out" by the very government
agency which had assigned him to conduct a penetration of the ongoing
activity. I can only say that Nagell impressed me as being utterly honest
and sincere in his account.[1]

After the late August 1963 meeting among Oswald, Nagell, Angel, and
a fourth individual whom Nagell has not identified, Nagell appears to have
traveled immediately to Mexico City. Apparently cut off from his CIA
contact, Nagell was issued his orders from his Soviet control, "Oaxaca."

"In the summer of 1963," as Nagell wrote to Senator Richard Russell,
"I received instructions to initiate certain action against Mr. Oswald, who
was the indispensable tool in the conspiracy, and thereafter depart the
United States, legally."[2]

Nagell was to try to persuade Oswald "that the deal was phony and if
this didn't work, and if it looked like things were going to progress beyond
the talking stage, to get rid of him."[3]

On several occasions when we met, Nagell emphasized that the KGB
was the last intelligence outfit that wanted to see Kennedy assassinated.
The Soviets had come out of the Cuban Missile Crisis with what they
considered a good deal. Relations between the United States and Cuba
were on the upswing by the summer of 1963. "If anybody wanted to stop
the assassination, it would be the KGB," Nagell told me in October 1977.
"But they didn't do enough."[4]

It appears that Nagell then made a journey from Mexico to Cuba. Except to admit having made what he calls an "unauthorized trip," Nagell
has said only that it took place before September 1963.[5] Ricard von
Kleist's correspondence with attorney Fensterwald told of Nagell having
traveled to Cuba from Mexico's Yucatán peninsula, in the fishing boat
partially owned by the Hotel Luma's bartender, Franz Waehauf. "This is
and was known by J. Edgar Hoover and the FBI," von Kleist reported.

Nagell indicated to me that he met personally with Fidel Castro,[6] apparently to inform the Cuban premier of what was transpiring—a "domestic-inspired, domestic-formulated, and domestic-sponsored" plot to assassinate Kennedy, where the intent was to make it look like Castro had
engineered it. "Cuban authorities had been informed of his [Oswald's]
association with anti-Castro elements (posing as pro-Castro agents) in the
USA before September 1963," Nagell has written.[7] During one interview,
when I asked him whether Castro ever knew what was going on, Nagell
replied: "That's a loaded question."

Professor Richard Popkin's notes on his conversations with Nagell recounted that both the "Cubans and Russians wanted to stop it [the conspiracy]."

Upon returning to the United States, Nagell briefly went back to Los Angeles. There, according to a letter he wrote to El Paso attorney Calamia while incarcerated, ". . . the main reason for my predicament is resultant from my unsuccessful efforts to get admitted to a Veterans Administration hospital in September 1963."[8] It was, as we have seen, a strategy Nagell had utilized prior to both the December 1962 (Miami) and June 1963 (Los Angeles) discussions about killing JFK.

Nagell went to see his L.A. friend Frederick H. John, asking him to safeguard negatives of the photographs of Angel and Leopoldo he had taken in June and in August, as well as the tape recording he had made of the late August discussion among the conspirators and "some other material."[9] In his Court of Claims case, Nagell would write "that I had made arrangements in the event of my demise by accident or other cause, to have my past illegal services performed for defendant [the Pentagon], the services I suspected I had performed for a foreign nation, and other illegal activities on the part of defendant [Pentagon] and the CIA, made public and verified by evidence that I had secreted at various locations in the United States."[10]

After this, Nagell went back to New Orleans.

Oswald's Whereabouts

After August 17, Oswald communicated no more with V. T. Lee of the Fair Play for Cuba Committee. After writing at the end of August to inform both the Communist Party, U.S.A., and the SWP of his plans to move to the Washington-Baltimore area, he did not communicate with any American-based "leftist" organization again until November 1.

According to the Warren Commission's exhibits, the FBI briefly sought to keep track of him. On August 28 an FBI agent checked court records in New Orleans for mention of Oswald.[11] One day later, WDSU Radio's William Stuckey made a transcript of his Oswald debate available to the FBI—for a second time—and spoke with the FBI on August 30.[12]

But the public record on where Oswald was for most of the first two and a half weeks of September is all but nonexistent. First Garrison, and later the House Assassinations Committee, did learn that, one morning at the beginning of September, Oswald showed up in the little Louisiana township of Clinton, about ninety miles north of New Orleans. There, the

Congress of Racial Equality (CORE) was organizing a black voter-registration drive.

It was an auspicious time for the civil rights movement. On August 28, 1963, more than 250,000 people from across the nation had marched on Washington and listened to Martin Luther King, Jr.'s, "I have a dream" speech at the Lincoln Memorial. Kennedy had personally committed himself to Congress's passage of a landmark bill that would finally guarantee blacks the right to vote. Especially in the South, the atmosphere was tense. CORE representatives were not sure what would happen when they started their voting drive in Clinton. When a black Cadillac arrived on the scene around midmorning, their first fear was that the FBI was paying an unwelcome visit.

Then a slim young white man emerged from the car, his two companions staying inside. For several hours he would wait patiently—the only white face—in the line of prospective voters. When he finally made it inside the office, as registrar Henry Palmer later told author Anthony Summers, "I asked him for his identification, and he pulled out a U.S. Navy ID card. I looked at the name on it, and it was Lee H. Oswald with a New Orleans address." Oswald told the registrar he figured he had a better chance of getting a job at the nearby East Louisiana State Hospital if he registered as a voter in Clinton. Palmer found the request strange, finally told Oswald that his time in the area was too short to qualify for registration, and Oswald thanked him and left.

Six witnesses told the House Assassinations Committee of seeing Oswald in Clinton that day. Several of these also got a good look at his two companions waiting in the Cadillac. The driver was a big, gray-haired man with a ruddy complexion. Garrison became convinced it was Clay Shaw, the key figure in the DA's conspiracy case. But the description was actually a closer match for Guy Banister. And the other passenger was positively identified by CORE chairman Corrie Collins as David Ferrie. "The most outstanding thing about him was his eyebrows and hair," he said. "They didn't seem real." Both Banister and Ferrie were outspoken opponents of actions like the CORE campaign.[13]

Also in the late summer of 1963, Oswald is said to have shown up in Bay Cliff, Texas, a little town between Houston and Dallas, at the home of Robert Ray McKeown. In the 1950s, McKeown had lived for a while in Havana and then shipped arms from Houston to the Castro revolution. He was well known among the Cuban exiles. In 1975 McKeown agreed to appear on a CBS News special about the assassination, where he told Dan Rather about Oswald and a Latin man who came to see him concerning the purchase of four high-powered automatic rifles.

In 1976 I interviewed McKeown at the little wooden house where, at sixty-five, he lived with his daughter in South Miami. There were some matters, McKeown told me, that he hadn't confided to CBS. "One thing is, I knew that Cuban with Oswald from before. Knew him from Cuba. 'Cept he didn't know I knew. His name was Hernandez." McKeown said that Hernandez drove the light-colored car, twice bringing Oswald to his door. Oswald was in shirtsleeves, Hernandez wearing a coat and tie.

McKeown remembered: "Guy said, 'My name's Oswald. Just call me Lee. My contacts have a big opportunity to take over Salvador. I want to know if you'd be interested in furnishing some arms.' "

McKeown said he refused, only to have the pair return half an hour later. The second time, Oswald offered $10,000 for four .300 Savage semi-automatic rifles with telescopic sights. "Oswald said, 'You're the man that run all the guns to Castro and got caught with the cache here in Houston, aren't you?' 'Yeah,' I says, 'but that's all in the past.' I told him I didn't want no part of this kinda business."[14]

Hernandez is, of course, a common Hispanic name. But there was a "Hernandez" conspicuously in the proximity of Oswald in New Orleans at the time. This was Celso Hernandez, secretary of Bringuier's New Orleans DRE chapter, who was arrested along with Bringuier during the August 9 street altercation.[15]

Another Hernandez—identified only as "A" in the congressional investigation's reports—was involved "with anti-Castro exiles and underworld figures who were operating the guerrilla training camp in New Orleans in July, 1963," according to CIA files. In June 1963 in Collinsville, Illinois, Victor Espinosa Hernandez purchased twenty-four hundred pounds of dynamite and twenty bomb casings meant to be dropped on Cuban targets. His contact was Richard Lauchli, a cofounder of the paramilitary Minutemen group. After Hernandez transported the matériel to the New Orleans camp, it was seized on July 31 in an FBI raid. Hernandez, Lauchli, and nine other men were temporarily detained.[16]

There seems to have been something strange about the raid itself. Nagell told me he had heard that Guy Banister was "partially responsible" for its occurrence.[17] Could the raid, for some reason, have been a setup? Not long thereafter, in early September with great fanfare, some Miami exiles went to the press telling of how their New Orleans camp had been infiltrated by a member of Castro's spy network. A letter purportedly written by the "spy" (Fernando Fernandez) to a contact at the Cuban embassy in Mexico City, was provided to a *Time* magazine reporter.[18]

Victor Hernandez was a lifelong friend of Rolando Cubela, who was a physician, former commander of Castro's rebel forces, and still closely associated with the Cuban premier in Havana in 1963. In 1961 Cubela had approached the CIA about defecting but was persuaded to stay on and spy in Havana. The CIA gave him a code name, AM/LASH. By the late summer of 1963, Cubela indicated he was ready to "do something really significant for the creation of a new Cuba" and wished to help "eliminate" Fidel Castro. Desmond FitzGerald, receiving approval from Richard Helms, was preparing to move this forward.[19]

The AM/LASH Plot

Communication between the CIA hierarchy and the Kennedy administration was virtually nonexistent by September 1963. On the one hand, William Attwood, a U.S. delegate to the United Nations, was preparing an unprecedented diplomatic approach to Castro. On September 5, Attwood had been informed by an ABC News correspondent who had recently interviewed the Cuban leader that Castro sought "to restore communications with the United States." By the end of the month, Attwood would meet with Robert Kennedy about whether to pursue this and would receive a go-ahead.[20]

As Attwood explained to me in 1976: "Bobby Kennedy was the original hard-liner. But now he realized that the Cubans wanted to settle on terms which would be favorable to both countries. Castro was offering an agreement that he would not try to subvert Latin America. In return, we would lift our economic blockade. Castro would give compensation for the companies that he had expropriated, and in exchange we might unblock the Cuban assets in America. In other words, normal relations—no longer a cancer on our shores."

But, as Attwood recognized in hindsight, "there were several tracks happening at once. The State Department had sort of a frozen, do-nothing policy towards Cuba. They were unaware of what we were doing because the whole thing had so many political overtones; it was all highly classified. Then there were very many people who were hired, you might say, as part-timers for the Bay of Pigs and kept their ID cards—who were pretty well committed to the cause of invasion or liberation. And there were CIA people who really believed this could be done, and were frustrated by their failures in the past. The gung-ho types.

"It was quite obvious to me that, at that time, Castro wasn't playing any game. He sincerely wanted to normalize relations with us. I've always felt if there was any Cuban involvement at all in the Kennedy assassination, it would have been on the part of the anti-Castro Cubans, who might have been fearful that this kind of normalization was in the works—and wanted to prevent it."[21]

While Attwood's delicate diplomacy was getting under way, at CIA headquarters on September 7, 1963, Desmond FitzGerald received a cable from a case officer in São Paulo, Brazil: "AMLASH still feels there only two ways accomplish change either inside job or invasion he realistic enough to realize latter out of question. . . . AMLASH still awaiting for U.S. reveal plan of action."[22]

That same evening, Fidel Castro walked into a party at Havana's Brazilian embassy. Taking aside a startled Associated Press reporter named Daniel Harker, the Cuban premier warned against "terrorist plans to eliminate Cuban leaders." His eyes ablaze, Castro added: "United States leaders should think that if they assist in terrorist plans to eliminate Cuban leaders, they themselves will not be safe." The story appeared two days later in newspapers across the United States.[23]

The synchronous timing of the cable from Brazil and Castro's comments at the Brazilian embassy reportedly sent tremors through the CIA's Cuban Special Affairs Staff (SAS). Was Castro sending a message that he knew about AM/LASH? If so, was Cubela really Castro's "double agent"? Joseph Langosch, FitzGerald's chief of counter intelligence on the SAS, later told the House Assassinations Committee that he believed Cuban G-2 intelligence was quite possibly aware of AM/LASH and his CIA association as of 1962. Thus Langosch felt the AM/LASH operation was "insecure," and such knowledge "was available to senior-level CIA officials, including Desmond FitzGerald. My disapproval of it was very strong. Des FitzGerald knew it . . . and preferred not to discuss it anymore with me."[24]

Later, Castro's remarks that September evening would be a red flag for those looking to postulate a Cuban plot against JFK:

* In March 1964, the Christian Nationalist Crusade's *Cross and the Flag* magazine stated: "We need to know more about a news conference which was held in the Brazilian Embassy reception in Havana where Castro when interviewed warned that John F. Kennedy and Robert Kennedy were not immune to assassination."
* In the extremist *Manion Forum* of March 25, 1964, Leopoldo Aguilera, Jr., quoted verbatim from Castro's "deadly threat" at the Brazilian embassy: "We are prepared to fight them and answer in kind. . . ." At the end of the interview, Dean Manion concluded "that this young man has made a very interesting prima facie case against Fidel Castro as the directing Communist genius behind the assassination of the President of the United States. The horrible realization that this International conspiracy that has sworn to bury us has its obedient criminal agents like Lee Harvey Oswald stationed in our midst should serve to shatter some of the complacency that, unfortunately, still prevails in this country. . . . Mr. Aguilera asks me to express his gratitude to this country for the refuge it has afforded for him and for his fellow exiles from

Castro's Red terror. But he wants to know where we expect to go for refuge when the terror strikes here, as it certainly will unless we stop it."

- In one of my interviews with James Angleton in 1976, he echoed much the same sentiments. "Castro was aware that the CIA was trying to assassinate him, and said he'd retaliate," Angleton said. "The *New Orleans Times-Picayune* picked this up, made a big to-do over it. It was a very important statement timewise. Oswald was in the area at the time, I think you'll find."[25]

On September 7, the same day that FitzGerald received the cable about AM/LASH and Castro made his reported remarks in Havana, the FBI sent a report on Oswald's latest activities to the CIA. Another FBI-to-CIA report on Oswald and the Fair Play for Cuba Committee followed on September 10, after information from the New York field office reached FBI headquarters—allegedly for the first time—that Oswald had communicated with the FPCC way back in April.[26]

At about this same time in September, Cubela's friend—anti-Castro arms dealer Victor Espinoza Hernandez—contacted the Immigration and Naturalization Service (INS) with information about the AM/LASH plan. Hernandez suggested a link between this latest operation and the earlier CIA anti-Castro plots involving the underworld. The information was passed by the INS to the FBI and on to the CIA. There followed an undated memo written by FitzGerald's counter intelligence chief: "The AMLASH circle is wide and each new friend of whom we learn seems to have knowledge of plan. I believe the problem is a more serious and basic one. Fidel reportedly knew that this group was plotting against him and once enlisted its support. Hence, we cannot rule out the possibility of provocation."[27]

Sometime that September, Rolando Cubela requested the CIA to arrange a personal meeting with Robert Kennedy. FitzGerald, according to a CIA inspector general's report, then went to meet with clandestine affairs chief Richard Helms. The two officials agreed that FitzGerald himself should see Cubela. Helms decided that "it was not necessary to seek approval from Robert Kennedy for FitzGerald to speak in his name."[28] Kennedy's CIA director, McCone, was not informed. McCone had not even been made aware of the earlier CIA-Mob plots against Castro until August 16, 1963—when, after reading an article in the *Chicago Sun-Times* that claimed the CIA had some connection with Sam Giancana, McCone asked Richard Helms for a report on what this was all about.[29]

Since FitzGerald was the CIA official directly involved with the AM/LASH anti-Castro operation, and given Nagell's allegation that he was himself in touch with FitzGerald on August 27, the question is whether these matters overlapped. Did Nagell, or Oswald, know about AM/LASH? What was going on?

When I showed Nagell a photograph of Cubela at one of our meetings, a glimmer of recognition showed in his face. But all he would say was, "AM/LASH—now, *that* sounds like a CIA code name."[30]

Alas, a closer look at Cubela's connections only raises even more questions. José Aleman, Jr., a Cuban exile who testified before the House Assassinations Committee, spoke of a link between Cubela and Florida's Tampa-based Mob boss Santos Trafficante, Jr. When Trafficante was briefly jailed by Castro in 1959, Aleman noted that Cubela had been among those looking to secure the mobster's release. Later, Aleman said, Trafficante "was in some way trying to get Cubela from Cuba."[31] In the meantime, Trafficante admitted to the House Assassinations Committee to having served as "interpreter" at a March 1961 Miami meeting among some Cuban exiles, Vegas mobster Rosselli, and Hughes's aide Robert Maheu. The men discussed "any kind of way that was possible to get rid" of Castro—"a cannon, pills, tanks, airplanes, anything," Trafficante said.[32]

Trafficante also admitted having met Cubela "after the revolution in Cuba," but claimed it was "just a hello and good-bye." He conceded that a Cuban exile associate of his was well acquainted with Cubela. "He [Cubela] was some kind of a [Cuban] diplomat. He was of stature enough to be able to travel to Madrid and Paris and all those places. In my opinion, he was not a Communist. I always believed sooner or later he would react against Castro."[33]

Reacting against Castro—and assassinating Kennedy in the process—was rapidly moving forward in September 1963. And the burden of doing something about it was squarely on the shoulders of Richard Nagell.

Nagell's Warning to Oswald

On August 12, 1974, Nagell wrote one of the most important of all his letters to Fensterwald, who had recently become Nagell's attorney-of-record in the Court of Claims lawsuit seeking a full disability compensation from the Pentagon. Three weeks earlier, Fensterwald had written to Nagell:

The Army seems to be playing its usual "game" of infinite delay. . . . I expect to publish a book based primarily on Oswald's trip to Mexico City, where, I believe, final plans for the assassination were hatched. Although you were in Texas at the time (Sept. 26–Oct. 3), it is my hunch that you know a good deal about the background of his trip, the reason for it, who was there, etc. Any details that you feel you can impart to me will be greatly appreciated.[34]

Nagell wrote back:

Regarding Oswald's trip to Mexico (9/26/63–10/3/63), I am of course limited in the amount of background information that I can supply, for a number of obvious reasons. I can, however, furnish a few facts, together with some opinion based on facts, although I'm afraid that what I have to offer will hardly bolster your belief that plans for the assassination (at Dallas) were finalized in Mexico City. But here goes anyway, written right off the top of my head:

In September 1963, "Laredo" (a code name unknown to Oswald) met with Oswald at Jackson Square in New Orleans, where both were photographed. ["Laredo," as described in Chapter Thirteen, was Nagell's admitted code name for meetings with his Soviet contact.] Photos of two of Oswald's associates, whom I shall call "Leopoldo" and "Angel," were displayed to Oswald. Oswald was informed that neither Leopoldo nor Angel were agents of Cuban G-2 (as the Dirección General de Inteligencia was then called), a story they had strapped on Oswald the previous month. He was informed that the two were in fact counterrevolutionaries known to be connected with a violence-prone faction of a CIA-financed group operating in Mexico City (and elsewhere), that in 1962 both of them had participated in a bomb-throwing incident directed against an employee of the Cuban Embassy there, that both were well-known to Cuban and Mexican authorities and, of course, to the CIA. He was informed in so many words that he was being "used" by fascist elements in an attempt to disrupt the Cuban revolution, to ruin chances for a contemplated rapprochement between Cuba and the United States, probably to incite the U.S. government to initiate severe retaliatory measures against Cuba (in the form of an invasion), etc. He was asked some subtle questions relating to his discussions with Leopoldo and Angel, about his pending move to Baltimore, Md., why he was going there without his wife and child, etc. His replies were evasive and in some instances untruthful. Despite evidence to contrary, he denied that there had been any serious discussion to kill President Kennedy, Robert Kennedy, or anybody else. He seemed genuinely upset and visibly shaken when a query was made in that direction. He stated that he was a friend of the Cuban revolution, that he leaned toward Cuban Marxism, but not Soviet Leninism, whatever that meant. . . .

Caught in the Web

In the event that Nagell failed in his attempt to get Oswald to back away from the "phony deal," he was supposed to meet with him—and then kill him—in Mexico City. Nagell has indicated he was to use the Colt .45 pistol he had borrowed from his California friend Bill Lynn.[35] According to a Fensterwald memo of a 1973 conversation with Nagell, "The USSR ordered Nagell to eliminate Lee Harvey Oswald because they thought it might be an extreme embarrassment to them if he was caught, not because he was one of them, but because of his history."[36]

But somehow Nagell had reached the conclusion that he had been conned. His CIA contact was suddenly nowhere to be found. In his "double agent" role, he believed he was being left out in the cold by the CIA. "Oaxaca," his Soviet contact, was calling the shots—and apparently had been for a long time.

At our first interview in 1975, Nagell had spelled out his realization that "some things I did [in 1962–63] were not for the CIA" (see Chapter Two). "I was trusting," he added. "But I had no reason to be, because in this dirty business I was involved in, *I* was certainly deceitful. It was just stupidity."[37]

In his Court of Claims case, Nagell wrote: "Plaintiff [Nagell] submits that if he was led to believe that he was functioning for the Central Intelligence Agency, and subsequently he discovered that instead possibly he was functioning on behalf of a foreign power or was being 'used' in other ways, then such a discovery would have caused stress sufficient to adversely affect plaintiff's mental condition in 1963."[38]

Just how Nagell arrived at this conclusion is not known, though he has written that it occurred after having investigated Hotel Luma bartender Franz Waehauf, Cuban exile leader Manuel Artime, L.A.'s FPCC executive Vaughn Snipes [Marlowe], and Lee Harvey Oswald.[39] On June 24, 1967, in his correspondence with Georgia senator Richard Russell, Nagell elaborated:

> . . . I want to state for the record that when I signed papers in 1962 acknowledging I was employed by the Central Intelligence Agency, I did so in good faith and with a clear conscience, and I did not then know or even suspect I was working for other interests.
>
> Later, when I became cognizant of my actual employer, I made every reasonable effort to correct the situation. I initiated a number of approaches to both the C.I.A. and the F.B.I. in Mexico and in five different

locales within the United States. When these agencies demonstrated they considered me just another crank, or, in the case of the F.B.I. specifically, when its agents seemed more bent on tying me into a violation of the law than helping me, I took other steps to neutralize the capacity in which I was acting. I might add here, that I do not feel the nature of my employment was in any way related to the national security of the United States. And, although several attempts were made by persons I suspect were associated with my employer to persuade me to engage in activities inimical to the national security, I refused to do so.[40]

Over the years, Nagell often raised the subject of the signed statement he provided the FBI, on January 6, 1964, from his El Paso cell. This document, he said, was central to understanding his motivation in taking himself out of the picture by getting himself arrested—which, he added, "had nothing to do with the assassination, at least not on my end."[41] It concerned another matter, but one that also involved Oswald.

The last time I spoke to Nagell was in late March 1990, when he talked by phone about that January 6 statement. The FBI had refused to produce it at either of his El Paso trials. "They denied it existed," Nagell said. "Later the FBI sent me a letter, saying they couldn't find it. [Agent] Lawrence W. Gorman wrote it in his own handwriting, as I dictated it. Then I signed it—I even initialed the mistakes on each page—and two FBI agents also signed it as witnesses. But there are reasons why the government does not want it to exist."[42]

Early that summer I contacted the U.S. District Court in El Paso and learned that all court records dating back to that era had been placed in storage at an archive in Fort Worth. I did not expect to find Nagell's statement among his case files. To my surprise and excitement, it was there —three pages long, signed by Nagell, with FBI special agents Edward Joseph Murphy and Lawrence W. Gorman as witnesses.

Portions of the statement have been quoted earlier in this book. They pertained to Nagell's having been first approached in September 1962, in Mexico City, when "a representative of a foreign government proposed to me that I participate in an act; such act being a criminal offense and inimical to the best interests of the United States. At that time I refused such proposal." That period, of course, had marked the beginning of what Nagell assumed was a CIA assignment to work as a "double" and approach the Soviets. Then, Nagell went on in his statement to the FBI,

in May, 1963, another representative of the same foreign government made the same proposal to me. At that time I agreed to such a proposal. In Sept., 1963, I was informed by an American, known to me as an agent of the same foreign government, that arrangements for my participation in the aforementioned act were completed. At this time I refused the aforesaid proposal.

Approximately one week later I was instructed by this same person to either participate as previously agreed or derogatory information pertaining to me would be disclosed to the Federal Bureau of Investigation. Thereupon I agreed to follow her [word crossed out] the instructions of this person, although I did not intend to do so. This existing situation actuated my conduct of September 20, 1963, for which I was arrested and am presently charged.

I did not actually attempt to rob any bank. I thought that my arrest would provide an immediate, though temporary, solution to the problem with which I was confronted.

I might be guilty of a more serious offense, but [entire previous phrase crossed out] I am not guilty as charged. . . .

Richard Case Nagell

In May 1978, Nagell told me that "the FBI called it a 'confession,' but I wasn't confessing to anything really. They wanted names and I wouldn't say. They would've gone to the people. Somebody in Juarez and somebody in El Paso, two people."[43]

In his Court of Claims case, Nagell had added: "In the Gorman FBI document . . . plaintiff [Nagell] detailed his reasons for effecting his arrest by federal authorities. The instructions plaintiff described therein as having been received in Mexico pertained to Lee Harvey Oswald, and, he believed at the time, originated with either the CIA or Soviet intelligence."[44]

Whatever else Nagell may have been involved in with Oswald, Nagell has never been willing to say. He seems to have thought, until the late summer of 1963, that it was sanctioned by U.S. intelligence. But the nature of the counterespionage business is a tricky one. As Christopher Felix described it in his 1963 book *The Spy and His Masters*, "The decisive question is precisely which turns are genuine and which are false. This is but one of the problems which makes C.E. an extraordinarily complex affair; the determination of which turns are genuine and which false is a painstaking exercise in the control of information, of who knows what when, that requires constant alertness and a simultaneous grasp of both large perspective and detail. It is obviously an intellectual exercise of almost mathematical complexity."[45]

What alarmed Nagell was that he found himself caught in the middle of something going on between American and Soviet intelligence. "Everyone was penetrating everyone else," he told me in 1977. "The CIA had its informants. Of course, everybody was using the Mexicans. And I'm *sure* the Soviets had a few high-level penetrations. At the operational level, it could be anybody. Both sides played footsies on occasion, made their little deals if it was to their advantage, and that's one of the things that bothered me most. You have to draw a certain line. There are certain principles you don't sacrifice for any reason at all."[46]

At this point, Nagell met with Oswald again. He arranged with a vendor in New Orleans' Jackson Square to take a photograph of the two of them secretly. That "faded Polaroid pic," Nagell wrote me in 1976, still existed "amongst my belongings in another country."[47]

As Nagell described the meeting in his 1974 letter to Fensterwald: "Shortly before 9/20/63, Oswald was again contacted by Laredo. Laredo advised that 'Oaxaca' (a code name unknown to Oswald) wanted to speak with Oswald at Mexico City, that Oaxaca could not leave Mexico City and therefore Oswald should visit him there. The identity of Oaxaca was unknown to Oswald also. Oswald was asked to depart the United States before 9/26/63, to register at either the Hotel New Gran Texas or another hotel whose name I do not recall (though it was not the Hotel del Comercio) upon his arrival at Mexico City, where he would be contacted by Laredo on 9/26/63 and introduced to Oaxaca the same day. He was instructed not to go near the Cuban or USSR embassies. Oswald agreed to do so when he was advised that he would be provided with more than sufficient funds to make the trip to and from Mexico City by plane. He was told where and how he was to pick up the money on 9/24/63, his expected date of departure from New Orleans. On 9/20/63 arrangements were made for the funds, consisting of $500.00 in U.S. currency, to be paid to Oswald."[48]

Sometime before noon on September 17, as he had been instructed to do by Nagell, Oswald went to the Mexican consulate in New Orleans to obtain a fifteen-day tourist permit. He presented not his passport, but his birth certificate for identification. He listed himself as a "photographer" and said he was taking $300 to Mexico as an "in transit" tourist.[49] Standing right in front of Oswald in line for a tourist permit was William George Gaudet, the New Orleans-based CIA agent who admitted to having watched Oswald pass out his FPCC leaflets—but who later insisted that his presence alongside Oswald at the Mexican consulate was merely coincidental.[50]

Alerting the FBI

Nagell then made his move—and dispatched a registered letter to J. Edgar Hoover. As Nagell wrote years later, "What it all boils down to (the impetus behind the government's diligent prosecution of me in the 1960's, the true reason for my lengthy imprisonment, all of this injustice) can be explained in one sentence: I informed the Director of the Federal Bureau of Investigation, *and others,* as early as September 17, 1963, that Lee Harvey Oswald and two of his Cuban associates were planning to assassinate the President of the United States . . . and nothing was done about it."[51]

As Nagell wrote to Robert Kennedy from jail on January 8, 1967: "The deed was done; and it could have been prevented. The Federal Bureau of Investigation was apprised of enough data to warrant the arrest and detention of Mr. Oswald, at least until an investigation disclosed sufficient evidence to sanction an indictment. To my knowledge he was not even picked up for questioning."

Nagell has never revealed the full contents of his letter (see Chapter One for the contents of his 1976 affidavit concerning as much as he has put on record). He did say that it included telling the FBI that he "had received instructions 'to take care of' Lee Oswald, that is, to kill him, in September 1963."[52] The letter was composed in a style "done to persuade the reader that its sender was familiar with CIA procedure, that it was not a crank letter."[53] By using the alias of "Joseph Kramer," the pseudonym of a known Soviet agent, Nagell also seemed to have been informing the FBI that Soviet intelligence was simultaneously aware of such information.

Yet, at this same moment in time, the CIA and FBI were colluding in an operation surrounding the Fair Play for Cuba Committee—one that might have been continuing to utilize Oswald. According to FBI documents, on September 16, 1963, the CIA advised the FBI that the "Agency is giving some consideration to countering the activities of [the FPCC] in foreign countries." The CIA specifically wanted the FPCC's foreign mailing list and other documents sent over by the FBI.

The FBI memorandum, dated September 18, continued: "Pursuant to a discussion with the Liaison Agent, [name deleted, identified only as a middle-level CIA official working on anti-Castro propaganda] advised that his Agency will not take action without first consulting with the Bureau, bearing in mind that we wish to make certain the CIA activity will not jeopardize any Bureau investigation."[54]

So if Nagell's letter was indeed received and ignored by the FBI, it could well have been because of the ongoing back-and-forth with the CIA over a separate Oswald-related operation—over which elements within both intelligence agencies might have *thought* they had control.

A "Second Oswald"

There has long been speculation among assassination researchers that an Oswald look-alike or "double" was impersonating him in the immediate months prior to Dallas, the purpose being to establish a fake Oswald persona—for example, as a sharpshooter practicing on a rifle range. The first to put forward this thesis in detail was Professor Richard Popkin in his 1966 book *The Second Oswald*. This book inspired Nagell to write Popkin from prison, telling him that there was some truth to this matter.

Oswald was certainly of a physical "type" for which others might be mistaken. (George de Mohrenschildt even told this writer, much to my dismay, that *I* bore a resemblance to Lee Harvey Oswald.) And, in the summer of 1963, Nagell says there was someone else—a Leon Oswald—who showed up on the periphery of the burgeoning conspiracy.

"I knew both of them," Nagell told me in 1975. "I have been trained in observation, and there is no mistaking who was who. The other Oswald was working with anti-Castro Cubans. He was not pro-Castro. This Leon Oswald, the second Oswald, allegedly registered at a hotel in Mexico City where I had once registered under a different name. Don't ask me the date, but it was sometime between July 4 and September 20. I told Popkin he ought to check with the State Department, because somebody's got a picture of him. But Leon Oswald, in my opinion, did not resemble Lee Harvey Oswald. He was somewhat taller, and not as articulate or intelligent. I have no idea whether or not he was personally acquainted with Lee Harvey Oswald."[55]

A Nagell-related memorandum in the Garrison files added this: "Leon Oswald—Male, Caucasian, American, 24–26, 150 lbs., 5′9″. Alive on September 14 or 15, 1963. Not alive after Sept. 19, 1963."

In my 1976 outline, which Nagell amended, he wrote: "The second Oswald, Leon, apparently was eliminated by mistake."

Who "eliminated" Leon Oswald, Nagell would not say. But since Nagell's orders to eliminate the *real* Oswald came from the KGB, it would make sense it was the Soviets' mistake. And, given what took place in New Orleans in mid-September 1963, the JFK plotters may even have designed such a mistake.

One of the key witnesses in Jim Garrison's conspiracy case was Perry Russo, a young insurance agent and acquaintance of David Ferrie. Russo told a reporter in February 1967 of a party he had attended at Ferrie's apartment, placing the date at probably September 15. There Ferrie introduced him to a "Leon Oswald," whom Russo could not positively identify as being Lee Harvey. Nagell told Garrison that it assuredly was not, since the real Oswald had been in his own company on the night in question. This was a major reason, Nagell believed, why Garrison did not call him as a witness at the Clay Shaw trial; Nagell's testimony might have cast doubt on Garrison's case.

Russo maintained that, after a long night of drinking, Ferrie, "Leon," several anti-Castro Cubans, and a tall, distinguished-looking, white-haired man introduced as "Clem Bertrand" began discussing how to assassinate Castro. Ferrie spread a map of Cuba out on a table, pointing out potential landing areas onto the island. Then, after the Cubans left, Ferrie reportedly began pacing the room, a perpetual mug of coffee in his hand, talking of a plan to get rid of JFK and blame it on Castro. He spoke, said Russo, of a "triangulation of crossfire" as the best means to assassinate the president. At the Garrison trial, where "Clem Bertrand" was alleged to be business leader (and CIA contact) Clay Shaw of the International Trade Mart, a three-judge panel concluded that Russo was telling the truth.[56]

A few days after the meeting with Ferrie, "Bertrand," and "Leon" that Russo described, Leon Oswald was killed, according to Nagell.[57] As we shall see, he was not the last Oswald "double" to surface before the assassination.

Countdown

On September 17, when Oswald went to pick up his Mexico tourist card and Nagell mailed his letter to Hoover, Nagell departed New Orleans. En route to El Paso, on September 19 he sent what was apparently his last communication to the Soviets. "I think you should also be apprised," he wrote to Senator Russell in 1967, "that all information resulting from my surveillance of Mr. Oswald's activities, including his involvement in a conspiracy to murder President Kennedy, was passed on to Soviet officials without delay. In fact, my last report concerning him was dispatched the evening before my arrest."[58]

D-day was approaching for Nagell. He assumed that the FBI would take some action on his letter. Nagell's inner dilemma was whether to follow through on the Soviet order to follow Oswald to Mexico City, kill him, and then depart this hemisphere—"no doubt permanently," he has said.[59] An FBI file of February 4, 1964, describes an undated bureau interview with a Nagell "cellmate" in El Paso. It quotes the cellmate as saying that Nagell apparently "decided everything was against him in Los Angeles and made arrangements with Communist Party in Los Angeles to pick up visa and passport from contact in El Paso and eventually end up in Czechoslovakia."[60]

I do not know why it was deemed essential that Nagell not set foot again in his native land. One reason could be that it was the only way, after murdering the conspiracy's essential fall guy, that Nagell could protect himself from the plotters. Another reason may have been his involvement in whatever other "inimical act" the Soviets had cooked up for him, which Nagell believed could subject him to prosecution—since he had been left twisting slowly in the wind by the CIA.

At any rate, his Soviet contact wanted Nagell to disappear. When I asked him in 1978 why he didn't follow through on their orders, his face took on a pained expression. "What can I say? The answer did not sit well with certain people. But I was honest. Honesty doesn't pay sometimes, it's subject to misinterpretation. It's said I was so emotionally unstable. Well, probably I was. My reasons centered around my children at that time."[61]

Nagell says he demanded that somehow he be able to take custody of his two young children from his estranged wife, and bring the children with him into imposed exile. As he would testify at his 1964 trial, ". . . if I had been allowed to take my children with me, I would have taken them but the circumstances were such at the time that I was told because I was not leaving the country through legal channels . . . I could not take my children with me."[62]

Later, from prison, he would write to Greenstein: "Keeping one in doubt about welfare and whereabouts of children cruel but effective device (supposedly stimulates spirit to cooperate). . . . Holdover from Stone Age. . . . Used successfully at LUBIYANKA [the KGB's Moscow headquarters] and other places . . . occasionally fails to produce desired results."

In our 1978 interview, Nagell added: "If I could have left the United States in September 1963 with my children, I would have. At that time, they told me my being without them was only temporary. I'll never know. But I'll tell you this, too: I'd rather my kids had been brought up in the Soviet Union than this country. I was in a quandary, I didn't know what to do."[63]

On September 20, 1963, Nagell arrived in El Paso. Someone, he says, was waiting for him across the border, in Juárez.[64] But Nagell had come to a decision. He cruised the streets for a while, then parked his Ford Fairlane next to a "No Parking" sign in the alley between Oregon and El Paso streets. Then he walked into the downtown post office.

There he mailed three letters. One was to Desmond FitzGerald. Another was "a nastier note" to another, unnamed CIA official at Langley headquarters. In an envelope, Nagell mailed five $100 bills—and, he says, an airplane ticket to Mexico City.[65] At his trial the following June, when asked about the intended recipient of the money, Nagell said: "I think that at this time the Federal Bureau of Investigation knows to whom I mailed it but I am not going to state it."[66]

Later, he would reveal that the $500 was the "expense money" for Oswald's Mexico trip. But in 1974, when Fensterwald wrote Nagell asking whether Oswald had gone by bus instead of plane to Mexico in an effort to "make a few bucks," Nagell wrote back: "I doubt it, mainly because I have cause to believe that he was never given, or did not receive, the five hundred dollars."[67]

There may have been a witness when Nagell mailed his package in El Paso late that afternoon. Awaiting trial on April 7, 1964, Nagell wrote a letter to one of his El Paso attorneys, asking that a $50 money order be telegraphed to Vaughn L. Snipes (Marlowe). "If you do not have the money left," Nagell wrote, "I have the money available in my jail account. This request is in conjunction with my obtaining a deposition and witness to the fact that I mailed $500.00 from El Paso on the date of my arrest."[68] Marlowe, however, did not remember ever receiving any $50 money order from Nagell. And he said he had no idea why Nagell would have made such a request of him, or what "witness" Nagell could have been describing.[69]

Action in the Bank

Having completed his business at the El Paso post office, Nagell had then walked across the street to the State National Bank and fired his two shots into the wall. "There was a reason for having myself arrested in the manner I did," Nagell told me in 1975, "which I thought would turn into a misdemeanor. It wasn't because of the Kennedy assassination, in that sense, but for a reason I've never disclosed to anybody in the United States. I certainly wasn't trying to establish an alibi, as some of these researchers have written. I didn't *need* an alibi. I was on my way out of the country, to Mexico and then somewhere else, and I did not plan to return."[70]

His actions inside the bank were all by design, intended as a signal to whomever was waiting for him right across the Mexican border. When he asked teller Patsy Gordon for $100 in *American Express* traveler's checks, this was intentional. At our last meeting, Nagell suggested I reexamine his trial transcript and think about why the prosecution raised such an objection to his specific mention of American Express.[71] In a letter to Greenstein, he indicated that it was through American Express that he was supposed to receive payment for his intelligence work in 1962–63—money that Nagell said had "failed to materialize."

Nagell also wrote to Fensterwald: "And then there is the instance of that .45 calibre pistol which destroyed two cubic centimeters of federally-insured plaster inside an El Paso bank. I understand that in a way it bore a remarkable resemblance to the weapon that was (supposed) to be used to dust a little rabbit."[72] The "little rabbit," Nagell seemed to be saying, was Oswald.

Nagell had surrendered casually to the young policeman James Bundren. "Why did you try to rob the bank?" Bundren asked. "I didn't know there had been any robbery," Nagell replied. Everything moved forward according to Nagell's desperate plan. All the "evidence" was removed from his trunk—the notebooks, the pamphlets about Cuba and China, the photographs and camera equipment. There were also, Nagell has written, two Mexican tourist cards hidden inside the lining of a dark brown suit jacket that bore the label of a Mexico City clothing store. One of them was in the name of "Joseph Kramer," Nagell's (and, according to him, Mark Gayn's) alias. The other was in the name of Oswald's alias, under "Albert Hidel" or "Aleksei Hidel." Policeman Bundren turned everything over to the FBI.[73]

The first FBI report about Nagell's questioning, which I found in the archives of his court case in Fort Worth, states:

. . . NAGELL requested permission to telephonically contact an attorney in Los Angeles, California at about 5:00 p.m. This request was immediately granted by SA White, upon which NAGELL stated, "No, I don't want to call that shyster." He then asked the time on the West Coast and on the East Coast.

Although refusing to directly discuss the attempted hold-up of the State National Bank, El Paso, NAGEL [sic] stated that he had fired two shots in the bank "to keep anyone from following me." He stated that he was an excellent shot, and the fact that he had fired the two shots into the ceiling proved he had not been trying to hit anyone. He stated that he was certain that "all of my problems have been solved for a long time, and now I won't have to go to Cuba." This statement was not further explained. When requested to explain this statement, NAGELL refused, stating "I can see this is going to be a frame, which is to be expected in our capitalistic system. . . ."

NAGELL advised he had been living in Mexico until a short time ago. . . .

He advised that he had been trained in the Army Counterintelligence School. He said that he had been assigned to Field Operations Intelligence and had taught interrogation.[74]

The clues were there. Nagell was making a point of dropping them. If the El Paso FBI was baffled by his initial statements, its agents would assuredly have done some checking on his record at headquarters. The fact of two Mexico tourist cards inside his jacket, in the names of "Joseph Kramer" and "Albert Hidel" or "Aleksei Hidel"—both of which also appeared in Nagell's warning letter to Hoover—would, one would imagine, also have been passed along to Washington.

When agent White testified at a preliminary hearing on November 4, he recalled Nagell making one very direct statement: "What would you have done if you were going to be followed out of the bank?"[75]

Nagell would write in 1966 of his belief "that it was . . . a direct result of my arrest that this conspiracy did not materialize."[76] The JFK conspirators would soon have become aware of Nagell's arrest—or at least his disappearance from the scene and inability to play whatever role he was cast to play. And, since they had no way of determining what he might be saying to the authorities, the plotters might reasonably have postponed their plans and waited for any reaction.

Yet the FBI did not move. Nor did the CIA. Or the KGB. Or the Cuban government. Richard Nagell cooled his heels in jail as the calendar progressed toward November 22.

Summary

Nagell found himself in an impossible situation in September 1963. Suddenly unable to locate his CIA contact, he came to the realization that he had been deceived: Much of his intelligence work, for the past year, had actually been on behalf of the Soviets, not the CIA. Now his Soviet contact instructed him either to convince Oswald that he was being set up in the JFK conspiracy—or kill Oswald in Mexico City and then take up residence abroad. Nagell appears to have gone to Mexico for his instructions, then possibly to Cuba to alert the Castro government, and returned to Los Angeles to stash his evidence with a friend. Then he met twice with Oswald in New Orleans and, unable to sway Oswald that he was being used by "fascist elements," instructed him to meet with "Oaxaca" in Mexico City. Caught in a compromising situation over his work for the Soviets, Nagell sent his warning letter to Hoover about the conspiracy. Then he drove to El Paso, dispatched Oswald's expense money for his trip to Mexico and letters to the CIA, and got himself arrested outside the State National Bank.

In the meantime, Oswald went to a black voting-registration drive with

David Ferrie and showed up with a Hispanic man looking to buy arms from Robert McKeown. As the Kennedy administration approached delicate negotiations to reopen relations with Cuba, the CIA enlisted Rolando Cubela in yet another assassination plot against Castro. The Cuban premier seems to have been alerted about it, and issued his own warning of possible retaliation. The CIA and the FBI remained in communication about Oswald, and efforts to target the Fair Play for Cuba Committee. The federal agencies may have believed that Oswald was still under their control, as part of an ongoing intelligence operation. In truth, as Nagell tried to tell them, everything was moving rapidly out of control.

Chapter Twenty

CIA vs. KGB: Mysteries of Mexico City

The dilemma facing Richard Case Nagell in September 1963 clearly traced back to the CIA contract he signed in Mexico City a year before. It was in Mexico where he was approached by the Soviets, then received the go-ahead from his CIA contact "Bob" to become a double agent. It was to Mexico where Nagell and Oswald journeyed in the summer of 1963, and where plans for the Kennedy conspiracy apparently moved forward. American and Soviet intelligence out of Mexico both seem to have been monitoring the operation.

I cannot claim to have sorted out everything that was going on. It may be that the CIA itself did not fully know. As author Anthony Summers surmised in his 1980 book *Conspiracy,*

> What we have of the jigsaw may mean that, perhaps because of an opera-
> tion against Fair Play for Cuba, one branch of the CIA was isolated from
> information on Oswald held by another department. . . . In the interests

of security, intelligence agencies do often run compartmentalized operations. It might have been undesirable, after the assassination, to reveal what some CIA "dirty tricks" department was up to—against Fair Play for Cuba or simply against Castro's Cuba.[1]

It would also have been "undesirable" for U.S. intelligence to reveal what I believe was another purpose of the whole Nagell-Oswald scenario —which was to determine, by observing the people around Nagell and Oswald, who was really working for whom. In other words, who among the Cuban exiles were secretly working for Castro? Who among the SWP, the Communist Party, U.S.A., or the FPCC might either be serving—or willing to serve—the Soviets or the Cubans? And who inside the CIA itself might actually be Soviet penetrations, or "moles"?

It is quite conceivable that Military Intelligence was also seeking answers to these "internal security" questions. As we saw in Chapter Nine, the military probably dispatched Nagell on his summer 1962 trip to Mexico. Journalist Joseph J. Trento, broadcast director for the nonprofit National Security News Service in Washington, discovered a joint FBI-Army intelligence operation that successfully "dangled" Ralph Sigler at Mexico's Soviet embassy in 1966. (In 1976 Sigler was found dead in his El Paso home; his story forms a major part of the 1989 Trento-William Corson book *Widows*.)

"Starting in the late '50s, the Soviets became extraordinarily active out of Mexico City," Trento told me. "Army Intelligence, out of Fort Meade, Maryland, set up teams for a joint program there in conjunction with the FBI. Its intent was to dangle agents, looking to find people whom the Soviets might think a vulnerable person to try to recruit. Often, the Army and the FBI did not tell the CIA what they were doing—because they were also trying to figure out exactly what the CIA was up to in Mexico."[2]

It is possible that Nagell, and even Oswald, were part of such a "dangle" scheme. Such a hypothesis concerning Oswald was outlined to me by Ronald Augustinovich, who claimed to be a former CIA contract agent and who was a licensed private investigator in Arizona when I met with him in 1975. He had come forward in 1967 to Garrison's investigators, who pursued some of Augustinovich's leads but did not call him as a witness at the Clay Shaw trial. One thing was quite clear: He was well aware of some of the Cuban exiles involved with Alpha 66.

Augustinovich was a big man—upward of 250 pounds on a five-foot, nine-inch frame—who looked and spoke a little like actor Andy Devine. He purported that he knew of Nagell, but he would not talk about him. Augustinovich said that he himself had been part of a CIA team that was trying to find the source of an intelligence leak. "We'd been plagued by this," Augustinovich said. "The agency, including probably the State Department and Military Intelligence, was just getting killed with a high-level intelligence leak. With Cuban affairs, everybody knew who we were and what we were doing almost before we did. They got our *orders* before we did."

Oswald—and a young fellow who looked just like him—were said by Augustinovich to have been "part of a penetration team directed against Castro's intelligence to find out where that leak was coming from. It had nothing to do with a plot to assassinate the president. I was part of that penetration."

Augustinovich indicated this had all been arranged before Oswald came back to the United States in June 1962. "I know Oswald was employed by American intelligence. And he had already managed to connect up with Castro's intelligence. There were five of Castro's people at an initial meeting, waiting for Oswald to return from Russia, in an apartment building on Ninety-ninth Street in New York. The group believed I was working for Castro's intelligence. I fed them a lot of good information, which I was told to do. I met with Oswald alone in New York—except I don't know if it was really him or the guy who looked like him. The operation was coordinated somehow so that if one of the two of them disappeared, we'd have something to go on. I made a report on my meeting with Oswald to the FBI in New York City. They claim there are no copies of that report, but that's a lie. I talked on two occasions to an FBI expert on Latin America."

Augustinovich warned me from the start: "Half of what I'll tell you might be truth, and the other half bullshit. But all of it is what I was told. That's part of the game in the intelligence business. You confuse your own operatives with false information; maybe *nobody* knows the full truth about a particular assignment."

So it was impossible to ascertain Augustinovich's credibility. Still, I include his account here, as one way of looking at Oswald's otherwise inexplicable relationships with anti-Castro Cubans and pro-Castro groups, with left-wing leaders such as V. T. Lee and right-wing extremists such as Guy Banister.

Nagell, working in an arena whose very foundation is deception, felt himself betrayed when he shot up the El Paso bank. He had found himself cast adrift—unable to communicate with his CIA contact, taking (and ultimately refusing) orders from his Soviet contact, involved at least peripherally in an assassination conspiracy against Kennedy, and enmeshed in other activities for which he feared prosecution.

The man he primarily blamed for his predicament was "Bob," whom Nagell has indicated he came to believe was really working for the Soviets all along. If this was true, then CIA operations in Mexico were obviously severely compromised. Mexico seemed a major key to unlocking the mystery and, in 1990, I made a springtime trip to Texas, where several people knowledgeable of the CIA's 1962–63 activities there were now living in retirement.

Clark Anderson, the FBI's legal attaché in Mexico City during that critical period, proved vague and unforthcoming. For example, when I mentioned a personal file that I had heard might have been kept on Oswald by Winston Scott, the CIA's station chief, Anderson quickly side-stepped the question. "I know nothing about it," he said. "If I did, I could not comment."[3] Anne Goodpasture, who had been Scott's personal aide-de-camp for years, was now living in Dallas, but she refused to be interviewed.

But when I drove on to Austin, where former U.S. ambassador to Mexico Thomas Mann resided, my luck was about to change.

Memories of an Ambassador

A native Texan, Thomas Mann was a career diplomat who had served in the Eisenhower administration as assistant secretary of state for inter-American affairs. When Kennedy took office, he removed Mann from that post, fearing that his strongly held anti-Communist opinions might make the president's new Latin American Alliance for Progress more difficult to get off the ground. Mann instead became JFK's Ambassador to Mexico, only to be reappointed by Lyndon Johnson to the same high State Department job he had held under Eisenhower. On December 14, 1963, Mann became the new president's first political appointment.[4]

When I met with Mann, he was living in gracious retirement in a ranch-style suburban home in Austin. Though now in his eighties, his mind remained sharp. And he was still puzzling over certain events that took place in Mexico City nearly thirty years before.

"You know, I don't think the United States was very forthcoming to me about Oswald," Mann reflected. "The great puzzle in all this, for me, is why J. Edgar Hoover would say, 'Leave it alone.' "

What do you mean? I asked.

"Basically, the message I received from Hoover, very soon after the assassination, was, 'We don't want to hear any more about this case. And tell the Mexican government not to do any more investigating, we just want to hush it up.' Well, I hadn't reached any conclusions, and that's why it surprised me so much. It was the only time anything like this ever happened to me in all my years in government."

"Did this word come down to you only from the FBI, or the CIA as well?" I asked.

"Well, I got it on instruction, because I think I had already protested, mildly, that not enough investigation was being done in Mexico. Here an American president had been killed, and this Oswald—an American citizen—was in and out of Mexico. Then just to be told not to investigate something like this, and to ask the Mexican government not to look into it! After that, dead silence. It was the strangest experience of my life.

"I think if the Mexican government had known much more than I knew, they would have told me. Lyndon Johnson had lines into Mexico that I knew nothing about. I knew he had information, he had his own sources, and I didn't know who they were. He was an amazing man. He didn't speak Spanish, but he was a good friend of [Gustavo] Díaz Ordaz, who became president of Mexico. He used to come down and see Johnson at the ranch several times, and Johnson would have me down to translate. I was born and reared in Laredo, right on the border, and if you didn't learn to say *pan,* you didn't get the bread."

Mann paused a moment, then went on: "Now there may be a perfectly logical explanation for all this. Hoover may have had a very legitimate reason. Maybe there were just too many rumors, and he wanted to cut it off. I never talked to him about it, because I respected him. But as I say, nothing like this had ever happened to me. I knew Allen Dulles fairly well, but we never spoke about it either. Dulles would have known, he was smart as hell."

I decided to tell Mann a little of what I knew, without mentioning my source. First, that the intelligence agencies may well have sought to cover up something about an earlier trip Oswald had made to Mexico. Second, that Hoover might have been warned beforehand about Oswald and two of his coconspirators but had not acted on the information. "That could have been very possible," the former ambassador said.

I told him more about Nagell's letter to Hoover and his use of the alias of a known Soviet agent. "That spy world is very bizarre, you don't know what to believe and what not," Mann responded. "Even talking to our own people, I was never quite sure, because they deliberately cover up and mislead sometimes."

Had Mann been privy to many of the intelligence-related activities going on in Mexico City? I wondered. "I don't know how to answer that truthfully," Mann replied. "I was briefed from time to time. I think with Win Scott and an FBI man there, too, we had very brief staff meetings every day. Senior officers, head of the [CIA] political section, that sort of thing. Just so I could have a feel of what was going on."

And could Mexico City be described as a kind of hotbed of intrigue? "It was unusual, yes. Because of the two-thousand-mile frontier with the

United States, there were many more agents there than was normal. It was the only post I was ever in, where there was an FBI man stationed." Clark Anderson? "I think that was his name. He would know more about this than anybody, I expect."

"Except he doesn't feel like saying much," I said.

"Well, I respect that, they take an oath."

I then asked Mann about Desmond FitzGerald—had he traveled often to Mexico City? "Yes, well, I don't remember if he ever came to Mexico City or not, but I knew him.[5] I thought he was a pretty sensible guy, in everything we talked about. But the caveat to all CIA people is, if you're smart you never know whether you're being told something or fed something. I frankly think anybody who wasn't aware that any CIA person might be disguising his status was naive. Or anybody who believed everything they told him was naive. I mean, it's really a bizarre world, a different world, a make-believe world."

The ambassador continued to muse about the CIA. "Yes, it was a very strange outfit in those days. They're sort of inoculated and I don't think they'll come completely clean with anybody outside the CIA. If they didn't take the vaccination, they didn't last very long. They had their own laws, you see."

Mann paused again, deliberated, then decided to continue: "Very strange things happened to people in that service. I had an official of the same agency [CIA] working for me when I was ambassador to Salvador, earlier. Several ministers, or the wives of ministers, were complaining that this man wasn't normal sexually. And I reported that, because I thought it should be reported. He was called to Washington immediately—and allegedly committed suicide right away. I always had a guilty conscience about that. I didn't think the fellow should be shot for whatever his sexual preference was. Well, either he died right away or was killed, I don't know what happened to him."

Then the ambassador added: "But that was one of the things that makes me a little bit suspicious about Win Scott dropping dead like he did."

Scott? I said, struggling to retain my composure. The CIA station chief in Mexico City? I told Mann what I had heard, that Scott had fallen off a ladder and died sometime in the late 1960s or early 1970s.

"Well, I always suspected he might have been murdered," the ambassador continued. My tape recorder was still running, but he said nothing about going off the record. "He left the agency sometime in the late '60s but he stayed on, went to work for people who had been connected with the Mexican government. He started running some kind of his own personal intelligence organization. They wanted to use his expertise and knowledge of Mexico, especially the intelligence side of it. When you get involved in that sort of thing, one is not surprised, if you know that world,

when people drop dead real quick. I wouldn't want to write a life insurance policy on some of the people I've known connected with that organization."

Evening was coming on in Austin; Mann's wife was due home anytime,
and they had plans to go out. As I prepared to depart, I mentioned that it
would be interesting to know who Mann spoke with in the immediate
aftermath of the assassination. "Well, I still have all my old diary appointment books upstairs," the former ambassador said. "We can go take a
look."

As we combed the bookshelf together, all of Mann's calendars were
there—except for one. The year 1963 was missing, and Thomas Mann said
he had no idea what could have happened to it.

A Well-Connected Station Chief

After the remarkable conversation with Ambassador Mann, I determined
to find out everything I could about Winston Mackinley Scott. It was not
easy. Like Desmond FitzGerald (and James Angleton before he left the
CIA), Scott basically remained an unknown personage outside his own
circle. Existing histories about the CIA very rarely mentioned him. But I
eventually came to learn quite a bit about the CIA's man to know in
Mexico, and I came away convinced that Scott probably took a number of
secrets about Oswald, and the CIA-KGB spy wars, to his grave.

Born in Alabama in 1909, Scott was named after the nineteenth-century
general Winfield Scott. A strapping six-foot-two and 210 pounds, he
played football and baseball at the University of Alabama, then got his
Ph.D. in mathematics from the University of Michigan. The New York
Giants had just offered catcher Scott a baseball contract when the FBI
recruited him at the onset of World War II.

"I think the reason the FBI hired him was, he could fiddle around with
probabilities on code-breaking," retired CIA officer James Flannery, who
worked under Scott in 1964–65, told me in a telephone interview. Flannery also recalled Scott as being a published poet, "probably under a
different name." Family members verified that Scott had published poetry,
as well as math textbooks, under the name "Ian Maxwell."[6]

Originally stationed by the FBI in Havana, Scott moved over to become
a lieutenant commander in the Navy as World War II progressed. His
adopted son Michael, now a film producer in Hollywood, related to me
that the OSS then recruited his father. "He was one of the first men sent
to London to train with British intelligence, to learn the methods they had

been devising for years. I remember my dad telling me that he traveled extensively throughout Europe, overseeing operations in many different countries."

Scott went on to be the CIA's first station chief in London (1947–50). In the late 1940s he met a beautiful Irishwoman named Maev Paula Murray, divorced his first wife, Bessie, and remarried. "His second wife was a nun, she left the order to marry him," according to Flannery. "He had that charisma, you know, very unusual guy." Scott was then called to Washington in 1950, where he became the CIA's inspector general, whose mandate was to investigate internal problems within the agency. Ferguson Dempster, a British intelligence official who was one of Scott's closest friends, first got to know him "when Win was chairman of some important talks over trying to redress the situation with the West in Southeast Asia."[7]

Then, in 1956, as the Eisenhower presidency was about to enter its second term, Allen Dulles named Scott the CIA's Mexico station chief. "It was basically a transfer for life, which was what he wanted," according to Michael Scott. "I was told by an old friend of my father's that nobody with CIA got to make such an arrangement, so somebody must have owed him big."

Scott soon developed remarkable connections within the Mexican government. "My dad spoke very broken Spanish, but I think was very respected by the Mexicans because he always made the effort," Michael Scott recalls. Joseph B. Smith, then a CIA officer in the Western Hemisphere Division, remembers: "The most fabulous story we all told was that, when Win got married again in Mexico [in December 1962], the future president [Gustavo Díaz Ordaz] was his best man. And he wasn't the only one in the wedding photo. So was Adolfo López Mateos [Mexico's president, 1958–64], and Luis Echeverría [then minister of government and eventually head of state]. The picture was supposed to have been buried in the archives of local newspapers, but all three of them were definitely prominent at the wedding."[8]

Such fertile sources provided a boon for American foreign policy. One of the most enlightening stories of Scott's influence dates from 1968, when Mexican foreign minister Antonio Carillo Flores made a trip to Moscow. This was not long before the first Strategic Arms Limitation Talks (SALT) were to begin with the United States, and nuclear weapons came up in Flores's discussion with President Leonid Brezhnev and Foreign Minister Andrei Gromyko of the USSR. The Soviet leadership made two strong points with Flores. One was their concern about China's nuclear capability. Brezhnev even raised the possible necessity of a joint U.S.-Soviet strike against the Chinese. While indicating that the Soviets would never contemplate the use of nuclear force in protecting a Western Hemisphere ally—namely, Cuba—Brezhnev also made it clear that a certain problem nation in Eastern Europe was going to have to be dealt with. The obvious reference was to Czechoslovakia, where reformer Alexander Dubcek was then intent on pulling away from the USSR.

Flores returned to Mexico, passing word along to President Ordaz, who in turn immediately phoned Winston Scott. Thus it was that the CIA knew, two months in advance, that the Soviets were planning their August 1968 invasion of Czechoslovakia. The CIA also knew that the Sino-Soviet split was definitely real, and insiders believe that Scott's tip paved the way for President Nixon's strategic American opening of diplomatic relations with China in 1971.[9]

Scott was known as a "string-saver." He never threw anything out and, as James Flannery remembers, "Win had the old FBI way, I understand, of keeping files. By name. You created a file every time a name came up. Christ, there in Mexico City, pretty soon you had files proliferating all over the place. In the mid-'60s, I think it was, we went to a centralized computer system in the agency, where the station files would mesh with the central files back at Langley instead of being on an independent track. Well, Win wouldn't play. And it drove them crazy at headquarters. He just went on with his own filing system. Then after he retired, there was a great flushing out, I presume, of the Mexico station's files and resetting them up."

After his retirement from the CIA in 1969, Scott set up a company in Mexico City called Diversified Corporate Services. But he did not leave all his files behind. In a closet of the den where he sometimes worked at home, there were four metal cabinets full of his most closely held secrets. And, in the two "retirement" years before his death, Scott also began working on a manuscript. It was a memoir—some call it an autobiographical "novel"—of his long life and times in the FBI, the OSS, and finally the CIA.

In this instance, Scott was vague even with his immediate family about what he was writing. "I understood it was basically a history of intelligence-gathering," his stepson Gregory remembers, "going all the way back to Cardinal Woolsey, who was Henry VIII's chief of intelligence. I never knew what it was really about until later."

In 1971 Scott completed his manuscript and apparently made plans to fly to Washington for an April 30 meeting with then CIA director Richard Helms. Those two men went way back, to the OSS days of World War II. Both had been assigned to the OSS by the Navy, and received some of their intelligence schooling from the British in London.

Helms was a tall, lean, sharp-featured man who, with his slick black hair and square jaw, bore a resemblance to the comic-strip character Dick Tracy. Like his longtime friend Desmond FitzGerald, he stayed in shape on the tennis court. Grandson of a former president of the Federal Reserve Bank of New York, he had attended prep schools in the United States and Europe, gone into journalism with United Press, and obtained an exclusive breakfast interview with Adolf Hitler in 1937. Once Helms caught the spy bug during the war, he also captured the eye of Allen Dulles, joining the CIA at its inception in 1947. During the 1950s he helped oversee the agency's illegal mail-opening program and helped supervise the digging of the Berlin Tunnel. Though rarely then in the public eye, Helms had shown up for Senate Foreign Relations Committee hearings in 1960 into the shooting down of the U-2 spy plane over the Soviet Union. After the Bay of Pigs failure, Helms was named by John McCone to take over the agency's "dirty tricks" division, under the title of deputy director for plans. In 1963 he worked as Desmond FitzGerald's immediate superior for the CIA's Cuban operations—and no doubt stayed in touch with Winston Scott.[10]

Cuba was right at the top of Helms's list. Years later, he would say that the CIA's decision to enlist organized-crime figures in plotting against Fidel Castro was "one of the greatest regrets of my life. It was a mistake, a case of poor judgment." Helms would also testify in 1978 before the House Assassinations Committee that another "mistake" was failing to inform the Warren Commission about the agency's anti-Castro machinations. "If I had to do it over again, I would've backed up a truck, taken all the documents down, and shoved them onto the Warren Commission's desk."[11]

In late June 1966, Lyndon Johnson appointed Helms as the seventh director of the CIA. He would remain there until February 1973, when he was fired by Richard Nixon as the Watergate scandal began to mushroom. Sometime during the week before he left, Helms is known to have systematically obliterated a huge volume of material he had collected over the years. He also ordered the destruction of records from the MK-ULTRA program he had initiated during the early 1950s, the secret testing of LSD and other drugs on unwitting civilians and military personnel (see Chapter Sixteen).[12] "The man who kept the secrets," as Helms was called, made sure that many would never surface.

When Win Scott set about arranging to see Helms in 1971, the main purpose seems to have been to let the CIA director read his finished memoir before doing anything further with it. Scott never made it to Washington. A week prior to his scheduled trip that April, the 62-year-old Scott suddenly fell off a gangplank in his backyard.

It was late on a weekend night and, the way family members recall it, Scott had gone outside alone and climbed up the gangplank to get a better look at a new brick wall that was being built in the backyard. His tumble into the rose bushes seemed more embarrassing to him than anything else.

He went to bed, awoke in some pain with bruises and cuts, then experienced trouble breathing at breakfast. His stepson Gregory and the Scotts' driver took him to the hospital, where a doctor found nothing seriously wrong and sent him home. All weekend Scott was uncharacteristically quiet, reading rather than playing his customary round of golf. On April 26, 1971, as he was preparing to go to his office, his wife, Janet, found Scott slumped over on a chair at his breakfast table. No autopsy was performed, and a postmortem suggested he had apparently suffered a blood clot to his heart during the fall.

His closest relatives, unlike Ambassador Mann, did not suspect that Scott's death was due to anything other than natural causes. But Michael Scott, who was away at boarding school when his father died, was told by an ex-CIA official who had known Scott that "certain people" had come by to see him when he was bedridden after the backyard fall—and the CIA source had expressed strong doubt that his death was an accident.

Somehow, CIA headquarters had learned very quickly of their retired official's demise. Michael Scott continued: "I was told that James Angleton was on a plane to Mexico within an hour of my dad's death, so quickly that he carried no visa or passport and was held for a while at customs. He finally arrived pretending to be there for my father's funeral. But he had really come to get at his files."

There was a rumor that Lyman Kirkpatrick, then the CIA's inspector general, might have accompanied Angleton to Mexico City. When I telephoned Kirkpatrick to ask about this, he denied it, saying only, "Count me out. If anybody went down there, it would have been Angleton."[13]

Angleton's Mission

The CIA's counter intelligence chief had been Johnny-on-the-spot before, concerning a mysterious death and privileged information. In 1976 the *National Enquirer* broke a story—later confirmed by other journals—about a Washington socialite named Mary Pinchot Meyer. She had been walking along a towpath near the Potomac River on October 12, 1964, when she was shot and killed by an unknown gunman. She had been divorced for some years from her husband, Cord Meyer, a high-ranking CIA official in various departments, including "dirty tricks." But Mary had remained close to some CIA people, particularly a fly-fishing partner of her ex-husband's—James Angleton. After moving next door to Robert Kennedy, she became closer still to someone else. Between January 1962 and the assassination, Mary Meyer had an affair with John F. Kennedy.[14]

She was a beautiful woman, a painter with friends in many circles. One of these was Timothy Leary, soon to become renowned as a "psychedelic guru" for the 1960s generation. In the midst of his earliest experiments with LSD, Leary would later write, Mary Meyer had come to see him at Harvard University in the spring of 1962. She had expressed interest in the mind-altering drug and seemed to know quite a bit about its secret uses in Washington. "The guys who run things—I mean the guys who *really* run things in Washington—are very interested in psychology, and drugs in particular," Leary remembered Meyer telling him. "These people play hardball, Timothy. They want to use drugs for warfare, for espionage, for brainwashing, for control." She and Leary discussed by contrast "drugs for peace"—wild ideas like "turning on" the Cabinet or maybe even the president, though Leary says she did not mention her affair.

The day after the assassination, according to Leary, Mary Meyer had called him, barely audible and sobbing profusely. "They couldn't control him [Kennedy] anymore," Leary would later quote her saying. "He was changing too fast. He was learning too much. . . . They'll cover everything up. I gotta come see you. I'm scared." The line went dead, and she never called back. The next Leary heard about Meyer, her body had been discovered on the Potomac towpath.

Sometime in 1963, Mary Meyer had confided in two friends about her liaisons with JFK—and the existence of a diary that included a recounting of some of their evenings together. In the event of her death, Mary told James and Ann Truitt shortly before their departure for Tokyo, where James was to become *Newsweek*'s bureau chief, she wanted them to preserve the diary and show it to her son when he came of age. When the Truitts received word of her murder while in Tokyo, responsibility for the diary was somehow communicated to their mutual friend James Angleton. The weekend after Meyer's death, five people gathered at her Georgetown home and tore it apart looking for the diary. Cord Meyer was there. So was Mary's sister Tony Bradlee, the wife of *The Washington Post*'s editor Ben Bradlee. And so were James Angleton and his wife, Cecily.

None of them could find the diary. Only later did her sister locate it in Mary's studio, inside a locked steel box containing hundreds of letters. She turned everything over to Angleton, who took the material to CIA headquarters. Later, according to James Truitt, he received a letter from Angleton that said: "As to the diary and related papers, I burned them."

With the exception of the Timothy Leary portion of this saga of the Camelot years, much of this story had appeared in print by the time I met with Angleton for the second time, in April 1976. When I asked him about the episode, Angleton replied that he had been acting in a private capacity for the family, and in no way for the CIA, which he hastened to add had nothing to do with her death. He then proceeded to relate a strange and fascinating epilogue. He and his wife had planned to go out to dinner and a show with Mary Meyer that October evening in 1964. When news came over the radio that someone had been killed in a park near where she lived, Cicely Angleton had a premonition that it was Mary. That evening they drove over to her house, but it was completely dark. A terrible foreboding grew stronger in Angleton's wife. Angleton called Meyer's answering service, which at first simply said that Mary wasn't in. But when Angleton explained they had a date with her, and that his wife was hysterical in the car, he was informed of Meyer's death.[15]

The entire time Angleton was relating this story, he dug his fingers into the wooden arm of the chair in the Army-Navy Club. He was dead by the time I learned of his similar quest in 1971 in Mexico City, in pursuit of the papers of Win Scott.

Even before Scott's funeral, once the customary amenities were ended Angleton made no bones about the real reason he had come. He wanted the manuscript, and right away, threatening a family member that "we have ways of getting it from you."

"Otherwise," said Michael Scott, "they were going to rescind a plaque that was planned to honor my dad at CIA headquarters because, Angleton said, obviously his intentions were not honorable."

The trouble was, the family apparently didn't know what Angleton was talking about. It took several days for them to find the manuscript, which had been hidden in Scott's study. Not far away was a penciled note in Scott's handwriting on a yellow legal pad. It was addressed to Richard Helms, but apparently had never been sent. "Dear Dick," it read, "I am coming to Washington, bringing the manifest. You may delete or destroy it in its entirety. Win."[16]

In the meantime, Angleton apparently put out a search team for a Mexican woman who had typed Scott's work, to see if she had a copy. He went through whatever files were in Scott's office, and demanded that any additional material at his home be brought there, too. The family complied. "I wasn't there, but I heard from my family that they loaded cratefuls of stuff," said Michael Scott. "I wonder what else they confiscated out of his study."

After Angleton received, by way of the CIA's new Mexico station chief, the manuscript that Scott's family had turned over, Angleton shipped all of Scott's files through diplomatic pouch and returned to Langley. "After this," added Michael, "I understand the CIA revised their rules about allowing station chiefs to keep files in their homes."

Michael Scott did not know this, but among the items Angleton is said to have retrieved was a tape recording, akin to a 45 rpm record—bearing the voice of Lee Harvey Oswald. Scott had kept it in his home since 1963.[17] Until 1976 the CIA would never acknowledge that such voice recordings—reportedly picked up through bugging the phone lines at the Soviet and Cuban diplomatic missions—had ever existed. When the agency did concede this, Scott's old friend David Phillips was the spokesman. The sound tapes, he falsely testified before Congress, had been "routinely destroyed" a week or so after Oswald's visit to Mexico City in the autumn of 1963.[18]

The Manuscript

In 1985, Michael Scott set out to try to obtain a copy of his father's manuscript from the CIA. So much about his dad's mysterious life continued to baffle him. Ironically, in 1987 Michael would work on a documentary segment for the *Unsolved Mysteries* TV program that unveiled new information about the 1968 assassination of Robert Kennedy. And he still remembered, as a young boy, being held in John F. Kennedy's arms when the president made a 1962 visit to Mexico City; Win Scott had been among the people in charge of JFK's security.

"So I wrote the CIA, saying I would love to get ahold of a manuscript that I understood had been confiscated from my dad's estate," Michael remembered. "Within a few weeks, I get a letter back saying my request was being processed. Then came a phone call one day from two CIA agents who said they were in San Francisco on business and wanted to meet me at some hotel or parking lot in L.A. When I said I couldn't do that, they told me if I was ever on the East Coast, feel free to come by headquarters.

"A few months later, I happened to be back East doing a film and I called up and went out to Langley. I was introduced to a high-ranking officer who had obviously read the manuscript. He spoke about how great my father had been for the agency, how much respect they had for what he did, and said they would honor my request. He was dangling the pages in front of me, saying 'There may be information you know from outside sources that might seem to be public knowledge, but we can't officially release it to you.' He said they had been forced to delete portions of the manuscript for reasons of national security.

" 'I thought this was supposed to be a personal story,' I said. 'I know my dad was trying to write this for the public, so what could possibly be so sensitive?'

"And he said, 'Well, there was some mention of Lee Harvey Oswald in some area, and we don't want to make that public.'

"Well, this didn't really surprise me. He handed me the thing. There were about 150 pages missing, chapters 13 to 26 were deleted in their entirety. Everything after 1947. Actually, they did leave in the Epilogue."

The manuscript was titled "It Came to Little." Michael Scott agreed to share the final chapter with me, saying that he believed his father had intended it to see the light of day. It was much about "burnout," how particularly a clandestine operations officer was forced to lead a "schizoidal" life where he could never discuss his vocation beyond a limited circle of people engaged in the same activity. In Scott's view, early retirement should be the rule.

This was particularly true for a counterespionage officer. Scott wrote,

At times these officers are assigned the task of protecting the security of operations and operations personnel from their own organization, and they can find personnel of their own organization either acting as traitors, or, for some less vile reason, breaking security. . . .

I believe that, in the case of a good and active counter-espionage [CE] officer, the individual's self-relationship becomes a pseudo personal one; and that his true self treats his false self as though his false self were another person . . . the ce officer's true self could become depersonalized. The false-self which becomes dominant could think, "He (the true self) is too cautious, too frightened and not daring enough." For, after a few successes, a ce officer is inclined to believe (or to have his false (ce) self) that his opponents are incapable of beating him. The false (ce) self comes to believe, "I am too smart for my opponents; they can never outwit me."

This "danger of conceit," Scott continued, had destroyed many of the best "long before they had reached their peaks as officers, and long before their successes warranted even the slightest conceit." Or they "are frequently so shocked by a failure so deeply that they are useless, at least temporarily, as clandestine operations officers. Some such failures have been said to have developed microcosms within themselves; and, as a result of such an autistic, private self-contained life, they cannot be used— since, for a time, they cannot associate themselves with a life of reality, which must be lived with, and to a degree, shared with others."

Besides the "problem of double lives," Scott concluded that there was one final reason for necessary early retirement. ". . . [That] they arrive at a point in life—having met and dealt with so many dishonest people, and having, themselves, in their demanding and dominating (false) selves, lived a lie—where they mistrust almost everyone, look for the hidden meaning and motives behind even the most sincere statements of friends and loved ones."

That was the last line of the book. Scott's Epilogue was, I thought, as honest a look at the inner life of the counterspy world as anything I had ever seen. It summarized a great deal that I had felt, and come to know, about Richard Nagell. And I wondered how much it might even pertain to a counter intelligence operation that once surrounded Lee Harvey Oswald —the conceit, the dishonesty, the failure.

Double Agent

Writing a memoir had first been suggested to Win Scott by John Barron. He was an author and friend who also used the former station chief's recollections about Soviet operations in Mexico as background in preparing his own book, *KGB: The Secret Work of Soviet Secret Agents.* Barron was (and still is) a senior editor in the Washington office of *Reader's Digest* magazine, as well as a former veteran of the Naval Intelligence School (specializing in the Russian language) who spent two years as a military intelligence officer in Berlin.[19]

Barron himself retained interesting connections, inside and outside the CIA. He became, for example, a friend of Soviet defector Yuri Nosenko— the KGB official who came over to the American side soon after the assassination, with the news that Soviet intelligence had never had much interest in Lee Harvey Oswald. Unlike the Angletonian crowd, Barron believed that Nosenko's "bona fides" were 100 percent genuine. According to Barron, they had met in May 1970, when Nosenko "walked unannounced into our Washington offices, stated he had read of our project in the *Reader's Digest,* and offered his assistance."[20] That project was *KGB,* published in 1974.

Barron was in Mexico City when Scott died. In recent days they had dined together on two occasions, and Scott had confided in Barron at some length. They had another appointment scheduled but, when Barron came to the house, he was informed that Scott had died that morning.[21]

From two other sources I learned that Barron may have been the person who contacted the CIA about Scott's death. Noteworthy here is something that happened to author Edward Jay Epstein a few years later, when in 1975 he was approached by *Reader's Digest* to write a book which became *Legend: The Secret World of Lee Harvey Oswald.* Epstein told me that he was promised two "exclusives" by the *Digest:* access to defector Yuri Nosenko, and a chance to hear the officially nonexistent CIA voice recordings of Oswald in Mexico. Both were to come through the auspices of John Barron. "Barron did provide me Nosenko," Epstein says (he did not trust the defector's account of the KGB-Oswald relationship), "but never the tapes. I was then told they had disappeared."[22]

I had heard another story, impossible to confirm until the CIA releases Scott's entire manuscript, that a considerable portion of his writing had to do with the "double" role alluded to in his Epilogue. In June 1992 I spoke by phone to Cleveland Cram, a longtime CIA official who had been called out of retirement in 1976 to spend four years compiling a secret, four-thousand-page study of Angleton's counter intelligence staff between 1954 and 1974.[23] When I raised the subject of Scott's manuscript, Cram replied that he had read part of it. "It was given me to examine and comment on," he said, "a very interesting section about the last days of the OSS and the early days of our London station, Kim Philby, and so on. Whether there were other chapters, I don't know."

I told Cram of a rumor that Scott may have written about a curious relationship he had with someone in Soviet intelligence. "I think I know what you're referring to," Cram said. "There was a double-agent operation in London, but I don't know the exact details well enough to comment much on that. It was not a Soviet approach to Win in the sense he was some sort of easy mark and they were out to recruit him. But Win took advantage of it to try to play the Soviets along. He did not do this on his own, or off the cuff. British MI-5 [England's counterespionage unit for its home territory] were fully knowledgeable of the whole thing, in on it practically from the start. And [CIA] headquarters I'm sure approved it. In those days after World War II, we were feeling our way with the RIS [Russian Intelligence Service]. We didn't know much about them, and some still felt we could get along. Others, like Win, were more clear-eyed and hardheaded and willing to take chances. This would have been sometime in the late '40s."

Cram said he did not know who Scott's Soviet contact was or how it all turned out. "I can tell you this," he added, "if Win had been involved in an operation like that, Angleton would have known about it. Because they were very close collaborators."

Clare Petty, who joined the CIA at its inception, had been brought onto Angleton's CI staff late in 1966. Angleton gave Petty a single mission: Find the KGB's "mole" inside the CIA.[24] Now living in retirement outside Washington, Petty had been personally instructed by Angleton to retrieve the Scott manuscript from the Western Hemisphere Division's archive and read through it.

"Scott was not writing this as though it was himself," Petty says, "though the facts concerning his life and service were so absolutely identical that there was not the slightest doubt it was autobiographical."

Petty verified that the manuscript described a relationship between Scott and a KGB official—"The fellow's name began with an M, he also had a cryptonym as I recall. It began in London and then Scott came back to Washington. Whereupon, the Soviet was also assigned to Washington. Ostensibly, Scott then got permission from a top-level group in the CIA to reinstate what developed into a very close relationship."

The result, Petty said, was that Scott took the bait offered by the KGB —and became a double agent.

"The manuscript gets kind of weird from that point onward," Petty continued. "In the process of all this, the Soviet falls in love with Scott's wife. Then Scott comes home one night and discovers his wife murdered in the bathtub. He knows who did it, and so Scott then ostensibly murders the Soviet—takes him down Highway 90 someplace or at least southward out of Washington, and dumps him over a culvert."

All of this, according to the manuscript's timetable, took place when Scott was stationed in Washington in the mid-1950s. Yet, in real time, his second wife, Maev Paula Murray, did not die until September 1962; she had a drinking problem and, as far as the family knew, overdosed on a combination of pills and alcohol, possibly having done so intentionally. If the incident Scott was describing did in fact happen, it would have taken place not in Washington, but in Mexico City—the very month when Richard Nagell signed his own contract with the CIA and became a double agent.

This raised all kinds of questions in my mind. Was the CIA's station chief compromised by the KGB? If Nagell's CIA contact "Bob" was in fact himself working for the Soviets, did Winston Scott know it? Or, if Scott did not know about Bob's purported true allegiance, could Bob have been part of a Soviet operation aimed at Scott? Bob's description, according to Nagell, was of a man in his middle to late thirties who spoke Japanese. This would not apply to Scott's linguistic background, and the station chief was fifty-two years old in 1962. Yet, according to what Nagell told Arthur Greenstein, Bob passed himself off as the CIA's Mexico station chief when they met in September 1962.[25]

Former ambassador Mann had also brought up the subject of Scott's personal life, but in another context. This had to do with the woman Scott married in Mexico City only three months after his second wife's alleged suicide. His new wife was the former Janet Leddy. Until her divorce in 1962, she had been the wife of Raymond Leddy, himself a very good friend of Scott dating back to their mutual employment with the FBI in World War II.

"If I were going to conduct an investigation into what happened to Win Scott," Mann said, "I would sure want to look into that whole mess. I remember Ray Leddy coming to me at the embassy, thinking that somehow as ambassador it would be possible for me to stop his wife from marrying Scott. He wanted me to move Scott out of Mexico. But I told

Leddy I had no authority to do something like that, and I couldn't go interfering with everybody who committed adultery, assuming he [Scott] had been. Leddy was very angry at me when I wouldn't take action.

"Leddy was a Foreign Service officer, not a CIA man, but he had very close connections with the CIA—much more so than the ordinary officer. He and Win were both very mysterious guys—true intelligence people, if you know what I mean. They played their cards very close to their vest. Raymond Leddy died under strange circumstances, too, I think."

Raymond Leddy and Winston Scott had met while with the FBI in Havana in 1941. Both had then gone into the Navy and then the OSS. After the war, as noted in Chapter Nine, Leddy had established the CIA's entire Latin American network. That was when he met and married Janet Graham, also hiring her onto his CIA staff. She was originally from Lima, Peru, where, oddly enough, she had gotten acquainted with Warren Broglie, future manager of Mexico City's Hotel Luma. It was Broglie who gave Janet her first job in New York, in the Latin American department of the Waldorf-Astoria Hotel.[26]

Spruille Braden, a State Department official who like Ray Leddy was a fervent anti-Communist, had suggested to Leddy that he switch over to the diplomatic side. In 1948 the ex-FBI/OSS/CIA man was posted first to Caracas, Venezuela, and then to Buenos Aires—where he oversaw American oil interests in Argentina, Chile, and Brazil. He and Janet then came back to the Central American desk at the State Department in Washington, where Leddy was called on by Allen Dulles to orchestrate the overthrow of the Arbenz government in Guatemala in 1954. In 1957, the year after Scott became CIA station chief there, Leddy was posted to Mexico as a counselor in the U.S. embassy. That went on for four years, with Leddy returning Stateside in 1961 to become State Department adviser to the U.S. Army War College in Carlisle, Pennsylvania. In that capacity he instructed Army officers on international affairs and diplomacy.[27]

During that period, the Leddys' marriage went sour. Janet left for Florida, and was heading back to Lima by way of Mexico City when she stopped by to seek help from Scott. Shortly thereafter, in 1962, came Ray Leddy's visit to Ambassador Mann. After Scott's second wife died in September, and he married Janet at the lavish ceremony in December, Scott officially adopted the five Leddy children. Leddy put investigators on their trail, threatening to kidnap them back. He and Win Scott had become bitter enemies.

Leddy, who remarried in 1969, became assistant secretary of defense for Latin America for the first three years of the Nixon Administration. Leddy died of a heart attack at age sixty-three while on a Florida vacation in 1976. Family members did not recall anything unusual about his death. But Ambassador Mann, who was not even aware of Scott's mysterious

manuscript, says he still "puzzled about it all." Mann added: "There was
the whole Oswald thing coming down in Mexico, at the same time back in
'63. Then later on, strange things happening, people like Scott and Leddy
dying pretty young and in apparently good health. If either of them had a
bad heart, I didn't know about it."

Were it not for the fateful timing of this knot of relationships, I would
not have chosen to write about them. Whether all this is germane historically, one could only speculate, or simply puzzle, as Ambassador Mann
did. Ray Leddy, during the Guatemalan coup planning in 1954, had
worked directly with two of the CIA men whose names keep cropping up
in our story: Tracy Barnes was the CIA's officer in charge; David Phillips
was the propaganda master.

And Leddy's path is quite likely to have crossed that of Oswald's friend
George de Mohrenschildt, since Leddy was the "petroleum attaché" in
the 1950s when de Mohrenschildt was doing oil-related consulting in two
countries directly under Leddy's purview, Venezuela and Argentina. Between 1954 and 1958 de Mohrenschildt also worked as a leading consultant for Sharmex S.A., an independent American oil company building up
ventures in Mexico.[28] In addition, in 1960 de Mohrenschildt came through
Mexico City (see Chapter Eleven), where he saw Soviet deputy premier
Mikoyan before advancing through Guatemala on his "walking tour" that
passed right near the Bay of Pigs invasion force's training camp.

And if Scott's relationship with a Soviet intelligence agent did continue
into his years in Mexico, this could add a whole new dimension to the
Nagell/Oswald story. Did Leddy know of this aspect of Scott's life? Could
people besides the KGB—such as the FBI, or Army Intelligence—also
have manipulated matters going on around the CIA's Mexico City battle
station?

The Clare Petty Study

"I had the feeling there was a little something more to the whole thing
Scott wrote up in that manuscript," Clare Petty was saying in our 1992
conversation. Angleton had recruited Petty onto his CI staff in 1966 after
Petty, while stationed for years in West Germany, helped expose several
major KGB penetrations into Reinhard Gehlen's network. For the next
seven years, Petty and a small staff pored over thousands of pages of CI
files about defectors and agency employees. In the course of doing so, he
spent some time studying the early career of Winston Scott.

Petty found that while Scott was station chief in London, he had developed a "very good friendship" with Kim Philby, then a senior officer with Britain's MI-6 [foreign] intelligence. When Scott came to Washington late in 1950, Philby was also stationed there as MI-6's American liaison, where he was among James Angleton's closest British friends. "The three of them were pretty close pals," according to Petty. Scott was also a friend of one of Philby's colleagues, Guy Burgess.

Then, in May 1951, Burgess and another British intelligence officer, Donald Maclean, suddenly defected to Moscow. Philby was recalled to London for questioning as the suspected "third man" who had managed to tip his countrymen that they were on the verge of being exposed as longtime Soviet agents. But concrete evidence against Philby was lacking, and it would be nearly twelve more years before he, too, fled to sanctuary in the USSR.[29]

In 1951, everyone at the CIA who knew Philby and Burgess were asked, in Petty's words, "to give a complete accounting of their relationship." Angleton and Scott each submitted memos. "Yet Angleton did not mention Scott having been present at a meeting in Georgetown and a couple other things," Petty continued. "He seemed not to want Scott involved in it. Looking back, you had Scott's very broad connections in London, and the fact that he did have a liaison with a Soviet case officer there and in the United States. Then he decided to write this 'novel,' which involved this guy. It's all rather bizarre."

Eventually Petty's quest to find a CIA mole would come to focus on Angleton himself. "It all involved a tremendous amount of detail, on Angleton's movements and other people. To say there was no penetration of CIA is rather like saying gravity does not exist because nobody ever held any in their hands. There were, of course, various penetrations, and logically you would have to consider the possibility of a long-term high-level penetration. The fact is, the Soviets went after the chiefs of counterespionage, or people high up in that area. Philby is the prime example; in Germany, Hans Felfe filled the bill. There is a great difference of opinion about a Canadian case, but at any rate Leslie Bennett, who did come under suspicion, was head of counterespionage there."

Petty carefully reviewed Angleton's career, focusing on the spate of Soviet defectors who began making themselves known in 1959—the same year that Oswald and a number of other Americans "defected" to the USSR. First there was Michal Goleniewski, who in 1959 began sending a series of letters to the CIA under the name "Sniper," and who defected in West Berlin late in 1960. Goleniewski provided leads that helped unmask several Soviet agents, including a key subordinate to Reinhard Gehlen.[30]

"From the start, Angleton thought Goleniewski was a fraud," says Petty. "But in my opinion, he was the most valuable defector we ever had. This case was extremely closely held, as much as anything I can ever remember.

Yet, within a matter of just a few weeks, the Soviets were aware that somebody had come to us with valuable information—and they knew the nature of it. This is an indicator, if you adopt my solution, as to where the penetration was. Eliminate everyone who didn't know about Goleniewski, and you end up with the fingers of one hand."

In 1961 Anatoly Golitsin, said to be a major in the KGB's First Chief Directorate, defected to the CIA. Golitsin announced that the KGB had an agent somewhere in the highest ranks of American intelligence; further, that future Soviet-controlled agents arriving in the guise of defectors or double agents would supply disinformation to build up the credibility of the "inside man." Angleton believed Golitsin, with a vengeance.[31]

Petty examined Angleton's "adherence to all of Golitsin's wild theories, his false accusations against foreign services and the resulting damage to our liaison relationships, and finally his accusations against innocent CIA Soviet Division officers."[32] Petty also looked at the failed counter intelligence cases, such as the exposure of Oleg Penkovsky during the Cuban Missile Crisis.

Then there was the internal battle over Yuri Nosenko's bona fides, which divided the CIA against itself. Petty believed that both Golitsin and Nosenko were Soviet "plants." He figured the Soviets had arranged Nosenko's defection to seem to counter Golitsin—and, in the process, arrive in January 1964 disclaiming any KGB interest in Oswald. The Americans already suspected Nosenko's legitimacy, but a defector bearing such alleged knowledge so soon after the assassination simply had to be received by the CIA. Richard Helms had already assigned Angleton to look into possible Soviet connections to Oswald. In turn, Angleton's staff became the CIA's liaison to the Warren Commission.

"The thing I've always wondered," says Petty, "is if Angleton really believed so strongly that Oswald was a Soviet agent, why did he never make any effort in that respect with the Warren Commission? And he absolutely for sure didn't. There was this inconsistency with how Angleton handled the Nosenko case, being so adamant that Nosenko was a fraud. There had to be something deeper involved."

What sealed Petty's suspicions about Angleton was a trip that the CI chief had made to Australia in 1967, for an international conference with his counterparts from several nations. "He used a false passport in the process, which was totally unnecessary," Petty said. "Then after the meeting, he returned alone on a flight that went across to Acapulco. Angleton was in Mexico City for a couple days, during which nobody had any idea what he did or bothered to look. I found out purely by accident that there was a very senior KGB officer who had also come to Mexico City on temporary duty at that particular point."

In the meantime, Angleton's own mole search honed in on CIA officers of Eastern European descent, or who had served in Moscow, or who were part of the agency's Soviet Russia Division. Eventually his suspicions came to focus on David Murphy, who had risen through the ranks to become head of that division in November 1963.[33] Petty scrutinized Murphy's career and concluded that Angleton was wrong. Cleveland Cram, who conducted yet another massive retrospective study of the CIA "molehunt" in the post-Angleton era, told me: "On the whole business of a mole in CIA, God knows maybe there was one and we didn't know about it. But the people Jim focused on as his candidates, none of those panned out."

Most recent research into Angleton's career has viewed his paranoia as stemming from the "betrayal" of friendship that he suffered at the hands of Kim Philby. Petty's report, which he presented in June 1974, was never officially deemed legitimate. But the fact remains that Angleton was fired by William Colby six months later.

When I spoke with Petty about Angleton's persistent finger-pointing at the Soviets and Cubans in our interviews about the assassination, Petty basically viewed this as all part of Angleton's game. "Because he's the expert, in control of everything that had to do with Soviet espionage," Petty said. In other words, he had to play the role to the hilt.

It was an astounding matter to contemplate. I thought back to Angleton's alleged early relationship with John Paisley (see Chapter Eight)—and Angleton's purported lack of suspicion about Paisley, at least with me. I contemplated the friendship between Angleton and Scott, and their mutual close relationship with Philby. Angleton, by so adamantly seeking to discredit Yuri Nosenko—and anybody in the CIA who believed Nosenko—had, in Petty's view, neutralized the Soviet defector. "Nosenko's information was cranked into the mill," Petty said, "but it became essentially unusable. Everyone was left hanging in the air. The general CIA inclination was to believe the Soviets had nothing to do with Oswald."

When I once asked Nagell for his impressions of Angleton, he wrote back that Angleton "strikes me as a typical armchair, pipe-smoking, retired 'gentleman spy,' who likely knew no more about certain matters than John McCone . . . or Jim Garrison."[34]

At a 1977 interview I specifically asked Nagell whether Soviet penetration of the CIA in Mexico City figured into the assassination picture. "Of course the CIA was penetrated backwards and forwards, as was the State Department," he replied. "Even little outfits like the U.S. Bureau of Narcotics and Dangerous Drugs, which was actually in the American embassy annex across the street. Most of these were penetrated by the Mexican authorities, who in turn were penetrated, so . . ."

His voice trailed off, and I pursued the matter by wondering whether such penetration reached a high level at CIA headquarters. "I don't know, but I could formulate some conclusions," Nagell said. "Like, do you mean was Desmond FitzGerald a KGB officer?"

"Yes," I said, holding my breath, "was he?"

"No," Nagell said, and laughed.[35]

But he did add one additional telling statement on this subject. "Domestic Operations was a division of the CIA, never at Langley but at 1750 Pennsylvania Avenue," he told me. "And it was very well penetrated by the Soviets."[36]

The Domestic Operations Division

Domestic Operations, as we have seen, was the division established in 1962 by Tracy Barnes—the CIA official whom Robert Morrow asserts not only received Oswald's material from the Soviet Union but also dispatched Nagell to New Orleans in the summer of 1963. The very title "Domestic Operations" amounted to a violation of the CIA's original charter. Time and again, the agency had assured Congress that it did not engage in domestic-based activities. *The Espionage Establishment,* a 1967 book by David Wise and Thomas B. Ross, notes that Barnes indeed operated out of a new office building at 1750 Pennsylvania Avenue, only a block from the White House. At 1750 Pennsylvania Avenue the CIA's new branch occupied the entire fifth floor under the cover designation "U.S. Army Element, Joint Planning Activity, Joint Operations Group (SD 7753)."[37]

A handsome six-footer who excelled as an athlete at Groton and then Yale, Barnes was another of the CIA's Ivy League lawyers who married well. His wife, Janet, was an Aldrich, related to the Rockefeller family; Barnes's sister was married to the prominent novelist John O'Hara. Joining the OSS in World War II, Barnes ended up assigned to Allen Dulles's "Operation Sunrise" mission in Switzerland. Like Desmond FitzGerald, Barnes temporarily resumed his law practice after the war, also becoming president of the Urban League of Rhode Island. In 1950 he was working in Washington as legal counsel to the under secretary of the Army when Dulles enlisted him as a CIA deputy director of the Psychological Strategy Board at the onset of the Korean War.

Late in 1953, when Barnes worked with Raymond Leddy and David Phillips in the CIA's Guatemalan coup d'état, Barnes also selected E. Howard Hunt, Jr., as his political action chief. It was a relationship that would continue, off and on, through the Bay of Pigs and into 1963, when Hunt became Barnes's covert-action man in the Domestic Operations Division. Barnes rose steadily through the CIA's ranks—posted to Frankfurt, Germany, then as the London chief of station in 1957, and back home by 1960 to be deputized as No. 2 man for the Bay of Pigs planning.[38]

According to Thomas Powers's biography of Richard Helms, a number of clandestine types "either disliked Barnes or distrusted his judgment and ability, and regarded his succession of top-level jobs as due to Dulles's weakness for an old friend and dashing figure."[39] Cleveland Cram, who worked under Barnes in London and during the Bay of Pigs period, adds: "Opinions of Tracy varied pretty widely. Some people were very critical of him, from the point of view that he never focused on the main problems, was too easy and too willing to go along with people and not tow a hard line."

By the early 1960s, Barnes certainly showed distaste for some of the CIA's more extreme activities. In the summer of 1960, headquarters cabled its Havana station that "Possible removal top three leaders [Castro, his brother Raul, and Che Guevara] is receiving serious consideration." Howard Hunt pushed the notion hard with Barnes. A Havana case officer set about making the arrangements, only to find another cable soon awaiting him: "Do not pursue ref. Would like to drop matter." It was signed by Tracy Barnes.[40]

He was sometimes called "the soul of vagueness." Angleton called him "principally an expediter, not a formulator. Very high-grade man, courageous type. Tracy was a real gent. No axes to grind there."[41]

Barnes retired from the CIA in December 1966, returning to his alma mater, Yale, to become a special assistant to President Kingman Brewster, Jr. By the late 1960s Barnes was the university's consultant to the local black community. Barnes died of a heart attack at age sixty, in his Rhode Island home, on February 18, 1972.

There is not a whit of public evidence that Barnes was ever suspected, by Angleton or anyone else, of having been recruited by the Soviets. Nor am I suggesting this. Still, there were questions about Barnes that troubled me as I assembled the Nagell narrative. First, by Morrow's account, Barnes was the first recipient of intelligence data from Oswald in Minsk— information that would, in the normal chain of command, probably have passed to the desk of John Paisley for analysis. Second, there was Barnes's Morrow-alleged role in coordinating Nagell's activities.

Also according to Morrow, the FBI's counterespionage chief, William Sullivan, had removed Oswald's name from the FBI's Security Index. "This request—for Sullivan to delete Oswald's name—had come directly from Tracy Barnes," Morrow has written.[42]

Finally, there was Barnes's closeness to E. Howard Hunt, Jr. On August 20, 1978, in the midst of the House Assassinations Committee's probe, an article appeared in the *Wilmington* (Del.) *Sunday News Journal.* It described a secret CIA memorandum of 1966 that stated that Hunt had been in Dallas on the day of the assassination. Said to have been initialed by Angleton and Helms, the memo was about keeping the importance of Hunt's presence there a secret. A cover story providing Hunt an alibi for being elsewhere "ought to be considered," it reportedly said.[43]

The memo's date of origin was some years before Hunt became infamous as one of the Watergate burglars in 1972. In 1966 Hunt was little known outside the CIA—having worked undercover in Mexico City and Tokyo and as station chief in Uruguay during the 1950s, authoring more than forty novels about the spy trade under various pseudonyms, even helping Allen Dulles prepare his own memoir, *The Craft of Intelligence.*[44]

Joseph J. Trento, who wrote the Wilmington news story, says that his source was none other than Angleton. "In 1978, Angleton called and asked me to come down for lunch at the Army-Navy Club," Trento recalls.[45] "He said he wanted to talk to me about something. This was as the House Committee's investigation was winding up, and he told me a number of things concerning the Kennedy assassination and its aftermath.

"Then he explained some very complicated counter intelligence operations. 'Did you know Howard Hunt was in Dallas on the day of the assassination?' he said. I said, 'So what? So was Richard Nixon, for a Pepsi-Cola convention.'

"Angleton said, 'What I'm trying to tell you is, some very odd things were going on that were out of our control.' Then he added the possibility that Hunt was there on orders from a high-level KGB mole inside the agency—and that this should have been looked into at the time."

If that was true, it seemed plausible that any "orders" given to Howard Hunt might have come from his boss at Domestic Operations, Tracy Barnes. Hunt has denied under oath that he was in Dallas on the fateful day. According to Trento, after his conversation with Angleton, the ex-CI chief then arranged for the internal CIA memo to be delivered to him. Angleton simultaneously alerted the House Assassinations Committee, using Tennessee senator Howard Baker as his intermediary, and the committee also received a copy.

"It was all handled in such a way that Angleton was not the source," Trento adds. "I later came to conclude that the mole-sent-Hunt idea was, to use his phrase, disinformation; that Angleton was trying to protect his own connections to Hunt's being in Dallas. You see, Angleton was aware of a serious counterintelligence problem with the Cubans. They were making these crazy movements all over Texas and New Orleans. You couldn't tell who was who, and he knew the exiles were heavily penetrated by Castro's intelligence. Things were getting out of hand, and Angleton was trying to find out what was going on at the time of the assassination. My guess is, it was Angleton himself who sent Hunt to Dallas, because he didn't want to use anybody from his own shop. Hunt was still considered a hand-holder for the Cuban exiles, sort of Helms's unhousebroken pet."

The godfather of Hunt's youngest son was Manuel Artime, the Cuban exiles' invasion leader for the Bay of Pigs.[46] Nagell's 1963 investigation into Artime was one of the reasons that he became convinced by September that he, Nagell, "may have performed intelligence services for a foreign nation." Nagell told me that while Artime was not directly involved in the assassination, "he may have been in meetings with certain people."

In another interview, Nagell commented that "one guy who's a well-known exile leader was definitely with Cuban intelligence." And, in one of Nagell's question-marked references to Art Greenstein, he wrote: "Was MANUEL ARTIME nash?"[47] The word "nash," as explained earlier, is the Russian word for "ours."

When Artime died, at age forty-five in 1977, before he could be questioned by the House Assassinations Committee, Miami-based committee staffer Gaeton Fonzi wondered about it. "There are some what I call mysterious deaths," Fonzi said. "Artime fits into that category—he got cancer awfully fast." Fonzi added that he, too, had heard "scuttlebutt" that Artime, after his release from a Cuban jail in the Bay of Pigs prisoner exchange, might have become a double agent for Castro.[48]

This endless spiral of possibilities would converge, in late September 1963, around Lee Harvey Oswald in Mexico City.

Summary

Nothing can be taken for granted in the realm of counterespionage. Inside this web, we now consider the possibility that Oswald was part of a penetration team looking for the source of an intelligence leak relating to Cuba. Military Intelligence may even have teamed up with the FBI to examine the CIA's mysterious dealings with Soviet intelligence in Mexico City. Orders received by Ambassador Thomas Mann from FBI director Hoover, to shut down the Mexico end of the postassassination investigation, indicate concerns at the highest levels of what might be exposed there.

And there were certainly abundant avenues to worry about. If Nagell's CIA contact "Bob" was in fact a Soviet "mole," what are we to make of station chief Winston Scott? CIA analyst Clare Petty suspected Scott— and even James Angleton—of finagling with the Soviets. Scott's relationship with a KGB official, dating back to London in the late 1940s, has been verified from several sources. Did this continue into Mexico, culminating in the death of Scott's second wife? Is Scott's triangular relationship with the ex-wife of his old friend Raymond Leddy germane to Nagell's simultaneous acceptance of a double-agent mission?

The answers may lie in Scott's manuscript, which Angleton whisked away in the immediate aftermath of the station chief's death. Whatever Scott's memoir contains about Oswald must also await the CIA's willingness to release this potentially vital document.

In a world where nothing is quite what it appears, the CIA's Domestic Operations Division also falls under the looking-glass. What was Angleton's purpose in asserting that E. Howard Hunt went to Dallas on instructions from a KGB mole? As Nagell has hinted, what if Hunt's Cuban exile associate Manuel Artime was in fact a Castro agent?

Many people in the CIA had reasons to cover up their own relationship to Oswald, even if this had nothing to do with an assassination conspiracy. In considering this plethora of possibilities surrounding Oswald, Nagell, and the assassination, what cannot be overlooked is that a "third force" was aware of the counterspy web—and seized on it to their own advantage.

Chapter Twenty-one

Oswald's Strange Voyage:
September 1963

━━━━━━━━━━━━━━━━━━━━◇━━━━━━━━━━━━━━━━━━━━

A few days after Richard Case Nagell's arrest in El Paso on September 20, 1963, Lee Harvey Oswald was on the move. Marina's friend Ruth Paine, who arrived that same day in New Orleans after a vacation, helped pack Oswald's wife's possessions. Marina was pregnant with a second child, and she and Lee had decided she should live with Paine in Irving, Texas. Marina knew—but Lee had warned her "not to tell anyone about it"— that her husband was soon bound for Mexico City. Since obtaining his tourist card on the seventeenth, Oswald had been writing a summary of his achievements in the service of Marxism. After cataloging his years in the Soviet Union, Oswald placed particular emphasis on his one-man Fair Play for Cuba Committee in New Orleans.[1]

On September 24, according to Senate investigators, the FBI's New Orleans office advised headquarters that its investigation into Oswald's FPCC activities was continuing and that a report detailing the findings would be presented. On the same day, FBI headquarters sent another report on Oswald to the CIA.[2]

Sometime that night, Oswald left New Orleans. What he did for the next twenty-four hours remains murky. The Warren Commission concluded that he had boarded a bus for Houston, but no documentary evidence exists to substantiate this, nor could bus line personnel or passengers be found who saw him.[3]

On the evening of September 25, three visitors showed up unexpectedly at the apartment door of Silvia Odio in Dallas.[4] She was a twenty-six-year-old Cuban exile who had come to Dallas a few months earlier from Puerto Rico, where she had helped establish a new group called Junta Revolucionaria (JURE). Now, as her sister Annie, seventeen, stood just behind her, the strangers introduced themselves. Two were either Cuban or Mexican—the sisters weren't sure which—and identified themselves by their "war names"; "Leopoldo," and either "Angel" or "Angelo." They introduced their partner, a quiet young American, as "Leon Oswald."

Leopoldo told the Odio sisters that the trio were fellow members of the new JURE exile group. They were on a trip from New Orleans and wanted Silvia's help in raising funds for anti-Castro operations. They seemed familiar with recent plots to assassinate Castro and claimed to know her father, Amadar. The father was then imprisoned on Cuba's Isle of Pines, arrested in 1961 for having harbored a fugitive who had attempted to assassinate Castro. The fugitive was Reinaldo Gonzalez, and his coconspirator in that plot had been the future leader of Alpha 66, Antonio Veciana.

When Silvia Odio told the strangers she wanted nothing to do with a campaign of violence, they departed. Then, within forty-eight hours, Leopoldo phoned her. "What did you think of the American?" he asked. Odio replied that she really had no opinion.

"Well, you know, he's a Marine, an ex-Marine, and an expert marksman," she remembered Leopoldo saying. "He would be a tremendous asset to anyone, except that you never know how to take him. He's kind of loco, kind of nuts. He could go either way. He could do anything—like getting underground in Cuba, like killing Castro. The American says we Cubans don't have any guts. He says we should have shot President Kennedy after the Bay of Pigs. He says we should do something like that."

A frightened Silvia Odio "immediately suspected there was some sort of scheme or plot." When the president was killed in the same city less than two months later, she was sure of it. When Oswald's picture flashed across a TV screen, both sisters gasped. Although Silvia had discussed the strange visit with a friend before the assassination, for some months after the assassination the Odio sisters were afraid to come forward. Finally they testified before the Warren Commission, which, then trying to wind down its investigation, concluded that Oswald could not have been at the Odios' apartment because he was en route to Mexico City at the time. The House Assassinations Committee would reach a different conclusion, finding the Odio testimony credible and "a situation that indicates possible conspiratorial involvement."[5]

All official inquiries in search of Angel and Leopoldo have begun, and reached a dead end, with Silvia Odio. In 1976 I spoke to her by phone in Miami. "I know this was part of something big, and for some reason I was made part of it," she said. "All I can tell you is that what came out in the Warren [Commission] Report was distorted. I *know* it was Lee Harvey Oswald, not someone posing as Oswald, at my door. But I was very confused and the FBI took advantage of that. I really don't want to know any more than I said about it then. Miami is a very dangerous place, that's why my phone is unlisted."[6]

The FBI's False Trail

Nagell's September 1963 warning letter to Hoover had already brought Angel and Leopoldo to the FBI's attention long before Silvia Odio. But in 1964, in looking to close the door on the most tantalizing evidence of a conspiracy around Oswald, the FBI seems to have taken advantage of more people than Silvia Odio. In September 1964, as the Warren Commission Report was being finalized, chief counsel J. Lee Rankin wrote to J. Edgar Hoover, "It is a matter of some importance to the Commission that Mrs. Odio's allegations either be proved or disproved."

Hoover reported back to Rankin that his agents had traced down Loran Eugene Hall, a "participant in numerous anti-Castro activities." According to Hoover, Hall had admitted visiting Odio in Dallas at the relevant time along with two colleagues, one of whom looked like Oswald. It was, Hoover added, basically much ado about nothing. The Warren Commission went along with this explanation.[7]

The FBI's version sounded plausible enough. Loran Hall was often mistaken for a Mexican, and he used the "war name" of "Lorenzo." One of his traveling mates, Lawrence Howard, Jr., was Mexican and used the alias of "Alonzo." They, as well as the alleged Oswald look-alike William Seymour, were all anti-Castro activists. But the FBI did not tell the commission that Howard and Seymour had both denied ever visiting the Odio apartment, after which Hall retracted his own story of having gone there.[8]

According to Nagell, Leopoldo "resembled one photo that I've seen of Loran Hall, but definitely was not Hall. Hall was involved at a low level with anti-Castro Cubans. And from what I know of the two suspects, the other was not Lawrence Howard. Even the FBI told me he was not there [at Odio's]."[9]

I interviewed both Hall and Howard in the late 1970s and came away convinced that the FBI had concocted the whole bit about them. "What happened," Hall told me, "was an FBI agent came to see me in '64. He said, 'Your name has been brought up concerning an incident that could have happened in Dallas, concerning the Kennedy assassination. Did you know a Mrs. Odio?' I said the name did not strike a note to me, did he have a picture? He showed me one, and I did not recognize her. Then the FBI said, 'Well, could there be a *possibility* that you'd met her?' I said, sure, there's always a possibility, I met hundreds of people in Dallas. I did tell the FBI that I'd driven from L.A. to Dallas somewhere around the time this was supposed to have been, with Larry Howard and Celio Alba. When I read my supposed statements in the Warren [Commission] Report, not one thing resembled what I'd said or the questions I'd been asked."[10]

The story got even stranger. Hall had passed through Dallas with Howard, and later with Seymour, in the autumn of 1963—but never as a trio. Hall and Seymour had stayed at the Dallas YMCA, but someone changed the register to erase Seymour's name and substitute Howard's. On their way out of town about a month before the assassination, a policeman had pulled Hall and Seymour's trailer over, reached into the glove compartment, pulled out a bottle of Dexedrine pills—and arrested the pair. Hall said they were held in jail for a day, and visited by agents from the CIA, the FBI, and Military Intelligence. For what purpose, he said he hadn't a clue, except the military man "wanted to know some areas where I'd been inside Cuba."[11]

Hall alleged in 1968—and repeated the story in our interviews—that right after being released from jail, he had been offered $50,000 to assassinate JFK at an October 17 Dallas meeting where he was seeking funds for guerrilla raids into Cuba. The offer, Hall said, "came from right-wing radicals who also had Robert Kennedy and Martin Luther King on their kill list. . . . They were lunatic, fanatical right wingers—Klansmen and Fascists—who had the means, the men, and their own twisted reasons for wanting to kill our leaders" and included "ex-military officers." Hall said he immediately turned down the offer and that the wealthy Dallas trucking executive in whose office the meeting took place sided with him.[12]

Then, after the assassination, a soldier-of-fortune acquaintance of Hall's in Miami put out two stories. One was that Hall had departed Florida for Dallas with three rifles shortly before November 22, 1963.[13] The other was that Hall "had plans to see Santos Trafficante, Jr.," on the way. When I interviewed Hall in 1977, shortly before he was to testify before the House Assassinations Committee, he admitted having known Trafficante. They had been in the same jail cell together in Havana in 1959. Then, in the spring of 1963, Hall said he had gone to a meeting in Miami Beach where the Florida Mob leader was assisting in plans for an exile raid into Cuba.[14]

In retrospect, both Hall and Howard believed that they were being set up in advance—as readily discernible "fall guys," if necessary, in an Oswald-oriented conspiracy. "I'd go so far as to say I probably sat as close as I'm sitting to you now, to some people who had a part in it," Hall opined. "I did hear Oswald's name mentioned before the assassination. It was right before I left Dallas that October. I passed an exile I knew, Nico Crespi, on the street, and he says, 'We're going downtown, Oswald's giving a talk and we're going to harass him.' The day of the assassination, I was in Monterey Park, California, shaving and in my shorts, when the news came on TV. I'd just taken my wife to her job and was getting ready to go apply for some work. But I'll tell you, I'm sure someone was out to implicate us. It's goddamned unreal."[15]

Besides all the weirdness surrounding the falsely identified "Angel" and "Leopoldo," there may have been an underlying motive for the two Cuban exiles' selection of Silvia Odio for their September visit. The JURE group in which she was active was headed by Manuel Ray, one of the more politically progressive exile leaders. As noted earlier, Ray was one of three prominent exiles apparently targeted for elimination by the CIA's "Operation 40" team after the Bay of Pigs—put under CIA house arrest in Miami until President Kennedy got wind of what was afoot.

Along with hard-line elements of the CIA and Alpha 66, the radical right despised Manuel Ray. As the Liberty Lobby wrote in its May 1963 newsletter: "There are those who believe that the Administration's policy on Cuba is to replace Castro, considered to be too pro-Russian, with a Tito type. The man whom these people watch closely is Manuel (Manolo) Ray. This veteran communist has 'broken' with Castro and is hopefully waiting in the wings for the State Dept's. blessing. He is presumed to be in Puerto Rico. . . . Without a revolutionary change in Washington the future of Cuba is Red."

It was true that Robert Kennedy and the State Department wanted Ray to have a role in any post-Castro government that might occur. As 1963 progressed, Ray was not immune from working with more extremist types in looking toward Castro's overthrow. According to an FBI file, "On August 16, 1963, CIA reported RAY arrived in Miami and met with . . . leader of Cubanos Libres [who] committed himself to JURE."[16]

Nagell has told me that members of Angel and Leopoldo's group had associations with JURE in San Juan, Puerto Rico. Nagell had himself traveled to Puerto Rico in the course of his investigations.[17]

When Ray was interviewed by the FBI in September 1964, he advised "that he never knew an individual by the name of Leopoldo connected with JURE," though he had met Silvia Odio on a number of occasions.[18] Yet Angel and Leopoldo passed themselves off to Odio as members of JURE, and even knew the "war name" of her father, who was then imprisoned in Cuba. When Silvia wrote to Amadar Odio about the strange visit, he responded: "Tell me who this is who says he is my friend—be careful. I do not have any friend who might be here, through Dallas, so reject his friendship until you give me his name."[19]

So, in addition to establishing Oswald in Silvia Odio's mind as a potential assassin who "could do anything," Angel and Leopoldo may have staged the incident as a subtle but deliberate means of later implicating Manuel Ray's JURE group.

The Old Preacher on the Bus

Apparently sometime on the night of September 25, Oswald placed a phone call to Houston. He told Estelle Twiford that he was hoping to discuss some ideas with her husband, Horace, "before he flew down to Mexico." Horace Twiford, a member of the Socialist Labor Party, had sent some pamphlets at Oswald's written request in November 1962. Otherwise he had neither seen nor heard of Oswald. A merchant seaman, Twiford was away, but his wife wrote down the message that Lee Oswald of the Fair Play for Cuba Committee had called.[20]

By 6:00 A.M. on the morning of September 26, Oswald was seen by a touring British couple aboard a Houston-to-Laredo bus. "He said he was the secretary of the New Orleans branch of the Fair Play for Cuba organization, and that he was on his way to Cuba to see Castro if he could," said John and Meryl McFarland in an affidavit for the Warren Commission.[21]

At midafternoon on the twenty-sixth, Oswald boarded another bus, at Laredo, heading for Mexico City. That night he struck up a conversation with two Australian girls, making a point of telling them that he had lived in Japan and Russia. Sitting next to Oswald, the girls remembered, was an Englishman who looked to be in his late sixties. En route, the Englishman told the girls of his seatmate: "This young man appears to have been in Mexico before."[22]

The Englishman's real name was Albert Alexander Osborne, although, when the FBI tracked him down early in 1964, he first claimed to be John Howard Bowen. He also insisted he had never met Oswald and never sat next to him on any bus. The McFarlands, sitting right in front of the pair, would recall Osborne telling them he was a retired schoolteacher who had taught in India and Arabia and who was writing a book about the Lisbon earthquake of 1775. In fact, he was an itinerant preacher who traveled widely, without any apparent source of income other than sporadic donations to his mission in Oaxaca, Mexico. Supposedly he ran a school there for twenty-five to thirty impoverished Mexican youths.

Osborne is one individual to whom the FBI devoted considerable man-hours of investigation after the assassination.[23] What they determined, and what I have been able to learn about him independently, marks Osborne as one of the most bizarre figures in this whole phantasmagoria. Consider the following:

1. According to Nagell, Oswald used not only "Alex" but also "Albert" as a false first name in the course of his 1963 activities. When ordering his Fair Play for Cuba leaflets that spring, Oswald did so under the name "Osborne." That means he utilized, at different times, all three parts of Albert Alexander Osborne's name. On occasion, in writing to a newspaper in Knoxville, Tennessee, Osborne used the alias "Hidalgo"[24]—not that dissimilar from the "Hidell/Hidel" pseudonyms adopted by Oswald and Nagell.

2. There was an actual John Howard Bowen, also a missionary in Mexico with whom Osborne was acquainted. They were about the same age and looked very much alike. Seemingly around 1958, when Mexican authorities were considering deporting Osborne for having improper papers, he ended up with all of Bowen's ID. Lola Loving, a woman who knew and contributed to the "missions" of both Osborne and Bowen, told me that Bowen had died "probably in 1958." Prior to that, according to Mrs. Loving, the two had "worked together."[25]

3. Osborne resided in the early 1960s on both sides of the border—in the Mexican state of Oaxaca, and at a hotel in Laredo, Texas, where he also kept a post office box. "Oaxaca" was the code name of Nagell's KGB contact, and "Laredo" his own code name in communicating with the KGB.

4. For years, Osborne had cashed numerous postal money orders—under the Bowen name—in small amounts at an American Express office in Mexico City. He later claimed that American Express had agreed to honor the payments because Bowen had died and Osborne was carrying on his missionary work.[26] In some mysterious fashion, American Express also figured into Nagell's actions in the El Paso bank (see Chapter Nineteen).

While Bowen was an American citizen born in Pennsylvania in 1885, Osborne's origins went back to Grimsby, England, in 1888. Osborne had served in the British Army before coming to the United States in 1914, after which he ended up traveling across the country as a journeyman rug cleaner. Claiming to be an ordained Baptist minister—for which there was no evidence—he settled in Mexico in 1939.

When Osborne journeyed to Canada in 1958, Mexican authorities suspicious of his "bona fides" queried the Royal Canadian Mounted Police to find out more about this potentially "undesirable alien." An FBI file about Osborne dated April 1, 1958, from its legal attaché in Ottawa to "Director, FBI, Attention: Foreign Liaison Unit," has since been publicly released—but all information in it is deleted.

Another FBI file records that Osborne "had apparently effected many entries into the United States, most of them from Mexico, but there is no indication that he was ever in possession of a valid immigrant visa, Form I-151 or re-entry permit." Generally, he came into the United States as Bowen through Laredo or El Paso, and the FBI found that he had at some point resided in Dallas—though no date was given.

On September 26, 1963, Osborne produced a counterfeit birth certificate to obtain his Mexico tourist card in Bowen's name, saying he was a resident of Houston.[27] Some fellow passengers believed that Osborne may have been accompanied on the bus by a companion or two. But only the baggage list from that particular trip has survived. The passenger list, the bus company manager said later, had been "borrowed by investigators of the Mexican government soon after the assassination." The acting minister of government—future president (and Winston Scott's close friend) Luis Echeverría—directed that "every effort to locate the passenger list" be made, but none was ever found for Flecha Roja No. 516 for that date.[28]

Though there is no known sighting of Oswald and Osborne together after the bus ride, only twenty-four hours separated their departures from Mexico City in early October. On October 2, Osborne crossed back into Texas at the Laredo border and journeyed on to New Orleans. On October 3, Oswald crossed back into Texas at the Laredo border, and was in Dallas by that same afternoon.[29]

On October 10, Osborne showed up at the Canadian consulate in New Orleans, producing a true birth certificate (and false record of service in the Canadian armed forces) to obtain a new passport in his own name. He told Canadian officials he had just arrived by bus from his residence in Montreal and was en route to Mexico City for a vacation. Instead, he set off on a lengthy trip across the southern United States, "visiting churches and collecting religious books," he would tell the FBI.

Then Osborne wrote to the *Knoxville Journal.* A short article that appeared on November 14, 1963, is headlined: "Bowen Leaves for Overseas." It went on: "John Howard Bowen, organizer of Boys' Club here and missionary to the Mixteca Indians in Mexico for the past 20 years, left

New York yesterday for a speaking tour in England, Spain, Portugal and Italy. . . . Bowen was invited by evangelical groups of each country."

The day after that article appeared, Osborne, not Bowen, wrote to American Express in Mexico requesting that all letters to "Bowen" be forwarded to him at their offices in New York City. Then he departed on an overseas trip, but there is no record that Osborne did any speaking that autumn of 1963. When first questioned by the FBI, he sought to conceal the fact that he had been out of the country for the three weeks shortly before and after the assassination. He had flown first to Scotland, then traveled some three hundred miles to Grimsby, England, to stay with his sister and visit a brother at a home for the elderly. "This was the first time his relatives in England had seen him in about 40 years," according to the FBI.

After staying three days in Grimsby, Osborne left shortly before the assassination, telling his sister he was going to London. On November 22, 1963, from an English town a short distance from Grimsby, a mysterious phone call was made to a newspaper in Cambridge about twenty-five minutes before the president was shot. "The caller said only that the reporter should call the American Embassy in London for some big news and then rang off," a CIA cable released in 1976 reports.[30]

On November 28, Osborne postmarked a letter from Madrid, Spain, noting that he planned to return to the United States in a week. Records show that he arrived in New York on December 5 and proceeded directly to Texas. After a considerable search, the FBI found him in Mexico in January 1964, and conducted the first of four interviews. Only at the final session in March did he admit that he was not "Bowen," but Osborne. The FBI, while having "established he is a con-man and an inveterate liar," found "no data of a subversive nature. Since no connection between Osborne and Oswald has been established, no additional investigation re Osborne will be conducted."

That is unfortunate, since Osborne's suspicious trail through Mexico, New Orleans, Texas, and abroad bore all the earmarks of someone who might have been able to tell us quite a bit more. He is said to have died in Texas sometime in the early 1970s. Hugh McDonald, an ex-CIA contract agent who wrote two books on the assassination, claimed to have uncovered information that Osborne was a KGB courier who operated for years in Spain, Canada, Mexico, and the southwestern United States.[31] But as an "itinerant preacher," there is no ruling out that he rode a similar circuit as Billy James Hargis—or, for that matter, David Ferrie, who set up his own branch of the Orthodox Old Catholic Church of North America. During World War II, Osborne was discovered by the FBI to have been a near-fanatical supporter of Nazi Germany.[32]

When I wrote Nagell asking him if he might have been acquainted with

"Albert Osborne aka John Howard Bowen," his response was as odd as everything else about the elderly "preacher." Nagell stated that to his knowledge he "was not acquainted with anyone named Albert Osborne, if he is aka John Howard Bowen."[33]

Oswald at the Soviet Embassy

On September 26, FBI headquarters wrote its New York field office about the CIA's request for all documents on the Fair Play for Cuba Committee —part of the CIA's "consideration to countering the activities of FPCC in foreign countries . . . [and] planting deceptive information which might embarrass the Committee. . . ." New York, of course, was FPCC director V. T. Lee's base. "New York should promptly advise whether the material requested by CIA is available or obtainable," the FBI headquarters memo stated, "bearing in mind the confidential nature and purpose of CIA's request. If available, it could be furnished by cover letter with enclosures suitable for dissemination to CIA by liaison."[34]

Early the next morning, September 27, Oswald checked into the Hotel Comercio in Mexico City.[35] Shortly before lunchtime, he showed up at the Cuban embassy, ostensibly in pursuit of an immediate Cuban transit visa en route to his final destination, the USSR. It has long been believed that this was Oswald's first of a series of alleged encounters with Cuban and Soviet authorities in Mexico City. Not so, according to Richard Nagell.

In a letter to Fensterwald in 1974, Nagell added this previously unknown piece of information: "I have hesitated saying this before, but since you, yourself, are bent on publishing a book, I feel that I must: LHO [Oswald] definitely visited the USSR Embassy at D.F. in September 1963, the first time on the morning of the 27th, where he was photographed, seated and standing, inside the visitors waiting room. Please accept this as fact."[36] The Soviets, Nagell added, also snapped a photo of Oswald leaving their Mexican headquarters.[37]

The reader may recall that Nagell had specifically instructed Oswald at their last meeting in New Orleans "not to go near the Cuban or USSR embassies." At that Oswald-Nagell rendezvous on September 15, Nagell advised Oswald that "Oaxaca" wanted to speak to him there. But Oswald was apparently not following the course that Nagell had mapped out for him. Even the hotel he checked into was not where Nagell had told him to register. Nagell elaborated to Fensterwald:

> In my opinion, Oswald's visit to Mexico was not made with the intent or
> for the purpose of applying for or obtaining a visa to either Cuba or the

USSR. He did not need the former, at least ostensibly, and he did not want the latter. In this regard, it is my considered opinion that Oswald was about as honest with his wife as he was with the authorities later at Dallas. Further, Oswald had been apprised of the legal requirements for travel to Cuba as early as May 1963, including the travel restrictions imposed by the Department of State, the length of time it would take to obtain a visa from the Cuban government, and the fact that the visa would not be stamped on his U.S. passport, but rather would be issued to him as a separate document. It is also my opinion that Oswald's Mexican trip at that time did not entail his participation in the finalization of any plans at Mexico City to assassinate President Kennedy. Notwithstanding his known or suspected movements and confrontations at Mexico City during the period 9/27/63–10/2/63, I have cause to believe that he visited there either to confer with Oaxaca or, possibly, for another reason that I deem inadvisable to mention. I have no idea why he visited the Cuban or USSR embassies at that particular time, though it is interesting to note that I am informed he was interviewed alone by a Soviet official who was not V. Kostikov or P. A. Yatskov.[38]

Valery Kostikov and Pavel Yatskov are the two Soviet officials who have long been known to have spoken with Oswald when he went to the Soviet embassy claiming to want a visa. But who was the third man? Was it Nagell's Soviet contact in Mexico, the man he has identified only by the code name "Oaxaca"?

In January 1992, a third Soviet came forward. At a press conference in Moscow, retired KGB officer Oleg Maksimovich Nechiporenko revealed that he and two other agents had met Oswald on September 27 and 28, 1963, at the Soviet embassy in Mexico City. Nechiporenko would say only that he had "historical information" that would "be useful for the analysis of what happened" on November 22, 1963. He described his information as a "commercial secret," suggesting that he was now willing to talk in exchange for money. "What happened in the United States of America in 1963 is not only an (unsolved) element of American history, but . . . a gap in world history," Nechiporenko was quoted by the Associated Press.[39]

The only other time that Nechiporenko's name had surfaced in connection with the Kennedy assassination was in a 1978 novel by former CIA contract agent Hugh McDonald. McDonald had wide-ranging associates in the intelligence community up to the time of his death in the late 1980s. In the book he names Nechiporenko as "a perfect selection to direct, at the regional level, those preliminary events that would lead to the assassination of John F. Kennedy."[40] (The novel sets forth a scenario of a KGB-inspired plot, with President Johnson a willing accessory to the cover-up.)

In 1963, Nechiporenko was assuredly well known to the CIA. In fact, John Barron's book *KGB*—using Winston Scott as his primary source on Mexico—offered more background on Nechiporenko than has been published before or since. He was, Barron wrote, considered "the most skilled and dangerous" KGB man in all Latin America.

Arriving in Mexico City with his wife and two children in 1961, Nechiporenko spoke flawless Spanish. Barron described him as "slender and darkly handsome" with a debonair mustache, wavy black hair, and an olive complexion that made him look "utterly Latin." Mexican authorities believed that Nechiporenko was either the child of Spanish Communists who had fled to Russia after the Spanish Civil War, or perhaps the scion of a Russian father and a Spanish mother. At any rate, often he was known to don the clothes of a *campesino* and journey into the countryside, where farmers or laborers accepted the KGB spy as one of their own. Many of his working hours were spent looking to recruit students at Mexican universities. Chameleonlike, Nechiporenko could also adopt the manners of a bright young Mexican professional man. Westerners, Barron added, found him charming, quick-witted, and inordinately aggressive.

The KGB, under Nechiporenko's hand, according to Barron "was trying to establish its own private detective force, composed of a corrupt ex-police official and cashiered cops. Through them it planned to gather data for blackmailing Mexicans, to harass anti-Castro Cuban exiles, and to execute 'wet affairs.' " The latter term was a phrase that meant "liquidation," or assassination.

On March 12, 1971—six weeks before Winston Scott's death—Barron recounted how "five of the most important men in the government of Mexico met at the National Palace." President Luis Echevarría (one of Scott's close Mexican associates) was shown documents obtained by his security service. These, according to Barron, "revealed a KGB plot conceived in Moscow to plunge Mexico into a civil war and destroy its government by armed force." Echevarría demanded decisive action, at which point his intelligence adviser recommended: "Strike at the embassy, Mr. President. All begins with the embassy. And with Nechiporenko. He is *número uno*."

Shortly thereafter, Nechiporenko and four other Soviet "diplomats" were expelled from Mexico, departing by plane on March 21. "Their enforced departure was probably regretted most by Nechiporenko," Barron wrote, "whose life had been so intimately intertwined with a country he would never be allowed to see again. But he was a good actor to the end, smiling and bantering with reporters." The Soviet Union, however, did not retaliate in kind but "swallowed its humiliation without protest."[41]

Barron's long chapter titled "The Plot to Destroy Mexico" and filled with details of how Mexico (and Mexico alone) had uncovered the KGB's nefarious plot, is not the way former clandestine officer Joseph B. Smith remembers it. When I asked Smith about Nechiporenko, he responded: "We had great admiration for Nechi, he was tremendous. One day he came into the American embassy, ostensibly to do some consular business and simply roamed all over the place until he was finally spotted. A great feat. It was a CIA operation that finally got him kicked out. There were a few Mexican students who had apparently received some guerrilla training in Russia. They got together and convinced Echevarría that this whole thing was a tremendous plot throughout the whole KGB station. Then we elaborated a little on how dangerous this was, letting all these very bad people operate freely in his country. We gave him the names of people he should throw out—and he did."[42]

In 1992 I found out that Nechiporenko had contracted with a Hollywood agent—of the literary variety—and was planning to write a book. Through the agent, Brian Litman, I was able to get a series of questions through in writing to Nechiporenko in Moscow. He responded, but declined to answer on several important points. He would not say whether he was familiar with the Cuban exile group Alpha 66, or whether Yuri Nosenko was a bona fide defector. As for whether the KGB had managed to penetrate the CIA: "This was of operative value, I am not prepared to discuss it."

Nechiporenko also refused to state whether he believed the assassination was a conspiracy, adding that this question would be addressed in his book. On an American TV program about the assassination, however, Nechiporenko stated his certainty that a conspiracy took place—and that Oliver Stone's movie thesis was going in the right direction, if a little too broadly.

Nechiporenko claimed that he was unfamiliar with either the "Oaxaca" or "Laredo" code names. "There is no strict organized system of assigning code names to operatives or recruits," he continued. "It was entirely up to the individual officer." He also alleged that the KGB's Mexico operation "in the early '60s . . . had no direct contacts with G-2 [Cuban intelligence]. Any such questions that occurred were solved via Moscow Center. Direct contact between the stations was established in the early '70s."

Finally, Nechiporenko maintained that he had never heard of Oswald before the ex-Marine walked into the Soviet embassy late that September of 1963. The other two officials present for that meeting, Kostikov and Yatskov, are still alive and collaborating with Nechiporenko on his book.[43]

Pavel Yatskov, who left Mexico in 1967, was considered by the CIA to be possibly the KGB's *rezident* (chief) in the capital. In his book *Inside the Company: CIA Diary,* Philip Agee tells the story of how the CIA's Soviet Russia Division considered offering Yatskov $500,000 to defect, setting him up "with an elaborate cover as the owner of an income-producing fishing lodge in Canada. The reason this plan wasn't adopted," Agee says, "was that we feared that our own man [an undercover CIA agent posing as an English teacher in Mexico] may have been a double agent, secretly recruited by Yatskov."[44]

Kostikov had been officially listed as consul since September 1961, but the CIA identified him at the time as "a staff officer of the KGB. He is connected with the Thirteenth, or 'liquid affairs' department, whose responsibilities include assassination and sabotage."[45] Kostikov departed Mexico in late September 1971, after the KGB feared exposure of operatives like himself when another member of Department 13 defected in Great Britain.[46]

Under normal circumstances, one would expect that any American—let alone Oswald—who was meeting with a trio including the KGB's chief (Yatskov), assassinations specialist (Kostikov) and "most dangerous" operative in the Western Hemisphere (Nechiporenko) would have raised all kinds of alarm bells at the CIA and the FBI. Well before the assassination, both agencies were aware of Oswald's having met with at least Yatskov and Kostikov.

In a copyrighted article published December 8, 1980, former Dallas FBI agent James P. Hosty, Jr., gave an exclusive interview on this subject to *Dallas Morning News* reporter Earl Golz. Hosty, the agent assigned to the Oswald "internal security" case in Dallas, revealed that the FBI's preassassination investigation of Oswald did unveil information about the Kostikov meeting. Nothing that filtered down to Hosty's own desk from the CIA, however, indicated Kostikov's actual responsibilities. Then, only hours after the assassination, Hosty discovered that all documents about Oswald's Mexico trip had been secretly removed by someone at the FBI from the Dallas bureau's Oswald file.[47]

The Warren Commission Report mentioned Kostikov only in passing as "one of the KGB officers stationed at the embassy." No comprehensive information about Kostikov's credentials was submitted to the commission until the CIA finally sent a report to counsel Rankin a week before the Warren Commission Report went to press.[48] Likewise, the House Assassinations Committee's report glossed over the Kostikov incident, leaving out any mention that he even worked for the KGB. This was despite its hearing testimony from lawyer David Slawson, who had explored foreign conspiracy theories for the Warren Commission and who believed this was "obviously . . . a suspicious circumstance" that warranted further scrutiny. The committee's three-hundred-page report titled "Lee Harvey Oswald, the CIA, and Mexico City" is still classified.[49]

After the assassination, investigators on Angleton's counter intelligence staff were immediately assigned to run down all prior contacts of Yatskov and Kostikov in Mexico City. One name they turned up was Rolando

Cubela.⁵⁰ The Cuban whom the CIA code-named AM/LASH, who was privately meeting in the fall of 1963 with Desmond FitzGerald about assassinating Castro, was in direct touch with the KGB hierarchy in Mexico City! The date of any meetings between them has never been made public.

In 1975, the *Los Angeles Times* published an interview with Ernesto Rodriguez, said to have been a former CIA contract agent in Mexico City. Rodriguez said that Oswald, in the course of his September voyage, spoke with Fair Play for Cuba Committee members about a planned assassination attempt against Castro—and offered the same information to both the Soviets and the Cubans.⁵¹

In 1976, Nagell wrote me one last message about all this. "I am curious as to just where in the KGB's organizational structure the CIA placed that '13th Department' (under what directorate, if under any). And, someday," he added, "I would like to see a photo of 'Valery Kostikov.' "⁵²

Was Kostikov "Oaxaca"? I wondered, but if Nagell knew, he would never say.

Oswald at the Cuban Embassy

After Oswald, according to Nagell's information, went first to the Soviet embassy on the morning of September 27, he then showed up at the Cuban embassy. Oswald introduced himself to Sylvia Duran, a young Mexican woman working as the consul's assistant. He brought out his FPCC membership card and a news clipping about the New Orleans street demonstration that resulted in his August arrest. Pridefully, he showed Duran passports, letters from the American Communist Party, and old documents from his time in the Soviet Union. But Duran told Oswald that no transit visa could be issued to him without first getting clearance from the Soviet embassy.

When Oswald returned with the required visa photos a few hours later, Duran accepted his application and asked him to call in about a week. "Impossible," she remembered Oswald saying. "I can only stay in Mexico three days." Duran again explained how the system worked, and Oswald again departed, returning for a third time after hours. This time he asserted he had been to the Soviet embassy and knew his Soviet visa would be granted. Duran telephoned over. Yes, the embassy knew about Oswald, but a spokesman said that Moscow could take as long as four months to make a decision.

Then Oswald flew into a rage, shouting that he couldn't wait that long. Eusebio Azcue, the consul, came out of his private office and entered into an angry argument. "As far as he was concerned, we would not give him a visa," Duran recalled. "A person like him [Oswald], in place of aiding the Cuban Revolution, was doing it harm."[53]

According to Nagell, Cuban authorities had already been alerted before September about Oswald's involvement in the JFK plot. And, Nagell wrote, "this fact may have prompted the reception that he encountered at the Cuban Embassy."[54]

Early in 1964, J. Edgar Hoover sent an FBI informant to Havana. He was Communist Party, U.S.A., member Morris Childs, code-named "Solo." Childs returned to tell Hoover that Castro had personally informed him of his knowledge that Oswald "vowed in the presence of Cuban consulate officials [in Mexico] to assassinate Kennedy." Hoover sent a Top-Secret memo on Childs's report to Warren Commission counsel Rankin in June 1964; it was declassified in 1976.[55]

In 1967, according to British reporter Comer Clark, Castro said much the same thing to him in an impromptu interview. Castro was quoted: "Lee Oswald came to the Cuban embassy in Mexico twice. The first time, I was told, he wanted to work for us. He was asked to explain, but he wouldn't. He wouldn't go into details. The second time he said something like: 'Someone ought to shoot that President Kennedy.' Then Oswald said —and this was exactly how it was reported to me—'Maybe I'll try to do it.'

"Yes, I heard of Lee Harvey Oswald's plan to kill President Kennedy. It's possible I could have saved him. I might have been able to—but I didn't. I never believed the plan would be put into effect."[56]

In the late 1970s, when author Anthony Summers interviewed in Havana both ex-Cuban consul Eusebio Azcue and his assistant Sylvia Duran, neither was any longer certain that the fellow who came to their embassy was really Oswald. Azcue said that the Oswald he saw on a newsreel soon after the assassination "in no way resembled" his visitor, whom the consul recalled as "maybe thirty-five years old," of "medium height" with "dark blond hair" and a "deeply lined face." Duran, shown a film by Summers of Oswald in New Orleans, responded: "The man on the film is not like the man I saw here in Mexico City," whom she remembered as being blond and about three inches shorter than Oswald.[57]

Yet Oswald's signature has been authenticated on the visa application form, which the Cuban government released in 1978. His picture also appears on the application.[58] So this question arises: If it wasn't really Oswald making a direct appearance, was someone acting as a courier to get the proper forms—and then seeking out Oswald to get the signature and photograph?

Sylvia Duran was taken into custody by the Mexican police the day after the assassination. A CIA headquarters memo to the Mexico station on November 23, 1963, records: "Arrest of Sylvia Duran is extremely serious matter which could prejudice U.S. freedom of action on entire question of Cuban responsibility. With full regard for Mexican interests, request you ensure that her arrest is kept absolutely secret, that no information from her is published or leaked, that all such info is cabled to us, and that fact of her arrest and her statements are not spread to leftist or disloyal circles in the Mexican government."

Duran was detained until after midnight and questioned extensively— "brutally," the Cuban government said in making an official complaint to the Mexicans—about her ties to left-wing circles in Mexico. Then, as she was about to depart for Havana four days later, Duran was picked up for questioning again. Richard Helms cabled Winston Scott: "We want to insure that neither Sylvia Duran nor Cubans get impression that Americans behind her rearrest. In other words, we want Mexican authorities to take responsibility for whole affair."[59]

The CIA and Oswald in Mexico

For years, the CIA stonewalled on its knowledge of Oswald's September trip to Mexico City. Asked by the Warren Commission to provide all its files, on Mexico in particular, CIA memorandums from 1964 reveal a desire to "wait out" the commission's probe. Richard Helms would later say that the agency was afraid full disclosure would compromise its espionage sources and methods.[60]

In November 1975, *The Washington Post* verified that two calls made by Oswald to the Soviet and Cuban embassies had been secretly taped by the CIA. With the full cooperation of the Mexican government, the agency had installed wiretaps on both embassies' phone lines. David Phillips would recall Oswald telling the Soviets: "I have information you would be interested in, and I know you can pay my way to Russia." Winston Scott, according to the *Post*, personally reviewed the transcripts, and a CIA translator remembered them as arousing keen interest. "They usually picked up the transcripts the next day. This they wanted right away."[61]

But the FBI, when alerted by the CIA on October 10 about Oswald's phone call to the Soviets, was apparently told nothing about the "deal" the ex-Marine was trying to cut. Complete transcripts were never turned over to either the FBI or the Warren Commission. Phillips testified that the tape was routinely destroyed before the assassination. But, as we saw in the previous chapter, Scott kept at least one audio "record" of Oswald's voice among his private files.

The phone call the CIA eventually admitted monitoring from Oswald to the Soviet embassy described the American speaking "in very poor Russian."[62] Oswald, however, spoke the language quite fluently, well enough for Marina to believe when she first met him that he was a native. So, as Duran and Azcue believed occurred at the Cuban embassy, was it an impostor claiming to be Oswald in communication with the Soviets by phone?

Still locked away in the classified House Assassinations Committee report on Mexico is an account about no less than *eight* Oswald phone conversations with the Soviet embassy having been taped, and transcripts made. Two of these, on September 27, were reportedly in Spanish; several others were in Russian. Nothing about these, the committee learned, was apparently passed on by the Mexico station to CIA headquarters prior to the assassination.[63]

Then there was the matter of an Oswald picture. Despite its known photographic surveillance of the two embassies, the CIA still officially claims that nothing was ever snapped of Oswald entering or leaving either one. This is not true.

The House Assassinations Committee spoke with three CIA officials who saw a picture of Oswald in Mexico, and two more had heard about it.[64] The way Joseph B. Smith remembered it, according to a committee interview with him, "the discovery of the picture was supposed to have greatly pleased President Johnson and made Mexico City station chief Win Scott 'his number one boy.' He [Smith] said the story was that someone remembered seeing Oswald's face somewhere in the photo coverage of the Cuban or Russian embassy, went back through the files and found the picture. Smith said he heard that story certainly more than once, at least, when he got to Mexico City and perhaps when he first got into the WH [Western Hemisphere Division]." Smith believed Desmond FitzGerald might have mentioned it when he came through Smith's base in Argentina early in 1964.[65]

Winston Scott was said to have kept a copy of the photo, a right-hand profile taken from above when Oswald visited the Cuban embassy.[66] Why, then, did David Phillips claim in sworn testimony in 1977 that the CIA's camera broke down the day Oswald called there?[67] Was the CIA still hiding "sources and methods"? Could someone else have been in the frame with Oswald?

The Unidentified Man

Another CIA memorandum makes reference to twenty photographs of Oswald taken in Mexico City.[68] But only twelve pictures have ever been released—and they are all of the wrong man.

This mystery originated in the immediate aftermath of the assassination. "Copies of photo of Oswald reproduced for use of [FBI] legal attaché with Mexican police," notes an undated CIA file declassified in 1976. Penciled in handwriting on the same page: "We made fifty (50) copies of each of these (which we got from legal attaché) for leg. attaché to use with Mexican police."[69] The implication seems to be that the FBI's man in Mexico had provided an Oswald photo to the CIA, which in turn duplicated and returned it to the FBI there.

Another CIA memo, dated November 22, 1963: "Reference is made to our conversation of 22 November in which I requested permission to give the [FBI] Legal Attaché copies of photographs of a certain person who is known to you." A special flight with these photos was then made from Mexico City to Dallas via a naval attaché, and more to CIA headquarters by pouch that night.[70]

A memo written by J. Edgar Hoover described what happened when the CIA's material from Mexico arrived the night of the assassination at Dallas FBI chief Gordon Shanklin's office. According to Hoover, Dallas agents looked at the pictures and "listened to a recording of [the] voice" —and, in both instances, quickly reached "the opinion that the above-referred-to individual was not Lee Harvey Oswald." Later, both Shanklin and the CIA would deny that any sound recordings had been sent.[71]

If not Oswald, then who was "a certain person who is known to you"? It came out in 1975 that the mystery man was photographed outside the Soviet embassy on October 1, the same day that Oswald was known to have made another visit there. On October 10 the CIA had sent a cable to the FBI, the State Department, and the Navy headed "Lee Henry [sic] Oswald." It read: "On 1 October 1963 a reliable and sensitive source in Mexico reported that an American male, who identified himself as Lee OSWALD contacted the Soviet Embassy in Mexico City inquiring whether the Embassy had received any news concerning a telegram which had been sent to Washington. The American was described as approximately 35 years old, with an athletic build, about six feet tall, with a receding hairline."[72]

That fit the description of the man in the picture, but it was obviously not the slender, twenty-three-year-old Oswald. But whoever it was, he appeared to have been impersonating Oswald at the Soviet embassy gate. And there is no doubt that the CIA knew the man's identity. On July 23, 1964, Helms sent this memo to Rankin at the Warren Commission: "The Central Intelligence Agency recommends that this photograph not be reproduced in the Commission's report. It could be embarrassing to the individual involved who as far as this Agency is aware, had no connection with Lee Harvey Oswald or the assassination of President Kennedy." At the time, Helms claimed the picture had been taken on October 4—the day after Oswald left Mexico—thus leading to the innocent explanation of a clerical error. Not until much later did a Freedom of Information Act (FOIA) lawsuit uncover that it was taken on the first, while Oswald was still in town.[73]

At any rate, the commission complied with the CIA's request not to reproduce the picture. Not until 1974, through a FOIA suit filed by Bernard Fensterwald, was the CIA forced to let go of twelve pictures of the "unidentified man." Even then, it would not name him. The then CIA director, William Colby, still maintained afterward: "To this day we don't know who he is."[74] To the House Assassinations Committee, Phillips and others explained that someone at the Mexico station mistakenly "guessed" back in October that the other American—"a person known to frequent the Soviet embassy"—was actually Oswald. And, the agency spokespeople confabulated, since there was no known photo of Oswald in the files, this was simply attributable to human error.

The only lead the House Assassinations Committee came up with was that the man may not have been an American at all but a Soviet seaman.[75] This was a possibility that Richard Nagell first raised with me in a letter dated February 21, 1976, some time before the committee independently heard such news. Nagell had first shed new light on "the man who was not Oswald" in a letter to Fensterwald on May 8, 1975:

> . . . I would guess that he was photographed as he was exiting the main entrance to the Soviet Embassy compound by a hidden surveillance camera situated on the second floor of a building located across the street (some guess, eh?). If the CIA thought he was in some way associated with Oswald, this would account for it acknowledging that the original photograph was taken in Mexico City on October 4, 1963, the day after Oswald supposedly returned to the United States. It would also indicate that Oswald, himself, had been under CIA surveillance while in Mexico City. The phraseology of the CIA's 23 November 1963 message to the Secret Service (". . . several photographs of a person known to frequent the Soviet Embassy . . .") infers that his (the unidentified man) visits took place over a longer period of time than one week. One does not "fre-

quent" a place for one week; he makes a specific number of visits. Anybody who is familiar with CIA reports will grasp this nuance. One thing is certain, the CIA is not going to identify the man, even if he is not KGB.

I wrote Nagell about eight months later, wondering about a rumor that the "mystery man" was an American soldier of fortune type named Johnny Mitchell Devereaux. In his response, Nagell added an entirely new dimension to the CIA's "mix-up." The photos were not merely of *one* unidentified man, but two. Nagell wrote:

> The "mystery man" photographed at the instance of the CIA coming out of the *Cuban* Embassy at Mexico (identified as being "attired in a dark shirt with white collar buttons and apparently walking along with the thumb of his left hand hooked into the top of his left-hand trouser pocket") was not "Johnny Mitchell Devereux [sic]." He was a Cuban. The "mystery man" shown in two other publicized photos (identified as being "attired in a white shirt and tan trousers, holding what appears to be a courier-type pouch under his left arm and examining a wallet-type folder which it appears may contain one or two documents resembling passports," and also identified as being "attired in the same dress described above and holding the wallet-type folder in his left hand and inserting this folder into the courier-type pouch held in his right hand") exiting the *Soviet* Embassy at Mexico was neither Devereux [sic] nor Cuban, nor was he the same man depicted in the initial photograph, despite that he was identified as such by the FBI. The Cuban is dead. The second guy may have been a merchant seaman, possibly an American, more likely a European. I wouldn't know for sure, but I'm sure that somebody knows.[76]

Since Nagell seemed to know who the mystery men were, the question is: Did the CIA realize, from the outset, that making such identities public would reveal either Oswald's confederates—or a team that was busy setting Oswald up as someone in constant touch with the Cubans and the Soviets?

The Disinformation Machine?

By November 27, 1963, rumors were rampant about Oswald's involvement with Castro-oriented Cubans in Mexico City. One CIA informant claimed that Oswald had attended a "twist party" at the home of a relative of Sylvia Duran. Another asserted that Oswald had met with several Cuban intelligence agents at the embassy there. One of David Phillips's agents,

Salvador Díaz Verzon, alleged a restaurant meeting among Oswald, Cuba's ambassador, and a KGB official. Oswald was said to have touched base with a pro-Castro group at the University of Mexico campus.[77]

Then there was a Nicaraguan named Gilberto Alvarado, who walked into Mexico's U.S. embassy the day after Oswald was shot and demanded to see the ambassador. Alvarado claimed to have been at the Cuban embassy in mid-September, furnishing a false ID in an attempt to get a Cuban visa for a "penetration mission for the Nicaraguan secret service." While there, he said he had observed Consul Azcue conversing with a tall, thin black man and a young American he now recognized as having been Oswald. Alvarado overheard the black man say, "I want to kill the man." To which Oswald replied: "You're not man enough. I can do it." Then Alvarado said he saw the black man give Oswald $5,000 in American currency of large denominations as "advance payment."[78]

Oswald's supposed words were very close to those that "Leopoldo" had "confided" over the phone to Silvia Odio in late September ("He says we Cubans don't have any guts. He says we should have shot President Kennedy after the Bay of Pigs."). After extensive questioning, Alvarado admitted he had made the whole story up—but not before it had caused considerable consternation in Ambassador Mann, who strongly urged that Alvarado be flown to the United States for further questioning. He wasn't. Alvarado soon vanished into the Latin capital, leaving the question open of who had been writing his (and perhaps Leopoldo's) script.

The Russell Memorandum

Mann wasn't the only high official concerned about the goings-on in Mexico City. Back in Washington, Georgia senator Richard Russell was keeping abreast of the Mexico investigation. On November 29, 1963, Russell had been named by Lyndon Johnson to the eight-member Warren investigative panel. As chairman of the Senate Armed Services Committee, Russell's responsibilities included oversight of the CIA. And, on December 5, 1963, the senator wrote a memorandum that was later found in the top right-hand drawer of his desk and placed in his Memorial Library at the University of Georgia.

I had been in touch with the Russell Library in obtaining the 1967 correspondence between the senator and Nagell. Early in 1992, archivist Sheryl Vogt also mailed to me a copy of the handwritten note that Russell left behind upon his retirement. It has never before been made public.

And, as the archivist wrote me, "The note certainly hints at a cover-up from the beginning."

The senator scrawled:

> Warren asked about C.I.A. "Did they have anything." When I told of Mexico & Nicaraguan *NOT mentioning sums*—He mention 5G [$5,000] as McCone had told me. He [Warren] knew all I did & more about CIA. Something strange is happening—W. [Warren] & [Deputy Attorney General Nicholas] Katzenbach know all about F.B.I. and they are apparently through psychiatrists & others planning to show Oswald only one who even considered—This to me is untenable position—I must insist on outside counsel—"Remember Warren's blanket indictment of South—"

The last phrase seems to refer to Chief Justice Warren's stand on civil rights. What this remarkable document shows is that Senator Russell, very soon after the assassination, sensed something was terribly wrong with the government's version of events. Not long before his death in 1971, the senator would tell a reporter of his conviction that "someone worked with Oswald on the planning."[79]

Summary

From the moment Oswald left New Orleans on September 24, 1963, a conscious effort to portray him as a potential assassin for Castro went into high gear. First came the visit by Angel, Leopoldo, and Oswald to Sylvia Odio's door in Dallas. After this, Leopoldo planted the seeds with Odio about an ex-Marine, "kind of nuts" and capable of anything. An effort to place future stigma upon Manuel Ray's moderate exile organization seems to have been part of the scenario. After the assassination, the FBI sought to dismiss the incident by falsely fingering three other "soldier of fortune" types as the Odio visitors.

It is difficult to believe that Oswald's fellow passenger on the bus trip to Mexico was simply making an innocent journey. Not only did Oswald use pseudonyms from all three segments of Albert Alexander Osborne's name, but also the elderly preacher later sought to cover up his own true identity—and made conspicuous journeys to New Orleans and Europe shortly before the assassination.

Oswald's six-day stay in Mexico City is right out of a Franz Kafka novel. Two Cuban embassy officials who received a visit from Oswald now believe it was really an impostor. The voice on a CIA tape recording of an Oswald conversation with the Soviet embassy also appears to have been that of someone else. While the CIA falsely claimed it took no photographs of the real Oswald during his visits to those two embassies, the pictures the CIA sent to Dallas the day of the assassination were of the wrong man. According to Nagell, there are really *two* "mystery men"—both of whom may have had some involvement with Oswald. For some reason, Oswald's meeting with three KGB officials at the Soviet embassy raised no alarm bells at either the CIA or the FBI. After the assassination, his Mexico journey was used in a propaganda campaign to link Oswald to the Communists. Through a recently discovered memorandum, it is now apparent that Warren Commission member Richard Russell sensed a government cover-up from the beginning.

IV
The Deed

A man feared that he might find an assassin;
Another that he might find a victim.
One was more wise than the other.
—Stephen Crane, from *The Black Riders and Other Lines,* #56

Chapter Twenty-two

The Colonel, the Cuban Exiles, and the Mob

In the spring of 1990, former CIA contract agent Robert Morrow revealed to me that he had a second source on Richard Case Nagell. This was a man Morrow had first met in the early 1960s; the man was then training a group of anti-Castro Cuban exiles at a Florida camp called No Name Key. Morrow knew him by his "war name"—Oscar del Valle Garcia—but had been told his true name was Bill Bishop. When Bishop telephoned Morrow out of the blue in February 1983, it came as a considerable shock: Morrow had previously been told by a retired Army colonel that Bishop had died about ten years before.[1]

Bishop told Morrow he had just finished reading his book *Betrayal,* and remembered him from their mutual association with the CIA and Cuban exiles. "He said he had tracked me down through a mutual friend," Morrow says. "And the reason he gave for calling me was that he was dying of terminal cancer and, since I had come close to portraying what he knew about the assassination of President Kennedy, he wanted to set the record straight."

Morrow had agreed to fly down to Cleburne, Texas, a suburb of Dallas, where he conducted a series of tape-recorded interview sessions with Bishop. One name that came up was the fellow Morrow had pseudonymously called "Richard Carson Fillmore" in his 1976 novel.

"The story I got," Morrow said, "was that Bishop was under contract to CIA, working with this group of Cuban exiles and maybe some Mafia people. They had some kind of test they were doing, a fake assassination attempt against Kennedy, I think it was in Washington. That summer in New Orleans, they had discovered what Bishop called 'a rat in the pack.' This was Richard Nagell. Evidently these Cubans called Bishop about it, put the finger on Nagell, and Bishop then put a Cuban onto him—who was following Nagell when he walked into that bank in El Paso. Well, the story matched pretty close with the one I'd heard from Tracy Barnes. Except I hadn't known of Bishop's involvement."[2]

Morrow had not communicated with Bishop in several years, but believed that he was still alive and in touch with an assassination researcher who also lived in Cleburne, Gary Shaw. I telephoned Shaw, an architect and one of the founders of the JFK Assassination Information Center and museum in downtown Dallas. Yes, he said, Colonel Bishop was still waging his ongoing struggle with bone cancer, and Shaw knew how to locate him. He would ask if Bishop might be willing to see me. "It appears he was some kind of contract killer for the CIA," Shaw added.

Early that summer of 1990, I flew off for a week-long research trip across Texas. Shaw provided me his "William Bishop" file to peruse, prior to an interview arranged for the following morning at Shaw's home. Included was a certificate indicating that Colonel William C. Bishop had been a "Military Intelligence Aide" on the General Staff of General Douglas MacArthur's Army Intelligence team during the Korean War period. If true, that would mean Bishop had served under MacArthur's intelligence chief, Charles Willoughby.

Confirming Bishop's connections to the Cuban exiles during the early 1960s were two government documents and a set of notecards he had provided Shaw. An FBI file identified "Colonel BILL BISHOP" as having "been the military leader and instructor of the group at No Name Key." Another FBI document listed a "William Bishop" as a crony of Rolando Masferrer in anti-Castro activities and an attempted 1967 invasion of Haiti.[3]

Bishop's notecards were even more enlightening. They included Robert Morrow's name and address. In addition to a listing for "MASFERRER, ROLANDO (TIGER LEADER)," there were also phone numbers for numerous other prominent exiles. Among them were: (1) Carlos Prio, president of Cuba before Batista; (2) Antonio Varona, now known to have been part of the CIA-Mob plots against Castro; (3) Mario Garcia Kohly, Sr., nabbed with Morrow by federal authorities in October 1963 in a counterfeit-peso operation aimed at Cuba; and (4) Eladio del Valle, the Miami friend of David Ferrie whom Nagell was investigating in January 1963.

There were, as well, the office and home phone numbers of then CIA director John McCone. And a listing for General Edwin A. Walker of Dallas. I had seen enough to become very eager to meet Colonel Bishop.

A Visit with the Colonel

It was midmorning, coffee and sweet rolls had been served, and the sixty-seven-year-old Bishop fixed me with a steely glare as we faced one another across researcher Shaw's dining-room table. Bishop was a husky six-footer with a ruddy, bulldog countenance and a low, gravelly voice. He told me that he'd first gotten involved with the CIA after his service in the Korean War, using a Military Intelligence cover.

Among his CIA assignments, he said casually, was the 1961 assassination of Dominican Republic dictator Rafael Trujillo. "That's one mission I'm kinda proud of, because a lot of my associates said it couldn't be done," Bishop added. "Both the CIA and the Pentagon wanted Trujillo dead, and it's more effective to kill one man than it is to lose a thousand with an all-out invasion. I made the hit on Trujillo. Patriotism didn't have a damned thing to do with it. You hear the story time and again of men who were in combat, motherhood and apple pie, well, that's a buncha shit. You're trying to stay alive, pure and goddamned simple. In my case, I was good at my job. To this day, even after my stroke, I can still hit a playing card at five hundred yards with a rifle or a machine gun. It was a professional challenge for me, no more and no less. The only way you can live with it is, you look upon your target as a tin can, a silhouette. You don't allow yourself to become emotionally or psychologically involved. It's detached, okay?"

Bishop's words were chilling, and I sat in silence for a moment. What I needed to establish from the outset was why he was willing to talk. "That's a good question, and you're entitled to a straight answer," he said. He went on to describe how he had suffered from bone cancer since 1975, endured numerous chemotherapy and cobalt treatments, "and currently it has been in arrest for a little over three years." At the same time, he had a serious heart condition.

"There are those of us, as you well know, who collectively in all probability could correct many, many misconceptions about our American history during a certain point in time," Bishop continued. "Up to a point, when it does not—and I emphasize this—create personal jeopardy, legally or otherwise, I will tell you what I can. Because I feel an obligation, within reason, to help bring about some realistic approach to our history. The country deserves it. There are certain things that will come out only after I'm dead and gone. But what I'm telling you is, I'm not doing this for the dollar. I live comfortably, on a very limited income. I firmly believe that, in our system of government, if you don't like the man, then vote him out of office. Don't shoot him out. And we had a coup d'état on November 22, 1963.

"In many instances, what I picked up was after the fact. I did look into Oswald's background. I'd never met him, but I'd seen him in a training film in New Orleans the past summer. He just happened to be in the group out there at the Pontchartrain camp. Trying to get in with the anti-Castro exiles. I thought even then [after the assassination] that Oswald was a decoy. There's no way in hell he could have fired three shots in that space of time, with that accuracy, with that weapon.

"Of course, when Oswald was killed, the Warren Commission's investigation was a big joke. The whole bit—Military Intelligence, CIA, FBI. Where the mistake was made, the intelligence reports coming in from various men in the field were not assimilated and categorized and broken down to get some logical conclusion. The Warren Commission went into this thing with a preconceived idea. Overly simplified, in Oswald's case they tried to take a round peg and drive that son of a bitch into a square hole. And they did it."

I brought out a photocopy from a 1962 passport photograph of Richard Nagell, without offering his name, and passed it across the table. The colonel studied it for a moment, then said: "Where did you get this?"

"He gave it to me," I replied.

"I know him," said Bishop. "What about him? What do you want to know?"

"Did you know him under that name?"

"No, we all used code names back in those days. Well, he was with Alpha 66. Does he admit that?"

I replied that I knew Nagell had some cognizance at least of the Alpha 66 exile group in 1962 and 1963. Then Bishop changed the subject.

"Have you ever heard of Operation 40?" he asked.

Yes, I had read about Operation 40, the then ultrasecret CIA "hit squad" set up before the Bay of Pigs invasion. Frank Sturgis, a member of the team that broke into Democratic National Committee headquarters at the Watergate complex in 1972, later admitted to having been part of Operation 40. As Sturgis said in an interview, "this assassination group would upon orders, naturally, assassinate either members of the military [or] the political parties of the foreign country that you were going to infiltrate, and if necessary some of your own members who were suspected of being foreign agents. . . . We were concentrating strictly in Cuba at that particular time. Actually, they were operating out of Mexico, too."[4]

A 1981 history of the Cuban exile movement, *The Fish Is Red*, elaborated on Operation 40:

> Its hard core was made up of dice players at the foot of the cross— informers, assassins-for-hire, and mob henchmen whose sworn goal was to make the counterrevolution safe for the comfortable ways of the old Cuba. They were the elite troops of the old guard within the exile movement, who made an effective alliance with CIA right-wingers against CIA liberals. . . .[5]

Bishop brought out a series of photographs of Latin-looking individuals. On the back of each picture were the words "Special Talent 1960–65" —and the descriptions were frightening. "Ice pick man . . . Butcher . . . Sniper and demo expert . . . Prop[aganda] . . . Knife man . . . Pilot & navigator . . . Mutilator."

"We weren't playing a nice game," Bishop said.

On some of the pictures were inscribed two more words: "Destino— Mexico." I asked whether this meant that these particular people had operated out of Mexico. "Yep," said Bishop. "Lotta times they would cover their tracks by declaring themselves as nationals of Mexico or Nicaragua, Panama, didn't make any difference."

Bishop conceded having himself been to Mexico City "two or three times in 1963." But when I asked him for what purpose, he replied: "I'd rather make no comment on that. It was national security. It had something to do with Cuba, but not as such." I asked if Bishop had ever heard of the Hotel Luma. "Yeah, I had a few drinks there, fact I stayed there one time—'62 or '63, one or two nights, just a place to stay."

Bishop and Nagell

Much later in the interview, I carefully steered the subject back to Nagell. Bishop claimed to have met him "when he was an associate of Rolando Masferrer. I was introduced to him as a bodyguard of Masferrer. Rolando had another guy, typical rassler type and partial to .45 automatics. They had come to a headquarters on Flagler Street, Miami, where I was staying.

Later your man in the picture here came by and was introduced as additional security for Rolando."

My mind flashed back to several things Nagell had said. First, there was the .22-caliber revolver equipped with a silencer that he had obtained in Mexico City in the fall of 1962 and whose original target was to have been Masferrer. In 1976 Nagell had made another reference to Masferrer in a letter to me. It was not long after the exile was blown to bits by the dynamite bomb planted in his car. "Pleased to read that the tiger finally got his," Nagell wrote. "I assume that it was difficult to get to him at close quarters, 'cause his bodyguard used to carry around a cigar box containing a .45 automatic."[6] I thought, too, of Nagell's reference to conducting surveillance on Miami's Flagler Street in January 1963. Might Nagell have infiltrated Masferrer's entourage as part of his intelligence assignment?

Colonel Bishop was still talking into my tape recorder. "Later, I began realizing that this guy"—he pointed again at Nagell's picture—"was with intelligence, under CIA contract. But you see, Rolando Masferrer was deeply involved with Alpha 66. So it is safe to assume that your man was also involved with Alpha 66."

I asked Bishop if he had been in New Orleans in the late summer of 1963. "It had to be August or September of '63," he said. Shaw passed Bishop a large blowup of another photograph of Nagell, and I told the colonel I had been searching for years for someone to help corroborate what this man had been doing during that period. Again, I did not offer Nagell's name.

"Where is he now?" Bishop asked.

"I think he's in California," I said.

"When I got to New Orleans, within a matter of days, this fellow's presence came up. He had been there several times before I ever went there and got involved, okay? He was trying to get into the inner workings of the anti-Castro movement. Asking about the various and sundry pro- and anti-Castro groups in the New Orleans area. The training camps. Who was doing the training, who was putting the money up for 'em, all that kind of stuff. The exiles I was working with asked, did I know him? They were trying to check him out. He was asking too many pointed questions about things he had no business knowing. My end of it was to try to determine who the hell he was.

"I mean, it wasn't an unusual thing. From time to time, we would have Americans that would try to get involved in the inner sanctum of one group or another. It was standard operating procedure that we would try to find out where they were coming from, what they were after. That's when I called Bill Colby at CIA. We went back to paratrooper training together at Fort Benning in 1940. Colby ended up in OSS. He had a knack for languages."

I knew that William Colby, in 1963, had replaced Desmond FitzGerald as head of the CIA's Far Eastern Division.[7] During the Vietnam War, Colby had supervised the Operation Phoenix program—basically a "hit squad" aimed at suspected Viet Cong. Between 1973 and 1976 Colby had served as director of the CIA—the man who forced out James Angleton after leaking to the media that Angleton had been in charge of the agency's CHAOS operation, targeting domestic "subversive" groups.

"So I asked Colby," Bishop was continuing, " 'who the hell is this?' He said, 'I don't know the man. Use discretion.' Because of that, I was taking a very leery position as far as this guy was concerned."

Bishop said he did not recall Nagell using the name "Joseph Kramer," nor did he remember any other name. I told Bishop what Morrow had indicated, that Bishop had then assigned a Cuban exile to follow Nagell— all the way to the bank. "That's not what happened," Bishop said. "I put somebody on him to check him out—*in* New Orleans. The exiles brought up a name, a man I didn't know but was said to be responsible, that they wanted to put on this guy's trail. I said okay, use him.

"But don't confuse the issue. You're talking about two different operations altogether. I don't know who the hell was following him in El Paso. It wasn't my people. It was several months after that when I heard about your man here shooting up this bank. I do know there was a Cuban after him. Antonio Veciana told me this, word of mouth. And there were rumors that he'd stumbled onto the fact that there was an assassination seriously planned. Because of that knowledge, he was in jeopardy. So the deal in El Paso, in my opinion, was a means for him to get picked up and protected. At the same time, myself and others, nobody would believe that the assassination talk was something real."

"What were you doing in New Orleans that summer?" I asked. Bishop paused and took a deep breath, pushing his glasses back above his nose. He turned to give a hard look at Gary Shaw. "How far can I really trust him?" Bishop asked, casting a finger in my direction. "Tell him anything you'd tell me," Shaw replied.

Bishop nodded and continued: "I was to obtain additional funding, I'll say this and no more, from the [crime] Syndicate out of New Orleans, for Alpha 66. At that point in time, Rolando Masferrer was the key bagman, for lack of a better term, for Alpha 66. Primarily the funding came through the Syndicate, because of Masferrer's connections with those people back in Cuba. He had ties with Santos Trafficante, Jr., and other criminal elements. Organized crime, pure and simple. He also had different ties with Jimmy Hoffa [the Mob-affiliated Teamsters union leader]. As far back as 1962, I think.

"But Rolando, from time to time when it came to large sums of money, had sticky fingers. I think that's why he was killed, eventually. Either that, or the Kennedy assassination. Because he knew about it."

The colonel stopped talking again, sat in silence for a time, then resumed in low tones. "By 1963, the Cuban element—see, Kennedy had gone to Miami, to the Orange Bowl down there, and made this statement that the brigade's flag would fly over Cuba and all this crap. That was a stopgap. The exiles for a time believed him. Then shortly after that, a presidential executive order came out that no military-style incursions into Cuba based from the United States would be tolerated. The end result was complete distrust and dislike for Kennedy and his administration by the Cuban exiles. You take Tony Varona and Rolando Masferrer to name but two—and there were many, many more—when serious talk began to happen about the possibility of assassinating Kennedy."

Bishop, Angel, and Leopoldo

As my several hours of conversation with Bishop proceeded, I knew that this was the interview I had been waiting for—someone who, without prompting, was backing up in numerous ways what Nagell had imparted. I wondered whether Desmond FitzGerald had been involved in Bishop's activities. "He was in on the planning stage of operations, as against the field stage. In other words, he would get reports from operatives in the field. Then his aides would dissimulate this and come to a conclusion. After the conclusion was presented to him, he made the final decision in that area."

Bishop also claimed to have known two other key players in this terrible drama. He said he had worked closely with David Phillips. "I never really trusted him," Bishop said. "Because Phillips was the kind of man—well, a lot of us were, I'm not knocking him—but, for example, he would have a project and he was willing to get it done one way or another. He didn't give a damn who he hurt or how he did it—even if it meant sacrificing lives. So in that sense I didn't trust him."

"What was Phillips's main base in 1963?" I asked. "American embassy in Mexico." "Had Bishop known a number of the CIA's people there?" "No, not a lot. It doesn't operate that way. You are involved in a particular segment or phase of something, and you are only told what you need to know."

Bishop said he had personally served, along with David Phillips, as a case officer for Alpha 66's Antonio Veciana. But the colonel added that he himself was not the man who was alleged to have been in Veciana's presence with Oswald in the summer of 1963. I showed Bishop the sketch of "Maurice Bishop" that Veciana had provided to me and the House Assassinations Committee.

Bishop studied it, then said: "Bear in mind, when he did this sketch, Veciana was under a helluva lot of pressure. He was just out of jail, and under threat of having to go back. What he did was really make a composite of several people. Myself, Dave Phillips, and I'll let it go at that. But suffice to say that he was trying to cover his ass with both hands. He came up with this, and it worked. My own dealings with Veciana were straight up-and-up. He never lied to me, never cheated me, never hurt me."

Later, Robert Morrow would provide me with a tape recording that Bishop had made of a phone conversation between himself and Veciana. It took place sometime in the mid-1980s, and Veciana's voice was clearly nervous when the colonel contacted him without warning. "Why are you not talking in Spanish?" Veciana asked. "You are William Bishop? I need to talk to you personally." Bishop had taped this conversation to lend credibility to his having been well acquainted with Antonio Veciana.

Toward the end of our interview, I asked if Bishop had ever heard of two Cuban exiles who used the "war names" of Angel and Leopoldo. I specified that both had been with the CIA and that one was trained at Fort Jackson.

"What about 'em?" Bishop growled back.

"Do you know who they really were?" I asked, my heart pounding as I wondered if my long quest for their true identities was over.

"No comment," said Bishop.

I asked if it was safe to say they were with Alpha 66.

"Absolutely," said Bishop.

"But they also had affiliations with certain other exile groups?"

"There's something you should realize," Bishop continued. "In those days, damn near any Cuban could set up a splinter group, and as long as he could provide rice and beans to that particular crew, they would accept him as a leader. We had fifty or sixty of these groups, for chrissakes. But the one that did the most as far as organization and acceptance by various intelligence agencies was Alpha 66."

I asked Bishop whether Angel and Leopoldo may have operated off and on out of Mexico City.

"I can tell you that much," he replied.

When I asked for a physical description of Angel, Bishop glowered at me: "You're trying to come in the back door is what you're trying to do." Then he offered basically the same height and weight for Angel as Nagell had provided—"five-ten, 160–165 weight, swarthy complexion"—before cutting himself off, saying, "I think I'd better stop at that."

I kept pressing him, and Bishop motioned for me to shut off the tape recorder. Then he lowered his voice and, as I took notes, added: "There was talk as early as 1962 about assassinating Kennedy, doing it right after his speech at the Orange Bowl. And about doing it in Los Angeles. Nothing ever came of that. Nothing *serious* ever came of it."

Once again, without my prompting him, Bishop was corroborating Nagell's story. Did Bishop think it was conceivable that Angel and Leopoldo might have convinced a young fellow named Oswald that they were supposedly working for Castro?

Bishop uttered a long sigh. "I don't know that for a fact, but it's a good possibility. At that point, it would have been relatively simple if Angel and Leopoldo dealt with Oswald. 'How can you prove you're Cuban intelligence? Do you know so-and-so?' Yeah, it's possible it was a set-up deal. I've done it myself. They could have been double agents and convinced Oswald, falsely, that they were Cuban intelligence or associated with it. I'll tell you one damn thing, whoever set up that poor little son of a bitch did a first-class job.

"Look, Angel and Leopoldo had direct ties with Santos Trafficante and Rolando Masferrer. That's where their money came from. Bear in mind, the Cubans [exiles] were doing it for one reason. The Syndicate had an entirely different reason. They wanted the pressure off, because Bobby Kennedy was after organized crime all the way. Particularly they wanted the pressure taken off Jimmy Hoffa, because if he got nailed, it was only a matter of time before they nailed somebody else. Like the domino effect, all right? So when organized crime, through Trafficante in Tampa, eventually provided the money for carrying out the assassination, the Cubans fell right into it. What they didn't know then was that they were really pawns of organized crime. Not until later, after the actual event."

Again, there was a pregnant pause. Colonel Bishop fixed his eyes on mine. He seemed to have decided to divulge far more than I had anticipated.

"Hoffa gave Masferrer $50,000," he went on. "Expense money. To partially set up the assassination team. I didn't realize until later that's what the money was for. I didn't *see* the money, but I heard that from reliable sources.

"It was later, not too long before the assassination, that Masferrer made the statement—more than once, not only to me but to others—that Kennedy was gonna be hit. But hell, I had heard that before, from any number of people, I didn't pay no mind to it. I mean, it wasn't unusual for Jimmy Hoffa or Trafficante to come up with X number of dollars to support the exiles' operations, okay? I repeat, Alpha 66 was the biggest recipient of the funding that was channeled through Rolando Masferrer.[8] You're looking in the right direction."

The Mob and the Kennedys

Before JFK became president, only 35 convictions had ever been handed down to persons connected with organized crime. In 1963, through the impetus of Robert Kennedy's Justice Department, there were 288. His primary targets were several of the same mobsters who worked with the CIA in the anti-Castro plots—Giancana, Trafficante, Marcello. Tangling the web was the president's relationship with Judith Campbell, who was simultaneously Giancana's mistress. Further complicating matters was JFK's affair with actress Marilyn Monroe, whose California home is now known to have been wiretapped by associates of Jimmy Hoffa, looking for "blackmail" on the Kennedys.[9]

Robert Kennedy had been trying to put Hoffa behind bars since 1956, when he served as staff counsel for a Senate subcommittee examining the influence of the Mob in the American labor movement. "No group better fits the prototype of the old Al Capone syndicate than Jimmy Hoffa and some of his chief Lieutenants,"[10] Kennedy wrote in his 1960 best-selling book *The Enemy Within*.

In late September 1962, Edward Grady Partin, a Teamster official in Baton Rouge, Louisiana, approached a member of Robert Kennedy's special unit with information of a "security nature." Partin had been indicted that July on twenty-six counts of embezzlement and falsification of union records, and he seems to have been looking for a deal. He proceeded to keep the Justice Department apprised of Hoffa's effort that December to pay off members of a federal jury in Nashville; the jury refused to indict Hoffa on an illegal-payoff scheme in December 1962. Based on Partin's tips, on May 9, 1963, Hoffa was indicted for jury tampering and convicted the following March.

In April 1964, the sensational "security nature" information Partin had provided was revealed on page one of *The New York Times*. "James R. Hoffa has been under investigation since September, 1962, by the Department of Justice," the *Times*'s story of April 12, 1964, began, "on a charge of allegedly plotting the assassination of Attorney General Robert F. Kennedy."[11]

Partin provided more details to *Life* magazine, which verified his story to its satisfaction with a polygraph examination. Partin wrote in *Life*'s May 15, 1964, issue that he had been talking alone with Hoffa at Teamsters union headquarters in Washington in midsummer of 1962 when the boss brought up the subject of Robert Kennedy.

According to Partin: "He said, 'Well, somebody needs to bump that son of a bitch off. . . . You know, I've got a run-down on him. His house sits here, like this, and it's not guarded.' Jimmy was making kind of diagrams with his fingers and I remember being surprised about the Attorney General's house not being guarded. Then Hoffa said, 'He drives alone in a convertible and swims by himself. I've got a .270 rifle with a high-power scope on it that shoots a long way without dropping any. It would be easy to get him with that. But I'm leery of it: it's too obvious.'

"He wasn't quite ready to give up thinking about the rifle, though, because then he asked, 'Do you know where I could get a silencer for it?'

"But then he went on, thinking it out some more, and he said, 'What I think should be done, if I can get hold of these plastic bombs, is to get somebody to throw one in his house and the place'll burn after it blows up.' "

Partin said that the thought of what would happen to Kennedy's children made him sick. Partin also felt he had himself been double-crossed by Hoffa, leading to his own indictment, and therefore decided to go to the Justice Department.

The timing of Partin's revelations—the early fall of 1962—coincided with FBI informant Edward Becker's account of a similar threat against the Kennedys being made by New Orleans Mob boss Carlos Marcello (see Chapter Eighteen). It also coincided with Nagell's original briefing in Mexico City from the Soviets about a Cuban exile plot. And it overlapped with yet a third story, told to the House Assassinations Committee by Cuban exile José Aleman, Jr.

In 1976 an article in *The Washington Post* quoted José Aleman, Jr., about an evening he spent in a Miami hotel room with Trafficante sometime in September 1962. Aleman was in financial debt and went to see Trafficante, whom Aleman said owed his cousin a favor, about getting some help. According to Aleman, Trafficante agreed to help bail him out by arranging a loan through Jimmy Hoffa. During the course of a long conversation "about democracy and civil liberties," Aleman recalled Trafficante suddenly launching into a vehement attack on President Kennedy.

"Have you seen how his brother is hitting Hoffa, a man who is a worker, who is not a millionaire, a friend to the blue collars?" Trafficante told Aleman. "He doesn't know that this kind of encounter is very delicate. Mark my words, this man Kennedy is in trouble, and he will get what is coming to him."

Aleman answered that Kennedy would most likely be reelected. "No, José," Trafficante is said to have replied, "he is going to be hit."[12]

Aleman was interviewed early in 1977 by House Assassinations Committee investigator Gaeton Fonzi. Fonzi's report stated: "Aleman said in more than one way that Trafficante did specifically tell him that Kennedy 'is going to get hit. . . .' Aleman said he got the impression that Trafficante was hinting that Hoffa was going to make the hit, not him, and that Kennedy would never make it to the election because of Hoffa."[13]

Aleman said he had reported the conversation in 1962 to two Miami FBI agents, George Davis and Paul Scranton, whose primary charge was keeping tabs on the Cuban exile community.[14] (Whether these were the two FBI agents code-named the "TACOS" with whom Nagell was in touch in January 1963, I've been unable to determine.)

Called before the House Assassinations Committee in 1978, Trafficante conceded having met Aleman "two or three times, perhaps," also verifying that he had sought to arrange a loan for the exile through the Teamsters union. But Trafficante claimed the entire conversation was in Spanish, "and in Spanish there was no way I could say Kennedy is going to get hit. I didn't say that. I might have told him he wasn't going to get reelected."[15]

In his testimony, Trafficante admitted to a thirty-year relationship with Carlos Marcello.[16] And Marcello's links in New Orleans to Oswald's uncle "Dutz" Murret, David Ferrie, Guy Banister, Sergio Arcacha-Smith, and other New Orleans characters around Oswald have also become abundantly clear. So far the FBI has refused to release 161 reels of its wiretap-obtained Marcello tapes, as ordered by a federal judge in Washington in May 1991 after a Freedom of Information Act suit by author John Davis.[17] In his book *Mafia Kingfish,* Davis wrote about an FBI informant, Joe Hauser, who alleged having made secret recordings in the 1970s in which Marcello alluded to involvement in the assassination. Hauser also told Davis that Marcello freely admitted having known Lee Harvey Oswald.

The theory of Mob involvement in the assassination has certainly become the most widely accepted in recent years. The House Assassinations Committee concluded in 1979 that while no concrete evidence existed to implicate Hoffa, Trafficante, and Marcello, all three had the "means, motive, and opportunity" to have taken part in a conspiracy.[18]

The latest account of such a possibility appeared in January 1992, in a *New York Post* series by investigative reporter Jack Newfield, based on his interviews with Frank Ragano, former attorney for both Trafficante and Hoffa. Ragano recalled a meeting he had had with Hoffa early in 1963 at Teamsters union headquarters. Hoffa knew that the lawyer was about to fly to New Orleans to meet with Marcello and Trafficante "to coordinate strategy against various federal investigations." And, according to Ragano, Hoffa asked him to deliver a message that he wanted the president killed. Ragano thought Hoffa was joking but did pass the word along. The two Mob leaders' wordless glances at one another, Ragano recalled, "scared me. . . . They made me think they already had such a thing in mind." When, a few weeks later, Hoffa asked Ragano, "Did you give them the message?," the lawyer said the Teamster boss expressed confidence that the deed would be done.[19]

Among the Cuban exiles, the Mob certainly had abundant inroads. Trafficante was a major player in the international heroin trade. In the early 1960s, the Federal Bureau of Narcotics (now called the Drug Enforcement Agency) estimated that more than 30 percent of the heroin entering the United States came through Latin America and the Caribbean, with Miami as the port of entry.[20] Cuban exiles often acted as couriers to New York and points beyond. Operation Eagle, a 1970 federal roundup of 150 suspects and considered to be the largest in the history of government law enforcement, discovered that an incredible 70 percent had been part of the CIA's Bay of Pigs invasion force. Grayston Lynch, a retired CIA officer from Miami's JM/WAVE station, has termed drug smuggling "child's play" for exiles who had made as many as several hundred raiding missions into Cuba.[21] The Miami Organized Crime Bureau had much evidence that Eladio del Valle, the friend of David Ferrie whom Nagell was shadowing in Miami in January 1963, was heavily involved in drug trafficking.[22]

Yet nowhere in the Warren Commission's entire record is there a single mention of Carlos Marcello. Nor, apparently, did the commission look into Hoffa, despite the Partin story about the Teamster leader's threat against Robert Kennedy coming to light in the midst of its investigation. The commission, however, was never informed by the CIA or the FBI about the anti-Castro plots involving the Mob and Cuban exiles. Spokespeople from both agencies were well aware of those conspiracies. Indeed, J. Edgar Hoover's office knew about the Hoffa, Trafficante, and Marcello threats against the president and his brother Robert long before November 22, 1963.

But Hoover never pursued organized crime with anything close to the vigilance he devoted to anticommunism. Early in 1963, Robert Kennedy had personally taken Hoover to task for failing to assist in the Marcello cases.[23] The FBI director is now known to have maintained a friendship with New York Mafia boss Frank Costello, who helped fix horse races for Hoover on occasion. When Marcello was rising to power in the early 1940s, he had been Costello's protégé in Louisiana.[24]

Richard Nagell had his own admitted associations in the Cosa Nostra world. He was a friend of two big-time New York gangsters: Salvatore "Tom Mix" Santoro, who has been imprisoned since 1986, and Joseph "Joe Beck" DiPalermo.[25] The latter was a onetime "enforcer" for Lucky Luciano and Vito Genovese, who operated out of New York's Little Italy —specifically, according to Nagell, the Thompson Social Club at 23 Prince Street. A 1964 Senate report listed DiPalermo as a key figure, along with Trafficante, in the Miami-based heroin traffic.[26]

In 1975 Nagell wrote to Fensterwald that "I have a friend who is familiar with both John Rosselli and Carlos ('The Little Man') Marcello."[27] As mentioned in Chapter Nine, Nagell was greatly disturbed when he received his FBI files under the Freedom of Information Act—because they had him "all tied in" with Rosselli and Sam Giancana, a claim he said was false. Yet, at our last rendezvous in 1984, Nagell again said he had a number of friends among the New York Syndicate—and was even thinking of going to work for them.

Yet, at the same time, Nagell has consistently stated that organized crime had no direct involvement in the assassination. His strongest statement along these lines appears in a July 9, 1979, certified letter he sent to the House Assassination Committee's chairman, Ohio congressman Louis Stokes.

Nagell wrote:

I am advised that the Committee will release its final report this month on its investigation into the assassination of President John Kennedy, and that such report will conclude that the murder may have been "arranged" by members of organized crime and their associates, namely, by James Hoffa, Carlos Marcello or Santos Trafficante, et al.

I doubt that there is any person alive today, at least not in the United States, who knows more about Lee Oswald's associates, activities and frame of mind during the months of July, August and September 1963 (the period when certain well-laid plans were formulated) than I do, and I state for the record that none of the aforenamed individuals or their alleged associates (including Jack Ruby, Charles Murret and Nofio Pecora) influenced or bore even the slightest responsibility for the later actions of Mr. Oswald.

Tentacles of an Octopus

Despite Nagell's disclaimer about organized crime, there was far too much evidence for me to disavow the likelihood of Syndicate involvement. Yet the Mob, by itself, simply did not have the power to tamper with all the physical evidence eventually used to incriminate Oswald as a lone gunman—or the autopsy results on the president's body, which author David Lifton amply documented as having been falsified in his book *Best Evidence*. A cover-up of the dimensions that ensued had to originate at a high governmental level—either the White House, the Pentagon, the CIA, or the FBI, maybe all four. And maybe this was pushed forward by certain "friends" much more closely aligned with government agencies than were members of the Syndicate.

It is worth a close look at the Mob's ties, through Hoffa and Marcello, into the realm of Texas oilmen and their powerful associates in government. One of Hoffa's closest consultants in Washington was I. Irving Davidson, who was not only the Teamsters' registered lobbyist but who also performed the same services in the early 1960s for the CIA, three Central American dictatorships (the Somozas of Nicaragua, the Duvaliers of Haiti, and the Trujillos of the Dominican Republic), and Dallas oil millionaire Clint Murchison. Through Hoffa, Davidson arranged a huge Teamsters' pension fund loan to the Murchisons. Through Davidson, the Murchisons later ended up doing considerable business with Marcello.

It was Davidson, in fact, who provided Marcello with an initial entrée into the CIA and other realms of Washington. In 1961, after Robert Kennedy temporarily deported Marcello to Guatemala, Davidson was the only person in Washington who had the mobster's phone number there. Edward Partin alleged that Davidson had been witness to a secret Marcello-Hoffa meeting in 1960, where "a $500,000 cash payment to the Nixon [presidential] campaign was made. Davidson was a good friend of Nixon, as well as of J. Edgar Hoover, who was said to rely on him for inside information.[28]

The House Assassinations Committee, when it was probing the background of George de Mohrenschildt in 1978, called Davidson in to testify. The committee was curious about a 1964 *Washington Post* article that stated that Davidson had visited Haiti in May 1963 with two Dallas arms suppliers—the same month that de Mohrenschildt was headed toward that Caribbean nation.

Davidson denied ever participating in Haitian arms deals. He did concede having a close friendship with dictator François ("Papa Doc") Duvalier. Indeed, the committee came across a CIA Office of Security memo dated January 7, 1964, wherein an informant advised that Duvalier had "sent a confidential message to Davidson during the last week of December 1963; the contents of the message were not known." According to Davidson, "his [Davidson's] business deals also involved working with the American Embassy in Port-au-Prince."

The lobbyist said he had met Clemard Charles—de Mohrenschildt's springtime 1963 companion in Washington at meetings with U.S. intelligence officials (see Chapter Thirteen)—on one occasion when visiting Duvalier. But Davidson alleged that he was not even aware of de Mohrenschildt until 1978, when a newspaper article "suggested that he had approached the FBI to find out what information the Bureau had on de Mohrenschildt in connection with the Kennedy assassination."[29]

Yet an FBI memo of November 1, 1967, reported Davidson having recently called the FBI and requested a meeting with Hoover's second-in-command, Clyde Tolson. The reason was that Davidson had been approached by two men—ex-CIA contract agent Hugh McDonald and Leonard Davidov—who asked him to make some inquiries into de Mohrenschildt's background. According to the FBI, Davidson "alleged his only concern was that of protecting President Johnson from being 'smeared,' however, it is strongly believed that his real motive was that of seeking information on de Mohrenschildt and McDonald." The FBI file went on that Davidson had spent the previous weekend in Dallas, allegedly to attend a football game.[30]

The House Assassinations Committee seems not to have pursued Davidson's intriguing relationships with Hoffa, Hoover, Nixon, Marcello, and the Murchisons. (In fairness, the long-standing Marcello-Davidson relationship did not become known until 1979, through an undercover FBI investigation; Davidson was indicted, along with Marcello and several others, on racketeering and bribery charges, but was acquitted in 1981.)[31]

The Murchison link alone was certainly worth pursuing. Clint Murchison, Sr., who died in 1969, was cut from the same political cloth as H. L. Hunt. Back in 1951, after General Douglas MacArthur was relieved of his Korean command by President Truman, H. L. Hunt accompanied MacArthur on a flight to Texas for a speaking tour. Hunt and Murchison were the chief organizers of the pro-MacArthur forces in Texas. They would always remember the general standing bareheaded in front of the Alamo, urging removal of "the burden of taxation" from enterprising men like themselves, charging that such restraints were imposed by "those who seek to convert us to a form of socialistic endeavor, leading directly to the path of Communist slavery." Hunt went on to set up a MacArthur-for-president headquarters in Chicago, spending $150,000 of his own money on the general's reluctant 1952 campaign, which eventually fell apart as MacArthur adopted the strident rhetoric of the right wing.[32] Still, connections were made; Charles Willoughby, for example, was a regular part of the MacArthur-Hunt entourage and undoubtedly was acquainted with Murchison as well.

At least on paper, the Hunts and the Murchisons were rivals in the Texas oil business. But both cultivated not only powerful people on the far right but also J. Edgar Hoover, Richard Nixon, organized-crime figures, and Lyndon Johnson, whose rise to power emanated directly from his friends in Texas oil. Like Hunt, Murchison was an ardent supporter of Senator Joseph McCarthy's anti-Communist crusade. McCarthy came often to the exclusive hotel that Murchison opened in La Jolla, California, in the early 1950s. So did Richard Nixon and J. Edgar Hoover. In 1961, after Nixon had lost the presidential election to JFK the previous year, Murchison sold Nixon a lot in Beverly Hills for only $35,000—a lot Murchison had financed through a Hoffa loan—which Nixon sold two years later for $86,000.[33]

As James Reston, Jr., wrote in his biography of another Texas politician, John Connally: "At the [Murchison] Hotel Del Charro, the FBI and the underworld and the oil business coexisted in a nervous axis of collegiality. When Hoover came, as he did every summer between 1953 and 1959, Murchison picked up his tab. That amounted to about $19,000 of free vacations for the FBI Director over those years."[34] Whether Hoover knew it or not, almost 20 percent of the Murchison Oil Lease Company in Oklahoma was then owned by Gerardo Catena, chief lieutenant to the Genovese crime family.[35]

In 1992 I asked former H. L. Hunt aide John Curington about the oil family's possible ties to organized crime. He answered: "Hunt used to gamble a lot with Lucky Luciano and Frank Erickson, another big-time gambler there in New York." And did he know Carlos Marcello? "Yeah," Curington said, "but that gets into a whole different ball game," and refused further comment.[36]

By the autumn of 1963, while the Willoughby crowd assailed JFK's policies for political reasons, things were coming apart, financially and otherwise, for many others in this nexus of alliances. Organized crime's problems with the Kennedys were but the tip of an iceberg. A major scandal was brewing around Bobby Baker, whom Vice President Johnson had made secretary of the Senate Democrats in 1955, when LBJ was majority leader. LBJ called Baker "my strong right arm, the last man I see at night, the first I see in the morning." Baker's duties, which he assumed at age twenty-five, ranged from counting heads for close votes on important issues to fixing parking tickets. Unofficially, he controlled the flow of legislation and campaign contributions. On October 8, 1963, he was forced to resign, as a Senate investigation of his outside business activities began producing sensational testimony on numerous questionable deals.[37]

Baker's deals were tightly interwoven with the Murchison family—and the Mob. What first attracted the attention of Senate investigators was a lawsuit brought against Baker in 1963 by his associates in a vending company, alleging that he had failed to live up to certain bargains. Those associates were, for the most part, Las Vegas gamblers; one of them, Edward Levinson, was a lieutenant of Florida mobster Meyer Lansky, whose Fremont Hotel in Vegas was financed through a Hoffa loan. Baker, it later turned out, did considerable business with the Mob in Las Vegas, Chicago, Louisiana, and the Caribbean. Through Baker, Levinson had also gotten to know Clint Murchison.[38]

Here things started to get very sticky. Clint Murchison, Jr., tried to persuade the Senate Rules Committee in 1964 that his own real-estate dealings with Jimmy Hoffa in Florida were "hardly relevant" to the Baker investigation. The Murchisons had already been revealed as "the money partners" in a meat-packing plant in Haiti that was kicking back thousands of dollars to Baker in return for using his influence to speed the granting of an export certificate.[39]

Then there was LBJ's own history with Carlos Marcello. Biographer John Davis was told by a former Justice Department official that at the time of the assassination, Robert Kennedy had a thick investigative file on his desk on the Marcello-LBJ connection. In the 1950s, Marcello's Texas "political fixer" Jack Halfen had reportedly arranged to siphon off a percentage of the mobster's racing wire and slot machine profits for LBJ's Senate campaigns. In exchange, according to journalist Michael Dorman in his book *Payoff,* LBJ had helped kill certain antiracketeering legislation in committee.[40]

Nor were these the only scandals looming in the autumn of 1963. Roy Cohn, former chief counsel to Senator Joe McCarthy—and a close friend of both Hoover and H. L. Hunt—was indicted by a federal grand jury in September 1963 on eight counts in a stock-fraud case. Cohn and Robert Kennedy were longtime enemies, dating back to when they nearly came to blows over the handling of the Army-McCarthy hearings in 1954. Cohn's Lionel Corporation was deeply enmeshed with Las Vegas gambling interests, which provided the basis for his indictment.[41]

Then there was a defense contract scandal wherein Secretary of the Navy Fred Korth was accused by members of Congress with conflict of interest in ensuring that the TFX fighter plane would be developed by General Dynamics. Korth resigned at the Kennedy administration's request on October 18, 1963, allegedly because of an "indiscretion" involving Navy stationery.[42] One of Bobby Baker's associates, Donald Reynolds, later told Congress of a $100,000 payoff involved in the contract award.[43] Korth, also a Texan, was another LBJ friend. Korth had been present at a June 1963 meeting when JFK decided to make an autumn trip to Texas. Strangely, back in 1948 Korth had been the attorney for Edwin Ekdahl, Oswald's stepfather, in a divorce settlement with Marguerite Oswald.[44]

So all this was mushrooming in the two months preceding Kennedy's death. And afterward, things quickly began to change. Though Bobby Baker was finally convicted in 1967 of tax evasion, theft, and conspiracy, he didn't take anybody else with him. As a Justice Department lawyer complained to *The New York Times,* after the assassination "the next day we stopped getting information from the FBI on the Bobby Baker investigation. Within a month the FBI men in the field wouldn't tell us anything. We started running out of gas."[45]

The Kennedys had been stepping on some very powerful toes.

Summary

The remarkable account of Colonel William Bishop served to verify much of what Nagell had already said: the Miami (December 1962) and Los Angeles (June 1963) discussions about killing JFK; the direct involvement of Cuban exiles, including Angel and Leopoldo; and Mexico as a locale for the CIA's Operation 40 assassination squad. A self-avowed hit man himself, Bishop claimed to have been introduced to Nagell as "additional security" for Rolando Masferrer. Then, in New Orleans, at the request of some exiles, Bishop had authorized surveillance on Nagell.

According to Bishop, Masferrer dispatched funds to Alpha 66 directly from organized crime. A $50,000 payoff from Jimmy Hoffa was said to have helped fund the assassination. Although Nagell has disclaimed Mob involvement, he had a number of Syndicate acquaintances—and the evidence of an organized-crime link to the assassination is strong. Hoffa, Marcello, and Trafficante are all alleged to have made threats against the president and/or his brother Robert in September 1962—the very period when Nagell was briefed by the Soviets about a plot. Oswald, through his uncle, may have had direct ties to the Marcello organization.

But the Syndicate network extended into high places—to the oil-rich Murchison family in Dallas, to LBJ's protégé Bobby Baker. J. Edgar Hoover had vacationed alongside gangsters at Murchison's California hotel. By the autumn of 1963, scandal threatened many of the wealthy and powerful. The nefarious dealings of McCarthy's anti-Communist right arm Roy Cohn, and Secretary of the Navy Fred Korth were also publicly exposed. LBJ's past connections to Marcello, and Richard Nixon's to Hoffa, threatened to come to light. All this was coming to the fore as November 22, 1963, approached. Beyond that date, along with Robert Kennedy's pursuit of organized-crime figures, the scandals soon faded into oblivion.

Chapter Twenty-three

Countdown to Dallas:
October–November 1963

◇

Inside his cell at the El Paso County Jail, Richard Case Nagell paced and waited. He waited through the last days of September 1963 as President Kennedy embarked on a five-day conservation tour through the western states before returning to Washington on the twenty-ninth. The FBI, the CIA, the KGB, and Cuban intelligence all knew at least bits and pieces of the secret Nagell was carrying. Perhaps, he must have thought as the September plan did not materialize, something had been done.

On October 10, Nagell wrote to his sister:

Dear Eleanore. . . .

I have hesitated to write you as I did not want you to become involved in my present situation. I have requested the F.B.I. not to contact you and to the best of my knowledge they have cooperated thus far. . . .

At this time I ask of you only two things. . . . *First,* please believe that I did what I did because I had to, but that I am *not* guilty of bank robbery or anything related. *Second,* I ask that you do not become involved in this matter in *any way whatsoever.* I base these two requests on the affection which you have displayed as a sister throughout the years and all of the assistance given me by both you and Lou subsequent to my marriage.

Please forget that I exist at present. As for the embarassment [sic] caused by the charges filed against me, I can only say I am sorry.

It is not necessary, or desired, that you answer this letter as I will know whether or not you receive it.

With love,
Dick

The next day, Dr. R. J. Bennett, a neuropsychiatrist at the El Paso Medical Center, wrote a letter to Judge R. E. Thomason, who was then presiding in Nagell's case:

I have attempted to examined [sic] Mr. Nagell on two occasions, both times he has been unwilling to give information. The first time he said he had no attorney and since he knew "nothing" of the proceedings [sic] in Texas, he did not care to discuss anything about his case.

He was assigned an attorney, Mr. J. Hammond. The latter called and said that he had advised Mr. Nagell to cooperate with me but that information about the bank episode should not be discussed.

I returned to examined [sic] Mr. Nagell on 10-10-63 but he informed me that he wanted to see his attorney again before answering any questions as he wanted to know what information to give me and how to answer my questions. He wanted to know whether the information would be presented in court. He pointed out that it was "priviledged [sic] information" and wanted to know if he could choose a psychiatrist to examined [sic] him and report to the court. . . .[1]

Oswald in Dallas

On October 2, Lee Harvey Oswald had departed Mexico City by bus, arriving in Nuevo Laredo and going straight to Dallas. Early on the afternoon of the next day, he applied for unemployment insurance at the Texas Employment Commission and registered at a downtown YMCA as a serviceman. On a JOBCO application, he stated that he had lived in Dallas for fifteen years and listed George de Mohrenschildt as his closest friend.[2]

Going to see Marina at Ruth Paine's home in Irving, Texas, Oswald told his wife "that he had visited the two embassies [in Mexico City], that he had received nothing, that the people who are there are too much—too bureaucratic." Oswald added that he had attended a bullfight and seemed "disappointed at not being able to get to Cuba."[3]

On October 5, a story appeared in the *Dallas Morning News* announcing that President Kennedy would visit the city in November. Oswald moved alone into a small rooming house two days later.[4] After the assassination, a Dallas citizen reported seeing a man "identical" to Oswald at an October 13 meeting of the DRE. This was the same anti-Castro exile group that Carlos Bringuier served as New Orleans' delegate and that would lead the way in Miami spreading the Castro-did-it rumors. That same October meeting was admittedly attended by General Edwin Walker.[5]

The next afternoon, Paine and Marina went to the home of an Irving neighbor for coffee. The subject of Oswald's looking for work came up. As Paine later testified to the Warren Commission, "Mrs. [Bill] Randle mentioned that her younger brother, Wesley Frazier, thought they needed another person at the Texas School Book Depository, where Wesley worked." When Marina and Ruth went home, Marina asked her friend to call and see about the possibility of an opening. Roy Truly, the depository superintendent, suggested that Lee come see him.

Truly later recalled Oswald having told him he had a wife and child to support, with another baby due in a few days; that he had received an honorable discharge from the Marines and had never been in any trouble with the police. He would be glad to do any kind of work offered. "He looked like a nice young fellow to me—he was quiet and well-mannered," Truly felt.[6]

So, on October 16, Oswald started his fateful job filling orders at the Texas School Book Depository. He moved alone to another small room, in Dallas's Oak Cliff section, where the rent was $8.00 a week. For the first time in over a year of renting rooms, he used an assumed name—"O. H. Lee."[7] Two days later, he celebrated his twenty-fourth birthday at the Paines. And two days after that, Marina gave birth to the couple's second child, another daughter.

Then, on October 23, General Walker addressed a downtown rally of the Dallas United States Day Committee. Adlai Stevenson, U.S. ambassador to the United Nations, was coming to town, and Walker was intent on preempting him. "Tonight we stand on a battleground identified on this stage as U.S. Day—the symbol of our sovereignty," Walker told a crowd of a thousand people. "Tomorrow night there will stand here a symbol to the Communist conspiracy and the United Nations." In the audience was Lee Harvey Oswald.[8]

Extremist Conclaves

At the same time, a major gathering of some of Walker's ideological comrades was taking place in Lucerne, Switzerland. It was the annual congress of Charles Willoughby's International Committee for the Defense of Christian Culture (ICDCC), and MacArthur's former intelligence chief was speaking on what he called "an 'old theme': the Sorge espionage case." Presiding at the October 14–16 affair was José Solis Ruiz, a minister in the Spanish cabinet of dictator Franco[9] and a leading member of a secret Catholic order called Opus Dei.[10]

Among the speakers was Dr. Theodor Oberlander, a former German officer who had led the Ukrainian Nightingales in World War II (see Chapter Ten). Oberlander had served as West Germany's minister of refugee affairs until 1960, when details of his wartime role became public and he was forced to resign. He was also a delegate to the Asian people's Anti-Communist League.[11] Herman Punder, the ICDCC's outgoing international president, was an ex-Nazi Abwehr agent. Both Punder and Oberlander had direct connections into the Munich-based newspaper that, the day after the assassination, would contact General Walker—and then somehow "scoop" the world on the previously unknown news that Oswald had fired on Walker in April.[12]

In the United States, both before and after his autumn European sojourn, Willoughby was in the midst of a steady correspondence with Colonel Charles Thourot Pichel. Thirty years earlier, when Hitler first came to power in Germany, Pichel had written the Führer's close associate Ernst Hanfstaengl, requesting that he, Pichel, be appointed official American liaison to Hitler.[13] In 1963 Pichel was grand chancellor of a mysterious sect called The Sovereign Order of Saint John of Jerusalem, also known as the "Shickshinny Knights," after the Pennsylvania town where Pichel based.

Pichel's group claimed to be the legitimate Knights of Malta, a Catholic order dating back to the Crusades. During the French Revolution, when Napoleon occupied Malta, the existing Knights scattered. One group was reconstituted later under the sovereignty of the Vatican. Another sought sanctuary under Czar Paul I in Russia, remaining there until the Russian Revolution of 1917, when they resettled once more in White Russian communities in America and Europe. Many came to the sleepy Pennsylvania town of Shickshinny.[14]

It is not clear from Willoughby's papers just how he happened to hook up with Pichel. But by September 1963 he had become the order's "security general." As he wrote to Pichel: "I shall be honored to be of service. I am familiar with the tradition and ethical purposes of your Order." He said he anticipated contributing his "specialized knowledge and experience in the field of intelligence, counterintelligence and security surveillance." For a time he even merged his *Foreign Intelligence Digest* into the Knights' own publication. On his autumn 1963 trip he informed Pichel that he would see about gaining recognition for the order from Generalissimo Franco in Madrid.[15]

Willoughby was in auspicious company, for the Shickshinny Knights had an "Armed Services Committee" that in 1963 read like a *Who's Who* of retired military men at the extremist fringe. All these "Knights" had been "singled out for their brilliant and outstanding careers as Soldiers of Christ and Advocates of a Free World." Besides Willoughby, they included a number of other members of MacArthur's old team—Brigadier General Bonner Fellers, Lieutenant General Pedro del Valle, Marine general Lemuel Shepherd. British admiral Sir Barry Domville, jailed in England during World War II as a Nazi agent, was also on the list.[16]

So was Colonel Philip J. Corso, a twenty-year Army Intelligence career man until his retirement in August 1963. He had been the military Operations Coordinating Board's delegate to the CIA group planning the 1954 Guatemalan coup. In 1956 Corso had sought to reactivate fifty surviving garrisons of East European paramilitary units still hanging on in West Germany and tied to the Gehlen spy network. When his Volunteer Freedom Corps, dedicated to rolling back communism, was scuttled as too radical by the Eisenhower administration, Corso attributed the defeat to "lies by our liberal darlings." A staunch foe of what he considered a laissez-faire CIA, Corso testified before Congress on "military muzzling" after General Walker was kicked out of West Germany in 1961. Upon leaving Army Intelligence, Corso went to work in 1963 as a "research assistant" for segregationist senator Strom Thurmond of South Carolina. And, after the Kennedy assassination, Corso was among the first to spread rumors hinting that Oswald was tied to a Communist ring inside the CIA —and doubling as an informant for the FBI.[17]

Oswald and the FBI

At about noon on November 1, Oswald walked over to a post office on his lunch-hour break from the Texas School Book Depository and rented another post office box. He listed "Fair Play for Cuba Committee" and

"American Civil Liberties Union" (ACLU) as organizations on the form. Then he mailed three letters. One was a change-of-address card to Consul Reznichenko at the Soviet embassy in Washington. Another was a membership application to the ACLU. The third was Oswald's alerting Communist Party, U.S.A. headquarters that his September plans had changed about moving to the Philadelphia-Baltimore area. He described having attended an ACLU meeting on October 25 where "a film was shown and afterwards a very critical discussion of the ultra-right in Dallas." He also told of having gone to "a ultra-right meeting headed by Gen. Edwin A. Walker. . . . As you can see, political friction between 'left' and 'right' is very great here."[18]

In the meantime, Dallas FBI agent James P. Hosty, Jr., had been trying to find him. The day after Oswald's return from Mexico, Hosty was notified of Oswald's disappearance from New Orleans by the FBI's field office there, and later testified that he checked the couple's former neighborhoods in Dallas and Fort Worth with negative results.[19] On October 25 the Dallas FBI office received word, again from New Orleans, that Oswald had been in contact with the Soviet embassy in Mexico City. Hosty says he then placed a higher priority on locating Oswald and, after receiving another communication from New Orleans with a change of address to Irving, he drove out to Ruth Paine's home on November 1.

At Hosty's request, Paine told him that Oswald was working at the book depository and living somewhere in Oak Cliff. Marina was alarmed when she saw Hosty at the house, and he sought to reassure her "that it wasn't the job of the FBI to harm people." Sometime during Hosty's visit, Marina jotted down the FBI agent's license plate number.

Hosty verified Oswald's place of employment by telephone, then advised both the New Orleans office and FBI headquarters that Dallas was assuming control of the "internal security" case "because he had now been verified in our division." Again on November 5, Hosty dropped by the Paine home; again he says he was told that Oswald's precise whereabouts were unknown. Since the agent had twenty-five to forty cases going at the time and "had now established that Lee Oswald was not employed in a sensitive industry," he let the matter rest.[20]

Marina's news of Hosty's visits is said to have plunged Oswald into a dark mood. He jotted down the agent's name, and the license plate number Marina had obtained for him, in his address book.[21] On November 9 Oswald wrote a very strange letter to the Soviet embassy in Washington:

> This is to inform you of recent events since my meetings with comrade Kostin [apparently Kostikov] in the Embassy of the Soviet Union, Mexico City, Mexico.
> I was unable to remain in Mexico undefinily [sic] because of my Mexi-

can visa restrictions which was for 15 days only. I could not take a chance on requesting a new visa unless I used my real name, so I returned to the United States.

I had not planned to contact the Soviet embassy in Mexico so they were unprepared, had I been able to reach the Soviet Embassy in Havana as planned, the embassy there would have had time to complete our business.

Of course the Soviet Embassy was not at fault, they were, as I say unprepared, the Cuban Consulate was guilty of a gross breach of regulations, I am glad he has since been replaced.

The Federal Bureau of Investigation is not now interested in my activities in the progressive organization "Fair Play for Cuba Committee," of which I was secretary in New Orleans (state Louisiana) since I no longer reside in that state. However, the FBI has visited us here in Dallas, Texas, on November 1st. Agent James F. Hasty [sic] warned me that if I engaged in F.P.C.C. activities in Texas the F.B.I. will again take an "interest" in me.

This agent also "suggested" to Marina Nichilayeva that she could remain in the United States under F.B.I. "protection," that is, she could defect from the Soviet Union, of course, I and my wife strongly protested these tactics by the notorious F.B.I.

Please advise us of the arrival of our Soviet entrance visa's as soon as they come.

Also, this is to inform you of the birth, on October 20, 1963, of daughter, AUDREY MARINA OSWALD in DALLAS TEXAS to my wife.[22]

Oswald left the draft of his letter on Ruth Paine's desk, where she discovered it. Later she would testify that Oswald's "false" statement that the FBI was no longer interested in his activities upset her. So she secretly made a copy of the letter, which the day after the assassination Paine would turn over to the FBI.[23]

At about the time Oswald wrote to the Soviet embassy, he dropped by the Dallas FBI office and left a note for agent Hosty. Its contents can never be known, since Hosty was ordered to destroy it within hours of Oswald's death. In 1975, after a retired agent tipped a journalist about this incident, the note's destruction became the basis for a congressional investigation by the House Subcommittee on Civil and Constitutional Rights.

Hosty testified that he had simply placed the note in his workbox, where his supervisor found it on the afternoon of the assassination. J. Gordon Shanklin, in charge of the Dallas FBI office, asked Hosty to prepare a memorandum detailing all facts about the note's contents. Then, about two hours after Jack Ruby silenced Oswald, Shanklin called Hosty into his office. "Jim, I don't ever want to see that Oswald note again,"

Hosty recalled Shanklin saying. "Oswald's dead and there can't be a trial now." Hosty went into the men's room and flushed the note down the toilet.

As best Hosty said he could recall in 1975, the note said something like: "If you have anything you want to learn about me, come talk to me directly. If you don't cease bothering my wife, I will take appropriate action and report this to proper authorities." An FBI receptionist, Nancy Fenner, believed the contents were more dramatic: "Let this be a warning. I will blow up the FBI and the Dallas Police Department if you don't stop bothering my wife."[24]

Hosty remembered also showing to Shanklin the Oswald letter to the Soviet embassy that Ruth Paine had passed along to him on November 23. Shanklin, according to Hosty, "became highly upset and highly incensed." Hosty added that he and a colleague decided to preserve the letter to the embassy, despite his supervisor's apparent intent that it, too, be destroyed.[25]

But it was Hosty himself who ended up being censured by his superiors. In early October 1964, after the Warren Commission Report offered mild criticism of the FBI's failure to keep better track of Oswald, Hosty was suspended from duty for thirty days without pay on direct orders from Hoover. After that he was transferred to Kansas City, where he continues to reside in retirement.[26]

I called Hosty there in 1981. What I wanted to know was whether he was ever alerted before the assassination about Richard Nagell, confined in the El Paso County Jail after sending his warning letter to Hoover on September 17. "I think I've heard of that deal, yeah," Hosty said. "As I recall, isn't he something of a mental case? I have heard of him." But Hosty maintained he did not remember ever being contacted about Nagell by either headquarters or the El Paso office.[27]

Nagell and the FBI

Late in October 1963, Nagell has written that while discussing his contemplated defense with James E. Hammond, a court-appointed counsel, he had revealed having made an unauthorized trip to Cuba. Several days later, Hammond was said to have admitted to Nagell that he had disclosed "this privileged communication and other information given him in confidence" to the FBI.[28]

On Monday morning, November 4, a habeas corpus hearing for Nagell took place at the district courthouse. Nagell requested that attorney Hammond be discharged; Judge Thomason granted the request. Nagell told the court that he did "not intend to disclose my motive at this time" but that it was not to hold up the bank.[29] It was at this hearing that Nagell let policeman Jim Bundren know that he "wouldn't want to be in Dallas" (see Chapter One).

On November 19, El Paso FBI agents Edward J. Murphy and George E. Aiken visited Nagell at the county jail. He had been alleging certain violations of his constitutional safeguards by the authorities, and he wanted to offer a statement in that regard. Signed by the two agents as witnesses, it read:

> . . . On September 24, 1963, the U.S. District Court ordered that I be given a psychiatric examination to determine my mental competency to stand trial, and that if determined necessary by the examining psychiatrist to conduct such examination, to be committed to the Federal Correctional Institution, La Tuna, Texas, for a period not exceeding two weeks.
>
> On November 4, 1963, the court nullified that part of the aforesaid order, pertaining to the committment [sic] and reordered that I be committed to Beaumont Army Hospital, El Paso, Texas, for psychiatric examination.
>
> On September 24, 1963, and again on November 4, 1963, the U.S. District Court ordered that further prosecutive action against me be deferred until such time as the Court is in receipt of the results of said psychiatric examination.
>
> As of this date I have not received the aforementioned psychiatric examination nor have I been committed to either of the aforementioned institutions for such examination, nor have I been indicted by the Federal Grand Jury.
>
> I believe that an unnecessary and undue delay has occurred in bringing me to trial, as a result of my reluctance to participate in a psychiatric consultation and/or examination. I believe that this is a violation of my right to a speedy trial as guaranteed to me by Amendment 6 of the Constitution. . . .
>
> An attempt has been made to indirectly coerce me to incriminate myself, by a court appointed psychiatrist known to me as Doctor Bennett, in that he queried me as to my motive for committing the alleged offense and stated to me that if I did not give him such information, I was being uncooperative, and that I might have to be sent to Springfield Medical Center. . . .[30]

At the close of the interview, Nagell handed a note to agent Murphy, requesting that it be given to Thomas B. White, Jr., the agent who had first questioned him on September 20.

To: Mr. Thomas B. White
      F.B.I. El Paso

When one's actions are motivated by an ideological conviction, he cannot deviate from his pursued path simply because society may censure it as wrong. But when one becomes disillusioned with such ideology, and an existing situation so dictates, he must initiate immediate corrective action as befits circumstance and as best he knows how.

I have always acted from a principle of love for my country and the same principle actuated my conduct of September 20th, however inappropriate or incomprehensible it may appear.[31]

Three days later, John F. Kennedy was shot.

Desmond FitzGerald and AM/LASH

Desmond FitzGerald's stepdaughter Barbara Train remembers being "aware of tension between he and Bobby Kennedy. I don't think he trusted Bobby," she told me in 1992, "and felt manipulated by him. Part of it was that it was sort of a social thing to put down the Kennedys, among snotty upper-class WASPs like my stepfather. He had a much better relationship with Jack, but viewed Bobby as sort of a weasel. They certainly weren't friends, not by a long shot."[32]

All through the six weeks that led up to the assassination, the CIA's secret plotting against Castro with Rolando Cubela (AM/LASH) was continuing. Desmond FitzGerald's first meeting with Cubela occurred on October 29 in Paris, where FitzGerald falsely claimed that he was Robert Kennedy's "personal representative." Cubela was assured that the attorney general had committed the U.S. government to the project. Cubela wanted an arms cache, including grenades and high-powered rifles, to be waiting for him inside Cuba. He also requested, according to the CIA, that the agency "devise some technical means of doing the job that would not automatically cause him to lose his own life in the try."

So FitzGerald went to the CIA's Technical Services Division, which manufactured a ballpoint pen rigged with a hypodermic needle. The needle's point was designed to be so fine that the victim would not notice its insertion.

On the Paris evening of November 22, 1963, FitzGerald and his case officer met to finalize plans with AM/LASH. The CIA officials used a speech made by JFK in Miami four days earlier as evidence that the president supported a coup against Cuba. The speech had described the Castro government as a "small band of conspirators" who formed a "barrier" that "once removed" would ensure American support for progressive goals in Cuba. The case officer lied and told Cubela that FitzGerald had helped write it.

FitzGerald then proferred the poison pen, recommending that Cubela use Black-Leaf 40, a poison that was commercially available. Cubela, the unidentified case officer would later recall, complained that the CIA could surely "come up with something more sophisticated than that." Both CIA officials assured AM/LASH "that CIA would give him everything he needed (telescopic sight, silencer, all the money he wanted)." The cache would be dropped in Cuba, Cubela was told.[33]

Years later, Cubela would tell journalist Anthony Summers that Fitz-Gerald had pretended to be a senior U.S. senator, that the CIA fountain pen contained not poison but a "special chamber with a .45-caliber bullet in it," and that it was the CIA—not he—who brought up the idea of assassinating Castro in the first place.[34]

The two CIA men and the Cuban emerged from their final Paris meeting—whatever its content—to learn some earthshaking news: President Kennedy had just been assassinated in Dallas.

FitzGerald flew back to Washington immediately. He was watching television on Sunday, November 24, when Ruby pumped a single deadly bullet into Oswald's stomach. Barbara Train remembers: "My mother told me that when Oswald was shot, this was the only time she ever saw Dezzy cry. He said to her, 'Now we'll never know what happened.'"

Today Train believes it quite conceivable that her stepfather may have had some advance knowledge of Oswald's activities. "I'm convinced he was somehow involved," she says, "but that somehow he didn't understand the seriousness of it—and wrote Oswald off as a joke."[35]

There was certainly something FitzGerald knew about the whole AM/LASH business that he later feared revealing, even within the CIA. After Angleton's counter intelligence staff came across Cubela's name among the contacts of KGB official Valery Kostikov at the Soviet embassy in Mexico, they requested any information available from FitzGerald's Cuban task force. But the operational file on AM/LASH—which contained details of FitzGerald's autumn 1963 meetings with Cubela—was withheld from Angleton's staff. Nor was any information about AM/LASH, or the CIA-Mob plots against Castro, ever made available to the Warren Commission.[36]

The Cubela operation continued for nearly nineteen months after the assassination. Cubela received shipments of guns and ammunition in March and June of 1964, and his case officer asked the CIA's Technical Services Division to make a silencer for Cubela's rifle "on a crash basis." In Madrid the following winter, Cubela met twice with exile leader Manuel Artime, who provided him with a telescopic sight and silencer for his rifle. The "hit" was then scheduled for Easter weekend of 1965, after which Artime and five hundred Cuban commandos were to launch a mini-invasion and take over the government. It failed to go forward. That June, according to the Senate Intelligence Committee, "CIA terminated all contact with AM/LASH and his associates for reasons related to security."[37]

On March 1, 1966, Cubela and another ex-Cuban Army major were arrested in Havana for plotting to assassinate Castro. A government communiqué charged that the plot was hatched in Spain with the help of Artime and the CIA. Nine days later, Cubela went before a revolutionary tribunal. No mention was made of his pre-1964 involvement with the CIA. He was convicted but not executed,[38] serving some eighteen years in prison before being released. Today Cubela is said to reside in Madrid.

Former U.S. senator Robert Morgan, a member of the Senate Intelligence Committee, came away convinced in 1976 that Cubela "was nothing but a double agent" for Castro all along.[39]

We have already looked in this book at Cubela's connections to a Cuban exile, Victor Hernandez, who worked with Minuteman leader Richard Lauchli in transporting arms to the New Orleans training camp. We have also looked at the testimony of Cuban exile José Aleman, Jr., about a possible Cubela relationship with Florida mobster Santos Trafficante, Jr. Aleman, who revealed Trafficante's threat against JFK to the House Assassinations Committee, also advised that "it was very important to pay attention of the possibility of Castro being mixed in with Santos Trafficante."[40]

What did Aleman mean? Trafficante had lost millions in his casino investments when Castro took over Cuba. Castro had even had the Mob leader briefly imprisoned in 1959. Yet a Federal Bureau of Narcotics report on Trafficante in July 1961 reported "unconfirmed rumors in the Cuban refugee population in Miami that, when Fidel Castro ran the American racketeers out of Cuba and seized the casinos, he kept Santo [sic] Trafficante Jr. in jail to make it appear that he had a personal dislike for Trafficante, when in fact Trafficante is an agent of Castro. Trafficante is allegedly Castro's outlet for illegal contraband in the country."

During the early 1960s, Castro is said to have relied on Cuban Mafia contacts for much of his intelligence about Miami's exile community. According to Aleman, the Florida numbers racket known as "Bolita" was a method of payment for Castro's agents there. Another Narcotics Bureau report from the period says the same thing: Cuban G-2 intelligence operatives in Tampa and Miami were allegedly placing bets with Trafficante's numbers operators, and Trafficante's payoffs were pegged to the Cuban lottery drawings. The Castro agents were communicating to Havana information about which numbers were getting the heaviest play.[41]

Trafficante denied before the House Assassinations Committee that there was any "affiliation whatsoever between Castro government and myself. There never has been."[42]

Ominous possibilities arise when we consider that Trafficante could have been simultaneously in touch with Castro, aware of the CIA's AM/LASH plot—and of Oswald, through the mobster's New Orleans associates. The manipulation of Oswald by Angel and Leopoldo, posing as Castro agents supposedly bent on revenge for American plots against the Cuban leader, would fit readily into this picture.

Two of FitzGerald's children—his daughter Frances and stepdaughter Barbara—each recall the CIA official expressing concern in the early 1960s about the Cuban exiles. "I just remember a letter my father wrote," Frances told me, "about how working with the exiles was really a nightmare. Because they had their own paranoias and hostilities, and made things very large in their imagination."

Barbara Train reflected on sitting at the breakfast table one morning, and FitzGerald talking about how "the exiles were trying to engage particular people in Texas, hoping to get financial and military commitments to go back into Cuba and wrench Castro out of his nest. I know he was very concerned not just about Castro, but about the exiles."[43]

The Exiles on the Move

Not long before his arrest on October 1, 1963, for his involvement in a scheme to flood Cuba with counterfeit pesos, ex-CIA contract agent Robert Morrow says he received a phone call at his Baltimore residence. It was Eladio del Valle, David Ferrie's friend in Miami. "He asked me to get ahold of some electronics equipment, communications gear," Morrow told me in 1992. "Eladio wondered if I could supply four small walkie-talkies that could not be traced. Very-low-frequency transceivers, good at one-quarter mile at just below audio range. Del Valle was Mario Kohly's right-hand man there in Miami. He was also a liaison to Rolando Masferrer, and the Mafia, and all those crazy Cubans. I told him I'd take care of his request—and I did. Later, when I saw some pictures that had been taken November 22 in Dealey Plaza, I saw one of my radios hanging out of some guy's back pocket."[44]

On November 1, 1963, according to the sworn testimony before a Dade County, Florida, judge by Mrs. Lillian Spingler, a Cuban man entered the Parrot Jungle gift shop where she worked in Miami. Spingler said "he initiated a conversation . . . in which he stated that he could write with both hands simultaneously and that he was a sharpshooter." Also, "that he had a friend named Lee who could speak Russian and German and was living in Texas or Mexico, and that Lee was also a sharpshooter." Mrs. Spingler said she had related the incident to the FBI in late December 1963 but, after a quick investigation, agent James O'Conner told her to "just drop it and not mention it."[45]

All through November, as far as Oswald's landlady knew, when he was not at work he spent most of his time alone at the rooming house. Four days before the assassination, he made an angry phone call to Marina, telling his wife that he was "using a different name" and that she shouldn't have tried to reach him the day before at the North Beckley address.[46]

The next day, November 19, in Abilene, Texas, a commercial photographer named Harold Reynolds was showing some pictures to his neighbor Pedro Gonzalez. Reynolds had befriended a small group of Cuban refugees in the area. "There were about 20 Cubans here in '62 and '63," Reynolds wrote me in 1979. "There was a regular route through here, exiles traveling through from Dallas, New Orleans, even Chicago."[47]

As Reynolds reported the story to Dallas reporter Earl Golz, Pedro Gonzalez's landlady knocked at his door and handed Reynolds a note that she had seen wedged in the exile's mailbox for a couple of days. "In handwriting," according to Reynolds, "it said something like 'call me immediately, urgent,' and had two Dallas numbers on it. I noticed the name 'Lee Oswald' and asked Gonzalez who he was. Seems like he said, 'some attorney from Dallas.' He looked nervous and sweat started appearing on his forehead."

A little later, Reynolds noticed Gonzalez's car a few blocks from his house "and him standing in a pay phone booth." Right after the assassination, his exile friend disappeared from Abilene. Reynolds then twice sought to tell the FBI about this and other curious incidents—including cars arriving from Louisiana and Florida for exile group meetings at Gonzalez's apartment. Both times, the FBI agents showed no interest because, Reynolds said, no pro-Castro Cubans seemed to have been involved.[48]

At about the same time, in Miami, an anti-Castro activist named Rolando Otero alleged that there was a meeting of some exiles tied into "intelligence and counter intelligence." Otero told the story to a House Assassinations Committee investigator in 1977, while imprisoned for having taken part in a rash of terrorist bombings. "They had a rumor in the Cuban community, like Kennedy was a Communist, he's against us, he's messing up the whole cause. Before the Kennedy assassination, they called a meeting of these people, and they said they had to be ready because there was going to be a coup d'état in the United States. . . . They didn't give a reason for it, how it was going to happen or when it was going to happen, they just said it was going to happen."[49]

Gerry Patrick Hemming, the soldier of fortune who first encountered

Oswald outside L.A.'s Cuban consulate in 1959 (see Chapter Seven), told me a similar story in 1992. "The week before the assassination, Felipe Vidal Santiago told my group that some people had approached him to go to a big meeting in Dallas that week," Hemming said.[50] "We warned him and some other people not to go, that something funny was up. I'd heard of other meetings, where the conversation got steered around toward hitting JFK instead of Fidel. I'm talking about some friends of [Nicaraguan dictator Anastasio] Somoza, and about some people in Dallas.

"It's hard to say exactly who this select group of Cuban exiles was really working for," Hemming continued. "For a while, they were reporting to Bill Harvey's ex-FBI CIA guys. Some were reporting back to Hoover, or the new DIA [Defense Intelligence Agency]. There was a third force— pretty much outside CIA channels, outside our own private operation down in the Keys—that was doing all kinds of shit, and had been all through '63.

"Then after the assassination, a lot of us presumed that somewhere down the line, the KGB was orchestrating with Fidel to do the Dallas job. Not until later did we figure out that most of the exiles being approached were being set up as patsies themselves. And not by Castro or the Russians. It was domestic. Somebody like J. Edgar Hoover. Who else had the power?"

Hemming remembered having helped introduce some of his exile friends to General Walker in the summer of 1963. Another man who was brought into the circle was John Martino. Martino had worked for the Trafficante interests in Havana's casinos before Castro's takeover. Later incarcerated by Castro for entering Cuba illegally and engaging in an effort to overthrow him, Martino was released with the Bay of Pigs prisoners and wrote a book called *I Was Castro's Prisoner.*

FBI reports state that Martino remained close friends with Trafficante.[51] In September 1963, Martino had gone to Dallas to speak at an anti-Castro rally. In the Warren Commission volumes, it is noted that Martino mentioned at that time knowing Amadar Odio and that Odio's daughter Silvia was living in Dallas.[52] Not long after Martino's appearance in Dallas, Angel, Leopoldo, and Oswald showed up at Odio's door just before Oswald's late September trip to Mexico. After the assassination, Martino was among those spreading rumors about Oswald's alleged contacts with Cuban G-2 intelligence.[53]

In 1978, Texas businessman Fred Claasen provided some information about Martino, a former close business associate, to journalist Earl Golz. According to Claasen, this is what Martino told him in 1975, in a phone conversation in which Martino also admitted having been a CIA contract agent:

"The anti-Castro people put Oswald together. Oswald didn't know who he was working for—he was just ignorant of who was really putting him together. Oswald was to meet his contact at the Texas Theater. They were to meet Oswald in the theater, and get him out of the country, then eliminate him. Oswald made a mistake. . . . There was no way we could get to him. They had Ruby kill him."

Martino died soon after talking to Claasen. Martino's widow told reporter Golz that "the Company [CIA] or the government" came for his body to establish the cause of death, and determined it to have been a heart attack. After Claasen sent his information along to the House Assassinations Committee, he left his previous place of employment, and the committee was unable to trace where he had moved.[54]

Alpha 66 and the House on Harlandale

The day Ruby shot Oswald, a classified teletype went from FBI headquarters in Miami to J. Edgar Hoover. Released in 1976, it reads:

> . . . Speculation on future U.S. policy re Cuba is currently topic of discussion among exiles. Rumors are now circulating among exile Cubans re possible GOC [Government of Cuba] involvement in Pres Kennedy's death. Authors these rumors not identified but it clear this being done primarily in attempt provoke strong U.S. action against Cuba. . . .
>
> "A" reported hearing from "B" whose sister's husband "C" is member SNFE [Second National Front Escambray, an offshoot of Alpha 66] that Eloy Gutierrez Menoyo commented 21 Nov 63 that "Something very big would happen soon that would advance Cuban cause."[55]

Menoyo, along with Antonio Veciana and Tony Cuesta, was one of the founders of Alpha 66. In October 1963, an FBI file placed Menoyo in Los Angeles, announcing that his "organization would be in Cuba in less than six months."[56] The exiles' "Omega Plan," a joint effort of SNFE, Alpha 66, and the MRP, involved "a specialized reserve brigade [trained] in various types of guerrilla warfare."[57]

The day after the assassination, Dallas deputy sheriff Buddy Walthers filed a police report stating that he had informed the Secret Service about weekend meetings "at 3128 Harlandale" of "some Cubans." These, he added, were "possibly connected with the 'Freedom for Cuba Party' of which Oswald was a member."[58] Coincidentally, perhaps, Walthers helped arrest Oswald and collect his belongings in Ruth Paine's garage.[59]

It was Fair Play for Cuba, of course, to which Oswald "belonged." "Free Cuba," or "Cuba Libre," was at the opposite end of the spectrum. Indeed, it was Jack Ruby who first pointed out the discrepancy, as he stood in the back of the room of the Dallas police station when Oswald was brought out briefly to meet the press on the night after the assassination. In his introduction of Oswald, Dallas DA Henry Wade had identified him as a member of the Free Cuba Committee. Ruby then piped up to correct Wade, saying, "That's Fair Play for Cuba, Henry."[60]

On November 26, Dallas policeman Walthers made a second report, noting that at some point between November 15 and 23 "these Cubans moved from this house" on Harlandale. "My informant," Walthers added, "stated that subject Oswald had been to this house before."[61] While both of Walthers' reports appear in the Warren volumes, he was never questioned about them when testifying before the commission.

Lonnie Hudkins, then the Texas-based reporter who broke the story on Oswald's FBI ties as a sometimes informant, also knew of the Harlandale house. "T. George Harris, the ex-senior editor of *Look* [magazine], and I went all through the Little Cuba district in Dallas," Hudkins said, "and found people who said Oswald and others had attended a party the Wednesday night before the assassination at the Harlandale house."[62]

The Harlandale address was known to the FBI, very soon after the assassination, as the Dallas headquarters of a joint Alpha 66/SNFE/MRP Cuban exile operation. In June 1963, Andres Sargen of Alpha 66 had written Manuel Orcarberro Rodriguez requesting that he form a Dallas chapter of the organization. Formerly a dishwasher at a Miami hotel, Rodriguez was already living in Dallas and proceeded to register with immigration authorities as an alien on September 6. It was Rodriguez who got the house on Harlandale. On November 24, 1963, a Dallas FBI memo to Hoover concluded: "[Informant] 'D' reports one Manuel Rodriguez. . . . Living Dallas, Texas was known be violently anti-President Kennedy. . . ."

A Secret Service memorandum of April 24, 1964, is devoted entirely to Manuel Rodriguez, whom that agency had considered enough of a threat to the president to place on its "Protective Research" list. The Warren Commission had also learned that Rodriguez, "apparently a Cuban survivor of the Bay of Pigs episode, was attempting to purchase arms in Dallas for Alpha 66. Rodriguez is also a member of the DRE [the Carlos Bringuier group]."[63]

Rodriguez's name came up in the autumn of 1963 in conjunction with an undercover investigation of arms trafficking being conducted by Frank Ellsworth, an agent with the Treasury Department's Alcohol, Tobacco, and Firearms (ATF) Division in Dallas. Ellsworth's primary focus was a young Dallas gun shop owner, John Thomas Masen, under investigation for violations of the National Firearms Act. Masen had admitted to the agent that Rodriguez "was attempting to buy arms—machine guns, bazookas, and other heavy equipment."[64]

Reports about Masen in the National Archives were equally as intriguing as those about his would-be client Rodriguez. An FBI file dated March 27, 1964, began:

"Mr. John Thomas Masen, Owner, Masen's Gun Shop . . . advised he purchased about ten boxes of 6.5mm Mannlicher-Carcano, Western Cartridge Company, ammunition from Johnny Brinegar in early 1963 and that he sold these 10 boxes to individuals. He stated he was not able to recall the identity of any persons to whom he sold the ammunition. . . ."

The rifle that Oswald had ordered in March was, of course, a 6.5mm Mannlicher-Carcano. And there was more about Masen in the FBI's records: He spoke Spanish fluently, and "during the summer of 1963 he made an extensive vacation trip to Mexico, visiting friends in various places." He was also, according to agent Ellsworth, "an ardent member of the Minutemen."

Ellsworth, in a Warren Commission file dated April 16, 1964, was quoted as revealing:

"An organization known as the Minutemen is the right-wing group in Dallas most likely to have been associated with any effort to assassinate the President.

"The Minutemen are closely tied to General [Edwin] Walker and H. L. Hunt."[65]

Early in 1976, on a trip through Dallas, I arranged an interview with ATF agent Ellsworth. As we sat in his downtown office, he unfolded a remarkable tale that I first broke in *The Village Voice* that April. Ellsworth told of having been called to the police interrogation room to question Oswald about the rifle found on the sixth floor of the book depository. When he walked in, Ellsworth was certain that he had made one of history's most tragic mistakes.

A "Twin" Among the Minutemen

"Oswald was sitting in a chair about ten feet from the doorway," Ellsworth remembered. "And all I could see was headlines that I'd just turned loose the man who'd killed the president."

He hadn't. However, only a few days before, Ellsworth had given a routine okay to release on bond a young man who was allied with the local Minuteman group and had been charged with a violation of the National Firearms Act. He was, said Ellsworth, "an absolute dead ringer for Oswald—identical build, weight, coloring, facial features, hair. They were like identical twins; they could've passed for each other."

Almost from the moment of Oswald's arrest, perfectly credible witnesses claimed to have seen him driving a car (though Oswald didn't drive). They had also seen him in a gun shop, at a rifle range, and cashing a check in a grocery store. The problem was, especially in the month of November, wherever "Oswald" was supposed to have been, he was really somewhere else.

Ellsworth broke a twelve-year official silence to confirm a look-alike's existence. While refusing to divulge the look-alike's name and passing off the incident as "sheer coincidence," the ATF agent admitted that the man was still alive, well, and living in Dallas; that he had been interrogated by federal authorities shortly after the assassination and found to have been "nowhere near downtown Dallas"; and that several witnesses who believed they had seen Oswald (notably practicing at a Dallas rifle range) had actually seen his "twin."

If not for several other Ellsworth revelations, the "twin's" existence might be dismissed as a curiosity of history. But while the real Oswald was purportedly a fanatic leftist and member of the Fair Play for Cuba Committee, his "double" was an equally fanatic right-winger and member of the Minutemen. Like Oswald, he traveled in and out of Mexico. Like Oswald, he associated with Cuban exiles.

I realized, but did not push Ellsworth to say so, that the look-alike was most probably John Thomas Masen.

"Quite a number of officials—state, federal, and local—were aware of this situation, because we talked about it," Ellsworth continued. "We laid it to rest, and satisfied ourselves it was merely coincidence. I have a vague recollection that this man was questioned about the assassination, but not by me. Possibly nobody paid much attention because we had Oswald in custody. We weren't looking for a fugitive.

"I'd tracked this other fellow undercover through another man for several months before I actually met him. I think this began sometime in the summer of 1963. When I finally made contact with him, I led him to believe I was a crook. He claimed to have done some arms smuggling in and out of Mexico, but not when I was dealing with him. And yes, there were rumors that he had some connection with the family of H. L. Hunt.

"I do remember two instances where Oswald was supposed to have been at someone's house in North Dallas, and I was able to ascertain after the assassination that it was actually the look-alike. I wasn't keeping notes of where he was minute by minute, but these were instances where witnesses thought they saw Oswald in the company of several Minutemen. One of these times did involve a group of Minutemen at a rifle range. The look-alike knew all those people. Several of their names came up in my conversations with him, and I'd noted at the time that he was out shooting with them."

The look-alike was eventually convicted on "one of the gun violations," but Ellsworth said he could not remember the sentence. Subsequently, the man gained his release, and Ellsworth remained in occasional contact with him over the years. Despite considerable prodding, Ellsworth refused to name him, saying only that "he's straightened out and has a right to privacy."

I did not bring up John Thomas Masen's name at our initial meeting. But after reviewing the three documents about gun shop owner Masen, the Minutemen, and the Cuban exiles, I went back to see Ellsworth again. When I mentioned the information he had provided the Warren Commission and Secret Service about Masen, Ellsworth did a double take. At first he issued a hesitant denial that Masen was the Oswald "twin." Then, at the end of our interview, suddenly the agent said: "Look, you've got me boxed in. You're trying to get me to tell you something I'm not at liberty to tell without grossly jeopardizing myself and my agency. But if you can find Masen, the answer to what you've been trying to worm out of me will become immediately apparent."

Masen's name was not listed in the Dallas phone book. But, I learned from a local assassination researcher, he did still work there—a gunsmith, apparently one of the best in town, operating in the back room of a sporting goods store in a North Dallas shopping center. Early one evening, I drove out and found Masen working alone.

According to Ellsworth, the Oswald look-alike had put on about thirty pounds over the years. So, it seemed, had Masen. In 1976 he was a stocky, brown-haired thirty-six-year-old, about the same height as Oswald. The moment we shook hands, an uneasy feeling settled over me. If you looked closely, you could still see the resemblance.

"If I saw a picture of Lee Harvey Oswald, I could probably pick it out," Masen said, carefully smoothing some oil along the sight of a rifle. "But I can't really visualize his face."

When I mentioned the name of Frank Ellsworth, Masen's eyes flashed and his reply was acrid.

"I got set up on that situation," he said. "There was an agent from New Mexico who represented himself as a buyer for the Cuban revolution against Castro. I sold him a couple automatic arms. They entrapped me into buying some parts. They finally dropped all charges except failure to keep proper records. I paid a $200 fine, but they took my firearms license away. And this has cost me an enormous amount of money, not being able to deal in firearms. I recently applied for a presidential pardon and was turned down."

Had he ever associated with the Minutemen? I asked. "I'd been to a couple parties. I knew some of the group. I realized they were gonna try to help take Cuba back and I was very sympathetic to the cause."

What about General Walker? "I met him back there. When things are unpleasant, you block them out. You try to forget. This has cost me $20,000 or $30,000 over the past twelve or thirteen years. I don't know if I did any business with his people."

And H. L. Hunt? "Mr. Hunt was a fine man. One of my dear friends lived next door to them. But did I ever work for him? No. Did I ever receive money from him? No. Although I might have said I did at one time. You see, one of my dearest friends was in a sorority with a daughter. I met a good deal of the Hunts. I have some friends who were under the impression that the Hunts poured a lot of money into their coffers."

For a moment Masen paused. He gave me a long, probing look, as if he knew precisely what I was driving at. "Look, as I told them back then, if there was a Minutemen situation I'd been connected with, I couldn't have told 'em anyway. My life wouldn't be worth a penny. Realistically, that's what it amounted to.

"You know," he went on, "I wouldn't be in your shoes. Going around asking people about the Cubans, the Kennedy assassination. Why should people talk to you? There's no way they can do anything but lose. One thing you should remember: What may be a living to you"—he paused, giving me another long look—"can be a life to them.

"But if you want my opinion, to think the assassination was the act of one man, well, it'd be a very hard thing to do. I've got some friends who are top marksmen who say it couldn't have happened like they said. I really don't believe this was the brainstorm of one deranged man. I think it was the sophisticated work of someone with a great deal of money, who could buy a life."

Summary

The clock was ticking toward November 22. Nagell sat in his jail cell, dismissing a court-appointed attorney for informing the FBI that he had made a trip to Cuba. When two FBI agents came to see Nagell three days before the assassination, he wrote a statement questioning the delay in bringing him to trial—and hinted that his real motive for shooting up the bank was a patriotic one.

Oswald returned to Dallas from Mexico City, attended at least one rally where General Walker spoke, and renewed his correspondence with leftist groups and the Soviet embassy. In mid-October he landed his fateful job at the Texas School Book Depository. Twice in early November, FBI agent Hosty visited Marina. A note that Oswald then delivered to Hosty was ordered destroyed by the agent's superiors immediately after Oswald was killed by Jack Ruby.

The international right wing, the CIA, and the Cuban exiles were equally busy. In mid-October Charles Willoughby's organization met in Switzerland, where the attendees included several Germans linked to the Munich newspaper that would break the Oswald-Walker story after the assassination. Desmond FitzGerald pretended to be a representative of Robert Kennedy (with whom he did not get along) at two Paris discussions with Rolando Cubela about assassinating Castro. Two of FitzGerald's children recall him expressing concern about the Cuban exiles, including their association with wealthy Texans.

Eladio del Valle received communications gear from Robert Morrow; meetings among the exiles took place in Miami and Dallas; an Abilene exile, Pedro Gonzalez, reportedly received a note from Oswald on November 17. Years later, Mob/CIA affiliate John Martino would reveal that Oswald was set up by anti-Castro agents. Manuel Rodriguez had set up an Alpha 66 chapter in Dallas in September, and engaged in arms negotiations with John Thomas Masen—a young Minuteman member and alleged associate of the Hunt oil family. Treasury agent Frank Ellsworth remembered Masen as an Oswald look-alike who was mistaken for Oswald while target-shooting at a Dallas rifle range before the assassination.

Chapter Twenty-four

Warnings: The Right Wing and the Pentagon: November 1963

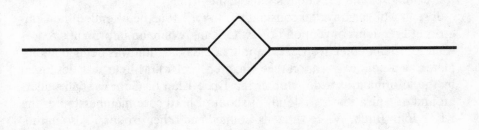

Joseph Adams Milteer, sixty-one years old in 1963, was a man of inherited wealth who lived in a ramshackle mansion in Quitman, Georgia. He was a stocky five feet, four and 160 pounds, generally wore old-fashioned clothes and a hunting cap—and also wore a number of hats in ultraright circles. One was as regional director of the Constitution Party, which was pushing South Carolina senator Strom Thurmond to run for president on its 1964 ticket.

Out on the West Coast, Milteer's counterpart as Constitution Party chairman in California was retired colonel William P. Gale—also the one-time MacArthur guerrilla commander in the Philippines and organizer of a Minuteman offshoot in Southern California. According to Garrison investigation files, Gale often played host to anti-Castro "freedom fighters." He was also friendly with General Walker, reportedly staying at his house in Dallas in July 1963.

Colonel Gale's political ambitions were strongly endorsed by the National States Rights Party (NSRP), of which Milteer was a leader.[1] The NSRP was formed in 1958, quickly coming to national attention when five of its members were arrested for the dynamiting of an Atlanta synagogue. Its constitution noted that "Without the Jews, there would be NO Communism!," and proposed the expulsion of all such individuals from American shores. The NSRP's publication *The Thunderbolt* set out to prove "scientifically" that "the Negro actually is a higher form of gorilla. God did not wish for the white race to mix with these animals." In 1960, when the NSRP fielded a national slate of electoral candidates, its vice presidential choice was retired admiral John Crommelin, whose connections also stretched to Colonel Gale in California. Crommelin spoke around the country on what he called "The Hidden Force," a giant "Jewish-Communist-Integration Conspiracy." Six months after JFK was elected, the NSRP was calling for the president's impeachment.[2]

Joseph Milteer traveled constantly. In April 1963 he attended the Congress of Freedom convention in New Orleans, where an informant's report went to Miami detective C. H. Sapp that assassination was being contemplated as a political weapon (see Chapter Twelve). Milteer was described by the informant as a director of the Dixie Klan of Georgia, "an underground organization . . . [and] offshoot of hard core membership of the KKK, John Birch, White Citizens Council and other groups." Also authorized under its nonprofit charter to conduct business in Virginia, the Dixie Klan was said to be "pushing for" the elimination of undesirable politicians. "It is his [the informer's] considered opinion that for assassinations through rifles, dynamite and other types of devices, this is the worst outfit he has ever come across."[3]

At the New Orleans gathering, Milteer ran into an old friend his same age, Willie Somersett, a union organizer from Miami and member of the Ku Klux Klan. The "patriot" organizations, Milteer told Somersett, needed to act fast, because Kennedy was on the edge of turning the government over to the United Nations.

What Milteer did not know was that Somersett had been acting as an FBI informant for nearly a decade. In February 1962, alarmed by a series of bombings in Miami, Somersett had offered similar services to the Miami police. After the New Orleans meeting, he would inform Circuit Judge Seymour Gelber (today the mayor of Miami Beach) that something very dangerous was in the works. Describing Milteer as "the most violent man I know," Somersett elaborated: "Those people are people of means, financially, and educationally. . . . I will bet my head on a chopping block there will be some people killed by this time next year and it will be in high places."

In June 1963, Milteer went to Dallas, where he would later tell the FBI he tried to persuade Dan Smoot to run for vice president on the Constitution Party's next national ticket. Smoot, an FBI agent for ten years, had ended up in the Dallas bureau, from which he resigned in 1951 to work for Facts Forum—the political propaganda operation of H. L. Hunt. By the mid-1950s, Smoot had gone off on his own and, by 1963, the *Dan Smoot Report* was being widely distributed nationwide.[4]

Informant Somersett ran into Milteer again early in October 1963, at a meeting in Vero Beach, Florida. Milteer was there promoting an upcoming convention of the Constitution Party. According to Somersett, Milteer helped formulate "plans to put an end to the Kennedy, [Martin Luther] King, Khrushchev dictatorship over our nation."

Somersett accompanied Milteer on the long drive to the Constitution Party's gathering in Indianapolis on October 18–20. Not long before, on September 15, the Sixteenth Street Baptist Church in Birmingham, Alabama, had been dynamited and four black children killed. According to Somersett's next report to the Miami police, Milteer had confided to him in Indianapolis that the Dixie Klan's imperial wizard, Jack Brown, had been responsible for the church bombing.

After that, Judge Gelber suggested that Somersett secretly tape-record his next meeting with Milteer. A Miami detective, Everett Kay, set up the recorder in a broom closet of Somersett's home shortly before Milteer was to come for breakfast on November 9, 1963. The content of this conversation was revealed first by *Miami News* reporter Bill Barry early in 1967, then in a copyrighted article by *Miami Magazine* reporter Dan Christensen in September 1976.

SOMERSETT: I think Kennedy is coming here on the 18th to make some kind of speech. I imagine it will be on TV.

MILTEER: You can bet your bottom dollar he is going to have a lot to say about the Cubans. There are so many of them here.

SOMERSETT: Yeah, well, he will have a thousand bodyguards. Don't worry about that.

MILTEER: The more bodyguards he has the more easier it is to get him.

SOMERSETT: Well, how in the hell do you figure would be the best way to get him?

MILTEER: From an office building with a high-powered rifle. . . .

SOMERSETT: Boy, if that Kennedy gets shot, we have got to know where we are at. Because you know that will be a real shake.

MILTEER: They wouldn't leave any stone unturned there. No way. They will pick up somebody within hours afterwards, if anything like that would happen, just to throw the public off.

Alerting the Authorities

While Miami authorities immediately alerted the Secret Service about the Somersett/Milteer tape, Somersett also went to the FBI. An FBI file declassified in the 1970s reads: "On November 10, 1963, a source who has furnished reliable information in the past . . . advised SA LEONARD C. PETERSON that J. A. MILTEER on November 9, 1963, at Miami, Florida, made a statement that plans were in the making to kill President JOHN F. KENNEDY at some future date . . . and that he (MILTEER) would be willing to help. . . . U.S. Secret Service was advised of the foregoing information."

President Kennedy arrived in Miami on November 18, to give the speech that Desmond FitzGerald's case officer would use as justification to AM/LASH of JFK's approval of the CIA's anti-Castro plot. The Secret Service had the president abandon a planned motorcade, and JFK took a helicopter instead to Miami Beach.[5]

Gerry Patrick Hemming told me in 1992 that he and some of his associates were called to the airport to be part of a security team. But Hemming said they were told nothing about any threat against the president emanating from right-wing extremists. "The FBI sent us over there," according to Hemming. "We were told they were afraid of terrorism by Castro, because there were a lot of Castro agents in town."[6]

Hemming says that Milteer sought to make contact with Cuban exiles in Miami around August or September. "He persisted in wanting to talk to us, but we had reason to believe he might be linked to a couple of people doing local bombings. So we were very cautious with the guy. In November, he talked to some of us in a parking lot about getting some weapons. As I later found out, that was the same night he was being taped about the plans to hit JFK."

Judge Gelber, who kept a diary of these events, wrote that a detective assigned to the case assured him the Secret Service knew the whereabouts of Milteer. But *Miami Magazine* writer Christensen was told in 1976 by Bob Newbrand, a local Secret Service spokesman, that "I know for sure we didn't put him [Milteer] under surveillance. We were never that much involved with that. If anybody made a threat we wouldn't put him under surveillance, we'd lock him up!"

Yet, according to Warren Commission Exhibit 762, the Secret Service had information similar to Somersett's from yet another source. A Secret Service report listing "Date of Origin" as November 15, 1963, concerns "information received telephonically from FBI headquarters, Washington, D.C." It was about an unnamed subject who had been arrested on September 30 in Piedras Negras, Mexico, for stealing three automobiles. The subject told the FBI on November 14 "that he is a member of the Ku Klux Klan; that during his travels throughout the country, his sources have told him that a militant group of the National States Rights Party plans to assassinate the President and other high-level officials. He stated that he does not believe this is planned for the near future, but he does believe the attempt will be made. . . ."

The report went on that the FBI believed "the subject was attempting to make some sort of deal with them for his benefit in the criminal case now pending against him. There was no information developed that would indicate any danger to the President in the near future or during his trip to Texas."[7]

The afternoon after the assassination, Somersett met Milteer again in a train station in Jacksonville, Florida. They then drove together to Columbia, South Carolina, where Milteer had a session planned with some Klan members. "During the journey," Somersett told the Miami police upon his return, "he [Milteer] told me that he was connected with an international underground. He said there would be a propaganda campaign put on how to prove to the Christian people of the world that the Jews, the Zionist Jews, had murdered Kennedy. He was very happy over it and shook hands with me. He said: 'Well, I told you so. It happened like I told you, didn't it? It happened from a window with a high-powered rifle.' "

According to the FBI's report from informant Somersett: "When questioned as to whether he was guessing when he originally made the threat regarding President KENNEDY, MILTEER is quoted as saying, 'I don't do any guessing. . . .' During this trip [to South Carolina], Milteer stated that he had been in Houston, Ft. Worth, and Dallas, Texas, as well as New Orleans, Louisiana, Biloxi and Jackson, Mississippi, and Tuscaloosa, Alabama. . . . MILTEER related that MARTIN LUTHER KING and Attorney General ROBERT KENNEDY are now unimportant."

It was the next morning, only hours before Oswald was shot, when "MILTEER advised that they did not have to worry about LEE HARVEY OSWALD getting caught because he 'doesn't know anything' and that the 'right wing' is in the clear. MILTEER further related that, 'The patriots have outsmarted the communists and had infiltrated the communist group in order that they (communists) could carry out the plan without the right wingers becoming involved.' "

What Somersett told the Miami police was phrased somewhat differently. "From the impression he gave me, and what he told me," Somersett said, "the Oswald group was pro-Castro. This group was infiltrated by the patriot underground who arranged from there to have the execution carried out and drop the responsibility right into the laps of the Communists. I don't think there was any agreement with this little flim-flam organization [the Fair Play for Cuba Committee] that Oswald belonged to."

On November 27, 1963, the FBI went to see Milteer, who "emphatically denies ever making threats to assassinate President KENNEDY or participating in any such assassination. He stated he has never heard anyone make such threats."

At the time, Miami authorities were trying to have Somersett entice Milteer and his Dixie Klan partner, Jack Brown, to come to the city in hopes of obtaining more tape recordings. But when the informant called on December 4, Milteer let Somersett know that the FBI had come around. The pair would never meet again. Judge Gelber recorded in his diary:

"Somersett is extremely concerned about this turn of events. Milteer did not accuse him of being an FBI informer, but inasmuch as the questioning appeared to be based on the statements made to Somersett, suspicion would inevitably rest on him. . . . There is no chance of getting Milteer and Brown to Miami now. . . . I wonder why the FBI picked these people up after the President's assassination rather than before the act? All this manages to do is jeopardize the safety of our undercover agent. . . . It ruins our investigation."

The FBI did not pursue the Milteer matter further, although twenty-six pages of its Milteer file remain withheld from public view. Willie Somersett died on May 7, 1970, in Goldsboro, North Carolina. Joseph Milteer died under mysterious circumstances on February 28, 1974, reportedly after suffering severe burns when a gas heater exploded in his home. According to Judge Gelber, between 1971 and 1976 the Dade County state attorney's files on the Milteer case disappeared from a North Miami warehouse where they had been stored. They had consisted of thousands of pages of transcripts and documents.

The Dinkin Dossier

It is staggering to consider how many warnings the FBI received that something dire was being planned for President Kennedy. Besides the Milteer case, informants had revealed threats from Carlos Marcello and Santos Trafficante, Jr. Garrett Trapnell had volunteered an account of a Cuban-related plot. And Richard Case Nagell had provided enough information, so he figured, to warrant the arrest of Oswald, Angel, and Leopoldo.

Nor was the FBI the only government agency alerted. Through Nagell at least, so was the CIA. And, through an Army private first class stationed in 1963 in Metz, France, so was the Pentagon.

Eugene B. Dinkin studied psychology at the University of Illinois and, after enlisting in the Army in 1961, was sent to Fort Gordon, Georgia. There he was trained as a cryptographic code operator, which in effect made him part of the National Security Agency, the CIA's Top-Secret communications counterpart. In March 1962 Dinkin was assigned to the 529th Ordnance Company in France "as a crypto operator [who] was awarded the requisite security clearances," according to Lieutenant Colonel John C. Lippincott of the Pentagon's Legislative Liaison Office.[8] A crypto clearance is among the highest that the military gives.

Then, as Lippincott wrote in a February 1964 letter to Senator Everett Dirksen, Private Dinkin allegedly began to behave strangely in the late summer of 1963. "During a troop information class on the subject 'Duty, Honor, Country,' Private Dinkin made a 25-minute speech on the government's stockpiling of atomic bombs. . . ." On September 24, 1963, Lippincott wrote that Dinkin "was given a psychiatric evaluation which revealed doubts as to the advisability of entrusting him with classified material." Thus was Dinkin transferred to other duties, and his security clearance was subsequently revoked.

We saw, in Nagell's case in the Far East, how a psychiatric evaluation and removal from classified duties followed close upon his having decided to reveal certain clandestine military activities that his superior officers wanted kept quiet. With Private Dinkin, we may be looking at a similar situation—and a far more frightening one.

Until 1976, when portions of some documents on Dinkin were finally released, everything supplied to the Warren Commission about him was withheld from the public. But an FBI report of April 3, 1964, recounted Dinkin's projection—several weeks before the assassination—"that a conspiracy was in the making by the 'military' of the United States, perhaps combined with an 'ultra-right economic group.' . . ."[9]

According to since-declassified CIA files, Dinkin's warning was known to a number of people before November 22, 1963. He told his version in a civil action lawsuit filed in 1975, charging the Pentagon and the CIA with having violated a number of his constitutional rights.

It began on October 22, 1963, when Dinkin writes that he mailed a letter to Attorney General Robert Kennedy.

Dinkin said,

I did offer in this letter a warning that an attempt to assassinate President Kennedy would occur on November 28th, 1963; that if it were to succeed, blame would then be placed upon a Communist or Negro, who would be designated the assassin; and believing that the conspiracy was being engineered by elements of the Military, I did speculate that a military coup might ensue. I did request of the Attorney General that he dispatch a representative of the Justice Department to Metz, France to discuss this warning. . . .

Dinkin realized, he continued, that his letter to Robert Kennedy had an "extremely minimal . . . probability of . . . coming into the direct attention of the Attorney General." So Dinkin suddenly left his unit. On October 25, he set out to try to contact certain European ambassadors in the nearby nation of Luxembourg, in hopes that his message would then filter through their intelligence networks back to the United States. Nobody would give him the time of day except the Israeli ambassador to Luxembourg, who, Dinkin writes, advised him how best to present his case at the American embassy there. Dinkin says,

At the U.S. Embassy I was interviewed by Chargé d'Affaires Mr. [first name unknown] Cunningham, who told me that the Ambassador was playing tennis and was therefore unavailable. I did relate to Mr. Cunningham that I had information indicative of a political assassination to occur in late November in the United States, and he did then guarantee to convey this message to Ambassador [FNU] Rivkin, who would notify me at my military base of an appointment.

A week passed, and no such notice came. Then, Dinkin explains,

I did however learn through the military grapevine that I was to be locked up as a psychotic. I did on November 2nd, 1963 obtain a signed and officially stamped leave permit from the commanding officer of Metz General Depot, and when summoned back to the CO's office to be told that the leave was cancelled, having concealed the signed form, I did then tear up a blank form. That evening I left Metz, France by train and used the signed leave permit to gain entry to Switzerland on the morning of November 3rd, 1963.

Thus Private Dinkin went AWOL, and his quest grew stranger still. On November 6 he showed up at the U.N. press office in Geneva where, failing to find the American correspondent he was seeking, he told his tale to "the owner-editor of the *Geneva Diplomat.*"

The CIA verified this in a document prepared for the Warren Commission by Richard Helms on May 19, 1964, and released in 1976 with Dinkin's name deleted. "Immediately after the assassination the CIA [deleted] reported allegations concerning a plot to assassinate President Kennedy that were made by Pfc. [deleted], U.S. Army, serial number [deleted] on 6 and 7 November 1963, in Geneva while absent without leave from his unit in Metz, France." In other words, someone with the CIA was aware, at least "immediately after the assassination," that Dinkin had made such "allegations" two weeks prior.

After describing Dinkin's appearance at the press office, the CIA file continued:

> Around 26 November 1963, after President Kennedy had been assassinated, a Geneva journalist named Alex des Fontaines, stringer for Time-Life and correspondent for Radio Canada, was reported to be filing a story to the Paris office of Time-Life recounting Private [deleted] visit to Geneva and quoting [deleted] as having said that "they" were plotting against President Kennedy and that "something" would happen in Texas. . . .

The CIA file concluded: "All aspects of this story were known, as reported above, by U.S. military authorities and have been reported by military attaché cable through military channels."

Another since-declassified CIA "IN CABLE No. 56631," dated November 7, 1963, also reported on Dinkin's background and allegations of conspiracy. At the end of the cable, the CIA's Geneva office asked: "DIRECTOR: ADVISE ANY ACTION DESIRED. WILL CONTINUE TO MONITOR DEVELOPMENTS VIA ARMY ATTACHE, F.B.I., GENEVA CONTACTS, BUT WILL NOT BECOME INVOLVED VISAVIS SWISS UNLESS SO DIRECTED."

On the evening of November 6, Dinkin writes that he left Switzerland by train and arrived in Frankfurt, West Germany, the following morning. "I proceeded on that date to speak to the editor of the *Overseas Weekly*, who did regard my warning to be farfetched, and did recommend that I return in haste to the military base to avoid an AWOL charge being converted to a Desertion charge."

So Private Dinkin journeyed on to Bonn, where the next afternoon he again

> went to the U.S. Embassy . . . signed the visitors roster, and requested to be seen by an aide of the Ambassador to discuss an urgent political matter. The person who attended this request insisted that I prove the authenticity of my leave, give proof of my military ID and place of military assignment. I left the Embassy without attempting to convey the warning.
>
> I had decided that the only remaining alternative would be to return to Metz General Depot and try to deceive the authorities with a story that I had been successful in attending to a "political matter" in Switzerland.

Upon my return to Metz on the evening of November 8th, 1963, I did maintain this line with CIC [Army Counter Intelligence Corps] officer Mr. [FNU] McNair, who had been assigned to conduct the investigation [into Dinkin's disappearance]. I was then notified that I was under arrest and spent the next five days in the depot jail.

On November 13th, 1963 I was "hospitalized" at Landstuhl General Hospital in a closed psychiatric ward and was kept virtually incommunicado for approximately one week.

Private Dinkin was still in the hospital ward when, on the evening after the assassination, he says he was visited

by a gentleman claiming to be a "Secret Service agent" who had flown to Europe to interview me regarding the letter written to the Attorney General. He asked the following questions and my answers were as follows:

(1) "Do you believe it was the Right or the Left?"

Answer: "The Right."

(2) "Why was the date changed from November 28th to November 22nd?"

Answer: "I knew of no exact date and gave November 28th as an approximate date."

I then informed the gentleman that under the circumstances of being locked up in a psychiatric ward I would give the government absolutely no information.

Warren Commission Document 1107 reports that Colonel W. L. Adams, Jr., of Army Intelligence, stated in 1964 that Dinkin "was the subject of a closed investigation by the Office of the Assistant Chief of Staff, G-2, United States Army Communications Zone, Europe. He advised further that according to." The file ends there. The next page, at the request of the FBI, has never been released.

Dinkin continues,

Upon being transferred on December 5th, 1963 to Walter Reed Hospital in Washington, D.C. I began receiving "therapy" to help me understand that my warning of the assassination had been "coincidental" and represented a projection of hostility toward authority figures in my family and a displacement of my internal conflicts about inability to adjust to military life. In order to "get well" I was to understand that in approaching European ambassadors I was "really looking for attention and assistance to obtain psychiatric treatment." . . . I was led to understand that if my condition did not improve that I could be treated with ECT [electric shock treatment], and I consequently feigned cooperation and understanding of my unfortunate condition (schizo-assassination prognostication) and pretended to participate in group therapy and pharmacological treatment (I faked swallowing pills throughout). . . .

I was given an injection of a strong drug which left me dazed and was then introduced to a "psychologist from Case Institute of Cleveland" and told that he was conducting a research project requiring my cooperation. I was then required to free associate to a list of words while a tape recorder was in process of recording. . . .

What was happening to Private Dinkin? Was his "free association" intended to alter or nullify what he may have known in advance about the assassination? Shortly thereafter, he was released from Walter Reed—and the U.S. Army—on a medical discharge.

Dinkin's name first came up in the Garrison investigation, wherein interviews with some of Dinkin's former Army associates led to the conclusion that he had been hospitalized until he memorized a cover story. By the time he filed his lawsuit in 1975, Dinkin was maintaining that he had somehow discerned images in news photographs that led him to the advance conclusions he once drew about the Kennedy assassination.

As Garrison's people pieced the story together, however, one of Dinkin's duties as a code breaker had been to decipher telegraphic traffic that originated with the French OAS.[10]

U.S. Intelligence, the OAS, and the Radical Right

The OAS, or Secret Army Organization, was a cadre of disaffected right-wing French military officers who had come together early in 1961 to fight President Charles de Gaulle's decision to give colonial Algeria its independence. They sought, and in some cases received, aid from both the CIA and the U.S. military. Several OAS attempts were made on de Gaulle's life and later became the subject of the famous Frederic Forsyth novel *Day of the Jackal*. Technically, the OAS ceased to exist after June 1962, with Algeria's independence. But many of the group's hard-core veterans joined up as mercenaries in a worldwide anti-Communist alliance.

One of these was a man named Jean René Souetre, who was thirty-three years old in 1963. According to a since-released CIA file, upon his escape from a detention camp the OAS captain "was alleged to have been involved in an assassination attempt against de Gaulle." In May 1963, a Richard Helms memo notes, Souetre had approached the CIA and identified himself as the OAS's "coordinator of external affairs. . . . Souetre explained that he traveled on various passports, one of them being a U.S. passport. He claimed to be documented as a naturalized citizen from Martinique. He stated that he had U.S. contacts who could arrange documentation." The CIA file goes on, oddly in a different typescript, that a "[deleted] representative told Souetre . . . that the U.S. had absolutely no intention of working with any person or group against the duly constituted government of France."

Another CIA file on Souetre (June 25, 1963) has him apparently offering the CIA its "list of the Communist penetrations of the French government" and expressing the OAS's belief "that the de Gaulle government was aiding the Communist takeover by seeking a rapprochement with the USSR." Souetre went on that de Gaulle "was an old man [who] could easily meet with an accident" and the OAS was "prepared to counter a Communist plot at any time"—even to "the expedient of preventing the [next French] election from taking place."[11]

By this time, the CIA—particularly James Angleton—was quite concerned about alleged KGB penetration of NATO and the SDECE French intelligence service. Angleton's only trusted defector, Anatoly Golitsin, had informed the counter intelligence chief in 1963 that the SDECE had been penetrated by a KGB spy ring of some twelve agents. More KGB spies were said to be concealed within the top echelons of several French ministries, and Golitsin claimed that even de Gaulle's entourage had been penetrated by a senior KGB official. The result of Golitsin's charges was Angelton's recruitment of the SDECE's intelligence boss in Washington, Philippe de Vosjoli, to spy on his own embassy and pass along classified information. Sometime in mid-1963, de Vosjoli even allowed Angleton inside the French embassy to perform a personal after-hours "black bag job"—purloining French cipher traffic and other data.[12]

So, while there is no evidence that the CIA took Jean Souetre up on his offer, it doubtlessly would have had interest in the OAS officer's "list" of alleged Soviet penetrators into the French government.

The next known official word on Souetre appeared in a CIA memorandum dated April 1, 1964. When Texas researcher Mary Ferrell discovered it among some fifteen hundred CIA documents on the assassination released in 1977, the largely excised file was so faint that she needed a magnifying glass to read it. Once she did, however, researchers would come to consider this one of the more significant pieces of paper yet released by the U.S. government. It said:

> Jean SOUETRE aka Michel ROUX aka Michael MERTZ—on 5 March [deleted] the FBI advised that the French had [deleted] the Legal Attaché in Paris and also the [deleted] had queried the Bureau in New

York City concerning subject stating that he had been expelled from the U.S. at Fort Worth or Dallas 48 hours after the assassination. He was in Fort Worth on morning of 22 November and in Dallas in the afternoon. The French believe that he was expelled to either Mexico or Canada. In January he received mail from a dentist named Alderson living at 5803 Birmingham, Houston, Texas. Subject is believed to be identical with a Captain who is a deserter from the French Army and an activist in the OAS. The French are concerned because of de Gaulle's planned visit to Mexico. They would like to know the reason for his expulsion from the U.S. and his destination. . . .[13]

Thus began the hunt for a possible French connection to Dallas. That the CIA used foreign mercenaries, at least in its successful 1960 assassination of the Congolese leader Patrice Lumumba, had been well documented in 1975 by the Senate Intelligence Committee. The identities of the CIA hit men code-named QJ/WIN and WI/ROGUE have never been revealed. The former was described only as "a foreign citizen with a criminal background, recruited in Europe." The latter was called an "essentially stateless" soldier of fortune, "a forger and former bank robber" who "learns quickly and carries out any assignment without regard for danger."[14]

The House Assassinations Committee was working on the "French connection" angle when it closed up shop. Committee investigator Mike Ewing told me in 1980 that Jean Souetre "was connected with people involved in murders or political assassinations in Europe. He was most definitely in the same circles of OAS-connected killers. The agency admits that its own handlers of WIN and ROGUE were afraid of them, that they were not following CIA directives and were off on assassination plots of their own. The CIA was trying to keep them on a leash, because it was afraid to cut them off. So Jean Souetre is not the kind of guy you like to see was arrested and deported from Texas that day."[15]

Souetre, Mertz, and Roux

The trouble is, as with so much else on the assassination, the CIA's file on Souetre's deportation raised more questions than it answered. That is because the names listed for him as "AKA," or "also known as," are both real people.

Michael Mertz had been a leader of the French Resistance movement in World War II; his exploits were recorded in a number of books. A former intelligence agent with the French SDECE, by the late 1950s

Mertz had turned to smuggling narcotics on a vast scale from France to both the United States and Canada. Called back into uniform in 1961, he was assigned by the SDECE to infiltrate the OAS.

Eventually Mertz had learned details of an OAS plan to assassinate de Gaulle. A bomb planted at Pont Sur Seine was rendered harmless by the government, and Mertz was credited with having saved the French president's life. He then went back into the drug business and, between late 1961 and 1969, he and his colleagues were said to have moved two tons of heroin across the North Atlantic. U.S. officials noted Mertz's ties to the Trafficante organization in Florida and, several times during the decade, asked France to take action against him. But because of his SDECE and Gaullist connections, Mertz was considered "untouchable."[16]

Michel Roux had once served with the French Army in Algeria, and received an honorable discharge. Like Souetre and Mertz, he spoke French, German, and English. In October 1963, Roux was the assistant manager of a Paris hotel when he struck up with American tourist Leon Gachman and expressed a desire to visit the United States; Gachman invited him over. Roux showed up in Texas on November 20. According to Gachman, whom I interviewed by phone, Roux listened to JFK's speech as it was broadcast in a Fort Worth parking lot on the twenty-second and then went with Gachman's son to sit in on some classes at Texas Christian University. Immigration records show that Roux departed the United States into Mexico, through normal channels, on December 6. The FBI twice came to see Gachman about Roux in 1964 and, according to Gachman, said they had finally determined "that the man they were looking for had apparently assumed Roux's name."[17]

Virgil Bailey, a former official with the Immigration and Naturalization Service in Dallas, told me in 1981: "We picked up a Frenchman, I can remember that. I don't remember it being the day of the assassination, it might have been right before or right after, but I don't recall any correlation to the assassination. It seems to me that this man had already been under some kind of deportation proceedings."[18]

In 1981 I also had an extensive conversation with Dr. Lawrence Alderson, the Houston dentist referred to in the CIA's file on Souetre. Alderson told me that he had met Souetre in the early 1950s, when both were stationed in Metz, France—Alderson as a U.S. military security officer, Souetre his counterpart with the French Air Force. After Alderson returned Stateside and Souetre went off to Algiers—"in 1955 or '56 at the latest"—they had corresponded in a few subsequent letters. "The last letter I had was from Jean's wife, who said he was very upset because the French government was giving Algiers to the Communists. That was why he deserted, and went underground with the OAS."

Almost immediately after the Kennedy assassination, Alderson said he received a visit from two FBI agents, who were very vague about their purpose in seeing him. Then the dentist noticed he was under surveillance. "I could hear them on the telephone, see them out in the alley. It didn't really bother me—I did it for two years in France—but I didn't know what the heck it was about."

About a month later, the FBI dropped by again. After considerable hedging, Alderson was told that they had traced him to Souetre "through a Christmas card I'd sent that was undelivered a few years before that. They admitted they had been observing me, and tapped my telephone, for nearly a month."

The agents informed Alderson that they were investigating the Kennedy assassination. "They told me that Souetre was in Dallas that day, and was flown out that afternoon by a private pilot. As far as they were concerned, in a government plane. But there was no record whatsoever of the plane being there. They said Jean was a very questionable character, a free-lance soldier of fortune. They had known he was in the United States, and had traced him as far as Dallas the day before the assassination.

"They kept saying, 'If he contacts you, we want to talk to him. And he can lay the ground rules. We don't care where he is, or what country it's in. You be a go-between.' In other words, they were not saying he killed Kennedy. Because at that point, everyone was totally convinced it was Oswald. But they sure wanted to talk him, anywhere, anytime. I told them truthfully that I hadn't seen Jean in years, and that's where the matter ended."[19]

Souetre's American Connections

Next to Richard Nagell, the French Connection was what most intrigued Bernard Fensterwald, Jr., in the decade before his death in 1991. He spent countless hours seeking government documents, largely without success, on Souetre, Mertz, and the OAS-CIA-Pentagon relationship. On a ten-day trip to Paris in 1982, among Fensterwald's meetings was one with Jean Claude Perez, former chief of the OAS's intelligence branch. Perez confirmed that the OAS dispatched a three-man team to try to assassinate de Gaulle in Mexico City in March 1964, and further, that the OAS had contact in New Orleans with an anti-Castro group.[20]

Assassination researcher Peter Dale Scott uncovered that, after de Gaulle reached a truce with the OAS early in 1963, the French president helped arrange for its members to start going to other parts of the world. Some turned up in Latin America. At the same time, certain Cuban exiles have said they were transferred from CIA case officers to new handlers—some of them OAS veterans.[21]

At the same time, the OAS was a "darling" of the radical right. The John Birch Society, in their July 1962 *White Book,* described de Gaulle as a "Comsymp" [Communist sympathizer] and compared the OAS to the "Hungarian Freedom Fighters" and "the Cuban patriots betrayed in the fiasco of the Bay of Pigs." It continued: "Now, however, we have the OAS, led by the finest and most patriotic officers of the French army, many of whom—on de Gaulle's orders—gave their word of honor to the inhabitants of Algeria that they would never pull out and leave the country to the mercy of the Communists. These men and their followers are willing to give their lives to back up their word of honor. . . ."[22]

Gilbert Le Cavelier, a well-connected Frenchman who arranged many of Fensterwald's interviews, conducted an unofficial investigation overseas for the Washington attorney. Le Cavelier found that Jean Souetre traveled widely in Latin America and the Caribbean between 1962 and 1971. Souetre's official residence was Madrid, which under the Fascist dictatorship of Franco was a center for the international right wing—including, as we have seen, a site of occasional visits by General Charles Willoughby.

"Extremely close ties have always existed between the anti-Castroites in Florida and the French extreme right," Le Cavelier wrote Fensterwald in 1982, "through the intermediary of ex-O.A.S. members who emigrated to Argentina, Paraguay and to Venezuela. In March–April 1963 Souetre met Howard Hunt in Madrid."

Hunt, as noted earlier, was then Tracy Barnes's clandestine-affairs chief in the CIA's Domestic Operations Division. Also at this meeting, Le Cavelier continued, were OAS intelligence director Jean Claude Perez and several Hungarians looking to expand the global anti-Communist network. Several of those present proceeded "in the direction of the Caribbean, then towards New Orleans. They rediscovered someone called Bringuier, director of the Free Cuba Committee." Bringuier, of course, was the exile whom Oswald also encountered in the summer of 1963.

Le Cavelier continued: "Then Souetre met—still around April–May 1963—with General Edwin A. Walker at Dallas. [Souetre was] at the training program of Anti-Castro groups, Alpha 66 and the 30 November group" [the latter then led by Rolando Masferrer]. "Arms were furnished by the intermediary at the [American] Guantánamo naval base [in Cuba]. Training took place at the New Orleans region of Mandeville. Their Q-G ('Quartier General' or 'Headquarters') was 544 Camp Street." That was Guy Banister's office, and the address stamped on Oswald's Fair Play for Cuba literature.

At a tape-recorded session in Paris, Le Cavelier told Fensterwald that Banister was "former FBI, he was with Carlos Quiroga, and in the World

Anti-Communist League." OAS veterans, he said, had a "cell" at Mandeville, Louisiana, the site of an exile training camp. And, while E. Howard Hunt, Jr., was a CIA contact for Souetre and OAS intelligence, Le Cavelier said that ex-OAS officers also worked closely with elements of the Pentagon's Defense Intelligence Agency (DIA).[23]

If Le Cavelier's information was true, then the circle of American and international right-wing extremists, dissident CIA and Pentagon types, and Cuban exiles with Oswald connections was coming into much sharper focus.

Jean Souetre was tracked down in 1983 by first the *National Enquirer* and then a French newspaper, working at a casino in the French town of Divonne les Bains. Souetre denied being in Dallas on November 22, 1963, and speculated that it might instead have been "agent provocateur" Michael Mertz—"passing himself off as me, [who] started the rumor that the OAS was in on it just to make things look black" for the group. "It would be interesting to question Michael Mertz on this matter," Souetre added, "a guy who has had a lot of publicity in the past, at the time of the discovery of a drug network between France and the U.S."[24]

This was correct. Mertz's heroin-smuggling world was the Corsican Mafia in Marseilles, with which the CIA admits establishing a relationship in 1947 to help secure the docks from Communist influence. A parallel investigation in France, conducted in the 1980s by independent researcher Steve Rivele, pointed at Kennedy's assassins having been spirited into Dallas via Mexico from Marseilles, provided with weapons, hidden in a Dallas "safe house" for ten days, and then flown out. They had been hired, according to what several witnesses told Rivele, by the Santos Trafficante network.[25]

"Souetre also had ties to the Corsicans," Rivele told me in 1992. "I spoke with an undercover narcotics agent in Marseilles who had followed him for years, and there is no question he was on the Paris end of the drug traffic."

Rivele went on to say that before he ceased his investigations in 1988, he had written a letter to Richard Nagell. "Nagell called me a couple of times after that," Rivele said, "and said he would be in touch. He gave me the impression that I was on the right track."[26]

Summary

It is astonishing how much advance knowledge there was of plans to assassinate JFK. The FBI and Secret Service both knew by mid-November, from two separate sources, that members of an ultraright group (the National States Rights Party) were holding such discussions. One of these people, Joseph Milteer, was even captured on tape by an FBI informant. After the assassination, Milteer described himself as part of an "international underground"—and allowed that Oswald knew nothing, that the right wing had infiltrated the Communist group around him and set the plot in motion. Why did the tight security surrounding JFK in Miami on November 18 become so lax in Dallas? And why did the FBI suddenly visit Milteer on November 27, effectively scuttling plans by Miami officials to get his further revelations on tape?

In the meantime, in France, code breaker Eugene Dinkin of the Army suddenly went AWOL and alerted various embassies across Europe about a conspiracy involving the military and perhaps an "ultraright economic group." Picked up and hospitalized on November 13, Dinkin ended up in Walter Reed Army Hospital—where it appears that a "cover story" may have been induced to obfuscate whatever legitimate advance knowledge he possessed.

Dinkin's deciphering had focused on cable traffic emanating from the French OAS underground, one of whose leading members was apparently expelled from Dallas right after the assassination. Jean Souetre, later investigation revealed, had been in touch with General Walker and Cuban exiles in New Orleans during 1963. The FBI let a Houston dentist acquaintance of Souetre's know that the Frenchman was desperately being sought for questioning after the assassination. There is some doubt whether Souetre or Michael Mertz was the man deported. But if it was Mertz, a heroin trafficker tied into the Trafficante network, his Dallas presence is no less significant than Souetre's.

Chapter Twenty-five

The Deed: November 22, 1963

On Friday morning, November 22, 1963, President Kennedy returned to his hotel suite after giving a speech in Fort Worth and perused the *Dallas Morning News*. "Nixon Predicts JFK May Drop Johnson," read the headline of one article, which described the former vice president's trip to Dallas as a lawyer attending a Pepsi-Cola bottlers' convention.

There was also a full-page advertisement. "WELCOME MR. KENNEDY TO DALLAS," it said, and there was a black border around it. It asked why JFK had allowed "thousands of Cubans" to be jailed by Castro and why JFK had "scrapped the Monroe Doctrine in favor of the Spirit of Moscow."

Kennedy shook his head and turned to his wife. "We're going into nut country today," he said, and began pacing the room. "You know, last night would have been a hell of a night to assassinate a president," he continued. "There was the rain and the night, and we were all getting jostled. Suppose a man had a pistol in a briefcase."

Jacqueline Kennedy felt that the fantasy was her husband's way of shaking off the ad. On the flight to Dallas, Kennedy asked one of his aides, Kenneth O'Donnell: "What kind of journalism do you call the *Dallas Morning News?* You know who's responsible for that ad?"

The president looked through his morning *Intelligence Checklist.*[1] One of the situation estimates concerned South Vietnam, where more than 16,000 American "military advisers" were then in place. The buildup had occurred with JFK's approval; when he was elected president in 1960, only 685 U.S. personnel had been stationed there. But the president was having second thoughts about the wisdom of deepening American involvement in South Vietnam's battle with its northern Communist neighbor. On September 2, 1963, he had told the American people: "In the final analysis, it is their war. They are the ones who have to win it or lose it." In October Kennedy had quietly approved the withdrawal of 1,000 advisers by the end of 1963, the first stage of a total phasedown of the American military presence planned by 1965.[2]

Then, on November 1, the dictatorship of Ngo Dinh Diem had been overthrown by a team of South Vietnamese generals—backed by the CIA and U.S. ambassador Henry Cabot Lodge. Robert Kennedy would say in 1965 that Lodge, who had been Nixon's running mate in the 1960 presidential election, was "the individual that forced our position really at the time." Lodge refused to respond to the president's messages and, Robert Kennedy said, "wanted a coup. . . . It was an impossible situation." Things got so bad that the president decided in November to call Lodge home, and discussed with his brother "how he could be fired, because he wouldn't communicate in any way with us."[3]

Someone who *was* in communication with Lodge was Charles Willoughby. In a letter to the ambassador on October 3, 1963, Willoughby wrote: "I understand your position completely. As MacArthur's Chief of Intelligence, I had to cope with it from 1939 to 1951. You are enmeshed in a web of empire builders that once frustrated [General Albert] Wedemeyer in China and when they could not handle MacArthur, they intrigued against him. He [MacArthur] fought for an important principle: The control of all 'agencies' within his area as a function of normal command *responsibility*. It applies everywhere, in peace or war, from G.H.Q. [General Headquarters] to Embassies. Congratulations that you have met this 'fifth column' head on!"[4]

On November 21, 1963, Lodge was in Honolulu for a "summit conference" on Vietnam with several members of Kennedy's cabinet and military advisers. While the others stayed in military quarters, the ambassador took up residence at the Royal Hawaiian Hotel. There, shortly after lunch on the day before the assassination, he was noticed by a reporter for the *Honolulu Star-Bulletin* putting coin after coin into a pay phone in the lobby. The newspaper found this incident worthy of remark, since Lodge had ready access to phones in the privacy of his room or through military circuits.[5]

Three days later, the eulogy for JFK had just been conducted when President Johnson met with Lodge, instructing him to return to Vietnam and inform the Saigon government that the United States was now going to provide strong military support.[6]

Meanwhile, in Havana, French journalist Jean Daniel was meeting with Fidel Castro on November 20–22. Prior to his departure, Daniel had met with JFK, who keenly wanted to know whether Castro was serious about renewing relations. As Daniel later recounted his conversations with the Cuban premier, Castro spoke admiringly of the president's change of heart. Kennedy, Castro said on November 20, had "the possibility of becoming the greatest president of the United States, the leader who may at last understand that there can be coexistence between capitalists and Socialists, even in the Americas." Castro added that he had received the impression, "from all my conversations with Khrushchev," that "Kennedy is a man you can talk with. . . . Since you are going to see Kennedy again, be a messenger of peace in spite of everything."

As Castro and Daniel finished a lunch-hour meal together on November 22, a Castro aide rushed in with a radio tuned to a Miami station. He translated the words to Castro as they came over: "Wounded in the head. . . . Pursuit of the assassin. . . . President Kennedy is dead." Castro stood up and began muttering over and over, *"Es un mala noticia"* ("This is very bad news"). Then he turned to Daniel and said: "There is the end to your mission of peace. Everything is going to change." Twenty long minutes passed. Then Castro asked Daniel: "Who is Lyndon Johnson? What authority does he have over the CIA?"

News reports indicated that the authorities were in hot pursuit of a possible suspect in the slaying. "They will have to find the assassin quickly, but very quickly," Castro said. "Otherwise you watch and see—I know them—they will try to put the blame on us for this thing."[7]

Dealey Plaza and Its Aftermath

Lee Harvey Oswald arose before 7:00 A.M. on the morning of November 22. He was staying with Marina at Ruth Paine's home. Unseen by his wife, he removed his wedding ring and dropped it into an antique Russian teacup on a bureau.[8] Then, carrying a package in a heavy brown bag, he rode with fellow employee Wesley Frazier the fifteen miles to the book depository. "What's the package, Lee?" Frazier asked. "Curtain rods," Frazier remembered Oswald saying.[9]

The shots rang out at 12:30 P.M., just after the president's limousine made the turn onto Elm Street at Dealey Plaza. Of 178 witnesses at the scene, 61 would later say they believed that at least some of the gunfire had originated in front of the presidential motorcade. Nearly all of the dozen or so people standing on an area known as the "grassy knoll" were convinced that shots had come from directly in back of them—where a wooden picket fence took a right angle a mere thirty-five yards from the oncoming motorcade.[10]

But the attention of the authorities focused immediately on a large warehouse, the Texas School Book Depository (TSBD) building, at the right rear of the motorcade. One witness, Arnold Rowland, said he saw *two* men in sixth-floor windows, one of them with a rifle across his chest, at 12:15 P.M.[11] About a half hour after the assassination, three spent rifle cartridges were found by a policeman near an open window on the TSBD's sixth floor.[12]

Fifteen minutes before that, a radio dispatcher at Dallas police headquarters had already sent out a description of a man wanted for questioning: "an unknown white male approximately 30, 165 pounds, slender build, armed with what is thought to be a 30-30 rifle. . . ."[13] Within the hour, a small army of police closed in on the Texas Theater, a couple of miles away. "CRY OF BATTLE—WAR IS HELL," the theater's marquee announced. It was a double feature. Inside, a close match for the police dispatcher's description—twenty-four-year-old ex-Marine Lee Harvey Oswald—was handcuffed and driven to headquarters.

At about the same time as Oswald's arrest, Deputy Sheriff E. L. Boone said he discovered a rifle stashed inside a rectangle of boxes on the TSBD's sixth floor. Some of the original police reports described it as a 7.65mm German Mauser—not the 6.5mm Italian Mannlicher-Carcano that Oswald owned.[14] And, as Frank Ellsworth of the federal Alcohol, Tobacco, and Firearms (ATF) Division told me in 1976—and reiterated during a 1992 telephone conversation—the Mannlicher-Carcano was actually found on a *lower* floor of the building.[15]

Ellsworth had been in his office not far from Dealey Plaza when news of the shooting came over the radio. He recalled at our interview in 1976: "I immediately took off running, and got there the same time [Dallas police captain] Will Fritz did. He motioned me to follow him into the book depository. To my knowledge, I was the only federal officer in the building."

Ellsworth then aided in the authorities' search of the depository. "We didn't know what we were looking for, we picked up and tagged as evidence all sorts of stuff. I went up in the false ceilings, figuring whoever did the shooting might still be hiding in the building. We found a lot of whiskey bottles up there. Because of my assigned location, I happened to be the individual who found where Oswald had done the shooting. There were a number of boxes over by the sixth-floor window, which appeared to have been the sniper's nest.

"We started at the top of the building and worked our way down," Ellsworth continued. "The gun was not found on the same floor, but on a lower floor by a couple of city detectives. If I recollect right, there was an elevator shaft or stairwell back in the northwest corner. The gun was over near that, just south of it behind some boxes." Ellsworth recalled the weapon as being an Italian Mannlicher-Carcano.

In 1992 I asked Ellsworth, now retired from the ATF, about this matter again. He added: "I think the rifle was found on the fourth floor. I have a vague recollection that the position it was in, and where it was found, led to the conjecture that as Oswald came down the stairs, he probably pitched it over behind these books."

Ellsworth was never called to testify before the Warren Commission. "Which suited me fine," he added, "because I was just a spear-carrier; there were other people who were the lead players in the investigation." But while Ellsworth has never seen any reason to question the Warren Commission Report's findings, what he witnessed would have cast an entirely different light on the physical evidence.

For one thing, it raises the possibility that not one but two rifles were actually found in the TSBD—a Mauser on the sixth floor (perhaps while Ellsworth himself was looking in the false ceilings), and a Mannlicher-Carcano on the fourth floor. But even if there was no second rifle in the TSBD, the fact that a rifle found on the fourth floor then "officially" ended up on the sixth floor is equally significant.

The Military on-Scene

As it happens, Frank Ellsworth was not the only federal official inside the TSBD. An Army Intelligence officer, special agent James Powell, was found trapped inside the TSBD after the building had been sealed. Powell later told researcher Penn Jones that he had "worked with the sheriff's deputies at the rear of the Texas Book Depository for about six or eight minutes" and had then ordered a newsman to hang up a telephone on the first floor so that he, Powell, might use it.

Powell had been in Dealey Plaza when the shooting occurred and had taken several photographs with a 35mm Minolta camera. One of these, which shows the full length of the TSBD, was released in 1976 by the FBI. An unidentifiable object—perhaps a man's shoulder—is visible in the sixth-floor southeast window, where Oswald allegedly fired. Powell said he took the photo from the corner of Elm and Houston streets about thirty seconds after the president was shot.[16]

Why Powell was in the vicinity at all was never ascertained by investigators, though it was customary for the Secret Service to receive protective assistance from elements of Military Intelligence on presidential trips. Jack Revill, then in charge of the Dallas police's Criminal Intelligence Division, told the Warren Commission that an Army Intelligence officer had ridden with him from Dealey Plaza to the station that afternoon.[17] Before Oswald's capture, it was Revill who submitted a list of employees at the TSBD. The first name on Revill's list was "Harvey Lee Oswald," with an address given as 605 Elsbeth in Dallas. Oswald had lived at 602 Elsbeth in late 1962 and early 1963, but this address was not known to Oswald's employers at the TSBD.

Where, then, did Revill get his information? It turned out that the 112th Military Intelligence Group—which, as reported in Chapter Six, maintained an Oswald/Hidell file that was "destroyed routinely" in 1973— possessed information on a "Harvey Lee Oswald" who resided at 605 Elsbeth. Thus the probability arises that Revill, and therefore the Dallas police, obtained their first data on Oswald from Military Intelligence.[18]

One minute *before* the shooting, in Washington, D.C., there had occurred an astonishing breakdown of the telephone system. The official explanation was overloaded lines. But it was almost an hour before full service could be restored,[19] while the Pentagon was placing American troops on a worldwide alert. After the assassination, when Pentagon officials reaching the White House switchboard set up at the Dallas-Sheraton Hotel asked who was in command, a military man grabbed the phone and made a curious remark. The secretary of defense and the Joint Chiefs of Staff, he said, "are now the president."[20]

Over at Dallas's Parkland Hospital, where doctors sought in vain to save the president's life, another military man was standing in the doorway to Trauma Room 1. This was Colonel William Bishop, who had been working for months with the anti-Castro Cuban exiles on behalf of the CIA. "I had been in Palm Beach at the Berkeley Hotel," Bishop told me in 1990, "when I received a phone call telling me to be in Dallas on the morning of November 21. I wasn't the only Army officer called, that's all I can say about that. I was flown to Dallas by military aircraft and checked into a Holiday Inn, at which time I received instructions that I was to make sure the press had proper credentials at the Trade Mart when Kennedy came to speak the next afternoon. I was in position and waiting for his arrival, when I heard over a squad car parked at the curb that shots had been fired in Dealey Plaza. I commandeered a police car and ordered the driver to take me directly to Parkland Hospital. With the ID I had, that was not a problem. There the Secret Service instructed me to secure the area outside the Trauma Room and make myself available to the First Lady or medical staff."[21]

Inside Trauma Room 1, Dr. Charles Crenshaw, a resident surgeon, had been called in the absence of his superior to try to save the president's life. Standing over the fallen leader, Dr. Crenshaw immediately observed that JFK had been struck twice from the front: once in the neck, once in the right side of the head. Shortly after the president was pronounced dead, the emergency room's director, Dr. Charles Baxter, issued an edict of secrecy to all physicians in attendance. It would be almost thirty years before Dr. Crenshaw decided to break what he now calls the "conspiracy of silence."[22]

That night, at the Bethesda, Maryland, Naval Hospital, three military physicians conducted an evening autopsy on the body of the late president. Two of them had no firsthand experience with bullet wounds. They stood surrounded by military superiors, who basically directed them, as well as by FBI and Secret Servicemen.

"Who's in charge here?" Navy commander James J. Humes is said to have asked at the outset. "I am," an unidentified Army general replied.

Army lieutenant colonel Pierre Finck was the only member of the autopsy team who was a member of the American Academy of Forensic Sciences. Yet he was told not to track the neck wound through the president's body to examine its precise path. His request to examine the president's clothing, a standard autopsy procedure, was also denied. Finally, the three attending doctors were instructed not to talk about what they had seen in the autopsy room. "When you are a lieutenant colonel in the Army," Finck would recall, "you just follow orders."[23]

When the autopsy ended, two FBI agents took possession of "a missile" removed from the president's body. Yet, according to the official record, both of the bullets that struck him had also exited the body at the time. The existence of "a missile" clearly indicated a fourth bullet.[24]

Late that night, Commander Humes burned his original autopsy notes in a fireplace.[25] He said he did so because they were stained with Kennedy's blood, and he did not want the notes to become a ghoulish collector's item.[26]

In 1972 Dr. Cyril Wecht, a former president of the American Academy of Forensic Scientists, was allowed to examine the autopsy photographs and X rays. Wecht determined that JFK had been hit from behind, but concluded that only a study of the president's brain could show whether another bullet had entered from the right front. When Wecht asked to make such a study, the National Archives made a startling discovery: The President's brain was missing.[27]

In 1978, when the House Assassinations Committee was keeping the X rays and ballistics evidence in a locked safe inside a special room, it was discovered that these had been tampered with. A fingerprint check traced to Regis Blahut, the CIA liaison officer assigned to help safeguard the agency's own secret material on the committee's premises. Caught red-handed and fired by the committee, Blahut admitted the deed. The CIA told the committee he had acted out of "mere curiosity." In his one brief statement to a reporter, Blahut said only: "There's other things involved that are detrimental to other things."[28]

Nagell and the Mystery of the Rifle

Some six hundred miles away from Dallas on November 22, 1963, Richard Case Nagell heard the news over a radio in the El Paso County Jail. At approximately 1:00 P.M., he scrawled a note on a slip of paper and handed it to a jailer, asking that it be taken immediately to the jail captain. It was a request to speak to the Secret Service as soon as possible.[29]

"The conspiracy I was cognizant of," Nagell said at our first interview, "I'm not saying is the same one that resulted in the president's death, although I'm sure the same people were involved."[30]

As Nagell wrote in two letters to Fensterwald, "Even if LHO missed JFK, that doesn't mean that he did not fire shots from the Texas School Book Depository with the intent and for the purpose of killing or assisting in the assassination. . . . Every outspoken critic of the Warren [Commission] Report (not excluding the clods on the Commission), it seems, missed the point as to why LHO was recruited in the first place. It certainly was not because of his expertise with a 6.5mm Mannlicher-Carcano rifle."[31]

When I met with Nagell in 1984, he had reached the conclusion that Oswald definitely did not kill the president, although he stuck to his belief that he "probably" did shoot. A "marksman," he pointed out, is a very low level of expertise in the military, even below the rank of "sharpshooter."[32]

In 1967, at a meeting with a Garrison investigator, Nagell had queried "if the District Attorney's Office was aware of a man in San Antonio who owned a 6.5mm Mannlicher-Carcano rifle." Nagell had "stated that this man had known Lee Harvey Oswald and had been seen with him. . . ."[33]

In 1971, Nagell had elaborated in a letter to Fensterwald about what he called "the old substitution trick. . . . I understand that a rifle quite like the one picked up at a certain school book depository was discovered the following day, abandoned, in a hotel room at Terre Haute, Indiana. Its ownership was traced to a person then residing in San Antonio. . . ."[34]

Sure enough, buried away in the Assassination Archives Research Center, I found an article from the *Los Angeles Herald-Examiner* of April 8, 1967, datelined Putnamville, Indiana, and headlined: "JFK-TYPE SNIPER RIFLE APPEARS." It described an Associated Press interview with Frank Riddle, who had retired that February after sixteen years as Terre Haute's police chief. Riddle revealed that a 6.5mm Mannlicher-Carcano had indeed been found in a Terre Haute hotel room and traced to a salesman from San Antonio.

"Riddle said San Antonio authorities informed him the salesman had no criminal record, was a member of the Young Communist League and an expert rifle marksman. He declined to name the salesman. Riddle said the salesman registered at the Terre Haute House Nov. 25, 1963 and, according to the desk clerk, was carrying a 'long package.' Shortly after noon on Nov. 26, he checked out without the package. . . . The rifle, found by a maid, bore no fingerprints, Riddle said."

Riddle told the AP reporter that all his information about the rifle had been turned over to the Warren Commission, and the rifle itself was taken away by Secret Service agents.

I went to the National Archives and found a document about the incident that had been declassified in 1970. The rifle owner was identified as Harry L. Power, described as a twenty-year-old Army veteran, standing a stocky five feet, six inches and with dark hair. He was determined to have been a painter for a neon sign company in San Antonio but had allegedly left the Texas city late in 1962, leaving a forwarding address in Manila, West Virginia.

According to the file, policeman Riddle insisted that Power had been investigated in connection with the shooting attempt on General Walker.[35] Other documents in the assassination archives indicated a brief FBI investigation of people in the San Antonio area, but all names were blanked out.

In response to my question about Harry Power, Nagell wrote back in May 1976: "I know little about the fella who once resided in San Antonio. I think he was a Trotskyist or Maoist type."[36]

The effort to use the "far left" as a decoy, it seemed, had extended beyond Lee Harvey Oswald.

David Ferrie's Midnight Ride

Robert Kennedy, who had just turned thirty-eight, spent the morning of November 22, 1963, at the second day of a conference assessing the results of his Justice Department's ongoing battle against organized crime. At the top of Kennedy's agenda were four Cosa Nostra leaders: Chicago's Sam Giancana, Florida's Santos Trafficante, Jr., Teamsters union boss Jimmy Hoffa, and New Orleans' Carlos Marcello. A southern jury was expected to reach a verdict that afternoon in the government's conspiracy and perjury case against Marcello. And the attorney general was hopeful that victory would pave the way for Marcello's permanent deportation from the United States.[37]

By one-thirty that afternoon in New Orleans, the closing arguments in *United States* v. *Carlos Marcello* were over. The jury was about to be handed the case when a bailiff suddenly entered the courtroom and handed Judge Herbert Christenberry a note. A cacophony of voices erupted as the judge made the announcement about President Kennedy. A brief recess was called. Marcello showed no emotion as he filed out with his brother Joe and his lawyers. Accompanying Marcello was a local "strategist" in his case—free-lance pilot, amateur hypnotist, anti-Castro fanatic, and CIA contract employee David Ferrie.

By three-fifteen the jury returned a verdict of complete acquittal on the government's charges against the Marcellos.[38] David Ferrie left the Federal Courthouse and, sometime before early evening, telephoned a Marcello-owned Houston motel to make reservations for the night for himself and two young male companions. Then he picked them up in his new Comet station wagon and, through the most violent thunderstorm that anyone could remember, drove nonstop the 356 miles to Houston. It was four in the morning when the trio arrived at the Alamont Hotel. The next day, from the Winterland Skating Rink, Ferrie spent several hours at a pay phone, making and receiving calls. One of these was collect to Carlos Marcello's Town & Country Motel headquarters back in New Orleans.[39]

Then, for reasons Ferrie would never explain, he drove on again on the evening of November 23 to the southeastern Texas city of Galveston. Checking into a hotel at about 10:30 P.M., he immediately headed out again until the wee hours of the morning. A friend of Jack Ruby, Breck Wall, had arrived in Galveston at about the same time, from Dallas. And, at about 11:00 P.M. that night, the Warren Commission learned that Ruby began frantically trying to reach Wall by phone. Wall later explained that

Ruby finally reached him, shortly before midnight, to discuss "union business" concerning Ruby's Carousel Club.[40]

By the time David Ferrie arrived back in New Orleans on November 25, he would learn from Marcello's attorney, G. Wray Gill, that his own library card had apparently been found on Lee Harvey Oswald after the alleged assassin's arrest. Yet in the Dallas police inventory of Oswald's effects, no mention was ever made of it. Two witnesses—Oswald's former landlady and an Oswald neighbor—later told the House Assassinations Committee that a panicked Ferrie came by their houses asking if they knew anything about the library card. Several former members of the Civil Air Patrol also recalled Ferrie getting in touch to find out if they recalled Oswald having been in Ferrie's squadron.[41]

In 1975 I paid a visit to Ferrie's former roommate, a gay activist named Raymond Broshears. In the heart of San Francisco's Tenderloin district, Reverend Broshears (ordained by the Universal Life Church) had a storefront office called Helping Hands. It was a place where the city's gays could find refuge when troubled by the law or by straights. Broshears was a large man with a neatly trimmed, downturned mustache and brown eyes. He dressed completely in black, with a white clerical collar and a handsome cross around his neck. He had once been called in to talk to the Garrison investigators but revealed little. Now, at the end of a long day, he sat behind his desk and hesitantly, nervously, agreed to speak into my tape recorder about his days with David Ferrie.

"He called me here in San Francisco shortly before his death [in February 1967]. He said he was going to be killed. I said, 'Oh, sure, what are you drinking? 'No,' he said, 'really.' I said, 'Why don't you come out here?' He said, 'I can't really leave the South. I don't want to come out there with all those Communists.' That was it. The next thing I knew, he was dead. They said he killed himself. But he didn't. You know it, and I know it."

Broshears became silent, then continued: "David believed Kennedy was a Communist, or being controlled by the Communists. David wasn't a redbaiter; he really believed this. He had a deep love for his country. And he believed we were in danger of being invaded, that the missiles had never been removed from Cuba and there was going to be an all-out atomic holocaust in the U.S. When you can understand that, and his religious part—he would wear priest robes and perform a Mass, you see—well . . ."

What was the point, I asked, of Ferrie's sudden trip to Texas on the night of November 22, 1963? Broshears considered for a long moment, then said:

"David was to meet a plane. He was going to fly these people on to Mexico, and eventually to South Africa, which did not have an extradition treaty with the United States. They had left from some little airfield between Dallas and Fort Worth, and David had a twin-engine plane ready for them, and that was the purpose of his mad dash through a driving rainstorm from New Orleans. But the plane crashed off the coast of Texas near Corpus Christi. That was what David was told in the telephone booth that day. Apparently they had decided to try to make it to Mexico on their own. They did not."

There was substantiation for what Broshears had to say about a plane at "some little airfield between Dallas and Fort Worth." At about 1:00 P.M. on the afternoon of November 22, half an hour after the president was shot, neighbors who lived along the road that runs by the little Redbird private airport began calling the police. A twin-engine plane, they reported, was out there behaving very peculiarly. For an hour it had been revving its engines, not on the runway but parked at the end of the airstrip on a grassy area next to the fence. The noise prevented nearby residents from hearing their TVs, as news came over about the terrible events in downtown Dallas. But the police were too busy to check it out, and shortly thereafter the plane took off.[42]

Had David Ferrie ever told Broshears who was on the plane he was supposed to meet elsewhere?

"They had code names. The only one I remember was Garcia."

What did Ferrie tell you about Oswald? I asked. Another pause. "Oh, lots of things, some of it very personal. But he certainly knew Lee Harvey Oswald when he was chicken [a gay phrase that means, basically, a teenage boy]. And knew him later. I myself met a person who was introduced to me as Leon Oswald. A very fleet passing meeting, I had sex with him. He looked a helluva lot like him, but it's highly unlikely to me this was the same Lee Oswald.

"David told me Lee Harvey Oswald did *not* kill the president. He was very adamant about it, and I believed him. All the things he told me about Oswald, I doubt he could have shot a rabbit standing fifty feet away."

Did Broshears get the impression that Oswald may have believed he was working for Castro, but in fact was being used by anti-Castro Cubans? "I would imagine that's what happened to him, he was sold out at the end. I know the whole plan was to make it look like a Communist conspiracy.

"David said four people were going to shoot. He told me this in 1963, before the assassination. Then we talked later, in '64. He said one of them fired from a sewer opening along the parade route, another from the grassy knoll, and someone from behind."

Was there money involved? "Well, it had to come from someplace and I want to tell you it didn't come from any of the people that hung around David Ferrie. Because they didn't have any visible means of income. Yet they did have money."

"Then who put it up? Did Ferrie tell you?"

"Oh, yes. Carlos Marcello. The first time I ever heard his name was late '63. David told me that the man Garrison went after, Clay Shaw, knew a lot of things, but primarily things that people had told him. But Clay Shaw did not engineer the killing of Kennedy. Carlos Marcello is the person most closely aligned with the people who actually did engineer the killing. But how are you going to get him? He'll kill you. That man is really dangerous!"

Broshears became more agitated, and when he finally spoke again, his voice carried strong emotion. "I'm very distressed," he said. "I'm trying at this moment to find out who is still alive, besides myself, that knew David Ferrie at that particular time in history. I don't know why I'm talking to you at all, but . . . Some people said David was an ugly man, but he was a beautiful person. David never said he worked for CIA. You know, you can work for the CIA and never know. I have since learned some of the places I worked in New Orleans were CIA front businesses. But David was working for people he saw as patriotic Americans."

As I got ready to leave Helping Hands that evening, Raymond Broshears got out a shotgun and put it on his desk—"for show, in case that big dope pusher standing right outside my door there gets ideas." He said if Congress tried to subpoena him to testify, he would refuse. They never tried.

"Please understand," Broshears concluded our interview, "this was a very patriotic thing to David. It was a conglomerate of different ideologies pushing on a few people, and it all came together at the same time. The government knows how to manipulate groups on both the left and the right. Some of these people, as they were brought together on November 22, 1963, there was no way they could have been working in concert with one another. I think they were all manipulated very cleverly—by somebody in the government pulling the strings."

Oswald in Custody

Lee Harvey Oswald was first booked by the police on suspicion of having shot and killed Dallas policeman J. D. Tippit in the Oak Cliff vicinity near the Texas Theater where he was captured.[43] Oswald's initial interrogation, lasting from 2:15 to 4:05 P.M., was handled by Captain Will Fritz, who would later claim that he took rough notes, then and at his subsequent discussions with Oswald—but these were never turned over to government investigators. Fritz recalled Oswald frantically denying shooting policeman Tippit, or the president, and saying he would not take a polygraph examination without the advice of an attorney.[44]

However, ATF agent Frank Ellsworth, who was present for part of the interrogation, does not recall any panic in Oswald. "He appeared to be awfully pleased with himself," Ellsworth told me in 1992, "which struck me as incongruous for a man sitting there in police headquarters who had just assassinated one of the most popular presidents in American history."[45]

Just as the interrogation began, Gordon Shanklin, the FBI's special agent in charge of the Dallas office, called over to ask that agent James P. Hosty, Jr., be allowed to sit in as the bureau's "Oswald expert." The moment Hosty told Oswald his name, the ex-Marine is said to have responded: "Oh, so you are Hosty. I've heard about you." He banged his fist on the desk, accusing the agent of having twice accosted his wife. If Hosty wanted to know something about him, Oswald reportedly said, the FBI man should have spoken to him directly.

"Have you ever been to Mexico City?" Hosty finally asked. Oswald rose to his feet and demanded, "How did you know about that?" Captain Fritz ordered him to sit down and answer the question. Oswald vehemently denied ever having been in Mexico City.

Then Fritz asked Oswald about his role in the Fair Play for Cuba Committee. Oswald pointed his finger at Hosty and said: "Ask Hosty. He seems to know everything!"

When the first interrogation ended, Hosty emerged to find himself confronted by a senior member of the FBI field office, W. Harlan Brown, who informed him that he would not be permitted to attend the next interrogation session. Nor was he to divulge anything to the Dallas police or cooperate with them in any way. He should return immediately to Dallas's FBI headquarters.[46] There, Shanklin confronted him with the note from Oswald that had been found in Hosty's workbox. Shanklin wanted a memorandum detailing all facts about the note's contents and the police interrogation of Oswald. Two days later, as we have seen, Shanklin told Hosty: "Jim, I don't ever want to see that Oswald note again."

Shortly after midnight, on November 23, Oswald faced the press for the first time in a basement assembly room at police headquarters. Jack Ruby mingled in the crowd, correcting District Attorney Henry Wade's explanation that Oswald was a member of the "Free Cuba Committee" by shouting out: "Henry, that's the Fair Play for Cuba Committee."[47]

A bruised-faced Oswald maintained he had not been allowed legal representation at his arraignment. "I really don't know what the situation is about," he asserted. "Nobody has told me anything except that I am accused of murdering a policeman. I know nothing more than that and I do request someone to come forward to give me legal assistance."

"Did you kill the president?" a newsman shouted.

"No, I have not been charged with that," Oswald said. "In fact, nobody has said that to me yet. The first thing I heard about it was when the newspaper reporters in the hall asked me that question."

A policeman standing nearby said quickly, "You have been charged with that."

More reporters' questions: "What did you do in Russia?" "How did you hurt your eye?"

"A policeman hit me."[48]

At 12:20 A.M., Oswald was placed in a maximum-security cell on the fifth floor of the jail. A representative of the American Civil Liberties Union came to the station, asking to visit with Oswald, but was rebuffed by the FBI.[49] In the middle of that first long night, Oswald would finally be arraigned for the assassination. Less than forty-eight hours later, he would be dead.

His final shouted words to reporters had been: "I'm just a patsy!"[50]

The Mob, the CIA, and the Cuban Exiles

Richard Nagell says he never heard of Jack Ruby before the nightclub owner somehow made his way into the Dallas police basement and silenced Oswald forever on Sunday afternoon, November 24. Over the years since, Ruby's associations with organized crime—dating back to his Chicago days in the 1930s—have been documented in numerous books. Some of the strippers at his Carousel Club were recruited from a New Orleans bar operated by Carlos Marcello's brother. Ruby's telephone records show that he called a Marcello lieutenant, Nofio Pecora, on August 4 and October 30; spoke to two of Jimmy Hoffa's known hoodlums two weeks before the assassination;[51] and remained in close touch with Lewis McWillie, a friend of Santos Trafficante since their Havana casino days.[52] The FBI has admitted that at least in 1959, Ruby acted as an FBI informant.[53] Ruby had also made at least one trip to Cuba, in 1959, and was rumored to have run guns to Castro before the Cuban revolution.[54]

On November 22, 1963, attorney Frank Ragano said he received a phone call from an exuberant client. "Have you heard the good news?" Hoffa reportedly said. "They killed the son of a bitch. This means Bobby is out as attorney general. Lyndon will get rid of Bobby." Indeed, Robert Kennedy's organized-crime strike force would never meet again.

The evening of the assassination, Ragano had dinner in Tampa with Trafficante, who raised a toast to the president's demise and said: "Our problems are over now. . . . We're out of trouble now. We will build hotels. We will get back into Cuba now." Two weeks later, in New Orleans, Ragano saw Marcello, who was angry because he had yet to receive a $3 million loan he had requested from the Teamsters pension fund. "Jimmy owes me and he owes me big," Ragano remembered Marcello saying. Sometime in December 1963, Hoffa told Ragano: "I'll never forget what Carlos did for me."

In February 1987, as Trafficante lay dying of heart disease, Ragano says he was summoned for one last conversation and told: "Carlos fucked up. We shouldn't have gotten rid of Giovanni. We should have killed Bobby." This convinced the lawyer, once and for all, that his clients Trafficante and Hoffa had plotted with Marcello to kill the president.[55]

They are all gone now, the Syndicate leaders who may have known just how far the conspiracy went. The first to die was Chicago Mob boss Sam Giancana. On the night of June 19, 1975, shortly after he was publicly linked to the CIA-Mafia plots against Castro, Giancana was shot seven times with a .22-caliber, silencer-equipped pistol in his basement kitchen. Six of the bullets formed a neatly stitched circle around his mouth, a seeming message that Giancana was no longer available to talk. He was just about to be subpoenaed before the Senate Intelligence Committee. The gun, it was determined, had originally been purchased in Miami.[56]

Next came Hoffa, who disappeared on July 30, 1975, last seen getting into a friend's car at midafternoon in Detroit. His body has never been found.[57]

The body of Johnny Rosselli was discovered on August 7, 1976, stuffed inside a fifty-five-gallon oil drum in a bay near Miami. He had testified three times before congressional investigators, the last time (in April 1976) in a secret session focusing on the JFK assassination. Twelve days before he vanished from a friend's fishing boat, he had dined with Trafficante in Fort Lauderdale.[58]

At my last face-to-face interview with Richard Nagell in 1984, he reiterated his belief that organized-crime figures were not the real masterminds behind the assassination. But Giancana and Rosselli knew a lot, he volunteered, Rosselli probably more than the Chicago boss—and both men were eliminated not by the Mob but by the CIA. Nearly everybody on the periphery of the conspiracy was dead, Nagell pointed out. "Somebody has been tying up loose ends over the years," he added.[59]

As for the two Cuban exiles who, according to Nagell, were central to the conspiracy, Nagell wrote Fensterwald in 1975: "Leopoldo is dead. . . . So I am told." Later he added: "I heard several stories. That he was a suicide. That he was executed. For something else, nothing to do with this." By 1984, Nagell had concluded, or received word, that Leopoldo was murdered within the United States.[60]

Of Angel, Nagell wrote to Fensterwald in 1975: "A friend out here, formerly connected with Alpha 66, advises that an Angel was apprehended in Cuba while I was on ice, possibly in 1965 or 1966. This Angel was found in possession of .45 calibre ammunition containing (?) or coated with cyanide. . . . He is said to have copped out that he and several cohorts were on a CIA-sponsored mission to assassinate Fidel."[61]

In 1984, Nagell hinted to me that Angel might have been among forty-eight political prisoners released by Castro that June, in what was termed by the Cuban premier as a "personal gesture" triggered by a visit from Jesse Jackson.[62]

Were Angel and Leopoldo part of the CIA's scheming with organized crime? We may never know, although Colonel Bishop certainly allowed that such was the case (see Chapter Twenty-two). At my last meeting with James Angleton, in October 1976, the former counter intelligence chief had spoken in what he considered pragmatic terms about the CIA-Mob relationship. "From a straight intelligence point of view, the Mafia were people who knew a great deal about Cuba," Angleton said. He added that William Harvey, FitzGerald's CIA predecessor on Cuban matters, had "made one mistake. You never become involved, at his level, with the operators. You put people between you."

Angleton held the Senate Intelligence Committee "responsible" for what happened to Giancana and Rosselli. "Because there was a helluva lot more leaking out of that committee than anyone has ever put together," he said, "and they dramatized it. There's no question the Mafia could not tolerate testimony under oath which could go far beyond the agenda. You see, the Mafia is based on, number one, never forcing a person to become a member; there's no coercion. It has very simple articles of faith that are well known to everybody. The basic one is *omerta,* secrecy. But the Senate Committee, in its handling of all this, placed Rosselli in a situation of closed hearings.

"If you go back to the original stories," Angleton continued, "you find that when Giancana was shot, the Chicago police said it couldn't be organized crime because the caliber of bullets were .22s. Well, I deny any police force in the United States to know the modus operandi of the Mafia, period. Bill Harvey called me not long before it happened. I warned Bill that Giancana would not appear [before the Senate]."

We had just ordered dinner that night at the Army-Navy Club, and Angleton asked me to put down my notepad. "This is off the record," he said. "Don't write it down." He went on to tell me that the murders of Giancana and Hoffa were committed by the same people, inside the New York and Chicago Mob families. Hoffa's body, he added, was in concrete somewhere between Detroit and the Canadian border.[63]

James Angleton died in 1988, and I no longer feel under any obligation to keep secret what he told me. What I will always wonder is where Angleton got his information, and whether his statements about the Mob's responsibility for the killings—diametrically opposed to Nagell's statements about the CIA being behind them—were, to use one of Angelton's favorite words, "disinformation." I also wonder why he warned Wiliam Harvey that Giancana would never testify before the Senate.

Harvey died of a heart attack on June 8, 1976, at age sixty, shortly before Rosselli's murder. That autumn, Harvey's widow told a journalist: "Up to his last breath Bill told me never to talk to anyone." Her Indianapolis home had been the object of two attempted break-ins shortly after Harvey's death. "They're after his papers," Mrs. Harvey said. "But I burned everything."[64]

Around the World: November 22, 1963

Washington, midafternoon: Before Lee Harvey Oswald was officially charged with any crime, J. Edgar Hoover issued an internal FBI memo. It stated that the Dallas police "very probably" had the president's assassin in custody, an individual "in the category of a nut and the extremist pro-Castro crowd . . . an extreme radical of the left."[65]

Mexico City, early evening: Winston Scott received an urgent teletype from CIA headquarters asking the station chief for all relevant information developed on Oswald's September trip. Scott either already knew or was suddenly made aware of one very salient fact: The photo of "Oswald" that his office had dispatched to Langley back in October was not really Oswald. Now Scott put out a request to the Office of Naval Intelligence to send him a legitimate picture. By eleven o'clock that night it would arrive on his desk.[66]

Washington, 7:00 P.M.: Lyndon Johnson, having arrived by plane an hour before, had his first appointment as president with CIA director John McCone. What they discussed remains unknown.[67] At 9:10 P.M., LBJ conferred by phone for fifteen minutes with J. Edgar Hoover.[68]

Havana: Alone in his office in the Palace of the Revolution, Fidel Castro lit one of his famous cigars and worked into the night drafting a two-hour speech he would give the next day. Of Oswald, he wrote: "Is he really guilty? Is he a scapegoat? Is he a psychopath? Or is he perhaps a tool of the most reactionary U.S. circles? Who is this man? Why did he go into action precisely when circumstances were least favorable for a left-wing fanatic to assassinate the U.S. president?"[69]

Moscow: The next day's newspapers were being put to bed. *Pravda* assembled a large front-page photo of President Kennedy, noting his "steps toward cleansing the international situation" and how these had "met with sharp attacks from American 'madmen.' "

The *Izvestia* story read: "All the circumstances of President Kennedy's tragic death give grounds for believing that the assassination was conceived and executed by ultraright-wing fascist and racist circles . . . displeased by any step aimed at relaxing international tension and improving Soviet-American relations."[70]

Dallas: The most famous "home movie" in history—an eighteen-second-long, 8mm film taken by Dallas dressmaker Abraham Zapruder in Dealey Plaza—was being processed at Jamison Film Labs. Zapruder knew he may have captured something momentous the moment the motorcade passed, sirens blazing en route to Parkland Hospital, and his secretary had immediately alerted the authorities.

Except for a few moments when a street sign obscures the view of the president's limousine, the Zapruder film depicts almost the entire horrifying scene of the assassination. Few who watch the frames of the fatal shot —where the president's head is blasted to the rear and left—can avoid feeling that the bullet came from the right front, the area known as the grassy knoll.[71]

This, it would seem, is proof positive of at least a second gunman. But government investigations have not come to that conclusion. The House Assassinations Committee's analysts concluded that the motion of the president's body might have been a neurological spasm. Hence "the rearward movement of the president's head would not be fundamentally inconsistent with a bullet striking from the rear."[72]

The Warren Commission had not even mentioned the left rearward head snap in any of its evidentiary volumes. In fact, when it did publish stills of a portion of the Zapruder film, the vital frames showing the impact of the fatal head shot were reversed. In 1965 J. Edgar Hoover— whose FBI reviewed the film before passing it on to the commission— called the transposition that removed the perception of a front-to-rear shot "a printing error."[73]

By November 25, 1963, *Life* magazine was said to have purchased the original copy, negotiating through the Passman/Jones law firm to pay Zapruder at least $150,000 for all rights. The man who made the deal was *Life*'s publisher, C. D. Jackson, who said he was so horrified by what he saw that he decided the film must be permanently locked away from public view.[74] It was revealed years later that Jackson, who died in 1964, had been *Time-Life* founder Henry Luce's personal emissary to the CIA— approving specific arrangements to provide CIA employees with *Time-Life* cover.[75]

In its December 6, 1963, issue, *Life* sought to explain away the view of some of the Dallas doctors that a small wound observed in the president's throat was an entrance wound. The *Life* article said: "But the 8mm [Zapruder] film shows the President turning his body far around to the right as he waves to someone in the crowd. His throat is exposed—toward the sniper's nest—just before he clutches it."[76]

That account was patently false, since the film clearly showed that the president had never made such a turn. But, at the time, nobody outside *Time-Life* or the government had seen the film. Only after Jim Garrison won a lawsuit to obtain a copy—which *Time-Life* fought all the way to the U.S. Supreme Court—was the Zapruder movie finally shown at the Clay Shaw trial. It aired for the first time on national TV in 1975.

Robert Groden, who worked for almost nine years studying a bootleg copy he had managed to obtain, discovered that in fact there were ten missing or damaged frames in the film. Certain key moments, which might have proven the existence of more than three shots, had been spliced out.[77]

But a pristine copy of the Zapruder film may still exist. In 1992, Paul Rothermel, Jr., a former chief aide to Dallas oil billionaire H. L. Hunt, told me an incredible story. Rothermel said he was dispatched by the Hunt family, in the late afternoon following the assassination, "with a substantial amount of money, to buy the original. I got the first copy, as far as I know."

"Before *Time-Life* negotiated for theirs?" I asked. "Yeah," Rothermel said.

"Why?" I persisted. "Why did the Hunts so badly want this film?"

"Well," Rothermel replied, "it was pretty hard to believe that, with as little moxie as Oswald had, he did it all by himself. There was a lot of speculation about how all this happened, who was really behind it. I think certain people wanted to find out who did it."[78]

Summary

The terrible day of the assassination is riddled with mysteries. Not least of these is how Oswald came so quickly to the authorities' attention, and the likelihood that Military Intelligence had a hand in alerting the Dallas police. At least two MI officials—James Powell and Colonel William Bishop—were on hand in Dealey Plaza. That night, a military autopsy would be conducted in Washington, and numerous questions remain about its legitimacy.

There is also the matter of the assassination rifle or rifles, as the case may be. In these pages, Frank Ellsworth has revealed for the first time that Oswald's alleged weapon was not found by the sixth-floor window. This raises the question of whether another rifle, perhaps a Mauser, was also discovered by authorities. Yet another Mannlicher-Carcano turned up abandoned the next day in an Indiana hotel room. Nagell has said that its owner, Harry L. Power, was associated with Oswald.

David Ferrie's ex-roommate Raymond Broshears has shed new light on Ferrie's drive to Texas immediately after the acquittal of mobster Carlos Marcello. According to Broshears, Ferrie was scheduled to fly some of the assassins out of the country. Broshears pointed at a Marcello connection, something that attorney Frank Ragano has also revealed in describing the relationships among Marcello, Trafficante, and Hoffa. Jack Ruby was in direct touch with lieutenants of these Mob figures shortly before the assassination.

In assessing the demise of Giancana, Hoffa, and Rosselli in the mid-1970s, we find the Nagell and Angleton views diametrically opposed. Nagell is sure the CIA was behind the deaths; Angleton believed it was the Syndicate itself. As for the two Cuban exiles working directly with Oswald, Nagell has indicated that Leopoldo is dead and Angel (as of 1984) still alive and just released from a Castro jail.

The Soviets and the Cubans—perhaps with considerable "inside" knowledge—began pointing at a right-wing conspiracy immediately after the assassination. And, in the later afternoon of November 22, we now know that the H. L. Hunt family purchased the first copy of the remarkable Zapruder film.

Chapter Twenty-six

Patriot Games: The Hunts and the Assassination

———————◇———————

At a few minutes past noon on November 22, 1963, Haroldson Lafayette Hunt watched the presidential motorcade pass to tumultuous acclaim down Main Street, right below his seventh-floor office in the Mercantile Bank building. Not long after the news bulletins started coming over the radio, someone from the FBI called his office. Because of his prominence as a Kennedy critic, the seventy-four-year-old Hunt was advised, his family might now be facing threats. It would be best if Hunt left town as soon as possible. According to the 1981 biography *Texas Rich,* Hunt initially objected to going into hiding. But another Hunt son, Herbert, and the family's security chief, Paul Rothermel, Jr., were said to have urged him to follow the FBI's dictum. "I believe I can do better going to Washington to help Lyndon," Hunt finally agreed. "He's gonna need some help." Rothermel ordered two plane tickets to the nation's capital for Hunt and his wife, under assumed names.

Hunt biographer Harry Hurt III writes that the oilman and his wife,

Ruth, took a suite at Washington's Mayflower Hotel, where, after a couple of weeks, Hunt tired of his exile "and told the FBI he was returning to Dallas for Christmas. The bureau protested vigorously, but Hunt would not be deterred."[1]

Along with J. Paul Getty, Daniel Ludwig, and Howard Hughes, H. L. Hunt was one of the wealthiest men in the world in 1963. A financial supporter of Senator Joe McCarthy's anti-Communist crusade in the 1950s, Hunt continued to pour about $2 million a year into the *Life Line* radio program. It was his own weekly fifteen-minute ideological "advertisement," broadcast over more than four hundred stations, on which he regularly railed against the Kennedy brothers and "the myth of the indispensable man."[2]

Particularly irksome to Hunt and other Texas oilmen, such as the Murchisons, was JFK's assault on the oil industry's time-honored tax status. At that time, Texas accounted for half of the proven oil reserves on U.S. soil, and six giant companies in Texas controlled 80 percent of it. Government controls had long been in place to maintain artificially high domestic petroleum prices. Then, in October 1962, a law known as the Kennedy Act had removed the distinction between repatriated oil profits and profits reinvested overseas, making both subject to U.S. taxation. In January 1963, the president voiced a plan to reduce the oil depletion allowance—which had long permitted anybody who struck the "black gold" to keep 27.5 percent of the return tax-free. If enacted, *World Petroleum* magazine predicted that Kennedy's reforms might cost the U.S. oil industry as much as $280 million in profits annually.[3]

Hunt called these moves "criminal offenses against the American system. . . . We are losing the right to keep a fair share of the money we earn and a fair share of the profits we make."[4] In October 1963 the president had singled out the Hunts for particular scorn, telling a newspaper columnist that they "paid small amounts in federal income tax last year" and used "various forms of tax exemption and special tax allowances to subsidize the ultraright on television, radio, and in print."[5]

The Warren Commission would find that Nelson Bunker Hunt, one of the patriarch's five sons, had been among "three wealthy businessmen" who financed the full-page, black-bordered anti-Kennedy advertisement that appeared in the *Dallas Morning News* the morning of the assassination. Besides attacking Kennedy's policies in Cuba and Vietnam, the ad accused him of permitting his brother Robert "to go soft on Communists, fellow travelers, and ultraleftists," and raised the specter that the Communist Party, U.S.A., had "praised almost every one of your policies."[6]

More alarming was the Warren Commission's finding that on the day before the assassination, Jack Ruby had driven a young woman over to the Hunt offices for a job interview.[7] After Ruby shot Oswald, Dallas police found two scripts from H. L. Hunt's *Life Line* radio program among his possessions.[8] The FBI also reported that the telephone number of another son, Lamar, appeared "in a book which was the property of Jack Ruby." Questioned about this on December 17, 1963, Lamar replied "that he could not think of any reason why his name would appear in Jack Ruby's personal property and that he had no contact whatsoever with Ruby to the best of his knowledge."[9]

The Warren Commission never bothered to question anyone in the Hunt clan. H. L. Hunt died on November 29, 1974, at age eighty-five, leaving behind a fortune estimated as high as $5 billion.[10] The following summer, an anonymous letter dated August 18, 1975, written in Spanish, and with a Mexico City postmark, arrived in the mailbox of Texas assassination researcher Penn Jones, Jr.

The Oswald Letter

The letter contained an enclosure, a scribbled note dated November 8, 1963, which read:

Dear Mr. Hunt,
I would like information concerding [sic] my position.
I am asking only for information. I am suggesting that we discuss the matter fully before any steps are taken by me or anyone else.
Thank you,
Lee Harvy [sic] Oswald

The typewritten cover letter, translated from the Spanish, described how the sender had provided a copy to FBI director Clarence Kelley late in 1974. The anonymous writer said: "To my understanding it (the Oswald note) could have brought out the circumstances of the assassination of President Kennedy. Since Mr. Kelley hasn't responded to that letter, I've got the right to believe something bad might happen to me, and that is why I see myself obligated to keep myself away for a short time. . . ."

The FBI denied any record of such a delivery to Director Kelley. Researcher Jones tried in vain to correspond back to the Mexico City return address. Then he passed a copy along to Dallas reporter Earl Golz, who sent it over for comment to Paul Rothermel, who in turn passed the letter on to the FBI. (Rothermel had been fired by the Hunts in 1969.) Two FBI agents then came to question Golz, seeking to find out whether the Oswald note was genuine.

The *Dallas Morning News* contracted with three handwriting analysts—two in Texas, one in Canada—"all members," Golz says, "of a national organization of the highest repute." All three experts concluded that the signature was indeed Oswald's. The House Assassinations Committee's handwriting analysts, however, reported that they "were unable to come to any firm conclusion" in 1978. (Oswald, a notoriously poor speller, did misspell the word "concerning" as "concerding" in another of his letters. Comparison with his other known signatures reveals he was also known to have left out the "e" in Harvey.)[11]

In 1983, an FBI document disclosed through a FOIA request showed that the bureau had, in 1977, investigated the Oswald note in terms of its being intended for a Hunt son, Nelson Bunker Hunt. Results of the FBI's investigation have never been made public.[12] Assuming Oswald did write the note to "Mr. Hunt" two weeks prior to the assassination, its purpose remains a mystery.

The Hunts' Own Private Investigation

This much is for certain: The Hunt family maintained an extremely active interest, through 1969, in keeping tabs on what was coming out about the assassination. In fact, they put their own private investigator, Paul Rothermel, on the case. A tall, brown-haired man with square features, Rothermel had gone to work as Hunt's security chief after leaving the FBI in 1957. He was one of about half a dozen ex-FBI agents on the oilman's staff—and was well wired not only into the FBI, but into the CIA and the Dallas police as well.[13]

In 1976 I came into possession of a series of nearly one hundred largely typewritten memorandums written by Rothermel to Hunt and his sons between November 4, 1963, and September 29, 1969. These memos concerned Rothermel's ongoing probe, on behalf of the family, into the assassination. While there was nothing among the memos that incriminated the Hunts, they provided considerable insight into the Hunts' concerns—and wide-ranging network.

The first memo, which the Hunts were said to have rushed around gathering up after the assassination, was dated November 4, 1963. Under the heading *"POLITICS,"* it concerned JFK's upcoming trip to Dallas and "unconfirmed reports of possible violence during the parade. The F.B.I. and Police Department each have planted an informant in the General Walker group here in Dallas. . . ." The memo went on to describe a possibility that a left-wing group might start an incident and seek to drag the right wing into it. "If an incident were to occur," the memo concluded, "the true story of who perpetrated it would never come out."

The next memo was dated January 3, 1964: "The FBI has instructed its agents not to discuss the Oswald-Ruby case, even among themselves, as there has been a leak of some information which has caused embarrassment to the Bureau."

February 6, 1964: "Lyndon B. Johnson is mortally afraid of being assassinated and does not trust the Secret Service to protect him. He has ordered the FBI to be present everywhere he goes with no less than two men and more when there is any possibility that he will be exposed. Johnson has confidentially placed a direct telephone line from his office to J. Edgar Hoover's desk."

A February 10, 1964, memo provided information about a planned invasion of Cuba, backed by the CIA and headed by the "extremely left-wing" Manuel Ray group. The plans, Rothermel wrote, were being "closely scrutinized by John Martino." The reader may recall that the visit of Angel, Leopoldo, and "Leon Oswald" at Sylvia Odio's door sought to identify the trio with Manuel Ray's JURE organization. Also, that John Martino was the CIA contract agent/organized-crime associate who later described to businessman Fred Claasen how Oswald was set up by the anti-Castro Cubans. Apparently, according to the memo, the Hunt organization was already aware of both Ray and Martino.

A February 21, 1964, memo reported Dallas sheriff Bill Decker's having "cooperatively indicated that there was nothing to the story that any prisoners had seen the Kennedy assassin or assassins." The Dallas County Jail was directly across the street from the Texas School Book Depository. "The only possibility," the memo concluded, "is one Trustee who has since been talked to several times by both the Sheriff's office and FBI agent, Wallace Hietman. The Trustee was not in that part of the jail at the time where he could see anything."

Undated, 1964: ". . . A rifle with a silencer has been found. There is no information which would indicate that this is so, but it is still being checked. . . ."

On May 18, 1964, it was noted that Nelson Bunker Hunt had been interviewed by the FBI about the black-bordered ad. But after the Warren Commission Report was released in September 1964, the memos ceased until Jim Garrison's investigation in New Orleans heated up in 1967.

Rothermel's memos on the Garrison period reveal the Hunt family's persistent concerns that the New Orleans DA might link them to the assassination. They also reveal how the Hunts moved to head off the effort.

The first warning from Rothermel came on October 16, 1967, when he wrote to H. L. Hunt: "I have information to the effect that Garrison is

referring to either you or Bunker as the wealthy oil man in his probe."
Then: "On 12-6-67 I warned Mr. Hunt about the possible consequences of
going into New Orleans. I suggested he might either be arrested or subpoenaed. On the basis of my discussion he called McConnell with [Louisi-
ana Senator Russell] Long's office."

January 26, 1968: "JIM GARRISON: We have extended our cooperation to Garrison in his probe hoping to help guide his investigation. . . ."

April 3, 1968: "GARRISON PROBE: A C.I.A. agent in Houston, Texas
has indicated that an effort is being made to have a lunacy hearing on Jim
Garrison, the New Orleans District Attorney. The informant said he did
not know who would push the lunacy charges but that the C.I.A. seems
concerned enough to be behind the movement."

April 4, 1968: "THE GARRISON PROBE: Bill Wood, former CIA
man and investigator for Jim Garrison, came to see me today. He said that
he had heard that I was incensed with him for having made investigations
which tended to indicate that he Wood was checking on Mr. Hunt as
involved in the assassination. . . . Wood was here with hat in hand to try
to explain that Garrison was in no way concerned with H. L. Hunt and
that Garrison further wanted my personal cooperation as I had given
valuable information to him in the past. He said that Garrison will prove
that the assassination was a plot by officials in the Federal Government
and consisted of CIA, Secret Service, FBI, and one or two military men.
. . . he hoped that we realized that Garrison had to come forward with
statements which would bring him both leads for investigation and throw
off the CIA which was trying to thwart his investigation. . . ."

December 16, 1968: *"JIM GARRISON INVESTIGATION:* Garrison
has, over the weekend fired William Wood (also known as William
Boxley), on the grounds of Boxley being a CIA agent. I am told that
Boxley's theory is that H. L. Hunt was the key man in the assassination of
President Kennedy, and that he has others underneath Mr. Hunt on a
chart. I am making efforts to get this chart. . . . We have over the years
cooperated with Garrison in every way and, of course Garrison's investigators, including William Boxley, had full access to the information we provided. I am reassured by Garrison's staff that he has no intention of embarrassing Mr. Hunt. . . ."

There followed letters from Rothermel to J. Gordon Shanklin, special
agent in charge of the Dallas FBI, and to U.S. Congressman Earle Cabell,
who had been the mayor of Dallas when the assassination occurred.[14] To
both of them, Rothermel enclosed Garrison's chart of suspects (including
Shanklin himself). Cabell replied on January 10, 1969, assuring Rothermel
"that contents will be kept confidential" and adding that he "would be
interested in knowing of any further developments on this."

Shortly after this exchange, the memos describe how Garrison's former investigator Bill Wood had come around to explain the chart. Wood insisted "that he was not antagonistic toward Mr. Hunt" and "was broke and needed a job." Rothermel recommended two people "who might need some private detective work done."

The memos go on to describe interchanges with or about several other people who had come under scrutiny by private assassination researchers. One was Carlos Bringuier, the Cuban exile who headed New Orleans' DRE delegation and engaged Oswald in the August 1963 street scuffle. Bringuier wrote to H. L. Hunt on January 28, 1969, looking for some financial assistance to help publish his book on the assassination, *Red Friday*.

Two others were fellow Texas oilmen. On February 12, 1969, Rothermel wrote of Bill Wood's having informed him about "a big leak in the oil fraternity. . . . He said it was the wife of a well-known oil man who maintained an apartment in Paris, France. While he did not identify this woman, I asked him if Houston was the correct identity of the oil man's residence, and he indicated that it was. By process of elimination, it would appear that this might be John Mecom." Mecom, a friend of George de Mohrenschildt, also had close ties to the Hunts.

The last piece in the file was a September 29, 1969, letter from Rothermel to Clint Murchison at Dallas's First National Bank building. It read: "I am enclosing a copy of a letter with an attached page, which I obtained from a source of information, who desires to remain anonymous. I have other material which may or may not be of interest to you. I doubt that anything further will ever come up on the Kennedy assassination, but I did want to send this to you for your evaluation. As a former F.B.I. agent, I run into this type of material, but do not consider it to be of much consequence." A copy of whatever Rothermel sent to Murchison was not included in the file.

Not too long after Garrison's celebrated case against Clay Shaw bit the dust in 1969, Rothermel's onslaught of memos to the Hunt clan also ceased. Garrison never did make any accusations against the Hunts.

The Hunts and Eugene Hale Brading

By the summer of 1969, the Hunts were worried about the efforts of another investigator besides Garrison: attorney Bernard Fensterwald, Jr. The family's files include a letter from Rothermel to Lieutenant George Butler of the Dallas police—who had known Jack Ruby for many years, defended Ruby against charges of involvement with the Mob, and was part of the basement security operation just before Ruby shot Oswald.[15]

On June 2, 1969, Rothermel wrote Butler: "I do greatly appreciate your sending me the Bernard Fensterwald material which I found highly enlightening and amusing. . . ." Attached to the correspondence was Butler's note to Rothermel: "Subject has been in town several days. He talked to me twice and finally gave up. . . . For your files." Butler had enclosed Fensterwald's curriculum vitae, and a list of all affiliates of his private Committee to Investigate Assassinations.

The Hunts appeared particularly concerned about Fensterwald's inquiries in Dallas into one of their former associates. On July 10, 1969, Rothermel's memo noted: "James Braden was arrested on the day of the assassination. He was on parole from the State of California. He had been in both prior to and after the assassination to see us on an oil deal. . . . It may be that Fensterwald is going to write a new book, pointing the finger at the Hunts."

"James Braden" was actually an alias for Eugene Hale Brading. Within minutes after the assassination, he had been among a dozen or so people rounded up for questioning, after the police found him having taken an elevator to the ground floor of the Dal-Tex Building, across the street from the book depository. He said he had gone inside to try to make a phone call on the third floor, and that he was in the oil business in Beverly Hills.[16] The police soon released "Jim Braden," unaware that he had a rap sheet listing thirty-three arrests under his real name of Brading—and a long history of associates in the criminal underworld.[17] Indeed, Los Angeles TV newsman Peter Noyes devoted a large portion of his 1973 book *Legacy of Doubt* to Brading. Besides Brading's sudden interest in oil speculation in Louisiana and Texas during the fall of 1963, Noyes discovered that Brading had worked a few feet away from David Ferrie's office that October in New Orleans' Père Marquette Building.[18]

On November 21, 1963, Brading had checked in with a Dallas probation officer, provided his real name, and "advised that he planned to see Lamar Hunt and other oil speculators while here." Later, Brading would deny to the FBI having gone to the Hunt offices, saying that one of his California traveling companions went instead. But Rothermel told author Noyes that he was sure Brading had indeed dropped in. The visitors' log for that day showed that three other men "and friend" visited both Lamar and Nelson Bunker Hunt. While in Dallas, Brading was staying at the Cabana Motel—where Jack Ruby also visited late on the night of November 21. Brading also told the FBI that he departed Dallas for Houston right after his brief time in custody on November 22. Records checked by the authorities, however, did not show him arriving in Houston until four days later.[19] Hence the Hunt internal memo that Brading had come in "both prior to and after the assassination" appears to have validity.

The Hunt-Willoughby Letters

When I first came upon the Hunt memos, I thought that there might well be some innocent explanation for all this. It was not illogical that the Hunts, in their concern about being linked to a right-wing conspiracy, would want to keep up with any ongoing investigations. Still, their remarkable intelligence-gathering apparatus and connections to the power center —along with the "coincidences" of Ruby and organized-crime associate Brading visiting the Hunt offices just before November 22, 1963—troubled me even in 1975. My suspicions were not allayed by the surfacing of the Oswald letter to "Dear Mr. Hunt."

Then, as I was putting this book together, I received copies of extensive correspondence between Charles Willoughby and the Hunt family from the Douglas MacArthur Archive in Norfolk, Virginia. I already knew that H. L. Hunt and Willoughby went way back. Hunt's former chief assistant, John Curington, had told me: "Mr. Hunt and I lived in New York one time for several months, at the same time General MacArthur was staying at the Waldorf-Astoria. As such, Mr. Hunt knew a lot of his top generals— Albert Wedemeyer, Courtney Whitney, Charles Willoughby; several people from whom we had access to their information and data."

By mid-1966, Willoughby had gone to work directly for Nelson Bunker Hunt, in helping arrange the acquisition of offshore oil rights in the Portuguese colony of Mozambique. Getting along in years, Willoughby was also looking to have Nelson take over major responsibility for his International Committee for the Defense of Christian Culture (ICDCC). As Nelson Bunker Hunt wrote to Willoughby on November 28, 1966: "It seems, as of course you told me was the case, that the COMITÉ does make available a lot of avenues which otherwise are difficult." On December 4, 1966, Willoughby responded that he was sending along enclosures concerning "the 'master plan' centering control of *Comité* affairs in Dallas."

Then, in 1967, the Hunt empire seemed potentially threatened by looming disclosures in the Garrison investigation. That September, Willoughby wrote to the Hunts: "My Comité sources fortunately can offer a sensational intelligence that will relieve Dallas. My study on it is entitles [sic]: 'Murder to Order: Stashinsky and Oswald.' You know my work and my connections. That is what the Dallas Comité could do for its hometown and to the image of N. B. Hunt in defense of a cruel historical hoax. . . . Details by mail."

Willoughby's reference was to a matter that certain right-wing circles had first seized on some years earlier as a prime example of Soviet skulduggery. This was the apparent confession of a Soviet defector, Bogdan Stashinsky, that he had personally murdered two Ukrainian émigré leaders on behalf of the Soviet MVD secret police. "There is no difference between Stashinsky and Oswald," Willoughby also wrote to H. L. Hunt, ". . . in an obvious parallel of training and planning and direction." And, in yet another memo: "The similarity with the Oswald case is irresistible. . . . The case should be widely publicized to remove the leftist smear on Dallas. . . . I recommend patriotic residents of Dallas to handle this project under your leadership."[20]

The Stashinsky case is indeed extremely interesting as it might relate to Oswald—but not for the reasons that Willoughby described. On October 15, 1959—the very day that Oswald arrived in the USSR—Stepan Bandera was found dead in his Munich apartment. During World War II, Bandera had collaborated with the Nazis as a leader of the Ukrainian Nightingales. Afterward, he continued to work with two of Willoughby's closest European associates among the international right wing, Jaroslaw Stetzko and Theodor Oberlander. Hundreds of Bandera-Stetzko followers had been recruited by U.S. Military Intelligence and the CIA in the late 1940s to assist in fighting the Cold War in Europe against the Soviets.[21]

The initial press speculation in Eastern Europe was that Bandera's murder had been ordered by Oberlander himself, who reportedly feared that Bandera was about to provide information to West German authorities then probing Oberlander's Nazi past. In fact, not long after Bandera's death, Oberlander was dismissed in 1960 from his seven-year-long position as West Germany's minister of refugee affairs—when his Nazi ties became public knowledge.[22]

Then, in August 1961, Bogdan Stashinsky defected to the Americans in West Berlin, bearing news that it was he who killed exiled Ukrainian publisher Lev Rebet in 1957, and then Stepan Bandera in 1959, with the same weapon.[23] The CIA described the weapon, in a report provided to the Warren Commission on Soviet Use of Assassination and Kidnapping, as "a gun which fired vaporized poison which killed almost instantly upon being inhaled. The properties of the killing agent were such that, until the defection of the assassin, both victims were officially believed to have died from heart attacks."[24]

There was something strange from the beginning about Stashinsky's "defection." American authorities had doubts about his veracity and, when his case was turned over to West German criminal investigators, they at first believed the whole Stashinsky story to be fictitious.[25] But right-wing extremists—such as Willoughby and his Ukrainian-American friend Lev Dobriansky—seized upon Stashinsky's alleged confession as a means of opposing any rapprochement between the United States and the Soviet Union.[26]

As we saw in Chapter Ten, it was Spas T. Raikin, an affiliate of Bandera's Ukrainian émigré underground, who first greeted Lee and Marina Oswald on their return from the USSR in June 1962. They were coming home from Minsk, in the heart of Soviet Belorussia (now Belorus). There, Oswald had recorded in his diary that his monthly subsidy had been provided by the Soviets' internal security network, the MVD.[27] There, too, Marina's uncle Ilya Prusakov was an official with the MVD (see Chapter Eight). And, when Bogdan Stashinsky went on trial in Karlsruhe, West Germany, he would take pains to implicate the MVD in his activities.

The seven-day trial took place in October 1962, just when the Cuban Missile Crisis was coming to a crescendo and when Oswald moved alone to Dallas. Traveling to West Germany to be the attorney for Stepan Bandera's widow was Charles Kersten, a former Republican member of the U.S. House of Representatives, from Wisconsin, and then America's chief member of the World Anti-Communist Steering Committee.

In his summation, Kersten noted that "this trial has clearly demonstrated that practically any nation of the free world can be the hunting ground of the KGB. . . . It is the Council of Ministers of the Soviet Union which has been found guilty of murder in this case. It is true that this court cannot impose the sentence which the real criminal should receive, but it can pronounce an historical judgment in declaring the Soviet government guilty of the murder."[28]

The presiding judge, a Dr. Jagusch, reiterated Stashinsky's description of how the Soviet intelligence had won him over as an "easily influenced young person . . . a man who has first been indoctrinated with the propaganda of hate and is then degraded to having to commit murder." From a spy against Ukrainian underground groups, Stashinsky was said to have turned into an assassin. But because "Stashinsky's frank confession has helped to uncover and lay bare the criminal methods of the political struggle," the judge meted out only an eight-year prison sentence.[29]

A year went by. In October 1963, Willoughby, Oberlander, and other International Comité members met for an annual conference in Switzerland (see Chapter Twenty-three). Very soon after that, Charles Kersten, the ex-congressman and Bandera's widow's lawyer, wrote a letter to JFK. "Fifteen days before he was shot down," reported Washington-based columnists Robert S. Allen and Paul Scott in the *Philadelphia Daily News* of November 26, 1963, "President Kennedy was warned that assassins were being trained in Russia to commit murders in the U.S. and England. . . .

The burden of Kersten's letter was an effort to obtain Administration help in focusing public attention on the assassination of Stepan Bandera, the Ukrainian underground leader, by Communist agents."

The Allen-Scott column went on to cite Kersten's concerns that a hearing then being sought by the Senate Internal Security Subcommittee into the Stashinsky-Bandera affair had been delayed by the Kennedy State Department. "It was a bizarre assassination," Kersten was quoted as having written the president, "illustrating the subversive operations of the Soviet police in the free world."[30]

After the Kennedy assassination, the *Ukrainian Bulletin* was the first to try to draw a parallel between Stashinsky and Oswald, speculating in January 1964 that both had been trained at the same "Department 13" school for assassins.[31] And, in Willoughby's attempts to give the Hunts solid ground to stand on against Garrison's potential accusations, it was the former general's friends—the "sophisticated" Europeans—who "have refused to accept the juridical whitewash of the Oswald case."[32] Specifically, he was referring to ex-Nazi Oberlander's émigré network.

All of this could perhaps be dismissed as an expected propaganda attempt by the right wing to link Oswald with a Soviet-inspired plot. But given the revelations that Paul Rothermel, Jr., began to offer in the mid-1970s, I came to believe that the Willoughby-Hunt correspondence—and the whole Bandera-Stashinsky affair—had a much deeper meaning than that.

The Hunt Security Man

In 1975, right around the time that the Oswald note to "Dear Mr. Hunt" showed up in researcher Penn Jones's mailbox, a most unusual wiretapping case was unfolding in Texas. Its genesis went back to 1969, just as Paul Rothermel wound up his role as the family's information-gatherer on the assassination. That was when several of the Hunt sons alerted their octogenarian father that they suspected Rothermel and John Curington of embezzling funds from the family's food business. H.L. refused to believe that his two most trusted associates would do such a thing. Nelson, Tom, and Herbert Hunt then went around the old man, hiring a private detective agency to look into the matter. Learning about this, Rothermel and Curington both resigned from the Hunt Oil Company on November 14, 1969. Two months later, a pair of Hunt gumshoes were caught with wiretapping and electronic surveillance equipment outside Rothermel's home in a Dallas suburb.[33]

Later, Bunker Hunt would testify at his trial that he simply didn't know such wiretapping was illegal.[34] Rothermel charged that the bugging effort was not really aimed at uncovering his suspected embezzling but rather because he had been "lobbying" with H.L. to leave control of Hunt Oil to the children of his second wife—cutting Bunker, Herbert, and Lamar out of that picture.[35] (This seemed plausible, since the Hunt empire was divided into eleven separate fortunes by two marriages, and the rival siblings had been jockeying for position for many years.)

After H.L. died in 1974, the scandal mushroomed. In July 1975, when Bunker and Herbert Hunt were indicted for obstructing the government's wiretap investigation, they suddenly charged that the CIA had infiltrated the family oil empire with "secret agents" who embezzled over $50 million from them. Strongly hinting that Rothermel was one such spy, the brothers said their refusal to allow the CIA to use Hunt Oil overseas as an espionage front had led to the wiretap charges against them.[36]

Coincidentally, perhaps, less than a month later came the Oswald note out of Mexico City. It had yet to surface when the Hunt brothers went on trial in Lubbock, Texas, in mid-September 1975. In a surprise move, the government announced it would not call either Rothermel or Curington to the stand. One CIA memo, dated December 1965, surfaced at the trial. The memo was about asking Bunker Hunt whether his Middle Eastern oil operation might be used as a cover. It noted that the agency had "had good cooperation . . . on our routine requests but have no way of judging possible reaction to operational requests. Our estimate is that we see no reason we should not make a cautious approach." The CIA declined to let the family see nearly all of the twelve items it said were in its Bunker Hunt file, since this would imperil "intelligence sources and methods."[37]

After three years of rumors about payoffs to politicians and a bargain with the Nixon Justice Department,[38] the Hunt brothers were acquitted after a two-week trial. Bunker cockily told the press that their success was based simply on having the financial means to hire the legal talent and investigation needed to offset the government's case.[39] The Hunts then pretty much dropped from notoriety—until 1988, when a federal jury in New York ruled that Bunker and Herbert had conspired in a racketeering scheme to corner the world silver market in 1979–80. The Hunts, ordered to pay $130 million in damages, soon filed for bankruptcy.[40]

Long before the Hunts got their comeuppance, I had wondered whether the wiretaps on Rothermel might have been about more than embezzling or a family feud over H.L.'s will. Rothermel knew plenty about particularly Nelson Bunker's affinity for right-wing causes, which was said to have been far more active than his father's propagandizing.

In 1976 I received access to a file that had been sent to Fensterwald's Committee to Investigate Assassinations. It was titled "AVG (American

Volunteer Group)."[41] Although it was undated and unsigned, I knew it
had been prepared by newsman Peter Noyes in pursuing his investigation
of Eugene Hale Brading, alias "Jim Braden"—the fellow taken in for
questioning on the day of the assassination. Through the California attorney general's office, Noyes had uncovered that Brading apparently worked
for Bunker Hunt—and had helped establish a secret, paramilitary organization called the AVG on the West Coast.[42]

Noyes recounted in the AVG file that after writing Rothermel, he,
Noyes, had received a collect call from the ex-Hunt security man on August 19, 1970.

> He said he was calling me from a phone booth because he was frightened
> for his life and said he had to be extremely careful. Rothermel seemed
> astounded that I should know about AVG. He said some years ago, when
> he was in Nelson Hunt's confidence, a most unusual conversation took
> place. He said Nelson announced his intention of forming a group known
> as AVG and intended to draw on the ranks of General Edwin Walker's
> cell of the John Birch Society in Dallas.
>
> Rothermel said Nelson's plans sounded bizarre. He said Nelson
> planned to form a para-military group for political purposes, and hoped
> to obtain a certain type of gas gun from Europe which would kill people
> and make their deaths appear to be heart attacks. . . . He said that
> Nelson proceeded with his plans to set up AVG and bought a ranch
> through a real estate broker. . . . He also said Nelson Hunt had set up a
> similar organization in Europe known as Der Burd and that it had taken
> several assignments from the CIA. . . .

The "gas gun" being described was the same type of weapon that was
allegedly used by Stashinsky in his murders of Rebet and Bandera for the
Soviet MVD. And "Der Burd" ("The Bird") appeared to be a derivation
of "Nightingale"—the European émigré group used by U.S. intelligence
and Charles Willoughby, and "whose cohesiveness was greatly enhanced
by the financial support they got from a multimillionaire American who
was involved in a one-man crusade against the 'evils of communism' " (see
Chapter Ten). It was the group of Russian émigrés in Dallas, largely of
similar outlook, who had first taken the Oswalds under their wing in the
summer of 1962.

Rothermel had gone into private law practice in Dallas when he agreed
to see me for an interview in July 1976. He refused to comment on the
Hunts' possible subsidizing of refugee groups at home and abroad. "I am
presently reassessing my position," he said, "whether or not, under the
circumstances, it is in the public interest for me to remain silent."

"What about Bunker Hunt looking into how to obtain a certain gas gun from Europe?" I asked, telling Rothermel that I had seen a researcher's memo about this.

"That information is maybe out of context," Rothermel said. "There was an article that appeared in 1960, in a magazine published in Europe, that showed the Russians used a gas gun to assassinate a Ukrainian leader. The Hunts were familiar with the fact that the Communists had developed such a weapon. There were papers about it circulated among the top echelon of Hunt Oil."

"What about the American Volunteer Group, or AVG?"

"I've always said that all such groups that advocate violence have no place in our society," Rothermel replied carefully. Was Bunker Hunt involved with it? "I don't know that to be a fact. I'd believe Pete Noyes, whatever was said about it."

I brought up the name of Eugene Hale Brading. "I truthfully do not know what his connection in Dallas really was."

"Did he work for the Hunts in California?"

"I've heard that."

Then I asked why the Hunts spent so much time having Rothermel look into the Kennedy assassination. "While I was privy to a great deal of highly confidential information and in on most of the thoughts of those people, I cannot speculate why so much time was spent on it. I was trying to sell Mr. Garrison on the idea that the assassination was concocted by leftist Cubans. Other investigation was planted to convince Mr. Garrison that the people I was associated with had nothing to do with the assassination. I was trying to snow Mr. Garrison. Al Hill [H. L. Hunt's son-in-law] told me once that it was imperative Garrison not get the idea that anybody of our family and friends had anything to do with the Kennedy assassination. I presume he said that in good faith."

Of Oswald and a Hunt connection, Rothermel said: "I don't recall anybody I met of the description of Oswald being up there."

Then Rothermel volunteered what he knew about Jack Ruby. "I was told within an hour after the execution of Oswald by Ruby that he was a PCI [potential criminal informant] of the FBI. I was told a file was destroyed, and told the name of the agent who developed him as a PCI, who received a letter of reprimand and was told never to divulge this."

It was not until 1992, when I recontacted Rothermel by telephone, that he told me about having purchased the first copy of the Zapruder film.

The Reminiscences of John Curington

In May 1992 I also managed to track down H. L. Hunt's former chief aide, John Wesley Curington, in a small town in Texas. Now sixty-four and retired, Curington was a young attorney when he first went to work for Hunt Oil in 1955. Between 1960 and when he was forced out by the sons at the end of the decade, he had worked directly for the family patriarch. As Hunt biographer Harry Hurt III writes: "By his own account, the things Curington did for Hunt ranged from running HLH Products (the 'food division') to covering up tax-evasion schemes, collecting gambling debts . . . and carrying out covert political operations."[43]

The remarkable telephone interview that I had with Curington must, I realize, be seen in the context of a disaffected former employee. The same must be said of Rothermel, although his memorandums verify the Hunts' ongoing fascination with the assassination. But long after the dust had settled over the internal brouhaha between the Hunts and their chief employees, I saw no particular motive for Rothermel or Curington to be making anything up. Indeed, both men remained extremely careful about offering any sinister tinge to their recollections. And Curington's memories proved even more startling than Rothermel's, leading to questions that only a legitimate official investigation might yet answer.

Curington remembered: "About five-thirty or six o'clock on the Saturday afternoon after the assassination [November 23, 1963], Mr. [H. L.] Hunt called me and asked that I go down and see what kind of security they had surrounding Oswald in police custody. I had no more than hung up the phone when a lady called who did ironing for my family. She said her husband was in jail on a DWI charge and asked if I could go down and get him out. I jumped at the opportunity, because that gave me a respectable reason for being at the jailhouse.

"So, on that particular night, I went in and out of the Dallas County Jail on three separate occasions. I had my briefcase with me, and at no time was I ever stopped or asked any questions. On one of these trips I got on the elevator—the prison was up on the third floor, I believe—and the old homicide captain, Will Fritz, got on with Oswald. I had known Fritz. All he said was, 'Meet the blankety-blank who shot the president.' We rode on up, Fritz, Oswald, and myself. Then I got my laundress's husband out of jail.

"Mr. Hunt had told me, regardless of what time it was, to come by the house and tell him what I witnessed. It was a little bit after midnight when

I reported to him that, in my opinion, there was no security whatsoever around the jailhouse. A lot of newspeople, but nobody too concerned with security. We did not discuss the merits of this, and I left."

My mind raced back to another of Richard Nagell's cryptic pieces of "trivia" sent to Arthur Greenstein: "Was Lee Harvey Oswald silenced by the KGB, the CIA, the Dallas PD, H. L. Hunt enterprises, or a weirdo named Jack Ruby acting on his own volition?"

Curington went on to relate the story recounted in Chapter Thirteen, that he had "run across Oswald" before the assassination—when General Walker mentioned Oswald's name in connection with the sniping incident against him.

It was shortly after Curington made his report to H. L. Hunt about the poor security at the jail, he said, that the oilman left Dallas for Washington. Curington confirmed that the Hunts had stayed for a while at the Mayflower Hotel, "but he wasn't gone a full month there." Curington believed that Hunt had returned in less than a week, for, on what he recalls as "probably the Saturday morning a week after the assassination, about ten-thirty or eleven, Mr. Hunt asked me to go downstairs and stay in the lobby. We were at that time officed in the Mercantile Bank building downtown, and also had offices in the adjoining Mercantile Securities building. There was a common door between them, which required a passkey to go through.

"Mr. Hunt asked me first to secure the door between the two buildings, then stay in the lobby and not let any Hunt employee come up to the seventh floor, where our offices were, which in itself seemed a little unusual of a request. I hung around there for fifteen or twenty minutes and nobody came in or out. Mr. Hunt said he would come down and get me, when he got through with what he was doing. Then the elevator door opened up and Marina Oswald stepped off. I recognized her from the photos on TV and in the newspapers. I hadn't seen her go up.

"I followed Marina to the exit of the building there. She got into an unmarked car and I took the license number, and had it run through the Dallas police. Turned out the car was registered to the FBI. I never asked Mr. Hunt whether he had seen Marina. He was difficult to work with and for, most people did not have a longevity with him, but I survived almost twenty years without cross-examining him on anything."[44]

In June 1992, I spoke with Marina—remarried to Kevin Porter and still living in Dallas—by phone. "I was taken to somebody's office, but I have no idea what I went there for. I don't think it was the FBI that took me. Yes, it is very possible I went to see the oil millionaire, but I can't remember the face. Everything is so vague about that time. I was a walking zombie. I just know that all the different agencies were fighting with each other. What it was all about, I don't know.

"There has been a lot of misinformation poured out for people to look in different directions," Marina continued. "Both Lee and I were put through the sifter, and it is time for people to look in different directions. I don't really care who did it. I just want Lee to be exonerated if he is not the guilty party."

She added that in the years since, she had come to "assume" that her late husband had some connection to the CIA. "I see history unravel in front of me," Marina added with a tangible sadness in her voice. And she believed that there had never been a legitimate investigation by or into "the real government, which is faceless."[45]

Curington's Context

"Very few people have ever put all this into proper perspective," John Curington was saying. "To do that, you have to go back before 1960. Lyndon Johnson wanted to be president, and [House Speaker] Sam Rayburn [from Texas] wanted him to be, and at that time he [Rayburn] was the most powerful man in Congress. Rayburn and LBJ thought they were strong enough, because political climates and conventions back in the '60s were run different than today; the press dictates who gets elected now.

"Mr. Hunt and I went to the [1960 Democratic] Convention in L.A. Up to within ten days of the nomination, nobody on earth could have convinced LBJ he wasn't gonna get it. But I had enough information and knowledge that I concluded, if he ever wanted to be president, he had to take the second spot. So Mr. Hunt and I started a campaign, we went to Lyndon and outlined this. One of Mr. Hunt's selling points to Johnson was, he had to take a calculated risk that Kennedy would not be nominated in '64 and that would give him the opportunity to be president.

"Jack and Bobby Kennedy hated LBJ. We went to Bobby first, who said he wouldn't have that blankety-blank on the second spot under any consideration. Jack didn't want him either. Finally, we went to Joe [the Kennedys' father], and he had enough gumption to know they needed LBJ on the ticket because he was from the right geographical area, the South.

"Then in '64, they were not gonna keep Johnson on. Bobby Baker was LBJ's bagman there with the Senate, and common sense will tell you, they were going to indict Baker, causing sufficient embarrassment for LBJ to be dropped. With that premise in mind, the only way Lyndon gets to be president is if something happened to John F. Kennedy.

"Lyndon did not talk to H.L. immediately after the assassination, but I have reason to believe they did communicate on it there."

Somewhere around this time, Curington said, the Hunt family hired Booth Mooney, a longtime administrative assistant for LBJ. "He was directly on our payroll, but always maintained a close personal relationship with Lyndon. In this way we were able to have memos or anything hand-carried to Lyndon, or talk to him anytime we wanted.

"We maintained a very active file on the assassination, and had people in Washington that were giving us reports. Jim Garrison was later a visitor to our office, and did avail himself of the various files we had available."

Curington said Hunt also knew J. Edgar Hoover. He had been in Hunt's presence at meetings with Hoover in several locations during the early 1960s.

Then I brought up the Oswald note to "Dear Mr. Hunt." Curington said he could "only make a theory on it. There's no question in my mind that Oswald had been stalking Kennedy for a long time, if our information was correct. And I think the climate was such at that time that all the Hunts were pretty well known for their political philosophies and vocal that they didn't like Kennedy as president. Yes, I do think Oswald wrote that letter and, yes, to Mr. Hunt. But I think that was only a cover-up, or a letter he would have used should he have ever gone to a defense posture in the courts there. In my opinion, it would just have been a self-serving letter."

Curington added that he knew of no relationship between the Hunts and George de Mohrenschildt or any Cuban exiles. The latter was not quite accurate. In 1968, H. L. Hunt's name came up in a conversation tape-recorded by FBI informant Ricardo Morales and an exile terrorist named Orlando Bosch. It was in the context of a Miami court case, where nine exiles had been charged with conspiring to bomb the ships of nations trading with Cuba. Asked about this by the *Fort Worth Star-Telegram*, Hunt replied that he had had no contact with the Cuban exiles "in years."[46]

I had heard from another source that Nelson Bunker Hunt might have kept a list of undesirable politicians, and when I asked about this, Curington's response was frightening. "I called it a kill squad. Bunker had a program where there were certain leaders he thought should be gotten rid of. One was Sukarno of Indonesia, Juan Bosch of Santo Domingo, and a few of those real left-wing liberal senators—[J. William] Fulbright out of Arkansas, [Jacob] Javits from New York. Castro would have fit into the same category. Those kind of people you cannot vote out of office, so the only way is to remove them from existing there. Well, Bunker might have talked a good game, but I don't think he would ever have actually done anything like that."

What about something called the American Volunteer Group? "Well, training operations," Curington said. "I saw certain checks and moneys going out, into the California area. In the early '60s, yeah."[47]

To Curington's knowledge, the Hunt family did no oil business in Mexico but was well connected to business interests in New Orleans—including Carlos Marcello.

At the end of our conversation, I mentioned the name of Richard Nagell. "The name rings a bell. I cannot pinpoint any specific remembrance of him." I told Curington about what happened at the El Paso bank. "I recall the shooting incident, but really nothing else on it."

When I began looking into the Willoughby-Hunt connection, I called both Curington and Rothermel back. Both former Hunt employees were aware that members of the family knew Willoughby, but could offer little more.

In 1968, Willoughby had left Washington and moved with his wife, the former Marie Antoinette Becker, to Naples, Florida. His mentor, Douglas MacArthur, had died not long after the Kennedy assassination, on April 5, 1964. And, in August 1972, Willoughby sent Nelson Bunker Hunt his piece of MacArthur's legacy. It was Willoughby's own twenty-one-volume *Intelligence Series* on the MacArthur era. The MacArthur Archive was not even aware that this many volumes existed, until it came across the thank-you letter from Hunt among the Willoughby papers.

On October 25, 1972, William J. Sebald, political adviser to MacArthur during the occupation of Japan and who lived next door to the eighty-year-old Willoughby in Florida, wrote a letter to Nelson Bunker Hunt. It said:

"I am writing to convey to you the sad news that our good friend General Willoughby passed away this morning. His end was peaceful and he simply died in his sleep, after his lengthy illness during the past four months. . . . I would be most appreciative if you would be good enough to convey the above information to your father of whom General Willoughby often spoke in the most friendly terms."[48]

Corroboration from LBJ's Mistress

As I was completing the manuscript of this book, it was suggested that I get in touch with Madeleine Brown. Between 1948 and 1969, Brown maintains that she was a mistress of Lyndon B. Johnson. LBJ's handwriting on numerous letters to Brown has been verified by analysts, and today it is generally accepted that her son Steven, who died of cancer in 1990, was a son of the former president.[49]

Brown, today sixty-seven, came from a wealthy Dallas family, the Duncans, which made its money in real estate and ranching. Today, she looks back on her relationship with LBJ, whom she met at a hotel party celebrating his election to the Senate, as "a Texas romance." She decided to go public with what Johnson once imparted to her about the Kennedy assassination because, Brown told me on August 4, 1992, "I felt the world needs to know the truth and how Texas oil money has controlled Washington."

Before the assassination, according to Brown, "Lyndon told me that the Kennedys would never embarrass him again. It was not a threat, but a promise." Then, as 1963 passed into history, they were together at a New Year's Eve party. "I said, Lyndon, I've got to have my mind put at ease," Brown remembers. "People are saying you are responsible for the assassination, and I've got to know. Well, he had a terrible temper tantrum, as he often did. Then he told me: It was the oil people and the CIA."

Brown already knew the H. L. Hunts socially, as well as in her professional capacity with Dallas's Glenn advertising agency. "Mr. Hunt and I parked our cars in the same lot," she said, "and three days before the assassination, H.L. called me over and said he wanted to give me something. It was that 'Wanted for Treason' poster with Kennedy's face on it, which got circulated all over Dallas. I said, 'H.L., you're gonna get in trouble.' And he said, 'I'm the richest man in the world and nobody's going to do anything to me.'

"I knew John Curington and Paul Rothermel," Brown continued. "And I knew that John had gone down to check on the security around Oswald at the jail. Of course, there wasn't any security. I think it's quite possible that H.L. called Jack Ruby and said, 'Get rid of that Communist sonovabitch.' Because Hunt knew Ruby. He was real fond of one of Ruby's girls, her name was Lacey. He himself wouldn't go into the Carousel Club, but he would meet Lacey for rendezvous at the King's Club, where your affluent people met.

"I mean, Ruby knew everybody. I used to go to his club, gambling and playing cards in the afternoon before the strip part opened at night. Ten days or so before the assassination, he showed me a copy of the president's motorcade route. I said, 'Jack, where did you get that?' He didn't answer me.

"Look, all these people interlocked," Madeleine Brown added. "The oil people, organized crime, the politicians. Dallas was a wide-open city. H. L. Hunt, because of his oil operations, you know, trained assassins in Mexico. If he wanted something, and they wouldn't let him buy it with a dollar, he took it. After Kennedy was elected, I remember him saying, 'We may have lost a battle—but there's a war to win.'"

Summary

It is abundantly clear that the H. L. Hunt oil family was either involved in the JFK conspiracy and cover-up—or mortally afraid that someone would try to connect them to it. There is no other explanation for their intensive private investigation. We cannot really know the meaning behind Oswald's letter to "Dear Mr. Hunt," and Jack Ruby's appearance at the Hunt offices the day before the assassination. It could be that the actual conspirators were looking to blaze a false trail in the Hunts' direction. However, the family's alleged purchase of the first copy of the Zapruder film; the dispatching of their chief assistant to the jail to check out security around Oswald; and the visit of Marina to the Hunt offices soon after the assassination raise grave questions that have never before been asked.

There is also the Hunts' closeness to Lyndon Johnson, and their convincing him to accept the vice-presidential spot on the 1960 national ticket. There is Charles Willoughby's later association with Nelson Bunker Hunt—and Willoughby's urging, in the midst of the Garrison investigation, that the Hunts make a strong case for Soviet involvement in the assassination. The entire Bogdan Stashinsky-Stepan Bandera case has a suspicious tinge, not the least being the warning letter from attorney Charles Kersten to the Kennedys about Soviet assassins, only two weeks before Dallas. Was the international right wing building a prima facie case against the Communists?

Finally, a future investigation must look into Nelson Bunker Hunt's alleged ideas about assassinating undesirable political leaders; his funding of paramilitary activities in Southern California; and his interest in obtaining a similar weapon as was allegedly used by Stashinsky in the murder of Bandera.

V

The Cover-up

I am sentenced and I have no pardon to ask. But in the name of my honor which I hope will be accorded me someday, I have the duty of respectfully requesting you to pursue your investigations. Sent away, as I shall be, I beg that the search continue forever. That is the sole favor I beg of you.

—Alfred Dreyfus, French military officer
falsely accused of treason, 1894

Chapter Twenty-seven

Nagell and the Government Cover-up: November 1963–May 1964

One man, perhaps the most important man, who could have opened the door on what happened to John F. Kennedy sat idle in a jail cell in El Paso. Despite his continuing efforts to bring some things to light during the life of the Warren Commission, Richard Case Nagell's communications—to the El Paso FBI, to Hoover, to counsel Rankin, and to others— never even received a response.

In a letter of May 5, 1986, I received my last communication of significance from Nagell. Here he offered a terse summary of what he might once have said.

"NO MOMMA, NO POPPA, NO UNCLE SAM": A Case Study in International Bungling, Embarrassment, Axe-Grinding, and Stupidity—a very short story by Richard Case Nagell

The GRU/KGB (?) didn't want me because it was apprised about LHO and the plan, and (as I found out much later) it failed to pass the data upstairs. [Also, I suppose, somebody became angry when I didn't keep a certain appointment in Juarez.]

Mother Rusher didn't want me because it learned about LHO's intentions, and the plan, too late . . . and the buck was passed to me.

The CIA didn't want me because it was apprised about LHO and the plan, and (as I found out much later) it failed to pass the data upstairs. [Or did it? Did a certain secret die with Dizzy Fitz on the tennis court? Or did that secret become known to then DCI John McCone and/or Richard Helms of Operations fame?]

The FBI didn't want me because its Top Dog was apprised about LHO and the plan, and (as I found out quite early) he did nothing or little* about it.

Bigfoot Jim Garrison and all of the so-called Assassination Buffs and journalists didn't want me because I insisted that LHO was in it up to his ears and that necessarily he must have fired (at least some of) the shots.

Uncle Sam (the Commission, Committees, Senators, Congressmen) and the rest of the journalists didn't want me because of the successful disinformation campaign that was launched against me.

AND NOW, I DON'T WANT THEM, BECAUSE THEY ALL TURNED OUT TO BE ASSHOLES.

(*There *was* an FBI interview of LHO after my *first* letter was mailed on *9/17/63)*

On the afternoon of the assassination, Nagell maintains he wrote an urgent request to speak to the Secret Service as soon as possible, and handed it to a senior jailer whom he knew as "Chuy." Returning to El Paso in 1990, I found "Chuy"—Jesus Mendoza—living in a ranch-style home on the outskirts of the city. "I was working when the assassination happened, yes," he remembered. "If Richard Nagell did give me a note, I'd have gave it to Captain [Raymond] O'Rourke. I can't remember, it's way back, but with something like that we never handled it ourselves. It's a very touchy deal. The captain knew more than we did, because he probably had more conversations with the Secret Service and the FBI."[1] (Captain O'Rourke, however, had turned down my initial request to interview him in 1975 and had since died.)

In a memorandum he wrote in prison in 1967, Nagell recalled that not long after the assassination, El Paso FBI agent Thomas B. White, Jr., came to see him. Nagell told White he had sent a letter to the FBI in Washington prior to his arrest "about Lee Oswald," but that the FBI had neglected to do anything about it. Nagell said White asked him where and how he had met Oswald, and other questions. Nagell answered a few, refused to answer others, and said he had asked to speak to the Secret Service, not the FBI. Whereupon White became angry and left the interview room.

A few days later, Nagell received another visit from White, accompanied by an FBI agent who said he was handling the bureau's assassination investigation, and another man who identified himself as being with the Secret Service. Because of the presence of the FBI, Nagell says, he "refused to answer any questions truthfully or elaborate on any answers he gave."[2]

That same night, Nagell "wrote a letter to the Chief, Secret Service Division, U.S. Treasury Department, Washington, D.C., advising that there had been a conspiracy to murder President Kennedy and other government officials" and that he "would be willing to give information in regard thereto."[3] Nagell never received a reply. I have tried in vain to locate such a letter in the National Archives.

At a court hearing on December 4, 1963, Nagell requested that the FBI return all personal effects seized from him when arrested. The then presiding judge, R. E. Thomason, instructed Assistant U.S. Attorney Fred Morton to see to it that this was done. Ten days later, according to Nagell, agent White brought most of these effects to the jail and permitted him to inspect them, but refused to give back the items Nagell said he needed for his trial. These included the receipt for his September registered letter to Hoover and, among other things, his personal notebook.[4]

It is on record that the FBI came to see Nagell on December 12 and December 19, 1963, and January 2 (accompanied by Secret Service agent George Weisheit), and January 6, 1964.[5] In 1990 Fred Morton, formerly of the U.S. attorney's office, told me he was "not aware of the fact that the FBI interviewed him at all. If they were, it was without my knowledge basically."[6]

It was on January 6, 1964, when Nagell dictated and signed the three-page statement outlining the situation that actuated his conduct in the bank (the "inimical act" about which he had been approached by representatives of "a foreign government"). At this same visit with FBI agents Edward Murphy and Lawrence Gorman, Nagell says he "was accused of having acted as an 'unregistered agent' for a foreign power and of aiding and abetting in the commission of a capital offense." He was also "accused of having resigned his commission from the Army for reasons not included in his Letter of Resignation."

Nagell wrote that Murphy had said words to the effect that Nagell had "something you want to get off your chest. . . . We are glad we got to you before you did anything to yourself." In the latter regard, Murphy drew a comparison between Nagell and Jack Dunlap, a suspected Soviet spy who allegedly committed suicide the previous October. Then, according to Nagell, the FBI man asked whether he would be willing to go to "Springfield" for a while.[7]

The Medical Center for Federal Prisoners at Springfield, Missouri, it would later be revealed in a congressional investigation, was an institution where "a prototype behavior modification program" was conducted. Though the Senate Judiciary Committee inquiry did not predate 1972, at least at that point Springfield's Project START "was based on classical concepts of behavior modification involving the use of both positive and negative reinforcement as a means of altering behavior."[8]

Nagell told Murphy that he would not go to Springfield, that he wanted to stand trial because he was innocent of the charges. After this, Murphy allegedly said, "Well, you might have to go to prison for a while." Nagell became angry and accused the FBI of "trying to cover everything up." Murphy answered, "What do you mean?" Nagell retorted, "You know damn well what I mean."[9]

My attempts to interview White, Murphy, and other FBI agents involved in the Nagell case basically met with a stone wall. Murphy, for example, said his discussions with Nagell "had nothing to do with any foreign entanglements that I can recall." White suggested that I "contact the headquarters, and see what they'll come up with for you."[10]

Origins of the Cover-up

Late on the morning after the assassination, J. Edgar Hoover sent a teletype to all FBI field offices: "In view of developments, all offices should resume normal contacts with informants and other sources. . . . Daily teletype summaries may be discontinued. All investigation bearing directly on the President's assassination should be afforded most expeditious handling and Bureau and Dallas advised."[11]

At CIA headquarters, Richard Helms called a meeting to outline responsibility for the CIA's investigation of the assassination. James Angleton was told that a desk officer in the Western Hemisphere Division (Desmond FitzGerald's bailiwick) would be placed in charge. After the Warren Commission's formation, however, all CIA research for its purposes would be turned over to Angleton's Counterintelligence Division.[12]

In Dallas, control of Marina Oswald fell immediately to two members of the city's Russian expatriate community, for purposes of translating her statements. Eventually Marina's testimony would provide the strongest support for the official conclusion that her husband was a maladjusted loner who not only shot at Walker but even considered assassinating Nixon.

Five hours after the assassination, Ilya Mamantov, who had never met Oswald, received a phone call from Jack Crichton asking him to serve as "interpreter" for the first interrogation of Marina.[13] Crichton was in 1963 the president of Nafco Oil & Gas, Inc., and a former Military Intelligence officer still connected with Army Reserve Intelligence.[14] According to information uncovered by the Garrison investigation, Crichton had been among a small group of Army Intelligence officials who met with H. L. Hunt soon after the assassination.[15]

Ilya Mamantov was a geologist with Sun Oil Company, whose owners, the Pew family, were later known to have donated well over $1 million to right-wing organizations such as the Christian Freedom Foundation.[16] George de Mohrenschildt, in his Warren Commission testimony, would describe Mamantov as the one "excessive rightist" of Dallas's Russian émigré community.[17]

Interestingly, Mrs. Igor Voshinin told me in 1992 that Mamantov "knew George Bush very well." Bush was president of Zapata Oil in Houston in 1963. "Mamantov died recently," said Voshinin, "but he told me that he had received a very charming letter from President Bush. I remember one line: 'You and I did it.' " (She could not recall the context.)[18]

It was Mamantov's mother-in-law, Dorothy Gravitas, who had first warned the Voshinins and other émigrés to steer clear of Oswald back in the late summer of 1962. "She told us immediately that the town where Oswald lived in Russia had the KGB Academy, and that it took exactly two years to graduate it," Mrs. Voshinin remembered.[19]

Now it was Mamantov who, at the request of an Army Intelligence Reserve officer, went to the first postassassination session with Marina. Also present was Marina's protector since April 1963, Ruth Paine, whose tutor in learning the Russian language that year was Dorothy Gravitas. Mamantov was, curiously, the one member of the Russian community besides de Mohrenschildt who knew the allegedly ultraliberal Paine.[20]

No transcript exists of Marina's first questioning by Mamantov, Paine, and the Dallas police. Her second interpreter on Sunday, November 24, was Peter Gregory. Right after the Oswalds' return from the USSR, Gregory, a petroleum engineer and Russian-language instructor, had been the first member of the Dallas-Fort Worth expatriate community whom Oswald met. Oswald had listed Gregory as a reference in obtaining his first job in the region, at Leslie Welding. Gregory's son Paul became the couple's first friend, having long discussions with Lee on political philosophy. But Peter Gregory had not seen Oswald since October 1962. Then he and his Secret Service agent friend Mike Howard came to spend the entire day of Oswald's death with Marina and Oswald's mother, Marguerite—under circumstances that were never adequately explained.[21]

Researcher Peter Dale Scott, who studied the transcripts of Gregory's several translations with Marina, noticed numerous inconsistencies. Six days after the assassination, in the presence of Gregory and Russian-speaking Secret Serviceman Lee Gopadze, Marina contradicted her testimony of three earlier interviews. At first she had said she could not describe Lee's rifle, nor had she ever seen a gun with a telescopic sight. Then, on November 28, Marina allowed that she could recognize the rifle without question and admitted taking the famous photograph of Oswald holding the weapon, including the scope that she had allegedly never seen. On December 3, Marina "revealed" that her late husband had also fired at General Walker—an allegation that the Munich newspaper had published a week earlier.

The Oswald women were sequestered at the time in an Arlington, Texas, motel, the Inn of the Six Flags. Its manager, James Herbert Martin, soon became Marina's business agent, even temporarily lodging her in his home early in 1964. It was Martin who negotiated the sale of the photograph of Oswald posing with his rifle and two left-wing newspapers, which appeared on the cover of *Life* magazine on February 21, 1964.

All of this convinced Scott, and other researchers, that Marina—barely able to speak English, terrified of being deported back to the USSR—was manipulated by her "handlers" to incriminate Oswald in the proper manner.[22]

Hours after Oswald was slain by Ruby on November 24, Hoover had a telephone conversation with LBJ aide Walter Jenkins. "The thing I am concerned about," the FBI director said, "and so is [Deputy Attorney General Nicholas] Katzenbach, is having something issued so we can convince the public that Oswald is the real assassin."[23]

The next day, Katzenbach wrote the following memo:

> It is important that all of the facts surrounding President Kennedy's assassination be made public in a way which will satisfy people in the United States and abroad. That all the facts have been told and that a statement to this effect be made now.
>
> 1. The public must be satisfied that Oswald was assassin; that he did not have confederates who are still at large; that the evidence was such that he would have been convicted at trial.
>
> 2. Speculation about Oswald's motivation ought to be cut off, and we should have some basis for rebutting thought that this was a Communist conspiracy or (as the Iron Curtain press is saying) a right-wing conspiracy to blame it on the Communists. . . .[24]

• *November 28, 1963:* Richard Helms sent a cable to CIA station chief Winston Scott in Mexico City. It read: "For your private information, there distinct feeling here in all three agencies [CIA, FBI, State] that Ambassador [Thomas Mann] is pushing this case too hard . . . and that we could well create flap with Cubans which could have serious repercussions."[25] Shortly thereafter, Ambassador Mann was recalled to Washington by Lyndon Johnson.

- *November 29, 1963:* According to a Hoover memo, LBJ told the Director that he wanted to "get by" on just the FBI report. "I told him," Hoover wrote, "I thought it would be very bad to have a rash of investigations. He then indicated the only way to stop it is to appoint a high-level committee to evaluate my report and tell the House and Senate not to go ahead with the investigation." Hence LBJ's creation of the Warren Commission the day before.[26]

- *December 9, 1963:* The FBI completed its five-volume report on the assassination. Katzenbach wrote the newly formed Warren Commission recommending that it immediately state the FBI report clearly showed that Oswald was a "loner."[27]

- *January 22, 1964:* From a transcript of an executive session of the Warren Commission, counsel J. Lee Rankin speaking: "They [the FBI] would like us to fold up and quit. . . . They found the man. There is nothing more to do. The Commission supports their conclusions, and we can go on home and that is the end of it."[28]

- *January 23, 1964:* Yuri Nosenko, a lieutenant colonel in the KGB, sat down with the CIA in Geneva, Switzerland, and informed the agency that he wanted to defect. He had been in personal charge of the KGB's Oswald file, Nosenko said. "It was decided that Oswald was of no interest whatsoever, so the KGB recommended that he go home to the United States." After Oswald departed the USSR with Marina—whom Nosenko described as having "anti-Soviet characteristics—the Soviets were glad to get rid of them both"—the next he claimed to have heard about Oswald was in the early fall of 1963. When Oswald came to the Soviet embassy in Mexico City seeking a visa, a superior had asked Nosenko whether this should be allowed. Nosenko said he had advised that the "unstable" Oswald should not be allowed back inside the USSR.[29]

- *January 27, 1964:* From a transcript of an executive session of the Warren Commission, declassified in 1974:

  SENATOR RICHARD RUSSELL: If Oswald never had assassinated the President or at least been charged with assassinating the President and had been in the employ of the FBI and somebody had gone to the FBI they would have denied he was an agent.

  ALLEN DULLES: Oh, yes.

  SENATOR RUSSELL: They would be the first to deny it. Your agents would have done exactly the same thing.

  ALLEN DULLES: Exactly. . . . That is a hard thing to disprove, you know. . . . The record may not be on paper. But on paper you would have hieroglyphics that only two people would know what they meant, and nobody outside of the agency would know; and you could say this meant the agent and somebody else could say it meant another agent.

HALE BOGGS: . . . The man who recruited [the agent] would know, wouldn't he?

ALLEN DULLES: Yes, but he wouldn't tell.

EARL WARREN: Wouldn't tell under oath?

ALLEN DULLES: I wouldn't think he would tell under oath, no. . . . He ought not tell it under oath. . . . What I was getting at, I think, under any circumstances, I think Mr. Hoover would say certainly he didn't have anything to do with the fellow.[30]

A New Judge for Nagell

When Richard Nagell came before the court for the first time in the new year, on January 24, 1964, suddenly another U.S. District Court judge was presiding over his case. His name was Homer Thornberry, and he was a longtime close personal friend of Lyndon Johnson. Born to poverty in Austin, Texas, Thornberry had worked his way through school and into politics. In 1948, when LBJ was elected to the Senate, Thornberry had succeeded to LBJ's seat in the House. Johnson called him "my congress-man" and introduced him to Sam Rayburn—the powerful House Speaker who had helped his own career—and Rayburn made sure Thornberry got on the right committees. "It's just unbelievable how many things he [Lyn-don] and Mrs. Johnson did to help us when we went to Washington," Thornberry would say later.

In 1965, standing on the front porch of his ranch, LBJ would swear in his friend as judge of the U.S. Court of Appeals for the Fifth Circuit. And when LBJ's nomination of another old friend, Abe Fortas, as U.S. Su-preme Court chief justice foundered in 1968, Thornberry became his next choice. He didn't make it only because, as one White House official put it, it would have looked like "old crony week."[31]

I have not been able to learn how Thornberry came to replace the previous judge, R. E. Thomason, in the Nagell case. Fred Morton of the U.S. attorney's office began the January 24, 1964, hearing by requesting that Nagell be "sent to Springfield for observation for thirty days so the psychiatrist there could determine whether or not he is competent to stand trial."[32]

Asked by Thornberry if he had any statement, Nagell responded that he did. He defended his mental competency, saying that he "knew exactly what I did on that day [in the bank], and I have a reason for doing exactly what I did. . . . I have talked extensively to the Federal Bureau of Investigation and also the Secret Service Division of the Treasury Department regarding certain things which I do not honestly know whether the U.S. Attorney is cognizant of or not."

Nagell then made reference to the verbal court order, issued by Judge Thomason in December, that the government return his documents and photographs. "I have been questioned by the Federal Bureau of Investigation regarding alleged subversive activities and possible activities of a nature inimical to the best interests of the United States in which I allegedly participated in previously and up to the date of my arrest. I have been asked questions by the Secret Service regarding Lee Harvey Oswald. I have been asked questions by the F.B.I. regarding things which I do not think have anything to do with this charge. Now, I very strongly feel that either the Federal Bureau of Investigation through the U.S. Attorney should charge me with some crime related to these documents or they should return them to me or they should get a warrant or a Court Order to keep these documents. . . .

"I would like to ask Mr. Morton this question," Nagell continued, "if he received a copy of the statement which I gave to the Federal Bureau of Investigation about a week ago, a signed statement?"

Morton said that he had not. Judge Thornberry then cut off the conversation. "Mr. Nagell," he said, "the Court believes that the record speaks for itself. The Court is convinced that in order to see to it that you are protected, that you are competent to stand trial and understand the charges and your rights as an American citizen . . . all this will be done by granting the motion of the United States Attorney. It is so granted."

Nagell saw the handwriting on the wall, responding, ". . . Now, certainly if I am sent by the Court to some place to undergo psychiatric observation, I will have no alternative but to go there and to conduct myself in accordance with their rules and regulations but I definitely will make no statement, and I wish to make it a matter of record at this time that I violently object because I think there are many things that even the U.S. Attorney has not been notified about, one thing, why hasn't this statement been made available to the U.S. Attorney, my last confession to the F.B.I.?"

THORNBERRY: The record will show that you object to this and the Court will assure you that your rights will be protected under these proceedings and the Court appreciates your statement that you will abide by the rules and regulations.

NAGELL: But I will not participate in any psychiatric examination or consultation.

THORNBERRY: Well, the motion is granted. The court is now adjourned.

That day after adjournment, an FBI file on Nagell, later released under a FOIA to attorney Fensterwald, was sent from El Paso "To DIRECTOR AND DALLAS" under a heading of "MOST URGENT." Dated January 24, 1964, it read:

. . . Upon subject's being removed from US Courthouse to El Paso County jail for incarceration and while in custody of deputy US Marshals, he made wild accusations to newspaper reporters accusing FBI of not attempting to prevent the assassination of President Kennedy and stating the FBI had questioned him concerning Oswald. These statements made by the subject yelling on the elevator en-route to El Paso County Jail in ear shot of newspaper reporters. . . .

TV coverage of Nagell's hearing and statements after hearing has been afforded. Only one press inquiry received with no comment answer given which will be adhered to strictly should any subsequent inquiries be received. . . .[33]

Three days later, Nagell wrote to his sister Eleanore about his commitment to the Springfield Medical Center.

. . . But will it be for 30 days? I, *and others,* know that my situation is indicative of what happens to "uncooperative" persons. And why is this action being taken so late in the game? Aside from casting the obvious dispersions [sic] on my character (or what I may say in the future), could it be that my admission to Springfield would provide the prosecution with a certain advantage? Or, could it be that the F.B.I.—and hence the prosecution, has an ulterior motive for such action? Well, I believe that both reasons apply! . . . If the American people think that only the Chinese are experts at brainwashing, subterfuge, trickery and deceit, then I am afraid someday they will be in for a big surprise when it is discovered that the F.B.I. is not too far divorced from Hitler's gestapo, the M.V.D. or like agencies. . . .

The government is going to put me away for as long as they can, by *any* means that they can, but not necessarily because they think I am guilty as charged. For the F.B.I. knows otherwise.[34]

On February 3, Nagell was admitted for psychiatric evaluation at Springfield. Dr. H. Wayne Glofelty, chief of the Psychiatric Service, wrote in a February 10 memo: "It is not known if this man has a mental illness but from his actions here and in this interview, it is believed he can factually understand the charges against him and assist in his defense. . . . He states that he has worked as an Intelligence Officer in the past and he realizes how various government agencies will use and imply the use of psychiatric reports."[35]

A report of a February 14 neuropsychiatric staff examination noted that Nagell "has consistently but pleasantly refused to take part in any psychological testing nor psychiatric examination," since his "extensive experience as a Government investigator" caused him to believe that "any confidential information would be forwarded to the judge and thence to the U.S. Attorney's office and would be investigated extensively through collateral sources. . . ." Nagell went on that his previous self-admissions to a psychiatric hospital were "part of a necessary farce." Staff psychiatrist Gustave J. Weiland found Nagell "consistently rational and coherent" and "the findings would support an adjudication of competency."[36]

By now, his sister had alerted Nagell that the FBI had been to see her. On February 15, Nagell wrote back that he was in need of "assistance and obviously it is not going to come from any of my prior associates. However, I have plenty of 'bargaining power' available if I can communicate with them. It is impossible for me to contact anyone by mail. This is where you can help me." He asked that Eleanore try to come see him if possible.

After being returned to the El Paso County Jail on about March 12, Nagell proceeded to write the letter cited earlier in this book to the Warren Commission's Rankin. He sought to contact Vaughn Marlowe, trying to locate a witness to his having mailed the $500 destined for Oswald on the day of his arrest. Still more delays in bringing him to trial ensued.

Nagell's "Irrelevant Material"

On April 10, 1964, Nagell went before Judge Thornberry again, in a hearing held at the prisoner's request. Nagell asked that "all F.B.I. reports and data which is pertinent to the charge against me for attempted bank robbery be subpoenaed for my trial." Morris Raney, assistant U.S. attorney for El Paso, responded: "May it please the Court, we would controvert and oppose such a motion and such a far-reaching and broad subpoena as this defendant has just requested."[37]

Judge Thornberry said: "The Court has a feeling that in addition to the reasons advanced by counsel for the Government, it would not be in the interest of your defense for irrelevant material to be introduced in the Court or for it to be paraded before the jury, and the Court respectfully overrules it."

Nagell argued that his statements provided the FBI on November 19, 1963, and January 6, 1964, were extremely pertinent to his motive. "Now, if these things are not relevant simply because the F.B.I. knows that it is going to perhaps mushroom into a national security matter which will be embarrassing to them and to the Military Intelligence Department, I think something is wrong someplace. . . ."

The transcript of these proceedings quotes Nagell as then elaborating: "I think I am being railroaded because I am a Communist and because I have been accused of being an espionage agent." Later, Nagell would say that he had been misquoted, that he had said he was being railroaded "because I'm an *accused* communist." Yet Nagell noted that this "errone-ous statement was made public in and around El Paso" and had never been corrected despite his repeated efforts "to have court-appointed counsel entertain an affidavit affirming to the contrary."[38]

After Nagell's statement, Judge Thornberry replied: "Well, Mr. Nagell, that is the very reason that the Court is here to see to it that you are not railroaded." Nagell then demanded to know why FBI agent Murphy was not in the courtroom.

Prosecutor Raney said: ". . . Whatever his life may have contained outside of his actions down there on September 20 are immaterial to me in connection with this charge. . . . If Mr. Nagell has made a confession, it is strange to me." Then Raney turned to FBI agent White, saying: "I understand he has made two statements, is that correct?" "Yes," White said. Raney asked: "Has he made a statement pertaining to this case to you?"

> WHITE: He made a statement to justify his actions.
> NAGELL: It wasn't to justify anything, it was to explain my motives.
> THORNBERRY: Well, just a minute, now, I think we are getting out of order. . . . The Court at this time will not grant the motion of the defendant with the understanding from the Government that any state-ment that the defendant, Mr. Nagell, has made pertaining to this case will be made available at the time.

In essence, Thornberry had now made moot the intent of the first judge, Thomason, that Nagell's personal property be returned to him. And the statements Nagell had given to the FBI were never "made available" at his June trial. Although I found the January 6, 1964, statement in the archives of his case in 1990, the FBI continued to deny its very existence.

On April 16, 1964, Nagell sent another registered letter to Hoover, cited in Chapter Four ("The Joseph Kramer Connection"). The letter was never acknowledged—although the FBI did release a copy of it, without comment, from its files in the mid-1980s.

In April 1990 I reached now retired Judge Thornberry by phone in Austin, Texas. After some prodding, Thornberry seemed to recollect the Nagell case quite well. "I recall it as being odd, yes," he said. "There is no question he went into the bank with a gun. I never was convinced he was mentally competent, but he thought he was."

I asked Thornberry if he had been in personal communication with the FBI about the case. "I don't believe the FBI talked to me about him, no. It would not have been proper. It was a rather peculiar circumstance. He seemed to want to call attention to himself. Nevertheless, he did it in such a strange way. I don't know, I don't know. I thought there was something the matter with him. It worried me a little bit at the time, whether or not I could really have found him unable to stand trial. There was nothing to indicate a lack of intelligence at all."

Did Thornberry remember anything relating to news articles about Nagell having previously passed "highly confidential information" to the FBI? "Yes, I think there was something where he had wanted to help the FBI." He added he recalled nothing about any intelligence agency contacting him about Nagell, reiterating, "it would not have been proper to talk to me about it."

In response to another question, Thornberry said he did "not remember" anything coming up about the Kennedy assassination.

I allowed that the ten-year sentence meted out by Thornberry after Nagell's conviction seemed rather stiff. "I don't know why that seemed extreme, because he went in with a gun. Some thought it was too lenient, in fact. Most people who use a gun consider it pretty dangerous. There was some doubt in my mind, but I was not ready to turn him loose on the community. I was convinced he was dangerous, though apparently he was not.

"My problem was, I had to appoint several lawyers for him, because he would not cooperate with them. One time I appointed two and he would not talk to them. I said to them, 'You're gonna come in here and tell me all these wild things he said'—but he's entitled to a fair trial. One said, 'Judge, he does not have any confidence in me.' Finally, I found one who stuck with him, Joe Calamia. I thought he would have even less success, but Calamia gained his confidence."[39]

Nagell and His Lawyers

It was true that Nagell proved quite cantankerous about his legal representation. At yet another hearing, on April 20, 1964, he asked that the latest court-appointed attorney, Richard B. Perrenot, be dismissed.[40] When I interviewed Perrenot in 1990, he remembered:

"The whole deal was a little screwy. Nagell always hinted there was something else involved. Obviously there was, because as a bank robbery it didn't make any sense at all. One day when I was chatting with Nagell— you could meet with a prisoner in a private room—he said something about Cuba and Castro. Like what a great guy Castro was. I said, 'I don't agree with you.' At that time, my brother-in-law was in prison there in Cuba. Nagell might have said he'd made a trip to Cuba, because I'd just come back from there. It seems like he told me he had been in Mexico, for example, at the Cuban embassy in Mexico City.

"Then at the arraignment, Nagell stood up and said he did not think I could represent him because I didn't like his politics. Judge Thornberry said that was no big problem, they'd just have the next lawyer on the list."[41]

The next lawyer was Joseph A. Calamia, or "Calamity Joe," as I was told he was affectionately known. He worked in conjunction with attorney Gus Rallis and, on May 1, three days before the trial, Nagell later wrote that both counsel "attempted to persuade him to submit to an indefinite commitment to the U.S. Medical Center for Federal Prisoners in lieu of standing trial. Mr. Calamia advised that he had spoken to the district court judge [Thornberry] about this and that the judge said he would agree to such a commitment. . . ." According to Nagell, Rallis warned that Nagell would be tried before a "blue-ribbon jury" and doubtlessly convicted otherwise. Nagell was adamant that he had been found medically competent to stand trial and that both counsel knew he was "being framed."

The day before the trial, Calamia, Rallis, and El Paso psychiatrist Dr. Manuel Hernandez, who had examined Nagell previously, again visited the jail. "Mr. Calamia stated," Nagell would write, "that he was going to hold a sanity hearing 'tomorrow' and that he intended to show [Nagell] was not mentally competent to stand trial." Nagell objected strenuously again. The trio left and returned an hour later, with Calamia saying he would abandon the "sanity hearing" plan but needed Nagell's "complete cooperation on the defense of insanity."[42]

And so it went. The defendant's "requested instruction to jury," as submitted by Calamia and Rallis, went as follows: "The term 'insanity' as used in this defense means such a perverted and deranged condition of the mental and moral faculties of an accused, as to render a person incapable of distinguishing between right and wrong, or unconscious at the time of the nature of the act he is committing, or where, though conscious of it and able to distinguish between right and wrong and know that the act is wrong, yet his will, by which is meant the governing power of his mind, has been otherwise than voluntarily so completely destroyed, that his actions are not subject to it, but are beyond his control. . . . The defendant makes the claim in this case that he is not guilty by reason of insanity."[43]

The trial took place over three days. According to Nagell, the prosecution requested that FBI agent White be permitted to sit at its counsel table, and Judge Thornberry allowed this. Despite Nagell's insistence to his lawyers that White be called to testify, he never was.[44] Four psychiatrists were called to the stand, two by each side. Dr. Hernandez thought "the defendant was a schizoid personality with rather strong paranoid features." The defense's other medical witness, Dr. R. J. Bennett, opined that Nagell suffered from a paranoid condition but was able to distinguish between right and wrong on September 20, 1963. For the prosecution, Dr. Martin L. Schwartz, who had interviewed Nagell when he admitted himself into the Bay Pines Veterans Administration Hospital in Florida in December 1962, testified that Nagell was not psychotic, showed no bizarre behavior, was in good contact with reality, and would know right from wrong. Dr. Weiland, Springfield's staff psychiatrist, offered much the same view.[45]

Nagell's hints about his real motivation, as outlined in Chapter Two, were ignored. On May 6, 1964, a ten-person jury found him guilty as charged of "entering a federally insured bank with intent to rob." Calamia immediately announced an appeal would be made on behalf of his client.[46]

When I went back to El Paso for the third time, in June 1990, Calamia refused to be reinterviewed. I did manage to meet with coattorney Rallis, who called Calamia "one of the top five criminal appellate lawyers in Texas; Richard was very lucky to have Joe in his case.

"Anybody that knew Nagell probably liked him," Rallis said. "He was a bright guy, except where it was concerned with disagreeing with the strategy of the trial. He obviously wanted his own agenda. I felt he was not guilty of what he was charged with, that's for sure. He just did not fit the profile of a bank robber, let's face it.

"I've always assumed that the government knew a helluva lot about him. *Brady* v. *Maryland* was a landmark decision which I don't think existed at the time, that the government was required to tender all information bearing on the innocence of a defendant."[47]

In Austin, Texas, I also met with Ed Sherman, now a professor at the University of Texas; he had worked as a paralegal aide to Calamia for the 1964 trial. "I haven't had a lot of contact with Joe in the last twenty years," Sherman said, "but he had a reputation of being straight and honest. He was a good, tough criminal lawyer. That wouldn't mean, I guess, that he or any other lawyer, if somebody came by and said there is really nothing the FBI knows that could help your case but it may jeopardize national security, well, Joe's a veteran and a patriotic person. I don't think he would ever suppress something he thought would help his client, but I can imagine him not pursuing something like that, if he was told the national security was at stake."[48]

On the night of his conviction, Nagell sent a handwritten note to attorney Calamia. *"Some day,* if you ever have the opportunity, will you please give the 'Ode' I have written to the foreman of the jury which convicted me."

The "ode," which I came across in attorney Calamia's files in 1976, read as follows:

> My Trial
> By Richard Case Nagell
> A law I scoffed, but did commit no sin;
> A cause I lost and yet I could not win;
> The truth was known, though by lies concealed;
> My eyes were moist and to my peers appealed;
> They heard my story, yet it was not told;
> I wished to speak and still my tongue did hold;
> I had a tale, but dared not I retort;
> Such silence was for guilt, so judged the court;
> I pondered justice, yet I thought in vain;
> My heart is heavy and it suffers pain.

Summary

Nagell, whose warnings to the FBI and CIA had been ignored—and whose Soviet employers failed to act—made continuing attempts after the assassination to communicate with the investigative authorities. He wrote letters to the head of the Secret Service, to the Warren Commission, again to J. Edgar Hoover. All these pleas fell on deaf ears. Crucial statements provided by Nagell to the FBI would never be introduced in court.

While the FBI moved quickly to seal its case against Oswald, and while Marina changed her statements many times through her translators from Dallas's Russian community, LBJ's friend Homer Thornberry suddenly became the judge in the Nagell case. After Nagell made open statements about his questioning by the FBI and the Secret Service, Thornberry ordered Nagell sent to a federal medical center for psychiatric evaluation, where he was judged perfectly competent to stand trial. At another hearing, Thornberry refused to allow Nagell to introduce any "irrelevant material" seized from him at the time of his arrest. Delay after delay ensued before his trial began in early May. Over Nagell's objections, court-appointed attorney Joseph Calamia introduced an insanity defense. But Nagell was found guilty, as charged, of "entering a federally insured bank with intent to rob."

Chapter Twenty-eight

The Railroading of Richard Case Nagell: May 1964–April 1968

The case of *United States* v. *Nagell* ranks as one of the most bizarre courtroom dramas in American history. In my view, the machinations that went on behind the scenes, between 1963 and Nagell's sudden release from prison in April 1968, represent a travesty of the criminal justice system. They also reveal the lengths to which the U.S. government went to silence and destroy the credibility of a man who might otherwise have revealed the conspiracy to assassinate President Kennedy.

Immediately after Nagell's conviction, attorney Joseph Calamia wrote to Nagell's sister Eleanore Gambert on May 11, 1964: ". . . After much reluctance on the part of Dick, we nevertheless raised the issue that he was not criminally responsible at the time alleged in the indictment because of mental illness. The jury nevertheless returned a verdict of guilty as to both counts." The lawyer informed Eleanore that the next step would be filing for a new trial. "It will also be necessary to conduct more medical tests and examinations on Dick. Even if the motion for a new trial is overruled, we hope to make a good record for the appellate court. . . ."

In the meantime, Nagell's estranged wife, Mitsuko, and their two children were being kept in the dark about Nagell's whereabouts. In a letter written to Eleanore on May 26, 1964, Mitsuko said: "I have not heard from Dick for over 6 month have you heard from him? I wonder what he is doing? And where he is? Few month ago F.B.I. were looking and questioning about him. I hope he is not in trouble."

When I reinterviewed former assistant U.S. attorney Fred Morton in 1990, he recalled: "It was a strange case. Calamia didn't figure it out until after the first trial, when the guy [Nagell] finally started telling about his extensive psychiatric history. Joe dug out the whole records and found out a helluva lot—which nobody knew anything about when we tried him the first time. My recollection is that Joe filed a motion for a new trial based on newly discovered evidence."[1]

That much was true. The "crucial evidence newly discovered," as the appeal put it, centered around a renowned neurological specialist who was prepared to testify about "organic brain damage" suffered by Nagell in the 1954 crash of a military aircraft. But, in fact, Dr. Edwin A. Weinstein's name had come up long before. An FBI report dated September 21, 1963 —the day after Nagell's arrest—notes the prisoner having advised the FBI that Dr. Weinstein, "a civilian doctor assigned to the Neuropsychiatric Center at Walter Reed [Army] Hospital had treated him and had a considerable amount of information as to his mental condition. Continuing, he [Nagell] advised that he [Weinstein] did not think he was crazy. . . ."[2]

The FBI had then interviewed Dr. Weinstein in Washington on September 30, 1963. After the plane crash in which Nagell was the sole survivor, Weinstein said he had been

called into the case by the military authorities to offer his assistance in aiding the recovery of Nagell. . . . NAGELL manifested a suspicious attitude of questions asked him by Dr. WEINSTEIN. Dr. WEINSTEIN said as the consultations continued NAGELL's suspicions and hostility lessened. Dr. WEINSTEIN stated that he felt that at least some of the suspicion and hostility exhibited was the result of NAGELL feeling that Dr. WEINSTEIN was attempting to pry information from NAGELL who had been previously associated with the intelligence branch of the Army. Dr. WEINSTEIN stated that he last saw NAGELL about a month after his first consultation [in 1955]. . . . NAGELL's responses at that time were regarded as normal. . . .

Weinstein added that his files contained a report about Nagell dated January 29, 1963, emanating from the Veterans Administration Hospital in Bay Pines, Florida. It was also on FBI record that on October 16, 1963, a letter detailing the bureau's interview with Weinstein was sent to Assistant U.S. Attorney Morton by Herbert Hoxie, the head of the FBI's El Paso office. So, at best, Morton's 1990 recollection was faulty when he told me that "nobody knew anything" about all this when Nagell went on trial for the first time.

On February 5, 1964, the FBI had contacted Dr. Weinstein again. "Dr. WEINSTEIN stated that the information he had furnished concerning NAGELL was from records he maintained as consultant for the Walter Reed Army Institute of Research. He said that as a result he requested that the information be made available only through issuance of a subpoena."

No such subpoena was ever forthcoming from the government. According to Nagell's version, he had provided attorneys Calamia and Rallis with Weinstein's name and address ten days prior to his trial, along with information that he "had suffered a negligible amount of organic brain damage as the result of a head injury received in the plane crash."[3] According to the attorneys' version, once Nagell "consented" to raising the insanity defense, they had announced intent to subpoena all relevant V.A. medical files.

"On three different occasions, the U.S. Attorney told the court that he would or had opened his complete files to the defense," Calamia's appeals brief stated. "The record shows necessary reliance by the defense upon the good faith and diligence of the government. . . ."[4]

The motion for a new trial was scheduled to be heard by Judge Thornberry on June 7, 1964. Shortly before this, Nagell maintains that Calamia came to see him. The lawyer "inferred" that if Nagell "would testify that he had not mentiond Dr. Weinstein's name, the aforesaid plane crash, or the possible existence of brain damage to him until after the trial . . . there would be good grounds for a reversal of [his] conviction on appeal." With this in mind, and wanting out, Nagell took the stand and says he "perjured himself"—falsely maintaining that he had not disclosed the "existence" of these matters to his counsel before his trial. Later he would write that this "was in every sense of the word coerced testimony and wholly untrue."[5]

FBI agent White also took the stand on June 7. Calamia pressed him about three FBI reports that the lawyer said had not been made available previously to the defense. Calamia's conclusion was that "they reek of abnormal behavior." The prosecution objected. White allowed that when he saw Nagell the day after his arrest, "he had cut wounds on I think it was his left wrist, if you are asking me for my opinion, that isn't normal. . . ." Calamia asked if Nagell had sweated profusely; White said he did not recall. The agent also denied having "personally" examined Nagell's belongings or possessions.

The prosecution then took over questioning, asking White about the FBI's interviews with Weinstein. The agent said he had initiated these interviews the previous fall. "And have we ever directed you," U.S. Attorney Morris Raney said, "or instructed you to withhold any information from us or to hold back any information concerning this man's physical or mental condition?" White replied, "Never at any time." All such information, he added, had been made available to the U.S. attorney's office immediately upon receipt of it.

With the government off the hook, Dr. Weinstein was called by the defense. He testified that Nagell very likely suffered from a disease that compelled him to hide his condition and to mislead psychiatrists who possessed no intimate knowledge of his case history. At the time of Nagell's alleged crime, Weinstein offered his opinion that his "judgment and perception of reality was seriously disturbed so that he could not accurately differentiate right from wrong," and this was directly connected with his mental disorder.

Judge Thornberry proceeded to overrule the defense's motion for a new trial and immediately sentenced Nagell to ten years.[6] Branded as a convicted felon—and a man with serious mental problems—Nagell was transported to Leavenworth Federal Penitentiary on July 22, 1964.[7] Nagell says he was never allowed to see the appeal brief submitted in his behalf.

Confined at Leavenworth for the remainder of that year, Nagell wrote that after his refusal to answer questions, he "was subjected to coercion, duress and cruel and unusual punishments; that on one occasion he was stripped naked and made to lie and sleep on a tile floor for ten days . . . never permitted to wash any parts of his body or perform other necessities of personal hygiene . . . never provided with any toilet paper [and] not furnished an adequate supply of water to drink." Still refusing to talk after being put in solitary confinement, he "was forcibly administered a dangerous drug . . . until his physical condition commanded that it be stopped."[8]

The months went by. On March 5, 1965, there appeared this statement in a report on Nagell prepared at Leavenworth: "There is a Notify being placed by the United States Secret Service requesting that their office be notified if this man is released or transferred to another institution."[9]

Eleanore Gambert continued her private crusade seeking justice for her brother. In December 1965 she wrote to President Johnson, sending along copies of Nagell's Korean War citations and records about the head injuries from the plane crash. She stated, quite truthfully at the time, that she did not "know positively why my brother attempted to rob a federal bank. But he did write me to say that it was an overt act, he wanted to be arrested. . . . I feel that he should be free of all charges or released so that he can be rehabilitated through the VA Hospital. Our former President Kennedy said, 'Ask not what your country can do for you, but what you can do for your country.' My brother gave very much to his country. Now it is time for his country to help him in my opinion. . . ."[10]

Very soon thereafter, on January 4, 1966, the U.S. Court of Appeals for the Fifth Circuit, in New Orleans, reversed Nagell's conviction, with instructions for a new trial. It was this same court to which LBJ's friend Judge Thornberry had recently been appointed. The decision was rendered on the basis of crucial new evidence "unknown to the trial judge or defense attorneys until after the trial"—concealed by Nagell, the opinion said, "as the result of a damaged brain and a diseased mind." Judge Thornberry was held blameless for having denied the 1964 motion for a new trial, while formerly with the district court.[11]

Grim Prelude to a Second Trial

On February 15, 1966, Nagell was released from Leavenworth and returned to the El Paso County Jail. Despite specific instructions by the appeals court that his new trial proceed with dispatch, there were again many months of delay. Nagell sent a letter to the district court requesting permission to act as his own counsel at all future legal proceedings. He received no reply. On February 28, Nagell says Calamia came to see him. If Nagell would allow him to make arrangements for a voluntary commitment to a V.A. hospital, Calamia said, "the government would dismiss the charges pending against him." Nagell, viewing this as "a deal" of which he wanted no part, refused.[12]

On March 24, 1966, Nagell's twenty-two-page letter to his sister—which she then burned in a fireplace, as per his instructions—marked the first time he had spelled out any details about his 1962–63 activities.[13] Nagell had come to a decision: At his second trial, he was planning to talk about Oswald and the JFK conspiracy.

He began writing his "proposed testimony," two pages of which survive. In these he began by describing how his testimony would "necessarily link me, however obliquely, with a domestic-inspired, domestic-formulated, and domestic-sponsored conspiracy to assassinate a Chief Executive of the United States and other highly-placed government officials. But I want it to be clearly understood that this link stemmed from my cognizance of the conspiracy rather than my participation in it. . . . I made every reasonable effort, under the prevailing circumstances, to testify before the Warren Commission when it was in session."[14]

More attempts were made, both by his attorneys and by two deputy U.S. marshals, to convince Nagell to commit himself to a V.A. hospital. Still, he refused. On April 4, 1966, he wrote to Harry Lee Hudspeth, then an assistant U.S. attorney in El Paso, advising that further representation by his counsel was without his authorization. Hudspeth responded in writing that this was a matter for the court to decide.[15]

In 1990 I interviewed Hudspeth, by then a prominent district court judge, inside his chambers in El Paso. He had played a minor role at Nagell's 1966 trial, "cross-examining the psychiatrists, things like that." Hudspeth recalled "the facts of the case were fairly screwy, he really didn't act like a very accomplished bank robber."

I asked whether Hudspeth ever received any indication, from perusing the files, that this case involved more than met the eye—perhaps a pretense on Nagell's part, perhaps ties to the world of intelligence. Hudspeth said: "I know, just from general gossip, that they found a bunch of pictures and stuff in his briefcase or pocket that the FBI thought had some kind of intelligence significance."

"But you never looked into that?" I asked.

"Not at all. It was just vague generalities."

Had Judge Hudspeth ever heard that Nagell claimed to have foreknowledge of the Kennedy assassination? "If I did, I don't recall. I guess what you're saying is, there was one story that he was supposedly on his way to Mexico City to engage in some dealings with some embassy there. Of course, all that kind of stuff always comes up when you talk about the Kennedy case. But it just didn't have anything to do with my representation of my phase of the Nagell case, so I didn't delve into that."

Then Hudspeth asked me a question: "Is there a story that he chitchatted with some of the jailers about other things or something?" I said yes, and told Hudspeth about the 1969 Military Intelligence document I had, stating flatly that Nagell had been an intelligence officer and had investigated Lee Harvey Oswald.

"I suspect that's true," Hudspeth said, then quickly added: "Well, he had a good military record and career going apparently, I don't remember the details, but then I heard there was an accident of some kind that resulted in a head injury."[16]

On April 7, 1966, a hearing was held at the U.S. district court. Judge Dorwin K. Suttle ordered Nagell committed to Springfield Medical Center for a period of psychiatric observation to determine his competency to stand trial. The judge also ruled that any new attorneys retained by Nagell (his sister was then seeking a new attorney) would have to act under the supervision of court-appointed counsel. "This is a mockery of justice!"

Nagell cried out. He was ordered escorted from the courtroom by U.S. marshals.[17]

On April 9, the day Nagell was to be transported back to Springfield, he took his blankets and sheets, bound them to his cell door and the adjacent bars, and refused to come out. According to the *El Paso Times,* Nagell had acquired four razor blades and threatened to slash his jugular vein if any effort was made to remove him from behind his barricade. "Attempts to pacify Nagell had proved fruitless," the newspaper reported, "even to the extent of administering knockout drugs through his food."[18]

After a nine-day siege, Nagell finally emerged on April 18, after Jesse Dobbs, chief U.S. marshal for the Western District of Texas, came to see him. According to Nagell, Dobbs was bearing a message from Judge Suttle. If Nagell would agree to take part in all requested examinations at Springfield, Dobbs's indication was that the judge would order a verdict of acquittal should he be found competent to stand trial.[19]

So Nagell was transported to Springfield for the second time. A letter from Calamia instructed him to cooperate with all examinations, or the court could issue an order that he remain there until he did.[20] Nagell submitted to an EEG, skull X rays, and a series of psychological tests.

A report of a psychiatric staff examination conducted at Springfield on June 13, 1966, states:

> Nagell presented himself to the NP staff neatly groomed. He appeared to be somewhat guarded throughout the interview although he was quite cooperative in answering questions. He became some annoyed at the consultant, Dr. [George] Parlato, when Dr. Parlato asked if his job as investigator could be construed as being that of a similar nature to a spy. He also became annoyed at Dr. Parlato when an implication was made that he might have Communist feelings. . . .[21]

Another psychiatric report, dated June 17, contains this sentence: "Although competency at the time of the alleged crime has not been requested, an opinion will be offered in this regard. . . ." But determination of competency was supposedly the specific *reason* for Nagell's being shipped off again to Springfield.

The report continues:

> The record also alleges that he [Nagell] worked for approximately one year for an unpopular political party. The unpopular political party being implied as the Communist Party. Nagell, in the course of his interview, emphatically stated that he was not and has never been a communist. . . .
>
> Psychological testing failed to show any evidence of an active psychotic

process or show any evidence of an impairment suggestive of a cortical brain damage. . . . I can point out that on the basis of my examination and my laboratory findings including an EEG and psychological testing that I did not find any evidence or finding suggestible of brain damage.

The report was signed by Joseph F. Alderete, M.D., chief, Psychiatric Service. It was not submitted at Nagell's second trial by either the prosecution or the defense.[22]

While Nagell was spending this two-and-a-half-month stint at Springfield, another prisoner was suddenly moved to the cell directly across from him. He was Abraham Bolden, who in 1961 had been the first black man ever assigned to the Secret Service detail guarding American presidents. In May 1964, Bolden made an attempt to contact the Warren Commission concerning two matters he felt should be brought to light: (1) a rumored plot to assassinate JFK at a college football game in Chicago on November 2, 1963, which rumor Bolden and other Secret Servicemen had investigated (the president ended up canceling his trip) and (2) heavy drinking and "general laxity" among the Secret Service agents assigned to Kennedy. Suddenly Bolden found himself under indictment for allegedly selling evidence to a counterfeit ring. Convicted in August 1964 on what Bolden claimed were trumped-up charges to keep him away from the Warren Commission, he ended up serving a six-year sentence—a portion of it across from Nagell, who told me he ignored Bolden for fear he was a "plant" seeking information.

On July 9, 1966, Nagell was removed from Springfield and driven back to Texas by way of the Bexar County Jail in San Antonio. There he alleges he was badly beaten by a uniformed deputy sheriff and placed in solitary confinement for four days. He claims a deputy marshal said to him, "We are doing our best to get you into a state hospital so you won't have to stand trial."[23] Upon his return to El Paso, Nagell says that Calamia told him the government intended to dismiss the charges and instead file a motion that Nagell be committed to a Texas state mental institution "and there was nothing he [Calamia] could do about it."[24]

The government's motion was presented, and denied, on July 29. More efforts were then made to convince Nagell to commit himself to a state mental hospital, or face conviction once again. At one such meeting, Nagell says that jail captain O'Rourke interrupted Calamia. O'Rourke allegedly stated his belief that Nagell's first conviction was because of "the Kennedy assassination." But, despite O'Rourke's sympathy for Nagell—"I sure hate to see you get fucked around like this"—he would not get further involved.[25]

Finally, in August, Nagell says Calamia told him that Judge Suttle would wait no longer for Nagell to change his mind about going into a

hospital—but the lawyer would see the case through if Nagell would cooperate in an insanity defense. "Mr. Calamia said there was the possibility he
could win an acquittal if he could show the jury that [Nagell] was presently
insane." In that event, Nagell replied, he would "personally object to the
introduction of such a theme." After much argument, the lawyer reportedly agreed to stick to a plea of "temporary insanity" at the time of the
bank incident.

Then Nagell demanded that the psychiatric reports from his recent incarceration at Springfield be admitted into evidence. Calamia is said to
have replied that he did not think this was possible "because the government will object." Nagell asked why the government would object to "its
own evidence" being shown the jury. Then, according to Nagell, "Counsel
said he could not afford to permit [him] to testify, that he was 'too convincing and might destroy your defense,' or words similar and to that
effect." Nagell objected angrily, saying that he "surely intended to testify
and that for once he was going to see that the truth came out"—as well as
about the "screwing around" he felt he had been getting for three years.

At this point Nagell says that Calamia "became incensed" and stated
that if Nagell testified to "anything the judge doesn't like," the trial would
be stopped and Nagell shipped back to Springfield. More arguing ensued.
"I'm not going to go along with the program," Nagell insisted. "Come hell
or high water" he was going to tell the truth at his second trial. Nagell says
Calamia's reply was that he "was cutting off his nose to spite his face."[26]

On September 7, 1966, Louis and Eleanore Gambert came to see
Nagell. He told his sister it looked like he was "to be railroaded again,"
and gave her thirty pages of his unfinished "proposed testimony." It was
academic in any case, he added, for he would not be allowed to take the
stand.[27]

And he wasn't. More than eight months past the date that the appellate
court had instructed a new trial be granted, one finally convened on September 19. Once again, the insanity defense was raised, against Nagell's
will. Once again, he was promised that FBI agents White and Murphy
would be called, but they weren't.

Dr. Weinstein, the key witness for the defense, read aloud letters from
Nagell complaining of severe headaches, blackouts, recurring dreams of
falling and hitting the ground, reliving the plane crash, having nightmares
about Korean combat. Weinstein termed his actions in the bank "like a
delusion with gestures. . . . This was a dramatic way of expressing his
acute problems and conflict, in character with his bizarre thinking and
mental condition." Nagell was simply too disassociated with reality to
know the nature of his act.

Calamia asked Weinstein: "Under the stress of conditions at that time he was not able to refrain from doing wrong and did not possess a substantial capacity to conform to the requirements of law?"

"Yes," Weinstein replied.

A jury of six men and six women deadlocked for several days. Their upholding of the original guilty verdict was returned on September 27, 1966. Judge Suttle sentenced Nagell to ten years, with credit for the three years already served. Calamia announced he would file another appeal.[28]

Recollections of Dr. Weinstein

By the time I went to see Dr. Edwin Weinstein, in May 1990, he was in his eighties and retired in Bethesda, Maryland. I was aware that he had conducted a most unusual study for the federal government. Word of it had first appeared in an Associated Press article in 1969:

> A psychiatrist who studied 137 persons linked with threats to U.S. presidents says [that] the would-be assassins generally are social misfits and loners unconsciously trying to gate-crash into immortality.
>
> And, adds the researcher, they view the threatened act as a "stroke of national policy or patriotic heroism."
>
> Dr. Edwin A. Weinstein's just completed study came to light when it was mentioned last week by another psychiatrist testifying at the Los Angeles trial of Sirhan B. Sirhan.
>
> The witness, Dr. Eric Marcus, said Weinstein's study was commissioned by the Secret Service. Weinstein, contacted at his New York office, refused to say who requested or financed the survey. . . .[29]

As Dr. Weinstein recounted it in our interview, his relationship with Richard Nagell was an entirely separate matter from his federal study of "would-be assassins." Weinstein added that his entire career with the Army had been devoted to studying the aberrations of the human mind. Nagell, whom he had not seen in some years, had vacillated, Weinstein said, "between a very close relationship and thinking me the worst doctor in the world."

Weinstein still believed that Nagell's actions inside the El Paso bank were "a gesture, a dramatic representation of something." He said that Nagell's organic brain damage concerned "emotional and social behavior, rather than memory and calculation. Patients after a head injury will confabulate stories of things that never happened, usually in terms of how they happened to get into the hospital. They usually don't hold on to them as long as Nagell does, just a few months. But it seems to me, on the basis of the whole clinical picture, I would be very suspicious about any story about Oswald.

"On the other hand," Weinstein continued, "having the effects of that head injury from the plane crash, he could have gotten himself involved in certain things later on. I have this article that was in *Ramparts.*"

The doctor passed over to me the 1968 story on the Garrison investigation, the first national attention drawn to Nagell and the Kennedy assassination. In turn, I handed Weinstein the 1969 Military Intelligence file on Nagell, which openly stated that he had worked for the CIA, looking into Oswald.

"Well, he could have been an informant and/or investigator for the CIA," Weinstein said. "He says he shot that pistol off in the bank to attract attention?"

I replied that he had wanted himself placed in federal custody. "Well, that's pretty crazy," Weinstein said. "I use 'crazy' in the colloquial sense. You know, he used to talk about the capitalistic swine."

Well, did the doctor have the impression that Nagell was sincerely left-wing in attitude? "Yeah. Well, not so much left-wing in a sense of political conviction, but that communism and violence and patriotism were strong symbols for him. Another thing, Oswald knew his way around"—this was the first of several times in our conversation when Dr. Weinstein inadvertently referred to Nagell as Oswald—"like who to go to in the intelligence community, the law enforcement community, the military. He didn't have to get attention to get access to the system. See, another strong thing in Nagell is just denial that there was anything the matter with him. Just because someone has brain damage doesn't mean he doesn't know down from up. But these fantasies of adventure and violence and death all seem to fit into a pattern."

Weinstein never wavered from his contention that Nagell had "confabulated." "He did go to the Cuban embassy in Mexico City. I remember he said something about that. But I'm just extremely reluctant to believe things are as Nagell says. As I say, parts of it may be so. But I really think there ought to be some kind of independent confirmation."

Though Weinstein would not allow me to make copies or take notes from his Nagell file, he did let me look through it. It contained a number of reports, many concerning visits the doctor had paid to Nagell in jail between 1964 and 1966. Here are some highlights:

• Nagell became very nervous when Weinstein asked him about his association with Oswald. He replied that he had known Oswald in Japan and thus could say that Oswald knew nothing about real Marxism. Nagell indicated to Weinstein that he personally became interested in Marxism at about the end of his Korean War service in 1953.

- After a meeting with the FBI late in 1962, Nagell checked himself into the V.A. Hospital in Bay Pines, Florida, because of a fear of something that he chose not to name.
- Nagell made a list of all the jobs he tried and failed to get during the 1962–63 period. The period ended in May 1963, when he finally accepted a job from a foreign government.
- Nagell referred at least twice to plans he had made to depart the United States for Cuba in the fall of 1963. He implied that he had come close to acting on these plans before finally staging the incident in El Paso.
- When inside the bank, he said he thought he might be shot and killed.
- The $500 that Nagell mailed from El Paso just before his arrest—which, as we have seen, was intended to be Oswald's expense money for his Mexico journey in late September—was sent back to someone in Mexico City who had apparently loaned it to Nagell previously.

But all of this, as Weinstein claimed to see it, was really of little consequence. "You see, the facial disfigurement he suffered was another stress-producing factor. I imagine that at times this seems very real to people. I wouldn't be surprised if Nagell really thinks all this happened. There are a lot of people who are obsessed with the CIA, the FBI, or ideas about the president. I don't know, maybe Nagell ought to write a book himself."

Nagell Contacts the "Critics"

Once his second trial ended, on September 27, 1966, Nagell was returned to Leavenworth. But while he still vacillated on what he could say, he soon became more determined than ever to speak out. On October 7, he wrote to his sister:

> . . . As concerns the later developments in 1963, including those instances where I tried to talk sense into some thick, misguided heads, I shall be quite willing, when the time is ripe, to lay my cards on the table—face up—come hell or high water. And if the hell comes first, I am prepared to flip through the pages of my mental notebook for some very interesting names, dates, places, and events which ought to cause somebody to wonder about the reliability and integrity—if not the efficacy—of the Bureau and a number of its agents. (In this respect, I might add, with a calculated promise, that if anything happens to me before I obtain my freedom—for example, if I should succumb to one of those accidents that occasionally happen to uncooperative prisoners—the cat will jump out of

the bag so quick that every official who has helped keep it inside for three years will be promptly scratched on that part of the anatomy where it hurts most).

Nagell then directed Eleanore to try to get in touch with attorney Mark Lane, whose book attacking the Warren Commission, *Rush to Judgment,* had just become a best-seller. If Lane seemed like the right person to represent him, Nagell added, he could direct his sister and the attorney "to a location where I have photographic *evidence* relating to the Main Topic."[30] But Lane was on the road promoting his book, and Eleanore's efforts to get in touch with him came to no avail.

Letter from Nagell to Eleanore, November 11, 1966:

> Concerning the latest surreptitious intrusion into your home (it sounds more like the C.I.A. than the F.B.I.—the Bureau seldom botches a job so badly); well, Eleanore, about the only thing I can say, aside from offering an apology, is that now you know precisely how much weight your Constitutional safeguards carry. I often wonder what you would think if it seeped out that every word spoken (or whispered) inside your house and over your phone has been duly recorded through some of the sophisticated listening devices employed by both agencies. My chief regret is that I am the cause of your lack of privacy and all the inconvenience, embarassment [sic], and trouble you have endured and may yet face.

Nagell continued to reach out—writing to Richard Popkin, author of *The Second Oswald,* then to Senators Richard Russell and Robert Kennedy shortly after Jack Ruby's death in January 1967. Nagell had by then been placed in "locked status" inside Leavenworth's C cellhouse, forbidden to speak to other inmates. On February 2, 1967, he was transferred for a third time to the Springfield Medical Center. The day before he departed, Nagell says he was informed that if he would cooperate in answering questions, he would probably be "cut loose in a couple of months."[31] At Springfield, put in a maximum-security ward, Nagell somehow got a letter out to Jim Garrison.

The Mob/CIA/FBI and Jim Garrison

The year 1967 was a critical one for keeping the lid on the assassination cover-up. The advent of Garrison's New Orleans probe sent a chill down certain corridors in Langley, Virginia. And two weeks after Garrison's investigation was made public—and after David Ferrie and his friend

Eladio del Valle had been silenced forever—Jack Anderson broke a nationally syndicated column on March 3. "President Johnson is sitting on a political H-bomb," Anderson wrote, "an unconfirmed report that Sen. Robert Kennedy may have approved an assassination plot which then possibly backfired against his late brother."

Anderson went on to make the first public mention of the CIA-Mafia schemes to kill Castro, who, "with characteristic fury . . . is reported to have cooked up a counterplot against President Kennedy. . . . This report may have started New Orleans' flamboyant District Attorney Jim Garrison on his investigation of the Kennedy assassination, but insiders believe he is following the wrong trails."[32]

The "insiders" was really a single man, Johnny Rosselli—as part of what now appears to have been a conscious disinformation campaign begun by the mobster late in 1966, right after Garrison took Ferrie in for questioning. Rosselli had first gone to a powerful Washington lawyer, Edward P. Morgan, telling him that Castro had infiltrated teams of marksmen into the United States to retaliate against Kennedy. Morgan then called Jack Anderson, who arranged for his boss, Drew Pearson, to come see the attorney. There Morgan suggested that Pearson's friend Earl Warren would know best how to handle this explosive new information. The word traveled fast. Warren passed the information along to Secret Service chief James Rowley, who turned the matter over to the FBI. Here again, Hoover failed to respond. Then Rosselli decided to go public via Anderson.[33]

The column had the desired effect. LBJ demanded a full report on the CIA-Mob plots and ordered the FBI to investigate the source of the Castro-did-it report. Whether the CIA, or the Mob, or both floated the story —to deflect Garrison's effort—remains unknown.

Columnist Anderson's involvement did not end there. A few years ago, an April 4, 1967 FBI interoffice memo was declassified. It was written by Cartha DeLoach to Hoover's right-hand man, Clyde Tolson.[34] "Jack Anderson came in to see me at 11:55 A.M. today," it began. "He has just returned from New Orleans where, at the invitation of District Attorney Jim Garrison, he interviewed Garrison for approximately six hours at his home. Anderson and Garrison later had dinner at the Latin Quarter restaurant in New Orleans.

"Anderson stated that he went to New Orleans fully prepared to present a hostile viewpoint to Garrison. After listening to Garrison for approximately 90 minutes he began to believe Garrison's story. Anderson describes Garrison as a very convincing talker who has considerable facts at his disposal. Anderson now believes there is some authenticity to Garrison's claims and future plans. . . ."

The memo went on to describe Anderson's report to the FBI about Garrison's belief that Ferrie and Clay Shaw had become aware of Oswald's "ties and background which would lend themselves to gaining easy access to Cuba. Shaw at this point already had been approved by the CIA, through an appropriate cut-out, to engineer a plot that would result in the assassination of Fidel Castro." It had been arranged for Oswald to obtain an office, and the idea was conceived "of sending Oswald to Mexico in a fake attempt to obtain permission to re-enter the Soviet Union. Garrison, according to Anderson, can prove that Oswald did this merely to establish a good atmosphere so that he could gain ready access to Cuba. Garrison claims that it was at this point that Oswald became disillusioned and refused to go through with the plot to assassinate Castro." After this, he was sent to Dallas and engineered as the "patsy" to assassinate JFK.

According to Anderson, Garrison had said he was "more than willing to give the FBI everything I have and let them finish the investigation if they so desire." DeLoach's memo records: "I told Anderson that the FBI would not under any circumstances take over the case." Anderson told the FBI that he had also "discussed the entire matter with George Christian, the President's Press Secretary, at the White House. He stated that Christian was also convinced that there must be some truth to Garrison's allegations."

DeLoach continued: "In this connection, Marvin Watson [a leading LBJ staffer] called me late last night and stated that the President had told him, in an off moment, that he was now convinced that there was a plot in connection with the assassination. Watson stated the President felt that CIA had had something to do with this plot. Watson requested that any further information we could furnish in this connection would be most appreciated by him and the President. . . .

"ACTION: For record purposes. There is no need to make further contact with Anderson."

Garrison's CIA Infiltrator

Right about the same time all this was going on, Nagell also made himself known to Garrison—and started the elaborate arrangements, through his sister, to turn over the tape recording he had made of the JFK conspirators and then stashed with his friend Fred John prior to his arrest. Precisely how William R. Martin came to join Garrison's staff, or become the designated investigator to visit Nagell in Springfield, Garrison does not remember. But when I separately interviewed Garrison and Bill Wood, once Garrison's chief investigator, about this in 1980, both men were convinced that Martin had been secretly working for the CIA.

"I think Nagell was able," Garrison told me over the phone, "because of his experience in the field of intelligence, to make a quicker and more professional evaluation of Martin than we were. Martin spoke Spanish very fluently, which is almost too much of a coincidence. I remember vaguely something about his going to L.A. to pick up a tape, but I have the impression that by then Nagell realized that Martin was intelligence and sent him on a wild-goose chase. Martin was one of many people who successfully penetrated my office. As I recall, I think he was allowed to just slide away. I don't remember how it came about, he just didn't turn out to be useful in a constructive way. And people that we sensed did have possibilities of being useful witnesses were increasingly turned off by him. The few on my staff who had been exposed to the intelligence community 'made' Martin [as CIA] right away."[35]

One of those was Bill Wood, better known as Bill Boxley, himself an ex-CIA officer. "When I arrived, Martin was sort of assigned as my supervisory guide at the office," Wood recalled. "He got me through all the administrative procedures. At first I thought he was kind of an addleheaded Maxwell Smart type. During one of our conversations, he mentioned that the CIA had attempted to recruit him or somehow he had discovered a shipment of arms into the Caribbean somewhere, when he was a lawyer for a client down there. That was the only personal contact with the CIA that he mentioned to me. But he was also quite willing to show me a letter to him from Maurice Brooks Gatlin, deploring Martin's resignation as 'chief investigator' for the Anti-Communist League of the Caribbean. That was Guy Banister's group in New Orleans, we eventually found out.

"Then as I began traveling more and more out of town, I became aware that a feeling was coming to the front among the staff that Martin was possibly a CIA plant. I must say he did some awfully stupid things, outstandingly stupid. I would say the odds are good that he was connected with the CIA, probably on a contract basis, because he didn't strike me as a man who had been through case officer training. He was a fairly young man, in his thirties. One time, I returned from a road trip and Martin was no longer around. I tried to get in touch with him several times thereafter, but he had left his apartment and there was no forwarding address. His parents said he was in Hammond [Louisiana] somewhere, but I couldn't locate him at the number they gave me. He just up and disappeared."[36]

But not before he had carried out part of his mission. His memorandums to Garrison of his visits with Nagell at Springfield contained some damaging and, according to Nagell, blatant disinformation. "The CIA has copies . . . and so do I," Nagell later wrote to Fensterwald. "I don't know what the scam was, but some pertinent info contained in them is distorted. I never stated that I 'had worked under the specific control of the Soviet Embassy in Mexico City, functioned as a watchdog for the Soviet Embassy,' etc., or even disclosed to Mr. Martin whom I contacted. For that matter, I never stated or disclosed to anybody whether (or not) I functioned for the Soviets, Cubans, Chinese or what-have-you. A hell of a lot was twisted around, including some pertinent dates, I feel purposefully."[37]

After Martin, for whatever reason, confided to Nagell that he was a "former" CIA officer assigned to "Latin American operations," Nagell made sure that the tape recording Martin was avidly seeking would not be made available to him. It was after he was out of prison when Nagell found out that Martin was a past associate of Desmond FitzGerald, Tracy Barnes, and an FBI man in Mexico City named Harry White.[38]

In the midst of Nagell's contacts with Martin, FitzGerald dropped dead on the tennis court on July 23, 1967.[39]

Nagell had provided Martin several important documents, instructing him to turn copies over to his sister and to Art Greenstein. Martin failed to do so in a timely fashion, later offering the written explanation that there were "security considerations involved." In a letter of July 30, 1967, to Martin, Nagell concluded:

> Finally, in terminating our business and knotty association, I am going to venture that the future will show you people need me much more than I need you; that D.F. [David Ferrie] and his friends were nothing but peripheral characters, always expendable, who didn't really know the scheme of things, and couldn't tell you anything even if they were around to do so, which they are not; and that while you people may have set sail in the right direction you are now (from what I hear) about 180 degrees off course . . . but then, that is how it was meant to be.

Martin wrote Nagell back that he was returning to private law practice on September 1.[40]

Countdown to Release

Feeling himself deceived by Garrison's investigator, Nagell began in the late summer of 1967 to deluge his old Mexico acquaintance Art Greenstein with veiled information about the assassination conspiracy. Greenstein, determined to help Nagell obtain his release, began passing the pieces on to Fensterwald and to William Turner, an ex-FBI agent who was preparing an article for *Ramparts* magazine on the Garrison case.

The January 1968 edition of *Ramparts* marked the first national awareness of Nagell's case.[41] "The main ingredients of the patsy theory are wrapped up in a story that has gradually filtered out of Leavenworth Penitentiary," Turner wrote. "The story is that of inmate Richard Case Nagell, and paradoxically, the most cogent confirmation for it is the manner in which he wound up sentenced to ten years in federal custody."

The article went on to describe Nagell's warning letter to Hoover, and the brief FBI reports on Nagell's having told El Paso agents of a "purely social" relationship with Oswald in December 1963. It wrote of how "the government threw the book at Nagell, a first offender who says he expected to be charged only with discharging a firearm on government-protected property. Since his sentencing, he has been shuttled between Leavenworth and the federal medical center (a euphemism for mental institution) at Springfield, Missouri. While the government has suggested in court that his airplane crash mentally affected Nagell, the fact remains that he was given intelligence training *after* the crash. What Nagell alleges is damning not only to the FBI, but to the CIA. . . . When Nagell complains he has been 'salted away' because of what he knows, he just might be making the understatement of the year."

Not long thereafter, on April 3, 1968, the U.S. Court of Appeals for the Fifth Circuit handed down its decision on Nagell's latest appeal.[42] A portion of it read:

> We feel constrained to emphasize the particular and peculiar facts of this case reinforcing psychiatric testimony that Nagell was symbolizing, projecting, dramatizing, and/or confabulating when he entered the bank. Nagell demanded travelers' checks, not cash. He asked for a specific (and relatively small) amount. He said "this is a real gun," not "this is a stick-up." He fired two shots into the wall, not at anyone and for no apparent reason. And he was not at all evasive when he left the bank.
>
> The peculiar facts of this case also suggest error in the charge of the court. . . . A *specific intent* to rob is required under 18 U.S.C. 2113. The trial court instructed the jury that it might infer intent from Nagell's conduct in the bank. Viewing the totality of Nagell's conduct, and in light of the strong evidence of his insanity at the time, we observe that it was error for the court not to instruct the jury in terms of the more restrictive specific intent required by the statute. . . .
>
> Considering the facts of this case and the evidence in the record, we conclude that the evidence introduced by the Government is not sufficient to sustain the conviction. While in some of the cases in which the appellate courts have reversed convictions on this ground the cases were remanded to allow the Government an opportunity to strengthen its position, we feel that "no good purpose could be served in ordering a new trial" in this case. [Precedents followed.]
>
> The judgment of the conviction is reversed and the case is remanded to

the district court with directions to vacate that judgment and to enter an order granting the defendant's motion for acquittal and a judgment acquitting the defendant.

When I asked Judge Hudspeth about this in our 1990 interview, he recalled: "As far as the law existed on the insanity defense at that time, this was one of the few-and-far-between cases where any appellate court ever issued such a ruling. It was very, very unusual."

On April 29, 1968, Richard Case Nagell walked through the gates of Leavenworth after four and one-half years of imprisonment, and caught a plane to New York City.

Summary

The astounding machinations in the Nagell case went on for several years. At the time of his first conviction, his estranged wife was not even aware that he was in jail. Suddenly, defense lawyers appealed on the grounds of newly discovered evidence—specifically, the findings of Army neuro-specialist Dr. Edwin Weinstein. In truth, Weinstein was known to the defense and prosecution before Nagell's first trial. Judge Thornberry refused the appeal and sentenced Nagell to ten years.

Faced with deplorable conditions in Leavenworth Federal Penitentiary, three times Nagell was also sent to the Federal Medical Center in Springfield, Missouri, for psychiatric tests. Soon after his sister wrote to LBJ, Nagell's conviction was overturned early in 1966. But more months of delays ensued before he came to trial again, as his own lawyers sought to have him commit himself to a mental hospital. At one point Nagell barricaded himself in his El Paso cell for a nine-day siege.

Although he planned to testify about the conspiracy, a concerted effort was made to prevent him from doing so. At Nagell's second trial, Dr. Weinstein testified that Nagell was unable to distinguish right from wrong when he entered the El Paso bank. Even today, Weinstein, who also met with then accused assassin Sirhan Sirhan, claims to believe that Nagell was confabulating about the conspiracy.

After being found guilty a second time, Nagell intensified his efforts to speak out—through letters to two senators and to Jim Garrison. As Garrison's probe became public in 1967, targeting the CIA and its associates, once again an effort was made to point a conspiratorial finger in Castro's direction. Garrison investigator William R. Martin, who was dispatched to meet with Nagell, turned out to be an ex(?)-CIA associate of Tracy

Barnes, Desmond FitzGerald, and the Guy Banister group. Nagell ended up refusing to turn over his tape of a conspiracy, and he terminated the Martin relationship.

Not long after a *Ramparts* magazine article brought Nagell's case to national attention, his conviction was overturned in April 1968 and Nagell was ordered released.

Chapter Twenty-nine

Nagell's Disappearance Behind the Iron Curtain: 1968–70

On April 29, 1968, as a plane from the Midwest approached New York's Kennedy International Airport, Garrison investigator Bill Wood was already in the city. He was awaiting a call from Nagell's sister, who was to put them together. "She called late with word that Nagell had called her," Wood recalled, "said that he had landed but that he couldn't visit her because he had been met by a couple of 'friends.' She told us that she had asked him to bring them out with him and that he had replied: 'They're not *good* friends. . . .' "[1]

What may have happened to Nagell was described in an article about him published in 1969 in *The Family,* an obscure German-based magazine for American servicemen: " 'We pulled a lot of strings to get your freedom,' said a man who met Nagell when he landed at Kennedy International Airport. The man and his nontalking partner gave Nagell $500 in $20 bills. 'More will come where this comes from,' the unidentified man promised. 'We appreciate your cooperation in prison.' "

Nagell would later set down in his Court of Claims case: "On 29 April 1968 and during the succeeding three weeks plaintiff [Nagell] was provided with a total of $15,000.00 in increments of $500.00, $4,500.00 and $10,000.00 by one of two persons who identified themselves as representatives of the Central Intelligence Agency. Part of this money was deposited in a New York City bank by plaintiff [Nagell]."[2]

For the next month, Nagell would base out of his sister Eleanore's home in Elmhurst, Queens, New York City. There he got back in touch with Art Greenstein, who remembers: "Nagell called me before he came to see me. I think the general thrust was, he didn't have the Kennedy case solved but he said, 'Believe me, I have something'—something that would expose United States politicians. When he came to Wilmington, he told me that in effect I was the one who'd gotten him out of jail—by writing all those letters, to *Ramparts,* to Arlen Specter [formerly a staff member for the Warren Commission], and others."[3]

On May 10, Greenstein gave Nagell a manila envelope that came from Bernard Fensterwald. Nagell later wrote that it "contained a number of photographs, mostly of so-called anti-Castro Cuban refugees, whom it was alleged were 'prime suspects,' supposedly involved in the assassination of President Kennedy."[4]

"My recollection is that he made two comments which I passed on to Fensterwald," says Greenstein. "Seems to me they were anti-Castro militants practicing in the jungle. Nagell acted like he knew one person. He said, 'There's Leon.' He pointed to someone else and said, 'He could tell us a lot.' But he was very cool about it, as if he was used to looking at these kind of pictures all the time."[5]

Two days later, Nagell agreed to see political researcher Jones Harris, who then set up Nagell's two meetings with Garrison on May 14 and 16. He and Garrison first conversed for some hours in the lobby of the Algonquin Hotel. The second time, their encounter was arranged at the Central Park Zoo—"a hop, skip, and a jump from the Cuban mission," Nagell would recall. "That whole area was being watched. There were a lot of men in suits and neckties hanging around, whom I presume were Garrison's people."[6]

Nagell elaborated in a 1978 sworn affidavit:

Mr. Garrison's questions centered on the nature of my contacts with Lee Harvey Oswald in Japan and in the United States, and on the CIA. I advised Mr. Garrison that he had been misled during the course of his investigation, and that one of his staff had been a CIA case officer under Desmond FitzGerald. At one point Mr. Garrison told me that he had reason to believe that my life was in danger. I replied that I had no fear of being killed, particularly by the CIA or by a foreign intelligence organization which I named. I asked Mr. Garrison if he wished to speak with a representative of that organization who was then in New York City, presumably at the instance of the CIA, but he declined.

When I asked Garrison about this in 1980, he said he did not recall Nagell's offer. "It doesn't sound completely foreign to me, though," he said. "But I think it would have been my inclination not to get involved, because by that time it was apparent to me that any Soviet involvement in the assassination was an American intelligence fiction. And I think my attitude would have been not to want to contribute to developing that fiction, by a misinterpretation of my meeting with any Soviet official.

"Never at any time in our conversations did Nagell make any overt reference to KGB," Garrison continued, "but it was certainly something I surmised. From him, I felt that if there was a Soviet connection, their interests would have been to prevent the assassination—because they would know that otherwise the reaction would have been against *them*. I think there probably was an effort of some sort in that regard. But Nagell was very careful. He never even indicated precisely what American agency he was associated with. He was a man most desirous of wanting to be truthful, but at the same time not wanting to complicate his life by becoming a target of whatever his parent agency was. He knew he was walking a tightrope wire. But I still believe that Nagell is the closest thing to the key [to the assassination mystery] that there is in one man, if he wanted to be."[7]

When I spoke with Nagell about his "offer" to Garrison to meet with a Soviet official, Nagell expressed puzzlement about why the New Orleans DA had not chosen to take him up on it. "Maybe Garrison knew more than I thought he did," Nagell said. "Maybe he was afraid for his reputation. I'd stuck my neck out asking this guy if he would talk to Garrison, and frankly it really pissed me off when he wouldn't. Anyway, the CIA and the FBI knew the man was here, and I doubt if he was in this country before or since. He had no diplomatic immunity because he was not a member of the United Nations mission. He came to the United States and went back. In fact, he was in Switzerland when I was there that June, though he wasn't on the same plane I was."[8]

In 1984, Nagell added that the foreigner was a high-ranking official of the KGB.[9] If this man was in New York "at the instance of the CIA," then I wondered what "segment" of the CIA Nagell was talking about. Once, almost offhandedly, he told me of his understanding that "a big meeting" between certain CIA and KGB officials had been the spark that finally triggered his freedom from prison.[10]

There was one thing that Nagell wanted to make sure I remembered, during a May 1978 conversation where he presented me with a three-page affidavit that harkened back to his meetings with Garrison. "After my release from Leavenworth," he said, "I believed that I had been either the victim in a trade-off or a casualty of plausible denial. I was discarded and disowned by both sides."

He stopped to let the message sink in, then went on: "Now that's not true, per se. Certainly by the Americans. Honestly I was not, by other people. So then your question is, why? It's a question of what did they do for you. Read my affidavit carefully, consider what I *didn't* say which, under normal circumstances, I should have said. Like the phrase, 'I functioned in the capacity of what is commonly called a "double agent." ' The logical question is, for who? I would only go so far. I won't cut off my nose to spite my face."

What was he going to do with the affidavit? I asked. "It's going to the CIA, for one," Nagell replied. "I hope it might reach the right people, and maybe someone will realize they shouldn't keep saying bad things about me." Then he smiled. "And it's going someplace else."[11]

Departure for Europe

When the overseas *Family* published its 1969 article about Nagell, it was written (and copyrighted) by Thomas C. Lucey, a former member of the Army's Counter Intelligence Corps. The article relied heavily on an unnamed source who was quite familiar with Nagell's history, past and present. It was the first—and, until now, the only—published mention that Nagell had worked with the Army's "then super hush-hush Field Operations Intelligence in Japan and Korea."

Sometime soon after the article came out, Nagell wrote: "I shall not at this time attempt to affirm or deny any of the particulars contained in the OVERSEAS FAMILY article. May it suffice to say that the author has referenced a number of inaccuracies . . . yet, in essence he has depicted the truth. Perhaps the article would be best described as a thumbnail sketch of the whole, which, someday, must be told."[12]

The copy of the article I received contained a two-page typewritten addendum offering certain corrections to Thomas Lucey's article. This addendum, Nagell says, "was written by a former friend in New York. I did make some of the statements attributed to me in the addendum, but many were twisted around. The conversation was taped, so there was no excuse for error."[13]

With these semidisclaimers in mind, I believe that allegations from both the article and the addendum are important to set forth in this narrative.

They portray a much more complete picture than anything else available about what happened to Nagell after his release from prison.

"In New York," the article in *The Family* says, "Nagell kept an appointment with a CIA official he knew only as Buehel. The CIA official told Nagell he had heard that his wife had divorced him while he was in Leavenworth. 'It might be true,' the source noted, 'but wouldn't it be nice for Nagell to know for sure. He assumes his children are still with his wife.'

"Nagell met Buehel to be briefed for another CIA assignment. Why did he go back to the CIA? 'It was the only practical thing to do,' the source said, 'because of his financial situation. . . .' "

The addendum offers this elaboration:

While my return to the fold of the CIA in May 1968 may have been the only "practical thing" for me to do, it definitely was not predicated on my financial situation, as a few old bank account passbooks will substantiate (I am not quite the mercenary that Mr. Lucey has portrayed). Nor was it because of any peculiar allegiance to those who had tossed me on the scrap heap for the sake of expediency 4½ years earlier. . . . I agreed to go back out into the cold, so to speak, strictly for personal reasons and I think the explanation is wisely left at that for now.

Those "personal reasons" centered, in part, on Nagell's desire to be reunited with his children. "During the period 1963 to 1970," Nagell would write in his Court of Claims case, he "was involuntarily separated from and unknowing of the whereabouts, health, safety and welfare of his two minor children, and unknowing of the fact that his wife had been granted a divorce during plaintiff's [Nagell's] incarceration, on 4 January 1964." He added that his children "were reported by a State Department official as living in Europe."[14]

On May 24, 1968, Nagell was issued U.S. passport number J543069.[15] Greenstein came to see him, and Nagell invited his old friend to accompany him on a trip to Switzerland. "I knew he'd been in touch with Garrison right before he went," Greenstein remembers. "And I knew he'd squirreled some stuff away in Europe. But I decided not to go. I drove him to the airport."[16]

On May 30, Nagell left New York for Zurich, where, he later wrote, "arrangements had been made for [him] to take up temporary residence."[17] Garrison investigator Bill Wood remembered: "Jim said that he had offered Nagell funds, which the latter declined with the comment that he had plenty of money to get out of the country—and that if he made it, he would let Garrison know by a code-word communication. Later still, Jim and I were conferring at a table in the New Orleans Athletic Club one Saturday afternoon when Lynn Loisel brought over a stack of mail from the office. In it was a picture postcard postmarked Zurich, Switzerland. On the back was written: 'Knickerbocker sends greetings to Jim Garrison.' Jim smiled and said, 'Nagell made it,' and explained the card."[18]

Both CIA and State Department telegrams have since been declassified concerning Nagell's next known move in Europe. He had walked into the U.S. consulate in Zurich on June 4, where he was "interviewed by vice consul." The CIA described Nagell as having "told incoherent story about 'working for US Government secret agency on mission to Geneva where [he was] to meet Japanese." The State Department cable contains the same sentence, except it calls Nagell's story not "incoherent," but "coherent."

Both documents go on that Nagell "wanted ConGen [consul general's] assistance to get money which claims had deposited New York bank before departure US. Subject was told by Vice Consul Congen could not assist." Nagell then returned the next day and "asked for political officer, thus was referred to [excised] by receptionist," says the CIA file. "Subj[ect] made assumption political section CIA, which denied. Subj quite incoherent, in fact, appears psychotic, possibly dangerous. Claims was interviewed by New Orleans District Attorney Garrison 14–16 May in connection 'CIA and Pres Kennedy assassination.' Subj claims Garrison told him he in danger being killed. Therefore wants 'inform CIA he in Zurich.' "

The State Department telegram went on that Nagell "also said 'US Government had previously withheld passport from him.' . . . Did not seem know of Senator Kennedy shooting, hence his conduct apparently not provoked by this. [Robert Kennedy had been assassinated in Los Angeles on June 4.] Dept requested provide telegraphically any background info available on [Nagell] and advise whether ConGen should inform police or take other action."

According to two FBI memos of June 7—one of which went straight to Hoover from a blanked-out source—the bureau was immediately apprised of Nagell's actions at the consulate in Zurich.[19]

It was the public release of the CIA cable in 1978 that prompted an angry Nagell to write the sworn affidavit about which he elaborated with me that spring. In it, Nagell offered additional comment about his consulate visit on June 4–5:

> . . . I spoke with a female vice consul named Martin and with an individual in the consulate's political section named James A. Treichel. Prior to my visits, Mr. Treichel had been identified to me as a longtime member of the American intelligence services and an officer of the Central Intelligence Agency assigned to the U.S. Department of State as a Foreign Affairs Political Analyst. Although I did request the assistance of

the consul general in arranging for the transfer of some funds which I had deposited in a New York bank before departing the United States (which assistance was indeed granted) and although I did request that CIA headquarters be notified that I was in Zurich, I did not do so for the reason stated in CIA document number 1123-424. It was an entirely separate matter that comprised the purpose of my visits to the consulate.

With regard to the allegations in CIA document number 1123-424 that I told an incoherent story about working for a U.S. government "secret agency," that I said that I was on a mission to Geneva to meet "Japanese," and that I appeared "quite incoherent," psychotic and possibly dangerous, I state only that anything I said or did was said and done with full intent and purpose.

As for the declassification and release of CIA document number 1123-424 (and likewise, the numerous fabrications about me that have been entered in various official records and fed to the news media and selected "journalists" and authors over the years), it is my opinion that such action was designed to discredit me and impeach any testimony that I may have given or might ever give regarding the assassination of President Kennedy.

Looking back, I must add that this made me wonder about the timing of the State Department's decision to declassify its own Nagell cable, making him out once again to be a kook. It was declassified on April 29, 1992, as I was preparing this book, and sent with some other assassination files to researcher Harold Weisberg.

Coinciding with Nagell's European trip in the summer of 1968, there had appeared two articles on the Garrison investigation that certainly would have had the effect (if not the purpose) of discrediting him. The first appeared in the July 13, 1968, *New Yorker* magazine, where Edward Jay Epstein described Nagell as "another witness found in the mail (of crank letters, publicity seekers and bogus tips) . . . an inmate of a Federal institution for the criminally insane, in Springfield, Missouri. . . . court records indicated that Nagell had suffered brain damage in an airplane crash in 1957."

The next was in the August 2, 1968, edition of *Time,* a blatant hatchet job on Garrison titled "Jolly Green Giant in Wonderland." It referred to how Warren Commission Report critic Epstein had just "systematically shredded almost every piece of evidence that Garrison has put forward," and went on: "Richard Case Nagell, an inmate in a hospital for the criminally insane, said he had got himself jailed so that he would not have to carry out his part of the plot, which was to kill Oswald: Garrison repeated the tale until he was finally convinced that Nagell was not credible." That was not only a distortion of Nagell's incarceration but also of Garrison's strong belief in Nagell's legitimacy.

By the time those articles appeared, Richard Nagell was incommunicado. On June 10, four days after all the government cable traffic out of Switzerland, he boarded a train in Zurich. While en route to West Berlin through East Germany, Communist authorities detained and then imprisoned him—"on charges," Nagell later wrote, "that he had been a member of a now-defunct U.S. intelligence organization which had conducted 'criminal intelligence activities against a Socialist State.' "[20] I presumed that that "now-defunct" organization was Field Operations Intelligence (FOI).

Behind the Iron Curtain

The Thomas Lucey article picks up the story:

"During his last week of discussions with Buehel and another man in New York," THE FAMILY's source said, "it was Nagell's understanding that he was to have himself arrested by East German authorities. All he had to do was buy a train ticket from Zurich, Switzerland, to East Berlin. The train would go through East Germany and he would be arrested. . . ."

"The main objective of his imprisonment was twofold: one concerned a U.S. naval officer who had allegedly defected and Nagell had to find out if he was there. But his main purpose was to get as much information as possible on techniques of interrogation and methods of treatment of the MfS [East German Ministry for State Security]."

The typewritten addendum to the article offers this:

My mission inside East Germany—if indeed it was a mission—was neither as well-defined nor as elementary as Mr. Lucey has perceived. I am sure the CIA knows all it needs to know about American defectors in Berlin and the modus operandi of the MfS. In fact, the mission was not directed against East Germany, per se. Preparations bore the trademarks of an authentic, even typical Agency project targeted in the main to another nation. That I was unable to comprehend the German language, that I had been a recent, unwilling guest of the U.S. Attorney General, branded a Communist in the public records, etc., merely served to strengthen an already plausible cover built up by chance rather than by design. Paradoxically, the chinks in the armor were that the cover was not wholly untrue. . . . In the past I had engaged in certain covert intelligence activities hostile to other socialist states, to which—as an integral part of my cover—I freely confessed. Oddly enough, however, my mentors from Langley had neglected to tell me during the briefings that these previous activities constituted a violation of the criminal statues of the GDR [German Democratic Republic—i.e., East Germany], warranting a maximum penalty of death upon conviction. By inadvertence or by plan I found myself in a not altogether unfamiliar predicament. If I had confessed to my real mission, assuming it was genuine, without doubt I would have been spared execution, probably even escaped long-term imprisonment. Instead, I selected what I considered to be a better alternative . . . and gained my freedom. As for my treatment by the MfS, from beginning to end it was far more gentle than that experienced beneath the cudgel of the U.S. Department of Justice.

Nagell added a telling remark about these events in his amendment to my 1976 "outline" of his life and times: "Back in the United States, the FBI suggested that his arrest had been 'arranged' so that he could be 'debriefed' by a foreign power without suspicion."

Nagell later told me this "wasn't exactly the case," but in his question-mark-type "cerebrations" to Greenstein, he certainly made overtures about CIA-KGB collusion regarding his East Berlin voyage. "Was 'Mr. Buehel' CIA or KGB? . . . Was it the looney CIA or the sly KGB that sent me to East Germany? Was I on a mission for the CIA or was I sent there after volunteering to appear as a prosecution witness at the Clay Shaw trial or was I sent there to get debriefed by the KGB, MfS, DSE, Cuban G-2, BND, Hai Wai, or what have you?"

Here is Art Greenstein, looking back on what Nagell later told him about his being taken off the train: "A remark I can remember is, he said, 'I should have known I was being set up'—when the train stopped and the East German security people marched back right to where he was sitting. He said he'd been sitting next to a person who led him to say things that didn't reflect well on East Germany. He told me, in hushed tones, that he was then sent to Russia for interrogation. But that he was treated very well, much better than in Leavenworth. And I think that one of the Communist countries did give him a brain test, trying to see if or prove there was something wrong with him. They checked him out, for their purposes. But there wasn't any [brain] damage."

What did Greenstein believe was the real purpose of Nagell's arrest there? "Well, the most favorable thing to me was, they were trying to find out what he knows about the assassination."[21]

The unidentified source for the *Family* article told of Nagell's CIA contact at the Zurich consulate having asked him the train compartment number on his reservation. Nagell told him No. 46. It was after midnight when the train suddenly stopped after crossing the East German border. "He could hear people get on the train and clump down the aisle, directly to his compartment. There were two men in uniform and two men in civilian clothes. They asked Nagell for his passport—by name. Then they asked for his transit visa."

Since he didn't possess a valid transit visa, he was removed from the train. "They drove to Erfurt, where Nagell was held for three days in a safe house. There some men in civilian clothes questioned Nagell. Next he was driven to an East Berlin political prison for extensive interrogation. They accused him of espionage and said they were going to try him.

"Nagell had been told that if he was in East Germany for over three months, his release would be effected by the agency [CIA], but he was not told how. On his own he started to play crazy because he was there over four and a half months and he began to think there was another reason for his being there. He felt the CIA had deserted him and that, quite frankly, he had been sent to Germany to get him out of sight or to get rid of him."

Little more is known about Nagell's time behind the then Iron Curtain. In 1977 we were watching the traffic go by along Sunset Boulevard when Nagell told me that he had already put much of his historic tale on the record.

"Do I have most of that?" I asked naively.

"No," Nagell replied. "The Soviets have a lot of it, in my own handwriting."

"Oh," I said, "from when you were in East Germany."

"I didn't spend all my time in East Germany," Nagell said evenly.[22]

Nine months later, he went into slightly more detail about his time spent with the KGB in the USSR. We were talking of his decision not to carry out the Soviets' assignment to leave the United States and eliminate Oswald, instead "busting two caps" inside an El Paso bank. He said: "The big question put to me was—why did you do it? Yet it was understood why. Once they said to me, 'You could have had your kids.' Well, *that* was a lie. They told me that later when it didn't count, and I resented it. 'Well,' they said, 'maybe you *were* flipping your lid.' And maybe I was. I was in a quandary. I didn't know what to do at that time."[23]

Nagell was also questioned in the USSR about a KGB lieutenant colonel, Yevgeny Runge, who had sought asylum from the CIA in West Berlin in the early fall of 1967. Runge's defection was said to have exposed the widespread uses of "illegal" agents, unattached to any embassy, by Soviet intelligence (Runge himself had posed as a traveling jukebox salesman).[24]

I made two futile attempts to garner the secrets of Nagell's 1968 sojourn. While in Moscow for the first time in March 1990 to cover an environmental conference, I went to KGB headquarters and was allowed to visit with two unnamed officials inside the notorious walls of Lubiyanka. I told them that I understood the KGB may have tried to prevent the assassination of President Kennedy and that perhaps the time was right historically for this information to come out. Questioned about my sources, I did not name Nagell but said I had learned this from someone "who once worked for the CIA—and perhaps the KGB." This remark certainly raised eyebrows, but did not elicit my desired response. I was politely asked to drop a letter of inquiry in a box at 22 Kuznetsky Most, which I did, and then they would see about someone getting back to me in the United States. As of this writing, no one has.

I also sought access to files now being released by the former "Stasi," or East German MfS. But I was told that while citizens of the former Communist nation are being allowed to see material compiled about them, no such information was being released on international matters like that of Richard Case Nagell.

Free at Last?

On October 23, 1968, after four and one-half months in captivity, Nagell was released into the waiting arms of the Americans at a bridge between the two Berlins. *The Family*'s source continues: "He didn't know he was going to be released until he was taken out of prison and driven to a Berlin checkpoint identified to him as Sandkrugbruecke."

What Nagell called a "sanitized" Associated Press story about his release mentioned that the man involved in helping arrange it, on the Communist side, was East German lawyer Wolfgang Vogel. The story did not mention, however, that Vogel was no ordinary attorney. He was brought in on only the most sensitive "spy exchanges," his specialty since negotiating the 1962 deal where downed U-2 pilot Francis Gary Powers was swapped for Soviet colonel Rudolf Abel.[25]

When I sent a letter to Vogel in 1990, he wrote back that he would be unable to provide any information on the Nagell case. I did, however, manage to interview two other men who had been present at the border. One was Ricey S. New, Jr., a Washington-based attorney who, according to Nagell in his Court of Claims case, "stated to me that he had handled negotiations for the CIA and the Army in effecting the releases and exchanges of other American prisoners held by the East Germans, that he was one of the few Americans permitted to enter the confines of the MfS (Ministry for State Security) prison at which I had been incarcerated." Nagell says that, upon his query, New stated "that I could consider him as a representative of the CIA."

I spoke with New by telephone in September 1978, from his small law office ("basically just my wife and myself," he said). When I asked whether he was acting on behalf of the CIA in the Nagell case, New said, "Certainly not, I never had any connection with them." (Former Garrison investigator William Wood, however, said that he understood New to have been connected with the CIA as far back as 1951.)[26]

How then, I wondered, had New become involved in Nagell's release?

"Well, I'd gone over in 1965 in another case and become associated with Mr. Vogel. I'm an attorney-at-law, just you could say a friend of Mr. Vogel's. I kept up the contact throughout the years. I'm not trying to be vague on purpose, just to call a spade a spade. Vogel notified me of the pending release and wanted me to come over. At that time we had no [legal] representation at the U.S. mission in Berlin."

What did New remember about the Nagell matter? "As I vaguely recall, I think he had gotten off a train in East Germany and was wandering around the station there in an unauthorized area. They questioned him and kept him, on a violation of their laws. Most of the Americans who were detained over there throughout the years have been represented by Mr. Vogel."

And what was his impression of Nagell after he was set free? "Well, he seemed to be a highly intelligent person. He could remember facts, things like that. I didn't attempt to go into it in depth, otherwise."

Did New hear anything about Nagell's background? "Well, just what I read after he was released. Apparently he was in intelligence over in the Orient. I think he was married to an Oriental girl and had some children, was trying to get in touch with them."

I mentioned that it had been written of Nagell that he alleged to possess some knowledge about the Kennedy assassination. Did New recall anything about that?

There was a pause. "No, just what I read, he was . . . he was, uh. . . . That article, I guess you read the same one. That's all I know about that. Then I've seen his name crop up since then, he claims that he knew something about it and I imagine they've questioned him. I think that's the reason he said he put himself out of circulation for a while, got himself in prison so he wouldn't be implicated because he knew too much."

"But you never asked him anything about that?"

"No, I didn't ask him. All of mine was just a courtesy thing. I wasn't his attorney, but then again he might claim that I was. I did try to help him after his release there. I mentioned that if he ever came to Washington, he might get in touch with me and we'd see about these extra veteran's benefits that he thought he was entitled to. As I recall, he was in a severe plane accident near Washington and I don't know whether that had any effect on him mentally or not. That's a psychiatric question. Anyway, in dealing with him, don't accept carte blanche anything he says. I mean, investigate it."

New suggested that a fellow named Andor Klay, who had then been head of the Eastern Affairs Section at the U.S. mission in Berlin, "might be in a position to tell you something more about this. He knows about these things in depth, the psychological and other reasons, you know. Sometimes he opens up."

I phoned Klay, by now retired from the State Department and living in suburban Washington, at his home that night.[27] I told him that Ricey New had suggested I call, and he described the attorney as "a very dear friend" who was "the attorney of record in many, many of these cases. Ricey had established a wide and excellent reputation as a specialist in this field. There was usually a humanitarian touch. Ricey is a very warmhearted man and a wealthy man.

"Nagell, yes!" Klay remembered right away. "The Nagell case. Well, the question is not what he was doing over there, the question is what he was charged with. They can charge a man with anything. They probably thought at first that he was some kind of spy—a military or CIA agent— and then later on perhaps they reached the conclusion that he was a nut. So they released him. This is just my speculation, you realize, speaking from the top of my head across the span of so many years now behind us. But this is my impression—that at first he got himself involved in some shady activities so the East German police went after him and slapped him in jail, and then possibly it was during his trial there that his mental shape became questionable.

"There is, of course, intervention on our part for any and every American citizen. We went out of our way, either to try to get this man out or have some kind of exchange deal, or have the sentence reduced. It could well be the latter, some manipulations about reducing the sentence, or a realization on the part of the East Germans that the man was worthless. Or both. That is the answer to your question why he was let out after a relatively short time."

But there was never any indication that he was indeed a spy? I asked.

"No, not on *my* side," Klay said. "I mean, I can only tell you that from the files I had, this was just a visionary sort of individual. I am not competent to judge his mental condition, but assuming that he's okay mentally, then I would say there is probably a kind of morbid ambition to get on the front page of the papers or have himself accepted as a man who can perform great services for *us*. And I certainly don't want to go so far as to suggest that failing all this, he might offer his services elsewhere. I have no grounds *for* that, but we have had cases in the past, you know that. So I think that is about *all* in the way of real meaningful comment that I can make to you. Unless you have further questions, let's see."

Klay added that neither Military Intelligence nor the CIA had ever contacted him about the Nagell case. "Never, never, there was no need for that." But why was it considered important enough, on the other side, for Wolfgang Vogel to get involved? "Well, as I said, there could well have been a supposition at first that this was an important case, an important man. If that was the idea the East Germans had, it's a logical thing that Vogel enters the picture immediately. But, except for the liquidation of the case, which would still call for Vogel in a sort of supervisory capacity, I doubt very much that he had anything in the meantime to do with it. From his point of view, as soon as it turned out that the man is releasable shortly —because the story won't hold water and he is really a nobody—then Vogel is simply too important a man to carry on."

I asked Klay about what happened when the Americans met Nagell at the border.

"I think that this was a somewhat confused man. I only supervised the release, you see. I didn't want to send any of my officers because the matter had these shady overtones, so I decided to go myself to the bridge-head with Ricey New. We even had with us, I recall, the physician from the mission, ready to administer injections of appropriate medication to calm him down. They figured that he might well become ferocious—and they were not wrong. I think that Nagell was the man who started running back."

"Running back?" I asked.

"Running back! The East German people—the police, officials, and so on—let him out and he started coming over to us, the distance was maybe twenty yards. Then suddenly, in the middle of the bridge, he stopped and yelled something, then turned and ran back to the East Germans! So we had a very odd experience. We struggled with him physically, finally, to put him in the car and take him out. It did not come to giving any injection. We tried to calm him down and I think that simply eventuated.

"But then he took his revenge in suggesting, giving all kinds of information—of course, most of it quite false—to this long overseas weekly newspaper that was published. We could never really make head or tail of it. The whole thing is full of spies and complex machinations and plots and CIA and Army."

Under Western Eyes

Nagell, and the article in *The Family*, told a very different story about his relationship with America's representatives involved in his release. Ricey New, Nagell wrote in his Court of Claims case, had from the outset promised legal assistance in obtaining a disability retirement from the Army . . . out of the clear blue sky, so to speak, first when I was discussing the 1954 B-25 Bomber crash with Captain George R. Babineau (a U.S. Army psychiatrist wearing civilian clothes) at the U.S. Mission in West Berlin and then outside the TWA office near the Berlin Hilton, confirming the offer as a promise if I stayed away from the West German news media. He repeated the promise at Tempelhoff [sic] Airport, where he had accompanied me to see me off on my return to Switzerland.

He seemed in a terrible hurry to get me out of Germany (I flew to Switzerland only several hours after my release, with a 1-hour stopover at Stuttgart). He indicated that the promise also was based on my staying clear of the Swiss news media and on my early return to the United States from Zurich. He gave me his telephone number at the Berlin Hilton and told me to call him when I arrived at Zurich. He suggested that I not talk to anyone at the U.S. Consulate in Zurich, indicating that he might visit me at Zurich. (The following day when I called him from Zurich at the Berlin Hilton, I was told that he had already checked out. Later, back in the United States, he told me that he had left West Berlin for Amsterdam, that he had decided it was not advisable for me to call him, because the MfS might have tapped the lines.)

I accepted Mr. New's promise of legal assistance in good faith and did as he suggested; I stayed away from both the West German and Swiss news media and returned to the United States ten days later, on 2 November 1968. Meanwhile, unknown to me, unnamed "American spokesmen" in West Berlin had told the Associated Press the day after my exchange that I had already returned to the United States. A sanitized AP dispatch from West Berlin, containing fabrications about me and the circumstances leading to my apprehension by the MfS, appeared in major American newspapers throughout the United States on 25 October 1968, and I have cause to believe that the information given to the AP was concocted at the instance of both defendant [Pentagon] and the CIA. Later, while visiting Mr. New's office at Suite 522, 1250 Connecticut Avenue, N.W., Washington, D.C. 20036, he stated that I should stay away from the American news media too, indicating that if I discussed the truth about my imprisonment by the MfS, that it might delay the release of other American prisoners believed held in East Germany. . . .

The Family's source told much the same story but filled in some details. While at the U.S. mission at 170 Clay Allee in West Berlin, "somebody brought Nagell a cup of coffee." He drank a small portion, finding it tasted very bitter, and after about five minutes "began feeling sleepy and thought that he was under the influence of a drug." (The psychiatrist present denied to the magazine that any substance had been put in Nagell's coffee.)

"New spoke to the doctor in a corner—the doctor kept shaking his head no—and then New told Nagell, 'I think you ought to leave for the United States. The German newspapers are going to pick this thing up any moment and might want to talk to you. I don't think you should talk to them.

"Nagell said he wanted to go back to Zurich first to pick up his belongings . . . certain documents in a safe deposit box. Nagell keeps records, plenty of them." New saw him to the airport, waiting until he boarded the plane. By the time Nagell reached Zurich around 4:00 A.M., "he was feeling extremely sick. He rested for a few hours and went to the U.S. Consulate General. New had told him to stay away from the consulate in Zurich because 'they will question you and send it to Washington.' " But Nagell "was drastically sick and wanted a doctor. He thought he was dying." Referred to a civilian physician, Nagell was told "he had been given an overdose of Seconal, a most potent sleeping drug." He remained ill for about six days.

Nagell had told New that he wanted a search for his missing family to be agreed upon before he returned to the United States. When he could not reach the attorney at the Berlin Hilton, Nagell then violated his instructions and went to the consulate for help. On his first visit, Nagell found "they had a classified file on him and knew he had been in East Berlin. But he refused to answer questions about his imprisonment and told them about New's promise. The next time he told the consulate he was angry that he had not heard from New and that if he didn't get help he was going to the news media. This is when he was offered State Department help in locating his family—predicated on his early return to the United States. Nagell agreed and flew back to New York."

For several weeks Nagell waited to hear from the State Department. Then he went to Washington, where the State Department told him it "didn't have the facilities to search for the children, but on account of the circumstances surrounding the case and 'because one of our employees apparently made a promise in Zurich,' they would conduct a search for his children and determine whether he was married or divorced. He never heard from them again. When he called they were quote unavailable unquote."

Nagell says he paid a number of visits to New's Suite 522 during the months of November and December 1968 and January 1969. New put him in touch with John H. Gullett, a former naval commander in his office who was to help with Nagell's attempt to get a full disability retirement. But eventually the promise of assistance was withdrawn and "Mr. New accompanied me to the elevator, apologizing for 'the misunderstanding' in West Berlin" regarding it.[28]

In Search of the Kids

Nagell wrote in his Court of Claims case: "On 12 February 1969, following an incident at New York City, in which a practice Mark IV hand grenade was thrown at me from a speeding automobile, I flew to Mexico City via New Orleans, Louisiana." The day before heading south of the border, Nagell had stopped off to see if William R. Martin "indeed had occupied an office at the new International Trade Mart" and been told by the building manager that the former Garrison "investigator" had not. Nagell then proceeded "to inform Mr. Garrison that I felt it inadvisable for me to appear as a prosecution witness at the Clay Shaw trial, which was then in progress. I turned over what remained of the practice grenade to Mr. Garrison in the presence of one of his investigators."

Nagell spent nine days in Mexico City. Here he renewed his acquaintance with two people so pivotal to his activities in 1962–63: Maria del Carmen and Franz Waehauf, the latter having found employment at the Restaurant Fritz and "trying to get into Florida," according to Nagell.[29] In Mexico, Nagell told me, he verified a number of things about the events leading up to the assassination. He then flew to Montreal and onward to Zurich on February 21, 1969. From Switzerland he commenced sending a series of photocopied travel vouchers back to Greenstein, substantiating his whereabouts over the next several months.[30]

Nagell was still in search of his children. Writes Thomas Lucey:

> But the vice-consul who had promised State Dept. help last fall [in Zurich] was no longer there. Nagell asked for the man he claimed to be the CIA station chief. He, too, was gone. Sent to the consulate's political section, Nagell told them of the promises he'd been given and threatened to go to Swiss newspapers about a CIA agent in Bern, the Swiss capital.
>
> "A member of the consulate asked Nagell to give them two weeks and telexed Washington," the source said. "But then one night there was an attempt on Nagell's life and he left for Barcelona the next day. There he contacted the U.S. Consulate General and told them why he had left Zurich and asked that Zurich's reply from Washington be sent to Barcelona. Nagell was in Barcelona for two weeks. But then he realized he was being watched and left to see an ex-Army intelligence officer at the American Embassy in Madrid."

Nagell writes:

. . . on 7 March, 1969, I was shot at by a person unknown to me. The next day, I departed Switzerland for Spain, where I stayed for one month. Following a conversation with Colonel Cecil K. Charboneau, the U.S. Army Attaché at Madrid, during which he told me, none too subtly, that "You should know that anybody can be made to disappear in Spain and never be heard from again," or words similar and to that effect, I departed Spain for West Berlin, on 8 April 1969.

If he couldn't find his children, the article in *The Family* says that Nagell promised himself he would go to the news media. Back in Berlin, he was referred to Andor Klay and Bruce Flatin, two of the men who had met him upon his return from East Berlin. According to the article's source, "A week or two later, they finally got confirmation from Washington that they had been unable to locate Nagell's children so far but were continuing their efforts. So he finally agreed to go back to the States."

Then, Nagell writes: "On 22 April 1969, I was attacked by one of two men, both unknown to me, and rendered unconscious by a blow to the head." *The Family* relates that Nagell had realized two days earlier that he was under surveillance.

"Around 10:30 on the night of April 22, Nagell was walking down Kurfuerstendamm when he lost his tail," the [magazine's] source continued. "They just disappeared. He didn't try to lose them. Nagell then went down a side street and into a small restaurant with a bar. He ordered a beer and was standing at the bar, talking to a guy on his right, when he saw the door open and two men came directly toward him. Nagell was getting ready to tell the men he didn't speak German when he saw one pick something out of his pocket and swing at him. Nagell turned and was hit on the back of the head."

Police took Nagell to the Albrecht Achilles Hospital. When he told the Germans he thought he had been hit by the CIA, "they called an American from the CID [Criminal Investigation Division], a British representative (apparently the side street was in the British Sector) and a member of the Berlin political police."

Around midnight Nagell went to the U.S. Mission and asked for [Kenneth] Hill in the passport section. Instead, he got the Army staff duty officer and a CIC agent. "He gave his bloody shirt and T-shirt in a bag to the CIC agent," the source said, "and told him to give it to Hill. 'If something happens to me,' he told the agent, 'the responsibility is going to be pinned because I'm going to the papers.' Back in his hotel, Nagell was worried that he was going to be killed."

In the morning he went to the Army hospital and then to Hill in the consulate. "Hill had the bloody clothing. 'You must get out of Berlin,' he told Nagell. 'We cannot give you protection here. The German police think it's either mistaken identity or the MfS.'

" 'Last night I thought somebody wanted to kill me,' Nagell replied. 'Now I take it as (only) a warning.' "

(Later, Hill told *The Family* he considered Nagell merely "a private American citizen traveling abroad." He added: "Ninety-nine and a half percent of his story is fantasy." Hill confirmed that he had received Nagell's bloody clothing and that Nagell had come to him with a stitched-up head wound. But he would only say that the attack "is his story, not that I have any other story about it.")

Nagell writes: "On 26 April 1969, I traveled to East Berlin in the company of a U.S. Army major (whom I can identify) in uniform. I met a GDR official who assured me that the MfS was not behind the recent attempts to frighten or intimidate me, not that I suspected the MfS."

The FAMILY adds: ". . . shortly after that Nagell was placed on orders as an ambulatory patient and sent on the Berlin duty train to Frankfurt. His orders also put him on a military flight back to the States."

When he departed West Berlin on the twenty-sixth, bound first for Frankfurt—"travel is deemed necessary in the public service," says an Army file of that same date[31]—Nagell was en route back to McGuire Air Force Base in New Jersey, from where it was recommended his injury be checked at a V.A. hospital. But before his flight home, it was in Frankfurt where he paused to speak with the serviceman's overseas *Family* journal.

His reason, as he wrote to Greenstein,

was for the purpose of getting the ball rolling, not with the aim of having it publish a maudlin story in its family supplement. . . . if Overseas broke the latter part of the story in Deutschland, then Ricey New, et al, well-knowing there was more that could be told, might have second thoughts about leaving me high and dry, a rusty, useless old piece of junk protruding from the scrap heap. . . .[32]

Another Nagell letter from the period:

I arrived at McGuire Air Force Base, New Jersey, during the evening of April 29. Since nobody was there to meet me (as purportedly had been arranged at Frankfurt), I was billeted overnight. . . . After waiting most of the following day for the person who was supposed to meet me, I took a train to New York since I was still experiencing a severe headache.[33]

A telegram about his predicament, sent to Greenstein:

He finally gets to see V.A. doctor on 2 May. Doctor questions him first about imprisonment in East Germany and in U.S.A. and fails to even look at wound in head. When vet refuses to discuss reasons for imprisonment doctor becomes angry and instructs him to return 5 May saying if you don't feel better then we'll see about getting you admitted to a hospital. Vet now threatens to catch first plane back to Berlin.[34]

May 7, a telegram from Nagell to Alfred G. Ennulat, an FBI agent in the New York field office: "Re our conversation this date—when I am apprised of the whereabouts of my children I shall be willing to discuss the circumstances regarding the person empl[oyed] at 45 East 49th Street."

In 1990 I tracked down Ennulat at his retirement home in Silver Spring, Maryland, and showed him the telegram. "If anything," he said, "I probably would have talked with Nagell briefly on one occasion at our office, I don't recall just why. He might have told us about East Germany. Nothing ever came of this [telegram], because he never came back. I don't remember what it's all about. And how Nagell came to our attention, I don't know. Our interest, I'm sure, was based on the fact that he was in East Germany for any period. He lived in Queens, on Elmhurst Avenue if I remember. He used to travel around the world, you never knew where he was from one day to another. He used to get military checks, was always getting on and off planes. But if he received a military annuity and was still under that, the military would have had responsibility; they would have briefed and debriefed him."

When I brought up the Kennedy assassination, Ennulat added only that such a subject—"and any counterintelligence investigation"—would have been an entirely separate unit of the FBI than his.[35]

Nagell writes:

On May 8 [1969], no doubt because of an inquiry initiated into the matter from the New York Daily News, I received a telegram indicating that I would be admitted to the Manhattan VA hospital that day. Thus it was that sixteen days after my head injury in Berlin the Veterans Administration graciously reeled in its red tape and finally decided that it just might be advisable to examine me. I reported to the hospital, had the sutures removed from my scalp and walked out disgusted, wondering how many other veterans who have a lesser disability rating than myself (100%) get the same brand of treatment at New York.[36]

Nagell continued to pursue his two quests: finding his children, and getting full compensation for his disability retirement from the Pentagon. That November, he was advised that the Army Board for Correction of Military Records (ABCMR) was the ultimate authority in the latter matter. On April 7, 1970, he went to the Pentagon and submitted a handwritten application to the ABCMR.[37] Then, one more time, he left the country.

From Switzerland on April 14, Nagell wrote to Francis X. Plant, then special assistant to the under secretary of the Army, and with whom he had met shortly before his departure:

> Enclosed are five (5) documents, ranging in classification from "Secret" to "Top Secret," that I believe can be considered as evidence in my case, since I was directly involved in the operations referenced during the official performance of my assigned duties. Anybody with even a shallow sense of moral convictions would develop a "nervous disorder" after participating in these illegal operations.
>
> Please advise me immediately by telex in care of the person whose name and address is listed on the envelope by stating either "YES" or "NO" as to whether or not these documents constitute the hard evidence you said on 6 April was needed by the ABCMR.

After a salutation of "Very truly, Richard C. Nagell," he added "P.S. I have not signed my name to this letter for obvious reasons."

Receiving no reply, Nagell journeyed on to West Berlin. From there, another letter from Nagell to Plant followed on April 24, enclosing more "xerox copies of several documents, which your housecleaning office might find of interest. The originals, together with numerous other documents and the details about them, are safely locked away. . . ." If he did not receive the money due him, Nagell added, "then you can pass on to the Secretary that before my case is closed the Army will be confronted with a scandal that will make France's Dreyfus affair seem inconsequential by comparison. I am not quite the fool that apparently I have been taken for."[38]

On May 1, according to Nagell, Plant wrote him back to his P.O. Box in New York City that he had never received his "communication" of April 14.[39]

Nagell was apparently still working for someone, in an intelligence capacity, during another 1970 trip to West Berlin. One piece of paper I came upon in Fensterwald's files is dated April 26, a page-long list of twenty-two photographs he had taken that "cloudy-dull" afternoon with a Minolta II camera.

Although Nagell's disability claim battle with the Pentagon would go on for many years, it was the spring of 1970 in Berlin when he was finally somehow informed of the whereabouts of his two children. If they had previously been in Europe, by this time they had returned to Los Angeles. A June 19, 1970, letter from L.A.'s director of the Department of Public

Social Services let Nagell know that the case record had been reviewed and the staff "will proceed without delay to contact Mrs. Nagell and develop a plan to provide you the opportunity to visit [his son] Robert. I specify Robert is under our supervision and his sister is not. We are further prepared to return to Juvenile Court if Mrs. Nagell does not cooperate with us."[40]

Reunited with his children late that month, Nagell would take legal custody of Robert and Teri Nagell on August 17, 1971.[41] I knew that his ex-wife, Mitsuko, had since remarried, but I was unable to find her. Trying to find out more about this most bizarre of circumstances surrounding Richard Case Nagell, through a university alumni office I was able to locate Robert Lamont Nagell by phone in February 1992. Now thirty-two and working as a veterinarian in California, he said:

"I saw my father for the first time in 1970. And I lived with him for a number of years, until eventually he decided he was not into parenting. He was a very secretive man. Do you know I don't even know where he was born? Or his mother's maiden name? He was never willing to have a photo of himself taken with the family.

"I haven't spoken to my father in eleven years. The last talk we had was amicable enough, it closed a chapter and I've never really looked back. If I had a relationship with him, it might be worthwhile for you to talk to me. But our family is completely split up. Nobody talks to anybody, except me and my mother. I don't really want to delve into my past. I would be interested in what really went on myself, but my mother will not even talk to me about it. My father always told me that someday the truth would be known."[42]

Summary

The two-plus-years after Nagell gained his freedom from prison did not see any letup in the turmoil surrounding him. As soon as he was free, he was gone again—first to New York, where two CIA men met him at the airport and gave him a down payment on $15,000 he would soon deposit. Meeting with Jim Garrison, Nagell offered the DA an opportunity to meet with a KGB official who was then in the city. Nagell also received another assignment from a "Mr. Buehel," got a new passport, and headed off for Europe. The FBI was alerted as soon as he showed up at the U.S. consulate in Zurich. A few days after that, Nagell simply disappeared into East Germany.

Although more mystery surrounds his four and one-half months behind the Iron Curtain, apparently Nagell was taken to Moscow and provided the KGB with the full story behind his actions (or lack thereof) in September 1963. His return to the American fold at the Berlin border is right out of a John le Carré novel. Although U.S. representatives Ricey New and Andor Klay have described their reception of Nagell as routine, the ex-Army captain seems to have been drugged and warned to stay away from the media. Involved in his release was East German spy exchange master Wolfgang Vogel.

Early in 1969, the peripatetic Nagell was gone again: meeting certain old acquaintances in Mexico City, ultimately returning to Europe. Three attempts were made on his life during this period. Upon his return this time to an American military base, he was back in touch with the FBI. Nagell's quest for his two children did not culminate until the summer of 1970, by which time he was also pushing the Pentagon to grant him a full disability retirement. Even Nagell's son Robert, who went to his father's custody in 1971, finds him as much of a mystery man as so many others have.

Chapter Thirty

Orchestration of the JFK Conspiracy

When Richard Nagell was with Oswald in New Orleans, he discovered that Oswald was "undergoing hypnotherapy" from David Ferrie. Nagell dropped this potential bombshell in a single phrase in one of his letters to Arthur Greenstein. In a set of "cartoons" that Nagell also mailed to Greenstein from prison, one sequence shows Oswald, armed with a secondhand rifle, at the sixth-floor window of the Texas School Book Depository, when he suddenly "awakens from [a] hypnotic trance."

Ferrie's former roommate Raymond Broshears told me in 1975 that hypnosis was part of Ferrie's general interest in the occult—"spiritualism, voices from the other side, all of that."[1] The reader may recall the House Assassinations Committee's mention that Ferrie "frequently practiced" techniques of hypnosis on his young associates (see Chapter Seventeen). Jack Martin, an associate of Ferrie and Guy Banister, told the FBI three days after the assassination "that he believed Ferrie was an 'amateur hypnotist' who may have been capable of hypnotizing Oswald."[2] And, when the New Orleans police discovered Ferrie dead in his apartment in 1967, they found several voluminous abstracts on posthypnotic suggestion amid a veritable library on hypnotism.[3]

Was Oswald manipulated through applications of "mind control" techniques? Is this possible? It smacks of something so fantastic that even raising the question seems incredible. At first it confronted me with a challenge that I honestly did not want to face. Yet I came to feel that I had no choice. The fact is, the CIA and Military Intelligence worked diligently for years on the manipulation of human behavior, even the creation of a "Manchurian Candidate." So did the Soviet Union. And, in this book, I have introduced this as a recurring theme, on the periphery surrounding Oswald, since his years in the Far East.

1. The CIA's reported LSD experiments, under the MK-ULTRA program, at the Atsugi base; and the interest of Mark Gayn, Dr. Chikao Fujisawa, and MIT's Center for International Studies in Japanese "thought control" methods (Chapters Four and Five).
2. The "brainwashing" expertise of Charles Willoughby's associate Edward Hunter (Chapter Seven).
3. The experiences of U-2 pilot Francis Gary Powers, and the Rand Corporation's studies of hypnosis (Chapter Eight).
4. The focus on ideological conversion at the April 1963 Hunter-Willoughby "psychological warfare" seminar (Chapter Thirteen).
5. The CIA's 1954 effort to create a "Manchurian Candidate," a crossover between its personnel in charge of the MK-ULTRA and assassination programs, and mind-control experiments in Mexico City (Chapter Sixteen).
6. Oswald's strange behavior in the office of Edward Gillin in New Orleans, and the CIA's sudden concern in the summer of 1963 about its MK-ULTRA experiments (Chapter Seventeen).
7. The apparent knowledge by JFK's mistress Mary Meyer about the government's mind-control program; and the 1973 destruction of records by Richard Helms (Chapter Twenty).

As set forth in the 1975 report, "CIA Activities Within the United States," by a presidential commission, 152 files concerning drug testing and "a much larger program to study possible means for controlling human behavior" had disappeared. The commission mentioned that these other studies "explored the effects of radiation, electric shock, psychology, psychiatry, sociology and harassment substances."[4]

The U.S. military had long been intrigued by the same means. "The Hypnotic Manipulation of Attitudinal Effect," for example, was part of the title of a 1957 research contract granted by the Office of Naval Research. W. H. Bowart, in researching his 1978 book *Operation Mind Con-*

trol, found references to several similar military contracts in a book *(The Manipulation of Human Behavior)*—but discovered that these hypnosis studies had been erased from the record in the Military Intelligence Classified Index.[5]

In 1968, Dr. Joseph L. Bernd of Virginia Polytechnic Institute questioned authorities on hypnosis about whether the creation of a "Manchurian Candidate" was really feasible. As author Bowart recounted one expert's response to Dr. Bernd: "I would say that a highly skilled hypnotist, working with a highly susceptible subject, could possibly persuade the subject to kill another human. . . ." Another believed it was even possible, through posthypnotic suggestion, to make a subject unable to recall such an act: "There could be a conspiracy, but a conspiracy of which the principal was unaware."[6]

So I do not believe we can rule out this insidious possibility in terms of Oswald. It might explain Nagell's inability to convince Oswald in September 1963 that he was being set up as a "patsy" in the assassination conspiracy by Angel and Leopoldo, the conversation wherein Nagell told Oswald he was being "used by Fascist elements." It might also explain Oswald's remarkably nonchalant attitude after his arrest on November 22, 1963. One policeman described his behavior on the ride to the station as akin to someone who had just been picked up for a speeding ticket, and Frank Ellsworth described to me his own mystification at Oswald's "cool" behavior during his initial interrogation.[7]

And "mind control" was not a subject that the Warren Commission ignored altogether. It first arose in the testimony of J. Edgar Hoover on May 12, 1964—when the FBI director raised the specter of a programmed assassin, pointing cryptically but directly at the alleged capabilities of the Soviet Union.

"Just the day before yesterday," Hoover told the commission, "information came to me indicating that there is an espionage training school outside of Minsk—I don't know whether it is true—and that he [Oswald] was trained at that school to come back to this country to become what they call a 'sleeper,' that is, a man who will remain dormant for three or four years and in case of international hostilities rise up and be used."[8]

One week later, commission counsel Rankin requested from the CIA all "materials relative to Soviet techniques in mind conditioning and brainwashing." Richard Helms, later known to have supervised the CIA's MK-ULTRA program, responded on June 19, 1964, with an agency-prepared memorandum titled "Soviet Research and Development in the Field of Direction and Control of Human Behavior." Regarded as too sensitive to declassify until 1974, the memo says as much about America's "research and development" as it does about the USSR's:

There are two major methods of altering or controlling human behavior, and the Soviets are interested in both. The first is psychological; the second, pharmacological. The two may be used as individual methods or for mutual reinforcement. For long-term control of large numbers of people, the former method is more promising than the latter. In dealing with individuals, the U.S. experience suggests the pharmacological approach (assisted by psychological techniques) would be the only effective method. Neither method would be very effective for single individuals on a long-term basis. Soviet research on the pharmacological agents producing behavioral effects has consistently lagged about five years behind Western research. They have been interested in such research, however, and are now pursuing research on such chemicals as LSD-25, amphetamines, tranquilizers, hypnotics, and similar materials. There is no present evidence that the Soviets have any singular, new, potent drugs, or that they are particularly expert in the use of such drugs to force a course of action on an individual. They are aware, however, of the tremendous drive produced by drug addiction, and *perhaps* could couple this with psychological direction to achieve control of an individual [emphasis in original].

The memo goes on to describe the Soviet interest in such modern marvels as cybernetics, information inputs, and so on. It concludes: "In summary, therefore, there is no evidence that the Soviets have any techniques or agents capable of producing particular behavioral patterns which are not available in the West."[9]

The Warren Commission did not pursue particulars about the CIA/ Pentagon's own mind-control efforts, with Helms or anyone else.

The "Black Book"

In 1967, a little-known 173-page volume was published by University Books of New Hyde Park, New York. Its author wrote under the pseudonym of "Lincoln Lawrence," and said at the outset that he wished to spell out the structure of a "deadly rumor" that had come to his attention. The book was titled *Were We Controlled?*

"Lawrence" began his chronicle on March 30, 1961, when Oswald was admitted to the Third Clinical Hospital's Ear, Nose, and Throat Division in Minsk. He had been suffering "complaints about suppuration from the right ear and weakened in hearing," and the diagnosis called for an adenoid operation. Marina, whom he had recently met, came regularly to his bedside during his eleven-day stay in the hospital.

"After he was placed under anaesthesia," Lawrence wrote, "advanced technique was employed to implant a miniaturized radio receiver which would produce a muscular reaction in his cerebral region." Thus, upon leaving the hospital, Oswald would "remain for the rest of his life—without his knowledge—a completely efficient human tool . . . subject to 'control'!"

The author went on to describe two devices implanted in Oswald's brain. One was R.H.I.C. (Radio-Hypnotic Intracerebral Control), "the ultra sophisticated application of post-hypnotic-suggestion *triggered at will* by radio transmission. It is a recurring hypnotic state, re-induced automatically at intervals by the same radio control" (emphasis in original).

The other was E.D.O.M. (Electronic Dissolution of Memory), which "enables man to juggle with other men's sense of time . . . through the use of radio-waves and ultra-sonic signal tones. . . . It in effect blocks memory of the moment."[10]

On record in the National Archives is a government memo dated March 3, 1964, from CIA director McCone to Secret Service chief James Rowley, which makes a remarkably similar speculation. Following his surgery at the Minsk hospital, McCone wrote, Oswald might have been "chemically or electronically 'controlled' . . . a sleeper agent. Subject spent 11 days hospitalized for a 'minor ailment' which should have required no more than three days hospitalization at best."[11] (This would lead to the conclusion that the CIA was Hoover's source for his subsequent revelation to the Warren Commission.)

But "Lincoln Lawrence" did not see Oswald ultimately as a pawn of the Soviets. Rather, he wrote that Oswald was later "high-jacked," or "maneuvered into the orbit of *another* group which trained and prepared him for work in the future when they (the second group) might have need for his 'special' qualifications" (emphasis in original). This second group then asserted control of Oswald upon his return to the United States in the summer of 1962.

The idea is not unlike that posed in Richard Condon's 1958 novel *The Manchurian Candidate,* wherein an assassin is programmed by Korean Communists but used by the hapless Army sergeant's own mother to try to achieve presidential ambitions for her husband. It was also raised in ex-CIA contract agent Hugh McDonald's 1975 book *Appointment in Dallas.* Here, McDonald describes a conversation with a former high-ranking CIA official, Herman Kimsey, who claimed to have inside knowledge on the assassination.

"Hugh, Oswald was programmed to kill," McDonald quotes Kimsey as saying. "Like a medium at a séance. Then the mechanism went on the blink, and Oswald became a dangerous toy without direction. . . ."[12]

Three weeks after making these statements to McDonald, Kimsey died from reported heart failure, at age fifty-five, on January 24, 1971.[13]

Kimsey also told McDonald that the actual JFK assassin was a European contract killer code-named "Saul," hired by "a private group, but that group had strong government connections." When McDonald set out to find Saul—which he eventually managed to do—he went through an émigré network in Europe that he called by the code name "Blue Fox."[14] McDonald's description of this group was very close to what is known of the Gehlen-White Russian-Ukrainian underground—with its connections to Charles Willoughby and the CIA. Herman Kimsey, interestingly enough, was, like Willoughby, a member of the Military Affairs Committee of the Shickshinny Knights of Malta.[15]

According to Lincoln Lawrence, Oswald was not the only manipulated cog in the wheel. Another was Jack Ruby, "placed under hypnosis . . . perhaps at a party or perhaps by some 'performer' who was pretending to offer a casual audition for the Carousel Club." The entertainer at Ruby's club the week of the assassination was, in fact, a hypnotist, William Crowe, whose stage name was Bill DeMar.

In Lawrence's astonishing summary of "evidence," he noted the psychiatric report on Ruby by Dr. Walter Bromberg: "Definitely there is a block to his thinking which is no part of his original mental endowment." Lawrence noted, too, Ruby's strange testimony to the Warren Commission: "Very rarely do I use the name Oswald. I don't know why. I don't know how to explain it."

I set out to learn more about the origins of *Were We Controlled?* In October 1976 in New York, I tracked down the man who had been contacted by "Lincoln Lawrence" and whom I was told ghost-wrote the book based on Lawrence's information. He was Art Ford, a prominent radio announcer and longtime student of parapsychology with many connections in the publishing world.[16]

"I never met Lawrence," Ford told me. "Whoever he was, he was very clever. He covered himself well. The only reason I am sure the man actually existed is, I got a telegram from him and then he managed to reach me by phone. I received payment, in cash, for helping him research his book. The research I did all went to a certain mail drop and was picked up. When he first contacted me, he told me to look into mind-control techniques. I said, you mean mind therapy, psychology. No, he said, start with Vasilyev in Russia, work your way to Delgado, go from there."

A. T. Vasilyev was the chief of the Russian secret police, the Okhrana, at the time of the 1917 Revolution. Dr. José Delgado was a well-known neurophysiologist at the Yale University School of Medicine; his experiments with electronic stimulation of the brain were supported by the Office of Naval Research.[17]

"I let a lot of time go by before I'd even talk about it," Ford continued. " 'Lawrence' had a lawyer, Martin Scheiman, whose role was to pay out royalties up to a certain point. He was found dead in the *Time-Life* Building, with a gun beside him and a bullet through his head after the book was published, a supposed suicide. Damon Runyon, Jr., did a condensation of the book for the *National Enquirer,* which never published it. He was the only person to ever receive a written communication from 'Lawrence.' He ended up being pushed off a bridge in Washington, D.C."

Ford was right about Runyon's strange demise. I went to the clipping files of *The New York Times* and found that on April 14, 1968, the son of the famed newsman "fell to his death from an overpass in Rock Creek Park here today. The police tentatively ruled Mr. Runyon's death a suicide."[18]

Someone else had quite a frantic reaction to the "Lincoln Lawrence" book. Late in 1967, Dallas assassination researcher Mary Ferrell received a call from Oswald's mother, Marguerite. "She called me the minute she read *Were We Controlled?,*" Mrs. Ferrell remembers. "She said, 'I've got to find out who wrote this book, because he knew my son.' I asked her why. Marguerite said, 'I can't divulge that.' But she started calling me day and night, saying if I was so smart, why couldn't I find Lincoln Lawrence?"

Mrs. Ferrell got a copy of the book and read it "until I almost memorized it, because I could not figure what would cause her to say that the author knew her son. Then I went back and reread all of Marguerite's testimony to the Warren Commission. Somewhere in there is a statement that when Lee and Marina came back from Russia, Marguerite would sometimes stand behind Lee's chair as he played some board game and rub his back and head. And she said the texture of his hair had changed, it wasn't soft like it used to be. Suddenly it came to me: What if, when she was doing that, she felt a little scar up inside the hairline? Then she read this book about implanting an electrode in his brain. That was the best I could come up with."[19]

Oswald's brother Robert apparently had similar concerns. As described by author Epstein in his book *Legend,* Robert was shocked at Oswald's appearance on his return from the USSR. "The most marked change . . . was his hair. Not only had it thinned almost to the point of baldness on top, but the texture had changed from soft to kinky. Struck by this loss of hair, Robert couldn't help wondering what happened to his brother during the intervening years in the Soviet Union . . . [and] later speculated that it might have been caused by medical or shock treatments."[20]

In 1973, Mary Ferrell met with Art Ford in New York. "He showed me his notes from communications with the man who told him this story. I believed him, and I'm a skeptic on many of these wild claims. I got the feeling that the storyteller was dead, that something horrible had happened to him. And Art Ford wanted me to understand that he felt his life was in danger, too."[21]

The Hypothesis Brought Forward

Both James Earl Ray, the accused and convicted assassin of Martin Luther King, Jr., and Sirhan B. Sirhan, who definitely did fire at Robert Kennedy, had a known fascination for hypnotism.

When Ray was arrested at London's Heathrow airport in June 1968, Scotland Yard found in his luggage well-worn copies of three books on "self-improvement." One was titled *Self-Hypnotism: The Technique and Its Use in Daily Living.* It was later revealed that Ray, an escaped convict, had paid a visit earlier that year to Reverend Xavier von Koss, head of the International Society of Hypnosis in Los Angeles. Despite this lofty title, von Koss was unknown in reputable scientific circles, and his number wasn't even listed in the L.A. phone book. Interviewed by William Bradford Huie, one of Ray's biographers, von Koss did not recall exactly how or why Ray had called him for an appointment. He did remember that Ray "had several books on the subject and was impressed with the degree of mind concentration which one can obtain by the use of hypnosis." Von Koss also admitted having "tested him for hypnosis," but having "quickly encountered very strong subconscious resistance." Not much more is known about von Koss. Four months to the day after Ray's visit to the hypnotist, Martin Luther King, Jr., was gunned down in Memphis.[22]

The Sirhan case is even more telling. When taken into custody that June 1968 night in Los Angeles, the young man who fired point-blank at Robert Kennedy in the kitchen of the Ambassador Hotel appeared disoriented, seemed to be trembling, and his pupils were dilated. A common enough reaction for a deranged assassin—except that when later placed under hypnosis by psychiatrists looking for his motive, Sirhan exhibited the exact same symptoms. The defense psychiatrist, Dr. Bernard Diamond, became convinced that Sirhan had prior experience experimenting with "hypnotic states of mind." So suggestible was Sirhan, said Diamond, that he obeyed a hypnotic command to climb the bars of his cell like a monkey.[23]

At Sirhan's trial, Diamond testified that Sirhan may well have shot Robert Kennedy while in a trance, self-induced by using the mirrors on the walls at the hotel. In six of Diamond's eight sessions with Sirhan, the psychiatrist admitted placing him in a hypnotic state. This led another psychiatrist, Dr. Eduard Simson, to conclude that Sirhan might even have been programmed by Dr. Diamond to *accept* the idea of being a lone gunman. Simson later conducted extensive tests on Sirhan inside San Quentin Penitentiary. The young Arab, he believed, was the ideal Manchurian Candidate—"easily influenced, no real roots, and looking for a cause."

Sirhan later told his biographer Robert Blair Kaiser that he had visited the Philosophical Research Center of Manley Palmer Hall, one of Southern California's biggest names in hypnosis.[24] Whoever might have been dabbling with Sirhan's mind, he remembered nothing of having fired those eight shots at Robert Kennedy. Asked by a reporter whether he had planned the assassination, Sirhan had replied: "Only in my mind. I did it, but I was not aware of it, sir." His last recollection was of meeting a girl in a coffee shop of the hotel and handing her a cup of coffee. Shortly before Sirhan opened fire, several witnesses recalled seeing a young lady in a polka-dot dress standing next to him and possibly whispering something into his ear. But the "girl in the polka-dot dress" has never been identified. She remains as enigmatic as the page of Sirhan's diary where he inscribed over and over in a kind of automatic writing that "RFK must die." At the bottom of the page, there occurs this passage: "practice practice practice practice Mind Control Mind Control Mind Control."

The Military, the CIA, and the German Scientists

Retired colonel L. Fletcher Prouty, former Pentagon liaison officer to the CIA, pondered my question in 1992 on the intelligence agencies' use of mind-control methods. "It was pretty well organized," Prouty said finally. "If you get ahold of a directory for the American Psychiatric Association in around 1956 or 1957, you'll be surprised to find that an enormous percentage of the individuals listed are foreign-born. Mostly they came out of Germany and Eastern Europe in a big wave. They were all called technical specialists, but really they were psychiatrists. They went into jobs at universities mostly—but many were working on these 'unconventional' mind-control programs for U.S. intelligence. A lot of the contracts were written by James Monroe, who was with CIA but concealed as an Air Force lieutenant colonel. These would go to people like Dr. [D. Ewen] Cameron in Canada, or the [M. D.] Anderson Foundation in Texas. That's where the money goes blind, you don't know what happened to it."[25]

Dr. Cameron's "pioneering" in the covert uses of LSD and what he called psychic driving—a way to make "direct, controlled changes in personality"—has been documented in several books.[26]

Houston's M. D. Anderson Foundation was revealed in 1967 to have long been a CIA conduit.[27] One of its leading trustees was Leon Jaworski, a prominent trial lawyer who served as president of the Texas State Bar Association in 1962–63. Jaworski was a good friend of Lyndon Johnson, having successfully challenged two lawsuits filed against LBJ in the 1960 campaign to prevent him from running simultaneously as a vice-presidential and senatorial candidate. The attorney based himself out of Houston but also had offices in Washington and Mexico City. After the Kennedy assassination, Jaworski was appointed special counsel to the Texas Board of Inquiry, which briefly conducted its own investigation until soon after the Warren Commission's formation. Jaworski then moved over to become special counsel to the commission, where his primary assignment was checking out Oswald's possible links to the CIA.

In August 1964, *The New York Times* announced that the fifty-nine-year-old Jaworski was LBJ's leading candidate to replace Robert Kennedy as attorney general. This did not take place, for reasons that were never explained.[28] Then, in 1968, when LBJ sought to appoint another friend, Homer Thornberry, to the U.S. Supreme Court, Jaworski investigated Thornberry's credentials and gave a "highly acceptable" rating. It was the same service Jaworski had performed on Thornberry's behalf in 1963, when Thornberry was named to the Federal District Court in El Paso— and shortly thereafter became the judge in the trial of Richard Case Nagell.[29]

In 1973 Jaworski achieved his strongest notoriety when Richard Nixon appointed him special prosecutor in the Watergate investigation—after firing Archibald Cox in the famous "Saturday Night Massacre." A book by James Doyle, the former press chief in Jaworski's prosecutor's office, described the staff's suspicions that Jaworski sought to dispose of the Watergate case "with a quick stroke."[30] Then, when Gerald Ford nominated George Bush as director of the CIA in 1976, Jaworski came forward again to maintain that Bush had "no involvement" in illegal political fund-raising activities that were then being raised by the press.[31]

But Jaworski really got his start in law after World War II, when, as a military colonel, he was named Chief of the War Crimes Trials Section of the U.S. Army in occupied Nazi Germany.[32] At the same time, the U.S. Joint Intelligence Objectives Agency began bringing over to the United States dozens of Nazi scientists to work on a variety of projects under "Operation Paperclip." These projects included extensive research, first begun by the Germans during the war, into the uses of drugs and hypnosis. A number of psychochemical experiments were conducted at the Edgewood Arsenal or the nearby Army intelligence base at Fort Holabird, Maryland.[33]

One of those who took part was, by his own account to researcher Gary Shaw, Colonel William Bishop—the man who was so deeply involved with Cuban exiles, and aware of Richard Nagell, in 1963. As I was completing this book in July 1992, Bishop died of heart failure at his home in Cleburne, Texas. Only days before his death, Bishop had authorized Shaw to release to me a tape recording made in 1983 about his participation in the CIA's MK-ULTRA program.

"That was how, after the Korean War, I got involved with CIA," Bishop said. "I have been subjected to every known type of drug. The medical doctors connected with the agency found that certain drugs work quite well in conjunction with hypnosis—hypnotic power of suggestion—with some subjects. It did with me. I speak with absolute certainty and knowledge and experience that this is not only possible, but did and is taking place today.

"I never understood why they selected me personally," Bishop continued. "There were any number of psychological or emotional factors involved in people's selection. Antisocial behavior patterns, paranoid or the rudiments of paranoia, and so on. But when they are successful with this programming—or, for lack of a better term, indoctrination—they could take John Doe and get this man to kill George and Jane Smith. He will be given all the pertinent information as to their location, daily habits, etc. Then there is a mental block put on this mission in his mind. He remembers nothing about it.

"Perhaps a month or a year later—rarely over a year, at least back in those days—the phone rings. A code word will be read to him in a voice that John Doe recognizes. That will trigger the action. John Doe will commit the assassination, return home, and remember absolutely nothing of it. It is totally a blank space.

"Now, there is a problem with this, and they never found a way that I know of to overcome it. From time to time—it happens to me now—I will see faces, names, places, gunfire, for which there is no rational explanation. I went back for deprogramming. In these sessions, they explain that this does happen from time to time, not to worry about it, just clear your mind and forget it.

"I know men who gradually lost their sight, or some of their hearing, or the use of their vocal cords. Some had chronic constipation. For entirely psychological reasons, not physical, because inadvertently these mental blocks developed. I myself became totally impotent. For obvious reasons, I don't care to go into this in any greater detail."

After Bishop's death, Gary Shaw recalled: "I got the feeling many times with him, he wanted to tell me more and either he couldn't or wouldn't.

Either his mind wouldn't let him tell me, or he felt somewhat threatened if he said more. He was obviously, for years, a man that was tormented."

Another figure who ended up deeply tormented was Frank Wisner, the CIA's original man in charge of bringing over the Nazi scientists under "Paperclip," and with establishing the Gehlen, Ukrainian, and White Russian underground movements in Europe. In 1961, after suffering two nervous breakdowns in recent years, Wisner left the CIA but kept his interest in agency affairs.[34]

Apparently sometime not long after the Kennedy assassination, as Wisner's daughter Wendy recalled to author Burton Hersh, her father became obsessed with the world he had been so enmeshed in creating. Wisner began talking about his belief that Martin Bormann, Hitler's leading henchman, had escaped Berlin at the end of the war and resettled in Latin America. "He was on a thing about this," Hersh quotes Wendy Wisner in his 1992 book *The Old Boys*, "that we should pool our sources and resources and get Bormann. He talked about the 'mysterious and sinister figure of Martin Bormann.' He wrote millions of letters. If there really was a CIA connection to Bormann in South America, who knows if he wasn't feeling terrible about it? If he's starting to yell and scream about these Nazis, who in the CIA is starting to get worried about it?"

On October 29, 1965, Frank Wisner put a twenty-gauge shotgun to his head and pulled the trigger.[35]

The Testament of Jack Ruby

After the assassination, many publications of the radical right took a long look at Jack Ruby. While raising the specter of his alleged Communist sympathies, above all they stressed his Jewish heritage. Ruby, it was noted time and again, was a shortened form of "Rubenstein."

Indeed, one of Ruby's first statements in explaining his motive for killing Oswald had been: "I wanted to show them a Jew had guts." It was grist for the mill of anti-Semites such as Tulsa preacher Billy James Hargis—traveling companion of General Walker, sponsor through the Christian Crusade of Charles Willoughby's *Foreign Intelligence Digest*.

A child of Chicago's Jewish ghetto with an alcoholic father and a mother who went mad, Ruby had always been sensitive about his heritage. When he showed up at the Oswald press conference on the night of the assassination, and was asked what he was doing there, Ruby replied: "Translating for a Jewish newspaper."[36]

A close examination of Ruby's testimony before the Warren Commission, taken at the Dallas County Jail on June 7, 1964,[37] reveals that he was obsessed with the black-bordered anti-Kennedy advertisement that appeared in a Dallas paper the morning of the assassination—because of the Jewish name at the bottom. On the morning of November 23, 1963, Ruby had gone to the post office "to find out his box number of this Bernard Weissman." Ruby's testimony was rambling, seemingly unable to follow any logical time sequence concerning his movements. But it was the Weissman ad, he remembered, that caused him to awaken his roommate in the middle of the previous night.

Ruby implored the commission to get him to Washington, the only place he said he could talk freely. Toward the end of the interview, he suddenly said that if the commission had only come to see him earlier, "a certain organization wouldn't have so completely formed now, so powerfully, to use me because I am of the Jewish extraction, Jewish faith, to commit the most dastardly crime that has ever been committed. Can you understand now in visualizing what happened, what powers, what momentum has been carried on to create this feeling of mass feeling against my people, against certain people that were against them prior to their power? That goes over your head, doesn't it?"

> CHIEF JUSTICE WARREN: Well, I don't quite get the full significance of it, Mr. Ruby. I know what you feel about the John Birch Society.
> RUBY: Very powerful.
> WARREN: I think it is powerful, yes I do. Of course, I don't have all the information that you feel you have on that subject.
> RUBY: Unfortunately, you don't have, because it is too late. And I wish that our beloved President, Lyndon Johnson, would have delved deeper into the situation, hear me, not to accept just circumstantial facts about my guilt or innocence, and would have questioned to find out the truth about me before he relinquished certain powers to these certain people.
> WARREN: Well, I am afraid I don't know what power you believe he relinquished to them. I think that it is difficult to understand what you have to say.
> RUBY: I want to say this to you. The Jewish people are being exterminated at this moment. Consequently, a whole new form of government is going to take over our country, and I know I won't live to see you another time. . . .[38]

The commission neither took Ruby to Washington as he asked, nor ever saw him again. On January 31, 1966, a year before he died of cancer, Ruby wrote in a letter confiscated by one of Ruby's guards and subsequently smuggled from the jail:

. . . don't believe the Warren [Commission] Report, that was only put
out to make me look innocent. . . . I'm going to die a horrible death
anyway, so what would I have to gain by writing all this. So you must
believe me. . . . that is only one kind of people that would do such a
thing, that would have to be the Nazi's, and that is who is in power in this
country right now. . . . Japan also is in on the deal, but the old war lords
are going to come back. South America is also full of these Nazi's. . . . if
those people were so determined to frame me then you must be convinced that they had an ulterior motive for doing same. There is only one
kind of people that would go to such extremes, and that would be the
Master Race. . . ."[39]

What Ruby had to say has largely been dismissed as the rantings of a
sick mind. But could he have been trying to tell the world far more than
was ever realized?

The reader may recall the tape-recorded statements by Joseph Milteer
that a propaganda campaign would ensue from "an international underground" seeking to prove "that the Jews, the Zionist Jews, had murdered
Kennedy." An examination of certain "propaganda" that came out after
the assassination points in precisely that direction. Here are excerpts from
Gerald L. K. Smith's *Christian Nationalist Crusade* magazine from March
1964:

When Oswald was arrested, why did he ask immediately for a certain
Jewish lawyer, John Abt? . . . He has been the legal defender of many
Communists and was associated closely with the Jew, Lee Pressman, formerly attorney for the National Labor Relations Board. [Abt, whom Oswald did request represent him for unknown reasons, was in 1963 a leading attorney with the American Civil Liberties Union in New York.]

Why do the editorialists of Egypt and Middle Eastern papers insist that
the assassination was a Zionist plot because President Kennedy recently
made decisions which were very favorable to the Arabs and very unfavor-
able to the Israelis?

Why did a man who signed his name Bernard Weissman buy a paid ad
in a Dallas paper challenging President Kennedy and bordering the ad
with a wide black border similar to the border which surrounds death
notices? Was the extreme right wing contents of the ad designed to cast
suspicion in the wrong direction? [As we have seen, Larrie Schmidt, alleged to have been involved with Oswald, put Weissman up to signing the
ad.]

Walter Winchell reported that the Jew, Stanley Marcus, head of the
much advertised Neiman-Marcus mercantile company, pled with President Kennedy not to come to Dallas. What did he know, if anything, that
panicked him concerning this matter?[40]

But what can best be described as "Jew-baiting" was not the only target of propaganda by the radical right. Another, and more successful campaign, was directed against the Fair Play for Cuba Committee (FPCC).

The Demise of the FPCC

From Billy James Hargis's *Weekly Crusader*, December 1963:

> Christian Crusade has tried for years to offer factual information about these "communist fronts." . . . Ironically, Congressman Cramer made a speech on the floor of the House on March 15, 1962, criticizing the Department of Justice for not listing the Fair Play for Cuba Committee as being subversive "in spite of overwhelming evidence" to that effect produced at "hearings by the Senate Subcommittee." On my spring tour of the nation conducting Christian Crusade rallies, I called upon the U.S. Government to enforce the law of the land, that is, to arrest those communists who had refused to register as agents of the Soviet Union and put them on trial for treason. If the law had been enforced our President would probably be alive today.

Dorothy Healy, for years a leading member of the Communist Party, U.S.A., and now living in Washington, recalls a "very conscious and very heavy" attempt to make the assassination look like a leftist conspiracy. "It sure scared the left, too," she added. "Both the CP and the Socialist Workers Party were just terrified. The SWP had all its membership go underground for a week, not be seen anywhere—because Oswald had been photographed holding a copy of *The Militant.*"[41]

Al Lewis, executive secretary of the Los Angeles FPCC in 1963 and now a retired psychiatrist, remembered: "The FBI called me after Kennedy was assassinated, and apparently wanted to involve me in it some way. They tried to pin a relationship with Oswald on me, because apparently I'd been in Mexico at the same time he was, on my way to Cuba. Well, that was the first I heard about it. And I never heard of Oswald and the New Orleans Fair Play for Cuba Committee in the movement. That whole thing to me was a setup of some kind by the intelligence services."[42]

If the FBI, the CIA, and others were looking to destroy the FPCC, the president's assassination did just that. The first nail in its coffin, of course, came when Oswald's affiliation was touted in the headlines. Then, in what seems an oddly synchronous event, on December 20, 1963, the Secret Service filed charges "of threatening to kill President Johnson" against twenty-nine-year-old Robert Beaty Fennell, "who claims membership in the Fair Play for Cuba Committee."

According to a *Los Angeles Times* account, police in Berkeley, California, had picked up Fennell on a vagrancy charge and found a note in his pocket reading: "My immediate goal: the assassination of President Johnson." In Sioux City, Iowa, in October, Fennell had picketed the Municipal Auditorium, urging permission to travel to Cuba and supporting interracial marriages, telling newsmen at the time that he belonged to the FPCC. His father said his son had been working on a Texas ranch several hundred miles from Dallas on November 22, 1963. Fennell, the article noted, had received an honorable discharge from the Air Force five years before. Curious parallels, indeed, to the short life of Lee Harvey Oswald.[43]

That was the coup de grace for the FPCC. By the end of December 1963, V. T. Lee had resigned his chairmanship and the organization vanished from the political map.[44]

The Radical Right Targets the CIA

The first clue of what was to come appeared in the famous black-bordered ad. As it was about to go to press the day before the assassination, Bernard Weissman later recalled for the Warren Commission that the John Birch Society's Joseph Grinnan had handed him a scrap of paper saying, "This has to be in. Go back and have them change the ad."[45] The insert, part of a long list of questions about Kennedy policies, read: *"WHY* has the Foreign Policy of the United States degenerated to the point that the C.I.A. is arranging coups and having staunch Anti-Communist Allies of the U.S. bloodily exterminated."[46]

In the aftermath of Dallas, the CIA itself became a target of the radical right. The Liberty Lobby's newsletter in January 1964 picked up where the black-bordered ad left off: "It is high time that Americans begin to state some very unpleasant facts. It is no more moral for the CIA to assassinate the anti-communist President of the Dominican Republic [Trujillo] and South Viet Nam [Diem] than it is for a communist to assassinate the President of the United States. What is sauce for the goose is sauce for the gander."

At that time, the CIA's involvement in assassination plots against foreign leaders was still a well-kept secret from the general public. But, curiously, the radical right seemed to know a great deal of "inside information" about the CIA. The possibility that the agency had been penetrated by the Soviets—again, something that was rarely mentioned beyond closed doors in those days—was widely trumpeted. The primary purveyor was Revilo Pendleton Oliver, a professor of languages at the University of Illinois. Oliver's three-part series on the assassination for the John Birch Society's *American Opinion* magazine was so eyebrow-raising that the Warren Commission saw fit to call him in to testify on September 9, 1964.

Oliver, a native Texan, had been a code-breaker for the Army Security Agency in Washington during World War II. There he came to believe that the nation's capital was permeated with Communists. A regular contributor in the 1950s to William F. Buckley, Jr.'s, *National Review,* Oliver attended the 1958 meeting that established the John Birch Society and soon transferred his major writing to its monthly journal. In January 1963 he began a cycle of articles on race and history. To meet the threat of the Black Muslims, Oliver counseled that conservatives should consider eugenic solutions to the deterioration of racial stock in America.

Oliver was a featured speaker—and recipient of an award "for outstanding service to the cause of freedom"—at the Congress of Freedom's meeting in New Orleans that April. This was the same gathering where an informant afterward told the Miami police that plans to assassinate political leaders was being discussed, and where Joseph Milteer renewed his friendship with Willie Somersett. In the summer of 1963, Oliver served as speaker and instructor at the Christian Crusade's annual seminar.[47]

In his 1964 trilogy on the assassination, Oliver declared that the Warren Commission was planning a cover-up of a Communist conspiracy by declaring Oswald a loner, suppressing the FBI's report, and smothering evidence connecting "Jakob Rubenstein" with Oswald and Cuba. If Oswald had not been found, Oliver continued, the American right would have been blamed and destroyed in the first phase of the Communist "coup."

The professor described Oswald's having been trained at the Soviet "school for sabotage and terrorism" in Minsk, and Marina's having been "an adopted daughter for practical purposes with the colonel of the Soviet military intelligence." When the Warren Commission asked for Oliver's source, he replied that it came from his "research consultant"—a man named Frank Capell, "who, I understand," Oliver added, "has the cooperation of many former intelligence officers of the Army and former members of the FBI."

Capell published a biweekly periodical on Staten Island, New York, called the *Herald of Freedom,* and was listed on the masthead of Willoughby's *Foreign Intelligence Digest.* Oliver further described Capell's vast files and "contacts with the Cuban underground, in fact with several Cuban undergrounds, and various other sources which enable him to obtain information which he believes to be reliable and accurate. He will indicate to me the nature of the information that he has, although over the telephone he will not usually disclose a source that he regards as confidential."

Oliver was questioned by the commission about another of his statements in *American Opinion:* "In June of 1963 an experienced American military man made a careful analysis of the situation at that time, and in his highly confidential report concluded, on the basis of indications in Communist and crypto Communist sources, that the conspiracy's schedule called for a major incident to create national shock before Thanksgiving."

Asked to identify the military man, Oliver said it was a retired Air Force colonel, Chesley Clark, who discussed this matter with him "a month or 6 weeks before" the assassination. Oliver explained that "his [Clark's] estimates were made entirely from, what should we say, experience in psychological warfare and in reading the indications in the sequence of events and the form the propaganda was taking, and that he obviously had not, so far as I know, no inside information."

The commission quoted to Oliver from a *Washington Post* story recounting one of his speeches late in August 1964, saying: "I don't know whether Oswald was paid by the CIA or by the Soviet secret police—and it is just a matter of bookkeeping anyway."

Oliver then launched into a heavy-duty attack on the CIA, speculating that the agency was behind the funding of the Frankfurt-based *Overseas Weekly* (which broke the 1961 story resulting in General Walker's dismissal from Germany). The professor went on to describe the death of Povl Bang-Jensen:

"He is the member of the United Nations staff who attempted to communicate to the Central Intelligence Agency the names of certain Soviet agents in the United Nations who were, (A) willing to defect, in fact eager to do that; and (B) willing to identify agents of the Soviet Secret Police in the State Department and CIA. He is reported to have communicated his information in confidence to an officer of the CIA and very shortly thereafter he met his death in what was called a suicide although most improbably such. The CIA is reported to have been shadowing him at the time of his death.

"On those principal data, my statement here is an inference. If they can assassinate General Trujillo in the Dominican Republic there is nothing impossible about their doing something similar on American soil."[48]

Oliver was not alone in raising questions about the CIA's penetration by the KGB. H. L. Hunt's research-gatherer on the assassination, Paul Rothermel, somehow came up with additional data, which he passed along to Garrison investigator William Wood in 1967. Rothermel began by citing an article appearing in the *Washington Observer* (the Liberty Lobby's publication) that said: "Three loyal employees of CIA are alleged to have discovered the existence of a Soviet spy ring inside the CIA. They reported this to their superiors, and subsequently each one met a violent or mysterious death."

Rothermel then provided Wood with three names: Josephine Berkovic, employed by the CIA's Yugoslav Section, "who leaped or was pushed from the roof" of her Washington apartment in 1964; Ivan [last name illegible], station chief of the CIA's Bulgarian Section, "found in 1963 with his throat slashed in Madrid, Spain"; and Stephan Gidaly, "former chief of the Hungarian Section, who died in 1956–57, immediately following discovery of the Communist Cell in CIA, of a heart attack."[49]

The point is, this network had remarkable sources—and was not circumspect about pushing forward a particular thesis: that the Kennedy assassination might have been engineered by a Soviet spy ring operating within the CIA.[50] I believe the evidence revealed in this book indicates that such a "ring" did exist, and was involved in the intrigue surrounding Oswald and Nagell. It is also pretty clear that certain people who were well wired into military and FBI circles knew about this—and, from all their propagandizing after the assassination, used it as a means of intimidating the CIA. In short, keeping the CIA from poking into their own affairs—and thus removed from scrutiny those who might really have been behind the assassination.

Charles Willoughby sat on the sidelines, saying nothing publicly about the events in Dallas. It was left to his associate Frank Capell to raise the question of whether Oswald had been trained at the KGB's school for assassins in Minsk. In Capell's January 17, 1964, *Herald of Freedom,* he looked back at "the confessions and trial of Soviet Intelligence Agent Bogdan Stashinsky (using the alias of Josef Lehmann) . . . for the murder of Ukrainian anti-Communist leaders. . . . Stashinsky, an admitted Soviet assassin, stated he had been studying English and, after one more Ukrainian murder, was to be sent to England or the United States. It was learned also that other Soviet agents were in training for assignments to murder anti-Communist leaders and officials in the United States and England."[51]

Willoughby and the Cuban Exiles

On November 24, 1963, a long-distance telephone operator in Mexico City monitored an international phone call and alerted U.S. authorities. She had overheard one of the voices saying: "The Castro plan is being carried out. Bobby is next. Soon the atomic bombs will begin to rain and they won't know from where."

The telephone numbers were traced. One of them belonged to Emilio Núñez Portuondo, the Cuban ambassador to the United Nations during the Batista regime. Portuondo was a well-known figure in the Cuban exile community and whom the Secret Service noted had recently "become bitter at the United States"—to the point where the Secret Service's Protective Research Division kept a file on him as a presidential threat.

The other number belonged to José Antonio Cabarga of Mexico City. When Portuondo was asked about the call, he simply explained: "Cabarga was in close contact with the U.S. embassy in Mexico City and was a good investigator who could develop information in the event the plans to assassinate the president were formulated in Mexico City." No government follow-up investigation was done on either man.[52]

At the time, Portuondo headed a list of members of the United Organization for the Liberation of Cuba, formed on May 20, 1963. This was Mario Garcia Kohly's group,[53] and Kohly was the Cuban exile for whom CIA contract agent Robert Morrow worked as case officer until both men were arrested that October as masterminds of a plan to flood Cuba with counterfeit pesos. According to Morrow, Rolando Masferrer was "the financial conduit for Kohly's Miami exile groups and Mafia mercenaries from No Name Key, and David Ferrie for Kohly's exile groups at Lake Pontchartrain, Louisiana."[54] The New Orleans branch was affiliated with Alpha 66. Their plan was to launch an invasion of Cuba in December 1963. After the Kennedy assassination, Kohly was counseled to go "underground" and thereby avoid being called to testify before the Warren Commission. The man who advised him, Morrow writes in his book *The Senator Must Die*, was Richard Nixon.[55]

Emilio Núñez Portuondo was also the Latin American Affairs editor of Charles Willoughby's *Foreign Intelligence Digest*, and in regular correspondence with the former general. They had considered forming a foundation, according to a Portuondo letter to Willoughby, "to uphold our ideals in the Western Hemisphere, specifically in the Caribbean area."[56] Portuondo may have worked toward those "ideals" with someone else. A British publication, which had access to House Committee files, identifies Portuondo as having been an "agent" of the CIA's Cuban specialist in Mexico City—David Atlee Phillips.[57]

Mario Kohly had paid a personal visit on H. L. Hunt in Texas in December 1962 (see Chapter Twelve). At least in later years, Kohly would also be in touch with Willoughby. In a letter of March 23, 1970, he wrote the retired general in Florida: ". . . As I explained over the phone I would like to be received by Mr. Edgar Hoover of the F.B.I. whom I understand is a good friend of yours."[58]

Anonymous Letter

Early in September 1975, after my article about Professor Richard Popkin and his theory of a "Manchurian Candidate" appeared in *The Village Voice,* I received an anonymous letter:[59]

> . . . You are now part of the great game of solving the JFK assassination riddle. The danger to those involved is immense tantamount to playing Russian Roulette which the writer played while brainwashed and in the programming process in Red China. [Richard] Condon's "Manchurian Candidate" starring Laurence Harvey and Frank Sinatra. . . . is there or was there a Robot killer????
>
> . . . Prior to his death some time ago I spent several days with TSCHEPPE WEIDENBACH, a famous American general who was born in Heidelberg Germany in 1892. He was one of our foremost experts in intelligence, particularly in the Far East. . . . we questioned my programming as I still speak fluent Mandarin Chinese . . . 25 YEARS later. . . . An enlightened [sic] conversation . . .
>
> The enclosed was written in the King Edward Sheraton Hotel, Toronto, Canada almost ten years ago. . . . on your copy one name is blocked out. . . . you may want to research down to the name which is part of the game we can't make it too easy. . . .

The enclosure, on a letterhead from the above-mentioned hotel, read as follows:

> YOUR CANADIAN COMPUTERS RESEARCHING THE ASSAS-SINATION OF JOHN KENNEDY DEVELOPED LEADS TO A MAN NAMED TSCHEPPE-WEIDENBACH BORN IN 1892 IN HEIDEL-BERG, GERMANY AS HAVING MASTERMINDED THE ASSASSI-NATION WITH THE APPROVAL. "THE" MAN WHO COULD DO NO WRONG IN AMERICAN HISTORY?
>
> YOUR GEN [EASY RESEARCH] MIGHT WELL PROVIDE A LEAD TO THE CLEVER MIND FROM HEIDELBERG.
>
> THE TITLE "THE MANCHURIAN CANDIDATE" COMES OUT LINKED TO THE WORD "BIBLE" AND SOMETHING NAMED "WHITE."
>
> RAYMOND SHOT HIS MOTHER AND SENATOR ISELIN. AS IN "THE MANCHURIAN CANDIDATE" JUSTICE MUST TRIUMPH. EVEN PATRIOTS CANNOT TAKE THE LAW INTO THEIR OWN HANDS—

"Raymond shot his mother and Senator Iselin" refers to the conclusion of *The Manchurian Candidate,* when the programmed protagonist realizes he is being manipulated for political ends—and strikes back at those who would "control" him.

Many years went by before I found out who "Tscheppe-Weidenbach" was. It happened by chance, perusing a history of the MacArthur period— an obscure mention that Adolf Tscheppe-Weidenbach of Heidelberg, Germany, had changed his name, upon arrival in the United States shortly before World War I, to Charles Willoughby.[60]

Summary

A Manchurian Candidate? Was it really possible in Oswald's case? At first glance, this seems like something out of science fiction. But Nagell's allegation that Oswald was undergoing hypnotherapy from David Ferrie is only the tip of the iceberg. The directors of both the CIA and the FBI wondered whether Oswald might have been "programmed" while in the Soviet Union, causing the Warren Commission to request a full report on such techniques from the CIA. No direct mention was made by Richard Helms, however, of his own MK-ULTRA operation.

In 1967, the book *Were We Controlled?* took this scenario to new heights. At that time, little was known about such government experiments. Yet "Lincoln Lawrence" postulated that Oswald had received an electronic implant in his brain in Minsk, then been maneuvered into the orbit of another group after he returned to the United States. Similar speculation was made by former CIA official Herman Kimsey. The fact that at least two people directly connected to the book's appearance met mysterious ends is no more fantastic than Oswald's mother's belief that author "Lawrence" must have known her son. By the end of the 1960s, researchers learned of the fascination with hypnosis of two more assassins—James Earl Ray and Sirhan Sirhan; indeed, the subject was conspicuously raised at Sirhan's trial. Years later, Colonel William Bishop would reveal that he, too, had undergone programming by U.S. intelligence.

Jack Ruby was alleged by "Lawrence" to have been subject to similar "mind control." To the Warren Commission and afterward, Ruby fixated on the notion that Nazi-type elements were behind his utilization. Strangely, CIA official Frank Wisner—who set up the agency's use of ex-Nazis in the Cold War—committed suicide after a similar fixation. In the ultraright's postassassination propaganda, we witness concerted anti-Semitic attacks, as well as allegations about Communist involvement and

CIA penetration by the KGB—for example, the remarkable Warren Commission testimony of Revilo Oliver, based on a source linked to Charles Willoughby. The Hunt family, too, had an inside track on the CIA's odd tangled relationship with its Soviet counterpart.

In the end, we are left with this terrible question: Was the CIA's relationship with Oswald—even the CIA's experiments with mind control—usurped by another group? A group that was aware of Soviet penetration of the CIA? A group, as Eugene Dinkin warned, that was part of a Pentagon/"ultraright economic" apparatus?

Chapter Thirty-one

Conclusion

The last time I spoke to Richard Case Nagell was by phone in March 1990. He was living at the time in a Holiday Inn just outside Los Angeles, and had finally received his CIA and FBI files under the Freedom of Information Act. "I know the CIA withheld things," he said, "but I can't come out and say this or I'm in a trap. The FBI sent a whole lot, but somebody really did a number on those files. They've got me pegged as a racketeer and associated with people I never even heard of."[1]

I implored Nagell, once again, to sit down and lay out his full story for the sake of history. Some years ago, he had indicated that once his lawsuit seeking a full disability retirement from the Pentagon was settled in the Court of Claims, he would finally be in a position to come clean. On October 6, 1982, after a twelve-year fight, he won his case.[2] Now I learned that there were strings attached to his victory.

"I'm not going to take a chance on losing my money from the government," Nagell admitted. "I assisted in the destruction of my own credibility, or I would not be getting what I am getting. I went along with the program. I had to, in order to live the way I do. I was sitting there smiling, and they were smiling, and we all knew."

Nagell was saying, in a less veiled manner than usual, that he had made a deal: Stay silent and get your benefits from the military.

"The truth will come out if I die," Nagell continued, "and the government is well aware of that. Some want me alive, others don't. So I can't give you a time when I'm going to open up. I would need a guarantee of immunity from prosecution and also against administrative sanctions being taken against me by the military, in terms of my benefits. And the government is well aware of that, too. I'm not going to put myself in a bind."

A few months later, in late June 1990, Nagell sealed his lips formally in a letter. "All that I have to say at this point in time regarding the subject we once discussed already has been said," he wrote me. Despite several attempts by mail to recontact Nagell and let him review what I was writing about him prior to publication of this book, my efforts received no response.[3]

The Enigma of Richard Case Nagell

What, finally, are we to make of the man who knew too much? Nagell was certainly not a man who lacked courage. What he went through even in his first thirty-three years staggers the imagination: wounded three times in battle, sole survivor of two military plane crashes, counterspy in the Far East, investigator of organized crime in the liquor industry, wounded by a gunshot near a California beach, part of a dangerous netherworld filled with Cubans and others whose motives and very identities were ever in question. As the years passed, there was scarcely any letup. Under what crossed stars does a single man see the inside of both American and Communist prisons?

I knew Nagell well enough to believe him a man of principle. But the espionage world in which he operated was one disengaged from the human heart. Nagell's plight could be compared to that of Kirk Douglas in the movie *Detective Story*. Like Nagell, Douglas's character compensated for the pain of his past by making principle supreme. William Bendix warns the detective in a memorable rooftop scene, "don't be such a monument"—but to no avail. Ultimately, as happened to Douglas's detective, Nagell could not break free from the world he was caught up in, and it destroyed him.

I believe that Nagell's disenchantment with the American military establishment was genuine, even at the same time this disenchantment was used to help establish a good cover as a CIA double agent. For Nagell, idealism transcended "national security." He seems to have been of a breed who operated in an in-between realm where the compelling motivation was that communism and democracy would someday find common ground. Nagell worked for both sides, and had since Tokyo, for what he saw as a "just cause."

This is not to say that he was a devoted Communist, but rather that his particular brand of patriotism did not preclude taking part in an effort by, for example, the KGB or Castro to expose or head off the ongoing CIA plots to disrupt Cuba and eliminate its leadership. Nagell prided himself on being in the fray but above it, working for what he viewed as higher goals. He was so brilliant—as evidenced by his ability to master complex languages—that he thought he was in command of his own destiny.

Yet deception was intrinsic to the big leagues of counterespionage. When Nagell realized that somebody had slipped a blindfold over him in the course of the game, and that people he trusted were not who they purported to be, he found himself all alone.

If Nagell had been a "triple agent" all along, feigning allegiance to the CIA but knowingly serving the KGB, then coming to learn somehow that his CIA contact ("Bob") was really a Soviet agent would not have pushed Nagell over the edge. They would simply have been part of the same apparatus. They could just have gone on working together, not at cross purposes. But in realizing that he had engaged in certain illegal actions (precisely what they were, Nagell has never specified) that he had falsely believed were sanctioned by the CIA in his double-agent role vis-à-vis the KGB, Nagell found himself in an unconscionable bind. Unknown to him until September 1963, he had been basically operating for the Soviets ever since signing his CIA contract the year before.

Nagell has always dreaded revealing whatever else he was involved in with Oswald for the Soviets—something apart from the assassination. Until we know what the "inimical act" was that Nagell spoke about to the FBI on January 6, 1964, the picture will remain fuzzy. All that seems clear is that certain plans went awry in the summer of 1963. What began as a separate intelligence operation utilizing Oswald ended up with Oswald and Nagell becoming enmeshed in a plot against JFK.

It is unsettling to consider that Nagell himself was probably the go-between who led to Oswald's recruitment into the conspiracy. Nagell had the existing relationship with Angel and Leopoldo. Nagell befriended Vaughn Marlowe at the same time that Angel and Leopoldo were checking out Marlowe as a rifleman with a left-wing background. Nagell had been observing Oswald's activities for some months when Angel and Leopoldo hooked up with the ex-Marine that summer. Then Oswald agreed, or at least Nagell saw him as agreeing, to go along with the exiles' plan. Nagell viewed Oswald as being duped into thinking he was serving the interests of Castro, and reported as much back to his superiors.

But if Oswald was the essential tool of the JFK conspirators, and Nagell could not bring himself to kill him, as the Soviets ordered, why didn't Nagell at least shoot Oswald in the foot in September 1963?[4] Only Nagell could answer that haunting question. My conclusion is that when he found himself left out in the cold by the CIA, something in him snapped. Coming to the realization that he was being used, already aware that Oswald had long been in a similar boat, Nagell simply opted out. He couldn't pay the price of committing murder, because nobody was looking out for him. He was essentially a man without a country.

The pressure on Nagell was immense. He was being ordered by a foreign government to kill an American citizen who had CIA/FBI connections. He was being threatened with exposure of other illegal acts that he had performed, wittingly or unwittingly, on behalf of the Soviets. He was being told to leave his country for good, faced with the prospect of never seeing his two young children again. For someone to whom the Army had been the only family he ever really knew, leaving his kids behind was probably the most chilling prospect of all.

So perhaps Nagell did all that he could do. He alerted the FBI and the CIA in registered letters. The Soviets and the Cubans also knew what was on the horizon. Nagell, believing that his own life was in jeopardy—no doubt with legitimacy—placed himself in federal custody in a bizarre manner that was apparently calculated to send a loud message. And yet nobody moved to stop the assassination.

The Enigma of Lee Harvey Oswald

In a way, Oswald may be seen as a younger alter ego of Richard Nagell. Their life paths are similar in so many ways it is eerie: both from broken homes, both military men who were students of Marxism, both walking down the perpetually winding corridors of American and Soviet intelligence agencies, both caught up in a conspiracy to assassinate JFK. Like Nagell, Oswald seems fiercely idealistic. Unlike Nagell, he was not wise to the ways of counterespionage.

When an ex-Marine "defector" has the names of Soviet officials and the secretary of the American Nazi Party (Dan Burros) in his personal notebook, what are we able to discern about who he really was? Maybe he never knew. It is frighteningly clear that many parties utilized Oswald for their own purposes. But even with a scorecard, it was often hard to tell who the players were. In Tokyo there was a Japanese scholar who once served the imperial warlords and then loomed as a Soviet agent; and a Soviet colonel whom the CIA had targeted for defection. In the USSR there were reports from a young "defector" working in an electronics factory that ended up being analyzed by a Soviet mole inside the CIA. In Dallas there was a baron once thought to be a Nazi agent, later thought to be a Communist, who debriefed the "defector" for the CIA.

At the same time that Oswald corresponded feverishly with representatives of the "left"—V. T. Lee, the Socialist Workers Party, the Communist Party, U.S.A.—he came to be surrounded by denizens of the "right"—Cuban exiles, Guy Banister, David Ferrie. At the same time that Oswald apprised the Soviet embassy of his interests and activities, he was regularly visited by agents of the FBI. While he passed out Fair Play for Cuba Committee leaflets on street corners, the FBI and the CIA were busily scheming how to disrupt the committee's activities.

Was Oswald a rebel looking for a cause? Did he believe that he was working for Castro, hooking up with extremist elements to find out about their plans against Cuba? Was he a loyal employee of some U.S. government agency, on a fact-gathering, penetration, or provocateur mission? Was he, as Nagell believes, involved in the assassination plan "up to his ears," ready and willing to take aim from the Texas School Book Depository or wherever? Or was he a potential "Manchurian Candidate" who had undergone a CIA, military, or perhaps Soviet mind-control program?

It is quite possible that Oswald was indeed "fashioned" in the mind-control testing grounds of the era. Such techniques were real and very much in use in the 1950s and 1960s. I have offered such a thesis in this book as a way of looking at Oswald's otherwise so inexplicable behavior at so many stages of his life. It explains his pretense of ideological conviction, but the lack of legitimacy observed by many people. The fact is, Oswald often did not seem to know what he really believed or what he was really doing.

The purpose of this book, however, is not to come to definitive answers about Oswald, or even Nagell. It is the world around these men that I have sought to portray. The overwhelming evidence is that a conspiracy—a big conspiracy containing numerous levels of intrigue—led to the Kennedy assassination. Whether Oswald fired shots, or even what motivated him, becomes incidental to the maelstrom that enveloped him.

The Kennedy conspiracy is a fundamental mystery of our century. Everywhere you look, there is another hall of mirrors. Over the years, as our government and other governments have sought to make their lies consistent about this seminal event, it has become virtually impossible to see what the truth is. Where is the wizard, the wicked witch? All of the above, or none of the above? It is a maddening multiple-choice test. Yet are we still, as F. Scott Fitzgerald once wrote, "borne back ceaselessly into the past."

What ultimately faces us is a hydra-headed beast, but it is possible to come to grips at least with its claws. Always remembering that the intrinsic nature of this beast is fog and smoke, nevertheless this is not a wholly ambiguous and unknowable world. Over the years a number of people have begun to come forward, a record of out-of-school testimony has developed. By coordinating stories like Nagell's with a review of the public record, we are able to see connections and make limited, reasoned judgments about how certain organizations and individuals were involved in the conspiracy.

The Role of Soviet Intelligence

Since Nagell says that his assignments to monitor an assassination plot and the activities of Oswald both came originally from Soviet intelligence, the possibility must be considered that the KGB (or maybe the GRU) was manipulating the situation from the beginning. In this scenario, the KGB's eventual order to Nagell that he kill Oswald and scuttle the plot could be viewed as a sham. By treating Nagell so badly—having people threaten him with exposure as one of theirs, telling him he couldn't depart the country with his children—the KGB knew that Nagell would balk. But they themselves were covered. If necessary they could say, and Nagell could substantiate, that they made the effort.

Just as the CIA had its "rogue" elements, so undoubtedly did the KGB. Such individuals would have seen the growing détente between JFK and Khrushchev as a threat to communism. It may be remembered that Khrushchev himself was overthrown less than a year after the assassination, and replaced by hard-liners who remained in power until Gorbachev.

But the Soviet Union long produced the world's greatest chess players, masters of moves and countermoves. Were Oswald ultimately their pawn, the Soviets put themselves in immediate checkmate. Oswald was blatantly conspicuous—a two-and-a-half-year resident of the USSR, married to a Russian woman, in communication with Soviet officials in Washington and Mexico. Had the KGB decided to eliminate Kennedy, would they not have selected a totally anonymous assassin with an untraceable identity? A highly trained, thoroughly tested killer who could be counted on not to bungle the job and who had a reasonable chance for escape?

Nagell believes that the Soviets were sincere in giving him his mission to get rid of Oswald. In Nagell's words, they were the last intelligence outfit that wanted to see Kennedy killed. It may not be out of any particular admiration for Kennedy that the KGB would have set out to stop the plot, but rather that they understood the perpetrators would seek to lay the blame at their doorstep (or Cuba's). They would not countenance such a maneuver.

The question then becomes: Why didn't the Soviets take additional steps after Nagell removed himself from the picture?

1. A nation, particularly an "enemy" nation, can only go so far in interfering with the internal politics of another country. Assuming Nagell's Soviet contact knew that the plot against JFK was an "inside job," "Oaxaca" could not have done more except pass the word to the highest official levels of his own government. But according to what Nagell was told long afterward, for some reason the word never went out from Mexico City to the Kremlin.

2. Perhaps, after Nagell so publicly took himself out of the loop, his Soviet contact believed that the conspiracy would not proceed. After all, it did not go forward as scheduled in late September.

3. The KGB could not risk exposing its moles inside the CIA. If John Paisley, Nagell's Mexico contact "Bob," and perhaps others were part of a KGB apparatus within the CIA—and these same people had been involved with Oswald at one time or another—then the KGB had no choice but to protect them.[5]

Castro's Knowledge

It is certainly true that the highly trained Cuban intelligence service had the exile community well penetrated. If, as Nagell has hinted, even CIA "golden boy" Manuel Artime was really a double agent for Castro, we once again enter a realm where anything is possible. Among Nagell's contacts, Franz Waehauf and Maria del Carmen apparently worked with Cuban intelligence. That the Cubans, through Nagell or others, could have used Oswald in certain ways is a conjecture that probably has validity.

But as 1963 progressed, Castro's intent to reestablish relations with the Kennedy government appears to have been quite sincere. Castro's comments to French journalist Jean Daniel, both before and after the assassination, indicate that the Cuban leader was fully prepared to reach accommodation with JFK and was deeply disturbed by the assassination.

While many postassassination efforts were undertaken to point blame in Cuba's direction, this smacks more of a "disinformation" campaign than anything to do with reality. For Castro or his aides to have enlisted Oswald to assassinate Kennedy would have been flirting with disaster. Since Oswald's paper trail was so obviously that of a Castro sympathizer, what better pretext could there be for an invasion and overthrow of Castro's government? This may have been the aim of the conspirators: Kill two birds with one stone.

Nagell admittedly made a trip to Cuba, and has indicated that the Castro government was apprised about Angel and Leopoldo posing as Cuban agents in bringing Oswald into the JFK plot. But, as with the KGB, Cuba was hamstrung in what it could reveal for fear of jeopardizing other of its American operations. Castro and Kennedy were on the verge of burying the hatchet, but they could scarcely be considered friends. So, the United States would legitimately have asked, if Cuba knew of such a nefarious plot, *how* did it know? Since it is doubtful that Castro knew exactly where the conspiracy was coming from, any answer he gave would be suspect. Thus silence was golden—and both countries have lived in a stalemate ever since.

The Role of the CIA

The Central Intelligence Agency is now known to have plotted against foreign leaders, made bargains with drug dealers and unreconstructed Nazis, and orchestrated a wide-ranging mind-control program. And the long arm of the CIA extends across the course of this narrative.

According to Nagell, Oswald had CIA connections while stationed in Japan—and the Soviets knew it when the Marine "defected" to the USSR. Information from Oswald is alleged by Robert Morrow to have been couriered out from Minsk, destined for review by Tracy Barnes and analysis by John Paisley. George de Mohrenschildt maintained that he was asked to "debrief" Oswald by the CIA's man in Dallas, J. Walton Moore —and Nagell confirmed this.

Since Nagell was assigned to watch Oswald as part of his double-agent mission out of Mexico City, we must assume that his CIA contact "Bob" was privy to the situation. Nagell has said that he "complained" to Desmond FitzGerald on August 27, 1963, apparently about the Oswald-related operation having gone out of control. Since a FitzGerald-Nagell relationship dates back to Tokyo, it may be that FitzGerald's awareness of

Oswald also began at the time of the CIA's plan to get Soviet colonel Nikolai Eroshkin to defect.

CIA contract agent Robert Morrow claimed that Tracy Barnes knew about certain goings-on in New Orleans, that a rifle shipment picked up by David Ferrie might have another purpose than the overthrow of Caribbean leader Juan Bosch. Thus, according to Morrow, Barnes dispatched Nagell to New Orleans to check things out. There, another CIA contract man, Colonel William Bishop, picked up on Nagell's presence and put a Cuban exile onto his trail.

In the meantime, Antonio Veciana's case officer, "Maurice Bishop," reportedly had a meeting with Oswald in Dallas in the presence of the Alpha 66 leader. Both Angel and Leopoldo were said by Nagell to have been former employees of the CIA, tied in with Alpha 66. William Bishop knew of Angel and Leopoldo, expressed knowledge of the Miami and Los Angeles discussions to kill the president, and was aware through Rolando Masferrer that an autumn plot was in the works. Morrow has admitted that he, too, was informed of the plot in advance by refugees Eladio del Valle and Mario Garcia Kohly, Sr.

In ferreting out the meaning behind all this, we must keep in mind that the CIA was highly compartmentalized. For reasons of security—and "plausible denial"—officials and agents often did not know the scope of what was going on. JFK's CIA director, John McCone, insisted under oath before Congress that he was kept in the dark about his underlings' ongoing plans to assassinate Castro. By 1963, the CIA seems to have been fragmented, with employees such as "Maurice Bishop" running off-the-shelf operations that were not reported to superiors.

When the specter of KGB moles within the agency is brought into the equation, the potential for internal CIA confusion escalates to near-unfathomable proportions. From Nagell's perspective, John Paisley, "Bob," and elements within Tracy Barnes's Domestic Operations Division were actually part of a Soviet apparatus. We have examined CIA analyst Clare Petty's consideration that James Angleton himself was a KGB mole. As revealed publicly for the first time in this book, even the CIA's Mexico City station chief, Winston Scott, had at least a prior history as a CIA double agent involved with Soviet intelligence.

So various individuals within different branches of the CIA would have had their own reasons for disassociating themselves from any knowledge of Oswald or Nagell. To protect themselves, they would have lied to one another. The CIA's oversight, through Nagell, of Oswald's one-man Fair Play for Cuba Committee may have started out innocently enough as a counterespionage venture—and then been usurped by another faction.

Did a section of the CIA put Oswald together with Angel and Leopoldo by design, as part of a counterintelligence operation over which the agency hierarchy believed it had control? If so, then why didn't FitzGerald or Barnes take steps to stop it? Even if they were deceived by men supposedly under their command, their lack of action is a sign of either stupidity or gross negligence—and, ultimately, complicity.

As an institution, the CIA grew accustomed to operating beyond the law. In the end, the agency appears to have fallen prey to its own internal turmoil. The tools of its trade were readily available to mavericks within the agency—and to outsiders well positioned to capitalize on its chaos.

The Base of the Pyramid

Among elements of the Cuban refugee population with strong CIA, FBI, military, Mob, and right-wing connections, bitterness against the Kennedy administration was rampant by 1963. It began with the failed Bay of Pigs invasion, and it crescendoed after JFK's post-Cuban Missile Crisis agreement to leave Cuba alone. The violent propensities of organizations such as Alpha 66 were no secret. And there is strong evidence that the Cuban exiles had a part in the planning, if not the execution, of the assassination.

Oswald was seen in the company of Hispanic acquaintances many times in New Orleans, and at the doorsteps of Robert McKeown and Silvia Odio. A note from Oswald was reportedly found in the mailbox of an Abilene, Texas-based exile, Pedro Gonzalez, only three days before the assassination. According to one exile's account, a Miami meeting took place where a forthcoming coup d'état was privately discussed.

At the forefront were Angel and Leopoldo. Not only Nagell, but also Odio and Colonel William Bishop have substantiated these two mystery figures' role with Oswald. On the periphery, many other names have come to the surface: Masferrer, del Valle, Veciana, Kohly, Sergio Arcacha-Smith, Tony Cuesta, Carlos Bringuier, Carlos Quiroga.

We cannot necessarily presume, however, that the New Orleans exiles were consciously setting up Oswald to take the fall. They may simply have been following orders. Oswald's busy three weeks creating a public image as a Castro supporter proceeded step-by-step through the street altercation, the trial, and the radio debate. The FBI was kept apprised of every footfall. A noose was tightening around Oswald, and it is very doubtful that the exiles alone were holding the rope.

Gerry Patrick Hemming, who still keeps his ear to the ground in Miami's Little Havana, maintains that some of the exiles who thought they knew the score in 1963 have today become convinced that they were being used. They were incited to an anti-Kennedy fervor by being let in on the secret knowledge that Kennedy was seriously exploring accommodation with Castro. They were told that their dream of retaking their homeland was dead—unless something drastic was done. They took the bait.

Should it have become necessary in the design of the behind-the-scenes planners, the exiles were also expendable. Implicating a few Cuban refugees in the assassination was not desirable, but it would not come at a high cost, especially if, in the case of Angel and Leopoldo, they had worked diligently to build a cover as Castro agents. Small cogs in the wheel, they could also be made to disappear.

So Cuban exiles were merely the base of the pyramid. They had no power to initiate the cover-up that followed.

And neither did organized crime.

The Mob and the Assassination

In recent years, the majority of theories about the assassination have pointed in the direction of the Mob. A strong case can certainly be made for this. Carlos Marcello, Santos Trafficante, Jr., and Jimmy Hoffa were all under fire from Robert Kennedy's Justice Department. All three are said to have made threats against the Kennedys. This coincided with Nagell's assignment from the Soviets to monitor a plot emanating from a group of Cuban exiles, and many of the exiles had connections to the Mob. In Miami, according to Colonel Bishop, Rolando Masferrer acted as a conduit for Syndicate funds going to Alpha 66. In New Orleans, David Ferrie and Guy Banister had ties to the Marcello organization, along with Oswald's uncle Charles Murret. Jack Ruby's links to the Mob are undeniable.

Then there were organized crime's connections to government agencies and other people in high places. Some of the Mob's members were enlisted by the CIA in the anti-Castro effort. Others were acquainted with J. Edgar Hoover, through the FBI director's penchant for the racetrack. LBJ reportedly received under-the-table money from Marcello in his senatorial campaigns, and the vice president's close associate Bobby Baker did business with the Syndicate. The Mob hooked up in other business ventures with the Murchison oil interests, and probably with the Hunts. Even JFK, through singer Frank Sinatra and the mistress (Judith Campbell) he shared with Sam Giancana, is part of this web.

So none of the above-named parties would have wanted to have their own dirty laundry aired in a courtroom, as was likely to occur if organized crime were implicated in the assassination. Nagell has insisted, however, that Syndicate figures were not the masterminds behind the conspiracy.

And I believe the evidence supports this, up to a point. It is quite likely that the mob had foreknowledge, and indeed welcomed Kennedy's demise. As Colonel Bishop alleged, certain members probably served as conduits passing the word (and money) along to some Cuban exiles.

But to blame the Mob per se is, in my mind, too simplistic, a kind of good-guys versus bad-guys mentality. The scheme was far more devious and complex than organized crime could have conceived. Nor did the Mob have the power to tamper with the physical evidence used to implicate Oswald, or make the autopsy results fit the lone-assassin scenario. In examining the pyramidal structure of the conspiracy, organized crime enters at a layer right above Oswald and the exiles.

J. Edgar Hoover and the Assassination

Almost from the moment of Oswald's arrest, the FBI director led the charge toward the lone-nut, single-assassin conclusion that the Warren Commission adopted. Hoover, who built his reputation as a Red-hunter, never sought to portray Oswald as part of any Communist design. He simply moved to shut down any bona fide investigation from the outset. Anyone who stood in the way, even Ambassador Mann in Mexico City, was ordered to back off.

A benign explanation for Hoover's response would be that he did not wish to look deeply into Oswald's history with the Soviets or the Cubans, for fear of sparking World War III. But in the final analysis, the FBI's reaction can scarcely be viewed as benign—because its own fingerprints were all over Oswald.

Since-declassified documents show that Oswald agreed to keep the FBI apprised of any suspicious contacts with the Soviets, almost immediately upon his return from the USSR in the summer of 1962. The FBI regularly monitored his mail to the Soviet embassy and to domestic left-wing organizations. The fact that Oswald's name did not appear on the FBI's massive Security Index boggles the mind—unless, of course, he was functioning periodically in some capacity for the FBI.

After the Warren Commission Report came out, Dallas FBI agent James Hosty became Hoover's scapegoat. Hosty was reprimanded for alleged lack of diligence in keeping tabs on Oswald, and was transferred to Kansas City. Nothing became public until 1975 about Hosty's being ordered to destroy crucial evidence, in the form of the note Oswald left for him shortly before the assassination. And Hosty seems to have been kept in the dark about the FBI's intensive scrutiny of Oswald in New Orleans the previous summer. Informants had kept the FBI apprised of Oswald's every move with his Fair Play for Cuba Committee. Guy Banister's role with Oswald, given Banister's former position as head of the FBI's Chicago bureau, is particularly suspect.

In this book, we have looked at five warnings received by FBI headquarters about threats against the president's life. Two of these reportedly came from organized-crime figures Marcello and Trafficante. Another alert was provided by Garrett Trapnell, an associate of Cuban exiles, in August 1963. The fourth, Nagell's, provided details on Oswald, Angel, and Leopoldo. A fifth concerned right-wing extremist Joseph Milteer. Every one of these warnings was ignored.

Nagell was in regular communication with the FBI during 1962–63 in a number of cities. And, after his arrest, it is clear that the El Paso field office received orders to keep Nagell under wraps. The evidence among his belongings, being held by the FBI since the bank incident on September 20, 1963, was not returned to Nagell for presentation in court. Nor did any FBI agents testify at Nagell's trial, despite his request that they be called to the stand. The FBI denied the very existence of Nagell's January 6, 1964, statement about his motives—which this author discovered filed in the archives of his court case. And, of course, the FBI officially denies ever having received Nagell's registered letter to Hoover about the pending conspiracy.

This weight of evidence suggests that Hoover's FBI was actively working to cover up the true facts behind the assassination, as well as the FBI's advance knowledge of a conspiracy. In effect, this makes Hoover an accomplice. His antipathy toward the Kennedys was well known. So was his long-standing disdain for the CIA. At the same time, the director retained friendships with the Murchison and Hunt oil interests. Between Hoover and Charles Willoughby, correspondence exists only for the year 1951 among the general's papers. But in a 1970 letter to Willoughby from Mario Garcia Kohly, the Cuban exile refers to Hoover as "a good friend of yours." How close the Hoover-Willoughby relationship was remains unknown, but they were certainly cut from the same cloth.

Texas Oil and the Ultraright Underground

The hardest evidence of a conspiracy that has ever come to light is informant Willie Somersett's tape-recorded conversation of November 9, 1963, with Joseph Milteer. The Dixie Klan member spoke openly about assassinating JFK from a window with a high-powered rifle. Right after the event in Dallas, Milteer described himself as part of an "international underground" that used Oswald as a dupe to put the blame on the Communists.

Was the H. L. Hunt oil family part of this "underground"?[6] Their funding of American paramilitary and East European émigré groups, the Oswald letter to "Dear Mr. Hunt," and the visits of Jack Ruby and Eugene Hale Brading to the Hunt offices shortly before the assassination certainly raise questions that were never carefully examined. The actions taken by the Hunts in the assassination's aftermath are even more incriminating. As two former high employees of their oil empire have alleged, the Hunts purchased the original copy of the Zapruder film; dispatched John Curington to check out the security surrounding Oswald the night before he was shot; and received a visit from Marina Oswald (which she herself vaguely remembers).

During the spring of 1963, meetings of two ultraright organizations took place: the Congress of Freedom convention in New Orleans, where an informant reported discussions about eliminating "undesirable" political leaders; and the Anti-Communist Liaison in Washington, where the Willoughby crowd outlined psychological-warfare strategies. The shooting incident at the home of General Walker took place at this same time—and new information makes this event loom large in bringing Oswald to the fore as a tool of the ultraright. Bradford Angers's revelation about Conservatism, U.S.A.'s leader Larrie Schmidt being involved with Oswald in the Walker attempt—and Walker's own belief that this was a distinct possibility—brings the circle around to Schmidt's connections with the Hunts and, according to Angers, Charles Willoughby.

Willoughby's "old boys" were a vastly different breed from the old-school-tie, Ivy League crowd who ran the CIA. Their enmity went back to a battle for hegemony between Military Intelligence and the OSS in World War II. While the CIA's power base expanded, the MacArthur-Willoughby team's very existence was challenged. One Democratic president, Harry Truman, pushed them out of the Far East. But Willoughby and his ilk did not fade away. They melded into global alliances, extending from a quasireligious order such as the Shickshinny Knights of Malta to the Reinhard Gehlen-Otto Skorzeny spy team in Europe.[7] Then the policies of the next Democratic president, Kennedy, threatened this fanatically anti-Communist network with oblivion.

The case for Willoughby's involvement in the Kennedy conspiracy can be no more than circumstantial. But Willoughby was a master of intrigue who established Nagell's Field Operations Intelligence unit in the Far East and played a major part in forming the basis for the Asian People's Anti-Communist League. Willoughby was in regular correspondence with Allen Dulles—before JFK fired Dulles—and with ex(?)-Nazis who ran the CIA's European-based spy network.[8] Willoughby's domestic associations extended from the Cuban exile community to the H. L. Hunt family. He and other of MacArthur's former top generals undoubtedly retained a strong bond with right-wing elements of the Pentagon. MacArthur's "little fascist," as the general once described him, was assuredly in a position to make the right connections from his Washington domain.

The Military and the Assassination

The message that Army code-breaker Eugene Dinkin tried to send in a variety of European capitals in October–November 1963 is the strongest, if most bizarre, indication of a possible high-level military role in the assassination. Then, on November 22, we find:

1. Army Intelligence officer James Powell taking pictures in Dealey Plaza.
2. The likelihood that Oswald's name first came to the attention of the Dallas police through Military Intelligence.
3. A file on Oswald/Hidell being scrutinized by Army Intelligence official Robert Jones in San Antonio, the file later to be "routinely destroyed."
4. An Army Intelligence reserve officer, Jack Crichton, making the first arrangements for Marina Oswald's translators.
5. A military autopsy at Bethesda Naval Hospital during which, as researchers such as David Lifton have painstakingly discovered, a concerted attempt was made to back up the government's lone-assassin-firing-from-behind scenario.

When the House Assassinations Committee sought to get to the bottom of what the military knew about Oswald, committee investigator Edwin Lopez described to me what happened: "We talked to a number of people, but our leads went nowhere fast. Since we had no enforcement power, we couldn't get half the information we wanted. Army Intelligence basically told us to go screw ourselves."

Nagell seems to have embarked on his CIA-KGB mission at the original behest of Military Intelligence. The Robert Nolan pseudonym he used in 1962–63, and previously with FOI in the Far East, was, Nagell says, authorized for his use "by an intelligence organization operating under the control of responsible officials of the United States Department of Defense."

Nagell has offered a number of hints about a Pentagon role in the conspiracy. The CIA, as Nagell wrote to Arthur Greenstein, would have done well to check in with a certain "right-wing clique in the Pentagon" concerning Oswald. Nagell has also written: "It is no secret in the intelligence community that this clique has been pressing for some time to have the DIA [Defense Intelligence Agency], the CIA's chief competitor, take over the black operations of the CIA."

Did one of those "black operations" center around Oswald and Nagell and result in the assassination of our thirty-fifth president?

The Specter of November 22, 1963

Everything changed after Dallas. Within a month, Lyndon Johnson embarked on the course that would plunge America into the Vietnam War. The new president also reviewed the Kennedy administration's Cuban policies, and the anticipated rapprochement with Castro was permanently shelved.

What did LBJ know about the Kennedy conspiracy? FBI files reveal that he confided to a staff assistant, Marvin Watson, in 1967 that he was convinced there had been a plot and that somehow the CIA was involved. LBJ said the same, and more, to his mistress Madeleine Brown soon after the assassination—indicating that the very Texas oil interests who had fueled his career were, at least in part, responsible.[9]

Nor is LBJ the only president for whom what happened in Dallas became a ghostly presence. After the Watergate break-in where several ex-CIA men and Cuban exiles were caught in 1972, Richard Nixon expressed worry on the White House tape-recording system that this might open up "the whole Bay of Pigs thing." Nixon's chief of staff, H. R. Haldeman, later wrote of his belief that the president was really talking about the Kennedy assassination.[10]

Gerald Ford, who became president after Nixon resigned in August 1974, had been named to the Warren Commission while a U.S. congressman, and he became a vigorous defender of the lone-assassin theory. In 1978 the FBI released files revealing that Ford was the bureau's personal pipeline into the commission. A memo to Hoover from an aide, Cartha DeLoach, noted on December 12, 1963: "Ford indicated he would keep me thoroughly advised as to the activities of the commission . . . on a confidential basis."

George Bush, a Texas oilman in 1963, is also found on the periphery of the assassination. As noted earlier in this book, his name appeared in George de Mohrenschildt's personal notebook and Bush was a friend of Marina Oswald's translator, Ilya Mamantov. When George Bush became

CIA director (1976–78), Nagell is on record as having written to him about Robert Morrow's book *Betrayal.*

The White House has denied that the president was the "Mr. George Bush of the Central Intelligence Agency" identified in a November 29, 1963, FBI memorandum as having been briefed by the FBI on the reaction of Miami's Cuban exiles. But there is no denying the existence of another recently released FBI memo, which begins:

"On November 22, 1963, Mr. GEORGE H.W. BUSH, 5525 Briar, Houston, Texas, telephonically advised that he wanted to relate some hear say that he had heard in recent weeks, date and source unknown. He advised that one JAMES PARROTT had been talking of killing the President when he comes to Houston."[11]

An FBI investigation into Bush's charge failed to turn up any connection whatsoever tying James Parrott to the assassination. Parrott was then an active member of Houston's Young Republicans, who had been involved in picketing members of the Kennedy administration. Bush was then serving as campaign manager for future Republican senator John Tower. Since Parrott's group had come out strongly against a then nascent alliance between Texas Republicans and representatives of the petroleum industry, Bush and Parrott were political enemies.

This makes no less than four of the past six American presidents who either expressed doubts about the Warren Commission's conclusions or had some kind of direct role in postassassination events.

Where Do We Go from Here?

It is time for our government to release all existing files on the assassination of President Kennedy.

Beyond that, armed with the realization that these files will not provide the complete picture of what happened on November 22, 1963, we must demand a new investigation with the appointment of a special prosecutor.

Many of the most important witnesses are dead. But quite a few are still living, and should be deposed. These include:

- Former Military Intelligence officer and CIA contract agent Richard Case Nagell[12]
- Nagell's known associates (e.g., Vaughn Marlowe, Arthur Greenstein, John Margain), and the individuals involved in his arrest and incarceration in El Paso and East Germany (e.g., policeman James Bundren,

attorney Joseph Calamia, FBI agent Edward J. Murphy, Judge Homer Thornberry, and attorney Ricey New)
- Texas oilman Nelson Bunker Hunt
- former CIA contract agent Robert D. Morrow
- former manager of the Hotel Luma Warren Broglie
- former ambassador to Mexico Thomas Mann
- members of the Charles Murret family, New Orleans
- members of Dallas-Fort Worth's Russian community (e.g., Mrs. Igor Voshinin and Peter Gregory)
- retired CIA officials, including Richard Helms, E. Howard Hunt, Jr., and Clare Petty
- retired military officials and personnel (e.g., Eugene B. Dinkin)
- retired Treasury agent Frank Ellsworth
- Cuban exiles Sergio Arcacha-Smith, Antonio Veciana, Tony Cuesta, and others
- Dallas gun dealer John Thomas Masen
- prisoner Garrett B. Trapnell

The trails are fresh. The clues are current. The case is open.

Until more of the truth is known about what really happened in Dallas, we the people will remain unable to reclaim the heritage that made this country what it was. This great trauma of modern American history has affected all aspects of our political and social life. Our democracy has never recovered from the Kennedy assassination and the terrible events that followed in the 1960s: the Vietnam War, the assassinations of Malcolm X, Martin Luther King, Jr., and Robert Kennedy.

John F. Kennedy once foresaw, prophetically, that "we shall have to test anew whether a nation organized and governed such as ours can endure. The outcome is by no means certain."

Today we live in a nation far removed from the "New Frontier" that JFK envisioned. Racism, poverty, homelessness, drugs, and violence permeate our republic. The seeds of a government completely removed from the real concerns of the people, with control concentrated in the hands of a powerful few, were planted in the coup d'état that overthrew John F. Kennedy.

This book was written to expose those forces that tore this nation apart and whose hold on America has brought us to our current impasse.

Time Line of Primary Events

1889
H.L. Hunt is born in Illinois.

1892
Charles Willoughby is born in Heidelberg, Germany.

1895
January 1: J. Edgar Hoover is born in Washington, D.C.

1909
Mark Gayn is born near Manchurian-Mongolian border.

1911
Jack Ruby is born in Chicago.
George de Mohrenschildt is born in Russia.

1917
Russian Revolution occurs.
May 29: John F. Kennedy is born in Brookline, Massachusetts.

1930
August 5: Richard Case Nagell is born in Greenwich, New York.

1935
Mark Gayn, Harold Isaacs reside in Shanghai.

1939
October 18: Lee Harvey Oswald is born in New Orleans.

1941
Charles Willoughby becomes General Douglas MacArthur's chief of intelligence in the Far East.
George de Mohrenschildt forms film partnership with Nazi espionage agent.
July 17: Marina Prusakova is born at Arkhangeloblast, USSR.
December 7: The United States enters World War II.

1945
June: Mark Gayn is arrested in *Amerasia* case.
August 14: Japan surrenders, ending World War II.

Late August: Hitler's spymaster Reinhard Gehlen makes agreement with U.S. intelligence officials to establish anti-Communist espionage network in Europe.

1946
Charles Willoughby begins establishing liaison with Japanese war criminals.
November: Mark Gayn encounters Chikao Fujisawa in occupied Japan.

1947
Central Intelligence Agency (CIA) is authorized by Congress.

1948
August 5: Nagell enlists in the Army.

Late 1940s
Winston Scott, future station chief in Mexico City, begins relationship with Soviet official in London.

1950
June: Korean War begins; Charles Willoughby sets up Field Operations Intelligence.

1951
Desmond FitzGerald joins the CIA.
April: MacArthur is relieved of Pacific command by President Truman; Willoughby also returns Stateside. H. L. Hunt, Clint Murchison set up welcome-MacArthur committee in Dallas.
May: Soviet spies Burgess and McLean defect from Great Britain; Kim Philby is recalled from United States. CIA's James Angleton and Winston Scott write memos describing relationships with Philby.
Autumn: Nagell arrives in South Korea.

1953
John Paisley joins the CIA.
April 13: CIA's MK-ULTRA mind-control program is authorized by Director Allen Dulles.
July 27: Korean War ends. Nagell becomes the youngest American to receive battlefield promotion to captain, is assigned to Army Language School.

1954
Asian People's Anti-Communist League is established.
CIA begins studying possibility of creating "Manchurian Candidate." CIA-backed coup overthrows government of Guatemala.
November 28: Nagell is sole survivor in crash of B-25 military bomber, is hospitalized four months.

1955
July: Oswald joins New Orleans' Civil Air Patrol, commanded by David Ferrie.
August 12: Nagell is designated military Counter Intelligence officer, assigned to Los Angeles, where he also works for the CIA. Granted "Top-Secret" security clearance in September.

1956
FBI establishes COINTELPRO operation.
Winston Scott becomes CIA station chief in Mexico City.

May 5: Nagell is assigned to Field Operations Intelligence in the Far East.
October 24: Oswald enlists in the U.S. Marines.

1957

George de Mohrenschildt travels to Yugoslavia, is debriefed upon return by CIA.

February 7: Nagell is transferred out of FOI at his request, and is reassigned to Counter Intelligence Corps in Tokyo.

Spring: Oswald receives "Confidential" security clearance.

September 12: Oswald arrives in the Far East and is assigned to the Atsugi U-2 spy base outside Tokyo as a radar operator.

October: Global anti-Communist alliance is formed in Taiwan.

October–December: Nagell supervises review of Top-Secret Military Intelligence files in Tokyo.

November: Nagell is recruited into CIA project aimed at getting Soviet colonel Nikolai Eroshkin to defect.

Probably early November: Oswald is photographed entering Soviet embassy in Tokyo by national police; meets with Colonel Eroshkin.

Exact date unknown: Nagell and Oswald meet with Professor Chikao Fujisawa, also involved in Eroshkin plan.

Exact date unknown: Oswald and Nagell frequent the Queen Bee nightclub; Oswald allegedly recruited by U.S. intelligence.

November 20: Oswald ships out to Cubi Point, Philippines.

1958

Richard Condon novel *The Manchurian Candidate* is published.

January 5: Marine private Martin Schrand dies under strange circumstances in Philippines. Oswald is later alleged to have been involved, giving CIA a "handle" on him.

January 5: Nagell begins his crusade against U.S. military injustices.

Cir. January 10: Nagell drops out of Eroshkin defection plan.

March: World Anti-Communist Congress is formed in Mexico City.

March 12: Master Sergeant (and FOI agent) Emmett Dugan's body is discovered in Tokyo Bay. Nagell had witnessed his execution by U.S. authorities as a suspected Chinese spy.

March 18: Oswald returns to Atsugi from Philippines.

March 24: Nagell marries Mitsuko Takahashi, whose father he was investigating, at U.S. embassy in Tokyo.

April 11: Oswald is allegedly court-martialed for illegal possession of a pistol; gets suspended sentence.

April 21: Nagell is informed he is being investigated for compromise of classified material.

June 20: Oswald enters brig for forty-five days after court-martial over altercation with a sergeant.

July 15: Nagell and his wife return to the United States; he is assigned to Fort Dix, New Jersey, as an infantryman.

August 28: Nagell brings long "contestation" about illegal Army activities to inspector general in Washington.

October 5: After a brief stay in Taiwan, Oswald returns to Japan and is reassigned to Iwakuni.

October 5: Nagell writes first letter of resignation to the Army.

November 2: Oswald returns to the United States.

Late December: Oswald is reassigned to radar duties at Santa Ana, California, base.

1959

January 1: Fidel Castro takes power in Cuba.

Early 1959: Oswald is seen by Gerry Hemming at Cuban consulate in Los Angeles.

March 11: Jack Ruby is recruited as FBI informant.

April 14: Army declares Nagell ineligible for further duty with CIC.

April–June: Nagell meets with Professor Fujisawa twice in New York; Fujisawa seeks to recruit Nagell as Soviet agent.

June: The first of five American defectors over a four-month period arrive in the USSR.

Late summer: Oswald's cousin Marilyn Murret leaves for extended overseas journey.

August 17: Oswald requests dependency discharge from Marines.

August 31: Nagell sends another letter of resignation to Army.

September 10: Oswald gets a passport; he is discharged from Marines the next day.

September 20: Oswald sets sail from New Orleans.

Early October: Ex-Navy man, Rand Development technician Robert Webster defects in Moscow.

October 15: Ukrainian leader Stepan Bandera is found dead in Munich.

October 16: Oswald arrives in Moscow.

October 17: John Paisley, recently made chief of CIA Soviet Electronics Branch, embarks on long European trip.

October 29: Nagell receives honorable discharge, moves with family to Los Angeles.

October 31: Oswald announces intent to "dissolve his American citizenship" at U.S. embassy in Moscow.

December 11: CIA director Allen Dulles approves plans to eliminate Castro.

1960

Cuban exile Antonio Veciana meets "Maurice Bishop" in Havana.

January: Nagell takes job as investigator for state of California, allegedly working for CIA at the same time.

January 8: Oswald arrives in Minsk, is provided job in radio-TV factory.

Early 1960: George de Mohrenschildt meets with Soviet deputy premier Anastas Mikoyan in Mexico City.

April 6: Fair Play for Cuba Committee makes its public debut in New York.

Spring: Professor Fujisawa departs United States.

May 1: Francis Gary Powers's U-2 spy plane is shot down over the USSR.

May: Mark Gayn visits the Soviet Union.

Summer: H. L. Hunt convinces LBJ to accept vice-presidential nomination.

Late September: Initial meetings take place between CIA and organized-crime figures in plots to assassinate Castro.

October: Mario Garcia Kohly, Sr., meets with Vice President Nixon about a plan to eliminate other Cuban exile leaders and have Kohly take power in Cuba after Castro's overthrow.

1961

KGB officials Oleg Nechiporenko and Valery Kostikov take up residence in Mexico City.

January 20: John F. Kennedy is inaugurated president.

February: Oswald writes to U.S. embassy in Moscow, expressing desire to return to the United States.

March: George and Jeanne de Mohrenschildt arrive in Guatemala, near Bay of Pigs training ground.

Mid-March: Marina Prusakova meets Oswald at a dance; courtship proceeds as Oswald is hospitalized for eleven days after adenoid operation.

March 31: Nagell is transferred to California's Department of Alcoholic Beverage Control.

April: General Edwin Walker is relieved of command in West Germany by JFK administration for indoctrinating his troops.

April 6: Robert Kennedy has mobster Carlos Marcello deported to Guatemala.

April 15–17: Bay of Pigs invasion fails.

April 30: Oswald marries Marina in Minsk.

May: CIA begins working with FBI in targeting Fair Play for Cuba Committee.

August: Bogdan Stashinsky defects, claiming he was Soviet assassin.

September: Plans to form "secret fraternity" to coordinate right-wing activities are announced by Billy James Hargis.

October 1: Defense Intelligence Agency (DIA) is formed.

October: FBI approves forty-five actions against Socialist Workers' Party under COINTELPRO.

October: Assassination attempt planned by Veciana and "Bishop" is discovered by Castro; Silvia Odio's father is imprisoned for harboring a perpetrator.

November 29: John McCone succeeds Allen Dulles, fired by Kennedy, as CIA director.

Late 1961: CIA contract agent Robert Morrow receives data in Madrid from "Harvey in Minsk," passes it along to Tracy Barnes.

Late 1961: CIA official J. Walton Moore discusses agency "interest" in Oswald with George de Mohrenschildt.

1962

February: David Ferrie goes to work in New Orleans as investigator for Guy Banister and Carlos Marcello.

March 21: Anti-Communist Liaison holds private meeting in Washington.

March 22: Hoover lunches with JFK, informs president his girlfriend Judith Campbell is also mistress of Sam Giancana.

Spring: Mark Gayn publishes article about Southern California Minutemen.

April–May: Having trouble with his marriage, Nagell twice checks himself into Veterans Administration psychiatric hospital.

May: Marina Oswald is examined at U.S. embassy in Moscow by Air Force doctor Alexis Davison, who is simultaneously involved with CIA spy Oleg Penkovsky.

Mid-May: Soviet defector Robert Webster returns to United States.

June 2: Soviet defector Oswald departs USSR with Marina.

June 8: Nagell is fired from his job with California Department of Alcoholic Beverage Control.

June 13: Oswalds are met in New York by Spas Raikin, who is connected with extremist Ukrainian underground; Oswalds arrive in Fort Worth next night.

July: Nagell contacts FBI in Los Angeles.

July 1: Marina writes to Soviet embassy in Washington.

July 16: Nagell is shot in his car at a Southern California beach; he drives himself to a V.A. hospital.

Summer: Cuban exile organization Alpha 66 is formed under CIA auspices.

July 26: FBI agent John Fain questions Oswald in Fort Worth.

Early August: Oswald writes to Soviet embassy in Washington, subscribes to "leftist" periodicals.

August 16: FBI agent Fain interviews Oswald again; Oswald agrees to report any suspicious Soviet contacts.

August 17: Nagell gets Mexican tourist card in Los Angeles.

August 24: Nagell crosses Mexican border at El Paso.

Late August: After discussing Oswald with the CIA's J. Walton Moore, George de Mohrenschildt befriends Oswald.

August–October: Vaughn Marlowe, Harriett Buhai, and other American "leftists" are in Mexico City, making plans to visit Cuba.

August–October: Cuban Missile Crisis occurs.

September: New Orleans Mob leader Carlos Marcello makes alleged threat against JFK. Florida Mob leader Santos Trafficante, Jr., tells José Aleman, Jr., that JFK is "going to be hit." Edward Grady Partin tells Justice Department of Jimmy Hoffa threat against Robert Kennedy.

September: Nagell indicates he plans to renounce U.S. citizenship at American embassy in Mexico City. Nagell refuses offer from "representative of foreign government" to participate in criminal offense against United States. Nagell contacts FBI in Mexico City.

September: Nagell becomes "double agent" under CIA contract.

September 30–October 1: General Edwin Walker is arrested by federal authorities for insurrection against enrollment of black student James Meredith at University of Mississippi. Walker is sent to federal medical center for mental tests.

October: Nagell receives assignments from Soviets to monitor JFK assassination plot and Oswald's activities.

October: Bogdan Stashinsky trial takes place in West Germany.

October: Larrie Schmidt, founder of Conservatism U.S.A., arrives in Dallas from Munich.

October 10: Oswald moves alone to Dallas, gets job two days later with Jaggers-Chiles-Stovall photo-lithography firm.

October 21: Nagell leaves Mexico City for the United States.

October 22: JFK reveals existence of Soviet missiles in Cuba to American people. Nagell arrives in Dallas, checks into Oswald.

Late October: JFK and Khrushchev reach agreement ending Cuban Missile Crisis; JFK agrees to leave Cuba alone. Operation MONGOOSE is terminated in November.

November 16: Nagell contacts FBI in New York, begins surveillance of Cuban exiles.

November 25: Nagell seeks commission in Army Reserve. He is turned down December 7.

December: Cuban exile Mario Kohly meets with H. L. Hunt in Dallas.

Early December: Nagell is in Washington and is contacted by Soviets; he touches base with CIA.

December 15: Nagell contacts FBI in Jacksonville, Florida.

December 20: Nagell checks into Bay Pines, Florida, Veterans Administration Hospital.

December 29: JFK addresses returning Bay of Pigs prisoners in Miami. First scheduled plot against his life does not proceed.

Late December: Oswald meets Yaeko Okui and soon begins an affair with her.

1963

Chikao Fujisawa dies.

January: Oswald's cousin Marilyn Murret returns to the United States.

January: JFK announces plan to reduce oilmen's tax breaks.

January 1: Oswald steps up his correspondence with Trotskyite organizations.

January 2: Nagell writes to JFK from the V.A. hospital.

January 4: Advisers propose JFK consider opening communications with Castro.

January: CIA's Desmond FitzGerald secretly explores ways to assassinate Castro.

Mid-January: Exile leader Manuel Artime meets with Robert Kennedy.

January 22: Nagell is discharged from the hospital, registers under false name at Miami hotel the next day.

January 24: Nagell contacts FBI in Miami, using "Joseph Kramer" alias; discusses his Cuban and Soviet sources and illegal armaments.

January 27: Oswald uses "Hidell" alias for first time, in filling out mail-order coupon for a revolver. Nagell admits to having used the same alias.

Late January: Nagell investigates various members of Miami Cuban exile community, including Artime, Rolando Masferrer, Sergio Arcacha-Smith, and Eladio del Valle.

Late January–early February: Rolando Masferrer turns over weapons to exile group looking to infiltrate Cuba.

Late January–early February: Mark Gayn visits Mexico City and Cuba.

February: CIA officially sets up new Domestic Operations Division, under Tracy Barnes. In Mexico City, David Phillips takes over Cuban operations on orders from Desmond FitzGerald.

Early February: Nagell spends a few days inquiring about Oswald in Dallas. Nagell apparently meets his Soviet contact in Nuevo Laredo, Mexico.

February 17: Marina Oswald writes the Soviet embassy about returning to her homeland.

February 22: Ruth Paine meets the Oswalds.

Late February: General Walker leaves with Billy James Hargis for cross-country "Operation Midnight Ride" speaking tour.

March 25: Oswald's mail-ordered Mannlicher-Carcano rifle arrives for "Hidell" at Dallas P.O. Box.

March 30: After a series of unauthorized attacks on Cuba, U.S. government announces crackdown on Cuban exiles.

March 31: Oswald has Marina take photographs of him holding weapons and leftist newspapers. Oswald initiates correspondence with V. T. Lee of Fair Play for Cuba Committee.

April: CIA takes pictures of Nagell outside Soviet embassy in Washington.

April: Nagell conducts an inquiry in Dallas and San Antonio into Marina's reported desire to go back to the USSR.

April 2: Oswald meets Michael Paine; they discuss General Walker.

April 3: Walker-Hargis tour comes to rousing finish in Los Angeles.

April 4: Miami police discover exile plans to direct violence against the United States.

April 4–5: V. T. Lee of Fair Play for Cuba Committee speaks in Los Angeles.

April 4–6: Wealthy right-wing extremists meet in New Orleans for annual Congress of Freedom.

April 10: Oswald, allegedly accompanied by Larrie and Bob Schmidt, fires a shot at General Edwin Walker in Dallas.

April 12: George de Mohrenschildt asks Oswald how he happened to miss General Walker.

Mid-April: The Igor Voshinins report to the FBI de Mohrenschildt's statement to them about Oswald firing at Walker.

Mid-April: While Oswald intensifies communications with V. T. Lee, the FBI simultaneously steps up surveillance on Lee.

Spring: Garrett Trapnell "penetrates" Alpha 66 group for Castro intelligence, is soon approached in Miami about participating in plot against Kennedys.

April 18: Alpha 66 announces formation of Los Angeles chapter.

April 19: Nagell, in Los Angeles, contacts FBI.

Cir. April 19: De Mohrenschildts leave Dallas for the East Coast.

April 24: Oswald moves alone to New Orleans, moves in temporarily with Murret family.

April 26–27: Anti-Communist Liaison holds strategy seminar in Washington.

Spring: French OAS captain Jean Souetre reportedly meets with General Walker, goes on to New Orleans.

May: De Mohrenschildts meet with U.S. intelligence officials in Washington.

May: FBI scrutinizes the activities of Alpha 66.

May: Nagell says Oswald is apprised of legal requirements for travel to Cuba.

May: In Los Angeles, Nagell commences investigating Vaughn Marlowe of the Fair

Play for Cuba Committee, who is being considered by Cuban exiles for "recruitment" in assassination attempt against JFK. Nagell gets a job driving a cab. Nagell agrees to proposal made by "representative of foreign government" to participate in criminal offense against the United States.

May: French OAS captain Jean Souetre approaches CIA about de Gaulle government.

May 9: Oswald gets a job with Reily Coffee Company, whose owner is leading backer of anti-Castro causes.

May 9: Jimmy Hoffa is indicted for jury tampering.

May 19: Alpha 66 issues a call to arms in Los Angeles.

May 20: Mario Kohly forms United Organization for the Liberation of Cuba.

June: Colonel Chesley Clark tells ultraright's Revilo Oliver of likely Communist conspiracy to create "major incident" before Thanksgiving.

June: Nagell takes still photographs of Angel and Leopoldo in Los Angeles.

June 2: The de Mohrenschildts move to Haiti.

June 3: Oswald rents New Orleans P.O. Box, moves ahead setting up one-man chapter of Fair Play for Cuba Committee.

June 4: Nagell requests admission to V.A. hospital in Los Angeles. FBI gets a report on this.

June 7: JFK arrives in Los Angeles for fund-raising dinner. Second scheduled plot against his life fails to materialize, at Beverly Hilton Hotel.

June 25: One day after applying, Oswald is issued a new passport in New Orleans.

Late June: Marina Oswald writes Soviet embassy that she and Lee wish to return to the USSR.

July: Nagell communicates about Oswald with Steve Roberts, Socialist Workers Party and FPCC functionary.

July 1: British government announces that intelligence official Kim Philby has fled to the USSR.

July 1–2: Nagell monitors a witness at House Un-American Activities Committee hearings in Los Angeles.

Cir. early July: Adrian Alba observes Oswald receiving a document from an FBI agent.

Cir. July: Oswald and a Mexican visit attorney Dean Andrews, from whom Oswald seeks advice on his dishonorable discharge.

July 10: Oswald and Nagell are turned down, by the Marines and the Army, respectively, on their separate requests to have their service records changed.

July 19: Oswald is fired from his job at the Reily Coffee Company.

July 19: Navy yeoman Nelson Drummond is convicted as a Soviet spy. His name appears in Nagell's notebook.

July 24: Ten Cuban exiles arrive in New Orleans from Miami, go to a training camp. Oswald makes contact with Arnesto Rodriguez, who runs local Spanish-language school.

Probably late July: Angel and Leopoldo meet Oswald in New Orleans. Oswald goes to exile training camp to take rifle practice with David Ferrie.

July 27: Oswald travels with the Murrets and Marina to give a speech in Mobile, Alabama, returns to New Orleans next day.

July 30: Foreign correspondent Anita Ehrman is found dead in her Washington apartment. Her name appears in Nagell's notebook.

Midsummer: Tracy Barnes asks Robert Morrow to buy four 7.35mm Mannlicher-Carcano rifles. David Ferrie flies three of these weapons to New Orleans.

Late July: Nagell contacts FBI in Dallas.

July 31: Oswald is reportedly seen at Selective Service office in Austin, Texas.

July 31: Cuban exile training camp outside New Orleans is raided by FBI.

July: CIA conducts MK-ULTRA "mind control" field test in Mexico City.

Late July–early August: Nagell, and apparently Oswald, travel to Mexico City. Robert Clayton Buick probably encounters Oswald and Nagell at the Hotel Luma at this time, reports to intelligence contacts in Garibaldi Park.

August: Oswald's cousin Marilyn Murret travels through Mexico and Central America.

Early August: Nagell returns to Los Angeles from Mexico City. Renews his passport on August 6. Borrows Colt .45 pistol from Bill Lynn. Departs abruptly, leaving cryptic note for Vaughn Marlowe. According to Robert Morrow, Nagell is on CIA/DIA assignment to penetrate Banister-Ferrie group in New Orleans.

Early August: Oswald goes into the office of Edward Gillin in New Orleans, talking about a spectacular drug offering a view into the future.

August: CIA inspector general Lyman Kirkpatrick warns Richard Helms about experiments in manipulating human behavior.

August 4: Jack Ruby makes phone call to Marcello lieutenant Nofio Pecora in New Orleans.

August 5: Oswald goes to see Cuban exile Carlos Bringuier, offers to train anti-Castro guerrilla fighters.

August 7: Oswald is seen in New Orleans's Habana bar with two Hispanic acquaintances. Oswald is using offices of Guy Banister for his FPCC organization.

August 9: Oswald, while passing out Fair Play for Cuba Committee leaflets, has a street altercation with Bringuier and is arrested. In New Orleans jail, Oswald asks to see FBI. Bond is paid next day by mobster lieutenant of Carlos Marcello.

August 12: After pleading guilty at his trial, Oswald sends news clips to FPCC and Communist Party, U.S.A.

August 16: Oswald does more street leafleting, is visited by exile Carlos Quiroga, an FBI informant. CIA director John McCone learns of CIA-Mob plots through a newspaper article.

August 19: Garrett Trapnell alerts FBI that Cuban group had solicited him to take part in a plot to assassinate JFK.

August 20: Nagell takes photographs of Angel and Leopoldo.

August 21: Oswald participates in radio debate with Carlos Bringuier and Ed Butler. Transcript is provided to FBI.

Late August: In Dallas, Antonio Veciana is introduced to Oswald by "Maurice Bishop."

Late August: Colonel William Bishop places Nagell under surveillance in New Orleans.

August 23–27: Nagell makes secret tape recording of JFK conspiracy discussion among himself, Oswald, Angel, and a fourth party. Plan is for late September in Washington, D.C.

August 27: Nagell makes "complaint" to Desmond FitzGerald about his own situation with Oswald. FBI checks court records in New Orleans on Oswald.

Probably late summer: Nagell discovers Oswald undergoing hypnotherapy from David Ferrie.

Late August: Nagell makes possible trip to Mexico City and Cuba. Gets orders from "Oaxaca" either to convince Oswald he is being set up, or to kill him in Mexico.

August 29: Garrett Trapnell is reinterviewed by FBI.

August 31: Oswald writes to Communist *Worker* newspaper, announcing he is relocating to East Coast.

September 1: Oswald writes to Socialist Workers Party, asking how to contact representatives in Washington-Baltimore.

Early September: Nagell stashes evidence of conspiracy with a friend in Los Angeles.

Early September: Oswald goes to black voting-rights drive in Clinton, Louisiana, with Ferrie and possibly Banister.

Probably early September: Oswald and "Hernandez" try to purchase weapons from Robert McKeown in Bay Cliff, Texas.

September: Tracy Barnes tells Robert Morrow of concern about possible plot to kill JFK.

September: Charles Willoughby becomes "security general" for Shickshinny Knights of Malta.

September: Nagell realizes that much of his intelligence work has not been for CIA but for a foreign nation. Decides against proposal made to him to participate in criminal offense against the United States. Nagell contacts FBI in New Orleans, using "Kramer" alias.

September 5: JFK representative gets word Castro is ready to restore communications with United States.

September 6: Manuel Rodriguez registers as alien in Dallas, sets up local chapter of Alpha 66.

September 7: Desmond FitzGerald gets cable from Brazil stating Rolando Cubela (AM/LASH) is prepared to assassinate Castro. At Brazilian embassy in Havana, Castro warns U.S. leaders against plotting to kill him. FBI sends report on Oswald to CIA.

Cir. September 10: Nagell meets with Oswald in New Orleans, warns him he is being used by "fascist elements."

September 15–16: Nagell meets with Oswald again, instructs him to meet "Oaxaca" in Mexico City. Arranges for picture of himself and Oswald to be taken. Perry Russo hears conspiracy discussion among Ferrie and "Leon Oswald." CIA advises FBI it is planning to counter FPCC activities in foreign countries.

September 17: Oswald gets Mexican tourist card. Nagell writes warning letter to Hoover, leaves New Orleans.

September 19: "Leon Oswald" is killed by mistake.

September 20: Nagell gets himself arrested by firing two shots inside the State National Bank of El Paso. Mexican tourist cards for "Hidel" (Oswald) and "Joseph Kramer" are concealed in his luggage.

September 24: Oswald departs New Orleans. FBI and CIA communicate about Oswald and Fair Play for Cuba Committee.

September 25: Angel, Leopoldo, and Oswald visit Silvia Odio in Dallas.

September 26: Oswald travels by bus to Mexico, with preacher Albert Osborne as his seatmate. FBI writes to CIA about FPCC.

September 26–29: The third plot against JFK is scheduled but does not materialize.

September 27–October 2: Oswald is in Mexico City. Visits Soviet and allegedly Cuban embassies.

Before October 1: Robert Morrow receives request for communications equipment from Eladio del Valle.

October: JFK approves phased-down withdrawal of American advisers from Vietnam.

October 2: Robert Morrow and Mario Garcia Kohly, Sr. are arrested by Secret Service in Cuban counterfeit-peso scheme.

October 2: Oswald returns to Dallas.

October 5: Dallas papers announce JFK will visit in November. Oswald moves alone into rooming house.

October 8: LBJ aide Bobby Baker is forced to resign over financial improprieties.

October 10: Albert Osborne gets new passport in New Orleans.

October 10: CIA alerts FBI about Oswald contacting Soviets in Mexico.

Mid-October: CIA claims "sound tapes" of Oswald speaking to Soviet and Cuban embassies in Mexico were destroyed. In truth, station chief Winston Scott kept at least one.

October 14–16: Charles Willoughby's International Committee for the Defense of Christian Culture meets in Switzerland.

October 16: Oswald starts working at Texas School Book Depository.

October 18: Secretary of the Navy Fred Korth resigns in midst of defense contract scandal.

October 22: Army code breaker Eugene Dinkin writes Robert Kennedy from France about military plot against JFK, soon goes AWOL to offer warning at various embassies.

October 23: Oswald attends speech by General Walker.

October 29: Desmond FitzGerald meets with Rolando Cubela in Paris about assassinating Castro.

October 30: Jack Ruby makes phone call to Marcello lieutenant Nofio Pecora.

October–November: Harold Isaacs visits Tokyo.

October–November: Rolando Masferrer tells Colonel William Bishop that JFK is going to be assassinated.

November 1: South Vietnam's president Diem is assassinated in CIA-backed coup.

November 1: Cuban man enters Miami gift shop, talks about sharpshooter friend named Lee who speaks Russian and German.

November 1: Dallas FBI agent Hosty visits Ruth Paine and Marina Oswald.

November 2: Secret Service investigates alleged plot against JFK in Chicago.

November 4: Nagell tells policeman Jim Bundren about an imminent event in Dallas.

November 4: Internal memo to H. L. Hunt family describes possible incidents during JFK trip to Dallas.

November 5: Hosty returns to see Marina Oswald.

November 7: Letter from former congressman Charles Kersten warning of Soviet assassins is allegedly received by Kennedys.

November 7–8: Jack Ruby has long phone calls with two associates of Jimmy Hoffa.

November 8: Oswald writes note to "Dear Mr. Hunt."

November 9: Oswald writes to Soviet embassy in Washington about his Mexico City trip. The letter is discovered by Ruth Paine; a copy is provided the FBI a day after the assassination.

November 9: FBI informant Willie Somersett tapes conversation with Joseph Milteer about plans to kill JFK.

November 13: Army code breaker Eugene Dinkin is taken into custody by Army officials and hospitalized.

November 13: Albert Osborne leaves the United States for Europe.

November 14: Ku Klux Klan member tells FBI of right-wing plan to assassinate the president and other government officials.

Mid-November: Meeting of Cuban exiles allegedly takes place in Miami; told to be prepared for coup d'état in United States.

Mid-November: Several Cubans leave Dallas headquarters of Alpha 66, where Oswald is said to have been seen.

November 18: JFK comes to Miami under tight security.

November 19: In Abilene, Cuban exile Pedro Gonzalez allegedly receives note from Oswald in his mailbox.

November 19: Nagell is visited by two FBI agents in jail.

Probably November 19: Treasury agent Frank Ellsworth releases from custody gun dealer/Minuteman John Thomas Masen—an Oswald look-alike.

November 19–22: Castro confers with French journalist Jean Daniel about reducing tensions between the United States and Cuba.

November 21: Jack Ruby and Eugene Hale Brading go separately to the offices of H. L. Hunt.

November 22: Black-bordered anti-Kennedy ad appears in the *Dallas Morning News*.

November 22: Morning: General Walker flies to Shreveport, Louisiana.

November 22, cir. 12:30 P.M.: JFK is assassinated in Dallas.

November 22: Military Intelligence officer James Powell and organized crime/Hunt family associate Eugene Brading are observed inside buildings at Dealey Plaza.

November 22, 1:00 P.M.: Nagell makes urgent request to speak to Secret Service.

November 22, cir. 1:30 P.M.: Lee Harvey Oswald is arrested in the Texas Theater.

November 22, midafternoon: U.S. Military Intelligence in San Antonio sends data from Oswald/Hidell file to Dallas authorities.

November 22, midafternoon: Mobster Carlos Marcello is acquitted in New Orleans.

November 22, late afternoon: Carlos Bringuier's group in Miami indicates to Clare Boothe Luce and Daniel James that Oswald may have worked for Castro.

November 22: In Paris, Desmond FitzGerald provides poison pen to Rolando Cubela to assassinate Castro.

November 22: French underground figure (either Jean Souetre or Michael Mertz) is expelled from Dallas.

November 22: CIA sends photo from Mexico City of "unidentified man," not Oswald, to Dallas authorities.

November 22, evening: David Ferrie drives to Houston, then on to Galveston.

November 22, evening: Santos Trafficante, Jr., toasts death of Kennedy at dinner in Tampa.

November 22, evening: Zapruder film's original copy is purchased by aide to H. L. Hunt.

November 22, evening: Marina Oswald is taken under wing of Dallas's Russian community.

November 22, midnight: Jack Ruby makes sure everyone knows Oswald was connected with Fair Play for Cuba Committee at press conference at jail.

November 23: Hoover teletype instructs FBI agents to resume normal contacts.

November 23: Jack Martin calls New Orleans DA, links Guy Banister and David Ferrie to the events in Dallas.

November 23: Mannlicher-Carcano rifle is found abandoned in Indiana hotel room of Harry L. Power.

November 23: JFK mistress Mary Meyer calls Timothy Leary about assassination plot.

November 23: Joseph Milteer tells FBI informant that patriot underground "outsmarted Communists," killed JFK.

November 23: Cuban embassy employee Sylvia Duran is arrested by police in Mexico City and held for interrogation.

November 23: H. L. Hunt asks John Curington to check out security surrounding Oswald at the jail. Hunt then leaves for Washington.

November 24: Jack Ruby kills Oswald in Dallas police basement.

November 24: FBI agent Hosty is ordered by superiors to destroy a note Oswald left for him a week to ten days before assassination.

November 24: Mexico City phone operator overhears conversation where Emilio Portuondo, a Willoughby associate, alludes to a conspiracy.

November 25: Nicaraguan Gilberto Alvarado tells U.S. embassy officials in Mexico City he saw Oswald receive $5,000 from Castro Cubans.

Late November: Nagell writes to Secret Service chief James Rowley advising there was a conspiracy to kill JFK.

Late November: Ambassador to Mexico Thomas Mann is told by Hoover to cut off investigation into JFK assassination.

Late November: Marina Oswald visits the offices of H. L. Hunt.

November 28: LBJ creates the Warren Commission.

November 29: First public report of Oswald shooting attempt on General Walker appears in right-wing Munich newspaper.

December: U.S. military investigative team flies to Japan to look into Oswald's background.

December 4: FBI again interviews Garrett Trapnell about assassination.

December 5: Senator Richard Russell, a Warren Commission member, writes memorandum indicating concerns about a cover-up.

December 9: FBI completes five-volume report on assassination, showing Oswald as lone assassin.

December 12: FBI visits Nagell in jail.

December 14: Ambassador to Mexico Thomas Mann is recalled by LBJ and appointed to a high State Department post.

December 19: Nagell tells the FBI he had met Oswald in Mexico City and Texas.

December 20: Fair Play for Cuba Committee member is arrested for allegedly threatening to kill LBJ.

December 31: Fair Play for Cuba Committee disbands.

1964

Early 1964: "Maurice Bishop" instructs Antonio Veciana to pay his cousin, a Cuban intelligence operative in Mexico City, to say that Oswald worked for Castro.

January: Japanese government sends security agent Atsuyuki Sassa to join U.S. intelligence assassination probe.

January 2: FBI and Secret Service visit Nagell in jail.

January 4: Nagell's wife, Mitsuko, is granted a divorce, unknown to Nagell.

January 6: Nagell provides three-page statement to FBI outlining his motive for shooting up the State National Bank of El Paso.

January 18: Marina Oswald is questioned about Nagell for two hours by a Secret Service agent.

January 23: KGB official Yuri Nosenko defects to the West, saying he personally supervised its Oswald file.

January 24: Nagell reveals in court that the FBI and Secret Service have questioned him about Oswald. Judge Homer Thornberry, a friend of LBJ's, enters Nagell case, orders Nagell sent to federal medical center for psychiatric tests.

January 27: Warren Commission considers a rumor that Oswald was an FBI informant.

February 14: Nagell is found competent by medical center psychiatrists.

March 3: CIA director McCone speculates Oswald may have been mind-controlled Soviet agent.

March 12: Nagell is returned to El Paso County Jail.

March 20: Nagell writes the Warren Commission about his attempt to alert authorities about the assassination.

April: Vaughn Marlowe receives messages about the assassination from Nagell in jail.

April 5: General Douglas MacArthur dies.

April 10: Judge Thornberry turns down Nagell request for return of his belongings, citing "irrelevant material."

April 16: Nagell writes another letter to Hoover about the conspiracy.

April 20: Joseph Calamia becomes court-appointed attorney for Nagell.

May 6: Nagell is found guilty of "entering a federally insured bank with intent to rob."

May 12: Hoover raises possibility to Warren Commission that Oswald was a Soviet "sleeper" agent.

May 26: Nagell's ex-wife indicates she has no idea what has become of him.

June 7: Defense motion for new Nagell trial is denied by Judge Thornberry. Nagell gets ten-year sentence.

June 7: Jack Ruby begs Warren Commission to take him to Washington to get the truth of his testimony. Alludes to ultraright conspiracy.

June 19: CIA sends memorandum on Soviet mind-control techniques to Warren Commission.

July 1: Guy Banister dies of a reported heart attack.

July 22: Nagell is sent to Leavenworth Federal Penitentiary.

September 27: Warren Report is publicly released.

October 12: JFK mistress Mary Meyer is murdered in Washington.

October 16: Soviet premier Khrushchev is overthrown.

1965

March 5: Secret Service asks to be notified if Nagell is transferred to another prison or released.

December: Nagell's sister writes plea to President Johnson.

1966

January 4: U.S. Court of Appeals reverses Nagell's conviction, orders new trial.

January 31: Jack Ruby letter describes ultraright plot.

February 15: Nagell is returned to El Paso jail.

March 1: Rolando Cubela is arrested in Havana for plotting to assassinate Castro.

March 24: Nagell writes letter to sister outlining his role in the JFK conspiracy, makes plans to testify.

March 29: Robert Clayton Buick is captured after bank robbery spree and is incarcerated with Nagell temporarily in El Paso.

April 9: Nagell barricades himself in cell for nine-day siege after being ordered sent back to federal medical center.

April 20: Nagell is sent to federal medical center for more psychiatric tests.

Mid-1966: Charles Willoughby becomes consultant to Nelson Bunker Hunt.

June: LBJ names Richard Helms CIA director.

July 9: Nagell is driven back to Texas.

August: Efforts are made to have Nagell committed to a V.A. psychiatric hospital.

September 19: Second Nagell trial begins, in El Paso. Dr. Edwin Weinstein is key witness for insanity defense.

September 27: Nagell is found guilty a second time.

November: Jim Garrison begins investigating JFK conspiracy in New Orleans.

1967

"Lincoln Lawrence" book *Were We Controlled?* is published, speculating that Oswald and Ruby underwent mind control.

January 3: Jack Ruby dies of cancer. Nagell writes letter about the conspiracy to Senator Richard Russell.

January 8: Nagell writes letter about the conspiracy to Senator Robert Kennedy.

February 2: Nagell is transferred again to federal medical center.

February 17: Jim Garrison's investigation becomes public in New Orleans newspaper article.

February 20: David Ferrie has a long meeting with Carlos Bringuier.

February 22: Deaths of David Ferrie (in New Orleans) and Eladio del Valle (in Miami) occur.

March 1: New Orleans businessman Clay Shaw is arrested by Garrison and charged with conspiracy.

March 3: Jack Anderson column makes first public mention of CIA-Mafia plots against Castro, speculates about Castro's retaliation.

March: Nagell writes Garrison about willingness to turn over a tape recording of JFK conspiracy.

March 23: Vaughn Marlowe writes to Garrison about Nagell, using an alias.

March 23: Richard Helms assigns CIA inspector general to prepare report on assassination attempts against Castro.

April 3: President Johnson tells staff aide Marvin Watson he is convinced there was a conspiracy to assassinate JFK, including CIA involvement.

April 4: Columnist Anderson sees FBI about Garrison.

April 10: Garrison investigator (and ex?-CIA man) William R. Martin visits Nagell in prison for first time.

May 23: Richard Helms orders destruction of all notes and source material on inspector general's report.

July 23: CIA's Desmond FitzGerald collapses on tennis court and dies.

July 30: Nagell cuts off relationship with investigator Martin.

August: Nagell begins sending "cryptograms" about the conspiracy to Arthur Greenstein.

September: Charles Willoughby writes to H. L. Hunt about linking Oswald to Soviet assassin.

October 16: Nagell's "leftist" friend Steve Roberts dies in Los Angeles after a long illness.

1968

January: *Ramparts* magazine article appears with information on Nagell case.

April 3: U.S. Court of Appeals reverses Nagell's second conviction, orders him set free.

April 4: Martin Luther King, Jr., is assassinated in Memphis.

April 29: Nagell is released from prison confinement, flies to New York City. Two CIA employees meet him at airport with first of three payments totaling $15,000.

May 14 and 16: Nagell meets with Jim Garrison in New York. High KGB official is also in the city.

May 24: Nagell gets passport.

May 30: Nagell flies to Zurich, Switzerland.

June 4 and 6: Nagell visits U.S. consulate in Zurich. FBI is apprised June 7.

June 5: Robert Kennedy is assassinated in Los Angeles.

June 10: Nagell is arrested by East German authorities on a train. Eventually ends up in Moscow.

Summer: Mark Gayn visits West Berlin and Soviet Union.

October 23: Nagell is released at Berlin border to American authorities. Associated Press story appears next day.

November 2: Nagell returns from Europe to the United States.

1969

Winston Scott retires as CIA station chief in Mexico City and begins working on a memoir.

February 12: Attempt is made to kill Nagell in New York. He flies to New Orleans, then Mexico City, Montreal, and Zurich. Arrives in Switzerland on February 21.

March 1: Clay Shaw is acquitted on Garrison's conspiracy charges.

March 7: Nagell is shot at in Switzerland, leaves for Madrid.

April: CIA releases defector Yuri Nosenko from security restrictions.

April 8: Nagell leaves Spain for West Berlin.

April 22: Nagell is attacked in Berlin and is hospitalized.

April 29: Nagell returns to the United States, at McGuire Air Force Base.

May 2: Nagell communicates with New York FBI agent Alfred Ennulat.

May 2: A Military Intelligence file describes Nagell having investigated Oswald for the CIA.

June 20: Article about Nagell's East German imprisonment and release appears in overseas *Family,* Frankfurt, West Germany.

1970

April 7: Nagell submits application at Pentagon seeking full disability retirement.
   April 14: From Switzerland, Nagell sends Top-Secret documents to Pentagon official.
   Late June: Nagell is reunited with his children in Los Angeles.

1971

March 21: Oleg Nechiporenko and other KGB officials are expelled from Mexico in CIA "disinformation" plan.
   April 25: Winston Scott dies of a heart attack in Mexico City. James Angleton comes from Washington to retrieve Scott's autobiographical manuscript and other files.
   August 17: Nagell obtains legal custody of his children.

1972

February 18: Tracy Barnes dies at sixty of a heart attack.
   May 1: J. Edgar Hoover dies.
   June 17: Watergate break-in occurs.
   June 23: President Nixon expresses concern that Watergate will open "the whole Bay of Pigs thing."
   October 25: Charles Willoughby dies, at eighty, in Florida.

1973

Oswald's Military Intelligence file is "routinely destroyed" by the Pentagon.
   Late January: Fired as CIA director, Richard Helms orders destruction of records on mind control.

1974

February 28: Joseph Milteer dies in mysterious fire.
   Mid-March: Nagell authorizes Bernard Fensterwald, Jr., as his attorney in lawsuit against Pentagon seeking full disability retirement.
   June: Clare Petty presents CIA report concluding that James Angleton may have been a Soviet "mole."
   Summer: John Paisley retires from the CIA.
   August 9: Richard Nixon resigns as president.
   September: The FBI returns some of Nagell's personal belongings seized on September 20, 1963.
   November 29: Texas oil billionaire H. L. Hunt dies at eighty-five.
   December 23: Angleton is asked to resign by CIA director William Colby.

1975

Mobster/CIA contract agent John Martino tells business associate how anti-Castro exiles set up Oswald; Martino dies soon thereafter.
   January 27: Senate Select Committee on Intelligence Activities is formed.
   February 3: Pentagon moves to dismiss Nagell's pleadings in U.S. Court of Claims as "immaterial, impertinent, and scandalous." Pleadings include details on FOI, CIA, Oswald.
   February 28: First public revelation that CIA has plotted to assassinate foreign leaders.
   June 19: Chicago mobster Sam Giancana is murdered.
   July 30: Teamsters boss Jimmy Hoffa disappears.
   Late August: Oswald note to "Dear Mr. Hunt" surfaces.
   October 26: The author meets Nagell for the first time.
   October 31: Rolando Masferrer is killed by dynamite bomb in his car.
   November 21: Nagell writes U.S. congressman Don Edwards about his warning letter to Hoover.

1976
June 8: CIA's William Harvey dies after heart surgery.
   July: Johnny Rosselli has dinner with Santos Trafficante, Jr.
   Summer: Robert Morrow's book *Betrayal* is published, containing information on Nagell ("Richard Carson Fillmore").
   August 7: Rosselli's body is discovered in bay in Miami.
   September: Congress authorizes investigation by House Select Committee on Assassinations.
   October: Congressional investigators bring Antonio Veciana face to face with David Phillips, seeking identification of "Maurice Bishop."

1977
March 29: George de Mohrenschildt dies of gunshot to head in Florida.
   November 18: Cuban exile leader Manuel Artime dies, at forty-five, of "inoperable cancer."

1978
September 23: Former CIA director Richard Helms testifies before House Assassinations Committee on defector Yuri Nosenko's captivity.
   October 2: John Paisley's body is discovered in Chesapeake Bay.

1979
March 29: House Assassinations Committee issues its report.
   July: Antonio Veciana is shot in the head in Miami.
   July 9: Nagell writes to House Assassinations Committee, avowing their conclusions about organized-crime involvement are wrong.

1981
December 17: Mark Gayn dies.

1983
March 2: U.S. Court of Claims awards Nagell full disability retirement in his lawsuit against Pentagon.

1987
May 11: James Angleton dies.

1988
July 10: David Phillips dies.

1992
July: Colonel William Bishop dies.

Appendix A: Nagell and Oswald's ID Card

In 1976, after Richard Case Nagell provided written authorization for my access to the files on him maintained by attorney Bernard Fensterwald, Jr., I flew to Washington, D.C. Going through a thick sheaf of correspondence and other documents in Fensterwald's office, I came across a poor photocopy of a "Uniformed Services Identification and Privileges Card" bearing Lee Harvey Oswald's picture and apparent signature. It was inside the Nagell file, but no other notation appeared with it.

Neither Fensterwald nor I could recall ever seeing this particular Oswald ID card among any of the Warren Commission exhibits. The attorney said he had no idea how it had come into Nagell's possession and could not remember why or when Nagell sent it to him.

I made a copy of the card and later, when passing through Dallas to do more research, showed it to Mary Ferrell. For years, Mrs. Ferrell had labored to assemble the most comprehensive assassination research library in existence. She was astounded at this "find," and shortly thereafter described why in a letter to Fensterwald:

> Dear Bud:
> Dick Russell is here now, visiting and working in my files. He showed me something yesterday which I consider very important. From your Richard Nagell files, he made a Xerox of an "identification card" for Lee H. Oswald bearing a number starting with N 4 etc., with the "signature" of Lee H. Oswald. . . .
> Dick had called me from New York several months ago and asked for the numbers of Lee's two passports and I assured him the number on this card was not on either of the passports. But, yesterday I recognized the Xerox of the card (with the exception of the picture and the dubious signature). It is a replica of the "Uniformed Services Privilege Card" issued to Oswald on September 11, 1959, in California. (I may have the title of the card slightly off.)
> The card has been pictured only *one time anywhere*. This is in Judy Bonner's book, *Investigation of a Homicide*, published in 1969. I believe it is on page 129, but that too may be wrong. The picture of the card has Lee's photograph on it and a signature, neither of which are on the card Dick Russell copied from your file. However, the most important thing is that the copy in Judy's book has stamped over the card what appears to be a postmark "October 1963." This does *not* appear on the Nagell card.
> Question: Where in the world did Nagell get the copy he possessed? Assuming he obtained the original card and Xeroxed it adding a different picture and different signature, how did he obtain it before it had the postmark (or whatever that stamp is) put on it? I stress the point that this card does not appear in anything else—not the [Warren Commission] Report, not the [commission] volumes, in no other book. . . .
> I really believe this is important.

The military ID card shown in the Bonner book was in Oswald's wallet when he was arrested on November 22, 1963. Bonner was able to obtain it from the Dallas police. The picture on Nagell's Oswald card, it turns out, is the same photograph that appears on a Marine Notice of Classification bearing the name of "Alex J. Hidell." Oswald is believed to have fabricated the "Hidell" card by altering his own Notice of Classification and adding the picture, service number, and fictitious name.

Published in the photo section of this book, for the first time, is a reproduction of the Oswald ID card which originated with Richard Nagell. We must recall that Nagell was in jail after September 20, 1963—which means that he is likely to have had this card in his possession at or before that time.

Also pictured here is another card—Oswald's Social Security Card—a photocopy of which was sent by Nagell to Arthur Greenstein. This is a card already known to exist, but for some reason a separate Oswald signature appears four times below it, on the copy Nagell mailed to Greenstein. Does this mean that someone—perhaps Nagell—was practicing how to write Oswald's signature? And, assuming that Nagell did not simply photocopy the card out of the Warren Commission volumes, how did he get it?

Appendix B: Nagell on Oswald and the Soviets

In 1978 I received from Richard Case Nagell a typed statement he had written in response to someone's request that he comment on the allegations made about Oswald and the Soviets in John Barron's 1974 book *KGB: The Work of Soviet Secret Agents*. Although portions of what Nagell said have been quoted elsewhere in this book, I believe it is significant enough to reproduce here in full.

First, author John Barron's statements:

> The Party oligarchy and the KGB are sensitive and in some cases responsive to foreign opinion when it becomes forceful enough to threaten Soviet interests. Their sensitivity is well illustrated by the abject fear shown by the KGB leadership after Lee Harvey Oswald was arrested as the assassin of President Kennedy. The reaction has been disclosed by Yuri Nosenko, who, as deputy director of the American section of the Seventh Department, became involved with Oswald when he requested Soviet citizenship in 1959. Nosenko states that two panels of psychiatrists independently examined Oswald at KGB behest, and each concluded that though not insane, he was quite abnormal and unstable. Accordingly, the KGB ordered that Oswald be routinely watched, but not recruited or in any way utilized. Oswald returned to the United States in June 1962, then in September 1963 applied at the Soviet Embassy in Mexico City for a visa to go back to Moscow. On instructions from the KGB, the embassy blocked his return by insisting that he first obtain an entry visa to Cuba, through which he proposed to travel. The Cubans, in turn, declined to issue a visa until he presented one from the Russians. Shunted back and forth between the two embassies, Oswald finally departed Mexico City in disgust and on November 22 shot the President.
>
> With news of his arrest, the KGB was terrified that, in ignorance or disregard of the headquarters order not to deal with him, an officer in the field might have utilized Oswald for some purpose. According to Nosenko, the anxiety was so intense that the KGB dispatched a bomber to Minsk, where Oswald had lived, to fly his file to Moscow overnight. Nosenko recalls that at the Center officers crowded around the bulky dossier, dreading as they turned each page that the next might reveal some relationship between Oswald and the KGB. All knew that should such a relationship be found to have existed, American public opinion would blame the KGB for the assassination, and the consequences could be horrendous.

Nagell's response:

> Re your memo of February 19, 1974, with copy of page 335, *KGB*, by John Barron:
>
> I doubt seriously that the KGB leadership displayed either intense anxiety or abject fear after Lee Oswald was arrested for the assassination of President Kennedy. I have substantial cause to believe that at the time neither the Soviet government nor the KGB hierarchy were overly concerned with American public opinion; certainly, neither were fearful of any "horrendous consequences" developing from accusations that the KGB was peripherally involved (as was the FBI) from the standpoint of having been apprised of LHO's intentions. It was taken for granted that fascist elements in the USA would in some way attempt to place the blame on the USSR. Thus, to surmount such a probability LHO's dossier was revealed to U.S. authorities. Any nation finding itself in a similar situation would have done the same.
>
> As for dispatching a bomber to Minsk to fly LHO's file to Moscow overnight, while such action might very well have occurred, it speaks more of efficiency than it does of panic. Incidently [sic], the file referenced could not have been his main KGB dossier, because that file was already at the Center. Likely, the source of that information was referring either to a personnel file maintained at the factory in Minsk at which LHO had been employed or to a counterintelligence file that may have been kept at Minsk, for any number of reasons, by a sub-section of a subordinate department of the KGB's political directorate.
>
> I cannot accept that the KGB was "terrified" that in ignorance or disregard of the Center's orders "an

officer in the field might have utilized Oswald for some purpose." To assume otherwise is to underestimate the extent and efficacy of the KGB's surveillance system at home and abroad and to minimize the control that it exerts over its own officers (vis-á-vis agents). Rather, the KGB may have been worried—if it was worried at all—about another matter. But the KGB was not worried about that matter being disclosed to the American public anymore than it was concerned about some of the remarks made in LHO's soon-to-be-discovered "Historical Diary."

In order to view in a proper perspective the KGB's reluctance to recruit or utilize LHO, one must realize that almost since the day he first met with a GRU representative in Tokyo, he was suspected of being an agent of one of the U.S. intelligence services. Without doubt information regarding this suspicion was passed on to GRU headquarters. And since the KGB had the responsibility of conducting military counter-intelligence (security) operations, it too would have become aware of such information at that time. So I doubt that the KGB's order not to recruit or utilize him stemmed solely from the results of psychiatric examinations given him later in the USRR. This in no way implies that the KGB would refrain from talking to him, or listening to him talk, or keep him under surveillance subsequent to his return to the USA, particularly after he sent letters to the USSR embassy in Washington.

When LHO approached the USSR embassy in Mexico City for a visa, he was not turned down in the manner that Mr. Barron describes; nor do I believe that his return to the USSR was blocked on instructions from the KGB. He was simply advised that if he wished to apply for a visa his application would be processed in a routine fashion. Nor did the Cuban embassy decline to issue him a visa for the reason stated. Cuban authorities had been informed of his association with anti-Castro elements (posing as pro-Castro agents) in the USA before September 1963 and this fact may have prompted the reception that he encountered at the Cuban embassy.

Just who is this Yuri Nosenko anyway? I don't recall that the KGB had an American Section of the Seventh Department in its organizational structure circa 1959 (though the U.S. intelligence services, including the CIA, never seem to have been able to accurately keep track of KGB organization; it changes so regularly). Perhaps Mr. Barron's source is referring to the latterday Directorate of Counter-Intelligence (Kontrrazvedyvatelnoe upravlenie), a Chief directorate of the KGB, or to the Foreign Directorate (Inostrannoe upravlenie), also a Chief directorate, both of which had American "departments." Or maybe the mixup can be attributed to semantics or incorrect translation of Russian into English. In this vein, many U.S. intelligence officers do not even know the distinction between such commonly used American intelligence terms as "counter-intelligence" and "counterintelligence."

In closing, I would be interested in knowing where Mr. Barron got his information, so sanctimoniously recited, that KGB "wet affairs" (Mokryye) were curtailed in 1962 as the result of Bogdan Stashinsky's "confessions." It sounds to me like that spiel was written off the top of his head. Next, I anticipate his writing that the American intelligence services do not engage in political murders or murders for expediency.

NAME OF SUBJECT OR TITLE OF INCIDENT

NELL, Richard Case
B: 5 August 1930
B: Greenwich, New York, USA

2. DATE SUBMITTED
2 May 1969

3. CONTROL SYMBOL OR FILE NUMBER

REPORT OF FINDINGS

October 1959, promoted SUBJECT, retroactively, to the rank of permanent Captain, as of 1 August 1959. On 29 October 1959, SUBJECT received an Honorable Discharge.

From 14 December 1959 through 22 June 1962, SUBJECT was employed as a special investigator for the State of California, Fraud Section, Department of Employment, and the Department of Alcoholic Control. On 8 June 1962, SUBJECT was suspended for unauthorized release of information to the newspapers and the Los Angeles Police Department. During the period from August 1962 to October 1963, SUBJECT was intermittently employed as an informant and/or investigator for the Central Intelligence Agency (CIA). In April 1963, SUBJECT conducted an inquiry concerning the marital status of Marina Oswald and her reported desire to return to the USSR. During July, August, September, and on one occasion prior to this, SUBJECT conducted an inquiry into the activities of Lee Harvey Oswald, and the allegation that he had established a Fair Play For Cuba Committee in New Orleans, Louisiana. SUBJECT stated that while working for the CIA, HE had operated in Mexico, Florida, Louisiana, Texas, California, Puerto Rico, and New York. HE was primarily concerned with investigating activities of Anti-Castro organizations and their personnel in the United States and Mexico. On 20 September 1963, SUBJECT was arrested in El Paso, Texas on the charge of entering a Federal bank with the intent to commit a felony. In May 1964 and September 1966, SUBJECT was twice tried and twice convicted on this charge. The conviction of the May 1964 trial had been subsequently reversed, thus the reason for the second trial. SUBJECT was sentenced to a maximum of ten years imprisonment, but was released after four and one-half years. SUBJECT claimed that HIS conviction and subsequent incarceration was a result, not of HIS supposed intent to commit a felony, but rather as a result of HIS knowledge of Lee Harvey Oswald and the assassination of President Kennedy. SUBJECT claimed that while HE was in prison HE was beaten, intimidated, threatened, tortured, and kept incommunicado. SUBJECT stated that this treatment resulted from HIS refusal to "talk," although SUBJECT did not make clear exactly what it was that HE was being asked to talk about. SUBJECT also claimed that HE was denied due process of law during HIS respective trials. On 29 April 1968, the US Court of Appeals for the Fifth Circuit at New Orleans acquitted SUBJECT, due to insufficient evidence. On 30 May 1968, SUBJECT was given $500 by two people who refused to identify **BULLSHIT** themselves, and told to leave the US. SUBJECT went to Geneva, Switzerland, though HIS reasons for picking Geneva were never made clear. SUBJECT was apparently trying to determine the location of HIS family. SUBJECT next

PAGE 2 OF 4 PACES

TYPED NAME AND ORGANIZATION OF SPECIAL AGENT

6. SIGNATURE OF SPECIAL AGENT

This Military Intelligence file on Nagell (see pages 53–55) is the only official reference known to exist that Nagell investigated Oswald, Oswald's wife Marina, and anti-Castro Cuban exiles on behalf of the CIA. The penned notations ("MI" for Military Intelligence and "Bullshit" in the right margin) were added by Nagell in the copy that he sent to the author.

r U-JU_ ,H*v. I-ZS-b_,   FEDERAL BUREAU OF INVESTIGATION

Date __December 20, 1963__

1
—

      RICHARD CASE NAGELL incarcerated in the El Paso County
Jail on a complaint charging him with Bank Robbery advised
that "For the record he would like to say that his association
with OSWALD (meaning LEE HARVEY OSWALD) was purely social and
that he had met him in Mexico City and in Texas."

      NAGELL stated he decided to "clear the record up".
since his fingerprints were taken on December 12, 1963 by
Special Agents WHITE and BOYCE.

      Although questioned as to where and when his
contacts with OSWALD were made, he refused to comment further
and said he had nothing more to say.

On __12/19/63__ at ___ El Paso, Texas ___ File # __ EP 105-1264 __

by SA HAROLD H. BOYCE & ,
SA THOMAS B. WHITE, JR./st   -3-   Date dictated __12/19/63__

An FBI file, found in the National Archives but not appearing in the Warren Commission
volumes, concerning Nagell's statements about having met Oswald in two locations. (See page 51).

F. M. 14.

Nº 152087

SECRETARIA DE GOBERNACION

TARJETA DE TURISTA PARA MULTIPLES VIAJES

FOTO

VIAJE EN AUTOMOVIL

BUENA HASTA

X

(Firma del turista ante el funcionario que expide este)

AUTORIZACION PARA UN NUMERO ILIMITADO DE VIAJES A LA
DEL PLAZO DE SU VIGENCIA:

SEIS MESES:

EXPEDIDA POR .... CONSULADO GENERAL DE MEXICO ....
EN LOS ANGELES, CALIF., E.U.A.

AUG 17 1962 .... P. O. El Cónsul General .....
(Lugar y fecha)

(Firma del funcionario que expide este documento)

DATOS DEL TITULAR

NOMBRE Y APELLIDOS .... RICHARD CASE NAGELL ....

.... SEXO HOMBRE .... EDAD **32** AÑOS ..
(Años cumplidos)

ESTADO CIVIL DIVORCIADO .... RELIGION ....

OCUPACION .... ESCRITOR. ....
(Dígase la actual)

NACIO EN GREENWICH, NEW YORK, E.U.A.

NACIONALIDAD ACTUAL NORTEAMERICANA (PAS. No. C526729) ....

DOMICILIO 4037 LEEWARD AVE, LOS ANGELES, CALIFORNIA ....

ANOTAR NOMBRE, EDAD Y PARENTESCO DE LOS MENORES DE 15 AÑOS QUE LO ACOMPAÑAN

....

EL TITULAR ENTRO AL PAIS, EN EL PRIMER VIAJE QUE AUTORIZA ESTA TARJETA.

POR ....

FECHA ....

(Firma del funcionario de la Oficina)

(Firma del turista ante el mismo funcionario)

Nagell's tourist card for entry into Mexico on August 17, 1962 (see Chapter Nine).

HEADQUARTERS
U. S. ARMY COMMAND RECONNAISSANCE ACTIVITY, FAR EAST
APO 613

22 March 1957

C-E-R-T-I-F-I-C-A-T-E

This is to certify that RICHARD C. NAGELL, Captain, 02028346,
was granted a Top-Secret security clearance on 22 September 1955.

ROBERT W. BURGNER
Major, Arty
Adjutant

D# 1-73

An official Army notificiation concerning Nagell's having been granted a Top-Secret clearance,
filed by Nagell in the U.S. Court of Claims. (See Chapters Three and Four).

ISSUE SLIP								PAGE **1** OF **1**		PAGES	

<table>
<tr><td rowspan="2">FROM</td><td colspan="3">BASE OR STATION ACCOUNTABLE OFFICER
MAJOR PAUL O KUKER
AFU 301 COORDINATING DET TEAM 26</td><td colspan="3">ISSUE SLIP NO.</td><td colspan="4">PROPERTY
SOA</td></tr>
<tr><td colspan="3"></td><td colspan="3">TYPE OF ISSUE</td><td colspan="4">PROPERTY CLASS
EXP</td></tr>
<tr><td rowspan="2">TO</td><td colspan="3">ORGANIZATION NAME
CAPT ROBERT NOLAN
ARMY COORDINATING DET TEAM 26
AFO 301</td><td>INITIAL</td><td>REPLACE-MENT</td><td>MEMO RECEIPT</td><td colspan="4">ACCOUNT SYMBOL</td></tr>
<tr><td colspan="3"></td><td></td><td></td><td></td><td colspan="4">WORK ORDER NO.</td></tr>
</table>

ITEM NO.	STOCK OR PART NO.	NOMENCLATURE	AUTH. ALLOW.	ON HAND AND DUE IN	UNIT	QUANTITY REQUESTED	UNIT COST	TOTAL COST	ACTION
1	NSN	CIGARETTES, American			pkg	500			500
		//Only Item //							

To be expended through US Inteligence activities.

AUTHORITY

ISSUANCE OF QUANTITY IN "QUANTITY REQUESTED" COLUMN IS AUTHORIZED. ITEMS MARKED "DUE OUT" WILL BE ORDERED AND WHEN RECEIVED ORGANIZATION WILL BE NOTIFIED.

FOR THE COMMANDING OFFICER:

_____
(DATE)   (ORGANIZATION SUPPLY OFFICER)

QUANTITIES SHOWN IN "ACTION" COLUMN HAVE BEEN RECEIVED:

_____
(DATE)   (FOR THE BASE OR STATION ACCOUNTABLE OFFICER)

QUANTITIES SHOWN IN "ACTION" COLUMN HAVE BEEN ISSUED:

Robert C. Nolan
2 Aug 56   NOLAN ROBERT   CAPT   INF
(DATE)   (AUTHORIZED REPRESENTATIVE)

VOUCHER NO.

_____
(DATE)   (STOREKEEPER)

DA FORM 446   Edition of 1 Mar 47 may be used.

A 1956 "Issue Slip" to "Robert Nolan," an alias used by Nagell while with Field Operations Intelligence in the Far East and later under contract to the CIA in 1962–63.

Nov. 8, 1963

Dear Mr Hunt,

I would like information
concerning my position.

I am asking only for information
I am suggesting that we discuss the
matter fully before any steps are
taken by me or anyone else.

Thank You
Lee Harvey Oswald

Oswald's letter to "Dear Mr. Hunt," written two weeks before the assassination and mailed anonymously from Mexico City to Texas researcher Penn Jones, Jr., in 1975. (See pages 588–89.)
J. GARY SHAW COLLECTION

Notes

Abbreviations used in the Notes:

- RCN stands for Richard Case Nagell.
- LHO stands for Lee Harvey Oswald.
- CC stands for Court of Claims.
- GPO stands for Government Printing Office.
- AARC stands for Assassination Archives Research Center, Washington, D.C.
- CIA stands for Central Intelligence Agency document.
- ROK stands for Republic of Korea.
- MI stands for Military Intelligence.
- Citations from the twenty-six volumes of Hearings and Exhibits published by the Warren Commission are referred to by volume and page (e.g., WC VII, 160).
- Warren Commission Documents and Exhibits, on file at the National Archives, are referred to by abbreviation and document number (e.g., WCD 55 or WCE 20).
- Citations from the House Select Committee on Assassinations' twelve volumes of Hearings and Appendices are referred to by volume and page (e.g., HSCA VII, 240).
- References taken from Charles Willoughby's correspondence, on file at the MacArthur Archives in Norfolk, Virginia, are referred to as CW Papers.
- In some cases, particularly with newspaper and magazine articles that were photocopied by the author some years ago, page numbers were not available for listing.

Chapter I

The account of Nagell's action inside the El Paso bank and his arrest is derived primarily from the transcript of *United States* v. *Richard Case Nagell,* U.S. District Court, El Paso (May 4–5, 1964), and testimony of Nagell and policeman Jim Bundren. The information about Nagell's effects comes from the official police report signed by officer Bundren on September 20, 1963, the policeman's testimony, and the author's interviews with Bundren (October 21, 1975, and May 11, 1990). At the latter interview, Bundren revealed Nagell's foreknowledge of what was to happen in Dallas.

The author's interview with Nagell in a West Los Angeles bar took place on May 19, 1978.

A copy of Nagell's notebook is on file at the Assassination Archives Research Center, Washington, D.C. Numbered notes are as follows:

1. In a draft copy of Nagell's "Memorandum in Support of Petition for Writ of Habeas Corpus" (June 6, 1967), he writes that he may instead have said, "I would rather be arrested than commit treason." The same statement is mentioned by Nagell's attorney Joseph Calamia in questioning officer Bundren at Nagell's trial (p. 308, transcript). However, in reviewing and amending an outline prepared by the author in 1976, Nagell did not correct his original statement to the FBI as having been, "I would rather be arrested than commit murder and treason."

2. Fensterwald on RCN: written statement sent to author, 1981.

3. Garrison on RCN: author's interview, New Orleans (October 16, 1975).

4. The author's article about Professor Popkin appeared in *The Village Voice* (September 1, 1975).

5. LHO's address book: WC XVI, p. 54.

6. Nagell's notebook contains many intriguing notations. Listed on one page are the following names of CIA officials, as follows:

C.I.A.
1. MR. F. PARKER
2. MISS GUTHRIES

3. MR. C. CHURCHILL
4. MR. J. DA VANON
5. MR. J. SLOSS
6. MR. E. LEIBACHER

The Parker and Sloss names have check marks beside them. Da Vanon and Leibacher are described more fully in Chapter Three. The author has been unable to determine who the others are.
At the bottom of the same page there appears:

RICHARD FECTEAU, LYNN, MASS.
(DAC) (C.I.A.)

"DAC" stands for Department of the Army Civilian. Fecteau and his pilot, John Downey, were shot down over Manchuria by the Communist Chinese in November 1952. Accused of espionage, Fecteau was released late in 1971 after nineteen years in prison.
"A. DOAK BARNETT," listed on another page of RCN's notebook, was a China-born former State Department employee who in 1963 was on the faculty of Columbia University.
A number of other citations from the RCN notebook are referred to elsewhere in this narrative.
7. RCN on Oswald: FBI file ("EP 105-1264") in National Archives (December 20, 1963) by SA [special agent] David J. Reid and SA Richard K. Graham.
8. RCN's letter to Rankin is in a "Citizen's Correspondence" file on the assassination in the National Archives; no reply from Rankin is attached.
9. RCN's correspondence with Senator Russell, which begins with this January 3, 1967, letter, is on record in the Richard B. Russell Memorial Library, University of Georgia Libraries, Athens, Georgia.
10. FBI Security Index and LHO: *Supplementary Detailed Staff Reports on Intelligence Activities and the Rights of Americans,* Book III, *Final Report of the Select Committee to Study Governmental Operations with Respect to Intelligence Activities,* U.S. Senate (Washington, D.C.: U.S. GPO, April 23, 1976), pp. 467–69.
11. RCN on FBI letter: letter to author (May 13, 1976).

Chapter II

The author's interviews in El Paso were conducted with Joseph Calamia and Fred Morton (October 20, 1975); Edward J. Murphy, Raymond O'Rourke, Juan L. Medina, and Jim Bundren (October 21, 1975).
The author's first two meetings with Richard Case Nagell took place in Manhattan Beach, California, and Los Angeles on October 26 and 28, 1975, respectively.
Numbered notes are as follows:
1. Early articles about RCN in the El Paso newspaper archives are: Ramon Villalobos, "Veteran Tries Daring Bank Holdup," *El Paso Times* (September 21, 1963), p. 1; "Bank Robber Wants to Kill," *El Paso Herald-Post* (September 21, 1963); Ramon Villalobos, "Nagell Pleads Not Guilty," *Times* (September 22, 1963), p. 1; "Bank Holdup Suspect Remains Sullen," *Herald-Post* (September 23, 1963); "E.P. Bank Robber Decides to Eat," *Herald-Post* (September 24, 1963); "Nagell to Take Sanity Test at La Tuna," *Times* (September 26, 1963); "Nagell Balks on Sanity Test," *Herald-Post* (October 1, 1963); "Attorney Named in Robbery Case," *Herald-Post* (October 2, 1963); "Set Nagell Appearance in Court," *Times* (October 3, 1963); "Holdup Suspect Accepts Attorney," *Herald-Post* (October 3, 1963); "Nagell Claims Cooperation," *Times* (October 4, 1963); "Habeas Corpus Hearing Set for Accused Bandit," *Times* (November 1, 1963); "Bank Holdup Suspect Says Motive Is Secret," *Times* (November 4, 1963); "Says Bank Holdup Try Patriotic," *Times* (December 10, 1963), p. 1.
2. RCN testimony: transcript, *United States* v. *Nagell,* pp. 343–415. Records on RCN case on file in archives of U.S. District Court, Fort Worth, Texas. See also "Robbery Try Trial Marked by Outbursts," *El Paso Times* (May 5, 1964), p. 1. Cliff Sherrill, "Bandit Suspect 'Wanted Arrest,'" *El Paso Herald-Post* (May 5, 1964); "Trial Ends; Nagell Jury to Be Charged," *Herald-Post* (May 6, 1964).
3. RCN's remarks after conviction: "'Bank Bandit' Is Found Guilty," *El Paso Herald-Post* (May 6, 1964), p. 1. "Nagell Guilty of Robbery," *Times* (May 7, 1964).
4. RCN's appeal: appellant's opening brief, *Richard Case Nagell* v. *United States,* U.S. Court of Appeals, Fifth Circuit. "Judge to Rule on Motion for New Trial for Nagell," *El Paso Times* (June 9, 1964); "Nagell's Brain Injuries Cited," *El Paso Herald-Post* (June 9, 1964).
5. RCN sentencing: "Nagell Given Ten Years; Appeal Set," *El Paso Herald-Post* (June 10, 1964).
6. RCN 1966 conviction: "Jury Finds Nagell Guilty in Holdup," "Nagell Again Sentenced to 10 Years," *El Paso Times* (September 27 and 28, 1966, respectively).
7. RCN conviction overturned: U.S. Court of Appeals, Fifth Circuit, No. 24152 *Nagell* v. *United States.* On file in archives, U.S. District Court, Fort Worth, Texas. See also 392 F.2d 934–38.
8. FBI and COINTELPRO: See *Supplementary Detailed Staff Reports on Intelligence Activities and the Rights of Americans,* Book III, *Final Report of the Select Committee to Study Governmental Operations with Respect to Intelligence Activities* (Washington, D.C.: U.S. GPO, April 23, 1976), pp. 467–69.
9. Hoover and the Mob: Ovid Demaris, *The Director: An Oral Biography of J. Edgar Hoover* (New York: Harper's Magazine Press, 1975), pp. 35–46. See also *Time,* "The Truth About Hoover" (December 22, 1975), p. 20.
10. JFK/Judith Campbell Exner/Hoover: See *Interim Report of the Select Committee to Study Governmental*

Operations with Respect to Intelligence Activities, U.S. Senate, *Alleged Assassination Plots Involving Foreign Leaders* (1975), p. 129; *My Story* as told by Judith Exner to Ovid Demaris (New York: Grove Press, 1977).

11. Hoover and call to Robert Kennedy re assassination: Arthur M. Schlesinger, Jr., *Robert Kennedy and His Times* (New York: Ballantine Books, 1978), pp. 655–56.

12. Hoover on LHO: FBI memo, Hoover to Tolson, Belmont, et al. (November 22, 1963). Cited in Henry Hurt, *Reasonable Doubt* (New York: Holt, Rinehart, & Winston, 1985), p. 19.

13. Hoover memos on assassination investigation: *The Investigation of the Assassination of President John F. Kennedy: Performance of the Intelligence Agencies,* Book V, *Final Report of the Select Committee,* p. 39.

14. FBI awareness of LHO: memorandum from Belmont to Soviet Section supervisor (November 4, 1959). *Investigation of the Assassination,* p. 87.

15. LHO as FBI informant rumor: transcript cited in Harold Weisberg, *Whitewash IV: Top-Secret JFK Assassination Transcript* (self-published, 1974), pp. 129–130.

16. Agee on CIA: Philip Agee, *Playboy* interview (August 1975), p. 52.

17. CIA agents worldwide: James Hepburn, *Farewell America* (Vaduz, Liechtenstein: Frontiers, 1968), p. 312.

18. Dulles quote: Leonard Mosley, *Dulles: A Biography of Eleanor, Allen, and John Foster Dulles and Their Family Network* (New York: Dial Press/James Wade, 1978).

19. While the CIA's covert involvement in numerous foreign countries has been documented in many books, the Truman quote is taken from Sterling Seagrave, *The Marcos Dynasty* (New York: Harper & Row, 1988), pp. 53–54.

20. Eisenhower advisers' quote: cited in Arthur Schlesinger, Jr., "The Eisenhower Presidency: A Reassessment," *Look* (May 14, 1979), p. 46.

21. Truman on Eisenhower: *Where the Buck Stops: The Personal and Private Writings of Harry S. Truman,* comp. and ed. Margaret Truman (New York: Warner Books, 1989). Excerpt taken from *The New York Times Magazine.*

22. Eisenhower farewell address: Schlesinger, "The Eisenhower Presidency," p. 42.

23. Pentagon budget: *Farewell America,* p. 132. JFK's final days found the projected 1964 budget pared down to $49.9 billion, a nearly $2 billion slash since 1962. The president had begun closing fifty-two military installations in twenty-five states, and twenty-one bases overseas (p. 151). At the same time, Congress was starting to take a hard look at a munitions industry that received 86 percent of its contracts without competitive bidding (p. 133).

24. For further reading on the Cuban invasion, the most contemporary account is Peter Wyden, *Bay of Pigs: The Untold Story* (New York: Simon & Schuster, 1979).

25. Robert Kennedy made his remark about "treason" in an interview for the JFK Oral History program with John Martin (March 1, 1964). President Kennedy's reaction to the CIA after the Bay of Pigs is cited in numerous books and articles. The version used by this author is found in Anthony Summers, *Conspiracy* (New York: McGraw-Hill Book Company, 1980), pp. 255–56.

26. CIA-Mafia alliance against Castro: *Alleged Assassination Plots.* Also, HSCA V, 257. For further reading on American intelligence and organized crime, see Thomas Sciacca, *Luciano* (New York: Pinnacle Books, 1975); *The Secret War Report of the OSS,* ed. Anthony Cave Brown (New York: Berkley Publishing Corporation, 1976); and Richard Harris Smith, *OSS: The Secret History of America's First Central Intelligence Agency* (New York: Dell Books, 1973).

27. RCN letter to author (January 16, 1976).

28. RCN authorizations: January 26 (Fensterwald) and January 29 (Calamia), 1976.

29. RCN letter to Clarence Kelley (June 28, 1976); Kelley reply to Nagell (July 8, 1976).

Chapter III

The author's interview with Louis, Robert, and Roger Gambert took place in Tarpon Springs, Florida, on February 16, 1990.

The interview with John Margain took place in Baldwin Park, California, on April 7, 1991.

The interview with Colonel John B. Stanley, former commander of Field Operations Intelligence, was conducted by telephone on January 5, 1992.

Numbered notes are as follows:

1. Eleanore Gambert/Joseph Calamia correspondence: August 6 and 11, 1964, respectively. All of Mrs. Gambert's correspondence cited in this book was sent to the author from Nagell (January 16 and 19, 1976).

2. Nagell's statement here about his early years, and other statements quoted from Nagell about the course of his service in the Korean War, are taken from the transcript of his testimony, May 5, 1964, in *United States* v. *Nagell,* U.S. District Court, El Paso, pp. 344–76.

3. This information about Nagell's early years is on record at the U.S. Court of Claims, Washington, D.C., Case No. 1-73.

4. RCN and early Army years: Author's interview with José Ibarra, Jr. (May 12, 1990). The S-2 branch of Military Intelligence, according to a military historian the author spoke with at the National Archives, involved intelligence activities "at a lower level." S-2 generally specified the command level, while G-2 was Military Intelligence's division level.

5. RCN's early intelligence background: interview with author (May 19, 1978), Los Angeles.

6. For further contemporary reading on the Korean War, see Clay Blair, *The Forgotten War: America in Korea, 1950–1953,* (New York: Times Books, 1987) and Barton I. Kaufman, *The Korean War: Challenges in Crisis, Credibility, and Command* (Philadelphia: Temple University Press, 1986).

7. RCN on combat experience: handwritten letter (January 25, 1965) to attorney Joseph A. Calamia.

8. RCN language training: Army records on file in Case No. 1-73, U.S. Court of Claims, Washington, D.C.

9. The story of the military plane crash in which Nagell was the sole survivor is derived from articles on November 29, 1954, in the *Baltimore Sun* ("Five Dead in Bomber Crash," p. 1), *Baltimore News-Post* ("5 Die, 1 Hurt as Bomber Falls Near Airport"). Also, *Baltimore Evening Sun*, "B-25 Survivor 'Holding Own'; Probe Starts" (November 30, 1954), p. 26; and *The Washington Post* "B-25 Which Crashed Nov. 28 Had Full Power, AF Believes" (December 1954) as well as in Nagell's May 4, 1964, court testimony cited above and in an "Accident" report and hospital "Summary-Chart" that appear in his file in the Court of Claims case.

10. Nagell's recounting of his early assignment with the CIC, and subsequent difficulties due to his appearance, are derived from "Defendant's Motion to Strike Plaintiff's Second Amended Petition," pp. 4–8, filed with U.S. Court of Claims (February 3, 1975).

11. For further contemporary reading on the McCarthy period, see Robert Griffith, *The Politics of Fear* (University Press, 1970) and David M. Oshinsky, *A Conspiracy So Immense: The World of Joe McCarthy* (New York: Free Press; Collier-Macmillan, 1983).

12. RCN on CIC mail-opening operation: interview with the author (October 26, 1975).

13. RCN statement about CIA recruitment: typewritten "Addendum" dated January 28, 1970, to a 1969 pamphlet about Nagell titled "Man in the Middle." Nagell says that he himself did not write the addendum, that while it originated from a tape-recorded conversation with him, someone else had assembled it and portions of it were inaccurate. Since Nagell did not specify which portions, the author has decided to include this quotation.

14. CIA in Los Angeles: author's telephone interview with Herbert E. Leibacher (January 30, 1992). Additional corroboration was obtained in a telephone interview with Joseph Da Vanon (February 9, 1992).

15. RCN as CIA informant: Typewritten "Addendum."

16. RCN Army assignments/reports 1955–56: documents on file in U.S. Court of Claims, Case 1-73.

17. Oswald's early years have been documented in many books. Among those consulted by the author were Henry Hurt, *Reasonable Doubt* (New York: Holt, Rinehart, & Winston, 1983), p. 195, and Anthony Summers, *Conspiracy* (New York: McGraw-Hill, 1980), p. 143.

18. RCN and statement to FBI: September 21, 1963, FBI report on file, U.S. District Court archives, *United States* v. *Nagell*, Fort Worth.

19. RCN and FOI background: Plaintiff's Motion to Terminate the Administrative Proceedings and Reinstate the Judicial Proceedings, p. 4, filed April 16, 1974, U.S. Court of Claims, No. 1-73.

20. RCN, FOI/CIA, Berlin Tunnel: quoted in Defendant's Motion to Strike Plaintiff's Second Amended Petition, pp. 8–9, filed February 3, 1975, U.S. Court of Claims, No. 1-73.

21. FOI in Germany: Sanche de Gramont, *The Secret War* (New York: G. P. Putnam's Sons, 1962), p. 476.

22. For a fascinating account of the Berlin Tunnel story, see David C. Martin, *Wilderness of Mirrors* (New York: Harper & Row, 1980), pp. 59–90.

23. Victor Marchetti quote: author's telephone interview (January 28, 1977).

24. William Bishop quote: author's interview (May 8, 1990).

25. FBI official Bill Child: author's telephone interview (July 4, 1992).

26. Colonel Robert Roth: author's telephone interview (January 6, 1992).

27. RCN on FOI/assassination devices: Plaintiff's Motion, April 16, 1974, p. 5.

28. Robert Nolan pseudonym: record on file, U.S. Court of Claims, No. 1-73.

29. RCN on Team 26: Plaintiff's Motion, April 16, 1974, pp. 6, 7, 9.

30. An explanation about why Team 26 would have been secretly spying on its South Korean ally: By the mid-1950s, President Syngman Rhee was seeking complete domination over the ROK military, in itself an American creation. According to Se-Jin Kim, *The Politics of Military Revolution in Korea* (Chapel Hill, N.C.: University of North Carolina Press, 1971), pp. 75–76:

> Rhee asked more than mere loyalty from the favored officers—he asked for financial contributions that were used to shore up the sagging popularity of the President. The military, which dispensed over 40 percent of the national budget and roughly 400 million dollars of annual aid from the U.S. in arms and other commercially valuable goods, became the major supplier of political funds for Rhee's vast political machine.
>
> Among many unlawful plans to raise money, the most frequently used method was the outright marketing of such commercially valuable war materials as petroleum, automobiles and their parts, and most vital foodstuffs. A more ingenious method—and one which yielded a tremendous amount of money—involved the diverting of monetary allowances designated for the purchase of secondary foodstuffs for 600,000 soldiers. Also, kickbacks were openly demanded, not only for granting a contract, but also for allowing goods of inferior quality to pass inspection.
>
> The gravitation of the senior officers into the world of politics and financial irregularities led them to increasingly shady operations. . . . The financial and material misappropriation rapidly spread at all levels of the military; low-ranking officers began to imitate their superiors. Indeed, the corruption within the military was rampant.

The same book, in a footnote (p. 97), notes that when Rhee was overthrown in a 1961 military coup, the Korean intelligentsia speculated "that the coup had been supported either directly or indirectly by some agency of the United States, because the revolution could not have been successful without American sanction."

31. In David E. Kaplan and Alec Dubro's book *Yakuza* (Reading, Mass.: Addison-Wesley Publishing Com-

pany, 1986), the authors write on pp. 189–90: "The KCIA, established in the wake of Park [Chung Hee's] 1961 coup d'état, had become the most feared means of repression wielded against South Korea's 35 million people. The organization employed more than 100,000 agents, according to some estimates, and its influence extended to every walk of Korean life. Few doubted the allegations of torture, kidnapping, and murder made against the corrupt agency."

It has also been written that the Unification Church—the worldwide religious cult of South Korean Sun Myung Moon—was first founded with help from both the American CIA and its stepchild the Korean CIA. See *Yakuza*, p. 192, and Sterling Seagrave, *The Marcos Dynasty* (New York: Harper & Row, 1988), p. 363.

32. In Defendant's Motion to Strike, February 3, 1975, Nagell's petition is quoted describing other FOI/HID operations as follows:

The ingress and egress of FOI agents (as distinct from HID agents) into North Korea and China (Manchuria) and their debriefings and reports, were handled by Team 26, an FOI unit operationally subordinate to the ACD [the Army Coordinating Detachment, another FOI unit in Korea]. Other FOI agents were launched to China proper and to the USSR by teams situated on Okinawa and the Japanese mainland. Some of FOI's Chinese agents were recruited in Taiwan for training in Japan, but were prohibited by Japanese law from entering Japan. This ban was circumvented by furnishing the agents with American identification cards covering them as U.S. Department of the Army civilian employees, DAC's. Some were furnished U.S. passports in violation of State Department regulations, though with the connivance of that agency. By claiming American citizenship, at least one embarrassing incident was avoided when several of these agents went AWOL from their training facility and were apprehended in Yokohama by the Japanese police. HID agents that were launched to North Korea, China (Manchuria) and occasionally to the USSR (Southern Siberia) were handled by the HID, subject to the approval and often under the supervision of Team 26. Copies of selected HID agent reports were turned over to or otherwise obtained by Team 26, translated into English, and forwarded to FOI Far East headquarters [in Japan] by courier and other means. Whereas FOI acted as an organizational cut-out for certain CIA operations, the HID acted as an organizational cut-out for certain FOI operations.

[From Plaintiff's Motion, April 16, 1974, pp. 7–8:] On one occasion when our source of supply to North Korean currency was temporarily cut off, the HID counterfeited such currency under Team 26 supervision, using plates furnished by the FOI, which, I was advised, were engraved in the United States by the U.S. Treasury Department, but which I believed actually were engraved by the CIA's technical division. The plates were hand-carried to Korea from ACRAFE. . . . However, because of a slight flaw on one of the plates, which in turn showed up on the reverse side of the counterfeit notes . . . some of the agents launched to and through North Korea were apprehended. Shortly thereafter, I was instructed . . . to consult . . . concerning the feasibility of obtaining genuine North Korean currency by (1) A drug smuggling operation to be conducted through the demilitarized zone between the HID and North Korean underworld elements, [of] which allegedly North Korea was in short supply, would be purchased in Japan by ACRAFE [U.S. Army Command Reconnaissance Activities, Far East] and furnished by Team 26); (2) An incursion across the DMZ to Pyongyang by HID personnel and/or agents . . . disguised as North Korean soldiers to rob a North Korean Army payroll; and (3) The robbery of a bank at Pyongyang by civilian agents of the HID. HID headquarters turned down all three proposals, recommending instead that a gold-smuggling operation be put into effect, a recommendation that was turned down at ACRAFE (so I was told . . .) because it was felt that the gold would never reach its destination.

(Author's note: In the above-cited statements by Nagell, I have chosen to eliminate all names of American and Korean military personnel said by Nagell to have been involved, since verification is impossible to obtain.)

33. There are several threads to an explanation of why both U.S. Field Operations Intelligence and the HID Korean intelligence branch would have been mutually interested in spying on nearby Japan. Between 1910 and 1945, Korea had been a Japanese colony. After the Second World War, in 1952 South Korea and Japan confronted each other over private claims. "The South Korean side was determined to elicit penitence from Japan and the return to Korea of gold reserves and art treasures taken during the 36 years of colonial rule." The talks eventually collapsed in acrimony. See Chong-Sik Lee, *Japan and Korea: The Political Dimension* (Stanford, Calif.: Hoover Institution Press, 1985), pp. 38–39.

In May 1955, a third unofficial Japan-Communist China trade agreement was concluded. By May 1956 Japan had signed a fishery agreement with the Soviet Union and, in October 1956, came a joint declaration on the restoration of formal diplomatic relations between Japan and the USSR. See James W. Morley, *Japan and Korea: America's Allies in the Pacific* (New York: Walker & Company, 1965), p. 71.

34. A UPI story of December 15, 1977, quoted Stanford University history professor Bartin Bernstein, who had seen recently declassified U.S. government documents, about a Top-Secret U.S. plan to overthrow ROK president Syngman Rhee—"a very troubling, often unreliable ally"—during the Korean War. "Plan Ever Ready" was apparently revived several times during the first year of the Eisenhower administration. Rhee resigned as president in April 1960, in the wake of massive public demonstrations; less than a year later, General Park took command in a military coup. In 1979, Park himself was assassinated by six members of the Korean CIA.

Nagell also has written in his Court of Claims filing of April 16, 1974, that on a Friday in August 1956 (I do not have the precise date readily available), there was an assassination attempt sponsored by the HID on the life of the ROK Vice President, Chang Myun (who, paradoxically, was the chief political opponent of President Rhee), in which as far as I knew the FOI took no part, but about which some personnel in Team 26 had prior knowledge that was not reported to ACRAFE until after the assassination was bungled by one Kim Sang Poong.

After Rhee's resignation, Chang Myon was elected prime minister by the National Assembly before his own government was ousted in 1961. See Morley, *Japan and Korea,* p. 124.

35. *The Politics of Military Revolution in Korea* describes the assassination of Major General Kim Chang-yong (pp. 58–59, 73) and notes that the chief of the Counter Intelligence Corps had been "Rhee's hatchet man." Author Se-Jin Kim writes: "It was later revealed to this author by a high-ranking officer who wishes to remain anonymous that General Kim was eliminated because he planned to enhance his position by investigating the leading generals who were presumed to have engaged in unsavory conduct."

Nagell, in the Court of Claims filing cited above, adds that he "was not in the Republic of Korea at the time" but "later became cognizant by reading a TOP SECRET—EYES ONLY report that the FOI was suspected by the American 30th Service Battalion (actually the 308th CIC Detachment)" of participating in the Kim Chang-yong assassination—"notwithstanding the confessions beaten out of Lieutenant Colonel Paik Hak Kyoo, Colonel Huh Tai Yung and other Second ROK Army officers who were arrested and tried for the crime."

36. CIA assassination plots: See *Interim Report of the Select Committee to Study Governmental Operations with Respect to Intelligence Activities,* U.S. Senate, *Alleged Assassination Plots Involving Foreign Leaders* (1975).

Chapter IV

The author's telephone interview with Suzanne Gayn in Toronto was conducted December 2, 1991.

All references to the Mark Gayn papers were made by the author during a visit to the Gayn archive at the Thomas Fisher Rare Book Library, University of Toronto, April 2, 1992.

The referenced Charles Willoughby-Allen Dulles correspondence is on file among the Willoughby papers, Douglas MacArthur Archives, Norfolk, Virginia.

Numbered notes are as follows:

1. RCN reassignment: Plaintiff's Motion to Terminate the Administrative Proceedings and Reinstate the Judicial Proceedings, p. 12, filed April 16, 1974, U.S. Court of Claims, No. 1-73.

2. RCN and CIC files: quoted in Defendant's Motion to Strike Plaintiff's Second Amended Petition, pp. 18–19, filed February 3, 1975, U.S. Court of Claims, No. 1-73. Quotes from Nagell about information in these files are drawn from the same account.

3. The most detailed account of the Kaji Wataru affair and links to the Canon group appears in Chalmers Johnson, *Conspiracy at Matsukawa* (Berkeley: University of California Press, 1972), pp. 367–73. See also David E. Kaplan and Alec Dubro, *Yakuza* (Reading, Mass.: Addison-Wesley, 1986), pp. 60–61.

4. The Yuri Rastvorov affair is mentioned in Richard Deacon, *A History of the Japanese Secret Service* (London: Frederick Muller, 1982), p. 235. In 1956 and 1957 Rastvorov testified at a series of hearings, "Scope of Soviet Activity in the United States," before the Senate Judiciary Subcommittee to Investigate the Administration of the Internal Security Act and Other Internal Security Laws.

According to information uncovered by Joseph J. Trento of the National Security News Service in Washington, Rastvorov was originally interrogated on the island of Saipan by Army CIC officers. At this interrogation, the defector allegedly demanded of a security officer that two CIA officials—David Murphy and Arseny "Andy" Yankovsky—be removed from the room. Rastvorov claimed that Yankovsky was a double agent for the Soviet Union and, since Murphy was his sponsor, Murphy, too, could not be trusted.

Yankovsky, a White Russian raised in North Korea, had been recruited into the CIA by Murphy. During the Korean War, according to CIA official Newton "Scotty" Miler's account to author David Wise, *Molehunt* (New York: Random House, 1992), pp. 220–25, the majority of Yankovsky's agents sent behind enemy lines were captured. Yankovsky was fired from the CIA in 1959 in the agency's first "molehunt." David Murphy became chief of the CIA's Soviet Russia Division the same month that JFK was assassinated, and later came under suspicion by James Angleton as a KGB mole because of his prior relationship with Yankovsky. Murphy was forced out of the Soviet Russia Division in 1968 and transferred to Paris; he is now retired.

5. The author's discussion with Robert Gambert took place at the family interview, February 16, 1990, and was reviewed by telephone on several occasions. There have been a number of books written on the Richard Sorge espionage case, the most recent of which is Far Eastern scholar Chalmers Johnson's *An Instance of Treason* (Stanford, Calif.: Stanford University Press, 1990).

6. RCN on Gayn: Plaintiff's Motion, April 16, 1974, p. 19.

7. RCN and "Hidel" tourist card: "Memorandum in Support of Petition for Writ of Habeas Corpus" (June 6, 1967).

8. RCN and "Kramer" letter to FBI: Interview with author (October 26, 1975).

9. RCN and FBI letter: notarized affidavit (November 21, 1975).

10. Barros quote: author's interview, Toronto (April 3, 1992). A former high official with the Royal Canadian Mounted Police substantiated that Gayn was under suspicion as a Soviet agent but added that nothing could ever be proven.

11. Gayn's arrest in the *Amerasia* case: The quote is taken from *The Amerasia Papers: A Clue to the Catastrophe*

of China, Vol. I, prepared by the Subcommittee to Investigate the Administration of the Internal Security Act and Other Internal Security Laws of the Committee on the Judiciary, U.S. Senate (Washington, D.C.: U.S. GPO January 26, 1970), p. 41. The same report describes Gayn as "a dedicated Marxist in thin disguise" (p. 40). Gayn's arrest was described in "3 Here Deny Plot on State Secrets," *The New York Times* (June 9, 1945), p. 1.

12. A number of books reference the *Amerasia* case, including Ross Y. Koen's *The China Lobby in American Politics* (New York: Octagon Books, 1974), pp. 60–66.

13. Gayn obituary: David Crane, "Mark Gayn: Journalism Was His Mission," *Toronto Star* (December 18, 1981).

14. Gayn and pseudonyms: Graham S. Bradshaw, "Biographical Sketch," *Guide to the Mark Gayn Papers,* p. viii, Thomas Fisher Rare Book Library, University of Toronto.

15. Gayn trip to Mexico/Cuba: Gayn archive, Box 50, No. 6.

16. Gayn trips to USSR: Gayn archive, Box 31, No. 1 (1960), and Box 33, Nos. 1, 2, 3 (1968).

17. Gayn and Strategic Air Command: Gayn archive, Box 50, No. 3.

18. Gayn and Dulles: Gayn archive, Box 50, No. 1.

19. Charles "Dutz" Murret and Marcello: John H. Davis, *Mafia Kingfish* (New York: McGraw-Hill Book Company, 1989), pp. 122–23.

20. Murret and Pic: WCD 942; CIA 1294–481; Knoxville *Journal* (April 11, 1973).

21. FBI interview with Murret: WCE 3119, p. 10.

22. Hudkins on Murret: interview with author, Baltimore (May 12, 1976).

23. Gaudet on Murret: interview with Bernard Fensterwald, Jr., and Allan Stone, Waveland, Mississippi (May 13, 1975).

24. Murret and Isaacs: FBI document, WCD 942. Cited in Michael Canfield and Alan J. Weberman, *Coup d'État in America* (New York: The Third Press, 1975), pp. 21–22.

25. Isaacs background: WCD 1080, FBI file (May 22, 1964). First page reprinted in Canfield/Weberman, p. 269.

26. Smedley and Sorge: Janice R. Mackinnon and Agnes Smedley Stephen, *The Life and Times of an American Radical* (London: Virago Press, 1988), p. 148.

27. Isaacs and Chinese Communists: WCD 1080.

28. Isaacs as "Trotskyist": Freda Utley, *The China Story,* (Chicago: H. Regnery, 1951), p. 210, and Freda Utley, *Lost Illusion,* (Philadelphia: Fireside Press, 1948), p. 247.

29. Giesbrecht and Isaacs: WCD 645 and 866.

30. Harold Isaacs's papers are on file at the Institute Archives and Special Collections Library, Massachusetts Institute of Technology, Cambridge, Mass.

31. Isaacs and Smedley: Isaacs's papers, MIT.

32. Isaacs in address book: *The Amerasia Papers,* p. 1711.

33. MIT and Isaacs: WCD 1080.

34. MIT Center and CIA: David Wise and Thomas B. Ross, *The Invisible Government* (New York: Random House, 1964), p. 243.

35. Isaacs's 1963 trip: "long journey," Isaacs's letter to Shigeharu Matsumoto (August 10, 1963); "students . . . China," letter to Isaacs from Charles B. Fahs, minister-counselor for cultural and public affairs, U.S. embassy, Tokyo (October 3, 1963), Isaacs papers, MIT.

36. Matsumoto hostelry/Ozaki: David Bergamini, *Japan's Imperial Conspiracy,* Vol. II (New York: William Morrow & Company, 1971), p. 866.

37. Nagell's handwritten letter from jail, referencing Amendments IV, V, and XIV, Section 1 of the U.S. Constitution, asked for return of his private property, including:
"Four individual photographs, approximately 4″ × 6″ in size of:
(a) Akiyama Jiro
(b) Sugaya Eijiro
(c) Fukuhara Yukinori
(d) Matsumoto Shogo"

38. Willoughby's heritage: Frank Kluckhohn, "Heidelberg to Madrid: The Story of General Willoughby," *The Reporter* (August 19, 1952), pp. 25–30.

39. Willoughby's background: *The Reporter,* ibid; Bruce Cumings, *The Origins of the Korean War,* Vol. II (Princeton, N.J.: Princeton University Press, 1990), pp. 104–6.

40. MacArthur's Willoughby quote: Cumings, *Origins,* p. 104.

41. Willoughby on Mussolini: Meirion Harries and Susie Harries, *Sheathing the Sword* (New York: Macmillan, 1987), p. 222.

42. Willoughby on Soviet bloc: Cumings, *Origins,* p. 104.

43. Also enlightening on the CIA-MacArthur/Willoughby battle is Joseph C. Goulden, "CIA's Korean Capers," *Soldier of Fortune* (May 1983); e.g., "Willoughby took the CIA's insistence on running its own intelligence networks in Asia as a personal affront."

44. Willoughby and Japanese military: *Sheathing the Sword,* pp. 222, 227.

45. Willoughby and biological warfare criminals: Mae Brussell, "The Nazi Connection to the John F. Kennedy Assassination," *The Rebel* (November 22, 1983), p. 26.

46. Gayn article on Japanese drug trafficking: *Coronet* (November 1942), pp. 22–26.

47. Willoughby and Kodama: Sterling Seagrave, *The Marcos Dynasty* (New York: Harper & Row, 1988), p. 120. See also Kaplan and Dubro, *Yakuza,* p. 57.

48. Gayn on war criminals: *Yakuza,* p. 62.

49. Hattori: *Sheathing the Sword,* p. 226 (quote); *Yakuza,* pp. 60–61.

50. Hattori real estate: Jones Harris's discussion with former Marine lieutenant John Donovan, related to author.

51. Hattoris and Oswald: author's interview with Jones Harris (May 12, 1992).

52. Willoughby and Canon: CW Papers, MacArthur Archives, Norfolk, Virginia.

53. ZED: Brussell, "The Nazi Connection," p. 33.

54. FOI and Willoughby: author's telephone interview with Colonel John B. Stanley (June 25, 1992).

55. Willoughby and CIA: CW letter to Allen Dulles (December 28, 1960).

56. Willoughby and Pentagon: "General Willoughby, Spy Hunter, Has a Thriller to Tell Congress," *U.S. News & World Report* (May 25, 1951), p. 36.

57. Willoughby and Nixon: "Footlocker Preview: Red Spy Files from Orient," *Newsweek* (May 28, 1951), p. 24.

58. Willoughby on Isaacs: Charles Willoughby *Shanghai Conspiracy* (New York: E. P. Dutton & Company, 1952), p. 308.

59. Iron Triangle quote: *The Marcos Dynasty,* p. 112.

60. Kishi history: *Yakuza,* pp. 81–82.

61. Willoughby and Franco: *The Reporter,* p. 25.

62. Background on Otto Skorzeny was derived from Glenn B. Infield, *Skorzeny: Hitler's Commando* (New York: St. Martin's Press, 1981), pp. 215–17, and Henrik Kruger, *The Great Heroin Coup* (Boston: South End Press, 1980), p. 205. On Reinhard Gehlen, from E. H. Cookridge, *Gehlen: Spy of the Century* (New York: Random House, 1971), pp. 237–42, and Carl Oglesby, "The Secret Treaty of Fort Hunt," *Covert Action* (Fall 1990), pp. 8–16.

63. Willoughby speech: "Soviet Espionage: The American Communist Party," delivered before the Twenty-seventh Annual Convention of the American Coalition of Patriotic Societies, Washington, D.C. (January 31, 1957).

64. Taiwan meeting and American Security Council: Peter Dale Scott, "The Dallas Conspiracy," unpublished manuscript (1971), Chap. II, pp. 25–29.

65. Oswald "confidential" clearance: WCD 978.

Chapter V

The author's interview with Frances FitzGerald took place in New York on March 16, 1992. Interviews with James Angleton were conducted in Washington, D.C., on December 17, 1975; April 2, 1976; and October 22, 1976.

Numbered notes are as follows:

1. MacArthur-Smith meeting: Joseph C. Goulden, "CIA's Korean Capers," *Soldier of Fortune* (May 1983), p. 70.

2. CIA and LSD at Atsugi base: The manuscript of a 1981 article that later appeared in *Rolling Stone,* "Did Lee Harvey Oswald Drop Acid?," by Martin Lee, Robert Ranftel, and Jeff Cohen, quotes an ex-Marine who served in the same unit as Oswald that two CIA officials gave him a variety of drugs in an effort to recruit him. "They wanted to find out how well you could stand up under pressure," said the Marine, who asked that his name be withheld. "This guy says, 'We just want to see how you'll react. If you're going to be a spy, don't you want to be informed about every mind-altering drug there is?' " The ex-Marine, eighteen at the time, recounted how his CIA contacts paid for prostitutes, bought him drinks, and put LSD and other "weird drugs" into his beverages.

3. Prouty quote on Atsugi: telephone interview with the author (June 20, 1992).

4. The author's background information on Oswald in Japan is drawn from Jim Marrs, *Crossfire: The Plot That Killed Kennedy* (New York: Carroll & Graf, 1989), p. 103; Henry Hurt, *Reasonable Doubt* (New York: Holt, Rinehart, & Winston, 1985), pp. 199–200; Anthony Summers, *Conspiracy* (New York: McGraw-Hill, 1980), pp. 144–45; and Edward Jay Epstein, *Legend: The Secret World of Lee Harvey Oswald* (New York: Reader's Digest Press/McGraw-Hill, 1978), pp. 68–69.

5. HSCA quote: *Report of the Select Committee on Assassinations, U.S. House of Representatives: The Final Assassinations Report* (New York: Bantam Books, 1979), p. 282.

6. Willis quote: Telephone interview with the author (January 6, 1992).

7. RCN on Japanese police/Oswald: Interview with the author (October 26, 1975). In the chapter "Japanese Intelligence Organizations" in Jeffrey T. Richelson's book *Foreign Intelligence Organizations* (Cambridge, Mass.: Ballinger, 1988), the author writes: "The Foreign Affairs Section of the National Police Agency is concerned with operations carried out by China, North Korea, the Soviet Union, and other nations from the East Bloc" (p. 265).

8. Nagell's reference to having "been introduced to Mr. Oswald long before the Fair Play for Cuba Committee came into existence, albeit under an assumed name" is taken from the typewritten "Addendum" (June 20, 1969) to an article about Nagell appearing in *Family,* an English-language magazine for U.S. servicemen stationed in Germany. It is the author's inference that this refers to Japan, since that is where RCN says he met LHO for the first time. Nagell has stated that the "Addendum" was based on a tape-recorded conversation with him but that he did not personally author it and that not all of its statements are accurate.

9. Oswald at Embassy/Eroshkin: Memo of conversation with RCN by Bernard Fensterwald, Jr. (May 31, 1978).

10. Eroshkin background: Plaintiff's Motion to Terminate the Administrative Proceedings and Reinstate the Judicial Proceedings, p. 16, filed April 16, 1974, U.S. Court of Claims, No. 1-73.

11. Soviet GRU: Harry Rositzke, *The KGB: The Eyes of Russia* (Garden City, N.Y.: Doubleday, 1981), pp. 61–62.

12. RCN on Soviet suspicions of LHO: RCN "critique" of the book *KGB* by John Barron, sent to the author with letter dated February 27, 1978.

13. Nagell's account of the Eroshkin defection project and his enlistment of Chikao Fujisawa is all drawn from his April 16, 1974, Court of Claims filing, pp. 13–17.

14. Oswald and U-2: The CIA's Richard Helms, in a May 13, 1964, memorandum to J. Edgar Hoover ("Lee Harvey OSWALD's Access to Classified Information About the U-2," on file in National Archives), maintained that since the U-2 flights "were conducted from a classified hangar area at one end of the flight lines," Oswald would not have had access to it. Helms did concede that Oswald "could have heard such gossip" about the U-2's.

15. RCN's "casual, but purposeful acquaintance": interview with the author (October 26, 1975).

16. RCN on Fujisawa/LHO: interview with the author (May 19, 1978).

17. RCN on Eroshkin project: Court of Claims filing, pp. 13–17. There may have been more involved in the CIA's targeting of Eroshkin. According to what intelligence sources imparted to investigative journalist Joseph Trento, the GRU colonel had had an affair in Tokyo with Anastasia (Nata) Sokolovskaya. She was the White Russian stepdaughter of Andy Yankovsky, and a translator/interpreter for the CIA in Japan. In 1954 she married another CIA official, Edgar Snow, in Tokyo. Soon after their marriage, Snow and his wife reportedly returned to CIA headquarters, where Snow—a close associate of David Murphy—rose to become chief of operations in the Soviet Russia Division by 1959. According to the book *Molehunt,* Snow came under internal investigation because of his marriage to Nata, and was fired along with Andy Yankovsky. According to Trento's sources, the CIA's strong suspicions of Nata focused on her stepfather, Yankovsky—and her previous affair with Colonel Eroshkin.

18. Fujisawa letter to RCN: April 14, 1959, in author's possession.

19. RCN/Fujisawa meeting: interview (May 19, 1978).

20. Fujisawa's attempt to recruit RCN: Court of Claims filing, pp. 14–15.

21. O'Toole and Fujisawa: interview with author (December 18, 1975).

22. Fujisawa in the war: Ben-Ami Shillony, *Politics and Culture in Wartime Japan* (Oxford: Clarendon Press, 1981), pp. 113, 152.

23. Fujisawa's booklet: Otto Tolischus, *Tokyo Record* (New York: Reynal and Hitchcock, 1943), Appendix B, "The Great Shinto Purification Ritual and the Divine Mission of Nippon," pp. 429–49.

24. Tolischus on Fujisawa: *Tokyo Record,* pp. 399–400.

25. Fujisawa quote: Chikao Fujisawa, *Zen and Shinto: The Story of Japanese Philosophy* (Westport, Conn.: Greenwood Press, 1959), pp. 33–34.

26. Thornley quote: WC XI. 87, 97. For a fascinating look at Thornley's own life, see Jonathan Vankin, *Conspiracies, Cover-ups, and Crimes* (New York: Paragon House, 1991), pp. 3–18.

27. Thornley on LHO: Secret Service report (November 23, 1963), National Archives.

28. De Mohrenschildt quote: WC IX. 242.

29. Gayn on Fujisawa: Mark Gayn, *Japan Diary* (New York: W. Sloane Associates, 1948), pp. 448–49.

30. Gayn notebook quote: Gayn archive, Thomas Fisher Rare Book Library, University of Toronto, Box 40, No. 7.

31. Gayn activities: ibid.

32. MIT Japanese studies/Isaacs: author's telephone interviews with researcher Kevin Coogan (January 5 and May 10, 1992).

33. RCN/LHO and Queen Bee: Fensterwald memo of conversation with RCN (May 31, 1978).

34. LHO and Queen Bee: Edward Jay Epstein, *Legend: The Secret World of Lee Harvey Oswald* (New York: Reader's Digest Press/McGraw-Hill, 1978), pp. 71–72.

35. Bucknell on LHO: Mark Lane, "The Assassination of President John F. Kennedy: How the CIA Set Up Oswald," *Hustler* (October 1978), p. 50.

36. LHO and gun: Epstein, *Legend,* pp. 72–73.

37. RCN on FitzGerald: typewritten page, Nagell file, Assassination Archives Research Center, Washington, D.C.

38. RCN on FitzGerald death: ibid.

39. Flannery on FitzGerald: Author's telephone interview (February 13, 1992).

40. Background on Desmond FitzGerald is drawn from several sources, including his obituaries in *The New York Times* and *The Washington Post,* p. B2 (July 24, 1967); *Time* magazine files (July 27 and 28, 1967) from the *Time-Life* Library; the obituary of Marietta Tree, *The New York Times* (August 16, 1991), p. C16; and the following books: Thomas Powers, *The Man Who Kept the Secrets* (New York: Alfred A. Knopf, 1979), p. 323; David Wise and Thomas B. Ross, *The Espionage Establishment* (New York: Random House, 1967), pp. 140–41; and John Ranelagh, *The Agency: The Rise and Decline of the CIA* (New York: Simon & Schuster, 1987), p. 223.

41. Smith on FitzGerald/Willoughby: author's telephone interview (June 29, 1992).

42. Train on FitzGerald: author's telephone interview (June 11, 1992).

43. For fascinating reading on James Angleton's life and times, see the following books: Tom Mangold, *Cold Warrior* (New York: Simon & Schuster, 1991); David Wise, *Molehunt* (New York: Random House, 1992); and Edward Jay Epstein, *Deception* (New York: Simon & Schuster, 1989).

Chapter VI

The author's discussions about Nagell with New York political researcher Jones Harris were conducted in person (October 8, 1986, and April 22–23, 1992) as well as in a number of telephone conversations.

Numbered notes are as follows:

1. The Rhodes quote appears in Jim Marrs, *Crossfire* (New York: Carroll & Graf, 1989), p. 107, and was first reported in Edward Jay Epstein, *Legend* (New York: Reader's Digest Press/McGraw-Hill, 1978), p. 81. There is considerable doubt, however, whether Oswald ever went with his unit to Formosa. The HSCA (pp. 280–81, Final Report) stated that its "review of his military records, including unit diaries that were not previously studied by the Warren Commission, indicated, however, that he had not spent substantial time, if any, in Taiwan." However, I have elected to go with the Rhodes account, as being at least indicative of Oswald's state of mind at the time.

2. LHO's "medical treatment": HSCA IX. 603; HSCA VIII. 313–15; HSCA XIX. 601.

3. LHO on Iwakuni: Epstein, *Legend*, pp. 82–83.

4. Wilcott testimony, LHO/CIA: HSCA Report, pp. 198–200.

5. Wilcott telephone interview with author (October 22, 1986).

6. Besides WC VIII. 316, XXV. 862, 865, and HSCA XI. 542, a possible link between LHO and the death of Private Schrand has been meticulously explored in an article by Jerry D. Rose, "Martin Schrand," *The Third Decade*, (January 1988), pp. 15–19.

7. RCN and Dugan execution: Plaintiff's Motion to Terminate the Administrative Proceedings and Reinstate the Judicial Proceedings, p. 9, filed April 16, 1974, U.S. Court of Claims, No. 1-73.

8. Military Dugan investigation: A "Synopsis" of the Military Police's investigation (July 3, 1958) notes that Dugan "was a consistent gambler on various club slot machines and, during the period of 30 November 1957 and 4 February 1958, had lost the approximate sum of $355." The same report adds that Dugan "had sold his personal typewriter" to a Japanese company "on the same day that he disappeared." While Dugan's death was officially "from unknown causes," Nagell has hinted on a page of *"TRIVIA"* sent to Arthur Greenstein that something else was involved. Nagell writes: "Was Emmett Dugan given a drink of conium maculatum? No? How about a brew of colchicum autumnale?" Both references are to lethal poisons. In 1991 the author contacted a Maude Dugan by telephone in Crafton, Pennsylvania, but the woman stated she "was not married" and denied any knowledge of Emmett E. Dugan.

9. RCN quote on Dugan: Letter to Arthur Greenstein (October 14, 1970).

10. RCN Army file: USAREUR Liaison Team, Headquarters USA INTC, Fort Holabird, Maryland, report on Nagell sent to Berlin Station, (April 24, 1969) on file CC, No. 1-73.

11. Army records cited are on file at CC. Also see February 3, 1975, filing, p. 4. The "Narrative Summary" of a February 13, 1958, report on Nagell by Army captain/psychiatrist Carl L. McGahee notes that ". . . the patient had made certain allegations to the Department of the Army directly, circumventing ordinary channels in the chain of command. The allegations are supposed to deal with security violations and other infractions or inefficiencies in his organization." This document is on file in the U.S. Court of Claims case.

12. Investigation of RCN: quote from CC files, memorandum addressed to "Commanding Officer, United States Army Intelligence Support Center" (April 30, 1958).

13. Army file quoted: in CC case files.

14. Garrison on RCN: transcript of Round-Table Conference, New Orleans, Louisiana (September 20–24, 1968) p. 68.

15. Von Kleist letter to Fensterwald (February 7, 1969). An FBI document dated February 2, 1972, from its Albuquerque, New Mexico, office also notes that "August Ricard Von Kleist" had advised the previous day that he had "certain information concerning a plot to assassinate President John Fitzgerald Kennedy."

16. RCN on "distortion": CC (April 16, 1974). In a registered letter of November 29, 1968, addressed to John Malone, assistant director in charge of the FBI's New York City field office, Nagell called von Kleist's allegations "inaccurate and distorted in almost every respect" but added that von Kleist "nonetheless cites references that could only have been derived from official sources, that is, from the FBI, the CIC or the CIA, and, in one area, only the FBI. That area pertains to information that I had provided only to the FBI, information that was not revealed to any other agency, at least not by me." Nagell told the author that he had known Malone personally since October 1955, when the FBI and Army CIC reached a "delineation agreement" and Malone lectured to Nagell's group.

17. RCN on Far East service: author's interview (May 19, 1978).

18. RCN on loyalty oaths: This statement, handwritten and undated, was found by the author in U.S. District Court archive on *United States* v. *Nagell*, Fort Worth.

19. RCN and Soviets: Fensterwald memo of conversation (May 31, 1978).

20. De Mohrenschildt/Okui testimony: WC IX. 319.

21. Marina and Okui: Priscilla Johnson McMillan, *Marina and Lee* (New York: Harper & Row, 1977), pp. 245–46.

22. George De Mohrenschildt on Okui: HSCA XII. 170–73.

23. LHO and pamphlets: Epstein, *Legend*, p. 202.

24. Okui in Japan: ibid., pp. 202, 317.

25. LHO and Japanese card: WC XVII. 770.

26. RCN on LHO Tokyo residence: letter to author (March 29, 1976).

27. Japanese at leafleting: WC XXVI. 773. An "Ehara" is mentioned in WCD 75. 693.

28. Gaudet and tourist card: Anthony Summers, *Conspiracy* (New York: McGraw-Hill, 1980), pp. 363–65.

29. Gambert on RCN's wife: author's interview (February 16, 1990).

30. Margain on RCN and Japanese: author's interview (April 7, 1991).

31. Marlowe on RCN calling card: author's interview (August 2, 1990).

32. RCN on intelligence "advice": undated letter to Arthur Greenstein.

33. Huff allegations: HSCA XI. 539–51.

34. Sassa stories: Glenn Troelstrup, "New Light on the Assassination: A Secret Agent's Story," *U.S. News & World Report* (June 8, 1964), pp. 38–39; "Assassination Story—The Reaction in Japan," *March of the News* (June 15, 1964).

35. Oswald/Hidell gun orders: WC XVI. 511; VII. 295, 366; XVII. 635, 677; XXIV. 19.

36. Hidell and Fair Play for Cuba Committee: WC XI. 328, XVII. 760.

37. A record of Oswald's effects after the assassination may be found in former Dallas police chief Jesse Curry's book *JFK Assassination File* (Dallas: American Poster and Publishing, 1969).

38. The Warren Commission Report concluded (p. 14) that "Hidell was a completely fictitious person created by Oswald." For a full account of all the discrepancies about the Hidell name, see Sylvia Meagher, *Accessories After the Fact* (New York: Vintage Books, 1976), pp. 181–99.

39. RCN on Hidell alias: author's interview (October 26, 1975).

40. RCN statement on Hidell: from an outline of "highlights" sent by the author, and returned from Nagell with corrections (March 22, 1976).

41. RCN question-mark statements on Hidell: from his "Trivia" in letters to Arthur Greenstein.

42. RCN on CIA/Soviet cryptonyms: interview with author (May 19, 1978).

43. RCN and origins of Hidell: interview with author (April 11, 1977).

44. CIA/Japan/Korean CIA: Richard Deacon, *Kempei Tai* (New York: Beauford Books, 1983), p. 243.

45. ROK military Se-Jin Kim, *The Politics of Military Revolution in Korea* (Chapel Hill, N.C.: University of North Carolina Press, 1971), pp. 37–43.

46. APACL and Pentagon/John Birch Society: Peter Dale Scott, *The War Conspiracy* (Indianapolis, Ind.: Bobbs-Merrill, 1972), p. 204. The probable role of CIA official Ray Cline with the APACL is described in Scott Anderson and Jon Lee Anderson, *Inside the League* (New York: Dodd, Mead, 1986), pp. 55–58.

47. Szulc on KCIA: Tad Szulc, "Inside South Korea's CIA," *The New York Times Magazine* (March 6, 1977), p. 41.

48. KCIA and Korean Yakuza: David E. Kaplan and Alec Dubro, *Yakuza* (Reading, Mass.: Addison-Wesley, 1986), p. 192.

49. Agee on CIA/KCIA: Philip Agee, *Inside the Company: CIA Diary* (New York: Bantam Books, 1976), p. 541.

50. Graef on LHO/Korea: WC X. 189.

51. Military Intelligence/LHO/Hidell: HSCA, *The Final Assassinations Report* (New York: Bantam Books, 1979), pp. 282–86.

Chapter VII

The author's interview with John Margain and members of his family was conducted in Baldwin Park, California (April 7, 1991).

The author's interview with Charles W. (Bill) Lynn was conducted in Los Angeles (July 29, 1977).

All cited Charles Willoughby correspondence is on record at the MacArthur Archives, Norfolk, Virginia.

Numbered notes are as follows:

1. The additional information on RCN's military background in this chapter, and more, is on file at CC, No. 1-73.

2. Donovan quote: WC VIII. 290. Oswald's "secret" clearance: WC VIII. 298 (Donovan) and VIII. 232 (Delgado).

3. Call quote: WC XXIII. 322. See also testimony of James Anthony Botelho, WC XXIII. 315, about "Oswald-skovich" nickname and interest in Russian music.

4. Thornley on LHO/1984: Kerry Thornley, *Oswald* (Chicago: New Classics House, 1965), pp. 25–34.

5. Rankin on LHO/languages: Harold Weisberg, *Whitewash*, Vol. IV: *JFK Assassination Transcript* (Hyatt-stown, Md.: self-published, 1965, 1967), p. 101 (January 27, 1964 Executive Session of Warren Commission).

6. The author interviewed Gerry Patrick Hemming in January, March, June, and October 1976, by telephone and in person. Hemming told a similar story about meeting Oswald in 1959, to investigators for the Senate Select Committee on Intelligence Activities on May 23, 1975. Some of this material from the author's Hemming interviews appeared in *Argosy* magazine (April 1976).

7. Delgado on LHO/Cuba: WC VIII. 232–63.

8. Bucknell on LHO: Mark Lane, "The Assassination of President John F. Kennedy: How the CIA Set Up Oswald," *Hustler* (October 1978).

9. Oswald's travel plans and his mother's injury are described at length in his brother Robert L. Oswald's book *Lee: A Portrait of Lee Harvey Oswald*, with Myrick and Barbara Land (New York: Coward-McCann, 1967).

10. RCN and LAPD: Letter from Nagell to LAPD seeking applicant and employment records (November 16, 1975).

11. RCN on CIA service: addendum January 28, 1970, to pamphlet, "Man In the Middle: The Inside Story."

12. CIA's Domestic Division: Robert D. Morrow, *The Senator Must Die* (Santa Monica, Calif.: Roundtable, 1988), p. 60.

13. In Dr. I. I. Morris, *Nationalism and the Right Wing in Japan* (London: Oxford University Press, 1960), p. 267, Mr. Ryutaro Takahashi is identified as Japan's former minister of commerce and industry. The author was unable to determine if this man is the father of Mitsuko Takahashi Nagell.

14. The story of "Yamashita's Gold" is well documented throughout Sterling Seagrave, *The Marcos Dynasty* (New York: Harper & Row, 1988). Besides Singlaub, the roles of CIA officials Ray Cline and Theodore Shackley are explored in the book.

15. Clinical Report: on file, CC No. 1-73.

16. RCN losing ABC job: MI file (May 2, 1969), report of Thomas J. Hench, 766th military detachment; transcript, *United States* v. *Nagell*, p. 383; 1975 FBI synopsis of report by special agent David J. Reid, El Paso (February 4, 1964), released under the Freedom of Information Act to Fensterwald.

17. RCN and the Mob: interview with author (July 27, 1984).

18. Spotts on RCN shooting: interview with author (October 21, 1986). Nagell told the FBI after his arrest in El Paso that "the shooting was a result of a private matter and he did not care to discuss it further." FBI report (September 25, 1963) on file, *United States* v. *Nagell*, U.S. District Court archives, Fort Worth.

19. Clinical worker's report: on file, CC No. 1-73.

20. Gambert on RCN visit: author's interview (February 16, 1990).

21. Greenstein quote: author's interview (February 10, 1990).

22. RCN on Steve Roberts: author's interview (October 26, 1975).

23. SWP quote: *International Socialist Review* (Spring 1960) p. 52.

24. Steve Roberts background: "Communist and Trotskyist Activity Within the Greater Los Angeles Chapter of the Fair Play for Cuba Committee," Report, Committee on Un-American Activities, House of Representatives, 87th Congress (November 2, 1962), p. 1522. Washington, D.C.: U.S. GPO.

25. Richard Gibson and the CIA: Several people connected with the Fair Play for Cuba Committee in the early 1960s voiced this suspicion to the author. The above-cited report noted that Gibson was "president of the New York chapter of FPCC from the time of its chartering in September 1960" and " 'acting' executive secretary of the national organization since January 1961." The same report noted that Gibson had "supplied an admittedly incomplete list" of FPCC chapters in response to a Senate Internal Security Subcommittee request, and specifically identified Steve Roberts as a West Coast representative whose " 'expenses' were reimbursed by the New York headquarters."

26. LA FPCC: report, "Communist and Trotskyist Activity. . . . ," pp. 1569–70.

27. Eastland quote: "U.S. Newsman Listed on Castro's Payroll," AP article in *Los Angeles Times* (April 3, 1961).

28. CIA and FPCC in 1961: The Investigation of the Assassination of President John F. Kennedy: Performance of the Intelligence Agencies, Final Report, Book V (April 23, 1976), p. 66.

29. FBI and SWP: *Supplementary Detailed Staff Reports on Intelligence Activities and the Rights of Americans* Book III, U.S. Senate (1976) pp. 17–18.

30. Roberts testimony: "House Anti-Red Quiz Turns to Cuba Group," *Los Angeles Times* (April 28, 1962).

31. Plans to assassinate exile leaders: Robert D. Morrow, *Motivation Behind the Assassination of John F. Kennedy* (July 1976), pp. 1–6. The notarized affidavit of Mario Garcia Kohly, Jr. (July 15, 1976), states: "In October 1960, in a conversation between my father in Washington, D.C. and myself in Miami between two predesignated pay telephones, I was told that Vice President Nixon had agreed to the elimination of the leftist approved Cuban Revolutionary Front leaders at a time when the island would be invaded by the exile groups trained under the direction of the Central Intelligence Agency. . . ."

32. This account of the detainment of exile leaders Antonio Varona, Manuel Ray, and José Miro Cardona is drawn from Peter Wyden, *Bay of Pigs*, (New York: Simon & Schuster, 1979), pp. 207–8, 290–91.

33. Operation 40: According to the Warren Hinckle and William Turner history of the exiles *The Fish Is Red* (New York: Harper & Row, 1981), one of the secret operation's political functions was "to purge the Cuban exile ranks of the anti-Castro left, the exponents of *Fidelismo sin Fidel*. . . . After the Bay of Pigs, the CIA kept Operation 40 intact in Miami." (p. 308). "By 1967 Joaquin Sanjenis had expanded the group to the point where it received more than $2 million a year from the CIA, in addition to extensive logistical support." (p. 310). Howard Kohn, "Strange Bedfellows" (*Rolling Stone*, May 20, 1976), notes that Florida Mob leader Santos Trafficante, Jr., "infiltrated Operation Forty with Syndicate money and henchmen."

34. White House on right wing: "Memorandum for the President, Subject: Right-Wing Groups" (August 15, 1963). On file at Political Research Associates, Cambridge, Massachusetts. The author's other background information on the ultraright is drawn from numerous sources cited in the Bibliography.

35. A fact sheet on Willoughby, compiled March 11, 1963, by Group Research, Inc., a private monitoring organization in Washington, describes his affiliations in 1961–62, including: National Advisory Committee and Washington representative, Hargis's Christian Crusade; National Advisory Board, Young Americans for Freedom; Committee of Endorsers, John Birch Society; National Advisory Board, Conservative Society of America; National Advisory Committee, Committee on Pan American Policy; member, American Committee for Aid to Katanga Freedom Fighters.

36. Background on Hargis's Christian Crusade and his founding of the Anti-Communist Liaison is derived from Arnold Forster and Benjamin R. Epstein, *Danger on the Right* (New York: Random House, 1964), pp. 68–86.

37. Edward Hunter and intelligence: OSS work described in congressional testimony March 13, 1958—"Communist Psychological Warfare (Brainwashing)," consultation with Edward Hunter, Committee on Un-American Activities, U.S. House of Representatives, p. 6. Hunter never officially acknowledged continuing as a CIA

contract agent while a "roving correspondent" for the Cox newspapers, but several sources have verified this to the author.

38. Hunter quote on brainwashing: Edward Hunter, *Brainwashing from Pavlov to Powers* (Linden, N.J.: The Bookmailer, 1971), p. 203.

39. Bonner Fellers background: Bruce Cumings, *The Origins of the Korean War,* Vol. II (Princeton, N.J.: Princeton University Press, 1990), p. 101. As of June 1962, Fellers was also national director, For America; national director, Citizens Foreign Aid Committee; Committee of Endorsers, John Birch Society; National Advisory Committee, Christian Crusade; vice chairman, Americans for Constitutional Action; and National Advisory Board, Young Americans for Freedom, Inc. (9/29/62 fact sheet on Anti-Communist Liaison, Group Research, Inc.).

40. John Rousselot background: Group Research fact sheet. Other Anti-Communist Liaison Committee Members as of June 1962 were Benjamin Gitlow, Bella Dodd, and Karl Hess.

41. William Gale background: Derived from Cheri Seymour, *Committee of the States: Inside the Radical Right* (Mariposa, Calif.: Camden Place Communications, 1991).

42. Ibid, pp. 229–30. The Arch Roberts book cited by author Seymour notes that Lieutenant General Charles B. Stone, Third Air Force; General Albert Wedemeyer, former General Staff officer on War Plans at the Pentagon; and Lieutenant General John O'Daniel, military attaché, U.S. embassy in Moscow (1948–50), were among Willoughby's and del Valle's compatriots in "backing a tactical guide, or manual of arms for the future, called *The John Franklin Letters*. . . ." No specific reference is made to Colonel Gale's Rangers; however, the Gale group was established almost simultaneously.

43. California report on Rangers: Seymour, *Committee of the States,* pp. 67–71. In a closing "Commentary" section, the report notes:

> This organization is designed as a secret underground guerrilla force, yet it is linked with other non-military organizations by a common ideology and leadership. The California leaders of the group have intimate connections with the Ku Klux Klan, the National States Rights Party, the Christian Defense League, and the Church of Jesus Christ—Christian. They are associated with these groups both in California and in the Southern United States.

44. Ibid., p. 71, Seymour citing California report.

Chapter VIII

The author's interviews with James Angleton were conducted on December 17, 1975; and April 2 and October 22, 1976.

The *Nightline* program on the KGB files aired on November 22, 1991, on ABC-TV.

All referenced CIA files about John Paisley were released under the FOIA to attorney Bernard Fensterwald, Jr., representing Paisley's widow, Maryann, in 1980; the author received Fensterwald's permission to review and photocopy the files at the attorney's office.

The author's interview with Robert Morrow about Oswald in Minsk was conducted on August 8, 1976.

Numbered notes are as follows:

1. Angleton and Nosenko: See Edward Jay Epstein, *Legend* (New York: Reader's Digest Press/McGraw-Hill, 1978), pp. 3–50; also, HSCA XII, "Oswald in the Soviet Union: An Investigation of Yuri Nosenko," pp. 475–644.

2. LHO's Soviet visa: WC XXVI. 32; HSCA Final Report, pp. 267–69 (Bantam edition) also raises questions about his rapid trip to Helsinki.

3. For more on LHO's early days in Moscow, see Jim Marrs, *Crossfire* (New York: Carroll & Graf, 1989), pp. 118–19.

4. U.S. consul Richard Snyder and the CIA say that Snyder resigned from the CIA in 1950. But a HSCA review of Snyder's CIA file noted that "a matter of cover" existed after that time concerning the U.S. embassy employee (Final Report, pp. 272–47). A book published by Julius Mader, *Who's Who in CIA,* in East Berlin in 1968, lists Snyder as having been with the CIA since 1951.

5. McVickar's reaction: WC XVIII. 153.

6. Snyder cable: HSCA Report, p. 252; quoted on *Nightline* broadcast (November 22, 1991).

7. Marine lieutenant John Donovan told the Warren Commission that Oswald's knowledge about West Coast air bases included "all radio frequencies for all squadrons, all tactical call signs, the relative strengths of all squadrons, number and type of aircraft in a squadron," as well as "the authentication code for entering and exiting" [the air defense zone] and "the range of surrounding units' radio and radar" (WC VIII. 298).

8. McMillan interview with LHO: She describes her November 16, 1959, visit in *Marina and Lee* (New York: Harper & Row, 1977), pp. 69–72.

9. *Nightline* broadcast (November 22, 1991).

10. Oswald's arrival in Minsk and employment: WC XVI. 99, 121, 287.

11. U-2 background: "C.I.A. Operations: A Plot Scuttled," *The New York Times* (April 28, 1966), p. 1.

12. Prouty on U-2: interview with *Gallery* magazine, (November 1975), p. 47–48.

13. U-2 and stocks: V. Chernyavsky, "U.S. Intelligence and the Monopolies," *International Affairs* (January 1965). The article notes that two months after the U-2's demise, Eisenhower allocated the biggest military allocations ever approved at that time, $48,300 million for fiscal 1960–61.

14. U-2 discrepancies: See Michael R. Beschloss, *Mayday: Eisenhower, Khrushchev, and the U-2 Affair* (New York: Harper & Row, 1986) p. 358.

15. Powers on LHO: WC VIIIH. 298; interview with *The Times* (April 20, 1971); also cited in Anthony Summers, *Conspiracy* (New York: McGraw-Hill, 1980), p. 206, and Philip H. Melanson, *Spy Saga: Lee Harvey Oswald and U.S. Intelligence* (New York: Praeger, 1990), pp. 17–18. According to a Yale alumni book, U.S. consul Snyder described himself as having been "in charge of the Gary Powers U-2 trial matters" after the plane was shot down (Melanson, *Spy Saga*, p. 16).

16. Net damage assessment on LHO: Epstein, in *Legend*, quotes the Department of the Navy's responding to his question that ". . . no formal damage assessment was conducted because of his low level of clearance" (p. 366). Melanson, in *Spy Saga* (p. 16), points out that damage assessments were, however, conducted "in the cases of the only two U.S. enlisted men who defected to communist countries before Oswald" and at least two cases after Oswald.

17. Hunter on Powers: *Brainwashing from Pavlov to Powers* (Linden, N.J.: The Bookmailer, 1971), p. 321.

18. Bryan on Powers: cited in W. H. Bowart, *Operation Mind Control* (New York: Dell Publishing, 1978), pp. 47–48.

19. Powers on treatment: ibid., pp. 48–49.

20. Hunter on U-2: *Brainwashing*, p. 320.

21. U-2 and possible sabotage: The author is indebted to Matthew A. Coogan, who provides a full chapter on the U-2 incident in his unpublished manuscript "Thirty Years of Deception." See also Marrs, *Crossfire*, p. 115, concerning Powers' radio interview.
In examining the role of the CIA's Office of Security with the U-2, Coogan notes that the security chief in 1960 was Sheffield Edwards, who arranged the original CIA-Mafia assassination attempts against Fidel Castro. Watergate burglar James McCord and Edwin P. Wilson, later convicted of illegal arms deals with Libya, were also with the Office of Security at that time.

22. Buckley/Eden books: cited in Coogan, "Thirty Years of Deception."

23. LHO on Powers: Epstein, *Legend*, pp. 121, 300. Marina Oswald noted that Oswald was honeymooning with her in Minsk on May Day 1961, and in 1962 preparing to return to the United States.

24. Bernard Drell on CIA's ORR Division: author's telephone interview (March 5, 1992).

25. Paisley as "nash": RCN mailing postmarked October 11, 1978, to author.

26. RCN on "nash": author's interview (May 19, 1978). The use of "nash" as a Soviet intelligence code name meaning "he works for us" is also mentioned by ex-FBI agent Robert J. Lamphere in his book *The FBI-KGB War*, coauthored with Tom Schachtman (New York: Random House, 1986), p. 83.

27. Questions about Paisley: Tad Szulc, "The Missing CIA Man," *The New York Times Magazine* (January 7, 1979), p. 13.

28. Fensterwald on Paisley: author's interview (December 1, 1980).

29. Paisley duties: CIA "Fitness Report" on Paisley covering January 4, 1962–March 31, 1963, released to Fensterwald in 1980.

30. CIA and Minsk radio factory: HSCA *Final Assassinations Report*, p. 264.

31. LHO "Diary": HSCA XII. 236. It was based partly on this diary that the CIA's Richard Helms assured the Warren Commission there was nothing unusual about LHO's defection (XXVI. 146).

32. LHO on Minsk plant: WC XVI. 349 (CE 94).

33. RCN on "Diary": critique of John Barron, *KGB* (New York: Reader's Digest Press, 1974). For more on LHO's "Historical Diary," see Epstein, *Legend*, pp. 144–45, 149–50, and Anthony Summers, *Conspiracy* (New York: McGraw-Hill, 1980), pp. 182–85. The complete transcript of the Diary appears in WC XVI. 94–105 (CE 24).

34. Background on Paisley: author's article "The Spy at the Bottom of the Bay," *Gallery* magazine (May 1981), p. 36; and William R. Corson, Susan B. Trento, and Joseph J. Trento, *Widows* (New York: Crown, 1989).

35. Angleton recruiting Paisley: Szulc, "The Missing CIA Man."

36. Crowley quote: Corson, Trento, and Trento, *Widows*, p. 26.

37. Paisley's 1959 travels: from CIA file, released in 1980 to Fensterwald.

38. Paisley's travels: Corson, Trento, and Trento, *Widows*, p. 30.

39. Defectors in 1959: *The New York Times* (July 20, 1959), p. 4.

40. Defectors' histories: Peter Dale Scott, "The Dallas Conspiracy" (unpublished manuscript, 1971).

41. Webster's defection: *The New York Times* (October 20, 1959), p. 3.

42. Rand Development ties: WCE 915, WC XVIII. H113; Summers, *Conspiracy*, pp. 177–78.

43. Bird background: A. J. Weberman "Mind Control: The Story of Mankind Research Unlimited, Inc.," *CovertAction* (June 1980), p. 17.

44. Rand and hypnosis/drugs: Seymour Fisher, *The Use of Hypnosis in Intelligence and Related Military Situations*, Study SR 177-D, Contract AF 18 (600) 1797, Technical Report No. 4 (Washington, D.C.: Bureau of Social Science Research, 1958). Study is in author's possession. See also Bowart, *Operation Mind Control*, pp. 67–72, on Rand.

45. Webster/LHO parallels: cited in Summers, *Conspiracy*, pp. 177–78.

46. Webster State Department file: CE 915, cited by Michael Canfield and Alan J. Weberman, *Coup d'État in America* (New York: The Third Press, 1975), p. 25.

47. LHO on Webster: McMillan, *Marina and Lee*, p. 107.

48. Marina and Webster: Summers, *Conspiracy*, p. 191; CIA Document 624-823.

49. Marina on meeting husband: WC V. 259 (FBI report on Katya Ford).

50. RCN on Paisley: author's interview (July 27, 1984).

51. Maryann Paisley comments: author's interview (December 3, 1980).

52. Paisley and boat near Nosenko: Szulc, "The Missing CIA Man."

53. CIA on Paisley/Nosenko: memo released to Fensterwald, 1980.

54. Helms on Nosenko: Helms's elaborate testimony about Nosenko and other matters appears in HSCA IV. 5–250.

55. Sword on Paisley boat: author's article. "The Spy at the Bottom. . . ." At the time of his death, Paisley had come out of retirement to coordinate a Top-Secret reevaluation of Soviet strategic capabilities and intentions. He became the go-between for an "A Team" of intelligence community specialists and a "B team" of civilian experts (such as Paul Nitze, who had been the chief U.S. negotiator at the Strategic Arms Limitation Talks). Basically, Paisley's job was to provide the B team with classified CIA documents. The two teams feuded over whether to take a hard line. Paisley was considered a dove, and a B team academician who disagreed with his views leaked Paisley's name to *The New York Times*. Paisley's wife, Maryann, remembers George Bush, then the CIA director, following up by sending Paisley a sweatshirt with "A team" on the front and "B team" on the back—an attempt to humor Paisley's anger over the leak.

In April 1978 Paisley, now separated from his wife, moved into a Washington apartment complex on whose floor also lived eight employees of the Soviet embassy. The CIA was simultaneously responding to a request from President Jimmy Carter to close security breaches following the loss of a Top-Secret manual detailing the operations of the KH-11 surveillance satellite to the Soviets (CIA employee Thomas Kampiles was arrested and received a forty-year sentence for selling the manual; Paisley had been briefed about the KH-11 by the CIA late in 1977).

56. Maryann Paisley on Angleton: author's interview (December 3, 1980).

57. Angleton on Paisley: author's telephone interview (October 1, 1986).

58. Angleton on Paisley: Edward Jay Epstein, *Deception* (New York: Simon & Schuster, 1989), p. 272.

59. Angleton as mole: Tom Mangold, *Cold Warrior* (New York: Simon & Schuster, 1991), pp. 299–303.

60. Tracy Barnes's background can be found in a number of books about the CIA, including David Wise and Thomas B. Ross, *The Espionage Establishment* (New York: Random House, 1967) and *The Invisible Government* (New York: Random House, 1964); Peter Wyden's *Bay of Pigs* (New York: Simon & Schuster, 1979); Robert D. Morrow's *The Senator Must Die* (Santa Monica, Calif.: Roundtable, 1988); and John Raelagh, *The Agency* (New York: Simon & Schuster, 1987).

61. CIA memo on Soviet women marrying foreigners: cited in Summers, *Conspiracy*, p. 192.

62. The most detailed background on Marina is found in McMillan, *Marina and Lee;* curiosities about Marina's background are duly noted in Summers, *Conspiracy*, pp. 189–93. The story of Marina's first meeting with "Alik" is described in Marrs, *Crossfire*, pp. 124–25.

63. LHO and mother: State Department file, declassified 1992; author's conversation with researcher Mary Ferrell. Marguerite Oswald long suspected that her son was a government agent. "Lee went to many, many a school, gentlemen," she testified before the Warren Commission.

64. Oswald getting passport back: WC XVIII. 131, 137, 160–62; XVI. 705–6; V. 284. Marina visa: XVIII. 158.

65. Immigration/State Department on Marina: Warren Commission Report, pp. 671–73.

66. Marrs quote: *Crossfire*, p. 127.

67. Prusakov farewell: Epstein, *Legend*, p. 150. Additional background on Prusakov appears in the same book, on pp. 133–34, 144–45.

68. The CIA chronology of Oswald's life in the USSR was sent from Richard Helms to Warren Commission counsel J. Lee Rankin on August 13, 1964.

69. Nosenko as "Alex": David Wise, *Molehunt* (New York: Random House, 1992), p. 78.

70. Penkovsky/"Alex," Kisevalter/"Alexander": Nigel West, *The Circus* (Briarcliff Manor, N.Y.: Stein and Day, 1984), pp. 142–43.

71. The Oswalds' visit with Alexis Davison: HSCA Final Report, pp. 274–75. Davison explained to the House Assassinations Committee that his providing his mother's name and address in Atlanta was merely a gesture to Marina, "since his family had always been very hospitable to Russians who visited Atlanta." The Oswalds' return flight to Dallas: WC XVI. 616; XVIII. 16. Robert L. Oswald, with Myrick and Barbara Land, *Lee*. (New York: Coward-McCann, 1967), p. 117.

72. Background on the Penkovsky case was drawn from a number of sources, including *The Circus* and *Molehunt*. The ouster of Alexis Davison from the USSR, in connection with the Penkovsky case, was recounted in *The New York Times* (May 14, 1963), p. 1.

73. Davison's HSCA testimony: Final Report, p. 275. "Davison denied under oath participating in any other intelligence work during his tour in Moscow."

74. Paisley and Penkovsky case: author's telephone interview with Victor Marchetti (March 7, 1992).

75. Paisley's access: Corson, Trento, and Trento, *Widows*, p. 34.

76. KGB files: Author's telephone interview with Forrest Sawyer (February 5, 1992).

77. Helms's testimony before HSCA: excerpt cited in Melanson, *Spy Saga*, p. 153.

78. John McCone interview: conducted for Lyndon B. Johnson Library, Austin, Texas, by Joe B. Frantz (August 19, 1970).

79. LHO and Naval Intelligence: Henry Hurt, *Reasonable Doubt* (New York: Holt, Rinehart, & Winston, 1985), p. 243.

80. CIA and LHO in Minsk: *The Final Assassinations Report* (New York: Bantam Books, 1979), pp. 263–65. The HSCA notes that the CIA has long admitted having a "201 file" on Oswald, opened "when a person is considered to be of potential intelligence or counterintelligence significance." This took place in Oswald's case on December 9, 1960, allegedly after the CIA received a State Department request for information on American

defectors. The HSCA, in reviewing the file, discovered "an unsigned memorandum to the Chief of Counterintelligence, Research and Analysis, dated February 20, 1964, which stated that 37 documents were missing from Oswald's 201 file." (See *The Final Assassinations Report,* pp. 251–63.)

Chapter IX

The author's interview with Arthur Greenstein took place on February 10, 1990.
   The author's interview with Edward Lansdale was conducted in McLean, Virginia, on May 14, 1976.
   Numbered notes are as follows:
   1. RCN on correspondence with Greenstein: letters to author (January 29 and May 13, 1976).
   2. RCN Mexico tourist card: document in author's possession.
   3. FBI file on Nagell: July 30, 1975 "Synopsis" of report by special agent David J. Reid (February 4, 1964), p. 3. This file was released to attorney Bernard Fensterwald, Jr., under a Freedom of Information Act request.
   4. RCN quotes on Mexico: 1967 correspondence with Greenstein.
   5. CIA in Mexico: Philip Agee, *Inside the Company: CIA Diary* (New York: Bantam Books, 1976), pp. 538–39.
   6. Phillips on CIA: David Atlee Phillips, *The Night Watch: 25 Years of Peculiar Service* (New York: Atheneum, 1977), pp. 113–14.
   7. KGB and Cuba in Mexico: Agee, *Inside the Company,* pp. 536–38.
   8. State Department Mexico Airgram: on file at John Fitzgerald Kennedy Library, Boston, Massachusetts.
   9. McCone on Mexico and the Cuban Missile Crisis: interview with Joe B. Frantz for Lyndon B. Johnson Library, Austin, Texas (August 19, 1970); also on file at JFK Library.
   10. DIA background/officials: David Wise and Thomas B. Ross, *The Invisible Government* (New York: Random House, 1964), pp. 211–16.
   11. Quinn's instructions: William R. Corson, *The Armies of Ignorance* (New York: Dial Press/James Wade, 1977), p. 279.
   12. Hoover agents in SSI: ibid., pp. 286–87.
   13. Leddy and Guatemala: ibid., pp. 356–57.
   14. Disbandment of émigré units: Burton Hersh, *The Old Boys* (New York: Charles Scribner's Sons, 1992), pp. 410–11.
   15. Smith on Pentagon clique: author's telephone interview (April 8, 1992).
   16. Phillips on Mexico: Phillips, *The Night Watch,* p. 114.
   17. Phillips on FBI in Mexico: ibid.
   18. COINTELPRO in Mexico: Ronald J. Ostrow and Robert L. Jackson, "10-Year FBI Effort to Disrupt Communists in Mexico Disclosed," *Los Angeles Times* (November 22, 1977).
   19. RCN as FBI informant: Plaintiff's Motion to Terminate the Administrative Proceedings and Reinstate the Judicial Proceedings, p. 3, filed April 16, 1974, U.S. Court of Claims, No. 1-73.
   20. Harry White/Harry Johnson: RCN interview with author (October 5, 1977) and RCN letter to Fensterwald (May 20, 1974) (White); RCN letter to Greenstein (September 20, 1967) (Johnson).
   21. RCN on CIA/FBI contacts: author's interview (October 5, 1977).
   22. RCN on events leading to Mexico: letter to Eleanore Gambert (October 7, 1966).
   23. RCN on trip to Mexico: letters to Greenstein (September 12 and 17, 1967).
   24. RCN on offer from foreign government: statement handwritten by FBI special agent Lawrence W. Gorman and signed by RCN, also witnessed by FBI special agent Edward J. Murphy (January 6, 1964). On file, archives U.S. District Court, *United States* v. *Nagell,* Fort Worth.
   25. Broglie background/quotes: author's telephone interview (March 8, 1992).
   26. Waehauf background: derived from RCN, Plaintiff's Motion, Court of Claims; author's interviews with Broglie (March 8, 1992), Greenstein (February 10, 1990).
   27. Czech intelligence: Agee, *Inside the Company,* p. 537.
   28. RCN investigating Waehauf: Plaintiff's Motion, Court of Claims.
   29. RCN on "Bob": author's interview (May 19, 1978). Discussion with "Bob" about the Eroshkin defection project: RCN letter to attorney Ricey New (November 11, 1968).
   30. Double-agent operations in Mexico: Melvin Beck, *Secret Contenders: The Myth of Cold War Counterintelligence* (New York: Sheridan Square Publications, 1984), pp. 98–99.
   31. RCN on CIA "disinformation" project: filing with U.S. Court of Claims (July 14, 1969).
   32. Identity of "Bob": One man whom I was told had been with the CIA in Japan, become Scott's deputy chief in Mexico, and worked closely with FitzGerald, was Stan Watson. Like Nagell, he had also married a Japanese, a ballerina. But Watson, now in retirement in Mexico, refuses to talk to journalists—and I could not pinpoint whether he had been in Mexico prior to 1964.
   There was a Robert Shaw, the man Phillips replaced in 1963 as Mexico's Cuban specialist; but Nagell has written that, while he knew of Shaw, "he was not involved in my activities." In Philip Agee's book *Inside the Company* I came across the name Bob Driscoll, who in 1966 was "a retired operations officer now working under contract" as a CIA case officer—his specialty being agent penetrations against Communist Party organizations in Mexico City.
   Another CIA official in Mexico during that period was Robert H. Feldmann, a close friend of station chief Winston Scott. According to the 1964 *Foreign Service Registry,* he did not arrive in Mexico City (from Hamburg, West Germany) until December 9, 1962. Agee's book describes Feldmann as "Mexico City station officer in

charge of penetration operations against the Institutional Revolutionary Party (PRI) and the Mexican Foreign Ministry." Feldmann, now retired in the Washington area, refused the author's request for an interview.

It is also possible that "Bob" was not officially connected with the CIA through the American embassy. As Philip Agee recounts in his book *CIA Diary,* Desmond FitzGerald, on one of his trips to Mexico, "decided to make an experiment to see just how productive a group of CIA officers could be if they worked from a commercial cover office with very little direct contact with the CIA station under State cover in the Embassy." Three of these operations officers, according to Agee, were set up undercover as import representatives.

33. Phillips background: obituary, *The New York Times* (July 11, 1988); "Brief Notes on Mexican Material Supplied by Tony Summers," AARC files (January 24, 1983).

34. Phillips on military officer/Soviets: Phillips, *The Night Watch,* pp. 127–28; author's telephone interview (January 28, 1977).

35. RCN on CIA contacts: author's interview (October 5, 1977).

36. Smith on Scott: author's telephone interview (April 8, 1992).

37. Flannery on Scott: author's telephone interview (February 13, 1992).

38. Soviet missile delivery and blockade concern: RCN letter to author (April 18, 1976).

39. Definition of "EEI": author's telephone interview with Wayne Barker (January 5, 1992). Barker's publishing house, Aegean Park Press, of Laguna Hills, California, specializes in books about intelligence and codebreaking.

40. Operation MONGOOSE discussion about assassinating Castro: *Alleged Assassination Plots Involving Foreign Leaders: An Interim Report of the Select Committee to Study Governmental Operations with Respect to Intelligence Activities, United States Senate* (Washington, D.C.: U.S. GPO, 1975), pp. 161–70.

41. Lansdale quote: ibid., p. 167.

42. Lansdale and Willoughby: Sterling Seagrave, *The Marcos Dynasty* (New York: Harper & Row, 1988), p. 143.

43. Lansdale background: Richard Drinnon, "Who Is Edward G. Lansdale?," *Inquiry* (February 5, 1979).

44. CIA's Cuban sugar contamination and Kennedy reaction: "C.I.A. Operations: A Plot Scuttled," *The New York Times* (April 28, 1966), p. 1.

45. Schlesinger/Kennedy memos on Cuban uprising: Michael R. Beschloss, *The Crisis Years: Kennedy and Khrushchev, 1960–1963* (New York: Edward Burlingame Books, 1991), p. 412.

46. Pentagon and the Cuban Missile Crisis: James G. Blight and David A. Welch, *On the Brink* (New York: The Noonday Press, 1990), p. 330.

47. Possibility of military coup: ibid., p. 264.

48. Harvey and Cuban Missile Crisis/transfer: David C. Martin, *Wilderness of Mirrors* (New York: Harper & Row, 1980), pp. 143–47.

49. Pentagon's hopes to start small war: Nagell letters to author (January 29 and February 21, 1976).

50. Soviets and blockade: author's interview with Nagell (July 27, 1984).

51. Kennedys and KGB: author's interviews with Nagell (May 19, 1978, and July 27, 1984).

52. Kennedys and Bolshakov: Arthur M. Schlesinger, Jr., *Robert Kennedy and His Times* (New York: Ballantine Books, 1978), pp. 537–40. Also see Beschloss, *The Crisis Years,* particularly Chapter 7, "The Secret Agent," pp. 152–81.

53. Nagell on Cuban Missile Crisis's aftermath: letter to the author (April 18, 1976).

54. For further reading on the Cuban Missile Crisis, see Beschloss, *The Crisis Years;* David Detzer, *The Brink: Cuban Missile Crisis, 1962* (New York: Thomas Y. Crowell, 1979); and Robert F. Kennedy, Thirteen Days (New York: W. W. Norton, 1969). The latest book, by former intelligence officer Dino A. Brugioni, is *Eyeball to Eyeball: The Inside Story of the Cuban Missile Crisis* (New York: Random House, 1992).

Chapter X

Charles Willoughby correspondence quotes are from Willoughby papers, MacArthur Archives, Norfolk, Virginia.

Author's interview with Arthur Greenstein was on February 10, 1990.

Author's interview with Barney Hidalgo was on July 3, 1990.

Numbered notes are as follows:

1. RCN's KGB assignment: letter to Arthur Greenstein, (September 17, 1967).

2. RCN on "Bravo Club": outline returned to author (March 22, 1976).

3. Alpha 66 background: "Castro Foes Plan Five Raids Soon," *The New York Times* (September 14, 1962), p. 13; Daniel James, "Vow New Attacks on Ships for Castro," *New York Journal-American* (September 28, 1962), p. 2; "Exile Unit Vows New Raids," *The New York Times* (October 15, 1962).

4. Beck on double agents: Melvin Beck, *Secret Contenders* (New York: Sheridan Square Publications, 1984), pp. 98–99.

5. RCN on LHO assignment from Soviets: RCN interview with author (October 26, 1975); amended outline sent to author (January 1976).

6. Spas Raikin background: Warren Commission Report, p. 173; Peter Dale Scott, "From Dallas to Watergate," *Ramparts* (November 1973), p. 12 and passim.

7. ABN background: Russ Bellant, *Old Nazis, the New Right, and the Republican Party* (Boston: South End Press, 1988), pp. 67–78; Scott Anderson and Jon Lee Anderson, *Inside the League* (New York: Dodd, Mead,

1986), pp. 33–38. The spelling of Stetzko's name is taken from his letters to Charles Willoughby. Stetzko and his wife were guests at the Reagan White House in July 1983.

8. Willoughby/Dobriansky/ABN background: Peter Dale Scott, "The Dallas Conspiracy" (unpublished manuscript, 1971). Dobriansky, while chairman of the Ukrainian Congress Committee of America, was named Ronald Reagan's ambassador to the Bahamas in 1983 (Bellant, *Old Nazis,* p. 69).

9. Mexico City 1958 conference: Scott, ibid.

10. Diaz Verson: AARC files, Washington, D.C.

11. ABN lobbying: Scott "The Dallas Conspiracy."

12. Raikin on LHO: author's telephone interview (March 17, 1992).

13. Pierre and LHO: Edward Jay Epstein, *Legend* (New York: Reader's Digest Press/McGraw-Hill, 1978), pp. 156–57.

14. Raikin quote: author's interview, March 17, 1992.

15. Cato and defector: Epstein, *Legend,* p. 310.

16. LHO quote: WC 1.233, cited in Tom Miller, *The Assassination Please Almanac* (Chicago: Henry Regnery, 1977) p. 96.

17. LHO and FBI: Norman Kempster, "Warren Report Omitted Oswald Offer to FBI," *Washington Star* (October 8, 1975).

18. LHO letter to Soviet embassy: WC XVIII. 486.

19. CIA on Gerasimov: Epstein, *Legend,* pp. 164–65.

20. KGB and Oswald: RCN letter about John Barron's book *KGB* (New York: Reader's Digest Press, 1974), enclosed with cover letter to the author (February 27, 1978).

21. Fain visit to LHO: WC 1. 20; IV. 421; XVII. 736.

22. FBI on LHO: Kempster, "Warren Report Omitted."

23. Tolstoy Foundation subsidy: WC IX. 5.

24. Bouhe on Raigorodsky: WC VIII. 358, 453.

25. Bouhe on LHO: author's telephone interview (July 12, 1976).

26. "Nightingale"/CIA/Hunts: Miles Copeland, *Without Cloak or Dagger* (New York: Simon & Schuster, 1974), pp. 239–41.

27. Solidarists: E. H. Cookridge, *Gehlen: Spy of the Century* (New York: Random House, 1971), pp. 243–45.

28. Vlassov Army/Gehlen: Carl Oglesby, *The Yankee and Cowboy War* (New York: Berkley Medallion, 1977), pp. 38–43, 106.

29. Gehlen background: obituary, "Gehlen Dies at 77; Bonn's Ex-Spy Chief," *The New York Times,* (June 10, 1979); Carl Oglesby, "The Secret Treaty of Fort Hunt," *CovertAction* (Fall 1990), pp. 8–16; *Time-Life* library archives.

30. Voshinin on LHO: author's telephone interview (April 5, 1992).

31. Hoover on Minsk espionage: WC V. 105.

32. RCN on Maria del Carmen: author's interview (May 19, 1978).

33. Assassination attempt against Masferrer: RCN amendment of author's outline, March 1976. In an undated, typewritten page of "Trivia" sent to Greenstein, RCN alluded to a .22-caliber weapon being used not against Masferrer but possibly JFK. Nagell wrote: "Do you lurch violently backward when hit in back of the head with a 6.5mm bullet? [the alleged caliber of LHO's fatal shot]. Which way does your head bounce if you are hit in the front with a .22 caliber hornet hollow-point? . . . backward? Foreward? Sideways? Up? Down? Who did Franz Waehauf refer to the lil' ol' Silencer Maker? Does smokeless powder give off a gigantic white puff?"

34. Masferrer's death: "Ex-Batista Aide Killed by Bomb As He Starts His Auto in Miami," *The New York Times* (November 1, 1975).

35. RCN letter seeking "certain witness": Sent by Nagell (April 12, 1967) to "Fred J. Benjo," an alias used by his friend. In documents mailed to the author in January 1976, Nagell wrote concerning this letter that it "was returned marked 'not here' and 'moved.' "

36. RCN on contacting Waehauf: letter to Bernard Fensterwald, Jr. (April 22, 1974).

37. RCN quotes on trip to Texas, LHO: author's interview (October 26, 1975) amended outline sent author (see above).

38. RCN on CIA duties: "Man in the Middle" Addendum, January 28, 1970, to *Family* article. The addendum also notes: "My assignments required and necessitated travel to three Latin American nations and many states, including the Commonwealth of Puerto Rico. They also necessitated my taking on cover employment in New York and for about ten weeks in Los Angeles. . . ."

39. RCN on FBI approach: letter to Arthur Greenstein, October 8, 1967.

40. FBI file on RCN: July 30, 1975, referencing Reid report of February 4, 1964.

41. RCN on Cuban exiles: memorandum (April 18, 1967) from William R. Martin, assistant district attorney, to Jim Garrison, district attorney. Subject: Richard Case Nagell, Federal Prisoner No. PMB-A-16606-H Medical Center for Federal Prisoners, Springfield, Mo., pp. 5–6.

42. FBI file on RCN: July 30, 1975.

43. Amtorg background: Richard Deacon, *A History of the Russian Secret Service* (London: Frederick Muller, 1972) reports (p. 378) that the Soviets "established the Amtorg Trading Company which was financed by the sale of Romanoff jewels smuggled into America by merchant seamen. . . . Amtorg was manned by Soviet spies who were given the job of recruiting agents in the U.S.A."

44. Kornienko background: Hency Raymont, "Russian Is Ousted by U.S. In Spy Case," *The New York Times* (July 2, 1963), p. 1; *Time* (November 21, 1969), p. 34; "Soviet Specialist on U.S. Made Deputy to Gromyko," *The New York Times* (October 21, 1975).

45. FBI file on RCN: July 30, 1975, referencing 1964 report.
46. Bay Pines VA report on RCN: clinical social worker report (January 18, 1963), on file Court of Claims No. 1-73.
47. Bay Pines "Psychological Report": Court of Claims No. 1-73.
48. RCN on bomb plot against JFK: amended outline returned to author, 1976.
49. JFK trip to Florida, December 1962: "Kennedy to Address Rally of 'Bay of Pigs' Veterans," *The Philadelphia Inquirer* (December 28, 1962), p. 1; "The Return of Brigade 2506," *Time* (January 4, 1963), p. 13.
50. RCN and plot: letter to Greenstein, 1967; amended outline sent author, 1976. A William R. Martin memorandum of April 18, 1967, to Garrison notes that according to RCN, the first plot "had never really become serious and the plans never did reach more than just the talking stage."

Chapter XI

The author's interviews with George de Mohrenschildt were conducted on November 3, 1975 and July 14, 1976, in Dallas.
Numbered notes are as follows:
1. Oswald in Dallas: Background is derived primarily from Albert H. Newman, *The Assassination of John F. Kennedy: The Reasons Why* (New York: Clarkson N. Potter, 1970), pp. 261–62; Edward Jay Epstein, *Legend* (New York: Reader's Digest Press/McGraw-Hill, 1978), pp. 191–92 (wage at JCS).
2. JCS work/"microdots": Epstein, *Legend*, pp. 193–96; WC XVI. 53.
3. LHO, film, cameras: Earl Golz, "Dallas Camera Disappeared During FBI Investigation," *Dallas Morning News* (June 15, 1978), and Golz, "Oswald Pictures released by FBI," *Dallas Morning News* (August 7, 1978). Also, Anthony Summers, *Conspiracy* (New York: McGraw-Hill, 1980), pp. 231–32.
4. De Mohrenschildt getting LHO job: Warren Commission Report, p. 719; Summers, *Conspiracy*, p. 230. According to Epstein, *Legend* (p. 189), Oswald's mother also had the impression the baron had arranged for her son's employment.
5. De Mohrenschildt background: WC IX. 166–285 (his testimony); Summers, *Conspiracy*, pp. 222–26; Epstein, *Legend*, pp. 177–83.
6. Voshinin on Houston: WC VIII. 469–70.
7. De Mohrenschildt and John Mecom: WC IX. 211. And Brown brothers: WC IX. 17, 214. According to Rowland Evans and Robert Novak's book *Lyndon B. Johnson: The Exercise of Power* (New York: New American Library, 1966), p. 332. the Brown brothers "became Lyndon Johnson's personal vehicle for a lateral movement into the center of the new oil power." The Brown Foundation in Houston was later identified as a conduit for CIA funds.
8. De Mohrenschildt and De Menil: WC IX. 16 notes that De Menil was a "very close friend" of Paul Raigorodsky, who arranged for de Mohrenschildt to meet De Menil on a business matter in 1962. In April 1961, David Ferrie and others raided an explosives bunker owned by De Menil in Houma, south of New Orleans, taking land mines and hand grenades and storing them.
9. De Mohrenschildt-LBJ White House letters: December 27, 1966, and January 6, 1967, respectively. A State Department memorandum of January 14, 1967, from executive secretary Benjamin H. Read to Walt W. Rostow notes: "The Department's reply to Mr. de Mohrenschildt should be considered a *de minimus* response to his letter of December 27 to the President. A lengthy file in the Office of Special Consular Services clearly indicates that de Mohrenschildt is an unstable and unreliable individual who would not hesitate to misuse or misrepresent even the slightest expression of interest."
10. Bush name in de Mohrenschildt notebook: Mark Lane, *Plausible Denial* (New York: Thunder's Mouth Press, 1991), p. 332. Lane also notes odd similarities among Bush's Zapata Offshore oil company, the "Operation Zapata" code name given the Bay of Pigs, and the names of two of the invasion's ships: *Barbara* (Bush's wife's name) and *Houston* (Bush's business abode).
11. Bush-de Mohrenschildt relationship: Anthony L. Kimery, "In the Company of Friends," *CovertAction* (Summer 1992), pp. 60–66. Kimmery maintains that Bush and de Mohrenschildt met through the auspices of Henry Neil Mallon, board chairman of Dresser Industries, in the late 1940s.
12. De Mohrenschildt and Mikoyan: Tad Szulc, "Friend of Oswalds Knew Mrs. Kennedy," *The New York Times* (November 24, 1964).
13. De Mohrenschildt walking tours: WC IX. 213–17.
14. De Mohrenschildt letter to State: CIA file No. 431-154B (December 30, 1963); declassified May 1976.
15. De Mohrenschildt early history/CIA ties: CIA file, ibid.; CIA file No. 18-522, declassified April 1976; Epstein, *Legend;* author's telephone interview with Clare Petty (July 4, 1992). See also HSCA XII. 49–52.
16. De Mohrenschildt on Moore: Edward Jay Epstein, *The Assassination Chronicles* (New York: Carroll & Graf, 1992), pp. 555–69.
17. Moore on de Mohrenschildt: HSCA XII. 54–55.
18. Epstein, *The Assassination Chronicles*, p. 559.
19. Natasha Voshinin on de Mohrenschildt: author's telephone interview (April 5, 1992).
20. Jeanne de Mohrenschildt as accused Comunist: WCD 533.69; 539.1, as reported by Robert LeGon to Dallas special agents Hosty and Kuykendahl.
21. De Mohrenschildt on Jeanne and LHO: HSCA XII. 185.
22. De Mohrenschildt on LHO in Japan: ibid., p. 83.
23. De Mohrenschildt on LHO/Cuba: ibid., pp. 308–9. The baron's manuscript contains many interesting "anecdotes" about LHO, pp. 69–315.

24. RCN on de Mohrenschildt: author's interviews (October 26 and 28, 1975).

25. RCN on de Mohrenschildt/LHO relationship: letter to author (April 8, 1976).

26. Fensterwald memo: May 31, 1978.

27. Bouhe on de Mohrenschildt: author's telephone interview (July 12, 1976).

28. Oltmans on de Mohrenschildt: Willem Oltmans, "The Missing General," *Gallery* (March 1978), p. 43–.

29. De Mohrenschildt death: Robert Barkdoll, "Kennedy Case Figure Died as He'd Lived," *Los Angeles Times* (April 3, 1977); "Assassination: Now a Suicide Talks," *Time* (April 11, 1977), p. 20; Mark Lane, "The Mysterious Death of a Key JFK Witness," *Gallery* (November 1977), p. 41–.

30. Jeanne de Mohrenschildt on husband's death: author's telephone interview (September 1, 1978).

31. RCN on de Mohrenschildt death: author's interview (July 27, 1984).

32. Oltmans testimony: Wendell Rawls, Jr., "Witness Ties Oswald to Oilmen and Cubans," *The New York Times* (April 2, 1977), p. 1.

33. Fonzi on Oltmans: author's telephone interview (April 15, 1977).

34. FBI on Oltmans: Bishop to DeLoach memo re I. Irving Davidson (obtained by author from Edward Cohen).

35. Oltmans background: Wendell Rawls, Jr., "Dutch Journalist in Kennedy Case Is 'Half Showman,' Colleague Says," *The New York Times* (April 12, 1977).

36. Oltmans on Donaldson/Japanese article: Oltmans, "The Missing General."

37. Auchincloss letter: WC XIX. 557.

38. De Mohrenschildt on assassination: testimony of Mrs. Igor Voshinin, WC VIII. 446–47. On March 29, 1964, de Mohrenschildt's son-in-law Gary Taylor testified before the Warren Commission: "Well, the only thing that occurred to me was that—and I guess it was from the beginning—that if there was any assistance or plotters in the assassination that it was, in my opinion, most probably the de Mohrenschildts." (Cited in Lane, "Mysterious Death.")

Chapter XII

The documents, both Nagell's letters and official hospital reports, dating from RCN's stay at the Bay Pines Veterans Administration Hospital were all found by the author in records of Court of Claims Case No. 1-73.

The author's interviews with Cuban exile Antonio Veciana were conducted in Miami on June 15, 17, and 19, 1976. Some of this material appeared in articles by the author for *New Times* magazine, "Three Witnesses" (June 24, 1977), p. 31–36, and *The Village Voice,* "This Man Is a Missing Link" (August 14, 1978), p. 1.

Numbered notes are as follows:

1. RCN on JFK letter: letter to author (February 27, 1978). RCN's original letter is on file at the John F. Kennedy Memorial Library, Boston, Massachusetts.

2. RCN hospital discharge: In a filing at the CC, Nagell states he was discharged on January 20, 1963.

3. RCN on hospital diagnosis: letter to attorney William Ohlhausen (May 18, 1975).

4. RCN at Holiday Inn: author's interview (October 28, 1975).

5. RCN contacting FBI: comments on William R. Martin memorandum to Garrison, sent to author January 1976.

6. FBI on RCN: Reid report (February 4, 1964) referenced in 1975 FBI file.

7. RCN on "tortillas": letter to Greenstein, 1967.

8. RCN on The Tacos: Comments on Martin memo.

9. RCN using "Kramer" alias: notarized affidavit (November 21, 1975).

10. Military Intelligence file: "Agent Report" (May 2, 1969) (see Chapter One).

11. RCN on monitoring exiles: author's interview (October 5, 1977).

12. Castro reaction to Cuban Missile Crisis: Daniel Ellsberg, "The Day Castro Almost Started World War III," *The New York Times* (October 31, 1987). Michael R. Beschloss's *The Crisis Years* (New York: Edward Burlingame Books, 1991), p. 543, reports Castro's reaction to the settlement: "Kicking the wall, shattering a mirror, Castro denounced the Chairman [Khrushchev] as a 'son of a bitch . . . a bastard . . . an asshole,' a leader with 'no cojones' and later, a 'maricon' [homosexual]. He refused Alexeyev's desperate telephone calls." At a 1989 conference on the Cuban Missile Crisis in Moscow, Khrushchev's son Sergei recounted that Castro had even urged Khrushchev to fire nuclear weapons at the United States. Bill Keller, " '62 Missile Crisis Yields New Puzzle," *The New York Times* (January 30, 1989).

13. CIA plots against Castro: *Alleged Assassination Plots Involving Foreign Leaders,* U.S. Senate (1975), pp. 85–86.

14. Exiles' reaction to JFK: *Time* archives file (February 13, 1963); Tad Szulc, "Cuban Exile Leader Out in Rift with U.S.," *The New York Times* (April 10, 1963), p. 1; Max Frankel, "Cuban Exiles Near Total Break with Washington," *The New York Times* (April 17, 1963), p. 1.

15. Artime on RFK meeting: author's interview (October 1976), Miami.

16. Artime and bases: Warren Hinckle and William Turner, *The Fish Is Red* (New York: Harper & Row, 1981), pp. 148–49.

17. Artime on Kennedy betrayal: author's interview.

18. RCN on surveilling exiles: addendum "Man in the Middle," January 28, 1970, to *Family* article.

19. Del Valle and Trafficante: Hinckle and Turner, *The Fish Is Red,* p. 206.

20. Tarabocchia on del Valle: author's interview (December 19, 1975).

21. Del Valle/Ferrie: Hinckle and Turner, *The Fish Is Red,* p. 206. See also Robert Morrow, *The Senator Must Die* (Santa Monica, Calif.: Roundtable, 1988), pp. 31, 73.

22. Del Valle's force: Joseph Martin and Phil Santora, "Countdown for Castro," New York *Daily News* (January 8, 1961).

23. Del Valle/Free Cuba: Anthony Summers, *Conspiracy* (New York: McGraw-Hill, 1980), p. 347.

24. Del Valle's death: ibid., p. 498. See also Charles Golden, "Mystery Miami Murder Linked to JFK Plot," *National Enquirer* (April 30, 1967).

25. Ferrie's death: Jim Garrison, *On the Trail of the Assassins* (New York: Sheridan Square Press, 1988), pp. 140–44.

26. Ferrie background: HSCA X. 105–22.

27. Arcacha-Smith background: ibid., pp. 109–12. Trips to Mexico: Memo from Frank Klein to Jim Garrison re interview of Carlos Quiroga (January 13, 1966).

28. Tarabocchia on Masferrer: author's interview.

29. Masferrer background: Humberto Cruz and Hilda Inclan, " 'El Tigre' Died as He Lived—by Violence," *Miami News* (November 1, 1975); Morrow, *The Senator Must Die,* pp. 14–17.

30. RCN on Angel/Leopoldo: amended outline returned to author (March 22, 1976).

31. RCN on Angel in Miami: letter to Fensterwald (March 21, 1975).

32. RCN on "Rangel/Wrangel" surname: letter to Fensterwald (May 8, 1975).

33. Description of Angel: March 1, 1969, memo by Jones Harris (lists Angel as "Wrangel").

34. RCN on Angel/Leopoldo: author's interviews (October 5, 1977 and May 19, 1978).

35. For the HSCA's account of its interviews with Veciana, see HSCA X. 37–56.

36. Veciana and Alpha 66: "Castro Foes Plan Five Raids Soon," *The New York Times* (September 14, 1962); "Exile Unit Vows New Raids," *The New York Times,* October 15, 1962); Daniel James, "Vow New Attacks on Ships for Castro," *New York Journal-American* (September 28, 1962), p. 2.

37. Hidalgo on Alpha 66: author's interview (July 3, 1990).

38. Exile commando raids: "U.S. Curbs Miami Exiles to Prevent Raids on Cuba," *The New York Times* (April 1, 1963), p. 1; Tad Szulc, "British Capture 17 Cuban Exiles and Raiding Boat," *The New York Times* (April 2, 1963), p. 1; "U.S. Strengthens Checks on Raiders," *The New York Times* (April 6, 1963); "Chronology of Cuban Incidents," *The Christian Science Monitor* (April 4, 1963).

39. Andres Nasario Sargen: author's interview (June 15, 1976).

40. Exile violence: City of Miami interoffice memorandum, "Information concerning Cuban activity," from Detective Sergeant C. H. Sapp, Intelligence Unit, to A. W. Anderson, assistant chief of police (April 4, 1963).

41. Congress of Freedom meeting: "Third Decade Document Discovery: the Congress of Freedom Papers," *The Third Decade: A Journal of Research on the John F. Kennedy Assassination,* Vol. 2, No. 2 (January 1986).

42. Texas flyer: William Manchester, *The Death of a President* (New York: Harper & Row, 1967), p. 46.

43. Willoughby on Bay of Pigs: letter to Allen Dulles (June 2, 1961).

44. Cubans fleeing island: RG-23, Willoughby papers, Series 1, *Foreign Intelligence Digest,* Miscellaneous.

45. Kohly letter to H. L. Hunt: Robert Morrow files. For an enlightening view of the Vatican's secret ties to U.S. intelligence and underground groups through the years, see "Special: Nazis, the Vatican, and CIA," *CovertAction* Information Bulletin No. 25 (Winter 1986), p. 27–38.

46. Exiles and Texas money: author's telephone interview with Gerry Patrick Hemming (April 4, 1992).

47. RCN on Tony Cuesta: author's interviews (October 5, 1977, and May 19, 1978).

48. Arcacha-Smith at Hunt offices: author's interviews with Paul Rothermel, Jr. (July 12–13, 1976).

49. Gaudet on Arcacha-Smith: transcript of taped interview with Fensterwald and Allan Stone (May 13, 1975).

50. Arcacha-Smith and Walker: author's interviews with Paul Rothermel, Jr.

Chapter XIII

The author's interviews with General Edwin A. Walker were conducted in Dallas (November 2, 1975) and by telephone (March 23, 1976; June 24 and July 15, 1992).

The author's interviews with Bradford Angers were conducted by telephone (March 24, June 24, and June 27, 1992).

Numbered notes are as follows:

1. RCN-Pentagon correspondence: on file Court of Claims, No. 1-73.

2. LHO pistol order/loan repayment: Edward Jay Epstein, *Legend* (New York: Reader's Digest Press/McGraw-Hill, 1978), p. 203.

3. LHO and SWP, August 1962: Albert H. Newman, *The Assassination of John F. Kennedy* (New York: Clarkson N. Potter, 1970), pp. 246–48, citing WC XIX. 571, 576.

4. LHO application rejected: Warren Commission Report, VI. 289.

5. LHO offer to SWP, pamphlet orders, missing correspondence: Newman, *Assassination,* pp. 292–95; Epstein, *Legend,* p. 202. Author Newman points out that Bob Chester, a volunteer worker at the SWP's New York headquarters, acknowledged receiving a sample of Oswald's photographic reproduction, which he vaguely recalled "were of headlines from *The Militant.*" Oswald, however, did not subscribe to *The Militant* until December 17, 1962, nine days after his letter offering help to the SWP. This raises the question of where he obtained the headlines to photograph. "A reinvestigation of the John F. Kennedy case must examine this period with the greatest care," Newman writes.

6. RCN on Soviet code names: author's interviews (May 19, 1978, and July 27, 1984).

7. Marina on LHO wanting her to return USSR: WC I. 10, 12.

8. Marina quote: WC I. 35.

9. Marina letter to Soviet embassy: WC XVIII. 501–2.

10. Gerasimov: Epstein, *Legend,* p. 207.

11. Reznichenko reply: WC XVIII. 503–5.

12. Hosty visit: Newman, *Assassination,* p. 319.

13. Marina sending items to embassy: WC XVIII. 506–13.

14. CIA photos of RCN outside Soviet embassy: Fensterwald memo (May 31, 1978).

15. RCN Soviet assignment on Marina: Fensterwald memo (December 5, 1973).

16. Military Intelligence on RCN/Marina: 1969 "Agent Report", Thomas J. Hench, 766th Military Detachment.

17. RCN on Marina: author's interview (October 26, 1975).

18. RCN in Los Angeles: FBI 1964 Reid report, cited in FBI report, July 30, 1975.

19. FBI on RCN/Secret Service/Marina: Report by special agent Thomas B. White, Jr. (January 2, 1964) File EP 105-1264.

20. Weisheit on RCN: author's telephone interview (December 10, 1976).

21. Secret Service detail report: WCD 379; SS CO-2-34,030.

22. RCN on Secret Service/Marina: letter to Richard Popkin (June 30, 1975).

23. Walker's manifesto: *Time* "Chronology of Walker Case," file (November 29, 1961).

24. McNamara directive: Seymour Martin Lipset and Earl Raab, *The Politics of Unreason* 2d ed. (Chicago: University of Chicago Press, 1978), p. 314.

25. Thurmond/John Birch Society on Walker: ibid., pp. 314–15.

26. Walker in politics: "Another Lost 'Cause,' " *New York Journal-American* (October 2, 1962).

27. Walker in Mississippi: Newman, *Assassination,* pp. 254–55, citing "Thousands Coming to Aid Mississippi, Walker Says," *Fort Worth Star-Telegram* (September 30, 1963).

28. Walker to Springfield: Newman, *Assassination,* p. 255.

29. Gale on Walker: Cheri Seymour, *Committee of the States,* (Mariposa, Ca.: Camden Place Communications, 1991), p. 89.

30. Walker's return, Oswald's move: Newman, *Assassination,* pp. 256–7.

31. A Mississippi grand jury's refusal to indict Walker was headlined on the front page of the *Dallas Morning News* (January 22, 1963). On February 14, Dallas papers reported that Walker would join Hargis's tour in Miami on February 27.

32. Volkmar Schmidt and LHO: Epstein, *Legend,* pp. 203–5, 318. Marina meeting Paine: pp. 206–7. Author Epstein elaborated to me about Schmidt's interest in hypnosis, which is not mentioned in *Legend*.

33. Paine on LHO: author's interview (August 6, 1976), Philadelphia.

34. LHO at Walker house/mailing for rifle/taking it to work: Epstein, *Legend,* pp. 209–10.

35. LHO's firing: WC XXII. 161, XXIV. 872; Graef testimony, WC X. 184–88.

36. LHO photos: WC XVI. 510. Marina testimony: WC I. 15–16. When arrested for the assassination and confronted with a blowup of the picture, Oswald claimed that his face had been superimposed over someone else's torso and that he had never seen the photo before. Despite conjecture for years over their authenticity, an HSCA panel of experts concluded in 1979 that the pictures were authentic. See Anthony Summers, *Conspiracy* (New York: McGraw-Hill, 1980), pp. 94–99 for the most detailed analysis of the faked-photographs possibility.

37. LHO letter to FPCC: Newman, *Assassination,* p. 328.

38. HUAC on Lamont: *Guide to the American Left* (Kansas City, Mo.: Laird M. Wilcox, 1969) p. 410.

39. Lamont on "Crime Against Cuba": author's telephone interview (January 4, 1992).

40. RCN and Lamont pamphlet: discovered by author among RCN case files, office of attorney Joseph Calamia, El Paso, in 1976; photocopy in author's possession.

41. LHO and photos: Epstein, *Legend,* p. 210. That the picture was indeed sent to *The Militant* was confirmed in 1992 to researcher Gus Russo, who in turn shared this information with the author.

42. Michael Paine on LHO/Walker: WC II. 402–4.

43. Ruth Paine on LHO and *The Militant:* author's interview, ibid. There has been some question about when this conversation with Michael Paine took place, but Ruth Paine indicated to me that it probably was in the spring of 1963.

44. LHO and rifle: Epstein, *Legend,* p. 211. Leaving JCS: Newman, *Assassination,* p. 333.

45. Surrey sighting: WC V. 446–49 (Surrey testimony).

46. Coleman testimony: HSCA Report p. 98, n. 4; WC XXVI. 437ff.; XVI. 753. Detailed in Summers, *Conspiracy,* pp. 243–44.

In the AARC files there is an unsigned letter from an ex-serviceman that relates to the Walker shooting—and the possibility that its origin emanated from the military or the CIA. The letter states:

I enlisted in the Army, March 18, 1962 and after basic and advanced infantry training at Ft. Ord, Calif. I was transferred to Ft. Benning, Ga. for jump school. September of 1962 I was assigned to Ft. Bragg, NC (2/501st HQ co.—that was the system at the time). . . .

During October 1962 and again in Feb. 1963 I was interviewed by two warrant officers at Ft. Bragg. After several meetings at a small Spanish type cafe near the train station I agreed to undergo some special weapons training for an overseas assignment. They explained that I would be given additional up to date briefings in Germany and that from there I would be flown into Riga, Latvia USSR for an assassination case. As I had a confidential clearance, they stated it was all right for them to discuss the basic details with me and also said that I could refuse the assignment, but in any case I would have to remain quiet about it. The Riga operation entailed some Colonel in the Soviet Army that was infiltrating a CIA team which was supplying some weapons for a rebellion. The warrant officers said that no one would believe me if I said anything anyway, and that after I did, I would be placed incommunicado and given "treatment." I had no reason to say anything at that time to anyone, but within the last few years I believe that an effort has been made to seriously neutralize my position. They attempted to say I was incompetent once in 1969 and after a transfer to Springfield Medical Center their assertions were proven untrue.

During Feb. 1963 I was told that my assignment was going to be in the United States and that the target was Major General Edwin Walker. Then, late in that month, I was told to forget that assignment, that someone else had been chosen. . . .

47. Marina on LHO and Walker: WC I. 16. Warren Commission Report conclusions: Ch. IV. 183, 187. LHO keeping material: Epstein *Legend,* p. 213. The HSCA looked into the dispute over whether Oswald actually fired at Walker, and concluded in *The Final Assassinations Report* (New York: Bantam Books, 1979), p. 59: "The committee's firearms panel examined the bullet fragment that was removed from the wall in the home of General Walker and found that it had characteristics similar to bullets fired from Oswald's Mannlicher-Carcano rifle. In addition, neutron activation analysis of this fragment confirmed that it was probably a Mannlicher-Carcano bullet. . . ." The HSCA also verified Oswald's handwriting on the note to Marina and concluded "that the evidence strongly suggested that Oswald attempted to murder General Walker. . . ."

48. Car photograph mystery: Summers, *Conspiracy,* pp. 244–45; WC XVI. 7 (missing tag), XXII. 582 (police testimony); Jesse Curry, *JFK Assassination File* (Dallas, Texas: American Poster and Printing, 1969), p. 113, exhibit 55.

49. Munich newspaper: Peter Dale Scott, "The Dallas Conspiracy" (unpublished manuscript, 1971).

50. "Colonel Caster": WC testimony of Mrs. C. L. Connell, cited in Paris Flammonde, *The Kennedy Conspiracy* (New York: Meredith, 1969), p. 125.

51. Castorr and Walker: transcript, Harold Weisberg interview, Colonel and Mrs. Robert Castorr (January 30, 1968), p. 39.

52. Curington on LHO/Walker: author's telephone interview (May 12, 1992).

53. Marina on de Mohrenschildt's remarks: WC V. 619. At earlier testimony, Marina recalled the baron saying: "Lee, how is it possible that you missed?" (WC I. 18).

54. De Mohrenschildt's explanation to WC: Epstein, *Legend,* p. 213.

55. Voshinin on de Mohrenschildt/reporting to FBI: author's interview (April 5, 1992).

56. De Mohrenschildt on CIA knowledge/LHO and Walker: Edward Jay Epstein, *The Assassination Chronicles* (New York: Carroll & Graf, 1992), p. 560.

57. CIA expedite check: CIA memo, No. 431-154B (December 30, 1963); declassified May 1976.

58. Kail quote: HSCA XII. 57.

59. Prouty on Matlack: author's telephone interview (June 19, 1992).

60. De Mohrenschildt in D.C.: HSCA XII. 57.

61. Pierce on de Mohrenschildt/Charles/RCN: Fensterwald memo to Gary Shaw, Mary Ferrell (June 30, 1983).

62. RCN on de Mohrenschildt/Haiti: letter to Fensterwald (February 26, 1975).

63. De Mohrenschildt/Dulles: Author's interview with Fletcher Prouty, June 10, 1992.

64. De Mohrenschildt in Haiti: HSCA XII. 57–61.

65. De Mohrenschildt reaction to assassination: WC. IX. 274.

66. Larrie Schmidt background: Patricia Swank, "A Plot That Flopped," *Look* (January 26, 1965), pp. 28–29.

67. Schmidt letters: WC XVIII. 836–63 (CEs 1032–40).

68. Willoughby and YAF: Group Research, Inc. (GRI), fact sheet on CW (March 11, 1963).

69. Willoughby and Larrie Schmidt: Source of author's interview requested anonymity.

70. International Committee geographical links: Bruce Cumings, *The Origins of the Korean War,* Vol. II (Princeton, N.J.: Princeton University Press, 1990), p. 105.

71. Hargis/Hunt/ICDCC: CW papers, MacArthur Archives.

72. Willoughby and H. L. Hunt: author's telephone interviews with Paul Rothermel, Jr., and John Curington (June 1992).

73. Walker on Willoughby: telephone interview (July 15, 1992). Walker added: "He knew Asia better than anybody in the whole Washington setup." According to GRI files, Willoughby preceded Walker as military editor of the John Birch Society's *American Mercury* magazine.

74. Walker on Hunt: author's telephone interview, ibid.

75. Willoughby and Schmidt: anonymous author's source.

76. Schmidt in Munich PIO: author's telephone interview with Bernard Weissman (June 29, 1992).

77. Walker in Germany: Newman, *Assassination,* p. 205.

78. Bob Schmidt hired by Walker: Swank, "A Plot That Flopped."

79. Schmidt letters: WC XVIII. 836–63 (CEs 1032–40).

80. Weissman and black-bordered ad: WC V. 487–535 (on Grinnan, 504–6). See also XI. 428–34 on CUSA.

81. Schmidt on Weissman's name: Swank, "A Plot That Flopped," p. 29.

82. Weissman on Schmidt and ad: author's interview.

83. This section is all derived from two Group Research, Inc., Washington, D.C., reports on the Anti-Communist Liaison's two-day strategy seminar.

Chapter XIV

The majority of this chapter focuses on Vaughn Marlowe, whom the author interviewed by telephone (December 10, 1976) and at Newport, Oregon (August 2, 1990).

Numbered notes are as follows:

1. Alpha 66 in L.A.: FBI file (May 28, 1964), "Second National Front of Escambray (Operation Alpha 66)", CD 1085C3; declassified 1970.

2. In the amended outline RCN returned to the author early in 1976, there is this sentence: "He also conducted surveillances on or was briefed about Angel/Leopoldo, though not in Florida [January 1963], and not until much later." Since both exiles came to be involved in the June 1963 plot to assassinate JFK, the author believes this briefing must have taken place in the spring.

3. RCN on Leopoldo training: author's interview (April 11, 1977).

4. Exiles and Fort Jackson: author's conversation with Peter Dale Scott (January 16, 1981).

5. Fort Jackson commandos: attachment to Miami police memo (April 4, 1963), from Detective Sergeant C. H. Sapp to A. W. Anderson.

6. Leopoldo description: Jones Harris memo to Garrison (March 1, 1969).

7. Origin of Leopoldo name: RCN letter to author (May 5, 1976).

8. FBI on Valdes/Howard: FBI file, Los Angeles, "Second National Front of Escambray (Operation Alpha 66)" (May 2, 1963).

9. Alpha 66 branches: FBI file, ibid. (May 8, 1963).

10. Unity efforts: FBI file No. 105-112098, San Juan, Puerto Rico, report of John L. Spurgers, Jr., p. 3. Eloy Gutierrez Menoyo was identified as "in charge of military operations for this combined group." Amaury Fraginals was identified as having replaced Veciana, then confined to Miami, as "spokesman and fund-raiser" in San Juan.

11. Sargen in L.A.: FBI file, Los Angeles (May 21, 1963).

12. Valdes as G-2 agent: FBI file (May 28, 1964).

13. RCN and inquiry into Communist Party, U.S.A.: memo from RCN to Los Angeles Police Department Organized Crime Intelligence Division, Attn.: Sgt. Neil K. Spotts and Sgt. John White (August 6, 1971).

14. RCN on JFK plot in L.A.: Amended outline returned to author, March 1976.

15. Marlowe letter to Garrison: March 23, 1967.

16. RCN on Marlowe investigation: letter to Fensterwald (April 1, 1974).

17. Marlowe-RCN correspondence: December 13, 1975; RCN reply on January 22, 1976.

18. RCN photos of Angel/Leopoldo: letter to Fensterwald (March 21, 1975). On March 6, the attorney had written Nagell, asking: "Was one of the two [exiles] in the June, and September, projects photographed in Mexico City?" Nagell responded in his March 21 letter:

I assume that we were all photographed in Mexico at one time or another by the Mexican intelligence/security services. If so, I would further assume that both the CIA and the FBI (and probably State's Bureau of Research & Intelligence) were automatically furnished photos of "Angel," "Leopoldo" and Oswald. However, I don't know this for a fact. I have no idea where or when the photo that my contact had of Oswald was taken, though it did not appear to be posed. . . .

In 1962 and 1963 Mexican authorities (presumably at the instance of the CIA) had a camera positioned across the street from the main entrance to the Cuban Embassy compound. This camera photographed everybody who entered and exited the premises; it was equipped with an infra-red device.

19. RCN on L.A. plot: amended outline.

20. RCN at L.A. VA Hospital: RCN filing in Court of Claims No. 1-73; FBI February 1964 Reid report; cited in FBI report, July 30, 1975; FBI file, September 25, 1963, report of special agent Thomas B. White, Jr., dictated September 23, 1963.

21. JFK trip to L.A.: Tom Wicker, "Navy Demonstrates Might to President," *The New York Times* (June 8, 1963), p. 1.

22. JFK in L.A.: Don Irwin, "President Wooing the West," New York *Herald Tribune* (June 8, 1963).

23. JFK and pickets: Associated Press, "Kennedy Lands on Roof, Avoiding Racial Pickets," *The New York Times* (June 8, 1963), p. 8.

24. JFK dinner: Wicker, "Navy Demonstrates," p. 1.

25. RCN driving cab: letters to Greenstein, undated.

26. RCN and foreign proposal: January 6, 1964, statement to FBI, on file in archives U.S. District Court, *USA v. Nagell*, Fort Worth, Texas.

27. RCN on conspiracy: two-page typewritten "Proposed Testimony," Richard C. Nagell (September 19, 1966), U.S. District Court, El Paso, Texas.

Chapter XV

Numbered notes are as follows:

1. The old envelope from the FPCC to Oswald is FBI exhibit 413 in the National Archives.

2. V. T. Lee background: *Time* file from Fred Smith, Tampa (October 4, 1962); Guy Richards, "Mystery N.Y. 'Contact' of Oswald Revealed," *New York Journal-American* (December 8, 1963), p. 1. At testimony before the Senate Internal Security Subcommittee on February 14, 1963, Lee was asked if he was Clarence Theodore Lee, but he took the Fifth Amendment. The *Time* correspondent lists Lee's real name as V. T. Tappin, born to Mr. and Mrs. Charles Tappin in New York City in 1927.

3. Lee in L.A.: "Cubans Freer Under Castro, Backer Claims," *Los Angeles Times* (April 5, 1963).

4. LHO letter to FPCC and reply: WC X. 87.

5. FBI on Lee: WCD 1085E1, p. 4.

6. FBI/LHO/FPCC: HSCA V. 90.

7. LHO arrival New Orleans: Edward Jay Epstein, *Legend* (New York: Reader's Digest Press/McGraw-Hill, 1978), pp. 215–16.

8. FBI Lee files, May 6–7: WCD 1085E1, p. 4.

9. Reily and Cuban exiles: Anthony Summers, *Conspiracy* (New York: McGraw-Hill, 1980), p. 313.

10. LHO references: Albert H. Newman, *The Assassination of John F. Kennedy* (New York: Clarkson N. Potter, 1970), p. 354.

11. LHO to FPCC: Newman, *Assassination,* p. 356.

12. LHO/*The Militant:* WC XIX. 567.

13. LHO FPCC membership: WC XX. 512–13 (Lee exhibit 2).

14. Hosty visit: HSCA V. 90.

15. Lee response: WC XX. 514–16 (Lee exhibit 3).

16. LHO ordering handbills: WC XXII. 796–98.

17. Lee on FPCC: WCD 6, p. 481.

18. LHO P.O. box: Newman, *Assassination,* p. 360. LHO order: WC XXII. 800–801.

19. FBI Security Indexes: *Supplementary Detailed Staff Reports on Intelligence Activities and the Rights of Americans,* Book III. Final Report of the Select Committee to Study Governmental Operations with Respect to Intelligence Activities, U.S. Senate (April 23, 1976), pp. 467–69.

20. RCN letter to Senator Russell: January 3, 1967.

21. RCN on FPCC: author's interview (October 26, 1975).

22. RCN on FPCC "scam": letter to author (May 13, 1976).

23. Police on FPCC: "Letter from J. S. De la Llana, Sgt., Supervisor, Intelligence Unit to Joseph I. Giarrusso, Superintendent of Police, New Orleans, Attention: Capt. P. J. Trosclair, Re: Fair Play for Cuba Committee" (December 17, 1962). AARC files.

24. Police interview with LHO: "Interoffice Correspondence, To: Major Presly J. Trosclair, Jr., From: Sgt. Horace J. Austin & Patn. Warren Roberts" (August 12, 1963). AARC files.

25. Trosclair on LHO: author's telephone interview (March 2, 1992).

26. Smith on FPCC: "Memorandum, May 8, 1978, To: G. Robert Blakey from Gaeton Fonzi Re: Interview with Joseph Burkholder Smith." Author's telephone interview (April 8, 1992).

27. Cuban/Chinese plot allegations: CIA/FBI files (December 6 and 7, 1963). Individuals named in government documents include Raul Savedra, "a high official in the Cuban Ministry of Interior for Commerce"; Fernandez Feito; and a Mexican called "Camacho"—"small, fat, with lots of black hair. Under a respectable business cover he appears to be the real head of an 'action-reseau' (action net) covering all of Texas and even, perhaps, part of Mexico. . . . CAMACHO also seems to be a close friend of two Mexican millionaires named PASQUEL or PASCUAL, who are involved in Mexican and/or Texan petroleum and who do not know the secret real activities of the former." (Quotes are from April 15, 1964, CIA file.)

28. V. T. Lee: Guy Richards, "Mystery N.Y. 'Contact.' "

29. China reaction to Cuban Missile Crisis: John Gittings, *Survey of the Sino-Soviet Dispute* (Oxford University Press, 1968), p. 183.

30. Mao backing Castro: ibid., p. 384.

31. Khrushchev letter to Castro: David Binder, "In Letter, Khrushchev Tells of Mockery Over Cuba Crisis," *The New York Times* (January 22, 1992).

32. China on Test-Ban Treaty: *Peking Review* (August 2, 1963). In the author's interview with Oswald acquaintance Ruth Paine, she noted "the possible connection between the timing of Cuba endorsing China and Oswald's application for a visa" [to Cuba, in Mexico City that September].

33. Consideration of bombing China: author's conversation with Jones Harris, citing 1963 article (April 20, 1990).

34. RCN on Mexico City principals: letter to Greenstein, undated (1967).

35. RCN on Ben Tue Wong: author's interview (July 27, 1984).

36. China-Cuba drug smuggling: *Time* file (October 4, 1962) from José Ferrer (New York Bureau), cites Enrique Abascal as source on Cuba financing: ". . . the Fidelistas have turned to dope peddling. Their source of the stuff is Communist China through Castro, says Abascal. Narcotics, unattributively, says pro-Castroite, traffic mostly in cocaine grown in South America. The Fidelistas move into the dope market has forced them further underground. Not only is the Narcotics Bureau after them; they have also earned the wrath of the Mafia,

who resent having the market cut in on. Other Castro exiles unanimously agree with Abascal that the Fidelistas are pushing dope. And it now seems to be their primary source of money."

37. Japanese Communist Party: "Young Bae Kim, The Japanese Communist Party and the Soviet Union: A Pattern of Coalition and Conflict, 1945–69" (master's thesis, University of Kansas, 1974).

38. L.A. left and Cuba: author's interview with Vaughn Marlowe (August 2, 1990).

39. RCN on missing items/Roberts: letter to Fensterwald (September 11, 1974).

40. Roberts obituary: Milton Alvin, "A Socialist Fighter Dies," *The Militant* (October 30, 1967), p. 6.

41. Al Lewis on Roberts: author's telephone interview (October 28, 1986).

42. RCN on Roberts: author's interview (October 26, 1975).

43. RCN monitoring HUAC witness: author's interview (October 28, 1975).

44. HUAC hearings: Gene Blake, "Cuba Travel Probe in Stormy Session," *Los Angeles Times* (July 2, 1963), p. 1; Blake, "12 Who Defied Red Hearing to Be Cited to Justice Dept.," *Los Angeles Times* (July 3, 1963), p. 1.

45. RCN on Buhai/Lewis: memo to LAPD, August 6, 1971. Arnett Hartsfield verified in a March 21, 1992, telephone conversation with the author that he had represented Harriett Buhai at the 1963 HUAC hearing.

46. Philby defection: "Spy Cases Reported in '63," *The New York Times* (October 31, 1963).

47. Soviet expulsions: Henry Raymont, "Russian Is Ousted by U.S. in Spy Case," *The New York Times* (July 2, 1963), p. 1.

48. Nelson Drummond: "Spy Cases Reported." See also J. Bernard Hutton, *Struggle in the Dark* (London: George G. Harrap 1969), pp. 88–95, and Pierre J. Huss and George Carpozi Jr., *Red Spies in the U.N.* (New York: Coward-McCann, 1965), pp. 215–39.

49. Anita L. Ehrman: "Ex-Reporter Found Dead in Washington," *The New York Times* (August 1, 1963). Author's interview with Mrs. Frederick L. Ehrman (April 11, 1992). The late Frederick Ehrman was a partner in the Lehman Brothers investment banking firm in 1963; other major posts had included chairmanship of the Monterey Oil Company and membership on the boards of Continental Air Lines, the TXL Oil Corporation, and Park & Tilford Distillers Corporation (*Times* article).

50. LHO leafleting at docks: WC XXII. 806 (Patrolman Girod Ray report).

51. Marina on Hidell forgery: WC V. 401.

52. LHO getting new passport: WC XVII. 666–67. A number of researchers have questioned how Oswald, as a former "defector" listing the USSR among his planned places to visit and even referring to a previous "cancellation" of his passport, could so readily get a new one and—for the third time—escape notice of American authorities, since the Passport Office was then headed by the staunchly anti-communist Miss Frances Knight. Ordinarily, a State Department "lookout card" is posted for such individuals.

53. Marina letter to Soviet embassy: WC XVI. 25–29, 520–26.

54. LHO note to embassy: WC XVI. 30 (CE 13).

55. RCN on LHO's Cuban visa: letter to Fensterwald (August 12, 1974).

56. Alba on LHO: Taped interview with Kevin Walsh (May 1976) provided to author.

57. LHO fired: Warren Commission Report Appendix XIII. 726. Researcher Philip H. Melanson notes in his book *Spy Saga* (New York: Praeger, 1990), p. 87, that four fellow employees who worked with Oswald at the Reily Coffee Company all went on to jobs at the National Aeronautics and Space Administration's (NASA) plant in New Orleans later that summer. Oswald himself is said to have told Alba that he anticipated getting a job at NASA. As Melanson writes, "Whatever went on inside Reily Coffee, the firm seems to have been a primary recruiting ground for the aerospace industry. It is not clear how a coffee company would train its personnel in such a way that several of them could make an easy transition to aerospace work."

58. Alba quoting LHO: Summers, *Conspiracy,* p. 313.

59. Arnesto Rodriguez and LHO: WC XXIV. 659; CD4. 819. Golz interviewed Rodriguez on March 7, 1979. Cited in Summers, *Conspiracy,* pp. 318–19, where Rodriguez added that it was he who originally sent Oswald to see Carlos Bringuier (see Chapter Seventeen).

60. FBI informant on LHO: WC XVII. 769 and 754.

61. LHO name in museum registry: WCD 1066. 612; 897. 506.

62. LHO speech in Mobile: WC XXV. 919 (Eugene Murret invitation to LHO, July 6); WC XXV. 926 et seq. (speech).

63. RCN comments on LHO: amended outline sent to author, March 1976; author's interview (October 5, 1977); author's interview (October 26, 1975); Richard Popkin notes on conversation with RCN (1975).

64. Dean Andrews testimony: WC XI. 325–39.

65. Andrews on LHO/"The Mex": To Jim Garrison from Harold Weisberg, "Dean Andrews" (March 17, 1968). Copy provided author by Weisberg.

66. LHO whereabouts late July–early August: analysis derived from chronology compiled by Mary Ferrell, Dallas. See WC XXIII. 711, XIX. 212, XXII. 82.

67. LHO in Austin: WC XXIV. 733. Also, *Dallas Morning News* (December 25, 1963), Sec. 1, p. 4. There is some confusion as to when Oswald may have been in Austin. A memorandum supplied to the WC by Mrs. Lee Dannelly, assistant chief of the Administrative Division, State Selective Service Headquarters, stated that on the basis of reviewing her records, Oswald came either on July 31 or September 25.

68. LHO military status: WC XIX. 688–89. Cited Newman, *Assassination,* p. 374.

69. RCN on military status: Court of Claims No. 1-73 filings by plaintiff.

70. RCN contacting Dallas FBI: Court of Claims (April 16, 1974).

Chapter XVI

The author's interview with Nagell described at the beginning of the chapter took place on October 5, 1977.

The author's interviews with Robert Clayton Buick occurred by telephone (September 14, 1981) and extensively in La Crescenta, California (May 5, 1991).

Numbered notes are as follows:

1. RCN on his motivation: letter to author (January 29, 1976).
2. RCN on LHO as subject: author's interview (October 26, 1975).
3. All quotes are from RCN letter to Arthur Greenstein (October 8, 1967).
4. LHO recommending Mexico hotel: WC XI. 223 (Mumford testimony).
5. Roberts on another LHO trip: interview with Anthony Summers cited in Anthony Summers, *Conspiracy* (New York: McGraw-Hill, 1980), p. 370.
6. LHO two trips to Mexico: *Time-Life* library archive, file to *Time* Nation Section, from Jerry Hannifin, Washington (October 23, 1975).
7. Leopoldo Aguilera: *Manion Forum* (March 22, 1964), interview with "prominent exile leader."
8. Anderson on LHO trips: author's interview (May 9, 1990), San Antonio, Texas.
9. Mann on LHO trips: author's interview (May 9, 1990), Austin, Texas.
10. RCN on LHO in Mexico: author's interview (October 26, 1975).
11. Margain on RCN/LHO/Mexico: author's interview (April 7, 1991). Former CIA clandestine official Joseph B. Smith told me that there was an ultraright extremist group in Guadalajara, known as the Tecos, which "some people in the agency [CIA] were definitely inclined to see as something they could work with. But I received an admonition when I was there to stay away from these guys, have nothing to do with them. That was in the late sixties or early seventies. They [the Tecos] had existed for quite a while." The Tecos group, and its connection to the international right-wing, is described in Scott Anderson and Jon Lee Anderson's *Inside The League* (New York: Dodd, Mead, 1986), p. 71–81.
12. Garrison on RCN/LHO/Mexico: transcript, roundtable discussion, New Orleans (September 21, 1968).
13. Hudkins background: George O'Toole and Ron Rosenbaum, "Was Fidel on the Grassy Knoll?," *New Times* magazine (July 11, 1975), p. 13–14.
14. Hudkins on LHO in Mexico: author's interview (May 12, 1976), Baltimore.
15. Andrews on LHO and "CIA whore": Harold Weisberg memo to Jim Garrison, March 17, 1968.
16. RCN on LHO in Mexico: letter to Fensterwald (August 9, 1974).
17. On CIA and murder: In a registered letter sent to the *Los Angeles Free Press* (August 12, 1975), Nagell wrote: "The main distinction between some American intelligence officers that I knew and hired killers were the procedures utilized in murdering their victims and/or the methods used to disassociate themselves and the U.S. government from their crimes."

At our second interview (October 28, 1975), Nagell compared the assassination capabilities of the Soviets and the Americans as follows: "They [CIA] play it up like the Russians are a bunch of killers. But it's CIA more than the Russians. I could tell you instances where the CIA killed their own people. That's one of the main differences I see between American intelligence affairs and foreign. I'm not talking about efficiency. They [CIA] are so interested in this plausible denial, disassociating themselves and their boss. If they want to knock a guy off, they use cutouts. Somewhere along the line, somebody will be dead. The case officer will be scot-free—and the U.S. government will be scot-free. I'm not saying the Soviets don't do it, but when they do something, they do it right. We have so many amateurs who are supposed to be experts."

However, in terms of the JFK assassination, Nagell also wrote in a June 30, 1975, letter to Richard Popkin: "I want to emphasize that it is also my opinion—based on what I knew then and know now—that the CIA, as such, did not plan or carry out the assassination of President Kennedy."

18. Von Kleist: The statement quoted is undated, but von Kleist repeated basically the same information in a letter to Fensterwald of February 7, 1969, where von Kleist also notes having "advised Robert Buick to write you as suggested. . . ."
19. Buick statements: Fensterwald notes on conversation with Robert Buick (April 1, 1969). Copies of Buick's registration record at the Hotel Luma in 1962 are in the author's possession.
20. FBI release on Buick and arrest: Mark Sabljak and Martin H. Greenberg, *Most Wanted: A History of the FBI's Ten Most Wanted List* (Bonanza Books, New York: 1990), pp. 117–18. The book also notes that Buick was born in Pennsylvania and "spent much of his life in Mexico."
21. RCN and Buick: In a letter of November 29, 1968, to John Malone, special agent in charge of the FBI's New York office, Nagell wrote: "Mr. Buick was once a bullfighter in Mexico and apparently is familiar with some of the people I knew there in 1962–63. . . . I have met him before, but I am not the source of his information. . . ."
22. RCN on hypnosis: author's interview (October 28, 1975).
23. Marks documents: Nicholas M. Horrock, "C.I.A. Data Show 14-Year Project on Controlling Human Behavior," *The New York Times* (July 21, 1977), p. 1.
24. Korean War BLUEBIRD project: John Marks, *The Search for the "Manchurian Candidate"* (New York: W.W. Norton, 1991), p. 25.
25. CIA assassin study: Nicholas M. Horrock, "C.I.A. Documents Tell of 1954 Project to Create Involuntary Assassins," *The New York Times* (February 9, 1978). In 1975 *The Sunday Times* of London broke a story that Navy psychologist Thomas Narut had told an international conference that the Navy had taken convicted

murderers from military prisons, trained them as political assassins, and placed them in American embassies around the world. After the article came out, Narut labeled it "blatantly false and absurd." Associated Press, "Training of Assassins by U.S. Navy reported," *Chicago Sun-Times* (July 7, 1975), p. 1. In that same year, the Army admitted having given LSD to 585 unwitting men over a twelve-year period. "More Guinea Pigs," *Time* (August 4, 1975), p. 66.

26. Edwards as Artichoke officer: Horrock, "CIA Documents Describe . . ."

27. Siragusa involvement: "Senate Panel to Focus on Abuses Linked to C.I.A. Drug Testing," *The New York Times* (September 20, 1977), p. 1. Siragusa is linked to George White, an ex-OSS man in World War II who went on to become a senior Bureau of Narcotics official. Another *Times* article—"Files Show Tests for Truth Drug Began in O.S.S." (September 5, 1977), p. 1—noted that one of White's papers maintained "that August Del Gracio, whom it identifies as a 'well-known New York hoodlum' with whom Colonel White had become acquainted in another context, was used as an unwitting 'guinea pig' in the 1943 experiments." Del Gracio sought to negotiate with White and others for the 1943 prison release of "Lucky" Luciano in return for cooperation with Allied intelligence services.

28. The author's account of the CIA's assassination plans and methods is drawn from the 1975 U.S. Senate report *Alleged Assassination Plots Involving Foreign Leaders*. The Antonio Varona/Juan Orta plot is described in Charles Rappleye and Ed Becker, *All American Mafioso: The Johnny Rosselli Story* (New York: Doubleday, 1991), pp. 192–93. Those authors tell of Varona's having met with Florida mobster Meyer Lansky to secure financing for anti-Castro activities.

29. Helms and plots/mind control: "Alleged Assassination Plots," p. 83; *Foreign and Military Intelligence,* Book I, Final Report of the Select Committee to Study Governmental Operations with Respect to Intelligence Activities, U.S. Senate (April 26, 1976), pp. 389–90; Marks, *Search.* "He would become the most important sponsor of mind-control research within the CIA, nurturing and promoting it throughout his steady climb to the top position in the Agency." Marks, *Search,* p. 14.

30. MK-ULTRA by 1963: *Foreign and Military Intelligence,* p. 392. For a fascinating account about one of the CIA's experimental subjects, see Donald Bain, *The Control of Candy Jones* (Chicago: Playboy Press, 1977). Jones was the wife of radio talk-show host Long John Nebel, who, interestingly, Oswald is said to have telephoned in the summer of 1963, asking to appear on his program.

31. CI hypnosis: Marks, *Search,* p. 202.

32. Beck on Mexico experiment: Melvin Beck, *Secret Contenders* (New York: Sheridan Square Publications, 1984), pp. 109–14.

33. Marks on Mexico experiment: Marks, *Search,* pp. 202–4.

Chapter XVII

Numbered notes are as follows:

1. Gillin on LHO visit: Garrison investigation files. Gillin confirmed the basic details in a 1992 telephone conversation with the author.

2. Estabrooks on programming: cited in W. H. Bowart, *Operation Mind Control* (New York: Dell Publishing, 1978), p. 59, 230–31; G. H. Estabrooks with Leslie Lieber, "Hypnosis: Its Tremendous Potential as a War Weapon Is Revealed Here for First Time," *Argosy* (February 1950), pp. 26–29, 90–92.

3. Marks's source on control: John Marks, *The Search for the "Manchurian Candidate"* (New York: W. W. Norton, 1991), p. 203.

4. Kirkpatrick memorandum: *Foreign and Military Intelligence,* Book I, Final Report of the Select Committee to Study Governmental Operations with Respect to Intelligence Activities, U.S. Senate (April 26, 1976), p. 390.

5. Programmed patsy: Marks, *Search,* p. 204.

6. RCN on LHO's instructions: letter to Arthur Greenstein (October 8, 1967).

7. Bringuier background: WC X. 34. Name in LHO notebook: XVI. 67. *The New York Times* (August 7, 1962) (DRE goal). Taylor Branch and George Crile III, "The Kennedy Vendetta," *Harper's,* (August 1975), p. 60 (JM/WAVE and Helsinki). Bringuier's newsletter, *Crusade,* which he founded upon arriving in New Orleans in 1961, was aided by support from the Crusade to Free Cuba Committee, among whose financial angels was Oswald's New Orleans employer William Reily.

8. Bringuier on LHO coming to store: WC X. 35–36.

9. LHO on "Cosa Nostra": WC X. 77.

10. Raid on exile camp: Anthony Summers, *Conspiracy* (New York: McGraw-Hill, 1980), p. 346; FBI memo from New Orleans to headquarters (May 11, 1964) (Bringuier). Warren Hinckle and William Turner, *The Fish Is Red* (New York: Harper & Row, 1981), pp. 198–99.

11. LHO and Hispanic man in bar: WC XI. 343, 356; XXV. 671; XXVI. 358. Summers, *Conspiracy,* p. 311.

12. Bringuier on LHO in bar: WC X. 45; XI. 349, 351, 637. Journalist Lonnie Hudkins also described the FBI's awareness that Oswald had been "running quite a bit prior to the assassination" with "a guy who was Secretary of the Texas Communist Party and of Mexican ancestry." Hudkins said he himself had met this individual in Texas. Author's interview (May 12, 1976).

13. An August 12, 1963, New Orleans police report quotes Bringuier that the sign was given to him by Arnesto Rodriguez, who encountered Oswald on July 24.

14. Bringuier on street fight: WC X. 37–38.

15. LHO comment to Bringuier: WC X. 38.

16. Gaudet on CIA/LHO: interview with Bernard Fensterwald, Jr., and Allan Stone (May 13, 1975).

17. Police reaction to LHO: Summers, *Conspiracy,* p. 301. Martello testimony, WC X. 53–56.

18. LHO letter to FPCC: WC XX. 524–25 (Lee exhibit 5).

19. Marina on LHO/FPCC: Paris Flammonde, *The Kennedy Conspiracy* (New York: Meridith, 1969), p. 122.

20. LHO request to see FBI: FBI item No. 100-16601-18; declassified 1977.

21. Quigley report on LHO: FBI file No. 100-16601 (CE 826). Oswald showed Quigley his FPCC chapter card, which falsely listed the membership number as 33. Oswald said he had never seen "A. J. Hidell" in person but that Hidell contacted him by letter or phone to let him know the agenda of political activities and the time and place of meetings. Philip H. Melanson, *Spy Saga* (New York: Praeger, 1990), pp. 65–66.

22. Quigley and LHO Navy file: WC IV. 432, 438.

23. Martello on Murret/LHO interview: WC X. 53–54.

24. Bruneau/Marcello/LHO bail: HSCA cited in John H. Davis, *Mafia Kingfish* (New York: McGraw-Hill, 1989), p. 128.

25. LHO visit with Murret: WC VIII. 145 (Lillian Murret testimony).

26. DRE word to CIA: HSCA X. 81 n.

27. LHO trial/letter to Lee: WC X. 39 (Bringuier testimony); XX. 526–28 (Lee exhibit 6). Uncle with associate of Nofio Pecora: John H. Davis, *The Kennedys: Dynasty and Disaster* (New York: McGraw-Hill, 1984), p. 509.

28. LHO letter to CP: WC XX. 261.

29. LHO calling Nebel: Lincoln Lawrence [pseud.], *Were We Controlled?* (New Hyde Park, N.Y.: University Books, 1967), p. 66.

30. Gaudet on FPCC: Fensterwald/Stone interview, May 13, 1975.

31. 544 Camp St. address on leaflet: WC XXVI. 783.

32. Banister background: This account is drawn primarily from Summers, *Conspiracy,* pp. 319–26. See also HSCA X. 123–36.

33. HSCA X. 123 notes that the Cuban Revolutionary Council rented space at 544 Camp Street from October 1961 through February 1962, when Bringuier was affiliated with the CRC. Arcacha-Smith moved into the building in 1962 (X. 110).

34. Arcacha-Smith and Banister: Summers, *Conspiracy,* p. 326.

35. RCN on Arcacha-Smith: letter to author (May 5, 1976); author's interview (May 19, 1978).

36. Arcacha-Smith's move and funds: A CIA file of October 26, 1967, notes: "Some Cubans said Arcacha SMITH stole money entrusted to him for the counterrevolution. When he left New Orleans, the rent for the FRD [Friends of Democratic Cuba] office in the Newman Building [544 Camp Street] was unpaid." As of January 19, 1963, Arcacha-Smith's registration card showed a Houston address (memorandum to Garrison from Sergeant Fenner Sedgebeer, February 13, 1967). Another Garrison file, dated February 10, 1967, describes Carlos Bringuier living "next door to ARCACHA" in February 1962 in New Orleans.

37. RCN on Banister: author's interviews (October 26, 1975, and May 19, 1978).

38. Roberts/Nitschke on Banister and LHO: Summers, *Conspiracy,* pp. 323–26.

39. FBI Banister interview: HSCA X. 126.

40. Martin on Banister: HSCA X. 129–30; IX. 104.

41. Gatlin background: William W. Turner, "The Garrison Commission on the Assassination of President Kennedy," *Ramparts* (January 1968), p. 47. Jerry M. Brooks, a former Minuteman who worked for Banister on "anti-Communist" research in 1961–62, made the allegations about Gatlin.

42. Courtney background: Harry and Bonaro Overstreet, *The Strange Tactics of Extremism* (New York: W. W. Norton, 1964), pp. 230–35; Arnold Forster and Benjamin R. Epstein, *Danger on the Right* (New York: Random House, 1964), pp. 154–55; White House memorandum for the president (August 15, 1963), p. 54.

43. Oliver on LHO: WC XX. 720 (Oliver exhibit 2).

44. Oliver on Bringuier, LHO, and Courtney: WC XV. 720.

45. Banister files and Courtney: HSCA X. 130–31.

46. Background for the section on David Ferrie is derived from HSCA X. 105–22 and Summers, *Conspiracy,* pp. 326–29, 339–38.

47. LHO and Ferrie to training camp: Summers, *Conspiracy,* pp. 332–33.

48. Banister and Marcello: HSCA X. 127; Summers, *Conspiracy,* p. 338.

49. Arcacha-Smith and Marcello: Summers, *Conspiracy,* p. 326.

50. For a detailed analysis of LHO's possible ties to the Marcello organization, see Davis, *Mafia Kingfish,* pp. 118–33.

51. Becker on Marcello threat: ibid., pp. 107–11; also, Charles Rappleye and Ed Becker, *All American Mafioso* (New York: Doubleday, 1991), pp. 237–38.

52. RCN on Marcello: letter to Fensterwald (February 26, 1975); "cerebrations" to Greenstein.

53. LHO at Trade Mart: WC X. 61; XXVI. 771. Photo: XXI. 139. An FBI file of November 27, 1963 (CD 351), recounts the following information from Edward Butler (who debated LHO on the radio program): "He is of the belief that Oswald appeared on the campuses of Tulane and Loyola Universities trying to organize Fair Play chapters. In fact, the fellow who appeared with Oswald distributing Castro leaflets on a New Orleans street during August is believed to be a student at Tulane." Carlos Quiroga told Garrison investigator Frank Klein (January 13, 1967) that Oswald told him he was studying Russian at Tulane University.

And Oswald allegedly told both policeman Martello and his aunt Lillian Murret that he was acquainted with a Dr. Leonard Reissman at Tulane and that FPCC meetings were held at Reissman's home (WC XXVI. 763–66). At the time, scholar Reissman was not even in Louisiana, but on leave at Stanford University. However, Reissman's wife had enraged local racists by arranging for the first integrated birthday party at her daughter's school. And Oswald's information was used in a Martello memo to the Secret Service to link Reissman falsely to another integrationist, Dr. James Dombrowski of the Southern Conference Educational Fund. Dombrowski was arrested on October 4, 1963, for alleged criminal conspiracy in operating a subversive organization. After the assassination, the Louisiana Joint Legislative Committee on Un-American Activities issued a press release tying the FPCC to Dombrowski's group. As researcher Peter Dale Scott observes in the unpublished manuscript "Beyond Conspiracy" (1979–80), the Oswald-Reissman-Dombrowski linkage, which had no basis in reality, could lead to the conclusion that Oswald was "acting not as a left-wing ideologue but as a right-wing provocateur."

It is also interesting to note that Dr. Robert Heath, chairman of the Tulane University Department of Psychiatry and Neurology, was approached by a CIA doctor in November 1962 about experimenting with the "pain system" of the brain. Heath told *The New York Times*—"Private Institutions Used in C.I.A. Effort to Control Behavior" (August 2, 1977), p. C36—that he turned down the suggestion as "abhorrent." Dr. Heath was a pioneer in implanting "depth electrodes" in the brain and had agreed to a CIA research project in 1957, testing a purported brainwashing drug on monkeys.

54. Core as FBI source: FBI No. 97-74-67.

55. Quiroga infiltrating LHO: Klein interview; Fred Powledge, "Cuba Exile Tells of Oswald Boast," *The New York Times* (November 27, 1963).

56. FBI file, New Orleans: "Confidential Informant NO T-5 furnished the following on November 27, 1963" (in author's possession).

57. Stuckey-LHO radio interview: WC XI. 159–61 (Stuckey testimony). Transcript, XXI. 621–32 (Stuckey exhibit 2). Portions appear in Albert H. Newman, *The Assassination of John F. Kennedy* (New York: Clarkson N. Potter, 1970), pp. 390–93.

58. LHO to Lee: WC XX. 529–30.

59. Stuckey on giving tape to FBI/arranging debate: WC XI. 165–66. Edward Butler background: WC XI. 166–69; XXI. 637–40. Butler served as executive director of INCA. Its president was Dr. Alton Ochsner, a consultant to the U.S. Air Force "on the medical side of subversive matters" and a personal friend of the Somoza family of Nicaragua. Scott, "Beyond Conspiracy," p. 649.

60. Radio debate: WC transcript, XXI. 633–41. The discrepancy between the recorded version and the Warren Commission is described in Jeff Cohen, "The Oswald Tapes," *Crawdaddy* (August 1975), p. 40. After the assassination, it was learned that INCA (whose production manager, Manuel Gil, was a member of the Cuban Revolutionary Council at Banister's building, 544 Camp Street) owned the rights to the debate, as well as a second Oswald interview. Both were then released as commercial recordings, the debate by Key Records with a "dynamic documentary by Dr. Hargis," the Oklahoma preacher who was a close associate of Charles Willoughby and Edwin Walker. Peter Dale Scott, "The Dallas Conspiracy," unpublished manuscript (1971).

61. Bringuier call for LHO probe: WC XIX. 175.

62. WDSU giving tape to FBI: WCD 12. 11. On August 23, 1963, FBI headquarters instructed the New Orleans office to "submit results of their Oswald investigation to the Bureau." (HSCA V. 91).

63. Librarian Gallo: Garrison roundtable conference transcript, New Orleans, (September 21, 1968), p. 110.

64. Debate to media: HSCA. 85–86. The HSCA's interview with José Antonio Lanusa revealed that the DRE in Miami first "called a CIA contact," who instructed them he needed an hour "to contact Washington headquarters for instructions. . . . When the CIA contact called back, he told them the FBI would contact the group." The next day, Lanusa said the DRE turned over the debate tape and other material on LHO—including the Marine Corps training manual he had dropped off with Bringuier on August 6—to FBI agent James J. O'Conner.

An FBI file of November 27, 1963 (WCD 351), describes a conversation with Al Tarabochia (of the Senate Internal Security Subcommittee), recounting his telephone discussion with Carlos Bringuier. Tarabochia maintained that Bringuier had "identified Oswald as having been in New Orleans and an active leader of the Fair Play for Cuba Committee there" on the afternoon of the assassination after Oswald's arrest. The next day, "Tarabochia states that Bringuier told him he was threatened . . . by an unidentified man, believed to be American. . . . The unidentified man told Bringuier that Oswald did not kill President Kennedy and that the killing was done by a racist group rather than by a Communist or Marxist. He then said to Bringuier that he, Bringuier, would pay the penalty for accusing an innocent man. Bringuier had never seen the man before this occasion." (See Chapter Twenty-four for more on a possible link with a "racist group.")

65. James on Lanusa: FBI file (November 26, 1963) report (November 23, 1963) by special agent Stuart W. Angevine, WFO 89-75. Daniel James was the Citizens Committee to Free Cuba's executive secretary, as well as an author and newspaper columnist. A September 5, 1963, memorandum about his committee, on file at the JFK Memorial Library, quotes an unidentified source on James: "He said this fellow James needs to be watched. He said he hung with some pretty shifty people . . ." and had traveled to Cuba from Mexico City.

A State Department memo at the JFK Library, "Cuban Exile Plotting," dated July 19, 1963, described a source's information that John Birch Society types were backing "certain Cuban exiles of a militant bent," as well as being "the real movers and shakers behind Dan James and the Free Cuba Committee."

Along with James and Luce, the anti-Castro Citizens Committee included Paul D. Bethel, former press attaché at the American embassy in Havana, and listed on its letterhead Admiral Arleigh A. Burke, Brigadier Generals S.L.A. Marshall and Frank L. Howley, and newsman (and Miami-based CIA agent) Hal Hendrix. On the afternoon of the assassination, Hendrix provided immediate details on Oswald's past, his Soviet "defection," and his pro-Castro activities to another journalist, Seth Kantor. Hendrix also reported the coup that overthrew the Dominican Republic's Juan Bosch on September 24, 1963—the day *before* it happened. In 1976, Hendrix would plead guilty to withholding information from a Senate committee investigating ties between the CIA and multinational corporations. Summers, *Conspiracy*, pp. 134–35.

66. According to Garrison's files, Clare Boothe Luce called their office with this basic story on February 22, 1967. The HSCA's account of Luce's information is in X. 86–87. "The evidence indicates that the Luce allegations, although related to certain facts, cannot be substantiated in the absence of corroboration by other individuals," the HSCA concluded. The most in-depth treatment of Luce's allegations is found in HSCA investigator Gaeton Fonzi's article "Who Killed JFK?," *The Washingtonian* (November 1980), p. 167. Fonzi notes that Luce was on the board of directors of David Phillips's Association of Former Intelligence Officers. She was also a close associate of Miami's William Pawley, a former American ambassador in Latin America who persuaded Luce to finance anti-Castro guerrilla operations. Summers, *Conspiracy,* p. 450.

José Lanusa says of Luce's story: "That's not us; I think it's a lot of baloney." Lanusa told the author in a March 5, 1992, telephone interview that he met Mrs. Luce in the late summer of 1962, when she sought to purchase photographs taken by Lanusa's group during a commando raid into Cuba but had her plans scotched by her husband, Henry, *Time-Life*'s publisher.

In the summer of 1963, *Life* magazine became part of an expedition seeking to prove that Soviet missiles were still in Cuba. The alliance among *Life,* the CIA, the "Commandos L" (Tony Cuesta) exile group, and ex-diplomat Pawley was brought together by Mob-connected John Martino. Summers, *Conspiracy,* pp. 449–50; a detailed account of this expedition, "The Bayo-Pawley Affair: a Plot to Destroy JFK and Invade Cuba," by Miguel Acoca and Robert K. Brown, appeared in the Spring 1976 issue of *Soldier of Fortune* magazine.

67. Bringuier on Ferrie/FBI/CIA contacts: author's telephone interview (April 2, 1992).

Chapter XVIII

The author's interviews with Robert Morrow took place in Baltimore (August 8, 1976); by phone (April 2, 1990); and in Boston (March 27, 1992).

The author visited Garrett Brock Trapnell at the Marion Federal Penitentiary in Illinois (March 10, 1978).

The interviews with Antonio Veciana were conducted in Miami over a three-day period in June 1976.

Numbered notes are as follows:

1. RCN passport renewal: photocopy in author's possession.

2. RCN borrowing pistol: author's interview with Bill Lynn (July 29, 1977).

3. CIA and Trujillo assassination: *Alleged Assassination Plots Involving Foreign Leaders* an Interim Report of the Select Committee to Study Governmental Operations with Respect to Intelligence Activities, U.S. Senate (November 20, 1975), pp. 191–216.

4. Bosch overthrow: Tom Miller, *The Assassination Please Almanac* (Chicago: Henry Regnery, 1977), p. 117.

5. Morrow on "Fillmore": Robert D. Morrow, *Betrayal* (Chicago: Henry Regnery, 1976), pp. 120–28, 227.

6. RCN's instructions: letter to Arthur Greenstein (October 8, 1967).

7. RCN on Morrow book: letter to author (April 18, 1976).

8. Peña and de Brueys: "The American Assassins," *CBS Reports,* (November 26, 1975); de Brueys denial, HSCA Report, p. 193; Summers, *Conspiracy,* pp. 232, 310–11. It was de Brueys who took Oswald's possessions from Dallas to Washington after the assassination.

9. RCN on Barnes/Angel/Leopoldo: Jones Harris memo to Jim Garrison (March 1, 1969).

10. RCN on Morrow book: letter to George Bush (May 15, 1976).

11. RCN photos of Angel/Leopoldo: letter to Bernard Fensterwald, Jr. (March 21, 1975).

12. Cruz on Latin man near LHO: memo to Jim Garrison from Andrew J. Sciambra, interview with Miguel Cruz (March 19, 1967), in Baton Rouge.

13. Trapnell arrest: Robert D. McFadden, "Hijacker Is Shot at Airport Here After Freeing 93," *The New York Times* (January 30, 1972), p. 1. For more Trapnell background, see Robert Lindsey, "Sane or Insane? A Case Study of the TWA Hijacker," *The New York Times* (January 18, 1973); "Return of Dr. Jekyll," *Time* (January 29, 1972), p. 20.

14. Trapnell on Cuban G-2 affiliation: author's interview.

15. All government-derived information on Trapnell is taken from the following sources: Warren Commission No. 196, pp. 1–21 (FBI report of special agent J. Stanley Rotz, Baltimore [December 20, 1963], etc.); WCD 394, pp. 1–6 (FBI report of James J. O'Conner, Miami [January 24, 1964]; WCD 461, pp. 1–8 (FBI report of special agent Richard G. Sullivan, Jessups, Maryland [February 4, 1964]. Reports on file at National Archives, Washington.

Document 196, p. 10, notes: "On August 21, 1963, Mr. JOHN MARSHALL, Agent in Charge of Secret Service, Miami, Florida, advised that in January, 1962, AARON PAUL WILHEIT, FBI Number 1166538, wrote a letter to Secret Service and accused GARRETT BROCK TRAPNELL and JOSEPH ANTHONY LLANUSA, FBI Number 4244323B, who were both in jail in Miami at that time, of plotting to kidnap the children of President KENNEDY. Both TRAPNELL and LLANUSA were questioned by Secret Service and denied the accusation." (José Antonio Lanusa was the DRE's secretary for American Affairs in Miami; he appointed Carlos Bringuier delegate in New Orleans. The author has been unable to determine whether he might be the "LLANUSA" referred to in the FBI's Trapnell file. WCE 1138 makes the brief remark that "Oswald reportedly known to one JOSE LANUSA, Miami.")

16. Mauser as assassination rifle: Dick Russell, "What Was in the CIA's Declassified JFK File?," *The Village Voice* (April 16, 1976), pp. 17–20. The November 23, 1963, affidavit of Deputy Constable Seymour Weitzman stated: "This rifle was a 7.65 Mauser bolt action equipped with a 4/18 scope, a thick leather brownish-black sling on it." Deputy Sheriff Eugene Boone's report added: "I saw the rifle, that appeared to be a 7.65 Mauser. . . ."

17. Masferrer and Tokarevs: WCD 1085E11, pp. 1–2 (FBI file, New York, June 2, 1964, "Movimiento Revolucionario 30 de Noviembre").

18. Trapnell on exile involvement: letter to author (June 28, 1977).

19. Trapnell on FBI reports/Angel and Leopoldo: letter to author (July 27, 1977).

20. Trapnell rescue attempts: "Gun Found in Woman Hijacker's Car," *Los Angeles Times* (May 26, 1978), p. 4; Douglas E. Kneeland, "Girl, 16, Hijacks Jet and Holds 68 in Illinois in Effort to Free Prisoner," *The New York Times* (December 22, 1978), p. 1; "Skyjack Sequel," *Time* (January 1, 1979).

21. Trapnell and Hinckley: correspondence with Tom and Peter McCann, 1988.

22. Trapnell on Phillips: letter to author (July 27, 1977).

23. Schweiker on "Bishop": Gaeton Fonzi, "Who Killed JFK?," *The Washingtonian* (November 1980), p. 186.

24. Phillips background: obituary, Wolfgang Saxon, "David Phillips, 65, Former Agent and Public Advocate for C.I.A.," *The New York Times* (July 11, 1988); "Ex-Spy David Phillips Preaches the C.I.A. Story, but Can't Convince His Own Daughter," *People* (June 23, 1975), pp. 10–11; Linda Charlton, "Chief of C.I.A.'s Latin Operations Quits to Defend Agency Before the Public," *The New York Times* (May 10, 1975).

25. Phillips/Cuban affairs in Mexico: David Atlee Phillips, *The Night Watch* (New York: Atheneum, 1977).

26. "Bishop" and Phillips: Fonzi, "Who Killed JFK?," pp. 183–95.

27. Phillips and Chile task force: Thomas Powers, *The Man Who Kept the Secrets* (New York: Alfred A. Knopf, 1979), pp. 270, 273.

28. Lopez on Phillips/Veciana: author's telephone interview (November 21, 1989). The HSCA (X. 46–47) notes that when Veciana was introduced to Phillips by Fonzi, "there was no indication of recognition on Phillips's part."

29. Veciana on "Bishop": Fonzi, "Who Killed JFK?," p. 235. The HSCA (X. 50–51) noted a link between Veciana and Army intelligence: "Although file reviews of Maurice Bishop proved negative, the committee learned that Army intelligence had an operational interest in Antonio Veciana during one period. Veciana was registered in the Army Information Source Registry from November 1962 until July 1966. The nature of the Army's contact with Veciana appeared to be limited to attempting to use him as a source of intelligence information about Alpha 66 activities, with Veciana, in turn, seeking to obtain weapons and funds. Veciana acknowledged and detailed to the committee these contacts with Army intelligence and said that, aside from keeping Bishop informed of them, they had no relationship with his activities with Bishop."

30. McCone and CIA review on "Bishop": HSCA X. 50.

31. Beck on Phillips: author's telephone interview (February 13, 1992).

32. Smith on Phillips: author's telephone interview (April 8, 1992).

33. Veciana on "HH" memo: author's interview (June 15, 1976).

34. RCN on Phillips: letter to Greenstein (1975); author's interviews (October 5, 1977, and May 19, 1978).

35. Jack Anderson/Les Whitten column, "A Mr. X Enters the JFK Mystery," (January 19, 1977) (syndicated to various newspapers).

36. The author recontacted Veciana in 1990, but he expressed reluctance to meet again. Other journalists have told the author of similar experiences in seeking to interview Veciana since the attempt on his life, although he did make a brief TV appearance in 1992.

37. RCN instructions to sister: letter to Eleanore Gambert (March 13, 1967).

38. Martin on RCN and tape: memorandum to Jim Garrison from William R. Martin (April 18, 1967), pp. 9–12.

39. Letter to John: Sent by RCN to author (January 1976).

40. RCN on Martin: letter to Fensterwald (August 2, 1971).

41. RCN on tape's contents: "Comments by Richard Case Nagell on William R. Martin's 5-Page Memorandum Dated May 11, 1967, to Jim Garrison, District Attorney"; Martin memo of same date; RCN letter to Fred John (June 7, 1967); RCN letter to *The New Yorker* magazine (November 14, 1968).

In 1967, Nagell wrote to Greenstein: "The sum of things as I knew them were right [wing], generally speaking, as were the gusanos [Cuban exiles] who were making the watch tick. I'll add that the poor fool [Oswald] left holding the bag, as it was meant to be, was supposed to perform his task solaments [alone], though he was led to believe that assistance would be forthcoming from another angle. There was no egress worked out either, though, again, he thought there was. This was my understanding then and later."

42. LHO job applications: WC XIX. 234; XXIII. 711; XXV. 626 (FBI and signature).

43. RCN alerting FitzGerald: "Customer Experience Record" sent to Greenstein.

44. LHO letter to Communist Party, U.S.A.: WC XX. 262–64.

45. LHO letter to *Worker:* WC XX. 266–67.

46. LHO letters to Communist Party/Socialist Workers Party: WC XX. 270; XIX. 577.

Chapter XIX

Numbered notes are as follows:

1. Garrison on RCN: Jim Garrison, *On the Trail of the Assassins* (New York: Sheridan Square Press, 1988), pp. 184–85.

2. RCN on LHO instructions: letter to Senator Richard Russell (January 3, 1967).

3. RCN on persuading LHO: letter to Arthur Greenstein (August 27, 1967). (In this letter, RCN refers to LHO as "the ghoul.")

4. RCN on KGB effort: author's interview (October 5, 1977).

5. RCN on trip to Cuba: Memorandum in Support of Petition for Writ of Habeas Corpus, U.S. District Court, Western District of Missouri, draft copy (June 6, 1967); letter to *Los Angeles Free Press* (August 12, 1975).

6. RCN on Castro: At our May 19, 1978, interview, RCN mentioned that should I ever go to Cuba, Castro was an excellent Ping-Pong player—"and he'll play you, too." He added that I ought to brush up on my game.

7. RCN on Cuban knowledge of LHO: comments on John Barron's *KGB* sent to author (1978).

8. RCN on seeking V.A. admission: letter to Joseph Calamia, undated.

9. RCN stashing material with John: letter to Fensterwald (March 21, 1975).

10. RCN on arrangements: Court of Claims filing (April 16, 1974), *Nagell* v. *U.S.*, No. 1-73, "Plaintiff's Motion to Terminate the Administrative Proceedings and Reinstate the Judicial Proceedings."

11. FBI check on LHO: WCD 12:11; 1114.

12. Stuckey and FBI: WC XVII. 825–26.

13. LHO in Clinton: Anthony Summers, *Conspiracy* (New York: McGraw-Hill, 1980), pp. 333–36; *The Final Assassinations Report* (New York: Bantam, 1979), pp. 170–71.

14. McKeown allegations: The author's account of the 1976 McKeown interview appeared at greater length in "Three Witnesses," *New Times* (June 24, 1977). McKeown was a longtime close associate of Batista's predecessor as president of Cuba, Carlos Prio Socarras. Oswald's apparent knowledge of McKeown's having been "caught with the cache" of weapons traces back to a 1958 arms smuggling case that included charges against Carlos Prio and resulted in McKeown's being sentenced to six months in prison and fined $500. (WCE 3066).

McKeown, who had also been a personal friend of Castro, also recounted that Jack Ruby came by to see him soon after Castro took power in Cuba in 1959. "He told me his people were willing to give me $15,000 to help get five people outta Cuba," McKeown told the author. "He mentioned some Jewish-sounding names, and a fella in Las Vegas. And his people, he said, were the Mafia. That's what he called it, the Mafia, but he never did mention no names. Later he says he's gonna give me $25,000 for a letter of introduction to Castro, but he never did come up with the money." Ruby is known to have made a 1959 trip to Havana (Warren Commission Report, 801, 821, 370), and McKeown told HSCA investigator Fonzi that he met with Ruby on three different occasions. McKeown first told this story to the FBI in January 1964 (XXIII. 158ff.), and he is mentioned in HSCA Report, p. 152, and in Vol. IX.

McKeown also told this author in a spring 1977 telephone conversation that Oswald's older friend George de Mohrenschildt came to see him "one time, long time ago. Just to ask me a few questions, that's all." "Concerning Cuba?" I asked. "No, Oswald." After or before the assassination? "Oh, before. No, after. No, before— goddamn, after. It's been so long." And what did he want to know? "Well, none of your business," McKeown said. "I don't want to get all messed up in this." McKeown was an associate, too, of soldier of fortune Frank Sturgis.

15. Celso Hernandez: HSCA X. 86; WC XXV. 90. CIA/FBI on "A": *The Investigation of the Assassination of President John F. Kennedy: Performance of the Intelligence Agencies,* U.S. Senate (1976), Book V, p. 79.

16. "A" and "B" in arms deal: Book V, p. 12–13. The author independently confirmed the identity of "A" as Victor Espinosa Hernandez and "B" as Richard Lauchli. They are also named in Peter Dale Scott's unpublished "Beyond Conspiracy" (1979–80).

17. RCN on Banister and raid: letter to author (April 18, 1976).

18. Fernando Fernandez: *Time* files from Jay Mallin, Miami, and Jerry Hannifin, Washington (September 5, 1963). *Time-Life* library archive.

19. Cubela/AM/LASH: *Alleged Assassination Plots Involving Foreign Leaders,* Senate Select Committee on Intelligence Activities (1975), p. 86.

20. Attwood diplomacy: *The Investigation of the Assassination of John F. Kennedy: Performance of the Intelligence Agencies,* Final Report, Book V, of the Select Committee to Study Governmental Operations with Respect to Intelligence Activities, U.S. Senate (April 23, 1976), p. 20; Summers, *Conspiracy,* pp. 419–27. See also Attwood's book *The Twilight Struggle: Tales of the Cold War* (New York: Harper & Row, 1987).

21. Attwood on Cuban policies: author's telephone interview (June 3, 1976).

22. AM/LASH cable: HSCA X. 158.

23. Castro warning: *Investigation of the Assassination,* p. 14.

24. Langosch disapproval: ibid., p. 17; HSCA, X. 162–63, identifies Langosch, who is not named by the Senate.

25. Angleton on Castro retaliation: author's interview (April 2, 1976).

26. FBI-CIA reports on LHO: CIA document 590-352; CD 692. Cited in Summers, *Conspiracy,* pp. 388, 584.

27. Hernandez/AM/LASH circle: *Investigation of the Assassination,* p. 78.

28. Helms/FitzGerald decision: *Alleged Assassination Plots,* pp. 174–75.

29. McCone awareness: ibid., pp. 107–8.

30. RCN on AM/LASH: author's interview (May 19, 1978).

31. Aleman on Trafficante/Cubela: HSCA V. 314–15.

32. Trafficante on assassinating Castro: ibid., p. 361.

33. Trafficante on Cubela: ibid., p. 368.

34. Fensterwald letter to RCN: July 24, 1974.

35. RCN on pistol use: letter to Fensterwald (June 9, 1971).

36. USSR order to Nagell: Fensterwald memo (December 5, 1973).

37. RCN on being deceived: author's interview (October 26, 1975).

38. RCN on functioning for foreign power: Plaintiff's Reply Brief, Court of Claims, p. 46, mailed to author April 21, 1981.

39. RCN investigations: Court of Claims (April 16, 1974).

40. RCN letter to Senator Russell: on file, Senator Richard B. Russell Memorial Library, Athens, Georgia.

41. RCN on bank action: amended outline sent to author (March 1976).

42. RCN on FBI statement: author's telephone interview (March 21, 1990).

43. RCN on "confession": author's interview (May 19, 1978).

44. RCN on instructions: Plaintiff's Reply Brief.

45. Christopher Felix quote: cited in Robin W. Winks, *Cloak and Gown* (New York: William Morrow, 1987), p. 424.

46. RCN on penetration: author's interview (October 5, 1977).

47. RCN on photo with LHO: letter to author (April 8, 1976).

48. RCN on LHO instructions: letter to Fensterwald (August 12, 1974).

49. LHO and Mexican permit: WC XXV. 674–77.

50. Gaudet in line: HSCA Report, pp. 218–19. "Gaudet said he could not recall whether his trip to Mexico and other Latin American countries involved any intelligence-related activity."

51. RCN on informing FBI/others: page of letter sent author by RCN.

52. RCN on killing LHO: letter to *The New Yorker* (November 14, 1968).

53. Style of letter: amended outline sent author.

54. FBI/CIA and FPCC: *Investigation of the Assassination,* pp. 65–66.

55. RCN on Leon Oswald: author's interview (October 26, 1975).

56. Russo story: Garrison, *On the Trail,* pp. 151–56.

57. Leon Oswald death: Jones Harris memo to Garrison (March 1, 1969); also, amended outline.

58. RCN on apprising Soviets: letter to Senator Richard Russell (April 1, 1967).

59. RCN plans to depart: transcript of 1964 trial *United States* v. *Nagell,* T406; amended outline.

60. Cellmate statements: FBI July 30, 1975 report citing 1964 David J. Reid report.

61. RCN on not following Soviet orders: author's interview, May 19, 1978.

62. RCN on taking children: Trial transcript, T409.

63. RCN on kids: author's interview, May 19, 1978. An FBI report dated September 25, 1963, notes: "When asked for his motive in attempting to hold up the bank, NAGELL stated that he was unhappy with the American judicial system, because he had attempted, through judicial procedures, to get to see his two children, a girl 3½ and a boy 2½, in custody of his divorced [sic: estranged] wife, and the California court had not executed an order in keeping with his request."

64. Contact waiting in Juárez: amended outline; RCN letter to author (May 5, 1986).

65. RCN letters/plane ticket: letters to Greenstein (October 8 and 13, 1967); Fensterwald (August 12, 1974). In correspondence with Greenstein, RCN referred to FitzGerald as "Dirty Dick." The author's "translation" is based on numerous other references to FitzGerald.

66. FBI knowledge of $500: trial transcript, T398.

67. LHO failure to get $500: RCN letter to Fensterwald (August 26, 1974), responding to letter of August 21.

68. RCN seeking witness: letter to Burgess Perrenot (April 7, 1964).

69. Marlowe on RCN letter: author's interview (August 2, 1990); telephone conversation (January 29, 1992).

70. RCN on bank action: author's interview (October 26, 1975).

71. RCN on American Express: author's interview (July 27, 1984).

72. RCN on weapon used: Letter to Fensterwald (June 9, 1971).

73. Kramer/Hidel tourist cards: RCN Memorandum in Support (June 6, 1967), p. 4; amended outline, 1976; letter to Fensterwald (September 11, 1974). Bundren told the author that he had turned everything over to the FBI.

74. FBI on RCN in bank: FBI report, September 25, 1963, by special agent Thomas B. White, Jr., and special agent Harrel Leon Davis, on file *United States* v. *Nagell,* Fort Worth. In another FBI report of the same date, Nagell is said to have stated that "he had made an attempt to find a former war buddy of his named JOSE C. IBARRA, who formerly resided at 904 South Hill Street in El Paso. He stated that he had made inquiry at this address, but IBARRA had moved and he was not able to find out where he had gone. . . ."

75. White testimony: transcript, RCN Writ of Habeas Corpus hearing (November 4, 1963), p. 21.

76. RCN on effect of arrest: proposed testimony for second trial (1966).

Chapter XX

The author interviewed Ronald Augustinovich in Phoenix on October 22–23, 1975.

The author's interview with former ambassador to Mexico Thomas Mann was conducted in Austin, Texas, on May 9, 1990. Mann was reinterviewed by telephone, July 4, 1992.

The author's telephone interviews with Michael Scott took place on May 19–20, 1992; with Gregory Leddy, May 28, 1992.

Telephone interviews with former CIA official Clare Petty took place on June 9–10 and July 4, 1992; with Cleveland Cram on June 3, 1992.

Numbered notes are as follows:

1. Summers on FPCC: Anthony Summers, *Conspiracy* (New York: McGraw-Hill, 1980), p. 388.

2. Trento on Army/FBI and Mexico: author's telephone interview (June 3, 1992); on Sigler, see William R. Corson, Susan B. Trento, and Joseph J. Trento *Widows* (New York: Crown, 1989), pp. 266–396.

3. Anderson on Scott file: author's interview (May 9, 1990).

4. Mann background: Arthur M. Schlesinger, Jr., *Robert Kennedy and His Times* (New York: Ballantine Books, 1978), pp. 680–82.

5. According to FitzGerald's stepdaughter Barbara Train, he, too, was a good friend of Mexican president Díaz Ordaz. "He had a very close relationship with the president of Mexico, Díaz Ordaz, and he in fact told me he was briefing Díaz Ordaz on intelligence on a regular basis. There were these jokey stories about how my stepfather would take him presents—one time, it was a Polaroid camera tested by everybody in the CIA and, of course, it didn't work. Díaz Ordaz gave him a Mayan jade necklace, an amulet. There was also a really ugly picture of Díaz Ordaz on our mantelpiece." Author's telephone interview (June 11, 1992).

6. Flannery on Scott: author's telephone interview (February 13, 1992). Background on Scott is drawn primarily from family members, with dates verified through the Foreign Service Registers of the period.

7. Dempster on Scott: author's telephone interview (July 5, 1992). Dempster, who went into a private business with Scott in 1969, called his longtime friend "one of the most brilliant intelligence officers the CIA has produced."

8. Smith on Scott wedding: author's telephone interview (April 8, 1992).

9. Two sources told the author the story of Scott's being tipped off by the Mexican government about the Czech invasion and Soviet problems with China. Both sources requested anonymity.

10. Background on Richard Helms is drawn from a number of sources, including the Thomas Powers biography *The Man Who Kept the Secrets* (New York: Alfred A. Knopf, 1979); "Head of the CIA," *New York Post* (February 25, 1967), p. 26; and *Time* files (February 16 and 17, 1967).

11. Helms on anti-Castro plots: "'A Tremendous Insanity,'" *Newsweek* (October 2, 1978), p. 62; and Helms's interview for NBC-TV with David Frost. Helms's testimony before the HSCA is in IV. 5–250.

12. Helms's destruction of MK-ULTRA records: *Foreign and Military Intelligence,* Book I, Final Report of the Select Committee to Study Governmental Operations with Respect to Intelligence Activities, U.S. Senate (April 26, 1976), pp. 403–4. "According to Helms, Dr. Sidney Gottlieb, then director of TSD [Technical Services Division] '. . . came to me and said that he was retiring and that I was retiring and he thought it would be a good idea if these files were destroyed. And I also believe part of the reason for our thinking this was advisable was there had been relationships with outsiders in government agencies and other organizations and these would be sensitive in this kind of a thing but that since the program was over and finished and done with, we thought we would just get rid of the files as well, so that anybody who assisted us in the past would not be subject to follow-up or questions, embarrassment, if you will.'"

The report noted: "The destruction of the MK-ULTRA documents made it impossible for the Select Committee to determine the full range and extent of the largest CIA research program involving chemical and biological agents."

13. Kirkpatrick on Angleton's mission: author's telephone interview (February 8, 1992).

14. Background on Mary Meyer/Angleton/Leary is drawn from these sources: Philip Nobile and Ron Rosenbaum, "The Mysterious Murder of JFK's Mistress," *New Times* (July 9, 1976), pp. 22–33; Timothy Leary, "The Murder of Mary Pinchot Meyer," *The Rebel* (November 22, 1983), pp. 44–49; and Bernie Ward and Granville Toogood, "JFK 2-Year White House Romance," *National Enquirer* (March 2, 1976), p. 4.

15. Angleton on Meyer: author's interview (April 2, 1976).

16. Scott to Helms: This quote is the way a family member recalls it.

17. The source who told the author about the tape recording of Oswald's voice being in Scott's possession requested anonymity; I can only add that this source was well positioned to know about this and had no reason to fabricate the story. The same source suggested there was something very odd about the CIA's awareness of Oswald's Mexico City trip. "It had to do with some luggage that was found at the airport," which indicates that Oswald may have flown into (or out of) Mexico at some point. The source believed that Oswald may in fact have flown to Havana and back to Mexico City.

18. Phillips on LHO tapes: Summers, *Conspiracy,* p. 385.

19. Barron background: "About the Author" in John Barron, *KGB* (New York: Reader's Digest Press, 1974), last page. Barron's role with Scott was confirmed to the author by family members and other sources. The author attempted to reach Barron by phone on three occasions at Reader's Digest offices in Washington, but Barron never returned my calls.

20. Barron on Nosenko: author's preface, *KGB,* p. xv.

21. Barron in Mexico: Scott family interviews.

22. Epstein on Barron: author's telephone interview (May 26, 1992).

23. Cram CIA study: David Wise, *Molehunt* (New York: Random House, 1992), pp. 256–58.

24. Petty CIA study: ibid., pp. 159–60 (Petty background); 234–37.

25. Greenstein on "Bob": author's interview (February 10, 1990).

26. Janet Scott and Broglie: Scott family members, interviews.

27. Leddy background: Besides family interviews, material on Leddy was found in Burton Hersh, *The Old Boys* (New York: Charles Scribner's Sons, 1992), pp. 187, 340, 345, 410, and William R. Corson, *The Armies of Ignorance* (New York: Dial Press/James Wade, 1977), pp. 287, 356–57.

28. De Mohrenschildt in Latin America: résumé provided FBI by Lawrence Orlov (March 4, 1964); résumé sent by de Mohrenschildt to Lyndon Johnson (dated September 1966) (on file at LBJ Memorial Library, Austin).

29. The Kim Philby/Burgess/Maclean story has been documented in numerous books. The most current details on the Angleton-Philby relationship appear in Tom Mangold, *Cold Warrior* (New York: Simon & Schuster, 1991), pp. 63–70.

30. Goleniewski background: Wise, *Molehunt,* pp. 24–25. See also, Edward Jay Epstein, "The Spy War," *The New York Times Magazine* (September 28, 1980), for details on Goleniewski's claim to be the heir to Czar Nicholas of Russia. Author's note: Goleniewski's cause was taken up by elements of the ultraright, including the Shickshinny, Pennsylvania, Order of St. John of Jerusalem, to which Charles Willoughby was linked. One of

Goleniewski's staunchest supporters was ex-CIA official Herman Kimsey, who claimed knowledge about the JFK assassination to Hugh McDonald in *Appointment in Dallas* (New York: Zebra Books, 1975). According to former CIA official Clare Petty, "In the period when the CIA was having nothing to do with Goleniewski, the FBI continued to have a relationship with him, through the New York field office."

31. Golitsin and Angleton: See Mangold, *Cold Warrior,* pp. 71–90, and Wise, *Molehunt.*

32. Petty quote on Angleton/Golitsin: Mangold, *Cold Warrior,* p. 300.

33. David Murphy: The most detailed study of Murphy's career is in Wise, *Molehunt,* pp. 210–32. See also footnotes in Far East chapters of this book. Former CIA official Clare Petty told me that Murphy also knew Charles Willoughby.

34. RCN on Angleton: letter to author (May 5, 1976).

35. RCN on Soviet penetration of CIA in Mexico/FitzGerald: author's interview (October 5, 1977).

According to Ed Lopez, one of the HSCA's Mexico City investigators: "The CIA suspected that someone in Mexico was with the KGB. [David] Phillips himself told us that, they just didn't know whom."

36. RCN on Domestic Operations penetration: author's interview (October 28, 1975).

37. Domestic Operations background: David Wise, *The Espionage Establishment* (New York: Random House, 1967), pp. 144–45.

38. Barnes background: ibid., Powers, *The Man Who Kept the Secrets,* various pages; Peter Wyden, *Bay of Pigs* (New York: Simon & Schuster, 1979), pp. 38–39; obituaries, *The New York Times* (February 20, 1972), p. 68, and *The Washington Post,* February 20, 1972.

39. Clandestine view of Barnes: Powers, *The Man Who Kept the Secrets,* p. 121.

40. Barnes and anti-Castro plots: Wyden, *Bay of Pigs,* pp. 39–40; Powers, *The Man Who Kept the Secrets,* p. 147.

41. Angleton on Barnes: author's interview (October 22, 1976).

42. Morrow on Barnes/Sullivan/LHO: Robert D. Morrow, *The Senator Must Die* (Santa Monica, Calif.: Round-table, 1988), p. 95. Morrow writes: "I was originally told the story by Washington attorney Marshall Diggs; and I asked my former case officer, Tracy Barnes, about it in February 1964. . . . Barnes would not admit it, but his smile after I asked the question was confirmation enough."

43. CIA memo on Hunt in Dallas: Joe Trento and Jacquie Powers, "Was Howard Hunt in Dallas The Day JFK Died?," *Wilmington Sunday News Journal* (August 20, 1978). Reprinted in entirety in Mark Lane, *Plausible Denial* (New York: Thunder's Mouth Press, 1991), pp. 152–55.

44. Hunt background: See Tad Szulc's full-length biography *Compulsive Spy* (New York: Viking Press, 1974).

45. Trento provided background on the Angleton/Hunt in Dallas story to this author in a telephone conversation (June 3, 1992).

46. Hunt and Artime: George Volsky, "Manuel Artime Dies; Led Invasion of Cuba," *The New York Times* (November 18, 1977). Another *Times* article, "Cuban Reportedly Links Convicts' Funds to Hunt" (July 9, 1973), describes Artime's reported delivery of $24,000 in "support" money for the convicted Watergate burglars from Miami, which "came in cash either directly or indirectly from E. Howard Hunt, Jr." Artime was an organizer of the Miami Watergate Defense Relief Committee, and he visited the imprisoned Hunt on several occasions after the burglary.

47. RCN on Artime: Court of Claims (April 16, 1974); author's interviews (October 26, 1975, and April 11, 1977); letter to Greenstein (October 13, 1967).

48. Fonzi on Artime: author's interview (February 9, 1990). Whether or not Artime was a double agent for Castro, his "Second Naval Guerrilla Force" established in Central America in 1963 was a spectacular flop. In September 1964 it even attacked the wrong ship (a Spanish vessel) off Cuban shores. More blunders ensued, and a financial scandal wherein some $2 million in unvouchered CIA funding to Artime simply disappeared. See Warren Hinckle and William Turner, *The Fish Is Red* (New York: Harper & Row, 1981), pp. 238–39.

Chapter XXI

Numbered notes are as follows:

1. LHO's plans/Paine arrival: Albert H. Newman, *The Assassination of John F. Kennedy* (New York: Clarkson N. Potter, 1970), pp. 415–16; Edward Jay Epstein, *Legend* (New York: Reader's Digest Press/McGraw-Hill, 1978), pp. 229–30.

2. FBI reports on LHO: *The Investigation of the Assassination of President John F. Kennedy: Performance of the Intelligence Agencies,* Book V, Final Report, Senate Intelligence Committee (1976), p. 91; CIA document 590-252, cited in Anthony Summers, *Conspiracy* (New York: McGraw-Hill, 1980), p. 584.

3. LHO bus trip: Newman, *The Assassination,* pp. 419–20.

4. Odio visitors: Silvia Odio and her sister Annie could never be certain of the precise date, though Silvia was positive it was before October 1. She eventually estimated it was probably either September 26 or 27, but as the Warren Commission noted, "the only time not strictly accounted for during the period that Mrs. Odio thought Oswald might have visited her is the span between the morning of September 25 and 2:35 A.M. on September 26." So if it was the real Oswald—and not an impersonator, as some researchers have speculated—with Angel and Leopoldo at Odio's door, the visit would necessarily have taken place on the night of the twenty-fifth. Odio herself has remained adamant that her visitor was Oswald, not a look-alike. Hence the author has elected to put the real Oswald there on September 25.

5. The Odio account is drawn from several sources. See esp. HSCA X. 19–35; WC XI. 327/386; XXVI. 362/473; Summers, *Conspiracy,* pp. 411–18. The Veciana/Gonzalez link to her father appeared in George O'Toole and Paul Hoch, "Dallas: The Cuban Connection," *The Saturday Evening Post* (March 1976).

6. Odio comments: author's telephone interview (November 1976).

7. Rankin to Hoover/explanation: WC XXVI. 834.

8. Howard/Seymour/Hall denials: Summers, *Conspiracy*, p. 415.

9. RCN on Hall: letter to Fensterwald (August 26, 1974); author's interview (October 26, 1975, and October 5, 1977).

10. Hall on Odio: author's interview (October 1976, Los Angeles).

11. Hall, Howard, and a Cuban exile named Celio Alba arrived in Dallas, en route to Miami from Los Angeles, sometime in late September, and remained until about October 10. Then Hall and Seymour turned right around in Miami and went back to Dallas, where on October 18 they registered at the Dallas YMCA. Hall described what happened in Dallas at an interview with the author in Long Beach, California, on May 28, 1977.

12. Hall first told the story of the $50,000 offer to the *National Enquirer* (September 1, 1968). The trucking executive, in a telephone interview with the author in 1977, admitted knowing Hall but called Hall's allegation "a fabrication . . . a ridiculous charge."

13. Hall and rifles: Gerry Patrick Hemming, according to a Miami Police Intelligence Unit report of November 1, 1963, stated that Hall had stolen two rifles from his apartment the night before, as well as a third rifle in California (a jungle carbine, Savage .22 with scope, and Johnson 30.06). The latter weapon, according to WCD 1179 (pp. 295–98), was retrieved by Hall in Los Angeles on September 18, 1963, from a private detective, Richard Hatchcock, to whom Hall and Hemming had previously pawned it. Hall redeemed this rifle with a check drawn on the American Committee to Free Cuba, a group closely affiliated with Billy James Hargis's Christian Crusade. The FBI chose not to investigate the matter, after concluding "it is obvious that the rifle mentioned above was not used in connection with the assassination of President Kennedy."

However, the connections of Hall and Howard to ultraright groups backing the Cuban exile cause bear further scrutiny. Both men admittedly met separately with Colonel William Gale in Southern California in 1963, and both had acquaintances within the Alpha 66 exile group.

14. Hall and Trafficante: A more detailed analysis appears in the author's article "Loran Hall and the Politics of Assassination," *The Village Voice* (October 3, 1977), p. 23. Hall maintained that a meeting was held in Miami Beach in the spring of 1963, where Sam Giancana gave $30,000 to John Martino to finance the *Life* magazine/William Pawley/Cuban exile expedition to Cuba, seeking to prove the continuing existence of Soviet missiles there. The ten Cuban exiles who took part in Operation Red Cross disappeared from Pawley's yacht *Flying Tiger II* off the southeastern coast of Cuba in June 1963.

15. Hall on conspiracy/awareness of LHO: author's interviews (October 1976 and May 28, 1977). Hall alleged that Crespi introduced him to an "inhalation therapist at one of Dallas's children's hospitals" who kept weapons and "a mimeograph machine where he did anti-Kennedy shit" in his garage. "If you were to give a physical description of Oswald, that's the one you'd give of this guy."

16. FBI on Manuel Ray: HSCA file.

17. RCN on Ray group: amended outline. Addendum to *Family* article.

18. Ray on Odio/Leopoldo: HSCA file ibid, citing September 9, 1964, FBI interview with Ray. According to HSCA X. 31, "Ray told the committee that he knew of no members of JURE traveling through Dallas in September 1963 in search of money or arms. He does not recall anyone by the name of 'Leopoldo' or 'Angel' associated with JURE at the time. He said he had no American contacts in Dallas, nor did he receive any major financial support from anyone there."

19. Odio father letter: WC XX. 690; HSCA X. 29. The HSCA showed Sylvia Odio some three hundred photographs of Cuban activists, both pro- and anti-Castro, as well as other individuals who might have had some association with Oswald and the assassination. She was unable to identify Angel or Leopoldo. G. Robert Blakey, the HSCA's staff director, told me in 1980 that the CIA had provided photographs of several possibilities to the committee. "We concluded there were three people that Angel and Leopoldo could have been, but Mrs. Odio said she could not recognize any of them," Blakey said. "And we couldn't find them, I believe they are probably dead. The question is, on whose behalf were they acting? The report we got from the CIA indicated the background of the three possibilities was Cuban intelligence."

20. Twifords and LHO: WC XI, 179–80, 179.

21. British couple on LHO: WC XI. 214–15.

22. Australian girls on LHO: WC XI. 215–17 (Pamela Mumford testimony). On Englishman: FBI report of Chester C. Orton (December 18, 1963), Los Angeles (WCE 2194).

23. Except where otherwise noted, the author's background information on Albert Osborne is drawn from FBI and INS files released to Fensterwald under the FOIA in the 1980s and on file at the AARC in Washington. See also Michael Eddowes, *The Oswald File* (New York: Clarkson N. Potter, 1977), pp. 64–67.

24. Osborne/"Hidalgo": Garrison/AARC files.

25. Loving on Osborne/Bowen: author's telephone interview (1978).

26. American Express payments: WC XXV. 34.

27. Osborne falsification: Eddowes, *The Oswald File*, p. 64.

28. Missing bus passenger list: WC XXIV. 574; 623–24.

29. Osborne/LHO departures: Eddowes, *The Oswald File*, p. 70; WC XXV. 674–75.

30. Phone call about "big news": CIA document released 1976.

31. McDonald on Osborne: According to Fensterwald's notes of a October 16, 1981, conversation with McDonald, a Paris KGB man named "Tsymbal" was involved in a de Mohrenschildt-Osborne operation surrounding Oswald. Also see Hugh McDonald with Robin Moore, *L.B.J. and the J.F.K. Conspiracy* (Westport, Conn.: Condor, 1978). Reverend Walter Hluchan, who knew Osborne and Bowen, told me in a 1978 telephone interview: "I heard somebody say that they thought that they (Osborne) was a Communist."

32. It is possible that the Nazi supporter was Bowen, not Osborne.

33. RCN on Osborne/Bowen: letter to author (January 29, 1976).

34. FBI memo on FPCC/CIA: Book V, Final Report, Senate, pp. 65–66.

35. LHO registration: He signed the Hotel del Comercio register as "Lee, Harvey Oswald," conforming to his Mexican tourist card identification. Newman, *The Assassination,* p. 425.

36. RCN on LHO at Soviet embassy: letter to Fensterwald (September 5, 1974).

37. RCN on Soviet photo of LHO: Richard Popkin notes on conversation with RCN (June 1975).

38. RCN on LHO in Mexico: letter to Fensterwald (August 12, 1974).

39. Nechiporenko on LHO: "Ex-KGB Agent Claims to Have Information About JFK Murder," *Los Angeles Times* (January 10, 1992).

40. McDonald on Nechiporenko: McDonald with Moore, *L.B.J. and the J.F.K. Conspiracy,* p. 109.

41. Barron on Nechiporenko/expulsion: John Barron, *KGB* (New York: Reader's Digest Press, 1974), pp. 312–16.

42. Smith on Nechiporenko: author's telephone interview (April 8, 1992).

43. Nechiporenko comments: author's telephone conversation with Brian Litman (July 1992), responding to letter to Nechiporenko (April 24, 1992).

44. Yatskov background: Philip Agee, *Inside the Company* (New York: Bantam Books, 1976), pp. 544–45.

45. CIA on Kostikov: Norman Kempster, "Oswald Met Assassination Unit Agent, CIA Says," *Los Angeles Times* (April 4, 1976), p. 14.

46. Kostikov expulsion: Barron, *KGB,* pp. 413–14.

47. Hosty on Kostikov/LHO in Mexico: Earl Golz, "After 17 Years of Silence, FBI Oswald Agent Speaks Up," *Dallas Morning News* (December 8, 1980), p. 1.

48. CIA on Kostikov: Even when Richard Helms wrote a memo to Rankin on September 17, 1964, no mention was made of CIA suspicions about Kostikov being a member of Department 13. He was described as a known officer of the KGB, but Kostikov was mundanely cited as "one of several consular representatives who deal with visas and related matters."

49. HSCA on Kostikov: XI. 173–75 (Slawson testimony). Efforts to have the HSCA declassify its Mexico City report are continuing as of this writing.

50. Cubela as Yatskov/Kostikov contact: David C. Martin, *Wilderness of Mirrors* (New York: Harper & Row, 1980), pp. 151–53. Angleton testified before the Senate that he was not aware of the AM/LASH operation at the time (Final Report, Book V, p. 69).

51. Ernesto Rodriguez on LHO: Charles Ashman story cited by Summers, *Conspiracy,* pp. 389–90.

52. RCN on Department 13/Kostikov: letter to author (May 5, 1976).

53. LHO at Cuban consulate: This account is derived primarily from Summers, *Conspiracy,* pp. 371–72. See also WC XXV. 586–634; XXIV. 563, 570, 590; XVI. 33, and HSCA III. 1–194 (Duran interview, Azcue testimony).

54. RCN on Cuban foreknowledge: Comments on *KGB.*

55. "Solo" mission: "Lee Harvey Oswald in Mexico: New Leads," *Lobster* 6, (November 1984); "Hoover Is Said to Have Been Told Oswald Disclosed Plans to Cubans," *The New York Times* (November 12, 1976).

56. Castro on LHO: Comer Clark, "Fidel Castro Says He Knew of Oswald Threat to Kill JFK," *National Enquirer* (October 15, 1967). Clark also quoted Castro saying that he thought Oswald's "visits might be something to do with the CIA" and that "I think he [JFK] was killed by U.S. fascists—right-wing elements who disagreed with him." Castro denied to the HSCA having been interviewed by Clark and "also suggested that had such a threat been overheard by Cuban officials, they and he would have been morally obligated to transmit it to U.S. authorities." (HSCA Report, p. 122).

57. Duran and Azcue on false Oswald: Summers, *Conspiracy,* pp. 374–77.

58. LHO authentication: LHO's address book also contained Duran's name and phone number (XVI. 54), indicating certainly that he was aware of the Cuban consulate official.

59. Duran and CIA: Department of State airgram (December 2, 1963); Henry Raymond, "Havana Accuses Mexico of 'Plot,'" *The New York Times* (November 28, 1963) (cites Cuban complaint); CIA files declassified 1976.

60. CIA desire to "wait out": Summers, *Conspiracy,* p. 382; details on the CIA's relationship to the Warren Commission are found in Book V, Final Report, pp. 57–60.

61. LHO calls taped: "CIA Withheld Details on Oswald Call," *The Washington Post* (November 26, 1975).

62. LHO voice on tape: HSCA Report, p. 251; Summers, *Conspiracy,* p. 385.

63. Eight CIA tapes of LHO: material supplied by Anthony Summers (January 24, 1983) to Fensterwald. (Summers was able to read through the HSCA's still-classified Mexico City report, where this information apparently appears.)

64. Photo of LHO: ibid. In the Summers notes, the five CIA employees are identified as Philip Agee, Daniel Stanley Watson, Joseph B. Smith, Joseph Piccolo, and Daniel Niescuir.

65. Smith on photo: HSCA memorandum from Gaeton Fonzi to G. Robert Blakey (May 8, 1978), interview with Joseph Burkholder Smith.

66. Scott and photo: Summers material.

67. Phillips on LHO photo: In his book *The Night Watch* (New York: Atheneum, 1977), p. 142, Phillips wrote that the CIA "spent several days studying literally hundreds of photographs available to the CIA before and during Oswald's trip to Mexico City. He did not appear in any of them." The HSCA Report states that "The committee believed that photographs of Oswald might have been taken and subsequently lost or destroyed" (p. 125).

68. Twenty photographs: A CIA Memorandum for the Record, dated October 11, 1972, Subject: "Fensterwald

Request for 20 Photographs," describes a CIA discussion with a woman who "was assigned to the Mexican station during the Oswald investigation and was thoroughly familiar with the Mexican aspects of the case." (Author's note: This is probably Scott's assistant, Anne Goodpasture.) "I showed [deleted] the 24 February, FBI memorandum and she said that she could not identify any of the 20 photographs and doubted that they originated with the CIA." The indication is that all twenty photographs were of someone other than Oswald.

69. CIA file: Document No. 11-6A (undated), declassified April 1976.

70. CIA flight to Dallas: In ink on this 1976-declassified document is noted: "Letter informing [deleted] of transmittal of photos which were thought to be of Oswald." This indicates that the referenced photos were of someone other than Oswald, although the wording—"a certain person who is known to you"—also indicates that his identity was known to intelligence officials at the time.

71. FBI and sound tapes: Summers, *Conspiracy,* p. 386.

72. CIA description of LHO: CIA teletype, October 10, 1963: WCD 631.

73. CIA claims on photo date: WCD 1287.

74. Colby quote: Summers, *Conspiracy,* p. 380.

75. Soviet seaman: Summers material.

76. RCN on mystery man: letter to author (February 21, 1976).

77. Allegations on LHO/Cubans in Mexico: (1) "twist party": This came from Elena Garro, a Mexican woman whom the HSCA sought unsuccessfully to interview. A 1969 State Department report described Garro as "a professional anti-Communist." (HSCA III. 291). She apparently also had strong ties to the CIA (Summers, *Conspiracy,* p. 585). (2) LHO meetings with Cuban intelligence: Several 1976-declassified CIA files from May 1964 cite an unnamed "well-placed individual," with direct knowledge of Cuban intelligence personnel, who believed it likely that Manuel Vega Perez and Rogelio Rodriguez Lopez—DGI officials who screened visa applicants—would have seen LHO in Mexico. The source also mentioned a woman, Luisa Calderon. (3) Díaz Verson allegations: A January 29, 1964, CIA file describes him as the source but casts doubt on his credibility. Díaz Verson is identified as one of Phillips's agents in "Afterword: The Search for 'Maurice Bishop,'" *Lobster* 10 (January 1986). Díaz Verson was former Cuban president Carlos Prio's chief of Military Intelligence (1948–52) and sat on the steering committee of the World Anti-Communist Congress for Freedom and Liberation. (4) Oscar Contreras, part of a left-wing student group at Mexico City's National University, recalled a fellow who spelled out his entire name—"Lee Harvey Oswald"—approaching him and three friends, seeking help in getting a visa to Cuba. Oswald spent the night at their apartment. When Summers found Contreras in 1988, he described "Oswald" as short (about five-feet-six) and looking more than thirty. This, again, raises the question of an LHO imposter. (Summers, *Conspiracy,* pp. 377–78.)

78. Alvarado story: Book V, Final Report, pp. 28, 41; WC XXV. 647.

79. Senator Russell on conspiracy: Don Oberdorfer, "Oswald Had Help, Sen. Russell Says," *The Washington Post* (1970), quoting taped TV interviews for broadcast on WSB-TV, Atlanta.

Chapter XXII

The author's interview with William Bishop took place in Cleburne, Texas (May 8, 1990)

Numbered notes are as follows:

1. It is possible that Bishop was really John Adrian O'Hare, a CIA contract agent who reportedly died on March 23, 1975, in Florida. The mystery surrounding O'Hare's demise was detailed in a three-part series by Bob Martin in the magazine *Jacksonville Today* (March, April, May 1989). The possibility of a Bishop-O'Hare link is described in Part 3. Private investigator Kennard Smith also conducted an investigation of O'Hare in a November 30, 1975, report, on file at the AARC. Bishop denied he was O'Hare, but Bernard Fensterwald, Jr. (among others) believed he was.

William C. Bishop (or perhaps O'Hare) died in the summer of 1992 of heart failure. His obituary from the *Madisonville* (Texas) *Meteor* says:

Col. Bishop was born February 18, 1923 in Georgia and passed away July 2, 1992. He served in World War II, Korea and Viet Nam, retiring after thirty years of service. He was a paratrooper with Darby's First Rangers Battalion, and served twenty-three years in military intelligence. His expertise was in South and Central American and Cuban affairs. . . .

2. Morrow on Bishop: author's telephone interview (April 2, 1990).

3. FBI on Bishop: #105-126-39-149 ep. 2 (30-239); MM 2-156. Both pages from the FBI files are undated; the latter notes that Bishop "reportedly spent 17 years in the U.S. Army."

4. Sturgis on Operation 40: Michael Canfield with Alan J. Weberman, *Coup d'État in America* (New York: The Third Press, 1975), pp. 250–52.

5. Operation 40: Warren Hinckle and William Turner, *The Fish Is Red* (New York: Harper & Row, 1981), pp. 52–53.

6. RCN on Masferrer: letter to author (April 8, 1976).

7. Colby replacing FitzGerald: William Colby with James McCargar, *Lost Victory* (Chicago/New York: Contemporary Books, 1989), p. 120. Colby background (including OSS): Tom Mangold, *Cold Warrior* (New York: Simon & Schuster, 1991), pp. 309–10.

8. According to Latin affairs expert Thayer Waldo, Jack Ruby also claimed to be close to certain Cuban exiles,

including Masferrer. "The Garrison Commission on the Assassination of President Kennedy," *Ramparts* (January 1968) p. 61.

9. Kennedys/Monroe/Hoffa: Anthony Summers, *Conspiracy* (New York: McGraw-Hill, 1980), p. 277. Numerous books, including Jim Hougan's *Spooks* (New York: Morrow, 1978) and Summers's *Goddess,* (New York: Macmillan, 1985) have documented the Kennedy-Monroe relationship.

10. RFK on Hoffa: Robert F. Kennedy, *The Enemy Within* (New York: Harper & Row, 1960), p. 75. Considerable background on RFK's war against the mob is found in Arthur M. Schlesinger, Jr., *Robert Kennedy and His Times* (New York: Ballantine Books, 1978), pp. 280–307.

11. Partin on Hoffa plot: "Hoffa 'Plot' to Kill R. F. Kennedy Alleged," *The New York Times* (April 12, 1964), p. 1.

12. Aleman on Trafficante: George Crile III, "The Riddle of AMLASH," *The Washington Post* (May 2, 1976), p. C1. Reprinted in HSCA V. 308–11.

13. Fonzi report: HSCA V. 314.

14. Aleman and FBI agents: Crile, "The Riddle."

15. Trafficante on Aleman: HSCA V. 376.

16. Trafficante on Marcello: ibid., p. 372.

17. Marcello tapes: Jack Newfield, " 'I Want Kennedy Killed!' Hoffa Shouted . . . ," *Penthouse* (May 1992), p. 31.

Also of possible sifnificance are the ties of Marcello and Hoffa to the right-wing. Life Magazine noted in a September 8, 1987 article that Marcello was using "muscle provided by the Ku Klux Klan" for his operations in east-central Louisiana. Walter Sheridan, a former Justice Department staffer for Robert Kennedy, alleged in his book, *The Fall and Rise of Jimmy Hoffa* (New York: Saturday Review Press, 1972, p. 193), that the Teamsters boss contacted Klan figures during November 1961 "in connection with strategy" against federal scrutiny of his dealings with a development scheme in Florida.

18. Mob involvement: See esp. HSCA staff counsel G. Robert Blakey and Richard N. Billings, *The Plot to Kill the President* (New York: Times Books, 1981).

19. Ragano story: Newfield, " 'I Want Kennedy Killed!' "; "Hoffa Had JFK Killed," *New York Post* (January 14, 1992), p. 1.

20. Drug trade: *Newsday* Staff, *The Heroin Trail* (London: Souvenir Press: 1974), p. 167.

21. Operation Eagle/Lynch quote: Peter Dale Scott and Jonathan Marshall, *Cocaine Politics* (Berkeley, Calif.: University of California Press, 1991), pp. 26–27.

22. Del Valle: linked to Trafficante, Hinckle and Turner, *The Fish Is Red,* p. 206.

23. RFK/Hoover/Marcello: John H. Davis, *Mafia Kingfish* (New York: McGraw-Hill, 1989), p. 115.

24. Hoover/Marcello: ibid., p. 266.

25. RCN and Mob friends: author's interviews (October 26, 1975, and December 7, 1986). Of Santoro, Nagell said: "I knew Tom when I was on ice and saw him when I came back from Switzerland." An underboss in the Lucchese crime syndicate in New York, Santoro was convicted under the racketeering act on November 19, 1986.

26. DiPalermo background: Articles in *The New York Times* on organized crime Selwyn Raab, "Top Drug Dealers Named By Police," (December 9, 1975), p. 1, and Fred Ferretti, "How Wheels of Justice Turned For 8 Cogs in Traffic of Drugs" (January 25, 1977), p. 37. The 1975 article relates: "During his sentence at the Atlanta Penitentiary, another convict, Joseph Valachi, believed that Mr. DiPalermo had been ordered to kill him. In May 1962, Mr. Valachi mistakenly killed a prisoner who resembled Mr. DiPalermo. It was that murder that prompted Mr. Valachi to make extensive disclosures about the Cosa Nostra, or Mafia."

27. RCN on friend's Mob awareness: letter to Fensterwald (February 26, 1975).

28. Davidson background is drawn from Davis, *Mafia Kingfish;* see esp. pp. 425–26 ("cash payment" to Nixon).

29. Davidson and Haiti: HSCA XII. 57–59.

30. FBI on Davidson: Bishop to DeLoach memo re I. Irving Davidson (November 1, 1967).

31. Davidson indicted: Davis, *Mafia Kingfish,* p. 2.

32. Hunt/Murchison/MacArthur: Harry Hurt III, *Texas Rich* (New York: W. W. Norton, 1981), p. 164.

33. Nixon/Murchison: James R. Polk, "Murchison Is Said to Link Nixon to Role in Donation," *The New York Times* (July 19, 1974).

34. Hoover/Murchison: James Reston, Jr., *The Lone Star* (New York: Harper & Row, 1989), p. 166.

35. Murchisons/Catena: Dan E. Moldea, *The Hoffa Wars* (New York: Paddington Press, 1978), p. 104.

36. Curington on Hunt/mob: author's telephone interview (May 12, 1992).

37. Baker background: "He Got Things Done," *The New York Times* (January 6, 1966); "He Made At Least One Too Many 'Bargains,' " *The New York Times* (December 27, 1970) (LBJ quote).

38. Baker and the Mob: *The New York Times* (November 7 and 9 and December 18, 1963); Robert W. Winterberger, *The Washington Payoff* (New York: Dell Publishing, 1972), pp. 53–70; G. R. Schreiber, *The Bobby Baker Affair* (Chicago: Henry Regnery, 1964).

39. Murchisons/Hoffa/Baker: *The New York Times* (November 13, 1963); also in the *Times:* "Haiti Meat Concern Still Paying Baker for Aid on Exports" (November 14, 1963); "Inquiry May Call the Murchisons" (November 16, 1963); "Murchison Official Aided Baker in Purchase of Stock" (January 29, 1964); "Baker Made $8,000 in Fees in Haitian Meat Deal" (February 5, 1964); "A Timber Deal Interests Baker Investigators" (February 19, 1964). Davis, *Mafia Kingfish, p. 476; "Construction of the D.C. Stadium and Matters Related Thereto,* part 9, U.S. Senate hearing (February 4–5, 1965), p. 895 (Hoffa-Murchison).

40. LBJ and Marcello: Davis, *Mafia Kingfish,* pp. 272–73.

41. Cohn troubles: "A Decade Later, Roy Cohn Is the Accused," *National Observer* (September 9, 1963);

"Going Which Way?," *Time* (September 13, 1963), p. 27; "The View for Roy Cohn: Courtroom's Other Side," *New York Herald Tribune* (March 22, 1964).

42. Korth background: "Rancher on the Bridge," *The New York Times* (January 5, 1962); "Korth Reported Asked to Resign for 'Indiscretion,' " *The New York Times* (October 19, 1963), p. 1.

43. Reynolds on TFX payoff: Ovid Demaris, *Captive City* (New York: Lyle Stuart, 1969), p. 227.

44. Korth and LHO: WC VII. 475 (at June meeting); WC XXIII. 786 (LHO mother). When LHO wrote to the secretary of the Navy seeking reversal of his undesirable discharge, the responsibility fell to Korth, who had replaced John Connally (WC I. 450). Like the Baker case, soon after the JFK assassination, the Senate's investigation into the TFX contract was put to rest. Korth, who was scheduled as the next witness when hearings recessed on November 20, was never called to testify. The hearings, promised for "next week," did not resume for six years.

45. Baker case and assassination: *The New York Times,* cited in William Turner, *Hoover's FBI: The Man and the Myth* (Los Angeles: Sherbourne Press, 1970), p. 185.

Chapter XXIII

The author's interviews with Frank Ellsworth (July 13, 1976) and John Thomas Masen (July 14, 1976) were conducted in Dallas. The author first described this story in an article "Is the 'Second Oswald' Alive in Dallas?," *The Village Voice* (August 23, 1976) p. 23.

Numbered notes are as follows:

1. Bennett letter: October 11, 1963 (sent author by RCN, 1976).

2. LHO return to Dallas, first moves: WC XXV. 674–75; XIX. 193, 397; XX. 192; XXIII. 752; CE 1950 (de Mohrenschildt listing).

3. LHO on Mexico: WC I. 27–28, 59 (Marina Oswald testimony).

4. JFK visit article: "Connally Tells JFK Texas for Democrats," *Dallas Morning News* (October 5, 1963), p. 1; LHO to rooming house: WC VI. 401.

5. LHO at DRE meeting: WCD 205.646ff.

6. LHO getting TSBD job: WC III. 33–35 (Ruth Paine testimony); III. 213–14 (Roy S. Truly testimony).

7. LHO as "O. H. Lee": WC X. 294 (testimony of Mrs. A. C. Johnson, landlady at 1026 North Beckley). See also Warren Commission Report, App. XIII. 737.

8. Walker rally: *Dallas Morning News* story cited in Albert H. Newman, *The Assassination of John F. Kennedy* (New York: Clarkson N. Potter, 1970), p. 461. LHO attendance: LHO November 1, 1963, letter to Arnold Johnson, Communist Party, U.S.A. (WC XX. 271–74).

9. ICDCC conference: RG-23: CW Papers, Series 1 (conference program); CW letter to "The Hon. U. Alexis Johnson, Deputy Under-Secretary of State" (October 8, 1963), Douglas MacArthur Memorial Library, Norfolk, Virginia. To Johnson, Willoughby wrote: "I attend the Congress in a purely private capacity, as the editor-publisher of the "Foreign Intell Digest. . . . On return from Luzern, I expect to travel via Ascona, Madrid and Lisbon, where I will address similar organizations as well as interview important personages in order to obtain article material."

10. Opus Dei: See Fred Landis, "Secret Order Vies for Power," *CovertAction* 11, No. 18 (Winter 1983), p. 11–15. "By 1965, Opus Dei controlled half of Franco's Cabinet and about a third of its legislature."

11. Oberlander background: Scott Anderson and Jon Lee Anderson, *Inside the League* (New York: Dodd, Mead, 1986), pp. 44–45. The book notes Oberlander's "special relationship" with Ukrainian leader Yaroslaw Stetzko. "Oberlander is a high officer of the ABN's European Freedom Council and leads German delegations to World Anti-Communist League conferences." Peter Dale Scott, "The Dallas Conspiracy" (unpublished manuscript, 1971), p. I-4, cites him as an APACL delegate.

12. Punder background: author's conversation with Peter Dale Scott (June 1992). Scott noted the ties of Oberlander and Punder to the Munich newspaper.

13. Pichel and Nazis: Sander A. Diamond, *The Nazi Movement in the United States: 1924–41* (Ithaca, N.Y.: Cornell University Press, 1974), pp. 116–17.

14. Shickshinny Knights: "The 'Other' Orders of the Knights of Malta," *CovertAction* No. 25 (Winter 1986), p. 36.

15. Willoughby and Pichel: RG-23, CW Papers: correspondence ("Pichel, Charles L. T., Corr., 1931–1970"), CW letters to Pichel of September 1 and 21, 1963. In the latter, Willoughby writes of his upcoming European trip: "I will see Franco and Salazar [prime minister of Portugal]. It is all arranged. I will ascertain delicately their position on the Order. . . ."

16. The complete list of the "Armed Services Committee of the Sovereign Order of Saint John of Jerusalem," on file among the Willoughby correspondence, as of 1962–63 was as follows: General Lemuel C. Shepherd, USM Ret.; Lieutenant General Pedro A. del Valle, USMC Ret.; Lieutenant General Clovis E. Byers, USA Ret.; Major General Charles J. Willoughby, USA Ret.; Major General Allen DeLamater, USA Ret.; Major General Douglass Taft Greene, USA Ret.; Brigadier General H. Terry Morrison, USA Ret.; Brigadier General Bonner Fellers, USA Ret.; Brigadier General Edwin Cox, USA Ret.; Brigadier General J. Harry LaBrum, USA Ret.; Lord Malcolm Douglas-Hamilton, OBE, DFC, RAF; Marquis de Amodio, CB, CBE, MC; Colonel Philip J. Corso, USA Ret.; Colonel Catesby Jones, USA Ret.; Colonel George Stewart, USAF Ret.; Colonel John Monroe Johnson, USA Ret.; Sir Barry Edward Domville, KBE, CB, CMG; Vice Admiral Harold Davies Baker, USN Ret.; Rear Admiral Arthur A. de la Houssaye, USN Ret.; Rear Admiral Robert Lee Porter, USN Ret.; Rear Admiral Herbert S. Howard, USN Ret.; Rear Admiral Richard Blackburn Black, USN Ret.; Rear Admiral

Francis T. Spellman, USN Ret.; Rear Admiral Francis W. Benson, USN Ret.; and Commodore Howard H. J. Benson, USN Ret.

17. Corso background: Burton Hersh, *The Old Boys* (New York: Charles Scribner's Sons, 1992), pp. 347, 411; files of Group Research, Inc., Washington, D.C.

18. LHO on November 1: WC XX. 172 (rental of box 6225); XVIII. 536–37 (change of address to Reznichenko); XVII. 671 (ACLU membership); XX. 271–74 (letter to Arnold Johnson).

19. Hosty seeking LHO: Newman, *The Assassination,* pp. 430–31.

20. Hosty visit with Paine/Marina: WC IV. 447–59 (Hosty testimony). Marina taking license number: Newman, *The Assassination,* p. 477.

21. Hosty name in LHO address book: WC XVI. 64, V. 112, 242; HSCA Report, pp. 186, 327. The initial information that went to the Warren Commission about the contents of Oswald's address book conspicuously contained no reference to Hosty. Only later did the FBI confirm the existence of Oswald's Hosty notation.

22. LHO letter to Soviet embassy: WC XVI. 33. While it has been generally assumed that "comrade Kostin" is a reference to Valery Kostikov, author Michael Eddowes points out the existence of a "clandestine KGB officer" named Valeri Dmitrevich Kostin in his book *The Oswald File* (New York: Clarkson N. Potter, 1977). Eddowes writes (p. 69):

> According to a CIA memorandum to the Warren Commission, Kostin was not listed as working at the Soviet Embassy in Mexico City. It would seem, therefore, that Kostin came to Mexico City either from the Soviet Embassy in Havana or direct from the Soviet Union to confer with "Oswald" after the latter's failure to get to the Soviet Embassy in Havana. . . . it would seem that considerable secrecy had been maintained over the meetings between "Oswald" and Kostin.

23. Paine and letter: WC III. 13, 17–18.

24. Hosty and destruction of LHO note: Background is derived from Anthony Summers, *Conspiracy* (New York: McGraw-Hill, 1980), pp. 395–96; HSCA Report, p. 195; Senate Intelligence Committee, *Performance of Intelligence Agencies,* Appendix B; Hearings on FBI Oversight Before House Subcommittee on Civil and Constitutional Rights, Serial 2, pt. 3 (October 21 and December 11–12, 1975) (Hosty, Shanklin, Fenner testimony).

William Sullivan, then chief of the FBI's Counter Intelligence Division, told *Time* that at least ten top FBI officials in Washington knew of the Oswald note to Hosty ("FBI: Shaken by a Cover-up That Failed," *Time* [November 3, 1975], p. 9). Sullivan died in a hunting accident on November 9, 1977, when he was mistaken for a deer in the White Mountains of New Hampshire. Sullivan had become disenchanted with the FBI in his latter years. In 1973 he called Hoover "a master blackmailer" in an interview with the *Los Angeles Times.* Testifying before the Senate Intelligence Committee, Sullivan said Hoover had leaked the FBI's JFK assassination report about ten days after the shooting to "blunt the drive for an independent investigation of the assassination." See also J. Y. Smith article, *The Washington Post* (November 10, 1977); Jim Marrs, "Ex-Agent 6th to Die in Six-Month Span," *Fort Worth Star-Telegram* (November 10, 1977).

25. Hosty and LHO letter to Soviets: Summers, *Conspiracy,* p. 398. "In fact it would have survived in any case, because a routine FBI mail intercept turned up a copy Oswald actually mailed to the Soviet Embassy."

26. Hosty censure by FBI: Jim Lehrer, "FBI Agent Suspended for 30 Days," *Dallas Times Herald* (October 13, 1964), p. 1.

27. Hosty on RCN: author's telephone interview (1981).

28. RCN on Cuba trip: Memorandum in Support of Petition for Writ of Habeus Corpus, U.S. District Court, Western District of Missouri, draft copy (June 6, 1967), p. 2. Nagell writes that Hammond's disclosure "was later confirmed by persons not herein identified" and adds that Hammond denied Nagell's charge at a November 3, 1963, hearing but was nonetheless relieved as his counsel. According to the *El Paso Times* of November 4, 1963, "Judge Thomason granted the request, after telling Nagell that Mr. Hammond is considered an able, conscientious member of El Paso Bar. Nagell had refused to talk to Mr. Hammond before the hearing opened."

29. RCN at habeas corpus hearing: "Bank Holdup Suspect Says Motive Is Secret," *El Paso Times* (November 4, 1963).

30. RCN statement to FBI: four-page handwritten statement on file, *United States* v. *Nagell,* archives of U.S. District Court for the Western District of Texas, Fort Worth, signed by Edward Joseph Murphy and George E. Aiken as witnesses.

31. RCN note to White: written in undated letter from RCN to attorney Gus Rallis, wherein RCN notes that he had requested the court to order that the FBI turn it over to the U.S. attorney.

32. Train on FitzGerald/RFK: author's telephone interview (June 11, 1992).

33. Cubela/FitzGerald meetings: *Alleged Assassination Plots Involving Foreign Leaders,* Senate Intelligence Committee (1975), pp. 87–89; HSCA X. 157–58.

34. Cubela on meetings: Summers, *Conspiracy,* pp. 350–51.

35. FitzGerald reaction/involvement: Train interview.

36. AM/LASH file withheld: David C. Martin, *Wilderness of Mirrors* (New York: Harper & Row, 1980), pp. 151–53.

37. Cubela/Artime plotting: *Alleged Assassination Plots,* pp. 89–90. Artime is referred to as "B-1" in the Senate report, but his identity as "B-1" has been confirmed by many sources, including George Crile III, "The Riddle of AMLASH," *Washington Post Outlook* (May 2, 1976), p. C1; Frank Faso and Paul Meskil, "Operation Amlash," New York *Daily News* (January 27, 1977), p. 47.

38. Cubela arrest: The Crile article notes, "At his trial in 1966 no one condemned Cubela more harshly than

Cubela himself. He called for the maximum sentence for himself—to be shot against the wall—and he seemed to confess to everything. But he did not mention—nor did the prosecutors ask him about—his earlier CIA plots. There appeared to be a studied attempt to avoid any public mention of Cubela's plotting before 1964. Finally, Castro himself intervened on Cubela's behalf to ask for clemency." See also "Havana Accuses Seven Cubans of Plotting with C.I.A. Agents to Assassinate Castro," *The New York Times* (March 6, 1966), p. 25, and "Cuban Admits Plot to Murder Castro; Requests Execution," *The New York Times* (March 8, 1966).

39. Morgan on Cubela: Crile article.

40. Aleman on Trafficante/Castro: HSCA V. 315. On July 31, 1983, Aleman, then fifty, shot four relatives and then died in a volley of police gunfire in Miami. The *Miami Herald* observed: ". . . he had become a helpless, paranoid recluse who believed 'the Communists and the Mafia' were trying to kill him, intimate friends said."

41. Trafficante and Castro: George Crile, "The Mafia, the CIA, and Castro," *The Washington Post* (May 16, 1976), p. C4.

42. Trafficante on Castro relationship: HSCA V. 369.

43. FitzGerald and exiles: author's interview with Frances FitzGerald (March 16, 1992); Train interview. James E. Flannery, who knew FitzGerald well at the CIA, said of him in our February 13, 1992, telephone interview: "One time in Mexico City, I asked Des what he considered his biggest job in the division. He said, 'I consider my big job is to create the conditions that will make people reach.' And if you failed, well, there you were, you tried anyway. He would defend his people to the end of time."

44. Morrow on del Valle/radios: author's interview (March 27, 1992).

45. Spingler story: Dan Christensen, "JFK, King: The Dade County Links," *Miami Magazine* (September 1976), pp. 25, 42. The Cuban exile who came to the Parrot Jungle was identified as Jorge Martinez, who, according to Summers, *Conspiracy* (p. 447), "had been brought to the United States by Mike McLaney, one of the old Havana gambling bosses." Martinez denied being Spingler's source.

46. LHO call to Marina: WC I. 46. See also confirming testimony by Ruth Paine (III. 45).

47. Reynolds on Abilene Cubans: undated letter to author (1979).

48. Reynolds story: Earl Golz, "Cubans' Friend Believes Oswald Contacted Exile Leader," *Dallas Morning News* (June 10, 1979), p. 1AA. This author interviewed Pedro Gonzalez's 1963 Abilene roommate Raul Alfonzo on July 28, 1979, in Los Angeles. Alfonzo said Gonzalez had "no contact with Harvey Oswald whatsoever as far as I am concerned. Pedro and I were friends before, at the time, and still; he would have told me." Alfonso added that he believed Gonzalez was no longer in the United States.

49. Otero on meeting/coup d'état: HSCA interview with Rolando Otero (June 2, 1977), Lake Butler Prison Hospital, Florida. Otero was serving a thirty-year prison at the time for his involvement in a 1975 series of terrorist bombings in Miami.

50. Hemming on exiles: author's telephone interview (April 4, 1992). The name of Felipe Vidal Santiago also came up in Colonel William Bishop's interviews with researcher Gary Shaw. Bishop maintained that Vidal was an associate of General Walker, whom the exile kept apprised of goings-on in the anti-Castro community. Hemming confirmed to the author that Vidal was one of the Cuban exiles whom his own group, Interpen, introduced to Walker. An FBI file, #105-84265, states that Felipe Vidal Santiago was among the Cuban exiles confined (along with Antonio Veciana) to Dade County, Florida, by government order on March 31, 1963. Vidal was executed in Cuba in 1964 after being captured on an exile raid. Hemming's son is named after him.

51. Martino background: Summers, *Conspiracy,* p. 449; FBI document 64-44828 (July 31, 1959) (Martino-Trafficante connection).

52. Martino and Odio: WC XI. 380; XXVI. 738.

53. John Martino told the FBI that Oswald had contacted Cuban intelligence by phone from a private residence in Miami (see CD 1020, 691–92; Secret Service report CO234030; FBI document 105-82555-2704). FBI agent James J. O'Conner, in a March 24, 1964, report, adds: "Martino stated the information concerning such an alleged telephone call by Oswald to Cuban intelligence did not originate with his friend Felipe Vidal Santiago, a Cuban exile active in anti-Castro activities."

54. Martino on assassination: Summers, *Conspiracy,* pp. 451–52.

55. FBI teletype on exiles: also see CD 1553.

56. Menoyo: FBI file, "Second National Front of Escambray (Operation Alpha 66)" (May 28, 1964), Los Angeles.

57. "Omega Plan": FBI file 105-6243 also states that "ELOY GUTIERREZ MENOYO is in charge of military operations for this combined group." Another FBI file (Miami, June 3, 1964) states: "In June, 1963, the SNFE began publicizing 'Plan Omega' which was alleged to be a military operation which would overthrow the CASTRO government." The Senate Intelligence Committee took note that FBI reports to the Warren Commission on Alpha 66 "did not include the fact that the Alpha 66's leaders in September 1963 had been negotiating for the use of aircraft with which to conduct raids against Cuba, with those involved in a New Orleans anti-Castro training camp." (Book V, Final Report, p. 65).

58. Walthers on Harlendale meetings: WC XIX. 534.

59. Walthers and LHO: WC VII. 548.

60. Ruby comment: Warren Commission Report, p. 342; Summers, *Conspiracy,* p. 480.

61. Walthers on Cubans: WC XIX. 534 (Becker exhibit 5323).

62. Hudkins on Harlandale house: author's interview (May 12, 1976).

63. Rodriguez background: WCD 1085U (FBI Dallas file, May 26, 1964); WCD 853a, Secret Service file CO-2-34, 364, attached to memorandum to J. Lee Rankin. Michael Canfield with Alan J. Weberman, *Coup d'État in America* (New York: The Third Press, 1975), pp. 118–20. Those authors note that a photograph of Rodriguez, supposed to be part of an FBI file, was missing from the National Archives.

64. Masen and Rodriguez: WCD 853a, p. 2.

65. Masen and Mannlicher/Mexico: WC XXVI. 62–64 (WCD 778, pp. 11–15). On October 1, 1963, Ernesto Castellanos, a Cuban exile guest speaker at a John Birch Society meeting in Dallas, was secretly tape-recorded saying that he and other anti-Castroites "are going to give him [Kennedy] the works when he gets in Dallas." According to journalist Earl Golz, who broke the story in the August 14, 1978, *Dallas Morning News*, the tape had been made available "by a retired Dallas police intelligence officer" and was turned over to the House Assassinations Committee. Castellanos said in 1963 that he had lived in Dallas for three and a half years and "had flown in a plane during the abortive Bay of Pigs invasion. . . ."

Chapter XXIV

Except where otherwise noted, the Joseph Milteer story is drawn from the following sources: Dan Christensen, "JFK, King: The Dade County Links," *Miami Magazine* (September 1976), pp. 20–25; Robert J. Groden, "Argosy Discloses: 'The JFK Evidence That Nobody Wanted to Reveal!,'" *Argosy Magazine* (August 1977), pp. 28–34; Bill Barry, "Assassination Idea Taped," *Miami News* (February 2, 1967); WCD 20, FBI file (December 1, 1963), pp. 24–25; WCD 1347, FBI file ("Re: Threat to Kill President KENNEDY by J. A. MILTEER, Miami, Florida, November 9, 1963), pp. 119–24; and files on Milteer of Group Research, Inc., Washington, D.C.

The Eugene Dinkin story is derived from *Eugene B. Dinkin* v. *United States Department of Defense/Central Intelligence Agency/United States of America,* Civil Action No. 75C 1015, U.S. District Court for Eastern District of New York; CIA memorandum to J. Lee Rankin of May 19, 1964, and CIA file of November 26, 1963, both declassified 1976; and WCD 1107, pp. 353–62. The author also interviewed Dinkin in December 1975 in New York City.

Numbered notes are as follows:

1. Gale background: Anti-Defamation League of B'nai Brith *Extremism on the Right: A Handbook* (New York: 1983), pp. 86–87; letter from Steven J. Burton, Citizens' Committee of Inquiry, to William Boxley (March 13, 1968) (Garrison files); memorandum to Jim Garrison from Tom Bethell re: visit of Gerry Patrick Hemming and Roy Hargraves (September 18, 1967) (Gale and Walker).

2. NSRP background: George Thayer, *The Farther Shores of Politics* (New York: Simon & Schuster, 1968), pp. 34–48.

Further indication of a possible NSRP connection to the assassination is found in two FBI files. The first (WCD 1107, p. 374) reports an advisement to the FBI from a University of California, Berkeley, graduate student, Jerry Russell Craddock, on November 27, 1963, that "he contacted one ROBERT BROWN the last week of August, 1963, at Boulder, Colorado. BROWN was described as being anti-Castro, formerly a free-lance correspondent in Cuba and believed to belong to some anti-Castro organization. BROWN stated that, while in California raising funds for anti-Castro activities, a physician or dentist contacted him and told BROWN he was in the process of attempting to recruit an assassin for President KENNEDY."

Brown was interviewed by the FBI on December 4, 1963, in Columbus, Georgia (Commission No. 641). "Captain ROBERT KENNETH BROWN, The School Brigade, Fort Benning, Georgia, advised that he has been active in Cuban matters for several years and during the Spring of 1963, in connection with anti-Castro activity, he was in contact with the National States Rights Party in Los Angeles, California." In this connection, Brown "contacted Dr. STANLEY L. DRENNAN . . . who was active in the National States Rights Party. BROWN stated that once while a guest in Dr. DRENNAN's home, DRENNAN stated in general conversation that he could not do it, but what the organization needed was a group of young men to get rid of KENNEDY, the Cabinet and all members of Americans for Democratic Action. . . ." While Brown initially considered this a "crackpot" remark, "as DRENNAN continued the conversation, he gained the impression that DRENNAN may have been propositioning him on this matter." (Brown later went on to found *Soldier of Fortune* magazine.)

A letter in the Garrison investigation files notes that anti-Castro activists Loran Hall and Lawrence Howard stated they had been at meetings where Dr. Drennan was present; Howard indicated he heard Drennan make the JFK threat. Hall said he met Drennan at a gathering where Colonel William Gale was also present. (March 13, 1968, letter from Steven J. Burton to William Boxley.)

3. Informant's report: "Third Decade Document Discovery: The Congress of Freedom Papers," *The Third Decade,* Vol. 2, No. 2 (January 1986), p. 6–10.

4. Smoot background: See Arnold Forster and Benjamin R. Epstein, *Danger on the Right* (New York: Random House, 1964), pp. 132–43.

5. Miami motorcade change: Anthony Summers, *Conspiracy* (New York: McGraw-Hill, 1980), p. 430.

6. Hemming on Miami security: author's telephone interviews (April 4 and July 24, 1992).

7. Warning on JFK plot: WCE 762, U.S. Secret Service, Protective Research Section report from San Antonio office. William S. Walter, a night-duty security clerk at the FBI's New Orleans field office, charged in 1975 that he had received a TWX message from headquarters on November 17, 1963, that read as follows: "Bureau has determined that a militant revolutionary group may attempt to assinated [sic] President Kennedy on his proposed trip to dallas. . . . All receiving office shouls [sic] immediately [sic] contact all CIS; PCIS logical racial and hate group informants and determine if any basis for threat." This story was reported in an article by Barry Sussman, "New Probe into 'Lost Warning' on JFK," *New York Post* (October 1, 1975), p. 22. After hearing testimony from FBI officials, the HSCA "concluded that Walter's allegations were unfounded." *Report of the Select Committee on Assassinations,* U.S. House of Representatives (March 29, 1979), p. 192.

8. Lippincott on Dinkin: filed as Exhibit B, Dinkin lawsuit, February 10, 1964, letter from John C. Lippincott to Honorable Everett McKinley Dirksen, U.S. Senate.

9. FBI report: WCD 1107.

10. Dinkin as code breaker: transcript, New Orleans researchers' conference (September 21, 1968), pp. 73–75.

11. CIA Souetre files: declassified 1976.

12. Golitsin/Angleton/de Vosjoli: Tom Mangold, *Cold Warrior* (New York: Simon & Schuster, 1991), pp. 117–35. Considerably more intrigue surrounds Philippe de Vosjoli. As tension mounted over Anatoly Golitsin's claims about KGB penetration of the French SDECE, de Vosjoli received a cable on September 16, 1963, that he was being recalled to France after his refusal to spy on the Americans. He resigned instead and, after the CIA gave him a farewell party, de Vosjoli suddenly disappeared. As recounted in *Cold Warrior,* de Vosjoli was in New York that November when he spotted the SDECE's deputy chief, Colonel George de Lannurien, and followed him and another SDECE official to the Harvard Club. De Lannurien was then among the "mole" suspects and de Vosjoli, fearing his own life might be in danger, decided to flee to Mexico.

In May 1978, according to a document on file at the AARC, de Vosjoli was interviewed in Miami by an HSCA investigator. At that time, de Vosjoli was said to have elaborated that he observed Colonel de Lannurien having lunch at the Harvard Club "a few days before the JFK assassination . . . with a group of right-wing Texans." De Vosjoli also "talked generally about plots against Castro and an offer by French Intelligence to the CIA to carry out the Castro assassination for them." On November 22, 1963, the Mangold book points out, Colonel de Lannurien was in James Angleton's office at CIA headquarters when the JFK assassination occurred. Angleton told the HSCA that de Lannurien had come to complain about allegations that "his intelligence service's number two man" was suspected of ties to the Soviets.

13. CIA on Souetre in Dallas: CIA document 632-796 (April 1, 1964) declassified 1977 under the FOIA. An FBI file of May 7, 1964, also declassified in 1977, relates the story of Luis Fernandez Gonzalez, who claimed to be a citizen of Honduras and who appeared at the U.S. embassy in Mexico City on December 2, 1963, "and indicated he possessed information of interest concerning LEE HARVEY OSWALD." Fernandez "alleged that he had been arrested in Miami, Florida, in February, 1963, as a result of his having posed as a Cuban diplomatic official, and later he was deported from the United States to Mexico." He said he was a member of "the National Liberation Movement in Mexico and also a member of the 'Armed Forces of National Liberation' in Venezuela." Fernandez "claimed that about September 28, 1963, and again on or about September 29, 1963, he met an American male whom he had known as JOHN WHITE on the street in front of the Hotel Reforma, Mexico, D.F. FERNANDEZ stated that in his opinion the aforementioned JOHN WHITE greatly resembled newspaper photographs of LEE HARVEY OSWALD." The file goes on that an attorney, Santiago Ibanez Llamas, had told the FBI that Fernandez had been detained by Mexican Immigration authorities on March 4, 1964, "for questioning as a result of information received by Mexican authorities that he had claimed to have information concerning a planned attempt on the life of French President CHARLES DE GAULLE incidental to DE GAULLE'S March 16–19, 1964, visit to Mexico." The attorney related that a Mexican investigation had established that Fernandez's true name was Manuel Santamarina Mendez.

14. CIA and mercenary killers: *Alleged Assassination Plots Involving Foreign Leaders,* Senate Intelligence Committee (November 1975), pp. 43–46. Stephen Rivele, who traveled extensively across Europe researching the "French connection" to the JFK case, postulated that QJ/WIN may have been Robert Blemant, "an intermediary between the Marseille Mafia and the CIA" after World War II and a known narcotics trafficker. See Stephen J. Rivele, "Death of a Double Man," *The National Reporter* (Spring 1987), pp. 44–50. Other researchers have speculated that QJ/WIN was Joe Attia, a heroin financier and assassin for the French SDECE. For Attia background, see "The French Secret Service—6 Agents Have Sold Heroin," *Newsday* (February 13, 1973), p. 7. Jim Marrs of the *Fort Worth Star-Telegram* was told by ex-Army intelligence officer William Spector that WI/ROGUE's real name was Christian Jacques David. David is currently incarcerated in the Atlanta Federal Penitentiary for his part in a heroin-smuggling ring. In interviews with Stephen Rivele, David has claimed knowledge of a French team of assassins being involved in the JFK murder.

The HSCA looked into the allegation of journalist Seth Kantor, in his book *Who Was Jack Ruby?* (New York: Everest House, 1978), that a gun-running associate of Jack Ruby named Thomas Eli Davis III had been bailed out of jail in Algiers at the time of the JFK assassination by QJ/WIN. The HSCA reviewed FBI files stating that Davis "was being held by the Moroccan National Security Police because of a letter in his handwriting which referred in passing to Oswald and to Kennedy assassination." Mrs. Davis reported that her husband was a "soldier of fortune" who had "worked in Indochina, Indonesia, Algeria, and Cuba, always on the 'Western side.' She stated they left the United States on November 2, 1963, and arrived in Tangiers via London, Paris, and Madrid on November 28, 1963."

Davis, according to the FBI, "claims one month in Mexico in late 1962." Another FBI file reviewed by the HSCA noted that Davis was in Los Angeles in May 1963, seeking "an independent group to overthrow the Haitian President Duvalier." More FBI reports (not cited by the HSCA) note that Davis's Haitian recruitment venture was connected to the Cuban exile group Alpha 66. The registry of the Hotel La Salle in New Orleans shows that a "T. E. Davis" was registered there on August 8–9, 1963.

Davis, a native Texan, was discharged from a five-year Army stint in February 1958; he later told the FBI he had served in a Ranger battalion in Korea. In June 1958 he was arrested for attempted bank robbery in Detroit where, in a situation strikingly similar to Richard Nagell's 1963 arrest, Davis suddenly exclaimed "I can't do it," grabbed a note he had placed on the counter demanding money, and ran out of the bank; he was arrested a block away as he reached his car (FBI files). Davis died mysteriously in September 1973, electrocuted while stealing some copper wire from an abandoned rock crusher site in Wise County, Texas (Kantor, *Who Was Jack Ruby?,* p. 16).

15. Ewing on Souetre: author's telephone interview (December 1980).

16. Mertz background: *Gary Shaw* v. *Department of State et al.,* U.S. District Court for the District of Colum-

bia, Civil Action No. 80-1056, pp. 15–17. Published accounts about Mertz's exploits can be found in *Newsday* Staff, *The Heroin Trail* (New York: New American Library, 1974), pp. 109–29; Pierre Demaret, *Target de Gaulle* (New York: Dial Press, 1975), pp. 98–106; and Pierre Galant, *The Marseilles Mafia* (London: W. H. Allen, 1979), pp. 41–55.

17. Roux background: *Shaw* v. *Department of State et al.,* pp. 17–20; author's telephone interview with Leon Gachman (January 1981). I also spoke by telephone on January 21, 1981, to Roux, who found the entire incident "completely strange to me" and added: "Who knows, maybe I met somebody and somebody used my name."

18. Bailey on Frenchman in Dallas: author's telephone interview (January 13, 1981).

19. Alderson on Souetre: author's telephone interviews (January 13 and 18, 1981).

20. Perez on OAS: Bernard Fensterwald, Jr., *Summary of Paris Trip—November 13–22, 1982,* p. 4. Perez added that he met with Guy Banister in Madrid, but did not specify the date.

21. OAS and exiles: author's telephone conversation with Peter Dale Scott (January 16, 1981).

22. John Birch Society on OAS: John Birch Society, *White Book* (July 1962), pp. 7–9.

23. Lecavelier on OAS/American connections: interview with Gilbert Lecavelier, questions by Bud Fensterwald, interpretation by Alan Farrell, Paris (November 1982). Also, letter from Lecavelier to Fensterwald (January 11, 1982). On file AARC, Washington, D.C. Jim Gentry, a soldier-of-fortune type who once fought with Castro in the mountains, told me in 1984 that he "knew of an OAS man, strictly a behind-the-lines type from the word go, who was definitely tied into Oswald and the Kennedy affair. There was a connection with him and Oswald in Mexico City." (Gentry, who lived in Miami, has since died.)

24. Souetre comments: "Is This the Man Who Killed JFK?," *National Enquirer* (November 22, 1983); Jacques Chambaz, "This French Terrorist Accused of Murdering Kennedy," *Le Quotidien de Paris* (January 1, 1984).

25. JFK assassins from Marseilles: Stephen J. Rivele memos, 1986–87, on file at AARC, Washington.

26. Rivele on Souetre/RCN: telephone conversation with author (June 10, 1992).

Author's note: A possible "French connection" to the JFK case is well worth pursuing by future researchers. A Garrison investigation file (June 21, 1968, "Meeting with Representative of French Deuxième Bureau"), describes an interview between Garrison staffer Steve Jaffe and a Frenchman named "Phillipe" at the "Club KAMA in the Latin Quarter of Paris." They were introduced by Jaffe's contact, Herve Lamarre, who told Jaffe "that it was Phillipe who had been so instrumental in gathering information about the oil industry people involved in the plot against Kennedy. . . . At one time Phillipe had met with a man in Mexico who had been part of the ambush group which murdered the President in Dealey Plaza. . . . Phillipe had had this conference in a hotel in Mexico City in approximately 1966." (Phillipe's specialty was the international petroleum industry.)

"Although Phillipe had never admitted to this meeting to me," the Jaffe file continues, "he did confirm in subtle terms, always being careful to qualify his statements as 'his own personal opinions,' that he was aware of the Hotel Luna [sic: Luma], that it had been an important meeting place for the assassination and in 1963 it had certain residents who were Cuban. . . . He suggested that the hotel (LUNA) had a 'Cuban band' and after that the analogy became one of discussing musicians and 'their instruments.' " (See Chapters Nine, Ten, and Sixteen for more on the Hotel Luma.)

Chapter XXV

The author interviewed Raymond Broshears in San Francisco (October 31, 1975).

Numbered notes are as follows:

1. Background on JFK's last day is drawn from Michael R. Beschloss, *The Crisis Years* (New York: Edward Burlingame Books, 1991), pp. 670–71; and Albert H. Newman, *The Assassination of John F. Kennedy* (New York: Clarkson N. Potter, 1970), pp. 524–25.

2. JFK and Vietnam: Arthur M. Schlesinger, Jr., *Robert Kennedy and His Times* (New York: Ballantine Books, 1978), p. 768 (JFK quote), p. 772 (withdrawal). For the most extensive analysis to date, see John M. Newman, *JFK and Vietnam: Deception, Intrigue, and the Struggle for Power* (New York: Warner Books, 1992).

3. Kennedys and Lodge: ibid., p. 771.

4. Lodge and Willoughby: CW Papers, MacArthur Archives, Norfolk, Virginia.

5. Lodge in Honolulu: J. Gary Shaw with Larry R. Harris, *Cover-up* (Cleburne, Tex.: self-published, 1976), p. 200.

6. LBJ/Lodge meeting: Schlesinger, *Robert Kennedy,* p. 782. On December 6, 1963, Secretary of State Dean Rusk cabled Lodge, eyes only, that "The President has expressed his deep concern that our effort in Viet-Nam be stepped up to highest pitch." (p. 783).

7. Daniel-Castro meeting: Jean Daniel, "Unofficial Envoy: An Historic Report from Two Capitals," *The New Republic* (December 14, 1963), pp. 15–20; Jean Daniel, "Two Interviews: Castro's Reply to Kennedy Comments on Cuba," *The New York Times* (December 11, 1963). See also Schlesinger, *Robert Kennedy and His Times* (New York: Ballantine, 1979), pp. 596–600. Castro verified Daniel's statements in an interview with Tad Szulc published in *Parade* magazine (April 1, 1984).

Within a few weeks, however, President Johnson reversed the JFK rapprochement policy. As Max Frankel reported in "President Asks Review on Cuba," *The New York Times* (December 9, 1963), p. 1: "President Johnson has ordered a special review of United States policy toward Cuba. His purpose apparently is to determine whether any more can be done to encourage opposition to Premier Fidel Castro both on the island and throughout the Western Hemisphere." Then, on December 16, the United States moved to increase Castro's economic isolation "by instituting a new set of controls on Western shipping engaged in trade with Cuba."

Henry Raymont, "U.S. Revises Rules on Shipping to Cut Trade with Cuba," *The New York Times* (December 17, 1963), p. 1.

8. LHO on November 22: Newman, *The Assassination,* p. 525; WC I. 72–73 (Marina Oswald testimony).

9. Frazier on LHO: WC II. 222.

10. Direction of shots: Anthony Summers, *Conspiracy* (New York: McGraw-Hill, 1980), pp. 55, 58.

11. Rowland seeing two men: WC II. 169–83. When Rowland informed FBI agents over that weekend about the second man, "they told me it didn't have any bearing or such on the case right then." Summers, *Conspiracy,* p. 73.

12. Cartridges found: WC III. 284.

13. Radio description: WC XXIII. 916.

14. Rifle discovery: WCE 2003, p. 63. Deputy Sheriff Roger D. Craig, who was on the sixth floor during the search, wrote in 1975 that he and Boone discovered the rifle, "a 7.65 Mauser, so stamped on the barrel." Cited in Robert Sam Anson, *"They've Killed the President!"* (New York: Bantam Books, 1975), p. 77. Craig, who also maintained he saw Oswald run and get into a light-colored Rambler station wagon in Dealey Plaza a few minutes after the assassination, lost his job when he sought to bring his information to Jim Garrison's attention. He committed suicide in 1975. Anson, *"They've Killed the President!,"* p. 217.

15. Ellsworth on rifle: author's interviews, Dallas (July 13, 1976) and by telephone (July 19, 1992).

16. Powell at scene: WCD 354; Shaw and Harris, *Cover-up,* p. 31 (Powell photograph) and p. 194.

17. Revill and Army officer: WC V. 57.

18. Revill/Army/LHO address: WCE 709; WC XXII. 156–57; IV. 180–81; Anson, *"They've Killed the President!,"* p. 175.

19. Phone breakdown in D.C.: William Manchester, *The Death of a President* (New York: Popular Library, 1968), pp. 198–99.

20. Pentagon in command: Jim Bishop, *The Day Kennedy Was Shot* (New York: Random House, 1968), p. 271.

21. Bishop at Parkland: author's interview, Cleburne, Texas (May 8, 1990).

22. Crenshaw on wounds: See Charles A. Crenshaw, M.D., with Jens Hansen and J. Gary Shaw, *JFK: Conspiracy of Silence* (New York: Signet Books, 1992). At a press conference on May 19, 1992, five doctors who attended JFK at Parkland Hospital maintained that they observed nothing to contradict the findings of two pathologists who performed the autopsy that night—that the president was struck by only two bullets fired from above and behind. Lawrence K. Altman, "Doctors Affirm Kennedy Autopsy Report," *The New York Times* (May 20, 1992), p. 1.

23. JFK autopsy: transcript of interview with Colonel Pierre Finck by Jim Garrison's office, reprinted in Shaw with Harris, *Cover-up,* pp. 195–97.

24. FBI and "missile": Jim Marrs, *Crossfire* (New York: Carroll & Graf, 1989), p. 375. Marrs cites two documents, one from the FBI of November 22, 1963: "We hereby acknowledge receipt of a missile removed by Commander James J. Humes, MC, USN on this date." The other is a letter of receipt, dated November 26, 1963, from the Protective Research Section of the Treasury Department. It lists "One receipt from FBI for a missile removed during examination of the body." Marrs concludes: "All of this suggests yet another bullet was discovered but kept secret, since another bullet would have destroyed the lone-assassin theory. . . ."

25. Humes burning notes: WC XVII. 48.

26. Humes explanation: Altman, "Doctors Affirm."

27. Missing brain: HSCA VII. 25ff. Wecht: HSCA I. 349, 362; VII. 201. Cited in Summers, *Conspiracy,* pp. 45, 68–71.

28. CIA and HSCA evidence: Summers, *Conspiracy,* p. 46; George Lardner, Jr., "CIA Officer Rifled Assassination Files," *Los Angeles Times* (June 18, 1979); Janet Battaile, "C.I.A. Says It Ousted Officer After a Search of House Unit's Files," *The New York Times* (June 18, 1979).

29. RCN request: *Memorandum in Support of Petition for Writ of Habeas Corpus,* U.S. District Court, Western District of Missouri, draft copy (June 6, 1967). p. 3.

30. RCN on conspiracy: author's interview (October 26, 1975). At another interview, on October 5, 1977, when I asked Nagell about financial backing behind the assassination, he said: "There was no big money behind the assassination itself, though there was money involved in peripheral matters. The most I ever handled at one time was, I believe, five hundred dollars. I handled much more than that on other occasions. But there was no *contract,* is what I'm saying."

31. RCN on LHO: letters to Bernard Fensterwald, Jr. (March 21, 1975, and February 1, 1975).

32. RCN on LHO shooting ability: author's interview (July 27, 1984).

33. RCN on San Antonio man: "Comments By Richard Case Nagell on William R. Martin's 5-Page Memorandum Dated May 11, 1967, to Jim Garrison, District Attorney," sent to author in 1976.

34. RCN on rifle substitution: letter to Fensterwald (June 9, 1971).

35. Harry Power: Other files on Power, in the possession of Dallas researcher Mary Ferrell, describe the rifle found in his Indiana hotel room as a 7.65mm German Mauser. Terre Haute authorities noted they had "reason to believe this subject is using this name [Power] as an alias."

36. RCN on Power: letter to author (May 13, 1976).

37. RFK organized crime conference: John H. Davis, *Mafia Kingfish* (New York: McGraw-Hill, 1989), p. 180; Schlesinger, *Robert Kennedy,* p. 654.

38. Marcello trial: Davis, *Mafia Kingfish,* pp. 180–81.

39. Ferrie to Texas: ibid, pp. 186–87 (FBI file cited on call to Marcello headquarters).

40. Wall/Ruby/Ferrie: Summers, *Conspiracy,* pp. 482–83.

41. Ferrie and LHO card/inquiries: HSCA X. 113–14.

42. Plane at Redbird: author's conversation with Dallas researcher Mary Ferrell (May 12, 1992) concerning radio station reports about airplane complaints. An FBI file of March 10, 1967, describes statements made by Louis Gaudin, the government's air traffic control specialist at Redbird airport, who recalled observing three men in business suits board a Comanche-type aircraft at about 2:00 P.M. on November 22, head north, then return with only two occupants, where they were met by a Dallas policeman named Haake.

43. LHO and Tippit: There is considerable controversy over whether Oswald actually shot officer Tippit. One witness, Mrs. Acquilla Clemons, stated to independent investigators that she saw two men near the policeman's car just before Tippit was shot; another, Frank Wright, told researchers that he saw a man standing over Tippit who then drove rapidly away in "a little gray old coupe." See Henry Hurt, *Reasonable Doubt* (New York: Holt, Rinehart, & Winston, 1985), pp. 139–70, and Summers, *Conspiracy,* pp. 114–26, for thorough analyses of the Tippit shooting. Richard Nagell indicated his apparent belief, in a series of cartoons that he sent to Arthur Greenstein, that someone other than Oswald killed the policeman.

44. Fritz and LHO interrogation: Warren Commission Report, p. 180 (lack of notes). The Report's Appendix XI contains everything known on Oswald's statements following his arrest.

45. Ellsworth on LHO attitude: author's telephone interview (July 19, 1992).

46. Hosty at interrogation: This account is drawn primarily from Clarence M. Kelley and James Kirkpatrick Davis, *Kelley: The Story of an FBI Director* (Kansas City, Mo.: Andrews, McMeel, & Parker, 1987), pp. 289–93.

47. Ruby on FPCC: Warren Commission Report, p. 342.

48. LHO at press conference: Mark North, *Act of Treason* (New York: Carroll & Graf, 1991), p. 413; Newman, *The Assassination,* pp. 547–48.

49. ACLU rebuffed: Harold Weisberg, *Whitewash,* Vol. I (New York: Dell Publishing, 1966), p. 137.

50. "I'm just a patsy!": Summers, *Conspiracy,* p. 86, citing radio/TV tapes.

51. Ruby phone calls: HSCA IX. 190–96.

52. Ruby and McWillie: HSCA IX. 193; V. 370 (Trafficante testimony).

53. Ruby and FBI: Seth Kantor, *Who Was Jack Ruby?* (New York: Everest House, 1978), p. 87, quotes from a Hoover memo to Warren Commission counsel Rankin that "Ruby had been contacted nine times by the FBI in 1959, from March 11 to October 2, 'to furnish information' on criminal matters." Hoover requested that this fact be kept from the public, and the commission complied.

54. Ruby and Cuba: WC V. 200. And gun-running: WC XXIV. 345; HSCA IX. 188. The HSCA notes (IX. 176): "There is very strong evidence that Ruby made more than one trip to Cuba. . . ." It was alleged by John Wilson Hudson that Ruby visited Santos Trafficante, Jr., when the mobster was imprisoned by Castro in 1959; Trafficante denied the charge (V. 371).

55. Ragano on Mob involvement: Jack Newfield, " 'I Want Kennedy Killed!' Hoffa Shouted . . .," *Penthouse* (May 1992), pp. 31–32, 36, 102, 104, 106. A recently declassified FBI file on Trafficante, dated April 11, 1967, describes Ragano having written to Director Hoover on March 27, 1967. The letter was not made public, but the file quotes Ragano as stating "that some of the allegations involving TRAFFICANTE have been ridiculous" and depicts the attorney's seeking at that time to deflect any suspicion of Trafficante's involvement in the assassination. The FBI file, addressed from the Tampa field office to Hoover, also contains this curious notation: "TRAFFICANTE, on instructions of Attorney RAGANO, to utilize recorder on his person."

56. Giancana murder: Lawrence Meyer and Joel D. Weisman, "Giancana, Linked to CIA Plot, Slain," *The Washington Post* (June 21, 1975), p. 1; Summers, *Conspiracy,* p. 502.

57. Hoffa disappearance: "Jimmy Hoffa Vanishes," *Newsweek* (August 11, 1975), pp. 19–21.

58. Rosselli murder: Nicholas Gage, "Rosselli Called a Victim of Mafia Because of His Senate Testimony," *The New York Times* (February 25, 1977), p. 1.

59. RCN on Giancana/Rosselli: author's interview (July 27, 1984).

60. RCN on Leopoldo's fate: letter to Fensterwald (March 21, 1975); author's interviews (October 5, 1977, and July 27, 1984). Colonel William Bishop maintained in our 1990 interview that Leopoldo had been killed in an automobile accident in Mexico in 1978.

61. RCN on Angel: letter to Fensterwald (March 21, 1975).

62. RCN on Angel's release: author's interview (July 27, 1984).

63. Angleton on CIA-Mob/mobster's fate: author's interview, Washington, D.C. (October 22, 1976).

64. Harvey death/papers: David C. Martin, "The Life and Hard Times of 'America's James Bond,' William King Harvey," *The Washington Post* (October 10, 1976), p. C1. Some of Harvey's handwritten notes about the CIA's "ZR/RIFLE" assassination program have survived and were printed in HSCA IV. 197–204. They included this statement: "5. Cover: planning should include provision for blaming Sovs [Soviets] or Czechs in case of blow."

65. Hoover on LHO: Memo cited by Hurt, *Reasonable Doubt,* p. 19.

66. Scott and LHO: WCD 674 (p. 1) describes three cabled reports received from Mexico City on November 22–23. The interaction between the CIA and the Pentagon is described in the following cryptic Naval Intelligence memorandum: "Copy of photo to AMEMB Mexico City Winfield [sic] Scott. At 2315 received call from Lcdr. [Lieutenant Commander] Hamar directing me to send the copy of the file to Pentagon ASAP. File was held while checking w Capt Jackson. Second conversation w Lcdr Hamar revealed this had been cleared w/Adm Taylor. Then sent the file via Agent Roach. Roach to State w [with]/. Make sure Bliss brings two small copies of the picture." See also HSCA V. 24 for the early CIA reaction to the assassination.

67. LBJ meeting with McCone: interview with McCone by Joe B. Frantz, for Lyndon B. Johnson Memorial Library, Austin, Texas (August 19, 1970). "I saw him [LBJ] almost immediately upon his arrival in Washington," McCone said.

68. LBJ/Hoover call: North, *Act of Treason,* pp. 412–13.

69. Castro speech on LHO: Central Intelligence Agency memorandum (November 25, 1963), "SUBJECT: Fidel Castro's Speech," declassified 1976.

70. Soviet reaction to assassination: quoted in Michael R. Beschloss, *The Crisis Years* (New York: Edward Burlingame Books, 1991), pp. 677–78. A CIA memorandum of January 21, 1964, adds: "In the period immediately following the assassination of President Kennedy many Soviet officials are reported to have expressed their private opinions that Oswald was the tool of an ultra right-wing conspiracy in the United States which *interalia* plotted to murder the President, seize power, break relations with the Soviet Union, and invade Cuba." A December 14 article in the official Soviet Army organ *Red Star* is quoted as speculating that " 'Texas oil millionaires' contacted the Chicago underworld in order to arrange the assassination." The CIA also takes notice of "a Foreign Broadcast Intercept Service report" from Prague that quoted " 'an ultraright wing Italian paper *Secolon'* (Il Secolo) as stating that, 'President Kennedy fell victim to a gang of criminals linked with certain political circles in Texas.' "

71. Zapruder film background: Hurt, *Reasonable Doubt,* pp. 128–30; Summers, *Conspiracy,* p. 47.

72. HSCA conclusion: HSCA *Report,* p. 44.

73. Hoover on error: Sylvia Meagher, *Accessories After the Fact* (New York: Vintage Books, 1976), p. 22; HSCA I. 100. In a letter from Hoover to J. Lee Rankin on December 4, 1964, the director writes: "You previously have been informed that this Bureau is in possession of a copy of a film portraying the assassination of President John F. Kennedy. The film being referred to was taken by Adrian [sic] Zapruder who, after making a copy available to the FBI, sold the film to 'Life' magazine. . . . The Central Intelligence Agency has inquired if the film copy in possession of this Bureau can be loaned to that Agency solely for training purposes."

74. C. D. Jackson and film: Marrs, *Crossfire,* pp. 66–69.

75. Jackson and CIA: Carl Bernstein, "The CIA and the Media," *Rolling Stone* (October 20, 1977), p. 63. "While a *Time* executive, Jackson coauthored a CIA-sponsored study recommending the reorganization of the American intelligence services in the early 1950s," writes Bernstein, who adds that some of his "cover" arrangements for the CIA "were made with the knowledge of [Henry] Luce's wife, Clare Boothe."

76. *Life* magazine description: Paul Mandel, "End of Nagging Rumors: The Six Critical Seconds," *Life* (December 6, 1963).

77. Missing frames: Robert Groden, "A New Look at the Zapruder Film," *Rolling Stone* (April 24, 1975), pp. 35–36.

78. Rothermel on Hunt purchase of film: author's telephone interview (May 15, 1992).

Chapter XXVI

The author's interviews with Paul Rothermel, Jr., were conducted in Dallas (July 12, phone) and in person (July 13, 1976); also, in two more telephone conversations in 1992.

The interview with John Curington took place by phone (May 12, 1992), with two subsequent conversations to go over details.

The interview with Madeleine Brown was also conducted by phone (August 4, 1992).

The Rothermel memorandums and letters quoted in this chapter were obtained by the author in 1976 from a private source (not Rothermel) and were also provided by the author to Harry Hurt III, who included portions in his book *Texas Rich* (New York: W. W. Norton, 1981).

The Charles Willoughby correspondence with H. L. Hunt and his son Nelson Bunker Hunt is on file at the MacArthur Archives Norfolk, Virginia.

Numbered notes are as follows:

1. The account of the Hunts' leaving Dallas for Washington is drawn from Hurt, *Texas Rich,* pp. 231–33. H. L. Hunt verified the basic story in a 1966 interview with *Playboy.* Hunt claimed that his family had received warning threats right after the assassination and "We were sent out of town, and neither the police department nor the FBI would consent to us returning to Dallas until a few days before Christmas."

2. Hunt background: Besides *Texas Rich,* see "A Multimillionaire with a Right-Wing Mission," *The New York Times* (August 17, 1964); and Marquis Childs, "Oil $$ Putting McCarthy on TV," *New York Post* (June 18, 1953).

3. Oil industry: These figures are drawn from James Hepburn's *Farewell America* (Vaduz, Liechtenstein: Frontiers, 1968), pp. 234–38.

4. Hunt quote: ibid., pp. 245–52.

5. JFK on Hunts: Marquis W. Child's syndicated column "Washington Calling" (October 10, 1963). JFK's remarks may have been prompted by a White House "Memorandum for the President" (Meyer Feldman, August 15, 1963), which noted: "Hunt is a frank champion of plutocracy, and reputed to be the richest or second richest man in America. . . . In a Houston, Texas, speech, he said, 'It is just as well that the Cuban invasion failed, because it was just one Communist government trying to overthrow another. . . . *Life Line* is often sponsored by the Hunt Food Company and the cost is taken as a business deduction by the company, even though that company may sell no food whatsoever within 1,000 miles of the place of the broadcast. Contributions to the *[Life Line]* Foundation are tax-exempt, even though the Foundation uses the funds for purely right-wing propaganda purposes. Sometimes the Foundation receives funds from the business corporation by selling the business transcripts and 'talent' for its radio shows. The talent consists of an employee of the Foundation who reads the transcript." (The author obtained the memorandum from the files of Political Research Associates, Cambridge, Massachusetts.)

6. Nelson Hunt and black-bordered ad: Warren Commission Report, pp. 296–97.

7. Jack Ruby at offices: WC XXV. 194. Citing WC and HSCA files, David E. Scheim, *Contract on America*

(New York: Shapolsky, 1988), p. 240, adds: "According to an informant judged reliable by the Secret Service, Ruby had met H. L. Hunt in the early 1950s through some large football bets made between them. Two other sources confirmed Hunt's fondness for high-stakes gambling, and a third indicated that Ruby and Hunt had patronized the same Dallas gambling club in the 1940s." William McEwan Duff, who worked for General Edwin Walker between late 1962 and early 1963, told the Secret Service that Ruby also visited Walker "on the basis of about once a month, each time in the company of two unidentified white males." WCE 2389, cited in William W. Turner, "The Garrison Commission on the Assassination of President Kennedy," *Ramparts* (January 1968) pp. 59–60. The same article mentions the Warren Commission's finding that Ruby's notebook contained the name of Thomas Hill, an "official of the John Birch Society" in Belmont, Massachusetts.

8. Ruby and *Life Line* scripts: WCE 1322, pp. 734, 754, 757.

9. Hunt number in Ruby book: WCE 2980, p. 13.

10. Hunt death/fortune: "A Scandal for the Hunt Clan," *Newsweek* (March 24, 1975), p. 26.

11. LHO letter to "Dear Mr. Hunt": The letter is reprinted in HSCA IV. 337; testimony about the letter and the HSCA conclusions are in IV. 357–61. The author's account is drawn from Earl Golz, "Alleged Oswald Letter Checked for Its Authenticity by FBI Agents," *Dallas Morning News* (February 6, 1977); Mary Ferrell, " 'Concerding' the Oswald Letter," *The Continuing Inquiry* (March 1977), pp. 7–8, 13 (signature comparisons), and the author's telephone conversation with reporter Golz (June 11, 1992).

12. FBI investigation: Henry Hurt, *Reasonable Doubt* (New York: Holt, Rinehart, & Winston, 1985), p. 236, citing FBI memo Legal Counsel to Associate Director (February 9, 1977) (HQ 62-117290-161).

13. Rothermel background: Hurt, *Texas Rich*, p. 188.

14. Earle Cabell was also the brother of Air Force general Charles Cabell, a former CIA deputy director who resigned on January 31, 1962, after the Bay of Pigs disaster. It was revealed by *The Washington Post* (September 16, 1973) that Jim Garrison was preparing as late as March 1971 to accuse General Cabell of conspiracy in the JFK assassination. General Cabell died in 1970, Earle Cabell in 1975.

15. Butler background: Anthony Summers, *Conspiracy* (New York: McGraw-Hill, 1980), pp. 458–59, 490. Summers notes that Lieutenant Butler "had handled the exposure and prosecution of Ruby's friend Paul Jones when he tried to bribe Dallas officials into giving the Mafia free rein in Dallas. After the assassination it was Butler who, in contradiction of the former sheriff, declared that Ruby had been innocent of involvement in the Mafia operation. Just before the Oswald shooting Butler was sought out in the basement by a reporter who had found him especially reliable and controlled in the hectic hours since the assassination. Now, however, the reporter testified later, Butler's poise 'appeared to have deserted him completely. . . . He was an extremely nervous man, so nervous that . . . I noticed his lips trembling.' Today, Butler concedes that he had the jitters but says that it was because he was concerned that arrangements for Oswald's transfer was [sic] poorly organized."

16. "Braden" arrest: WC XXIV. 202, XXV. 626; WCDs 385/401/816.

17. Brading criminal record: Peter Noyes, *Legacy of Doubt* (New York: Pinnacle Books, 1973), pp. 28–29.

18. Brading in New Orleans: ibid., p. 158.

19. Brading at Hunt offices/Dallas departure: ibid., pp. 71–72, 75, 79, 81. Brading at Cabana/Ruby visit: Summers, *Conspiracy*, pp. 475–76. According to Noyes, Brading maintained that his business associate Roger Bauman and two other men, Morgan Holbert Brown and Duane Hermin Nowlin, had visited the Hunt Oil Company. All three of those men were discovered by Noyes to have underworld connections.

20. Willoughby/Hunt correspondence on assassination: CW memos to H. L. Hunt (September 7 and 8, 1965) (the memos are addressed to "L. H. Hunt," but the Dallas home address listed is the Hunts'). The September 1967 letter is undated. Willoughby makes another reference to the assassination in a letter to Hunt employee Austin B. Taylor (February 17, 1968).

21. Bandera background: Scott Anderson and Jon Lee Anderson, *Inside the League* (New York: Dodd, Mead, 1986), pp. 22–25 (World War II), p. 34 (recruitment). See also Russ Bellant, *Old Nazis, the New Right, and the Republican Party* (Boston: South End Press, 1991), pp. 69, 76.

22. Oberlander background: Anderson and Anderson, *Inside the League*, pp. 44–45. Involvement in Bandera murder: Karl Anders, *Murder to Order* (London: Ampersand, 1965), pp. 102–3.

23. Stashinsky defection: *Murder to Order*, pp. 77–85. Christopher Andrew and Oleg Gordievsky, *KGB: The Inside Story* (New York: HarperCollins, 1990), notes: "According to Anatoli Golitsyn, who defected four months after Stashinsky, at least seventeen KGB officers were sacked or demoted. More important, the [Nikolai] Khokhlov and Stashinsky defections led both the Politburo and the KGB leadership to reassess the risks of 'wet affairs.' After the worldwide publicity generated by Stashinsky's trial, the Politburo abandoned assassination by the KGB as a normal instrument of policy outside the Soviet Bloc, resorting to it only on rare occasions. . . ." (p. 465).

24. Stashinsky weapon: CIA report, *Soviet Use of Assassination and Kidnapping* (February 17, 1964), p. 15.

25. Doubts on Stashinsky: Anders, *Murder to Order*, p. 86.

26. Use of confession: Peter Dale Scott, "The Dallas Conspiracy" (unpublished manuscript, 1971), p. II-30.

27. LHO MVD subsidy: Edward Jay Epstein, *Legend* (New York: Reader's Digest Press/McGraw-Hill, 1978), pp. 107–8, 121, 170.

28. Kersten summation: Anders, *Murder to Order*, pp. 108–10.

29. Judge Jagusch: ibid., pp. 90–96.

30. Kersten letter to JFK: Robert S. Allen and Paul Scott column, *Philadelphia Daily News* (November 26, 1963) repr. *Ukrainian Bulletin* (January 1–15, 1964), p. 2, cited in Scott, "Dallas Conspiracy," p. II-31.

31. Stashinsky/LHO: Scott, "Dallas Conspiracy," p. II-30, citing *Ukrainian Bulletin*, ibid., and *New York Journal-American* (January 11, 1964).

Notes

32. Willoughby on Europeans/LHO: Willoughby memo to H. L. Hunt (September 7, 1965).

33. Background on the Hunt wiretap case is drawn from Hurt, *Texas Rich,* pp. 276–308. Houston lawyer Percy Foreman was indicted, along with the Hunt brothers, in a separate obstruction-of-justice case (the charges against Foreman were dropped in 1976; Nelson Hunt paid a $1,000 fine). Jon Kelly, one of the Hunt wiretappers, later claimed that when he told Foreman he was planning to testify against the family in exchange for immunity, Foreman "responded by telling him that the Hunts had the means to hire a Mafia assassin if they were double-crossed, and advised, 'The government can't help you if you are dead.'" (Hurt, *Texas Rich,* pp. 305–6). Foreman was also the attorney for James Earl Ray, convicted slayer of Dr. Martin Luther King, Jr., in 1968; Ray later charged that Foreman coerced him into entering a guilty plea, but the court ruled this was unfounded. See *The Final Assassinations Report* (New York: Bantam Books, 1979), pp. 416–20.

34. Bunker Hunt on taps: "Bunker Hunt Says He Was Unaware Taps Were Illegal," *The New York Times* (September 26, 1975).

35. Rothermel explanation: Hurt, *Texas Rich,* pp. 300–301; "A Scandal for the Hunt Clan," *Newsweek* (March 24, 1975), p. 26.

36. Hunt charges on CIA: "Hunt Sons Charge C.I.A. Used Agents to Embezzle Funds," *The New York Times* (July 23, 1975).

37. CIA and Hunts: Martin Waldron, "U.S. Inquiry on 'Theft' of $50 Million from Hunt Foods Reported Rejected," *The New York Times* (September 22, 1975).

38. Payoffs rumor: A Jack Anderson and Les Whitten column, "Cover-up Scandal Brewing in Dallas"—*The Washington Post* (January 27, 1975), p. D13—described the possibility that Mississippi senator James Eastland "may have 'received a $50,000 to $60,000 payoff' to intervene with the Justice Department in Hunt's behalf." It was alleged that Eastland called Deputy Attorney General Richard Kleindienst, after which the Nixon Justice Department stalled the case in 1973. Eastland denied the charge.

39. Acquittal/comments: Martin Waldron, "Hunt Says Oil Fortune Was the Key to Acquittal on Wiretapping Charges," *The New York Times* (September 28, 1975).

40. Hunts and silver: Thomas J. Lueck, "Hunts Are Ruled Part of a Scheme to Control Silver," *The New York Times* (August 21, 1988), p. 1; Mike Clancy, "A Beaten Hunt Emerges from Bankruptcy," *The Boston Globe* (December 18, 1989), p. 32.

41. AVG file: Available at the AARC, this seven-page file was received August 4, 1975, by Bernard Fensterwald, Jr.

42. Eugene Hale Brading has acknowledged that on June 4, 1968, the night Robert Kennedy was killed at the Ambassador Hotel, Brading was staying at the Century Plaza Hotel in Los Angeles—less than fifteen minutes away. (See Noyes, *Legacy of Doubt,* p. 72, re Brading interview with LAPD Homicide sergeant Chic Guitierrez.) John Curington told me during our 1992 interview that "Mr. [H. L.] Hunt and I were at the Ambassador Hotel in L.A. under assumed names for about a week, until a day or two before the [Robert Kennedy] assassination." Curington did not elaborate, except to say: "We were just out in California on other business activities and stayed there."

43. Curington background: Hurt, *Texas Rich,* pp. 188–89.

44. Curington first revealed portions of what he later told this author to the *National Enquirer*—"*JFK Assassins Got $$ From Kennedy-Hating Billionaire*" *(June 14, 1977), p. 4.* The Enquirer had Curington's statements "independently analyzed by two experts using the truth-detecting Psychological Stress Evaluator (PSE), a device so reliable that PSE results have been used in legal proceedings or accepted as court evidence in 14 states." One expert, Charles M. McQuiston, coinventor of the PSE, stated: "I concluded that he is telling the truth. He displayed no abnormal stress in stating the facts as he believed them." These included Curington's statements about Hunt ordering him to check police security surrounding Oswald, and Curington's having seen Marina Oswald get off an elevator at the Hunt offices. Curington also told the *Enquirer:* ". . . Hunt didn't just think there was a conspiracy—he knew."

A Secret Service file of November 27, 1963 (WCD 87, pp. 1–2), recounts allegations made by John Richard Salisbury, an engineer at Brown & Root construction in Houston, concerning a relative of his by marriage named Robert L. Norris. In September 1963, Salisbury related, he "spent an hour or so in the Norris residence. During this time Norris stated 'if Kennedy comes to Texas, he will get shot or killed.' Norris went on to say the only way to get rid of him was to kill him; that Kennedy was taking over complete control of the Government and other statements. Mr. Salisbury advised that Norris claimed to be very close to Mr. H. L. Hunt. . . . Salisbury states that Norris went to New Orleans, La. two or three months under unusual circumstances. . . . John Richard Salisbury states that it is his opinion that Robert L. Norris went to New Orleans and engaged Harvey Lee Oswald to assassinate the President. He also infers that Norris would not have had the money to arrange this on his own or had the courage to have done so alone. He therefore, suspects that H. L. Hunt or possibly one of Hunt's close associates sent Norris to New Orleans to hire Oswald."

Under *"SUSPECT,"* the Secret Service file describes Norris as having been "employed by H. L. Hunt Co. . . . as a law clerk," between twenty-six and twenty-eight years old and "allegedly extremely radical in his political views." The file concludes: "Two copies of this report are being furnished the Dallas office for whatever action they consider warranted. . . ."

45. Marina Oswald Porter's statements: author's telephone interview (June 15, 1992).

46. Hunt and Cuban exiles: Dick Russell, "Little Havana's Reign of Terror," *New Times* (October 29, 1976), p. 43.

47. California operations: Harry Dean, who claims to have been an FBI informant inside the Fair Play for Cuba Committee in Chicago and then the Minutemen and John Birch Society in Southern California, met with the author on October 25, 1975, in Alhambra, California. Dean believes that Oswald was part of the same FBI

informant network as he was. Dean maintains he heard in 1963 of an ultraright plot to assassinate JFK, which was originally scheduled during the president's trip to Mexico City in June 1962. Dean alleged that a California congressman and a former Army general were the architects/financiers of the assassination. In September 1976, Dean was quoted in *Argosy* magazine: "I was with a man in September 1963 when he picked up $10,000 in cash from the congressman at his home. The money was taken to Mexico City to help finance the murder of John Kennedy."

48. Willoughby death: Obituaries appeared in *The New York Times,* p. 46, and *The Washington Post,* p. C27 (October 26, 1972).

49. Background on Brown: See "Was LBJ's Final Secret a Son?," *People* (August 27, 1987); Glenn Troelstrup, "LBJ's Secret Mistress Tells All," *National Examiner* (February 6, 1990), p. 6, 7, 10.

Chapter XXVII

Numbered notes are as follows:

1. RCN and note: author's interview with Jesus Mendoza (May 11, 1990).

2. RCN and FBI: *Memorandum in Support of Petition for Writ of Habeas Corpus,* U.S. District Court, Western District of Missouri, draft copy (June 6, 1967), p. 3.

3. RCN and Secret Service: ibid.

4. RCN/hearing/request for effects: ibid., p. 4.

5. FBI files: in National Archives; released under FOIA; in author's possession and at AARC, Washington, D.C.

An FBI file on Nagell dated November 21, 1968, contains a penned-in notation linking Nagell through a cross-file reference to someone named "Gongora." The New York *Daily News* of March 2, 1967, describes a Gongora connection to the JFK assassination as follows:

A Cuban national who allegedly told Federal authorities President Kennedy would be murdered three days before his assassination is in Creedmore State Hospital in New York where he has been committed since 1964, it was learned yesterday.

A copyright story in the Spanish-language daily newspaper "El Tiempo" said Tuesday that Pascual Enrique Ruedolo Gongora told the FBI on Nov. 19, 1963 that Cuban Premier Fidel Castro had sent "six or eight teams" of assassins to the U.S. to kill Mr. Kennedy. . . .

An FBI file (WCE 1444) describes Gongora's arrest "on November 14, 1963, for carrying a concealed knife." Another FBI file on "RUEDOLO GONGORA" reveals that he "was deported to Madrid, Spain, on 11/28/63, but was returned to NY and custody of INS [Immigration and Naturalization Service] on 2/24/64, when Cuba refused to accept him from Spain." A CIA file dated December 9, 1963, adds that "Ruedolo was once in a training camp for the Bay of Pigs but was culled out."

6. Morton on FBI: Author's interview with Fred Morton (May 10, 1990).

7. RCN on January 6 meeting with FBI: *Memorandum in Support,* pp. 4–5. Jack Dunlap: Jack Healy, "Suicide Bares Soviet Spy in Our Code HQ," New York *Daily News* (October 11, 1963), p. 2. Dunlap was identified as "an Army sergeant who took $60,000 from the Russians for stealing highly secret U.S. documents over a period of two years" while "assigned to the supersecret National Security Agency." His body was found "early July 23 near Ferndale, Md., about a mile from his home, in one of his several Cadillacs. He had taken his life by running a hose from the auto's exhaust into a window of his car."

8. Project START: Staff of Subcommittee on Constitutional Rights of the Committee on the Judiciary, U.S. Senate, *Individual Rights and the Federal Role in Behavior Modification* November 1974, pp. 31–32.

9. RCN and Murphy: *Memorandum in Support,* pp. 4–5.

10. FBI agents: The author spoke by telephone with retired agents Thomas B. White, Jr., and Edward J. Murphy on April 26, 1978. In a letter to the author of April 18, 1978, responding to my request for an interview, White wrote: "As you are no doubt aware, I am prohibited by law to divulge information concerning an official investigation." The author also spoke by phone in May 1990 to retired agents Harold Boyce and Leon Davis, neither of whom offered anything of substance.

11. Hoover teletype: *The Investigation of the Assassination of President John F. Kennedy: Performance of the Intelligence Agencies,* Book V, Final Report of the Select Committee to Study Governmental Operations with Respect to Intelligence Activities, U.S. Senate (April 23, 1976), p. 39.

12. CIA investigation: ibid., p. 25 (Western Hemisphere officer in charge) and p. 57 (Angleton division takes over). In HSCA XI. 476, the Western Hemisphere Division desk officer "and headquarters Mexico branch chief" who was initially put in charge of the CIA's investigative effort is identified as John Scelso.

13. Mamantov call from Crichton: WC IX. 106 (Mamantov testimony).

14. Crichton background: The 1963 Dallas City telephone directory lists Crichton as president of Nafco Oil & Gas, Inc. A short article on Page 26A of the *Dallas Morning News* (February 16, 1975) identifies him as a "millionaire oilman." Researcher Peter Dale Scott's unpublished 1971 "The Dallas Conspiracy," pp. III-16–17, notes that Crichton until 1962 "was also a Vice-President of the Empire Trust Company, a firm whose leading shareholders, the inter-related families of Loeb, Lehman and Bronfman, are said by Stephen Birmingham to have maintained 'something very like a private CIA . . . around the world' to protect their other investments such as in Cuba, in Guatemala, and in General Dynamics." One of Empire Trust's directors was, Scott notes,

Lewis W. MacNaughton—the employer of George Bouhe, one of the first members of Dallas's Russian community to meet Oswald.

15. Crichton and Hunt meeting: transcript of Garrison roundtable conference in New Orleans (September 21, 1968), p. 121. According to William Boxley: "That group is the group that Hunt was suppose to have met with in the Bonn building. There was an army or intelligence group that met over there according to a guy who came down and told us about it. Crichton was in the group."

16. Mamantov background: Scott, "The Dallas Conspiracy," pp. III-15–16, citing Arnold Forster and Benjamin R. Epstein, *Danger on the Right* (New York: Random House, 1964), p. 267 and passim.

17. De Mohrenschildt on Mamantov: WC IX. 219. In IX. 125, Mamantov spontaneously denied being a member of the John Birch Society, even before de Mohrenschildt had suggested that he was.

18. Mamantov and Bush: author's telephone interview with Natasha Voshinin (April 5, 1992).

19. Dorothy Gravitas: ibid.

20. Mamantov and Paine: WC IX. 106–7.

21. Gregory background: Edward Jay Epstein, *Legend* (New York: Reader's Digest Press/McGraw-Hill, 1978), pp. 161, 165–67; WC II. 343; Scott, "The Dallas Conspiracy," pp. III-18–27.

22. Marina testimony discrepancies/James Martin: "The Dallas Conspiracy," III.

23. Hoover/Jenkins conversation: *The Investigation of the Assassination,* p. 33.

24. Katzenbach memo: ibid., p. 23.

25. Helms cable: ibid., p. 41.

26. Hoover and LBJ: HSCA III. 476.

27. Katzenbach recommendation: *The Investigation of the Assassination,* p. 23.

28. Rankin on FBI: transcript cited in Mark North, *Act of Treason* (New York: Carroll & Graf, 1991), p. 508.

29. Nosenko defection: cited in Epstein, *Legend,* pp. 8–9.

30. Dulles on agents: transcript reprinted in Harold Weisberg, *Whitewash,* Vol. IV (self-published, 1974), p. 143.

31. Thornberry background: Bruce Allen Murphy, *Fortas: The Rise and Ruin of a Supreme Court Justice* (New York: William Morrow, 1988), pp. 284–87.

32. The account of January 24, 1964, is drawn from *Transcript of Motion Proceedings, United States* v. *Nagell,* pp. 65–75.

33. FBI file on RCN: released under the FOIA to Bernard Fensterwald, Jr., and stamped "Mr. Belmont For The Director," with "CC-Mr. Rosen, CC-Mr. Sullivan."

34. RCN to sister: letter to Eleanore Gambert (January 27, 1964).

35. Glofelty memo: "Report of Neuropsychiatric Examination" on "NAGELL, Richard Case," on file, U.S. Court of Claims [CC], No. 1–73.

36. Weiland memo: "Report of Neuropsychiatric Staff Examination—2-14-64," Medical Center for Federal Prisoners, Springfield, Missouri, on file CC No. 1–73.

37. The account of the April 10, 1964, hearing is drawn from *Transcript of Motion Proceedings,* pp. 91–110.

38. RCN on misquote: *Memorandum in Support,* pp. 6–7.

39. Thornberry comments: author's telephone interview (April 28, 1990).

40. Perrenot withdrawal: *Memorandum in Support,* pp. 7–8. "Petitioner [RCN] alleges that the reason he asked for Mr. Perrenot's relief concerned his remark to petitioner, in the presence of Mr. Rallis, that he had heard petitioner was a communist and that he despised everything petitioner stood for, but that he would still represent him if he wanted his assistance. Petitioner did not feel he could safely go to trial with such counsel."

At the same hearing, Nagell stated to the judge: "I have had dealings with the Federal Bureau of Investigation, I have worked with them, I have also been an agent in the Counter Intelligence Corps, I know a lot of the dirty things that go on behind the scenes. In other words, if I can't be convicted I am not going to be put into some psychiatric institution on my own volition." *Transcript Of Court Proceedings,* pp. 129–30.

41. Perrenot on RCN: author's interview (May 12, 1990).

42. RCN on Calamia/Rallis: *Memorandum in Support,* p. 9A, handwritten insert.

43. Attorney's plea: "Defendant's Requested Instruction No. 3," *United States* v. *Nagell,* submitted by Joseph A. Calamia and Gus Rallis. On file, U.S. District Court Archives, Fort Worth.

44. RCN on FBI at trial: *Memorandum in Support,* p. 9.

45. Psychiatric testimony: 354 F.2d 441 (1966), *Nagell v.United States,* pp. 445–46.

46. RCN conviction: "'Bank Bandit' Is Found Guilty," *El Paso Herald-Post* (May 6, 1964).

47. Rallis on RCN: author's interview (May 12, 1990).

48. Sherman on Calamia: author's interview (May 9, 1990).

49. RCN "Ode": "My Trial By Richard Case Nagell," dated May 6, 1964, in files of attorney Joseph Calamia. The same file contained handwritten poems written to Nagell's children; sister Eleanore; wife, Mitsuko; and another titled "My Life."

Chapter XXVIII

Unless otherwise cited, the Richard Nagell letters from prison and other correspondence with Nagell's sister Eleanore Gambert quoted in this chapter were all sent to the author by Nagell in March 1976.

The author's interview with Dr. Edwin A. Weinstein was conducted in Bethesda, Maryland (May 26, 1990).

Numbered notes are as follows:

1. Morton on RCN case: author's interview (May 10, 1990).

2. FBI files concerning Weinstein: On file in U.S. District Court Archives, *United States* v. *Nagell,* Fort Worth, Texas.

3. RCN on attorneys: *Memorandum in Support of Petition for Writ of Habeas Corpus,* U.S. District Court, Western District of Missouri, draft copy (June 6, 1967), p. 10.

4. Attorney's intent: appellant's opening brief, *Nagell* v. *United States,* filed by Joseph A. Calamia, Gus Rallis, Edward F. Sherman. Copy obtained by author from Edward Sherman (May 1990), p. 37 and passim.

5. RCN on own perjury: *Memorandum in Support,* p. 11.

6. Appeal hearing: transcript, *Nagell* v. *United States,* pp. 575–82; 700–703 (White testimony); appellant's opening brief, p. 32 (Weinstein quote). See also "Nagell's Brain Injuries Cited," *El Paso Herald-Post* (June 8, 1964), p. 12; "Judge to Rule on Motion for New Trial for Nagell," *El Paso Times* (June 9, 1964); "Nagell Given Ten Years; Appeal Set," *El Paso Herald-Post* (June 10, 1964).

7. Prior to being transported to Leavenworth, Nagell says he "was taken to the hospital ward of the United States Correctional Institution, La Tuna, New Mexico, by ambulance." He initially signed papers "electing *not* to begin serving his sentence pending outcome of appeal from conviction." Only after his lawyers advised him that he "would not be sent to a penitentiary or any prison until and unless his conviction was affirmed on appeal" did Nagell sign the papers. Later he would write that such legal advice "constituted a usurpation and encroachment" of his rights under existing law. He was incarcerated for thirty-three days at the U.S. Public Health Service Hospital in Fort Worth and, he says, questioned repeatedly and "involuntarily" until being sent to Leavenworth. *Memorandum in Support,* p. 12.

8. RCN on Leavenworth confinement: ibid., p. 13.

9. Secret Service statement: "First Review," Special Progress Report on NAGELL, Richard Case, United States Penitentiary, Leavenworth, Kansas (stamped March 5, 1965).

10. Gambert letter to LBJ: provided to author by Gambert family (February 16, 1990).

11. RCN conviction reversed: 354 F.2d 441 (1966), *Nagell* v. *United States,* pp. 441–49; "Reverse Conviction of EP Bank Robber," *El Paso Times* (January 7, 1966).

12. RCN return to El Paso/Calamia visit: *Memorandum in Support,* p. 14; "Nagell Returns to El Paso From Leavenworth Prison," *El Paso Times* (February 19, 1966).

13. RCN letter: letter from Eleanore Gambert to RCN (March 30, 1966).

14. RCN "Proposed Testimony": sent to author (1976). Nagell also states: "I am not now, nor have I ever been, insane or otherwise devoid of my mental faculties; nor have I ever attempted suicide, though I have made gestures in that respect for good reason."

15. RCN on Hudspeth: *Memorandum in Support,* p. 15.

16. Hudspeth on RCN: author's interview (May 10, 1990).

17. 1966 hearing: *Memorandum in Support,* p. 15; "Judge Orders Examination in Springfield for Nagell," *El Paso Times* (April 8, 1966).

18. RCN barricade: *El Paso Times* and *El Paso Herald-Post:* "Prisoner Barricades Self in Cell" (April 12, 1966); "Prisoner Still Barricaded in Jail Cell" (April 14, 1966); "Maintain Close Watch on Nagell" (April 15, 1966); "Bank Robber Still Barricaded in County Jail Cell" (April 16, 1966); "Nagell Ends Prison Rebellion" (April 19, 1966).

19. RCN on agreement: *Memorandum in Support,* p. 16.

20. Calamia letter: The lawyer wrote: ". . . if you refuse to take the examinations which you have outlined in your letter, or to cooperate with the medical authorities there, the Court can enter another order that you remain there until you do; I believe this would be against your best interest." (letter dated May 19, 1966, from Joseph A. Calamia to Richard C. Nagell at Springfield, in author's possession).

21. Staff exam: "Report of Psychiatric Staff Examination—6-134-66," Special Progress Report, NAGELL, Richard Case, Medical Center for Federal Prisoners, Springfield, Missouri.

22. Alderete report: "Report of Psychiatric Examination" stamped 6-17-66, ibid. Material on Secret Service agent Abraham Bolden is drawn from: Bernard Fensterwald, Jr., Memorandum of Conversation, March 29, 1968; Bernard Fensterwald, Jr., "The Case of Secret Service Agent Abraham W. Bolden," *Computers and Automation* (June 1971), pp. 41–43; "Accused Agent Says JFK Guards Were Lax," *Washington News* (May 21, 1964); "Plot on Kennedy in Chicago Told," *The New York Times* (December 6, 1967).

23. Nagell transfer to Texas: *Memorandum in Support,* p. 17.

24. RCN on Calamia: ibid., p. 19.

25. RCN on O'Rourke: ibid., pp. 21–23.

26. RCN on Calamia meeting: ibid., pp. 27–29.

27. Gambert visit: ibid., p. 29.

28. RCN second trial: ibid., pp. 30–31; 392 F.2d 934–38; "Holdup Suspect Has 'Brain Injuries,'" *El Paso Herald-Post* (September 20, 1966); "Start Nagell Defense Testimony," *El Paso Times* (September 21, 1966, p. 1-B); *El Paso Times* and *El Paso Herald-Post,* "Jury Due Nagell Case Thursday" (September 22, 1966); "Bank Holdup Jury Remains Deadlocked" (September 24, 1966); "Nagel Jury Hopelessly Deadlocked" (September 26, 1966); "Jury Finds Nagell Guilty in Holdup" (September 27, 1966); "Nagell Again Sentenced to 10 Years" (September 28, 1966).

29. Assassin study: "Assassins are Misfits, Study Finds," Associated Press (undated on author's copy).

30. RCN on evidence: letter to Eleanore Gambert (October 16, 1966).

31. RCN on early 1967: *Memorandum in Support,* pp. 39–40.

32. Anderson column: cited in Charles Rappleye and Ed Becker, *All American Mafioso* (New York: Doubleday, 1991), pp. 270–71.

33. Details of the 1967 allegations are derived primarily from *The Investigation of the Assassination of President*

John F. Kennedy: Performance of the Intelligence Agencies, Book V, Final Report of the Select Committee to Study Governmental Operations with Respect to Intelligence Activities, U.S. Senate (April 23, 1976), pp. 80–86. See also Rappleye and Becker, *All American Mafioso,* pp. 268–75.

34. FBI memo quotes: Memorandum from C. D. DeLoach to MR. TOLSON, 4/4/67, "Assassination of President Kennedy," cc: Mr. DeLoach, Mr. Rosen, Mr. Sullivan, Mr. Wick, pp. 1–4.

35. Garrison on Martin: author's telephone interview (December 15, 1980). For whatever reason, Garrison does not mention William R. Martin in his book *On the Trail of the Assassins* (New York: Sheridan Square Press, 1988), although Garrison does write about his belief that Bill Wood (alias Boxley) was a CIA infiltrator on his staff (pp. 187–92).

36. Wood on Martin: author's telephone interview (December 16, 1980).

37. RCN on Martin memos: letter to Bernard Fensterwald, Jr. (March 21, 1975). Nagell added, in two pages of typewritten comments on Martin's May 11, 1967, memorandum (sent to the author in 1976): "My abrupt termination of the meeting that had been scheduled with Mr. Martin on April 25, 1967, resulted from my overhearing Mr. Bert Nicholas ask Mr. Martin if I had ever threatened to kill the President of the United States and the ensuing conversation, which Mr. Martin inaccurately described in his Memorandum merely as continuing 'in a very general and friendly tone.' I felt no animosity toward Mr. Nicholas personally, but as the Chief of Classification and Parole at the USMCFP [U.S. Medical Center for Federal Prisoners], he had no legal right to question Mr. Martin (who was acting under the pretense of being my legal counsel) on such matters, nor, for that matter, did Mr. Martin have any business discussing my case with him, particularly in view of the circumstances leading to my incarceration at the USMCFP. Incidentally, I am informed that Mr. Nicholas committed suicide three months later, in July 1967."

38. RCN on Martin intelligence connections: letter to Fensterwald (August 2, 1971).

39. FitzGerald death: "Desmond FitzGerald Dies at 57; Chief of CIA Secret Operations," *The Washington Post* (July 24, 1967), p. B2.

40. RCN-Martin correspondence: letters from May 19 to September 11, 1967, in author's possession.

41. *Ramparts* article: William W. Turner, "The Garrison Commission on the Assassination of President Kennedy," *Ramparts* (January 1968), pp. 56, 58.

42. Appeal decision: U.S. Court of Appeals For the Fifth Circuit, No. 24152, *Nagell v. United States:* "Sentence for Nagell Reversed," *El Paso Times* (April 5, 1968).

Chapter XXIX

The Thomas C. Lucey article " 'I Want to Find My Children' " appeared in the overseas *Family* (June 20, 1969), pp. 12–14, published in West Germany, and was provided to the author as part of a pamphlet, *Man in the Middle: The Inside Story (What the Controlled Press and Official Reports Forgot to Mention).* The pamphlet contained an unsigned cover letter dated January 28, 1970, with "R. C. Nagell" typed at the bottom, and a three-page addendum following the article.

Unless cited otherwise, references drawn from Nagell's Court of Claims case appear in his Plaintiff's Motion to Terminate the Administrative Proceedings and Reinstate the Judicial Proceedings, *Nagell v. United States,* Case No. 1-73, U.S. Court of Claims, Washington, D.C. (April 16, 1974), pp. 20–32. Where the author says "Nagell writes . . . ," the reference is to the above-named document.

The Nagell affidavit referenced was three pages in length, sworn to before Notary Public Lewis White in Los Angeles (May 18, 1978).

The author's interviews with Ricey New and Andor Klay were conducted by telephone (September 1, 1978). Numbered notes are as follows:

1. Wood waiting for RCN: Bill Wood letter to Bernard Fensterwald (April 6, 1970).

2. RCN on money provided: "Plaintiff's Requested Findings of Fact," *Nagell v. United States,* No. 1-73, U.S. Court of Claims (April 22, 1980), p. 24.

3. Greenstein on RCN: author's interview (February 10, 1990).

4. RCN on photos: May 18, 1978, affidavit.

5. Greenstein on photos: author's interview.

6. RCN meeting with Garrison: author's interview (May 19, 1978).

7. Garrison on RCN meeting: author's telephone interview (December 15, 1980).

8. RCN on Garrison and offer: author's interview (May 19, 1978).

9. RCN on foreigner: author's interview (July 27, 1984).

10. RCN on "big meeting": author's interview (October 5, 1977).

11. RCN comments: author's interview (May 19, 1978).

12. RCN on article: typed comment attached to bottom of copy sent to Arthur Greenstein.

13. RCN on addendum: letter to author (April 8, 1976). Nagell stated in a filing for his Court of Claims case that the addendum "was written and prepared by a former CIA case officer."

14. RCN on children: "Plaintiff's Requested Findings," p. 29. The last quoted statement is from a separate Court of Claims filing.

15. RCN passport: photocopy in author's possession.

16. Greenstein seeing RCN: author's interview.

17. RCN to Zurich: "Plaintiff's Requested Findings," p. 25.

18. Wood on RCN: letter to Fensterwald.

19. Government on RCN in Zurich: CIA Document No. 1123-424, incoming message No. 25955 (June 6,

1968); declassified September 1976; Department of State telegram "Paris for Hanley" (stamped June 10, 1968), declassified April 29, 1992; FBI memorandum to Director from [deleted] (June 7, 1968), "Subject: Assassination of President John Fitzgerald Kennedy, 11/22/63 Dallas, Texas—Misc.—Info. Concerning," declassified May 5, 1992; FBI memorandum (June 7, 1968), declassified September 5, 1988.

Nagell commented on the CIA files during a phone conversation in the spring of 1990: "It's an utter lie that I was demanding money from the State Department, asking State to get money sent to me in New York. So many of these reports are out-and-out lies, part of a ploy to discredit me."

20. RCN on arrest: Court of Claims filing.
21. Greenstein on East Germany: author's interview.
22. RCN on East Germany: author's interview (October 5, 1977).
23. RCN on interrogation: author's interview (May 19, 1978).
24. Nagell mentioned Runge, briefly and cryptically, in one of his letters to Greenstein. For background on the Runge case, see David Binder, "Bonn Experts Say Defector Was One of Soviets' Ablest Agents," *The New York Times* (October 26, 1967); "The Spies That Were Left Behind," *Time* (October 27, 1967), p. 35; Benjamin Welles, "Defection of a Soviet Spy Viewed in U.S. as Windfall," *The New York Times* (November 10, 1967), p. 1.
25. AP story on RCN release: "E. Germany Frees U.S. Ex-Officer," *The Washington Post* (October 25, 1968). Background on Vogel: Murray Seeger, "He's Tops in Global Trading of Men," *Los Angeles Times* (April 27, 1978), p. 12. See also E. H. Cookridge, *Spy Trade* (London: Hodder & Stoughton, 1971), pp. 124–35.
26. New as CIA: Memo from William Turner to Bernard Fensterwald (December 9, 1968): "Boxley [Wood] told me when I was in N.O. [New Orleans] that Ricey New is CIA; that he knew him as such back in '51."
27. Andor Klay is mentioned as "a State Department desk man" during the 1956 Hungarian crisis in Burton Hersh, *The Old Boys* (New York: Charles Scribner's Sons, 1992), pp. 400–401. Researcher Peter Dale Scott told me in 1992 that Klay was also involved in the defection case of alleged Soviet assassin Bodgan Stashinsky.
28. RCN to New's office: CC filing (April 16, 1974).
29. RCN seeing del Carmen, Waehauf in Mexico: author's interview (May 19, 1978). Waehauf working at Restaurant Fritz: CC filing (April 16, 1974).
30. Travel vouchers: The author was able to date RCN's 1969 movements in Europe through the vouchers; photocopies passed along from Arthur Greenstein.
31. Travel voucher: on file CC, "Exhibit D."
32. RCN on speaking to magazine: letter to Greenstein (May 16, 1969).
33. RCN on return to United States: letter to P. E. Howard, special assistant to the administrator, Veterans Administration, Washington, D.C. (May 15, 1969).
34. RCN on seeing VA: Telegram to Greenstein (May 3, 1969).
35. Ennulat on RCN: author's interview (May 27, 1990).
36. RCN on treatment: letter to P. E. Howard.
37. RCN to Pentagon: "Plaintiff's Requested Findings," p. 29.
38. Both letters to Plant bear a typed "Richard C. Nagell" but are unsigned. Each is addressed to "Francis X. Plant, Special Assistant, Office, Under Secretary of the Army, Room 1E520, The Pentagon, Washington, D.C."
39. Plant response: CC filing (April 16, 1974). A letter from Plant, filed November 20, 1979, in the Court of Claims, is dated July 20, 1970, and states: ". . . your conjecture that certain unnamed military intelligence officers have precluded your retirement for disability have been noted. Both are without foundation in fact." Plant also refers to "our conversation on 6 April 1970."
40. RCN informed of children: Letter signed by Frederick W. Gustafson II, program deputy, Public Inquiry and Appeal Section, for Ellis P. Murphy, director, Department of Public Social Services, County of Los Angeles (June 19, 1970).
41. RCN taking custody: "Plaintiff's Requested Findings," p. 30.
42. Robert Nagell on RCN: author's telephone conversation (February 27, 1992).

Chapter XXX

1. Broshears on Ferrie/hypnosis: author's interview (October 31, 1975).
2. Martin on Ferrie/hypnosis: HSCA IX. 104. Another FBI report from Los Angeles, of December 2, 1963, reported the remarks of NBC cameraman Gene Barnes: "Barnes said Bob Mulholland, NBC News, Chicago, talked in Dallas to one Fairy [sic] [who] said that Oswald had been under hypnosis from a man doing a mind-reading act at Ruby's 'Carousel.' " Mulholland later said he had been misquoted.
3. Hypnosis tracts: W. H. Bowart, *Operation Mind Control* (New York: Dell Publishing, 1978), p. 193.
4. Rockefeller report on mind control: *Report to the President by the Commission on CIA Activities Within the United States* (June 1975), p. 226.
5. Missing documents: Bowart, *Operation Mind Control*, p. 87.
6. Dr. Bernd comments: ibid., p. 169.
7. LHO's attitude: Anthony Summers, in *Conspiracy* (New York: McGraw-Hill, 1980), p. 128, offers additional statements on Oswald's remarkable coolness after the assassination. Former Dallas police chief Jesse Curry is quoted: "One would think Oswald had been trained in interrogation techniques and resisting interrogation techniques." Assistant District Attorney William Alexander told Summers: "I was amazed that a person so young would have had the self-control he had. It was almost as if he had been rehearsed, or programmed, to meet the situation that he found himself in."
8. Hoover on LHO as "sleeper": WC V. 105.

9. CIA on Soviet mind control: WCD 1131, declassified July 30, 1974.

10. See Lincoln Lawrence [pseud.], *Were We Controlled?* (New Hyde Park, N.Y.: University Books, 1967). James L. Moore, in the August 18, 1975, issue of *Modern People,* quoted from a CIA source in an article headlined "Oswald Was Brainwashed": "You'll find a lot of people at CIA who think Oswald was somehow brainwashed or electronically controlled when he was in Russia. If you look hard enough, you can find evidence of that yourself; I could get in a helluva lot of trouble if I came right out and told you—but it's there if you want to look for it. The CIA was in up to its neck in this Oswald thing." The *Modern People* saga, beginning in the July 20, 1975, issue ("The RHIC-EDOM Files: TOP SECRET Bombshell"), offers much the same scenario as that of "Lincoln Lawrence." The article claims that the CIA prepared a 350-page scientific report about RHIC-EDOM after the assassination.

11. In September 1962, a letter came to Lee and Marina from a "Pavel" in the city of Minsk. The Warren Commission published it as Exhibit 132 (WC XVI. 503–8), in translation. Pavel is asking Marina to send him "some technical article from the press about space ship 'Mariner 2.'" He then writes in great detail about the proper methods for remodeling a faulty record player, digresses to discuss the weather, then adds: "By the way, Marina . . . the basic idea of Pogodon's play 'A Man With the Rifle,' is contained in words: 'Now we do not have to fear a man with the rifle.' This, as doctors say, is a quintessence."

There is also a strange, perhaps innocuous, story told in Priscilla Johnson McMillan, *Marina and Lee* (New York: Harper & Row, 1977), pp. 458–59. Marina Oswald told her biographer that her husband "attributed an altogether magical significance to the number three and was obsessed by it." Marina noted that on the Fair Play for Cuba Committee card on which he asked her to forge the "A. J. Hidell" signature, Oswald had written the number 33 "to signify that he was the thirty-third member of his fictitious chapter—still another sign of the power he attached to the number three."

The day before the assassination, according to Marina, Oswald "had done everything in threes." The book goes on:

Marina had known of the peculiar importance which her husband attached to the number three from the outset of their marriage when Lee often used to sneak off to see the film version of the opera based on Pushkin's short story, "The Queen of Spades." In Minsk, he played music from the opera every night and, while listening to his favorite aria ("I would perform a heroic deed of unheard-of prowess for your sake . . ."), he fell into a reverie and imagined that he was the hero, Hermann. A young Russian Guards officer during the 1830s, Hermann thought that his life was determined by the powers of fate and was obsessed by the number three. Avid for money, he obtained what he believed to be the secret or three cards which, played one after the other, would win him a fortune at the gaming table. Hermann played the three cards, staked his love and his whole life on them—and lost.

Marina believes that on the evening of November 21 Lee was again seized by the fantasy that he was Hermann. That is why he asked her three times if he might kiss her and three times if she would move in with him to Dallas. Like Hermann, he staked his life on three cards. And, like Hermann, he lost.

Oswald had first attended the Belorussian Bolshoi State Theater of Opera and Ballet's presentation of the Tchaikovsky opera *The Queen of Spades* in June 1960. He kept the night's program among his personal effects, and the Warren Commission came across this odd phrase on the back of the front cover in Oswald's handwriting: "Then this means that you are pronouncing death sentence." The commission speculated this may have been a line from the aria, but considered the sentence significant enough to translate the program's scene-by-scene synopsis. (See WC XVI. 191.)

The protagonist of *The Queen of Spades* is a soldier named German, oddly enough the namesake of the girl with whom Oswald was then in love (Ella German) and who consistently refused his own advances. The soldier German is "a gloomy shadow, absorbed in his unhappy thoughts. He loves a girl . . . (who) cannot become his wife due to her position and wealth." Her grandmother is a countess, and German longs to meet with her. Somehow he "sees in her a gloomy personification of his fate," and believes that she is destined to "play a decisive role in his life." Spellbound, he listens to a friend tell an old legend about the countess's youth—how the Count St. Germain, seeking to win her favors, had named to her the secret of three magic winning cards; how she had revealed the secret first to her husband, then to a lover, and finally how a phantom of the count had come to warn her:

You will receive a mortal blow,
From the third one, who, ardently and
passionately in love,
Will come to extort from you by force
Three cards, three cards, three cards. . . .

In the left margin, opposite the third line of the phantom's warning, Oswald wrote: "You will receive a blow."

The scenes change. Jokingly, his friends suggest to German that he seek to learn the secret of the countess. And German, "shaken by the fact that Liza is to become the wife of another, decides to win Liza's love at any price, even at the cost of his own life." He sees his beloved once again at the celebration of her engagement to a handsome prince. Slowly, impulsively, German begins to fall into "the power of a fatal idea and sees in this the command of fate—to learn the secret of the countess." Now, on the program page, Oswald underlined two words: *poryv* ("impulse") and *taynu* ("secret").

That night, as the countess reminisces to her chambermaids about her lost youth, German enters her bedroom. He "begs, implores, and adjures her, invoking everything she holds most dear, to disclose to him her secret. Not getting any answer, German starts to threaten her and points his pistol at her. Countess dies." German's beloved Liza enters and, seeing him standing beside her grandmother, she flees. German returns to his barracks. "Staggered by his experiences, German tries in vain to forget and to sleep. In the howling of the wind . . . he hears the funeral dirges." In his sleep, "he believes he sees the ghost of the countess, who finally names to him the long-wished-for three cards. . . ." And so he comes, a man possessed, to a gambling house. "He wins two times in succession, astounding the players with his stakes. Jubilant, he compares life with a game and proclaims as the highest wisdom:

> Abandon the struggle,
> Grasp the moment of luck.

His challenge to put his entire winnings at stake is accepted by Prince Eletsky, who came to avenge Liza." As the fateful hand is played, all becomes still. But instead of an ace, German draws the queen of spades. He has lost. In a long and harrowing moment, he sees the visage of the old countess in the card. And, losing his mind, he stabs himself.

Below the text, Lee Harvey Oswald wrote three words in ink: *zakalyvatsya* ("to stab oneself") and *zakalyvaest-sya* ("stabs himself," repeated twice). The curtain closes.

For Richard Condon's fictional "Manchurian Candidate," the sight of the red queen in a deck of cards triggered the assassin into action. For Oswald, the dark queen seemed to possess a similar kind of fascination.

12. Kimsey on LHO programming: Hugh C. McDonald, *Appointment in Dallas* (New York: Zebra Books, 1975), pp. 107–8.

13. Kimsey death: obituary, "Herman Kimsey," *The Washington Post* (January 26, 1971). CIA files note that Herman Edward Kimsey was an agency staff employee from March 1953 until his resignation on July 16, 1962; prior to that he was a special agent with the Army's Counter Intelligence Corps, stationed for a time in Japan. For the CIA, he was chief of the Research & Analysis Branch for eight years. According to a CIA file declassified in 1983: "In 1960 he was of interest to the Office of Security following the receipt by the Armed Services Sub Committee, as well as by a Deputy under Secretary of Defense, of an anonymous letter which stated that Subject and [deleted] would be the next [deleted] employees to defect. . . . The Agency remained convinced that the bona fides of Subject [Kimsey] remained unimpaired. . . . In March 1963 it was learned that Kimsey was doing business under the title 'Security Associates Inc.' " in Washington, D.C. In 1964, Kimsey worked with Hugh McDonald as a security officer for Republican nominee Barry Goldwater during the presidential campaign.

14. "Blue Fox": McDonald, *Appointment in Dallas*, p. 71. The background of the alleged assassin, Saul, according to McDonald with Robin Moore in *L.B.J. and the J.F.K. Conspiracy* (Westport, Conn.: Condor, 1978), "lies in the Ukraine. The people of that area have a fierce addiction to nationalism and have never really felt a part of the USSR. He was born in the town of Mogilyov on the Dnieper River. During World War II Saul was trained by the KGB as an assassin. At seventeen he murdered his first victim. Then he deserted the KGB, and for a number of years was a fugitive. He traveled to the Western Front and at the end of the war wound up in a displaced persons lager near Augsburg, Germany." (The KGB, as such, did not come into being until 1954.)

15. Knights of Malta: Jonathan Marshall, "Brief Notes on the Political Importance of Secret Societies," *Lobster* 6 (1984), p. 3.

16. The author interviewed Art Ford on October 1, 1976, at the offices of *Circus* magazine, New York.

17. Vasilyev background: See Christopher Andrew and Oleg Gordievsky, *KGB: The Inside Story* (New York: HarperCollins, 1990), pp. 21, 27, 36; Delgado background: see Bowart, *Operation Mind Control*, pp. 249–51.

18. Runyon death: "Damon Runyon Jr., Is Killed in Plunge," *The New York Times* (April 15, 1968). A *Time* file of April 18, 1968, notes: "For several years, he was fascinated by the possibilities of atomic war and by the Jim Garrison theory of the assassination of President Kennedy."

19. Mrs. Oswald reaction: author's phone interview with Mary Ferrell (June 14, 1992).

20. Robert Oswald reaction: Edward Jay Epstein, *Legend* (New York: Reader's Digest Press/McGraw-Hill, 1978), pp. 157–58, 310.

21. Ferrell on Ford: author's interview.

22. Ray and hypnosis: Xavier von Koss is mentioned in Clay Blair, *The Strange Case of James Earl Ray; The Man Who Murdered Martin Luther King* (New York: Bantam Books, 1969), p. 134, as well as William Bradford Huie, *He Slew the Dreamer* (New York: Delacorte Press, 1970).

Bowart, *Operation Mind Control* (pp. 213–14), describes Ray visiting the office of a Beverly Hills psychologist, Dr. Mark Freeman, on November 27, 1967, and asking "to be hypnotized because he wanted to sleep better and remember things better." Dr. Freeman is quoted as having told author George McMillan: "I taught him eye fixation, bodily relaxation, how to open himself to suggestion." Ray told author Huie that he had been to as many as eight different hypnotists, having "read a lot about it in prison" and taking a course in Los Angeles.

23. Sirhan and hypnosis: See Robert Blair Kaiser, *"R.F.K. Must Die!"* (New York: Grove Press, 1970). The most recent, and most detailed, analysis of the possibility that Sirhan was programmed appears in Philip H. Melanson, *The Robert F. Kennedy Assassination* (New York: Shapolsky, 1991), pp. 167–215.

24. Sirhan and Hall: Kaiser, *"R.F.K. Must Die!,"* p. 284.

25. Prouty on mind control: author's telephone interview (June 10, 1990).

26. Cameron and mind research: See esp. John Marks, *The Search for the "Manchurian Candidate"* (New York: W. W. Norton, 1991), pp. 140–48.

27. M.D. Anderson as CIA: "This is How the Money Goes Round," *The Washington Post* (author's copy undated).

28. Jaworski background early '60s: Fred Powledge, "Texas Investigation into Kennedy Death Put Off Indefinitely," *The New York Times* (December 7, 1963); "Texan Is Under Consideration for Robert Kennedy's Position," *The New York Times* (August 24, 1964); Ted Lewis, "Capitol Stuff," New York *Daily News* (November 6, 1964); Linda Charlton, "Bar's President-Elect," *The New York Times* (February 25, 1970). Researcher Peter Dale Scott noted in his unpublished "Dallas Conspiracy" (1971) that Jaworski served on the board of the Houston Bank of the Southwest in 1968 with D. B. Marshall of the Marshall Foundation and Ernest Cockrell of the San Jacinto Fund, both CIA conduits.

Former Texas journalist "Lonnie" Hudkins, at an interview on May 12, 1976, brought up Jaworski's name and said: "Jaworski had a Mexico City law partner who's never been heard from since [the JFK assassination]. The little hotel where Oswald stayed there, his Mexican partner was in the same block or building." Charlton, "Bar's President-Elect," noted that Jaworski maintained offices in both Houston and Mexico.

29. Jaworski and Thornberry: Fred P. Graham, "Johnson Texas Lawyer Checked Thornberry for Panel of A.B.A.," *The New York Times* (August 3, 1968).

30. Watergate and Jaworski: Ronald J. Ostrow, "Staff Distrusted Jaworski, Talked of Tailing Him, Book Says," *Los Angeles Times* (May 31, 1977), p. 12.

31. Jaworski and Bush: James P. Sterba, "Jaworski Says He Cleared Bush," *The New York Times* (November 8, 1976), p. 28.

32. Jaworski in World War II: file in *Time-Life* archive, "Leon Jaworski: Biographical Data" (November 1, 1973).

33. U.S. Intelligence/Germans/mind control: See Linda Hunt, *Secret Agenda* (New York: St. Martin's Press, 1991), pp. 157–74.

34. Frank Wisner's background has been detailed in many books. His involvement in "Operation Paperclip" is outlined in Hunt, *Secret Agenda,* pp. 132–33, 138–39.

35. Wisner and Nazi fears: Burton Hersh, *The Old Boys* (New York: Charles Scribner's Sons, 1992), p. 439. The same basic story was confirmed to me by Wisner's son Graham during a June 1992 telephone conversation. Wisner's death is described in *The Old Boys,* p. 441.

36. Ruby on Jews: "A Letter from Jail by Jack Ruby." The *Ramparts* article notes: "Attorney Mel Belli [Ruby's lawyer] agreed in an interview last Christmas that Ruby 'very definitely had been told about a pogrom against the Jews, and told over and over again until he believed it."

37. Ruby testimony: See WC V. 181–213.

38. Ruby-Warren exchange: ibid., p. 210. Ruby also said during his testimony: ". . . there is a John Birch Society right now in activity, and Edwin Walker is one of the top men of this organization—take it for what it is worth, Chief Justice Warren. Unfortunately for me, for me giving the people the opportunity to get in power, because of the act I committed, has put a lot of people in jeopardy with their lives." (p. 198).

39. Ruby letter: "A Letter from Jail," pp. 20–21, addressed to "John."

40. Article quotes: Gerald L. K. Smith, "The Assassination," *The Cross and the Flag* (March 1964), pp. 3, 23–33.

41. Healy on left conspiracy: author's telephone interview (October 28, 1986).

42. Lewis on JFK case: author's telephone interview (October 28, 1986).

43. FPCC man and LBJ: "Iowan Jailed in Berkeley for Threats on Johnson," *Los Angeles Times* (December 21, 1963).

44. End of FPCC: "Fair Play for Cuba Unit Indicates Plan to Quit," *Los Angeles Times* (December 28, 1963).

45. Weissman on ad: WC V. 510.

46. The black-bordered ad is reprinted in WC XVIII. 835 (WCE 1031).

47. Revilo Oliver background is drawn from Frank P. Mintz, *The Liberty Lobby and the American Right* (Westport, Conn.: Greenwood Press, 1985), pp. 163–79, and files of Group Research, Inc., Washington, D.C.

48. Oliver's testimony appears in WC XV. 709–44. The Colonel Chesley Clark reference is on p. 729. Oliver's attack on the CIA is on pp. 735–36. The Capell connection to the Cuban underground is on p. 742–43. Oliver's articles for *American Opinion* are reprinted in WC XX. 692–735.

49. Rothermel on CIA deaths: June 5, 1967, memo from "Wm. C. Boxley," listing "Source—Rothermel."

50. KGB-CIA penetration: Shortly before the JFK assassination, State Department security officer Otto Otepka was dismissed by Secretary of State Dean Rusk for allegedly having turned over confidential documents on loyalty and security matters to a Senate subcommittee. Otepka was a longtime "Red-hunter," and his ouster enraged the radical right. A memorandum (July 30, 1970) of a Bernard Fensterwald, Jr./Hal Dorland lunch with Otepka notes his revealing that "there were three State Department files on Oswald" in separate departments. At the time of his ouster, Otepka said he "had been working on defectors to the Soviet Union. . . . He said it was not possible to determine how many or which ones of the 15–20 were CIA agents although he thought several were."

51. *Herald of Freedom* article: reprinted in WC XX. 745–48.

52. Portuondo/Cabarga phone call: Michael Canfield with Alan J. Weberman, *Coup d'État in America* (New York: The Third Press, 1975), pp. 131–32, citing WCD 453; SS report, Miami (November 24–December 4, 1963).

53. Portuondo and exile group: membership list from Robert Morrow files.

54. Morrow on Masferrer: Robert D. Morrow, *The Senator Must Die* (Santa Monica, Calif.: Roundtable, 1988), p. 73.

55. Kohly and Nixon: ibid., pp. 113–15.

56. Portuondo and Willoughby: Letter, CW Papers, MacArthur Archives, Norfolk, Virginia (October 8, 1957); masthead, *Foreign Intelligence Digest.*

57. Portuondo and Phillips: "Afterword: The Search for 'Maurice Bishop,' " *Lobster* 10 (January 1986), p. 13.

58. Kohly letter to Willoughby: RG-23, CW Papers, Series I.

59. Anonymous letter: dated August 30, 1975, sent to author at *The Village Voice.*

60. Willoughby as Tscheppe-Weidenbach: Bruce Cumings, *The Origins of the Korean War,* Vol. II (Princeton, N.J.: Princeton University Press, 1990), p. 104; Frank Kluckhohn, "Heidelberg to Madrid—The Story of General Willoughby," *The Reporter* (August 19, 1952), p. 26.

Conclusion

1. Last conversation with RCN: March 21, 1990.

2. Lawsuit victory: Judge David Schwartz's judgment read, in conclusion: "On the basis of the findings of fact and opinion herein, it is concluded that plaintiff [Nagell] is entitled to, and the defendant [Pentagon] is liable for, payment of a military disability pension appropriate to plaintiff's rank as of the time of his resignation for total mental disability, from the time of his resignation from the Army in 1959, and any other sums provided in such case by law, and that the case is set down under Rule 131 for proceedings for the determination of damages."

On March 2, 1983, the U.S. Court of Appeals for the Federal Circuit, in *Nagell* v. *United States,* Appeal No. 1–73, affirmed the judgment.

3. Nagell's last letter to the author was dated June 20, 1990. The author tried unsuccessfully to recontact Nagell in letters sent to his post office box in Los Angeles on January 19, February 27, April 2, and June 11, 1992. Nagell's son Robert told the author that this address is still good, and the author's letters were not returned by the post office.

4. Gilbert Offenhartz, a New York attorney whose name appears in Nagell's notebook seized by the FBI on September 20, 1963, was interviewed by the author on April 21, 1992. Offenhartz seemed to know a good deal about Nagell, based, he said, on a meeting with Nagell after his prison release. The lawyer said "there was no other way he could have protected himself" except to shoot up the El Paso bank in 1963. "I am morally certain," Offenhartz continued, "that Richard Nagell did not know who was running him [in 1963]. You need to find out who recruited him, and who his control was." The lawyer indicated that Nagell's "control" had worked for "the [H. L.] Hunts, or someone like them perhaps." When I asked if Nagell had ever mentioned the Hunt family to him, he replied: "I don't remember. I wouldn't remember—because it was irrelevant to our conversation—it may be that he could have mentioned something like this."

5. A May 15, 1973, memo in the files of researcher Richard Popkin recounts a conversation with former CIA official Victor Marchetti in which Marchetti reportedly offered "a theory he claimed to have heard that fits with his own picture of the chaos in the CIA; namely that the KGB has infiltrated the CIA and the CIA has infiltrated the KGB so it is impossible at the present stage to tell who is who (he mentioned a case of having been sent to meet somebody and being shown all sorts of identification and then being totally unable to tell whether he was dealing with a U.S. or Russian agent). Marchetti thinks it is the KGB branch of the CIA that killed Kennedy and that the U.S. CIA is too embarrassed to investigate and reveal the real state of affairs."

When I interviewed Marchetti in 1976, he indicated that the scuttlebutt was the CIA had been penetrated "somewhere near the top" in the Soviet Russia Division and that the chief suspect "had an Irish name."

6. The HSCA (IX. 532) notes: "Lonnie Hudkins, a reporter for the *Houston Post* in 1963, allegedly told Shirley Martin, a Warren [Commission] Report critic, that while he was employed as a public relations man for Hunt Oil Co., Hunt personally approached him about going to Mexico to help kill either Castro or Cheddi Jagan, former Prime Minister of Guyana. According to Hudkins, the project never went forward because he and two other individuals believed the operation was dangerous. In 1967, Hudkins revealed the identity of one of the other participants to be R. D. Matthews." R. D. Matthews, who "denied being present at any meeting where the possibility of killing Castro was discussed," was identified by the HSCA as a longtime acquaintance of Jack Ruby and other organized-crime members (HSCA IX. 524–32). Matthews had resided in Havana prior to Castro's takeover.

7. Nagell, in a page of *"TRIVIA"* sent to Arthur Greenstein in the 1970s, opened with a definition of the acronym "AGEA," which Nagell spelled out as standing for "Arbeitagemeinschaftehemaliger Abwehrangeneriger." In English, the meaning is "Working Association of Former Members of the Abwehr," the Abwehr being the intelligence service of Nazi Germany's wartime high command. Farther down the page, Nagell writes several sentences, all underlined, in the German language. They are a quote from someone's conversation, and the English translation reads:

"Yes, we know what kind of a mechanic he was. But do you know whether he accomplished a contract in Dallas? We never saw his calling card. Was he nameless?"

In a letter to Greenstein of April 30, 1974, Nagell writes: "As stated during our telecon of 4/13/74, ex-Wehrmacht Captain is 'Rudy Cleye' aka Heinrich Klyer (sp), current partner of the Blarney Castle, 601 So. Western Ave., L.A. Quite a story on this fella, one that needs bringing up to date."

The Blarney Castle was a bar frequented by Nagell, where we met for an interview on May 19, 1978.

8. A Robert S. Allen and Paul Scott column of April 10, 1963, described cause for considerable anger among East European exiles at the JFK administration:

President Kennedy's harsh crackdown on Cuban exile groups is being broadened to include the activities of the anti-Communist Eastern European refugee groups in the U.S.

Behind the scenes, and without taking the American people into his confidence, the President is drastically reversing U.S. policies which have importantly aided these exiles since the late '40s.

This undercover policy shift calls for hamstringing the efforts of the European refugees by sharply curtailing the "covert" funds supplied them by government agencies, among them the Central Intelligence Agency.

Although these financial curbs will not be fully effective until around July 1, the secret crackdown already is compelling Baltic and Russian exile groups to restrict their anti-Communist activities. . . .

9. LBJ's first major weekend appointments immediately after the assassination were with Robert B. Anderson, a fellow Texan who served as Navy and then Treasury secretary under President Eisenhower. After LBJ himself, Anderson was the most influential postwar representative of Texas oil interests. After calling Anderson to Washington, LBJ met with him for several hours on November 23–24, 1963. "The details" of the conversations "are not known," according to a *New York Times* account. Anderson went on to carry out numerous diplomatic tasks for LBJ. Anderson died in 1989, having pled guilty not long before to income-tax evasion and operating an illegal offshore bank. Edward Cowan, "R. B. Anderson Sees 2 Big Problems," *The New York Times* (December 8, 1963), p. 1; Eric Pace, "Robert B. Anderson, Ex-Treasury Chief, Dies at 79," *The New York Times* (August 16, 1989). Anderson was also a codirector of Dresser Industries, Inc., the oil equipment company that gave George Bush his start.

10. Nagell has indicated cognizance at least of one of the Watergate burglars. "Does James W. McCord, Jr., still reside at No. 7 Winder Court, Rockwell, Md. 20850?" he wrote to Greenstein; at the time, the address was correct. Also, in a March 28, 1973, note sent to a police acquaintance, Neill Spotts, then of the LAPD's organized-crime bureau, Nagell added: "I understand that the Watergate caper inquiry is going to stretch out as far as a little bar across the street from Ramparts Division [in Los Angeles or New Orleans], maybe even to San Francisco and Havana."

11. George Bush and JFK case: FBI No. 62-2115, on file at AARC, Washington, D.C. See also Mark Lane, *Plausible Denial* (New York: Thunder's Mouth Press, 1991), pp. 329–33.

12. During a telephone conversation of March 13, 1987, Nagell commented concerning his CIA dossier: "I honestly don't feel anything written about me would be complete without the knowledge of what is in those files. I want to see how they had me pegged, whether they honestly think I was working for the other side or whether they go along with Desmond FitzGerald. I'm not expecting to get anything that states that officially, but I'm sure I could glean some impression."

In his Court of Claims case, Nagell made note of the following government files concerning him, and where they were located:

Department of State: central file in Washington, D.C., offices in Los Angeles, Mexico City, New York, Zurich, Barcelona, Madrid, and U.S. mission, West Berlin.

Central Intelligence Agency: central file at Langley, Virginia, and CIA offices and stations in Los Angeles, Tokyo, Seoul, Mexico City, Zurich, Madrid, West Berlin.

Federal Bureau of Investigation: central file at Washington, and FBI field and area offices in Trenton, New Jersey; New York City; Jacksonville and Miami, Florida; El Paso, Dallas, Los Angeles.

U.S. Secret Service: central file at headquarters, Department of the Treasury, Washington, and offices in El Paso, Dallas, New York, and Los Angeles.

Bibliography

Books About the Assassination

Anson, Robert Sam. "*They've Killed the President!*": *The Search for the Murderers of John F. Kennedy*. New York: Bantam Books, 1975.

Bishop, Jim. *The Day Kennedy Was Shot*. New York: Random House, 1968.

Blakey, G. Robert, and Richard N. Billings. *The Plot to Kill the President: Organized Crime Assassinated J.F.K.* New York: Times Books, 1981.

Blumenthal, Sid, with Harvey Yazijian. *Government by Gunplay: Assassination Conspiracy Theories from Dallas to Today*. New York: Signet Books, 1976.

Canfield, Michael, and Alan J. Weberman. *Coup d'État in America: The CIA and the Assassination of John F. Kennedy*. New York: The Third Press, 1975.

Coogan, Matthew A. "Thirty Years of Deception." Unpublished manuscript, 1991.

Crenshaw, Charles A., M.D., with Jens Hansen and J. Gary Shaw. *JFK: Conspiracy of Silence*. New York: Signet Books, 1992.

Curry, Jesse. *JFK Assassination File*. Dallas: American Poster and Printing, 1969.

Davis, John H. *Mafia Kingfish: Carlos Marcello and the Assassination of John F. Kennedy*. New York: McGraw-Hill, 1989.

DeLillo, Don. *Libra*. New York: Viking Press, 1988.

DiEugenio, James. *Destiny Betrayed: JFK, Cuba, and the Garrison Case*. New York: Sheridan Square Press, 1992.

Eddowes, Michael. *The Oswald File*. New York: Clarkson N. Potter, 1977.

Epstein, Edward Jay. *Counterplot*. New York: Viking Press, 1969.

———. *Legend: The Secret World of Lee Harvey Oswald*. New York: Reader's Digest Press/McGraw-Hill, 1978.

———. *The Assassination Chronicles*. New York: Carroll & Graf, 1992.

Fensterwald, Bernard, Jr., with Michael Ewing. *Coincidence or Conspiracy?* (for the Committee to Investigate Assassinations). New York: Zebra Books, 1977.

Flammonde, Paris. *The Kennedy Conspiracy: An Uncommissioned Report on the Jim Garrison Investigation*. New York: Meredith, 1969.

Garrison, Jim. *A Heritage of Stone*. New York: G. P. Putnam's Sons, 1970.

———. *On the Trail of the Assassins: My Investigation and Prosecution of the Murder of President Kennedy*. New York: Sheridan Square Press, 1988.

Hepburn, James [pseud.]. *Farewell America*. Vaduz, Liechtenstein: Frontiers, 1968.

Hurt, Henry. *Reasonable Doubt*. New York: Holt, Rinehart, & Winston, 1985.

Jones, Penn, Jr. *Forgive My Grief*, Vols. I–IV, 1966, 1967, 1969, 1974; *Midlothian* (Texas) *Mirror*.

Kantor, Seth. *Who Was Jack Ruby?* New York: Everest House, 1978.

Lane, Mark. *Plausible Denial*. New York: Thunder's Mouth Press, 1991.

———. *Rush to Judgment*. New York: Holt, Rinehart, & Winston, 1966.

Lawrence, Lincoln [pseud.]. *Were We Controlled?* New Hyde Park, N.Y.: University Books, 1967.

Lifton, David S. *Best Evidence*. New York: Macmillan, 1980.

McDonald, Hugh C., as told to Geoffrey Bocca. *Appointment in Dallas: The Final Solution to the Assassination of JFK*. New York: Zebra Books, 1975.

McDonald, Hugh, with Robin Moore. *L.B.J. and the J.F.K. Conspiracy*. Westport, Conn.: Condor, 1978.

McMillan, Priscilla Johnson. *Marina and Lee*. New York: Harper & Row, 1977.

Manchester, William. *The Death of a President: November 20–25, 1963*. New York: Harper and Row, 1967.

Marrs, Jim. *Crossfire: The Plot That Killed Kennedy*. New York: Carroll & Graf, 1989.

Meagher, Sylvia. *Accessories After the Fact: The Warren Commission, the Authorities, and the Report*. New York: Vintage Books, 1976.

Melanson, Philip H. *Spy Saga: Lee Harvey Oswald and U.S. Intelligence*. New York: Praeger, 1990.

Miller, Tom. *The Assassination Please Almanac*. Chicago: Henry Regnery, 1977.

Morrow, Robert D. *Betrayal: A Reconstruction of Certain Clandestine Events from the Bay of Pigs to the Assassination of John F. Kennedy.* Chicago: Henry Regnery, 1976.

———. *Motivation Behind the Assassination of President John F. Kennedy,* July 1976.

———. *The Senator Must Die.* Santa Monica, Calif.: Roundtable, 1988.

Newman, Albert H. *The Assassination of John F. Kennedy: The Reasons Why.* New York: Clarkson N. Potter, 1970.

North, Mark. *Act of Treason: The Role of J. Edgar Hoover in the Assassination of President Kennedy.* New York: Carroll & Graf, 1991.

Noyes, Peter. *Legacy of Doubt.* New York: Pinnacle Books, 1973.

Oglesby, Carl. *The JFK Assassination: The Facts and the Theories.* New York: Signet Books, 1992.

———. *Who Killed JFK?* Berkeley, Calif.: Odonian Press, 1992.

———. *The Yankee and Cowboy War.* New York: Berkley Medallion, 1977.

Oswald, Robert L., with Myrick and Barbara Land. *Lee: A Portrait of Lee Harvey Oswald.* New York: Coward-McCann, 1967.

O'Toole, George. *The Assassination Tapes: An Electronic Probe into the Murder of John F. Kennedy and the Dallas Cover-up.* New York: Penthouse Press, 1975.

Popkin, Richard H. *The Second Oswald.* New York: Avon Books, 1966.

Report of the Select Committee on Assassinations, U.S. House of Representatives: The Final Assassinations Report. New York: Bantam Books, 1979.

Scheim, David E. *Contract on America: The Mafia Murder of President John F. Kennedy.* New York: Shapolsky, 1988.

Scott, Peter Dale, with Paul L. Hoch, Russell Stetler, and Josiah Thompson. "Beyond Conspiracy: The Hidden Dimensions of the John F. Kennedy Assassination." Unpublished manuscript, 1979–80.

———. "The Dallas Conspiracy." Unpublished manuscript, 1971.

———, with Paul Hoch and Russell Stetler. *The Assassinations: Dallas and Beyond—A Guide to Cover-ups and Investigations.* New York: Vintage Books, 1976.

Shaw, J. Gary, with Larry R. Harris. *Cover-up: The Governmental Conspiracy to Conceal the Facts About the Public Execution of John F. Kennedy.* Cleburne, Tex.: self-published, 1976 (available through JFK Assassination Information Center, Dallas).

Sprague, Richard E. *The Taking of America 1-2-3.* Privately published, 1976.

Summers, Anthony. *Conspiracy.* New York: McGraw-Hill, 1980.

Thornley, Kerry. *Oswald.* Chicago: New Classics House, 1965.

Torbitt, William. "Nomenclature of an Assassination Cabal." Unpublished manuscript, 1970.

Weisberg, Harold. *Oswald in New Orleans: Case for Conspiracy and the CIA.* New York: Canyon Books, 1967.

———. *Whitewash,* Vols. I–IV. Hyattstown, Md.: self-published, 1965, 1967, 1974; Vols. I and II, New York: Dell Publishing, 1966–67.

Books on Intelligence

Agee, Philip. *Inside the Company: CIA Diary.* New York: Bantam Books, 1976.

———. *On the Run.* Secaucus, N.J.: Lyle Stuart, 1987.

Allen, Thomas B., and Norman Polmar. *Merchants of Treason.* New York: Delacorte Press, 1988.

Anders, Karl. *Murder To Order.* London: Ampersand, 1965.

Andrew, Christopher, and Oleg Gordievsky. *KGB: The Inside Story.* New York: HarperCollins, 1990.

Ashman, Charles. *The CIA-Mafia Link.* New York: Manor Books, 1975.

Bain, Donald. *The Control of Candy Jones.* Chicago: Playboy Press, 1977.

Barron, John. *KGB: The Secret Work of Soviet Secret Agents.* New York: Reader's Digest Press, 1974.

Beck, Melvin. *Secret Contenders: The Myth of Cold War Counterintelligence.* New York: Sheridan Square Publications, 1984.

Beschloss, Michael R. *Mayday: Eisenhower, Khrushchev, and the U-2 Affair.* New York: Harper & Row, 1986.

Biderman, Albert D., and Herbert Zimmer, eds. *The Manipulation of Human Behavior.* New York: John Wiley & Sons, 1961.

Bittman, Ladislav. *The KGB and Soviet Disinformation: An Insider's View.* Elmsford, N.Y.: Pergamon-Brassey's International Defense Publishers, 1985.

Blum, William. *CIA: A Forgotten History.* London: Zed Books, 1986.

Bowart, W. H. *Operation Mind Control.* New York: Dell Publishing, 1978.

Bower, Thomas. *The Paperclip Conspiracy.* Boston: Little, Brown, 1987.

Churchill, Ward, and Jim Vander Wall. *The Cointelpro Papers.* Boston: South End Press, 1990.

Colby, William, with James McCargar. *Lost Victory: A Firsthand Account of America's Sixteen-Year Involvement in Vietnam.* (Chicago/New York: Contemporary Books, 1989).

Cook, Fred J. *The FBI Nobody Knows.* New York: Macmillan, 1964.

Cookridge, E. H. *Gehlen: Spy of the Century.* New York: Random House, 1971.

———. *Spy Trade.* London: Hodder & Stoughton, 1971.

Copeland, Miles. *Without Cloak or Dagger: The Truth About the New Espionage.* New York: Simon & Schuster, 1974.

Corson, William R. *The Armies of Ignorance: The Rise of the American Intelligence Empire.* New York: Dial Press/James Wade, 1977.

————, Susan B. Trento, and Joseph J. Trento. *Widows.* New York: Crown, 1989.

Deacon, Richard. *A History of the Russian Secret Service.* London: Frederick Muller, 1972.

Dunlop, Richard. *Donovan: America's Master Spy.* Chicago: Rand McNally, 1982.

Epstein, Edward Jay. *Deception: The Invisible War Between the KGB and the CIA.* New York: Simon & Schuster, 1989.

Estabrooks, G. H. *Hypnotism.* New York: E. P. Dutton, 1945.

Gentry, Curt. *J. Edgar Hoover.* New York: W. W. Norton, 1991.

Gramont, Sanche de. *The Secret War: The Story of International Espionage Since World War II.* New York: G. P. Putnam's Sons, 1962.

Hersh, Burton. *The Old Boys: The American Elite and the Origins of the CIA.* New York: Charles Scribner's Sons, 1992.

Hohne, Heinz, and Hermann Zolling. *The General Was a Spy.* New York: Coward, McCann, & Geoghegan, 1971.

Hougan, Jim. *Spooks: The Haunting of America—The Private Use of Secret Agents.* New York: William Morrow, 1978.

Hunt, Linda. *Secret Agenda: The United States Government, Nazi Scientists, and Project Paperclip, 1945 to 1990.* New York: St. Martin's Press, 1991.

Hunter, Edward. *Brainwashing from Pavlov to Powers.* Linden, New Jersey: The Bookmailer, 1971.

Huss, Pierre J., and George Carpozi, Jr. *Red Spies in the U.N.* New York: Coward-McCann, 1965.

Hutton, J. Bernard. *Struggle in the Dark: How Russian and Other Iron Curtain Spies Operate.* London: George G. Harrop, 1969.

————. *The Traitor Trade.* New York: Ivan Obolensky, 1963.

Kelley, Clarence M., and James Kirkpatrick Davis. *Kelley: The Story of an FBI Director.* Kansas City, Mo.: Andrews, McMeel, & Parker, 1987.

Lamphere, Robert J., with Tom Schachtman. *The FBI-KGB War.* New York: Random House, 1986.

Mader, Julius. *Who's Who in CIA.* East Berlin: Julius Mader, 1968.

Mailer, Norman. *Harlot's Ghost.* New York: Random House, 1991.

Mangold, Tom. *Cold Warrior: James Jesus Angleton: The CIA's Master Spy Hunter.* New York: Simon & Schuster, 1991.

Marchetti, Victor, and John Marks. *The CIA and the Cult of Intelligence.* New York: Alfred A. Knopf, 1974.

Marks, John. *The Search for the "Manchurian Candidate": The CIA and Mind Control.* New York: W. W. Norton, 1991.

Martin, David C. *Wilderness of Mirrors.* New York: Harper & Row, 1980.

Phillips, David Atlee. *The Night Watch: 25 Years of Peculiar Service.* New York: Atheneum, 1977.

Powers, Gary, with Curt Gentry. *Operation Overflight.* New York: Holt, Rinehart, & Winston, 1970.

Powers, Richard Gid. *Secrecy and Power: The Life of J. Edgar Hoover.* New York: The Free Press, 1987.

Powers, Thomas. *The Man Who Kept the Secrets: Richard Helms and the CIA.* New York: Alfred A. Knopf, 1979.

Prouty, L. Fletcher. *The Secret Team.* Englewood Cliffs, N.J.: Prentice-Hall, 1973.

Ranelagh, John. *The Agency: The Rise and Decline of the CIA.* New York: Simon & Schuster, 1987.

Reese, Ellen. *General Reinhard Gehlen: The CIA Connection.* Fairfax, Va.: George Mason University Press, 1990.

Rositzke, Harry. *The KGB: The Eyes of Russia.* Garden City, N.Y.: Doubleday, 1981.

Sabljah, Mark, and Martin H. Greenberg. *Most Wanted: A History of the FBI's Ten Most Wanted List.* New York: Bonanza Books, 1990.

Scott, Peter Dale, and Jonathan Marshall. *Cocaine Politics: Drugs, Armies, and the CIA in Central America.* Berkeley, Calif.: University of California Press, 1991.

Smith, Joseph B. *Portrait of a Cold Warrior.* New York: G. P. Putman's Sons, 1976.

Stockwell, John. *The Praetorian Guard: The U.S. Role in the New World Order.* Boston: South End Press, 1991.

Szulc, Tad. *Compulsive Spy: The Strange Career of E. Howard Hunt.* New York: Viking Press, 1974.

Turner, William. *Hoover's FBI: The Man and the Myth.* Los Angeles: Sherbourne Press, 1970.

West, Nigel. *The Circus: MI5 Operations 1945–1972.* Briarcliff Manor, N.Y.: Stein and Day, 1984.

Winks, Robin W. *Cloak and Gown: Scholars in the Secret War, 1939–1961.* New York: William Morrow, 1987.

Wise, David. *Molehunt: The Secret Search for Traitors That Shattered the CIA.* New York: Random House, 1992.

Wise, David, and Thomas B. Ross. *The Espionage Establishment.* New York: Random House, 1967.

————. *The Invisible Government.* New York: Random House, 1964.

Yakovlev, Nikolai. *CIA Target: The USSR.* Moscow: Progress Publishers, 1982.

Books on the Kennedy Era (General)

Attwood, William. *The Twilight Struggle: Tales of the Cold War.* New York: Harper & Row, 1987.

Beschloss, Michael R. *The Crisis Years: Kennedy and Khrushchev, 1960–1963.* New York: Edward Burlingame Books, 1991.

Davis, John H. *The Kennedys: Dynasty and Disaster, 1848–1983.* New York: McGraw-Hill, 1984.

Goodwin, Richard N. *Remembering America: A Voice from the Sixties.* Boston: Little, Brown, 1988.

Khrushchev, Nikita S. *Khrushchev Remembers.* Boston: Little, Brown, 1970.

Newman, John M. *JFK and Vietnam.* New York: Warner Books, 1992.

O'Donnell, Kenneth P., and David F. Powers with Joe McCarthy. *"Johnny, We Hardly Knew Ye": Memories of John Fitzgerald Kennedy.* Boston: Little, Brown, 1972.

Schlesinger, Arthur M., Jr. *Robert Kennedy and His Times.* New York: Ballantine Books, 1979.

———. *A Thousand Days.* Boston: Houghton Mifflin, 1965.

Books on Organized Crime (General)

Demaris, Ovid. *Captive City.* New York: Lyle Stuart, 1969.

Galant, Pierre. *The Marseilles Mafia.* London: W. H. Allen, 1979.

Giancana, Sam, and Chuck Giancana. *Double Cross: The Explosive, Inside Story of the Mobster Who Controlled America.* New York: Warner Books, 1992.

Kennedy, Robert F. *The Enemy Within.* New York: Harper & Row, 1960.

Kruger, Henrik. *The Great Heroin Coup: Drugs, Intelligence, and International Fascism.* Boston: South End Press, 1980.

McCoy, Alfred. *The Politics of Heroin,* 2d ed. New York: Lawrence Hill, 1991.

Messick, Hank. *Lansky.* New York: Berkley, 1973.

Moldea, Dan E. *The Hoffa Wars.* New York: Paddington Press, 1978.

Newsday Staff. *The Heroin Trail.* New York: New American Library, 1974.

Rappleye, Charles, and Ed Becker. *All American Mafioso: The Johnny Rosselli Story.* New York: Doubleday, 1991.

Winterberger, Robert W. *The Washington Payoff.* New York: Dell Publishing, 1972.

Books on Cuba and American Involvement in

Abel, Elie. *The Missile Crisis.* Philadelphia: Lippincott, 1966.

Blight, James G., and David A. Welch. *On the Brink: Americans and Soviets Reexamine the Missile Crisis.* New York: Noonday Press, 1990.

Brugioni, Dino A. *Eyeball to Eyeball: The Inside Story of the Cuban Missile Crisis.* New York: Random House, 1992.

Detzer, David. *The Brink: Cuban Missile Crisis, 1962.* New York: Thomas Y. Crowell, 1979.

Hinckle, Warren, and William Turner. *The Fish Is Red: The Story of the Secret War Against Castro.* New York: Harper & Row, 1981.

Hunt, Howard. *Give Us This Day.* New Rochelle, N.Y.: Arlington House, 1973.

Johnson, Haynes. *Bay of Pigs.* New York: W. W. Norton, 1964.

Kennedy, Robert F. *Thirteen Days: A Memoir of the Cuban Missile Crisis.* New York: W. W. Norton, 1969.

Mina, Gianni. *An Encounter with Fidel.* Melbourne, Australia: Ocean Press, 1991.

Wyden, Peter. *Bay of Pigs: The Untold Story.* New York: Simon & Schuster, 1979.

Books on the Right Wing and Associates

Anderson, Scott, and Jon Lee Anderson. *Inside the League.* New York: Dodd, Mead, 1986.

Anti-Defamation League of B'Nai Brith. *Extremism on the Right: A Handbook.* New York: 1983.

Bellant, Russ. *Old Nazis, the New Right, and the Republican Party.* Boston: South End Press, 1991.

Diamond, Sander A. *The Nazi Movement in the United States: 1924–41.* Ithaca, N.Y.: Cornell University Press, 1974.

Flynn, John T. *While You Slept.* New York: Devin-Adair, 1951.

Forster, Arnold, and Benjamin R. Epstein. *Danger on the Right.* New York: Random House, 1964.

Hurt, Harry III. *Texas Rich: The Hunt Dynasty from the Early Oil Days Through the Silver Crash.* New York: W. W. Norton, 1981.

Infield, Glenn B. *Skorzeny: Hitler's Commando.* New York: St. Martin's Press, 1981.

John Birch Society White Book, Belmont, Mass.: 1962.

Lipset, Seymour Martin, and Earl Raab. *The Politics of Unreason: Right-Wing Extremism in America, 1790–1977* 2d ed. Chicago: University of Chicago Press, 1978.

Mintz, Frank P. *The Liberty Lobby and the American Right.* Westport, Conn.: Greenwood Press, 1985.

Overstreet, Harry and Bonaro. *The Strange Tactics of Extremism.* New York: W. W. Norton, 1964.

Seymour, Cheri. *Committee of the States: Inside the Radical Right.* Mariposa, Calif.: Camden Place Communications, 1991.

Thayer, George. *The Farther Shores of Politics: The American Political Fringe Today.* New York: Simon & Schuster, 1968.

Turner, William. *Power on the Right.* Berkeley, Calif.: Ramparts Press, 1971.

Books on the Far East, and U.S. Military Role in

Ames, Walter L. *Police and Community in Japan*. Berkeley, Calif.: University of California Press, 1981.

Bergamini, David. *Japan's Imperial Conspiracy*, Vol. II. New York: William Morrow, 1971.

Cohen, Theodore. *Remaking Japan: The American Occupation as New Deal*, ed. Herbert Passin. New York: The Free Press, 1987.

Cumings, Bruce. *The Origins of the Korean War*, Vol. II: *The Roaring of the Cataract, 1947–1950*. Princeton, N.J.: Princeton University Press, 1990.

Deacon, Richard. *The Chinese Secret Service*. New York: Taplinger, 1974.

———. *A History of the Japanese Secret Service*. London: Frederick Muller, 1982.

———. *Kempei Tai*. New York: Beauford Books, 1982.

Deyo, Frederick C., ed. *The Political Economy of the New Asian Industrialism*. Ithaca, N.Y.: Cornell University Press, 1987.

Fujisawa, Chikao. *Zen and Shinto: The Story of Japanese Philosophy*. Westport, Conn.: Greenwood Press, 1959.

Gayn, Mark. *Japan Diary*. New York: W. Sloane Associates, 1948.

Gittings, John. *Survey of the Sino-Soviet Dispute: A Commentary and Extracts from the Recent Polemics, 1963–1967*. London: Oxford University Press, 1968.

Harries, Meirion and Susie. *Sheathing the Sword: The Demilitarization of Postwar Japan*. New York: Macmillan, 1987.

Hellman, Donald C. *Japanese Foreign Policy and Domestic Politics*. Berkeley, Calif.: University of California Press, 1969.

Jaffe, Philip J. *The Amerasia Case*. Self-published, 1979.

Johnson, Chalmers. *Conspiracy at Matsukawa*. Berkeley, Calif.: University of California Press, 1972.

Kaplan, David E., and Alec Dubro. *Yakuza*. Reading, Mass.: Addison-Wesley, 1986.

Kim, Se-Jin. *The Politics of Military Revolution in Korea*. Chapel Hill, N.C.: University of North Carolina Press, 1971.

Kim, Young Bae. "The Japanese Communist Party and the Soviet Union: A Pattern of Coalition and Conflict, 1945–69." Master's thesis, University of Kansas, 1974.

Koen, Ross Y. *The China Lobby in American Politics*. New York: Octagon Books, 1974.

Langdon, F. C. *Japan's Foreign Policy*. Vancouver, B.C.: University of British Columbia Press, 1973.

Mackinnon, Janice R. and Stephen R. *Agnes Smedley: The Life and Times of an American Radical*. London: Virago Press, 1988.

Manchester, William. *American Caesar: Douglas MacArthur, 1880–1964*. Boston: Little, Brown, 1978.

Morley, James W. *Japan and Korea*. New York: Walker, 1965.

Morris, Dr. I. I. *Nationalism and the Right Wing in Japan: A Study of Post-war Trends*. London: Oxford University Press, 1960.

Richelson, Jeffrey T. *Foreign Intelligence Organizations*. Cambridge, Mass.: Ballinger, 1988.

Scott, Peter Dale. *The War Conspiracy: The Secret Road to The Second Indochina War*. Indianapolis, Ind.: Bobbs-Merrill, 1972.

Seagrave, Sterling. *The Marcos Dynasty*. New York: Harper & Row, 1988.

Service, John S. *The Amerasia Papers: Some Problems in the History of U.S.-China Relations*. Berkeley, Calif.: University of California Press, 1971.

Shillony, Ben-Ami. *Politics and Culture in Wartime Japan*. Oxford, England: Clarendon Press, 1981.

Tolischus, Otto. *Tokyo Record*. New York: Reynal and Hitchcock, 1943.

Utley, Freda. *Lost Illusion*. Philadelphia: Fireside Press, 1948.

———. *The China Story*. Chicago: H. Regnery, 1951.

Willoughby, Charles A. *Shanghai Conspiracy: The Sorge Spy Ring*. New York: E. P. Dutton, 1952.

Other Books

Blair, Clay. *The Strange Case of James Earl Ray: The Man Who Murdered Martin Luther King*. New York: Bantam Books, 1969.

Condon, Richard. *The Manchurian Candidate*. New York: Dell Publishing, 1959.

Demaret, Pierre. *Target de Gaulle*. New York: Dial Press, 1975.

Evans, Rowland, and Robert Novak. *Lyndon B. Johnson: The Exercise of Power*. New York: New American Library, 1966.

Guide To the American Left. Kansas City, Mo: Laird M. Wilcox, 1969.

Huie, William Bradford. *He Slew the Dreamer*. New York: Delacorte Press, 1970.

Kaiser, Robert Blair. *"R.F.K. Must Die."* New York: Grove Press, 1970.

Melanson, Philip H. *The Robert F. Kennedy Assassination: Conspiracy and Cover-Up*. New York: Shapolsky, 1991.

Murphy, Bruce Allen. *Fortas: The Rise and Ruin of a Supreme Court Justice*. New York: William Morrow, 1988.

Reston, James, Jr. *The Lone Star: The Life of John Connally*. New York: Harper & Row, 1989.

Schreiber, G. R. *The Bobby Baker Affair*. Chicago: Henry Regnery, 1964.

Vankin, Jonathan. *Conspiracies, Cover-ups, and Crimes: Political Manipulation and Mind Control in America.* New York: Paragon House, 1991.

Government Reports and Documents

Alleged Assassination Plots Involving Foreign Leaders. Interim report of the Select Committee to Study Governmental Operations with Respect to Intelligence Activities, U.S. Senate. Washington, D.C.: U.S. Government Printing Office, 1975.

The Amerasia Papers: A Clue to the Catastrophe of China, Vol. I. Prepared by the Subcommittee to Investigate the Administration of the Internal Security Act and Other Internal Security Laws of the Committee on the Judiciary, U.S. Senate. Washington, D.C.: U.S. Government Printing Office, 1970.

Communist Psychological Warfare (Brainwashing). Consultation with Edward Hunter, Committee on Un-American Activities, U.S. House of Representatives, 85th Congress 2nd Session. Washington, D.C.: U.S. Government Printing Office, 1958.

Construction of the D.C. Stadium, and Matters Related Thereto, Part 9. U.S. Senate, 89th Congress, 1st Session, iii+827-975p., February 4–5, 1965 hearing (Bobby Baker).

FBI Oversight. Hearings Before the Subcommittee on Civil and Constitutional Rights of the Committee on the Judiciary, House of Representatives, 94th Congress, 1st and 2nd Sessions, Part 3. Washington, D.C.: U.S. Government Printing Office, 1976.

Individual Rights and the Federal Role in Behavior Modification. A Study Prepared by the Staff of the Subcommittee on Constitutional Rights of the Committee on the Judiciary, U.S. Senate, 93rd Congress, 2nd Session. Washington, D.C.: U.S. Government Printing Office, 1974.

"Investigation of the Assassination of President John F. Kennedy," appendix to *Hearings Before the Select Committee on Assassinations of the U.S. House of Representatives, 95th Congress,* Vols. I–XII. Washington, D.C.: U.S. Government Printing Office, 1979.

The Investigation of the Assassination of President John F. Kennedy: Performance of the Intelligence Agencies, final report, Books I, III, and V. U.S. Senate, Select Committee to Study Governmental Operations with Respect to Intelligence Activities, 94th Congress, 2nd Session. Washington, D.C.: U.S. Government Printing Office, 1976.

Report to the President by the Commission on CIA Activities Within the United States. Washington, D.C.: U.S. Government Printing Office, 1975.

Report of the President's Commission on the Assassination of President John F. Kennedy [Warren Commission Report]. Washington, D.C.: U.S. Government Printing Office, 1964. With accompanying twenty-six volumes of exhibits and testimony.

Fisher, Seymour. *The Use of Hypnosis in Intelligence and Related Military Situations.* Study SR 177-D, Contract AF 18 (600) 1797, Technical Report No. 4 Washington, D.C.: Bureau of Social Science Research, 1958.